1992

Byzantium and the Slavs

RENOVATIO 1

Harvard Ukrainian Research Institute — Cambridge

Istituto Universitario Orientale — Napoli

IHOR ŠEVČENKO

BYZANTIUM AND THE SLAVS

IN LETTERS AND CULTURE

HARVARD UKRAINIAN RESEARCH INSTITUTE
CAMBRIDGE, MASSACHUSETTS

ISTITUTO UNIVERSITARIO ORIENTALE
NAPOLI

The participation of the Ukrainian Research Institute of Harvard University in this project was made possible in part by a generous grant by the Reverend Gregory Lysko.

ISBN 0-916458-12-1
Library of Congress Catalogue Number 88-81196
Printed in the United States of America

Distributed in the USA by Harvard University Press
for the Harvard Ukrainian Research Institute

EDITORIAL STATEMENT

The purpose of the series *Renovatio* is to republish materials relating to Slavic, Byzantine, and Eurasian studies, especially those with a comparative focus, that arc cither scattered or not easily accessible. Three types of works are intended for republication: topically arranged collections of articles and essays; monographs; texts and documents. As a rule, each republished item will be provided with a retrospective essay on the developments in the given field.

The series is sponsored jointly by the Istituto Universitario Orientale of Naples and the Ukrainian Research Institute of Harvard University.

Thc Editors

TABLE OF CONTENTS

PREFACE

The thirty-five items contained in this volume deal mostly with Byzantino-Slavic literary and cultural relations. They were originally published between 1952 and 1984 and thus span a period of thirty-two years. Consequently, along with some more recent offerings, the reader is presented with many a vintage piece. This is less of a disadvantage than might appear at first sight.

For one thing, much of the volume's material consists of finds and establishes genetic relationships between Byzantine and Slavic texts; and the method predominantly employed is that of the critique of sources, with value judgments and programmatic statements only sparingly proffered. Time is usually slow in rendering products of such a method obsolete, except when these products are absorbed—with or without acknowledgment—into subsequent scholarship.

Secondly, history of scholarship is served by reprints of studies in which, to give two examples, signal contributions to the field were first brought to the Western public's attention (see chapter II), or in which new material was first identified and assessed (see chapter XXXIV).

Within the rules of the scholarly game that prevailed between the 1950s and the early 1980s, the studies of this volume represented what historians of scholarship call the "normal science." Their relevance was not questioned; nor were they considered especially controversial. Controversy, when it arose, turned around propositions that impinged upon national or parochial pride and prejudice (see chapters XVIII, XXVI, and XXVII), or upon a great scholar's firmly held beliefs (see chapter XXI). Controversy did not affect the method, which was used essentially for establishing dependencies among texts.

Some ten years ago, voices were heard to the effect that establishing genetic links was not the only way in which to investigate various aspects of cultural contacts between Byzantium and the Slavs. These were reasonable voices, and I myself said a supportive word on this topic in the final section of chapter I. Today, "normal science" has still a number of well-qualified and aggressive practitioners (the names of Francis Thomson and William Veder come to mind), and proponents of the newer approaches (such as Simon Franklin) continue to take the validity of the genetic method for granted.

There are signs, however, that things have moved towards a systemic change. In one recent study devoted to Muscovite culture the view was expressed that forging genetic links with Byzantium was of interest to the older generation of scholars, the implication being that such forging was no longer of special interest to the younger generation. In other writings, intertextuality—to use the current term—was as much a matter of alluding to late twentieth-century texts and concepts as that of establishing relations between medieval ones. These late twentieth-century texts came either from outside fields, such as cultural anthropology or literary theory *cum* semiotics, surely an excitingly tasty dish, provided it is served on a bed of well-prepared and well-understood sources; or they were texts produced by like-minded members of the craft.

The catch here is that statements that ostensibly refer to what went on in the minds of people of the medieval or early modern past may in fact refer, to a larger extent than admitted, to what is going on in the minds of modern researchers. The exhilarating freedom from doing the chores of source criticism has its price, for, as R. C. Lewontin, a forward-looking Harvard professor of biology, observed in 1990, one cannot predict where a system will end up if one does not know where it started.

Still, the recent change in the scholarly climate is a given, and no Jeremiads can wail it away. If it lasts, the present volume will serve as a compendium of the ways in which things used to be done. But if a new post-post generation realizes that much remains to be discovered, rolls up its sleeves and turns to digging again, the volume might serve as the young prospector's manual.

* * *

With the exception of chapter VI,[1] the present volume contains no studies that had been reprinted in other collections. Thus, it lacks one study reprinted in my *Society and Intellectual Life in Late Byzantium* (1981)[2] and five studies reprinted in *Ideology, Letters and Culture in the Byzantine World* (1982).[3] Furthermore, three items were omitted by design or

[1] Reprinted in Michael Cherniavsky, ed., *The Structure of Russian History. Interpretative Essays* (New York, 1970), pp. 80–107.

[2] Chapter XV, ''Notes on Stephen, the Novgorodian Pilgim to Constantinople in the 14th Century,'' originally published in *Südost-Forschungen* 12 (1953): 165–175.

[3] Chapter III, ''Agapetus East and West: The Fate of a Byzantine 'Mirror of Princes,' '' originally published in *Revue des Etudes Sud-Est Européennes* 16 (1978): 3–44; chapter IV, ''Three Paradoxes of the Cyrillo-Methodian Mission,'' originally published in *Slavic Review* 23 (1964): 220–236; chapter VI, ''The Christianization of Kievan Rus','' originally published in *The Polish Review* 5, no. 4 (1960): 29–35; chapter IX, ''Intellectual Repercussions of the Coun-

oversight;[4] finally, one article was published too late to be included in this collection.[5] On the other hand, chapter XXIII, entirely Slavic in scope, was thrown in for good measure.

Within the volume, the arrangement of articles is chronological. The only exception is the introductory essay, among the last to have been written down in its final form.

In making selections, I did not try to sweep anything under the carpet. Thus the early chapter III, containing an emendation to the text of the Igor' *Tale*, has been included, although today I have great difficulty in dating the *Tale* to the twelfth century. My assessment of the social standing of the father of Saints Cyril and Methodius has somewhat improved (see *Addendum* to chapter XXVII). On the other hand, some nuances apart, I continue to stand by chapter IX, even though, according to one early reviewer, the volume in which this item appeared belonged on the refuse heap of the cold war.

All items in the volume were reset in Italy, through the kind mediation of Professor Riccardo Picchio. This circumstance has enhanced the volume's outward appearance; it also has provided the opportunity for eliminating some typographical (and a few factual) errors and for harmonizing the terminology with standards followed by the Harvard Ukrainian Research Institute. No attempt was made, however, to standardize the various transliteration systems adopted by editors of individual pieces. Nor have I attempted to bring the studies up to date in terms of bibliography, for such an attempt might have delayed the publication of the volume indefinitely. Instead, I have provided a dozen pages or so of *Addenda* containing some random remarks, arranged by chapter. Most of these remarks are bibliographical, a few, substantive (as in *Addenda* to chapters XXI, XXVI and XXVII).

The resetting of all studies resulted in a new pagination, with the pagination of the originals indicated in pointed brackets. Many, but unfortunately not all, plates have been reproduced from original photographs, or were redone. The index went through several friendly hands (of Dr. Donald

---

cil of Florence,'' originally published in *Church History* 24 (1955): 291–323; chapter X, ''Byzantium and the Eastern Slavs after 1453,'' originally published in *Harvard Ukrainian Studies* 2, no. 1 (March 1978): 5–25.

4 Review of Francis Dvornik, *The Idea of Apostolicity in Byzantium and the Legend of Apostle Andrew* (1958), in *American Slavic and East European Review* 19, no. 1 (1960): 134–137; review of Oscar Halecki, *From Florence to Brest (1439–1596)* (1958), in *Slavonic Review* 20, no. 3 (1961): 523–527; my chapters in Hans Belting, ed., *Der Serbische Psalter. Faksimile-Ausgabe des Cod. Slav. 4 der Bayerischen Staatsbibliothek München* (1978), Textband, pp. 25–172.

5 ''Religious Missions Seen from Byzantium,'' *Harvard Ukrainian Studies* 12/13 (1988/1989): 7–27.

Ostrowski, Dr. Čelica Milovanović, and Dr. Maxim Tarnawsky) and was given the final touches and converted to the new pagination by Dr. Giorgio Ziffer.[6] Professor Mario Capaldo, Dr. and Mrs. Thomas Butler, Dr. George Mihaychuk, Ms. Kathryn Dodgson Taylor, and Mr. Robert De Lossa supervised the various stages of production. The volume itself would not have seen the light of day without the optimism and the gentle but persistent prodding that came from Professor Omeljan Pritsak.

Ihor Ševčenko
Cambridge, Massachusetts
March 1991

6 Names and items occurring in the *Preface* and in the *Addenda* could no longer be included in the index.

I

Byzantium and the Slavs*

To Cyril Mango

I

Throughout more than a thousand years of their history, the Byzantines viewed their state as heir to the Roman Empire, which pretended to encompass the whole civilized world. It followed that the Byzantine state, too, was a universal empire, claiming rule over the whole civilized world; that Byzantine emperors were by right world rulers; that the Byzantines were Romans; and that they were the most civilized people in the world. True, they had improved upon their Roman ancestors in that they were Christians; also, by the seventh century the Latin component had all but disappeared from their highbrow culture, which from then on was essentially Greek; but, like ancient Romans, the Byzantines felt entitled to pour scorn on those who did not share in the fruits of civilization, that is, on the barbarians. The best thing these barbarians could do was to abandon their bestial existence, and to enter — in some subordinate capacity of course — into the family of civilized peoples headed by the Byzantine emperor. The way to civilization led through Christianity, the only true ideology, of which the empire held the monopoly. For Christianity — to be more precise, Byzantine Christianity — meant civilization.

Throughout a millennium of propaganda, these simple tenets were driven home by means of court rhetoric — the journalism of the Middle Ages — of court ceremonies, of imperial pronouncements and documents, and of coinage. The Byzantine emperor claimed certain exclusive rights. Until the thirteenth century at least, he did not conclude equal treaties with foreign rulers; he only granted them privileges, insignia, or dignities. In correspondence with certain foreign states, he

* This essay is a reworking of a lecture written a number of years ago. Thus it has a number of layers. While the earliest of these layers owe a debt to the standard picture of Byzantium drawn by Franz Dölger and George Ostrogorski in their day, the later ones reflect my present views on the topic.

issued "orders", not letters. He claimed the exclusive right to strike gold coinage (other peoples' ⟨290⟩ gold coins were at first imitations or counterfeits; only in the thirteenth century did the western ducat replace the bezant, for almost one thousand years the dollar of the Mediterranean world). As the Byzantines were not blind, they had to accommodate themselves to the existence of other states besides their own. To fit them into their system, they elaborated the concept of Hierarchy of Rulers and States that, taken all together, ideally encompassed the whole world. The emperor headed this hierarchy; he was surrounded by subordinates, who would stand in an ideal family relationship to him: the English ruler was only his friend; the Bulgarian, his son; the Rus' one, his nephew; Charlemagne was grudgingly granted the position of a brother. Or else these rulers would be given titles of varying importance: ruler, ruler with power, king, even emperor. But never — not until the fifteenth century, if at all — Emperor of the Romans.

By the ninth century, the following truths were held to be self-evident in the field of culture: the world was divided into Byzantines and barbarians, the latter including not only the Slavs — who occupied a low place on the list of barbaric nations — but also the Latins; as a city, the New Rome, that is, Constantinople, was superior to all others in art, culture, and size, and that included the Old Rome on the Tiber. God has chosen the Byzantine people to be a new Israel: the Gospels were written in Greek for the Greeks; in His foresight, God had even singled out the Ancient Greeks to cultivate the Arts and Sciences; and in Letters and Arts, the Byzantines were the Greeks' successors. "All the arts come from us," exclaimed a Byzantine diplomat during a polemical debate held at the Arab court in the fifties of the ninth century. A curious detail: this diplomat was none other than the future Apostle of the Slavs, Constantine-Cyril. Cyril's exclamation implied that Latin learning, too, was derived from the Greeks. The Greek language, the language of the Scriptures, of the church fathers, also of Plato and Demosthenes, was rich, broad, and subtle; the other tongues, notably the Slavic, had a barbaric ring to them; even the Latin language was poor and "narrow".

The Byzantines maintained these claims for almost as long as their state endured. Even towards the very end of the fourteenth century, when the empire was little more than the city of Constantinople in size, the Byzantine patriarch lectured the recalcitrant prince of Muscovy on the international order. The prince should remember — so the patriarch explained — that he was only a local ⟨291⟩ ruler, while the Byzantine emperor was the Emperor of the Romans, that is, of all Christians. The fact that the emperor's dominions were hard-pressed by the pagans was beside the point. The emperor enjoyed special prerogatives in the world and in the Church Universal. It therefore ill behooved the prince to have discontinued mentioning the name of the emperor during the liturgy.

By the end of the fourteenth century, such a claim was unrealistic, and, as is to be deduced from the Byzantine patriarch's closing complaint, it had been challenged by the Muscovite barbarian. But throughout more than half of Byzantine history, such claims worked. Why?

The first reason why they worked was that for a long time the claims were objectively true. In terms of the sixth century, Justinian, under whose early rule the large-scale Slavic invasions occurred in the Balkans, was a world emperor, that is, a ruler holding sway over the civilized world. In the east, his dominions extended beyond the upper Tigris River; they skirted the western slopes of the Caucasus. In the north, Byzantium's frontier ran across the Crimea, and along the Danube and the Alps. The empire had a foothold in Spain, it controlled the coast of North Africa and much of Egypt, it dominated today's Israel, Lebanon, and a great deal of Syria. Now let us skip half a millennium. In the time of Basil II (d. 1025), under whose reign the Rus' accepted Christianity, the situation was not much worse: it was even better in the east, where the frontier ran beyond Lake Van; for a stretch, it hugged the Euphrates. Antioch and Latakia were still in Byzantine hands; in the North, the Crimea was still crossed by the Byzantine frontier, and the Danube and the Sava were the frontier rivers — thus in this sector, too, Byzantium possessed as much as Justinian did. In the West, parts of southern Italy with the city of Bari were under Byzantine sway. In the ninth and tenth centuries, which were decisive for the Byzantinization of the Slavs, the empire's capital at Constantinople was, with the possible exception of Baghdad and Cairo, the most brilliant cultural center of the world as not only the Slavs, but also western Europe, knew it. Its patriarchs were Greek scholars and politicians. Its prelates read and commented upon Plato, Euclid, and even the objectionable Lucian; its emperors supervised large encyclopaedic enterprises; its sophisticated reading public clamored for, and obtained, reeditions of old simple Lives of Saints, which were now couched in a more refined and complicated style. The Great Palace of Constantinople, ⟨292⟩ covering an area of ca. 100,000 square meters, was still largely intact and functioning. The pomp of the court ceremonial and of the services at St. Sophia, then still the largest functioning building in the known world, was calculated to dazzle barbarian visitors, including Slavic princes or their emissaries. Byzantine political concepts influenced western mediaeval political thinking down to the twelfth century; the western symbols of rule — scepter, crown, orb, golden bull — owe a debt to Byzantium. The mosaics of Rome, of St. Mark in Venice (thirteenth century) and of Torcello near Venice (twelfth century), of the Norman churches in or near Palermo (twelfth century), are reflections of Byzantine art, and some of them were executed by Byzantine craftsmen.

The renascence of theological speculation in the High Middle Ages was stimulated by the imperial gift which arrived from Byzantium at the court of Louis the Pious in 827. The gift was a volume of Dionysius the Pseudo-Areopagite, in Greek, of course. This work, translated twice into Latin, the second time by Johannes Scotus Eriugena (d. 877), spurred subsequent western theological speculation. It is difficult to imagine a western church without an organ — yet, this instrument, too, arrived from Byzantium in 757 and 812. On the latter occasion, the Byzantines refused to leave the organ with the Westerners, who attempted to copy it in secret, but only later successfully reproduced it. The silk industry was introduced to the West in the middle of the twelfth century, as a result of a Norman raid on Central Greece — the Normans abducted Byzantine skilled laborers from Thebes and settled them in their dominions. Even the fork seems to be a rediscovery of Byzantine origin — an eleventh-century Greek-born dogissa introduced forks to Venice, to the great horror of a contemporary ecclesiastic. No wonder that the Slavs experienced the influence of Byzantium: the West, which could fall back upon refined Latin traditions, experienced it, too, long after Byzantium's political domination over parts of Italy had ceased. So much for the first reason — Byzantine claims worked because they were objectively valid.

The second reason why the Byzantine claims of superiority worked was that they were accepted as valid by the barbarians, whether western or Slavic, even after they had ceased to be objectively valid. The usurpation of Charlemagne occurred in 800. But he, the ruler of Rome, did not call himself emperor of the Romans — he knew that this title, and all that it implied, had been preempted by the Byzantines. It was not until 982 that the ⟨293⟩ titulature "Imperator Romanorum" appeared in the West. And it was only with Frederick I Barbarossa (second half of the twelfth century) that a logical consequence was drawn from this titulature by a western ruler. Since there could be only one Emperor of the Romans, the Byzantine emperor should not be called by this title — he was to be called only what in fact he had been for a long time: the *rex Graecorum*. But did Frederick reflect that the very concept that there should be only one emperor was a Byzantine heritage? The Slavs were much slower to be weaned from Byzantium and never drew a conclusion similar to that of Frederick. With them, emulation of Byzantium was always but another form of Byzantium's imitation. True, Symeon of Bulgaria in the early tenth century and Stephen Dušan of Serbia in the mid-fourteenth assumed the title of Emperor of the Bulgarians and Greeks or of the Serbians and Greeks, respectively. But they did not think of proclaiming a Slavic counterpart to the Western doctrine *Rex est Imperator in regno suo* and thus downgrading the Byzantine emperor. Rather, they dreamed of supplanting him by taking Constantinople and seating themselves on his throne; and the same fantasy occurs in one text produced in thirteenth-century Rus', *Slovo o pogibeli russkoj zemli*.

Short of supplanting the Byzantine emperor, many a Balkan ruler aimed at securing for himself the prerogatives of that emperor, or attempted to imitate imperial pomp and usage. Ways of doing this were varied. One instance was by having a patriarch of his own: in the ninth century, the newly converted Boris of Bulgaria wanted to have one; around 900, Symeon of Bulgaria succeeded in setting one up; so did Stephen Dušan of Serbia in the mid-fourteenth century, not without resistance on the part of Byzantium. Another instance was by striking gold coins: the Bulgarian tsar Ivan Asen II (d. 1241) managed to do it, but he appeared on his coins in the garb of a Byzantine emperor with Christ on the reverse; another, by having the court hierarchy bear Byzantine aulic titles: Stephen Dušan named sebastocrators and logothetes; yet another, by assuming the epithet "second Justinian" on the occasion of the proclamation of new laws; still another, by looking to Byzantium as a reservoir for prestigious marriages — between the thirteenth century and the fall of Bulgaria in 1393, we count eight Greek women among 21 Bulgarian tsarinas; another, by patterning one's own capital after Constantinople: Symeon of Bulgaria's Preslav copied the Imperial City, as, by the way, did Prince Jaroslav's Kiev in the 1030s.

⟨294⟩ In fifteenth- and sixteenth-century Muscovy, the attitude toward Byzantium and its patriarchate was less than friendly; but when the Muscovite bookmen began to formulate an indigenous state ideology, they drew heavily upon Byzantine sources, in particular upon a Mirror of Princes written in Greek for the emperor Justinian in the sixth century; and they called Moscow "the reigning city," a formula by which the Byzantines usually referred to Constantinople. In sum, throughout their Middle Ages, the Balkan and to a considerable extent the East Slavic ruling elites were beholden to the Byzantine model in the matter of political concepts.

The Byzantine cultural impact did not presuppose the existence of friendly relations between Byzantium and the Slavs. Sometimes it looked as if the more anti-Byzantine the Balkan Slavs — like the Normans of Sicily — were in their political aspirations the more Byzantinized they became; they fought the enemy with the enemy's own weapons. What the Byzantine cultural impact did presuppose was the acceptance — both by the producers and the receivers of cultural values — of the Byzantine world view and civilization as superior to all others.

II

The Christianization and cultural Byzantinization of the Balkans was a pivotal event. It affected both the medieval and the post-medieval history of the Balkans and of eastern Europe; what is more, its effects are with us today. Whether the consequences of this event should be considered as beneficial or baneful is a matter of judgment that depends on the historian's own background and on the modern public's political views. It remains that the Christianization of the Balkans not only determined the cultural physiognomy of Serbia and Bulgaria, but also prepared and facilitated the subsequent Byzantinization of the East Slavs, an event which, along with the Tartar invasion, contributed to the estrangement of Rus' from the European West. In the light of the preceding remarks, however, the Byzantinization of the South and East Slavs should be viewed just as an especially successful and enduring case of Byzantium's impact upon its neighbors, whether in Europe or in the Near East.

It was an especially successful case on two counts. First, when we speak of those Balkan Slavs who experienced the strongest influence of the Byzantine culture, we mean Serbs and Bulgarians. ⟨295⟩ But we forget that these formed the rear guard, as it were, of the Slavic populations that had penetrated into the territory of the empire. In the late sixth century, the Slavs attacked the outer defenses of Constantinople; around 600, they besieged Thessalonica. About the same time, they reached Epirus, Attica, and the Peloponnesus; by the middle of the eighth century, the whole of Greece—or, at least, of the Peloponnesus— "became slavicized," to use the expression of a text written under the auspices of a tenth-century Byzantine emperor. Slavic raiders reached Crete and other Greek islands. We do hear of Byzantine military campaigns aiming at the reconquest of the lands settled by the Slavs, but judging by the paucity of relevant references in our sources, it is wise to conclude that these campaigns were not too frequent. And what remained of those Slavs? About 1,200 place-names, many of them still existing; some Slavic pockets in the Peloponnesus, attested as late as the fifteenth century; about 275 Slavic words in the Greek language; perhaps a faint Slavic trace or two in Greek folklore. Nothing more. In matters of cultural impact, the ultimate in success is called complete assimilation. When it comes to mechanisms that facilitated this spectacular assimilation, we must keep in mind the role played by the upper strata of the Slavic society, for by the end of the ninth century the Slavs were already socially differentiated. In my opinion, it was this Slavic elite, as much as the Byzantine missionaries, that served as a conduit in the transmission of Byzantine culture to the Slavic population at large.

Second, Byzantium held more than its own in its competition with Rome over the religious allegiance of the Balkan Slavs. For historical reasons, which had some validity to them, the Church of Rome laid jurisdictional claims to the territory of ancient Illyricum, that is, roughly the area on which the Serbs, Croats, and some Bulgarians (Slavic and Turkic) had established themselves. Croatia and Dalmatia were the only Byzantine areas where western Christianity was victorious in the ninth century. The Serbs were first Christianized by Rome about 640; but only the second Christianization took permanent roots there. It occurred in the seventies of the ninth century and it was due to Byzantine missionaries, later aided by Bulgarians. For a while, the newly converted Bulgarian ruler Boris-Michael flirted with Pope Nicholas I; but in 870, the Bulgarians entered the Byzantine fold, and they have remained there ever since.

⟨296⟩True, the Cyrillo-Methodian mission in Moravia and Pannonia, which originally was staged from Byzantium, ended in failure shortly after 885, when Methodius's pupils were expelled and supplanted by the German clergy of Latin rite. But if this was a failure, it was a qualified one: the Moravian and Pannonian areas had never belonged to Byzantium.

Before its collapse, the Cyrillo-Methodian mission did forge the most powerful tool for indirect Byzantinization of all Orthodox Slavs: it created — or perfected — the Old Church Slavonic literary language. The Byzantinized Slavic liturgy did continue in Bohemia — granted, in a limited way — until the very end of the eleventh century; and the expelled pupils of Methodius found an excellent reception in late ninth-century Bulgaria and Macedonia, in centers like Preslav and Ohrid, from where they continued and deepened the work of Christianizing and Byzantinizing the Bulgarian and Macedonian Slavs. Occasional attempts on the part of the thirteenth-century Serbian and Bulgarian rulers to play Rome against Constantinople had no durable effects. True, both the Serbian Stephen the First-Crowned and the Bulgarian Kalojan, tsar of Bulgaria, obtained their royal crowns from the pope (1217 and 1204, respectively). But their churches, although autonomous, remained in communion with the Byzantine patriarchate in exile (1220 and 1235, respectively); they even remained under its suzerainty, in spite of the fact that at that time the Latin Crusaders resided in conquered Constantinople and the Byzantine empire was just a smallish principality of Asia Minor, fighting for its survival.

The loss of Moravia and Pannonia by the Byzantine mission was amply compensated for by a gain in another area which (except for the Crimea) had never been under the actual Byzantine government: I mean the territories inhabited, among others, by the East Slavs. There, too, the field was not uncontested, for Rome had sent its missionaries to Kiev in the middle of the tenth century. In addition, Byzantium had to struggle there with other religious influences, Islamic and Jewish. It emerged victorious: the ruler of Kiev adopted Christianity for himself and his people in 988/9, and the act was sealed by the prince's marriage with the Byzantine emperor's sister. In retrospect, the Christianization and concomitant Byzantinization of the East Slavs was the greatest success of the Byzantine cultural mission. Churches in Byzantine style still stand in Alaska, and in Fort Ross in California; this marks the ⟨297⟩ furthest eastward advance of Byzantine Christianity under the auspices of a predominantly East Slavic state.

The cultural Byzantinization of the Orthodox Slavs was also an especially enduring case of the Byzantine impact on Europe. Chronologically speaking, this Byzantinization, as opposed to complete assimilation, started with the ninth or tenth century, depending on the area, and it lasted long after the fall of the empire in 1453, down to the eighteenth and the nineteenth century. Paradoxically enough, after 1453, new possibilities of expansion were opened to Byzantine culture, the culture of an empire that was no more.

Before 1453, the history of the relations between Byzantium and the Slavic churches and states was that of intermittently successful attempts to shake off the administrative tutelage of the Byzantines. Now, both the Balkan Slavs and the Byzantines were subjects of the Ottoman Empire; in the eyes of the Ottoman conquerors these peoples, all of them Christian, formed one entity, *Rum milleti*, that is, "Religious Community (or Nation) of the Romans" — a name coined in good Byzantine tradition. To the Ottomans, the patriarch of Constantinople was now the head (civilian and ecclesiastical) of all the Christians in the Ottoman Empire.

Although their circumstances were reduced, the patriarchs were in some areas of activity heirs to the Byzantine emperors, and the Greek church was a depository and continuator of many aspects of Byzantine culture. This culture had now the same, if not better, chances for radiation among the Balkan Slavs as before, because both the Greeks and the Slavs were now united within the same Ottoman territory.

The churches in the Balkans were administered from Constantinople, especially since the late seventeenth-century, when Phanariote Greeks had obtained great influence at the Sublime Porte. From that time on, native Greeks, rather than Hellenized Slavs, began to be installed as bishops. The historical Slavic Patriarchates of Peć and Ohrid were abolished in the second half of the eighteenth century (1766 and 1767, respectively). Dates marking the official independence of the Bulgarian and Serbian churches from Constantinople coincide roughly with the achievement of political independence by those countries. This rule of the Patriarchate of Constantinople, often unwisely exercised, created much bad blood between Greeks and Bulgarians in the nineteenth ⟨298⟩ century. By that time, the élite of the Balkans was looking to Vienna, Paris, and westernized St. Petersburg for inspiration. But down to the eighteenth century, Greek — that is, post-Byzantine — culture, largely represented by Greek or Hellenized churchmen, was the highest culture in the area.

Eastern Europe, too, very slowly moved away from Byzantium. The Tartar invasion of the 1240s first cut and then weakened contacts with the West, and brought about a falling back upon those forms of local cultural heritage that were in existence in the forties of the thirteenth century. This heritage had been mostly Byzantine; now, it was being preserved and elaborated upon, but not substantially enriched. The Ukraine and Belorussia were reopened to western influences somewhat earlier than other areas, as they gradually fell under the domination of Catholic Poland-Lithuania, especially from the fourteenth century on. But even there the union of Churches did not occur until some two hundred and fifty years later (I am referring to the Union of Brest in 1596), and it was only a limited success, even from the Catholic point of view.

In Moscow, the jurisdictional dependence on the Patriarchate of Constantinople continued until 1448. When the break came, it was motivated by the accusation that Byzantium was not Byzantine enough, that it had fallen away from the true faith by compromising with the Latins at the Council of Florence (1439), while the true Byzantine Orthodoxy was from now on to be preserved in Muscovy. The establishment of an independent patriarchate in Moscow had to wait until 1589. Its confirmation necessitated the assent of other patriarchs, but it was easily obtained from the impecunious Greeks. Western influences penetrating through the Ukraine were present in seventeenth-century Muscovy, but it was only Peter the First, ascending the throne as Tsar and Autocrat, Byzantine style, and leaving it in death as August Emperor, western fashion, who put an end to the Byzantine period in the history of the Russian cultural élite, but not in the history of the Russian lower classes.

III

The two main — but not the only—channels through which Byzantine influences entered the Orthodox Slavic world were the church hierarchy, secular and monastic (both for a long time largely Greek, even in eastern Europe), and the respective princely courts. Thus, Byzantium was imitated, above all, in those aspects of culture ⟨299⟩ in which the church, the state, or the upper layers of the Slavic society were interested: script, literary language, both sacred and secular, literature, ecclesiastical and secular learning, art (both in its ecclesiastical and aulic variety), ruler cult, state ideology, law, and the sphere of gracious living. But the upper layers of medieval Orthodox Slavic society were less refined than their Byzantine counterparts. There was much in Byzantine culture which they did not yet need; on the other hand, there were many elementary things not exactly belonging to the exalted sphere, that they had to learn. Thus while the most sophisticated products of Byzantine literature were never translated into medieval Slavic, the Bulgarian words for onions (*kromid*) and cabbage (*lahana*) and the Serbian expression for fried eggs (*tiganisana jaja*) have been taken over from Greek. Art is an exception, for there Byzantium gave the Slavs the best it had to offer. But art is not primarily an intellectual pursuit, and it can be appreciated even by newcomers to civilization; moreover, then as now, money could buy the best.

From the court and the episcopal residence, borrowed elements of Byzantine culture seeped down to the people. Also, pilgrims traveled to Constantinople and brought back with them both wondrous tales of the capital's splendor and objects of devotional art; monks moved to the Serbian, Bulgarian, and Rus' monasteries of Mount Athos and had Greek-Slavic conversation manuals composed for them (we know of one dating from the fifteenth century). In areas geographically closest to Byzantium, like Bulgaria, Byzantine direct domination, and later the post-Byzantine symbiosis under the Ottomans, brought close contacts on a popular level. Thus we have reflections of Byzantine influences in Slavic popular language and folklore: we know of at least 107 (perhaps as much as 245) proverbs that the Slavs borrowed directly from Greek. Eighty percent of these borrowings were preserved by South Slavs, twenty percent by East Slavs.

IV

The extent of Byzantine cultural impact upon the Orthodox Slavs can best be demonstrated by discussing two cases: that of literary language and that of literature. The Old Church Slavonic language was formed by two generations of Byzantine and Slavic missionaries in the second half of the ninth century and the very beginning of the tenth, originally as a vehicle for spreading the word of God in ⟨300⟩ Slavic. It was a tool with which to translate from the Greek. We do know of some original Slavic writings by the immediate pupils of Saints Cyril and Methodius, but the bulk of the literary activity of the Slavic Apostles and of their direct successors consisted in translations from Greek; excerpts from both Testaments (soon followed by the full translation of the Gospels), liturgical books, edifying sayings of the monks, codes of ecclesiastical and secular law. In late ninth- and early tenth-century Bulgaria, the situation was much the same. The most bulky literary products of John, the Exarch of Bulgaria, were interpolated translations of St. Basil's *Hexaemeron* and of John of Damascus's *Fountain of Knowledge*. The Mirror of Princes by Agapetus (sixth century) was most probably translated into Old Bulgarian at this same early period, and thus became the very first secular work of Slavic literature. This meant that Old Church Slavonic had to struggle with the world of theological, philosophical and political concepts and other notions, as they were expressed in Hellenistic, early Byzantine, and middle Byzantine Greek. No wonder that Old Church Slavonic teems with simple, semantic, and phraseological calques, that is, word-formations and expressions closely patterned on Byzantine Greek. To a linguist, the results of that patterning often look un-Slavic, even if the Orthodox Slavs of today no longer react to the Byzantine calques in Old Church Slavonic as un-Slavic — a thousand years of familiarity took care of that. For instance, Slavic makes little use of composite words: Greek, especially late antique and Byzantine Greek, loves them; accordingly, Old Church Slavonic abounds in composites like *blagosloviti*, *bogonosьcь*, *bogorodica*, *samodrъžьcь*, to mention those words which have survived in several modern Slavic languages, including modern Russian. This slavish adherence to Byzantine templates can be explained in part by the character of the originals selected for translation: the words of these originals were sacred or of high political importance, be they the words of God, of a church father, of a saint's Life, or of an imperial charter. They had to be rendered with the greatest exactitude, even at the price of doing violence to the tendencies prevalent in early Slavic.

The calque character of Old Church Slavonic was not exclusively a bad trait. Greek, the model of Old Church Slavonic, was a very highly developed and supple language; and the more sophisticated Byzantine writers intended to imitate Demosthenes and Plato, even if in fact they often imitated the much later and more mannered imitators of these authors. In wrestling with the complicated ⟨301⟩ Greek, Old Church

Slavonic acquired something of that language's quality and versatility. The impressive stylistic possibilities of modern literary Russian are due to the fact that much — some say roughly one-half — of its vocabulary is made up of Church Slavonic words, a feature that enables a Russian writer to play on two linguistic registers at will. Old Church Slavonic, with admixtures of respective vernaculars, remained the main literary vehicle for the Orthodox Slavs down to the sixteenth, seventeenth, or eighteenth century, depending on the geographical area and the literary genre. This language was Slavic according to its sound, but largely Byzantine according to its word formations and even its content.

The lexical borrowings from Greek in the languages of the Orthodox Slavs are legion. There are about fourteen hundred of them in Bulgarian, about a thousand each in Serbian and Russian. Their distribution is most dense in the area of Christian terminology, such as ecclesiastical dignities, ceremonies and activities, buildings, names of liturgical texts and songs, and names of months. The language of law, court, administration, education, and the army also abounds in borrowings from Greek. In a less exalted sphere, Greek provided the Slavs with many piscatorial and nautical terms, as well as terms of commerce, coinage and measurement, agriculture and horticulture, and, finally, with terms pertaining to civilized living. Thus the words for basin (*harkoma*), floor (*patoma, patos*), cushion (*proskefal*), breakfast (*progim*), desert (*glikizmo*), pan (*tigan*), bench (*skamija*), fork (*pirun*), drug (*voitima*) are Greek in medieval Serbian or Bulgarian. Even some expressions for family relationships (*anepsej, bratovčed*), some prepositions (*kata*, as in *kata· godina*), interjections (*elate*, originally an imperative), and morphological elements (the verbal suffix *-sati*) come from the Greek. Some other linguistic traits common to the Balkan peoples (Slavic and non-Slavic alike) are attributed by some to the impact of late (that is, in part Byzantine) Greek: I have in mind such phenomena as the lack of an infinitive, or forming the future with the Slavic equivalents of θέλω ἵνα.

When we speak of older Slavic literature, we think first of all of the creative effort of Slavic writers. Still, literature is not only what one creates, but also what one reads. When we are asked what was read, say, in an important Muscovite cultural center like the Kirillo-Belozerskij Monastery around the year 1500, we can give an answer, for we possess a catologue of this monastery's library dating ⟨302⟩ from that time. The answer is revealing. Out of 212 books listed in the catalogue, some 90 have a liturgical character; most of the others are translations from Byzantine homiletic, hagiographic, and ascetic texts. Not only fourth-to-ninth-century Greek fathers of the church appear on the shelves of the library of Kirillo-Belozerskij Monastery around 1500 (Gregory of Nazianzus, St. Basil, Ephrem the Syrian, John Chrysostom, Cyril of Jerusalem, Pseudo-Dionysius Areopagita, John of the Ladder, Theodore of Studios), but also Byzantine writers of the tenth and eleventh centuries (Symeon the Younger, the Theologian), the eleventh (Nikon of the Black Mountain), and even the fourteenth (Gregory Palamas). A few of these translations are explicitly described as coming from the Balkans. Only two texts in the library are written by Kievan authors (Hilarion's *Slovo* and Cyril of Turov's *Sermons*). One more treats a Rus' subject of interest to Muscovy (the Life of Metropolitan Peter [d. 1328], by Metropolitan Cyprian). Only two of the texts, Josephus Flavius's *Jewish War* and *Barlaam and Joasaph*, are secular, and even these were considered recommended reading in one's pursuit of sacred learning. Needless to say, both of them are translations from the Greek.

V

What has been said about language and literature (and could have been as convincingly said about art and music) should have suggested to us that Byzantium thoroughly dominated the cultural horizon of the Orthodox Slavic elite in the Middle Ages; and we should remember that for some of these Slavs the Middle Ages lasted down to the eighteenth century. Such is the truth, even if it is not the whole truth. For in the matter of the transfer of cultural goods from one society to another, telling about what was transferred and through what channels it was transferred amounts to showing only one side of the coin. The other side of the coin would consist in telling what was selected for importation and what happened to the imports once they reached the receiving society — how they were understood (or misunderstood) and for what purposes they were used. This, however, is subject matter for another essay.

Whether the Byzantine impact on the Slavs was a good or a bad thing is for a Slavicist, not a Byzantinist, to decide. True, when Machiavelli was writing his *Prince* and composing his *Discourses* on ⟨303⟩ Livy, Muscovite bookmen were still piecing together their political doctrines with some sixth-, ninth-, and twelfth-century Byzantine material. But it was not Byzantium's fault that the Orthodox Slavs took so long to break its spell.

II

An Important Contribution to the Social History of Late Byzantium

[Georgije Ostrogorski, *Pronija, Prilog istoriji feudalizma u Vizantiji i u južnoslovenskim zemljama*, — Srpska Akademija Nauka, Posebna izdanija, knjiga CLXXVI, Vizantološki Institut, knjiga I, Beograd 1951. (G. Ostrogorski, *Pronoia*, A Contribution to the History of Feudalism in Byzantium and in the South-Slavic Lands, Belgrade, 1951, 200 pp.)]

Conditional grants of land or other natural resources awarded by emperors to their subiects *eis pronoian* (for care) constituted one of the basic features of the economic and social order of the late Byzantine empire from the middle of the eleventh century. From Byzantium the *pronoia* system spread to other parts of the Balkans, especially to Serbian territory. There it outlived Byzantium itself, although in a somewhat modified form, and influenced in turn developments under Turkish rule. The living language preserves an inexact reminder of this feudal institution: in modern Serbian, *prnjavor* designates a village belonging to a monastery.

Pre-revolutionary Russian Byzantinologists, who made many a pioneer venture in the field of Byzantine social history, are to be credited with having grasped the essential characteristics of the *pronoia* system. Quite recently American scholarship[1] has also contributed worth-while general observations on the subject.[1a]

However, earlier research concentrated mainly on the Serbian phase of the *pronoia* system and could not draw upon the rich material

1. P. Charanis, "The Monastic Properties and the State in the Byzantine Empire," *Dumbarton Oaks Papers* IV (1948), 53-118; cf. *idem*, "The Aristocracy of Byzantium in the XIII Century," *Studies in Economic and Social History in Honor of Allan Chester Johnson* (Princeton 1951), 336-355.

1a. Western European Byzantinists as well have given precise, although succinct, definitions of the *pronoia* system: cf., p. *ex*., F. Dölger, "Die Frage des Grundeigentums in Byzanz," *Bulletin of the Intern. Committee of Hist. Sciences*, V (1933), 14.

published subsequently from the archives of the Athonite monasteries. One scholar, Mutafčiev, who utilized almost all the sources available to him, went much too far in denying the *pronoia* grants a military character.[2] Thus the need has remained for an exhaustive study, which would draw fully upon all the sources now available for clarification of the many problems raised by this ⟨449⟩ institution. Among the main problems are these: the features which distinguish a *pronoia* from other types of grants, such as *stratiôtika ktêmata* (military holdings) or *kharistikia* (lease of revenues from church or monastic property); the difference between a *pronoia* and private property; the services demanded in exchange for *pronoia* grants, the period of time for which they were bestowed and the type of revenue derived from them; the status of the peasants tilling the *pronoia* land; the ultimate ownership rights to the *pronoia*; and finally the history of the institution, especially the attempts made by *pronoia* holders to secure more control over the lands given them in trust, the vicissitudes of their struggle with the monasteries, which constituted the other principal class of landowners in Byzantium, and the attitude taken by the Byzantine state in this struggle.

Ostrogorski's book offers a definitive answer to most of these questions.[3] His conclusions are important to the student of history, though the language in which they are set down may be unfamiliar to him. Therefore a somewhat detailed summary may be advisable here.[4]

Ostrogorski views the *pronoia* as a temporary (pp. 22-3), revokable grant of state-owned land, usually awarded for life in exchange for the obligation of military service by the *pronoia* holder and by the peasants who cultivated the land allotted him. The difference between the *stratiôtika ktêmata* of the middle Byzantine Empire and the *pronoiai* lies not so much in their purpose, which is in both cases military, or in their

---

2. P. Mutafčiev, "Vojniški zemi i vojnici v Vizantija prez XIII-XIV v.," *Spisanije na Bŭlgarskata Akademija na naukite* XXVII (1923), 1-113, esp. pp. 37-61.

3. Some other questions are not discussed, however, such as the "social genealogy" of *pronoia*. Cf., on this subject, the interesting remarks by F. Dölger in *Byzantinische Zeitschrift* XXVI (1926), 108 f.

4. The author himself provided a German *resumé* of the results of his research (pp. 187-200). For another presentation of his main theses in a Western language, cf. G. Ostrogorski, "Le système de pronoia à Byzance et en Serbie médiévale," *Actes du VIe Congrès d'Études Byzantines* (Paris 1950), 181-189. A French translation of the complete book is being prepared by Professor H. Grégoire.

legal status, since neither grant constituted the unqualified private property of the holder, but in the social status of the recipients of these grants (p. 10). Whereas the hereditary "military holdings" were given to free peasant soldiers, the non-hereditary *pronoiai*, large and small, were allotted to feudal lords (p. 12). It is true, of course, that the *pronoiai* were not given exclusively to military persons, especially in the initial phase of the institution, which was a period of rule by the antimilitary bureaucracy. On the other hand, private property and even church and monastic possessions were burdened with certain military obligations. But the military purpose of *pronoiai* asserted itself quite soon and remained dominant thereafter (p. 15). Ostrogorski is able to trace this development definitively back to the time of Emperor Alexius I Comnenus, (d. 1118) (p. 24).

The feature which distinguishes a *pronoia* from the *kharistikion*, a counterpart of the western *beneficium*, is not the social status of the holders but the ⟨450⟩ lack of any obligation of public, especially military, service on the part of a *kharistikarios*. This differentiating principle was somewhat blurred by the initial use of the term *pronoia* for the *kharistikion* type of grants (pp. 11-12; 14).

A *pronoia* differs from private property in that it cannot be sold, bequeathed or even donated to a church of monastery. The Serbian Law Code of King Stephen Dušan (14th century) explicity forbids such donations (pp. 93, 134). When, in late fifteenth-century documents, the term *pronoia* comes to mean any type of land holding, including private property (pp. 172, 174), we may consider the history of the institution closed. For it was the state which remained the owner of the *pronoiai* (pp. 44-7), and the distinction between the *pronoia* and private property provided the legal basis for many a law suit (p. 47).

The *pronoiarios* (This term for *pronoia* holder, although standard in Serbian and Venetian documents under the form *pronijar, proniarius,* is all but absent from the Byzantine sources; p. 12) derived his revenue not from the direct exploitation of the land but mainly from the seignorial rent paid in money by the peasants (pp. 58, 66, 70). (Their obligations, which varied according to the size of their families and their possessions, were determined by imperial plenipotentiaries and set down in a charter called *praktikon*. The sum total of the data of the *praktikon* constituted *posotês*, the basic rent, of the *pronoiarios*). As the rent is the essential advantage derived from the *pronoia*, it follows that any grant from which a *posotês* is obtained may be given as *pronoia*. Thus, documents of the thirteenth century refer to fishing rights bestowed *eis pronoian* (pp. 55-58).

The fact that the rent of a *pronoiarios* is determined exclusively in money is a feature peculiar to the Byzantine *pronoiai*, for peasants attached to the monasteries were subject not only to payments in money but also to assessments in kind and to corvées (p. 77). On the other hand, at least in the one known case, the rent paid by the *pronoia* peasants was somewhat lower than that required from peasants attached to the monasteries or to privately owned land. This was due, Ostrogorski surmises, to the obligation of military service lying not only on the *pronoiarios* but also on his peasants (p. 80, cf. pp. 120-1).

On the whole, however, the exploitation of the *pronoia* proceeded along the same lines as the administration of monastic and private property. The *pronoiarios*, although a conditional owner, was the real lord of his estate and of the peasants, who were called his *paroikoi* (serfs) (pp. 23; 47-48). These basic similarities, Ostrogorski maintains, derive from the fact that all three types of property operated within the framework of feudal economy (p. 75). Ostrogorski's stand on the much discussed question of the existence of a feudal economy in Byzantium is firm and positive. He admits Byzantium differed in political structure from the western medieval world in not knowing the ⟨451⟩ western hierarchical gradation of feudal dependencies;[4a] thus, all Byzantine *pronoiarioi* held their grants directly from the emperor. But for all that, *pronoia* is for Ostrogorski (pp. 37ff) a counterpart of the western fief[5]. He corroborates this observation by citing the often quoted lines of the Chronicle of Morea, which show that the western occupation did not bring about any upheaval in the social structure of former Byzantine territories after 1204. The conquerors strove to acquire new fiefs, and the Byzantine lords were readily reconciled to the new regime provided their *pronoia* holdings were confirmed. As for Ostrogorski's contention that the oath of fidelity was not known to the Byzantines (p. 37), this is now subject to some qualifications.[6]

4a. As Byzantium thus lacked one of the essential feudal characteristics, it is quite probable that Ostrogorski's conception (a conception implied rather than explicitly stated) of what constitutes the determining traits of a feudal system will be challenged by some critics. We may gloss over this point, for the differences would be more of a terminological than of essential nature and would affect but little Ostrogorski's definition of *pronoia*.

5. For an example of similar views, followed by unexpectedly different conclusions, cf. E. Gerland, "Kannten die Byzantiner das Lehnswesen?," *Eis Mnêmên Sp. Lamprou* I (1935), pp. 52-54. This note on *pronoia* might have been mentioned in Ostrogorski's introductory chapter, where earlier literature on the subject is reviewed (pp. 1-5).

6. N. G. Svoronos, "Le serment de fidelité a l'Empereur Byzantin et sa

of the military obligations connected with it (pp. 89-91f, 125). The rare departures from this principle required special imperial permission (p. 87f).

Even in the first known *documentary* testimony on *pronoia*, dating from 1162, there are mentions of litigations between *pronoiarioi* and a monastery. These litigations are a salient feature of the subsequent history of the institution. As the bulk of our source material comes from the Athonite monasteries it may be argued that this circumstance favored the preservation of cases of lawsuits between "pronoiatic" and monastic property. Our direct documentary evidence on *pronoia* is extremely scanty. Only one *praktikon* for a *pronoiarios* has as yet been published (cf. pp. 75ff), compared with about thirty similar documents issued to monasteries. Even that one charter has been preserved in the dossier belonging to a monastery. This circumstance is due to the fact that a certain number of *pronoia* lands came into the possession of the monasteries together with their deeds. (This characteristic of our evidence may sometimes be misleading. Thus it is difficult to subscribe entirely to Ostrogorski's thesis that the earlier attempts at secularization of monastic properties and their transformation into *pronoiai*, attempts undertaken by the Byzantine state in the first half of the fourteenth century, were a failure because all the charters which have been preserved indicate that the monks had regained their properties [p. 108]. It is to be assumed that documents containing conditions favorable to the monasteries were kept with special care.)

However, there is much more than the peculiarities of the transmission of source material behind our information on the struggle between the monasteries and the *pronoiarioi*. Up to the beginning of the fourteenth century the inroads made by each upon the other's possessions were dictated by the expansionist tendencies of both of these feudal groups. The state intervened as an umpire. But the collapse of Byzantine sovereignty in Asia Minor spurred Andronicus II, a friend of the monks, into attempting to secularize some monastic properties to use them for military purposes (Pachymeres, II, 390, 3-7, Bonn). We hear more of these state attempts in documents from the second quarter of the fourteenth century (pp. 105-108). Finally we learn from ⟨453⟩ a charter of the year 1408 that soon after the battle of Maritsa (1371) the Emperor, aware of the imminent Turkish danger, ordered the secularization of half the monastic properties and their transfer to the *pronoiarioi* (pp. 109ff). This measure remained valid at least as late as the year 1420 (p. 117). Even when the rights to certain properties were returned to the monasteries, the seignorial rent derived from them augmented by some other taxes, normally reserved for the state, went to the *pronoiarioi*

The institution of *pronoia*, itself a symptom of the feudalization of the empire, added in turn to the weakening of the central authority in late Byzantium. The history of the *pronoia* system is also the history of independence gained progressively by the *pronoiarioi*. The fiscal immunity granted a *pronoia* meant that, in addition to seignorial rent, the state transferred to the *pronoiarios* its rights to most of the additional taxes required from the peasants. It is true that three *kephalaia* ("chapters", i.e. tax categories: indemnities for manslaughter, rape and for the finding of a treasure) were in most cases excluded from the immunity granted. But sometimes even the levying of a part of these "taxes" was left to the *pronoiarios*. The authorities thus gradually delegated to him partial or complete judiciary powers over the inhabitants of his *pronoia* (pp. 78-9). But, as a rule, the immunity did not free him from the obligation of (military) service (p. 84). The final stage of this development is reflected in the charters granted the great humanist, Gemistos Plethom, and his sons (15th century). We see there how large *pronoiarioi* supplanted the state authorities and becane *kephalatikeuontes* (governors) of the territories they held as *pronoia* (pp. 123-6; for similar developments in Zeta, cf. p. 150). Even in this double capacity, however, they were duty bound to perform *douleia* (service, which, it is to be noted, is not explicitly stated as being military). In Byzantium *pronoia* as an institution never turned into unqualified private property (p. 127).

⟨452⟩ But the decisive step in loosening the control of the state over the *pronoiai* was made when the emporors allowed them to become hereditary. It is no coincidence that our first sources on this transformation date from the reign of Michael VIII Palaeologus (d. 1282), a usurper whose success depended on his ability to secure for himself the support of the landed aristocrary (p. 62f). Nor is it due to chance that especially rich information on the changing of the *pronoiai* into hereditary possessions should be forthcoming from the period of the civil war (1341-1354) between John V Palaeologus and John VI Cantacuzenus, for both contending parties tried to satisfy their supporters and win waverers over to their side (pp. 83ff). A hereditary *pronoia* was still not identical with private property; as a rule it could not be sold or donated and was passed on to the male heir so as to guarantee, Ostrogorski adds, the fulfillment

---

signification constitutionelle," *Revue des Études Byzantines* IX (1951; appeared in 1952), 106-142, esp. pp. 136ff (Not all the conclusions of Svoronos' article can be accepted.) Cf. for the XIV century, A. V. Solovjev, in *Byzantinoslavica* IV (1932), 164.

(charter of 1409, pp. 111ff). These actions of pious Byzantine authorities do not represent an anti-monastic attitude. When the state finally sided with the *pronoiarioi* in their struggle with the monasteries, it was motivated by the consideration that the *pronoia* system was the most dependable basis for the military organization of the empire (p. 119). The disastrous experiences of fourteenth-century Byzantium with mercenaries must have the strengthened this belief. But Ostrogorski passes much sterner judgment on the system. While he warns against underrating the military efficiency of the *pronoia* institution, he sees a source of weakness for the state in the centrifugal tendencies engendered by it and considers *pronoiai* inferior to the middle Byzantine system of military holdings, whose successor the *pronoia* had been (pp. 118ff; cf. 9f).

The *pronoia* system in the medieval Serbian state (date of the first documentary mention is 1299-1300) and in Zeta under Venetian domination (where most of the evidence concerns the fifteenth century, although the *pronoiai* seem to have existed earlier, cf. p. 152) is fundamentally similar to its Byzantine prototype. This is only natural considering the manner in which the institution penetrated into Serbia. The conquering Serbian rulers assumed sovereign rights over the state-owned *pronoiai* previously granted by Byzantine emperors. Whether or not the *pronoia* system was known in Serbia much before 1300, as Ostrogorski suggests (p. 128), it is from these conquered territories that it spread into original Serbian lands. Here, as in Byzantium, *pronoia* remained a grant given conditionally in exchange for military service. The military character of *pronoia* is more explicitly stated in Serbian documents than in Byzantine sources. However, along with similarities we encounter significant differences. Seignorial rent was paid by Serbian serfs mainly in kind (p. 137), marking the more primitive economy prevailing in Serbia. Also, the *pronoia* here has an exclusively hereditary character from the outset (p. 129, cf. 135, 147f, 169ff). Moreover, we learn of *pronoiarioi* in the service of churches, for which they are bound to perform military duties (p. 129; cf. 143). In 1361 we even see an Epirote landlord of western origin who has a *pronoiarios* of his own (p. 141f). Ostrogorski refuses to attach too much weight to this isolated instance but concedes that under Serbian rule some western "hierarchical" feudal characteristics were grafted onto what was originally a Byzantine formation (p. 143). It is also to western influences that Ostrogorski attributes the facility with which the Bosnian king transformed a *pronoia* into private property in 1458 (p. 149). In Zeta, under the rule of the Serenissima, the *pronoiarioi*, whose Byzantine counterparts normally en⟨454⟩joyed immunity, were obliged to pay certain taxes (p. 163). This measure, by which Venice symbolically asserted its sovereignty over its *pronoiarioi*, was also practiced by Serbian kings (pp. 136; 164). In both cases, the real payers were the serfs, as the *pronoiarios* directed only a part of his seignorial rent to the state treasury (p. 165).

The Serbian *pronoia* policies in the time of the great expansion under Stephen Dušan are, one might say, somewhat similar to the policies of the lords of the fourth crusade. The Serbian conquest resulted in the expropriation of some Byzantine *pronoiarioi* and the allotment of their holdings to Serbian lords. Later, when the conquest was consolidated, the Law Code of Dušan guaranteed their possessions to Serbian and Greek landlords alike. As, however, the highest positions of the administration and church were reserved for Serbians, the losers in the change were Byzantine great nobles and high dignitaries of the church (p. 139). In this context we may find a clue to the favorable treatment accorded the Athonite monasteries by Dušan, especially those involved in litigations with the Byzantine *pronoiarioi*. The King, who for reasons of prestige aimed at the title of protector of orthodoxy, had no interest in favoring Byzantine landlords (cf. p. 140). Moreover, his monastic policies resulted indirectly in the weakening of the class which militarily and socially came to be the backbone of the Byzantine empire.

Most of Ostrogorski's conclusions are based on minute and penetrating analysis of a great number of charters, since the narrative sources are, as he himself points out (p. 17), notoriously vague in their terminology. Ostrogorski uses the historians whenever necessary; he also exploits literary texts. Thus a sad *scène de genre* from the correspondence of John Apocaucus (thirteenth century) enables him to depict the status of serfs on a *pronoia* in the despotate of Epirus (pp. 59-61). With the help provided by Ostrogorski's scrutiny of the documentary evidence, it is possible to connect other vague references in narrative texts with the *pronoia* problem, to understand them better and often confirm Ostrogorski's findings. One almost wishes Ostrogorski had done more of this work himself, especially as his book is an attempt at an exhaustive treatment of the subject. This can be illustrated by a few examples.

The frequent use of charters which employ the term *stratiôtês* (soldier) for a *pronoia* holder constitutes Ostrogorski's main argument as to the military character of *pronoia* grants (pp. 24, 38, 51 and *passim*). This is necessary if he is to prove his point, since in Byzantine official documents the "services" required from the *pronoiarioi* are very rarely specifically said to be military. Moreover, to prove the participation of *pronoia*-serfs in military campaigns, Ostrogorski had to use a charter issued by a large "regular" landowner (p. 120f). If the *pronoiai* are military in character, it follows that the "soldiers" holding them belong to the upper class.

On this latter point fourteenth-century narrative sources are quite explicit. In Cantacuzenus' History *stratiôtai* appear as a special group within the armed forces and are generally associated with the "best citizens", nobles and ⟨455⟩ "senators". Thus we encounter the distinction between *stratiôtai* on one hand and "other armored warriors" and "lightly armed bowmen" on the other.[7] After his proclamation as Emperor in 1341, Cantacuzenus catered to the "powerful ones of the cities and... the soldiers".[8] The protostrator Synadenos, who plots in Thessalonica against the popular government, has confidence in the "powerful ones" and the "army" of this city.[9] In the social struggle of the forties, the pro-Cantacuzenian "army", mentioned along with the "best among the citizens," is opposed to "the people", the lower classes.[10] In 1343, the great constable Michael Monomachus, a loyalist, expects that "most of the army" and "other elements of the Byzantine aristocracy" will go over to Cantacuzenus.[11] Elsewhere, Cantacuzenus mentions the "soldiers" as belonging to the Byzantine upper class.[12] The

7. *Cantacuzenus*, II, 187, 17 Bonn: *to Pamphilon hama khiliois phrourounta stratiôtais tên te akropolin heterois hoplitais kai psilois toxotais hekaton*.

8. *Cant*., II, 162, 8-9: *idia te tous dynatous ton poleôn kai tous par' hekastois stratiôtas grammasin hypepoieito*. In this passage, do the "soldiers" form the suites of the *dynatoi*?

9. *Cant*., II, 233, 19-21: *ou monon hê stratia hoi êsan ouk oligoi, alla kai tôn politôn hoi dynatoi... hois etharrhei*.

10. *Cant*., II, 297, 21-298, 2: *eis dyo diairetheisai* (sc. each of the cities) *stratia men kai hoi alloi aristoi ton politôn... hoi de dêmoi...*

11. *Cant*., II, 371, 7-10: *stratias te gar to pleiston kai hoi alloi ton Rhômaiôn aristoi ekeinô* (sc. Cantacuzenus) *prosekhousin*. The great constable Michael Monomachus is of course identical with the *pronoiarios* Michael Monomachus, whose *praktikon* is the only published example of its kind. It is difficult to follow Ostrogorski who says (book under review, p. 81f, and *Byzantinoslavica* IX [1948], 295) that the goverment of John V *confiscated* Monomachus' possessions at Chantax during the early stages of the civil war. The sources know him as a reasonable but never wavering supporter of John V (in spite of Dölger's interpretation of *Cant*., II, 191, 16ff.: cf. *Eis Mnêmên Sp. Lamprou* I (1935), 27). The only authentic — if it is authentic — Greek document on the transfer of Chantax (Act *Zographou* no. XXXIB) speaks of Monomachus as of *oikeios doulos tês basileias mou* (1. 19), hardly a description of a disgraced person.

12. *Cant*., II, 506, 7ff: Cantacuzenus' enemies are *polemioi tôn para Rhômaiois aristôn pantôn, ou monon hoson ên eugenesin ên, alla... kai stratiôtais kai tois ton politeiôn hekastês poleôs proekhousin*.

anti-Zealot assembly summoned in Thessalonica by the son of Apocaucus consisted of "aristocrats, army, other most influential people."[13] When reference is made to different elements of the population of Berrhoia, the phrase goes: "not only the vulgar mob, but also the soldiers and quite a few from among the members of the senatorial class."[14] The "soldiers" and the "army" of these and other passages[15] are not ⟨456⟩ common soldiery or mere army "officers." [16] The meaning of these terms here is no less technical than in the documents. They describe the class of feudal knights (cf. the western use of *miles*), serving on horseback (to be inferred e. g. from Nicephorus Gregoras, 708, 22ff, Bonn). At least some of them derive their yearly rent (*Cant.*, II, 81, 15; II, 367, 19 Bonn) from revokable land allotments (*Cant.*, I, 164-5, and 167, Bonn: Andronicus III asks his grandfather not to dispossess the "soldiers" he rewarded with land bringing in a yearly rent of ten *chrysia.*[17]) They are forbidden to practice agriculture and commerce, (*Cant.*, I, 238, 6, Bonn).

That exploitation of peasants provided revenue to these "soldiers" is borne out by a passage of Demetrius Cydones' Lament for the Nobles Killed in Thessalonica (during the popular uprising of 1345). Describing the "death march" of the prisoners, when usual social relations were turned upside down, he says: "Here, the slave pushed before him his master... the rustic, the commander, the peasant, the soldier."[18] To make sense, the translation of the last words should be : "the serf, his landlord" or rather "his *pronoiarios.*"

---

13. *Cant.*, II, 573, 10-12: *ekklêsian... synagagôn ek te tôn aristôn kai tês stratias kai tôn allôn politôn tôn malista en logô.*

14. *Cant.*, III, 120, 11: *ou dêmôdê monon okhlon, alla kai stratiôtas kai ouk oligous tôn synklêtikôn.*

15. *Cant.*, I, 322, 22; II, 84, 6; 179, 16; 311, 16, 574, 15.

16. Mutafčiev, *Vojniški zemi*, p. 50, had to resort to this artifice in order to dissociate the *pronoia*-holding "soldiers" from the elusive army of peasant-soldiers he postulated for the thirteenth to fourteenth centuries.

17. This low rate of rent should not dissuade us from considering these ex-mercenary soldiers as newly-backed *pronoiarioi*. From charters we know of small *pronoiarioi* whose rent amounted to 10-12 *nomismata* only (Act Kutlumus no. 20). Narrative sources mention different classes of *pronoiarioi* (*Cant.*, II, 81, 16: *to misthophorikon tês stratias kai tôn ek khôriôn tas prosodous ekhontôn tous dynatôterous paralabôn...*).

18. Migne, PG CIX, col. 648D: *entautha doulos men ton despotên ôthei... ton de stratêgon ho agroikos: kai ton stratiôtên, ho geôrgos.*

In his *Life* of the Patriarch Isidorus, Philotheos Kokkinos describes at length but rather obscurely the litigations connected with settlements between the victorious supporters of Cantacuzenus and the partisans of the official regime who had appropriated the confiscated possessions of the former.[19] It was the "vessel" of the senatorial class and of the army which was most troubled in the aftermath of the civil war.[20] From historical sources (*Cant.*, II, 614, 13; III, 11, 5-15, Bonn; *Nic.*, *Greg.*, 790, 16-791, 16, Bonn), somewhat imprecise on this important point, we learn that the restitution of landed property (*agroi, ktêmata*) was also involved in the moderate terms of the settlement. This in itself would be inconclusive, if we did not know that during the civil war many a *pronoia* changed hands (p. 82f). It seems that a more precise meaning may be implied in the word "army" in Philotheos' passage, namely ⟨457⟩ that of "*pronoia* holders". If so, we gain literary confirmation for an *a priori* plausible belief that *pronoiai* were among possessions restored to some of the supporters of Cantacuzenus in 1347.

Ostrogorski's discussion of the secularization measures employed by the state in the fourteenth century, by which parts of monastic possessions were allotted to *pronoia* holders, helps us to reinterpret one important *ineditum*. Ever since Sathas and, after him, Tafrali published excerpts from Nicolaus Cabasilas' *Logos peri tôn paranomôs tois arkhousi epi tois hierois tolmômenôn*, this pamphlet has been considered by all scholarship (including Ostrogorski, cf. *Geschichte des Byzantinischen Staates* [1940], 371) to be not only an attack on the revolutionary zealots of Thessalonica but also the chief source for the reconstruction of the Zealotic social program. The main reason for this assumption must have been that the expropriation of monasteries and churches, fought against in Cabasilas' *Logos*, could be imputed only to revolutionaries and in no case to pious Byzantine authorities. The study of Cabasilas' text reveals that it is more than doubtful that these adversaries (ecclesiastical as well as lay) were the Zealots. Moreover, none of their actions differs from the official measures and usages of the government under Andronicus III, John V or even Cantacuzenus. Cabasilas accuses the authorities in particular of secularizing the revenues of the land (*khôrôn tokous*) bequeathed to the monasteries by pious donors, sometimes even of con-

19. *Vita Isidori* §§57-60, ed. A. Papadopoulos-Kerameus, "Žitia dvukh vselenskikh patriarkhov XIV v., svv. Afanasia I i Isidora I," *Zapiski ist.-fil. fak. imp. S.-Petersburskago Universiteta* LXXVI (1905).

20. *Ibidem*, p. 125, 4-5: *tarakhês to koinon tês politeias kai malista tôn tês sygklêtou kai tou stratou peplêrôto skaphos.*

fiscating the land itself and appropriating it or giving it with its peasants to "others" (e.g. *Par. Gr.* 1213, fol. 245v). The official explained their actions by defense needs (*stratiôtas... hoplisomen*, we shall arm the solidiers, *ibid.* fol. 246v).[20a] All of this sounds like a literary parallel to the documents discussed in the ninth chapter of Ostrogorski's book. We shall have to look elsewhere for the sources of the Zealotic program, for Cabasilas' work belongs to the class of documents illustrating the endeavors undertaken by the Byzantine state to ward off its military collapse.[21]

In some parts of Ostrogorski's work one misses a discussion of narrative passages which might be at variance with his thesis. Such is the obscure but important sentence of Pachymeres (II, 209, 9-13 Bonn, *sub anno* 1296; cf. also II, 69, 2-5) referring to the measures taken by Andronicus II to stall the Turkish advances in Asia Minor. In quite technical terms it seems to speak of a contribution (*syndosia*, cf. *Pach.*, II, 293, 9, Bonn, where it is mentioned among the tax exactions of the government; cf. also F. Dölger, *Aus den Schatzkammern des Heiligen Berges* [1948], note *ad* no. 4, 86, with references) ruthlessly imposed (*anedên teloumenon*, cf. *telein tina*: impose taxes on one) on the *pronoiarioi* and being equivalent to the *dekaton* of the *pronoia* (tithe, cf. Dölger, *ibidem*, note *ad* no. 31, 12). Of course, the *pronoiarioi*, hardpressed (*sphôn ekneurizomenôn*: for the meaning cf. *Pach.*, II, 209, I) passed ⟨458⟩ this burden onto their *paroikoi*. Thus we may encounter taxpaying *pronoiarioi*, whose existence Ostrogorski postulates in Serbian and Venetian-dominated territories only, in Byzantium as well.

If rigidly adhered to, Ostrogorski's very definition of *pronoia* excludes, at least for the thirteenth and fourteenth centuries, the possibility of the existence of non-military, let alone that of monastic, *pronoiai* (pp. 33, 69, 97, 103, 114). One would expect a refutation p. ex. of *Pach.*, II, 390, 3-7 Bonn, where both these types of grants are implied as existing. Cantacuzenus II, 63, 12, mentions members of the senatorial class and great nobles, along with the "soldiers," among *pronoia* holders. Ostrogorski's stand on this point might have to be qualified, for the charters themselves mention *pronoiai* or *oikonomiai* (synonymous with the former, cf. Ostrogorski, pp. 6, 36) of monasteries (*ibidem*, p. 69f). In the charters the formerly "pronoiatic" lands are said to be given to

20a. Cf. fol. 253r: *stratiôtas trephousin*; fol. 253v: *naus ektêsanto kai hopla kai stratiôtas*.

21. I have prepared the text of Cabasilas' *Logos* for publication.

monasteries under the same conditions as those formerly enjoyed by their *pronoiarioi*. The conditional character of the *pronoia* grants, as opposed to monastic property, which was supposedly always granted unconditionally, cannot be considered a sufficient argument against the existence of monastic *pronoiai*. At least in the eyes of the fourteenth-century officials whom Cabasilas opposed, monasteries (or churches) did not have unlimited right of disposal of some of their property, while retaining the revenues deriving from it.[22]

The few examples quoted above suggest that while official documentary material must remain the basis for every socio-economic study of Byzantium, one need not be deterred by what often seems vagueness in the narrative sources. Ostrogorski's valuable contribution could perhaps profit from more liberal quotations from them, even if these quotations would more often confirm than modify the results of his study.

Many passages of Ostrogorski's book are indirect polemics against Mutafčiev, to whom we owe the most thorough earlier investigation of the *pronoia* system. Indeed, in their polemical form, Ostrogorski's and Mutafčijev's theses are diametrically opposed. For the latter,[23] there is no analogy between the western *beneficium* and the *pronoia*. This institution should not, in his mind, be connected with military considerations and needs. For Ostrogorski the feudal military character of *pronoia* is its most important feature. But if one goes into the details of the argument, one notices not only that the material covered by both authors is much the same, but also that qualifying state⟨459⟩ments bring their positions nearer together. Mutafčiev admits that some *pronoiarioi* belonged to the military class.[24] He even grants that under Manuel Comnenus they constituted an essential element of the military organization.[25] He believes that in late Byzantium the soldiers of the middle Byzantine type co-existed with the military *pronoiarioi*.[26] " On the other

22. *Par. Gr* 1213, fol. 248: *kai pôs an eiê despotas autous proseipein hôn ouden exestin autous apodosthai oute kharisasthai, oute agron oute oikian out' allo tôn anakeimenôn tois hierois?* Answer of Cabasilas: *ei men oun kai khôrôn kai oikôn kai tôn allôn ktêseôn despotas einai khrê toutous nomizein, mêpô zêtômen; hoti de kai tôn karpôn kai tôn prosodôn hai tôn ktêsamenôn entolai kyrious einai boulontai ta men eis tên autôn hekastou khreian, ta d'eis to koinon analiskein, ouk an deoi logou deiknynai.*

23. *Vojniški Zemi*, p. 53.

24. *Vojniški Zemi*, pp. 41-51.

25. *Vojniški Zemi*, p. 48.

26. *Vojniški Zemi*, p. 61.

hand, Ostrogorski, while stressing that the overwhelming majority of *pronoiai* were of military character, concedes the existence of non-military holders of these grants and that of military obligations imposed on other types of property. He does not deny that a few peasant-soldiers existed in the late Byzantine empire. It would be misleading, however, to reduce the two standpoints to mere differences in stress. By refusing to recognize the *pronoia*-holding *stratiôtai* as the chief element of the late Byzantine armed forces, and by forcing the meaning "peasant-soldier holding" on the word *pronoia* of the literary texts, Mutafčiev did confuse the issue. On the whole, Ostrogorski's position will now have to be adopted by scholarship.

It is impossible, even in a lengthy review, to do justice to all of the new views presented by Ostrogorski or to note all of the textual and chronological corrections he makes in passing. His book is not only a final word on most aspects of *pronoia*, it is also a tribute to the achievements of international Byzantine research. For it is from recent publications of documents that Ostrogorski has drawn a considerable part of his material. The synthesis in which he has used these elements is the most valuable single contribution to the social history of Byzantium made in the past several decades.

III

'To the unknown Land': A Proposed Emendation of the Text of the Igor' *Tale*

Conjectures that can lay claim to certitude are few. But all conjectures, including the wrong ones, are of some importance: they provoke objections, and they often attract attention to passages which might otherwise have been neglected by scholars. Thus it is better to attack a sound text unjustly than to allow a corrupt passage to go unnoticed.[1] A *fortiori*, attempting a conjecture in one of the admittedly corrupt passages of the Igor' *Tale* should be considered a legitimate pastime. This passage was early made plausible by philologists, at first sight at least, and did not attain the rank of "obscure", a circumstance that may explain why it has been taken for granted up to the present time.

Verse 168 of the Tale (as numbered by the editors of *La Geste du prince Igor'*[2]), opening Jaroslavna's plaint, has come down to us in the following form:

Jaroslavnynъ (*-nymъ* A) *glasъ slyšitь* (*slyšitъ* P) *zegziceju neznaemь rano kyčetь*

The impression is that of a text deformed in several places. As it stood in PA[3], the passage was found to be in obvious need of emendation. For the first part of the verse, sure conjectures have been provided by past scholarship. Differences of detail aside, a virtual consensus now reigns that we must read here, as do the editors of *La Geste*,

1. I am paraphrasing the view of P. Maas, *Textkritik*, 2nd ed., 1950, 13.

2. *La Geste du prince Igor... Texte... sous la direction d'Henri Grégoire, de Roman Jakobson et de Marc Szeftel, assistés de J. A. Joffe* [= *Annuaire de l'Institut de Philologie et d'Histoire Orientales et Slaves*, 8, 1945-47]. This book will be referred to throughout as *La Geste*.

3. P stands for the editio princeps of the *Tale,* by Musin-Puškin and associates, which appeared in 1800; A, for the ms. copy of the now lost manuscript of the *Tale* executed in 1795-6 for the Empress Catherine II.

Jaroslavny mi ⟨sja⟩ glasъ slyšit',
'But what I hear is Jaroslavna's voice'[4]. It is to be noticed that the error in the text is one of omission[5].

But what about the remaining part of the passage? Here the crux is the word *neznaem'*, 'unknown', which hardly makes sense in the context. Several attempts at eliminating the difficulty were undertaken, the readings proposed being *neznaema* (Buslaev 1861; Korš 1909); *neznaemě*, a hapax (Potebnja 1878); *neznaemъju [!?]* (Barsov 1887); *neznaemoju* [i.e., 'like an unknown cuckoo'] (Jakovlev 1891); while Ohonovs'kyj (1876) retained the reading of PA and con⟨357⟩sidered it as an "indeclinable adjective"[6]. Finally, Nahtigal (1950) reads *neznaemъ*, i.e., 'unknown voice'[7].

Most recent editors show a preference for one or the other of the first two conjectures. *Neznaema* (adj.), which suggests a literal translation 'Jaroslavna the unknown', is adopted by V. Peretc[8] and by the sesquicentennial commemorative edition of the Soviet Academy of Sciences[9]. The editors of *La Geste* read *neznaemě* (adverbialized locative), literally 'in an unknown (unknowing?) way'.

It is superfluous to insist that the literal meanings of these conjectures do not provide satisfactory sense. Any epithet but 'the unknown one' is more fitting for the spouse of Prince Igor' himself and a daughter of Jaroslav of Halyč. No wonder, then, that the supporters of the reading *neznaema* had to endow it with a somewhat special sense ("not seen by anybody, lonely, i.e. Jaroslavna", Buslaev 1888[10]) or to adopt in effect the risky conjecture *neznaemoju*[11] for translation purposes

4. For this and all other English renderings of passages of the *Tale* the translation by S. H. Cross (*La Geste*, 151-179) has been used.

5. The scribe must have been puzzled by the "free" position of the reflexive pronoun, which in the later language became inseparable from the verb. To remove the difficulty, he eliminated the pronoun altogether.

6. Enumeration of these readings in V. Peretc, *Slovo o polku Ihorevim*, 1926, 305.

7. *Slavistična Revija* 3, 1950, 378f., 390.

8. *Op. cit.*, 123.

9. *Slovo o polku Igoreve*, ed. V. P. Adrianova-Peretc, 1950, 26 (the text of the Tale has been edited by D. S. Lixačev).

10. F. Buslaev, *Russkaja xrestomatija*, 1888, 100.

11. V. Peretc, *Slovo o polku Ihorevim*, 305, finds it paleographically inadmissible.

(*kukuškoju bezvestnoju*, i.e. 'one that has no news', Lixačev 1950[12]), and to skip the problem altogether[13].

The reading *neznaemě* seems more satisfactory[14]. But it, too, often has as a point of departure the idea of Jaroslavna's being unaware of the fate of Igor' and his army. This is borne out by the rendering of the word in the various "literal" translations of the Tale; *v bezvestii* (Jakobson), *dans son angoisse* (Grégoire), without tidings (Cross)[15].

Taken out of context, these interpretations are possible, if slightly strained. But if we read Jaroslavna's plaint (vv. 168-183) we find that she is far from being ignorant of the circumstances of Igor''s defeat. Not only does she know the place of the battle (v. 170), but she is informed about the direction in which the wind blew during the struggle of the two hosts (v. 174); she is aware that Igor''s army suffered from thirst during the fight (v. 183), not to mention her knowledge of the wounds inflicted upon Igor' (v. 171)[16]. Far from being "without tidings", Jaroslavna is credited by the author of the tale with a minute ⟨358⟩ knowledge of the circumstances of the battle in which her beloved lost his liberty: a fine touch in the portrait of the wailing wife, who, the reader is led to infer, must have avidly interrogated every survivor about the details of the disaster[17].

After these considerations, we might feel more free to depart from interpretations connecting the unclear *neznaemъ* with Jaroslavna, and to look for the cue to the meaning of the passage elsewhere. We shall find it in the text of the *Tale* proper.

---

12. *Slovo...*, ed. Adrianova-Peretc, 70-98.

13. In the commentary to our passage, provided on p. 461 of the work quoted in the preceding note, there is not even a mention of the fact that *neznaema* is a conjecture.

14. By coincidence, as will soon be seen. Of course, we will not consider this form as an adverbialized locative. Such a postulated form, derived from a passive participle and having an active (?) meaning, besides being a hapax, is not a satisfactory remedy. A. Potebnja, *Slovo o polku Igoreve...* (Voronež 1878; 2nd ed., Xarkiv 1914), p. 136, who does not comment on his own conjecture, takes it in a passive sense.

15. *La Geste*, 197, 71, 173.

16. Some of the details are confirmed by the Hypatian and Laurentian Chronicles; cf. *La Geste*, 118, 144.

17. According to the Hypatian Chronicle, only fifteen Rus' warriors escaped death. We may assume that Belovolod Prosovič, mentioned in the same source, who brought the tidings of the defeat to Great Prince Svjatoslav (then in Novgorod-Seversk land), was one of the survivors.

Now, the *Tale* (and the Chronicles) use a technical term to designate Cuman territories, strange and inaccessible; *zemli neznaemě, na polě neznaemě, neznaemoju stranoju, na nevědomu zemlju* 'unknown land, plain'[18] are the expressions that we encounter in this special sense. It therefore seems that this "unknown land" was originally mentioned by the *Tale* in v. 168, and I propose to read its second part as follows:

zegziceju ⟨zemli⟩ neznaemě rano kyčet'

'like a cuckoo, in the morn she sends her song to the unknown land'.

The closest parallel provided by the Tale is v. 29, where we encounter a rather similar situation of the sending of a message towards the Cuman land. Here it is the birdlike demon Divъ who takes the place of Jaroslavna: *Divъ kličet' vrъxu dreva: velitъ poslušati zemli neznaemě* 'Div cries in the crest of a tree: bids the unknown land give ear'... (there follows the enumeration of place names and territories under Cuman domination). Cf. also the *Tale*, v. 128, where the Cuman victory over the princes Rjurik and David is deplored: it was obtained *na polě neznaemě.*

In order to explain the omission of *zemli* in the verse under discussion, it is not necessary to remind ourselves of the omission of *sja* a few words earlier and to think of an "error cluster". We need only assume that a single letter fell out: the name of the letter Z in the Slavonic alphabet was *zemlja*. Therefore it was by means of this letter with an abbreviation sign above it that the word 'earth, land' was often written[19]. Consequently, the omission of the word *zemlja* could ⟨359⟩ and did happen easily in our ms. Thus v. 152, where we have *Trojani* P: *Zojani*

18. The *Tale*, vv. 29, 67, 128; for examples derived from the Chronicles, cf. *Slovo...*, ed. Adrianova-Peretc, 394. The same technical term was used to designate the Cuman nation. When the author of the *Poxvala* of Feodosij Pečerskij referred to the havoc wrought by Cuman incursions towards the end of the eleventh century, he said that cities of Rus' had been taken *ot jazyka neznaema*, 'by the unknown people'. Cf. D. Abramovyč, "Kyjevo-Pečers'kyj Pateryk", in *Vseukrajins'ka Akad. Nauk, Pamjatky movy ta pys'menstva davnjoji Ukrajiny* 4, 1930, 93. For a similar expression, cf. a Prologue-type Life of St. Constantine-Cyril, where we read that this apostle *azbukvy neznaemi sъstavi dobrě* 'skillfully composed an unknown [i.e. hitherto unknown, unfamiliar] alphabet,' Lavrov, *Materialy po istorii vozniknovenija drevnejšej slavjanskoj literatury*, 1930, 104.

19. V. I. Borkovskij, "O jazyke suzdal'skoj letopisi po Lavrent'evskomu spisku", in *Akad. Nauk SSSR, Izvestija komisii po russkomu jazyku*, I, 1931, 10, where we find, for example: *b̄e (= bože)... sozdavyi n̄bo (= nebo) i.z̄. (= zemlju).* Cf. also E. F. Karskij, *Slavjanskaja kirillovskaja paleografija*, 1928, 243.

A, can be restored only by reading, with the editors of *La Geste*, *z⟨emli⟩ Trojani*. To take an analogous case: in one of the opening sentences of the Zadonščina the comparison of mss. readings *tugoju i pečaliju pokryšasja*[20]: *tugoju zemleju i pečaliju i pokryšasja*[21] led R. Jakobson to a sure reconstruction: *tugoju zemlja i pečaliju pokryšasja*[22].

The postulated dative without preposition to designate direction in which the action takes place is of current usage in the literature of the time[23].

The new reading is in agreement with the deliberately and skillfully handled principal formal device of the Tale. *Zegziceju zemli neznaemě* produces (not to say restores) a nice alliteration[24].

In Jaroslavna's Plaint, the attention of the princess is centered on the region in which her husband suffered the defeat and where he is detained — Igor''s wife's thoughts turn to the Cuman Land. She wants to fly like a cuckoo down the river (v. 169); to dip her sleeve in Kajaly, the river of the defeat (v. 170). With her mind's eye, she encompasses the battlefield (vv. 174, 183); if she apostrophizes the Dnepr, she does so to stress that it flows through the Cuman land (v. 177). Jaroslavna asks the

---

20. Undol'skij ms. Cf. J. Frček, *Zádonština*... (Prague 1948), p. 2 of synoptic texts.

21. Ždanov ms. Text in S. K. Šambinago, "Povesti o Mamaevom poboišče", in *Imper. Akad. Nauk, Sbornik ORJ aS* 81:7, 1906, 104.

22. A similar case is found in another passage of the Zadonščina (Frček, *op. cit.*, p. 17 of synoptic texts), where the ms. of the Kirillo-Belozerskij monastery omits the word *zemlja*, preserved in all other mss. The reconstruction of the Zadonščina is currently being undertaken by Professor Jakobson.

23. J. Tymčenko, "Nominatyv i datyv v ukrajins'kij *movi", in Ukrajins'ka Akad. Nauk, Zbirnyk istor.-filol. viddilu*, 32, 1925, 31. Cf. E. F. Karskij, "Nabljudenija v oblasti sintaksisa Lavrent'evskogo spiska letopisi", in *Akad. Nauk SSSR, Izvestija po russkomu jazyku i slovesnosti* 2: 1, 1929, 32-33 (of course, with verbs of movement). The closest parallel to our text is found in the so-called Christmas Sermon of John of Damascus (ed. A. Nikol'skaja, "K voprosu o pejzaže v drevne-russkoj literature", *Sbornik statej v čest'... A.I. Sobolevskogo*, 1928, 435 f.): *i slavii i lastovica pripěvajut goram*. J. Tymčenko, *op. cit.*, p. 36, adduces examples from Ukrainian folklore texts of the type *kozak orlu promovljaje*.

24. On alliterations in the *Tale* cf. D. Tschižewskij, *Geschichte der altrussischen Literatur im 11., 12. und 13. Jahrhundert*, 1948, 343f. and 414-16. Cf. also the same author's "On Alliteration in Ancient Russian Epic Literature", in *Russian Epic Studies*, edd. R. Jakobson and E. J. Simmons, 1949, 125-130.

"lordly river" to float her husband back to her, so that she may not "at morn send him... her... tears down to the sea" (v. 180), i.e., again towards the Cuman Steppe. She sends her plaint from the ramparts of Putivl' to the place where her captive husband is held: *zemli neznaemě rano kyčet'*.

Thus the proposed emendation can be defended on linguistic, paleographic and poetic grounds. What is more important, it makes better sense.

IV

Барська Євангелія початку XVII століття в Pierpont Morgan Library

Замітка, що її тут поміщаю, має за мету показати, що на давні україніка можна натрапити в досить несподіваних місцях. Може вона також заохотить наших дослідників систематично переглянути давні рукописні збірки США і Канади, про стан яких можна собі легко створити уявлення на підставі каталогу Seymour de Ricci[1].

The Pierpont Morgan Library в Ню Йорку відома передовсім колекцією західних середньовічних та коптійських рукописних матеріялів і автографів. Знаходиться там і декілька "слов'янських" рукописів різного походження[2]. На один із них, M 794, досить старанним півуста⟨193⟩вом написану тетраєвангелію[3] варто звернути ува-

---

1. Seymour de Ricci, with the assistance of W. J. Wilson, *Census of Medieval and Renaissance Manuscripts in the United States and Canada,* I (1935), II (1937), III (1940). Далі ортографія цитат спрощена усуненням "омеги" й "малого юса," а також нехтуванням графічними варіянтами літер (два "у").

2. Наприклад молдавського. Пор. рукопис M 694, Seymour de Ricci, *Census...* II (1937), p. 1483. Очевидно, рукопис цей не писаний "по російськи;" його дата не 1471, а 1492 рік, і він ніяк не "австрійського" походження. В дійсности, ця тетраєвангелія написана на 37-му році панування Степана Великого, воєводи молдавського, за справою його жінки Марії, в одному з сучавських манастирів. Про це говорять 4 колофони (заміщені після кожної євангелії, на фол. 63*, 118*, 207* і 287). Ось для прикладу один із них (фол. 63*): Въ дни блгочьстиваго и |хълюбиваго гна стефана воеводы господа|ріи въсеи молдовлахіискои| земли и блгочестивои его |господжи еже она желаніемъ въжделѣвши любви хвых| словесь рачительница потъчщався даде и списа сіи тетраеѵгль. в лѣт ,за и съвръшися| мца сентеврія въ л днь. Формула желаніемь въжделѣвши відзеркалює давню балканську традицію. Вона нагадує вислів присвяти Збірника 1073 року, де про Святослава (себто первісно Симеона болгарського) сказано, що він 'въжделанниемъ зѣло въжделавъ' і т. д. Походження вислову біблійне: пор. кн. Битія 31:30; Лука 22:15.

3. Рукопис M 794 не згаданий ще в каталозі Seymour de Ricci. Він увійшов у склад Pierpont Morgan Library після 1935 року, і також не охоплений каталогом нових набутків бібліотеки, що зупиняється на числі 793. Див. Seymour de Ricci, *Census...* II (1937), p. 2318.

гу, бо це робота українського переписувача. Мова її повинна стати предметом окремого дослідження. Нам тут цікаво те, що можна не лише докладно з'ясувати її дату і походження, але навіть простежити її долю аж у дев'ятнадцяте століття.

На фоліо 356 тетраєвангелії читаємо таку дуже нечітку замітку:

Б лѣто о(тъ) воплощения Сп(а)сителева, ,а|хи м(ѣся)ца Авгу(с)та є дня. |Молимъ любови по духу бра(т) нее или отца вся|кого хотящаго прочитати сию книгу: ключи(т) |лися изобрѣсти погрешение, исправля(й)те,| а не клѣнѣте, но паче бл(агосло)вѣте, да негли вашими |молитвами прощению сподоблю(сь). Написася |книга сия во граде Кроля Его М(илос)ти Баре, грѣшнымъ |и недо(с)то(й)ным Өеодоро(мъ) из Любартова[3a]**.**

Знавці історії початку сімнадцятого століття може знатимуть, хто такий Федір із Любартова, що займався переписуванням священних книг у Барі і що закінчив нашу євангелію 5 серпня 1608 року. З палеографічного погляду важливе те, що в наших руках датований примірник, який засвідчує переписування книжки у Барі.

Книга написана була для приватного (мабуть і світського) замовця, в якого пробула вона дуже недовго. Про це дізнаємося з запису нового власника на долішніх берегах чергових аркушів євангелії, миж 8 і 25. Тоді, коли Федір, хоч і за доброю візантійською традицією колофонів називав себе "недостойним", проте старався писати по книжному, "раб божий" Ілля менш вагається вживати тодішньої світскої мови з її полонізмами: **Воимя о(т)ца и с(ы)на и с(вя)т(а)го д(у)ха. Сталося ко вѣчно(й) памети |на честь и нахвалу Г(оспо)ду Б(о)гу во т(р)о(й)ци и свето(й) пречи(с)то(й) божо(й) м(а)т(е)ри |и всѣмъ светымъ уго(д)никомъ божиимъ. Рабъ божий илия |из жоною Своєю** [нечітке слово: **анною?**] **и Сынами Своими ио|а|номъ и маркомъ,** [другою рукою додано: **и з невѣсткою своєю м(а)р(иею) и з оунуками га(в)рило(мъ) дмитро(мъ) и з унукою своєю вѣркою**] **будучи побужо(нъ) милостю с(е)рдца и учи(н)комъ хр(ис)тия(н)скимъ, |о(тъ)мѣнили сию душеполезную и сп(а)сительную книгу| Рекомую Ева(н)гелиє Тетро Зао(т)⟨194⟩пуще(н)е грѣховъ своихъ.| И придали єє до храму а(р)хистра** (sic?) **г(о)с(под)ня михайла|. В селѣ мигаловцах(ъ) повѣту ба(р)ского. За державы |Кроля Зикгмо(н)та Третєго А пановання на то(т) ча(с) кгулского| старо(с)ти на баре и воєводы руского року**

3a. При транскрипції церковно-слов'янські літери: Омега, Ук і Малий Юс передані як О, У і Я.

о(т) воплоще(н)я| сп(а)сения (sic? сп(а)сителя?) нашого Г(оспо)да И(су)са Х(рист)а ,ахθ На де(нь) с(вя)т(о)го а(р)хистратига михайла.| А хто бы ся важил о(т)дати или продати или яким(ъ) |колвекъ обычае(мъ) о(т) далити о(т) сего светого Храма выш(е) помен(н)ого.| Той нехай будет проклят в сий вѣкъ и во будущи(й) и посме(р)ти не ра(з)рѣше(нъ).| А з нами з выш(е) менен(н)ыми о содѣян(н)омъ суд будет(ъ) мѣв| предъ нелицемѣ(р)ны(мъ) судиєю во второє прише(с)твие,| єгда при(й)де(тъ) воздати комуждо по деломъ єго. Аминь.

Знов же невідомо, хто був побожний власник, що надав євангелію церкві Арх. Михаїла в Мигаловцях 8 листопада (день архангела) 1609. Зате постать Станислава Гульського (пом. в 1612 р.), що ним додатково датований запис, часто зустрічається в документах епохи. Він згаданий під 1592 роком, коли, бувши ще тільки барським старостою[4]. Виступає як член королівської комісії для дослідження непокоїв, що недавно сталися на Україні. У 1596 р., Гульський бере участь, на цей раз як кам'янецький староста, в іншій королівський комісії, що мала утихомирити Україну. Під час походу на козаків, що відбувся в цьому ж році, гетьман Жулкевський доручив Гульському звернутися з листом до козаків, що відступали, заохочуючи їх зупинитися і дати цим змогу полякам оточити козацьке військо[5]. Несецький згадує Гульського у своїм Гербовнику як руського воєводу. Попередник його на цьому становищі помер у 1603 р.[6]. Яка б не була роля Гульського в епізоді 1596 р., він був відомий, як давній і довірений приятель козаків та дбав про розквіт барського староства. Може це, поруч з природним нахилом до докладности в пів-офіційному записі, вплинуло на поміщення його прізвища на берегах євангелії.

Ялщо не помиляюся, без нашого рукопису ми нічого позитивного не знали б про село Мигаловці. Воно засноване мабуть під сам кінець XVI століття, бо нема про нього ще згадки в описі сіл і міст барського староства, складеному в 1565 році[7]. В 1668 р., трохи

---

4. Гульський став барським старостою в 1588 році. Про його діяльність і кар'єру, див. Michał Rolle, *Z przeszłości. Okręg Rowski, Starostwo Barskie, (do r. 1774)*, стт. 142-150, розділ Zasługi Stanisława Golskiego około Starostwa (1588-1612).

5. М. Грушевський, *Історія України-Руси*, VII (1909) ст. 184; 213; 227, з вказівками на джерела.

6. Niesiecki, *Herbarz*... I (1839-1846), p. 173.

7. Опис друкований в *АЮЗР*, ч. VII, том 2 (1890), стт. 215-272.

більше, як за півстоліття після "християнського вчинку" покровителів церкви Арх. Михайла, воно вже спорожніло. В огляді місцевостей, що належали в цьому році до барського замку, складеному для встановлення висоти чиншів із них, знаходимо згадку про те, що Mihołowce... (та інші села)... te wszystkie puste są[8].

⟨195⟩ Проте, євангелія уціліла з руїни Мигаловців. На початку XVIII століття знаходимо її в інших руках. Хоч і новий власник, чи хтось із його попередників, "отдаливши" книгу від храму Арх. Михаїла, теоретично міг чекати зустрічі з рабом Божим Іллею на страшному суді — а може якраз через те — він сам кидає анатему на особу, що наважилася б оспорювати його право розпоряджатися євангелією. На долишніх крисах аркушів 26-38 читаємо таке: **Ія семио(н) колчицки(й) све(с)ченик| загалски(й) даю сие Єва(н)гелие| мое власноє за жывота моего| о(т)цу Іоа(н)ну колчицкому| све(с)ченику бабицкому до рук его вла(с)ных вѣчними часы;| теды позволяю по (с)ме(р)ти жывота моего| о(т)цу Іоану колч(ы)цкому свесченику бабицкому: |волно ему хочет у себе держат Албо і продат| і гъде хоче(тъ) его обе(р)ну(ть),| а єжелибъ хтобъся важи(л)ся за тое| ева(н)гелие о(т)ца Іоана Ко(л)цы(ц)кого све(с)ченика баби(ц)кого ту(р)бова(ть), теды буде(тъ) Анаθема прокля(тъ)| прокля(тъ)**[9].

Не зважаючи на врочистість цього прокльону, мабуть знайшлися завидющі люди, що сумнівалися в праві Івана Кольчицького (Кульчицького?) на книгу, бо в 1720 році він мусів підтвердити його присягою (аркуш 38-39):

Здакрету поприсягу (sic) **о(те)цъ иоанъ| сию книгу** (sic?) **евангелие мѣ(ся)ця юна дна аї ро** (sic) **року ,ажк яко его е(с)тъ правъдивая божъ неналезы доцерквы загалско(й).**

Спір був остаточно вирішений на користь Івана польським священиком, мабуть зверхником Кольчицьких, яких треба б тоді вважати уніятами. Проголосивши присуд (пор. вислів lator sententiae), він приклав свою руку на аркуші 40 євангелії:

iako Lator Sentenciae podpisuię X Woyciech Siennicki Kanonik y officiat Kijowski Proboszcz Wielednicki Komisarz.

На черговий, і останній, запис власника довелося євангелії чекати понад ціле століття. На цей рай раз вона попала в руки росіянинові. Його викриває не стільки прізвище, скільки правопис (чи

8. *Ibidem*, ст. 529.

9. Хоч і непевне, проте ймовірне припущення, що й ця нова передача відбулася на барщині. На мапі Н. Moll'а з 1710 р. зустрічаємо село Bubycze, 15-20 англійських миль на південний захід від Бару.

його брак: пор форму **мьсица**). Запис зроблений на долішніх крисах аркушів 8-24, себто — хто хоче, може добачити тут певну символіку — на місцях замітки першого власника українського раба божого Іллі. Він звучить:

сия|книга| Крыловского (?) |житиля| Якова александрова |сына| чернова |своєю| рукою |подъписана| 1831го года |мьсица |августа |шестаго|дня.

Про обставини, за яких євангелія дісталася Чернову можна лише здогадуватися, пов'язуючи їх, наприклад, з польським повстанням 1830-31 рр., що пройшло не без відгомону на Поділлі і могло призвести до руїни власника книги, унiята.

V

Harvard Slavic Studies I

HARVARD SLAVIC STUDIES I. Edited by H. G. Lunt, M. Karpovich, A. B. Lord, J. B. Hoptner, W. Weintraub. Cambridge, Massachusetts: Harvard University Press, 1953. Pp. 396.

THE appearance of this publication, established by the Department of Slavic Languages and Literatures at Harvard University, is an important event in the progress of Slavic studies in this country. Although it will appear periodically, *Harvard Slavic Studies* is not, strictly speaking, a journal. Insofar as it may be guessed from the first number, the *Studies* will consist of collections of articles, some of which amount to small monographs. As stated in the preface, the an⟨888⟩nual's 'scope will not be limited to a consideration of any single nation, area, or historical period but will encompass the cultural problems of all the Slavic peoples throughout their history, the interrelations of Slavic cultures and the mutual influences between Slavs and the rest of the world'. About one-fifth of the first volume is devoted to mediaeval topics. The second volume, to appear early in 1954, will contain a much greater amount of material of immediate interest to the readers of SPECULUM.

The question of comparative Slavic literature has been the subject of lively debate in the past few decades. Discussed is not only the advisability of singling it out as an autonomous field of investigation (some deny its autonomy) but also (among those who grant its autonomy) the criteria which should serve as the distinctive marks for establishing this separate field (some have sought it in a postulated Slavic 'ethical realism' or in the characteristics of the 'Slavic soul'). Roman Jakobson's 'The Kernel of Comparative Slavic Literature' (pp. 1-71) is a plea on behalf of autonomy: he enumerates objective structural and historical factors binding the Slavic literatures together and outlines a program for the comparative study of Slavic literatures.

The author's principal theses may be summed up as follows: The Common Slavic (i.e., linguistic in the widest acceptation of the term) patrimony is the 'hero' (common denominator) of comparative Slavic literature. (1) The linguistic communality decisively moulded the formal side of various Slavic literatures, and conditioned like responses to like formal problems diachronically. (2) By comparing Slavic areas between which no direct intercourse can be assumed at an early stage (e.g., Southern Slavs and Northern Russians) it is possible to reconstruct several basic metric patterns of Slavic oral poetry, to tie them up with Indo-European metrics, and to show that these patterns 'break through' or are consciously adapted in single Slavic written literatures of later days. (3) What is known as Old Church Slavonic language and literature was intended for all the 'Slavic lands' by the Slavic apostles of the ninth century and, in its local 'recensions,' was felt as a common possession by the vast majority of mediaeval Slavs (including some of the West). Literary relations between the Balkan and the Eastern Slavs in the Middle Ages are a matter of general knowledge. But recent research (of which, may it be added, Jakobson is one of the protagonists) has definitively established that until the end of the eleventh century a lively literary and cultural intercourse existed between the western and eastern parts of the Slavic world. Thus we find Bohemian hagiographical texts either preserved in eastern Church Slavonic manuscripts or influencing hagiographical writings of Kievan Rus'; Kievan saints were worshipped in eleventh-century Bohemia while other saints were popular in the West and East alike. Such, for example, was the case of Panteleemon (or Pantaleon, p. 47 — it might have been added there that the cathedral of St Sophia in Kiev has an eleventh century fresco of the saint). The dissolution of the literary unity of Church Slavonic did not put an end to its influence. Its linguistic patrimony was put to use by such modern poets as the Russians Tred'jakovskij (eighteenth century), Puškin and even Majakovskij (twentieth century), and the Cyrillo-Methodian ideology, stressing the rights of ⟨889⟩ the vernacular, was alive (of course partly in connection with the pre-Reformation and Reformation movements) as late as the seventeenth century. (4) In subsequent centuries, inter-Slavic contacts continued unabated (it is true, mostly on a two-by-two basis). Literary interpenetration even led to the formation of linguistic hybrids, as in the case of Czech and Polish (sixteenth century: Polish was the receiving side), Polish and Ukrainian (sixteenth to seventeenth centuries, Ukrainian being the influenced partner) and Ukrainian and Russian (sixteenth to seventeenth centuries, when Russian absorbed many Ukrainian and indirectly Polish elements). The feeling of kinship among the Slavs 'from the Adriatic to the White Sea,' based on the fact of linguistic proximity, has often been noted by Slavic intellectuals from the sixteenth century on and has led to attempts at creating a 'universal' Slavic language, and, on the political level, regional or 'pan-Slavic' unions.

This is a mere skeleton of the author's views. The illustrations provided to substantiate them, in part synthesizing Jakobson's own research of the past quarter century, are revealing in their acuteness and richness. It would take a modern Zoilus to try to point out some trifle. Thus, when the influence of grammatical gender on poetic imagery is discussed and the fact stressed that 'death' (feminine in Slavic) is depicted as a woman in Slavic literatures, while it appears as a man, for example, in German, it is perhaps worth mentioning that other associations may prove more decisive. In T. Ševčenko's poem *Ponad polem ide* (1847), where the word *smert'* is never mentioned, death appears as *kosar* (masc.), a man-reaper (cf. the English Grim Reaper), although women harvesters are a frequent feature in Ševčenko's poetry.

Unassailable as Jakobson's observations are, it may still be asked whether they alone are sufficient justification for comparative Slavic literature as an autonomous discipline. What seems essential for setting up boundaries of a field of comparative study are not only similarities and a certain number of discrepancies within the field, but also the realization that a large number of similarities selected as relevant are limited to the field — in scholastic terms, specific differences. Slavic linguistic affinity is undoubtedly one such relevant similarity. But not all of the more detailed criteria discussed by the author are. His mere use of time-honored terms of rhetoric in analyzing the effects of the similar 'verbal material or verbal art' (etymological figure, paregmena, polyptota) proves that we are dealing with general categories, by no means peculiar to Slavic literatures. Etymological figures are a device also used in primitive verbal art. But their abundance in Old Church Slavonic literature is also to be brought into connection with Byzantine letters, where they are a burdensome heritage of the second Sophistic. Hundreds of examples like John Chrysostom's ἵνα τῷ λόγῳ εὐλόγως χειραγωγούμενοι μηδὲν ἄλογον πράξωσιν might be easily provided at a moment's notice. Of course Jakobson's quotation (p. 10) from the Kievan Missal, where we find an etymological figure, while the corresponding Latin passage has none, is of great importance. But the frequent recurrence of *s'vět's'věščati* ('to hold counsel') in the fourteenth-century translation of the Byzantine writer Manasses is determined by the βουλὴν βουλεύεσθαι of the original. The device is also known in mediaeval Latin ⟨890⟩ poetry. In a twelfth-century poem taunting the avarice of the Roman Curia, we read: 'Romam avaritiae vitet manus *parca* | *parcit* danti munera, *parco* non est *parca*' (Utar contra vitia). As for polyptoton as a *poetic* device, Ps.-Herodian (ed. Spengel, *Rhet. Graeci*, III, 97) gives examples from Archilochus and Anacreon. Thus, while it is clear that such devices are alien to Western Indo-European languages which gave up the inflectional declensions (p. 15), it is also true that they are familiar to non-Slavic literatures whose languages retained flection. It is noteworthy that Bulgarian examples (flection has atrophied in Bulgarian) are seldom used in Jakobson's discussion.

While some of the author's observations apply equally well to certain non-Slavic literatures, some are valid with respect to only a few (or even a single) Slavic ones. It should be borne in mind that Russian is the only one of the modern Slavic languages where poetic adaptations of sacred texts can follow the Church Slavonic form rather closely, since it alone advantageously preserved its 'hybrid' character. As Jakobson remarks (p. 50), other Slavic languages have either shed their Church Slavonic elements, as the 'renaissances' of their peoples coincided with the romantic movement and its predilection for the popular tongue, or have lost the traces (if any) of their contact with Church Slavonic literature at an early stage. While in Tred'jakovskij's and Puškin's paraphrases (p. 51) we look for Russian words, lost among Church Slavonisms, the situation is reversed when we read T. Ševčenko's imitations of the Psalms or the Prophets. There, words like *vbohoduxi, vozplač, vesi, kryvodušije* are comparatively rare adornments embedded in Ukrainian vernacular. A mere mention of the sixteenth-century Pole Kochanowski's *Psałterz Dawidów* must suffice here to suggest the difference in treatment.

A postulate of comparative Slavic literature based on the common Slavic patrimony as its 'hero' is the more valid the further back we retreat towards this patrimony. Therefore Jakobson's observations are most illuminating and cogent when he speaks of the oral literature and the Church Slavonic written tradition. But obviously literature is more than the 'linguistic matrix out of which it is fashioned.' From the outset, the culture of Slavic peoples has borne the imprint not of the Greek and Latin cultures, but of the 'Latin' and 'Greek' mediaeval cultures. The Slavic peoples developed their literatures precisely at a stage when it dawned upon Rome and Byzantium that an unbridgeable gap seemed to have developed between them. As time went on, the gravitation towards the western and eastern centers respectively went at the expense of inter-Slavic contacts. Łukasz Górnicki's *Dworzanin Polski* (sixteenth century) is an important source for studying Czech-Polish cultural interpenetration (both countries were largely Catholic) but Górnicki's source is an Italian Renaissance work. And if we look for its contemporary parallels in the East, we find none, unless we want to consider the Muscovite *Domostroj* as such. The mere oddness of such a suggestion points to the latter's different inspiration and the different social set-up it reflects. Further discussion would force us beyond the mediaeval period.

Comparative Slavic literature is not an autonomous pre-existing field of study which has to be discovered, but a new way of looking at the existing Slavic liter⟨891⟩atures. The problem involved is methodological. If, to be justified, the comparative approach must enable us to see things which would escape our attention otherwise, then Jakobson's new vistas constitute a brilliant proof that such an approach is worth exploring. The author himself states that he has presented a 'kernel' of the question and implies a program of investigation (pp. 68 f.). It would be wise to follow his suggestions, for only after their elaboration will we be able to give a well-founded answer to the question of whether establishing comparative Slavic literature as a separate field is a methodological necessity, or only a didactic convenience.

There is no longer any need for defending the greatest work of Rus' literature, 'The Igor' Tale.' To the philologist, the mere comparison between the words of the Tale (vv. 32 and 47) *O Ruskaja zemle uže za šolomjanem esi* ('Oh Russian land, already art thou beyond the hill!') and the nonsensical deformation *Ruskaja zemlja, toti est kak za Solomonom carem pobyvalo* ('Russian land, it is unto you as it was in King Solomon's time') in the *Zadonščina*, a late fourteenth-century *pastiche* of the Tale, well attested by several manuscripts, is in itself a sufficient proof of authenticity. Still, the Tale appears as a jutting rock, lone and, but for *Zadonščina*, unheeded in the literature of the Kievan and Muscovite periods. Recently, Roman Jakobson undertook to prove that in its spirit, the Tale shares common traits with European literature of the twelfth century (SPECULUM, XXVII [1952], 45 ff.). A. V. Solov'ev's 'New Traces of the Igor Tale in Old Russian Literature' (pp. 72-81) is another attempt to free this work from its apparent isolation. The article lists and partly discusses the four known or already postulated cases of the familiarity of writers and scribes of the thirteenth to the sixteenth century with the Tale (*Slovo o pogibeli russkyja zemli*, the short reminiscence of 1307, *Zadonščina*, the now-lost sixteenth-century manuscript of the Tale) and adds a new one, the *Life of Jaroslav III*, written soon after 1246 and preserved (with modifications) in the *Stepennaja Kniga* (dating from the sixties of the sixteenth century). In a passage going back to the original thirteenth-century form of the *Life*, the Kursk people, proverbially despised in contemporary literary works, are unexpectedly referred to as *slavnii Kurjane*, glorious people from Kursk. The Tale is the only other work which refers to them as *svědomi kmeti*, glorious warriors. Also, the *Life's* reference to *slavnye rěki Dněpra*, the glorious Dnieper River, a formula not used elsewhere, has its parallel in the Tale's *Dněpr-Slovutič*. Solov'ev's thesis is plausible, provided the 'original' part of the *Life* is really free from later rhetoric. The parallels to the Tale, adduced from the *Slovo o pogibeli* are suggestive. The expression *železnymi voroty*, however (also occurring in *Zadonščina*), may have been inspired by the 'iron gates' by which, according to the 'Revelation' of Methodius of Patara, Alexander the Great shut off the bad people in the mountainous regions of 'the North' (ed. Istrin. p. 89; ed. Tixonravov, pp. 259, 273). That *Slovo o pogibeli* is a separate epic work must remain a hypothesis. The new manuscript discovery, where it appears as a preface to the *Life* of Prince Alexander Nevskij, should make us cautious. In Solov'ev's opinion (p. 80, n. 24), which is also that of the present reviewer, *Zadonščina* was written before 1383.

⟨892⟩ The typography of the first volume of the *Studies* is impeccable. Only two errors were noted: on p. 56 read *gmatwanina*, p. 79, n. 22, read *Bibliograf*, V, for ''Bibliografija, I.'

The other articles of the volume which fall beyond the period covered by SPECULUM, will only be mentioned. They are: D. Čiževsky's 'Comenius' *Labyrinth of the World*: Its Themes and Their Sources' (a very erudite investigation, dealing mostly with the antique — and a few mediaeval — sources of this baroque writer; the *Labyrinth* appears as a polythematic work, contrary to views held by previous scholarship). 'Adam Mickiewicz, the Mystic-Politician,' (Wiktor Weintraub), 'The Czechs on the Eve of the 1848 Revolution' (O. Odložilík), 'Russian Pan-Slavists and the Polish Uprising of 1863' (M. B. Petrovich) 'The Art of Ivan Bunin' (Renato Poggioli), 'The Letters of Maksim Gor'kij to V. F. Xodasevič' (Xodasevič, Yakobson, McLean), 'Marxist Theory in Czech Literature' (M. Součková), 'A Survey of Macedonian Literature' (H. G. Lunt) (where the mediaeval background is traced on the first three pages).

VI

A Neglected Byzantine Source of Muscovite Political Ideology

Poèty naši prozrevali značenie vysšee monarxa, slyša, čto on neminuemo dolžen, nakonec, sdelat'sja ves' odna ljubov', i takim obrazom stanet vidno vsem, počemu gosudar' est' obraz Božij, kak èto priznaet, pokuda čut'em, vsja zemlja naša...

Tam tol'ko iscelitsja vpolne narod gde postignet monarx vysšee značenie svoe—byt' obrazom Togo na zemle, kotoryj Sam est' ljubov'.

N. V. Gogol'*

It has long been a commonplace of historical writing that the Byzantine ideas on the character of imperial power influenced the political thought of the Kievan State and later, considerably more, the ideology of Muscovite Russia.[1] It is much more difficult to show — especially for the earlier period — precisely what this influence was, through what channels it passed, what the Byzantine literary models were which found their way into the works of the Kievan and Muscovite periods, and, finally, at just what time. The ⟨142⟩ chief obstacle is the vastness of the Byzantine and Slavic fields, but a recent article has shown what stimulating results

* "Our poets have discerned the highest significance of the monarch, sensing that he must inevitably become, at last, wholly and uniquely love. Thus it will become apparent to all why the sovereign is the image of God, as our entire land acknowledges, hitherto by instinct...
"The people will be entirely healed only where the monarch attains his highest significance — to be the image on earth of Him Who is Himself love." "O lirizme našix poètov," *Sočinenija*, ed. N. Tixonravov, IV (1889), 46, 47.

1. The literature on the subject is too vast to be adduced here in detail. The most recent publications in English which may serve as bibliographical introduction are the two following: William K. Medlin, *Moscow and East Rome* (= *Études d'histoire économique, politique et sociale,* I) (Geneva, 1952) — not always reliable — and D. Stremoukhoff, "Moscow the Third Rome: Sources of the Doctrine," *Speculum*, XXVIII (1953), 84-101. Also the well-written book by H. Schaeder, *Moskau das Dritte Rom* (Hamburg, 1929) contains a long list of works consulted by the author.

may be produced by collaboration between a Byzantine and a Russian historian. The findings, or rather the rediscoveries, made there will provide a point of departure for some remarks on the fate of quotations from a Byzantine political theorist of sorts in Kievan and Muscovite literature.

E. H. Kantorowicz, assisted by M. Cherniavsky, has shown[2] that a passage of the Laurentius Chronicle (*sub anno* 1175, where the murder of Prince Andrej Bogoljubskij is described), which asserts in substance that "though an Emperor in body be like all other, yet in power he is like God," has its exact counterpart in a Greek sentence, commonly attributed to Philo the Jew. Here are the texts:

est'stvom bo zemnym podoben est' vsjakomu čelověku cěsar', vlastiju že sana jako Bog. Věšča bo velikyi Zlatoustec' těmže protivjatsja volosti, protivjatsja zakonu Božiju.[3]	τῇ μὲν οὐσίᾳ τοῦ σώματος, ἴσος παντὸς ἀνθρώπου ὁ βασιλεύς, τῇ δὲ ἐξουσίᾳ τοῦ ἀξιώματος ὅμοιός ἐστι τῷ ἐπὶ πάντων Θεῷ.[4]

The complete correspondence between the two maxims is beyond doubt. What remains to be seen is how this piece of Greek wisdom spread into the Suzdal' Principality — where this passage was written — and exactly where it originated.

The Philo fragment reproduced in the text of the Chronicle is quoted by Kantorowicz from a collection of maxims gathered from earlier works of this type by an eleventh-century Byzantine monk, Antonius.[5] This kind of collection went under the name of Μέλισσα, the

2. E. H. Kantorowicz, "Deus per Naturam, Deus per Gratiam," *The Harvard Theological Review*, XLV (1952), 269, n. 55.

3. *Polnoe Sobranie Russkix Letopisej* I, 2nd ed. (1927), p. 370. The "message" of John Chrysostom seems to consist, for the author of the excursus, of Rom. 13:2. Some modern scholars have connected it with the preceding words and referred to a passage in Chrysostom's III Homily on Rom. 13:1. This attempt barred the way to the correct identification of the source of the excursus. Cf. H. Schaeder, *Moskau das Dritte Rom*, p. 46, n. 1, taken over by Medlin, *Moscow and the East Rome*, p. 57, n. 2.

4. Antonius called Melissa, p. ex. in Migne, *Patr. Graeca*, CXXXVI, col. 1012B: "By the essence of his body, an emperor is like any man. Yet in power of his office, he is like God, ruler of the All."

5. That there never was an Antonius, Melissa by name, has been known at least since Coxe; cf. R. Dressler, "Quaestiones criticae ad Maximi et Antonii

Bee. Antonius was not the only compiler of a *Bee*; at least three ⟨143⟩ other recensions of the Byzantine Μέλισσα have come down to us.[6] One of them (not that of Antonius) was translated into Church Slavonic. What is more important, the translation was made in Kievan Rus'.[7] Although by their very nature these anthologies fluctuated in their arrangement and contents, a great number of maxims are common to all of them. Accordingly, the Kievan *Bee* (*Pčela*) contains the sentence on the Divine nature of the Emperor's office:

> Plot'skym sušč'stvom raven est' vsěm čelověkom cěsar', vlastiju že sanovnoju podoben est' Bogu vyšnemu. Ne imat' bo na zemli vyš'šago sebe, *etc.*[8]

This Kievan *Pčela*, then, or some collection containing excerpts from it,[9] is the immediate source of the passage in the Laurentius Chronicle and such other chronicles as either share its source for the part comprising the year 1175[10] or have inserted the excursus on the murder of Andrej Bogoljubskij into their otherwise different narrative.[11] In the chronicles the saying was not copied verbatim. *Plot'skym* has been replaced by *zemnym*, possibly under the influence of *na zemli* of the following sentence, and *podoben est'* is connected with man instead of God. This

Gnomologias spectantes...," *Jahns Jahrbuecher... Supplementband*, V (1864), 311-314.

6. M. N. Speranskij, *Perevodnye sborniki izrečenij v slaviano-russkoj pis'mennosti. Issledovanie i teksty* (Moscow 1904) [also in *Čtenija v imp. obšč. istorii i drev. rossijskix pri Mosk. Univ.*, CXCIX (1901); CCXII (1905); CCXIII (1905)], p. 155ff., and especially p. 216ff. Speranskij's somewhat longwinded argument is well summarized in an otherwise disappointing book by S. A. Ščeglova, "Pčela po rukopisjam kievskix bibliotek," in *Pamjatniki drevnej pis'mennosti i iskusstva*, CLXXV (1910), 13ff.

7. M. N. Speranskij, *Perevodnye sborniki...*, p. 305ff.; 329.

8. V. Semenov, "Drevnjaja russkaja Pčela po pergamennomu spisku," *Sbornik Otd. Russ. Jaz. i Slov. Imp. Akad. Nauk*, LIV, 4 (1893), 111.

9. Perhaps similar to the later *Měrilo pravednoe*, see below.

10. These are in the first place the Radziwill Chronicle, the *Akademičeskij Spisok* and the *Letopisec Perejaslavlja Suzdal'skogo*. The readings of the first two may be conveniently reconstructed from the apparatus of the 1927 edition of the Laurentius Chronicle, cf. above note 3; for the *Letopisec Perejaslavlja Suzdal'skogo*, cf. the ed. by K. M. Obolenskij (Moscow, 1851), p. 84.

11. The Hypatian Chronicle, ed. of the Archaeographical Commission (1871), p. 402.

gives the impression of a quotation from memory, and perhaps indicates that at least certain parts of the *Pčela* had become familiar to learned scribes of Rus' by the time the ex⟨144⟩cursus on Andrej Bogoljubskij was composed. The original form of the *Pčela* quotation in the excursus must have been closer to its immediate source than is the text of the Laurentius Chronicle. Towards the end of this passage, the Hypatian Chronicle reads *vlastiju že sana vyš'ši jako Bog*, "By the power of his office he is higher than God," which remains a blasphemy in spite of the editors' efforts to save the situation by putting a comma after *vyš'ši*. In view of the *Bogu vyšnemu* of the *Pčela*, something like *vlastiju že sana jako Bog vyšnii* has to be postulated for the original text of the *excursus*.

The story of Andrej Bogoljubskij's murder, perpetrated in 1175, seems to have been incorporated into a historical work which was sponsored by Bogoljubskij himself and which was completed two years after his death.[12] In any case, it presents such a wealth of detail that it must have been written very soon after the event. M. N. Speranskij, in his lengthy considerations on the date of the translation of the *Pčela*, proposed either the late twelfth or the thirteenth century.[13] A more precise dating is now possible, as the passage of the excursus furnishes the year 1175 or 1177 as the *terminus ante quem* for the appearance of the Church Slavonic *Pčela* in Vladimir on the Klaz'ma. How much earlier than 1177 the Μέλισσα was translated must remain a matter of conjecture. If the supposition that the author of the excursus quoted from memory is true, the translation may have been in use for quite some time before that date.[14]

It is known that towards the end of the twelfth century — ca. 1193, if one adopts the opinion of M. D. Priselkov[15] — another quotation from the *Pčela* was introduced, this time with an indication of the

12. On this point, cf. D. S. Lixačev, *Russkie letopisi* (Moscow-Leningrad, 1947), p. 429, who sums up the results obtained by M. D. Priselkov, "Lavrent'evskaja letopis' (istorija teksta)," *Učenye zapiski Leningr. Gos. Univ.* no. 32 (1939).

13. M. N. Speranskij, *Perevodnye sborniki*, p. 305ff.; cf. p. 315.

14. M. V. Šaxmatov, *Opyty po istorii drevne-russkix političeskix idej* I. *Učenija russkix letopisej domongol'skogo perioda o gosudarstvennoj vlasti* (Prague, 1927), appendix, has collected parallels between a series of passages from Rus' chronicles and chapter nine of the *Pčela, O vlasti i knjaženii*, "On Power and Rulership." The few quite convincing parallels in Šaxmatov's list date from 1175 and later years.

15. M. D. Priselkov, *Učenye zapiski Leningr. Gos. Univ.*, no. 32 (1939).

source, into a historical work compiled in Vladimir. This work, among others, has been incorporated into the *Letopisec Perejaslavlja Suzdal'skogo* which notes under the year 1186: *jakože v Bčele glagolet':* ⟨145⟩ *bran' slavna luče mira skudna, s lživym že mirom živušče veliju pakost' zemljam tvorjat'.*[16] The fact that this *Letopisec* is the only one to give the source of its quotation correctly, while all the other chronicles reproducing the same recension (*svod*) give the vague *jakože prorok glagolet'*, should be well kept in mind. This one instance should suffice to prove the *Letopisec*'s high value not only for the reconstruction of the *Letopis' Perejaslavlja Suzdal'skogo* (= *Radziwill Letopis'* in modern terminology[17]), but also for ascertaining the original form of the recension (of 1193?) from which a part of the Laurentius Chronicle is derived.

The saying on the divine character of the emperor's office is attributed by the *Pčela* not to Philo, but to "Agipitos."[18] This is by no means an innovation of the Church Slavonic text. While no edition of the Μέλισσα is yet available, it is known that at least the MSS representing its so-called "long" recension make Agapetus the author of the maxim.[19] I do not know on what authority, except that of editions of Antonius, it found its way into Mangey's and Richter's collections of Philo's fragments[20] and even into a recent treatise on Philo's political theory.[21] It must be said in Antonius' defense, that he transmits the maxim anonymously. A cursory survey of his edition by Gesner[22] shows that

16. K. M. Obolenskij, *Letopisec Perejaslavlja Suzdal'skago* (Moscow, 1851), p. 99.

17. Cf. Lixačev, *Russkie Letopisi*, p. 434 and 436.

18. M. V. Šachmatov (*Opyty*, p. 160, n. on p. 162 and p. 561) quotes this passage from the *Pčela* and compares it with the Laurentius Chronicle. It is not clear whether he realizes who "Agipitos" was. It is noteworthy that although both Medlin, *op. cit.*, pp. 23-24 and V. Val'denberg, *Drevnerusskie učenija o predelax carskoj vlasti* (Petrograd, 1916), pp. 59-61 give long extracts from Agapetus, neither of the authors established the connection between the Deacon of Constantinople and the writings discussed in the present article.

19. M. N. Speranskij, *Perevodnye sborniki*, p. 237.

20. Thomas Mangey, Φίλωνος τοῦ Ἰουδαίου τὰ εὑρισκόμενα ἅπαντα... II (1742), p. 673, in the chapter "ex Antonio." Richter, *Philonis... opera*, V (1828), p. 235 copies Mangey.

21. E. R. Goodenough, *The Politics of Philo Judaeus* (New Haven, 1938), pp. 99-100, with conclusions on Philo's ideas drawn from the passage in question and a reproach directed against J. Rendel Harris for having omitted it from his collection of Philo's fragment.

22. On the three editions by K. Gesner, cf. R. Dressler, *Quaestiones criticae*, p.

the *lemma* "Philonis" there stands in the margin of the Latin translation of the saying: rather flimsy grounds for determining the authorship of the Greek text. The ⟨146⟩ maxim of the Μέλισσα and Antonius figures verbatim as chapter 21 in Deacon Agapetus' Ἔκθεσις κεφαλαίων παραινετικῶν.[23] Of course, this is not the only chapter of his *speculum principis* which entered into gnomic collections under the guise of Philo. Thus, to quote some examples, all the three "unidentified" passages of Harris' edition of Philonic fragments[24] coincide in full with the three respective chapters of Agapetus, two of which are also given as Philonic by the Μέλισσα.[25]

It would be idle to adduce detailed arguments proving that these "Philo" fragments also found in Agapetus are spurious and refuting an imaginary objection that they might be genuine Philonic passages taken over both by Agapetus, who concealed his borrowing, and, e.g., the Μέλισσα, which preserved the name of the author correctly. Not that Agapetus excelled in originality; many a source of his sometimes platitudinous precepts, sources ranging from Isocrates to St. Basil, has been identified.[26] But he had the ambition to be a brilliant writer and to

---

315ff. I was able to use only the last one, of 1609. The Migne text is a reprint from Gesner.

23. Most conveniently accessible in Migne, PG, LXXXVI, 1, col. 1163-1186. In all subsequent quotations from Agapetus, the Migne text will be used.

24. J. Rendel Harris, *Fragments of Philo Judaeus* (1886), pp. 104-105: "τοιοῦτος γίνου" = Agap. 23; "ὁ μὲν Θεὸς οὐδενὸς δεῖται" = Agap. 63; "πλέον ἀγάπα" = Agap. 50. [I see, after the completion of the present article, that K. Praechter, *Byzantinische Zeitschrift*, XVII (1908), 153, n. 2 has already identified a number of "Philonic" fragments of Antonius as borrowed from Agapetus.]

25. M. N. Speranskij, *Perevodnye sborniki*, pp. 232, 235.

26. K. Krumbacher, *Geschichte der byz. Litteratur* (2nd ed., 1897), p. 457; K. Praechter, *Byzantinische Zeitschrift*, II (1893), 455-458. Of course K. Emminger, *Studien zu den griechischen Fürstenspiegeln*, II, III (Munich, 1913), p. 49, n. 60 may be right in assuming that Agapetus took the royal road to erudition and found all his many sources in one florilegium which he had at his disposal. But it is also possible to think of several florilegia as Agapetus' sources. One of them may have been John Stobaeus (fifth century), who, among others, quoted the Neopythagorean theorists on kingship, Ecphantos, Diotogenes and Sthenidas. Compare Louis Delatte, *Les Traités de la royauté d'Ecphante, Diotogène et Sthénidas* (Liége-Paris, 1942), p. 36, 3ff. with Agap. ch. 11; 13; 41; p. 39, 18ff. with Agap. ch. 18; 68; p. 42, 7ff. with Agap. ch. 20; 62; p. 46, 4ff. with Agap. ch. 45.

improve upon his sources by turning his sentences into what he believed to be little jewels sparkling with punlike *paromoea*, assonances, and parallel constructions. All the "Philonic" sentences which reappear as Agapetus' chapters display the very mannerisms peculiar to the whole of his work. This is particularly true of chapter 21, which is the most interesting to us. Moreover, it is striking ⟨147⟩ that the boundaries of the suspect "Philo" fragments should in all cases exactly coincide with those of Agapetus' chapters and that we should precisely discover the "unidentified" Philo fragments in Agapetus, while no correspondence between him and some authentic saying of Philo can be established. Finally, at least the "Philo" fragment θεὸς οὐδενὸς δεῖται (Harris, p. 104 = Agapetus 63), sometimes attributed to Hippocrates, is definitely of gnomic origin and cannot be Philonic in its "Agapetian" form.[27]

Thus Agapetus, not Philo, made its first modest appearance in Rus' towards the third quarter of the twelfth century at the latest. This point is worth stressing, for the "Hortatory Chapters" of this sixth century Byzantine author were to stay there for well over five hundred years. The 72 chapters of this *opusculum*, rather loosely connected by an acrostic announcing that the humble Deacon (of the Great Church of Constantinople, Agapetus dedicated his works to the Very Pious Emperor Justinian,[28] could serve a fairly wide range of purposes. Those interested in extolling the ruler's position could find in Agapetus an ample supply of *dicta* on the divine nature of the emperor's office. But as the ruler, wielding godlike power, was, like all mortals, but dust that perisheth, he was reminded by the Deacon of the various duties he had towards his subjects and Him Who had placed him above all men. Agapetus' chapter 21, which epitomizes the twofold nature of the whole *opusculum*, runs as follows:

Τῇ μὲν οὐσίᾳ τοῦ σώματος, ἴσος παντὶ ἀνθρώπῳ ὁ βασιλεύς, τῇ ἐξουσίᾳ δὲ τοῦ ἀξιώματος, ὁμοιός ἐστι τῷ ἐπὶ πάντων Θεῷ, οὐκ ἔχει γὰρ ἐπὶ γῆς τὸν αὐτοῦ ὑψηλότερον. χρὴ τοίνυν αὐτὸν καὶ ὡς Θεὸν

Though an emperor in body be like all other, yet in power of his office he is like God, Master of all men. For on earth, he has no peer. Therefore as God, be he never chafed or angry; as man, be he never proud. For though

27. This has already been seen by J. F. Boissonade, *Anecdota Graeca* I (1829), p. 45, who gives a list of authors where this "Philo" fragment is found. Cf. *ibidem*, p. 127.

28. The acrostic runs: "τῷ θειοτάτῳ καὶ εὐσεβεστάτῳ βασιλεῖ ἡμῶν Ἰουστινιανῷ Ἀγαπητὸς ὁ ἐλάχιστος διάκονος."

μὴ ὀργίζεσθαι, καί ὡς θνητὸν μὴ ἐπαίρεσθαι. εἰ εἰκόνι θεικῇ τετίμηται, ἀλλὰ καὶ κόνει χοικῇ συμπέπλεκται, δι' ἧς ἐκδιδάσκεται τὴν πρὸς πάντας ἰσότητα.

he be like God in face, yet for all that he is but dust which thing teaches him to be equal to every man.[29]

⟨148⟩ The good ruler had to lend a willing ear to good counsels and shun flatterers. But foremost among his duties was that of charity towards the poor, and, we might almost add, that of liberality towards impecunious divines like Agapetus himself. Some of the emperor's virtues praised in the Hortatory Chapters could well adorn a man of less exalted rank. As will be seen, the authors of Kievan and Muscovite Rus' extracted now this and now that of Agapetus' precepts according to the main tenor of their writings and to the interests of the epoch into which these writings fall.

Some of Agapetus' chapters appeared once more on Kievan soil in the twelfth century, again through the intermediary of another work. The Greek text of the *Barlaam and Joasaph* novel contains two lengthy interpolations on the king's duties, both of which make liberal use either of Agapetus directly or, less probably, some source common to Agapetus and to them.[30] Both of these interpolations went into the Slavonic version of the novel and many sentences of Agapetus, transmitted anonymously, thus became available to Kievan and later to Muscovite *knižniki*. Curiously enough, most of these "Agapetus" passages of *Barlaam and Joasaph* seem never to have been used in writings of the Kievan Rus'. It is true that these excerpts stressed God's greatness and the ruler's humility and moderation rather than his splendor as God's imitator on earth. This, however, does not provide an adequate explanation for the neglect of the Kievan writers to take advantage of the presence of a ready set of political maxims and to adopt some of

29. This and all the other English renderings of Agapetus subsequently given in this article are based on the translation from Latin made by Canon Thomas Paynell sometime between 1532 and 1534. Cf. *Dict. of National Biography*, XLIV (1895), s.v. Paynell, Thomas. The Houghton Library, Harvard University, possesses a copy of the 1546 edition of Paynell's translation.

30. Cf. K. Praechter, "Der Roman Barlaam und Joasaph in seinem Verhältnis zu Agapets Königsspiegel," *Byzantinische Zeitschrift*, II (1893), 444-460. Praechter believes in a common source rather than in a direct use of Agapetus, since the Deacon's stylistic embellishments are never taken over liberally in the interpolations. This is hardly a decisive argument. In his Κεφάλαια, Pseudo-Basil, who depends heavily on Agapetus, almost never copies him verbatim.

them to local needs. "Agapetus" passages like *se bo ustav istin'nago carstva, eže carstvovati vozder'žatisja sladostej*: "This is the (chief) precept of a true Rulership, that the Ruler should abstain from voluptuous passions" (cf. Agapetus, ch. 18), [31] or *i pravda uže ispravisja emu* (i.e. the king) *jakože* ⟨149⟩ *věn'cem cělomudrija obolčenu i bagrjaniceju pravdy oděјanъ* (read, *oděјanu*): "And truth (justice?) was attained by him, who was adorned with the wreath of chastity and arrayed with the purple robe of justice" (cf. Agapetus, ch. 17),[32] or, finally, *těmže blagopristupen budi moljaščimsja i otverzaj uši obniščavšim, da obraštеši božie uxo otverstо*: "Therefore, be thou accessible to those who entreat thee and open your ears to the Poor, so that you may find God's ear open" (cf. Agapetus, ch. 8)),[33] were to be used by political writers of sixteenth-century Moscow, already able to quote from a full Slavonic translation of Agapetus. The rudimentary political theory of Kievan Rus' did not stress the exalted position of the prince, and it was many years before Agapetus' hour would come.

At least one twelfth-century author, however, utilized one of the Agapetus passages transmitted by the *Barlaam and Joasaph* novel. This was no less a figure than Cyril of Turov. Since M. I. Suxomlinov, it has been known that Cyril had made use of *Barlaam and Joasaph* in his *Address* to Vasilij, Abbot of the Kievan Monastery of the Caves.[34] There, Cyril paraphrased and adapted the simile — which he had found in *Barlaam and Joasaph* — on the otherwise good but pagan ruler, converted to the true faith by his wise councilor who showed him two poor people living in happiness, that is, having preferred eternal salvation to

31. The Slavic *Barlaam and Joasaph*, facsimile ed. of the *Obščestvo Ljubitelej Drevnej Pis'mennosti*, LXXXVIII (1887), 449. For the Greek original of the passage, cf., e.g., J. F. Boissonade, *Anecdota Graeca* IV (1832), 309; cf. Agap. 18: "βασιλέα σε κατὰ ἀλήθειαν ὁρίζομαι ὡς βασιλεύειν καὶ κρατεῖν τῶν ἡδονῶν δυνάμενον."

32. The Slavic *Barlaam and Joasaph, ibidem*, p. 449; cf. Boissonade, *ibidem*, p. 310; cf. Agap. 18: "καὶ τὸν στέφανον τῆς σωφροσύνης ἀναδησάμενον καὶ τὴν πορφύραν τῆς δικαιοσύνης ἀμφιασάμενον."

33. The Slavic *Barlaam and Joasaph, ibidem*, p. 485; cf. Boissonade, *ibidem*, p. 333; cf. Agap. 8: "εὐπρόσιτος δὲ γίνῃ τοῖς δεομένοις διὰ τὸ κράτος τῆς ἄνω ἐξουσίας, καὶ ἀνοίγεις τὰ ὦτα τοῖς ὑπὸ πενίας πολιορκουμένοις, ἵνα εὕρῃς τὴν τοῦ Θεοῦ ἀκοὴν ἀνεῳγμένην."

34. Ed. K. Kalajdovič, *Pamjatniki rossijskoj slovesnosti XII veka* (Moscow, 1821), pp. 117-125.

earthly pleasures.[35] What has not been seen up to the present time is the dependence of Cyril's *Address* on another part of *Barlaam and Joasaph* as well, the interpolation out⟨150⟩lining the duties of a ruler, which is found towards the end of the work. Of course, he applies the "Agapetus" passage to the ideal monk rather than to the ideal king when he writes *nъ sut'* (sc. the monks) *cělomudriem oblčeni i pravdoju pojasani, směreniem' ukrašeni*; "but they are clad in chastity and girdled with truth, adorned with humility."[36] For all that, his dependence on the *Barlaam and Joasaph* "Agapetus" passage, *jakože věn'cem cělomudrija oblčenu i bagrjaniceju pravdy oděјanu*: "who were adorned with the wreath of chastity and arrayed with the purple robe of justice," is unmistakable. In practice this means that Cyril of Turov used the full text of *Barlaam and Joasaph*.

The *Pčela*, which soon began a life of its own, absorbing elements of local literature, served in turn as an ideal source for compilers of specialized collections. Among them was an anthology of legal texts, called *Měrilo pravednoe*. It consists of two parts written simultaneously and complementing each other. The first one, a kind of introduction, is didactic and moralistic in character, although juridical in tendency; the second is an outright selection of juridical texts, some of them Byzantine. As none of the elements which found their way into the *Měrilo* is later than the first half of the thirteenth century, and as the oldest known manuscript of this work dates from the fourteenth, it is safe to assume that this compilation was put together in the second half of the thirteenth century and to reckon it among the products of Kievan literature.[37] The didactic part of the *Měrilo* contains a chapter entitled *ot bčely izbrano o knjažen'i* "Selections from the Bee on Dominion," in which the compiler, omitting the author's name, has placed the slightly mutilated sentence from Agapetus on the ruler's godlike power: *plot'ju roven est' vsěm čelověkom, a volost'ju sanovnoju podoben est' Bogu.*[38]

Nothing seems to be known of the fate of Agapetus quotations in

35. M. I. Suxomlinov, *O sočinenijax Kirilla Turovskogo* (1858), conveniently reprinted in "Issledovanija po drevnej russkoj literature," *Sbornik Otd. Russ. Jaz. i Slov. Imp. Akad. Nauk*, LXXXV (1908), 273-349; for dependence of Cyril on *Barlaam and Joasaph*, cf. pp. 325-331.

36. Ed. K. Kalajdovič, *Pamjatniki*, p. 123.

37. The results obtained by M. Speranskij, *Perevodnye sborniki*, pp. 316-320 have been summarized here with some modifications.

38. Speranskij, *Perevodnye sborniki*, appendix, p. 55.

fourteenth-century East Slavic literature, a period from which a relatively small number of writings has come down to us. Among these few, texts whose authors we might expect to turn to Agapetus for inspiration are extremely scarce.[39]

⟨151⟩ The fifteenth century is characterized by the consolidation of Muscovite predominance in Russia and by the first deliberate Russian (not exclusively Muscovite) attempts to transform Russian princes into the counterparts of Byzantine Emperors and, later, to claim the Byzantine heritage for themselves and their lands. It was at that time that panegyrists first coined hybrid epithets, calling their rulers *velikij knjaz'* (grand prince) and *bogověnčannyj car'* (Emperor Crowned by God = θεόστεπτος βασιλεύς) in the same breath, thus anticipating the developments lying a hundred years ahead. Following in the steps of time-honored Byzantine tradition, although possibly imitating South Slavic models,[40] the eulogists compared the subjects of their praise to Moses — a standing device of Byzantine imperial oratory since Constantine the Great — to Constantine himself — no novelty even of Rus' literature — or to other Byzantine emperors, like Leo the Wise. It is not surprising, then, that the full text of Agapetus' precepts should appear on Russian soil in a century which saw the beginnings of Russian "Imperial" ideology.

This text is transmitted anonymously in MS 202 of the former Synodal Library in Moscow, a manuscript containing (with one sure exception) various texts of East Slavic recension. Its title is *Poučenie*

39. Such is the short eulogy of Ivan Kalita, *Zapis' s poxvaloju vel. kn. Ioannu Kalite*, dating from 1339. Publ. by I Sreznevskij, "Svedenija i zametki o maloizvestnyx i neizvestnyx pamjatnikax," in *Priloženie k XXXIV tomu Zapisok Imp. Akad. Nauk* (1879), no. 86, pp. 145-148. Most of the quotations of the Eulogy come from Ezekiel and the Psalter. As for Byzantine references, Kalita is compared to Constantine and Justinian (on account of his piety), and, curiously enough, to Manuel Comnenus (on account of his love for books: *mnogim knigam napisanym ego poveleniem revnuja pravovernomu cesarju greč'skomu Manuilu*).

40. A good example of such models is the Praise of Tsar John Alexander of Bulgaria, written in 1337. ed. V. D. Stojanov "Bъlgarski star rъkopisen pametnik ot XIV vek," *Periodičesko spisanie na bъlgarskoto kniževno družestvo v Sredec*, XXI (1887), 267-277. This interesting *Res Gestae*-like document contains many overbearing anti-Byzantine passages. But the elements of this better-than-thou attitude come from the foe. John Alexander is called *car' carem', bogom' izbrannyj* and *bogom' ven'čenyj*; he is compared to "Alexander of old" and Constantine.

blagago cěsarstva, se že i k boljarom i k episkopom i ko igumenom, lěpo est' i čern'cem, "Admonition on Good Rulership, Also Addressed to Magnates, Bishops and Abbots, and Becoming to Monks."[41] In ⟨152⟩ the mind of the author of the title, Agapetus' chapters (the Slavic text has only 67 of them) were works of wide application. The readers followed the scribe's advice. Indeed, we shall see the *opusculum* used by an abbot, generously quoted by a metropolitan, and, finally, published under the auspices of another abbot. As for magnates, the first tsar of Muscovy was among its users.

The manuscript dates surely from the fifteenth century, since a note on the inner side of its back cover refers to "my lord, the abbot Ioachim of Pesnošsk." This abbot is mentioned elsewhere under the year 1468. Unfortunately, under present circumstances, no idea can be formed on this translation and we are reduced to the *incipit* given in the description of the manuscript by Gorskij and Nevostruev,[42] and to a few excerpts made from two sixteenth-century manuscripts by V. Malinin.[43] Nor can we say where the translation originated. It may have been made in Russia proper by a local *knižnik* anxious to add a useful piece to the Muscovite propaganda library or perhaps ordered to do so by Zoe Palaeologina, who may have brought Agapetus in her baggage. It also may have come, among the many translation from Greek imported in the late fourteenth and the fifteenth centuries, from the South Slavic lands, for instance from Bulgaria, where the writers of Tsar John Alexander's court (fourteenth century) were well acquainted with the Byzantine political jargon.

All we have to go by in trying to assess the influence of Agapetus in fifteenth-century Russia are the writings of contemporary ecclesiastical publicists, who were the chief mouthpieces of the new and still fluid

41. A. Gorskij and K. Nevostruev, *Opisanie slavjanskix rukopisej moskovskoj sinodal'noj biblioteki*, II, 2 (1859), p. 622 = ms. no. 202, fols. 33-47.

42. *Česti vsjakyja prevyše imějaj san carju, česti*, (read, *č'ti*) *pače vsego semu tja spodobivšago Boga*.

43. V. Malinin, *Starec Eleazarova monastyrja Filofej i ego poslanija* (Kiev, 1901), p. 548 and p. 85 of notes. The passages are: *nepriložen ubo esi čelověkom vysoty radi zemnago carstvia* (= Agap. 8), and the familiar *est'stvom ubo tělesnym točen vsjakomu čelověku car', vlastiju že sana podoben est' nad vsěmi Bogu, ne imat bo na zemli vyššago sebe. Podobaet' ubo emu jako smertnu ne v'znositisja i jako Bogu ne gněvatisja* (= Agap. 21). In note 2039 Malinin quotes the Laurentius Chronicle *sub anno* 1175 as a parallel to the Slavic Agap. 21. On principle, the present article could have been written by anyone since 1901.

ideology. Here, the results are disappointing. Of the two principal Muscovite political pamphlets of the period, the first one including a *Poxvala blagověrnomu velikomu knjazju Vasil'ju Vasil'eviču vseja Rusi*, "Eulogy to the Grand Prince Vasilij Vasil'evič ⟨153⟩ of All Rus'," was compiled in 1461 by an anonymous author — believed, on quite insufficient grounds, to have been Pachomius the Serb.[44] Its Byzantine elements boil down to a stress on the divine character of the ruler's office, expressed by an assiduous and repetitious use of epithets like *bogoukrašennyj*, "adorned by God," *bogověnčannyj*, "God-crowned," *bogom naučennyj*, "taught by God." These epithets are connected with the name of Prince Vasilij II, called tsar in some passages of the treatise. All this may have been learned from the Bulgarians. The most important contribution of the treatise, a first hint at the *translatio imperii*, the transfer of the ideal rule over the Christian world from Constantinople, now sullied by the Turkish conquest and moral surrender to the Papists, to Moscow, the upholder of the Pure Faith, cannot have been directly inspired by Byzantine sources.

Slightly less frustrating is the second pamphlet, the "Letter of Vas'jan (Rylo), Archbishop of Rostov... to Ivan Vasil'evič..."[45] written on the eve of the momentous, though bloodless, Russo-Tartar encounter on the Ugra (1480), which was to put an end even to the nominal dependence of the Muscovite Rus' on the Golden Horde. The purpose of Vassian's (d. 1481) appeal was to push the apparently inhibited Ivan III over the brink — to Liberty. The bishop, who took his task seriously, set about it with reference books at his side. One of these books was the *Pčela*, especially its ninth chapter on "Power and Rulership," *o vlasti i knjaženii*, from which Vassian got his heartening and appropriate quotation from "Democrat the Philosopher," i.e. Democritus, to wit: "It is becoming to a prince to show wisdom whenever the moment requires it, display strength, manliness and courage when facing the enemy," and so

44. Ed. A. Popov, *Istoriko-literaturnyj obzor drevne-russkix polemičeskix sočinenij protiv latinjan* (Moscow, 1875), pp. 360-395. Pachomius the Serb is held to be the author of the *Poxvala* by A. Pavlov in his critical review of Popov's work, cf. *Otčet o XIX prisuždenii nagrad grafa Uvarova* (SPb., 1878), p. 285ff. According to Pavlov the "imperial" ideas present in the *Poxvala* were unfamiliar to native writers of mid-fifteenth-century Russia. The Eulogy of Boris Aleksandrovič by Thomas the Monk, a text discovered after Pavlov had expressed his hypothesis, disposes of this kind of argument.

45. *Poslanie Vas'jana arxiepiskopa Rostovskago... Ivanu Vasil'eviču*, p. ex. in *Kniga Stepennaja, Poln. Sobr. Russ. Let.* XXI, 2 (1913), 557-564.

on.[46] The Agapetus quotation of the *Pčela* was about two folios away from the ⟨154⟩ one chosen by Vassian. There is little doubt of his having read it in the process of scanning chapter nine for fitting material to be used in his work extolling Ivan III as a ruler. Yet he has not quoted Agapetus, and it seems that his was a deliberate omission.

One of the psychological reasons for Ivan III's hesitation may be inferred from Vassian's text. Was not the word of the Holy Writ "Fear God. Honor the Emperor (in Slavic: *car'*)" (= I Peter 2:17), the cornerstone of the contemporary — and past — political thinking of Rus'? But in 1480, when the Byzantine tsar was no more, the only tsar ordained by God and therefore unassailable was the *car' ordyn'skij*, the Khan of the Golden Horde, and Moscow princes were the first to preach the doctrine that one should not oppose the powers that be. Vassian's course, therefore, was to present the Tartar pagan tsar as a usurper, and Ivan, the heir to St. Vladimir's tradition, as the more legitimate, because Christian tsar of the two. This, however, was easier proved than felt. The Agapetus quotation, insisting on a "tsar's" equality with God, could produce an adverse psychological effect and was out of place in a treatise virtually inciting to rebellion. The needs of the hour remain the ultimate reason for the rejection of acceptance of an "Ideal."[47]

Viewing the historical developments from the dubious vantage point of our time, we incline to take it for granted that Moscow, the victor in the struggle for supremacy over "All Russia," should have been the only power interested in furthering Byzantine autocratic political ideas. In the fifteenth century, however, this matter of predominance was by no means considered a foregone conclusion, at least in some quarters. Tver', whose princes had been the first to call themselves

46. *Poln. Sobr. Russ. Let.*, XXI, 2 (1913), 559. Cf. V. Semenov, *Drevnjaja russkaja Pčela*, p. 103; M. I. Suxomlinov had already realized that Vassian copied the *Pčela* when he quoted Democritus: "Zamečanija o sbornikax izvestnyx pod nazvaniem Pčel," in *Sbornik Otd. Russ. Jaz.*, LXXXV (1908), 494-509.

47. The "Demokrat" quotation in Vassian's letter has recently been discussed by I. M. Kudrjavcev, "Poslanie na Ugru Vassiana Rylo kak pamjatnik publicistiki XV v.," in *Trudy Otdela drevne-russkoj literatury Instituta russkoj literatury*, AN SSSR, VIII (1951), 158-186, cf. p. 174f. Kudrjavcev thinks that the words of Democritus suited the situation of 1480 better than any other saying of chapter nine of the *Pčela*. This is a matter of opinion. What seems sure is that some of the sayings were not quotable in the circumstances of 1480. Agapetus chapter 21 was one of them.

velikij knjaz' vseja Rusi, Grand Prince of All Rus',[48] ⟨155⟩ was not subdued until 1485. Until that date she could wishfully hope to wring the supremacy from her traditional rival. It is not surprising, therefore, to find a glorification *alla maniera bizantina* of a fifteenth-century prince of Tver', Boris Aleksandrovič (d.1461). It was written by Thomas (Foma) the Monk, the Tver' member of the Russian delegation to the Florentine Council, about 1453, several years earlier than the Muscovite praise of Vasilij II.[49] What is striking is the degree of similarity between the Tver' and the Muscovite eulogies. It starts with the title of both texts and the event they describe — the "Praises" are connected with a relation of what happened at the Council of Florence — but it does not stop there. Boris Aleksandrovič is treated like a Byzantine emperor. He is a prince, well known and admired in far away lands, and praised by the Emperor of Constantinople himself. He receives the various imperial epithets, is called *car'*, compared with Moses, Leo the Wise, Constantine, and represented as a righful successor of Vladimir and Jaroslav.[50] This identity of claims in itself pointed to an inevitable showdown. As earlier in the Balkans, so now in Russia, whoever accepted to play the imperial game, had to bear its merciless consequences. There is no place for two at the top of the pyramid.

Similar as Thomas's text is to its Muscovite counterpart, it is livelier, and, what is of interest here, it offers three short passages which may be considered as probably indirect reminiscences of Agapetus. When Boris is called "earthly eye" (as a counterpart to the "heavenly all-encompassing eye," a Byzantine paraphrase of God), *i iže byti emu zemnomu oku*, one is reminded of Agapetus's chapter 46, "as the eye is ensconced in the body, so is the God-sent ruler installed on earth," a phrase which we shall encounter again. The characteristic of the prince as "accessible to all," *vsim dobroprestupen* (read, *-pristupen*), already familiar from the discussion of the *Barlaam and Joasaph* novel, has a parallel in Agapetus, chapter 8, "thou art accessible (εὐπρόσιτος) to

48. M. D. D'jakonov, "Kto byl pervyj velikij knjaz' 'vseja Rusi'," *Bibliograf* V (1889), 11-17. (Mixail Jaroslavič of Tver', about 1315.)

49. N. P. Lixačev, ed., "Inoka Fomy slovo poxval'noe o blagověrnom velikom knjazě Borisě Aleksandrovičě," *Pamjatniki dr. pis'm. i isskustva*, CLXVIII (1908).

50. Boris called *car'*: N. P. Lixačev, *op. cit.*, p. 28; compared with Moses: *ibidem*, pp. 2, 13, 14; with Augustus and Justinian, *ibidem*, pp. 12, 16; with Leo the Wise: *ibidem*, p. 11; called New Constantine or compared with him: *ibidem*, pp. 2, 12; successor of Vladimir and Jaroslav; *ibidem*, pp. 2, 16.

those who entreat thee." Finally, Thomas's refer⟨156⟩ence to the purple garb of piety (or virtue) adorning Boris, *i čestnoju bagrjaniceju ego ukrašaema vidjašči*[51] is close to Agapetus' chapter 18, also mentioned in connection with *Barlaam and Joasaph*, "crowned with chastity, arrayed with the purple robe of justice." Of course, these parallels are not cogent: yet, as they occur in a cluster and are slightly less banal than the usual Byzantine clichés on similar topics, they had to be mentioned here. The provisional conclusion, then, is that although both an excerpt from and the full text of Agapetus were available in translation to some of the fifteenth-century Russian *literati*, little if any use was made of his "Hortatory Chapters" in the gestation period of the Russian Imperial ideology. The situation changes radically at the very beginning of the sixteenth century.

Joseph Sanin, Abbot of Volokolamsk (d. 1515), is generally considered as the author of the first important theoretical work of Muscovite Rus'. This work, in which the previous views on the princely power had been systematized, was to make a profound impact upon the political thought of the following two generations. Joseph's work is a collection of sixteen pamphlets (*slova*), composed at various dates and published under the title of *Prosvětitel'*, "Illuminator," after the year 1507. The pamphlets inveigh against the Sect of "Judaisers" of whom Joseph was the principal adversary. In good Byzantine tradition, the prince (Ivan III, d. 1505) was exhorted by Joseph to lend the secular arm to the work of extirpating the heresy and told that the persecution of heretics was among the chief duties of a good ruler, whereas failure to uphold the true faith would make him into a tyrant (*mučitel'*). This line of thought provided Joseph with an opportunity to state his views on the prince's office. A pregnant summary of these views is given in *slovo* 16, at the very end of the "Illuminator," a place which attests that we are presented with Joseph's later thought. The passage on the Divine character of the ruler's functions as opposed to his human nature is found there in the form familiar to us through the *Pčela* and the chronicles, and has become a stock phrase invariably quoted in modern historical works.[51a] We already know that it comes from Agapetus, chapter 21. But where did Joseph read it? To obtain a sure answer to this question, it suffices to go beyond the classical ⟨157⟩ phrase of Joseph

51. Cf. N. P. Lixačev, *op. cit.*, pp. 1, 2, 29.

51a. Cf., e.g., as two recent examples, I. U. Budovnic, *Russkaja publicistika XVI veka* (Moscow, 1947), p. 98, and W. K. Medlin, *Moscow and the Third Rome*, p. 89.

and to analyse the whole group of statements on the princely power inserted at the end of *Slovo* 16:

1. Vas bo Bog v' sebe město posadi na prestolě svoem. Cf. A. I. Ponomarev, ed., *Pamjatniki drevne-russkoj cerkovno-učitel'noj literatury*, III (1897), 117.	Cf., e.g., Agap. I: ἔδωκέ σοι τὸ σκῆπτρον τῆς ἐπιγείου δυναστείας, and Agap. 45: νεύματι Θεοῦ τὴν δυναστείαν παραλαβών. Cf. also Agap. 30.

These parallelisms alone are too general to be conclusive.

2. Sego radi podobaet carem že i knjazem vsjako tščanie o blagočestii iměti i suščyx pod nimi ot trevolnenija spasati duševnago i tělesnago.

A clear hint at Ivan III's duty to suppress the "Judaisers."

3. Solncu ubo dělo est', eže světiti suščix na zemli; carju že svoe est', eže peščisja o vsěx suščix iže pod nim.	= Agap. 51: ἡλίου μὲν ἔργον ἐστί, τὸ καταλάμπειν ταῖς ἀκτῖσι τὴν κτίσιν, ἄνακτος δὲ ἀρετή, τὸ ἐλεεῖν τοῖς δεομένοις.[52]

A simple translation of Agapetus, with *světiti* ruling the accusative, after the model of the Greek, and the substitution of *suščix iže pod nim*, "subjects," for Agapetus' "Those who entreat him" at the end.

4. Skipetr cěsarstvija priim ot Boga, bljudi kako ugodiši davšemu ti togo,	= Agap. 61: σκῆπτρον βασιλείας παρὰ Θεοῦ δεξάμενος, σκέπτου πῶς ἀρέσεις τῷ ταύτην σοι δεδωκότι.[53]

Coincidence literal.

5. i netokmo o sebě otvět dasi k Bogu,

A bridge.

52. Agap. 51: "The function of the sun is to illuminate the world; the emperor's virtue is to be merciful and to help those who entreat him.".

53. Agap. 61: "Having received from God the imperial sceptre, look Thou, endeavor Thyself to please the One who has given it to Thee.".

6. no eže inii zlo tvorjat, ty slovo otdasi Bogu, volju ž dav im.

= Agap. 30: ὧν γὰρ ἂν ἐκεῖνοι κακῶς διαπράξωνται, λόγον ὑφέξει Θεῷ ὁ τὴν ἰσχὺν αὐτοῖς δεδωκώς.[54]

⟨158⟩

7. Car' ubo estestvom podoben est' vsěm čelověkom, vlastiju že podoben est' vyšnemu Bogu.[55]

This is pratically a translation of Agapetus 21.

Joseph came to speak once more on the ruler's duties in his letter to a prince, the "Orthodox X, Who Had Asked Him for a Useful Admonition."[56] There Joseph declared that he had taken the liberty of writing down some sayings from the Holy Scriptures for the edification of the addressee. The sense in which Joseph understood the expression "Holy Scriptures" must have been quite broad, since his quotations included St. John Chrysostom, whom he mentioned, and Agapetus, whom he did not name. Here is the passage:

Poistině, iže veliku vlast' priem, datelju oblasti dolžen est' po silě podobitisja: ničemže tako moščno Bogu podobitisja, jakože milostiju.[57]

= Agap. 37: ὁ μεγάλης ἐξουσίας ἐπιλαβόμενος τὸν δοτῆρα τῆς ἐξουσίας μιμείσθω κατὰ δύναμιν... ἐν τούτῳ δὲ μάλιστα τὸν Θεὸν μιμήσεται, ἐν τῷ μηδὲν ἡγεῖσθαι τοῦ ἐλεεῖν προτιμώτερον.

Only the beginning and the end of Agapetus' chapter were used by Joseph. While Vasilij III was compared with God in *Prosvětitel'*, the middle of Agapetus' chapter 37, "For if the emperor represent God, Lord of all things and by His liberality has the governance of

54. Agap. 30: "For he that gave them power ⟨to act⟩ shall account before God for their evil deeds."

55. Quotations 1-7 in *Prosvětitel'*, (3rd ed., Kazan', 1896), p. 547.

56. Ed. G. Kuševel-Bezborodko, *Pamjatniki starinnoj russkoj literatury* IV (SPb., 1862), 192-193. For a discussion of the letter, cf. I. Xruščev, *Issledovanie o sočinenijax Josifa Sanina* (SPb., 1869), pp. 94-96. Xruščev's identification of the prince with a brother of Vasilij III is inconclusive. His dating of the letter (after 1505) depends on the identification and therefore cannot be more reliable than the latter.

57. Cf. G. Kuševel-Bezborodko, *op. cit.*, p. 192. Agap. 37: "He that has obtained high power should imitate, as near as he may, the Giver thereof... he will best imitate him by esteeming no thing more desirable than deeds of mercy."

everything," was omitted in the letter. A prince is not a tsar. Besides, in the "Illuminator," Sanin's purpose was to underscore the ruler's glory and might, in order to spur him into action against the heretics. In the letter, a didactic work, in spite of its mock deference, Joseph rather browbeat the addressee into mercifulness — and chastity.

Thus Joseph of Volokolamsk is the first author so far known who used the full Slavic translation of Agapetus for his outline of "im⟨159⟩perial" ideology.[58] True enough, his *Prosvětitel'* exerted a profound influence throughout the whole of the sixteenth century.[59] But as one of the most suggestive passages of this work is based on Agapetus, it will be seen that the similarity between Joseph's and his successors' opinions is partly due to the use of this common source. Joseph is only the first in a series of sixteenth-century writers who turned to the Deacon of Constantinople for ready formulas by which to articulate their views.

As the immediate roots of the State ideology of the *Roi Soleil* are to be sought under his father Louis XIII, so is the prefiguration of some of Ivan the Terrible's conceptions to be found in the writings of the time

58. This conclusion would not have been warranted, if we had to rely on the Agapetus passages in *Prosvětitel'* alone. There, they are embedded in an appeal which is announced as a quotation from the Emperor Constantine "*tako bo pišet'... car' velikii Konstjantin o carěx i o knjazex i o sudjax zemskix.*" Cf. Ponomarev, *op. cit.* p. 116. I. S. Volockij copies a *kormčaja*! As it is difficult to determine where this quotation ends, the suspicion might have arisen that Joseph found the Agapetus passages in his "Constantine" source. The independent use of Agapetus' chapter 37 in the letter to a Prince disposes of this doubt. The most recent treatment of Joseph's doctrine, A. A. Zimin's "O političeskoj doktrine Iosifa Volockogo," *Trudy Otd. drevne-rus. lit.., AN SSSR*, IX (1953), 159-177, seems to take a stand against those who suspected that the Volokolamsk abbot's views were not an original product of Russian thought (p. 160). In his otherwise quite interesting article, Zimin dates the theory of theocratic kingship, propounded by Joseph, as 1507-1511, and presents it as the result of Joseph's own searchings. It is in such a context that the passage derived from Agapetus ch. 21 is adduced (p. 174f.).

59. On Ivan IV's use of *Prosvětitel'*, cf. below, p. 166; Metropolitan Macarius transcribes some of Joseph's formulae in his *Admonition* to the newly crowned Tsar, inserted into the Coronation Ritual of 1547 [final version compiled about 1560; cf. M. V. Šaxmatov, "Gosudarstvenno-nacional'nyja idei Činovnyx knig venčanija na carstvo russkix gosudarej," *Zapiski russkago naučnago instituta v Belgrade*, I (1930), 245-278, cf. pp. 248-251]; about 1560, *Stepennaja Kniga* respectfully mentions Joseph's testament (*Poln. Sobr. Russ. Let.* XXI, 2 (1913), p. 505) and *Prosvětitel'* (*ibidem*, p. 568). Cf. also the *Stoglav* of 1551, chapters 1 and 79.

of his father Vasilij III (d. 1533) and of the regency. Next to the letters of Philotheus of Pskov, the most important ideological text of the period immediately preceding Ivan the Terrible's sole rule is the anonymous account of the birth of Vasilij's son, Ivan IV, the God-sent (*ot Boga darovana*), an account coupled with a posthumous eulogy of Vasilij III. The inclusion of almost the whole of this otherwise unpublished work into the *Kniga Stepennaja*,[60] a col<160>lection of legitimistic biographies of rulers and saints composed under the supervision of the metropolitan Macarius between 1560 and 1563, gave it official endorsement. The anonymous work could have been written at any time between 1533 and 1563, but its double contents seem to indicate that it was composed shortly after Vasilij's death, under the regency.

The treatise is strongly redolent of the lamp, and the lamp's oil is Byzantine. One may attribute its Greek clichés and bizarre composita to South Slavic influence,[61] and the puns on Ivan's "joyful" name[62] to the consultation of a Slavic reference work, giving the vernacular meanings of Hebrew names.[63] When, however, the author admits that he draws upon a source,[64] when his tone becomes suddenly "universal" — the birth of Ivan the Terrible "filled the Orthodox in all corners of the universe with joy"[65] — when he asserts that Vasilij III was loved by everyone and worshipped by people from near and far, to wit by inhabitants of Sinai and Palestine, Italy and Antioch,[66] — a perspective which suits the Byzantine picture perfectly, but is perfect nonsense for

60. *Poln. Sobr. Russ. Let.* XXI, 2 (1913), pp. 605-615.

61. P. 606: *ispravleniem blagočestija* = κατορθώμασι εὐσεβείας; p. 608: *pravoslavnyx ispolnenie* = τὸ τῶν ὀρθοδόξων πλήρωμα; p. 613: *skipetrokrestonosnyja*.

62. P. 606: Ivan is a *blagodatnoe imja*; cf. p. 609: *imja... Ivan... ego že... slyšanie veselit serdca*. Byzantines often indulged in puns resulting from their awareness that Ἰωάννης = Θεοῦ χάρις in Hebrew. A frequent Byzantine paraphrase of "John" is χαριτώνυμος. For other (fourteenth-century) examples, cf. e.g., Ed. Kurtz, "Emendationsvorschläge zu den Gedichten des Manuel Philes," *Byzantinisch-Neugriechische Jahrbücher*, IV (1923), 75.

63. For an example, cf. *Reč ' židovskago jazyka preložena na ruskuju...*, ed. as Appendix in K. Kalajdovič's *Ioann eksarx bolgarskij* (Moscow 1824), p. 193, where *Ioann* is translated by *blagodat'*.

64. P. 606: *o takovom carskom... roženii pisano bjaše někgdě ot někoix mudroljubnyx trudopolož'nikov... zde že o* (v.l. *ot*) *six v male javleno* (v.l. *-na*) *sut'*.

65. P. 606: *vsi pravoslavnii vo vsex kon'cyx vselennyja radosti ispolnišasja*.

66. P. 611.

Muscovy — we know he is copying a eulogy of a Byzantine emperor.[67] But he also has another source, Agapetus,[68] whom he adapts rather skillfully, toning down the By⟨161⟩zantine's references to the ruler's earthly nature and presenting as Vasilij's actual achievements those virtues which Agapetus postulated for an ideal emperor. It may be argued that this adaptation had already been performed by the hypothetical Byzantine panegyrist whom the Muscovite Anonymus copied. The question is difficult to decide. An analysis of Agapetus' passages, however, seems to indicate that the changes are due to the anonymous author himself. The texts are as follows:

1. I sego radi vsegda carskoe ego (*sc.* Vasilij III) serdce i um bdja i mudr'stvuja, okormljaja vsěx opasně vo blagozakonii, bezzakonii že potoki krěpce otganjaja, da ne pogrjaznet karabl' velikago ego deržavstva v volnax nepravdy.	= Agap. 2: ὡς κυβερνήτης ἀγρυπνεῖ διὰ παντὸς ὁ τοῦ βασιλέως πολυόμματος νοῦς, διακατέχων ἀσφαλῶς τῆς εὐνομίας τοὺς οἴακας, καὶ ἀπωθούμενος ἰσχυρῶς τῆς ἀνομίας τοὺς ῥύακας, ἵνα τὸ σκάφος τῆς παγκοσμίου πολιτείας μὴ περιπίπτῃ κύμασιν ἀδικίας.[69]

The adaptation is successful. Only the "many-eyed mind" of Agapetus' Emperor was evidently too much for the Anonymus, who replaced it with "heart and mind." What is more significant, the "universal empire" (παγκόσμιος πολιτεία) of the original was cut down to Muscovite proportions and rendered by "great rule," or "state." This detail speaks for a Russian adaptation rather than for a plagiarism from the supposed Byzantine eulogy already containing Agapetus. A Byzantine using Agapetus' text would have no reason to balk at a familiar reference to universal monarchy, a cornerstone of Byzantine political thinking. Official Moscow was reluctant to raise open claims to universality. True

67. This is yet to be found. The present remarks aim only at speeding up the identification.

68. M. D'jakonov, *Vlast' moskovskix gosudarej* (SPb., 1889), p. 107, n. 2, thinks that the eulogist of Vasilij III and Ivan IV was inspired by Pseudo-Basil's Κεφάλαια. This is an error. To clarify, it suffices to compare the treatment of Agapetus chapter 8 by Pseudo-Basil and the eulogist respectively.

69. Agap. 2: "Like the pilot of a ship, the emperor's many-eyed mind keeps a continuous watch, firmly handling the oars of equity and justice, and strongly repelling the vehement waves of iniquity, that the boat of this worldly commonwealth be not crushed by the waves of wickedness."

enough, Philotheus of Pskov, the mouthpiece of the doctrine of Moscow the third Rome, wrote to Vasilij III, about 1510, *edin ty vo vsei podnebesnoi xristianom car'*,[70] "Thou art the only Emperor unto the Christians under the vault of Heaven," but his was the voice of a quisling free-lance publicist. In a well known reply to Possevino, Ivan the Terrible declared that he did not aspire to temporal rule over the whole world: *zděšnjago gosudarstva vseě* ⟨162⟩ *vselennye ne xotim.*[71] By his adaptation of Agapetus, the Anonymus seems to have reflected the authoritative line more faithfully.

The use of Agapetus by the Anonymus does not stop with chapter two. His text continues as follows:

2. Takova bjaše mnogopopečitel'naja ego careva duša; po podobiju zercala vsegda isčiščaetsja i božestvennymi lučami vynu oblistaema i vešč'mi razsuženija ottudu naučaetsja,	= Agap. 9: τὴν πολυμέριμνον τοῦ βασιλέως ψυχὴν κατόπτρου δίκην ἀποσμήχεσθαι χρὴ, ἵνα ταῖς θείαις αὐγαῖς ἀεὶ καταστράπτηται, καὶ τῶν πραγμάτων τὰς κρίσεις ἐκεῖθεν διδάσκηται.[72]

3. Jako že něgdě pišet,

The device of announcing a quotation at this place is astute, as it creates the impression that everything but what follows is the author's own invention.

4. Iže ubo suščestvom tělesnym raven est' čelověkom car', vlastiju že dostojnago ego veličestva priličen vyšnemu, iže nado vsěmi, Bogu: ne imat' bo vysočajša sebe na zemli.	= Agap. 21. (For Greek text and translation, see page 147, above.)

70. V. Malinin, *Starec Eleazarova monastyrja Filofej* (Kiev, 1901), appendix, p. 50. Cf. *ibidem*, p. 63: *edin pravoslavnyi velikii russkii car' vo vsei podnebesnoi.*

71. Cf., e.g., N. S. Čaev, " 'Moskva-Tretij Rim' v političeskoj praktike mosk. pravitel'stva v XVI v.," *Istoričeskie Zapiski*, XVII (1945), 9, with indication of source.

72. Agap. 9: "The pensive soul of an emperor must be evermore as pure as the mirror so that it may continually send forth divine rays, and also that it may learn therefrom to acquire right judgment of things."

5. Ne prestupim (*read* nepristupim) ubo čelověki vysoty radi zem'nago carstvija, blagopim (*read* blagopristupim) že byvaet polučenija radi gornjago carstvija.

= Agap. 8: ἀπρόσιτος μὲν ὑπάρχεις ἀνθρώποις διὰ τὸ ὕψος τῆς κάτω βασιλείας, εὐπρόσιτος δὲ γίνῃ τοῖς δεομένοις διὰ τὸ κράτος τῆς ἄνω ἐξουσίας.[73]

Only the first part of Agapetus 21, the glorification of the emperor, has been taken over. Its second part, exhorting to humility, has been skillfully replaced by the beginning of Agapetus 8. The over-all effect is more stress on the ruler's lofty station. The text continues:

6. Jako že oko tělesi vodruzisja, sice i car' v mirě ustroisja ot ⟨163⟩ Boga darovannym emu pospěšeniem k poleznym, da promyšljaet ubo o čelověcěx i sam vo blagix da prebyvaet, vo zlyx že da ne pretykaetsja.[74]

= Agap. 46: ὥσπερ ὀφθαλμὸς ἐμπέφυκε σώματι, οὕτω βασιλεὺς ⟨163⟩ τῷ κόσμῳ ἐνήρμοσται, ὑπὸ τοῦ Θεοῦ δεδομένος εἰς συνεργίαν τῶν συμφερόντων. χρὴ οὖν αὐτὸν ὡς οἰκείων μελῶν, οὕτω πάντων ἀνθρώπων προνοεῖν, ἵνα προκόπτωσιν ἐν καλοῖς καὶ μὴ προσκόπτωσιν ἐν κακοῖς.[75]

7. Po istině ubo car' naricašesja, iže carstvuja (*read* carstvujaj) nad strast'mi i slastem odolěvati mogij, iže celomudrija ven'cem ven'čannyj i porfiroju pravdy obolčenyj.[76]

= Agap. 18: βασιλέα σε κατὰ ἀλήθειαν ὁρίζομαι, ὡς βασιλεύειν καὶ κρατεῖν τῶν ἡδονῶν δυνάμενον καὶ τὸν στέφανον τῆς σωφροσύνης ἀναδησάμενον, καὶ πορφύραν τῆς δικαιοσύνης ἀμφιασάμενον.[77]

73. Agap. 8: "Because of the loftiness of thy earthly empire, Thou art inaccessible; and yet Thou speedily admit'st supplicants (to Thine presence) by reason of the heavenly Power."

74. The final passage corresponds to a hypothetical ἵνα πάντων ἀνθρώπων προνοῇ καὶ αὐτὸς προκόπτῃ ἐν καλοῖς καὶ μὴ προσκόπτῃ ἐν κακοῖς. The modification, however, must be attributed to the Anonymus, whose chief purpose was to speak of the ruler, not of his subjects.

75. Agap. 46: "As the eye is ensconced in the body, so is the God-sent ruler installed in the world, to minister those things that may be profitable for man. Therefore he should provide for men as he would for his own limbs, that they may prosper in goodness and not stumble in doing evil.".

76. Passages 1-7 in *Vkratce poxvala samoderž'cu Vasiliju, Poln. Sobr. Russ. Let.*, XXI, 2 (1913), 610. M. D'jakonov, *Vlast' moskovskix gosudarej* (1889), p. 107, who read the full MS text of the *Poxvala*, quotes a passage from it which did not enter into *Stepennaja Kniga: Bog ne trebuet ni ot kogože pomošči, car' že ot edinago Boga*. This is of course the beginning of Agapetus 63: "ὁ μὲν Θεὸς οὐδενὸς δεῖται, ὁ βασιλεὺς δὲ, μόνου Θεοῦ." "God needeth nothing. An emperor hath only need of God."

77. Agap. 18: "For certain I affirm Thee to be an emperor, seeing Thou rulest

After this quotation, familiar to us from the earlier discussion of *Barlaam and Joasaph*, Cyril of Turov and Thomas the Monk, the author winds up saying "Such was also the pious Tsar of Tsars, Grand Prince Vasilij'."

Towards the middle of the sixteenth century, another Byzantine manual on the ruler's duties and prerogatives became fashionable with the *literati* of Muscovy. The authorship of these "Hortatory Chapters" is attributed — wrongly — to the ninth-century emperor Basil I. (According to the acrostic, Basil addressed his admonitions to his son, Leo VI.[78]) The author — probably Photius himself[79] — ⟨164⟩, who hints at his sources except for Agapetus, imitates and paraphrases him at length, in some instances closely following the wording of his model. Through Pseudo-Basil, ch. 51, a part of Agapetus' chapter 8 found its way into such venerable texts as the Coronation Ritual of Ivan IV, in which approximately one-half of the "Metropolitan's Admonition to the Great Prince," probably written by the learned Metropolitan Macarius, consists of literal excerpts from Pseudo-Basil's little work.[80] From there, Agapetus 8 wandered from one Ritual to another, and can be read, for instance, in the Metropolitan's "Admonition" prepared for the corona-

over and subduest Thy voluptuous passions, and That thou art crowned with the diadem of chastity and arrayed with the purple robe of justice."

78. Best edition by K. Emminger, *Studien zu den griechischen Fürstenspiegeln*, III: Βασιλείου κεφάλαια παραινετικά, (Munich 1913), pp. 50-73, with excellent indications of sources. Most accessible text in Migne, *PG*, CVII, col. xxi-lvi.

79. The authorship of Photius, at first rejected, since scholars were reluctant to attribute platitudes to their great colleague of the ninth century, now seems highly probable. Cf. K. Emminger, *op. cit.*, p. 49; I. Dujčev, "Au lendemain de la conversion du peuple bulgare. L'épître de Photius," *Mélanges de Science Religieuse*, VII (1951), 211-226; cf. p. 214. The only correct approach to solving this question is to compare Pseudo-Basil's *Chapters* with the second part of Photius' letter to Tsar Boris-Michael. The resemblance of the two texts is highly suggestive. Cf. p. ex., Photius § 41 with Pseudo-Basil, chapter 26; Photius § 109 with Pseudo-Basil, chapter 38.

80. First seen by X. Loparev, "O čine venčanija russkix carej," *Žurn. Min. Nar. Prosv.*, CCLIII (October 1887), 312-319. A Slavic translation of Pseudo-Basil was known in Muscovite Rus' since the fifteenth century at the latest. A. I. Sobolevskij, "Perevodnaja literatura moskovskoj Rusi," *Sbornik Otd. Russ. Jaz. i Slov.*, LXXIV, 1 (1903), 20 mentions three fifteenth century MSS of Pseudo-Basil's *Glavy nakazatel'nyja*. The dated one is of 1457.

tion of Peter II (d. 1730).[81] However as the dependence of the Russian coronation ritual on Pseudo-Basil is a known fact, it shall not be discussed here.

Ivan IV may have quoted Pseudo-Basil in his Testament.[82] It is possible to show for sure that Ivan's chief polemical writing, his first reply to Prince A. Kurbskij, a lengthy work so teeming with erudite quotations that the historian Ključevskij dubbed it *učennaja kaša*, ⟨165⟩ a learned medley, contains reminiscences from Agapetus. First, two passages reminiscent of Agapetus 21:

1. ašče bo i perfiru nošu, no obače vem se, jako po vsemu nemoščiju, podobno vsem čelovekom obložen esm' po estestvu.[83]	ašče ubo perfiru nosim, zlatom i biserom ukrašenu, no obače tlenny esmi i čelovečeskoju nemoščju obloženy.[84]

At first sight, it seems strange that the tsar, elsewhere so bent upon asserting his divine rights to rule, should treat this passage in the same way in which his adversaries were to treat it later. The equality with God is replaced by the "purple," and even this distinction is referred to in a concessive clause. This twist was necessitated by the general line of the argument. Ivan had to invoke his human weakness in order to prove that his sins did not make an apostate of the True Faith out of him, as Kurbskij contended. In fact, by this contention, the prince required Ivan to

81. Text, e.g., in E. V. Barsov, "Drevne-russkie pamjatniki svjaščennago venčanija carej na carstvo," in *Čtenija v imp. obšč. istorii i drevn. Rossijskix*, CXXIV (1893), 114f.

82. X. Loparev, *art. cit.*, p. 319, n. 1. Cf. The Testament of 1572: *ašče kto i množestvo zemli priobrjaščet i bogatstva a trilakotna groba ne možet izbežati* (p. ex. in D. S. Lixačev and others, *Poslanija Ivana Groznogo* (1951), p. 526; cf. p. 527) with Pseudo-Basil ch. 45: "εἰ τῆς γῆς ἁπάσης κατακρατῆσαι φιλονεικήσῃς, ἀλλ'οὐ πλέον τριπήχεως γῆς μετὰ θάνατον κληρονομήσεις." It is not sure, however, that Ivan quotes Pseudo-Basil, in whose passage there is no mention of a "grave." The motive of the inescapable "three-cubit-long grave" was known in Rus' literature, cf. a text of 1414: *...kamen' grobu Arilakotnago* (read, *trilakotnago*) *ne ubežiši*, quoted from Sobolevskij by H. Schaeder, *Moskau das Dritte Rom*, p. 53, n. 7. Cf. also V. Semenov, *Drevnjaja russkaja Pčela*, p. 136, Philistion.

83. D. S. Lixačev, J. S. Lur'e, V. P. Adrianova-Peretc, edd., *Poslanija Ivana Groznogo*, (1951), p. 49f.

84. *Ibidem*, p. 46. "Although I am wearing the purple robe, I know nevertheless that by nature I am perishable and weighed down with all human weakness."

show superhuman qualities, this being a heretical demand.[85] Further Agapetus reminiscences are:

2. Podovlastnyx že svoix blagix blagaja podavaem zlym že zlaja prinositca nakazanija.[86]	Cf. Agap. 28: καὶ τοὺς τὰ κάλλιστα ποιοῦντας προτίμα, καὶ τοῖς τὰ χείριστα δρῶσιν ἐπιτίμα.[87]
3. I vsegda ubo carem podobaet obozritel'nym byti, ovogda krotčajšim, ovogda že jarym.[88]	Cf. Agap. 48: γίνου τοῖς ὑπηκόοις, εὐσεβέστατε βασιλεῦ, καὶ φοβερὸς διὰ τὴν ὑπεροχὴν τῆς ἐξουσίας, καὶ ποθεινὸς διὰ τὴν παροχὴν τῆς εὐποιίας.[89]

The following passage goes back not immediately to Agapetus' chapter 30[90] but to Joseph Sanin's "Illuminator," which had excerpted from it:

4. *Ivan IV*: i ne tokmo o svoix, ⟨166⟩ no podvlastnyx dati mi otvet, ašče čto moim nesmotreniem pogrešitca.[91]	*Sanin*: i netokmo o sebě otvet dasi ⟨166⟩k Bogu, no eže inii zlo tvorjat, ty slovo otdasi Bogu, volju ž dav im.[92]

There is nothing extraordinary in the fact that Muscovite adherents of the theocratic imperial ideology should have drawn upon a Byzantine author who had dedicated his treatise on Rulership to a Justinian. Ivan the Terrible, however, like his counterparts in seventeenth-century France, had to assert himself against the anti-autocratic party of the nobility. Not only blood, but ink was spilled profusely in this struggle. What were the ideological arguments used by Ivan's opponents, what the authorities invoked by them? The question is worth investigating.

85. *Ibidem*, p. 46; 14; 15.

86. *Ibidem*, p. 61.

87. Agap. 28: "Honor them that do good and punish them that do evil."

88. *Poslanija*, p. 20.

89. Agap. 48: "Be thou, O most pious Emperor, to thy subjects, through the excellence of thy power, terrible, and by thy liberality, amiable."

90. "For he that gave them power (to act) shall give an account to God for their evil deeds."

91. *Poslanija*, p. 50f.

92. *Prosvětitel'* (3rd ed., Kazan', 1896), p. 547. Cf. above, p. 159.

Some of autocracy's adversaries like Kurbskij, were manoeuvered into exile and treason. But among those who defied the tyrant at home, the figure of Metropolitan Philip (Kolyčev) (1566-1568), towers above all the others. He fought the establishment of the *opričnina*, first tried to admonish Ivan, the "divider of the Kingdom," in private, then publicly upbraided him for his murders. For this, he was deposed, and as the story goes, strangled by Maljuta Skuratov (1569). The Russian Church made Philip a saint.

One of the two recensions of the Vita of Philip,[93] possibly written by a contemporary and an eye-witness to the events, [94] preserves three speeches allegedly delivered by the metropolitan. Up to the ⟨167⟩ present, they have been considered our most important source for the reconstruction of the ideas prevalent among the Russian ecclesiastical circles opposed to Ivan IV's system of values. If this opinion is upheld — and I think it should be modified — then these ecclesiastics had hardly an idea of their own. The first speech put in Philip's mouth was an inauguration address, supposedly delivered after his consecration. Be it said in advance that five-sixths of it is but a cento from various chapters of Agapetus. The compiler's originality is limited to choosing appropriate quotations and introducing slight changes into others. Here is the text of the address.

93. Cf. V. Ključevskij, *Drevnerusskija žitija svjatyx kak istoričeskij istočnik* (Moscow, 1871), p. 311 and n. 2; G. P. Fedotov, *Sviatoj Filipp, mitropolit moskovskij* (Paris, 1928), *passim*. Neither of the versions of Philip's Vita have been published. We are reduced to (a) a few excerpts made from one of them by N. M. Karamzin, *Istorija gosudarstva rossijskago*, IX, especially n. 178; (b) a few quotations in V. Malinin's *Starec Eleazarova monastyrja*, pp. 733-737; 743f; (c) a modern Russian paraphrase of the Vita, amounting to a translation, by A. N. Murav'ev '*Žitija svjatyx rossijskoj cerkvi. Janvar*' (SPb., 1857) (inaccessible to me); (d) a series of excerpts, apparently copied from Murav'ev, in G. P. Fedotov's work quoted in this note. In the present article, I am using Fedotov's excerpts and substituting for them Karamzin's (= K.) and Malinin's (= M.) original quotations whenever available.

94. Cf. Karamzin, *Istorija*, IX, n. 179: *ne ot inogo slyšax no* sam viděx. V. Ključevskij, *Drevnerusskija žitija*, p. 311, n. 2 points out, however, that only one version of the Vita's first recension has this remark and that the text of the Vita contains several errors of fact. At another place in the Vita, the author says that he had gathered his material from *iněix dostověrno predajuščix o něm* (sc. Philip).

1. O blagočestivyj car', Bogom sotvorennoe sokrovišče blagoj very, poskol'ku bol'šej spodobilsja ty blagodati, postol'ku i dolžen Emu vozdat'. Bog prosit ot nas blagotvorenij, ne odnoj liš blagoj besedy, no i prinošenija blagix del.

= Agap. 5: ἴσθι, ὦ εὐσεβείας θεότευκτον ἄγαλμα, ὅτι ὅσῳ μεγάλων ἠξιώθης παρὰ Θεοῦ δωρεῶν, τοσούτῳ μείζονος ἀμοιβῆς ὀφειλέτης ὑπάρχεις αὐτῷ... εὐχαριστίαν δὲ ζητεῖ παρ' ἡμῶν, οὐ τὴν διὰ ῥημάτων ἀγαθῶν προφοράν, ἀλλὰ τὴν διὰ πραγμάτων εὐσεβῶν προσφοράν.[95]

2. Postavlennyj nad ljud'mi vysoty radi zemnogo tvoego carstvija, (krotok budi deržavy radi gornija vlasti = K.). Otverzaj uši tvoi k niščete straždusčej, da i sam obrjaščeš slux Božij k tvoim prošenijam, ibo kakovy my byvaem k našim klevretam, takovym obrjaščem k sebe i svoego Vladyku.

= Agap. 8: ἀπρόσιτος μὲν ὑπάρχεις ἀνθρώποις διὰ τὸ ὕψος τῆς κάτω βασιλείας, εὐπρόσιτος δὲ γίνῃ τοῖς δεομένοις διὰ τὸ κράτος τῆς ἄνω ἐξουσίας. καὶ ἀνοίγεις τὰ ὦτα τοῖς ὑπὸ πενίας πολιορκουμένοις, ἵνα εὕρῃς τὴν τοῦ Θεοῦ ἀκοὴν ἀνεῳγμένην. οἷοι γὰρ ἂν τοῖς ἡμετέροις γενόμεθα συνδούλοις, τοιοῦτον περὶ ἡμᾶς εὑρήσομεν τὸν δεσπότην.[96]

The changes introduced by the Vita of Philip are small but noteworthy. They tone down the glorification of the emperor, and amplify the restraining notes present in Agapetus' text, a procedure of which ⟨168⟩ the later treatment of Agapetus 21 will be a perfect example. Here, ἀπρόσιτος ὑπάρχεις, "Thou art aloof," has been changed into the neutral "Thou art put over men," and "accessible," strengthened into *krotok*, "humble," a word Agapetus would not dare to use with respect to the emperor. The metropolitan's speech continues as follows:

95. Agap. 5: "Know, O God-wrought embodiment of piety, that the greater the gifts awarded to Thee by God, the deeper Thou art in His debt... God asks us for gratitude, not that expressed by gentle words, but that shown in offering Him good deeds."

96. Agap. 8: "Because of the loftiness of this earthly Empire, Thou art inaccessible; and yet thou speedily admit'st suppliants ⟨to thy presence⟩ by reason of the Heavenly Power. Thou doest listen to those who suffer poverty, that God may in Thy necessity kindly hearken to Thee. For as we are to our fellow servants of God, so shall we find the Heavenly Ruler disposed toward us."

3. Kak vsegda bodrstvuet kormčij, tak i carskij mnogoočityj um dolžen tverdo soderžat' pravila dobrago zakona, izsuščaja potoki bezzakonija, da ne pogrjaznet v volnax nepravdy korabel' vsemirnyja žizni.	= Agap. 2.[97]

The "many-eyed" mind of the emperor, which seemed disconcerting to the eulogist of Vasilij III, did not trouble the compiler of Philip's Vita. But παγκόσμιος πολιτεία, the "universal empire," fitted the Muscovite aspirations in the second half of the sixteenth century no better than it did in the first. In the rendering of the Vita, "all-world life," πολιτεία was taken to mean "life," since this was one of the acceptations of the Byzantine word. The error, however, may have been the Slavic translator's of Agapetus, not the compiler's. What follows in Philip's address is the admonition to choose right counselors and not to lend an ear to flattery (*laskatel'stva*). It seems that finally we have found an original allusion to the situation then prevailing at the court of Ivan IV. Kurbskij's contemporary diatribe against the Tsar's "flatterers" (*laskateli*), comes immediately to mind.[98] One scholar sees in this passage of the Vita a thinly veiled hint at the *opričnina*.[99] He may be right, only that the hint is not of Russian making. It is a literal translation of Agapetus' chapter 22:

4. Prinimaj xotjaščix sovetovat' tebe blagoe, a ne domogajuščixsja tol'ko laskatel'stv; ibo odni radejut voistinu o pol'ze, drugie že zabot⟨169⟩jatsja tol'ko o ugoždenii vlasti.	= Agap. 22: ἀποδέχου τοὺς τὰ χρηστὰ συμβουλεύειν ἐθέλοντας, ἀλλὰ μὴ τοὺς κολακεύειν ἑκάστοτε σπεύδοντας, οἱ μὲν γὰρ τὸ συμφέρον ⟨169⟩ συνορῶσιν ἐν ἀληθείᾳ, οἱ δὲ πρὸς τὰ δοκοῦντα τοῖς κρατοῦσιν ἀφορῶσι.[100]

97. "Like the pilot of a ship, the emperor's many-eyed mind keeps a continuous watch, firmly handling the oars of equity and justice, and strongly repelling the vehement waves of iniquity, so that the boat of this worldly commonwealth be not crushed by the waves of wickedness." For Greek text, cf. above, p. 161.

98. The epithet occurs towards the end of the first letter of Kurbskij to Ivan IV. Text, e.g., in *Poslanija Ivana Groznogo* (1951), p. 536.

99. G. P. Fedotov, *op.cit.*, p. 181.

100. Agap. 22: "Accept and favor them that desire to give Thee good counsel, but not those that strive to flatter Thee on every occasion. The former truthfully consider what is advantageous; the latter look after what may please those in power."

5. Pače vsjakoj slavy carstvija zemnogo ukrašaet carja venec blagočestija.

= Agap. 15: ὑπὲρ πάντα τῆς βασιλείας τὰ ἔνδοξα, τῆς εὐσεβείας τὸ στέμμα τὸν βασιλέα κοσμεῖ.[101]

6. (Ratnym pokazuet vlast', pokorlivym že čelověkoljubije, i poběždajušče oněx siloju oružija, nevooružennoju ljuboviju ot svoix poběždaetsja. = K.)

= Agap. 20: ...τοῖς πολεμίοις μὲν δεικνύει τὴν ἐξουσίαν, τοῖς ὑπηκόοις δὲ νέμει φιλανθρωπίαν, καὶ νικῶσα ἐκείνους τῇ δυνάμει τῶν ὅπλων, τῇ ἀόπλῳ ἀγάπῃ τῶν οἰκείων ἡττᾶται.[102]

7. Ne vozbranjat' sogrešajuščim est' tol'ko grex, ibo esli kto i živet zakonno, no prilepljaetsja k bezzakonnym, tot byvaet osužden ot Boga, kak součastnik v zlyx delax.[103]

= Agap. 28: ἴσον τῷ πλημμελεῖν τὸ μὴ κωλύειν τοὺς πλημμελοῦντας λογίζου. κἂν γάρ τις πολιτεύηται μὲν ἐνθέσμως, ἀνέχηται δὲ τῶν βιούντων ἀθέσμως, συνεργὸς τῶν κακῶν παρὰ Θεῷ κρίνεται.[104]

After this passage, which sounds so genuine in the mouth of an adversary of the *opričnina*, Philip's speech closes with a few lines exhorting the tsar to uphold the true faith and to keep it free from heresy.

Another part of the Vita in which Philip's "own" words are related, is a secret dialogue between the prince of the Church and the temporal ruler, supposed to have taken place towards the beginning of Philip's pontificate. In the dialogue, the metropolitan is made to proceed systematically and to start right away with Agapetus' chapter 1:

8. O deržavnyi, imeja na sebe san prevyše vsjakoj česti, počti Gospoda ⟨170⟩ davšago tebe sie dostoinstvo, ibo skipetr zemnoj est' tol'ko podobie

= Agap. 1: τιμῆς ἁπάσης ὑπέρτερον ἔχων ἀξίωμα, βασιλεῦ, τίμα ὑπὲρ ⟨170⟩ ἅπαντας τὸν τούτου σε ἀξιώσαντα Θεόν, ὅτι καὶ καθ' ὁμοίωσιν

101. Agap. 15: "Above all glorious ornaments of a Kingdom, the crown of piety does best ornate an emperor.

102. Agap. 20: "...he shows power to his enemies; but to his subjects, he shows humane kindness. Therefore, as he overcomes the enemies by strength of arms, so he is subdued by his subjects on account of his peaceful (= "weaponless") love for them."

103. Passages 1-7 in G. P. Fedotov, *Svjatoj Filipp*, p. 179f.

104. Agap. 28: "Not to chastise sinners is in itself a sin. For whosoever leads a lawful life, but suffers wicked livers, is before God held their accomplice."

nebesnago, daby naučil ty čelovekov xranit' pravdu.	τῆς ἐπουρανίου βασιλείας ἔδωκέ σοι τὸ σκῆπτρον τῆς ἐπιγείου δυναστείας, ἵνα τοὺς ἀνθρώπους διδάξῃς τὴν τοῦ δικαίου φυλακήν.[105]

Philip, however, does not stop with this borrowing from Agapetus. He goes on:

9. Zemnogo obladanie bogatstva rečnym vodam upodobljaetsja i malo-po-malu iždivaetsja; soxranjaetsja tol'ko odno nebesnoe sokrovišče pravdy.	= Agap. 7: τῶν ἐπιγείων χρημάτων ὁ ἄστατος πλοῦτος τῶν ποταμίων ῥευμάτων μιμεῖται τὸν δρόμον, πρὸς ὀλίγον μὲν ἐπιῤῥέων... μετ' ὀλίγον δὲ παραῤῥέων... μόνος δὲ τῆς εὐποιίας ὁ θησαυρὸς μόνιμός ἐστι.[106]
10. Esli i vysok ty sanom, no estestvom telesnym podoben vsjakomu čeloveku (ašče ubo, carju, i obrazom Božim počten esi, no persti zemnoj priložen esi. = M.).	Compare Agapetus 21, p. 147 above.

This was the familiar Agapetus chapter 21, with its "moderating" second part duly recorded and its first deifying clause provided, as it were, with a minus sign. By this device, a statement exalting the ruler's power has been turned into its opposite. It has been seen that Ivan the Terrible found it expedient to give this quotation the same twist in his polemics against Kurbskij. Incidentally, the comparison between *obložen* (*obloženy*), used by Ivan IV in the passage reminiscent of Agapetus 21, and *priložen* of the Slavic translation of Agapetus 21 inserted into the Vita of Philip, should remove all doubt as to the "Agapetian" origin of

105. Agap. 1: "Considering, O mighty emperor, that Thou hast the highest and most honorable dignity of all dignities, Thou shouldest above all honor God, Who has bestowed such honor upon Thee. For God, in likeness of His celestial empire has delivered to Thee the sceptre and governance of this world to teach men to keep justice."

106. Agap. 7: "The unsteadfast possession of earthly riches follows the course of flowing waters. For a short while, it floats to those who fancy themselves in their possession, but shortly after they float by and enrich others. The only permanent acquisition is the treasure of good deeds."

Ivan's passage, quoted by the tsar from memory. The metropolitan continued:

⟨171⟩

11. Tot po istine možet nazyvat'sja vlastelinom, kto obladaet sam soboju, ne rabotaet strastjam.	= Agap. 18.[107]

Finally, the tsar succeeded in breaking this chain of quotations and giving a retort, whereupon there ensued between the two a lively and interesting altercation on the metropolitan's right to intercede for the tsar's oppressed subjects. But even this part of the dialogue contains two gems from Agapetus:

12. Esli odin iz služitelej korablja vpadaet v iskušenie, ne bol'šuju delaet on bedu plavajuščim, no esli sam kormčij, to vsemu korablju nanosit on pogibel'.	= Agap. 10: ὅταν μὲν ὁ ναύτης σφαλῇ, μικρὰν φέρει τοῖς συμπλέουσι βλάβην, ὅταν δὲ αὐτὸς ὁ κυβερνήτης, παντὸς ἐργάζεται τοῦ πλοίου ἀπώλειαν.[108]
13. (Bogatstvo bo otxodit i deržava mimo grjadet = K.) bezsmertno tol'ko odno žitie po Boge.[109]	= Agap. 15: ...ὁ γὰρ πλοῦτος ἀπέρχεται καὶ ἡ δόξα μετέρχεται, τὸ δὲ κλέος τῆς ἐνθέου πολιτείας ἀθανάτοις αἰῶσι συμπαρεκτείνεται.[110]

The last speech attributed to Philip by the compiler of his Vita was delivered in the solemn setting of the Dormition Cathedral of the Kremlin in 1568. There the clash occurred which brought the tension between Philip and Ivan into the open and was followed by the metropolitan's deposition. The pontiff first refused to bless the tsar. Then he bitterly reproached him for spilling blood at the instigation of "flatterers," that is, Ivan's new creatures, who had replaced the council of magnates. A part of the reprimand was couched in terms avowedly borrowed from a "God-inspired chronicler" — this was the rank to which Agapetus had

107. "For certain I affirm thee to be an emperor seeing thou rulest over and subduest thy voluptuous passions." For text, cf. above, p. 163.

108. Agap. 10: "Whenever a sailor commits an error, he hurts but little those that sail with him. But if it is the pilot who goes off course, the whole ship goes to wrack."

109. Passages 8-13 in G. P. Fedotov, *Svjatoj Filipp*, pp. 142-144.

110. Agap. 15: ..."for why, earthly riches and glory do soon vanish away, but the renown of godly life is immortal for all time to come."

been promoted. *Istinu skazal bogoduxnovennyj letopisec*, Philip is made to say,

14. (otvraščajsja laskovcev lestnyx sloves; vrany xititel'nyja iskopyvajut tělesnyja očesa, sii že ⟨172⟩ duševnyja oslěpljajut mysli, ne popuščajušče viděti istiny. Ovii bo xvaljat suščaja xuly dostojnaja, druzii že xuljat mnogaždy xvaly dostojnaja. = K.)[111]

= Agap. 12: ἀποστρέφου τῶν κολάκων τοῦς ἀπατηλοὺς λόγους, ὥσπερ τῶν κοράκων τοὺς ἁρπακτι⟨171⟩κοὺς τρόπους. οἱ μὲν γὰρ τοὺς τοῦ σώματος ἐξορύττουσιν ὀφθαλμούς, οἱ δὲ τοὺς τῆς ψυχῆς ἐξαμβλύνουσι λογισμούς, μὴ συγχωροῦντες ὁρᾶν τὴν τῶν πραγμάτων ἀλήθειαν. ἢ γὰρ ἐπαινοῦσι ἔσθ' ὅτε τὰ ψόγου ἄξια, ἢ ψέγουσι πολλάκις τὰ ἐπαίνων κρείττονα.[112]

One other phrase of the metropolitan's reprimand is an echo of the second part of Agapetus's chapter 21: *ili zabyl, čto i sam ty pričasten persti zemnoj i proščenija grexov trebueš?*[113] "Hast thou forgotten that thou too art ⟨by nature⟩ a participant in the earthly dust, and needest thy sins absolved?" This echo, insignificant but unmistakable, will perhaps help to elucidate the question of the authenticity of Philip's speech. It may be asked whether the quotations from Agapetus put into Philip's mouth are entirely the product of a late sixteenth-century Muscovite scholar's zeal for copying, or whether some of them were uttered by the real metropolitan, for instance, at the moment of the clash in the Dormition Cathedral. At first, it seems more than improbable that Philip should have found nothing better to say on that occasion than to repeat the wisdom of the "God-inspired chronicler." Scholars, although unaware of the source of Philip's speeches, have expressed doubts as to their authenticity, preferring to see in them the reflection of opinions held by the anti-autocratic ecclesiastical circles of the late sixteenth century.[114] The present writer, all his insistence upon the cento character of Philip's

111. Karamzin, *Istorija*, IX, n. 178; cf. G. P. Fedotov, *op. cit.*, p. 147.

112. Agap. 12: "Thou shalt withstand the enticing words of flatterers, as thou wouldst eschew the ways of ravening crows. For crows peck out the corporal eyes. But flatterers blind the understanding of man's soul, since they will not suffer him to perceive the truth of things. For either they praise things that are worthy to be dispraised, or else dispraise things most worthy to be praised."

113. G. P. Fedotov, *Svjatoj Filipp*, p. 147.

114. G. P. Fedotov, *op. cit.*, p. 182; V. Leontovitsch, *Die Rechtsumwälzung unter Ivan dem Schrecklichen und die Ideologie der Russischen Selbstherrschaft* (Stuttgart, 1947), p. 45.

words notwithstanding, is inclined to believe that Agapetus' chapter 21 was really echoed by the walls of the Dormition Cathedral during the scene of 1568. Here is why.

Philip's Vita is not the only account of what occurred in the Cathedral. J. Taube and E. Cruse related the pontiff's speech in their ⟨173⟩ lampoon on Ivan IV which appeared in 1572, four years after the event.[115] It is safe to assume that Agapetus was not a *livre de chevet* with these international adventurers and cheats. And yet they make Philip say to the tsar: "Think that although God has put you high in this world, you nevertheless are a mortal man."[116] If it stood alone, this phrase would be commonplace enough. But, according to the Vita, the metropolitan quoted chapter 21, as well as another passage from Agapetus. Therefore Taube's and Cruse's version is to be evaluated as an echo of the same chapter. It is difficult to deny that very soon after the event of 1568 a tradition existed of Philip's having used the God-Man antithesis inspired by Agapetus to upbraid Ivan IV. This tradition may have had a foundation in fact.

It appears now that the adversaries of Ivan's absolutism used Agapetus to an even greater extent than did the apologists and theoreticians of the Muscovite imperial claims. This fact, if considered solely from the point of view of this author's usefulness for the "liberal" party, poses no problem. In Agapetus' work, praise is entwined with humble admonitions, the latter perhaps prevailing. This has even prompted the rather incongruous theory that the Deacon's chapters were but a veiled criticism of Justinian's reign.[117] The "liberals" had only to strengthen the admonitions and to weaken the praise. Such was, in fact, their procedure. A basic problem arises as soon as we turn to the political struggle of that time.

It has been recently maintained, on general grounds, that in sixteenth-century Muscovy the anti-autocratic party had no ideology of its own to distinguish it from the supporters of the Tsar's absolute rule.[118] It should be added that this weakness may have partly con-

115. Ed. G. Ewers and M. von Engelhardt, *Beiträge zur Kenntnis Russlands und seiner Geschichte*, I [= *Sammlung Russischer Geschichte*, X, 1] (Dorpat, 1816), 187-238.

116. Cf. Ewers and v. Engelhardt, *op. cit.*, p. 210: *Gedenck doch, ob Dich Gott in der Welt erhoehet, Du dennoch ein sterblicher Mensch bist.*

117. Proposed by A. Bellomo, *Agapeto diacono e la sua scheda regia* (Bari, 1906). (Cf. the destructive review by K. Prächter in *Byzantinische Zeitschrift*, XVII (1908), 152-164).

118. V. Leontovitsch, *Die Rechtsumwälzung*, pp. 44-51.

tributed to the "liberals" defeat. The extensive use of Agapetus by the anonymous eulogist of Vasilij III and by Ivan IV on one hand and by Philip or the compiler of his Vita on the other explains ⟨174⟩ the common traits in the ideological proclamations of both hostile camps, and provides a textual, and therefore cogent, argument converging with the recent thesis.

The first attempts to create a politically — and spiritually — independent center in the North in defiance of Kiev fall in Andrej Bogoljubskij's time. This development culminated in Ivan the Terrible's Moscow, where it received the articulate ideological form which was to endure until the twenties of the eighteenth century. Whatever the construction of late fourteenth- to sixteenth-century propaganda may have been, it is as plausible to maintain that the line of this development goes from twelfth-century Suzdal' to sixteenth-century Muscovy. It is hardly a coincidence that Agapetus should have entered Russian literature at both these historical junctures. No less significant is the vogue for Agapetus' chapter 21, whose boldness is by no means representative of the Byzantine standard doctrine of the emperor as the imitator of Christ.

Our investigation might well have ended at this point. But it is tempting to follow the somewhat different fate of Agapetus in sixteenth- and seventeenth-century Ukraine.

On the eve of the Union of Brest, in 1592, the Orthodox Stauropegiac Fraternity of Lwów (L'viv) petitioned Tsar Fëdor Ivanovič and some influential court personages for assistance in the construction of a church in that city. The letter to the tsar may or may not have been written by the metropolitan of Trnovo, Dionysius, Constantinople's exarch in "Great and Little Russia," but the approval of its final form certainly lay with the Fraternity. As the following passages prove, L'viv must have been aware that the correct approach in attempting to get money out of the heir to Ivan IV was to show that it knew what was, ideologically, the order of the day in Moscow:

> 1. Česti vsjakoja prevyše imja (*read* imějaj) dostojanie carju, počitaeši bo pače vsex sie tebě darovavšago Boga, jako i po podobiju nebesnago carstvija, dade tebě skipetr zemnago vlastitel'stva, da jakože nebesnyj car' Bog na nebesi, sice i ty tixoobrazně čelověky milueši na zemli i učiši six bljusti pravednaja...

This is almost word for word Agapetus chapter 1 (for Greek text, see above, page 165), only that the admonition has been changed into a statement of fact, a technique which will be repeated later, and, what is more important, the tsar is here likened to God not in power, ⟨175⟩ but in love. Centuries later, Gogol' will follow the same line of thought. The letter continues:

> 2. ...mnogobodrstvujuščim umnym carskim tvoim okom...

— this is the "vigilant and many-eyed mind" of the emperor which caused trouble to almost every Slavic excerptor of Agapetus —

> ...krěpko upravljaja ix na blagyja nažiti.

(Compare Agap. 2; for text see page 161, above.)

> 3. Neprikosnoven bo esi čelověkom vysokosti radi dol'njago carstvija, blagopristupen že moljaščimsja byvaeši vosprijatija radi gornjago i otverzaeši sluxi blagoprijatně iže v niščetě mnogobedstvujuščim, da obrjaščeši Božij slux tebě priklonennyj. I jako ubo milostiv ko prosjaščim milosti byvaeši, takova i sebe moljaščus' Vladyku milostiva obrětaeši.

This is almost word for word Agapetus 8 (for text, see p. 162, above), with its general tenor applied to Fëdor; a most appropriate choice in a petition asking for a subsidy.

Agapetus 21 follows a few lines later, with significant modifications:

4. Suščestvom ubo tělese raven esi čelověkom, o carju, dostojaniem že prevosxodiši vsjačeski: i jako blagonaučen ne gněvaešis', i jako tlěnen, ne voznosišis'.[119]	τῇ μὲν οὐσίᾳ τοῦ σώματος, ἴσος παντὶ ἀνθρώπῳ ὁ βασιλεύς, τῇ ἐξουσίᾳ δὲ τοῦ ἀξιώματος ὅμοιός ἐστι τῷ ἐπὶ πάντων Θεῷ. οὐκ ἔχει γὰρ ἐπὶ γῆς τὸν αὐτοῦ ὑψηλότερον. χρὴ τοίνυν αὐτὸν καὶ ὡς Θεὸν μὴ ὀργίζεσθαι καὶ ὡς θνητὸν μὴ ἐπαίρεσθαι.

The changes are worth discussing. Agapetus' "He is like unto God high above" has been omitted altogether; the words "Thou excellest all" seem to correspond to "He hath not his higher on earth" of the Greek; instead of "as God, he should not show anger," the Fraternity text reads "well instructed, Thou showest not anger."[120] The passage on the ruler's transient nature, which the eulogist of Vasilij III has omitted is included

119. Passages 1-4 in *Akty... Zapadnoj Rossii*, IV (1851), 47f. The petition contains one more familiar quotation, *car' ubo esi, iže věncem cělomudrija obložen i porfiroju pravdy oboločen* = Agap. ch. 18.

120. Unless one reads *Bogom naučen* for *blagonaučen*. Cf. *Bogom vrazumlevaem* in the fifteenth-century *Poxvala*, ed. A. Popov, *Istoriko-literaturnyj obzor*, p. 362.

here. All these omissions and modifications occur ⟨176⟩ not in a polemical anti-autocratic treatise but in an address intended to please the Tsar of Moscow. Here all may be in the nuances; but what is expressed is a different conception of the supreme ruler's office. No further conclusions are possible as long as the authorship of the Fraternity's missive remains in doubt. Although the changes may reflect the view of a high dignitary of the Patriarchate of Constantinople, they certainly did not contradict the opinions of the Ukrainian intellectuals of that time. They knew not only their Latin and their Polish, but also their Greek quite well and could have found the less extravagant forms of the Byzantine imperial doctrine more acceptable.

And yet, the first Slavic edition of Agapetus appeared in the Ukraine in the printing press of the Kievan Laura in 1628.[121] Unfortunately, no details can be given on this translation, as the pamphlet is not accessible in the West. It has been asserted that the translation was done by Peter Mogila (Mohyla), the later archimandrite of the Laura and metropolitan of Kiev, directly from the Greek in 1627.[122] The title of the 1628 edition announces that it is destined for "all those who righteously seek to rule over their passions." The intention is moralistic, not political. The archimandrite of the Laura, if he is the translator of Agapetus, is to be put on the same plane with Canon Thomas Paynell, who, approximately a hundred years earlier, declared in the preface to his English translation of Agapetus: "I saie it is a booke of great wysedome and learnying, conteyning all these preceptes, by the whiche not only a prince but all other estates may learne to do iustyce."[123] The closest parallel ⟨177⟩ to the Muscovite interest in Agapetus is not to be sought in the near seventeenth-century Ukraine, but in the faraway

121. *Ljubomudrejšago kyr Agapita diakona blažennejšemu i blagočestivejšemu carju Iustinianu, pače že vsěm pravedno xotjaščim nad strast'mi carstvovati, glavizny poučitelny*. Exact description of the print in F. Titov, "Materijaly dlja istoriji knyžnoji spravy na Vkrajini v XVI-XVIII vv.," *Ukr. Akad. Nauk, Zbirnyk ist.-fil. viddilu*, no. 17 (Kiev, 1924), p. 193f. Cf. also, I. Karataev, *Xronologičeskaja rospis' slavjanskix knig napečatannyx kirillovskimi bukvami 1491-1730* (1861), p. 40. It should be noted that Pseudo-Basil's Chapters were also first printed in the Ukraine, namely in Ostroh, in 1607. The text, in Slavonic and in the vernacular, appeared as an appendix to two sermons of John Chrysostom. It bears the title: *Testament hreckaho cesarja Vasylija do syna svojeho L'va*. Cf. A. S. Arxangel'skij, *Obrazovanie i literatura v moskovskom gosudarstve konca XV-XVII vv*. (Kazan', 1901), p. 428.

122. S. Golubev, *Kievskij mitropolit Petr Mogila i ego spodvižniki* I (1883), p. 400.

123. English ed. of 1546; cf. above, note 29.

seventeenth-century France. About the very time when the "Hortatory Chapters" were being translated in Kiev, the youthful Louis XIII improved his Latin by translating Agapetus into French under the guidance of his preceptor David Rivault, the same man whom he commissioned to publish the French version of the Chapters of Pseudo-Basil[124] which had so decisively influenced the Russian coronation ritual. In this context, the counterpart of the Metropolitan of Moscow, Philip, is not the Metropolitan of Kiev, Mohyla, but the Catholic Bishop Bossuet who said to the Dauphin "vous êtes des Dieux, c'est à dire vous avez dans vôtre autorité... un caractère Divin... mais, ô Dieux de boue et de poussière,"[125] amalgamating Ps. 81:6 with the second part of Agapetus 21. What all this means for the French State theory under Louis XIV is outside the scope of this article.

Muscovite autocracy was a native creation, although the garb it donned was of foreign making. Muscovite imperial ideology did not come into being because some *literati* chanced upon Agapetus' little work. Ideologies, more or less prefabricated, are found when they are needed. But there is a certain range of choice in the search for a ready ideological mold into which the still inarticulate tendencies can be forced. Its selection is a matter of importance. The mold, once chosen, predetermines the form and the modes of expression of certain desires and beliefs to which a political system corresponds. To some extent, this mold is a guaranty of the system's durability, since it determines the way of thinking even of its opponents. In Muscovy, the choice fell upon Agapetus with the chapters of Pseudo-Basil ranking next. By our standards, these texts were rather second-rate compendia. Even the Byzantines would agree that they ⟨178⟩ had better literature to offer on the subject of government and its ideological basis.

Whatever Agapetus' value was, he not only affected political thinking in Muscovy, but often proved almost a substitute for such thinking. Original Muscovite speculation on matters politic, if existent, will have to be sought outside the conventionally quoted Russian passages, unless

124. David Rivault, Sieur de Fleurance, *Remonstrances de Basile, Empereur des Romains, à Léon son cher fils* (2nd ed., Paris 1649). According to the title page, the translation was made *par l'exprés commandement du très-Auguste... Louis XIII*. The first edition appeared about 1613. The reëdition of 1649 was made in order to provide the young Louis XIV with a suitable textbook on government. Louis XIII's own translation of Agapetus appeared in Paris in 1612.

125. *Politique tirée des propres paroles de l'écriture sainte*, livre V, article IV, proposition I, *in fine*.

one wants to discover this speculation in their modifications of Agapetus' text. One more feature perhaps reflecting a general quality of the human mind has become apparent: the tenacity with which the same texts of Agapetus were used to express opposed views, or even any views at all. Herein lies the power, and the threat, of catechisms. It is as important to bring this point out as to have identified the source of a series of passages from Kievan and Muscovite literature.[126]

126. An investigation of seventeenth- and eighteenth-century Agapetian passages, although less important for the purposes of the present article, would be a worthwhile undertaking. With some authors, we could almost postulate the use of Agapetus. Ivan Timofeev, a staunch defender of absolute power, believed that no one but God could judge the Tsar's actions and he made a clear distinction between a sovereign's person, capable of error, and the ever immaculate throne, "animate" and innocent of sin. ["Animate" (*oduševlen*) corresponds to ἔμψυχος of the Greek and hearkens back to related antique and Byzantine notions on the ruler as "Living Law."] It is not surprising, then , that in his *Vremennik*, written about 1617 and dealing with the Time of Troubles, Timofeev quoted a part of Agapetus, chapter 21: *ašče i čelovek car' be po estestvu, vlastiju dostoinstva privlečen est' Bogu, iže nado vsemi, ne imat' bo na zemli vysočajši sebe* [= fol. 205^v of the MS. Cf. Deržavina, V. P. Adrianova-Peretc, edd., *Vremennik Ivana Timofeeva* (Moscow-Leningrad, 1951), p. 107]. It is more unusual to find a cento from Agapetus in a work dedicated to Peter the Great. Its author is the Ukrainian "Cossack-Versifier" Semen Klymovs'kyj-Klymov, who submitted his poems "On the Impartial Administration of Justice by Those in Office" and "On Humility of the High" to Peter during the latter's sojourn in Khar'kov in 1724. The prose "Preface to the Pious Reader" contains Agapetus' chapters 2, 46, 51, 37, 1, 8, 21 in that order. Texts in V. I. Sreznevskij, *Klimovskij-Klimov, "Kazak-Stixotvorec," i dva ego sočinenija* (Khar'kov, 1905) [an offprint from *Sbornik Xar'kovskago Ist.-Fil. Obščestva*, XVI]. Sreznevskij may go too far when he finds that Klymovs'kyj was "far from praising monarchs in general and the recipient of his poems in particular." Nevertheless, Klymovs'kyj, apparently wronged in the courts by a venal official of the Tsar, maintained a fairly independent attitute and arranged his Agapetian material (derived from the 1628 edition?) correspondingly. This is in line with the treatment of Agapetus by the Fraternity of L'viv. What is characteristic of the new situation is the fact that the first Tsar of Moscow to break with Byzantine traditions and to become Emperor of Russia, Western style, should be presented with sixth-century Byzantine arguments in the Ukraine from where the first strong wave of Western influences had reached Moscow less than a century earlier. I am indebted to Professor Čiževsky for drawing my attention to the texts of Timofeev and Klymovs'kyj.

[*Addendum*: I note with regret that V. Valdenberg's "Nastavlenie pisatelja VI v. Agapita v russkoj pis'mennosti," *Vizantijskij Vremennik*, XXIV (1923-1926), 27-34, has escaped my attention. At present I can only recommend that the reader consult Val'denberg's note.]

VII

Podil Jedynoji Xrystovoji Cerkvy

Mytropolyt Ilarion: Podil jedynoji Chrystovoji Cerkvy i perši sproby pojednannja jiji, istoryčno-kanonična monohrafija. [Metropolitan Hilarion (Ivan Ohijenko), The Division of the One Church of Christ and the First Attempts at Reunion, a Historical and Canonical Monograph]. Winnipeg, 1953, 381 pp.

Metropolitan Hilarion's book covers the two thousand years of Christian history; he begins with a discussion of the development of patriarchal and papal power, and then traces differences, controversies and attempts at reunion between the Eastern and the Catholic Church up to the present day, although his detailed presentation does not extend much beyond the Union of Florence. In his preface, the author deplores the lack of "truthful popular" literature on this subject and purports to fill this gap with his monograph, the first of its kind in the Ukrainian language. He promises to treat his subject matter in a scholarly but accessible manner, on the basis of "historical sources, the canons of the Church, and sound Christian logic". He takes care to define his Orthodox standpoint, i. e. that of a person for whom the dogmas and canons of the seven Oecumenical Councils are sacred and binding.

Within this framework and in spite of its more dignified tone and its documentation, the book has to be considered as a new link in a venerable tradition the antecedents of which are the treatises *Kata Latinōn*, with works *Contra errores Graecorum* as the latters' counterpart. The Metropolitan stands firmly on the ground of pentarchy (common and autonomous rule of the five patriarchs — of Rome, Constantinople, Alexandria, Antioch and Jerusalem) with only honorary priority accorded to the Roman bishop. He deals with all the problems conventionally to be disposed of in this type of literature: the Petrine succession, the 3rd canon of the second Oecumenical Council and the 28th canon of the fourth, making the see of New Rome equal and "second after" or equal "after" that of Rome, the canons of the Council of Sardica (considered a local one, therefore not binding for the East) instituting the Bishop of Rome as a source of appeal for other prelates, the pope's intervention in the Christological controversies of the 5th century, the dispute over the title of the "oecumenical" patriarch (end of the 6th century), the recognition of papal claims by Byzantine churchmen during the internal struggles of the 9th century (Studites, Ignatians), not to speak of the "Filioque" and the Unleavened Bread. The two latter, and other points related to western deviations, are treated more succinctly, since the author sees the real stumbling block to Reunion in papal claims of primacy.

The remedy to the present state of separation lies, according to the author, in the convocation of the 8th (counting with the Orthodox) Oecumenical Council (if need be, without Catholic participation), which alone could bring nearer the goal of Reunion, not of subordination, as Rome had repeatedly attempted in its unionist moves. Technically speaking there is no irrevocable necessity for the Orthodox and Catholics to consider each other heretics and schismatics, since no oecumenical council has yet pronounced itself on the differences between the two churches. Once more, the author ranges himself in a venerable Orthodox tradition, since from the 13th to the 15th century, Byzantines invariably countered papal advances with a demand for an oecumenical council.

As all specimens of its kind, the book suffers from its mixed "historico-canonical" character. There is no way of interpreting away the special position accorded to Peter in the New Testament (the author's exegesis, based on Photius', seems strained in places), and it is not astonishing that the Roman see should have exploited it. On the other hand, the tradition of Peter's founding of the Roman church and his martyrdom in Rome, although old, is (as the author does not fail to point out) by no means a guaranty of the historicity of the events themselves. Here an acquaintance with literature dealing with the recent excavations in the Vatican might have strengthened the author's hand. In attacking papal primacy, it is no longer necessary to expose at any length the spurious character of the Donation of Constantine and the Pseudo-Isidorian Decretals. Nor do, of course, numerous Byzantine texts in which papal primacy is recognized (often for partisan reasons) "prove" anything. Historically speaking, the separation between Rome and Constantinople was a result of the loss of the Byzantine grip over Italy, practically consummated with the Longobard invasion (third quarter of the 8th century) and of the emergence of the Caroligian west. A Justinian could still bring the pope into line; a Basil I no longer could. Canonically speaking, this separation is a consequence of Latin innovations, or of stubborn Greek refusal to see the Vicar of Christ in the pope, as the case may be. It is very difficult to reconcile a historical and a dogmatic approach in one book.

One other aspect of the mixed character of the book turns to its disadvantage. It is popular in tone, and yet it purports to be scholarly and gives a large amount of detailed information, buttressed by long bibliographical lists at the end of almost every chapter. Unfortunately the details are sometimes inexact (as when Basil I is said to be of Slavic origin; Constantinople is made to fall on May 25), the treatment anachronistic (as when "patriotic" and "unpatriotic" motives are imputed to the Photian and Ignatian parties) and the literature antiquated and limited mainly to works in Russian. Recent (and not quite so recent) non-Russian literature on the subject as well as the latest editions of texts, seem to be unknown to the author. Such editions of the proceedings of the councils as those by E. SCHWARTZ, HEFELE-LECLERCQ (better than the original Hefele), the old canonical Syntagma of RHALLES-POTLES and the abundant new literature on the Florentine Council, not to speak of articles or monographs like that of VILLER on the attempts at Union from the 13th to the 15th century (Rev. Hist. Eccl., XVII [1921]) or M. H. LAURENT's on Innocent V. (Studi e Testi 129 [1947]), are lacking in the bibliographical lists. The chapters on the so-called Photian schism could give the impression that the author has used the important work of F. DVORNIK (quoted as "a work which appeared in French in 1950"). This is doubtful, since the author asserts that Catholic literature has "invariably" been hostile to Photius. His views on the "liberal" and "conservative" parties in Byzantium go back to the articles of GERASIM (Jared) (Christijanskoe Čtenie of 1872-1873), with whose conclusions Dvornik agrees. It must be said, however, that the extensive bibliographies of Russian works and articles in his book may prove useful to the western reader. It is to be regretted that in the chapter on the oecumenical church conferences no literature concerning the latest one in Amsterdam (1949) is listed, nor is the conference itself mentioned at all.

In short, in the metropolitan's book we have an edifying compilation for the Ukrainian Orthodox reader, on the whole adequately, although in places passionately, expounding the conventional arguments of his Church.

VIII

The Definition of Philosophy in the *Life of Saint Constantine*

To a cultivated Byzantine of the ninth century, philosophy could mean at least two different things. It could be defined as the "discipline of disciplines" providing first principles for all the branches of knowledge, or it could be conceived as moral perfection based on the "true gnosis" of Being, that is to say, on the tenets of Christianity.[1] In the first case, philosophy meant primarily a technical rational activity, and the philosopher was a learned intellectual, dealing with a precious part of antique heritage which he might use for a better understanding of Christian truths. In the second, philosophy was synonymous with an intense spiritual life: the best philosopher was the ascetic monk, and his ancestors, the first true philosophers, were the disciples of Christ.[2]

Between these two extreme acceptations of this term, which in their polarity go back to the first Christian centuries, there lay a gamut of intermediate meanings.[3] From the sixth century on, all "technical" philosophers of Byzantium were Christians teaching Christian students.

1. This is the definition given by St. Nilus (fifth century), Λόγος ἀσκητικός, Migne, *PG*, LXXIX, 721B, quoted here since it was taken over by Georgius Hamartolus (ninth century), p. 345, 3-5, *ed.* de Boor. It also found its way into the encyclopaedias, like the *Suda* (Suidas) and the Lexicon of Zonaras (in both places s.v. φιλοσοφία). In an anonymous alphabetical collection of definitions of philosophical terms, preserved in *Parisinus Gr.* 2138 (13 c.), the formulation of Nilus is even improved upon: φιλοσοφία ἐστὶ ἠθῶν κατόρθωσις μετὰ δόξης τῶν (sic) περὶ τῶν ὄντων εὐσεβοῦς.

2. Nilus, Migne, *PG*, LXXIX, 720A; 721D-723AB, partly excerpted by Georgius Hamartolus, 343, 2f, *ed.* de Boor.

3. Cf., in this context, the interesting essay by F. Dölger, "Zur Bedeutung von φιλόσοφος und φιλοσοφία in byzantinischer Zeit," most conveniently accessible in the author's *Byzanz und die europäische Staatenwelt* (1953), p. 197-208. Dölger, however, concentrates on the non-technical aspect of the meaning of "Philosophy" (philosopher equivalent to monk, to a wise man, to an educated person, to a rhetorician, to a "city slicker" respectively).

Naturally enough, in defining philosophy they strove to harmonize its concepts with the body of Christian doctrine.[4] In view of this, it is noteworthy that throughout the centuries of Byzantium's history they should have clung to the several definitions of philosophy collected by pagan Neoplatonic ⟨450⟩ epigones. On the other hand, no matter how much scorn a religious author may have professed for "exterior" learning, he could not escape its prestige — he succumbed to it whether he was a Cappadocian Father or a ninth-century hagiographer boasting his ignorance of worldly disciplines. While ridiculing the futile pursuits of technical philosophers, Gregory of Nazianzus would slip in an allusion or two so as to let the initiated reader know that he himself was perfectly familiar with their nonsense.[5] While defining the "true philosophy" of his monkish hero, scornful of bookish learning and its vanities, a hagiographer would occasionally adapt for his purposes a definition culled from an introductory technical textbook.[6]

---

4. As an example, cf. the additions to the standard "Hellenic," i.e. pagan, body of definitions of philosophy made by John of Damascus in his "Philosophical Chapters" 3 and 67, Migne, *PG*, XCIV, 533C; 669D.

5. Εἰς Ἡρῶνα τὸν φιλόσοφον, Migne, *PG*, XXXV, 1205B: ταύτης καρπὸς τῆς φιλοσοφίας [i.e., of the ascetic Christian kind] οὐ λόγῳ πλαττόμεναι πόλεις, σκινδαψοί τινες, ὥς αὐτοί φασι [i.e. the "technical" philosophers], καὶ τραγέλαφοι, ἃ γλῶσσα μόνη συντίθησιν. Σκινδαψός, "what d'ye call it," and τραγέλαφος "goat-stag," an imaginary animal, are standard examples used in introductory treatises on philosophy. They are quoted as terms to which no reality corresponds: Elias, *Prolegomena philosophiae* [*Commentaria in Aristotelem Graeca*, XVIII, 1 (1900)], p. 3, 7-8; David, *Prolegomena philosophiae* [*Commentaria in Aristotelem Graeca*, XVIII, 2 (1904)], p. 1, 16-17. In subsequent notes, the *Commentaria* will be quoted as *CAG*.

6. Cf. P. Van den Ven, *ed.*, "La vie grecque de S. Jean le Psichaite," *Le Muséon*, N.S. III (1902), 109, 13-14. The author thunders against worldly learning (p. 109), but he does it in such a detailed manner that the invective amounts to a display of "technical" knowledge on his part. Ignatios, who wrote the *Life* of Patriarch Nicephorus (d. 829) soon after the latter's death, views learning as ancillary to the Christian "real knowledge." Still, in his description of "mathematics" he paraphrases introductions to philosophy: cf. *Vita Nicephori*, p. 149, 27-150, 2, *ed.* de Boor, with Ammonius, *In Porphyrii Isagogen Prooemium* [*CAG*, IV, 3 (1891)], p. 14; Elias, *Prolegomena* [*CAG*, XVIII, 1 (1900)], p. 29; David, *Prolegomena* [*CAG*, XVIII, 2 (1904)], p. 60-62. — An opposite combination occurs in *Parisinus Gr*. 1928, fol. 29v (the part of the *Prooemium* of Ammonius where definitions of philosophy are given). There a commentator added Nilus's formula in the margin.

In this business of definitions, then, much is in the nuances. But seeing our way clear in these matters is of some consequence for establishing a "philosopher's" intellectual position. Obviously somebody who gives a "technical" definition of philosophy with Christian modifications, dwells, intellectually, in different regions from those inhabited by a philosopher-monk or saint, whose philosophy is described in terms of ascetic life with additional embellishments of a "technical" origin.

Saint Constantine-Cyril (d. 869), the Byzantine Apostle of the Slavs, appears with the epithet "Philosopher" in Slavic, Greek, and Latin sources alike. We have seen that this term was ambiguous in Byzantine usage. What kind of a philosopher was Constantine? To clarify, it will be worthwhile to discuss the definition of philosophy attribued to him in his *Vita*. By guessing as to the character of the sources of this definition and assigning to it a place in the semantic spectrum of "philosophy," as the term was conceived in Constantine's time, a better insight may be obtained into the Saint's intellectual outlook.

The Slavic *Vita* of Constantine recounts how the logothete Theoctistus, impressed by young Constantine's learning and natural abilities, once asked him: "O Philosopher, I should like to know what philosophy is." "With a quick mind," the Saint, by then a freshly-baked graduate of the Imperial University, replied: "Knowledge (*razumъ*) of things Divine and human, as much as (*jeliko*) man is able to approach God, for it teaches man by deeds (*? dětěliją*) to be in the image and after the likeness (*po podobiju*) of the One who created him."[7] Had Constantine's words been preserved in Greek they would probably have read: θείων καὶ ἀνθρωπίνων πραγμάτων γνῶσις, καθ' ὅσον δύναται ἄνθρωπος προσεγγίσαι (πλησιάσαι) θεῷ, ὅτι πράξει διδάσκει ἄνθρωπον κατ' εἰκόνα καὶ καθ' ὁμοίωσιν εἶναι τῷ ποιήσαντι (πλάσαντι, κτίσαντι) αὐτόν.

The main ultimate sources of this composite definition are easy to ascertain. It was a Stoic belief that wisdom consisted in the knowledge of things Divine and human: οἱ μὲν οὖν Στωικοὶ ἔφασαν⟨451⟩ and τὴν... σοφίαν εἶναι θείων τε καὶ ἀνθρωπίνων ἐπιστήμην and τὴν σοφίαν [*sc.*

7. *I vъprosi ego jedinoją, glagolę: filosofe, xotelъ byxъ uvěděti, čьto jestь filosofija. On že skoromь umomь reče abije: božijamъ i člověčamъ věščьmъ razumъ, i jeliko možetъ člověkъ přibližiti sę božě, jako dětěliją učitъ člověka po obrazu i po podobiju byti sъtvorъšemu i.*

φασὶν] ἐπιστήμην θείων τε καὶ ἀνθρωπίνων πραγμάτων.[8] Philosophy viewed as man's approaching God according to his ability goes back to Platonic passages, especially to *Theaetetus* 176 AB, διὸ καὶ πειρᾶσθαι χρὴ ἐνθένδε ἐκεῖσε φεύγειν ὅτι τάχιστα. φυγὴ δὲ ὁμοίωσις θεῷ κατὰ τὸ δυνατόν: "Wherefore we must endeavor to fly from this world to the other as soon as we can. Now that flight [according to the Neoplatonic commentators of this passage "flight" here was equal to the pursuit of philosophy[9]] means the becoming like to God as much as possible."[10] The question as to the source of the part of Constantine's definition stating that philosophy teaches men to approach God *dětěliją* (by deeds?) will be left unanswered at this point in our discussion.

Finally, the words "in the image and after the likeness" are a quotation from *Gen.* 1:26. In my opinion, it is not necessary to consider this quotation as a third part of Constantine's definition. It is rather an elaboration on the Platonic formula where the word ὁμοίωσις occurs as it does in the Septuagint version of *Gen.* 1:26.

It is highly improbable that Constantine would have drawn his definition from several texts such as Pseudo-Plutarch and the *Theaetetus*. This brings up the problem of his more immediate sources. Here difficulties begin, since the question of late antique and Byzantine definitions of philosophy has not been systematically treated.[11] As several passages of the Slavic *Vita Constantini* depend on Gregory of Nazianzus,[12] and as the Stoic formula occurs in his writings,[13] this Father has been suggested as the source for the first part of Constan-

8. J. v. Arnim, *Stoicorum veterum fragmenta*, II (1923), p. 15, 3-5 (Ps.-Plutarch = Aëtius); p. 15, 12-13 (Sextus Empiricus).

9. David, *Prolegomena* [*CAG*, XVIII, 2 (1904)], p. 37, 11.

10. Translation quoted from B. H. Kennedy, *The Theaetetus of Plato* (1894), p. 161. Other pertinent Platonic passages are *Resp.* 500C (εἰς ὅσον δυνατὸν ἀνθρώπῳ ὁμοιοῦσθαι θεῷ) and 613A (ὅ γε φιλόσοφος... θεῖος εἰς τὸ δυνατὸν ἀνθρώπῳ γίγνεται).

11. In R. Eucken's *Geschichte der philosophischen Terminologie* (1879) the term φιλοσοφία is not even mentioned.

12. F. Grivec, "Vitae Constantini et Methodii; versio latina, notis ... de fontibus ... illustrata," *Acta Academiae Velehradensis*, XVII (1941), pp. 10; 12; 17; 55. This work sums up the author's earlier researches, devoted in part to the utilization of Gregory of Nazianzus in *Vita Constantini* and *Vita Methodii*.

13. Migne, *PG*, XXXV, 460A; XXXVI, 129A: σοφία δὲ ὡς ἐπιστήμη θείων τε καὶ ἀνθρωπίνων πραγμάτων.

tine's definition.[14] To make such an attribution is to underestimate the frequency with which the Stoic formula occurs in literature, Greek, Latin, and even Arabic. To give some instances, it is used by the Septuagint,[14a] Philo,[14b] Clement of Alexandria,[15] Origen,[16] Saint Basil[17] (from where it wandered to the *Melissa* of the eleventh-century monk Antonius[18]); under the guise of a definition of jurisprudence, it opens the Institutes of Justinian;[19] in the Latin West, the twelfth-century Dominicus Gundissalinus quotes it in his *De divisione philosophiae*.[20] One other point is more decisive. Gregory of Nazianzus (and all the other Greek Fathers) used the Stoic definition in the form transmitted ⟨452⟩ in Pseudo-Plutarch and Sextus Empiricus: They speak not of φιλοσοφία but of σοφία; for "knowledge" they put ἐπιστήμη.[21] Constantine's corresponding passage presupposes φιλοσοφία and has *razum* for "knowledge." Aside from its use for διάνοια, νόημα, σύνεσις "thought, understanding," *razum* translate γνῶσις of the Greek in most cases and I know of no instance in the earliest texts where

14. F. Grivec, "Vitae Constantini et Methodii," *Acta Acad. Velehradensis*, XVII (1941), 56, 170.

14a. Of course in the 'Hellenizing' *IV Macc.* 1:16.

14b. *De cong.* 79 = III, 88, 1 *ed.* Wendland.

15. *Paedag.* II, 25, 3 = I, 171, 16ff, *ed.* Stählin (for further parallels, cf. the apparatus to this passage); *Strom.* VI, 7 = II, 459, 9 *ed.* Stählin.

16. *Contra Celsum* III, 72 = I, 263, 24 *ed.* Koetschau.

17. *In princ. Proverb.*, Migne, *PG*, XXXI, 389C.

18. Migne, *PG*, CXXXVI, 798A.

19. *Inst.* I, 1, 1: *Iuris prudentia est divinarum atque humanarum rerum notitia* (taken over from Ulpian, cf. *Dig.* 1, 1, 10). *Notitia* is a routine rendering of γνῶσις, cf. *Corpus Gloss. Lat.*, *ed.* Goetz, II, 134, 37; 264, 12; 457, 69. It took the glossators until the sixteenth century to realize the connection between this definition and philosophy: Cuias said: *hoc commune est cum sapientia, cum philosophia*. Cf. *Glossa ordinaria* to *Inst.* I, 1, 1, s.v. *notitia*. I am indebted to Professor E. H. Kantorowicz for drawing my attention to this passage in the Institutes.

20. Ed. L. Baur, *Beiträge zur Geschichte der Philosophie des Mittelalters*, IV, 2-3 (1903), pp. 6, 1f; 7, 13f; cf. also pp. 168ff and 325ff of Baur's commentary.

21. The only exceptions I have come across are the passages *IV Macc.* 1:16 and *Strom.* VI, 7 in Clement of Alexandria, where γνῶσις is used. Clement seems to depend on the Septuagint: W. Völker, *Der wahre Gnostiker nach Clements Alexandrinus* (1952), pp. 310, n. 3; 382, n. 6 [*Texte und Untersuchungen zur Geschichte der altchr. Lit.*, V. Reihe, Bd. 2]. In both instances the word being defined is σοφία.

it would stand for ἐπιστήμη, which seems to be rendered in Church Slavonic by *xǫdožьstvo, xytrostь,* or *uměnije*[22] If we find a Greek text using both φιλοσοφία and γνῶσις in defining philosophy, we will be able to eliminate Gregory of Nazianzus as Constantine's prospective source.

As for the Platonic part of the Saint's definition, the *Theaetetus* passage is quoted or alluded to by a plethora of antique, patristic and Byzantine authors. K. Prächter[23] and H. Merki[24] collected a large number of names from Plutarch and Julian through a Pythagorean excerpted by Photius to an eleventh-century commentator of Aristotle, to which might be added such writers as Clement of Alexandria,[25] the author of the ninth century *Vita* of John the Psichaite,[26] Psellus,[27] the

22. V. Jagić considers *razumъ* for γνῶσις as a sign of the oldest layer of Old Church Slavonic vocabulary, *Entstehunsgeschichte der kirchenslavischen Sprache* (1913), p. 434. Cf. also F. Miklosich, *Lexicon Palaeoslovenico-Graeco-Latinum* (1862-65), K. H. Meyer, *Altkirchenslavisch-griechisches Wörterbuch des Codex Suprasliensis* (1935), I. I. Sreznevskij, *Materialy dlja slovarja drevnerusskogo jazyka* (1895-1912), s.v. *razumъ*. Only in the Russo-Slavonic translation of Hamartolus does *razumъ* appear as one of several possible renderings of ἐπιστήμη (cf. V. M. Istrin, *Xronika Georgija Amartola v drevnem slavjanorusskom perevode*, III [1930], 79), but inasmuch as this text dates from the eleventh century, it is unimportant for the ninth-century vocabulary of St. Cyril and his biographers. And even the Hamartolus translating team used *razumъ* in the translation of the St. Nilus definition given in note 1, above (*razuma istinnago*, Istrin, I, 239-20 = τοῦ ὄντος γνώσεως).

23. Review of *CAG*, XXII, 2 (Commentaries by Michael of Ephesus, eleventh century) in *Göttingische gelehrte Anzeigen*, CLXVIII (1906), 861-907, esp. p. 904 and n. 4; review of *Berliner Klassikertexte* II (an anonymous commentary to the *Theaetetus*), *Göttingische gelehrte Anzeigen*, CLXXI (1909), 530-547, esp. pp. 542, n. 2. and 543.

24. H. Merki, Ὁμοίωσις Θεῷ: *Von der platonischen Angleichung an Gott zur Gottähnlichkeit bei Gregor von Nyssa* (1952).

25. *Strom*. I, 52 = II, 34, 12 *ed*. Stählin; II, 167, 23ff, *ed*. Stählin; II, 388, 20ff, *ed*. Stählin.

26. For reference, cf. n. 6 above; quotation, n. 60 below. Therefore the statement by F. Dvornik, *Les légendes de Constantin et de Méthode vues de Byzance* (1933), p. 45, n. 1 is to be qualified.

27. E. Kurtz and F. Drexl, *edd., Michaelis Pselli scripta minora*, I (1936), 431, 24f.: ἡ μὲν [*sc.* philosophy] γὰρ τὸν ἄνθρωπον θεῷ προσαφομοιοῦν πραγματεύεται (from an *Essay on Philosophy*).

Melissa of Antonius,[28] and even the writer of the fourteenth century life of the Emperor John III Ducas Vatatzes.[29]

In the face of such an abundance it is impossible to pinpoint Constantine's sources without making certain specification. What are the ideal requirements for our postulated source of Constantine's definitions? It must be expressly a definition of philosophy, not wisdom; it has to use the word γνῶσις; it has to have both the Stoic and the Platonic variants, closely related to each other; preferably it should consist of them alone; in the best case the ὁμοίωσις-motif should be combined with *Gen.* 1:26.

These specifications once established, we shall return to our starting point — the fourth chapter of *Vita Constantini*, especially that part of it where the Saint's course of studies is described. It seems justifiable to connect Constantine's studies with his definition of philosophy, since the function of this definition in the economy of the fourth chapter of his *Vita* is to show the profundity ⟨453⟩ of learning he had acquired at the university. In the fourth chapter of the *Vita*, we learn that Constantine studied dialectic with Photius.[30] What did such a study encompass? To some of Constantine's contemporaries, dialectic was simply "called philosophy by experts in the matter."[31] According to other experts

28. Migne, *PG*, CXXXVI, 1116A (attribution to Justin Martyr more than doubtful).

29. Ed. A. Heisenberg, "Kaiser Johannes Batatzes der Barmherzige," *Byzantinische Zeitschrift*, XIV (1905), 219, 5-9. For quotation, see n. 58 below.

30. The Vita says that Constantine first mastered grammar; then, most of the mss proceed: "He learned Homer and geometry *both (i)* with Leo and (*i*) with Photius [he learned] dialectic, and all philosophical disciplines, moreover rhetoric, arithmetic, astronomy, music and all the other Hellenic arts." Only two mss omit "both." It still remains that Photius taught dialectic to Constantine. Leo the Philosopher was well versed in dialectic, too, for he was an admirer of Porphyry, cf. his epigram in the *Palatine Anthology*, IX, 214. — The sequence of studies, described in contemporary texts, is grammar, Homer, rhetoric, logic, philosophy, and the four mathematical disciplines, geometry, arithmetic, astronomy, music. In *Vita Constantini*, geometry and rhetoric exchanged places. The usual order is thus disturbed and the *quadrivium* appears incomplete. The slip may very well have been that of the author of the *Vita* and it would be too risky to change the text.

31. Michael the Monk, Βίος... Θεοδώρου... (the Studite), Migne, *PG* XCIX, 237B. This was not wrong, as the ultimate authority for the statement is Plato, *The Sophist*, 253CE. Cf. also *Respubl.*, 534E and Proclus, *In Eucl. Comm.*, p. 42, 15-16 ed. Friedlein (Dialectic = 'the purest part of philosophy').

dialectic was a subdivision of logic.[32] Logic in turn was usually defined in the Aristotelian sense: not as a part of philosophy but as its "tool". Dialectic, then, was introductory logic, an introduction to philosophy. One of the four parts of dialectic was the science of definition.

The standard textbook, declared as especially useful for the study of dialectic,[33] was the *Isagoge* of Porphyry (d. ca. 305). This introduction to Aristotle's *Categories* exerted an immense influence in the West, in Byzantium, and in the Islamic world. As the *Isagoge* served as an "introduction to all philosophy,"[34] it formed the basis for "freshman" university courses and gave rise to commentaries of which the three earliest preserved and most authoritative Greek examples are lecture notes from the courses of Ammonius Junior (late fifth century), Elias (sixth century) and David (sixth or seventh century).[35] These Neoplatonic commentaries on the *Isagoge* are prefaced by introductions to philosophy. Moreover, and this is a point to remember, they are alone in having such introductions.[36] Ammonius, Elias, and David provided the material for all the subsequent Byzantine commentators on Porphyry.

In combination with the *Isagoge* itself, the texts of these three authors form the basis of all the Byzantine introductory treatises on philosophy. The "Philosophical Chapters" of John of Damascus

---

32. So in a diagram illustrating the divisions of philosophy: *Cod. Monacensis Graecus* 222, fol. 3r; publ. in E. Wellmann, *Galeni qui fertur de partibus philosophiae libellus (Progr. des Königstädtischen Gymnasiums*, Berlin, 1892), p. 34: cf. also *Parisinus Gr.* 1868, fol. 3v. For dialectic proceedings = logical proceedings, cf. John of Damascus, "Philosophical Chapters," 68, Migne, *PG*, XCIV, 672B.

33. Ammonius, *In Porphyrii Isagogen* [CAG, IV, 3 (1891)], p. 34, 21-24; David, *In Porphyrii Isagogen prooemium* [*CAG*, XVIII, 2 (1904)], p. 90, 25f.

34. Ammonius, as in the preceding note; David, *ibidem*, p. 92, 7f; cf. p. 92, 24f.

35. Porphryry, *CAG*, IV, 1 (1887); Ammonius, *CAG*, IV, 3 (1891); Elias, XVIII, 1 (1900); David, *CAG*, XVIII, 2 (1904), all these texts edited by A. Busse. For information on the authors, cf. e.g. A. Busse, *Die neuplatonischen Ausleger der Isagoge des Porphyrius* [= *Wissensch. Beilage zum Programm des Friedrichs-Gymnasiums zu Berlin*, Ostern, 1892 (Berlin, 1892)], and M. Khostikian *David der Philosoph* (Leipzig, 1907). For more bibliography, cf. Überweg-Prächter, *Grundriss der Gesch. der Philosophie* (12th ed.), I (1926), p. 197*; O. Bardenhewer. *Geschichte der Altkirchl. Literatur*, V (1932), pp. 217-220, M. Plezia, *De Commentariis isagogicis* (Kraków, 1949) pp. 59-69.

36. K. Prächter, "Die griechischen Aristoteleskommentare," *Byzantinische Zeitschrift*, XVIII (1909), p. 527.

(significantly called "*Logica*" by one of the Western readers)[37] are a representative example of this syncretism.[38] In turn, John of Damascus yielded material for commentaries also drawing upon the conventional sources such as Ammonius and David: there was no end to contaminations, combinations and re-combinations. Some of these logical compendia ⟨454⟩ and philosophical encyclopaedias are unpublished and served as a quarry from which editors picked out parts of commentaries by the original trio; others, such as those by Psellus, Blemmydes, and Pachymeres, are accessible in old printed editions. Everywhere the core is the same: the *Isagoge* and its three commentators.[39]

What is most important for the present discussion is that Constantine's teacher himself tried his hand at commenting Porphyry. In some manuscripts, fragments of Photius' commentary to the *Isagoge* appear as scholia to Ammonius or even as parts of the latter's text.[40] These fragments are fairly independent, but they presuppose familiarity with the three classical commentators. Thus it is safe to assume that Saint Constantine was taught his dialectic and introductory philosophy from Porphyry and the commentators to the latter's *Isagoge*.

The prolegomena of Ammonius' commentary start as follows: "As we are about to begin [discussing] philosophical subjects, it is necessary to learn what philosophy can possibly be."[41] All the three commentators proceed by giving six definitions (ὅροι) of philosophy[42] and then discuss and repeat them *ad nauseam*. It is from them that these same definitions spread to all subsequent textbooks such as the "Philosophical Chapters" of John of Damascus (chap. 3 and 67) and the "composite" Byzantine treatises and commentaries. Two of these six definitions are the Stoic (γνῶσις θείων τε καὶ ἀνθρωπίνων πραγμάτων) and the Platonic

37. William Ockham, *Summa Logicae*, ed. P. Bochner [= *Franciscan Institute Publications*, Text Series, nr. 2 (1951)], pp. 81; 106; 111.

38. Cf. A. Busse in the preface to his edition of Porphyry's *Isagoge*, *CAG*, IV, 1 (1887), p. xlvf.

39. On various commentaries, cf. A. Busse in the preface to the edition of Ammonius, *CAG*, IV, 3 (1891), pp. xixf; xxxviif; a specimen of a mixed commentary on pp. xliii-xlvi; cf. also A. Busse in *CAG*, IV, 1 (1887), pp. XXXIV-L.

40. Cf. A. Busse in *CAG*, IV, 3 (1891), pp. XX-XXIII, with texts by Photius; also, combine Photius' text on bottom of p. XXI with apparatus to Ammonius, *ibid.*, *ad* p. 92, 26.

41. *CAG*, VI, 3 (1891), p. 1,2-3.

42. Ammonius, *CAG*, IV, 3 (1891), p. 2,22ff; Elias, *CAG*, XVIII, 1 (1900), p. 8,8ff; David, *CAG*, XVIII, 2 (1904), p. 20,27 ff.

(ὁμοίωσις θεῷ κατὰ τὸ δυνατὸν ἀνθρώπῳ).[43] In all cases, the ὅρος corresponding to the first Constantinian definition uses the term γνῶσις (in the formula of Ammonius, even the unusual word order is identical with that adopted by Constantine: φιλοσοφία ἐστὶ θείων τε καὶ ἀνθρωπίνων πραγμάτων γνῶσις); in all cases, the two Constantinian definitions appear either in sequence (as second and third) or close together (as second and fourth). This juxtaposition of Constantinian definitions with those given by standard commentators of Porphyry and their followers may be suggestive. Still the reason for Constantine's picking his two definitions among the six currently given is not apparent.

There exists a plausible explanation for the Saint's choice. The six definitions of philosophy given by the commentators are neatly divided into those viewing the subject matter of the *definiendum* (ἀπὸ τοῦ ὑποκειμένου), and those concentrating on its purpose (ἀπὸ τοῦ τέλους). The "more perfect" definition, however, so David informs us, is the one which encompasses both the subject matter and the purpose of the thing to be defined (ἀπὸ τοῦ συναμφοτέρου).[44] For philosophy, he gives the following example of this ideal definition: "Philosophy is the knowledge of things Divine and human, the becoming like God according to the ability of man."[45] Thus, ⟨455⟩ David singles out the two Constantinian definitions, and them alone, as the best double ὅρος of philosophy. His definition contains them in the same sequence in which they appear in *Vita Constantini*. All this adds weight to the contention that Constantine's definitions come from a milieu familiar with the standard commentaries to Porphyry's *Isagoge* or their "composite" derivations. David's version appears as the most likely source of inspiration.

43. In addition to references given in the preceding note, cf., for the Stoic definition, Ammonius, *CAG*, IV, 1 (1891), p. 5, 20; Elias, *CAG*, XVIII, 1 (1900), pp. 8, 32; 11, 16f; 24, 15; 27, 2; David, *CAG*, XVIII, 2 (1904), pp. 19,5; 22,6; 22,14; 23,18; 26,12; 28,25; 48,18; 77,24f; 78,10 for the Platonic definition, cf. Ammonius, *ibid.*, pp. 3,19f; 4,5f; 4,13f; 6,10; 6,22; 11,11; Elias, *ibid.*, 9,1f; 16,10; 18,1f; 24,21; 27,9; David, *ibid.*, pp. 16,25; 17,1; 22,9; 22,15f, 23,19; 26,20; 34,16; 36,3ff; 37,2ff; 48,20; 77,31f; 78,20.

44. David, *CAG*, XVIII, 2 (1904), p. 19,27f. ἰστέον ὅτι οἱ ἐκ τοῦ συναμφοτέρου ὅροι, ἤγουν οἱ ἐξ ὑποκειμένου ἅμα καὶ τέλους, μᾶλλον εἰσὶ τέλειοι.

45. David, *ibid.*, p. 18,6-11: οὕτως οὖν καὶ τὴν φιλοσοφίαν ὁριζόμεθα ἀπὸ μὲν τοῦ ὑποκειμένου, ὡς ὅταν εἴπωμεν 'φιλοσοφία ἐστὶ γνῶσις θείων τε καὶ ἀνθρωπίνων πραγμάτων' ἀπὸ δὲ τοῦ τέλους 'φιλοσοφία ἐστὶν ὁμοίωσις θεῷ κατὰ τὸ δυνατὸν ἀνθρώπῳ', ἀπὸ τοῦ συναμφοτέρου δὲ, ὡς ὅταν εἴπωμεν 'φιλοσοφία ἐστὶ γνῶσις θείων τε καὶ ἀνθρωπίνων πραγμάτων ὁμοίωσις θεῷ κατὰ τὸ δυνατὸν ἀνθρώπῳ'.

If this contention is accepted as plausible, it is in texts of this kind rather than in the patristic Sermons on *Gen.* 1:26 or treatises on Christian anthropology that we should look for clues as to the meaning of *dětěliję*, following Constantine's "Platonic" definition of philosophy. In Slavic translations of borrowings from Greek, *dětělь* is found for πρᾶξις "deed, action," of the original (so in the second chapter of *Vita Methodii*,[46] a work closely related to *Vita Constantini*) and for ἐνέργεια "act, activity." The most frequent use of this relatively rare word is in conjunction with the adjective *dobra* "good," as an equivalent of ἀρετή "virtue" or εὐεργεσία virtuous action."[47] *Dětělь* in the sense of πρᾶξις, ἐνέργεια apparently belongs to the oldest layer of Old Church Slavonic vocabulary, and since it early became associated with the idea of "good action, virtue," and is attested only in this meaning in later texts, some modern students of the *Vita Constantini* seem to hesitate when rendering this word or commenting upon it.[48] The meaning of *dětěliję* may be extricated from passages in Byzantine commentaries on the *Isagoge* which dwell on the "Platonic" definition of philosophy. When Ammonius discusses the relation between the division of philosophy into theoretical and practical on the one hand and the ὁμοίωσις-definition on the other, he concludes: "For through the theoretical [part of philosophy] we gain the knowledge of things that exist while through the practical [part] (διὰ δὲ τοῦ πρακτικοῦ) we take care of those [men] who are less perfect and

46. *Slovesьnyja* dětelьju *prěspěvъ*, *a* dětelьnyja *slovъmь* (cf. P. Lavrov, *Kyrylo ta Metodij*, p. 300) corresponds to τοὺς μὲν ἐν λόγῳ δεινοὺς τῇ πράξει, τοὺς πρακτικοὺς δὲ τῷ λόγῳ νικήσας in Gregory of Nazianzus, Migne, *PG*, XXXV, 1085C. The dependence of *Vita Methodii* on Gregory was established by Grivec and Gnidovec; for the present passage, cf. e.g. *Acta Acad. Velehradensis*, XVII (1941), 108, n. 4.

47. Although *dětělь* (with an alternate and doubtless later form *dětelь*) does not occur in the Gospels or the Psalter, it is found in the *Euchologium Sinaiticum* and in sermons in *Clozianus* and *Suprasliensis* which were translated early; cf. s.v. *dětělь, dětelь* in Miklosich, Meyer, Sreznevskij (quoted above in footnote 22) and in the *Slovník jazyka staroslověnského*. — For assessing the situation with respect to the equivalents of *razumъ* and *dětělь* I am indebted to Prof. H. G. Lunt.

48. P. Lavrov, *Kyrylo ta Metodij*, p. 244, translates; *česnotoju*, "through virtue." In his Latin translation, Fr. Grivec puts *opere*, but in commenting upon the passage, he adduces texts using the word ἀρετή (*Acta Acad. Velehradensis*, XVII, 55 and 206ff.), while in his Slovene translation he tries to take a middle way, "through (virtuous) deeds" — *s (krepostnimi) deli (Žitja Konstantina in Metodija*, Ljubljana 1951, p. 60). The Czech translator prefers "actions": *ve svém konání* (J. Vašica in *Na úsvitu křesťanství*, Prague 1942, p. 22).

in this manner we assimilate ourselves to God.[49] To David the Platonic ὁμοίωσις-definition shows that philosophy is "politic," for "the politic philosopher strives to imitate the Godhead in as much as it is possible for man, both through knowledge and deeds (κατὰ τὴν πρᾶξιν ἐφ' ὅσον ἐστὶ δυνατὸν ἀνθρώπῳ)."[50] Finally, in one of the Byzantine recensions of Ammonius, we read: "as has been said, philosophy is the becoming like God according to man's ability. The one who becomes like God strives to become like Him by use of reason: he also wants his actions to be his adornment (πράξεσι καλλωπίζεσθαι)."[51] The evidence of commentaries points to πρᾶξις as the Greek word to which Constantine's *dětěliją* hearkens back.[52]

⟨456⟩ What Constantine offered in his reply to Theoctistus was no poetical outburst but university textbook lore, which he learned in Photius's classes.[53] Still, we have to compliment the youth for his judicious selection: his answer reflected a definition of philosophy considered by the textbooks as the best one.[54]

---

49. *CAG*, IV, 3 (1891), p. 11, 14-16.

50. *CAG*, XVIII, 2 (1904), p. 78,1f. Cf. p. 78, 20ff: καὶ γὰρ ὁ θέλων ὁμοιοῦσθαι τῷ θεῷ ἐφ' ὅσον ἀνθρώπῳ δυνατὸν θέλει... ὁμοιοῦσθαι αὐτῷ καὶ κατὰ τὴν πρᾶξιν.

51. *CAG*, IV, 3 (1891), p. XLV.

52. Even Patristic texts based on *Gen*. 1:26 are ambiguous: John of Damascus, *De instit. element.*, Migne, *PG*, XCV, 97A: καθ' ὁμοίωσιν λέγεται ἄνθρωπος κατὰ τὸν τῆς ἀρετῆς λόγον καὶ τὰς θεωνύμους ταύτης καὶ θεομιμήτους πράξεις. Speaking of *Gen*. 1:26, Origen asserted (*De principiis*, III, 6,1 = p. 280, 16, *ed*. Koetschau) that man achieves perfect similitude with God *operum expletione*.

53. This opinion differs from the exalted remarks on the poetic spirit, ascetic character and "relative" originality of Constantine's definition, made by F. Grivec, *Acta Aced. Velehradensis*, XVII (1941), 20; 201; 203f. I believe, however, that in the long run it does the Saint more justice.

54. To say this is to imply that the fourth chapter of *Vita Constantini* is an echo of an event at the court and not merely a reflection of the learning of the *Vita's* author. Whether Constantine was really a mentor of Theoctistus is another matter. Theoctistus must have gone to college himself. The scene may have been a kind of examination, which the young man passed brilliantly, thus demonstrating his capacity for imperial service. A similar scene is reported in a late Byzantine hagiographical text: Philotheus, *Eulogy of Palamas*, Migne, *PG*, CLI, 559-560A. For a different opinion, cf. N. K. Nikol'skij, "K voprosu o sočinenijax, pripisyvaemyx Kirillu filosofu," *Akad. Nauk SSSR, Izvestija po russk. jazyku i slov.*, I, 2 (1928), 421f, who assumes that the definitions of chapter four were introduced by the author of Constantine's *Vita* merely in order

The second Constantinian definition differs somewhat from the wording usually given to the Platonic formula.[55] Moreover, it appears in a Christianized form, for it is amplified by a quotation from *Gen*. 1:26. An association between the two texts could easily have been made by a Christian thinker, especially since the word ὁμοίωσις occurs in both of them. Nor was combining the two of them original, relatively or otherwise. When describing the perfect virtue, Clement of Alexandria combined Plato's *Theaetetus* 176 AB with *Gen*. 1:26.[56] Origen did the same. He even maintained that the Platonic formula was a plagiarism from Genesis.[57] The fourteenth-century author of the *Vita* of the Emperor John Vatatzes may have alluded to *Gen*. 1:26 in giving the "Platonic" definition of the philosophy practiced by the emperor and his wife;[58] of

---

to give a concise idea of the Saint's way of thinking. As the source upon which the author drew, Nikol'skij suggests "Byzantine theological literature," especially the "Philosophical Chapters" of John of Damascus.

55. Byzantine "composite" commentaries to the *Isagoge* sometimes show slight deviations from the usual formula, so the recension in *Par. Gr*. 1973, fol. 14r: εἰ γὰρ τοιαύτη ἐστὶν ἡ φιλοσοφία, ὡς... ἐπιστήμην ἔχειν τῶν θείων καὶ ἀνθρωπίνων πραγμάτων καὶ μιμεῖσθαι θεὸν ὡς ἐνδέχεται ἄνθρωπον... (Again Constantinian definitions combined!), Text in *CAG*, IV, 3 (1891), p. XLV. — For an idea of what the Platonic definition becomes in a Western author (who got it through an Arab source), cf. Gundissalinus, p. 6,1f *ed*. Baur (for reference, cf. note 20 above): *philosophia est assimilacio hominis operibus creatoris secundum virtutem humanitatis*. By comparison, Constantine adhered relatively closely to his sources.

56. *Strom*. II, 22 = II, 185, 23-28, *ed*. Stählin: τοῦτο δὲ [*sc*. the perfect virtue] ἐν ἐπιστήμῃ τοῦ ἀγαθοῦ τίθεται [*sc*. Plato] καὶ ἐν ἐξομοιώσει τῇ πρὸς τὸν θεὸν... ἡ γὰρ οὐχ οὕτως τινὲς τῶν ἡμετέρων, τὸ μὲν 'κατ' εἰκόνα' εὐθέως κατὰ τὴν γένεσιν εἰληφέναι τὸν ἄνθρωπον, τὸ 'καθ' ὁμοίωσιν' δὲ ὕστερον κατὰ τὴν τελείωσιν μέλλειν ἀναλαμβάνειν ἐκδέχονται; cf. also *Strom*. II, 19 = II, 166, 1-3 *ed*. Stählin. This connection Clement took over from Philo: Völker, *Der wahre Gnostiker* (cf. n. 21 above), pp. 580; 582.

57. *De principiis*, III, 6,1 = p. 280, 2-8, *ed*. Koetschau: *summum bonum ... qui etiam finis* [= τέλος] *omnium dicitur a quam plurimis etiam Philosophorum hoc modo terminatur* [= ὁρίζεται] *quia summum bonum sit, prout possible est similem fieri deo* [= κατὰ τὸ δυνατὸν ὁμοιοῦσθαι θεῷ]. *Sed hoc non tam ipsorum inventum quam ex divinis libris ab eis adsumptum puto. Hoc namque indicat Moyses, cum primam conditionem hominis enarrat dicens*: *Et dixit deus*: *Faciamus hominem ad imaginem et similitudinem nostram* (*Gen*. 1:26). Of course, no dependence of Constantine on Clement of Alexandria or Origen is suggested.

58. *Ed*. Heisenberg, *Byzantinische Zeitschrift*, XIV (1905), 219, 5-9: προσῆν δὲ

course, he takes the philosophizing of his heroes in the sense of piety. Such a connection between the Platonic definition and the Genesis passage may have been made by some Byzantine compiler of definitions of philosphy.[59]

Saint Constantine's answer to Theoctistus' inquiry offered scholarly definitions with a Christian ⟨457⟩ tinge rather than monkish definitions with learned trimmings, like those quoted in the *Vita* of John the Psichaite,[60] written by a contemporary of Constantine, or in the later *Vita* of Vatatzes. From his university years on, St. Constantine belonged to the "intellectual" strain in the Byzantine milieu of the ninth century. He was a Christian philosopher-scholar, not a "philosopher" of the monkish ascetic kind.[61]

αὐτοῖς [*sc.* the emperor and his wife] καὶ τὸ τῆς εὐσεβείας ὁμότιμον καὶ φιλοσοφεῖν γνησίως ὡς ὁ τῆς φιλοσοφίας ὅρος ἀκριβῶς βούλεται, εἴ γε οὗτος ὅρος φιλοσοφίας ἡ πρὸς τὸ θεῖον ὁμοίωσις κατὰ τὸ ἐφικτὸν τῶν ἀνθρώπων τῇ φύσει· καὶ γὰρ δὴ καὶ οὗτοι εἰκόνες τῆς θείας ἐφάνησαν ἀγαθότητος. The use of the term ὅρος reveals the author's inspiration: a textbook or a collection of definitions of philosophy.

59. David compares a philosopher's similarity to God as that of an image to its original: ὥσπερ γὰρ τὴν εἰκόνα Σωκράτους λέγομεν ὅμοιαν εἶναι Σωκράτει... κατὰ τοῦτο τὸ σημαινόμενον λέγομεν τὸν φιλόσοφον ὅμοιον εἶναι τῷ θεῷ *CAG*, XVIII, 2 (1904), p. 35, 14-18. This is only one step removed from the utilization of *Gen*. 1:26, which was *the* text for all Christian authors treating the εἰκὼν θεοῦ-motif.

60. Ed. Van den Ven, *Le Muséon*, N.S. III (1902), 109, 13f: φιλοσοφίαν δὲ τὴν ἀνωτάτω ἀσκῶν ὡμοιοῦτο θεῷ κατὰ τὸ δυνατόν.

61. Fr. Grivec arrives at an opposite conclusion. He sees in Constantine a philosopher after the fashion of the Fathers who identified asceticism, sanctity and philosophy, and writers *quae philosophia Constantinum potius cum humilibus ascetis ac monachis quam cum superbis doctoribus sociabat*; "De ss. Cyrilli et Methodii amicitia dubia cum Photio," *Orientalia Christiana Periodica*, XVII (1951), 194. Cf. also the same author in *Orientalia Christiana Periodica* XVIII (1952), 119f. With all due regard to Grivec's undisputed contributions in the field of Constantinian studies, I find the general judgment on Constantine as reflected in the words of Fr. Dvorník to be more balanced.

IX

Byzantine Cultural Influences

I

The past decade has not been the first occasion upon which Rus' scholarship vigorously debated the question of Byzantine cultural influences in Rus'. Nor have Soviet scholars been the first Russian *literati* to cope with this fundamental aspect of Eastern European culture. The problem of the Byzantine impact upon Rus' and of the attitudes it provoked among her bookmen has a history of nine hundred years. It is against that background, however hastily laid, that the Soviet chapter, the most recent of this history, may be more advantageously narrated.

In the recension of 1118 the greatest historical work of early Rus', the *Tale of Bygone Years*, begins with a lengthy story of the partition of the earth after the Flood. The first part of this story was literally — although probably indirectly — derived from a ninth-century Byzantine monkish chronicler. The Chronicle's concluding entry makes mention of the de⟨144⟩cease of "Tsar Alexei," the Byzantine Emperor Alexius Comnenus. When the chronicler establishes the starting point of the *Tale's* chronology and the first precise date when "The land of Rus' began to be mentioned," he refers to the ascension of another Byzantine emperor, Michael III. The date itself, 852, is wrong, but it was arrived at by an intelligent use of indications contained in a chronological summary written by a ninth-century Patriarch of Constantinople.[1] The *Tale*'s dependence on Byzantine letters does not stop with more or less literal borrowings.[2]

---

1. These are not the only references to Byzantine historical events indirectly relating to the local history of Rus'. Nor are excerpts from George the Monk and the Patriarch Nicephorus the only Byzantine sources incorporated into the *Tale* by its compiler — or rather compilers. Others range from a life of a tenth-century saint through a seventh- or eighth-century collection of prophecies to one more, this time sixth-century, author of a Byzantine world chronicle.

2. It has been recently pointed out that the *Tale's* spiritual biographies of some eleventh-century Kievan monks are greatly indebted to motifs drawn from early

All this will hardly appear astonishing if we remember that the *Tale of Bygone Years* was composed and rearranged in the two most important monasteries of Kievan Rus'. Christianity came from Byzantium; Christianity meant civilization. Up to the beginning of the fifteenth century the metropoly (and later metropolies) of Rus' was legally an ecclesiastical province of Constantinople. Byzantine Christianity was inseparable from the Byzantine world view, its propaganda, and its artistic manifestations. The church hierarchy was headed by a Greek metropolitan from the beginning,[3] and it consisted, at least in the initial period, partly of ⟨145⟩Greek bishops. Its missionary and civilizing activities were carried on with the help of Byzantine literary technical works translated into Old Bulgarian in the ninth and tenth centuries. No wonder, then, that the "original" spiritual works of the early period of Rus' are often no more than simple compilations.

Where ecclesiastical and cultural activity was due to a prince's initiative, the source of inspiration was the same. The *Tale of Bygone Years* informs us expressly that the first stone church of Kiev, the Tithe Church, was built by masters brought by Vladimir "from among the Greeks." The Kievan church of St. Sophia, constructed during the reign of Vladimir's son Yaroslav the Wise, may be considered a worthy specimen of the Byzantine art of the Macedonian period;[4] at least to the same extent to which the twelfth-century Norman churches of Sicily must be viewed as reflecting the art of the Comneni, and Serbian frescoes that of the thirteenth- and fourteenth-century Palaeologian renaissance.

Among the works which we may attribute to the "Translation

Byzantine monkish histories. Cf. D. Čyževśkyj, "Studien zur russischen Hagiographie. Die Erzählung vom hl. Isaakij," *Wiener Slavistisches Jahrbuch*, II (1952), 22-49.

3. Within the framework of this short introduction, it is impossible to discuss the stand taken here on the controversial question of the origin of the church in Rus'. Suffice it to say that the present writer subscribes to the arguments of E. Honigmann, "Studies in Slavic Church History; A. The Foundation of the Russian Metropolitan Church According to Greek Sources," *Byzantion*, XVII (1944-1945), 128-62, esp. 142-58.

4. Not only did St. Sophia's interior religious decoration derive from Byzantine iconography and display exclusively Greek explanatory inscriptions, but its lay motifs, the Hippodrome frescos of the staircases, are also inspired by, if they are not even themselves specimens of, Constantinopolitan imperial imagery. Cf. A. Grabar, "Les fresques des escaliers à Sainte-Sophie de Kiev et l'iconographie impériale byzantine," *Seminarium Kondakovianum*, VII (1935), 103-17.

Commission" established in Kiev by Yaroslav the Wise in the second quarter of the eleventh century are renderings of Byzantine historical and "scientific" works, and of such Greek books as were among a cultivated Byzantine's obligatory reading, like Josephus Flavius' *Jewish War*. In early ⟨146⟩ secular literature, of which but little remains, less Byzantine influence should be expected *a priori*. Yet the famous *Igor Tale*, a work striking by its "pagan" character, makes use of Byzantine eschatological prophecies on the seventh millennium.

In the north, attempts at forming a new center in defiance of Kiev's ideal political and real ecclesiastical supremacy fall into the twelfth century, the time of Andrei Bogolyubsky. It was in the Suzdal principality that the political theme stressing the loftiness of the princely power first appeared, later to culminate in the imperial ideology of Ivan the Terrible's Moscow. The first articulate formulation of these claims, dating from about 1177 and stating in substance that "though an Emperor in body be like all other, yet in power he is like God," is a literal borrowing from a sixth-century Byzantine political theorist of sorts, Agapetus. Agapetus's admonitions were later to make a serious impact upon the political writings of Muscovy, but his hour did not strike until the very beginning of the sixteenth century.[5] In the meantime, thirteenth-century panegyrists of local princes mentioned the latters' great love toward the "Tsars of Greece" among their princely virtues.[6] The indirect "Byzantinization" of letters in fifteenth century Rus', due to the influx of Balkan intellectuals, is a matter of common knowledge. When Maxim ⟨147⟩ the Greek, the "Illuminator of the Russians," addressed Ivan the Terrible on matters of political theory a century later, he recommended to him assiduous reading of the famous epistle which the ninth-century Patriarch of Constantinople Photius addressed to the newly Christianiz-

5. Cf. I. Ševčenko, "A Neglected Byzantine Source of Muscovite Political Ideology," *Harvard Slavic Studies*, II (1954), 141-79.

6. Reference is made to the *Tale of the Sack of Ryazan by Batu*. For the relevant passage, see N. K. Gudzy, *Khrestomatiya po drevnei russkoi literature XI-XVII vekov* [Anthology of early Russian literature of the eleventh to seventeenth centuries] (5th ed., 1952), 153. A century later a Muscovite prince was compared not only to Constantine and Justinian, but even represented as an imitator of Manuel Comnenus on account of his love for books. Cf. *The Praise of Grand Prince Ivan Kalita*, ed. by I. Sreznevsky, "Svedeniya i zametki o maloizvestnykh i neizvestnykh pamyatnikakh" [Information and remarks regarding little known and obscure monuments] in *Prilozhenie k XXXIV tomu Zapisok Imp. Akad. Nauk* (1879), no. 86, 145-48.

ed barbarian ruler of the Bulgars Boris-Michael.[7] It is not known how Ivan reacted to this unwittingly tactless proposal. But we know that parts of another ninth-century Byzantine political admonition, said to have been written by Emperor Basil to his son Leo, were incorporated into Ivan the Terrible's coronation ritual.

When some hundred years later the Patriarch of Moscow, Nikon, tried to bolster up his aspirations with a theory of co-equality of the patriarchal with the tsar's power, he turned to the Donation of Constantine,[8] and to a ninth-century legal compendium, the *Epanagoge*, where the Byzantine equivalent of the western medieval doctrine of the "two swords" was expounded. But significantly enough for the change in the cultural climate, the *Epanagoge* was translated at Nikon's bidding from a printed edition, prepared in western Europe by a German humanist. And the translator was a Ukrainian scholar.[9] Only a few decades separated Nikon's time from the accession of Peter the Great, who began his rule as the Orthodox Tsar of Muscovy, crowned by God, Byzantine style, to end it as the August Emperor of Rus', Western fashion. The elite ceased to turn to Byzantium for cultural inspiration. This however was only the official aspect of things. In the old ⟨148⟩ times, Byzantium was so supreme in the political and cultural geography of the writers of Rus', that the relations of the sack of Constantinople in 1204 and 1453 are the two longest excursus on roughly contemporary events abroad to be read in Russian chronicles. Now the elite considered western capitals as the center of the world. But the Constantinople-centered world view continued its subterranean existence among the half-educated layers of the Russian people well into the nineteenth century.[10]

To present fairly adequately the manifold aspects of the cultural relations between Byzantium and the eastern Slavs, the above sketch

---

7. Cf. *Sochineniya prep. Maksima Greka* [Works of the reverend Maxim the Greek], II (1860), 351, ed. by the *Ecclesiastical Academy of Kazan*.

8. The Donation, whose authenticity nobody in Russia doubted at that time, was introduced there in the fifteenth century, through a late Byzantine legal text.

9. Cf. G. V. Vernadsky, "Die kirchlich-politische Lehre der Epanagoge und ihr Einfluss auf das russische Leben im XVII Jhdt.," *Byzantinisch-Neugriechische Jahrbücher*, VI (1928), 119-42.

10. A. N. Ostrovsky, the best expert on this crepuscular world, who immortalized the mid-nineteenth century merchant milieu of Moscow, will help to substantiate the point. In the first piece of the famous Balzaminov trilogy, *A Dream on the Eve of a Holiday Comes True Before the Midday Meal*,

needs to be corrected and supplemented. True, the *Tale of Bygone Years* derived its first precise date from a Greek source. But it did it in order better to establish the time of the first attack of the Russes on Constantinople. In the *Tale* the princess Olga, the grandmother of Vladimir the Great, is made to receive baptism in Constantinople, which hardly corresponds to reality. But we also are told with a somewhat naive pride that the Byzantine emperor himself was so impressed by her wisdom that he wanted to marry her; it was only Olga's witty repartee that put him in his place. After the description of a Byzantine cunning message, some recensions of the *Tale* add "for the Greeks are wise even to the present day," but two others substitute "crafty" for "wise" ⟨149⟩ and this seems to be the original reading.[11] Metropolitan Hilarion, an eleventh-century native of Kievan Rus', construes his *Sermon on Law* (i.e., the Old Testament) *and Grace* (i.e., the new Testament) after a Byzantine pattern and likens Vladimir to "New Constantine," an epithet of many a Byzantine emperor before and after this prince, but the *Sermon* contains a most proud eulogy of the "Rus' land." Hilarion's twelfth-century successor, Clement of Smolensk, a prelate who was acquainted with Plato and Aristotle through Byzantine compendia, was ordained metropolitan in open disobedience to the Patriarch of Constantinople. One of the arguments brought forward to justify his independent ordination was that Kiev's principal relic, the head of Pope Clement, was just as sanctifying as the hand of John the Baptist, by which metropolitans were consecrated in Constantinople.

A similar ambiguity prevailed upon the territories which were the cradle of the modern Russian nation. When the Muscovite Prince Ivan Kalita was likened to the Byzantine Emperor Manuel Comnenus (1143-1180), this was a compliment. A different type of compliment of Vladimir Monomakh (d. 1125) was meant by the thirteenth-century author of the *Tale of the Ruin of the Rus' Land*, perhaps a Novgorodian, when he said, somewhat twisting the chronology, that "Manuel of Constantinople, was afraid, wherefore he sent large gifts to him (i.e.,

Balzaminov is engaged in polite conversation with Nechkina, a Muscovite merchant's widow (Act III, Scene 3): "*N*. And Palestine, is it big? *B*. Sure. *N*. Is it far from Constantinople? *B*. Not too far. *N*. Must be sixty versts.... They say that the distance from all such places is sixty versts ... only Kiev is further away. *Jusha* (a thirteen year old boy): Constantinople, Auntie, this is the navel of the world, isn't it? *N*. Quite so, sweetie pie."

11. *Sub anno* 971.

Vladimir), so that the Grand Prince Vladimir would not take Constantinople away from him." Toward the middle of the fourteenth century, Simeon the Proud of Moscow could write the Emperor Cantacuzenus that "the Roman (i.e., Byzantine) Empire is the source of all piety and teacher of Law."[12] But towards the end of the ⟨150⟩ century, the Patriarch of Constantinople had severely to reprimand a Muscovite prince for having ordered his church to omit the name of the Byzantine emperor, the sole ruler of the Orthodox Christians, during liturgy.[13]

The first deliberate Russian attempts to transform Russian princes into the counterparts of Byzantine emperors fall into the middle of the fifteenth century. And it is at the very time that Byzantium was disavowed for its surrender to the Papists at the Council of Florence, and the first hints were made that the ideal rule over the Christian world passed from conquered Constantinople to Moscow, the upholder of the true faith. This development culminated in the well-known doctrine of Moscow the Third Rome, propounded by Philotheus of Pskov towards the beginning of the sixteenth century. Philotheus was by no means the official mouthpiece of the Muscovite princely court. At first Muscovite princes were not interested in officially assuming the Byzantine heritage. The only clear fifteenth-century statement that the rights to the Byzantine throne had passed to the Grand Prince of Moscow is to be read in a Venetian source, since it was by such means that the West thought to entice the Muscovite ruler into participating in an anti-Turkish crusade. Still, when Ivan the Terrible decided to have himself crowned tsar, he found it opportune later to secure the confirmation of his new title by the "Byzantine" Patriarch of Constantinople (1561).

Most of the expressions of national pride and attempts at asserting independence in church and cultural matters grew out of the desire to equal the corresponding Byzantine models. It was tempting to emulate the capital on the Bosporus. It was more difficult to be weaned from it. This kind of tension ⟨151⟩ between the giving and the receiving culture was strictly paralleled by the attitude of the Sicilian Normans in the twelfth century and of the Bulgarians in the tenth and the fourteenth. It

12. Simeon's declaration may be reconstructed from the reply Cantacuzenus made to his letter in 1347. Cf. Franz Miklosich and Joseph Müller, *Acta et diplomata graeca medii aevi*, I (1860), 263.

13. The famous letter of Patriarch Antonius IV to Grand Prince Vasily I of Moscow. Cf. p. ex. Miklosich and Müller, *Acta et diplomata* ... II (1862), 189-92. English translation of relevant parts in A. A. Vasiliev, "Was Old Russia a Vassal State of Byzantium?" *Speculum*, VII (1932), 358-59.

is in Norman Sicily that the following lines were written: "Cease to exist, Rome, and the City of Constantine ... your light and your pride is extinguished by the rising Sicilian brilliance" — only that the poem is written in Greek and in the purest Byzantine tradition.[14]

II

When the problem of the Byzantine impact upon Rus' became a subject for scholarly investigation, some of the tension between the giving and receiving cultures, which had permeated the attitudes of the learned men of Kievan Rus' and later of Muscovy toward Byzantine culture, was inherited by Russian scholarship. However, a distinction must be made at the very outset. The divergent opinions as to the cultural independence of early Rus' expressed in pre-revolutionary Russian scholarship remained within what by Western standards would be called differences in stress and interpretation. Soviet scholarship of the past few years has adopted a position which brings it nearer both in tone and exactitude to the thirteenth-century author of the passage on the fearful Manuel Comnenus.

In 1925 Uspensky, one of the two principal representatives of Russian pre-revolutionary Byzantine studies, wrote that this field of scholarship had and always would have special tasks of its own connected with the duty of the Russian people to know itself.[15] He went on to say that almost all Russian ⟨152⟩ Byzantinists chose subjects related to Slavic and early Rus' history. This was true. Along with the social and ecclesiastical history of the Eastern Empire, the fields of Byzantine relations with the Slavs and more particularly with Rus' were domains where pre-revolutionary Russian scholarship achieved such brilliant results that a western Byzantinist of Krumbacher's fame thought it necessary to

14. The quotation is from the poem by Eugenios of Palermo on William II (1166-1189). Cf. Leo Sternbach, "Eugenios von Palermo," *Byzantinische Zeitschrift*, XI (1902), 451.

15. F. Uspensky, "Notes sur l'histoire des études Byzantines en Russie," *Byzantion*, II (1925), 1-53, covering the period 1870-1914. For a brilliant characterization of Russian pre-revolutionary Byzantine studies, see H. Grégoire, "Les études byzantines en Russie soviétique," *Acad. Royale de Belgique, Bull. de la Classe des lettres*, V^{e} série, XXXII (1946), 194 ff., to be read along with the violent rejoinder by B. Goryanov, "Po povodu vystupleniya professora Greguara" [Concerning the article of Professor Grégoire], *Vop. Ist.*, IV, 1 (1948), 110-12.

master the difficult Russian language. But Byzantine-Rus' relations were by no means a monopoly of the Byzantinists. The direct and indirect Byzantine heritage of Kievan Rus' and Muscovy was also one of the central problems to occupy the attention of Russian philologists and literary historians, especially those studying the period prior to the middle of the seventeenth century. Outside the academic world, "Byzantinism" was also vividly debated, since its understanding was deemed of great importance for the assessing of Russia's origin, its cultural independence from the West and its national individuality. The evalution of "Byzantinism" did vary of necessity, but it was characteristic that in the nineteenth century the extent of Byzantine influence was not seriously questioned in the controversies raging among Slavophiles and the Westerners.

In Byzantine studies, there was no split comparable to that between the historical schools of the Normanists, who attributed an important role to the Scandinavians in the founding of the Rus' state, and the anti-Normanists, whose convictions and national pride led them to deny this role. In his doctoral dissertation of 1870 the Slavophile scholar Lamansky opposed the Greco-Slavic world which among other things he based on Byzantine Orthodoxy and mysticism to that ⟨153⟩ Hegelian construction, the Germano-Romanic world.[16] A Slavophile professor, Grigorovich, could extoll the originality and independence of the views held by ancient Slavs on religious, political and family matters. But he also was a first-rate expert on Byzantine sources, perhaps more a Byzantinist than a Slavicist, and had a deep reverence for the old Byzantine culture.[17] In the opposite camp, the Westernizer Granovsky declared in 1850 that it was the Russians' duty to evalute the history of Byzantium, to which they were so much indebted.[18] Herzen, another Westernizer, expressed the hope that Russia would take Constantinople, for it was only fitting — so he wrote in his Diary — that the place from which Russian culture had sprung should become the center of the future Slavic commonwealth. The greatest of the Russian Byzantinists, Vasilyevsky,

16. V. I. Lamansky, *Ob istoricheskom izuchenii Greko-Slavyanskago mira v Evrope* [On the historical study of the Greco-Slavic world in Europe] (St. Petersburg, 1871).

17. On Grigorovich, see I. V. Jagić, "Istoriya slavyanskoi filologii," [The history of Slavic philology], in *Entsiklopediya slavyanskoi filologii*, I (1910), 459, 479-84.

18. *Sochineniya* [Works], II (Moscow, 1856), 138-40. On Granovsky, see the now proscribed book by O. L. Vainshtein, *Istoriografiya srednikh vekov* [Historiography of the middle ages] (Moscow, 1940), 297-99.

refuted the patriotic anti-Normanist Ilovaisky by showing that for the Byzantines"Rus'" and "Varangians" were at first the same thing.[19] But Vasilyevsky also believed in the existence of "Russian"attacks on Constantinople prior to the one of 860, a view now abandoned by practically all Russian and non-Russian Byzantinists except the Soviets.[20] The literary historian Veselovsky, whose scholarly ⟨154⟩ horizon and fame transcended the boundaries of Russia and who felt equally at home in the Italian Renaissance and in Russian Romanticism, may have been in his youth an ardent reader of Feuerbach, Herzen and Buckle. But his studies on the Byzantine origins of Russian popular religious poetry, on the traces left by the Byzantine epos in the Russian epic, and on several Byzantine sources of early Rus' literature are among the masterpieces of his comparative historical research, which stressed the importance of the "wandering motifs."

The first attempts at a synthetic treatment of the Byzantine impact upon the culture or literature of Rus' date from the sixties. Ikonnikov's youthful essay entitled *An Investigation of the Cultural Importance of Byzantium in Russian History*,[21] about six-hundred pages long, happily leaned towards the dry-as-dust approach at an epoch when the scholarly treatment of Byzantine studies was at its beginnings in Russia. It

19. V. G. Vasilyevsky, *Varyago-russkaya i varyago-angliiskaya druzhina v Konstantinopole XI i XII v.* [The Varangian-Russian and Varangian-English guard in Constantinople in the eleventh and twelfth centuries], (1874-75); now in Vasilyevsky's *Trudy* [Works], I, (St. Petersburg, 1908), 174-377.

20. See Vasilyevsky's *Trudy*, II (1909), 297-427. Recently this question gave rise to a sharp, although somewhat one-sided, controversy between Henri Grégoire and his school and Soviet scholars, who seem to interpret doubts as to the authenticity of the "pre-860" attacks as a willful slighting of the Early Russes' valor; see G. da Gosta-Louillet, "Y eut-il des invasions Russes dans l'Empire Byzantin avant 860?" *Byzantion*, XV (1940-41), 231-48; E. E. Lipshits, "O pokhode Rusi na Vizantiyu ranshe 842 g." [On an expedition of Russes against Byzantium before 842], *Ist. Zap.*, XXVI (1948), 312-31; M. V. Levchenko, "A. Greguar i ego raboty po vizantinovedeniyu" [H. Grégoire and his work in the Byzantine field], *Vizantiiskii Vremennik*, III (1950), 230-45; *idem*, "Falsifikatsiya istorii vizantino-russkikh otnoshenii v trudakh A. A. Vasilieva" "The falsification of the history of Byzantine-Russian relations in the works of A. A. Vasiliev], *Vizantiiskii Vremennik*, IV (1951), 149-59. Neither the "pre-860" attacks nor the controversial one by Oleg of 907 will be discussed in the present article, as its scope is limited to the *cultural* aspects of Russo-Byzantine relations; see, however, note 121 below.

21. V. S. Ikonnikov, *Opyt izsledovaniya o kulturnom znachenii Vizantii v russkoi istorii* (Kiev, 1869).

deplored, somewhat naively, the low level, the restricted area of ⟨155⟩ penetration, and the uniformly ecclesiastical character of early Rus' culture. Arkhimandrite Amfilokhi's "On the Influence of Greek Script upon the Slavic between the Ninth and the Beginning of the Sixteenth Century"[22] was an article by a zealous dilettante. The Kievan university student Zavadsky-Krasnopolsky even risked a series of articles on the *Influence of the Greco-Byzantine Culture on the Development of Civilization in Europe*, in which he described Rus' as a Byzantine province and Byzantium as its intellectual mentor.[23] When the Kievan professor Ternovsky investigated the knowledge of Byzantine history in early Rus', he stressed the "tendentious" use to which it was put there.[24] Such syntheses were not undertaken at a later stage, for it was felt that they should be preceded by clearing up particular points. Among Byzantinists, it was Vasilyevsky who gave expression to this attitude in his whole scholarly activity, exclusively analytical.

The view of an undisputed and unilateral Byzantine influence was not absolutely predominant in pre-revolutionary Russian scholarship. Uspensky, a pupil of the Slavophile Lamansky, observed that this influence was paralleled by the impact exerted by Slavdom upon the Eastern Empire. In the field of the cultural history of early Rus', Priselkov put forward a highly ingenious, though hypothetical, interpretation of the literary and ecclesiastical events in the eleventh and twelfth centuries, according to which they had to be viewed as a ⟨156⟩ struggle between the pro-Byzantine and the anti-Byzantine trends at the princely court among the ecclesiastics and in the monasteries of Rus'.[25] It was of course essential for Priselkov's construction, published in 1913, that not only national, but also equally uncompromising pro-Greek,

---

22. "O vliyanii grecheskoi pismennosti na slavyanskuyu s IX v. po nachalo XVI veka," *Trudy pervago arkheologicheskago syezda* (Moscow, 1872), 860-73 and plates.

23. A. K. Zavadsky-Krasnopolsky, "Vliyanie vizantiiskoi kultury na razvitie tsivilizatsii v Evrope," *Universitetskie Izvestiya* of Kiev (June, 1866 and later issues of the year); see especially the issue of October, 1866, 11 ff.

24. *F. Ternovsky, Izuchenie vizantiiskoi istorii i eya tendentsioznoe prilozhenie v drevnei Rusi* [Study of Byzantine history in early Russia and its tendentious application there), I-II (Kiev, 1876). Ternovsky's work is useful even today.

25. M. D. Priselkov, "Ocherki po tserkovno-politicheskoi istorii Kievskoi Rusi X-XII vv." [Sketches of the ecclesiastical-political history of Kievan Rus' in the tenth to twelfth centuries], *Zapiski Ist.-fil. fakulteta Imp. S.-Peterburgskago Universiteta, CXVI* (1913).

tendencies should have left an imprint upon the literary documents of the early period.

Thus on the eve of the First World War the question of cultural relations between Rus' and Byzantium still awaited its solution. It is still regarded as very obscure by some today.[26] But in spite of the difficulties, some general propositions were widely adhered to by pre-revolutionary scholars. Byzantine influences were viewed as emanating from a cultural metropoly towards a "cultural colony." The Christianization of the Russes, an act by which Rus' joined the family of civilized peoples, was viewed as a decisive factor in the formation of early Rus' culture. This culture was considered to have been relatively low, at least at the beginning, and limited to a restricted milieu. Moreover, it was at a disadvantage as compared, say, with the Bulgarian culture of the First Empire, which could profit from its proximity to Byzantium. The "original" literature of Rus' owed its inception to Byzantine models, transmitted either by Bulgarian or local translations. Often, its originality consisted in combining patterns and motifs ultimately received from Byzantium. More particularly, the historical writings in Rus' were greatly indebted to Byzantine historiography. Even the very idea of composing ⟨157⟩ a chronicle was ascribed by some to the initiative of the Greek Metropolitan of Kiev.

The script of Rus', as that of many other Slavic countries, was of Byzantine origin in both its forms, glagolitic and cyrillic. Literacy in general started after 988 or 989, the date of adoption of Christianity by Prince Vladimir. It was agreed that in the domain of art the Byzantines gave Rus' the best the metropolis had to offer. In monumental art, Kievan Rus' owed to Byzantium the introduction of stone architecture. Up to the sixteenth century local, (if existent), Romanesque, Caucasian and later Renaissance elements were mere, and not frequent, additions to structures of a basically Byzantine type. Many scholars traced the Muscovite theory of theocratic absolutism back to Byzantium, and pointed to the Greek church hierarchy as a transmitter of Byzantine legal and state notions.[27]

---

26. V. Moshin, "Russkie na Afone i russko-vizantiiskie otnosheniya v XI-XII vv." [The Russes at Athos and Russo-Byzantine relations in the eleventh and twelfth centuries], *Byzantinoslavica*, IX (1947-48), 55.

27. M. Dyakonov, *Vlast moskovskikh gosudarei* [The authority of the Muscovite rulers] (St. Petersburg, 1889), *passim; Idem, Ocherki obshchestvennago i gosudarstvennago stroya drevnei Rusi* "Essays on the social and governmental structure of early Russia] (St. Petersburg, 1908), 399-405).

III

The First World War, the revolution, and the ensuing dozen years dealt a severe blow to Russian Byzantine studies.[28] The Russian Institute in Constantinople, founded in 1894, ⟨158⟩ had to be abandoned. At home, material conditions and the ideological climate were highly unpropitious. Byzantine studies were widely regarded as an offshoot of classical studies, the very pursuit by which some tsarist ministers of education had attempted to keep the minds of the youth off the revolutionary movement. For revolutionary leaders, "Byzantinism" was a term of abuse. Moreover, in those idyllic anti-imperialist days, a discipline which sometimes appeared as an ideological weapon in tsarist aspirations to rule over the Dardanelles was bound to be regarded with suspicion.[29] Between 1918 and 1928, only two volumes of the professional journal, *Vizantiiskii Vremennik*, appeared. Even this activity could not go on. In 1928, this journal, since 1894 a worthy competitor of *Byzantinische Zeitschrift*, ceased to exist with its twenty-fifth volume.

In a letter to the Academy of Sciences written in 1924, Uspensky used the ominous phrases "if Russian Byzantine studies are doomed to perish," and "in Europe they begin to count Russian Byzantine studies as dead." It is noteworthy that at a time when scholarly activity had to be reduced to a minimum, what remained as a core was the Russo-Byzantine Historical and Lexicographical Commission, whose main task, in addition to gathering material for a reshaping of Du Cange's late Greek dictionary, was the study of Russo-Byzantine relations.[30] This

28. See H. Grégoire's article quoted in note 15 above; A. A. Vasiliev, "Byzantine Studies in Russia, Past and Present," *Amer. Hist. Review*, XXXII, 3 (1927), 539-45; G. Lozovik, "Desyat let russkoi vizantologii (1917-1927)" [Ten years of Russian Byzantine studies (1917-1927)], *Ist.-Marks.*, No. 7 (1928), 228-38; N. S. Lebedev, "Vizantinovedenie v SSSR za 25 let" [Twenty-five years of Byzantine studies in the U.S.S.R.], in *Dvadtsat pyat let sovetskoi istoricheskoi nauki* (1942), 216-21. The latter report gives a rosier picture of Byzantine studies than the one presented here, since it stresses the developments since 1939.

29. Cf. the quotation of Uspensky in A. A. Vasieliev, *History of the Byzantine Empire* (Madison, 1952), 36, and Lozovik's article referred to in the preceding note, 228-9, 238.

30. V. N. Beneshevich, "Russko-Viz. Komissiya. Glossarium Graecitatis" [The Russo-Byzantine commission: The Greek glossary], *Vizantiiskii Vremennik* XX-IV (1923-26), 119-20, and his "Russko-Viz. istoriko-slovarnaya komissiya v 1926-27 g." [The Russian-Byzantine historical-lexicographical commission in 1926-27], *Vizantiiskii Vremennik*, XXV (1927), 165-70.

Commission was dissolved in 1930.[31] Eight years later, Ostrogorsky, today one of the leading Byzantine ⟨159⟩ historians, deplored the complete interruption of Byzantine studies in a country which brought forth a Vasilyevsky.[32]

If in the twenty years between 1918 and 1938, studies related to Russo-Byzantine cultural relations shrank in scope, they did not fundamentally change in character. True, we meet with a good deal of sociologizing, but interest in social problems and the social approach were characteristic of Russian pre-revolutionary Byzantine studies and Russian literary criticism as well. In the theory of literary influences, Veselovsky was still regarded as the leading authority. By 1929, if he was criticized at all, it was for using such "vague" sociological notions as "nation" or "national culture." As for foreign literary influences, it was believed that an independent literary development within one country was almost a nonexistent phenomenon, since in the final analysis, literary activity was international.[33] It is not difficult to speculate on the reason for such a state of things. The formative, and to a great extent the creative, years of scholars prominent in that field fell into the pre-revolutionary era. Such was, for example, the case of Istrin and Orlov in the field of early Rus' literature. On the other hand, questions of national or Slavic pride lay outside the ideological preoccupations of the hour. Among historians, Pokrovsky ruled supreme with his critical attitude toward the Muscovite state and what he termed the primitive intellect of its scholarly propagandists.[34]

⟨160⟩ In retrospect it seems ironical that in the 1920's it was a Western scholar who criticized his Soviet colleagues for adopting a too cautious attitude on the questions of the cultural independence of early

31. M. V. Levchenko in *Vizantiiskii Sbornik* (1945), 4.

32. G. Ostrogorsky, "V. G. Vasilyevsky kak vizantolog i tvorets noveishei russkoi vizantologii" [V. G. Vasilyevsky as a Byzantinist and creator of modern Russian Byzantine studies], *Seminarium Kondakovianum*, XI (1940, but written in 1938), 235.

33. *Literaturnaya Entsiklopediya* [Literary Encyclopedia], II (1929), col. 255 ff., article "Vliyaniya, literaturnye" [Influences, literary], by A. G. Tseitlin, see especially cols. 256, 263.

34. Pokrovsky, *Russ. ist. s drevneishikh vremen*, I, 126, 148. In 1930 a theoretical publication echoed the nineteenth-century views of Zavadsky-Krasnopolsky (cf. above, n. 23) when one of its contributors asserted that in the course of several centuries the history of eastern Slavic Europe could be largely considered as the history of a recondite Byzantine province. Cf. A. K. Berger in *Arkhiv K. Marksa i F. Engelsa*, V (1930), 450.

Rus', such as the "originality" of Kievan and Muscovite architecture, and for renouncing all nationalist tendencies.[35] It was also a Western scholar who pointed out in 1923 that Byzantine influence upon the *Tale of Bygone Years*, the greatest historical work of early Rus', was often over-estimated and who stated that Nestor's horizon was much broader than that of one of his Byzantine sources, George the Monk.[36]

In 1938, at the very time when Ostrogorsky regretted the demise of Russian Byzantine studies, the first attempts at resuscitating that discipline were being undertaken in the Soviet Union. In that year Zhebelev, a well-known classicist, published a dignified plea for rehabilitating Byzantine studies.[37] ⟨161⟩ A year later, a Byzantine section was created at the Institute for History of the Academy of Sciences,[38] and shortly after a brief *History of Byzantium* was published which proclaimed itself as "Marxian" but was in fact a very commendable piece of work.[39] The German invasion delayed the publication of a collection of Byzantine papers, which although ready by 1941 did not appear until 1945, but the voice of Russian Byzantinists was not absent from the patriotic upsurge in the latter phase of the war. In 1944, the leading historical journal, *Istoricheskii Zhurnal*, carried a number of articles advocating the renaissance of Byzantine studies and justifying the

35. Emmy Haertel, reviewing A. I. Nekrasov's *Vizantiiskoe i russkoe iskusstvo dlya stroitelnykh fakultetov vysshikh uchebnykh zavedenii* [Byzantine and Russian art for the departments of construction of higher educational institutions] (Moscow, 1924) in *Byzantinisch-Neugriechische Jahrbücher*, VI (1928), 560-62. About a quarter of a century later Haertel's wishes were more than fulfilled; see the remarks by V. V. Mavrodin, *Obrazovanie edinogo russkogo gosudarstva* [The formation of the unified Russian state] (1951), 285.

36. M. Weingart, *Byzantské kroniky v literatuře církevněslovanské. ...* [Byzantine chronicles in Church Slavic literature], II, 1 (1922-23), 120.

37. S. A. Zhebelev, "Russkoe vizantinovedenie, ego proshloe, ego zadachi v sovetskoi nauke" [Byzantine studies in Russia, their past and their tasks in Soviet scholarship], *Vestnik Drevnei Istorii*, No. 45 (1938), 13-22. It is interesting to note that the first articles extolling the "rejuvenating" role played in Byzantine history by the Slavs and their "autochthonous culture" appeared also in 1938 and 1939. Cf. V. I. Picheta, "Slavyano-vizantiiskie otnosheniya v VI-VII vv. v osveshchenii sovetskikh istorikov (1917-1947gg)" [Slavic-Byzantine relations in the sixth and seventh centuries as viewed by Soviet historians (1917-1947)], *Vestnik Drevnei Istorii*, No. 3 (1947), 95-99, esp. 97.

38. M. V. Levchenko in *Vizantiiskii Sbornik* (1945), 6.

39. M. V. Levchenko, *Istoriya Vizantii* (Moscow-Leningrad, 1940). A French translation appeared in Paris in 1949.

plea by purely scholarly arguments, and by stressing the undeniable contributions to Byzantine studies and the problem of Russo-Byzantine relations made by Russians in the past.[40] Finally, in 1947, after an interruption of twenty years, *Vizantiiskii Vremennik* resumed publication. As if to underline the continuity of the discipline in Russia, the volume of 1947 carried a double number: I (XXVI). Moreover, its leading editorial made it plain that students of Byzantium in Russia were rejoining the scholarly community of nations.

Again in its beginning this new phase hardly betrayed anything unexpected in approach, method, or conception. Soviet Byzantinists proclaimed themselves as adherents of the Marxian faith and this observance was to determine their choice of topics for research. This was a consistent attitude. The first innovation, as compared with the preceding two decades, was the accusation leveled at Pokrovsky's school, authoritative ⟨162⟩ until 1934, that it had deliberately stifled the pursuit of Byzantine studies in the Soviet Union.[41] It must be said in all fairness to Pokrovsky that he was, if anything, too pro-Byzantine on the subject of the Empire's impact on Rus'. He readily admitted Greek influences upon Slavs of the early Rus'. Following in the footsteps of his teacher Klyuchevsky and the church historian Golubinsky, he attributed the growth of the theory of political autocracy, unifying and formulating the instinctive "gathering of Russian lands" by Muscovite princes, to ecclesiastical literature and propaganda, which in turn was inspired by Byzantium.[42] Pokrovsky's real sins, it may be said, lay somewhere else, in the often too cavalier stand he took against Greater Russian jingoism.

Now the study of Russia's past, no longer to be mistrusted, but rather lovingly admired, required a closer interest in those Greeks of *Tsargrad* whose names appear so prominently in the early annals. Thus a second innovation of the early post-war period was the official endorsement with which Russia's cultural dependence on Byzantium was now to be investigated. In a programmatic article on "The Tasks of Contemporary Byzantine Studies," Levchenko informed his readers that Byzantium had exerted an immense influence upon the culture of early Rus', and that there was a time when Muscovite Russia as well experienced a

40. These contributions are reviewed in H. Grégoire's article, cited in note 15 above, on 207 ff.

41. M. V. Levchenko in *Vizantiiskii Sbornik* (1945), 4; editorial in *Vizantiiskii Vremennik*, I (XXVI) (1947), 3-4.

42. Pokrovsky, *Russ. ist. s drevneishikh vremen*, I, 11, 147, 155.

strong influence of Byzantine culture. Nor was an appropriate, if obvious, scriptural quotation found wanting. The readers were asked not to forget Marx's saying to the effect that "Russia's religion and civilization are of Byzantine origin."[43]

To the present writer's knowledge, this quotation never reappeared in any subsequent Soviet publication. About the year 1947, a sharp reversal occurred, dealing with various ⟨163⟩ aspects of Russo-Byzantine cultural relations. The astonishing new trend grew in intensity as the years went on, and remained, until 1953 at least, the official attitude.

IV

There was a reason behind the attention paid by recent Soviet scholarship to the otherwise academic question of Byzantine influence on Rus'. The answer to this question has a decisive bearing on the origin of what is officially considered "Russian" culture. And questions of origin are indissolubly linked with the problem of originality.

In a lecture on the "Basic Tasks in the Study of Early Russian Literature as Reflected in the Works of the Years 1917-1947," Adrianova-Peretts exposed as false the thesis of pre-revolutionary literary historians that the literature of early Rus' originated in the eleventh century under the influence of Byzantine-Slavic models. This might be true of religious and didactic literary works, but not of the historical writings which alone should be considered as the beginning of Russian literature and which were characteristic of it from the very origins up to the sixteenth century. These writings had deep popular roots and originated in the local oral literature. Thus the re-interpretation of the relationship between written and oral literature was declared to be among the urgent tasks of Soviet literary historians. Pre-revolutionary literary criticism was interested only in the way the Byzantine and South Slavic culture passed to Rus'. Yet in Rus' itself the assimilation of cultural achievements of its medieval neighbors was of a creative character. In fact, the early culture of Rus' had profound national peculiarities. True, Soviet literary historians had begun to study the mutual relationship between these cultures, and the influence of early Rus' literature on others. But even they were not free of error. They were burdened with a false approach to the problem of literary influences in

43. *Vizantiiskii Sbornik* (1945), 4-5.

⟨164⟩ their continued application of Veselovsky's comparativist methodology.[44]

In the Byzantine field proper, the delayed appearance of the new *Vizantiiskii Vremennik*, ready by 1944-1945 but printed in 1947, amounted to a major scandal, since it was reprimanded in numerous articles,[45] not to speak of the editorial of volume II (XXVII) (1949) recanting the sins of its predecessor. These sins, of a rootless cosmopolitan nature, were first, the thesis that Soviet Byzantine studies were the heir of the Russian bourgeois tradition in this field and, second, the attempt to establish a common front with Byzantine studies abroad, a discipline which represented a reactionary trend in scholarship. This was the more inadmissible as western bourgeois scholars denied the autochthonous character and the importance of the early culture of Rus'. In Byzantine studies, as elsewhere, the principles of objectivism had to be rejected and replaced by true Marxist-Leninist objectivity. Another pitfall the editors of the second volume of *Vizantiiskii Vre⟨165⟩mennik* promised to avoid was narrow empiricism and deadening factology.[46]

In the streamlined second volume of the *Vremennik*, Levchenko asserted that, however important Byzantine contributions to Russian culture may have been, one should not exaggerate them. The great Rus-

44. V. P. Adrianova-Peretts, "Osnovnye zadachi izucheniya drevnerusskoi literatury v issledovaniyakh 1917-1947 gg" [The basic tasks in the study of early Rus' literature as reflected in the works of the years 1917-1947], *Trudy Otdela drevne-russkoi literatury*, VI (1948), 5-14. The *Trudy* will be quoted in subsequent notes as *TODRL*.

45. Z. Udaltsova, "Obsuzhdenie pervogo toma 'Viz. Vremennika' na zasedanii gruppy po istorii Vizantii pri Institute istorii AN SSSR" [Consideration of the first volume of the *Byzantine Journal* by the Byzantine history group of the Institute of History of the Academy of Sciences of the U.S.S.R.], *Vop. Ist.*, IV, 1 (1948), 152-54; F. Rosseikin, "*Vizantiiskii Vremennik* ... t.I (XXVI)" [The *Byzantine Journal*, Vol. I (XXVI)], *ibid.*, IV, 3 (1948), 127-34; A. P. Kazhdan in *Izvestiya AN SSSR*, V; 1 (1948), 115-17; "V otdelenii istorii i filosofii AN SSSR. Sessiya po voprosam istorii Vizantii" [In the section of history and philosophy of the Academy of Sciences of the U.S.S.R. The session on problems of Byzantine history], *ibid.*, 127; "Protiv obʿektivizma v istoricheskoi nauke" [Against objectivism in historical scholarship], *Vop. Ist.*, IV, 12 (1948), 6.

46. "Protiv burzhuaznogo kosmopolitizma v sovetskom vizantinovedenii" [Against bourgeois cosmopolitanism in Soviet Byzantine studies], *Vizantiiskii Vremennik*, II (XXVII) (1949), 3-10. For a full French translation of this remarkable document, see M. Canard, "Vizantiiski Sbornik et Vizantiiski Vremennik, tomes I-XXVI (1947) et II-XXVII (1949)," *Byzantion*, XXI (1951), 471-81.

sian culture had an independent origin and a world importance of its own. Russia was made great by the Russian nation, not by Byzantine Orthodoxy.[47] Levchenko's statements of 1945 now belonged to the remote past. In his opening remarks pronounced at the Congress of Soviet Byzantinists late in 1950, Kosminsky noted that, while in their falsifications bourgeois scholars spoke almost exclusively of influence exerted by Byzantium upon other Slavic peoples, Soviet Byzantinists were bringing out the influences produced by Slavic and oriental peoples upon Byzantium.[48] Among those Slavic peoples, Rus' did much more than influence the Empire. In a 1951 version of what in historiographical folklore may be termed the *antemurale christianitatis* motif, a motif used at one time or another by historians living between the Volga and the Pyrenees, it was stated that by stopping the nomadic Pecheneg advance in the late eleventh century Rus' saved Byzantium and western Europe.[49]

⟨166⟩ The originality and high level of early Rus' culture became apparent in all domains. Rybakov, the author of a serious work on *Handicrafts in Early Rus'*,[50] was commended in 1949 for having convincingly refuted the reactionary theories of bourgeois scholars, who usually explained the high level of early Russia's material culture by foreign influences. Rybakov was said to have stressed the national and autochthonous character of this culture and its priority with respect to the material culture of various western states.[51] But not all authors had the advantage of having published their research at the right time. Lazarev's *History of Byzantine Painting*, one of the best works of its kind in the hands of scholars, was criticized in 1952 for exaggerating the extent of Byzantine and other influences upon the art of Kiev and Novgorod.[52]

47. M. V. Levchenko in *Vizantiiskii Vremennik*, II (1949), 337. By 1950, Levchenko reminded one of his opponents that Marx had called Byzantium "the worst of states," a strange quotation for a Byzantinist to use. See *Vizantiiskii Vremennik*, V (1952), 300.

48. *Vizantiiskii Vremennik*, V (1952), 292.

49. AN SSSR, Institut istorii materialnoi kultury, *Istoriya kultury drevnei Rusi. Domongolskii period* [A history of early Russian culture. The pre-Mongol period], II (1951), 512. This work will be referred to in subsequent notes as *Istoriya KDR*.

50. B. A. Rybakov, *Remeslo drevnei Rusi* (Moscow, 1948).

51. By G. B. Fedorov, in *Izvestiya AN SSSR*, VI, 2 (1949), 189-91.

52. By A. V. Bank, reviewing V. N. Lazarev's *Istoriya vizantiiskoi zhivopisi*, I-II (1947-48), *Vizantiiskii Vremennik*, V (1952), 266.

In the same year came the declaration by Likhachev, an able literary historian, to the effect that Byzantine culture represented only a thin layer in the body cultural of Rus', and that it underwent a sharp reinterpretation, becoming "Russian" in idea if not in form, because it was enlisted in the service of the early feudal state of Rus'. Even this formula of "Byzantine in form, Russian in content," reminiscent of a more famous prototype, was to be qualified with respect to certain genres of literature. True, literary works translated from Greek influenced the development of forms and genres of early Rus' literature. But even in its form, this literature reflected only the general ecclesiastical world-view and the demands of the local Christian cult, not directly Byzantine ⟨167⟩ models. Applied to hagiography in Rus', this meant that this most Byzantinized of all literary genres was in a sense original.[53]

We are told by a generally respected authority that the culture of early Rus', hitherto viewed as a result of the "grafting" of Byzantine culture, has a long east Slavic prehistory. For Grekov, the official historian of Kievan Rus', an original east Slavic, or Antes, or "Russian" culture expressed itself as early as the sixth or seventh century. It would, therefore, be grossly erroneous to assume that it was the Greek clergy who first taught the Russes to think and develop their culture. The first Greek metropolitans had already met with a "Russian" tendency towards shaking off the ecclesiastical dependence of Byzantium. Christianity of Rus' itself was an example of the Russian nation's ability to create its own culture and transform elements taken over from other nations.[54]

In writings dealing with the problem of Russo-Byzantine relations certain expressions appear with astonishing uniformity and simultaneity. Here belong the substitution of "interaction" for "influence," shibboleths like the device of putting the word influence in quotation marks, "creative reinterpetation," "originality," "elements of realism," "Russian reality," "patriotism," "progressive"; clever oxymora like "active reception," "creative assimilation," and above all the almost untranslatable *samobytnost* and *narodnost*, perhaps to be rendered by "autochthony" and "national character" respectively. The principal, though posthumous, villain of this period turned out to be Veselovsky,

53. D. S. Likhachev, *Vozniknovenie russkoi literatury* [The emergence of Russian literature] (Moscow, 1952), 126, 150-51. This work will be quoted in subsequent notes as *Vozniknovenie*.

54. B. D. Grekov, *Kievskaya Rus'* [Kievan Rus'] (new ed., 1949), 386, 372, 393, 387, 390.

the same scholar who in the late 1920's was mildly reproached for operating with such notions as "nation" and "national culture." Lately, however, it appears that ⟨168⟩ Veselovsky separated literary phenomena from their national and historical background by means of "borrowings," "influences," and "wandering motifs." Moreover, in his works, permeated with bourgeois and cosmopolitan ideas, he belittled the great role of Russian culture and in fact denied its national and autochtonous character.[55]

Official and still valid attitudes on the topic under discussion here were succinctly formulated in two works published in 1951: the new edition of the *Large Soviet Encyclopedia*, which for our purposes ranks as a primary source of great consequence, and in the second part of the *History of Culture in Early Rus'*, an impressive and useful volume edited under the auspices of the Academy of Sciences.[56] Discussing Russo-Byzantine relations from the ninth to the eleventh century in the *Encyclopedia*, Levchenko pointed out that Byzantium was in turn saved by Rus', scared by it, forced to yield to it, and treacherous to it on occasion.[57] Russes appear as powerful and victorious. As for Christianization, it was an ideological expression of the strengthening of the feudal class in Rus'. For Byzantium, it amounted to an attempt to subordinate Rus' politically and culturally. However these attempts failed and the autochthonous culture and state of Rus' developed independently. The passages related to Byzantium and Rus' are to be read in the concluding and synthesizing chapter of the second volume of the *History of Culture in Early Rus'*. The central one, a masterpiece of nuance and stylistic parallelism, deserves to be translated in its entirety:

> Yet, a separate and specific place in the formative process of Russian culture belongs to cultural and political relations with Byzantium. The old bourgeois and nobiliary scholarship viewed these as the *unilateral* influence of Byzantium, as a *contribution* ⟨169⟩ made by a leading civilization to the life of a "retrograde," "barbaric" land, as the *grafting* of the imperial culture upon Rus', as imitation of Byzantine models by the Russes. The art of Kievan Rus' was presented as a "provincial ramification" of Byzantine art on the soil of Rus'. The beginnings of literature in Rus' were presented as indebted to the Greek translation literature; Russian music and its oldest

55. *Bolsh. Sov. Ents.*, (2 ed.) VII, 543-44, article "Veselovsky, A. N." Veselovsky's official disgrace was proclaimed about 1948.

56. See note 49 above.

57. *Ibid.*, VIII, 33-34.

> written documents were attributed in their entirety to Byzantine influence, etc. To be sure, Rus' is indebted to Byzantine culture in many respects, but it is sufficient to observe how and what the Russian culture derived from that source in order to be convinced that these reactionary, cosmopolitan views are false and tendentious.
>
> Observing this process, we see how boldly Russian culture *takes in* new elements, how it assimilates progressive and enriching elements of the other nation's experience, elements that contribute to its growth and correspond to the needs and the level of development of society in Rus'. It is no accident that in its cultural construction the Kievan state turned towards the culture of Byzantium, the most *advanced* country of medieval Europe, towards the *most complicated and highest "models"*. This culture was a *match* to the people of Rus' and corresponded to the *high requirements* of its development. No less indicative is the active and creative character of this reception — Rus' employs the borrowings from Byzantium for the struggle with it, for the strengthening of its independence from "East Rome."[58]

Judging by the *Essays on the History of the U.S.S.R.*, a large synthesizing volume devoted to the feudal period, the militant phase in reevaluating the problem of Russo-Byzantine cultural relations seems to have been concluded by the middle of 1953. What in the immediately preceding period were polemically tinged new assertions are now taken for granted and form the background on which the picture of the autochthonous culture of Rus' and its prominent place in the medieval world is calmly outlined.[59]

⟨170⟩

V

Rapid as it was, the change in scholarly attitudes towards the assessing of the role of Byzantium in the culture of Rus' has a history of almost a decade and an even longer pre-history. Both deserve to be

58. *Istoriya KDR*, II (1951), 514. All the quotation marks and italics are those of the original.

59. *Ocherki istorii SSSR. Period feodalizma IX-XV* vv. (Moscow, 1953), B. D. Grekov's chapter on "The place of early Rus' in world history" (I, 258-64) devotes 9 lines to contacts between Byzantium and Rus', of which 4 are "anti-Byzantine." The provinces seem to lag slightly behind the center. *The History of the Ukrainian S.S.R.*, published in Russian by the Ukrainian Academy of Sciences and sent to the printer in December 1953, still vigorously inveighs against mendacious cosmopolitan inventions of bourgeois scholars who pretend-

outlined in some detail for, if true, the conclusions proposed during the last years would revolutionize our views on Kievan and Muscovite Russia. It might be convenient to enregister here the recent changes as reflected in the treatment of some particular aspects of our problem in Soviet scholarship. These are: the beginnings of early Rus' literature and especially its historiography, the origins of the use of the script in Rus', and the independence of early art in Rus'.

In 1900, Shakhmatov pondered over the origin of the *Hellenic Chronicle*, a Slavic compilation made on the basis of a number of Byzantine sources and transmitted in late manuscripts of Eastern European provenance. Was the compilation made in Rus' or in the Balkans? Assuming its Rus' origin, one would have to presuppose the presence of ten to fifteen different Byzantine sources in early Rus'. Should they even have been available, it is doubtful whether a local scholar would have been able to disentangle and use properly such variegated material. Therefore Shakhmatov attributed the *Hellenic Chronicle* to tenth-century Bulgaria.[60]

Shakhmatov's thesis was contested by Istrin, who postulated ⟨171⟩ a "local" solution. Istrin's general views, however, did not essentially differ from those of his older colleague. In his *History of Early Russian Literature in Outline*, Istrin observed in 1922 that proven "local" translations of Byzantine texts were few in number, the majority being of unknown origin. He had no illusions as to the erudition of early Rus' scholars. Tenth-century Byzantine theological controversies were incomprehensible to them, so that they confused the simplest things. The bulk of literature in early Rus' consisted of compilations, which outweigh original works several times. The tendency towards compilations appeared to Istrin as one of the distinguishing traits of that literature, as opposed to that of the south Slavs. Since the supply of Byzantine literature was not as plentiful in Rus' as it was in the Balkans, the bookmen of Rus' had to combine and rearrange the works once translated. Of the few "original" literary works of early Rus', all but the *Igor Tale* were based on ready material directly or indirectly Byzantine and often borrowed mechanically. Particularly in the lives of local saints, whole

---

ed that early Russian culture was formed as a result of Byzantine influence. Cf. AN USSR, Instytut Istorii, *Istoriya Ukrainskoi SSR*, I (Kiev, 1953), 82-86.

60. A. A. Shakhmatov, "Drevnebolgarskaya entsiklopediya X veka" [An early Bulgarian encyclopedia of the tenth century], *Vizantiiskii Vremennik,* VII, (1900), 1-35.

episodes were copied from Byzantine hagiographical texts. Of course, the simpler the content of the original works, the less dependent they were on Byzantine models. In some fields, such as natural sciences and geography, one could not, strictly speaking, postulate an influence, since in these matters no original activity was possible in Rus' for lack of knowledge on the part of local scholars. Works on these subjects were pure translations from Greek. But Istrin had a qualification to make: notwithstanding the Byzantine impact, almost all of the original works of the early literature of Rus' were prompted by events affecting contemporary society of Rus'. This was an obvious point which, however, was destined for an unprecedented career.[61]

⟨172⟩ Orlov's *Early Russian Literature in the Eleventh to Seventeenth Centuries* appeared in 1945. In fact the book was a revised edition of shorthand notes taken from the author's lectures delivered in 1934-35 — a period when Pokrovsky's disciples were still allegedly attempting to stifle Byzantine studies and Marr's followers were brazenly denying the existence of any kind of borrowing and influence. Orlov paid the required attention to the sociological aspects of literary creation. Otherwise his exposition was conventional and he often and freely stressed Byzantine influences. To Orlov, Byzantium and Bulgaria appear as organizers of the initial stage of early literature, since the overwhelming majority of texts imported into Rus' reflected Byzantine or Bulgarian ideology, and influenced local original and translated works. Even the "Russian alphabet was a facsimile of the Greek one, and had been perfected in Bulgaria. No less positive was Orlov's verdict on single original literary works, like the "Petition of Daniel the Prisoner" (*Molenie Daniila Zatochnika*), a somewhat enigmatic text of the twelfth or thirteenth century, whose very genre in Orlov's opinion was most probably taken over from Byzantine literature. Orlov judged the so-called second south Slavic influence of the fifteenth century positively. In this period, the south Slavic texts brought to Russia the last flourishing of Byzantine culture, and the rich rhetoric and political idea's of the Greco-Slavic states. Orlov regretted, however, that the level of Russian fifteenth-century imitations of south Slavic works was lower than that of the originals.[62]

61. V. M. Istrin, *Ocherk istorii drevnerusskoi literatury* (Petrograd, 1922), 7-53, *passim*.

62. A. S. Orlov, *Drevnyaya russkaya literatura XI-XVII vekov* (Moscow, 1945), 16, 136-37, 139-40, 209-10.

Adrianova-Peretts' interesting and useful *Essays on the Poetical Style in Early Rus'* may serve as an example of the rather short "transition period" to be dated about the year 1947. Her book is a hybrid formation in the sense that the material collected in it does not justify the assertions of the ⟨173⟩ preface or bear out the conclusions. Even in the body of the book one senses a dichotomy. The preface stresses the "national peculiarity" of the culture of early Rus', and the *narodnost* of the Russian literary process. But the author's thesis is a comparatively conservative one. She admits the impact of the heavily Byzantinized "bookish language" upon the style of early Rus', but she also postulates influences coming from the folklore, or as she puts it, the "indigenous oral poetics." She grants that the Byzantinized bookish culture provided the nascent "Russian" literature with models of literary genres, but she hastens to remark that at that early period the oral poetry already possessed a variety of lyrical and epical forms of its own. For instance, elaborate Byzantine forms were not taken over, because the chief subject matter of early ⟨174⟩ Rus' literature was historical and as such was modeled on the expressional devices of the historical epic poetry. For many metaphors, Adrianova-Peretts admits a double source, a Byzantine and a popular one. Such is the case with sun, moon, stars as metaphors for persons, or the eagle as the image of a hero. The difficulty is that as popular parallels she quotes late folksongs which may have been influenced by "bookish" literature. She herself grants such a possibility and later on ascribes certain types of metaphor, such as winter and summer allegories of paganism and Christianity respectively, and the sea-tempest-ship metaphor, to Byzantine influence alone.[63]

After all this, the reader is astonished to hear in conclusion that the metaphors of literature from the eleventh to the thirteenth centuries were a continuation of the devices used in oral poetry or were created in its spirit. Of course, the parallels at hand come from late folklore texts but as these parallels were absent from Byzantine literature, they must have come from the folklore. The stylistic development of early Rus' literature from the eleventh to the thirteenth centuries is in line with the national development of artistic style.[64]

Such ambiguous points of view disappear in later years. For reasons not devoid of a certain consistency, but hardly binding for

63. V. P. Adrianova-Peretts, *Ocherki poèticheskogo stilya drevnei Rusi* (Moscow, 1947), 10 ff., 18-19, 24, 30, 42, 48-49, 84.

64. *Ibid.*, 118 ff.

Western scholars, the conventional conception concerning the formation of Russian literature was scornfully rejected by Likhachev, one of the outstanding representatives of the younger generation, as shallow, naive, anti-scientific and directly contradictory to the methodological foundations of contemporary Soviet literary scholarship and the elementary requirements of Soviet historiography. The determining factor in the formation of the literature in early Rus' was "Russian" historical reality "in all the Russian autochthonous peculiarity of its aspects," rather than Byzantine influences. The role played by translation literature, although undeniable, was not so great as bourgeois scholars would have it. Moreover translations, if originating in Rus', sometimes bordered upon "creative reshapings." This meant that translators took great liberty in arranging, abbreviating, correcting, and interpolating their originals, in short, adjusting them to the needs of their readers. The very selection of translation was dictated by the demands of "Russian reality." The creative attitude of the *literati* of Rus' toward Byzantine historical sources also appears from the fact that compilations made from them were supplemented by extraneous material and rearranged, often with the elements of the very Byzantine chronicles. In conclusion we learn that the ***European*** literature which came to Russia through Byzantium, joined the wide current of the independent Russian literature, moving along independent channels of its own, having its sources in the pre-written, oral literature and folklore, and encompassing and reshaping works of translation literature in its powerful movement.[65]

⟨175⟩ As regards the origins of historical writing, Istrin assumed that historiography started in Rus' as a compilative arrangement of Byzantine sources such as George the Monk and Malalas, augmented by data referring to local history, mostly those connected with Byzantium, like the expeditions against Constantinople. These data were arranged within the framework of "universal," i.e. Byzantine, history. In time, Istrin speculated, entries of local interest were separated from this large compilative work under the influence of national aspirations, and formed the first recension of what later became the *Tale of Bygone Years*.[66] However widely this conception may have differed from Shakhmatov's elaborate and convincing reconstruction of the early

65. Likhachev, *Vozniknovenie*, 13, 120, 129, 131, 136-37; *idem*, chapter, "Literatura," in *Istoriya KDR*, II (1951), 167-68, 170 ff., 176.

66. V. M. Istrin, "Zamechaniya o nachale russkago letopisaniya" [Remarks on

stages of the *Tale*,[67] both views accorded an important place to Byzantine influence, since Shakhmatov established a connection between the earliest recension of the *Tale*, which he dated to 1039, and the foundation by Constantinople of the metropolitan see in Kiev, which he believed with the chronicle to have occurred about the same time. As late as 1940, Priselkov, a follower of Shakhmatov, went a step further. In his excellent *History of Annalistic Writing in Rus' in the Eleventh to the Fifteenth Centuries* he imagined that the *Tale's* first recension of 1037, in accordance with the customs of the Greek church, must ⟨176⟩ have been a memorandum on the history of the new metropoly. Following his earlier theory of alternate pro- and anti-Byzantine currents in the eleventh century, Priselkov saw in the recension of 1037, where he detected the scornful attitude of a Greek towards the people whose history he wrote, an expression of the point of view of a Greek institution. He similarly singled out as "Graecophile" certain sources supposed to have been incorporated into the recension of the *Tale* dating from 1093. As to the translation of Greek chronicles undertaken in the eleventh century, Priselkov attributed them to the initiative of the Greek Metropolitan of Kiev, who wanted to acquaint his flock with the greatness of the Empire.[68]

The contributions made by Byzantine chronicles to the cultural and literary development of Kievan Rus' could still be acknowledged in 1945.[69] Again, as elsewhere, 1947 is a liminary date. In the *Chronicles of Rus' and Their Significance for Cultural History*, published in that year, Likhachev, proceeding in a quite dignified although somewhat scholastic way, refuted Istrin's and Priselkov's theses.[70] Nevertheless, he admitted

---

the beginning of the annalistic writing in Rus'], *Izvestiya Otd. Russ. Yaz. i Slov. Rossiiskoi Akad. Nauk*, XXVI (1921), publ. 1923, 45-102; *idem, Ocherk istorii drevnerusskoi literatury*, 8, 142-45.

67. A.A. Shakhmatov, *Razyskaniya o drevneishikh russkikh letopisnykh svodakh* [Studies in the earliest recensions of the annals of Rus'] (1908). *Idem*, ed. of *Povest Vremennykh let* [Tale of Bygone Years], (1916). See for example D. S. Likhachev, "Shakhmatov kak issledovatel' russkogo letopisaniya" [Shakhmatov as a student of the annalistic writing in Rus'], *A. A. Shakhmatov* in *Trudy Komissii po istorii AN SSSR*, 3 (1947), 253-93.

68. M. D. Priselkov, *Istoriya russkogo letopisaniya XI-XV vv.* (Leningrad, 1940), 26, 28, 34, 29.

69. S. I. Maslov and J. P. Kyrylyuk, *Narys istoriyi ukrainskoii literatury* [A sketch of the history of Ukrainian literature] (Kiev, 1945), 41.

70. D. S. Likhachev, *Russkie letopisi i ikh kulturno-istoricheskoe znachenie* (Moscow-Leningrad, 1947), 60-62. The refutation is brought about by first

that the annalistic genre in Rus' "had ready-made models at its origins," but later changed under the impact of the "Russian" life. Modifying Shakhmatov's theories, Likhachev postulated a "Narrative on the Introduction of Christianity in Rus'" as the nucleus from which the *Tale of Bygone Years* ⟨177⟩ subsequently developed. He claimed the "Speech of a Philosopher before Vladimir," a part of the *Tale*, as the core of his hypothetical "Narrative." He vaguely doubted the originality of this "Speech," and declared that it belonged to a genre widespread in Greek literature. He quoted, not always pertinently, parallel Byzantine dialogues, and concluded that the author of his postulated nucleus of the *Tale* may have used ready-made models, unfortunately unknown.[71]

In Likhachev's opinion, the author of the postulated "Narrative" was anti-Greek. So was Nestor, one of the later editors of the *Tale of Bygone Years*. What is more, Nestor, the first Normanist in history, excogitated his theory of "the calling of the Varangian Princes" by the Slavs for the sole purpose of spiting the Greeks who claimed a decisive share in shaping the culture of Rus', and asserting her independence from Byzantium.[72] One cannot deny this hypothesis a certain ingenuity and even elegance, as with one blow it scored a victory on both fronts on which Soviet scholars had chosen to fight their battles.[73] It was duly appreciated by critics of Likhachev's book[74] and was repeated by him later.[75]

---

countering Istrin's and Priselkov's theses with the views of N. Nikolsky, who stressed the western Slavic influences in the *Tale of Bygone Years*, and then eliminating Nikolsky's views as unfounded. For a positive opinion on Nikolsky's findings, see R. Jakobson in *Harvard Slavic Studies*, II (1954), 45-46.

71. Likhachev, *Russkie letopisi*, 62, 73, 75.

72. *Ibid.*, 159 f.

73. Whether this anti-Scandinavian *and* anti-Byzantine battle array is correct scholarly strategy is open to question. It presupposes the existence of two independent cultural centers from which cultural influences could conceivably have radiated so as to converge in early Rus'. It is then asserted that influences originating from these centers were non-existent or negligible. This underlying assumption must be qualified since it has been proven that some legendary motifs common to Scandinavia and early Rus' wandered not from north to south, but from Byzantium via Rus' to Scandinavia. In some cases instead of two centers of potential influences on Rus' we obtain one, the Byzantine area; Rus' would only act as an intermediary to the north. For this important change in perspective, cf. Ad. Stender-Petersen, *Varangica* (Aarhus, 1953), 10-11, 241, and chapters X, XI.

74. S. Yushkov, reviewing Likhachev, in *Vop. Ist.*, III, 4 (1947), 111.

75. V. P. Adrianova-Peretts, ed., *Povest vremennykh let* [Tale of bygone years],

⟨178⟩ Likhachev is a prolific writer. Thus by necessity his works often incorporate with significant adjustments whole passages from the preceding ones. In the edition of the *Tale of Bygone Years* published in 1950, he took up again the question of its sources. As no new factual material had turned up since 1947, Likhachev operated with many of the same quotations. But his tone became virulent in exposing the errors of the "bourgeois" and "nobiliary" scholarship. The argument of the creative and "active" use of Byzantine sources made its appearance. Oral elements were held to be the main sources for the *Tale of Bygone Years*, whose authors were at the same time a match for Byzantine literature, the most highly developed in the European Middle Ages. The "ready-made models," which in the 1947 version might have been at the origin of annalistic writings in Rus', disappeared from an otherwise analogous passage in the 1950 book. As for the sources of the "Philosopher's Speech before Vladimir," the arguments professed were much the same but for a surprising conclusion: "Therefore, the Philosopher's speech is a Russian work." From now on, the only channel along which the *Tale* developed was "the channel of Russian reality."[76] By 1952 it became quite clear to Likhachev that the *Tale* was an autochthonous "Russian" genre of historical literature.[77]

As long as they remain in the realm of generalities, the findings of recent Soviet scholarship are not particularly disturbing to the professional historian, who is tolerant of broad hypotheses when they lack the rigorous apparatus of proofs and therefore avoid the danger of violating rules of the craft too flagrantly. When, however, the same type of speculation is applied to concrete points, where strict argumentation is a ⟨179⟩ prerequisite, the professional historian feels more uncomfortable. This is well exemplified by the new attitude towards the origin of the script.

Of the two Slavonic scripts, the glagolitic still presents a puzzling problem.[78] But the origins of the cyrillic seemed so obvious to the editors of the pre-revolutionaty *Encyclopedia of Slavic Philology* that they

---

II (1950), 113, with articles and commentaries by Likhachev.

76. *Ibid.*, 143 ff., 90, 330-31, to be compared with Likhachev's *Russkie letopisi*, 60-61, 62, 72-75.

77. *Vozniknovenie*, 166.

78. Cf., in the last instance, W. Lettenbauer, "Zur Entstehung des glagolitischen Alphabets," *Slovo*, III (1953), 35-50; a survey of previous theories and a new one, advocating a Western origin for the glagolitic script.

simply asked the famous paleographer Gardthausen to write a chapter on "Greek Script of the Ninth and Tenth Centuries." Gardthausen's starting point was the consideration that history knew no case in which a people received its culture from one nation and its script from another.[79] As for Rus', even Soviet scholars held that literacy as well as literature appeared there after the country's Christianization late in the tenth century. In Orlov's opinion, tenth-century eastern Europe possessed no alphabet corresponding to the phonetic particularities of the Slavic language, no literary language, no literary genres.[80] But already in 1936, Obnorsky, who analyzed the language of the Slavic version of treaties between the Russes and Byzantium, dated at 911 and 945 respectively, arrived at the conclusion that they were written not in Church Slavonic but in "Russian" with an admixture of Bulgarianisms, or Church Slavonisms, decreasing in number from one treaty to another.[81]

The implication of such a finding was obvious and soon it was taken up by Grekov. For him, the existence of literacy ⟨180⟩ among early tenth-century Russes became, as it were, certain.[82] The "Russian letters" with which St. Cyril is said to have come in contact in the Crimea in the latter half of the ninth century, may have been Greek letters, but the Psalter written in these letters and read by Cyril was obtained from a "Russian" and must have been written in "Russian."[83] Compared to what was to follow, Grekov's was almost a timid standpoint. In subsequent years it was asserted that the literary language of early Rus' was formed long before Christianization; that this language, it is to be assumed, developed when there already existed a standardized script; that the cyrillic script appeared in Rus' a few decades before Chris-

79. V. Gardthausen, "Grecheskoe pismo IX-X stoletii" [The Greek script of the ninth and tenth centuries], *Entsiklopediya slavyanskoi filologii*, III, 2 (1911), 37-50.

80. Orlov, *Drevnyaya russkaya literatura,* 14, 17.

81. S. P. Obnorsky, *"Yazyk dogovorov russkikh s grekami"* [The language of the Russian-Greek treaties], *Yazyk i myshlenie*, VI-VII (1936), 101 ff.

82. Grekov, *Kievskaya Rus* (3 ed., 1939), 11; the clause "as it were" disappeared from the 1949 edition of the book, 12.

83. *Kievskaya Rus* (new ed., 1949), 384. But there seems to have been nothing "Russian" about those letters which were most probably "Syrian letters." Cf. A. Vaillant, "Les 'lettres russes' de la Vie de Constantin," *Revue des Études Slaves*, XV (1935), 75-77; and R. Jakobson, "Saint Constantin et la langue syriaque," *Annuaire de l'Institut de Philologie et d'Histoire Orientales et Slaves*, VII (1944), 181-86.

tianization; that the treaty of 945 was undoubtedly written in Kiev; that "some indices" point to the fact that Eastern Slavic script was of local and even earlier origin; that this script was glagolitic, since the Psalter read by St. Cyril in the Crimea was written in glagolitic; that, consequently, the glagolitic script was created not by St. Cyril, but somewhere on the northern shores of the Black Sea as a result of a prolonged development; that the glagolitic alphabet stands in direct relationship to the cuneiform script and is also related to undeciphered signs of the northern Black Sea shore, dating from the first to the seventh century.[84] Concerning the cyrillic ⟨181⟩ script, Likhachev informed his readers that writing in Russia came about not as a result of individual inventions, but as a response to the needs which had appeared in a class society, although literacy itself did not have a class character. This need may have given simultaneous birth to scripts in different parts of the East Slavic world; thus the early script may have been polyalphabetical, cyrillic *and* glagolitic.[85] In other words, the way was paved to connect the invention of even the cyrillic script with the language of Rus'.[86]

All these were rather amazing assumptions. One would expect a more sober attitude in dealing with the tenth and later centuries in which our paleographic documentation is sufficiently abundant to leave but little leeway for extravaganzas. So close is the resemblance between the early cyrillic and Byzantine scripts that even a relatively trained eye wandering from a tenth-century Byzantine ⟨182⟩ uncial manuscript to some of the earliest specimens of the cyrillic uncial has to pause for a moment before deciding in which language the respective texts are composed. Until 1950 the reasons for this similitude seemed evident. But in that year Mrs. Granstrem raised the question of whether Slavic uncial manuscripts are an imitation of the Byzantine uncial or a product of independent development. Under the influence of other alphabets, she maintained, the Byzantine uncial script could assume local

84. See P. J. Chernykh, chapter "Yazyk i pismo" [Language and script], in *Istoriya KDR*, II (1951), 121-22, 130-31, 134; and V.V. Vinogradov's review of various recent hypotheses on the origin of literacy in Rus' in his preface to L. P. Yakubinsky, *Istoriya drevnerusskogo yazyka* [History of the early language of Rus'] (Moscow, 1953), 7 ff., based on lectures delivered in the thirties.

85. D. S. Likhachev, "Predposylki vozniknoveniya russkoi pismennosti i russkoi literatury," *Vop. ist.*, VII, 12 (1951), 34 ff., discussed by Vinogradov, in Yakubinsky, *op. cit.*, 10-11.

86. This is an observation of Vinogradov, Yakubinsky, 11. Vinogradov views such a procedure as lacking proof and not based on any new data.

characteristics as in the case of the Coptic, the western European, the Georgian, and finally, the postulated paleo-Slavic variant of the Byzantine uncial script. Although none of the specimens of this "paleo-Slavic" type of Byzantine uncial can be shown to come from Slavic territories, she reached the conclusion that the earliest Slavic cyrillic manuscripts are the product of an independent graphic creation of Slavic nations, and the type of Byzantine uncial from which the cyrillic uncial was believed to derive is on the contrary but a Byzantine reflection of the formative process undergone by the Slavic script.[87]

A similar attitude was displayed with regard to the art of early Rus'. In order better to acquaint his readers with the magnificence of early Rus' culture, Grekov invites them into the cathedral of St. Sophia in Kiev. This imaginary visit also serves the purpose of introducing the problem of the origins of Russian civilization. To Grekov's mind the solution to this problem would be incomplete if one explained the thriving state of eleventh-century architecture of Rus' by the activity of Greek architects alone. Architects are helpless without a host of skilled workers, and those must have been of local origin. Also a craftsman is only the executor of an order; the commission for a work like St. Sophia came not from Byzantium but from the Kievan state itself. Greek builders and artists of the tenth and eleventh centuries had to adjust themselves to the tastes of the prince of Rus' and his entourage.[88]

Again, these speculations of 1949 seem abstract enough. The next year, however, brought a technical article of a more disturbing nature, especially since it bore the signature of Brunov, a respected art historian trained in the pre-revolutionary school. The article's by now ritual preamble branded as false the views of the majority of "bourgeois" historians that St. Sophia of Kiev is a monument of Byzantine art on the soil of Rus', just as "bourgeois" scholarship was wont to ascribe all of the outstanding achievements of Russia's past to foreigners. ⟨183⟩ According to Brunov, St. Sophia is an architectural monument of independent artistic value and a creation made possible only by a previous architectural tradition in Rus' going back to pagan times.[89]

87. E. E. Granstrem, "O svyazi kirillovskogo ustava s vizantiiskim untsialom" [On the relations of the cyrillic script with the Byzantine uncial], *Vizantiiskii Vremennik,* III (1950), 218-29.

88. Grekov, *Kievskaya Rus* (1949), 368-69, 391.

89. N. I. Brunov, "Kievskaya Sofiya — drevneishii pamyatnik russokoi kamennoi arkhitektury" [St. Sophia of Kiev — the earliest monument of Russian stone architecture], *Vizantiiskii Vremennik,* III (1950), 154-200, esp. 155, 188, 199.

From the silence of the *Tale of Bygone Years* as to the importation of Greek architects to build St. Sophia, Brunov deduced that the cathedral was constructed by Russian builders, partly trained in the tradition of the large number of local craftsman who had assisted in the construction of the tenth-century Tithe Church, but mainly continuing the *millenary* tradition of the wooden architecture in Rus' and earth works, earthen fortifications, and funerary mounds. In all seriousness, sketches of pre-Christian mounds were provided by the author and juxtaposed with the silhouette of the Kievan cathedral in order to prove the derivation of its outline. Boasting such ancestry, St. Sophia was said to surpass Byzantine models and contain new characteristics peculiar to "Russian" architecture. Since a perfect artistic work must be not only national but also popular in its essence, we learn that St. Sophia's thick pillars express the sound popular feeling for the bodily principle and are closer to the ancient Roman architecture than are the more delicate but decadent Byzantine forms, far removed from the sources of popular creativity.[90] Brunov's melancholy performance still remains unsurpassed.

While the new views on St. Sophia's architecture appeared ⟨184⟩ in a developed form from the outset, it is possible to follow an evolution with respect to one particular problem, that of the contents of the "Hippodrome" frescoes decorating the cathedral's staircases. According to Orlov, Byzantine *jongleurs* were represented on the walls of St. Sophia;[91] in the art chapter from the *History of the Early Culture of Rus'* the question, Byzantine or "Russian", was left unsettled;[92] in 1952, Likhachev

90. *Ibid.*, 182, 199, 200 see also N. N. Voronin and M. Karger, "Arkhitektura" [Architecture], *Istoriya KDR*, II (1951), 249, 253, 261-62. Previous to his treatment of 1950, Brunov had dealt with the origin of St. Sophia in a number of articles dating from the late twenties. As between 1950 and the late twenties, his arguments are often identical, but his conclusions, vastly different. It is true that in these earlier essays Brunov denied a *direct* Constantinopolitan inspiration for the cathedral's architecture. But he looked for parallels in Asia Minor, viewed St. Sophia as a monument of Byzantine art, more exactly as a "Christian-Oriental" modification of the Constantinopolitan type. While he stated that the existence of important local features in St. Sophia could be proved, he also found a great affinity between this Kievan church and western Romanesque structures. Cf. as an example, Brunov's "Zur Frage des Ursprunges der Sophienkathedrale in Kiev," *Byzantinische Zeitschrift*, XXIX (1929-30), 248-59.

91. *Drevnyaya russkaya literatura* (1945), 139.

92. *Istoriya KDR*, II (1951), 351.

had no doubt that the scenes depicted games at the court of a Kievan prince.[93]

VI

A kind of textual criticism applied to modern Soviet works and practically amounting to a comparison between subsequent editions of the same book may best exemplify the direction in which the changing Soviet views evolve and illustrate the techniques by which this change is brought about. Gudzy's *History of Early Russian Literature*, [94] now in its fifth edition, is an aptly written textbook provided with a critical apparatus and destined for Soviet universities. For our purposes, the third edition, that of 1945, and the fourth, that of 1950, are of importance since the time elapsing between them encompasses the decisive turn of 1947. The changes to be ⟨185⟩ observed are not due to the accumulation of new factual material. Radical as they sometimes are, they occur mainly in the evaluating passages. Thus while in 1945 Gudzy thought that before the middle of the seventeenth century oral poetry only rarely found its way into written texts and only partly influenced the Byzantinized written literature, he omitted the latter passage from the fourth edition, added a chapter on oral poetry in early Rus', and concluded it with the assertion that there was no doubt but that the rich devices of Rus' folklore favorably influenced the literature of early Rus'.[95]

In the third edition, Veselovsky was praised at length as the principal literary historian of the past century who laid the foundations for a sociological study of literature.[96] Instead of eliminating the praise, the edition of 1950 omitted the whole chapter on the history of the studies of early Rus' literature, where Veselovsky figured so prominently. To take care of other references to the Byzantinizing Veselovsky — he was mentioned twenty-three times throughout the body of the 1945 edition — phrases like "we should assume, following Veselovsky..." were replaced by "we should assume that..."[97] In one place, the words "as Veselovsky has shown" were omitted in the 1950 edition, as was the footnote refer-

93. *Vozniknovenie*, 84.

94. *Istoriya drevnei russkoi literatury* (3d ed., 1945; 4 ed., 1950). There exists an English translation by S. W. Jones of the 2nd edition of 1941: N. K. Gudzy, *History of Early Russian Literature* (New York, 1949).

95. *Ibid.*, 3 ed., 11; 4 ed., 11, 14.

96. *Ibid.*, 24.

97. For example *ibid.*, 3 ed., 41; 4 ed., 27.

ring to his work, and the verbatim quotation was faithfully paraphrased and now appears as Gudzy's own words.[98] These were omissions for the layman, for whom Veselovsky should simply disappear as *damnatus memoriae*. For the refined reader, his spirit had to be exorcised. Thus even the words "wandering motifs," one of Veselovsky's pet terms, redolent of foreign influences, reappear in 1950 in the properly trimmed form "fairy tale motifs."[99]

⟨186⟩ In 1945, Gudzy praised Byzantine culture as much higher than pre-Christian culture of Rus'. As by 1950 Russian culture could be second to none, these words were changed at the corresponding page of the fourth edition into the assertion that "Christian literature was the product of a culture higher than the pagan culture."[100] Another change exhibited an even finer touch. According to Gudzy's view expressed in the third edition, the choice of Byzantine translations which found their way into Rus' was determined by the latter's cultural level. The implication of this pronouncement was obvious even to a university student who knew that the Greek works translated into Slavic did not on the whole rank highly in the body of Byzantine literature. The edition of 1950 replaced the embarrassing sentence by an enigmatic *dictum* that the choice of Byzantine translations was determined by "what Byzantium provided Rus' with."[101]

The evolution of the years 1945-1952 may best be summed up in the subsequent treatment of the two quotations found in the works of two Soviet historians. In 1945 Gudzy quoted from Marx and Engels that "Kiev imitated Constantinople in every respect, and was called the second Constantinople."[102] This remark, Gudzy thought, may have referred to Adam of Bremen's famous saying about Kiev's being a rival of the Constantinopolitan sceptre, and a brilliant adornment of Greece. This implied, it may be added, that in the medieval German chronicler's mind, Kiev belonged to the Eastern Empire's sphere of influence. Five years later, Gudzy, repeating the two quotations, omitted Marx's first clause concerning the imitation of Constantinople by Kiev.[103] In 1952,

98. *Ibid.*, 3 ed., 41; 4 ed., 28.

99. *Ibid.*, 3 ed., 255; 4 ed., 248.

100. *Ibid.*, 3 ed., 26 with 4 ed., 17.

101. *Ibid.*, 3 ed., 27 with 4 ed., 18; similar, although much milder changes may be found by comparing the different editions of Grekov's *Kievskaya Rus*: compare 249, 250, 252, of the 1939 edition, with 473, 471, 473 of the 1949 edition.

102. *Istoriya drevnei russkoi literatury*, 3 ed., 8.

103. *Ibid.*, 4th ed., 8.

Likha⟨187⟩chev, taking both authorities up again, proved even more succinct: to him, it was no chance that Adam of Bremen saw in Kiev a competitor of Constantinople and that Marx and Engels called it "the Second Constantinople."[104]

In reversing their views on the level and originality of the culture in Rus', Soviet scholars also resorted to techniques more sophisticated than doctoring up quotations or mere scissors and paste procedures. They extolled the neighbor's merits whenever they could not plausibly deny them or when they might even indirectly make Rus' appear in an advantageous light. Rus' may have withstood Byzantine attempts to enslave it culturally, but Byzantium was the most enlightened and advanced among Europe's contemporary states.[105] Learning in Rus' was influenced by Byzantium, but as a result it differed but little from that of the Eastern Empire; in fact, both were on the same level.[106] The influence of Byzantine translations upon local literature may have been grossly exaggerated by non-Soviet scholars, but it remained that the "Russian" language had thus assimilated the best works of European medieval literature.[107] To Istrin and Priselkov the few Byzantine world chronicles translated for the readers of Rus' were often ill-chosen, and all were of a popular and lowbrow character. Historical monographs for refined readers were not divulged since they described events not quite flattering to the Empire.[108] For once Likhachev ⟨188⟩ shows a distinct pro-Byzantine bias when he finds that, as a result of using Byzantine texts, world history was represented to "Russian readers" through skillfully executed compilations of all the best sources available at the time.[109] He comes close to his pre-revolutionary predecessors in maintaining that the twelfth-century Bishop Cyril of Turov not only used the skillful techniques of Byzantine preachers, but possessed a profound knowledge of the Greek

104. *Vozniknovenie*, 126.

105. For example Grekov, *Kievskaya Rus* (1949), 403.

106. N. S. Chaev, article "Prosveshchenie" [Education], *Istoriya KDR*, II (1951), 216 ff., 243; see also *Ocherki istorii SSSR*, I (1953), 223 (by Grekov). From the presentation of cosmological views attributed to people living in the Kievan period the uninitiated reader cannot realize that Grekov is quoting and paraphrasing a translation from a Byzantine source.

107. Likhachev, article "Literatura" [Literature], *Istoriya KDR*, II, 164.

108. Istrin, *Ocherk istorii drevnerusskoi literatury* (1922), 86-7; Priselkov, *Istoriya russkogo letopisaniya* (1940), 29.

109. *Istoriya KDR*, II, 174; *Idem, Vozniknovenie*, 136.

language.[110] The cathedral of St. Sophia may have surpassed its contemporary Byzantine counterparts, yet its builders were familiar with the newest achievements of Constantinopolitan architecture and art which, decadent as it may have been, was the best of Europe in the tenth century.[111]

Here also belongs the introduction of fine verbal distinctions which enable a Soviet author to maintain his surprising theses intact. In assessing Russo-Byzantine relations, we are told, the use of the term "influence" is inexact, as it presupposes an activity on the part of the giver and a passive attitude of the receiver. In Rus' the reverse was the case.[112] Whenever influences cannot be denied, they are localized and sanctioned. It becomes important to realize at what level they took place. Since in Rus' it was the feudal upper crust which turned to the Byzantine feudal ruling class for formulae of use for consolidating their "superstructure," it was not a question of a superior "national" culture influencing a less developed ⟨189⟩ national culture.[113] As in Soviet historiography the evershifting present seems to hold up its mirror to the past, which therefore shifts correspondingly, we hear that the grafting of Byzantine upper class cultural elements on the feudal culture of Rus' was a progressive phenomenon, because it strengthened the state of Rus' by increasing its *centralization*, in which not only the feudal lords but even the "people" were partly interested.[114]

Not all of the speculative techniques employed by Soviet scholars to enhance the self-sufficiency of the culture of early Rus' can be treated as verbal exercises. In the field of reconstructing the earliest period of historiography in Rus', where the main evidence available consists of one text and where hypothesis is pitched against hypothesis, it is impossible to reject any solution on the basis simply of its strange and speculative character. Thus the reconstruction attempted by Likhachev has to be given the same attentive consideration which, say, Shakhmatov's

110. *Istoriya KDR*, II, 196; that Cyril knew and read Greek, was asserted by M. I. Sukhomlinov, *O sochineniyakh Kirilla Turovskogo* [On the writings of Cyril of Turov] (1858), reprinted in *Sbornik Otd. Russ. Yaz. i Slov. Imp. Akad. Nauk*, LXXXV (1908), 275-349, but strongly doubted by A. Vaillant, "Cyrille de Turov et Grégoire de Nazianze," *Revue des Études Slaves*, XXVI (1950), 49-50, and G. P. Fedotov, *The Russian Religious Mind* (1945), 70-71.

111. Brunov in *Vizantiiskii Vremennik,* III (1950), 184; *Istoriya KDR*, II, 250.

112. Likhachev, *Vozniknovenie*, 125, 130, 154-55, 233.

113. *Ibid.*, 122 ff., 128.

114. Likhachev, *Vozniknovenie*, 127.

hypotheses received in their time. Still, it is essential to state, for the purpose of the present survey, that Likhachev's postulated nucleus of the *Tale of Bygone Years* is such as to be interpreted as anti-Byzantine and its composition dated into the forties of the eleventh century.[115] Shakhmatov, we remember, attributed to *his* nucleus the date of 1039 and connected its compilation with the establishment of the metropolitan see in Kiev by the Byzantine patriarchate. In two operations, a reconstructed document purportedly illustrating the impact of Byzantine culture was changed in Likhachev's system into an anti-Byzantine manifesto. The somewhat ironical element is that both Shakhmatov's hypothesis and Likhachev's rearrangement are closely con⟨190⟩nected with the belief, shared by both scholars, that the metropolitan see of Kiev was founded about 1037. As this no longer can be upheld with any certainty,[116] the main Soviet innovations appear irrelevant to the question of the pro- or anti-Byzantine attitude of the earliest chronicles of Rus'.

VII

No matter how improbable the Soviet hypotheses may appear, they should not in the last analysis be dismissed without a demonstration of their extravagance by proofs of universal cogency. This cannot be done within the scope of the present essay, and it should be noted that it is of slight use to refute the theoretical foundations on which Soviet scholars base their hypotheses in view of the basic divergencies between them and Western scholars in this area. It should nevertheless be added that such binding demonstration is quite feasible. Obviously, it can yield only limited results, for it implies the tackling of specific problems at a technical level where certain rudimentary methodological assumptions are professed in common. These include the validity of clear textual evidence and the importance of chronology, where proofs cogent for both sides appear possible.⟨191⟩

Faced with the remarkably synchronized and apparently general reversals in evaluating the whole field of Russo-Byzantine cultural relations, one cannot help looking for voices of dissent from the officially

---

115. Likhachev, *Russkie letopisi* (1947), 70-71, 76; edition of *Povest vremennykh let* (1950), 77; *Vozniknovenie*, 161, in a somewhat weakened form.

116. See E. Honigmann, "Studies in Slavic Church History; A. The foundations of the Russian metropolitan church according to Greek sources," *Byzantion*, XVII (1944-45), 128-62.

accepted interpretations and wondering about the attitudes and "real" beliefs of serious Soviet scholars. As for the first point, the present writer was able to discover, but not to explain, one non-conformist statement by a relatively obscure scholar made in passing but unmistakable in its tenor.[117] Among the more renowned scholars, a strange duality may sometimes be detected. In discussing various recent hypotheses dating the beginning of "Russian" script and literacy far into the pre-Christian era, the distinguished linguist Vinogradov called them "unfortunately as yet unfounded"; many of them, he thought, could not be ranged among the sure achievements of Soviet philology. He attacked some of Likhachev's statements on the subject as arbitrary, subjective and contradictory. And yet, in the same breath Vinogradov rejected the traditional viewpoint connecting the introduction of script with Christianization and Bulgarian-Byzantine influence as questionable and historically one-sided, since it did not take into account "the achievements of Eastern Slavs in the domain of script."[118]

One is reduced to guesses as to the reason which may have caused Vinogradov's surprising critique followed by a return into the fold of orthodoxy of the day. In another similar case, that of the art historian Igor Grabar, some plausible explanations can be offered. Reviewing Lazarev's valuable *Art of Novgorod*, Grabar stressed that Lazarev ascribed only the frescoes of the Saviour Church to the late fourteenth-century Byzantine Theophanes the Greek. Paintings in other churches are, in the author's opinion, to be attributed to Theophanes' Russian pupils. Grabar acknowledged that Lazarev's arguments were weighty, but remarked that this assumption would lead to a critical examination by specialists. Such a rather qualified adherence to a patriotic thesis is something unusual ⟨192⟩ in recent Soviet scholarship. As if to compensate for this, Grabar objected further on that Lazarev's book sometimes created the basically wrong impression that the chief impulses in the

117. Y. N. Dmitriev, "Meletovskie freski i ikh znachenie dlya istorii drevnerusskoi literatury" [The Meletovo frescos and their meaning for the history of early Russian literature], *TODRL*, VIII (1951), 403-12. On p. 410 we learn that the staircase frescoes of St. Sophia in Kiev were painted by a non-Rus' artist, do not represent scenes of local life, and therefore the jesters depicted there are not Russes.

118. V. V. Vinogradov in L. P. Yakubinsky, *Istoriya drevnerusskogo yazyka* (1953), 7, 10-11, 30.

history of Novgorod painting lay outside of Rus', especially in Byzantium.[119]

In order better to understand Grabar's somewhat contradictory attitude of 1949, it is worthwhile to remember his own field work in Novgorodian churches. In 1922 he published a pamphlet in which he praised Theophanes' influence on Russian art and credited him with bringing realistic and even salutary forces to the Russian north. Grabar claimed as a certainty that Theophanes was the author of frescoes in *several* churches of Novgorod.[120]

With the more important Soviet scholars, then, personal convictions can be discerned under the seemingly uniform façade of programmatic statements. In the Soviet Union as elsewhere, it seems easier to conform to new general trends than to discard one's personal scholarly findings. Freedom, the most human of passions, expresses itself, however faintly, in the protest against the unsound methods of those who violate the sacred rules of the art, and in the defense of one's own theories. Still, even in those cases a ransom in official theses must be paid for non-conformist hints if they are to be expressend at all.

This brings up the final question. To what extent do serious Soviet scholars believe in the patriotic assertions and anti-Western tirades which seem to contradict the previous stand of Russian or even Soviet scholarship and appear so outlandish to scholars outside the Soviet Union? Here the answer ⟨193⟩ should be very guarded. In East and West alike, patriotic feelings have often exerted a potent soporific effect upon the scholarly conscience. When Levchenko violently attacks Grégoire's theories on the spurious character of Prince Oleg's campaign against Constantinople of the year 907, it must be assumed that he performs this service with full conviction since he has behind him, aside from official sanction, a whole tradition of Russo-Byzantine studies, Soviet and non-Soviet, as well as a segment of Western scholarship.[121] Similar considera-

119. I. E. Grabar, review of V. I. Lazarev's *Isskustvo Novgoroda* (The art of Novgorod) (1947), in *Izvestiya AN SSSR*, VI (1949), 372-75.

120. I. E. Grabar, *Feofan Grek* (Kazan, 1922). I know this pamphlet only through J. Strzygowski's long review in *Byz.-Neugriechische Jahrbücher*, IV (1923), 153-58.

121. M. V. Levchenko, "Russko-vizantiiskie dogovory 907 i 911 gg." [The Russo-Byzantine treaties of 907 and 911], *Vizantiiskii Vremennik,* V (1952), 105-26; for orientation in the long controversy, see A. A. Vasiliev, "The Second Russian Attack on Constantinople," *Dumbarton Oaks Papers*, VI (1951), 163-225, and H. Grégoire, "L'histoire et la légende d'Oleg, prince de Kiev," *La Nouvelle Clio*, IV (1952), 281-87; cf. *ibid.*, 384-87.

tions apply to scholars like Lazarev, who seem to follow the official trends with some reluctance. But when a Brunov traces back the silhouette of St. Sophia in Kiev to the shape of a prehistoric mound, it must be equally strongly assumed that he is only desperate, since he himself knows better. Between these extreme examples lies a whole gamut of cases where academic considerations are mingled in an ever varying degree with extraneous motives which on occasion culminate in hoaxes. For all that, we must avoid passing judgment on a situation where individuals may be exposed to pressures which we ourselves would not be able to withstand.

What are then, from the Western point of view, the contributions of recent Soviet scholarship to the problem of Russian-Byzantine cultural relations? If we define this problem as one of assessing the impact of Byzantine culture upon Russia, then these contributions are of necessity of a limited scope. Looking everywhere for manifestations of original Russian or Slavic genius, Soviet scholars may conceivably be succesful in tackling anew still unsolved problems such as ⟨194⟩ that of the glagolitic script or correcting exaggerations of previous research, whenever it stressed Byzantine influences too much. Such results, however, will be accidental and will be paralleled by misconceptions arising from the prescribed negativistic attitude. The main positive contribution which may be expected from Soviet scholarship lies in adducing new evidence to corroborate the thesis of the high level of autochthonous cultural development in Russia. Here certain results have been achieved. Recent excavations in Novgorod have yielded ample material, justifying a revision of our views on the extent of literacy among Russian artisans and merchants,[122] and synthetic works like Rybakov's *Handicrafts in Early Russia* gave an impressive picture of the material culture of the early period.

In this connection, certain plans of Soviet scholars — in particular that of ultimately publishing a corpus of writings produced in early Rus'[123] — deserve general recognition. If carried out, they would benefit research in the Soviet sphere and the West alike. In recent years, investigations of manuscript collections have grown in intensity, as has the number of articles in which complete manuscript evidence for a text is enumerated. Still, to be performed well, the task of singling out original

122. See M. N. Tikhomirov, "Gorodskaya pismennost v drevnei Rusi XI-XIII vv." [Urban literacy in early Rus' of the eleventh to thirteenth century], *TODRL*, IX (1953), 51-66.

123. Cf. V. P. Adrianova-Peretts in *TODRL*, VI (1948), 7.

achievements of the culture of Rus' must be coupled with a thorough familiarity with its extraneous elements, which means a sound knowledge of things Byzantine. Unfortunately, Soviet scholars do not always meet this requirement, as witnessed by the number of factual errors contained in their works. Even when interesting finds are forthcoming, they are not put into their proper framework, since their Byzantine antecedents seem unknown to Soviet scholars. Such is the case of the "Oldest Russian Riddle" recently discovered ⟨195⟩ on a fourteenth- or fifteenth-century vessel in Novgorod, which is in fact a simple translation of a Byzantine one.[124] Finer "Byzantine" points in early texts of Rus' go unnoticed sometimes because of the inability of the commentators to cope with them. A propensity toward finding the culture of early Rus' original and ancient may be reinforced by the relative innocence of one of its important roots.

VIII

In the preceding survey of trends predominant in Soviet scholarship no attempt has been made to correlate Soviet works in Russo-Byzantine relations with developments in other areas of Soviet historical studies, or with simultaneous Soviet political pronouncements. But it should be apparent from other chapters in this volume that the ultra-patriotic tone in this field is only one aspect of a uniform pattern. That the ultimate inspiration for laying out this pattern is political can be read in as many words in programmatic articles appearing in *Voprosy Istorii*, the organ which serves as a relay between the party and the community of Soviet historians. In 1948 and 1949 *Voprosy Istorii* had some very precise things to say against what was termed the mendacious version concerning the lack of originality of Russian culture and the exaggeration of Byzantine influences upon Rus'.[125]

⟨196⟩ A Byzantinist is not qualified to juxtapose Soviet statements on Byzantine culture with Zhdanov's anti-cosmopolitan pronouncements

---

124. Published in A. V. Artsikhovsky and M. N. Tikhomirov, *Novgorodskie gramoty na bereste* [Novgorodian documents written on birchbark] (Moscow, 1953), 43. Cf. R. Jakobson, "Vestiges of the earliest Russian vernacular," *Slavic World*, VIII (1952), 354-55. Byzantine original version in C. F. G. Henrici, "Griechisch-Byzantinische Gesprächsbücher und Verwandtes..." *Abh. der Königl. Sächsischen Akad. der Wissenschaften, phil.-hist. Klasse*, XXVIII, 8 (1911), 37, 66.

125. "Protiv ob'ektivizma v istoricheskoi nauke," *Vop. Ist.*, IV, 12 (1948), 3-12, esp. 5-6, 10-11; "O zadachakh sovetskikh istorikov v borbe s proyavleniyami burzhuaznoi ideologii," *ibid.*, V, 2 (1949), 3-13, esp. 4 ff., 8, 13.

of 1946-47 or Stalin's linguistic revelations of 1950.[126] This is a task for contemporary historians. But another type of correlation remains to be hinted at, that with past Russian historical thinking, especially since the affinities may not always be felt by the Soviet scholars themselves.

The anti-Normanist theory is not a Soviet invention. Nor is the attempt to connect the Russes with peoples inhabiting the northern Black Sea shores in antiquity. As for the terms *samobytnost'* and *narodnost'*, so prominent in recent Soviet writings, they have a familiar ring for anyone even superficially acquainted with Russian nineteenth-century thought. The insistence upon the originality of "Russian" culture is curiously related to the proposition, advanced by a Russian about 1867, that cultures do not borrow essential elements from one another. Thus, if we choose to remain within the post-Petrine period, an ideal scholarly genealogy may be traced between Lomonosov, a historian by avocation, Russia's first anti-Normanist, who proudly pointed to the wars of Russia against the Byzantines and had the Slavs derive from the Sarmatians, the Slavophiles like the writer and scholar K. S. Aksakov, the Slavophile epigones Grigoryev and Danilevsky, and current Soviet scholarship. Of course, the Slavophiles took an extremely pro-Orthodox and therefore pro-Byzantine stand, mostly in order to create a counterweight against the ⟨197⟩ corrupt West. But their construction simultaneously extolled Slavic, meaning for them Russian, autochthonous qualities, and was therefore somewhat contradictory. This contradiction was resolved in the Soviet anti-Western and anti-Byzantine theories of recent years. Both the Slavophiles' and Soviet scholars' admiration for Lomonosov is no mere chance,[127] nor is it chance that an anti-Slavophile liberal literary

126. A Byzantinist, however, cannot dispense with the knowledge of Stalin's *Marksizm i voprosy yazykoznaniya* [Marxism and the problems of linguistics], if he is to grasp the finer points in recent Soviet publications on his subject. Likhachev's chapter "On the problem of the 'Byzantine influence' in Russia" (*Vozniknovenie*, 119 ff.) must be read along with Stalin's pamphlet. It is also in this light that we can understand why literacy in Russia is said not to have had a class character and why stress is laid on the active quality of early Russia's superstructure and the influence it exerted upon its base (*Ocherki istorii SSSR*, I [1953], 206).

127. See K. S. Aksakov, "Lomonosov v istorii russkoi literatury i russkago yazyka" [Lomonosov in the history of Russian literature and the Russian language], (written in 1846) in Aksakov's *Polnoe sobranie sochinenii*, II, 23-389; and D. Gurvich, "M. V. Lomonosov i russkaya istoricheskaya nauka" [M. V. Lomonosov and Russian historical scholarship], *Vop. ist.*, V, 11 (1949), 107-19.

historian of the last century like Pypin is frowned upon in Soviet publications.

For all its bizarrerie, the spectacle scholars have been witnessing for the past few years is to be taken seriously. This is a rewriting of the history of Russia's origins such as has not been seen since the late fifteenth and sixteenth centuries. At that time the activity passed almost unnoticed abroad. Only the sixteenth-century Polish poet Jan Kochanowski ironically referred to the historical validity of Ivan the Terrible's claims to descent from Emperor Augustus.[128] But Kochanowski's seems to have been a lone voice. Today historians have the opportunity to watch the birth of a new *vulgata*, and a duty to study its making closely.

Lomonosov is especially praised for unmasking the "false objectivism" of his eighteenth-century German opponents and inveighing against their "cosmopolitanism" and "anti-patriotic attitude" (110, 113). Cf. also P. K. Alefirenko and E. P. Podyapolskaya, review of the sixth volume (published in 1952) of Lomonosov's *Collected Works*, containing his historical writings, in *Vop. Ist.*, IX, 9 (1953), 136-41.

128. "Jezda do Moskwy": [Ivan claims to be] "the fourteenth descendant of the Roman Emperor Augustus. Who knows where he unearthed that chronicler." Cf. *Jana Kochanowskiego Dzieła polskie*, ed. Jan Lorentowicz (Warsaw, no date), I, 218.

X

Imagery of the Igor' Tale in the Light of Byzantino-Slavic Poetic Theory

JUSTINIA BESHAROV, *Imagery of the Igor' Tale in the Light of Byzantino-Slavic Poetic Theory*. (Studies in Russian Epic Tradition, II.) Leiden: E.J. Brill, 1956. Paper. Pp. 115.

At first glance, the *Igor' Tale* does not "byzantinize" to any considerable degree. The frequency of lexical or idiomatic clichés, which ultimately go back to "learned" Greek models, determines our first judgement on that aspect of a mediaeval Slavic text, and not many such clichés and other devices are attested in this late twelfth-century epic of Kievan Rus'. There are certainly more of them in the roughly contemporary texts of secular character, such as the *Supplication of Daniel the Prisoner* (twelfth-thirteenth century) and the story of Prince Vasil'ko's blinding (about 1110).

But we cannot be satisfied with first impressions, especially in the case of a work like the *Igor' Tale* where so much is concealed in cryptic allusions. In recent years, an analysis of these "puzzles" by Roman Jakobson has established conclusively that the author of the *Tale* was acquainted with Byzantine eschatological literature. Could we not go further and ask whether there is a relationship between the set of artistic devices employed in the *Igor' Tale* and the tropes and figures codified or repeated by Byzantine grammarians?

One could begin by exploring a possible link between these devices and the *Tale*: a short treatise on twenty-seven poetic tropes attributed to Georges Choeroboscus (sixth century: cf. *Hermes*, LIII [1918], 345-7). It was translated into Slavic in the tenth century and appeared in Kievan Rus' in a manuscript of 1073 (Svjatoslav's *Izbornik*). There are other copies of this manuscript, the oldest extant one being of the early fifteenth century. Writing on the *Igor' Tale* in SPECULUM, XXVII, 1 (January 1952), Professor Jakobson suggested (p. 44) such a genetic relationship between Choeroboscus' treatise and the practice of the Old "Russian" writers. He also thought that it would be worthwhile to "classify Old Russian poetic imagery in the light of this treatise".

Dr Besharov takes up this suggestion in the book under review, developed from a Harvard doctoral dissertation. Accordingly, her essay is divided into two roughly equal parts; the first is concerned with the texts of Choeroboscus; the second, with the imagery of the *Igor' Tale*.

The opening pages of the book, which are based on Krumbacher's *Geschichte*, ⟨539⟩ are a bit discouraging on account of the too numerous slips (once a reference to page 574 in Krumbacher has been transformed into the "year 574," supposedly the date of the tenth-century *Etymologicum Florentinum*). For first information on Choeroboscus and his date, the author might rather have turned to Cohen's article in Pauly-Wissowa's *Realenzyklopaedie*, III (1899), col. 2363 ff., or to W. von Christ's *Geschichte*, II, 2 (1924), p. 1079. But the remainder of the essay is more reliable and the texts discussed in the first part are interesting. With the assistance of Dr A. Kotsevalov, the author has published the ("Abridged") Greek version of Choeroboscus of which the Slavic text is a translation. Mr Milman Parry has translated the "Complete Greek Version" of Choeroboscus (e.g., in Spengel, *Rhet. Graeci*, III, 244-256). The author herself has translated the Slavic version. A facsimile of the pertinent pages in the Slavic *Izbornik* of 1073 is printed in an appendix. For the first time, the reader can conveniently study the technique of the Slavic translator, the degree to which the translator understood the original, and, finally, the degree to which the writer of the original understood what he was writing.

As a rule, the mediaeval Slavic translator renders word for word. Therefore it is often difficult to decide whether he understood his original or not. Such a decision is certain only in cases where his translation is not literal, or when he simply transcribes a Greek word. When he is not literal, he sometimes blunders; at other times, he shows himself quite intelligent, and more than once his solutions are superior to those of the English translators.

When compared with parallel Greek treatises, the Greek versions of Choeroboscus (both the "Abridged" and the "Complete") show a quite advanced state of erosion. We can assume for some parts of those texts that no clear understanding of the described tropes could have been derived from them by anyone either in Byzantium or in Kiev. To say this is to differ from the author's belief that Choeroboscus' was an ingenious code, cryptic to us but "immediately apprehended by the initiate" (p. 98).

The following remarks on the first part of Dr Besharov's essay are primarily of interest to the student of Choeroboscus' treatise. They may also be of some relevance to the profit, direct or indirect, which the author of the *Igor' Tale* might have derived from the Byzantine. Unless otherwise indicated, references are to page (or column) and line of the book.

A. *The "Abridged Greek Version."* This first edition is based on *Coislinianus* 120, known to Slavicists for over a hundred years. There is at least one other tenth-century manuscript, the *Vaticanus Gr. 423*, disregarded by Slavic scholars, which is almost identical with the *Coislinianus* in contents and arrangement. It would be interesting to investigate whether the Choeroboscus treatise as transmitted in the Vatican MS is not closer to the translation of the *Izbornik*. There are very few misprints in the edition; only p. 30, 11, *paismatos* for *ptaismatos* may prove bothersome. P. 16,2 ⟨*eis*⟩ has been added, probably because the "Complete Greek Version" (e.g., Spengel, III, 248,2) has it, although the *Izbornik*, p. 108a,8, presupposes a model without *eis*. To remain consistent, the editor should either have abstained from emendations or have corrected other errors of the *Coisl.* as well. But we read, p. 24,1, *autou*, although the correct *auto* stands in the ⟨540⟩ "Complete Version" (Spengel, III, 250,5) and is furthermore presupposed by the *Izbornik*, p. 109a,12: *samo*. Again, p. 14,3, *thymon* seems to be a *lectio facilior* when compared with *khymon* of the "Complete Version" (Spengel, III, 247,22 f.). But this time, *Izbornik*, p. 108a,1-2: *gněv'* presupposes *thymon*. P. 30,7, the defective *to antios kai to enanti kai katanti* juxtaposed with the "Complete Version" (Spengel, III, 252,9) and the *Izbornik*, p.110a,24, would require a correction into *to antios kai* ⟨*enantios kai*⟩ *to enanti kai kat* ⟨*en*⟩ *anti*. The best solution is to change nothing in the *Coislinianus*.

How should we evaluate the text of this manuscript? In places, it preserved more "original" readings. P. 18,4, *diairousa* may be better than the *di' heterou* of the "Complete Version" (Spengel, III, 248,12). On p. 32,1, the *Coislinianus* preserved the word *lexis*, omitted in the "Complete Version" (in Spengel, III, 252,18). P. 40,5, *proslēpsei* is better than *prolēpsei* of the "Complete Version" (as in Spengel, III, 255,3). Finally, p. 40,7, *eph'heautou* is better than *aph'heautou* of the "Complete Version" (Spengel, III, 255,6). Tryphon (Spengel, III, 205,12 ff.) defines urbanity as "irony... about ourselves," *to de eph'hemōn (autōn)*. Accordingly, his examples illustrating the concept of urbanity start with *egō* 'I' (Spengel, III, 206,12 ff.; already there, however, we read the expression *aph'heautou*).

But on the whole, the *Coislinianus* represents a shrunken reflection of "original" definitions. In several cases it is apparent that its scribe did not understand the subject matter of his compilation. Somewhat less frequently, this lack of understanding can be shown to occur in the "Complete Version" as well. Thus, on p. 40,7, last quoted, the Coislinianus illustrates urbanity with examples starting with *sy* 'you' (so does the "Complete Version"); he therefore no longer realized the meaning of *eph'heautou*. How, then, could the Slavic translator have guessed it? He puts *osob'* 'separately, alone' (*Izbornik*, p.112b,4). This is rendered in English by "particularly" (p. 41,22), perhaps under the influence of modern Russian *osobenno*. As things stand, neither the *Izbornik*, nor its Greek model can be translated at all. P. 8,12, "the sea saw and fled" is erroneously used in the *Coislinianus* as an example of "4.from the inanimate to the animate." In reality, it belongs with "3.from the animate to the inanimate" [cf. an analogous illustration of this transfer in Tryphon (Spengel, III, 192,17): "the shameless stone rolled"]. In the "Complete Version" (Spengel, III, 246,5 ff.) one still can see that it was originally meant as an addition to the "animate to inanimate" group of illustrations. The *Izbornik* follows the *Coislinianus*. The thinking reader of the *Izbornik* was faced with an inconsistency.

Tryphon (Spengel, III, 198,2) defines pleonasm as an expression "redundant either by itself or by some parts of itself." He says that in the *ektasis*-type of pleonasm, such as *thelēsi* (instead of *thelei*), there is a superabundant part (syllable), *-si* (he assumes an itacistic pronunciation *thelisi: theli*). This makes sense. The "Complete Version" (Spengel, III, 252,8 ff.) limits itself to the *ektasis*-type of pleonasm. It, too, makes sense since it says that there is pleonasm "when an expression is superabundant" and gives *antios: en-antios* and *enanti: kat-enanti* as examples. But the *Coislinianus*, p. 30, 6,f., says "when an expression is redundant by virtue of another expression," *pleonazei lexis lexei* and illustrates it by the garbled *to antios kai to enanti kai katanti*. This makes no sense. *Izbornik,* p. 110a,24, is not quite hopeless in this place; the Slavic translator might even have had a better, if curtailed, text before his eyes.

B. *The text of the Izbornik*. P. 106b,27 ff., the Slavic text goes back to the following hypothetical Greek: *ē gar apo empsykhōn epi apsykha metagetai, ē apo apsykhōn epi empsykha*. The net result is that two out of four categories of metaphor are absent from the preliminary enumeration of the *Izbornik*. Dr Besharov strives to maintain the four categories in her English translation (p. 9,8 ff.). To do so, she alters the arrangement of the *Izbornik* and adds an "or" (p. 8, 10) which is not in the Slavic. P. 107b,8, *někogo obyčaja* is a literal, if unclear, rendering of "by some customary usage" of the Greek (p. 10,1). The English translation stating the opposite, "which properly does not fit the usage" (p. 13,1) cannot be accepted. P. 107b,11, the difficult *to apo khalkou epiplates* 'a flat thing of bronze' is omitted in the *Izbornik*. P. 108b,6, *i d'vojem' ili o mnozě* misunderstands *kata dyo ē pleionōn* (p. 20,1) 'with respect to two or more.' The English translation does not signal the misunderstanding. P. 108b,24, the words *kai — onomazousa* of the *Coisl.* ⟨541⟩ (p. 22,3 f.) are omitted in the *Izbornik*. P. 109a,3, *perhaps* one should write [*po*] *podobiję* and assume a dittography, since *kata tina... homoiotēta* (p. 22,7 f.) is adequately rendered by *něpočesomu... podobiję*. P. 109a,20, *tožde*, normally an equivalent for *auto*, corresponds to *pros allēlous* (p. 24,4). P. 110a,24, *protiv'nik' i sę-protiv'nik'* corresponds to a hypothetical *antios kai en-antios* of the Greek model (cf. p. 30,7). The Slavic translator is to be commended for his rendering: he provided two words having identical meaning and shape, but for the "superabundant" first syllable in one of them. P. 110a,26, *porečenije* renders *epanalēpsis* 'resumption' of the Greek (p. 39,8). But *porečenije* means "reproach". Why should the Slavic translator have chosen this equivalent? In his Greek model he must have read, or misread, *epilēpsis* 'reproach'. The English translation calmly gives "*epanalepsis*" (p. 31,27). P. 110a,27, the word *dis*, 'twice,' (p. 30,8) is omitted in the *Izbornik*. P. 110b,9, *s' ob' štiim' naznamenanijem'* stands for *meta tēn koinēn sēmasian*: the translator was more familiar with "vulgar" than with "learned" Greek, for he took *meta* plus accusative to mean "with". P. 111b,12, *aky k' tělesi* 'as if to a body,' making little sense, stands for *prosōpa* of the Greek (p. 38,5) which should have been rendered, e.g., by *ličesa*. The translator must have mistaken the Greek word for *pros sōma* 'to a body.' P. 111b,14, *strina* should be read *stroina* 'fitting' (already seen by Karinskij, *Xrestomatija*...[1911], p. 212). P. 111b,20, *s' loženaago ukaza* is a literal rendering of *sygkritikēs deixeōs* 'showing by comparison' (p. 38,8). It is difficult to say whether the Slavic translator knew the meaning of what he wrote; it is impossible to derive "figurative" from his words, as does the English translation (p. 39,19). P. 111b,24, the words *kai — autou* (p. 38,10) are omitted in the *Izbornik*. P. 112a,14, *synyim' poxuxnani* does not make sense. Buslaev (*Istor. Xristomatija*...[1861], col. 272, n. 2) proposed *s' inyim'* 'with another,' which does not help. Karinskij (*Xrestomatija*...., p. 209) gives the passage up as corrupt. In view of the correponding *meta tēs rhinōn epimyxeōs* of the Greek (p. 40,1) and of the *poxuxnav'še nos' m', Izbornik*, p. 112a,17, I think that the original reading of p. 112a,14 was *s' nos' m' poxuxnanijem'*. P. 112a,17 *oneidizontes* of the Greek (p. 40,2) is omitted in the *Izbornik*. P. 112b,8 at first *selikzmiiot' imy* seems hopelessly garbled. Buslaev (*Istor. Xristomatija* ... col. 272, n. 3) divided *selik' zmii ot' imy* "so big a serpent from having (= ?)" and declared the passage corrupt on account of a lacuna. In reality this is a literal rendering of *soloikismos apologian ekhōn* (p. 40,8), the first word having been left untranslated (as already seen by Karinskij, *Xrestomatija*... p. 211), and the second, contracted by skipping from one *t'* to another. The original reading was, then, *solikizm' o⟨t'vě⟩t' imy*, "a soloecism having an answer," as *apologia*, which also means *answer*, is sometimes rendered by *otvět'* (spelled *ot'vět'* elsewhere in the *Izbornik*). P. 112b,11 *jegože pomilui* is corrupt. Whatever the original reading may have been (*jegože g̃ pomilujet'?*), we can hardly blame the Slavic translator for garbling the whole trope 26 (almost identical in both the "Complete" and the "Abridged" Greek Versions). The definition of *schema* as "soloecism with justification" can be properly understood only from parallel Greek passages (cf. Spengel, III, 9,21 ff.; 11,5 ff.; 44,18 ff.; 59,14; 85,5 ff.), and the illustration, "Mr John, God bless him, is a good man" proved too much even for the translators of the book under review (cf. pp. 41 f.). To understand, we must juxtapose this illustration with Gregory of Corinth's analogous example "Philip, whom everybody hates, is good" (Spengel, III, 226,8). Illustrated is a *schema* of irony: Mr John, like Philip, is really a scoundrel.

Using the newly published *Coislinianus* fragment, we can now explain some of the "crass barbarisms" and "obscurities" of the Slavic Choeroboscus which irked Buslaev a century ago (*Istor. Xristomatija* ..., col. 287). Still, his discomfort was much nearer the truth than is the singular view of Dr Besharov, who not only finds the *Coislinianus* (and the *Izbornik*) superior to the "Complete Greek Version" of Choeroboscus, but extolls it as a "work of vision" (p. 43).

C. *The English Translations*. For Church Slavic texts, the rule is: the best "translation" is the Greek original, whenever available. Unfortunately, the author sometimes acts as ⟨542⟩ if her own edition of the *Coislinianus* did not exist, not to speak of Mr. Parry's translation of the "Complete Greek Version." For the spirited note 2, p. 17, I would substitute the simple observation that the Slavic translator viewed *kaloumai* (p. 16,3) as passive voiçe, while it is middle. As for note 1, p. 19 (on *Izbornik*, p. 108a,21), I believe the Slavic translator understood the Greek. He even managed to put *do* and *dože* respectively for *heōs* occurring twice (p. 18,3), expressing like words by like in corresponding positions. P. 25,14, the rendering "on the basis of past experience" of *ot' s'lučiv'šiix' sę* (*Izbornik*, p. 109a,22) cannot be accepted, for the Slavic is a literal translation of *ek tōn symbebēkotōn* (p. 24,4) 'from the accidental (characteristics).' The same applies to p. 25,21, "when instead of the possessors we name the possessor." The Greek (p. 24,7), and therefore the *Izbornik* (p. 109b,2), which follows the Greek literally, requires "when we name the contained after the container." This meaning of the Greek is assured by a parallel example (Spengel, III, 233,32-234,1). Therefore Mr Parry's "when we use the general to denote the particular" (p. 25,21) must be discarded as well. P. 41,6, "drawled" is not satisfactory for *potęž' b'no* (*Izbornik*, p. 112a,13), declared obscure by Miklosich (*Lexicon*, s.v.). This word is a literal rendering of *diasyrtikos* 'disparaging' (cf. *tęzati* for *diasyrein*). Already Karinskij (*Xrestomatija...*, p. 209) was on the right track.

The translation of the *Izbornik* is smooth — at the price of several omissions, one of them of six lines, from the Slavic text; cf. p. 5,16, omitting p. 106b,12, *tol(kovanije)*; p. 7,2, omitting p. 106b,22, *zm'jem' naricajema*; p. 15,20, omitting p. 107b,25, *ot' sǫštaago istovoje* 'with the literal object;' p. 25,26, omitting p. 109b, 11-17, and wrongly referring the words "instead of — their habitat" to the previous passage; p. 33,13, omitting p. 110a,12, *v'slěd'neje ostaviv'* 'and then ceased;' p. 33,9, omitting p. 110b,13, *jemuže je lěpo* 'to whom it behooves ⟨to be so called⟩.' At times, it is too smooth, for it is given for passages which by the nature or state of the original cannot be translated at all (pp. 21,11 ff.; 31,23; 39,12 ff.; 41,5 ff.; 41,22; 41,26 ff.).

I shall mention only those passages in Mr Parry's translation which are relevant either to the *Izbornik* or to the *Coislinianus*. P. 13,3 ff. is a case where the Slavic translator saw things more clearly: difficulties vanish when we remember (as he did) that in Late Greek *pyxis* means not only box, but is an equivalent of *pyxion* 'tablet.' Thus we obtain the following tentative equivalent: "an example is when we call a flat thing of brass a brass table; for a tablet derives its name from table [The Greek has *pyxis* 'tablet' (of boxwood) and *pyxos* 'boxwood']; but since things made of any other material have no name of their own, we call them all tablets by a misuse of the word." P. 32,29, read "Irony is an expression of dissembling quality:" *hypokritikos*, not *hypokoristikos* is the correct reading; cf. *Philologus*, XXVII (1868), 543. P. 41,20, read "acquiring honors;" *proslēpsis*, not *prolēpsis*, is the correct reading; cf. Spengel, III, 214,1.

The second part of the book deals with the *Igor Tale's* imagery and will be of more interest to the literary critic than to the mediaevalist. An analysis of the *Tale's* imagery in the light of Choeroboscus' Slavic translation should make a connection between these two texts plausible; Dr Besharov did not successfully establish such a relationship. She grants that it is "of course" a matter of conjecture whether the author of the *Tale* ever read the treatise of Choeroboscus. What is important to her is that he "actualized the potency inherent in the figurative terms" (p. 44). A literary historian can do little with this statement. But he must object when he is asked, in a treatment of the *Tale* in the light of Choeroboscus' little work, to "reinstate the old division between tropes and figures *not* observed by Choeroboscus" (p. 46), or when he sees the author analyze the *Tale* in the light of a type of metaphor *not* mentioned in the Slavic translation of the Byzantine writer (p. 51). Tropes discussed by Dr Besharov are often defined not in the sense of Choeroboscus' definitions, but in that of the Ancients, of the text-⟨543⟩books, or of one particular school of literary criticism (cf. p. 48 on catachresis; p. 94 on exoche; p. 95 on paronomasia; p. 53 on verset 153; p. 60 on vv. 56 and 26; p. 66 on v. 60; p. 76 on v. 44; p. 99 on vv. 155-157, of the *Tale*). At one point, Choeroboscus is even said to express an opinion similar to that of André Bréton (p. 64). It would be amusing if it were true.

The author says that she attempted to "intuit" the *Tale* through a scheme of devices inherited by Kiev from Byzantium (p. 98). I do not think she did this. Her conceptual framework has other sources. It comes mainly from late Formalism-Structuralism, a significant twentieth-century theory of literary analysis. As Structuralism is a method claiming general applicability, it is legitimate to investigate a twelfth-century work in its light. Similar, if more balanced, attempts have proved interesting (cf. I. P. Erëmin's little book on the *Primary Chronicle: Povest' Vrem. Let* [1946]). But it would have been better if the author had laid bare her assumptions.

Such a clarification by the author of her use of the Structuralist's approach would have provided the reader with coordinates for appreciating a number of her astute observations. I have in mind her general remarks on the *Tale* — its polyphonic virtuosity (p. 59), its cross-references and allusions (p. 76), its breaking of the chronological continuity to stress the correspondence between events separated by time and space (p. 78), or breaking down distinctions between animate and inanimate (p. 64 f.) — and her interpretations of single versets of the *Tale* (e.g., v. 16, p. 72; v. 152, p. 67). Moreover, the reader would better know what to expect, had he been made aware of the author's approach. To a Byzantinist, for example, *tr'světloe*, "thrice bright" (sun) of verset

182 is valuable as one of the relatively few clichés in the *Tale* corresponding to *trilampes phaos* in the Church Fathers (but also occurring in the ninth-century Slavic *Vita Constantini*); to the author, this epithet expresses the "triplicity of pattern" — brightness, warmth, beauty, symmetrical with aorists of three verbs, and coupled with three alliterating nouns (p. 96).

The *Igor' Tale* may reflect the poetics of the eleventh and twelfth century. But the proof of this proposition cannot come from merely asserting the international character of twelfth-century poetry (pp. 69, 78, 99), and thus only restating Professor Jakobson's previous suggestion on the unity of eleventh- and twelfth-century poetics in East and West. Nor can this proof come from merely juxtaposing the *Tale* with Choeroboscus' treatise, if a different frame of reference is later used for discussing its imagery. Such a method can only show that Choeroboscus speaks of figures, while the *Tale*, like any literary work of any period or place, makes use of them. I think that little more can be said about the relationship between these two texts.

Dr Besharov has shown that she is thoroughly familiar with the *Tale's* intricacies. It is to be hoped that in her next study she will juxtapose this epic with other contemporary "Russian" and non-"Russian" literary works. This approach, I think, would be more suited for anchoring the *Tale* in the literary currents of the twelfth century.

XI

Mediaeval Slavic Manuscripts: A Bibliography of Printed Catalogues

David Djaparidzé, *Mediaeval Slavic Manuscripts: A Bibliography of Printed Catalogues.* (Mediaeval Academy of America Publication No. 64.) Cambridge, Massachusetts: The Mediaeval Academy of America, 1957. Paper. Pp. XV, 134; frontispiece, 8 plates.

Until recently, a western scholar, contemplating a critical edition of a mediaeval East or South Slavic text, or a study of its manuscript tradition, would have to be immune to frustrations and inclined to daydreaming. References to Slavic manuscripts in learned literature (especially Russian) are often inexact or ambig⟨391⟩uous; descriptions of manuscript collections are easy to miss without a guide to many obscure periodicals. If the desired manuscript was located in a collection, often no information on this collection's fate after the Revolution or the Second World War was available. Even the exact knowledge of a manuscript's whereabouts was of a little help, for many of them were locked away in Soviet libraries.

Now we are getting some microfilms from Moscow, Leningrad, and Warsaw. And, in the book under review, we have a tool with which to compile more easily complete and realistic lists of desiderata. The publication of this useful aid to researchers has been well timed with the resumption, however timid, of scholarly contacts with the Slavic countries.

The author implies (p.ix) that his work is not comparable to that excellent tool for Hellenists, M. Richard's *Répertoire* of libraries and catalogues of Greek manuscripts. On the grounds of scope alone, this is excessive modesty. True, Mr Djaparidzé gives only a bibliography of printed catalogues, not a full list of mediaeval Slavic manuscript collections, but in other respects his book offers as much as and even more than its Greek counterpart. First, it contains concise information (mostly historical) on collections, past and present, and often provides commentaries for single entries. Second, it opens with a list of some 113 general and reference works, dealing with bibliography, study of sources, auxiliary disciplines of history, historiography, history of mediaeval Slavic libraries, palaeography, facsimiles, watermarks, diplomatics and single manuscripts. The remaining material is arranged by country or area, within this by cities, within cities by libraries, and within the latter by collections. As expected, most entries refer to the USSR (some 388 items, while all the other countries combined yield some 161 items). All entries are provided with continuous numbering. There are two indices, one of authors, another of collections. Eight excellent plates reproduce manuscripts which range from the twelfth century to the seventeenth (Plate 8a is an autograph of the Protopope Avvakum).

Leafing through Mr Djaparidzé's bibliography one can reflect on the centralizing activity of the Russian State (e.g., the number of collections which ended up in Moscow) or deplore human folly (e.g., the destruction of Belgrade and Warsaw collections during the Second World War). But most of the book's users will open it for practical purposes and thus test the repertory's completeness, the uniformity in presentation of its materials, and the reliability of its indices. When this test was applied to Mr Djaparidzé's book, the results obtained were in most cases fully satisfactory. Difficulties were encountered only in the few instances which follow.

Test queries: 1. Sobolevskij (1903) refers to *Sinod.* 468, dated 1457. Identify and locate. Looking up in Djaparidzé No. 114, Gorskij and Nevostruev's Catalogue of the Synodal Library, is at first of no avail, since this book uses a new numbering, while 468 is the old number, that of the catalogue of 1823. This work is not listed in Djaparidzé (never published?). He should have indicated that Vol. III, 2 of his No. 114 contains a conversion table of old numbers into new ones. 2. Sobolevskij (same year) refers to *Troic.* 758. Identify and locate. Djaparidzé's index of collections has 3 "Trinity" (*Troick-*) entries, one of them in Koljazin, ⟨392⟩ but no reference to the famous *Troickaja* or *Troicko- Sergieva Lavra*, one of the richest manuscript repositories until 1917. In order to find relevant catalogues listed (Nos. 182 ff.), the user has to know that this collection belonged to the Moscow Ecclesiastical Academy. But his point of departure is the scholarly practice in quotations, not administrative divisions. Similarly, he will vainly consult the index for the *Kievo-Mixajlovskij Monastyr'* (cf. caption to Plate 6b), for it is listed only as *Michajlovskij Zlatoverchij Monastyr'*. 3. Find the manuscript catalogue of *Biblioteka Kórnicka*. The index is mute on this subject. In order to find No. 616, one must know that the Kórnik Castle is situated not far from Poznań. This is to overestimate the average user's knowledge of Polish geography.

Desiderata: Often, the author offers more than would be expected from a mere bibliography of catalogues. Thus he whets our appetite and prompts new, perhaps excessive, demands. He lists descriptions of single manuscripts (Nos. 489-492 are devoted to the Peresopnycja gospel of the Moscow Synodal Library — unfortunately it is not clear from these entries where this manuscript is at present; Nos. 87, 88, 93, 138, 242 deal with single miscellanies). But we look in vain under *Sinodal'naja Biblioteka* for a description of Metropolitan Makarij's huge (and not yet fully published) *Čet'i-Minei*, by itself a manuscript collection of works current in Old Russia. Mr Djaparidzé's decision not to quote seventeenth-century catalogues (cf. p. ix, n. 4) might justify the omission of the description by the Monk Evfimij [printed in *Čtenija v Imp. Obšč. Ist. i Drevn. Ross.* (1847), Book 4, pp. 1-78]. But both the (unfortunately incomplete) description by A. V. Gorskij and K. I. Nevostruev [*ibidem* (1884), Book 1, pp. i-xix and 1-65; (1886), Book 1, pp. 66-184] and the work of Arkhimandrite Iosif, *Podrobnoe oglavlenie Velikix Četiix Minej...*(Moscow, 1892) — 502 pp. of description, but no index! — deserved to be included. It is a pity that even the name of Metropolitan Makarij (sixteenth century) is missing from the index, and the only incidental reference to his *Čet'i-Minei* (p. 27) is listed under a nineteenth-century Arkhimandrite of the same name. In addition to Nos. 93a and 93b, dealing with the library of Muscovite rulers in the sixteenth century, one would expect Oskar von Gebhardt's "Zur Orientierung über die Moskauer Bibliotheken" [part of an article on C. F. Matthaei], *Zentralblatt fur Bibliothekswesen*, XV (1898), 393-420. The United States is not represented in the bibliography. But Seymour de Ricci's *Census of Medieval and Renaissance Manuscripts in the United States and Canada*, I-III (1935-40) lists some twelve Slavic items (including a fifteenth-century *Šestodnev* by John Ekzarx of Bulgaria) in nine North American collections. Ideally, these collections should have been entered separately; (Richard's *Répertoire* follows this method); at least a summary reference to the *Census* should have been made.

Minor flaws: No. 81 is a series of articles by A. Popov, which have the noncommittal title "Bibliographical Materials." Without a commentary, this is a dead entry, especially since there is no indication as to the year or volume of the periodical containing the first article of the series. It would perhaps have been better to list this article as No. 142a under the collection of the *Uspenskij Sobor*, for it is a long description (with excerpts) of the famous twelfth-century miscellany, the *Uspenskij Sbornik*. References to entries are sometimes false [under No. 5 read (16) and (18) instead of (15) and (17); under No. 645 read (504) instead of ⟨393⟩ (484)]. The abbreviation Z(apiski) A(kademii) N(auk) is used at least five times (Nos. 80 and 507), but it is not included in the list of abbreviations. Disturbing are misprints in Latin and Czech titles and the cavalier treatment of a dozen or só Ukrainian entries, among which only two are quoted without some error.

But the comparison of the present bibliography's 134 pages and over 664 neatly arranged entries with its only predecessor, Priest I. M. Smirnov's forty-six-page pamphlet published in 1916 (=No. 1 in Djaparidzé) gives a truer measure of Mr Djaparidzé's achievement than the above remarks. Slavicists will be grateful to the author for providing them with a needed reference work, and to the Mediaeval Academy of America for including it among its publications.

XII

Byzantine Elements in Early Ukrainian Culture

The Byzantine heritage is the most important non-Slavic component of early Ukrainian culture. It is not always easy to differentiate between Byzantine influences due to the direct impact of the Eastern empire and its Church on Rus'-Ukraine, and those coming through the mediation of the heavily Byzantinized Balkan countries such as Bulgaria, Serbia, and, perhaps later, Wallachia. From the fifteenth century on, and as long as the direct dependence upon the Constantinopolitan patriarchate existed, Byzantine influences continued to be felt in the Ukraine, in spite of its increasingly western orientation, although less strongly than in the Muscovite state.

Contacts before Christianization

Little is known of Byzantine cultural influences on the Ukrainian territories before the tenth century. Byzantine sources of the sixth and seventh centuries refer to military clashes and alliances between the Eastern empire and the Antes. There is evidence also that there were in the sixth century Byzantinized Antes in high commanding posts in the Byzantine army. A number of finds of remarkable Byzantine silverware and coins of the time of Emperor Heraclius (d. 641), made in Mala Pereščepyna, point to a lively trade and a refined, although restricted, buying public (possibly Avar). The evidence of such contacts stops in the seventh century when the Bulgarian migration across the Ukrainian steppe separated the northern Ukrainian territories from the Black Sea.

In the ninth and tenth centuries, contacts with Byzantium were renewed both in peaceful and military form. The two often went together, as commercial treaties followed predatory raids by the Ῥῶς (as the people of Rus' are called in Byzantine sources) on the Byzantine empire. However, relations of this type did not contribute decisively to cultural penetration. Only the acceptance by one partner of the other's world view as superior makes an assimilative process fully possible. The Byzantine world view was inseparable from Orthodox Christianity.

Rus': A Member of the Civilized World

The first precise reference to the spread of Byzantine Christianity among the Ῥῶς was made by Patriarch Photius (867). Thus it dates from the greatest ⟨18⟩ period of Byzantine missionary activity. The decisive step, however, was taken by Prince Volodymyr (Vladimir) only a century later (988 or 989).

By adopting Christianity and marrying Anna, the sister of Emperor Basil II, Prince Volodymyr became a member of the Byzantine imperial family, and his land was included in the ideal Byzantine family of states. At that time, this family of states was tantamount to the civilized world, for the only two recognized centers of civilization in the tenth century were Constantinople and Baghdad. Byzantium was at the peak of its military and cultural might. It is no wonder, then, that the civilization of early Rus' was derived to a great extent from that of the Byzantine empire.

It is noteworthy that later attempts by Kiev to assert independence in church and cultural matters often were but veiled desires to equal the corresponding Byzantine models. Kiev, "Mother of the Cities of Rus'" (cf. μητρόπολις and the feminine gender of πόλις, Kiev is masculine) has, like Constantinople, its Golden Gate, its churches of St. Irene, St. George, and, above all, St. Sophia. Its patroness is the Holy Virgin, protectress of Byzantium. Like Constantinople, Kiev is referred to as the "New Jerusalem." When a western source speaks of Kiev as *"aemula sceptri Constantinopolitani"*, it may reflect this competition with the capital on the Bosporus. Volodymyr, like many Byzantine emperors, was referred to as a new Constantine. An official formula used to describe the activity of a Byzantine emperor ("to accomplish unaccomplished things") is applied by Hilarion to Volodymyr's son, Yaroslav. One of the arguments brought forward to justify the independent ordination of Metropolitan Clement, a native of Rus' (middle of the twelfth century), was that Kiev's principal relic, the head of Pope Clement, could confer sanctification just as effectively as the hand of John the Baptist, by which metropolitans were consecrated in Constantinople. This fruitful tension between the giving and the receiving cultures was similar to that between the Byzantines and the Bulgarians in the tenth and the eleventh centuries, the Normans in the twelfth century, and the Serbians in the fourteenth century, and had at its roots the acknowledgement by Rus' of Byzantine cultural supremacy.

Church

Civilization meant Christianity. The new religious cult and the Church hierarchy were Byzantine. Kievan metropolitans (attested from

997 on) were, for the most part, of Greek extraction, as were many of the bishops in the earlier period; up to the fifteenth century, at least in theory, they had to be consecrated by the Patriarch of Constantinople. The first churches were built after ⟨19⟩ Byzantine models, initially by imported architects, later by local masters carrying on the Byzantine tradition. The interior decoration of the early churches not only duplicated Byzantine religious iconography and displayed Greek explanatory inscriptions, but also was inspired by Byzantine imperial imagery (for example, the Hippodrome frescoes in the St. Sophia Cathedral of Kiev). Ecclesiastical terms were borrowed either in the Greek form or as *calques*: *onoriia* (Gr. ἐνορία, diocese), *skhyma, epitymiia, skyt, otshel'nyk (Gr.* ἀναχωρητής, literally, "the one who moves away"). Matters of dogma and ritual observance were referred to Constantinople and were decided there; examples of this date from the eleventh and twelfth centuries. The organisation of the monastic life in Rus' followed closely the rules set out in the Byzantine *typika* (foundation charters regulating the life of monasteries). There are no Eastern Slavic contributions to Orthodox liturgy. A few prayers inserted in some manuscripts into the text of the liturgy are translations from Greek.

Language

The Church Slavonic language (imported to Rus' mainly from the Balkans) had acquired much of its specific character in the process of the translation from Greek texts. It teems with direct borrowings from Greek and with Byzantine loan translations (*calques*) in its vocabulary, phraseology, and syntax. With the adoption of the Church Slavonic Koine for original literary production in Rus', innumerable *calques* reflecting Byzantine patterns of thought, found their way into early Rus' literature. Some random examples follow: *ispravleniem* — κατορθώμασι (achievements); *vina* — αἰτία (cause); *beslovesna* — ἄλογα (animals); *o sikh* — ἐν τούτοις (thereupon); *yako i běgati* — ὥστε φεύγειν (so that they avoided) [all these instances are from the *Patericon* of the Kiev Cave Monastery] *pakybytiie* — παλιγγενεσία (resurrection) [Hilarion and Cyril of Turiv]; *yakozhe reshti* — ὡς εἰπεῖν (so to say) [Primary Chronicle and elsewhere]. A mere mention of the existence of numerous Byzantine lexical borrowings in the learned literature of the early period must suffice here.

Literature

The literature read and copied in Rus'-Ukraine consisted, for the most part, of translations from the Greek (see "Literature"). This may be deduced from the catalogs of diocesan and monastic libraries, dating from the fifteenth to eighteenth centuries.

The literary taste of the readers in Rus' was formed by the homilies of John Chrysostom (fourth and fifth centuries); they could, and did, have some inkling of Christian neo-Platonism through the works of Basil the Great (fourth century) and John of Damascus (eighth century). They learned world history and the Christian ⟨20⟩ philosophy of history through the mediocre models of John Malalas (sixth century) and George Hamartolus (ninth century). They discovered far-away lands with Cosmas Indicopleustes (sixth century), who informed them that the earth had the shape of a cylinder. In Johannes Moschus' writings (seventh century) they found stories of the record-breaking ascetic monks of the Egyptian desert. Johannes Climacus, or "of the Ladder", (sixth-seventh century) led the monks of Rus' up to paradise, rung by rung. As Byzantine prophecies, ascribed to Methodius of Patara (written in the seventh century) or to the Prophet Daniel, were geared to the Byzantine struggle with Islam, they lent themselves well to adaptation in a land where wars with the pagan (later Islamic) steppe were a problem of survival. The Byzantine epic of Digenis Akritas (ninth to tenth centuries[?]), the frontier hero and rebel of mixed origin, may have found willing ears in the courts of the princes of Rus', who defied the Kievan Grand Prince, fought with the Cumans but married their daughters.

Many of these translations were imported from Bulgaria. But a number of other translations are still claimed to have been the work of eleventh- and twelfth-century translators in Kievan Rus'. A source tells us expressly of a group of translators from the Greek appointed in Kiev by Yaroslav the Wise (*d.* 1054). It is unfortunate that most of our information on the twelfth-century Greek-speaking princes of Rus', on contemporary schools where Greek was taught, and on Greek books in thirteenth century Rus' should come from the sources quoted by Tatishchev (a not always reliable Russian historian of the eighteenth century). It may safely be surmised, however, that Greek was among the five languages spoken by Prince Vsevolod, the father of Volodymyr Monomakh.

It is not surprising, then, that there are many Byzantine elements in the original works, both sacred and profane, of the Kievan period. Metropolitan Clement (twelfth century, a native of Rus') was said to have quoted Homer and Plato (he may have learned his Platonism from Byzantine *Florilegia* and the Fathers of the Church); Byzantine influences are present in the sermons of Cyril of Turiv (twelfth century), but it is not clear whether he ever consulted Byzantine texts in their original Greek. Prince Volodymyr Monomakh (*d.* 1125) quotes St. Basil

in his didactic treatise and Byzantine ecclesiastical hymns in his Prayer. The Byzantine apocalyptic seventh millennium plays an important role in the Tale of Ihor. The Kievan Chronicles owe much of their chronological framework, form and material to Byzantine historiography, a genre in which Byzantium surpassed anything done in the Latin Middle ⟨21⟩
Ages. The Primary Chronicle's attitude toward the Byzantines is ambiguous; nevertheless, it draws on the work of the Byzantine chroniclers, Hamartolus and Malalas, and even derives its first historical reference to the *Rhōs* (allegedly 852) from a Byzantine source.

Law

Intimate ties existed between Byzantine law and the law of the old Kievan realm. Byzantine law collections such as the *Ecloga* (eighth century) and the *Prochiron* (ninth century) found their way into eastern Europe soon after its Christianization. A Slavic compilation of Byzantine laws (*Zakon sudny liudem*), which may go back to the Cyrillo-Methodian period, was known there in the twelfth century. The *Nomocanon* (first that of Johannes Scholasticus, later in the form attributed to the Patriarch Photius) was used to settle questions of ecclesiastical and canon law. The first translation of the *Nomocanon* into the literary language of Rus' belongs to the eleventh and twelfth centuries. About 1270 a Kievan metropolitan rejoiced over receiving a new adaptation of this text. As for the *Syntagma* of Matthew Blastares (1335) — a compilation of secular and ecclesiastical law that decisively influenced the codes of the Balkan countries — its presence in the lands of Rus' is attested only at a later date (sixteenth century).

In view of this impact of Byzantine legal models, it is the more remarkable that the rudimentary political theory of Kievan Rus' should have remained relatively unaffected by the Byzantine idea of the ruler as Christ's image and imitator on earth. The Kievan scribe could read the rudiments of Byzantine political theory in the *Novellae* inserted into the *Nomocanons*, or hear about it from Greek metropolitans. But the ideal ruler as depicted in the Kievan literature, had only to exhibit the qualities of a good Christian. In the principality of Muscovy theorists followed more closely the Byzantine models.

Art

Up to the sixteenth century, the art of Rus'-Ukraine was under pronounced Byzantine influence. It must be said, to the credit of the Byzantines, that in the domain of art they gave Rus' the best they had to offer. Rus' owes the introduction of stone architecture to Byzantium. In monumental art, a few local, Romanesque, and Caucasian elements were added to structures of a basically Byzantine type. Architects continued to be imported from "Greek lands" well after the initial period.

Thus in the middle of the thirteenth century, the *khytrec* (= τεχνίτης) Audios designed and built the cathedral church in the western outpost of Kholm. The huge double-headed eagle which adorned one of Kholm's towers has been connected with Audios's ⟨22⟩ activity there (A. V. Solovev).

The art of the icons, painted either according to the indications of the "Painter's Manual," of relatively late date, adapted from Greek, or by copying directly imported Byzantine models, reveals Byzantine characteristics down to modern times. Many techniques of the minor arts — for example, that of enamel, for which Rus' was so known in the Middle Ages — were learned in Byzantium (cf. the term *finipt* for enamel work, borrowed from the Byzantine χυμευτός).

It was natural that the princes and their entourages should import both objects of art and artists from Constantinople and have such objects made in Rus' according to Byzantine fashion. In 1135, for instance, Mstyslav of Kiev ordered from Constantinople a gospel with a luxurious binding; the same prince imported three singers to Kiev from Byzantium.

Ways of cultural penetration

The Church and the princely courts were the principal channels through which Byzantine cultural influences penetrated into the Ukrainian territories (most often directly from Byzantium, although occasionally from the Crimea, where the Byzantines held some cities up to the twelfth century). Not only did the Greek (or the Byzantinized Balkan) church hierarchy bring with it books and religious objects, it also introduced Byzantine manners, tastes, and administrative practices. The Fragments of Beneševič provide a glimpse into the workings of the metropolitan chancery under Theognostus (mid-fourteenth century) who often visited the Ukraine. The language of the chancery was certainly Greek, and thus some knowledge of Greek by native scribes may have been derived from this center.

We are well provided with data on the courtly contacts between Rus' and Byzantium. Intermarriage between the courts of Rus' and Constantinople is well documented for the eleventh and twelfth centuries. Nuns of high birth visited Byzantium. Undesirable princes of Rus' frequently were banished to Constantinople, although some of them returned to their native lands after having prospered in the empire. The reverse phenomenon was the prolonged sojourn at the court of Yaroslav Osmomysl of Halych of the fugitive Andronicus Comnenus, who later became emperor of Byzantium (*d.* 1185). The twelfth century was a period of animated Byzantine diplomatic activity in Kiev and in Halych as part of Byzantium's policy of encirclement toward Hungary.

The task of maintaining uninterrupted contact with Byzantium was recognized as a matter of importance to all Rus'. Caravans went to Byzantium along the Dnieper-Black Sea trade route in spite ⟨23⟩ of nomadic harassments. Thus, Rostyslav and other princes by common effort protected the Dnieper waterway from the Cumans in order that merchants trading with Byzantium (*hrechnyky*) could proceed unmolested (1166). Similar measures were taken by other princes later.

Some steps lower on the social ladder were the pilgrims from Kiev, who traveled, often in groups, to Constantinople or to the Holy Land, stopping en route in Constantinople. When they returned home, they spread their knowledge of Byzantine life. Many of them left written accounts of their experiences such as that of the "southerner" Daniel (from the Chernihiv region, beginning of the twelfth century).

Mount Athos, which attracted Kievan pilgrims at an early date (journey of Antonius of the Kiev Cave Monastery before 1033), soon saw the establishment of a permanent home for a number of Rus' monks, and became one of the important centers of translation activity from Greek into the language of Rus' as well as into Bulgarian and Serbian. A signature by an abbot of the ῾Ρῶς monastery in a document from the year 1016 may not be conclusive, but it is certain that the monastery Xylourgou (earliest of the preserved documents — 1030; first clear proof of its Rus' character — 1142), and later that of Panteleimon (monks from Rus' took possession of it in 1169) were centers from which Byzantine cultural influences reached old Ukraine. The exporting of Rus' books (most probably liturgical texts and translations from Greek) from these monasteries to Rus' may be inferred from a document of the year 1142.

Byzantium after Byzantium

The later political fate of the Ukrainian lands, which fell first under the domination of Lithuania and later under that of Poland, laid them open to western cultural influences. However, it would be an error to underestimate the survival of "Byzantium after Byzantium" in the Ukraine. Texts of Byzantine inspiration preserved in monasteries continued to be read; Greek was taught in the schools of the Stavropegian brotherhoods and in other church schools. The Ukrainian Church continued to depend upon the Patriarchs of Constantinople, who, however degraded they may have become under Turkish rule, were the heirs of the Byzantine emperors as protectors of Christianity. The religious struggle preceding and following the Church Union of Brest (Berestja) (1596) made Byzantine Christianity and Constantinople necessary points of reference for the Ukrainina Orthodox camp.

⟨24⟩ It was from the exhortations of the Patriarchs of Alexandria and Constantinople that Ukrainian princes, bishops, and the faithful gathered additional strength to withstand the Uniate movement (for example, the correspondence of Meletius Pigas with Prince Ostrozhsky, published by the latter in Greek; the letter of Cyril Loucaris to the Stavropegian brotherhood of "Leontopolis," Lviv, 1634). One of the polemicists (Smotrytsky) had to go to Constantinople before finally becoming convinced of the justice of the Uniate cause.

The literary controversy over the Union forced the Orthodox and the pro-Uniates alike to concentrate on certain problems of Byzantine history (the ecumenical councils, the "usurpation" of Charlemagne, the division of the Christian empire viewed by Orthodox polemicists through Byzantine eyes, and the Photian schism). It is true that this Orthodox polemical literature was permeated with western (often Protestant) elements, that it used the results of Catholic scholarship (Baronius), and that it was often written in Polish; yet the titles of most of the tracts and the pseudonyms used were Byzantine — for example, *Antirrisis, Antigrafi, Teraturgima* (all with itacisms); Θρῆνος, Λίθος (in Greek letters); *Feodul* (the Uniates wrote a *Parēgoria*, indicating the western humanistic pronunciation). The verbal abuse and the puns were ultimately of Byzantine inspiration (*mateolog, katolyk* — from λύκος [wolf], *Apollia Apologii* — effective only in "Byzantine" pronunciation, *apolia apoloiias* — plays on the name Zizania = darnels). Not only Fathers of the Church such as John Chrysostom and Gregory of Nazianzus (whose verses on "Two Romes" were cited in Greek), but also lesser Byzantine polemicists (Barlaam of Calabria, fourteenth century) were quoted. Sometimes Byzantine legends were used and erroneously transplanted from one century to another — for example, I. Vyshensky, an Athonite monk of Western Ukrainian origin, spoke of Catholic atrocities supposedly perpetrated on Athos after the Council of Florence (fifteenth century); however, the Byzantine legend referred to alleged persecutions under the Uniate emperor, Michael VIII (*d.* 1282).

From an examination of the publishing activity of the Kiev Cave Monastery (where a college was founded in Peter Mohyla's time), it appears that the majority of the books printed there were either liturgical texts or translations of Byzantine works: such were the *Speculum Principis* of Agapetus (sixth century — this work was popular also with the western Humanists); the novel of Barlaam and Ioasaph (because it was believed to be by John of Damascus); the *Nomocanon*; sermons of Macarius of Egypt; and a Gospel ⟨25⟩ commentary (in the form of sermons) attributed to Callistus, Patriarch of Constantinople (fourteenth century). In this way Peter Mohyla strove to raise the level of the cultural life of the Ukraine. He bought for his library, along with Latin classics, Greek Christian authors — some of them late Byzantine. Contemporaries were aware of Mohyla's complex tastes. In a dedicatory preface, written in 1630 and teeming with polonisms, the L'viv printer, A. Skulsky, recommended to the metropolitan a "Slavonic" version of Χριστὸς πάσχων (the Suffering Christ), a Byzantine *cento* (mainly from Euripides), written in the eleventh or twelfth century but attributed to Gregory of Nazianzus.

The end

In 1685 the metropolitan see of Kiev was made dependent upon the patriarchate of Moscow. This may be regarded as the final date in the history of Byzantine and post-Byzantine cultural influences in the Ukraine.

In Nizhyn, on Hetman Mazepa's territory, a churchman left a library containing many Byzantine works (Psellos, Planudes, etc.). In 1690, it was sent to Moscow upon the demand of Peter the Great. The catalog made on that occasion (both in Ukrainian and in Russian), points, albeit by its mistakes, to some knowledge of Greek in Mazepa's chancery (for example, *hotovoslovets'* stands for Etymologicum, as ἕτοιμος, ready, and ἔτυμος, true, were pronounced alike in Byzantine and later Greek). Ukrainian pilgrims visited the holy places of Greece, and learned the language and customs of the land (Hryhorovych-Barsky, *d.* 1747); Greek merchants passed through the Ukraine. One of the latter, Vatatzes, left a description of his journey (ca. 1710) in "political" verse, referring to the factual differences between Russia and the Ukraine. In the Ukrainian literature of the same period the Greeks were reduced to the level of humorous stage figures, appearing in the "intermedia."

The Ukrainian intellectuals of the eighteenth century showed occasional interest in Balkan and Byzantine subjects (*Photius* by G. Shcherbatsky, 1789). The dogmatic works of one of them (T. Prokopovych) were translated into "Byzantine" Greek, but their motivation and their cultural roots were already different.

The cessation of contacts with the post-Byzantine world may be exemplified by the title *Stephanotokos* of a panegyric on the Russian Empress Elisabeth (by I. Mihilevych, 1742). A monstrous misformation after the model of *theotokos* (Mother of God), it shows a total lack of feeling for the Byzantine language and culture. A century earlier, the term *porfirogenita* would have been used.

⟨26⟩ Religious and literary terms (*piit, spudei*) aside, the chief recipient of Greek vocabulary derived directly from Greece was Ukrainian slang: *khvyrka*—χείρ, χέρι (hand); *zitaty*—ζητῶ (to ask); *kryso*—κρέας (meat); *kimaty*—κοιμῶμαι, κοιμᾶμαι, κοιμοῦμαι (to sleep); *siuraty*—ξέρω (to know). The words were introduced probably by the *lirnyky*, wandering minstrels of dubious honesty.

Contemporary situation

On the surface little remains of the Byzantine heritage in present-day Ukraine. But its presence is still felt in many domains. The contemporary Ukrainian alphabet goes back ultimately to the Byzantine ninth-century uncial script.

The liturgy in its Church Slavonic form remained for the Ukrainians the permanent, though indirect, tie with Byzantium. The charming mistranslation, daily repeated in Ukrainian churches at the beginning of the Cherubic song (*izhe kheruvymy* — "which Cherubim" instead of simply "Cherubim"), reminds one of how close these links still are. The Ukrainian national banner (gold and blue) displays a typically Byzantine combination of colors.

The Ukrainian birthday song *Mnohaia Lita* (that is, πολλὰ τὰ ἔτη) is only a translation of the formula often repeated in a work by a tenth-century Byzantine emperor (also an expert on the Rus' problem) — a formula which was echoed for centuries through the halls of the imperial palace of Constantinople and through Byzantine cathedral churches, where it was applied to bishops. The present-day literary language preserves many scholarly terms borrowed directly or indirectly from Byzantium (*okean, leksykon, hramatyka, dohmat, piramida, stykhiia*), although in some cases these terms were later reintroduced from the West in a changed form.

Byzantine and post-Byzantine words are present in contemporary Ukrainian of common usage, although the question as to when and how these borrowings entered the language still needs clarification. The most likely candidates include names of foods (*palianytsia, knysh, kutia*), household objects (*makitra, myska, kadka, krovat'*), fabrics (*oksamyt*), structures (*terem, palata, komora, kolyba*), ships (*korabel', katorha*), places (*levada, lyman*), even an abstract (*khalepa*), and perhaps an adjective (*harnyi*).

XIII

The *Civitas Russorum* and the Alleged Falsification of the Latin Excommunication Bull by Kerullarios

The text known as the *Brevis et Succincta Commemoratio* or the "Short and Succinct Report on the Actions of the Legates of the Only Roman and Apostolic See in the Imperial City [of Constantinople]"[1] can be considered as the closing piece of the polemical *dossier* directly connected with the Schism of 1054. The second part of the *Commemoratio* describes the events immediately following July 16, the date upon which the Bull excommunicating Kerullarios was deposited upon the altar of St. Sophia at Constantinople. As the *Commemoratio* stems from the pen of Cardinal Humbert of Silva Candida, one of the protagonists of the Schism, it is an eyewitness account of first importance. Therefore each statement, however minute, of this document deserves close scrutiny. In this paper I shall propose the identification of a locality mentioned in the *Commemoratio*, namely the *civitas Russorum*. This identification, if accepted, will enable us to suggest an answer to a somewhat broader question, that is, the question of whether Kerullarios had indeed falsified the text of the Excommunication Bull, as Humbert and modern scholars following him assert, or whether such a falsification did not occur. I am inclined to believe that it did not.

In the *Commemoratio*, Humbert states that on their way home from Constantinople the Papal legates were overtaken by the imperial messenger (or messengers) who received from them the faithful copy of the Excommunication Bull and took it back to the imperial city. This encounter took place in the *civitas Russorum*.[2] When we look up one of the

1. Ed. *C. Will*, Acta et scripta quae de controversiis Ecclesiae Graecae et Latinae saeculo undecimo exposita extant... (1861), pp. 150-152, to be quoted henceforth as *Will*.

2. *Will*, p. 152b, 15-18 and Bernensis Lat. 292, fol. 60^{v}: *Verum imperator post nuntios Romanos directis suis exemplar excommunicationis veracissimum a civitate Russorum remissum sibi accepit*.

best and the earliest ⟨204⟩ witnesses for the text of the *Commemoratio*, the *Codex Bernensis Lat.* 292, an eleventh-century manuscript reproducing a collection compiled by Humbert himself, we find in it the words *a civitate Russor(um).*[3] Thus there is practically no reason to entertain the possibility of a corruption of the city's name in the manuscript tradition; instead we must look for the "*civitas Russorum.*" Where was it located?

The name suggests Rus' or some other Slavic area, or at least some place settled by "Russians" in the eleventh century. Therefore some scholars have attempted to localize this city somewhere in "Russia", in Kiev, the *civitas Russorum* par excellence, or in Preslav, a Slavic town.[4] A. Michel postulated that it was a camp of Catholic Varangian mercenaries just outside Constantinople. He assumed that these Varangians not only would have a whole city of their own, but also would be known as "Russes" to Humbert.[5] The "Russian" hypothesis, once accepted by the Russian church historian Golubinskij,[6] has had a most tenacious life. It appeared as late as 1954 in a work commemorating the nine-hundredth anniversary of the Schism.[7] Allegedly, the legates decided to take such a roundabout route to Rome in order to be the first to relate the events of 1054 in Kiev and thus to draw the Church of Rus' over to their own side.[8] Finally, in the latest general work on the history of the Schism of 1054, the *civitas Russorum* has been identified with Selymbria in Thrace.[9]

Several of these identifications were due to the feeling that the

3. Cf. the preceding note. On Bernensis Lat. 292, cf. *A. Michel*, Lateinische Aktenstücke und Sammlungen zum griechischen Schisma (1053/54), Historisches Jahrbuch, 60 (1940), 46-64, esp. p. 61.

4. Cf. *L. Bréhier*, Le schisme oriental du XIe siècle (1899), pp. 224-225: for other references, cf. *A. Michel*, Die Fälschung... (as in the next note), p. 318, n. 2.

5. *A. Michel*, Humbert und Kerullarios..., II (1930), [= Quellen und Forschungen... herausgegeben von der Görres-Gesellschaft, XXIII], p. 480 and n. 6; *Idem*, Die Fälschung der römischen Bannbulle durch Michael Kerullarios, Byzantinisch-neugriechische Jahrbücher, 9, (1931), 293-319, esp. p. 318 and n. 2; *Idem*, Schisma und Kaiserhof im Jahre 1054. Psellos, in 1054-1954. L'Eglise et les églises, I, (1954), pp. 351-440, esp. p. 425.

6. *E. Golubinskij*, Istorija russkoj cerkvi, I (1901), p. 595.

7. *P. Kovalevsky*, L'Eglise russe en 1054, 1054-1954. L'Eglise et les églises, I (1954), p. 482.

8. *Golubinskij*, Istorija... (as in note 6).

9. *Stephen Runciman*, The Eastern Schism... (1955), p. 49.

civitas Russorum must be somewhere in "Russia" or be connected with "Russians." None of them can muster any evidence on its behalf. We know nothing of a Varangian camp or barracks just outside Constantinople. As for Kiev, it seems that the legates had little interest in propagandizing the Church of Rus'. Their most urgent task was to return to Rome as quickly as possible.[10] ⟨205⟩ Lastly, the localization of the *civitas Russorum* in Selymbria is based on a misreading of Humbert's text. But this identification is closest to the truth as I see it.

We have reason to believe that coming to Constantinople the Papal legates took the *Via Egnatia*, which started at Durazzo and crossed Thrace before ending at the Byzantine capital.[11] It is permissible to assume that they took the same road on their way back, and hence to look for the *civitas Russorum* on the *Via Egnatia*. When we open the *Gesta Francorum*, an eyewitness account of the First Crusade written by an anonymous knight of Bohemund's entourage, we find that on their way to Constantinople Bohemund's contingent, proceeding along the *Via Egnatia*, stopped, on April 1, 1097, in the *Russa civitas: deinde pervenimus ad Russam civitatem.*[12] This *Russa* appears in a large number of tenth, twelfth, and thirteenth-century sources, Byzantine,

10. Of course, no trace of the legates' "Kievan" route has been preserved in the sources. They are supposed to have arrived back in Italy in August of 1054, cf. *H. Halfmann*, Cardinal Humbert, sein Leben und seine Werke... (Diss. Göttingen, 1882), pp. 14-15.

11. This, route, one of the two usual ways of reaching Constantinople from the West, would almost inevitably have to be taken by a party going to the Imperial City from Southern Italy. We know that at Christmas of 1053 the Papal Curia (from where the legates started their journey early in 1054, to arrive in Constantinople about April 1) was in Benevento or Bari. Cf., e. g., *A Michel*, Die Rechtsgültigkeit des römischen Bannes gegen Michael Kerullarios, Byzantinische Zeitschrift, 42 (1943-49), p. 198 and n. 3. — On the eastern leg of the *Via Egnatia*, cf. *Th. L. F. Tafel*, De Via Egnatia.... De viae Romanorum Egnatiae... parte orientali dissertatio geographica (Tübingen, 1841).

12. Gesta Francorum et aliorum Hierosolymitanorum, § 5, p. 26, ed. *L. Bréhier* (1924) = p. 10, 26-27, ed. *B. A. Lees* (1924). For the date, cf. *H. Hagenmeyer*, Chronologie de la première Croisade, Revue de l'Orient Latin, 6 (1898), 274 (no. 127). For the itinerary of Bohemund between Thessalonica and Constantinople, cf. *J. A. Knapp*; Reisen durch die Balkanhalbinsel während des Mittelalters, Mitteilungen der K.-K. geographischen Gesellschaft in Wien, 23 (New Series, 13) 180), 357.

Western, and Arabic, such as the Νέα Τακτικά,[13] Anna Comnena,[14] Nicetas Choniates,[15] histories of the First Crusade,[16] a description of the Third Crusade,[17] the *Partitio Romaniae* of 1204,[18] Henri de Valencien⟨206⟩nes,[19] Villehardouin,[20] and the Arabic geographer Idrisi.[21] It can, therefore, be easily localized: It is the Byzantine Rusion, once situated between Kypsala and Apros on the *Via Egnatia*. Rusion, the

13. *H. Gelzer*, ed., Georgii Cyprii descriptio... (1890), p. 59, no. 1181 (in the lists of archbishoprics depending on Constantinople): ιε' τὸ Ῥούσιον. No. 1180 is Apros, no. 1182, Kypsala.

14. VII, 9 = I, 254, 1-257, 21, ed. *A. Reifferscheid* (1884) = II, pp. 116-120 ed. *Leib* (1943): Ῥούσιον.

15. Hist., 830, 17 Bonn: τῷ Ῥουσίῳ.

16. Many of these histories depend on the Gesta Francorum. Cf. Raymond of Aguilers, Recueil des historiens des Croisades, Historiens occidentaux (to be quoted henceforth as RHC, H. Occ.), III (1866), p. 237c: *civitatem ... Rossam*; Albert of Aix, RHCn H. Occ., IV (1879), p. 560: *Rossa*; Baldricus, RHC, H. Occ., IV (1879), p. 24E: *Rusam civitatem*; Guibertus, RHC, H. Occ. IV (1879), p. 154 A: *quae dicitur Rusa civitatis fines*; Robertus Monachus, RHC, H. Occ., III (1866), p. 747 B: *civitatem quae Susa memoratur*; Petrus Tudebodus, RHC, H. Occ., III (1866), p. 18: *Rusam civitatem* (parallel: *Ruisam*); *ibidem*, p. 20: *civitatem... Rusam* (parallel: *Reusam*); Tudebodus imitatus, RHC, H. Occ. III (1866), p. 178: *Russam civitatem*.

17. Ansbertus, MGH, Script. Rer. Germ., Nova Series, V. pp. 70, 11 and 152, 17: *Rossa civitas*.

18. *G. L. F. Tafel* and *G. M. Thomas*, Urkunden zur älteren Handels- und Staatsgeschichte der Republik Venedig... I (1856) [= Fontes rerum Austriacarum, Zweite Abt., XII, 1], p. 484: *Catepanikium de Russa*; *G. L. F. Tafel*, Symbolarum criticarum geographiam byzantinam spectantium partes duae, Byzantine Bayerische Akad. d. Wiss., Philos.-hist. Abt., Hist. Kl., V, 3 Abt. (1849), p. 70 quotes Rhamnusius, a seventeenth-century Venetian editor, who writes: *cum catepanichio urbis Rusianae*.

19. Histoire..., ed. *J. Longnon* (1948), §566 = p. 58: Rousse (v. 1 Rouse).

20. La Conquête..., ed. *E. Faral* (1938-39), §402 [= II, p. 214]: cité... la Rousse (v. 1. Rousee): §§405, 406 [= II, p. 218]: Rosse (v. 1. Rosee), Rousse: cf. §409 [= II, p. 222] et 410 [= II, p. 224].

21. *P. A. Jaubert*, transl., Géographie d'Edrisi (1836), pp. 292 and 297: Rusio; *W. Tomaschek*, Zur Kunde der Hämus-Halbinsel, II. Die Handelswege im 12. Jhdt. nach... Idrisi, Sitzungsberichte der Kaiserl. Akademie d. Wiss. Wien, Phil.-hist. Klasse, 113 (1886), p. 334 (Rūsiō, between Kypsala and Apros); *K. Miller*, Arabische Welt- und Länderkarten, II (1927), pp. 129-130 and 124; Rūšiū (between Kobsila and Abrus); cf. *Idem*, Mappae Arabicae, I, 2, Die Weltkarte des Idrisi (of 1154) ... map V.

later Rusköy, is identical with the modern Keşan, a locality whose position is about two hundred kilometers west of Istanbul.[22] I believe that it is there, in Rusion, that the legates were overtaken by the imperial messenger and handed over to him another copy of the Excommunication Bull. There is nothing disturbing in the fact that the city of Rusion became *civitas Russorum* under Humbert's pen. The spelling of this city's name varies widely in our sources. It appears as Rusia, Russa, Rusa, Rossa, Reusa, Rousse, Rouse, Rosse, Rosee, Rūšiū, or even Susa.[23] The inhabitants of the town are called Rusiōtai in Anna Comnena.[24] Moreover, Humbert, who knew quite a bit of Greek, could have etymologized ῾Ρούσιον as a genitive plural of ῥούσιοι, the blond ones, one of the Greek names associated with the ῾Ρῶς and thus have obtained his *civitas Russorum*.[25]

I should like to add two further observations on behalf of my thesis. In the first place, Humbert describes the locality in which the imperial messenger overtook the legates as a *civitas*. The sources of the First Crusade, too, speak of the *civitas Russa*. In mediaeval Latin, this term has a precise meaning and is applied ⟨207⟩ to seats of a bishopric. Now, ever since the tenth century, if not earlier, Rusion was an archbishopric.[26]

Secondly, we know from Leo of Ostia that on the way back to Rome, the Papal legates Humbert and Frederick of Lorraine were am-

---

22. For localization, cf. commentaries to passages quoted in notes 12, 14, 18, 21 above, and, e. g., *E. Honigmann*, Le Synekdémos d'Hiéroklés (1939), p. 12; *P. Lemerle*, Philippes et la Macédoine orientale... (1945), p. 170; *Stephen Runciman*, The First Crusaders' Journey Across the Balkan Peninsula, Byzantion, 18 (1948), p. 218; *H. J. Kissling*, Beiträge zur Kenntnis Thrakiens im 17. Jhdt. (1956) [=Abhandlungen für die Kunde des Morgenlandes, 32, 3], pp. 57 and 110.

23. Cf. notes 16-21 above.

24. Cf. the apparatus to VII, 9 = I, p. 256, 25 and 26 ed. *Reifferscheid* (1882), and II, p. 119 ed. *Leib* (1943).

25. *Golubinskij*, Istorija... (as in note 6), p. 595 n. 2 knew that "some" had identified *civitas Russorum* with Rousion-Kesan. But he remarked that such an "error" in the *Commemoratio* was conceivable only if this text was transmitted in copies; if it was known in the original, it was impossible to assume the change from ῾Ρούσιον to (*civitas*) *Russorum*. The Bernensis Lat. 292 is practically as good as the original. Still, I do not see why Humbert could not have rendered ῾Ρούσιον by the form which we read in the *Commemoratio*.

26. Cf. note 13 above. Νέα Τακτικά dates from Leo VI or Constantine Porphyrogenitus' time.

bushed by Trasimund, the *comes Theatinus*, who robbed them of a part of the precious gifts which they were bringing back from Constantinople.[27] *Comes Theatinus* is the Count of Chieti, and Chieti is the Norman capital of the Abruzzi, over two hundred kilometers east of Rome, quite close to the east coast of Italy. One does not return from Rus' to Rome via Chieti. It is much simpler to assume that the legates reached the area of Chieti after having disembarked in southern Italy, that is, after having crossed the Byzantine territory along the *Via Egnatia*.

The imperial messenger who met the legates at the *civitas Russorum* received from them — so we learn from the *Commemoratio* — a faithful copy of the Excommunication Bull which they had deposited some days before in St. Sophia. The sending of the faithful copy was necessary, since in the meantime Kerullarios had falsified the Excommunication Bull in the process of translating it: *quam omnino corruperat transferendo*.[28] Here a difficulty arises, for we do possess the Greek translation of the Excommunication Bull.[29] This translation, preserved in an Act emanating from Kerullarios, is quite faithful. It contains no essential cuts,[30] has one addition unfavorable to Kerullarios,[31]

---

27. Leo of Ostia, Chronicle of Monte Cassino, II, 85-86, in MGH, Scriptores, 7, p. 686. Lampert of Hersfeld, however, says that upon his return to Rome, Frederick, one of the legates, gave the Roman Church *dona quae ab imperatore Constantinopolitano permagnifica deferebat*: Annales, edd. *Holder-Egger*, Script. rer. Germ. in usum Scholarum... (1894), p. 65.

28. *Will*, p. 152b, 1-2. Cf. ibidem, p. 152b, 19-20: the Emperor *Michaelem falsasse chartam legatorum comperit*.

29. *Will*, pp. 161a, 28-165a, 10.

30. Only the following Latin words have been omitted from the Greek version: *Will*, p. 153a, 1 *cardinalis*; *Will*, p. 153a, 19 *in domino*; *Will*, p. 154b, 11 *episcopus*; *Will*, p. 154b, 16-18 *Valesiis — Nazarenis*. As for the omission, *Will*, 153b, 17-18 *sicut Manichaei inter alia quodlibet* (this word is written *supra versum* in Bernensis Lat. 292, fol. 60^{v}) *fermentatum fatentur animatum esse*, an omission of which *Will*, p. 163 n. 60 makes so much, it is not too bad, for the equivalent Greek words appear in *Will*, p. 165a 5-7. There is no absolute warranty that the text of the Excommunication Bull transmitted by the Bernensis Lat. 292 is identical in all details with that which the Greek translators had before their eyes. (cf. *A. Michel*, Humbert und Kerullarios..., I [1925], pp. 91-92; *Idem*, Die Fälschung... [as in note 5 above], p. 299, n. 1: on Bruxell. 1360). This remark also applies to the Greek addition to be mentioned in the next note.

31. Instead of *Will*, p. 154a, 9-10 *et ecclesias ad missas agendum interdixit*, the translation has (*Will*, p. 164a, 8-10) οὔτε τῷ ὑγιεῖ βουλεύματι τῶν αὐτοκρατόρων καὶ τῶν σοφῶν νουθετούντων κατασπάσασθαι αὐτόν, οὐχ

one misplaced ⟨208⟩ sentence,[32] and one divergence in rendering a proper name;[33] as for translation errors, I found only four,[34], which for a text as extensive as the Bull is not an excessive number. The Act which contains the Greek translation of the Bull is the *Sēmeiōma* of the Patriarchal Synod.[35] This is a composite document, incorporating the story of the condemnation of the papal legates pronounced at a Synod held in the μέγα σέκρετον (thus in St. Sophia) on July 21[36] — it is in this part of the *Sēmeiōma* that we read the correct translation of the Bull — and adding that on July 24 it was decided to issue another — public — condemnation of the legates. The *Sēmeiōma*, dated by the month of July only, presents itself as the minutes of a Synod held in the "right part of the catechoumenaea" (of St. Sophia). In my opinion, "today",[37] when this second Synod took place, was July 24.[38] I have no reason to believe

---

ὑπήκουσεν. *A. Michel*, Schisma und Kaiserhof... (as in note 5), p. 434, n. 4 considers these words as a "quite freely [invented] insertion" by "the Emperor's" (?) translators. But this addition may go back to the Latin which once had been in the Bull. For the plural αὐτοκρατόρων, cf. *Will*, p. 153a, 16 *imperatores*; for σοφῶν, cf. *Will*, p. 153a, 22-23 *(cives) sapientes*; for νουθετούντων, cf. *Will*, p. 154a, 6 *admonitus*, rendered in *Will*, p. 164a 4 by νουθετηθείς. — Other additions of the Greek are insignificant: *Will*, p. 163a, 20 ὡς οἱ Ναζωρηνοί; *Will*, p. 164a, 7 παντελῶς.

32. Cf. note 30 above.

33. Compare *Will*, p. 154b, 12 *Constantinus* with *Will*, p. 164a, 35-36 Νικηφόρος.

34. *Will*, p. 164a, 14 αὐτοῦ (should be αὐτῆς): *Will*, p. 154a, 13 *suis*; *Will*, p. 164a. 18-19 ἐξάκουστον (famous): *Will*, p. 154a, 17 *inauditam*; *Will*, p. 164a, 25 ἀπό: *Will*, p. 154b, 3 *atque*; *Will*, pp. 164a, 36-165a, 1 προφανῶς (obviously): *Will*, p. 154b, 13 *profanis*.

35. *Will*, pp. 155-168. Cf. *V. Grumel*, Les regestes des Actes du Patriarcat de Constantinople, I, 3 (1947), no. 869.

36. The *Sēmeiōma* gives July 20, *Will*, p. 168a, 6-7: but the *Commemoratio*, *Will*, p. 152a, 24 has *sequenti die* after July 20, that is, July 21. I adopt this date with *A. Michel*, Die Fälschung... (as in note 5 above), p. 295 and Schisma und Kaiserhof... (as in note 5 above), p. 423. *V. Grumel*, Les regestes... (as in the preceding note), no. 867, adopts July 20.

37. Cf. *Will*, p. 168a, 9.

38. I interpret the crucial phrase, *Will*, p. 167a, 26-33 as follows: It was resolved on the fourth day after [i. e. after the first Synod held in the μέγα σέκρετον on July 20 or 21], which is [ἐστί] the first day [i. e. the Sunday] of the present [ἐνεστώσης] week (or the twenty-fourth [Allatius's κδ' is to be reintroduced here] of the present month), during which ⟨week⟩ also the ἔκθεσις of the Fifth Council

⟨209⟩ that this second assembly's minutes were drawn up much later. In any case, the *Sēmeiōma* as we read it today claims that the translation — the correct translation as we have seen — was available to the prelates of the Synod of July 21.

Which of the two witnesses should we believe, the *Commemoratio* or the text of the *Sēmeiōma* containing the correct translation? A. Michel, the modern proponent of the falsification theory, suggested that Kerullarios had originally falsified the translation (Michel even found traces of this original forgery in the opening parts of Kerullarios' *Sēmeiōma* and in the latter's letter to Patriarch Peter of Antioch), but then was confronted with the faithful copy obtained by the imperial messenger in the *civitas Russorum* and was forced to insert the correct translation into the *Sēmeiōma*.[39] The solution to the problem hinges

will be read according to custom [ἀναγνωσθῆναι μέλλει κατὰ τὸ σύνηθες], that the aforementioned impious writing should be anathematized once more." Since Sunday the twenty-fourth lies "in the present week," we are between July 24 and 30. But since the ἔκθεσις *will* be read according to custom (the customary date being July 25: cf. *H. Delehaye*, Synaxarium Ecclesiae Constantinopolitanae [1902], col. 842-843), we are in July 24. On that day the second Synod of which the *Sēmeiōma* is the minutes, decreed the second public condemnation of the Bull. Probably, this condemnation was to be pronounced on July 25, together with the ἔκθεσις of the Fifth Council. I do not think that any third Synod is referred to in the *Sēmeiōma*. This interpretation, which, I grant, is not absolutely sure, differs from that by *V. Grumel*, Les regestes... (as in note 35 above), nos. 867-869. Grumel dates the *Sēmeiōma* into the week after July 24, and assumes the date of the ἔκθεσις to have been July 24; tacitly correcting εἰκοστήν *Will*, p. 168a, 6, he refers the names of prelates mentioned at the end of *Sēmeiōma* (*Will*, p. 168a, 12-16) to a Synod of July 24 (instead of July 20 or 21), and thus obtains three Synods (July 20 = no. 867; July 24 = no. 868; sometime between July 24 and 30 = no. 869), instead of my two Synods (July 21 and 24). The reconstruction in *A. Michel*, Die Fälschung... (as in note 5 above) is not quite clear. On pp. 295-296 and 296, n. 1 he assumes two Synods (July 21 and 24), and seemingly a third one (undated), referred to by the word "today" in *Will*, p. 168a, 9. But on p. 310 he speaks of two Synods on the same day, July 21, and of a public Anathema (thus without a Synod?) on July 24. On p. 315, Michel places the first Synod in the *catechoumeneion*, while in reality it met in the μέγα σέκρετον. As for the names of the prelates mentioned at the end of the *Sēmeiōma*, Michel refers them to the Synod of July 24 (rather than to that of July 20 or 21). This he obtains by specifically changing εἰκοστήν *Will*, p. 168a, 6 into "24" (p. 296, n. 1). Finally, as already Michel justly pointed out, the dating in *Will*, p. 167, n. 80 is simply wrong. — I have not checked the manuscript tradition of the *Sēmeiōma*.

39. Die Fälschung... (as in note 5 above), passim, esp. pp. 317-319.

upon the localization of the *civitas Russorum*, and now you will understand why I insisted on this minor point in the opening part of this paper. Rather than to evaluate the honesty of the two protagonists, both of whom are known to have occasionally departed from truth, we should, I believe, count days and distances, in order to see whether the imperial messenger could possibly have brought the correct translation of the Bull back from the *civitas Russorum* in time for this translation to have been inserted into the definitive text of the *Sēmeiōma* drawn up on July 24 or soon after that date, for instance, by July 27. Given these dates, it is obvious that the falsification theory may be upheld only if we localize *civitas Russorum* quite near Constantinople, and Michel had to resort to this expedient in postulating his otherwise unknown Varangian camp.[40] But if the *civitas Russorum* is Rusion, at a distance of 200 kilometers west of Constantinople, the story becomes different.

I am going to submit to you the timetable for events in Constantinople, as well as for the movements of the legates and of the imperial messenger, between the Capital and Rusion. This timetable can be pieced together from Humbert's *Commemoratio*, from Kerullarios' *Sēmeiōma*, and from what we know from ⟨210⟩ mediaeval and later sources about the speed of travel in the area with which we are concerned. In computing this timetable, I shall assume the greatest speed of movement compatible with the data at my disposal. Thus I shall not follow such sources as Bertrandon de la Brocquière[41] or Henri de Valenciennes,[42] who imply that a distance usually travelled in one day along the route covered by the legates was about twenty-five kilometers. Instead I will assume that the legates spent about ten hours travelling each day, and that each day they covered about fifty kilometers.[43] As for the more

40. Having established his Varangian camp, Michel could state (Die Fälschung..., p. 319) that, as the *Sēmeiōma* was drafted on July 24 at the earliest, the true copy of the Bull could have reached Constantinople in ample time for insertion into this document.

41. Bertrandon (time: about 1433) says (169, ed. *Schefer*) that *Salubrie* (Selymbria, 50 kilometers west of Constantinople) was two days' journey from the capital.

42. Cf. the itinerary from Constantinople to Thessalonica, including Apros, "Russa" and Kypsala, in Histoire, 563-566, pp. 57-58, ed. *Longnon*.

43. The more frequent assumption is 40 to 45 kilometers per ten hours' traveling a day. Cf. *H. Hagenmayer*, Chronologie de la première Croisade, Revue de l'Orient Latin, 7 (1899), 277 (= no. 134) and 280 (= no. 139); *K. Zimmert* in Byzantinische Zeitschrift, 12 (1903), 46 and n. 1 (for a day's march in Odo of Deuil's De Profectione Ludovici VII in Orientem).

speedy imperial messenger, I will have him cover one hundred kilometers a day, a feat for which I find a parallel in one passage of Ducas.[44]

Here is the timetable:

July 18: The legates start their return journey from Constantinople.[45]

Before July 19: The Excommunication Bull is translated into Greek.[46]

July 19: The Emperor sends for the legates.[47]

July 20: The legates are in Selymbria (thus it took them two days to cover fifty kilometers). They are called back from there by the Emperor (thus it took a messenger one day to cover fifty kilometers), and reach *palatium Pighi*[48] on the same day.[49]

July 21: The legates refuse to appear at the Synod organized by Kerullarios. This Synod meets in their absence in the μέγα σέκρετον and excommunicates the Bull and those who had blasphemed against the Orthodox faith.[50]

July 22: Without delay, the legates leave Constantinople.[51]

⟨211⟩ July 22-23: A riot, instigated by Kerullarios, breaks out in Constantinople.[52]

July 23: The Emperor sends a messenger after the legates.[53]

---

44. XXIV, 4 = p. 187, 3-4, ed. *Grecu* (1958): distance between the Propontis and Adrianople covered in two days. *K. Zimmert* (as in the preceding note) assumes 70-80 kilometers a day for a courier.

45. *Will*, p. 152a, 15-16.

46. *Will*, p. 165a, 11-21. We do not know whether it was a faithful translation or not; Humbert implies that the translation had been falsified before July 21: *Will*, 152a, 24-152b, 2.

47. *Will*, p. 165a, 17-21.

48. This palace, situated outside of the city (cf. *Will*, p. 151b, 2-3) was more probably near the monastery of Pēgē, just west of the land walls of the city, cf. MISN, Ἡ Ζωοδόχος Πηγή (1937), p. 158, than in the quarter Pegai (at Kasımpaşa), where there was a palace, cf. *R. Janin*, Constantinople byzantine (1950), p. 423; *Idem*, La géographie ecclésiastique de l'Empire byzantin, I, 3 (1953), p. 237.

49. *Will*, p. 152a, 19-21.

50. Cf. note 36 above and *Will*, p. 167a, 21-26.

51. *Will*, p. 152b, 6-7: *confestim*.

52. *Will*, p. 152b, 8-15. The Commemoratio says only *porro*. I date the riot as soon as possible after the legates' departure.

53. *Will*, 152b, 15-16. The dating is conjectural. Again, I make the dispatch of

July 24: Another patriarchal Synod decrees a public condemnation of the Excommunication Bull.[54] Drafting of the *Sēmeiōma*?

25-26: The messenger receives the authentic copy of the Bull in the *civitas Russorum*, that is, Rusion.[55]

July 27-28 (not earlier than July 27 at night): the messenger returns to Constantinople with the *exemplar veracissimum* of the Bull.[56]

It appears from our timetable that the true copy of the Bull could not have reached the Emperor before July 28 or 29. The *Sēmeiōma* containing the correct translation of the Bull presents itself as the acts of the Synod which convened on July 24. If the date is meaningful, the "true copy" of the Bull could not have influenced the drawing up of the *Sēmeiōma*. We therefore have two choices: We must either agree that there is no proof, except for Humbert's word, that the Bull had ever been falsified by Kerullarios, or if we want to uphold the falsification theory, we must prove that the *Sēmeiōma* as a whole, including the story of the Synod of July 21, was drawn up several days after July 28.[57] I accept the first alternative. Kerullarios had no reason to falsify the text of the Bull. It was offensive enough to the Orthodox as it stood.

To say this is not to impute bad faith to Humbert. He wrote his *Commemoratio* away from Constantinople and had no means of knowing whether the Bull had really been falsified. Moreover, we do not know what kind of story the imperial messenger may have been commissioned to tell him. Nor do I want to make a sterling character out of

---

the messenger occur as soon as the text of the *Commemoratio* allows me to do so.

54. Cf. note 38 above.

55. *Will*, p. 152b, 16-18. Dating based on the assumption that the messenger had left on July 23. His postulated potential speed being 100 kilometers a day, he could have reached Rusion on July 24 at night. But the legates, to whom we assigned the considerable speed of 50 kilometers a day, could not have arrived in Rusion before July 25 at night. Thus July 25 or 26 are the earliest possible dates for the messenger's overtaking the legates, if *civitas Russorum* is Rusion.

56. Date of July 27 is based on the assumption that the messenger's actual speed was 100 kilometers a day. If it was only 80 kilometers (cf. note 44 above), then the messenger could not have returned to the capital before the evening of July 28.

57. Even if the dating of the *Sēmeiōma* on July 24 were disproved, no more than two or three days would conceivably remain for doctoring it up since, on the face of it, this document can under no circumstances be later than July 30, the last day of the week starting on July 24 (cf. ἐνεστώσης ἑβδομάδος in *Will*, p. 167a, 28).

Kerullarios. In summarizing the Bull in ⟨212⟩ the first part of the *Sēmeiōma* and in the letter to Peter of Antioch, he indulged in polemical exaggeration and some twists. By and large, however, he stopped short of outright misrepresentation.[58] When analyzed, the traces of his forgery postulated by Michel boil down to a distorted summary of the Roman position on the fascinating question of the bearded versus beardless priests.[59]

In any case, his distortions are not germane to the question of falsification, since no trace of the falsified text exists, and in the other part of the *Sēmeiōma* we read the correct translation of the Bull.

[*Additional note* 1, cf. n. 38 above: Texts published or adduced by *R. J. H. Jenkins* and *C. Mango* in Dumbarton Oaks Papers, 15 (1961), 226, 232 and n. 20 imply that in 1054 the *ekthesis* of the Fifth Council was pronounced on Sunday, July 24, rather than 25, as I assumed in n. 38 above. This considerably weakens my interpretation of *Will*, p. 167a, 26-33 given in that note. *Will*, p. 167a, 29 καθ'ἣν must mean "during which ⟨day⟩," the second anathema seems to have been planned for July 24, and the decision to pronounce it on that day may have been taken on July 21. Thus only the present ἐστί and the future ἀναγνωσθῆναι μέλλει (*Will*, 167a, 27 and 30-31) make me still reluctant to say with Grumel that the final Synod occurred between July 24 and 30.

Additional note 2, cf. n. 43 and 44 above: *J. W. Nesbitt*, Traditio, 19 (1963), 167-181, esp. p. 174 and n. 28, finds that speeds of crusading armies usually did not exceed 20-25 miles a day; individuals might cover 30-35 miles a day.]

58. Thus he insinuated (by means of μᾶλλον δέ), but never asserted, that the legates had excommunicated the whole Orthodox Church. Cf. *Will*, pp. 157a, 23-24 and 187a, 1-2.

59. *A. Michel*, Die Fälschung... (as in note 5 above), pp. 294, 299, 308. From there, the way is long to the postulated, and never proved, falsification of the text. In general, Michel's passionate arguments do not hold water, since he is not able to go any further than to show that the discursive parts of the *Sēmeiōma* and the letter to Peter of Antioch (which, by the way, paraphrases the *Sēmeiōma*, and not the Bull) display the usual barrister's tricks in giving exaggerated summaries of several of the Bull's points.

XIV

Yaroslav I

Yaroslav I [yŭ-rŭ-slåf'] (baptismal name *George*; called *the Wise*), grand duke of Kiev: b. about 982; d. Kiev, 1054. His father, Vladimir the Great (see Vladimir), made him vice-regent of Novgorod, where Yaroslav attempted to set himself up as an independent ruler in 1014-1015. On Vladimir's death in the latter year, Yaroslav became involved with his half-brother Sviatopolk the Accursed in a contest for the Kievan throne. Although Kiev itself was briefly occupied (1017-1018) by Sviatopolk's ally Boleslav (Boleslas) I of Poland, the war ended in a victory for Yaroslav, who assumed the throne in 1019. He next had to cope with several other brothers, especially Mstislav of Tmutorokan and Chernigov. After Mstislav won the Battle of Listven (1024), the two brothers divided their spheres of influence along the Dnieper River (1025), with Kiev and the territories of the right bank falling to Yaroslav. On Mstislav's death without issue (1036), Yaroslav became undisputed ruler of all Rus'.

Yaroslav warred against the Baltic and Finnic tribes, the Poles, the Turkic Pechenegs of the Steppe (ending in decisive victory in 1036), and Byzantium (the unsuccessful plundering raid of 1043). The most notable achievements of his reign, however, were internal. The Christian faith, established by his father (987/988), was propagated through the spread of book learning (Kievan commission for translations from Greek into Slavic?); and church architecture attained a high level. Among the outstanding structures of the period were the monasteries of St. George and of St. Irene and the Church of the Annunciation, in Kiev; the Church of St. Sophia (1045), in Novgorod; and above all, the magnificent Church of St. Sophia (c. 1037), in Kiev, containing the best-preserved examples of early 11th–century Byzantine art to be found anywhere. Letters flourished also, as witnessed by Metropolitan Hilarion's *Sermon on Law and Grace* (c.1040/1050), a work equal in quality to its Byzantine models. Some laws were written down: the core of the first recension of the "Russian Law" (*Pravda Russkaya*) may go back to Yaroslav's time. Under Yaroslav, the Kievan state lived through one of its two periods of greatness.

Judging by Hilarion's *Sermon* and the St. Sophia mosaics with their Greek inscriptions, Kiev's orientation under Yaroslav was Byzantine. This, however, is only part of the truth. Byzantium was defied militarily, and perhaps even ecclesiastically, since Hilarion was a native of Kiev and was elected metropolitan there. Marriage alliances in Yaroslav's family were often Western: his wife was the Swedish princess Ingigerðr-Irene, and his daughter Anna was married to the French King Henry I. The German Emperor Henry II was Yaroslav's ally in 1017. Contacts with Scandinavia continued: Yaroslav survives in Norse sagas, and kings of Norway spent some time at his court, which must have had an international flavor. His sarcophagus and skeleton are preserved in the Church of St. Sophia at Kiev.

XV

New Documents on Constantine Tischendorf and the *Codex Sinaiticus*

I

The *Codex Sinaiticus* was discovered by the Leipzig scholar Constantine Tischendorf in St. Catherine's Monastery at Sinai. This "incomparable gem for scholarship and the Church,"[1] dating from the middle of the fourth century, is one of the two oldest parchment manuscripts of the Bible in existence and, for the New ⟨56⟩ Testament, the more complete of the two.

The discovery of the *Sinaiticus* by Tischendorf occurred in two[1a] stages. In 1844, travelling under the auspices of the Saxon government, he found a part of the manuscript; it contained a portion of the Old Testament, and in all probability amounted to 130 folios.[2] He managed to obtain 43 of them, which he took back to Leipzig and offered to the Saxon king Frederick-Augustus II. In 1846 Tischendorf published these 43 folios in facsimile, but he kept their origin secret[3] until his second

---

1. The expression occurs in Tischendorfs letter to his wife Angelika, Cairo, February 15, 1859. Cf. slide 37 of *Tischendorfs Reise nach dem Sinai*, as in note 10 *infra*.

1a. We may disregard a small fragment (13×7 cm) which Tischendorf found during his second trip to Sinai in 1853. Most recent discussion of this fragment in E. Lauch, "Etwas vom Codex Sinaiticus," *Wissenschaftliche Zeitschrift der Karl-Marx-Universität Leipzig*; 3 (1953/54), Gesellsch.- u. Sprachwiss. Reihe, Heft I, p. 5-11.

2. The earliest mention of the number of folios seen by Tischendorf in 1844 occurs in his *Mémoire sur la découverte et l'antiquité du* Codex Sinaiticus, *Read at a Meeting of the Royal Society of Literature*, February 15, 1865, p. 2. I prefer the number quoted on that occasion (130 folios) to Tischendorf's later information (129 folios). Cf. H. J. M. Milne and T. C. Skeat, *Scribes and Correctors of the Codex Sinaiticus* (1938), p. 82.

3. *Codex Frederico-Augustanus... e codice Graeco omnium qui in Europa supersunt facile antiquissimo...* (1846); concerning the origin of his find,

discovery in February of 1859.[4] At that time Tischendorf, then travelling under the auspices of Tsar Alexander II of Russia, was shown, in addition to a part of the manuscript which he had seen but had not been able to obtain in 1844, additional parts of the Old Testament, the whole New Testament, the Epistle of Barnabas and a part of *Pastor Hermae*. Some months later he was permitted to take the entire 346 folios and a small fragment from the monastery and, in 1862, he presented them to the Russian Tsar, together with a four-volume edition of their contents.[5]

The intrinsic value of the *Sinaiticus* and the masterful publication of its text (completed in a record time of three years) accounted for the great admiration — and some envy — bestowed upon Tischendorf by his contemporaries. The *Sinaiticus* secured for him a prominent and permanent place in the history of scholarship. But the circumstances in which the manuscript had been removed from the monastery, offered to the Tsar, and finally obtained by Russia, aroused bitterness among Orthodox hierarchs and, according to travellers' reports, among the Sinai monks. These circumstances also produced some uneasiness among the Russians, the principal beneficiaries of Tischendorf's activities. The rumors, unfriendly to Tischendorf, concerning the legality — or at least the propriety — of the manuscript's transfer, subsided (in Europe at least) only after the monks of Sinai had finally been persuaded to sign

Tischendorf spoke of "the East," "disgraceful obscurity," "Egypt or its vicinity," "Lower Egypt." Cf. *ibidem*, title page and p. 5; also, "Die Manuscripta Tischendorfiana," *Serapeum*, 8 (1847), 52.

4. Tischendorf informs us that before his second trip to Sinai in 1853 he gave his secret away in a memorandum to von Beust, the Minister of Education of the Kingdom of Saxony; cf. *Die Waffen der Finsterniss wider die Sinaibibel* (1863), p. 11 and *Die Sinaibibel. Ihre Entdeckung, Herausgabe und Erwerbung* (1871), p. 5. [This work will subsequently be referred to as *Sinaibibel*.] In 1855, he declared that the 43 folios of the *Frederico-Augustanus* were but a part of what he had seen on his previous trip, but maintained silence as to where he had seen the manuscript: Cf. *Monumenta Sacra inedita. Nova Collectio*, I (1855, p. xxxx. However, he waited until March 15, 1859 before admitting in print that the *Frederico-Augustanus* was but a fragment of the manuscript he had found in Sinai. This, he said in a display of deadpan humor, had become clear to him beyond any doubt: Cf. "Ein Brief des Prof. Dr. Tischendorf an den Staatsminister v. Falkenstein," *Leipziger Zeitung*, Wissenschaftliche Beilage nr. 31, April 17, 1859, p. 137.

5. *Bibliorum Codex Sinaiticus Petropolitanus... Ex tenebris protraxit in Europam transtulit... Const. Tischendorf*, I-IV (St. Petersburg, 1862).

the manuscript away to Russia. This official donation occurred in 1869, a decade after Tischendorf's second discovery.[6]

Similar rumors were revived about 1933/4, soon after the British Museum acquired the *Sinaiticus* from Soviet authorities. These rumors were soon silenced. In a special pamphlet, the Trustees for the British Museum undertook to show that the £100,000 collected for the purchase of the *Sinaiticus* had not been paid for purloined goods.[7] In an article, the German biblical scholar A. Deissmann took upon himself the defense of Tischendorf's honor.[8]

The interest in Tischendorf and in the romantic circumstances surrounding his discovery have been revived in recent years. At least three books — two of them written by Tischendorf's relatives — have kept it alive among the German cultivated public;[9] a slide travelogue entitled ⟨57⟩ "Tischendorf Journey to Sinai" has been produced to be shown to interested, primarily religious groups,[10] and a Leipzig scholar has devoted much of his recent output to the *Sinaiticus* and its discoverer.[11]

---

6. Cf. documents in C. R. GREGORY, *Prolegomena* to the 8th ed. of TISCHENDORF'S *Novum Testamentum Graece*, III, 1 (1884), p. 351-353; IDEM, *Textkritik des Neuen Testaments*, I (1900), p. 27-28 (some kind of donation by July 15, 1869; definitive donation by November 18, 1869); cf. N. P. Ignat'ev's letters to Archimandrite Antonin, ed. A. A. DMITRIEVSKIJ, *Graf Ignat'ev kak cerkovno-političeskij dejatel' na pravoslavnom vostoke* (1909), p. 23-24 and 28 (donation after March 14, 1869, before January 7, 1870; document of donation forwarded to St. Petersburg about January 1870); N. P. Ignat'ev's letter to Tischendorf, *Universitätsbibliothek Leipzig*, MS 01029 (donation made and rewards in all probability paid to the monks by December 17, 1869). This letter has been (badly) published by PERADZE, *Dokumenty...* (as in note 22 *infra*), p. 149-150, and summarized in *The Mount Sinai Manuscript...* (as in the next note), p. 8.

7. *The Mount Sinai Manuscript of the Bible* (4th ed., 1935); cf. [H. J. M. MILNE and T. C. SKEAT], *The Codex Sinaiticus and the Codex Alexandrinus* (2nd ed., 1955).

8. «Entkräftung eines Kloster-Klatsches. Kampf um den Sinaiticus», *Deutsche Allgemeine Zeitung*, nr. 62 (Berlin, February 7, 1934). Much of DEISSMANN'S *Refutation* is a repetition of Gregory's statements.

9. O. SCHLISSKE, *Der Schatz im Wüstenkloster...* (1953); L. SCHNELLER, *Tischendorf-Erinnerungen. Merkwürdige Auffindung der verlorenen Sinaihandschrift* (1954); H. BEHREND, *Auf der Suche nach Schätzen...* (8th ed., 1960).

10. H. KUNTZ, ed., *Tischendorfs Reise nach dem Sinai* [= Nr. 182 of the Eichenkreuz-Bildkammer at Kassel-Wilhelmshöhe]; 50 slides and explanatory pamphlet.

11. E. LAUCH, «Nichts gegen Tischendorf», *Bekenntnis zur Kirche, Festgabe für Ernst Sommerlath zum 70. Geburtstag* (1960), p. 15-24, with a list of articles

These recent publications either repeat or corroborate with new arguments[12] the version of the story that has come to prevail in the literature on the subject ever since C. R. Gregory, the successor to Tischendorf's chair at Leipzig, cleared Tischendorf of any suspicion of improper dealings.[13] In the main, this version — one might call it the "vulgate version" — follows, and sometimes improves upon, Tischendorf's own story which that tireless scholar reiterated over and again.[14] Its proponents are legion,[15] and its pivotal argument is as follows: On September 28, 1859, Tischendorf received the 346 folios of the *Sinaiticus* against a receipt; the manuscript was loaned to him so that he might publish it and officially donate it to the Tsar in the name of the Sinaitic community. Thus the presentation of the manuscript to the Tsar by Tischendorf occurred in accordance with a previous agreement. In any case, an official donation took place in 1869; the Russians acknowledged it by sending nine thousand rubles and some medals to the monks. Thus throughout the *Sinaiticus* affair, Tischendorf's actions were above

---

devoted to the *Sinaiticus* by the same author, who also announced (*ibidem*), p. 24) that his *Codex-Sinaiticus-Bibliographie* was in press. I am indebted to Mr. Lauch for providing me with infomation concerning his writings.

12. Thus E. Lauch (as in the preceding note), p. 16, published the draft of the receipt of February 24, 1859, in which Tischendorf promised to return the *Sinaiticus* within a month and a half. This receipt refers to the first loan of the manuscript, to be copied by Tischendorf and aides in the Hôtel des Pyramides at Cairo.

13. Cf., in addition to the two works by Gregory quoted in note 6 *supra*, the same author's *Einleitung in das Neue Testament* (1909), p. 434-446.

14. Cf. «Ein Brief...» quoted at the end of note 4 *supra; Notitia editionis codicis bibliorum Sinaitici...* (1860), p. 5-7; *Bibliorum Codex Sinaiticus...* I (1862), as in note 5 *supra*, p. 1^r-4^v; *Aus dem Heiligen Lande...* (1862), p. 108-372; *Die Anfechtungen der Sinaibibel* (1863), p. 10 ff.; *Waffen der Finsterniss wider die Sinaibibel* (1863), p. 10-12; *Mémoire sur la découverte...*, as in note 2 *supra*, p. 2-14; *Sinaibibel, passim* (this is Tischendorf's principal work on the subject); cf. also *Codex Sinaiticus — Tischendorf's Story and Argument Related by Himself* (1934), p. 15-32 (a translation of TISCHENDORF'S *Wann wurden unsere Evangelien verfasst?*).

15. They include professional scholars like H. and K. Lake (as in note 25 *infra*), and all those who wrote popular accounts of Sinai — a multitude too overwhelming to be cited here. For the treatment of the Tischendorf story in two of the most recent examples of the latter genre, cf. H. SKROBUCHA, *Sinai* (1959), p. 107-108 and the excellent book by G. GERSTER, *Sinai, Land der Offenbarung* (1961), p. 172-174.

reproach and his account true, for "he attempts to conceal nothing."[16]

The documents about to be presented in this article indicate, to my satisfaction at least, that the vulgate story offers a too schematic and partly incorrect version of the events and that the conventional image painted in that story is not a portrait of the real Tischendorf. Answers to the following four questions are crucial to anyone attempting a plausible history of the *Sinaiticus* in the years 1859-1869; these answers furnish criteria for ⟨58⟩ judging Tischendorf's role in that history: (1) What were the exact conditions under which Tischendorf received the *Sinaiticus* on September 28, 1859? (2) By what authority did Tischendorf offer the *Sinaiticus* to the Tsar in 1862, if the official donation of the manuscript occurred only in 1869? (3) Why did this act of donation require a whole decade to be delivered by the monks? (4) How is one to explain the circumstance that Cyril, the Archbishop of Sinai, who let Tischendorf have the manuscript in 1859, did not issue the act of donation, while Callistratus, his successor and enemy, who had nothing to do with the negotiations of 1859, did? The circumstance is remarkable since Cyril is said to have been eager, in the beginning at least, to make a gift of the manuscript to the Tsar, and was otherwise notorious for squandering the monastery's property, while Callistratus was hailed as a stern guardian of that monastery's possessions.

In answering the first question, the adherents of the vulgate version improved upon Tischendorf's own story, for Tischendorf did not always imply that the intended donation to the Tsar was mentioned in the receipt of September 28, 1859.[17] The second question was not considered by the vulgate version at all. The third was answered by the allegation that all bureaucracies move slowly, and eastern bureaucracies even more slowly than others.[18] As for the fourth question, it was treated no more

---

16. *The Mount Sinai Manuscript...* (as in note 7 *supra*), p. 4.

17. I find such implications only in *Notitia editionis...* (1860), p. 7, in *Bibliorum Codex...* I (1862), p. 4^v, and in the ingenious wording of *Aus dem Heiligen Lande...* (1862), p. 371. For examples how unambiguously these implications were understood from the very outset, cf. S. P. Tregelles, *Poscript November 1, 1860*, in T. H. Horne, *An Introduction to the... Holy Scriptures*, 4 (New. ed., ... 1866), p. 776: "... the MS was put into the hands of Tischendorf, September 28, 1859, to be presented to the Emperor Alexander II," and the anonymous author of *Die Sinaitische Bibelhandschrift, Sächsisches Kirchen- und Schulblatt*, 13 (1863), 249: Tischendorf managed to get the *Sinaiticus* from the monastery as the monks' respectful gift for Alexander II.

18. *E. g.* C. R. Gregory, *Textkritik...*, p. 28; cf. Idem, *Einleitung...*, p. 436.

thoroughly than the second; moreover, the reader was not always explicitly informed that two Archbishops of Sinai were involved in the *Sinaiticus* affair.[19]

Better answers than those given in the vulgate version could have been obtained from the publications of Uspenskij,[20] Dmitrievskij,[21] Peradze[22] and Beneševič.[23] The views of these authors, all of them unfriendly to Tischendorf, are on occasion exaggerated, and their state⟨59⟩ments sometimes wrong. But these four writers offer significant information and documentation; it is regrettable that the proponents of the vulgate version have ignored them, garbled them, or shrugged them off.[24] The story of the *Sinaiticus* may be "one of the best-

---

19. *E. g.* GREGORY, *Textkritik...*, p. 28 fails to make the distinction.

20. Porfirij USPENSKIJ, *Kniga bytija moego*, I-VIII (1894-1902), esp. books VII and VIII, *passim; Pervoe putešestvie v Sinajskij monastyr' v 1845 godu* (1856), esp. pp. 225-238; *Vtoroe putešestvie arhimandrita Porfirija Uspenskago v Sinajskij monastyr' v 1850 godu* (1856), esp. p. 183; *Vostok Hristianskij. Egipet i Sinaj...* (1857), plates XV and XVI (= facsimiles of the *Sinaiticus*); P. V. BEZOBRAZOV, ed., *Materialy dlja biografii episkopa Porfirija Uspenskago*, I-II (1910), esp. II, p. 626-627; 681-684; 879-885; 912-922; 924-929. — I have not been able to consult USPENSKIJ's polemical pamphlet, *Mnenie o sinajskoj rukopisi, soderžaščej v sebe Vethij Zavet nepolnyj i ves' novyj Zavet...* (1862).

21. As in note 6 *supra*.

22. G. PERADZE, «Dokumenty, dotyczące zagadnień odnalezienia i tekstu kodeksu Synajskiego», Ἐλπίς, 8, 2 (Warsaw, 1934), 127-151.

23. V. N. BENEŠEVIČ (Bénéchévitch), *Les manuscrits grecs du Mont Sinaï et le monde savant de l'Europe depuis le XVIIe siècle jusqu'à 1927* [= *Texte und Forschungen zur byzantinisch-neugriechischen Philologie*, 21(1937)], esp. p. 33-51.

24. I have no quarrel with those who are influenced by familial piety, professional solidarity, local patriotism, or religious sentiment. My criticism is directed particularly to the two pamphlets published under the auspices of the British Museum in 1935 and 1955 respectively (cf. note 7 *supra*). There Uspenskij's claim to have seen the *Sinaiticus* (and written on it) before 1859 is discounted as the "Usual claim put forward... by someone 'who knew about it all the time'." In reality, one of them states, Uspenskij found (after Tischendorf) "fragments of two leaves... This was in 1845" (*The Mount Sinai Manuscript...*, p. 5, n. 2). Anyone familiar with the works quoted in note 20 *supra* (or even with A. RAHLFS' *Verzeichnis...* [1914], p. 226, no. 259, 2) knows that these statements are just not so. (I will grant that the treatment of USPENSKIJ in *The Codex Sinaiticus...*, p. 6, n. 1 is more equitable.) As for the "alleged admission by Count Ignatiew, in private letters" (and thus presumably of inferior value as testimony) to the effect "that he had 'stolen' the Codex," the pamphlet writes it off as a joke on the part of that astute diplomat (*ibidem*, p. 11). But that "alleg-

known stories in the history of palaeography;"[25] but, like all stories where the heroes and the villains are known in advance, it still remains a story told without too much care for detail.

The material offered in the present article brings us even closer to answering three of the four questions that have just been asked. Whether

---

ed" admission is printed for all to read in Dmitrievskij's work (as in note 6 *supra*), which the authors of the British Museum pamphlet did not directly quote, but of whose existence they were aware. If they took the trouble to read Ignat'ev's correspondence published there, they would have realized that Ignat'ev wrote in dead earnest and that, incidentially, he did not say that *he* had stolen the Codex, but that the Codex had been "stolen by us," i.e., by Russia. On this point, cf. p. 80 *infra*. Beneševič is said to have heard from the *skeuophylax* Polycarp in 1908 that the *Sinaiticus* itself came "to light among rubbish which his predecessor in office had been clearing out and burning in the bread ovens" (*The Codex Sinaiticus...*, p. 6, n. 1). What a marvelous confirmation of Tischendorf's story! Alas, when we turn to Beneševič (*Opisanie greč. ruk. mon. Sv. Ekateriny*, I [1911], p. xvi, n. 1), we read: "Quite recently, in order to get rid of 'rubbish,' they heated the bread oven with old books, among which were very rare editions." Thus the *Sinaiticus* is not mentioned in the passage adduced. What is more, no manuscripts at all are involved in the burning; and Polycarp's pyromaniac predecessor is a misunderstanding. Finally, since the statement is not Polycarp's, but Beneševič's (this appears with all clarity from the version of the same story the latter gave in *Les manuscrits grecs...* [as in the preceding note], p. 36), we are in the twentieth century, not in Tischendorf's times. *The Codex Sinaiticus...*, p. 8, reports that the troubles culminating in Archbishop Cyril's deposition in 1867 "were quite unconnected with the gift of the manuscript"; Beneševič, *Les manuscrits grecs...*, p. 48, thought otherwise; if not Beneševič, then *The Mount Sinai Manuscript...*, p. 8 should have given the authors of *The Codex Sinaiticus* food for thought; Ignat'ev's letter of December 17, 1869, which is summarized there, is explicit on the connection between "troubles" and "gift." *The Codex Sinaiticus...*, p. 8, n. 1 does quote Beneševič's *Les manuscrits grecs...* in passing, but only to remark that it unjustifiably questions Tischendorf's veracity; Peradze's *Dokumenty...* is quoted too (*ibidem*, p. 6, n. 2), as a publication not "adding anything of importance to the facts already known"; not a word is said of the six letters of Archbishop Cyril to Tischendorf which appear therein, and add a few things of importance on the manuscript's donation, one of these being that Cyril politely refused to make such a donation. In his *Text of the Greek Bible* (2nd ed., 1948), p. 78, n. 1, Sir Frederick Kenyon stated that "the fullest and fairest account of the whole [*Sinaiticus*] affair is to be found in the pamphlet, *The Mount Sinai Manuscript of the Bible*, published by the British Museum in 1934." It is difficult to subscribe to this view.

25. The formulation is by H. and K. Lake, *Codex Sinaiticus...* (Oxford, 1922), p. vii.

the vulgate story of the *Sinaiticus* still retains its basic validity in the light of this material is more a matter of opinion than of fact. In my opinion, it does not. But it will, I hope, be generally agreed that the story at least requires some retouching. The new documents also suggest that between ⟨60⟩ 1859 and 1869 the affair of the *Sinaiticus* produced repercussions not only beyond the awareness of modern research, but beyond that of Tischendorf himself.

II

Until recently, the receipt issued by Tischendorf on September 28, 1859 remained unknown to scholars, although it was said that it did exist somewhere either on Sinai or in Cairo.[26] The rumor proved to be correct, for when in November of 1960 I discussed the *Sinaiticus* with the then acting *œconomos* of the monastery Nicephorus, he claimed to have Tischendorf's receipt in his cell. Two days later he produced a sheet of four pages, with f. 1^r and 2^r empty (see Pl. 4). F.1^v contained the main text of the receipt in Tischendorf's own handwriting; f. 2^v bears remarks by two hands, identifying the document.[27] The main text runs as follows:

> Ἐγὼ ὁ ὑπογραφόμενος, Κωνσταντῖνος ὁ τοῦ Τισχενδόρφου, ἀπεσταλμένος νῦν εἰς τὴν ἀνατολὴν ἐξ ἐπιταγῆς Ἀλεξάνδρου τοῦ αὐτοκράτορος πασῶν τῶν Ῥωσσιῶν διαμαρτυρῶ διὰ τῆς παρούσης γραφῆς ὅτι ἡ Ἱερὰ Ἀδελφότης τοῦ ὄρους Σινᾶ κατὰ συνέπειαν ἐπιστολῆς τοῦ ἐξοχωτάτου Πρέσβεως Λοβάνωβ παρέδωκέ μοι λόγῳ δανείου χειρόγραφον ἀρχαῖον τῶν ἀμφοτέρων διαθηκῶν κατέχον φύλλα 346 καὶ κομμάτιόν τι μικρόν, ἀπόκτημα τοῦ αὐτοῦ μοναστηρίου, ὅπερ θέλω φέρειν μετ' ἐμαυτοῦ ἐν Πετρουπόλει πρὸς παραβολὴν τοῦ ὑπ' ἐμοῦ γενομένου ἀντιγράφου πρὸς τὸ πρωτότυπον ἐν καιρῷ τῆς ἐκτυπώσεως. Τὸ χειρόγραφον τοῦτο ἐμπιστευθέν μοι ὑπὸ τοὺς ἐν τῇ ῥηθείσῃ ἐπιστολῇ τοῦ Κυρ. Λοβάνωβ ἡμερολογουμένῃ ἀπὸ 10 Σεπτεμβρ. 1859. ὑπὸ ἀριθμὸν 510. ἐνδιαλαμβανομένους ὅρους ὑπόσχομαι ἀπο-

26. Cf. the hemming and hawing of Gregory, *Einleitung*... (as in note 13 *supra*), p. 437-38; cf. W. Hotzelt, "Die kirchenrechtlichte Stellung von Bistum und Kloster Sinai zur Zeit der Entdeckung der Sinaibibel," *Theologische Literaturzeitung*, 74 (1949), 462; E. Lauch, "Nichts gegen Tischendorf" (as in note 11 *supra*), p. 18 and 22 with notes 28 and 33.

27. First hand: ἀπόδειξις Τισσενδὸρφ διὰ τὸν Σιναϊτικὸν Κώδικα.
Second hand: εὑρέθη ἐν τοῖς ἐγγράφοις τοῦ Ἀρχιεπισκόπου Σινᾶ Κυρίλλου τοῦ Στρικίδου [?].

δοῦναι σῶον καὶ ἀβλαβὲς τῇ Ἱερᾷ τοῦ Σινᾶ Ἀδελφότητι εἰς πρώτην αὐτῆς ἀναζήτησιν.

Κωνσταντῖνος ὁ τοῦ Τισχενδόρφου.

Ἐν Καΐρῳ 16/28 Σεπτεμβρ. 1859.[28]

⟨61⟩ At first glance the text of the receipt is not too favorable to Tischendorf's cause, as it does not allude by a single word to the monks' alleged intention of donating the *Sinaiticus* to Alexander II, while it is quite explicit as to the manuscript's restitution which was to be made at the monastery's earliest request. But Tischendorf was a careful negotiator. The *Sinaiticus* — so the receipt states — was to be entrusted to him under the terms outlined in Prince Lobanov's letter of September 10.[29] In this letter, the Russian Ambassador did say that, from what he had heard, the monks intended to present the manuscript to the Tsar. Thus even today an admirer of Tischendorf might rise to the defense of this scholar's occasional hints[30] that a donation was mentioned or implied in the receipt of September 28. However, this defense will be weak indeed. In the same letter, Prince Lobanov goes on to state that the person who had enlightened him in regard to the monk's noble intention to donate the manuscript to Russia was none other than Tischendorf

28. I, the undersigned, Constantin von Tischendorf, now on mission to the Levant upon the command of Alexander, Autocrat of All the Russias, attest by these presents that the Holy Confraternity of Mount Sinai, in accordance with the letter of His Excellency Ambassador Lobanov, has delivered to me as a loan an ancient manuscript of both Testaments, being the property of the aforesaid monastery and containing 346 folia and a small fragment. These I shall take with me to St. Petersburg in order that I may collate the copy previously made by me with the original at the time of publication of the manuscript.

The manuscript has been entrusted to me under the conditions stipulated in the aforementioned letter of Mr. Lobanov, dated September 10, 1859, Number 510. This manuscript I promise to return, undamaged and in a good state of preservation, to the Holy Confraternity of Sinai at its earliest request.

Constantin VON TISCHENDORF.

Cairo, September 16/28, 1859.

The receipt found its way into Nicephorus' cell from the archives of Sinai's Cairene dependency. At present, it is exhibited in the visitor's room of the monastery's New Library. Several members of the 1960 expedition cooperated in having it mounted under glass.

29. Text in *Sinaibibel*, p. 22-23, and in BENEŠEVIČ, *Les manuscrits grecs*... (as in note 23 *supra*), p. 45.

30. Cf. note 17 *supra*.

himself, and the monks of Sinai had no reason to be bound by the statements of a Tischendorf concerning their intentions. They could very well let the reference to the "terms of Prince Lobanov's letter" stand in the receipt; the terms *they* had in mind were those by which the Ambassador undertook to restore the manuscript to the community and to assure them that, while on loan, the *Sinaiticus* would remain the monastery's property. That this was the monks understanding of these terms is evident from their reply, dated September 29, to Prince Lobanov's letter. This reply did not mention a donation; it spoke only of a temporary loan of the manuscript as a gesture of the community's special devotion to the Russian imperial house.[31]

Thus it must be granted that in 1859 the monks, too, turned out to be careful negotiators. The cautions leaders of Sinai did not commit themselves (in writing at least their words might have been more encouraging) to any offering of the *Sinaiticus* whatsoever.

III

While sifting through the material — ranging in date from the fifth to the twentieth century — contained in one of the chests which stand along the walls of the monastery's new library, I chanced upon an envelope inscribed Ἔγγραφα περὶ τοῦ δανείου τοῦ χειρογράφου τοῦ Σινᾶ. It yielded, among other things, the five documents transcribed and discussed in the following pages:

1. A letter from the monk Germanos to the Archbishop-Elect of Sinai, Cyril, then in Constantinople. Date: Cairo, October 28, 1859.

⟨62⟩ Cyril, the Archbishop-Elect of Sinai, was the chief spokesman for the monks in the negotiations with Tischendorf. About October 5, 1859,[32] a week after the conclusion of these negotiations, Cyril left Cairo for Constantinople in order to further his cause at the Oecumenical Patriarchate, at the Sublime Porte, and at the Russian Imperial Embassy. This journey was deemed necessary, since the Patriarch of Jerusalem, who by tradition performed the ordination of Sinai's archbishops, was violently opposed to Cyril. To keep informed of the events and the climate of opinion back home, Cyril enlisted the services of a confidential informant Germanos. Germanos' letter of October 16/28

31. Cf. French version in Beneševič, *Les manuscrits grecs*... (as in note 23 *supra*), p. 46; Greek (original?) version in *Cyril's Draft*, reproduced p. 69-70 *supra*.

32. Date to be inferred from Document 2, p. 63 *infra*.

1859 (see. Pl. 5 and 6) was his very first report to Cyril. After vividly describing the disorders which had erupted in the monastery's Cairene dependency on account of the "accursed winebibbing," τὴν ἐπάρατον οἰνοποσίαν, Germanos turned to the subject of Tischendorf, who had left Alexandria on October 9,[33] a few days after Cyril's departure:

> [p.2] Ὁ Τίσχενδορφ, ἀπ' ἐναντίας τῶν ὑμετέρων συστάσεων καὶ τῶν ὑποσχέσεών του, ἅμα εἶχε λάβει τὸ βιβλίον εἰς χεῖρας, ἔσπευσε νὰ τὸ διακοινώσῃ εἰς ὅλον τὸ Κάϊρον, εἴτε ἀπὸ ματαιότητα, εἴτε ἀπὸ ἄλλην τινὰ αἰτίαν. ἐμάθομεν δὲ ὅτι ὁ ἴδιος εἶχε καταχωρήσει [sic] ἐπὶ τοῦ ἀντικειμένου τούτου προλαβόντως ἓν ἄρθρον εἰς μίαν Ἀγγλικὴν ἐφημερίδα[34]. Καὶ ἐπειδὴ ὁ κόσμος ἐδῶ [sic] δὲν ἔχει ἄλλην ὁμιλίαν ἤδη παρὰ τὰ Σιναϊτικά, [p. 3] ἠγέρθη μεγάλη κατακραυγὴ κατὰ τῶν Σιναϊτῶν διότι ἀπεξένωσαν τὸ χειρόγραφον τοῦτο, ἐπειδὴ ὁ Τισχενδόρφ διεκήρυξεν ὄχι ὅτι τὸ ἐδανείσθη, ἀλλ' ὅτι τὸ ἔλαβεν ὁριστικῶς διὰ νὰ τὸ προσφέρῃ εἰς τὸν Αὐτοκράτορα. ὅθεν ἐδῶ [sic] εἶναι γνώμη ὅτι τὴν προσφορὰν ταύτην ἐκάματε ἡ Σεβασμιότης Σᾶς διὰ νὰ προσλάβητε τὴν ὑπεράσπισιν τῆς αὐτόσε Ῥ. Πρεσβείας. Τοῦτο ἤκουσα παρὰ πολλῶν, καὶ παρὰ τοῦ Εὐγενίου, ὅστις πρὸς τοῖς ἄλλοις μοι εἶπεν ὅτι τοῦτο τὸ περιστατικὸν δύναται νὰ φέρῃ σκάνδαλόν τι, διότι βεβαίως οἱ ἐνταῦθα ὑπεναντίοι δὲν θέλουν λείψει ἀπὸ τοῦ νὰ γράψουν τῷ Ἱεροσολύμων, χαρακτηρίζοντες τὴν πρᾶξιν ταύτην ὅπως τοῖς συμφέρει. Ὁ Σπανόπουλος μᾶς ἐπεσκέφθη καί μᾶς εἶπε μὲ ἄλλους λόγους, καὶ μὲ πνεῦμα ἐναντίον, τὰ αὐτά. ἡμεῖς ἠρνήθημεν καί ἀρνούμεθα πάντοτε τήν ἐκδίδοσιν τοῦ χειρογράφου λέγοντες ὅτι τὸ ἀπεστείλαμεν εἰς τό Μοναστήριον. Μολαταῦτα ἐνεκρίναμεν νὰ προλάβωμεν διά τοῦ ἐσωκλείστου πᾶν ἐνδεχόμενον, δημοσιεύοντες τὸ δάνειον τοῦτο. ἀποστέλλομεν δέ τὴν ἐσώκλειστον διατριβὴν τῇ Ὑ. Σεβασμιότητι, ὥστε ἂν ἐγκρίνῃ αὐτήν, νὰ τὴν δημοσιεύσῃ. νομίζω ὅτι ἡ δημοσίευσις αὕτη δύναται νὰ ἀμβλύνῃ τοὐλάχιστον τὰς ἐπὶ τοῦ ἀντικειμένου τούτου προσβολὰς τῶν ἐναντίων καὶ πρέπει νὰ θεωρήσητε τὴν ὑπόθεσιν ταύτην μὲ τὴν ἀνήκουσαν σπουδαιότητα, καθότι ἂν αἱ φῆμαι αὗται φθάσωσιν εἰς τὰ ὦτα τῆς Ῥ. Πρεσβείας, θέλουσι τὴν δυσαρεστήσει βεβαίως.[35]

---

33. Cf. *e.g. Sinaibibel*, p. 25.

34. This must have been a false rumor. Or did Germanos confuse an English with a German newspaper? Tischendorf, fearing that the *Sinaiticus* might be bought right from under his nose, announced his find in the April 17, 1859 issue of the "Scientific Supplement" to the *Leipziger Zeitung*; cf. end of note 4 *infra*.

35. Contrary to Your recommendations and to his own promises, Tischendorf, as soon as he put his hands on the book, hastened to spread the news throughout the whole of Cairo, either out of vanity or for some other reason. We also learned that he had beforehand published an article on this subject in an English

⟨63⟩ There is little love for Tischendorf in this report, written only a month after the *Sinaiticus* had been handed over to him. Tischendorf had not kept his part of the bargain, he had been indiscreet, he was vain. Instead of stating that the manuscript had been loaned, he claimed that it was to be donated to the Tsar. This was either not true or at least not the version agreed upon.

But was the manuscript to be donated, or was it not? On this point, Germanos' letter does not afford absolute clarity. Rumor had it that it was, as the price to be paid for Russian support. Cyril's enemies would exploit these rumors; the Russians, too, might be displeased. Therefore Germanos penned a special tract, unfortunately lost, in which these rumors were denied.

2. Tischendorf's note to Cyril. Date: Alexandria, October 4, 1859.

Monseigneur,

Empêché de venir ce matin, comme j'avais annoncé par Mr. le Consul Général, pour vous répéter mes adieux, je m'empresse de vous envoyer ce billet pour le Prince Lobanow, devant accompagner la petite caisse à son adresse. En même temps je me permets de renouveler à Votre Éminence l'hommage de mon dévouement respectueux et de toute ma gratitude. Vous savez que mon cœur vous suivra fidèlement à Constan-

---

daily. Since by now people here have no other subject of conversation than the affairs of Sinai, a great outcry arose against the Sinaites for having alienated this manuscript, since Tischendorf announced not that he had borrowed it, but rather that he had taken it for the definite purpose of offering it to the Emperor. Therefore people here are of the opinion that this offering had been arranged by Your Eminence in order that you might acquire the protection of the Russian Embassy there. I heard this said by many, and particularly by Eugenios. Among other things, he told me that this incident may cause some trouble, since the local adversaries surely will not abstain from writing to the Patriarch of Jerusalem, and from characterizing this action in accordance with their purposes. Spanopqulos paid us a visit and told us the same thing, although in other words and in an opposite spirit. We have been and still are denying all along that the manuscript had been given away, saying that we have sent it back to the monastery. Nevertheless, we thought it wise to anticipate all the eventualities in making this loan public by means of the enclosure. We are sending the enclosed essay to your Eminence so that it might be published, should it meet with Your Eminence's approval. I believe that such a publication might at least take the edge off the enemies' attacks in that matter. You should give this affair the serious consideration it deserves, for, should these rumors reach the ear of the Russian Embassy, they will surely cause displeasure there.

tinople et partout; veuillez bien aussi m'accompagner dans mon long chemin avec vos prières et votre bénédiction.

De Votre Éminence
le tout dévoué serviteur
C. TISCHENDORF

Alexandrie
ce 4. Oct(o)bre
1859

With the *Sinaiticus* in the bag, there was no urgent need to pay personal respects to Cyril, who was on the point of leaving for Constantinople. But Tischendorf was a man of good manners, and hastened to assure Cyril of his gratitude. It would be interesting to know the contents of the "little box" sent to Ambassador Lobanov's address.

⟨64⟩ 3. Letter of Tischendorf to Cyril, with "Tischendorf's Draft," an enclosure written in Tischendorf's own hand (see Pl. 7a and 7b). Date: Leipzig, January 21, 1864.

[p. 1]

Monseigneur,

C'est avec une véritable satisfaction que j'ai reçu de Vos nouvelles. Elles n'étaient pas des meilleurs [*sic*]; mais elles me renouvellent Votre amitié, Votre bienveillance: voilà pourquoi j'en suis charmé. Avant tout il faut me plaindre de ce que mes derniers envois à ce qu'il paraît, ont manqué Votre Éminence. Après Votre dernière lettre, remise au mois de Déc(em)bre 1861, je Vous ai adressé une lettre au mois de Mai ou Juin 1862; plus tard je Vous ai envoyé par un missionnaire protestant, qui allait aux Indes un exemplaire de mon ouvrage allemand: "Aus dem heiligen Lande" ("De la terre Sainte") qui s'occupe tant de Votre couvent et de ses affaires, ainsi que de mon vénérable protecteur l'archevêque Cyrille. Plus tard, je pense au mois d'Avril 1863, je Vous ai écrit une longue lettre, en Vous rapportant l'accueil que l'Empereur m'avait fait en recevant la grande édition du Codex[36] et l'entretien que j'avais eu avec S.M.I. sur le MS original. Aussi je vous ai envoyé ma brochure contre Porphyrios — devenu bien doux après — et contre Simonides, intitulée: "Die Anfechtungen der Sinaibibel" (Les attaques contre la bible du Sinai). Enfin au mois de Mai ou Juin 1863 je vous ai envoyé le premier exemplaire du

36. After this word, a sign refers to the following insertion at the bottom of the page: Tout dernièrement même le Pape m'a écrit une lettre avec les plus grands éloges sur l'édition. Cette lettre, imprimée partout, a fait une grande sensation, aussi à St. Pétersbourg.

"Novum Testamentum Sinaiticum."[37] Eh bien, serait-il possible que rien de tout cela ne soit parvenu à Votre adresse? Tous les envois de poste étaient cependant "recommandés au [*sic*] soins obligeans du Consulat général de Russie en Égypte." S'ils [p. 2] ont été véritablement perdus, je tâcherai au moins de réparer les deux livres, qui forment une partie essentielle de mes publications "Sinaitiques."

Maintenant passons à Vos nouvelles. Les affaires des Principautés ne me sont pas restées inconnues, et les injustices du Gouvernement relativement au couvents [*sic*], m'affligent extrêmement. Mais dernièrement nos journaux ont rapporté que les Grandes Puissances, notamment la Russie, ont protesté contre ces actes arbitraires du Prince Couza. J'espère avec Votre Éminence, que le bon Dieu fera triompher enfin le bon droit et l'intérêt sacré de l'Église.

Quand [*sic*] au MS. biblique, je plains beaucoup la perte de ma dernière lettre, où j'en avais longuement parlé. Voilà quelques mots de cette lettre, tels qu'ils se trouvent dans mes brouillons:

"Quand [*sic*] à l'original, je l'ai remis, d'après le désir du Ministre, dans les mains de l'Empereur; l'Empereur l'a fait déposer dans les caves du Ministère des Affaires Étrangères, garanties contre le feu. Dans l'audience l'Empereur a vivement abordé la question de la donation du MS. La donation ne lui paraissait pas encore toute certaine, et il en était assez peiné; aussi faisait-il mention de l'opposition du patriarche de Jérusalem. Je lui répondis que ce patriarche n'a aucun pouvoir aux affaires du couvent, et que le prince Gortczakoff[38], co(m)me le Ministre m'avait dit quand je dînais chez lui, venait justement de lui envoyer l'ordre d'Alex. Newsky. Quant au couvent même, j'assurais Sa Majesté des meilleurs [*sic*] dispositions pour la donation; je faisais valoir que Vous ne Vous étiez nullement ⟨65⟩ opposé au titre: Codex Sinaiticus *Petropolitanus* — ce qui intéressait particulièrement l'Impératrice —; je lui rapportai aussi les déclarations bienveillantes [p. 3] que Vous aviez faites à cet égard à Mr. de Noroff[39] qui m'avait prié d'en faire part à l'Empereur; je déclarais enfin que d'après mon opinion il *ne fallait plus faire autre chose que m'envoyer au couvent, chargé des présents Impériaux*. L'Empereur ne me dit pas le contraire; mais il a cru devoir avant tout s'en rapporter à son ministre.

---

37. A copy of this book is still preserved in the Monastery's library.

38. Prince A. M. Gorčakov (1798-1883), the famous Russian diplomat and Minister of Foreign Affairs (1856-1882).

39. A. S. Norov (1795-1869), Russian Minister of Public Instruction (1854-1858), a personal friend and ally of Tischendorf. As an administrator, he was well-meaning but ineffective. This writer, polyglot, and amateur scholar, who was a member of the Imperial Academy of Sciences, had travelled to the Holy Land. He also was an acquaintance of Porfirij Uspenskij.

Celui-ci, Mr. de Golovnine[40], m'a dit qu'il fallait gagner du temps, mais qu'on écrira à Votre Éminence de temps à temps, pour demander Vos résolutions. Voilà une manière d'agir, que je ne trouve pas bonne. En retournant par Varsovie (au mois de Déc 1862) j'en parlais au Grand Duc Constantin[41], qui a un intérêt tout particulier pour cette affaire; il était parfaitement de *mon* avis, non de celui de Mr. de Golovnine — qui d'ailleurs du cabinet du Grand Duc est passé au Ministère."

Mr. de Golovnine, je n'en doute pas, n'est pas trop de *nos* amis, bien qu'il m'ait fait présent "en marque d'amitié" de ses propres insignes, lorsque l'Empereur m'a revêtu de la première classe (Grand'Croix et Gr. Cordon) de l'Ordre de S. Stanislas, et qu'il m'ait comblé d'attentions pendant ma présence à St. Pétersbourg.

Depuis mon retour à Leipzig je n'ai pas cessé de m'occuper de l'affaire. En envoyant à S.M.I. le "Novum Testamentum Sinaiticum" j'ai écrit à l'Empereur dans le même sens que je lui en avais parlé à Zarsko-Sélo. Mr. le [*sic*] Golovnine, par lequel j'ai fait transmettre la lettre, n'a pas manqué de dissuader l'Empereur d'exécuter tout de suite mes propos. Mais le Grand Duc Constantin m'a de nouveau fait savoir qu'il est tout d'accord avec moi et qu'il appuiera mes vues et mes propositions.

Voilà donc où nous en sommes. Votre lettre du 21 Déc./2 Janv., qui ne m'est parvenue qu'hier, doit redoubler mon zèle. Votre Éminence a commencé Sa lettre par les mots: [p. 4] "Je ne puis pas croire que vous m'avez oublié." J'y réponds, Monseigneur: Mon cœur n'a jamais cessé d'être tout à Vous; j'aurais honte de pouvoir jamais manquer à mon sincère dévouement envers Votre Éminence et de pouvoir jamais oublier les intérêts de la communauté du Sinai. Eh bien, je Vous prie de regarder l'affaire de notre MS. comme une telle qui attend son réglement. Mais ne différez plus la déclaration que la communauté désire en faire hommage à l'Empereur et chargez moi-même de présenter cette déclaration personnellement à S.M.I. Je prends la liberté d'ajouter à ma lettre une esquisse des termes de cette déclaration; peut-être aurat-t-elle Votre approbation. Quand j'aurai ce document dans mes mains, j'irai à St. Pétersbourg. L'Empereur, je n'en doute pas, sera vivement touché d'une telle marque de confiance de Votre part, et je mettrai tout mon zèle, toute mon in-

40. A. V. Golovnin (1821-1886), energetic and liberal Minister of Public Instruction (1862-1866; dismissed after the attempt at Alexander II's life). In earlier years, Golovnin had been a confidant and protégé of Grand Duke Constantine (see next note).

41. Constantine (1827-1892), brother of Alexander II, was made Viceroy of the Polish Kingdom in 1862. He resigned — or was made to resign — in the middle of 1863, having refrained from taking harsh repressive measures against the Polish insurrection of that year. In 1863-1864 he undertook a prolonged journey abroad, in the course of which he visited several German principalities.

fluence à ce que cette noble donation soit noblement récompensée, en déclarant ouvertement que l'honneur de l'Empereur, l'honneur de la Russie y est engagé. Aussi je ne doute point que je réussirai; les membres les plus influents de la famille Impériale m'ont constamment témoigné leurs vives sympathies; et l'Empereur ⟨66⟩ saura apprécier la justesse des propositions que j'aurai alors le droit formel de faire valoir. Tout prochainement j'irai à Bade, où le Grand Duc Constantin passe cet hiver; je le préviendrai de ces arrangements; ses conseils et sa protection me guideront dans les démarches qui seront à faire. Malgré les affaires si tristes de la Pologne je sais que l'Empereur est resté tout dévoué à Son frère.

Veuillez donc croire, Monseigneur, que cette affaire me tient profondément au cœur. C'est avec impatience que j'attends de Vos nouvelles, que j'attends Vos résolutions. En attendant agrèez, Monseigneur, l'assurance de ma gratitude inaltérable et de mes sentimens respectueux, ainsi que mes complimens empressés à tous Vos confrères —

Constantine TISCHENDORF
Conseiller du Roi de Saxe et
Professeur à L'Univ. de Leipzig.

[p. 5] Sire,

V.M.I. a gracieusement daigné m'envoyer pour les Monastères du Sinai, qui sont confiés à ma garde, deux exx. de la Bible du Sinai d'aprés l'admirable publication que Mr. Tischendorf en a exécutés sous les auspices de Votre Maj. Imp. En exprimant à V.M.I. nos remercîmens profonds pour ce don précieux, nous nous félicitons, moi et la communauté, d'avoir avec tout empressement prêté la main à cette publication, par laquelle un trésor unique de notre Sainte foi fut rendu à toute la Chrétienté.

D'après la stipulation, passée entre le Monastère et Mr. Tischendorf le 16/28 Sept. 1859, l'édition achevée, notre communauté a le droit de réclamer l'original. Elle n'a guère l'intention d'user de ce droit. Remplis du plus profond respect et dévouement pour le haut protecteur de notre Sainte Église orthodoxe, nous désirons déposer comme un hommage de piété et de confiance, la Bible du Sinai aux pieds de V.M.I. Qu'elle soit digne d'augmenter la gloire d'Alexandre II., digne aussi d'assurer la grâce et la protection bienveillante à la communauté des Sinaites.

La communauté a confié son précieux MS. à Mr. Tischendorf, lorsque en 1859 la mission, dont il était chargé par V.M.I., l'avait conduit dans notre couvent. Sur sa demande elle le charge maintenant de déposer le même MS. aux pieds de V.M.I. et d'être l'interprète de ses vœux et de sa dévotion auprès de V.M.I.

Nous implorons tous la grâce de Dieu sur la tête sacrée de V.M.I. C'est avec le plus profond respect et dévouement que j'ai l'honneur d'être, Sire,

de V.M.I.
le tr. humble ed tr. obéiss. serviteur,

When Tischendorf discussed the *Sinaiticus* with Alexander II, the donation of the manuscript "did not seem quite assured" to the Emperor. Assured indeed! There had been no donation at all, either in September 1859 or by November 10, 1862, when the conversation with Alexander took place, or, finally, by January 21, 1864, when the present letter was written: this is evident from the phrase "do not delay the donation any longer." As a matter of fact, there was to be no donation for as long as Cyril would remain Archbishop of Sinai.

When in his draft of Cyril's address to Alexander II Tischendorf summed up the terms of the agreement of September 28, 1859, he abstained ⟨67⟩ from mentioning any intended donation; on the contrary, he stated that the community of Sinai had the right to ask for the manuscript's return. He could not have done otherwise: "Tischendorf's Draft" was destined for Cyril, and Cyril would have rejected any other formulation.

In his *Sinaibibel*[42] which appeared in 1871, Tischendorf intimated that the putting of the *Sinaiticus* into the Emperor's hands on November 10, 1862 was his own idea. By 1871, the *Sinaiticus* had been legally donated, and Tischendorf, an honorable man by that time, could afford some boasting. But by 1864 it must have been clear to all, and especially to Cyril, that in 1862 Tischendorf had had no right to put the manuscript into any person's hands. Had Tischendorf felt that he had such right in 1862, he would not have been so eager to repeat the ceremony (with a slight variation) in 1864, this time by putting the *Sinaiticus* at His Imperial Majesty's feet. In the present letter Tischendorf was far from assuming full responsibility for his act of 1862 and attributed it to a Russian minister's prompting.

The words "you were in no way opposed to the title Codex Sinaiticus *Petropolitanus*" confirm the impression that Tischendorf was on somewhat slippery ground when he appended the attribute *Petropolitanus* to that of *Sinaiticus* on the title-page of his four-volume edition of 1862. By so doing, he implied that the manuscript would find its permanent abode in St. Petersburg. Tischendorf's sole authority for imposing the new adjective was Cyril's silence: Cyril had not answered the letter in which Tischendorf suggested the addition, and thus had not directly opposed the change. In Tischendorf's interpretation this meant that Cyril approved it.[43]

---

42. Pp. 86-87.
43. Cf. also *Sinaibibel*, p. 86.

The letter's euphemisms did not obscure the aims of both correspondents. Cyril hoped to obtain Tischendorf's support of Sinai's endeavors to retain its Romanian possessions, confiscated by Prince Couza's government in 1863.[44] Cyril's was a vain expectation, for neither Tischendorf nor his pious hopes could change anything in the course of events, especially since the Russians, with whom Tischendorf was reputed to be influential, had no intention of intervening.

Tischendorf's aim was twofold. First, he wanted to see the donation made in due form, and thus to be let off the hook. In exchange, he dangled the promise of a compensation before Cyril. Since this was an affair in which "Russia's honor was at stake," the compensation would be liberal. But Tischendorf had a second goal as well: to have the Russian government send him on one more scholarly and diplomatic trip to the Near East. Already in 1862, he had personally suggested to the Tsar that he should be sent to the monastery in order to bring the *Sinaiticus* affair to a conclusion: through the present letter and through "Tischendorf's Draft" he again ⟨68⟩ offered his services as intermediary. But the Russians were unwilling to incur unnecessary expenses. In 1862, Minister Golovnin was evasive and thus earned Tischendorf's displeasure. In 1868, the Russian Ambassador to the Porte Ignat'ev, who did not mince words, alluded to Tischendorf's proposed scheme and said that the "misunderstandings" connected with the *Sinaiticus* were created by "a German who had wanted to take another joyride to Sinai and Athos at the Government's expense and under the Russian flag."[45]

There is no need to dwell on Tischendorf's own reference to Mr. Tischendorfs admirable publication, or the various passages in which he displays his medals and describes his hobnobbing with the great, for these passages do not directly bear on the history of the *Sinaiticus*.

4. Letter of Tischendorf to Cyril. Date: Leipzig, March 23, 1864.

[p. 1] Éminence,

N'ayant pas encore reçu de réponse à ma lettre du 9/12 Janvier, je commence à craindre que cette lettre ou Votre réponse ne se soit perdue, comme il est arrivé aux envois précédents que j'avais faits à Votre Éminence. Je m'imagine aussi bien que ce n'était pas si simple, si facile d'exécuter incessamment ma proposition. Quoi qu'il en soit, je me résous à

44. Cf. also *Sinaibibel*, p. 88.

45. Ignat'ev to Archimandrite Antonin, June 30, 1868, in Dmitrievskij, *Graf Ignat'ev...* (as in note 6 *supra*), p. 27.

Vous adresser ce billet pour Vous dire que S.A.I. le Grand Duc Constantin, chez qui j'ai passé à Bade-Bade quelques jours au mois de Février, s'intéresse toujours le plus vivement à notre affaire et qu'il a pleinement approuvé les démarches que je Vous ai proposées. Il a jugé absolument nécessaire que Votre Éminence adresse une telle lettre à S.M.I. pour qu'on puisse engager S.M.I. à reconnaître hautement la noble libéralité de Votre part et de toute la fraternité envers l'Empereur. Le Grand Duc, [p. 2] par lequel le Ministre de l'Instruction Publique a obtenu son poste et qui n'a pas cessé un instant d'être dans la plus grande intimité avec l'Empereur, veut bien que dans cette affaire je m'attache tout à sa protection et à sa coopération. Voilà une véritable garantie d'un succès parfait. La santé délabrée de la Grande Duchesse le retient encore en Allemagne; mais à pâques (d'après le calendrier Russe) il compte se rendre à St. Pétersbourg. Je serai trop heureux d'y aller en même temps, chargé de Votre dépêche pour l'Empereur.

Je vous prie donc de me faire connaître Vos résolutions à cet égard, et je Vous supplie d'exécuter ma proposition, pour pouvoir enfin m'acquitter moi-même dignement de mes obligations envers Votre Éminence.

C'est avec le plus profond respect que je suis tout à Votre Éminence.

Const. Tischendorf

Leipzig ce 11/23 Mars
1864.

This letter adds little to the preceding one: Cyril continued his silence, Tischendorf, his entreaties and promises.

⟨69⟩ 5. "Cyril's Draft": a memorandum, outlining the history of the *Sinaiticus* affair from September 1859 on (see Pl. 8a). Date: after August 1867, perhaps as late as 1869.[46]

The draft is unsigned, but its handwriting is unmistakably Cyril's.[47]

46. Reference, towards the end of the Draft, to "men that are at present administering Sinai under the auspices of the Patriarch of Jerusalem" places "Cyril's Draft" subsequent to January 21, 1867 (deposition of Cyril by the monks of Sinai), perhaps after August 30 of that year (ordination of Callistratus, Cyril's successor, by the Patriarch of Jerusalem). Since, however, these present administrators of Sinai have displayed "their most recent behavior with regard to the manuscript," which reveals their baseness of character, we may be as late as 1869, the year of negotiations culminating in the donation of the *Sinaiticus* by Callistratus.

47. This can be established by comparing the Draft's hand to Cyril's signed letter to the monks of Djuvania, dated November 25, 1859 (see Pl. 8*b* for the letter's last page) and to his autograph letter to Tischendorf, published on p. 73, n. 53 *infra*. Similar comparison shows that the inscription on the envelope containing our documents (cf. p. 61) is, too, by Cyril's hand.

This document, illegibly scribbled, teems with insertions, deletions and additions. The text given below is essentially a fair copy of the draft; thus, except for the beginning of the text, a continuous narrative has been obtained. The actual situation in the manuscript is given in the *apparatus*.

[p. 1] Ἡ Ιερὰ Μονὴ τοῦ Σινᾶ Ὄρους κάτοχος οὖσα [sic] παναρχαίου τινὸς χειρογράφου ἀνήκοντος κατὰ τὴν γνώμην τῶν σοφωτέρων κριτικῶν εἰς τὸν β^{ον} ἢ γ^{ον} μετὰ Χριστὸν αἰῶνα καὶ περιέχοντος

Μέρος τῆς Παλαιᾶς Διαθήκης
Ἅπασαν τὴν Καινὴν Διαθήκην
Ἐπιστολὴν Βαρνάβα τοῦ Ἀποστόλου ἀνέκδοτον

καί τινα ἄλλα ἀποσπάσματα ἀγνώστων ἐκκλησιαστικῶν συγγραμμάτων συνιστάμενον ἐκ σελίδων 346 καὶ κομμάτιον τι μικρόν. Τὸ χειρόγραφον τοῦτο τῇ συστάσει τοῦ ἐν Κωνσταντινουπόλει ἐξοχωτάτου Πρέσβεως τῆς Ῥωσσίας Πρίγγιπος Λοβάνοφ δι' ἐπιστολῆς του πρὸς τὴν Σιναϊτικὴν Κοινότητα μηνολογουμένης 10: σεπτεμβ. 1859: καὶ Ἀριθ. 510 ἡ Ἱερὰ Σιναϊτικὴ Κοινόντης διὰ πράξεως της [?] ὑπογεγραμμένης παρ' ὅλων τῶν μελῶν αὐτῆς καὶ καταχωρηθείσης ἐν τῷ Κώδικι ὑπὸ Ἀριθ. 6 καὶ ἡμερομηνίαν 16 7βρ. 1859 διαλαμβανούσης αὐτολεξεὶ τάδε: "Σήμερον 16 σεπτεμβ. 1859 ὑπ' ὄψιν λαβοῦσα ἡ Ἱ. Σύναξις τὴν κάτωθι συναφθεῖσαν ἐνταῦθα ἐπιστολὴν τοῦ ἐξοχωτάτου Πρέσβεως πασῶν τῶν Ῥωσσιῶν παρὰ τῇ Α. Μ. τῷ Σουλτάνῳ Κ. Πρίγγιπος Λοβάνωβ, δι' ἧς ἡ Α. Ἐ^{της} προτείνει τῇ Ἱ. Ἀδελφότητι ἵνα ἐμπιστευθῇ λόγῳ δανείου τῷ Κ. ἱππότῃ Κ. Τισχενδόρφῳ παλαιὸν τὶ χειρόγραφον περιέχον μήρος τῆς Παλαιᾶς καὶ τὴν Καινὴν Διαθήκην, σκεφθεῖσα πρὸς τούτοις ὅτι τὸ προσωρινῶς παραχωρούμενον χειρόγραφον τοῦτο θέλει χρησιμεύσει ὡς ὑπογραμμὸς εἰς τῆν ἤδη γενομένην [?] ἐκτύπωσιν ἐν Ῥωσσίᾳ τῆς Παλαιᾶς καὶ Νέας Διαθήκης καὶ δύναται να παρέξῃ οὕτως ὅσην πλείστην ὠφέλειαν ἅπαντι τῷ χριστιανικῷ πληρώματι διὰ τὴν γνησιότητα τοῦ πρωτοτύπου· οὐχ ἧττον δὲ περιποιουμένη νὰ δώσῃ ἰδιάζον τι δεῖγμα ἀφοσιώσεως τῇ Α. Μ. τῷ Αὐτοκράτορι Ἀλεξ. β^{ῳ}, ἀποφασίζει να ἐμπιστευθῇ τὸ χειρόγραφον τοῦτο συνιστάμενον ἐκ σελ. 346 τῷ μνησθέντι ἱππότῃ Κ. Κωνστ. Τισχενδόρφῳ ὑπὸ ἀπόδειξίν τοῦ καὶ ὑπὸ τοὺς ὅρους τοὺς ἐνδιαλαμβανομένους ἐν τῇ ἐπιστολῇ τοῦ ἐξ. Κ. Λοβάνωβ. ἕπονται αἱ ὑπογραφαί.

Κατὰ συνέπειαν ἐνεπιστεύθη τῷ Ἱππότῃ Κυρίῳ Κωνστ. Τισχενδόρφῳ λόγῳ δανείου ὑπὸ ἀπόδειξίν του 16/28 7βρ. 1859 λέγουσαν αὐτολεξεὶ τάδε καὶ σύμφωνα καὶ μὲ τοὺς ὅρους τοὺς ἐνδιαλαμβανομένους ἐν τῇ ῥηθείσῃ ἐπιστολῇ τοῦ ἐξοχωτάτου Πρέσβεως ὅτι μετὰ τὴν ἀποπεράτωσιν τῆς ἐκτυπώσεως νὰ ἐπιστραφῇ αὖθις τὸ πᾶν [?] ἔντυπον [?] χειρόγραφον πρὸς τὸ μοναστήριον ὡς ἀναφαίρετος αὐτοῦ ἰδιοκτησία.

Ἔκτοτε καὶ μέχρι τῆς σήμερον οὐκ ἐπεστράφη πρὸς τὴν Ἱερὰν

μονὴν τὸ ῥηθὲν χειρόγραφον· [p.2] ἀλλ' οὔτε ἡ σιναϊτικὴ Κοινότης διενοήθη ποτέ, ἢ καθυπέβαλεν ὑπὸ ⟨70⟩ κοινὴν σύσκεψιν [?] ἰδέαν τινὰ περί προσφορᾶς αὐτοῦ ἢ δωρήσεως πρὸς τὴν Αὐτοκρατορικὴν ῥωσσικὴν Κυβέρνησιν. ἀπ' ἐναντίας μάλιστα οἱ πλεῖστοι ἐδυσχεραίνοντο καὶ διὰ τὴν προσωρινὴν παραχώρησιν αὐτοῦ καὶ ὡς [?] ἐκ τούτου εὕρισκον ἀπὸ καιροῦ εἰς καιρὸν αἰτίαν κατηγορεῖν κατὰ τοῦ 'Αρχιεπισκόπου των Κυρ. Κυρίλλου, μαθὼν [?] ὁ Πατριάρχης Ἱεροσολύμων κυρ. Κύριλλος, μὴ θέλων κατὰ τὸ 1859 διὰ νὰ προαχθῇ ὁ κυρ. Κύριλλος εἰς τὴν 'Αρχιεπισκοπὴν τοῦ Σινᾶ ἕνεκα τῶν ἰδιοτελῶν σκοπῶν του, πρὸς τὰς ἄλλας ἀνυπάρκτους καὶ ψευδεῖς κατηγορίας κατὰ τοῦ κυρ. Κυρίλλου, ὡς ἀπεδείχθησαν ἐπισήμως τοιαῦται, ἐκατηγόρησε τὸν κυρ. Κύριλλον, ὅτι δῆθεν ἡ Πανιερότης του ἐδωρήσατο τὸ περὶ οὗ ὁ λόγος χειρόγραφον εἰς τὴν ῥωσσίαν διὰ νὰ προστατευθῇ παρ' αὐτῆς καὶ ἐπιτύχῃ τὴν ἀποκατάστασιν καὶ χειροτονίαν του εἰς τὴν 'Αρχιεπισκοπὴν τοῦ Σινᾶ. συνεπείᾳ τῆς τοιαύτης κατηγορίας, ἐγένοντο τότε παρὰ τοῦ ἁρμοδίου ὑπουργοῦ πρὸς τὸν κυρ. Κύριλλον πικραὶ καὶ αὐστηραὶ παρατηρήσεις διὰ τὴν ἀποξένωσιν δῆθεν ἐκ τοῦ μοναστ. ἑνὸς τοιούτου πολυτίμου ἀρχαίου κειμηλίου καὶ παρ' [p.3] ἄλλων ἐπισήμων ὁμογενῶν. ἡ τοιαύτη διαγωγὴ τοῦ Ἱεροσολύμων ἐπροκάλεσε τὸ ὑπὸ ἡμερομηνίαν 1/13 Νοεμβρίου 1859 πιστοποιητικὸν τοῦ Πρίγγιπος Λοβάνοβ ὅτι [ὅτι] τὸ χειρόγραφον ἐδόθη τῷ Κ. Τισχεντόρφῳ προσωρινῶς καὶ ὅτι θέλει ἐπιστραφεῖ εἰς τὸ μοναστ. ὡς ἰδιοκτησία αὐτοῦ· καὶ οὕτως ἀπεδείχθη ἡ ἀλήθεια ἀπέναντι τῶν κατηγοριῶν.

'Ακολούθως, ὅτε κατὰ τὸ 1865 Δεκεμβ. ἐπανέστησαν τινὲς τῶν καλογήρων κατὰ τοῦ ἀρχιεπισκόπου των κυρ. Κυρίλλου τη ἐνπνεύσει [sic?] τοῦ Πατριαρ. Ἱεροσολύμων, οὗτοι τῷ 1866 κατα Φεβρ., ὡς ὑπήκοοι ἕλληνες οἱ πλεῖστοι, ἀνεφέρθησαν δι' ἀναφορᾶς των πρὸς τὸ ἐν Καΐρῳ ἑλληνικὸν ὑποπροξενεῖον, καὶ πρὸς τὰς λοιπὰς κατηγορίας κατὰ τοῦ ἀρχιεπισκόπου κυρ. Κυρίλλου, ἀνέφερον καὶ ὅτι ὁ κυρ. Κύριλλος ἐπώλησεν ἓν χειρόγραφον τοῦ μοναστ. πρὸς τὴν Κυβέρνησιν τῆς ῥωσσίας ἐπὶ ἀμοιβῇ πολλῶν χιλιαδ. καρποβόνων. ἀκολούθως εἰς τὰ Πρακτικά των καὶ εἰς τὰς πρὸς διαφόρους ἀρχὰς ἀναφορὰς των ἀναφέροντες ὅτι ὁ Σιναΐου κυρ. Κύριλλος ὑπεξῄρεσε πολύτιμα καὶ βαρύτιμα κειμήλια ἐκ τοῦ μοναστηρίου ἀνεπιστρεπτί, δὲν εἶναι ἀμφιβολία ὅτι ἐννοοῦσι τὸ χειρόγραφον αὐτό. ἐκ τούτων ἁπάντων τῶν γεγονότων, καὶ ἐκ τῆς τελευταίας των διαγωγῆς [p. 4] ὡς πρὸς τὸ χειρόγραφον ἕκαστος δύναται να κρίνῃ, ὁποίου χαρακτῆρος ἄνθρωποι εἶναι οἱ διέποντες σήμερον τὰ τοῦ Σινᾶ ὑπὸ τὰς ἐμπνεύσεις τοῦ Ἱεροσολύμων καὶ ὑπὸ ποίου πνεύματος ὁδηγούμενοι τεκταίνουσι τὰ τοιαῦτα ψεύδη διὰ να ἐπιτύχωσι τῶν σκοπῶν των [48].

---

48. The Holy Monastery of Mount Sinai, being in possession of a very ancient manuscript, in the opinion of more experienced critics going back to the second

⟨71⟩ 7 *post* συγγραμμάτων *vocabula* συγκείμενον τὸ χειρόγραφον τοῦτο *expuncta in ms.* ‖ συνιστάμενον *supra* συγκείμενον *ad l.* 7 *laudatum.* ‖ 8 *post* μικρόν *vocabula* το χ αὐτό *expuncta in ms.* ‖ τὸ — τοῦτο *supra vocabula expuncta ad l.* 8 *laudata.* ‖ 9 ἐν Κωνστ. *supra versum.* ‖ 10 *post* ʽΡωσσίας *littera K expuncta in ms.* ‖ 12 ὑπογεγραμμένης — 13 αὐτῆς *supra versum.* ‖ 14 *post* 1859 *asteriscus, ante* διαλαμβανούσης *in ms. pag.* 4 *iteratus.* ‖ 14 διαλαμβανούσης — 28 μνησθέντι *ad ms. infimam paginam* 4 *leguntur.* ‖ 15 1859 *e corr.:* 1869 *ante corr. ms.* ‖ 28 *post* μνησθέντι *asteriscus, ante* ἱππότῃ *in ms. pag.* 4 *iteratus.* ‖ 28 ἱππότῃ — 30 ὑπογραφαί *ad ms. mediam paginam* 4 *leguntur.* ‖ 31 κατὰ συνέπειαν *supra versum, post asteriscum ad l.* 14 *laudatum.* ‖ 32 λέγουσαν — 33 τάδε *supra versum.* ‖ 35 ἔντυπον] *vocab. lectu difficile;* ἔντυπον *sensu caret, nisi idem hic valeat ac "postquam typis expressum est."* ‖ 35 τὸ πᾶν — 36

---

or third century after Christ, and containing

A part of the Old Testament
The whole of the New Testament
The unpublished Epistle of the Apostle Barnabas,

and some other fragments of unknown ecclesiastical writings — consisting of 346 folia and a small fragment. — Upon the recommendation of His Excellency the Ambassador of Russia at Constantinople Prince Lobanov, made in the letter dated September 10, 1859, Number 510, and addressed to the Community of Sinai — this manuscript through an Act, signed by all of its members and inserted into the Minutes under Number 6 and the date of September 16, 1859. The text of the Act is *verbatim* as follows: "On this day of September 16, 1859, the Holy *Synaxis*, having considered the letter (appended below) of His Excellency Prince Lobanov, the Ambassador of All the Russias to H.M. the Sultan, by which letter His Excellency proposes to the Holy Confraternity that an ancient manuscript, containing a part of the Old Testament and the New Testament, should be entrusted, as a loan, to *Chevalier* C. Tischendorf; having furthermore considered that this manuscript, ceded *ad interim*, may be of use as a model for the printing, already undertaken [?] in Russia, of the Old and New Testaments, and that it thus may prove of the greatest usefulness for the whole Body of Christendom owing to the authenticity of the prototype, being no less eager to display a special token of its devotion to H.M. the Emperor Alexander II, decides that the manuscript in question, consisting of 346 folia, should be entrusted to the above-named *Chevalier* Const. Tischendorf upon receipt, and in accordance with the terms contained in the letter of His Excellency Mr. Lobanov." The signatures follow. Consequently, it was entrusted to *Chevalier* Const. Tischendorf as a loan against his receipt of September 16/28, 1859, stating *verbatim* the following, and being consistent with the terms contained in the above-mentioned letter of His Excellency the Prince: that after the completion of the printing the whole [?] ... manuscript should be returned to the monastery as its inalienable possession.

From that time until the present day the aforesaid manuscript has not been returned to the Holy Monastery. On the other hand, neither did the Community

χειρόγραφον *supra versum.* ‖ 38 *post* σήμερον *vocab.* δεν *expunctum in ms.* ‖ 40 *post* ἤ *vocab.* ἐπρότεινε *expunctum in ms.* ‖ 41 *post* περί *litt.* δω (*principium vocabuli* δωρήσεως ?) *expunctae in ms.* ‖ 42 *post* μάλιστα *litt.* οἱ πλ *expunctae in ms.* ‖ 43 *post* τήν *vocabb.* λόγῳ δαν (*principium vocab.* δανείου ?) *expuncta in ms.* ‖ 44 *post* εὕρισκον *litt.* πάντο *expunctae in ms.* ‖ 45 *post* Κυρίλλου *vocabb.* ὡς παραδ (*principium vocabb.* παραδείγματος χάριν ?) *expuncta in ms.* ‖ μαθών (*num* καθώς ?)] *supra vocabb.* ὡς παραδ *ad l.* 45 *laudata.* ‖ ὁ *e corr.*: ὡς *ante corr.* ‖ 47 *post* του *litt.* ἐκατηγο *expunctae in ms.* ‖ 49 *post* ἐπισήμως *litt.* διε *expunctae in ms.* ‖ τοιαῦται *supra* διε *ad l.* 49 *laudatam.* ‖ 50 *post* Κύριλλον *vocabula* πρὸς τὴν Κυρίαρχον Κυβέρνησιν τῆς Α. Μ. τοῦ Σουλτάνου *expuncta in ms.* ‖ *post* ἐδωρήσατο *vocabula* ἓν πολύτιμον καὶ ἀρχαιότατον χειρο *expuncta in ms.* ‖ 52 *post* του *vocabula* εἰς τὴν ῥω ἀρχαι ὡς *ex-*

---

of Sinai ever contemplate nor did it deliberate in common upon any idea of offering or donating it to the Russian Imperial Government. Quite to the contrary, many ⟨monks⟩ were displeased even with its temporary cession, and from that time forth found the pretext for launching periodic accusations against their Archbishop, Kyr Cyril. Kyr Cyril, the Patriarch of Jerusalem, having learned [?] ⟨of the affair⟩, and being opposed in 1859, for reasons of his own, to the promotion of Kyr Cyril to the Archbishopric of Sinai, in addition to leveling other vain and false accusations against Kyr Cyril — they were shown to be such after official investigation — also accused Kyr Cyril to the effect that His Grace had allegedly donated the manuscript in question to Russia in order to gain Her protection and to obtain his installation and consecration to the Archbishopric of Sinai. As a consequence of such an accusation as this, the competent ⟨Ottoman⟩ Minister, as well as prominent Greeks, made bitter and severe representations to Kyr Cyril on account of the alleged alienation of such a valuable ancient treasure from the Monastery. Such behavior on the part of the Patriarch of Jerusalem called forth an affidavit of Prince Lobanov, under the date of 1/13 November 1859, to the effect that the manuscript had been given to Mr. Tischendorf *ad interim*, and that it would be returned to the Monastery as its possession. In such a manner, the truth was revealed in face of the accusations.

Subsequently, when in December of 1865 some of the monks rebelled against their Archbishop Kyr Cyril upon the instigation of the Patriarch of Jerusalem, they addressed a report to the Greek Viceconsulate in Cairo in February 1866, inasmuch as most of them were Greek subjects; in addition to other accusations against Archbishop Cyril, they reported that Kyr Cyril had sold a manuscript of the monastery's to the Russian Government in exchange for many thousands in assignations [?]. Consequently, when in their Acts and in their petitions addressed to various authorities they report that the Archbishop of Sinai Kyr Cyril has irretrievably alienated exceedingly valuable treasures of the monastery, they doubtless have in mind the manuscript in question. From all these events, and from their most recent behavior with regard to the manuscript, anyone may judge as to the character of the men that are at present administering Sinai under the auspices of the Patriarch of Jerusalem, and as to the spirit that guides them when they concoct such lies in order to reach their goals.

puncta in ms. || εἰς τήν *supra* ἀρχαι ὡς *ad. l.* 52 *laudatum.* || *post* 'Αρχιεπισκοπήν *vocabula* Σινᾶ. διὰ τήν *expuncta in ms.* || 53 τοῦ Σινᾶ *supra vocab.* Σινᾶ *ad l.* 52 *laudatum.* || 53 *post* τότε *litt.* παρ *expuncta in ms.* || 54 *post* τόν *litt.* 'Αρχιεπι *expunctae in ms.* || 56 πολυτίμου ἀρχαίου *supra versum.* || ἐπισήμων *supra versum.* || 57 *post* ὁμογενῶν *asteriscus, ante* ἡ τοιαύτη *in ms. pagina* 3 *superiore iteratus; post asteriscum vocabula* ὥστε τότε ἠναγκάσθη ὁ 'Αρχιεπίσκοπος κυρ. Κύριλλος νὰ ζητήσῃ παρὰ τοῦ ἐξοχωτάτου πρέσβεως Πρίγγιπος Λαπάνοφ ἔγγραφον ἀπός πιστοποιητικόν *expuncta in ms.* || 57 ἡ τοιαύτη — 59 ὅτι *in pag.* 3 *superiore add. ms.* || 59 *post* Λοβάνοβ *vocab.* δι' οὗ *expunxit ms.* || ὅτι *supra vocabb.* δι' οὗ *ad l.* 59 *laudata*; *post* ὅτι *asteriscus ante* [ὅτι] τὸ χειρόγραφον *iteratus; vocabula* [ὅτι] τõ χειρόγραφον *sequuntur vocab.* πιστοποιητικόν ad l. 57 *laudatum.* || *post* χειρόγραφον *vocabula* δὲν ἐδωρήθη ἀλλ' ἐδανείσθη προσωρινῶς, ὅστις καὶ ἀπέλυσε τὸ καὶ τῷ ἐπεδόθη παρὰ τῆς ἐξοχότητός του τὸ ἀπό πιστοποιητικὸν ἔγγραφον, δυνάμει τοῦ ὁποίου ἀπεδείχθη ψευδόμενος ὁ 'Ιεροσολύμων *expuncta in ms.* || 60 *post* ὅτι *vocabb.* εἶναι παν *expuncta in ms.* || *post* ἐπιστραφεῖ *vocab.* ὡς *expunctum in ms.* || 59 ἐδόθη — 61 κατηγοριῶν *supra vocabula* δέν — 'Ιεροσολύμων *ad l.* 59 *laudata.* || 62 κατά — Δεκεμβ. *supra versum.* || 63 *post* τῇ *vocab.* προτροπῇ *expunctum in ms.* || 65 *post* ἀνεφέρθησαν *vocab.* εἰς *expunctum esse videtur in ms.* || 69 *post* ἀμοιβῇ *vocabb.* (δὲν ἐνθυμοῦμαι) *expuncta in ms.* || 70 ἀρχάς — 71 ὅτι] ⟨72⟩ *supra haec leguntur sequentia in ms.*: τὰς καταφορὰς των κατὰ τοῦ κυρ. Κυρίλλου. || 72 *post* ἀνεπιστρεπτί *vocab.* πάλιν *expunctum in ms.* || δέν — 73 ὅτι *supra* πάλιν (*ad l.* 72 *laudatum*) *et supra* ἐννοοῦσι. || 73 *post* ἁπάντων *litt.* δύ (*principium vocab.* δύναται ?) *expunctae in ms.* || 77 ὁδηγούμενοι *e corr.*: ὁδηγοῦνται *ante corr.* || τεκταίνουσι — 78 ψεύδη *supra versum.* ||

"Neither did the Community of Sinai ever contemplate, nor did it deliberate in common upon any idea of offering or donating ⟨the *Sinaiticus*⟩ to the Russian Imperial Governement." The present text is one more proof that Cyril never signed "Tischendorf's Draft" of 1864. In addition, this text makes abundantly clear that, after November of 1859, an official donation of the *Sinaiticus* had been the last act Cyril was interested in performing.

This is not to say that he acted necessarily out of righteousness. On the contrary, we may surmise that in October and November of 1859, Cyril was corruptible and willing to corrupt, happy to pay a handsome *baksheesh* to anyone who could secure for him the ordination as Archbishop of Sinai, and confirmation to that dignity from the Porte. But discretion was also of great importance. Thus when in November of 1859 his enemies asserted that the *Sinaiticus* had been such a *baksheesh* paid to the Russians, Cyril reacted promptly: on November 13, he obtained a written denial of such slander from Ambassador Lobanov, the same man with whom Tischendorf had engineered the transfer of the *Sinaiticus* about a month and a half earlier. But as the private arrangement had since become a diplomatic affair, Lobanov had no choice but to issue this statement, which he did on November 13. The statement — it has not come to light, but its contents can be reconstructed from three sources[49] — committed the Russian Government to the position that the *Sinaiticus* had merely been loaned, and that no offering to the Tsar was to be expected. This official denial explains the Russians' subsequent insistence upon an explicit act of donation, to be provided with as many signatures as possible.[50]

Lobanov's statement strengthened Cyril's bargaining position vis-à-vis Tischendorf and Russia. Unfortunately, from November 1859 on, Cyril was not quite free to bargain — too many eyes, so "Cyril's Draft" tells us, — were watching his every move regarding the manuscript: first and foremost, his enemies in the Patriarchate of Jerusalem; then the Turkish authorities at Istanbul (the Evkaf?), suspicious of any deal a Christian monastery might strike with Russia; finally, the Greeks from Egypt, Istanbul, and even the Kingdom of Greece, indignant that a Hellenic treasure had been whisked away to the Russian North.

⟨73⟩

IV

Cyril was to remain true to the position taken in his "Draft" even on a late, probably even the last, occasion when he dealt directly with Tischendorf. Toward the end of 1867, Tischendorf, anxious to have his name cleared, and probably despairing of Sinai's cooperation, decided to go to St. Petersburg in person in order to spur the Russians into action.[51] But before leaving, he made one more attempt to approach Cyril,

49. *Cyril's Draft*, l. 46-48, p. 70 *supra*; Cyril's letter to Tischendorf (date: December 16, 1859), ed. Peradze, *Dokumenty...* (as in note 22 *supra*), p. 145-146; Porfirij Uspenskij, *Kniga bytija...* (as in note 20 *supra*), VIII, p. 38-39, story told on January 10, 1863 by Isidore, metropolitan of St. Petersburg; in that story correct Isidore's (or Uspenskij's) lapse and read "Patriarch of Jerusalem" for "Patriarch of Constantinople." The complaint of the δικαῖος to Brugsch may also have referred to Lobanov's statement. Cf. note 72 *infra*.

50. Cf. Ignat'ev to Tischendorf (date: Pera, December 5/17, 1869), ed. Peradze, *Dokumenty...* (as in note 22 *supra*), p. 150; Ignat'ev to Antonin (date: January 7/19, 1870), ed. Dmitrievskij, *Graft Ignat'ev...* (as in note 6 *supra*), p. 28.

51. In fairness to Tischendorf, it must be pointed out that the initiative for reopening the question seems to have been his. He went to St. Petersburg in the spring (before April) of 1868, cf. *Sinaibibel*, p. 89 f.; he met Ignat'ev there. The

by then a deposed prelate and a resident of Constantinople. On January 24, 1868, Cyril responded with a long letter,[52] in which he gave his account of the quarrel with the Patriarch of Jerusalem and of the gloomy prospects of his own cause. In the course of the letter, the *Sinaiticus* was brought up only once:

> It is noteworthy that ⟨among⟩ the accusations contrived against me upon his ⟨i.e., the Patriarch of Jerusalem's⟩ instigation — accusations which he accepted without proof, going so far as to have me deposed — there is also one to the effect that I allegedly have purloined highly valuable treasures; hereby they have in mind the manuscript given to you, as you know, according to the common belief[53].

⟨74⟩ The passage in the letter is close to the corresponding part of

---

earliest mention of the Sinaiticus in Ignat'ev's correspondence with Antonin is on May 8, 1868, cf. DMITRIEVSKIJ, *Graf Ignat'ev...* (as in note 6 *supra*), p. 26-27. According to Porfirij Uspenskij, however, an inquiry concerning the *Sinaiticus* had been ordered by the Tsar by January 10, 1863, cf. *Kniga bytija...* (as in note 20 *supra*), VIII, p. 38-39.

52. *Universitätsbibliothek Leipzig*, MS 01030.

53. I am giving the integral text of the letter. The translated passage is on p. 3/4.

Κωνσ/λις 12/24 'Ιαννου (α)ρ(ίου) 1868.

[p. 1) Κύριε!

῾Ο ἐνταῦθα ἀνταποκριτής σας μοι διακίνωσε [sic] τὰ γραφόμενά σας τὰ ἀφορῶντα ἐμέ, καὶ τὴν προσεχῆ μετάβασίν σας εἰς Πετρούπολιν, καθὼς καὶ τὴν ἐπιθυμίαν σας τοῦ νὰ μάθετε εἰς ποίαν θέσιν εὑρίσκεται ἡ δυστυχῶς ἀναφυεῖσα διαφορὰ μεταξὺ ἐμοῦ καί τινων Σιναϊτῶν Πατέρων. Πρὸς ἐκπλήρωσιν οὖν τῆς περιεργίας σας σᾶς λέγω ὀλίγα [sic] τινά, ἐξ ὧν δύνασθε νὰ κατανοήσητε τὴν ἀρχικὴν αἰτίαν τοῦ κακοῦ.

Γνωρίζετε Κύριε τὰ πρὸ ὀκτὼ ἤδη ἐτῶν ἐν καιρῷ τῆς χειροτονίας μου ὡς 'Αρχιεπίσκοπος Σιναίου λαβόντα χώραν ἀηδῆ, ἕνεκα τῶν ἰδιοτελῶν σκοπῶν τοῦ Πατριάρχου 'Ιεροσολύμων, τοῦ ἀτομικοῦ μου κεκηρυγμένου ἐχθροῦ, καὶ ὁποία [sic] θεμιτὰ καὶ ἀθέμιτα μέσα μετῆλθε τότε διὰ νὰ ματαιώσῃ τὸν διορισμόν μου. 'Αλλ' ἀποτυχῶν [sic] τότε χάρις εἰς τὰς συνδρομὰς τῶν φίλων τοῦ δικαίου, οὐκ ἐπαύσατο καραδοκῶν τὸν καιρόν, ὅπως ἐπαναλάβῃ αὖθις τοὺς [p. 2] καταχθονίους σκοπούς του. ὅθεν καὶ δὲν ὄκνησε νὰ ἐνσπείρῃ ζιζάνια μεταξὺ τινῶν ἁπλῶν καὶ εὐπίστων Πατέρων, νὰ ὁδηγῇ αὐτοὺς διὰ τῶν ὀργάνων του τὸν τρόπον τῆς κατ' ἐμοῦ καταφορᾶς, καὶ νὰ ἐμπνέῃ [sic?] αὐτοῖς τὸ πνεῦμα τῆς ἀνταρσίας καὶ ἀπειθίας [sic], ἐξ ὧν ἀνεφύη τὸ πολύκροτον τοῦτο ζήτημα· καὶ ὕστερον ἀφ' ὅλα ταῦτα, ἐναντίον τῶν ῾Ιερῶν

"Cyril's Draft."[54] True, since the letter was addressed to Tischendorf, the person most directly involved, the passage is shorter, its language less precise and more moderate. But it says the same thing; it even repeats the "Draft's" peculiar expressions. The veiled accusation that Cyril has embezzled the *Sinaiticus* "without ⟨hope for its⟩ return" or "irretrievably" (ἀμεταστρεπτί in both texts) is false. That the manuscript

---

Κανόνων, ἐναντίον ὅλων τῶν νόμων τῶν ἐθνῶν, ἀνέλαβεν αὐθαιρέτως καὶ τὸ πρόσωπον τοῦ δικαστοῦ, ἐν ᾧ εἶναι καὶ κατήγορος, καὶ ἐδίκασεν· ἀπεφάσισε μετὰ πολλῆς βίας, καί με κατεδίκασεν ἐρήμην κηρύξας με ἔκπτωτον τῆς θέσεώς μου, ἀντικαταστήσας με δι' ἄλλου τῆς ἀρεσκείας του, παραβὰς ἅπαντα τὰ προνόμια καὶ τὴν τάξιν τοῦ Ἱεροῦ Μοναστηρίου. Εἰς μάτην διαμαρτύρωμαι [sic] κατὰ [p. 3] τῶν παρανομιῶν του τούτων, εἰς μάτην τόσοι Πατέρες Σιναΐται καὶ ἐκ τῶν ἐντὸς καὶ ἐκτὸς τοῦ Μοναστηρίου ῥίγνυσι [sic] τὰ ἱμάτιά των κατὰ τῶν ἐπεμβάσεων τοῦ Ἱεροσολ. καὶ ὁμολογοῦσι τὴν εὐχαριστίαν των ἀπὸ ἐμέ. Εἰς μάτην τὸ οἰκουμενικὸν Πατριαρχεῖον τὸν γράφει ἐγκαίρως τοῦ νὰ μὴ προβῇ εἰς καμμίαν ὁποιανδήποτε πρᾶξιν [sic], διότι ἡ ὑπόθεσις αὕτη δέον νὰ θεωρηθῇ δι' εὐρυτέρας σκέψεως ὑπὸ τῆς καθ' ὅλου [sic] ἐκκλησίας κατὰ τὰ προλαβόντα πλεῖστα παραδείγματα. Ἀλλ' οὐδὲν τούτων λαμβάνεται ὑπ' ὄψιν ἀπέναντι τῆς ἐμπαθοῦς κακοβουλίας τοῦ Ἱεροσολύμων. Σημειοτέον ὅτι αἱ κατ' εἰσήγησιν αὐτοῦ ἐξυφανθεῖσαι κατ' ἐμοῦ κατηγορίαι, τὰς ὁποίας καὶ ἀβασανίστως παρεδέχθη καὶ ἐπροχώρησε μέχρι τῆς παύσεώς μου, εἶναι μία καὶ αὕτη, ὅτι [p. 4] δῆθεν ὑπεξαίρισα [sic] βαρύτιμα κειμήλια ἀνεπιστρεπτί καὶ μὲ τοῦτο ἐννοοῦσι τὸ πρὸς ὑμᾶς δοθὲν χειρόγραφον, κατὰ κοινὴν γνώμην ὡς γνωρζετε. Ἐν τούτοις κραυγάζω, ζητῶ δίκην, καὶ δικαστὰς ἀμεροληπτους διὰ νὰ μὲ δικάσωσι· ἐπικαλοῦμαι τὴν δικαιοσύνην τῶν Ἱερῶν Κανόνων, τῶν νόμων ὅλου τοῦ κόσμου· ἡ φωνή μου ἀποβαίνει κύμβαλον ἀλαλάζον [1 Cor. 13: 1]. Τὸ οἰκουμενικὸν Πατριαρχεῖον μέχρι τοῦδε δὲν ἀνεγνώρισε τὰς πράξεις τοῦ Ἱεροσολύμων θεωρὸν [sic?] αὐτὰς ἀντικανονικάς. Ἀλλ' ἴδωμεν ἂν δὲν εἰσχωρήσῃ καὶ ἐν αὐτῷ ἡ ῥαδιουργία τοῦ Ἱεροσολύμων ἐπὶ τέλους.

Ἰδοὺ φίλε ἡ ἀθλία κατάστασις τῶν καθ' ἡμᾶς πραγμάτων, ἕνεκα τοῦ ὅτι ἐπιλήσμονες γενόμενοι τῆς ὑψηλῆς ἡμῶν ἀποστολῆς, παραγνωρίζωμεν τὰ [p. 5] καθήκοντά μας καὶ ὑπηρετοῦμεν τυφλῶς τὰ πάθη καὶ τὴν κακίαν μας, ὡς καὶ ἐπὶ τῆς περιστάσεως ταύτης ὁ Πατριάρχης τῶν Ἱεροσολύμων. Ἀλλ' ἔστι Θεός ὁ ἀποδίδων ἑκάστῳ κατὰ τὰ ἔργα αὐτοῦ. Συγχωρήσατέ με ὅτι σᾶς γράφω γραικικά, διότι δὲν εὑρέθη παρ' ἐμοὶ ὁ γράφων με γαλλικά, καὶ ὅτι σᾶς ἐβάρυνα μὲ τὴν πολυλογίαν μου. Ἐλπίζω ὅτι ὡς καὶ ἄλλοτε μοι ἐφάνητε χρήσιμος καὶ εἰς ταύτην τὴν περίστασιν δὲν θέλετε μ' ἀρνηθεῖ τὴν συνδρομήν σας, καὶ μάλιστα μεταβαίνοντες ἤδη εἰς Πετρούπολιν· περαίνων διαβεβαιῶ ὑμῖν, Κύριε, περὶ τῆς πρὸς ὑμᾶς ὑπολήψεώς μου, μεθ' ἧς καὶ διατελῶ,

Πρὸς Θεὸν διάπυρος ἱκέτης

† Ὁ Ἀρχιεπίσκοπος Σιναίου Κύριλλος Α [?]

54. Cf. end of p. 3 of the *Draft*.

was *given* to Tischendorf is only "common opinion"; reality, it is implied, was different.

Cyril's refusal to state that the *Sinaiticus* had been, or was to be, donated to Russia may have ruined his last chance to be reinstated as Archbishop of Sinai. At the end of his letter, Cyril asked Tischendorf, who "had been useful... ⟨to him⟩ in the past," to intervene on his behalf in St. Petersburg. Cyril must have lost his touch. After the declaration he had just made on the *Sinaiticus*, Cyril was of no more use. Tischendorf and the Russians dropped him.[55] The *Sinaibibel* does not even mention the contact Tischendorf made with Cyril late in 1867, nor does it mention Cyril's letter of January 1868.[56]

Cyril was not quite candid when he hinted that the accusations of embezzlement leveled against him were nothing more than reproaches for having permitted Tischendorf to take the *Sinaiticus* away. Lists of objects which Cyril was said to have robbed from the monastery or its *Skeuophylakion* include liturgical vestments, staffs and silverware.[57] But in the *Sinaiticus* affair the prevaricating Cyril's hands remained pure, not only to the very end of his pontificate, but even after his deposition. It was reserved for his ⟨75⟩ successor Callistratus, whose integrity met with the approval of the Patriarch of Jerusalem, to sign away the *Sinaiticus* to Russia.[58]

---

55. The resourceful Ignat'ev (and the central government) strove for a double gain; after all, the dropping of Cyril could be turned to Russia's advantage precisely in the *Sinaiticus* affair. Letter to Antonin (date: May 8/20, 1868), ed. Dmitrievskij, *Graf Ignat'ev...* (as in note 6 *supra*), p. 27: "Perhaps by promising to recognize the new Archbishop of Sinai [i.e. Callistratus, Cyril's foe] ... one could get off cheaply, i.e. by means of medals alone" [and thus obtain the donation]; Letter to Antonin (date: June 18/30, 1868), ed. Dmitrievskij, *ibidem*: "Such an operation, i.e. paying for the Bible with our consent to Cyril's deposition and by offering monies that do not belong to us, was to St. Petersburg's... great liking."

56. The mention of "continuous correspondence" between Tischendorf and Cyril (*Sinaibibel*, p. 87) refers to the period shortly after 1862.

57. Cf. P. Neokles, Τὸ κανονικὸν δίκαιον τοῦ πατριαρχικοῦ θρόνου τῶν Ἱεροσολύμων ἐπὶ τῆς Ἀρχιεπισκοπῆς Σινᾶ... (Constantinople, 1868), p. 236, 256-257, 304.

58. Cf. a similar observation in W. Holtzelt, "Die kirchenrechtliche Stellung..." (as in note 26 *supra*), p. 460. Holtzelt rightly connected the *Sinaiticus* affair with the quarrel between Sinai and Jerusalem; his (quite correct) intuition was that problems connected with the *Sinaiticus'* discovery had not yet been solved (*ibidem*, p. 459).

V

A full and fair account of the *Sinaiticus* story is yet to be written. To be complete, this account would have to rely upon all the previously known documents: Cyril's correspondence with Tischendorf, Tischendorf's letters to his wife Angelika,[59] Porfirij Uspenskij's utterances concerning Tischendorf and the *Sinaiticus*, Ambassador Ignat'ev's correspondence with Archimandrite Antonin, and the texts published here. In addition, this account would have to draw upon materials that perhaps still slumber in divers archives relating to the affairs of the Near East. The struggle for the *Sinaiticus* was both lay and ecclesiastical; affected as it was by Eastern Mediterranean and Balkan politics in the fifties and sixties of the past century, it must have left some traces in diplomatic or governmental records.

To be fair, an account of the *Sinaiticus* story should stress the following points:

Very soon after his discovery of the *Sinaiticus* in February 4, 1859, Tischendorf, on his own initiative, started suggesting to the monks that they should donate the manuscript to the Russian ruler.[60] The "donation," he hinted, would be reciprocated by Imperial liberality; the lavish *baksheesh*[61] which he dispensed among the monks might whet their appetite for things to come.

The monks did not reject Tischendorf's suggestion outright. It may ⟨76⟩ be assumed that in pourparlers they promised, more or less explicit-

59. The absence of an edition of these letters is to be regretted. At present, one has to rely upon excerpts appearing in H. Behrend's book (as in note 9 *supra*), and even on a slide (cf. note 1 *supra*: we have no full text of that letter, written a mere eleven days after Tischendorf's second discovery of the manuscript).

60. On March 30, 1859, Tischendorf wrote to Angelika from Cairo that he hoped to be able to take the *Sinaiticus* with him, in order to present it to the [Russian] Imperial Majesties. On March 20 "both abbots" of Sinai had confirmed this hope of his. Cf. also Tischendorf to Angelika (date: Alexandria, May 1, 1859), on "new Archbishop" Cyril's "firm promise" that the manuscript would be offered, through Tischendorf, as a gift to the Emperor. Cf. H. Behrend (as in note 9 *supra*), p. 49. At first, a less subtle approach was tried: "By the way, from the very start and quite overtly, I stated my intention to make acquisitions with [the help of] the Emperor's name and gold": Tischendorf to Angelika (date: February 15, 1859), cf. H. Behrend, *ibidem*, p. 43.

61. Tischendorf to Angelika (date: February 15, 1859); "I behaved more like a Russian prince than a Saxon professor. I distributed gifts on every occasion. They often sollicited my favors and asked me to intercede for them in Petersburg." Cf. H. Behrend (as in note 9 *supra*), p. 43.

ly,[62] to follow that suggestion in exchange for favors, among them Russia's aid in having Cyril confirmed as Archbishop of Sinai. But even if there had been an unambiguous *entente* on this point, it was never set down in writing; there was no reference to it at all in Tischendorf's receipt of September 28, 1859.

Cyril's — and Russia's — chances for implementing such a postulated informal understanding were thwarted when Cyril's enemies learned, perhaps through Tischendorf's own boasting,[63] of the rumored donation and exploited this information to undermine Cyril's position with the Sublime Porte. In general, the removal of the *Sinaiticus* produced a great deal of excitement and dissatisfaction in high ecclesiastical circles in the Orthodox East.[64].

The rumors had to be silenced, the Turkish authorities pacified; Prince Lobanov's statement of November 13, 1859 did just this. Although Tischendorf betrayed no sign of having realized it, all his subsequent efforts to obtain an act of donation from Cyril were doomed to failure. Taking the terms of Tischendorf's receipt at their face value, Cyril may even have asked for the restitution of the *Sinaiticus* shortly after the *de luxe* edition of its text had appeared in St. Petersburg in

---

62. Quite explicitly, according to Tischendorf's letter quoted in note 60 *supra*; but cf. Cyril's cautious letter to Tischendorf (date: July 17/29, 1859), ed. Peradze, *Dokumenty...* (as in note 22 *supra*), p. 146: in answer to a request by Tischendorf for an interview on the subject of the *Sinaiticus*, Cyril agreed to have "une explication ouverte" concerning the manuscript. To my knowledge, this is as close as Cyril ever came to an admission in writing that he was negotiating the transfer of the *Sinaiticus*.

63. Cf. Germanos' complaints in the letter published p. 62 *supra*. The Patriarch of Jerusalem Cyril, the mortal foe of our Cyril, was told about Tischendorf's discovery on May 16, 1859, cf. C. Tischendorf, *Aus dem Heiligen Lande...* (1862), p. 233.

64. Cf. Porfirij Uspenskij, *Kniga...* (as in note 20 *supra*), VII, p. 233, entry for January 1860: The Patriarch of Constantinople is reluctant to authorize the loan of a manuscript to Porfirij, "knowing how dissatisfied the whole Greek clergy was with Tischendorf's tricks in the East;" cf. *ibidem*, p. 284-286, entry for November 28, 1860: The Patriarch of Alexandria started the discussion on topics that were exciting him at the moment with the *Sinaiticus*: "We think that the Bible taken by Tischendorf from Sinai... should be returned... to its [original] place." Cf. *ibidem*, p. 297-298, entry for December 22, 1860: To Porfirij's question "What is the news of the local Orthodox clergy?," the Secretary of the Russian Consultate in Alexandria answered: "They regret the loss of the Sinai Bible, taken away by Tischendorf, and they curse Couza."

1862.[65] We know for certain that on other occasions, he either maintained silence or refused to yield to Tischendorf's entreaties, hiding behind the authority of the "Community of Sinai," over which he in fact exercised a despotic rule.[66] Not that Cyril seriously desired the return of the manuscript to the monastery, but by deferring a regular act of donation he not only refuted the accusations ⟨77⟩ of his enemies but was in possession of a bargaining point for other purposes. He could use it for soliciting a counter-gift (though here his, or the monks', appetite seems to have been exaggerated),[67] for obtaining Russian support in staving off confiscation of Sinaitic property in Romania,[68] and, finally, for securing through Tischendorf Russian backing in his struggle to maintain his throne at Sinai.[69]

---

65. To be deduced from *Sinaibibel*, p. 87.

66. Cf. Cyril to Tischendorf (date: Cairo, December 20, 1860): "Concerning the affair of that manuscript... I shall have the pleasure of informing you in time of the decision that the community will have taken on this matter." Cyril to Tischendorf (date: Constantinople, [month not indicated] 18, 1867): "Concerning the manuscript of the Bible, I regret... not to be able to pass on to you the intentions of the Community, whose decisions, in accordance with our rule, have always dictated my behavior." Texts in PERADZE, *Dokumenty...* (as in note 22 *supra*), p. 146-147.

67. In his review of the 1862 edition of the *Sinaiticus*, E. von Muralt reflected opinions as to the manuscript's fate held at St. Petersburg about that time. Whether the *Sinaiticus* would remain in St. Petersburg or would be sent back to Sinai depended, "it is rumored," on whether or not the monks would get, of all things, a steamship. — Let us remember that work on the Suez Canal was proceeding rapidly in 1862-63. — Cf. *Bemerkungen über den* Codex Sinaiticus, *Deutsche Vierteljahrschrift für english-theologische Forschung und Kritik*, V (1865), 193-196 [these pages were printed on May 30, 1863].

68. Cf. *Sinaibibel*, p. 88.

69. "Cyril to Tischendorf (date: Constantinople [month not indicated] 18, 1867): you know that the Community could not have given a greater proof of its respectful attachment to the Imperial House of Russia than by offering to it the patronage over the publication of this treasure [i.e.the *Sinaiticus*]. As for the rest, since no decision has been taken, you will understand that, given the state of affairs that has befallen the community, this is not the opportune moment to submit to it an affair of this nature. Consequently, I shall not be able to give you any positive information on this matter, until the reestablishment of order permits us to take it up." French original in PERADZE, *Dokumenty...* (as in note 22 *supra*), p. 147. Thus Cyril was holding out as late as 1867. His conditions were simple: if Russian support in the struggle with Callistratus were forthcoming, one could seriously discuss the donation (for the donation is meant by "the rest").

The offering of the *Sinaiticus* to the Tsar in 1862 by Tischendorf was an illegal act. That it had no legal value was clear to Russian authorities,[70] to Tischendorf himself,[71] and, of course, to the monks. In 1865, the monks' dissatisfaction with Tischendorf was revealed to Brugsch. Brugsch, although a friend of Tischendorf, reported these complaints in print[72] and thus made the European reading public aware of them. Tischendorf's good name was in jeopardy, and for good reason. He knew that he would remain under suspicion as long as no regular act of donation was forthcoming from Sinai. In the spring of 1868, he traveled to St. Petersburg — having failed to budge Cyril, he decided to cajole the Russians into loosening their purse strings. While there, he may again have offered his services as bearer of Imperial gifts to Sinai, but whatever the nature of his intervention, it seems to have set the Russian official machinery in motion.[73] In the end, however, it was this machinery, run by professionals like Count Ignat'ev and the Archimandrite Antonin Kapustin,[74] and not Tischendorf's ⟨78⟩ amateurish attempts, that obtained (by the use of pressures that deserve closer scrutiny)[75] the regular act of donation from the Sinaites.

---

70. Hence the consigning of the *Sinaiticus* to the vaults of the Ministry of Foreign Affairs.

71. Cf. p. 67 *supra*.

72. H. Brugsch, *Wanderung nach den Türkis-Minen und der Sinai-Halbinsel* (2nd ed., 1868; the trip took place in April-May, 1865), p. 47-48: The δικαῖος of the monastery was dissatisfied, for the *Sinaiticus* had not yet been returned, although the Russian Ambassador in Constantinople had guaranteed its restitution. Brugsch was sure that Tischendorf had concluded a confidential agreement with the head of the monastery, an agreement by which the *Sinaiticus* "did have a legal owner" by 1865. This was unclear language.

73. Cf. note 51 *supra*.

74. On this scholar, director of the Russian Ecclesiastical Mission in Jerusalem, and visitor to Sinai, cf. Archimandrite Kiprian (Kern), *O. Antonin Kapustin...* (Belgrade, 1934). On Antonin's mediation in the *Sinaiticus* affair, cf. *ibidem*, p. 138 and Dmitrievskij, *Graf Ignat'ev...* (as in note 6 *supra*), p. 27-29.

75. In 1867, Ignat'ev had Sinai's holdings in Russia sequestered pending clarification of Cyril's status. At that time, it seemed to have been a move on Cyril's behalf. This sequestration was still in force by June 18/30, 1868, when Ignat'ev told Antonin about a report that the Sinaites were willing to "donate the Bible without compensation, provided that Callistratus would be recognized and the Monastery given permission to draw on [its] monies sequestered by us..." The sequestration of Sinaitic property was lifted some time between June 18/30, 1868-1869 and June 10/22, 1870. "I like to push people against the wall," wrote

Callistratus, the Archbishop from whom the donation was finally obtained, continued to write Tischendorf sweet-sounding letters until the latter's death in 1874,[76] for the Archbishop always hoped for Tischendorf's assistance. But these letters are no proof that Tischendorf had been a perfect gentleman, nor even that Callistratus thought he had. Rightly or wrongly his feelings were hostile, for Callistratus, too, felt that the monks had been cheated.[77]

VI

It is easier to assess the part played by Tischendorf the scholar in the *Sinaiticus* affair: All one has to do is compare his instant realization of the manuscript's value to the long and irrelevant description of the *Sinaiticus* produced by Porfirij Uspenskij,[78] who saw it in 1845 and 1850 and who, on the latter date, was able to study it on Sinai at his leisure.[79] Uspenskij's subsequent attacks, occasioned by the alleged heretical traits in the *Sinaiticus*, were merely sour grapes. Until Tischendorf's announcement of 1860, the learned but confused Archimandrite had seen nothing amiss in that manuscript. He had been convinced that it was of

---

Ignat'ev on March 14/26, 1869, otherwise you cannot squeeze anything out of the obstinate." This was a footnote to Ignat'ev's information that he was withholding the medals and payment promised for the anticipated donation of the *Sinaiticus*. Cf. DMITRIEVSKIJ, *Graf Ignat'ev*... (as in note 6 *supra*, p. 23, 25-28.

76. The letter of July 15, 1869, stating that the *Sinaiticus* had been donated (ἐδωρήθη), but complaining that the medals had not yet arrived. Cf. GREGORY, *Prolegomena*... (as in note 6 *supra*), p. 352-53; G. EBERS, *Durch Gosen zum Sinai*... (2nd ed., 1881), p. 588-590; partial German text in *Sinaibibel*, p. 91-92. A letter of March 12/24, 1874 in PERADZE, *Dokumenty*... (as in note 22 *supra*), p. 148.

77. Cf. Ebers (as in the preceding note), p. 590, referring to Gardthausen and "other recent travellers": they heard Callistratus' "bitter complaints" against the "purloining" of the *Sinaiticus*.

78. *Pervoe putešestvie v Sinajskij monastyr' v 1845 godu* (1856), p. 225-238. Porfirij reports on the letter of Barnabas without being aware of the capital importance of the find.

79. Cf. *Kniga*... (as in note 20 *supra*), VIII, p. 56: "for a long time;" P. V. BEZOBRAZOV, *Materialy*... (as in note 20 *supra*), II, p. 881: "forty days;" this can hardly be true, since it appears from PORFIRIJ's *Vtoroe putešestvie*... (as in note 20 *supra*), p. 77, 162 ff., 193, that in 1850 he spent a total of 29 days on Sinai, out of which a maximum of four were devoted to the study of the *Sinaiticus* (which Porfirij specifically mentioned on p. 193).

importance,[80] but he never realized how great this importance was.

⟨79⟩ It is less easy to evaluate the part played by Tischendorf the man in the *Sinaiticus* affair. He was enough of a scholar never to say an outright falsehood in relating the story of the years 1844-1869,[81] but he was masterfully vague when he narrated some of the points crucial to our judgment of the propriety of his acts. In the quarrel with Porfirij Uspenskij over the priority of the manuscript's discovery, Tischendorf was hardly fair. In 1859/60, poor Uspenskij could — and did — quite sincerely believe that he had been the first to discover and describe the *Sinaiticus*, for he had seen it in 1845. He cannot he held responsible because Tischendorf, who had seen parts of the manuscript in 1844, kept their origin a secret for all practical purposes until 1860.[82]

---

80. Cf. P. V. Bezobrazov, *Materialy*... (as in note 20 *supra*), II, p. 681-684: reporting to Count A. P. Tolstoj on March 1, 1858, Uspenskij expressed a negative opinion on Tischendorf's intended trip to the Near East (the trip that led to the *Sinaiticus*' discovery). Instead, Porfirij suggested that three Russians should be sent on a mission, and that they should obtain permission from the Eastern Patriarchs to borrow (not without compensation) certain [important] manuscripts for a time, *e.g.* "the Sinai Septuagint of the fifth century," in other words, the *Sinaiticus*.

81. Our eyebrows tend to rise on only one occasion: Having described a fifteenth-century manuscript (the *Tomos* against Barlaam) which he had acquired on his trip of 1844, Tischendorf copied its curse formula: "the present book belongs... to Mount Sinai. ... whoever removes it from the... monastery, may be afflicted with the curse of the Holy Fathers and of the Burning Bush." Tischendorf added in brackets, for no apparent reason, "I found these leaves when I was already far away from Sinai." — The reliability of two important points in Tischendorf's own story had been impugned by Beneševič, *Les manuscrits grecs*... (as in note 23 *supra*), p. 34-39 and 68-72. The first point deals with the authenticity of the famous basket in which the first portion of the *Sinaiticus* was presumably found in 1844, and with the question of whether that portion was about to be burned; the second, perhaps more interesting, point is concerned with the motivation of Tischendorf's third trip to Sinai in 1859. Was he driven there by an unclear impulse, a "pressentiment dont je ne savais me rendre compte," cf. *Mémoire sur la découverte*... (as in note 2 *supra*), p. 4, or had he gotten wind, as early as the summer of 1857, of the presence of the manuscript's other parts still on Sinai through the publications of Porfirij Uspenskij (1856; cf. note 78 *supra*) and the interview with A. S. Norov (cf. note 39 *supra*)? The documents I have seen clear up neither of these points.

82. Strictly speaking, until April of 1859, cf. end of note 4 *supra*. For all that, the fact of Tischendorf's priority in having seen a sizeable portion of the manuscript is incontestable. Nonetheless, a recent appraisal of Porfirij Uspenskij states that "the honor of the discovery" of the *Sinaiticus* belongs to the Russian

To see flaws in Tischendorf's behavior is not to impugn the legality of the *Sinaiticus*'s ultimate transfer to the British Museum. This legality is unquestioned.[83] Scholars may understandably prefer to see this treasure exhibited in a great Western repository of learning rather than buried in the wilderness of a far country, but this is a poor reason for exculpating Tischendorf. Moreover, to find his actions correct from 1859 onward because ten years later, and after the deposition of the Archbishop with whom Tischendorf had been dealing, another Archbishop of Sinai made a gift of the manuscript to Russia, and made it as a result of pressures with which Tischendorf himself had very little to do, is a procedure the logic of which escapes my understanding.

⟨80⟩ The professionals who engineered the legal transfer of the *Sinaiticus* to Russian hands in 1869 were perfectly aware of the nature of their enterprise. In 1868, Ignat'ev wanted to put "an end to the story of the Sinai Bible stolen by us."[84] Of course one could do so by giving Russia's consent to Cyril's deposition and by "offering ⟨Sinai's own⟩ monies that do not belong to us"; but Ignat'ev preferred a more "decorous" course — that of giving the monks any sum, however modest, that would "belong to us, so that it would be possible to say that we had bought the Bible rather than purloined it."[85] As for Archimandrite Antonin, he later spoke of the "long and fairly mixed-up procedure by which we acquired the famous Sinai manuscript." This, he argued, encumbered the Russians with a special obligation to compile a catalogue of Sinai manuscripts,[86] and thus, we might add, to perform an act of expiation.

---

scholar. Cf. M. A. Korostovcev and S. I. Hodžaš, *Vostokovednaja dejatel' nost' Porfirija Uspenskogo, Bližnij i Srednij Vostok, Sbornik statej* (1962), p. 130.

83. Ignat'ev saw to it that the donation of November 18, 1869 was made in all due form. All that the authors of the British Museum pamphlets needed to do to make their point was to quote the letter of June 13, 1878 in which the Russian Ministry of Foreign Affairs replied to C. R. Gregory's inquiries concerning the *Sinaiticus*, cf. Gregory, *Prolegomena*... as in note 6 *supra*, p. 351; cf. also other works quoted in that note. Attempts to strengthen the case of legality by asserting — incidentally erroneously — that Tischendorf was beloved and revered by the Sinaites *after* 1859, were superfluous.

84. Ignat'ev to Antonin (date: May 8/20, 1868), ed. Dmitrievskij, *Graf Ignat'ev*... (as in note 6 *supra*), p. 26.

85. Ignat'ev to Antonin (date: June 18/30, 1868), ed. *ibidem*, p. 27-28.

86. *Trudy Kievskoj Duhovnoj Akademii* (1873), vol. I, p. 389. Cf. excerpts in V. N. Beneševič, *Opisanie grečeskih rukopisej mon. Sv. Ekateriny*..., I (1911), p. XVII, n. 1 and in Idem, *Les manuscrits grecs*... (as in note 23 *supra*), p. 82.

In this "long and fairly mixed-up procedure," Tischendorf appears as a brilliant, erudite, quick-minded, devoted, resourceful person, but also as a vain, cantankerous, and, on occasion, unfair man.[87] For years, he was caught in the trap which he had helped to spring by his acts of 1859 and 1862; he was released from it in 1869 by hands more experienced than his own and, incidentally, more interested in securing a treasure for Russia than in saving a German professor's honor. By 1869, Tischendorf was an honorable man. But between 1859 and that date, he can be called honorable only retroactively. This picture of events I find more plausible, and even more worthy of Tischendorf, than the prevailing *image d'Epinal*.

87. Cf. on this point S. P. Tregelles' remark of 1860, published in T. H. HORNE, *An Introduction...* (as in note 17 *supra*), p. 753-54: "That he [Tischendorf] always treats other writers fairly, or shows sufficient candour or exactitude in estimating what they have done or written, I shall hardly be expected to admit." Cf. also E. TISSERANT, "Lettres de Constantin von Tischendorf à Carlo Vercellone," *Studi e Testi*, 126 (1946), p. 479-498, esp. p. 498; in these letters Tischendorf appears "passablement orgueilleux et d'un caractère pas trop facile."

Pl. 4 — Sinaï, Couv. Ste-Catherine, Reçu autographe de Constantin Tischendorf, f. 1r. (Voir p. 55-80).

Pl. 5 — Sinaï, Couv. Ste-Catherine, lettre de Germanos du 28.10.1859, p. 2. (Voir p. 55-80).

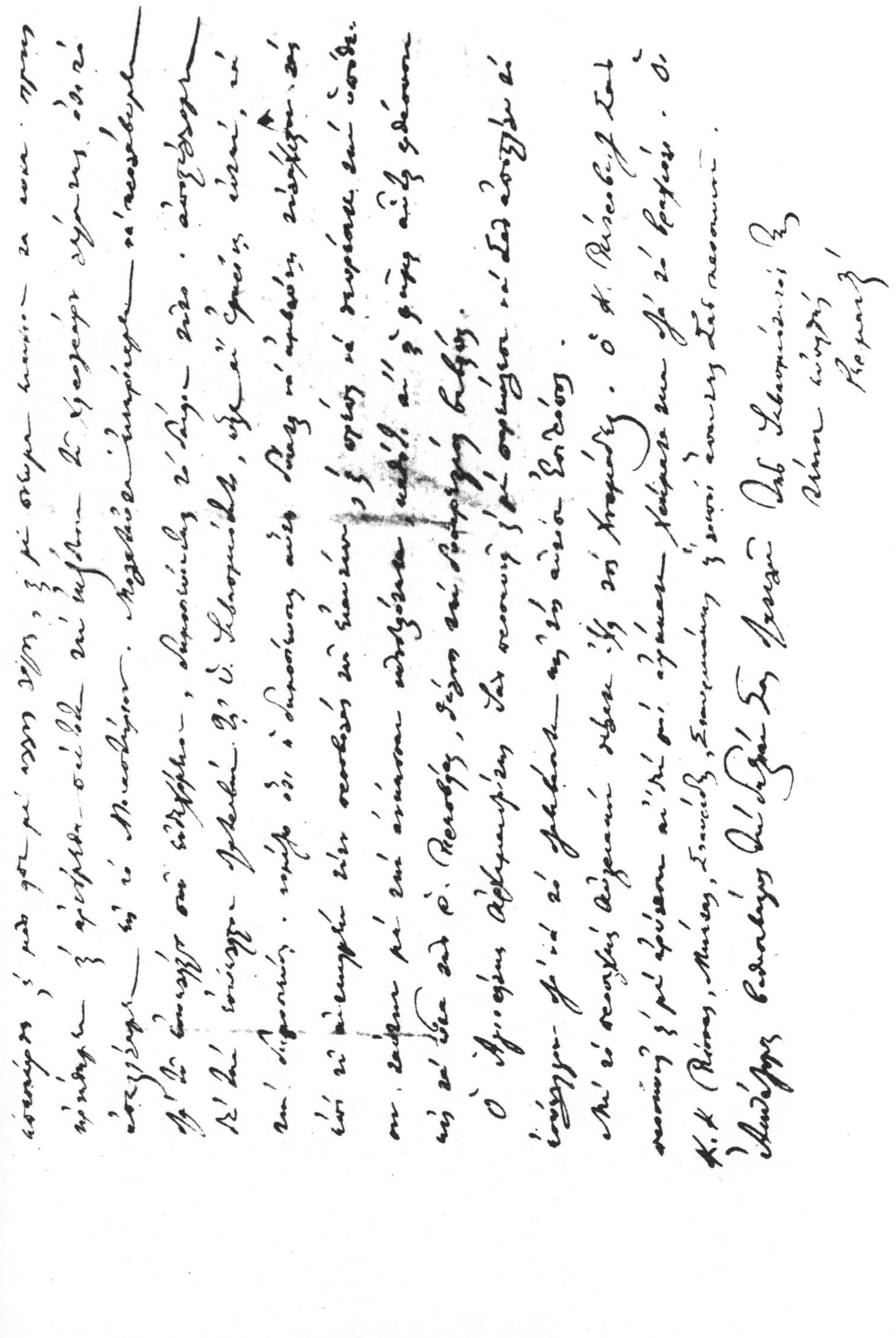

PL. 6 — Sinaï, Couv. Ste-Catherine, lettre de Germanos du 28.10.1859, p. 3. (Voir p. 55-80).

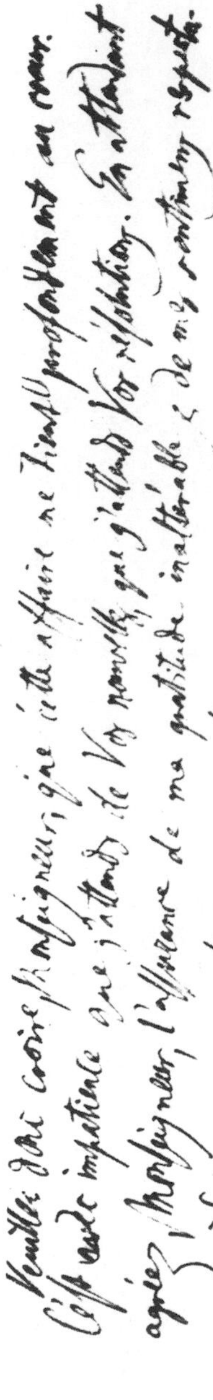

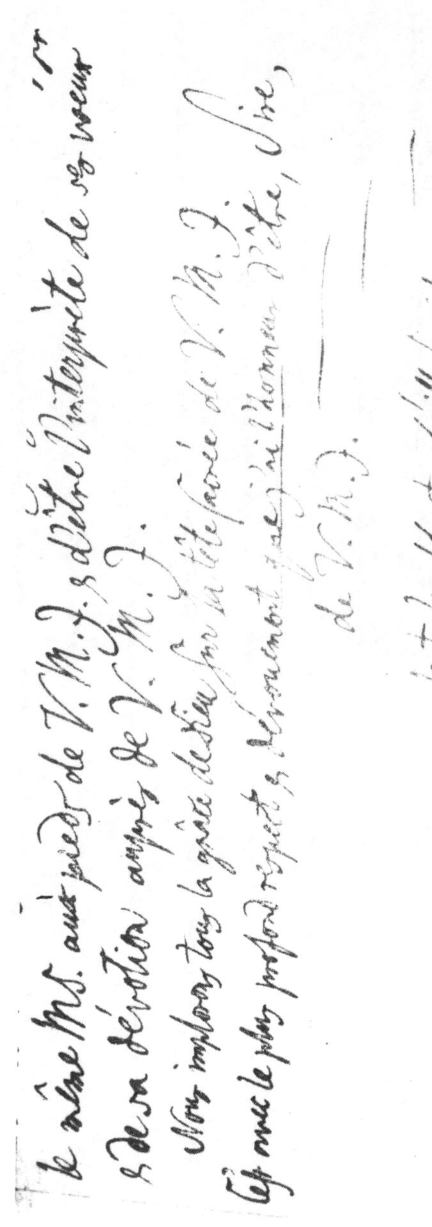

PL. 7 — *a*) Sinaï, Couv. Ste-Catherine,
Lettre de Constantin Tischendorf à Cyrille, archevêque du Sinaï, du 21.1.1864, p. 4;
b) *Ibidem*, Brouillon rédigé par Constantin Tischendorf pour Cyrille, archevêque du Sinaï.
(Voir p. 55-80).

PL. 8 — *a*) Sinaï, Couv. Ste-Catherine, Brouillon de Cyrille, archevêque du Sinaï, p. 2; *b*) *Ibidem*, Lettre de Cyrille aux moines de Djuvania, du 25.11.1895, p. 3. (Voir p. 55-80).

XVI

Obshchestvenno-politicheskaia mysl' drevnei Rusi

Obshchestvenno-politicheskaia mysl' drevnei Rusi (XI-XIV VV.) [Social and Political Thought of Ancient Russia (Eleventh to Fourteenth Century)]. By *I. U. Budovnits* (Moscow: Publishing House of the Academy of Sciences of the USSR. 1960. Pp. 486).

In 1947 the author published his ***Russkaja Publicistika*** XVI *v*. The present book covers the period from the eleventh to the fourteenth century. Several of its thirteen essays have appeared previously in various Soviet learned journals.

Few works dating from the eleventh to the fourteenth century, original or translated, deal expressly with sociopolitical subjects, and Mr. Budovnits discusses only a few of them. Consequently, most of his other texts are homiletic, literary, hagiographic, historical, and even folkloristic. The book's individual chapters center upon a text or event or deal with larger topics.

The author's general propositions are as follows: contrary to assertions by bourgeois historians, documents of sociopolitical thought in Rus' did exist between the eleventh and the fourteenth century, "long before" the investiture struggle in the West. These documents were autochthonous, original and often anti-Byzantine; deeply patriotic; and preoccupied with the notion of Russia's unity and with the establishment of centralized rule.

For the period prior to the Tartar invasion, these propositions are difficult to prove. Consequently, the first part of the book contains some shibboleths, contradictions, and plain errors.

For the period after 1240, Budovnits' main propositions do little or no harm to his narrative, for after that date and prior to the fifteenth century, the influx of translated literature came to a virtual stop. Thus, the second part of the book is a lively account of a fascinating ideological contest and contains many valuable observations.

Budovnits does not quote foreign authors, except for D. I. Čiževskij, castigated for a multitude of sins, including the one of not quoting Soviet scholars. Yet, Werner Philipp and Francis Dvornik deserve to be mentioned, and E. Honigmann, D. Obolensky, and T. Fijałek should have been used. The long years of Budovnits' journalistic and editorial career stood him in good stead: the book reads well and is written with gusto.

XVII

Sviatoslav in Byzantine and Slavic Miniatures

In the *Slavic Review* of September 1965 (XXIV, No. 3, viii) the editor invited the readers of Professor Terras' judicious article on "Leo Diaconus and the Ethnology of Kievan *Rus*"' (in the same issue) to help in a quest for an early picture of Grand Duke Sviatoslav's meeting with the Byzantine emperor John Tzimiskes. May I respond to the invitation and even go somewhat beyond its original tenor? In so doing, I hope not only to confirm what we have known all along — namely, that the Russo-Byzantine war of 967-72 left a considerable imprint on Byzantine and Slavic historiography — but also to remind readers that this war, its leader Sviatoslav, and the Varangians had a strong fascination for Byzantine and Slavic manuscript illuminators alike. Pictorial evidence will be offered here mostly for fun, but some of it has a bearing, however tenuous, upon Professor Terras' topic. I must leave to other readers the task of identifying nineteenth-century material; for my part, I shall set the year 1500 as my upper chronological boundary.

In his article Professor Terras quoted — or almost quoted — the quarry that yields a great deal of pictorial material on Grand Duke Sviatoslav. The quarry is the chronicle of Skylitzes, more precisely, the Madrid manuscript of this late eleventh-century Byzantine author.[1] With its 574 miniatures of secular content, this manuscript (*Matritentis Graecus Vitr.* 26-2) is a *unicum*, for no other extant Byzantine chronicle in Greek contains a sizable number of illuminations. Since, next to Leo Diaconus, Skylitzes is our most detailed source on the Russo-Byzantine war of 967-72 and on Sviatoslav's exploits, quite a large number of

1. See Sebastian Cirac Estopañan, ed., *Skylitzes Matritentis*, Vol. I: *Reproducciones y miniaturas* (Barcelona and Madrid, 1965). For discussion of the "Russian" miniatures in the Madrid manuscript (including some representing Sviatoslav), see N. P. Kondakov, "Grecheskie izobrazheniia pervykh russkikh kniazei," in *Sbornik v pamiat' sviatogo ravno-apostol'nogo kniazia Vladimira*, I (Petrograd, 1917), 10-20 (Vol. CXXXVII of the publications of the *Imperatorskoe Obshchestvo Liubitelei Drevnei Pis'mennosti*).

miniatures of the Madrid manuscript, twenty-one in all, illustrate the vicissitudes of this war, and five of them portray Sviatoslav. Once (Figure 1) we see the Grand Duke, seated on a throne, receiving an embassy sent to him by the Byzantine Emperor, who is challenging him to single combat (see *Georgius Cedrenus Ioannis Scylitzae ope ab I. Bekkero suppletus et emendatus* [Bonn, 1839], II, 408, 18-21). The back of Sviatoslav's throne ends in a carved ornament which looks like the head of a horse. This zoomorphic detail, which to my recollection does not occur in a similar context elsewhere in the manuscript, should merely be pointed out here, for neither the Normanists nor the anti-Normanists should be able to deduce much from it.

On another occasion (Figure 2) the miniaturist represents Sviatoslav ⟨710⟩ narrowly escaping disaster. A Byzantinized Arab warrior has just dealt the Duke a heavy blow on the head, and the stunned ruler is about to slide down from his mount; on the right, the Russes hasten to his rescue on what look like wooden horses, all this *pace* Leo Diaconus, who described the *Rhōs* invaders primarily as foot soldiers (see Skylitzes-Cedrenus, *Hist.*, II, 410, 11-19 Bonn).

The third miniature (Figure 3) is the answer to the editor's query: it depicts the meeting between John Tzimiskes and Sviatoslav. Readers reared upon Leo Diaconus' story of that meeting — and on illustrations like the one reproduced in the issue of September 1965 — will be greatly disappointed by the version reproduced here. In the Skylitzes miniature we miss the glitter of the Emperor's armor, we see no steed to carry him to the bank of the Danube — in fact, there is no Danube at all — nor do we see the modestly but cleanly clad noble barbarian, with a single earring, big moustache, shaven chin, and a big lock of hair. Instead, two seated personages, labeled "Emperor John Tzimiskes" and "Sfendosthlabos" respectively, are engaged in conversation. Within the framework of Byzantine one-upmanship, it is remarkable that Sviatoslav should be treated almost as an equal to the Emperor; only two traits seem to lend superiority to the latter: a scepter and a headgear which in the idiom of the miniaturist of this part of Skylitzes' manuscript represents an imperial crown. As for Sviatoslav, he dons a nondescript headcover, and sports a non-imperial looking goatee.

Our miniature lacks the colorful details of Leo Diaconus' narrative for the simple reason that it follows Skylitzes' shorter text, which merely states: "When peace had been ratified, Sviatoslav requested to see the Emperor and to converse with him. The Emperor granted this wish, and Sviatoslav came. They got together, talked on topics of their choice, and parted from each other" (Skylitzes-Cedrenus, *Hist.*, 412, 8-11 Bonn). However, our miniature does contain one curious element absent from

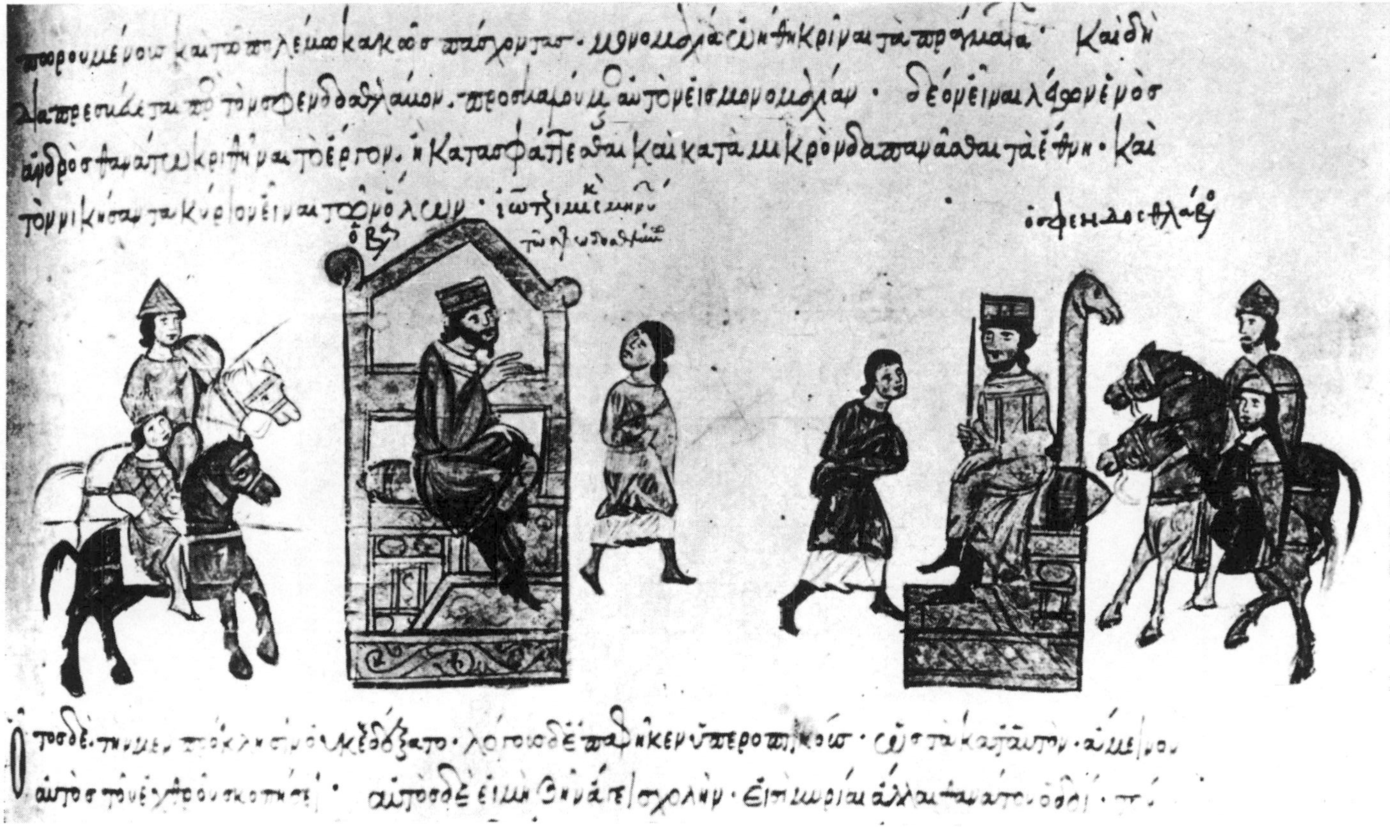

Figure 1: *Matr. Gr. Vitr.* 26-2, fol. 171r: John Tzimiskes sends an embassy to Sviatoslav

Figure 2: *Matr. Gr. Vitr.* 26-2. fol. 171v:
Sviatoslav, hurt, falls off his horse

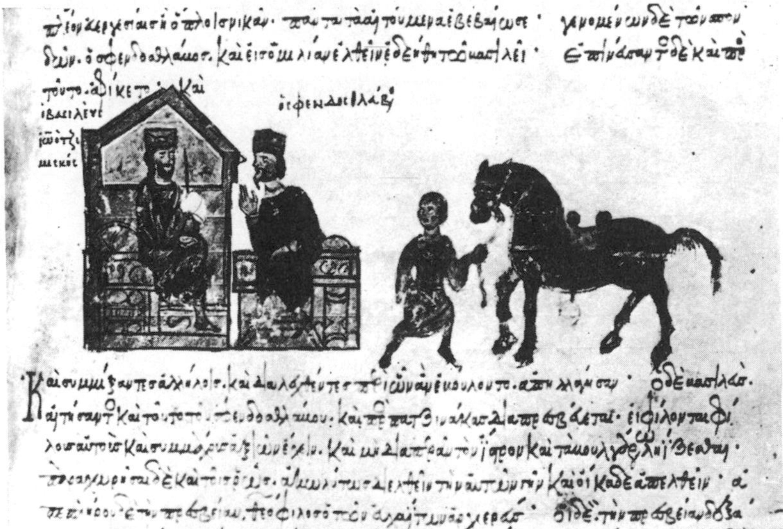

Figure 3: *Matr. Gr. Vitr.* 26-2, fol. 172v:
Interview between John Tzimiskes and Sviatoslav

Figure 4: Torcello, last Judgment mosaic, detail: The Damned

Figure 5: *Matr. Gr. Vitr.* 26-2, fol. 208^{r}: Varangians

Figure 6: *Vat. Slav.* II. fol. 178^{v}: Sviatoslav leads a foray

Figure 7: Radziwiłł Chronicle (Bibl. Akad. Nauk SSSR, 34.5.30), fol. 39ra: Exchange of embassies between John Tzimiskes and Sviatoslav

both Leo's and Skylitzes' passages: a groom of Sviatoslav is holding a fully saddled horse by the bridle. This may be a mere cliché, taken over from scenes depicting embassies where we usually see the ambassador's horse, and are thus reminded that the embassy has come from a faraway place. Let us speculate, however, that the saddled horse held in readiness at a meeting of the recent enemies may convey a different message as well. Byzantine chroniclers, including Skylitzes, tell in some detail how in 813 a trap was set for the Bulgarian Khan Krum at the very walls of Constantinople, how Krum was to be murdered during an interview with the Byzantine emperor Leo V or his high-ranking representatives, and how the alert Bulgarian escaped the snare — he had a horse kept in readiness during the interview; at the first sign of suspicious behavior on the part of the Byzantines, he mounted it and galloped away. In the miniature representing Sviatoslav's interview with John Tzimiskes, the ruler of the Russes may be credited with a similar precautionary measure.

We might declare the five[2] Sviatoslav miniatures of the Madrid manu⟨711⟩script moderately entertaining, and leave it at that. However, readers of Professor Terras' article are entitled to know how useful these miniatures are for reconstructing the world of the tenth century and elucidating the ethnology of Kievan *Rus'*. Here we have a new disappointment in store for them. Skylitzes wrote in Constantinople toward the end of the eleventh century, some one hundred and twenty years after the meeting between Sviatoslav and Tzimiskes. The Madrid manuscript of Skylitzes dates from the second half of the twelfth century, if not later. As for the miniatures, some of them, representing events of the ninth and tenth centuries, may go back to models earlier than the time of Skylitzes himself; but other miniatures depicting the same period may be inventions of twelfth-century illuminators. To complicate things further, I believe the Madrid manuscript to have been produced in Sicily, a meeting ground for Western — including Norman, if you will — Byzantine, and Islamic cultural strands, but an island far removed from Bulgaria, the Ukrainian steppe, and the Pechenegs. In sum, the five miniatures of the Madrid Skylitzes tell us nothing about Sviatoslav's actual appearance, let alone the ethnology of Kievan *Rus'*.

To find a Byzantinizing pictorial counterpart to Leo Diaconus' description of Sviatoslav's hairdress, moustache, and earring, we must

2. I have adduced only three out of five miniatures here, since I do not have good reproductions of fol. 170^r (Sviatoslav holding a council) and fol 173^v (Sviatoslav and his retinue killed by Pechenegs) at my disposal.

leave Skylitzes for a moment and turn to the famous twelfth-century mosaic of the Last Judgement in the Cathedral at Torcello near Venice. In the mosaic's right lower corner, there is a panel containing a dozen or so heads of the Damned (Figure 4). All of these heads have clean- shaven chins, several of them sport impressive moustaches, and several again show locks of hair separate from the rest of their coiffure. Finally, all of them have earrings hanging from one of their ears. We may only surmise the identity of these reprobates roasting in eternal fire. In my opinion, they are barbarian nomads, punished for the sin of having at some time waged war upon the God-protected Byzantine Empire. If this identification is granted, then the similarities between the Damned of the Torcello Judgement and Leo Diaconus' Sviatoslav lend further weight to Professor Terras' conclusion, which I have shared for some time, that by the late tenth century the Kievan ruling class, granted the Scandinavian descent of many of its members, had absorbed characteristics of the nomadic neighbors claiming the steppe for themselves.

We must return to one more miniature in the Madrid Skylitzes for a further corroboration of the view that Sviatoslav's — and presumably his retinue's — coiffure had been influenced by nomadic, rather than Norse, fashions. This miniature represents a group of Varangians, who since about the year 1000 formed the core of the Imperial Guard at Constantinople (Figure 5). We distinguish two scenes: in the first, a woman is killing a Varangian who made an attempt on her virtue; in the second, the Varangian's comrades are rewarding the woman with her justly punished assailant's earthly possessions (see Skylitzes-Cedrenus, *Hist.*, II, 508, 19-509, 4 Bonn). Our chief interest goes to a point extraneous to the lofty moral of the story: the Varangians shown on the miniature are no conventional mercenaries; their unique faces, for which there is no parallel elsewhere in the manuscript, must have been actually seen by the miniatur⟨712⟩ist or the painter of his model; and these faces are adorned with bushy, enormous moustaches, beards, and hair. In a word, Leo Diaconus' Sviatoslav did not look like the Varangians of the Skylitzes manuscript.

The anti-Normanists seem to have some point here, but to make it stick, they must be willing to concede — as often they are not — that in its early stages the Varangian Imperial Guard consisted mostly of Norsemen; as for us we should be willing to grant them that point only if we were sure that the Skylitzes miniature reflects the early "Norse" history of the Varangian mercenary body. This, of course, we do not know. The event depicted in the miniature occurred in 1034, at which time the Varangian Guard did consist mostly of Norsemen, sometimes alternating in the service of the rulers of Kiev and Constantinople. But we cannot be sure whether the twelfth-century miniaturist was copying portraits of early eleventh- rather than late eleventh-century Varangians, or even of "Varangians" of a still later date — a motley of various nationalities, including a strong contingent of Englishmen seeking employ in faraway Constantinople ever since some of them had been displaced after the débâcle of 1066.[3]

Until now we have been looking at the Russes, Sviatoslav, the Varangians, and nomadic barbarians through the eyes of Byzantine artists. In addition, we know two illuminated Slavic manuscripts with portraits of Sviatoslav and his Russes. The first is the Bulgarian translation of a twelfth-century Byzantine chronicle by Constantine Manasses. The original was made under the high patronage of the Bulgarian tsar John Alexander in the 1340s; we still possess a de luxe parchment copy of this work, made in the fourteenth century, now in the Vatican (*Vaticanus Slav*. II).[4] Since the high patron of the translation had an understandable interest in his own country's past, the Vatican manuscript displays two full-page miniatures (folios 178^r, 178^v) devoted to the "invasion of the Russes in Bulgaria" (*ruskyi plěn[ʻ] eže na Blʻgary*). Sviatoslav appears three times on these folios, either brandishing a sword, piercing a prostrated enemy with a lance, or just leading a Russian foray.

The second Slavic manuscript is a profusely, if indifferently, illuminated Rus' work going under the name of Radziwiłł or Königsberg Chronicle and executed toward the very end of the fifteenth century.[5] In its initial portion the Königsberg text follows the version of the Kievan Primary Chronicle, and thus devotes some space to Sviatoslav's campaigns in Bulgaria. Since the Chronicle version of events is more favorable to the Grand Duke than that of the Byzantines, the five miniatures which ⟨713⟩ the Königsberg Chronicle devotes to Sviatoslav (folios 38^r, 38va, 38vb, 39ra, 39rb) show wily Greeks sending embassies in

3. See V. G. Vasil'evskii, "Variago-russkaia i variago- angliiskaia druzhina v Konstantinople XI i XII vekov," in *Trudy*, I (St. Petersburg, 1908), 176-377; R. M. Dawkins, "The Later History of the Varangian Guard: Some Notes," *The Journal of Roman Studies*, XXXVI (1946), 39-46.

4. See I. Duichev, ed., *Miniatiurite na Manasievata Letopis* (Sofia, 1962); and Duichev, ed., *Letopista na Konstantin Manasi* (Sofia, 1963).

5. *Radzivilovskaia ili Kenigsbergskaia Letopis'*, Vol. I: *Fotomekhanicheskoe vosproizvedenie rukopisi* (St. Petersburg, 1902; Vol. CXVIII of the publications of the *Imperatorskoe Obshchestvo Liubitelei Drevnei Pis'mennosti*). Latest study is O.I. Podobedova, *Miniatiury russkikh istoricheskikh rukopisei: K istorii russkogo litsevogo letopisaniia* (Moscow, 1965), pp. 49-101.

order to mollify the Duke with gold and precious fabrics (which he spurns) or weapons (which he eagerly accepts). Even when Sviatoslav, locked up in Dristra, is forced to sue for peace, the corresponding miniature shows a Greek embassy bearing gifts, with Emperor Tzimiskes and Sviatoslav looking on.

The pictorial models of the Bulgarian Manasses chronicle do not go beyond the twelfth century. The Königsberg Chronicle may have preserved some traditions of the — otherwise hypothetical — Kievan illumination, but this can hardly be proven for the Sviatoslav cycle, and thus nothing can be gleaned from the Slavic miniatures for Professor Terras' immediate purpose. A cultural historian, however, should be excused for adducing two of these Slavic miniatures here. The one from the Bulgarian Manasses shows Sviatoslav leading the Russes in a foraging raid, Balkan style, the prize of which is summarily indicated by a few sheep and cattle (Figure 6). The miniature from the Königsberg Chronicle represents Emperor John Tzimiskes and Sviatoslav exchanging embassies (Figure 7); notice the un-Byzantine swords.

The other seven Slavic miniatures shall be left to the curiosity of *Slavic Review* readers, and of the editor. After all, we want to keep his hobby alive.

XVIII

On Some Sources of Prince Svjatoslav's *Izbornik* of the Year 1076

When, more than ten years ago, I was investigating the fate of Agapetus' *Hortatory Chapters* in Kievan and Muscovite political literature, Professor Čiževsky followed my work with friendly interest. It is, therefore, a special pleasure to return to Agapetus in this offering and to connect this Byzantine author with a Kievan text which Professor Čiževsky has treated with great fondness and sensitivity.

In the past decade scholars have often discussed the degree to which the literature and thought of the Kievan period were autochthonous and original. Like war, which is too serious a business to be left to generals, this problem is too delicate — at least in its preliminary stages — to be entrusted entirely to historians of Old Russian Literature. Byzantinists may put the problem of originality in a different perspective, provided they abstain from suspecting a Byzantine crib on the desk of every Kievan writer. For one thing, their vantage point lies outside the East Slavic area; for another, most of them are less involved in matters of ancestral pride, since their empire is no more.

I shall put these general statements to a test while discussing several passages of Prince Svjatoslav's *Izbornik* of the year 1076. This parchment manuscript, now in the Saltykov-Ščedrin Library of Leningrad (= *Èrmit.* 20), is appropriately called *Izbornik*, for it is a Miscellany comprising didactic, gnomic, spiritual, and moralistic pieces, and, less appropriately, of Svjatoslav, for it was copied during the rule of Svjatoslav, the Grand Prince of Kiev.[1] Thus the *Izbornik* is the third oldest dat-

1. *The manuscript*: E. È. Granstrem, *Opisanie russkix i slavjanskix pergamennyx rukopisej...* (Leningrad, 1953), p. 16; L. V. Čerepnin, *Russkaja paleografija* (1956), pp. 132-133. *Editions*: S. Šimanovskij, *K istorii drevnerusskix govorov* (Warsaw, 1887), the only edition available to me; second revised edition (Warsaw, 1894). *Bibliographies*: N. Nikol'skij, *Materialy dlja povremennogo spiska russkix pisatelej i ix sočinenij (X-XI vv.)* (1906), pp. 202-207; 484-486; N. N. Durnovo, *Vvedenie v istoriju russkogo jazyka*, I (1927) [= Spisy filosofické fakulty Masarykovy University v Brně, 20], p. 33; D. Tschižewskij, *Zwei*

ed manuscript ⟨724⟩ that has come down to us from the East Slavic area. It is only the second oldest dated Miscellany written in Kiev, but it is the more interesting of the two. The oldest one, Svjatoslav's *Izbornik* of the year 1073, presents no problem of originality: we know at least two Greek miscellaneous manuscripts[2] whose contents correspond to the *Izbornik* of 1073 almost word by word. In the case of *Izbornik* of 1076, however, the situation is much more complicated, since no Greek models have been hitherto adduced for a sizeable portion of this collection. It is thus not astonishing that this portion should have been considered original; it is, however, regrettable that this judgement was made without sufficient investigation. The *Izbornik* of 1076 was used for evaluating the original literary style of the Kievan period and, above all, for describing the autochthonous elements in Kievan social and political thought. The *Nakazanije bogatymъ*, or *Admonition to the Rich*, is one of the *Izbornik*'s chapters (fols. 24ᵛ-28)[3] upon which scholars drew for the latter purpose.

This chapter contains a simile not devoid of literary merit: отъвраштѧи сѧ ласкавьць льстьныих словесъ ꙗко и врановъ, искалаꙗть

russisch-kirchenslavische Texte [= Heidelberger slavische Texte, 4] (1958), pp. 9-19, esp. p. 11; L. Je. Maxnovec', *Ukrajins'ki pys'mennyky, bio-bibliohrafičnyj slovnyk*, I (1960), pp. 681; 682-684; I. U. Budovnic, *Slovar' russkoj, ukrainskoj, belorusskoj pis'mennosti i literatury do XVIII veka* (1962), pp. 113; 308; 335. — The following items might be added to the works mentioned in the bibliographies: M. S. Drinov, "O Sbornike Svjatoslava 1076 g.," *Sbornik xar' kovskogo istoriko-filologičeskogo obščestva*, 5 (1893), p. VIII; V. A. Jakovlev, "K literaturnoj istorii drevnerusskix sbornikov. Opyt issledovanija 'Izmaragda'," *Zapiski Imperatorskogo Novorossijskogo Universiteta*, 60 (1893), *passim*, esp. pp. 10; 14; 16; 20; 21; 24; 27; N. N. Speranskij, *Perevodnye sborniki izrečenij v slavjano-russkoj pis' mennosti* (1904), esp. pp. 505-515; A. Vaillant "Une source grecque de Vladimir Monomaque," *Byzantinoslavica*, 10 (1949), 1-15; D. Čiževskij, "K stilistike staro-russkoj literatury. Kenningar?," *Slavistična Revija*, 10 (1957), 102-110; Ja. N. Ščapov in *Vizantijskij Vremennik*, 16 (1959), 295-296; I. U. Budovnic, *Obščestvenno-političeskaja mysl' drevnej Rusi (XI-XIV vv.)* (1960), pp. 20; 103-148. Cf. also addition at the end of note 40 *infra*.

2. *Coislinianus* 120; *Vaticanus Gr.* 423.

3. I assume that the *Nakazanije* ends with творѧть on fol. 28. The chapter starting with Ѥже оубо правовѣрноу вѣроу имѣти (fol. 28ᵛ) is a separate entity, generally referred to as *Stoslovec Gennadija*. It is more difficult to say where the intervening two sayings (*inc*. fol. 28: ꙗко не достоить - *des*. fol. 28ᵛ: погынеши) belong. They, too, seem to be a separate entry, since the first of them starts with ꙗко (with a majuscule), a word usually introducing a new excerpt (cf. the Greek ὅτι in the same function).

бо очи оумънѣи, "Turn away from deceitful words of the flatterers as if they were ravens, for they gouge out the eyes of the mind" (fol. 25). The parallels flatterers — ravens and eyes of the flesh — eyes of the mind at once remind a Byzantinist of the *Gnōmika homoiōmata* or *Gnomic Similes*. Indeed, a close parallel to the flatterers — ravens passage of the *Izbornik* does exist in Byzantine gnomic texts.[4] However, no other sentence of the *Izbornik*'s *Admonition to the Rich* finds its counterpart in any of the published *Gnomic Similes*. For all that, the raven simile puts us on the right track, since it also occurs in the *Hortatory Chapters*, a kind of Mirror of Princes, which Deacon Agapetus, a lover of puns, acrostics and parallel constructions, addressed to Emperor Justinian (527-565).[5] It is from Agapetus that the simile found its way into the Slavic *Admonition to the Rich*. When we search further, we find that, except for one saying,[6] the whole of the *Izbornik*'s *Admonition* is a modified *cento* from seventeen chapters of Agapetus' *Mirror*, the sentences of the *Admonition* appearing on the whole in the sequence of ⟨725⟩ Agapetus' chapters.[7] The Agapetus text of the *Izbornik* is not a direct translation from the Greek; it adapts one of the Slavic translations of the *Hortatory Chapters*,[8] the one preserved, for example, in MS 202 of the former Synodal Library in Moscow.[9] A detailed proof of these assertions is no longer necessary, for with the full text of the Synodal MS 202 now at my dis-

---

4. Cf. A. Elter, "Gnomica homoeomata...," *Programm zur Feier des Geburtstages seiner Majestät des Kaisers und Königs am 27. Januar 1904* (Bonn), col. 14* = no. 69a: ὥσπερ οἱ κόρακες παρεδρεύοντες ἐξορύσσουσι τοὺς τῶν νεκρῶν ὀφθαλμούς, οὕτως οἱ κόλακες τοῖς ἐπαίνοις τοὺς λογισμοὺς διαφθείρουσι τῶν ἀνθρώπων. Cf. also L. Sternbach, *Gnomologium Vaticanum...* (1963), p. 83 = no. 206.

5. Text in Migne, *PG*, 86, 1, cols. 1163-1186.

6. In any case, not more than three sayings; cf. note 3 *supra*.

7. The compiler of the *Nakazanije* had apparently gone over the text of Agapetus twice, first excerpting chapters 5-68 (= sentences 1-13), then chapters 23-56 (= sentences 15-18). On both occasions, one chapters was inserted out of order (= chap. 25, corresponding to sentence 8, and chap. 14, corresponding to sentence 17).

8. The clinching argument is furnished by *Izbornik*, fol. 26v = Slavic Agapetus, fol. 45v (= chap. 59) = Greek Agapetus, chap. 64, where both Slavic texts end with the identical гнѣва бываѥть свобода which diverges from the φιλία καὶ οἰκείωσις of the Greek.

9. Gosudarstvennyj Istoričeskij muzej. Sinodal'naja biblioteka, no. 202, fols. 33v-47v: Пооученье бл(а)гаго ц(ѣса)рства, се же и к болѧромъ и къ еписко⟨по⟩мъ и ко игоуменомъ, лѣпо есть и черньцемъ. Cf. A. Gorskij and K. Nevostruev, *Opisanie slavjanskix rukopisej moskovskoj sinodal'noj*

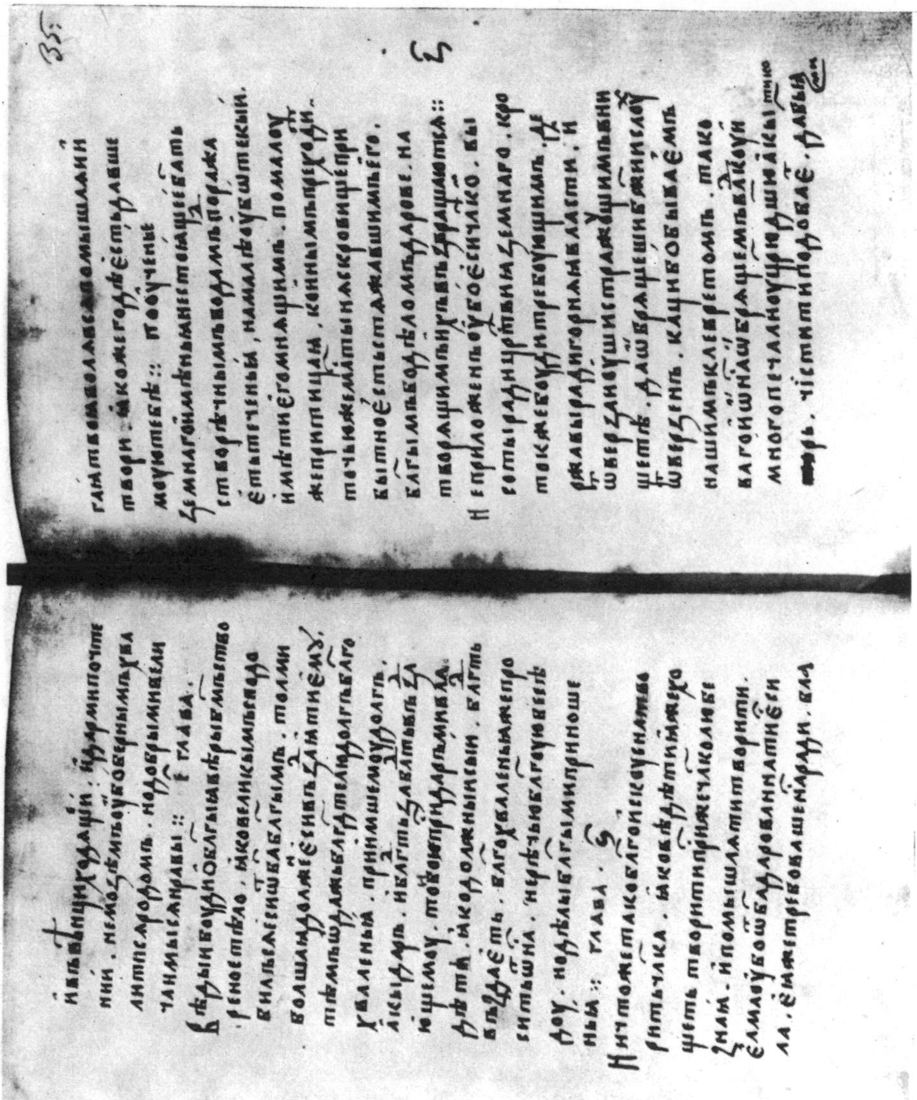

Moscow. Gosudarstvennyj Istoričeskij muzej. Sinodal'naja biblioteka, MS no. 202 (489). fols. 34v–35

posal, [10] I am able to present relevant passages from the *Izbornik*, from the full Slavic translation of Agapetus and from the Greek of the *Hortatory Chapters* in parallel columns:

Nakazanije bogatymъ (*Izbornik* of 1076)	Slavic Agapetus (Synodal MS 202)	Greek Agapetus (Migne, *PG*, 86, 1)
1. [Fol. 24^{v}] Ꙗко ѥлико великыимъ сьподобильсѧ ѥси отъ бг҃а благыимъ, тольма и большѧꙗ длъжьнъ ѥси въздаꙗти.	Fol. 34^{v} (= chap. 5): [Вѣдыи боуди о бл(а)гыꙗ вѣры б(ого)мъ створеное тѣло,] ꙗко великымъ сподобилъсѧ еси ωт б(ог)а бл(а)гымъ, толми болшаꙗ должен еси въздаꙗти емѹ...	Chap. 5: [Ἴσθι, ὦ εὐσεβείας θεότευκτον ἄγαλμα,] ὅτι ὅσῳ μεγάλων ἠξιώθης παρὰ θεοῦ δωρεῶν, τοσούτῳ μείζονος ἀμοιβῆς ὀφειλέτης ὑπάρχεις αὐτῷ ...
2. Отъвьрзаи оуши свои въ ништетѣ стражюштимъ, да обрѧштеши и ты бж҃ии слоухъ ωтвьрзенъ. Аци же оубо бываѥмъ нашiмъ повиньникомъ, тако и ω насъ обрѧштемъ нб҃сь [fol. 25] нааго	Fol. 35 (= chap. 8): [Неприложенъ оубо еси чл(овѣ)ком высоты ради ц(ѣса)рствиꙗ земнаго, кроток же боуди требоующимъ, державы ради горнѧꙗ власти, и] ωтверзаи оуши стражѹщимъ в нищетѣ, да ωбрѧщеши	Chap. 8: [Ἀπρόσιτος μὲν ὑπάρχεις ἀνθρώποις διὰ τὸ ὕψος τῆς κάτω βασιλείας · εὐπρόσιτος δὲ γίνῃ τοῖς δεομένοις διὰ τὸ κράτος τῆς ἄνω ἐξουσίας · καὶ] ἀνοίγεις τὰ ὦτα τοῖς ὑπὸ πενίας πολιορκουμένοις, ἵνα εὕρῃς τὴν τοῦ

biblioteki..., II, 2 (1859), p. 622. — In recent Soviet publications, this manuscript is given the number 489.

10. I wish to thank Mrs. Z. V. Udal'cova for her kind mediation, dating back to 1958, and the Photographic Division of the State Historical Museum for the execution of the microfilm (spring 1963). The same translation also appears in MS 1320, fols. 474^{v} sqq. of the former St. Sophia Cathedral in Novgorod, now in the Saltykov-Ščedrin Public Library, Leningrad. Unfortunately, I was not successful in obtaining a microfilm of this and other Leningrad texts. — As for the version contained in MS 158/522 of the former Volokolamsk Monastery, now in the Lenin State Library, Moscow, it seems to represent a different translation; if so, it is irrelevant to our purposes. Cf. P. M. Stroev, *Opisanie rukopisej Monastyrej Volokolamskogo*... [= Obščestvo Ljubitelej Drevnej Pis'mennosti, 98] (1891); p. 158 (= no. I, CCCLXI, fols. 305 sqq.) and a specimen of this version (= Agapetus, chap. 21) in Ja. S. Lur'e, *Ideologičeskaja bor'ba v russkoj publicistike konca XV — načala XVI veka* (1960), p. 478, n. 250. I am not able to determine the character of two other translations of Agapetus in the same collection, cf. Stroev, *Opisanie*..., no. I, 74 = p. 47 and III, 95 = p. 223.

	вл̃дкоу.	б(о)жии слоух ωтверзенъ. Каци бо биваемъ нашимъ клевретомъ, таковаго и ω нас ωбрѧщемъ вл(а)д(ы)коу.	θεοῦ ἀκοὴν ἀνεῳγμένην. Οἷοι γὰρ ἂν τοῖς ἡμετέροις γενώμεθα συνδούλοις, τοιοῦτον περὶ ἡμᾶς εὑρήσομεν τὸν Δεσπότην.
⟨726⟩ 3.	Отъвраштѧисѧ ласкавьць льстьныихъ словесъ ꙗко и враговъ (*leg.* врановъ); искалаѫть бо очи оумънѣи.	Fol. 36 (= chap. 12): ωтвращаꙗисѧ (*leg.* ωтвращаисѧ) ласкавець лестныхъ словес, ꙗко и враномъ [хыщныꙗ (*leg.* врановъ хыщныихъ?) нравъ; ови бо телеснаꙗ] ископаваютъ очеса, [друзии же д(оу)ш(е)вныꙗ ωслѣплѧють] мысли…	Chap. 12: Ἀποστρέφου τῶν κολάκων τοὺς ἀπατηλοὺς λόγους, ὥσπερ τῶν κοράκων [τοὺς ἁρπακτικοὺς τρόπους · οἱ μὲν γὰρ τοὺς τοῦ σώματος] ἐξορύττουσιν ὀφθαλμούς · [οἱ δὲ τοὺς τῆς ψυχῆς ἐξαμβλύνουσι] λογισμούς …
4.	Аште отъ вьсѣхъ хоштеші чьсть имѣти, боуди всѣмъ бл̃годѣтель обьшти.	Fol. 37^{v} (= chap. 19): Аще тоюже ωт всѣх хощеши имѣти ч(е)сть, боуди всѣмъ бл(а)годател ωбщь…	Chap. 19: Εἰ τὴν ἐκ πάντων βούλει καρποῦσθαι τιμήν, γίνου τοῖς ἅπασιν εὐεργέτης κοινός …
5.	Аште хоштеши всѧ соущѧꙗ подъ собою исправити, добротворѧштѧꙗ чьсти и зълотворѧштимъ запрѣщаи.	Fol. 39^{v} (= chap. 26): … аще ли хощеши добрѣ обоя искоусити, и добротворѧщаꙗ чти, и злотворѧщимъ запрещаи.	Chap. 28: … εἰ δὲ βούλει διττῶς εὐδοκιμεῖν, καὶ τοὺς τὰ κάλλιστα ποιοῦντας προτίμα, καὶ τοῖς τὰ χείριστα δρῶσιν ἐπιτίμα.
6.	[fol. 25^{v}] Пакы (*leg.* Такы) оубо себѣ дроугы и съвѣтьникы имѣи иже не вьсѧ гл̃емаꙗ тобою хвалѧть, нъ соудъмь правьдьныимь тъштатьсѧ ωтвѣштати ти.	Fol. 39^{v}-40 (= chap. 29): Разоумѣваи тыꙗ соуща дроугы истиньны, не хвалѧща всѧ тобою г(лаго)лемаꙗ, но соудомъ правымъ всѧ творити тщащасѧ…	Chap. 32: Ἡγοῦ τούτους εἶναι φίλους ἀληθεστάτους, μὴ τοὺς ἐπαινοῦντας ἅπαντα τὰ παρὰ σοῦ λεγόμενα, ἀλλὰ τοὺς κρίσει δικαίᾳ πάντα πράττειν σπουδάζοντας …
7.	Разоумьно послоушѧти подобаѥть пьрѧ соудиꙗмъ, не оудобь бо ѥсть пра-	Fol. 41^{v} (= chap. 38): Оумно послоушати подобаеть пьрю соудьꙗмъ, не оудобно бо есть правдоу изобрѣ-	Chap. 42: Νουνεχῶς ἀκροᾶσθαι δεῖ τοὺς τῶν πραγμάτων κριτάς · δυσθήρατος γάρ ἐστιν ἡ τοῦ δικαίου εὑ-

вьды изобрѣсти, скоро отьбѣгаюште или отъгонѧште.	сти, оудобь ѡтбѣгающе ѡт зѣло не внимающих.	ρεσις, ῥᾳδίως ἐκφεύγουσα τοὺς μὴ λίαν προσέχοντας.
8. Разоумѣваи пьрѧ мьдь[fol. 26] льно, твори же расоуждения не тьштасѧ (не *delendum ante* тъштасѧ?).	Fol. 38ᵛ (= chap. 24): Разоумѣваи пьрѧ моудно (*in margine inf.*: медлено), твори же расоуженьꙗ тощно...	Chap. 25: Βουλεύου μὲν τὰ πρακτέα βραδέως, ἐκτέλει δὲ τὰ κριθέντα σπουδαίως ...
9. Твьрдо разоумѣи сп҃сениꙗ своѥго хранилиште ѥже николиже людина обидѣти.	Fol. 42ᵛ (= chap. 43): Твердо мни сп(а)сеньꙗ твоего хранилище, еже николиже людина ѡбидѣти...	Chap. 47: Ἀσφαλεστάτην ἡγοῦ τῆς σωτηρίας σου φυλακήν, τὸ μηδέποτέ τινα τῶν ὑπηκόων ἀδικεῖν ...
⟨727⟩		
10. Боуди своимъ повиньникомъ страшьнъ сана ради, а любьзнъ поданиѥмь милостышѧ.	Fol. 42ᵛ (= chap. 44): Боуди своимъ людемъ, [бл(а)говѣрныи ц(а)рю,] и страшенъ сана ради и власти, и любсзснъ подаꙗньсмъ м(и)л(о)ст(ы)нѧ...	Chap. 48: Γίνου τοῖς ὑπηκόοις, [εὐσεβέστατε βασιλεῦ,] καὶ φοβερὸς διὰ τὴν ὑπεροχὴν τῆς ἐξουσίας, καὶ ποθεινὸς διὰ τὴν παροχὴν τῆς εὐποιίας...
11. Ѥлико силою прѣвышии ѥси вьсѣхъ, тольма и дѣлы добрыими свь [fol. 26ᵛ] тѣти ти подвизаисѧ паче вьсѣхъ.	Fol. 43ᵛ (= chap. 48): Елико сiлою всѣх прѣвыши еси, толми и дѣлы свѣтити подвизаисѧ...	Chap. 53: Ὅσον τῇ δυναστείᾳ πάντων ὑπερανέχεις, τοσοῦτον καὶ τοῖς ἔργοις ὑπερλάμπειν ἀγωνίζου ...
12. Проштениꙗ трѣбуꙗ грѣховъ, праштаи и самъ къ тебѣ съгрѣшаюштѧꙗ; ѥже бо на рабѣхъ нашихъ проштениѥ, бж҃иꙗ гнѣва бываѥть свобода.	Fol. 45ᵛ (= chap. 59): Прощеньꙗ требоуꙗ грѣховъ, пращаи и самъ к тобѣ съгрѣшающаꙗ; [ꙗко по прощеньꙗ въздаетсѧ прощенье, и] еже клеветъ наших прощенье, вл(а)д(ы)чнѧго гнѣва бываеть (*in margine additum*: свобода).	Chap. 64: Συγγνώμην αἰτούμενος ἁμαρτημάτων, συγγίνωσκε καὶ αὐτὸς τοῖς εἰς σὲ πλημμελοῦσιν · [ὅτι ἀφέσει ἀντιδίδοται ἄφεσις, καὶ] τῇ πρὸς τοὺς ὁμοδούλους ἡμῶν καταλλαγῇ, ἡ πρὸς θεὸν φιλία καὶ οἰκείωσις.
13. Тъгда наречетьсѧ къто оубо истинь-	Fol. 46ᵛ (= chap. 63): [Властелинъ оубо	Chap. 68: [Κύριος μὲν πάντων ἐστὶν ὁ

ныи властєлинъ, ѥгда самъ собою обладаѥть и нелѣпыимъ похотьмъ не рабо[fol. 27] таѥть.	всѣмъ есть ц(ѣса)рь, рабъ же съ всѣми есть б(ог)оу.] Тогда въистиноу наричетсѧ властелинъ, егда самъ собою обладаеть и нелѣпымъ похотемъ не работаеть…	βασιλεύς, δοῦλος δὲ μετὰ πάντων ὑπάρχει θεοῦ.] Τότε δὲ μάλιστα κληθήσεται κύριος, ὅταν αὐτὸς ἑαυτοῦ δεσπόζῃ, καὶ ταῖς ἀτόποις ἡδοναῖς μὴ δουλεύῃ …
14. Съмьрть и гонениѥ и напасть и вьсѧ видимаꙗ зълаꙗ прѣдъ очима тї да боудоуть по вьсѧ дьни и чѧсы.		
15. Такъ боуди о своихъ рабѣхъ, ꙗкоже молишисѧ тебѣ бо҃у быти.	Fol. 38ᵛ (= chap. 22): Такъ боуди ѡ своих рабѣх, ꙗкоже молишисѧ тобѣ вл(а)д(ы)цѣ быти…	Chap. 23: Τοιοῦτος γίνου περὶ τοὺς σοὺς οἰκέτας, οἷον εὔχῃ σοι τὸν Δεσπότην γενέσθαι …
16. Не оправьдаи неправьдьнааго аште и дроугь ти ѥсть, ти обидить правьдьнааго аште и вра[fol. 27ᵛ]гъ ти ѥсть	Fol. 41ᵛ (= chap. 37): … [понеже тогоже есть безаконьꙗ] и не ѡправдаи (*leg.* оправдати) неправеднаго, аще и дроугъ ти есть, ⟨и⟩ обидить праведнаго, аще и врагъ есть.	Chap. 41: […ἐπειδὴ τῆς αὐτῆς ἐστιν ἀτοπίας,] καὶ δικαιοῦν τὸν ἄδικον, εἰ καὶ φίλος ὑπάρχει, καὶ ἀδικεῖν τὸν δίκαιον εἰ καὶ ἐχθρὸς τυγχάνει …
17. Аште къто имать очиштеноу дш҃ѫ оть чл҃вчьскыꙗ прѣльсти и видить хоудость своѥго ѥстьства, оу⟨728⟩малениꙗ же и напрасноую съмьрть сего житиꙗ, въ брѣгъ гърдостьныи не въпадеть сѧ, аште и въ саноу ѥсть высоцѣ.	Fol. 36ᵛ (= chap. 14): Аще кто ѡчищеноу имать д(оу)шю ѡт чл(о)в(ѣ)чьскыꙗ прельсти и видить хоудость своего ества, ⟨728⟩оумаленье же и напрасноую см(е)рть сего житьꙗ [и припрѧженоую плоти скверноу,] въ презорь не впадеть брегъ, аще и в саноу есть высоцѣ.	Chap. 14: Εἴ τις κεκαθαρισμένον ἔχει τὸν λογισμὸν ἐκ τῆς ἀνθρωπίνης ἀπάτης, καὶ βλέπει τὸ οὐτιδανὸν τῆς ἑαυτοῦ φύσεως, τό τε βραχὺ ⟨728⟩ καὶ ὠκύμορον τῆς ἐνταῦθα ζωῆς, [καὶ τὸν συνεζευγμένον τῇ σαρκὶ ῥύπον,] εἰς τὸν τῆς ὑπερηφανίας οὐκ ἐμπεσεῖται κρημνόν, κἂν ἐν ἀξιώματι ὑπάρχῃ ὑψηλῷ.
18. Въ извѣстьнѣмь ср҃дцѧ твоѥго	Fol. 44 [= chap. 51): Во извѣстнѣмъ с(е)р-	Chap. 56: Ἐν τῷ ἀκριβεῖ τῆς καρδίας

съвѣтѣ разоумѣваи соуштиихъ съ то[fol. 28]бою норовы, да познаюешї въ истиноу съ любьвыѭ слоужѧштиихъ ти, или съ льстью ласкаюштиихъ. Мънози бо приꙗзиѭ (leg. приꙗзниѭ) лїцемѣрьною вельми извѣстьныимъ пакость творѧть.	дца твоего свѣтѣ [прилѣжнѣ] разоумѣваи соущих с тобою нравы, да познаеши въистиноу с любовью слоужащих и лестью ласкающих. Мнози бо приꙗзнью лицѣмѣрною велми извѣстым пакости творѧт.	σου βουλευτηρίῳ, [ἐπιμελῶς] κατανόει τῶν συνόντων σοι τοὺς τρόπους, ἵνα γινώσκῃς ἀκριβῶς καὶ τοὺς ἐν ἀγάπῃ θεραπεύοντας, καὶ τοὺς ἐν ἀπάτῃ κολακεύοντας· πολλοὶ γὰρ εὐνοεῖν ὑποκρινόμενοι, μεγάλα τοὺς πιστεύοντας καταβλάπτουσι.

Several conclusions must be drawn from this confrontation of texts.

1. Anyone using the *Admonition to the Rich* in order to reconstruct the contents of Kievan social thought may henceforth do so only with reservations and must first point to the *Admonition*'s Byzantine origin. In particular, one must not speak of the author of the *Admonition*, but only of a compiler working with a non-Kievan text, and one must state that the question of this compiler's origin — whether he himself was a Kievan or not — still awaits its solution.

2. Until now, the earliest traces of Agapetus' *Mirror* in the East Slavic area were found in texts dating from the twelfth century.[11] Now we know that passages from Agapetus were introduced into a Kievan manuscript written about a century earlier. We furthermore know that the excerpts from Agapetus appearing in the *Izbornik* presuppose the existence of the full Slavic translation of his *Mirror* by the year 1076. Previously I thought that, since this full translation was first attested in the Russian north and in the fifteenth century, it may have been made, perhaps there, at a relatively late date.[12]

3. The *Mirror* of Agapetus constituted an important quarry for ideological constructs erected both by the propagandists of Muscovite absolutism and by their opponents. In Kiev, I once maintained, the situation was different.[13] I do not think that this evaluation should be mo-

11. Cf. my "A Neglected Byzantine Source of Muscovite Political Ideology," *Harvard Slavic Studies*, 2 (1954), 144.

12. *Ibidem*, p. 152. — Lur'e, *Ideologičeskaja bor'ba*... (as in note 10 *supra*), p. 476 tentatively dated this translation to the sixties of the fifteenth century.

13. "A Neglected Byzantine Source...," pp. 148-149.

dified, now that we have found a portion of Agapetus' *Mirror* in a Kievan text. To see why, it is enough to observe the systematic changes, mostly omissions, introduced by the compiler of the *Admonition to the Rich* — or his model — into the chapters of Agapetus. The address to the Emperor, that ⟨729⟩ "monument of piety wrought by God," which opens chapter 5, has been eliminated from the very first sentence of the *Admonition*. The same was done in sentence 2, which has no trace of the "loftiness of Thy [i.e. the Emperor's] earthly Empire" mentioned at the beginning of Agapetus' chapter 8; in sentence 10, which omits the invocation to the "Most Pious Emperor" of the Slavic and Greek Agapetus (chapters 44 and 48 respectively); and in sentence 13, where instead of the Emperor, "Lord of All" (Slavic and Greek Agapetus, chapters 63 and 68 respectively), we have the pale къто оубо, "anyone."

In short, the compiler of the *Izbornik* — or his model — used Agapetus not to write a theoretical treatise, however rudimentary, on the ruler's power; he drew upon the Byzantine text to compose a purely moralizing tract, addressed to the upper classes in general. Whether these changes were made in Kiev or elsewhere must be left unresolved at this point. One thing can be safely stated: sometime before 1076, the Slavs had at their disposal the same full translation of Agapetus which later became so popular in Muscovite Russia. However, Slavs also adapted the text of Agapetus to achieve different, non-political, goals. Any East Slavic attempts to exploit Agapetus for ideological purposes, for instance to apply his exhortations and fawnings to the local ruler, would be unlikely in the eleventh century.[14] It is safer to assume that in that century the conceptions of the Byzantine hierarchy of states and the "family of princes" were accepted by the Slavs, however imprecise their understanding of these concepts may have been.[15] In them, the top rung of the ladder was reserved for the Byzantine Emperor and therefore a treatise like that of Agapetus could apply to him alone, or else have to undergo considerable modification.

4. The *Izbornik*'s *Admonition to the Rich is* not a Slavic translation of a moralizing adaptation, made by a Byzantine, of Agapetus' *Mirror*. It is rather an adaptation, made by a Slav, of the *Mirror*'s full Slavic translation. This much is clear. It is not clear, however, where and when this full Slavic translation was made. Phonetically and morphologically

14. But not in the tenth century in Bulgaria, as I shall presently suggest.

15. Cf., e.g., André Grabar, "God and the 'Family of Princes' Presided Over by the Byzantine Emperor," *Harvard Slavic Studies*, 2 (1954), 117-123, and the literature adduced *ibidem*, p. 117, n. 1.

speaking, the text of the Synodal MS 202 represents an East Slavic recension throughout, but this only shows that by the fifteenth century, the date of the manuscript, the Slavic Agapetus had had a long career on East Slavic soil. When it comes to the vocabulary, the picture is different. The translation contains many words absent from the East Slavic area or rarely occurring there, but well attested in texts of Old Church Slavonic provenance. Here belong words like бернье ~ πηλός and бернымъ ~ πήλινον (cf. OCS брьниѥ); тикорь, тикри (cf. OCS тикръ) ~ κάτοπτρον; покорникомъ ~ ὑπηκόοις; подрагъ ~ μίμησις; дрѧхльствоующимъ ~ ἐπιστυγνάζοντας; коурѣлкы ~ εἴδη; добраа дѣтель ~ ἀρετή; органъ ~ μουσική; извѣстым in the meaning of πιστεύοντας (cf. извѣстьныихъ оученикъ, "faithful disciples," in *Vita Methodii*, 17); бошию не (cf. OCS бъшиѫ) ~ μηδαμῶς; and сине ~ βύσσῳ.

These words point to the Balkans as the place of origin of our translation. For the time before 1076, this means Bulgaria. The most likely occasion anterior to 1076 ⟨730⟩ on which Bulgarian bookmen would show interest in Byzantine political literature are the reigns of Symeon (893-927) and Peter (927-969), the period of Bulgaria's own imperial ambitions, followed by her Byzantinization. I therefore assume that the Slavic translation of Agapetus which we read in Synodal MS 202 was made in Bulgaria in the tenth century. This, however, is a question which cannot be left to Byzantinists alone; to decide, we must await the concurring judgement of Slavicists. Still, the possibility that the vocabulary of the Slavic Agapetus reflects that of tenth-century Old Church Slavonic should make the edition of this text highly desirable. For the time being, a specimen page of the Synodal MS 202 (fols. 34^v- 35) is presented here (cf. fig. 1).

Like many of *Izbornik*'s chapters, the *Admonition to the Rich* entered other Russian miscellaneous manuscripts and collections. Thus parts of it were interpolated into the Слово св. отца нашего Василия, архиепископа Кесарийского, о судиах и властелех, *Speech of our Holy Father Basil, Archbishop of Caesarea, Concerning Judges and Those in Power*, a text transmitted in a number of Russian *Kormčie*, or Nomocanons.[16] This interesting pseudepigraphon admonished the judges to ad-

16. *Editions*: G. Rozenkampf, *Obozrenie kormčej knigi v istoričeskom vide* (Moscow, 1829), pp. 214-215 (excerpts); *Pravoslavnyj Sobesednik*, 1 (1864), 368-374, reprinted in A. I. Ponomarev, *Pamjatniki drevne-russkoj cerkovno-učitel'noj literatury*, III (1897), pp. 116-119; Makarij's *Velikie*

minister justice impartially, and the rulers to remain humble and to treat their subjects with kindness and charity. By relying on the *Admonition to the Rich*, the (Muscovite?)[17] compiler of the *Speech* showed a great deal of flair, for he recognized that the *Admonition* could be used to exhort rulers as well; thus he sensed the true character of Agapetus' *Mirror*, in spite of the moralizing disguise in which this text appeared in his source. Here are the parallel passages:

⟨731⟩

Slovo… Vasilija (Ponomarev, *Pamjatniki…* III)	*Nakazanije bogatymъ* (*Izbornik* of 1076)
[P. 118] Тѣмже рече великій Константинъ: да будеть судіа нелицемѣренъ, ни богата стыдяся, ни нища милуя на судѣ, яко Господень есть судъ;	
да творитъ разсужденіе на судѣ не тщася;	Fol. 26 (cf. Agap. 25): твори же расоуждения не тьштасѧ.
разумно и довольно послушати подобаетъ пря судіамъ; не удобь бо есть правды изобрѣсти; скоре	Fol. 25ᵛ (cf. Agap. 42): Разоумьно послоушѧти подобаѥть пьрѧ соудиꙗмъ. не оудобь бо ѥсть правды изобрѣсти. скоро…
не оправити неправаго, аще и	Fol. 27-27ᵛ (cf. Agap. 41): Не

Minei-četii, fascicule for December 31 (Moscow, 1914), cols. 2471-2476. For a shorter version (without the Agapetian passages; title: Слово свꙗтаго и великаго Васильꙗ о судьꙗхъ и о клеветахъ) of the *Speech's* final section, cf. N. V. Kalačev, ***Predvaritel'nyja juridičeskija svedenija dlja polnago obъjasnenija Russkoj Pravdy***, I (2nd ed. 1880), pp. 238-239 and the facsimile reproduction of *Merilo pravednoe*, ed. by M. N. Tixomirov (Moscow, 1961), pp. 39-40 (= fols. 20-20ᵛ). According to I. U. Budovnic, *Slovar'…* (as in note 1 *supra*), p. 313, the *Speech* occurs in the unpublished part of Makarij's *Velikie Minei-Četii*, among the entries for May 23. — Cf. V. Val'denberg, *Drevnerusskija učenija o predelax carskoj vlasti* (1916), pp. 126-128; Ja. S. Lur'e, *Ideologičeskaja bor'ba…* (as in n. 10 *supra*), p. 479.

17. The "Ponomarev" version of the *Speech* seems to be of a late date, since its Agapetian interpolation is absent from the recension published by Kalačev, *Predvaritel'nyja…* and from that of the *Merilo pravednoe* (cf. the preceding note). In both these recensions, господень (есть) судъ (= *Speech*, p. 118, 27) is immediately followed by тьмь недостоино слушати (= *Speech*, p. 119, 4). *Merilo pravednoe* was compiled towards the end of the thirteenth century. The "Ponomarev" version must date from the fourteenth or fifteenth.

другъ ти есть, ни обидить праваго, аще и брать (*leg.* врагъ) ти есть.	оправьдаи неправьдьнааго, аште и дроугь ти ѥсть, ни обидить правьдьнааго, аше и врагъ ти ѥсть.
Ты разумѣй твердо спасенія твоего хранилище, еже николиже человѣка обидѣти; буди къ своимъ повинникомъ добръ и тихъ в народѣ.	Fol. 26 (cf. Agap. 47 and 48): Твьрдо разоумѣи сп҃сениꙗ своѥго хранилиште, ѥже николиже людина обидѣти. Боуди своимъ повиньникомъ страшьнъ сана ради...
Елико силою превшелъ еси всѣхъ, толика и дѣлы добрыми подвизайся паче всѣхъ: милостыню твори по силѣ. Прощенія грѣховъ прося у бога, прощайся самъ согрѣшающая к тебѣ.	Fol. 26-26ᵛ (cf. Agap. 53 and 64): Ѥлико силою прѣвышии ѥси вьсѣхъ, тольма и дѣлы добрыими свьтѣти ти подвизаисѧ паче вьсѣхъ. Проштениꙗ трѣбуꙗ грѣховъ, праштаи и самъ къ тебѣ съгрѣшаюштѧꙗ.
Тогда наречется кто истинный властель, егда самъ собою обладаеть.	Fol. 26ᵛ (cf. Agap. 68): Тъгда наречетьсѧ къто оубо истиньныи властелинъ, ѥгда самъ собою обладаѥть...
Разумѣй же правы (*leg.* нравы) сущихъ во истину съ тобою, да познаеши съ вѣрою служащихъ ти, или лестію лицемѣрною ласкающихся тебѣ, довода дѣля, да погубять [p. 119] христіаны,	Fol. 27ᵛ-28 (cf. Agap. 56): [Въ извѣстьнѣмь ср҃дцѧ твоѥго съвѣтѣ] разоумѣваи соуштиихъ съ тобою норовы, да познаѥші въ истиноу съ любьвьѭ слоужѧштиихъ ти, или съ льстью ласкаюштиихъ.
яко не достоить ти послушати клеветника, сладко ти глаголющи (*leg.* глаголюща) или слышати на ближняго что, да не отпадеши любве; но воздержи клевещющаго во уши твои, да не с нимъ погыбнеши.	Fol. 28-28ᵛ (no equivalent in Agap.): Ꙗко не достоить послоушати клеветарѧ сладъко ти гл҃юшта, или слышати на ближьнѧго, да не отъпадеши бж҃иꙗ лѫбъве и цр҃ства. Въ (*leg.* Нъ) въздьржи клевештѫштааго въ оушию твоѥѧ, да не коупно съ нимь погынеши.

Comparison between p. 118, line 27-28 of the *Speech* (да творитъ разсуждение на судѣ не тщася), fol. 26ᵛ of the *Izbornik* (твори же расоуждениꙗ не ⟨732⟩ тъштасѧ) and chapter 24 (fol. 38ᵛ) of the Slavic translation (твори же расоуженьꙗ тощно) shows that the Agapetian passages in the *Speech* go back to the *Izbornik* or its source and not to the full Slavic translation of Agapetus preserved in Synodal MS 202. The fact that *Speech*, p. 119, lines 1-4 correspond to *Izbornik*, fol. 28-28^{v}, but have no counterpart in Agapetus, leads to the same conclusion. Thus passages from Agapetus had undergone a triple deformation (through the Slavic translation, through the adaptation in the *Admonition to the Rich*, and through the use of the latter in the *Speech*) when Joseph of Volokolamsk (d. 1515) read them while preparing the last of his pamphlets, later to be included into his major ideological work, the *Illuminator*. He must not have recognized these passages, for he did not use them in the portion of his pamphlet in which he copied other passages of the *Speech* extensively and almost verbatim.[18]

We should not accuse Joseph of lacking acumen. The Agapetian passages in the *Speech* were deformed out of recognition, and not even a modern scholar would realize that the phrase буди къ своимъ повинникомъ добръ и тихъ в народѣ (= *Speech*, p. 118, lines 33-34) ultimately goes back to γίνου τοῖς ὑπηκόοις... καὶ φοβερὸς διὰ τὴν ὑπεροχὴν τῆς ἐξουσίας of the Greek (= Agapetus, chapter 48), unless he were shown the intervening links боуди своимъ людемъ... и страшенъ сана ради и власти (= Slavic Agapetus, chapter 44) and боуди своимъ повиньникомъ страшьнъ сана ради (= *Izbornik*, fol. 26). С а н а р а д и, "on account of your rank," having become н а р о д ѣ, "people," by the *fiat* of a thoughtless scribe, the formidable holder of exalted power became in turn the good and serene lord of his subjects. Joseph, however, did make good his omission. He combined his borrowings from the *Speech* with quotations from the Slavic Agapetus,[18a] substituting direct and therefore more forceful excerpts from the Byzantine for the diluted Agapetian passages of the *Speech*. The *Speech*, the substitution made in it by Joseph of Volokolamsk, and other passages of Agapetus occurring in the recently published fragments attributable to him[19] should confirm, ra-

18. Cf. *Illuminator* (2nd ed., Kazan', 1882), pp. 339, 9-10; 14, 14-15, 15-17, 23-26, 26-27, 27-28, 28-29; 340, 7-10, with *Speech*, pp. 116, 5-6, 25-26, 10-11, 19-21; 117, 17, 19-21; 118, 12; 119, 14-17; 117, 22-23; 119, 16-19. Cf. also *Letter to Grand Prince Vasilij Against Heretics*, edd. N. A. Kazakova, and Ja. S. Lur'e, *Antifeodal'nye eretičeskie dviženija na Rusi XIV-načala XVI veka* (1955), p. 519, 10-11 with *Speech*, p. 117, 22-23. These correspondences were established at my Columbia seminar in 1958, and independently by Ja. S. Lur'e, *Ideologičeskaja bor'ba...* (as in note 10 *supra*), p. 479.

18a. Cf., e. g., my "A Neglected Byzantine Source..." (as in n. 11 *supra*), pp. 157-158.

19. Cf. the *Fragment of a Letter to the Grand Prince*, in effect a string of quotations from Agapetus (chapters 1, 2, 8, 9, 15, 48, 51, 53, 60 58, 61, 30, 21, as

ther than invalidate, the impression of Agapetus' ubiquity in Muscovite political literature.

The story of Sozomenus the Merciful (О милостивѣмь Созоменѣ и о томь како даıаи нищемоу сторицею прииме) is among the most charming chapters ⟨733⟩ of the *Izbornik* (fols. 269-274ᵛ).[20] It enjoyed some popularity and was repeated as a separate entry in other Russian manuscripts. Recently Professor Čiževsky found it worthy of a re-edition and a commentary.[21] Up to now, however, no clarity could be obtained on its origin and sources. Some assumed that the story must go back to a Greek original, but declared that the precise model of the Slavic text was unknown; others avoided discussing the subject. That the story of Sozomenus goes back to a Greek model is evidence itself. In the *Izbornik*, it is no more than a stylistic reworking of a chapter in the Byzantine *Life of St. Niphon*.[22] Since a Slavic translation of the *Life* is preserved in a relatively early Russian manuscript dated to the year 1219, it was well-known to pre-revolutionary philologists[23] and was last published, together with its Greek models, in the Soviet Union in 1928.[24] Thus it was a matter of oversight on the part of scholars that the connection between the texts of 1076 and 1219 has not hitherto been firmly estab-

established in my Columbia Seminar of 1958). First published in Kazakova and Lur'e, *Antifeodal'nye... dviženija...* (as in the preceding note) (1955), pp. 518-519, without awareness of the *Fragment's* Agapetian origin; then in A. A. Zimin and Ja. S. Lur'e, *Poslanija Iosifa Volockogo* (1959), pp. 183-184 (with full discussion of its Agapetian character, cf. pp. 260-262). Cf. also Ja. S. Lur'e, *Ideologičeskaja bor'ba...* (as in note 10 *supra*), p. 475 and n. 239.

20. Since there may be a lacuna between fols. 274ᵛ and 275, I am not sure whether the text on fols. 275-275ᵛ is a continuation of the Sozomenus story. The Greek and the Slavic parallel texts seem to indicate that it is not.

21. *Zwei russisch-kirchenslavische Texte...* (as in note 1 *supra*), pp. 12-19.

22. Cf. *Bibliotheca Hagiographica Graeca* (3rd ed., 1957), 1371z.

23. N. I. Kostomarov, "Mističeskaja povest' o Nifonte," *Russkoe Slovo* (March, 1861), 1-28, esp. 20-21; I. I. Sreznevskij, "Drevnie pamjatniki russkogo pis'ma i jazyka," *Izvestija Imp. Akad. Nauk po Otd. russ. jazyka i slovesnosti*, 10 (1861-63), 595-597; *idem*, same work (2nd ed., 1882), p. 93.

24. A. V. Rystenko, *Materijaly z istorii vizantijs'ko-slov'jans'koji literatury ta movy* (Odessa, 1928); cf. pp. 62-64 and 291-293 for the Sozomenus story. The Slavic *Life* is also to be read in Makarij's *Velikie Minei-Četii*, fascicule 12 (1907), among the entries for December 23; cf. cols. 1735-1737 for the Sozomenus story. — Cf. also N. N. Durnovo, *Vvedenie...* (as in note 1 *supra*; p. 42; Maxnovec', *Ukrajins'ki pys' mennyky...* (as in note 1 *supra*), p. 670; Budovnic, *Slovar'...* (as in note 1 *supra*), p. 91.

lished.[25] It is perhaps less easy to realize that the lifting of the Sozomenus story out of Niphon's *Life* and endowing it with an independent existence was not a unique feat performed by the compiler of the *Izbornik*. The story is transmitted as a separate edifying chapter in at least two Greek manuscripts, the *Canonicianus Graecus* 19 of the Bodleian Library, fols. 215-217^{v} (fifteenth-sixteenth century)[26] and in the *Vindobonensis Theol. Graecus* 10, fols. 195^{v}-196^{v} (tenth century), written in two columns).[27] But for insignificant variants, the text of the *Canonicianus* coincides with the corresponding portion of the Greek *Life* of Niphon published by Rystenko.[28] As for the text of the *Vindobonensis*, it differs somewhat from the versions published by him. Moreover, since the ⟨734⟩ *Vindobonensis* dates from the tenth century, it proves that the Sozomenus story had an independent life in Byzantium at least some hundred years before it had entered the *Izbornik* of 1076. I am therefore publishing the story as it stands in the Vienna manuscript, normalizing its negligent spelling and giving a few relevant readings of the Rystenko text.

[Fol. 195^{v}a] Κεφάλαιον πάνυ ὠφέλιμον περὶ τοῦ ἐλεήμονος Σωζομένου

Ἦν τις ἄνθρωπος εὐσεβῶς ἐν τῷ βίῳ ζῶν ἐν ταῖς ἡμέραις ὅτε ἔζη κατὰ τὸν βίον Κυριακὸς ὁ Ἱεροσολύμων ἀρχιερεύς, ἦν δὲ καὶ ἐλεήμων ἄκρως· ὄνομα δὲ αὐτῷ Σωζόμενος. οὗτος ὁ ἄνθρωπος ἐν μιᾷ διερχόμενος διὰ τῆς πλατείας τῆς πόλεως, ὁρᾷ πένητα γυμνόν, λίαν τρυχόμενον· οἰκτείρας οὖν αὐτὸν ὁ εἰρημένος Σωζόμενος, ἐκδυσάμενος δέδωκεν αὐτῷ τὸ ἱμάτιον αὐτοῦ καὶ ἀνεχώρησεν εἰς τὸν οἶκον αὐτοῦ· ἦν δε θέρος ὥρᾳ δείλης. καὶ μικρὸν ὑπνώσας, ὁρᾷ ἐν ὁράματι ὡς ὅτι εὑρέθη, φησίν, ἐν προαυλίῳ θαυμαστῷ, ἐν ᾧ ἦν φῶς 195^{v}b] ἄϋλον καὶ καθαρόν· καὶ ἄνθη πολυποίκιλα, ῥόδα τὲ καὶ κρίνα,

25. D. I. Abramovyč, "Do pytannja pro džerela Izbornyka Svjatoslava 1076 roku," *Vseukrajins'ka Akad. Nauk. Zbirnyk istor.-filol. viddilu* 74b, *Naukovyj Zbirnyk Leninhrads' koho Tovarystva doslidnykiv istorii*, 2 (1929), 65 and D. Tschiżewskij, *Zwei russisch-kirchenslavische Texte...* (as in note 1 *supra*), p. 15, n. 5 came closest to realizing this connection.

26. Cf. H. O. Coxe, *Catalogi codicum ... bibliothecae Bodleianae pars* III (1854), p. 26 D; cf. also *Bibliotheca Hagiographica Graeca* (3rd ed., 1957), 1372 d.

27. Cf. D. de Nessel, *Catalogus ... codicum ... Graecorum ... bibliothecae ... Vindobonensis*, I (1960), p. 27; cf. also *Biblioteca Hagiographica Graeca* (3rd ed., 1957), Appendix IV, no. 17.

28. The last six lines of the *Canonicianus* are a variation on the theme of the preceding passage; they provide the emancipated story with an ending of its own.

καὶ φυτὰ ὑψηλόκομα λίαν· ἄλλα τὲ φυτὰ βλέπει, καὶ ἰδοὺ ἦσαν ἀπὸ ἄνωθεν ἕως κάτω περικεχυμένα καρπὸν εὐωδίας· ἄλλα πλεῖστα φυτὰ ἑώρα ἔχοντα καρπὸν ὡραῖον τῷ εἴδει σφόδρα, καὶ τὰ κλάδη αὐτῶν ἕως τῆς γῆς χαλασμένα, καὶ ἕτερον τῷ ἑτέρῳ διαφέρον. ὄρνεά τε παμποίκιλα ἐκαθέζοντο ἐπάνω αὐτῶν, κελαδοῦντα μελίῤῥυτα, τοῦτο δὲ πρὸς ἐκείνῳ συνεσείετο, σιωπὴν μηδόλως ἔχοντα, ἄλλο δὲ τῷ ἄλλῳ ἀντέβλεπεν, καὶ ὡς μυριάδες τῷ πλήθει καθήμενα ἐπὶ τῶν φύλλων ἐκελάδουν ἀθάνατα ὥστε τὸν ἦχον ἀκούεσθαι ἀπὸ τῆς γῆς ἕως τοῦ οὐρανοῦ. τὰ δὲ φυτὰ ἐκεῖνα ἐκυμαίνοντο μετὰ περιφανείας πολλῆς, καὶ τὸ ἀκούειν καὶ βλέπειν τῶν φυτῶν καὶ τῶν πετεινῶν ἐκείνων ἀνείκαστον γλυκύτητα ἐνεποίουν τῷ ἀνθρώπῳ, ὥστε φρίττειν αὐτὸν ἐν ἡδονῇ μεγάλῃ. ὡς οὖν ταῦτα ἔβλεπεν, ἔρχεταί τις εὐνοῦχος καὶ λέγει αὐτῷ· "ἀκολούθει μοι." ἐκεῖνος δὲ εὐθὺς ὄπισθεν αὐτοῦ ἠκολούθει. ὁδεύσαντες δὲ μικρόν, ἔρ[196ʳa]χονται ἐπί τινα τόπον ἐν ᾧ ἦσαν στάβαρα χρυσᾶ· καὶ ὡς ἀνεπέτασαν ἀμφότεροι τοὺς ὀφθαλμοὺς αὐτῶν εἰς τὸ πέραν διὰ τῶν ὀπῶν τῶν χρυσῶν σταβάρων, βλέπουσιν ἐκεῖ πάλιν ἄλλην αὐλὴν καὶ παλάτια δεδοξασμένα καὶ περίβλεπτα σφόδρα σφόδρα. ἐν ὅσῳ οὖν ἔβλεπεν ὁ Σωζόμενος τὰ ἐκεῖ, ἰδοὺ ἐξέρχονται ἐκ τῶν παλατίων ἐκείνων ἄνθρωποι λάμποντες ὡς ὁ ἥλιος, ἐπτερωμένοι, φέροντες καμψάκια χρυσένδυτα τέσσαρα καὶ λαμπρά, τέσσαρις τέσσαρις κατὰ ἓν καμψάκιον ὑπουργοῦντες. ἐν ὅσῳ οὖν ἐδιέβαινον τὸ θαυμαστὸν ἐκεῖνο προαύλιον οἱ ἄγγελοι τοῦ θεοῦ, ὑπενόησεν ὡς ὅτι πρὸς αὐτὸν ἔρχονται ἐπειγόμενοι· ὅτε οὖν ἤγγισαν πλησίον τοῖς χρυσωρόφοις σταβάροις κατέναντι τοῦ Σωζομένου, ἔστησαν ἀποβιβάσαντες τὰ καμψάκια ἀπὸ τῶν ὤμων αὐτῶν, καὶ θέντες χαμαὶ ἐξεδέχοντο τινὰ μέγαν παραγενέσθαι πρὸς αὐτούς. ἐν ὅσῳ οὖν ἐξεδέχοντο, ὁρᾷ ὁ Σωζόμενος καὶ ἰδοὺ ἀνὴρ ὡραῖος πάνυ καὶ καλὸς τῷ εἴδει σφόδρα, ἐξελ[196ʳb]θὼν τῶν παλατίων ἐκείνων ἦλθεν ἔγγιστα τῶν ἀγγέλων τῶν φερόντων τὰ καμψάκια ἐκεῖνα καὶ λέγει αὐτοῖς· "ἀνοίξατε τοὺς καμψακίους τούτους καὶ δείξατε τῷ ἀνθρώπῳ ἐκείνῳ, τί φυλάττω αὐτῷ διὰ τὸν χιτῶνα αὐτοῦ, ὃν πρὸ ὥρας μοι ἐδωρήσατο διὰ τοῦ δεῖνα τοῦ πένητος." εὐθέως οὖν ἤνοιξαν τὸ ἓν καμψάκιον τὸ χρυσοῦν καὶ ἤρξαντο ἐκβάλλειν χιτῶνας καὶ ἱμάτια βασιλικὰ λευκάερα καὶ ποικίλα καὶ ὡραῖα τῷ εἴδει σφόδρα, καὶ ἥπλουν αὐτὰ κατενώπιον αὐτοῦ, λέγοντες· ⟨735⟩ "ἆρα, κῦρι Σωζόμενε, ἀρεστὰ εἰσὶν τοῖς ὀφθαλμοῖς σου;" ἐκεῖνος δὲ ἔλεγεν· "οὐκ εἰμὶ ἄξιος οὐδὲ κἂν τὴν σκιὰν τῶν ἱματίων τούτων θεάσασθαι." ὑποδεικνυόντων οὖν αὐτῶν τοὺς λαμπροὺς ἐκείνους καὶ ποικίλους χιτῶνας καὶ ὁλοχρύσους, ἀνέβη ὁ ἀριθμὸς ἕως τῶν χιλιοστῶν· ὅτε οὖν ἔδειξαν αὐτῷ τὸ ἑκατονταπλασίονα λήψεσθαι καὶ ζωὴν αἰώνιον ὑπὲρ τοῦ ἑνὸς χιτῶνος κληρονομεῖν, λέγει πρὸς αὐτὸν ὁ ἐπιτάσσων ⟨τ⟩οῖς ἀγγέλοις· "σοὶ λέγω, Σωζόμενε, ἰδοὺ πόσα ἀγαθὰ σοι ἡτοίμασα ὑπὲρ ὅσον [196ᵛa] ἰδὼν με γυμνὸν σπλαγχνισθεὶς ἐνέδυσας· πορεύου οὖν καὶ ποίει ὁμοίως, κἀγώ σοι ποιήσω ὁμοίως · σὺ δὸς πένητι ἓν ἱμάτιον, κἀγώ σοι ἑτοιμάσω ἑκατονταπλασίονα τούτων." ταῦτα ἀκούσας ὁ Σωζόμενος, λέγει αὐτῷ μετὰ φόβου καὶ χαρᾶς· "κῦρι μου, ἆρα οὕτως πᾶσιν τοῖς ποιοῦσιν ἔλεος μετὰ τῶν πενήτων ἑκατονταπλασίονα φυλάττεις καὶ ζωὴν τὴν αἰώνιον;'' λέγει αὐτῷ ἐκεῖνος· ''πᾶς ὅστις ἀφῆκεν οἰκίας, ἢ ἀγρούς, ἢ πλοῦτον, ἢ δόξαν, ἢ πατέρα, ἢ μητέρα, ἢ ἀδελφούς, ἢ ἀδελφάς, ἢ γυναῖκα, ἢ τέκνα, ἤ τι τῶν ἐπιγείων, ἑκατονταπλασίονα λήψεται καὶ ζωὴν αἰώνιον κληρονομήσει. τοῦτο δέ σοι παραγγέλλω, μὴ μεταμεληθῇς ποτὲ ἐπὶ ἐλεημοσύνην, ὀνειδίζων τὸν πένητα ὅτι ἔδωκας αὐτῷ τι, μήπως ἀντὶ μισθοῦ διπλὴν τὴν ζημίαν ὑποστῇς· πᾶς γὰρ ὁ παρέχων τὴν εὐποιΐαν καὶ μετανοῶν ὀνειδίζων, καὶ τὸν μισθὸν ἀπόλλυσιν καὶ κρίμα ἕξει ἐν τῇ ἡμ⟨έ⟩ρᾳ ἐκείνης κρίσεως.'' ταῦτα ἀκούσας ὁ Σωζόμενος, ἔξυπνος ἐγένετο καὶ ἐξίστατο [196ᵛb] ἐν ἑαυτῷ, θαυμάζων ὅπερ ἑώρακεν. καὶ ἀναστὰς τῆς κλίνης αὐτοῦ καὶ τὸν ὕπνον ἀποτιναξάμενος, ἄρας καὶ τὸ ἕτερον αὐτοῦ ἱμάτιον, δέδωκεν καὶ αὐτὸ τοῖς δεομένοις· καὶ τῇ αὐτῇ νυκτὶ βλέπει πάλιν τὸ τοιοῦτον ὅραμα. καὶ τῷ πρωῒ ἀναστάς, διέδωκεν ἅπαντα τοῖς πένησιν, καὶ ἀποταξάμενος τῷ κόσμῳ γέγονεν Θαυμάσιος μοναχός. ὅτε οὖν ἀπετάξατο, βλέπει πάλιν τὸ ὅμοιον ὅραμα, τό, ὃς ἀφῆκεν τὰ τοῦ κόσμου ἡδέα, ἑκατονταπλασίονα ἐπουράνια ἀγαθὰ ἑτοιμάζονται αὐτῷ καὶ ζωὴ αἰώνιος. αὐτῷ ἡ δόξα εἰς τοὺς αἰῶνας ἀμήν.

V = *Vindobonensis Theol. Graecus* 10, foll. 195ᵛ-196ᵛ; R = A. Rystenko, *Materialy ... (ut in nota* 24 *supra*).

Titulus in rasura V[2] 2 ἄκρως] ἄκρος V et p. 62, 21 R 9 ὑψηλόκομα *in lexicis non inveni*: ὑψίκομα p. 62, 28 R 11 τῷ εἴδει] τὰ ἴδη V, *sed cf. ad l.* 39 *infra* 26 χρυσένδυτα *malim* χρυσένδετα 38 λευκάερα quid? λευκότε ρα p. 63, 25 R 39 τῷ εἴδει] τῶ ἴδη V 58 ἐκεί τῆς V: ἐκείνης V[2] *e corr.*: *malim* ἐκείνῃ τῆς.

The extent of the Sozomenus story is the same in the two Greek manuscripts and in the *Izbornik*. For all that, the text as it stands in the *Izbornik* is not an independent translation of a chapter dealing with Sozomenus and culled from some Greek miscellaneous manuscript. The fact that the Sozomenus story existed independently in Greek manuscripts must have influnced the choice of the Slavic compiler, but his version appears to be but a shortening[29] and a ''Kievization''[30] of chapter 69 in the Slavic translation, made somewhere in Bulgaria, of the Greek Life of St. Niphon.

29. Juxtapose *Life* of Niphon, p. 292, 15-17 ed. Rystenko: и придосте къ стоборию златъмь покровеноу, и скважьнѧми златаго стоборіа оузрѣста ины двьри и полаты ины зѣло славны и красьны with *Izbornik*, fol. 270ᵛ-271: и придосте къ стоборию золотъмь покръвеноу, и полаты зѣло славьны и красьны.

30. Cf. the systematic substitution of the East Slavic (ultimately Scandinavian) ларь ''chest'' for ковчежьць of the Slavic *Life* (compare p. 292, 20, 21, 25, 28, 29, 32 ed. Rystenko with *Izbornik*, fols. 271, 271ᵛ, 272, 272ᵛ). This substitution merely points to a Kievan editor, not translator, of the Sozomenus story.

⟨736⟩ To have identified the models for two of the *Izbornik*'s chapters is to have made only a modest step towards solving the general problem of its sources. However, even this should give food for thought to the proponents of the *Izbornik*'s originality. The recent years have generated some controvertible writing on this subject. We are told that the *Izbornik* cannot be a translation from the Greek, and that "the core" or "the majority" of its entries are original Old Russian works.[31] The *Admonition to the Rich* is treated as if it were an original work and is used to determine the social standpoint of the *Izbornik*'s readers.[32] It is granted that names of Byzantine Church Fathers appear in the headings of many of the *Izbornik*'s chapters, but these headings are said to be pseudepigraph, and the chapters, essentially original. Even direct borrowings from the Greek have been so drastically edited and rearranged in our text, that they should be viewed as (quasi-?) original works.[33] The *Izbornik* of 1076, so the argument goes, is not only original, but close to the Kievan life of the eleventh century, and was compiled in answer to the burning questions of its times. In particular, the Kiev uprising of 1068 and other popular movements of that period influenced the contents of the *Izbornik*, the basic idea of our text being to promote class reconciliation between the rich and the poor at the time of exacerbated social antagonisms.[34] Since the *Izbornik*, so we further hear, is essentially an original work, it is legitimate to look for its author.[35] The earlier idea that the Metropolitan of Kiev Hilarion (fl. ca. 1050) was the author of much of the *Izbornik*[36] is rejected not because it is patent nonsense, but

31. Ja. N. Ščapov in *Vizantijskij Vremennik*, 16 (1959), 295-296; I. U. Budovnic, "'Izbornik' Svjatoslava 1076 goda i 'Poučenie' Vladimira Monomaxa i ix mesto v istorii russkoj obščestvennoj mysli," *Trudy Otdela drevnerusskoj literatury*, 10 (1954), 51; repeated in *idem*, *Obščestvenno-političeskaja mysl'* ... (as in note 1 *supra*), chapter IV "Teorija obščestvennogo primirenija," pp. 111-112; 114; 124.

32. Budovnic, *Obščestvenno-političeskaja mysl'* ..., p. 115.

33. *Ibidem*, pp. 111-113; 114; 115; 118. Accordingly, when citing *Izbornik*, fols. 98 and 102^v, Mr. Budovnic puts the names of John Chrysostom and St. Basil in quotation marks (p. 123). And yet, fols. 97^v-98^v = Ioh. Chrysost., *In cap. XVIII Genes. Homil. XLII*, Migne, *PG*, 54, 389 and fols. 101^v-8^v = Ps.-Basil., *Sermo de asc. disc.*, Migne, *PG*, 31, 648 C-652 D.

34. *Ibidem*; pp. 20; 111; 116-120; 136.

35. Also called "authors," "compiler" and "compilers." *Ibidem*, pp. 118; 119; 120; 123; 124; 126; 130.

36. N. P. Popov, "Les auteurs de l'Izbornik de Svjatoslav de 1076," *Revue des Études Slaves*, 15 (1935), 210-223.

because the flourishing culture of eleventh-century Rus' could have produced many other outstanding writers contemporaneous with him.[37]

Facts about the *Izbornik* are much simpler and pose a different set of problems. For some time, I have been able to provide Greek equivalents for 3842 out of the *Izbornik*'s ca. 7115 (or, if we count the colophon, 7130) lines. It follows that the majority of the *Izbornik*'s entries are not original Old Rus' works. Since a large portion of the unidentified passages is strongly redolent of Greek prototypes, the ⟨737⟩ task before the scholars is not to assert that the entries for which they have not found the Greek equivalents are Russian entries. The primary task in front of them is to undertake a search for these equivalents and to put source research ahead of careless procedure.[38]

Only after systematic attempts at establishing the sources of the *Izbornik* have been undertaken, can the question of its originality be sensibly discussed. The investigation may leave a residuum of entries for which no Greek counterparts have been found. I predict that this residuum, if at all existent, will be small indeed. But even if it were nonexistent, questions like "what is the extent to which the Slavic text adapts, rather than merely translates, the Greek originals?" and "what are the reasons why the compilers of the entries had chosen precisely these and not other translated texts available to them?" would still be legitimate, if perhaps less exciting, questions to ask.

In conclusion, a word of caution. We should think twice before linking the work of the *Izbornik*'s compiler or compilers with Kievan historical realities of the late eleventh century. True, we assume that the compilation was made in Kiev, but we do it mostly on the strength of the phrase избьрано из мъногъ книгъ кнѧжихъ, "It was selected from numerous princely books," standing in the *Izbornik*'s colophon. There is, however, no more than a reasonable presumption that the library of the Kievan Prince Svjatoslav was meant by this statement. The fact that some entries of the *Izbornik* — and the Sozomenus story is one of them — exhibit undoubtedly Kievan lexical elements and forms does not yet

37. Budovnic, *Obščestvenno-političeskaja mysl'* ..., pp. 125-126.

38. In Obščestvenno-političeskaja mysl' ..., pp. 120; 121; 122; 140; 143; 144, a string of quotations from Siracides [11:29 and 33; 4:1-2; 7:20-21; 31 (34): 21-22; 32 (35): 4-5; 2:14; 4:30 (twice); 7:21; 7:20] is attributed to the "Izbornik" or to the "compiler of the Izbornik" and used for reconstructing the social thought of this compiler, his connection with the life that surrounded him, and for comparing the compiler's thought with that of Vladimir Monomax's *Statute*. Had the late Budovnic bothered to consult a Concordance to the Old Testament, he would have done us all a better service.

prove that all of the text was put together in eleventh-century Kiev, or, if it was, that all of its entries were edited there. It can be argued that all or some of them could have been adapted from Greek originals or from Slavic translations in tenth century Bulgaria,[39] and that East Slavic linguistic traits and some new stylistic devices may have been introduced into the *Izbornik* more than a century later, when our text was copied or compiled in Kiev.

Thus, although at present we should continue to view the *Izbornik* as a Kievan text of the eleventh century, we may have to modify some of our opinions on this point. As for the current opinions concerning the *Izbornik*'s originality, they will have to undergo a more serious revision.[40]

39. Cf. M. N. Speranskij, *Perevodnye sborniki...* (as in note 1 *supra*), pp. 505-515; Speranskij's still remains the most reasonable statement I have read on the *Stoslovec Gennadija*.

40. A re-edition of the *Izbornik* by an international team of scholars could provide the opportunity for putting the divergent views on this text's originality to constructive use. Over one year after the present article had been sent to the printer, I came across two publications by V. F. Dubrovina: "O grečeskix paralleljax k Izborniku 1076 goda," *Izvestija Akademii Nauk SSSR, Otdelenie literatury i jazyka*, 22, 2 (1963), 104-109 and "O privlečenii grečeskix parallelej dlja pročtenija perevodnyx russkix tekstov," *Issledovanija po lingvističeskomu istočnikovedeniju* (Moscow, 1963), pp. 36-44. After what has preceded, these articles, cautious as they are in places, feel like a whiff of fresh air. In the first of them, the author did not directly dispute the *Izbornik*'s originality, a view which "as it were" was generally accepted "at the present time" (p. 104). Instead, she compiled, for various parts of the *Izbornik*, a list of Greek parallels previously established in scholarly literature. The list, considerable if not exhaustive (cf., to quote Soviet publications alone, D. I. Abramovyč's article mentioned in n. 25 *supra* and the same author's "Izbornyk Sviatoslava 1076 roku i pateryky," *Naukovyj Zbirnyk Leninhrads'koho Tovarystva doslidnykiv ukrajins'koji istorii, pys'menstva ta movy*, 3 [1931], 11-15), enabled Ms Dubrovina to re-establish the connection between the *Life of St. Niphon* and the Sozomenus story (p. 107); what is more important, it led her to the conclusion that Greek parallels had been found for "about one-half" of the *Izbornik*'s entries (p. 108). It was especially gratifying to read (p. 109) her tentative view that at least some of the *Izbornik*'s parts may consist of texts translated from the Greek at earlier dates (and presumably at places other than Kiev). Ms Dubrovina's second article is a sober discussion of textual questions, based mainly on Greek parallels to the *Izbornik*. Scholars everywhere will welcome these encouraging developments, and will hope that the forthcoming re-edition of the *Izbornik* (cf. Dubrovina, "O grečeskix...," p. 108, n. 40; "O privlečenii...," p. 37, n. 2) goes one step further and establishes previously unrecorded Greek (and Slavic) parallels to this text.

XIX

George Christos Soulis, 1927-1966

George Christos Soulis died of a heart attack in his Berkeley home on June 18, 1966, at the age of thirty-nine. He died young — some ancient Greeks taught that, until the age of forty-one, one was a *neaniskos*, a youth — and at the height of his intellectual powers and his academic career. This career was brilliant and rapid; it took him from his native city of Ioannina, where his father was the leading educator, to the United States, and there, rung by rung, from Tufts University (B.A., 1949) to Harvard Graduate School (M.A., 1950), Harvard Society of Fellows (Junior Fellow 1952-55), the Harvard Faculty of Arts and Sciences (1957), the Harvard doctorate (1958), and to Harvard's Byzantine outpost at Dumbarton Oaks (Librarian, 1957-62, Lecturer in Byzantine History, 1959-62). After the Harvard years Soulis moved to Indiana University (Associate Professor, 1962-65) and finally to the University of California at Berkeley (1965).

Soulis first appeared in print when he was a mere seventeen; by the time of his death, his bibliography comprised about forty items, not counting his major work on Stefan Dušan. His scholarly interests developed in four main directions. Possessed of a vast bibliographical knowledge, he had a liking for bibliographical surveys and what the Germans call *Gelehrtengeschichte* — one of his first articles was devoted to the famous neo-Hellenist and bibliographer Emile Legrand. He cherished the recent past of his native country — hence his notes on Chateaubriand and the ⟨721⟩ Greek Revolution, on Thessalonica in 1821, on Adamantios Korais, and on the nineteenth-century poet Solomos. He investigated the various tesserae of the Balkan demographic mosaic — hence his articles on Slavic and Albanian settlements in medieval Greece and his classic study on the gypsies in Byzantium and the medieval Balkans (1961). Soulis's chief concern, however, and his most lasting contribution to our discipline, was the study of Byzantino-Serbian relations in the fourteenth century, especially during the reign of Tsar Stefan Dušan (1331-55). Dušan's period was the topic of his doctoral dissertation, of a number of articles, and the complementary Report which he was still able to prepare for the Thirteenth International Congress of Byzantine Studies held in Oxford in September 1966.

Through his early education Soulis developed a love for his country's Christian past and acquired familiarity with Greek of all epochs. His Harvard years taught him to combine his love for Greece with sympathetic interest in her medieval Slavic neighbors; they gave him a thorough grounding in bibliography, and the Dumbarton Oaks Library reaped the benefit of this training during Soulis's librarianship there; finally, these years provided him with knowledge of Slavic languages and cultures. In addition to the Balkans, Soulis studied medieval Russia, an interest which deepened during a year's stay in Leningrad (1962-63).

Such outlook and equipment determined the quality of Soulis's scholarship: in a field where yesterday's concerns and mutual ignorance sometimes warp the views of the remote past, he was dispassionate, liberal, and thoroughly informed and served no cause except that of research. In a chapter of his unpublished work on Dušan, Soulis expressed doubt that the Tsar had aimed at creating a national state. Dušan, Soulis maintained, had rather conceived himself as the head of a universal Christian empire. This was in agreement with the tenets of Byzantine political theory, the only theory with which Dušan's milieu was familiar.

This liberal bent, impartiality, soft-spoken authority coming from competence, and total absence of self-centeredness — that professional weakness of academics — characterized Soulis as a man, colleague, and teacher.

In the recent past, Byzantine studies have suffered more than their share of tragic losses in the ranks of young and brilliant members of the discipline. The interwar years took away John Sykoutres. The Second World War claimed Otto Treitinger and Stephan Binon. In the 1950s, an airplane crash bereaved us of Jacques Moreau, and an illness contracted on an expedition, of André Maricq. Now George Soulis has joined those *aōroi*, the untimely dead. Those who remain, whether young or old, hope that his book on Stefan Dušan and Byzantium will soon be published. Byzantino-Slavic studies owe it to themselves and to Soulis's memory.

The *Dumbarton Oaks Papers*, Vol. XXI (1967), will carry a full bibliography of George Soulis's work. For the readers of *Slavic Review*, I append a list of Soulis's articles dealing with Slavic topics. "The First Period of the Serbian Domination of Thessaly, 1348-1356," *Epetēris Hetaireias Byzantinōn Spoudōn*, XX (1950), 56-73 (in Greek); "Tsar Stefan Dušan and the Holy Mountain," *ibid.*, XXII (1952), 82-96 (in Greek); "On the Slavic Settlement in Hierissos in the Tenth Century," *Byzantion*, XXIII (1953), 67-72; "On the Mediaeval Albanian Tribes of the Malakasioi, Bouoi, and Mesaritai," *Epetēris Hetaireias Byzantinōn Spoudōn*, XXIII (1953), 213-16 (in Greek); "Tsar Dušan and Mount

Athos," *Harvard Slavic Studies*, II (1954), 125-39; "The History of George Castriotes Scanderbeg in the Light of Recent Research," *Epetēris Hetaireias Byzantinōn Spoudōn*, XXVIII (1958), 446-57 (in Greek); "Notes on the History of the City of Serres under the Serbs (1345- 1371)," *Aphierōma M. Triantaphyllidē* (1960), pp. 373-79; "The Gypsies in the Byzantine Empire and in the Balkans in the Late Middle Ages," *Dumbarton Oaks Papers*, XV (1961), 141-65; "Historical Studies in the Balkans in Modern Times," *The Balkans in Transition*, ed. by C. and B. Jelavich (Berkeley and Los Angeles, 1963), 421-38; "The Legacy of Cyril and Methodius to the Southern Slavs," *Dumbarton Oaks Papers*, XIX (1965), 19-43; Supplementary Papers to Georges Ostrogorsky, "Problèmes des relations byzantino-serbes au XIVe siècle," *Thirteenth International Congress of Byzantine Studies, Oxford 1966,* Summaries of Supplementary Papers, pp. 11-15.

XX

Russo-Byzantine Relations after the Eleventh Century

I

Relations in General: Two Points of View

Ever since Tatiščev and Lomonosov in the eighteenth century, Russian scholarship has attempted to assess the extent and the character of Byzantine influence upon Rus', both that of Kiev and that of Moscow. Since the problem had two facets, influence and response, solutions proposed oscillated between two poles: the emphasis fell either on the magnitude of the Byzantine impact in all domains of culture and material civilization, or on the unique way in which borrowings from Byzantium, if at all admitted, were assimilated and transformed by the autochthonous culture of Rus'.

During the last quarter of a century, the latter solution prevailed in the works of Russian Byzantinists. However, in the past several years, the pendulum seems to have begun a swing towards a middle position, wherein two facets of Byzantino-Russian relations — imitation of the Byzantine models and local transformations of the impulses coming from the Empire — are being taken into account. The report which our Soviet colleagues have submitted to the congress is representative of this very welcome trend.

Particularly gratifying are the summaries of conclusions derived from hitherto unexploited written and archaeological sources. Such are the findings of G. G. Litavrin concerning Byzantine sovereignty over Tmutorokan' under Alexius I (Main Paper III, p. 77 and n. 4),[1] the ingenious interpretation of a letter by Michael Choniates by A. P. Každan (ibid., p. 73), and the discovery, reported by Ju. L. Ščapova, among others, of Greek workshops producing glassware in Kiev from the tenth

1. These findings were reported by Litavrin in 'A propos de Tmutorokan', *Byzantion*, xxxv (1965), pp. 221-34. For the full text of Straboromanos in Coisl. 139, on which Litavrin based his thesis, cf. now. P. Gautier in *Revue des Études Byzantines*, xxiii (1965), pp. 172-5, 178-93; esp. p. 190, ll. 26-27.

to the thirteenth centuries and offering objects of higher quality than those of their Rus' counterparts (ibid., p. 72 and n. 7). Finally, the authors of the main paper (p. 71 and n. 5) espoused the sound theory that the Rus' church hierarchy was established by the Patriarchate of Constantinople at the time of Vladimir's adoption of Christianity.[2]

⟨94⟩ The majority of the statements contained in the main paper, however, had perforce to rest on evidence, from Rus' and Byzantium, with which we have been familiar for a long time. And it is precisely in the interpretation of this familiar evidence that the difference between the 'autochthonous' and the 'pro-Byzantine' points of view becomes most apparent. While one scholar (ibid., p. 82) saw in Hilarion's *Sermon on the Law and Grace* an expression of national self-consciousness

2. Only in a few instances does the main paper seem unaffected by the new trend. 1. When one of its authors stresses the originality of early musical notation in Rus', both of the *krjuki* and the *kondakarnoe* varieties (p. 86), she differs not only from the views of non-Russian scholarship (Palikarová-Verdeil, Koschmieder, von Gardner), but also from what we read in the newest Soviet study of the subject (N.Uspenskij - Ju.Keldyš, *Drevne-russkoe pevčeskoe iskusstvo* (Moscow, 1965). That study points to similarities between the twelfth-century *krjuki* and the palaeobyzantine notations and shows the Byzantine origin of both the *kondakarnoe* notation and of its chant. The main paper's detailed evaluation of early Russian and Byzantine music (p. 86) assumes information which as yet does not exist, since by general admission neither the early *krjuki* nor the *kondakarnoe* notations have been deciphered (cf. N. Uspenskij - Ju. Keldyš, op. cit., pp. 7, 37). 2. One would wish to learn more about the statement (Main Paper III, p. 83) that at a very early period the Greek Nomocanon was translated in Rus' into "Old Russian", since this statement differs from the prevailing scholarly opinion. Of the two early types of the Slavic Nomocanon, the first type, best represented by the *Ustjužskaja Kormčaja* (thirteenth century, Rus' redaction), is universally considered to have been translated — most probably in Great Moravia — by Methodius or a member of his milieu; cf. the proofs in H. F. Schmid, *Die Nomokanonübersetzung des Methodius...* (= *Veröffentlichungen des baltischen u. slavischen Instituts a.d. Universität Leipzig* I; 1922), passim; J. Vašica, 'Metodějův překlad nomokánonu', *Slavia*, xxiv (1955), pp. 9-41. The second type, best represented by the *Jefremovskaja Kormčaja* (Russian redaction, twelfth century = *J.K.*) is said to go back to an Old Church Slavonic (or Bulgarian) original as well. This is implied in H. F. Schmid, *Die Nomokanonübersetzung...*, p. 48, in S. P. Obnorskij, *O jazyke Jefremovskoj Kormčej xii veka* (= *Imp. Akad. Nauk, Izsledovanija po russkomu jazyku*, iii, 2; 1912), pp. 36 (reference to the *'staroslavjanskij original'* of *J.K.*), 53, 57, and expressly stated in J. Vašica, *Literární památky epochy velkomoravské* (Prague, 1966), pp. 63-64 and in earlier works discussed by Ivan Žužek, *Kormčaja Kniga* (= *Orientalia Christiana Analecta*, clxviii; 1964), pp.

brought about by Byzantine attempts to subjugate Rus' spiritually, L. Müller found no anti-Byzantine tendencies in the same text, and, on the contrary, felt it to be friendly to the Greeks.[3] The canonization of Boris and Gleb may or may not have occurred against the will of the Byzantine Church (ibid., p. 82). It is certain, however, that in the twelfth-century *Skazanie* about these two Saints, people 'from Greece' are mentioned first among the *cognoscenti* who admired the beauty of their tomb. When the author of the *Skazanie* thought of a fabulous land to which his ⟨95⟩ heroes might depart on important business after announcing a miracle, he mentioned the 'Greek Land', that is, Byzantium.[4]

Andrej Bogoljubskij's attempt to wrest from the Byzantine Patriarchate permission to establish a metropolis of his own, and the publicistic

---

21-28. Cf. also S. S. Bobčev, *Starobŭlgarski pravni pametnici* (Sofia, 1903), pp. 24-25. The hypothesis that the *J.K.* reflects a translation undertaken in Rus' in the time of Jaroslav the Wise (d. 1054) is due to A. S. Pavlov, *Pervonačal'nyj slavjanorusskij Nomokanon* (Kazan', 1869), p. 56. However, Pavlov offered this hypothesis after much hesitation and admitted that *J.K.*'s prototype may date from the earliest period of Slavic letters, cf. ibid., pp. 33, 54, 58. To square his theory with the linguistic data contained in the *J.K.*, he had to assign the translation to Bulgarian scribes imported by Jaroslav the Wise, ibid., p. 58. No wonder that Pavlov found very few followers (and his view is explicitly rejected in Vašica, 'Metodějův překlad...,' p. 16, n. 21). On the originals of Slavic Nomocanons, cf. the summaries by Th. Saturník, *Příspěvky k šíření byzantského práva u Slovanů* (= *Rozpravy České Akad. Věd a Umění*, Tř. I, č. 64; 1922), pp. 15-22, by Žužek, *Kormčaja*, pp. 14-45, and by Vašica, 'Metodějův překlad,' pp. 9-10 and passim and *Literární památky*, pp. 63-70. I share the opinion of Vašica, 'Metodějův překlad,' p. 16 and P. Lavrov, *Kyrylo ta Metodij v davn'o-slavjans'komu pys'menstvi* (= *Ukrajins'ka Akademija Nauk, Zbirnyk istor.-filol. viddilu*, lxxviii; 1928), p. 202, that the most likely time for the Slavic translation represented by the *J.K.* is the Bulgarian Tsar Symeon's reign, since (*a*) the language of this document is archaic, but younger than that of the *Ustjužskaja Kormčaja* (cf. Vašica, 'Metodějův překlad', pp. 23-32, (*b*), *J.K.*, although it follows the Greek slavishly, attempts to 'nationalize' the technical terms often left untranslated in earlier texts; both these devices are characteristic of translators of Symeon's age. For an attempt to assign the prototype of *J.K.* to Prince Boris's period, cf. Žužek, *Kormčaja*, p. 24 and n. 31; for an (erroneous) attempt to assign it to Methodius, cf. A. Soloviev in *Bratstvo*, xxvi (1932), p. 26.

3. L. Müller, *Des Metropoliten Ilarion Lobrede auf Vladimir den Heiligen* (= *Slavistische Studienbücher*, ii; 1962), pp. 23-27, 31.

4. Cf. D. I. Abramovič, ed., *Žitija svjatykh mučenikov Borisa i Gleba* (= *Pamjatniki drevnerusskoj literatury, Vypusk* ii; 1916), p. 63, ll. 22-24; p. 61, ll. 28-29.

works written under this prince's auspices to enhance the prestige of his own principality, were expertly investigated by N. N. Voronin (ibid., p. 80 and n. 2). While he saw anti-Byzantine barbs in the Prince's actions and his bookmen's writings, it is well to remind ourselves of what, after others, Mr. Voronin has told us himself: that Our Lady of Vladimir is a Constantinopolitan icon; that the feast of the *Pokrov* (October I) was expressly modelled on a vision in the *Life* of the Prince's namesake, Andrew the God's-Fool (in Rus' October 2); that the legend of Bishop Leontij of Rostov, conceived to enhance the importance of this see, stressed its hero's Greek origin, and that the parallel to Andrej Bogoljubskij's expedition against the Bulgars in 1164 was the fictitious campaign of the Byzantine Emperor, Manuel I.[5] What in one perspective is a claim to equality, in another appears as an act of status-seeking; and the challenge which this act involves seems directed against Kiev rather than Constantinople.[6]

A different perspective — one viewing the Bogoljubskij episode from Constantinople and Kiev — helps us to rearrange our evidence and thus to go a step beyond the information contained in the Byzantine Patriarch's letter of 1168. The first securely known instance in which a

---

5. N. N. Voronin, 'Skazanie o pobede nad Bolgarami 1164 g. i prazdnike Spasa', *Problemy obščestvenno-političeskoj istorii Rossii i slavjanskikh stran ... k 70-letiju ... M. N. Tikhomirova* (Moscow, 1963), p. 91, attributes the passage 'Lord, grant repentance to *me* the sinner ... since ... I repulsed my guardian angel', occurring in the story of the campaign of 1164, to Prince Bogoljubskij himself: V. Ključevskij (ed.), *Skazanie o čudesakh Vladimirskoj ikony* ... (= *Obščestvo ljubitelej drevnej pis'mennosti i iskusstva*, xxx; 1878), p. 26. However, what follows immediately are the words 'I wrote by order of Emperor Manuel (*az' že napisakh' poveleniem' c̄r̄jā Manuila*)'. If the first passage is by Bogoljubskij, then these words, too, must be by him; and the Prince behaves as an antiquarian bookman invoking Byzantium's authority to endow a local Russian holiday with legitimacy, rather than as a ruler 'struggling against Byzantine "hegemony"' (Voronin, ibid.). Cf. also the statement (ed. Ključevskij, ibid., pp. 21-22) that the holiday was established by Andrej, Emperor Manuel (read *c̄r̄em̄' Manoilom* instead of *otcem' M.*), and 'by order of Lukas' (Chrysoberges) 'the Patriarch'. In fact, it is risky to look for Bogoljubskij's own prose in a text with as many anachronisms in prosopography and titulature as the story of 1164.

6. Another miraculous icon of Bogoljubskij's time, Our Lady *Znamenie* of Novgorod, copied the famous icon of the Blachernae. Some traits of the *Znamenie* legend were borrowed from Byzantine hagiography. Cf., e.g., A. Frolow, 'Le *Znamenie* de Novgorod: les origines de la légende', *Revue des Études Slaves*, xxv (1949), esp. pp. 50-67. The miracle performed by the

Rus' Metropolitan used the formula πάσης 'Ρωσίας occurs on a seal of Constantine II[7] who arrived in Kiev in 1168, just after ⟨96⟩ Andrej Bogoljubskij's attempts had been rebuked by Patriarch Lukas Chrysoberges. Another probable occurrence of the formula 'of All Rus'' on a Kievan Metropolitan's seal is to be dated to the rule of John IV (1164-6).[8] This second piece of evidence would also bring us into the period of the controversy between Bogoljubskij and the Patriarchate of Constantinople over the establishment of a new metropolis in Vladimir. All known earlier seals, including that of Constantine I (1156-9), lack the word 'All' before 'Rus'' while all purportedly earlier occurrences of the

---

Znamenie icon on the ramparts of Novgorod caused the rout of the besiegers led by Bogoljubskij's son in 1170. Thus not only Bogoljubskij, but also his enemies relied on Byzantium to enhance their status. The story of 1164 was revived in the years of Metropolitan Macarius — perhaps at his instigation — in an excursus written by the Serbian bookman Anikita Lev Filolog and inserted into his eulogy of Prince Michael of Chernigov. Filolog's purpose was to legitimize Bogolujbskij's supposed claims to a tsar's title: Andrew acquired 'an imperial name' on account of his courage (an erudite pun), 'for bonds of close frienship linked him to the Greek Emperor Manuel'. Cf. *Velikie Minei-Četii* (1869), September 20, col. 1319. Thus not even in the mid-sixteenth century, when the Muscovite political ideology was acquiring its final form, did the function of the story of 1164 go beyond status-seeking.

7. V. Laurent, *Le Corpus des sceaux de l'empire byzantin*, v, i (Paris, 1963), p. 606 = nr. 790. In the unpublished work by N. P. Likhačev, *Trudy Paleografii*, ii, Constantine II's seal is attributed to Constantine I (1156-9); cf. A. V. Soloviev, 'Metropolitensiegel des Kiewer Russland', *B.Z.*, (1962), pp. 293 and 296. V. Laurent's view is the correct one. For an authentic seal of Constantine I, cf. Laurent, *Le Corpus*, v, i, nr. 789.

8. Cf. Laurent, *Le Corpus*, v, i, nr. 781, *Nota* and v, 2, nr. 1605; Soloviev, *B.Z.*, lv (1962), p. 294. Laurent, and later Soloviev, *B.Z.*, lvi (1963), pp. 317-19, argue for attribution to John III (IV), rather than to any of John's earlier homonyms. The formula 'Metropolitan of All Rus'' occurs in Lukas Chrysoberges's letter to Prince Andrej, cf. *Russkaja Istoričeskaja Biblioteka*, vi (2nd ed., 1908), col. 65 = nr. 3. To avoid circular argument, I do not use its text as proof for the formula's existence in Lukas's time. Nor do I use the reference to a 'Kievan metropolitan of all Rus' in the Second Novgorod Chronicle *s.a.* 1165 (*P.S.R.L.*, (1841), p. 125); in this Chronicle, represented by a single manuscript of *c.* 1600, the 'full' formula occurs in an entry inserted by a hand different from that of the scribe. Similar considerations apply to the mention of 'Metropolitan Constantine of All Rus'' in the story of the campaign of 1164 (ed. V. Ključevskij, *Skazanie* [as on p. 95, note 2 *supra*], p. 22); the story is attested only in sixteenth- and seventeenth-century manuscripts, and there was no Metropolitan Constantine in 1164.

formula 'All Rus' in the title of the Kievan Metropolitan turn out to be later than the sixties of the twelfth century.[9] A Byzantinist, more sensitive to the claims issuing from the capital than to those raised by its ecclesiastical province, is tempted to interpret the introduction of the word 'All' before 'Rus'' in the Kievan metropolitan's title as a rebuke to Andrej Bogoljubskij and an assertion of the Patriarchate's advocacy of a sole metropolis for Rus'.[10]

II

Literary Relations: Two Perspectives

Opinions vary as to the principles which governed the selection of Byzantine works to be translated into Slavic. It has been observed that

---

9. 1. Seal Laurent, *Le Corpus*, v, i, nr. 791 (cf. Soloviev, *B.Z.*, LV (1962), pp. 293 and 297-8) belongs to Nicephorus II (*c.* 1182-97), rather than to Nicephorus I (1104-21). 2. An enigmatic seal, dating from the twelfth century, probably displays the name Constantine, cf. Soloviev, *B.Z.*, lv (1962), p. 297. If this is so, it should be attributed to Constantine II. 3. A reference to Metropolitan Nicephorus I 'of All Rus' occurs in a colophon quoted in the Nikon Chronicle, a sixteenth-century work (*P.S.R.L.*; ix (1862), p. 149), from where it was taken over by Tatiščev (*Istorija Rossijskaja*, ii (ed. of 1963), p. 132). The source from which the Nikon Chronicle derived its quotation is no longer extant. Since the formula 'of All Rus'' was familiar to all in the sixteenth century, I attribute no value to its occurrence in the Nikon Chronicle *sub anno* 1116. All known seals of Russian Metropolitans in the pre-Mongol period have been recently enumerated by V. L. Janin and A. A. Litavrin, 'Novye materialy o proiskhoždenii Vladimira Monomakha', *Istoriko-arkheologičeskij sbornik A. V. Arcikhovskomu* (Moscow, 1962), p. 207, n. 11. Nothing in their list invalidates the view proposed here.

10. In 1963, V. Laurent, *Le Corpus*, v, i, nr. 793, gave us the *editio princeps* of a late twelfth-century seal which may attest the existence of one Moses, Metropolitan of Vladimir on the Kljaz'ma, at the time (Main Paper, p. 80 and n. 3). If read correctly, this seal would show that Andrej Bogoljubskij did score an ephemeral success in his tug-of-war with the Patriarch Lukas Chrysoberges. However, personal inspection of the seal led me to believe that the reading ΠΟΛ[ε]ωC ΒΛΑΔΗ... is untenable. Would it not be possible to read ΠΟΛ[ε]ωC ΚΑΤΑΝ(ΗC) (cf. V. Laurent, ibid., nrs. 893-6), to date the seal to the eleventh century and to assign it to Sicily? The seal (American Numismatic Society, Mabbott Collection, nr. 302) was purchased from the Feuardent family. The firm of Rollin and Feuardent did obtain material from Sicily. Nothing in the Feuardent Collection struck Mr Mabbott as coming from Russia (information contained in Professor Mabbott's letters of 23 September, and 29 October, 1966). Cf., Figure 1 on p. 284.

this selection was haphazard, that the first-rate Byzantine texts were not translated at all, and that the works translated were out of date at the time of translation, the time lag sometimes amounting to five hundred years. To explain this, the main paper (pp. 90-1) ⟨97⟩ postulates a form of Byzantine censorship: the Byzantines, it states, were not interested in supporting translations of texts containing elements of free-thinking and of criticism levelled at the society of the time. The truth, in my opinion, seems to have been simpler. A glance at the six Byzantine chronicles translated by medieval Slavs — most of them were popular in medieval Rus' although for only one of these translations, that of George the Monk, can a Kievan origin be postulated — does show that, with the possible exception of Zonaras, the Slavs assimilated second-rate Byzantine historical literature. But the choice seems to have corresponded to their needs and interests. We may imagine these needs as the desire to obtain a chronological framework so that local history could be placed within it (hence the translation of Nicephorus's *Breviarium*); and the desire to obtain knowledge of world history (hence the exclusive reliance on world chronicles).

The other reason for the choice must have been the availability of works to be translated or used. We know nothing about Byzantine censorship, but we do know about the unsuccessful attempts by Grigorij, the Serbian compiler of Zonaras's *Paralipomenon*, to find the texts of Xenophon, Herodotus, Appian, Dio Cassius, Eusebius of Caesarea, Theodoretus of Cyrrhus, and even Nicetas David Paphlagon. By 1409, no friend of Grigorij knew where such authors were to be found.[11] What was true of the medieval Balkans and Mount Athos, where Grigorij was writing, may be inferred for medieval Rus'.

In one respect, however, the effect of the translated historical works was different in the Balkans and Rus'. In Bulgaria, Byzantium's closest neighbour, these translations were considered sufficient substitutes for local history, and thus stymied the development of local historiography. In Rus', Byzantine influence was strong enough to stimulate local activity and to provide some raw material for chronicle writing. But the Empire was far enough away for Byzantine histories to have been inadequate as a source of information on local events; hence the blossoming of local historiography in Rus', by far superior to that of other Orthodox Slavs.

11. Text e.g. in M. Weingart, *Byzantské kroniky v literatuře cirkevněslovanské*, i (Bratislava, 1922), p. 127.

In literary studies, we are accustomed to focus our attention on authors and translators. Literature, however, is not only something one writes but also something one reads. When we examine the reading matter available in medieval Rus', rather than the original literary output of Rus', we find the Byzantine impact to be quite considerable, no matter whether it was received directly from Byzantium or through the intermediary of the Balkans. The catalogue of the library of the Kirillo-Belozerskij Monastery gives us an insight into the reading tastes of a leading monastic community in late-fifteenth-century Rus'.[12] Out of two hundred and ⟨98⟩ twelve books listed in the catalogue, we may eliminate some ninety items of liturgical character. Most of the others were translations of Byzantine homiletic, hagiographic, and ascetic texts. In theology, the gap in time we observed in historiography does not occur. Not only ancient Fathers of the Church and authors of the tenth to eleventh centuries, but also translations of the 'latest' fourteenth-century writings of Gregory the Sinaite and Gregory Palamas appeared on the shelves of the monastery in the fifteenth century. Only two texts in the library were by authors of Rus' (Hilarion and Cyril of Turov), and one more (written by a Bulgarian prelate, Cyprian) treated a recent Russian, the Metropolitan Peter of Rus' (d. 1326). Only two among the two hundred and twelve volumes were secular in content and, needless to say, both of them were translations from the Greek. The holdings of the Kirillo-Belozerskij Monastery were very similar to those of the Patmos library, which we know through catalogues dating from 1103, 1200, and 1355.[13] The differences between the two collections, though slight, were significant. On Patmos, the number of manuscripts was higher (330) in 1200; so was the number of manuscripts of secular content (17); and by 1355 Patmos did boast a copy of Plato's *Dialogues*. For all that, the works of literature read in a prominent fifteenth-century monastery in Muscovy were almost exclusively Byzantine in content.

12. N. K. Nikol'skij, *Opisanie rukopisej Kirillo-Belozerskogo monastyrja, sostavlennoe v konce XV veka* (= *Izdanija Obščestva Ljubitelej Drevnej Pis'mennosti*, cxiii; 1897).

13. Catalogue of 1200 (on the date [1200, not 1201], cf. E. L. Vranoussi, Ὁ καθηγούμενος τῆς μονῆς Πάτμου Ἰωσὴφ Ἰασίτης καὶ ἡ ἀρχαιοτέρη ἀναγραφὴ χειρογράφων τῆς μονῆς, Δελτίον τῆς χριστιανικῆς ἀρχαιολογικῆς ἑταιρείας, iv, 4 [1964-5] (Athens, 1966), p. 350, n. 1): Ch. Diehl, 'Le Trésor et la bibliothéque de Patmos au commencement du XIIIe siècle', *B.Z.*, i (1892); pp. 488-525 (reprinted, without the text of the catalogue, in the same author's *Études byzantines* (Paris, 1905), p. 307 et seq.). Catalogue of 1355: *P.G.*, cxlix, cols. 1049-52.

Students of Russo-Byzantine literary relations should keep two rules in mind. Both of them are routine, but essential for progress in this field. In the first place, investigation of Rus' texts and concepts should begin with a search for their possible Byzantine sources. Observance of this old rule does yield fruitful results. The recent work on medieval Rus' lexicography by L. S. Kovtun,[14] the new edition of the *Izbornik of 1076*, and the articles by V. F. Dubrovina are cases in point, although these studies only sum up our previous knowledge concerning the Greek sources of Russian texts. Much remains to be done in the study of the *Izbornik*'s models.[15] For the later period, even occasional gleanings throw new light on important literary figures; for instance, we know now the Byzantine source of the text preserved in a manuscript of the year 1414 and misquoted by Philotheus of Pskov.[16]

In the second place, in their attempts at reconstructing the Rus' image of the Greeks, students of cultural history should make use of Rus' texts of semi-learned character — short chronicles, the *Rěč' tonkoslovia grečeskago*, and the *Azbukovniki*. These deserve closer study. The *Rěč' tonkoslovia*, a fifteenth-century word and phrase book, is a mine of information on the everyday life — and plight — of a hypothetical Rus' monk in a Greek milieu. It wavers between respect for the Greek tongue and resentment towards the difficult, unfriendly, and unloving Greeks. Moreover, it expresses the expatriate's disenchantment with social injustice in Rus' itself, and in one instance helps us understand the usage of a contemporary learned author, Epiphanius the Wise.[17] In the post-

14. L. S. Kovtun, *Russkaja leksikografija epokhi srednevekovija* (Moscow and Leningrad, 1963).

15. Cf. V. S. Golyšenko and others (edd.) *Izbornik 1076 goda* (Moscow, 1965); V. F. Dubrovina, 'O grečeskikh paralleljakh k Izborniku 1076 goda', *Izvestija Akad. Nauk SSSR, Otd. Literatury i Jazyka*, xxii, 2 (1963), pp. 104-9; eadem, 'O privlečenii grečeskikh parallelej dlja pročtenija perevodnykh russkikh tekstov', *Issledovanija po lingvističeskomu istočnikovedeniju* (1963), pp. 36-44. I tried to cover new ground in I. Ševčenko, 'On Some Sources of Prince Svjatoslav's Izbornik of the Year 1076', *Orbis Scriptus, Dmitrij Tschižewskij zum 70. Geburtstag* (Munich, 1966), pp. 723-38. Cf. also J. Lépissier, *Revue des Études Slaves*, xvl (1966), pp. 39-47 (parallel results).

16. Juxtapose A. I. Sobolevskij's review of V. Malinin, *Starec ... Filofej ...* (1901) in *Žurnal Min. Narodnogo Prosveščenija*, cccxxviii (1901, December), p. 490, with S. G. Mercati, 'Su una poesia giambica nel codice 605 del monastero di Dionisio nel Monte Athos', *B.Z.*, lii (1959), p. 11.

17. The best edition is by M. Vasmer, *Ein russisch-byzantinisches Gesprächsbuch...* (= *Veröffentlichungen des baltischen und slavischen Instituts*

Byzantine period, the *Azbukovniki* ⟨99⟩ which are a cross between dictionaries of foreign words and encyclopaedias, deplore the difficulty of the Greek tongue, and prove by their copious 'Byzantine' elements that Byzantinisms were felt to be worth knowing, but were unfamiliar to the semi-learned reading public of the late sixteenth and seventeenth centuries.[18]

III

Ecclesiastical Relations in the Fourteenth Century: Two Alternatives

The authors of the main paper chose to end their treatment of the subject in the middle of the thirteenth century. This was a wise decision, given the space which they had at their disposal and the wealth of previous investigations devoted to the twelfth century. Since, however, the original title of the subject is *Russo-Byzantine Relations after the Eleventh Century*, I shall interpret it as open-ended and conclude with some remarks on the skill and far-sightedness of the Byzantine Patriarchate's policy toward Eastern Europe in the fourteenth century. *Pace* the authors of the main paper (p. 69), Russo-Byzantine ecclesiastical relations *were* of importance; and in the fourteenth and fifteenth centuries this importance was political as well as ecclesiastical, since in the late Byzantine period the universal claims of the Byzantine Emperor — that politically impotent sovereign — were raised in alliance with the Church

---

an der Universität Leipzig, ii; 1922). Cf. esp. entries 341-2; 376-9; 384; 2756-830. Entry 941 *medvěd': arkuda* (in a distorted form *akrudo* already in *Greckoj jazyk*, ed. P. K. Simoni (*Izvestija Otd. Russ. Jazyka i Slovesnosti Imper. Akad. Nauk*, xiii, i [1908], p. 180, cf. p. 182) explains the gem *zvěr' rekomyi arkuda, eže skazaetsja medvěd* in Epiphanius the Wise's *Life* of Sergius of Radonež, in *Pamjatniki drevnej Pis'mennosti i Iskusstva*, lviii (1885), p. 55. Good lexicographical analysis of the *Reč' tonkoslovia* in L. S. Kovtun (as on p. 98 note 2 *supra*), pp. 326-89; 395-7.

18. On the difficulty of the Greek, cf. the quotation in A. I. Sobolevskij, 'Perevodnaja literatura Moskovskoj Rusi xvi-xviii vekov', *Imp. Akad. Nauk, Sbornik Otdel. Russ. Jazyka i Slovesnosti*, lxxiv, i, (1903), p. 284. The *Azbukovniki* absorbed the whole *Rěč' tonkoslovia*, cf. e.g., L. S. Kovtun (as in note 2 *supra*), pp. 375 et seq.; however, their Greek elements go beyond the borrowings from the *Rěč*: cf. the Homeric entry in the *Azbukovnik* of the Houghton Library, Harvard, fol. 30: *depas: čaša; depaesi; čašami*. Only Western material of the *Azbukovniki* has been systematically examined: M. P. Alekseev, 'Zapadnoevropejskie slovarnye materialy v drevnerusskikh azbukovnikakh xvi-xvii vekov', *Akademiku V. V. Vinogradovu k ego šestidesjatiletiju* ... (1956), pp. 25-41.

of Constantinople, protector of 'all the Christians'.[19] On the other hand, various political centres in Eastern Europe used the Church as a weapon in their attempts to hold on to or expand their power.

The vantage point of my remarks will be that of Constantinople, not that of various Rus' political centres; and I shall survey some of the alternatives which were facing the Byzantine Emperor and Patriarch and were conditioning their policy towards what today are the Lithuanian, Belo-Russian, Ukrainian, and 'Great Russian' territories.[20] Sources of the fourteenth century show that the Byzantines were aware both of Kiev's decay and the fragmentation of Rus' into warring principalities.[21] Still, for all their squabbles, these principalities were considered as parts of one whole. The Patriarchal Acts observed that the civil war in Byzantium ⟨100⟩ and the ensuing division of the originally unified metropolis of Kiev 'almost' led to civil wars among the Russes.[22] The division of *Rōsia*, as this word was understood by the Patriarchate of Constantinople, found its expression in the terms 'Little', 'Great', and 'All Russia', terms whose introduction is ascribed — rightly or wrongly — to the Byzantines of the fourteenth century.[23]

One curious problem arises in connexion with the Byzantine practice of subdividing *Rōsia*. In the fifties of the fourteenth century, the

---

19. Eastern European contemporaries were well aware of the Emperor's role in church affairs. Bishops assembled in Nowogródek to elect Gregory Camblak Metropolitan of Kiev in 1415 protested against 'the violence done by the Emperor [i.e. Manuel II] to God's Church' and refused to accept metropolitans 'ordained by the Emperor who is a layman', cf. *Russkaja Istor. Biblioteka*, vi (2nd ed., 1908), cols. 313-4. On the Greek side, Patriach Joseph II, too, stressed Manuel II's role in the Camblak episode, cf. ibid., cols. 357-60.

20. For a recent discussion of the same topic from the vantage-point of Moscow, cf. I. N. Šabatin, 'Iz istorii russkoj cerkvi. Ot dnja končiny sv. Mitr. Aleksija do osuščestvlenija russkoj cerkovnoj avtokefalii (1378-1448 g.)', *Vestnik russkogo zap.-evropejskogo patriaršego ekzarkhata*, xiii (1965), esp. pp. 36-45.

21. Kiev's decay: Nic. Gregoras, *Hist.*, iii, pp. 513 ll. 14-16 (Bonn ed.); F. Miklosich - J. Müller, *Acta Patriarchatus Constantinopolitani* ... (subsequently referred to as M.M.), ii (1862), p. 13 (a. 1380). Fragmentation: M.M., ii, p. 116 (a. 1389).

22. M.M., i (1860), p. 267 (a. 1347).

23. A Greek *Notitia episcopatum* of 1261-8 would be the earliest preserved text to use the term 'Little Russia': cf. H. Gelzer, 'Beiträge zur russischen Kirchengeschichte aus griechischen Quellen', *Zeitschrift für Kirchengeschichte*, xiii (1892), p. 248. However, the dating of this *Notitia* is hypothetical. The term oc-

historian Nicephorus Gregoras wrote a learned excursus on Rus'[24] in which he asserted that there existed four *Rōsiae*: three Christian ones and one pagan, which, so Gregoras added proudly, did not knuckle down to the Tartars. Of the three Christian *Rōsiae*, we can identify two with certainty. These are Moscow and Tver'. We are less clear about the third one — it may have been 'Little *Rōsia*' with Kiev as its centre. No shadow of doubt remains, however, when we come to the fourth *Rōsia*, the pagan one. It was Olgerd's Lithuania, for which Gregoras had strong sympathies.

The assumption that Lithuania's friends in Constantinople included it in the Rus' community is strengthened when we observe the hesitant way in which this question was treated in the Patriarchal Acts. More than that, the attitude of the Patriarchate towards the question of whether Lithuanian-held territories did or did not belong to '*Rōsia*' may be considered as a touchstone in our evaluation of the Byzantine ecclesiastical policy towards the Rus' lands in the fourteenth century. Patriarchal Acts which were favourable to Muscovite policy excluded Lithuania from the Rus' community and identified the latter with Moscow itself.[25] On the other hand, those charters — fewer in number — which leaned towards Lithuania, referred to it as to a part of *Rōsia*.[26]

---

curs in a charter issued 20 October 1335 by Boleslav-Jurij II Trojdenovič, *Dei Gratia natus Dux tocius Russie Mynoris*. Full text of the charter e.g. in the collective volume by O. Gonsiorovskij and others, *Boleslav-Jurij II, knjaz' vsej Maloj Rusi* (St. Petersburg, 1907), pp. 5-6, 154-5; cf. pp. 118-9, 209 and Pl. IX. Cf. also Karamzin, *Ist. Gos. Ross.*, iv, n. 276. For references to 'Little Russia' in the Acts of the Patriarchate from 1347 on, cf. M.M., i, pp. 262, 264, 265 and passim. As for the term 'Great Rōsia' (with Kiev as its centre) in a technical treatise, it is attested in *ca.* 1143 (*Taxis* of Nilus Doxopatres, ed. G. Parthey, p. 297, nr. 229), where, however, it had not yet acquired the later technical meaning. Cf. J. Fijałek, 'Średniowieczne biskupstwa Kościoła wschodniego na Rusi i Litwie na podstawie źródeł greckich', *Kwartalnik Historyczny*, x (1896), pp. 487-8; 490; A. Soloviev, 'Velikaja, Malaja i Belaja Rus'', *Voprosy Istorii*, vii (1947), pp. 24-38 (postulates the existence of the technical term 'Little Russia' from the very beginning of the fourteenth century, but does not adduce any text exhibiting this term prior to 1335); E. Borščak, 'Rus', Mala Rosija, Ukraina', *Revue des Études Slaves*, xxiv (1948), pp. 171-6.

24. Nic. Gregoras, *Hist.*, iii, p. 511, l. 16-p. 528, l. ii (Bonn ed.); cf. esp. p. 513, ll. 23-24; p. 514, ll. 4-6; p. 517, ll. 12-19.

25. Pagan neighbours of the Russian Church = Lithuanians: M.M. i, p. 426 (a. 1361); ibid., i, p. 435 (a. 1361).

26. M.M., i, p. 582 (a. 1371); ibid., i, pp. 320-22 (a. 1371); cf. ibid., ii, p. 120 (a. 1389). In a late equivocating document, the Patriarch used the term *Lit-*

In those Patriarchal Charters which were not antagonistic to Lithuania, metropolitan and princely titles as well were treated in a peculiar manner. Thus, in a decision dated 1387, the pro-Lithuanian Metropolitan Cyprian (d. 1406) was ambiguously referred to as 'Metropolitan of *Rōsia*' and not as 'Metropolitan of Lithuania and Little *Rōsia*'. The title of 'Metropolitan of all Rus'' was to be granted to Cyprian two years later in a charter bearing traces of his influence. In the ⟨101⟩ same text, Dmitrij Donskoj was called, contrary to previous practise, 'Grand Duke of Muscovy' (μέγας ῥὴξ τοῦ Μοσχοβίου) only and not 'Grand Duke of All *Rōsia*'.[27]

All this was more than an attempt to slip through between the Lithuanian Scylla and the Muscovite Charybdis. The Patriarchate of Constantinople showed a great deal of consistency in its policy towards the 'populous nation of Rus''. It insisted on the unity of the Metropolis of Kiev; it insisted on its rights of confirming, and, whenever possible, of nominating, the candidate to the metropolitan throne from among its own Greeks; and, finally, it clung to the claim of ideal supremacy over the Rus' Christians. Only the first of these points shall be illustrated here.

The failure of Andrej Bogoljubskij's ecclesiastical policy in the twelfth century shows that later Byzantine insistence on the unity of the metropolis was within the tradition of Russo-Byzantine relations. Patriarchal Acts of the fourteenth century frequently praised the wisdom of the ancestors who had established a sole metropolis in Rus' — an institution which united the quarrelling Rus' princes, and was responsible for much that was good for the Rus' land, while the division of the metropolis had brought this land many calamities.[28]

---

vorōsia among the titles of the Polish King Władysław Jagiełło: M.M., ii, p. 280 (a. 1397).

27. Vague title of Cyprian: M.M., ii, p. 98 (a. 1387). Curtailed titles of Princes Dmitrij and his father John ii: M.M.; ii, p. 117, 121 (a. 1389); in Acts friendly to Moscow, Dmitrij was called μέγασ ῥὴξ πάσης 'Ρωσίας, e.g. M.M., i, p. 516 (a. 1370); ii, pp. 12, 15 (a. 1380). Later on, Vasilij I enjoyed the full title: M.M., ii, pp. 177, 180 (a. 1393).

28. Principle of a sole metropolis: M.M., i, p. 265 (a. 1347); ibid., i, p. 268 (a. 1347); ibid., ii, pp. 120; 126-7 (a. 1389); cf. Nic. Gregoras, *Hist*, iii, p. 512, ll. 19-21 (turning the point against Moscow); one metropolis a blessing and a unifying factor among warring principalities: M.M., ii, pp. 116, 117, 126, 128 (a. 1389).

When Byzantium hoped — in vain, as the events were to show — to maintain the unity of the metropolis in the Rus' lands torn asunder by the struggle of several political centres, it faced the practical alternative of backing one or the other of the contestants. In 1370 Patriarch Philotheus declared that he loved Dmitrij Donskoj (d. 1389) more than he did other Christians on account of the great piety 'of the holy nation of Rus''.[29] The Patriarch permitted Metropolitan Alexius, Moscow's candidate, to turn to him not only in ecclesiastical but also in political matters, and gave him full powers to make use of Constantinople's authority in internal politics: whomsoever Alexius has excommunicated is excommunicated by the Patriarch.[30] The meaning of this sentence is clarified in other patriarchal charters. Some of them excommunicated Russian princes who in 1370 either did not follow Dmitrij Donskoj in his war with the 'worshipper of fire', the Lithuanian 'basileus' Olgerd, or, worse still, declared themselves on this pagan's side.[31]

The pro-Muscovite policy of the Byzantine Patriarchate rested on quite reasonable premises. Olgerd (d. 1377) was a pagan. This was bad enough; worse still, any day he might become a Catholic, as his son and his nephew were soon to become. These are no abstract considerations. The Patriarch feared that this might happen[32] and Olgerd himself threatened to take the Church of the Lithuanians and Russes over to the Latin side, if his wishes were not considered.[33] We read similar threats in the ⟨102⟩ letter ot the Polish king, Casimir the Great — in broken Greek, behind which I suspect a Slavic scribe's original — in which the king demanded the re-establishment of the Metropolis of Halyč.[34] Throughout the major part of the fourteenth century, the Patriarchate of Constantinople led, both at home and in Rus', an elastic defensive

29. M.M., i, pp. 516-17 (a. 1370).

30. Alexius invited to write on political matters: M.M., i, p. 517 (a. 1370); Alexius's excommunications confirmed by the Patriarch: ibid., 517 (a. 1370).

31. M.M., i, p. 518 (a. 1370); ibid., i, p. 520 (a. 1370); the Patriarch confirms Alexius's excommunications: ibid., i, pp. 523-4 (a. 1370); ibid., i, pp. 524-5 (a. 1370). Cf. J. Fijałek, 'Średniowieczne...' (as on p. 100, note 2 *supra*), p. 520.

32. M.M., i, p. 526 (a. 1364 or later); ibid., ii, p. 120 (a. 1389).

33. M.M., ii, p. 14 (a. 1380); ibid., ii, p. 119 (a. 1389); both texts give a survey of past events. Cf. J. Fijałek, 'Biskupstwa greckie w ziemiach ruskich'. *Kwartalnik Historyczny*, xi (1897), p. 17. Cf. a similar threat put into the mouth of the Novgorodians: M.M., ii, p. 177 (a. 1393).

34. M.M., i, p. 578 (a. 1370). Cf. Philotheus's remarks to Alexius, ibid., i, p. 583 (a. 1371).

against Unionist plans. In *Rōsia*, Moscow was the only entirely reliable centre which made use of Orthodox propaganda as an offensive weapon.

However, in its relations with *Rōsia* Byzantium could also consider a possible Lithuanian solution. The pro-Lithuanian policy held out the promise of including a young pagan nation in the sphere of Byzantine cultural influence, and Byzantium had a chance of returning to its great missionary traditions of the ninth century. Again, these seem to be more than theoretical considerations. In addition to the Muscovite silver, Lithuanian money was hardly unfamiliar to Patriarchal coffers. In the seventies of the fourteenth century, Lithuanian influence was on the increase on the shores of the Bosphorus. It reached its peak in the recognition of Cyprian as Metropolitan, and in his final victory in 1375. Thus it was with good reason that the Muscovites scorned the Byzantine Patriarch as 'a Lithuanian' in 1378.[35]

However, Byzantine groupings which showed pro-Lithuanian inclinations existed as early as the fifties of the fourteenth century. True enough, these Byzantines were prompted not by love for Lithuania, nor by determined views on Byzantium's religious mission, but by the desire to use the Lithuanian card in their struggle with their adversaries, who were leaning towards Moscow. It appears possible to connect the struggle which went on for 'All Rus'' in the mid-fourteenth century with the internal struggle which was going on for 'All Byzantium' at the same time. On at least one occasion the respective Muscovite and Lithuanian candidates for the Metropolitanate relied upon parties in Byzantium which were pitted against each other in the civil war between Emperors John V and VI and in the Palamite controversy. In the fifties, when pro-Lithuanian Metropolitan Romanus (d. 1361) vied with the pro-Muscovite Metropolitan Alexius (d. 1378) in Constantinople, the Patriarchs of the City were Palamites. But while one of them, Callistus, sided with John V Palaeologus, his successor Philotheus was not only among the most prominent theoreticians of Palamism, but also a devoted helper of John VI Cantacuzenus.

The chief mouthpiece of anti-Palamite circles was Nicephorus Gregoras. In one of the final parts of his *History*, which he devoted to his polemics against Philotheus and his protector Cantacuzenus, we find, for no apparent reason, a long excursus on Rus', from which I have

---

35. Letter of Cyprian to Sergius of Radonež, *Russkaja Istoričeskaja Biblioteka*, vi (2nd ed., 1908), col. 185.

already quoted.[36] This excursus had two heroes: Romanus and Olgerd. The latter desired nothing more than to see Romanus ordained Metropolitan of 'All Rus'', as a prelude to his own adoption of Orthodoxy.

The excursus had its villains as well. One of them was Alexius, presumably an upstart, appearing in Constantinople with his pockets full of gold. Another was Philotheus, suborned by Alexius, and, finally, Patriarch Callistus, who at first was willing to right Romanus's wrongs but then was unable to withstand the persuasion of Alexius's roubles. Discouraged by all this, Olgerd declared, or so Gregoras tells us, that he preferred worship of the sun to that of gold and silver, which were the gods ⟨103⟩ of Constantinople. He also felt released from his promise to adopt Orthodoxy together with his whole nation. This is how, in Gregoras's version, Patriarch Philotheus lost the chance of bringing the Lithuanian flock into the fold of Constantinople.

Gregoras's excursus is full of incongruities but offers extremely precious information. Gregoras had at his disposal details concerning Romanus: he knew that Romanus was a monk, that he was fifty-five years old when he arrived at Constantinople, and that he was related to the Prince Vsevolod Alexandrovič of Tver' through the latter's wife. This brings us into the sphere of Lithuanian influence, since Uljana of Tver', Olgerd's second wife, was the daughter of Prince Alexander of Tver'. For a long time Gregoras's information remained unique and historians attached no great importance to it. However, in 1922, it was brilliantly confirmed by the publication of the *Rogožskij Letopisec.*[37] This chronicle has pro-Tverian, and indirectly pro-Lithuanian, leanings, and it is the only one among the Russian sources to speak of Romanus the monk, a son of a Boyar of Tver'. Gregoras was not concerned with Romanus's victory over Alexius; his aim was to expose the villainy of Philotheus and Callistus, since the former wrote a polemical treatise against him, and the latter jailed him in one of the capital's monasteries. Still, Gregoras's precise data on Romanus suggest that the anti-

36. Cf. p. 100 3 *supra*; esp. p. 517, l. 24- p. 518, l. 7; p. 518, ll. 9-13; ll. 16-21; p. 520, ll. 3-5; ll. 11-15; p. 520, l. 26- p. 521, l. 3.

37. Rogožskij Letopisec, P.S.R.L., xv, i (2nd ed., 1922; reprint of vol. xv, 1965), col. 61; on Romanus's kinship with Vsevolod, cf. A. E. Presnjakov, *Obrazovanie velikorusskogo gosudarstva* (Petrograd, 1918), p. 199 (via Gregoras); for the recent use of *Rogozškij Letopisec*, cf. A. V. Čerepnin, *Obrazovanie russkogo centralizovannogo gosudarstva v XIV-XV vv.* (Moscow, 1960), p. 549.

Palamites may have been in touch with the Lithuanian Embassy, headed by Romanus, which visited Constantinople at least twice in the fifties of the century.

In Slavic sources, too, we find traces of similar contacts between the Lithuanian and Muscovite church factions and warring Byzantine groupings in the fifties of the fourteenth century. All Rus' chronicles which refer to events connected with Metropolitan Alexius's election in 1354 make a favourable mention of *Emperor* Cantacuzenus and Patriarch Philotheus. All — with one exception: the *Rogožskij Letopisec*, a pro-Tverian source. Under 1352/4 this chronicle mentions 'a confusion in Constantinople', that is, the civil war between John V and John VI. It is the only one to call John V Palaeologus, rather than John VI Cantacuzenus, Emperor. It is hostile in tone to Philotheus, but refers to Callistus in warm terms:[38] thus it parallels Gregoras's claim that at first Callistus had been favourable towards Romanus.

Russo-Byzantine ecclesiastical relations in the fourteenth century involve two territories, one of which symbolized the past, the other, the future. Byzantium was left with little more than prestige, and this prestige various political centres in Eastern Europe attempted to exploit for their own goals. In this endeavour, the principality of Moscow was more successful than others. Politically, it was often on the defensive — it had to ward off three campaigns by Olgerd, who, to quote the Acts of the Patriarchate, desired power over 'Great *Rōsia*'.[39] Ideologically, however, Moscow was on the offensive, for it skillfully played the All-Rus' card. It tenaciously maintained its grip over the metropolis, and succeeded in using the Patriarchate of Constantinople to bar the Lithuanian candidate from becoming Metropolitan of 'All-Rus'', and thus to isolate its Lithuanian foe. In turn, the Byzantine Patriarchate's predilection for Moscow showed a great deal of acumen ⟨104⟩ and sensitivity to new political trends. It foreshadows acts for which the Patriarchate of Constantinople was to provide a somewhat reluctant sanction some centuries later: the establishment of the Patriarchate of Moscow in 1589, and the subordination of the Metropolitan see of Kiev to that Patriarchate in 1685.

38. *Rogožskij Letopisec* (as in the preceding note), ibid.

39. M.M., ii, pp. 12-13 (a. 1380).

Figure 1: American Numismatic Society, Mabbott Collection, nr. 302; Seal of Metropolitan Moses (cf. p. 272, n. 10)

XXI

The Greek Source of the Inscription on Solomon's Chalice in the *Vita Constantini*

First impressions are often the strongest. I first heard Roman Osipovič lecture at the Dumbarton Oaks Symposium devoted to Byzantium and the Slavs. The year was 1952, the subject, Church Slavonic poetry, and the hero, Constantine-Cyril. My interest in the *Lives* of the Slavic Apostles was born at that lecture, and Roman Osipovič has ever remained my perceptive guide through the intricacies of *Cyrillo-Methodiana*; a generous guide as well, who encouraged — even prodded — me to present results which might lead to conclusions different from his own. The following observations on Solomon's Chalice in the *Vita Constantini* were promised to Roman Osipovič long ago; they are offered here as an homage to the ever youthful curiosity of his mind.

Chapter Thirteen of the *Vita Constantini* opens with a sentence on Constantine-Cyril's return from the Khazar Mission: "The Philosopher went to the Imperial City and, after an audience with the Emperor, established himself in the Church of the Holy Apostles, and led there a life of contemplation and of prayer to God."[1] The opening statement of Chapter Fourteen, in which the Moravian Mission is announced, reads like a direct continuation of that sentence: "While the Philosopher was rejoicing in God, another matter arose, and another labor ⟨i.e., the

1. *Filosofъ že ide vъ Cěsarь Gradъ, i viděvъ cěsarja živěaše bez mlъvy, Boga molję, vъ crъkъvi svętyixъ apostolъ sědę. Cf.* T. *Lehr-Spławiński, Żywoty Konstantyna i Metodego...* (Poznań, 1959), p. 63. In subsequent notes, I shall quote the *Vita Constantini* (= VC) after this edition, which gives a normalized text, rather than after the latest one by F. Grivec-F. Tomšič, *Constantinus et Methodius Thessalonicenses, Fontes* (1960), since the basis of the latter is a single manuscript of the fifteenth century. — On the translation "teaching" rather than "established" for *sědę*, cf., e.g., F. Dvornik, "Photius et la réorganisation de l'académie patriarcale", *Analecta Bollandiana*, 68 (1950), 122; *idem*, "Patriarch Photius, Scholar and Statesman", *Classical Folia*, 14 (1960), 13 and n. 47.

Moravian Mission⟩, no lesser than the previous ones ⟨i.e., the Arab and Khazar Missions⟩."[2]

These two statements, however, are not contiguous. The following story, constituting the rest of Chapter Thirteen, is inserted between them: "In ⟨the Church of⟩ St. Sophia there is a cup of precious stone, a work of Solomon, on which lines[3] ⟨1807⟩ are written in Jewish and Samaritan letters; nobody was able to read or explain them. But the Philosopher took the cup, read and explained the lines. The first line runs as follows: 'My cup, my cup, prophesy until the star; be unto a draught to the Lord, the first born, keeping vigil at night.' After that, the second line: 'created for the Lord's taste[4] ⟨from⟩ another wood, drink and be drunken from exultation (in revelry?), and cry out Alleluiah.' And after that, the third line: 'Lo the Prince, and the whole assembly will behold his glory and King David ⟨is⟩ among them.' And after that, the number 'nine hundred and nine' was written. The Philosopher computed ⟨it⟩ in detail and obtained nine hundred and nine years from the twelfth year of Solomon's reign to ⟨that of⟩ Christ's birth. And this is a prophecy about Christ."[5]

Until now, no parallels to this story were known outside the Slavic realm. Within that realm, however, two main versions of the story do occur in at least twenty manuscripts, all of east Slavic recension, either as separate narratives, or within an anti-Jewish polemical tract called *Sayings of the Holy Prophets*. They have been published — or re-published

2. C 14: *Veselęštu že sę o Bozě filosofu paky druga rěčь prispě i trudъ ne mьnьi prьvyixъ.*

3. The word *granъ* or *granь* does not mean a line of poetry, but is an equivalent of the Greek στίχος,which, *pace* the Russian word *stix*, means 'line, verse', the latter, for instance, in the sense of a verse in Scriptures.

4. VC 13: *vъkušenьje*. It is difficult to say what this word, which usually stands for γεῦσις, μετάληψις of the Greek, means here.

5. VC 13: *Jestъ že vъ svętěi Sofьi potirъ otъ dragaego kamene, Solomonьja děla, na njemьže sǫtъ pismeny Židovьsky i Samarěnьsky grani napьsani, ixъže ne možaaše nikъtožę ni pročisti ni sъkazati. Vъzьmъ že i filosofъ pročьte i sъkaza ję. Jestъ že sice prьvyi granъ: čaša moja, čaša moja, proricai, donьdeže zvězda; vъ pivo bǫdi gospodevi prьvěnьcu bьdęštu noštьją. Po semь že drugyi granъ: na vъkušenьje gospodьnje sъtvorjena drěva inogo, pьi i upьi sę veselьjemъ, i vъzъpьi alliluja. I po semь tretьi granъ: se kъnęzь i uzьritъ vьsь sъnьmъ slavǫ ego, i David cěsarь posrědě ixъ. I po semь čislo napьsano θ sъtъ i θ-ro. Rasčьtъ že je po tьnьku filosofъ obrěte otъ vъtorajego na desęte lěta cěsarьstva Solomonьja do roždьstva Xristova θ sъtъ i θ lětъ. I se jestъ proročьstvo o Xristě.*

— on at least eight occasions: by Sreznevskij,[6] Porfir'ev,[7] Petrov,[8] Istrin,[9] Lamanskij,[10] Evseev,[11] Lavrov,[12] and Tomov.[13]

Of the two versions, one agrees with Chapter Thirteen of the *Vita Constantini* almost verbatim,[14] while the other, and prevailing one, is expanded: it appends an ⟨1808⟩ exegesis, *tolkovanie*, to each of the three lines of the inscription.[15] According to the summary of one exegesis, "The first line speaks of the Nativity, the second, of ⟨Christ's⟩ Arrest, the third, of the Cross, of the Crucifixion, of the Death, of the Laying into the Grave, and of the Resurrection."[16]

---

6. I. I. Sreznevskij, *Svedenija i zametki o maloizvestnyx i neizvestnyx pamjatnikax*, I-XL [= *Sbornik statej, čitannyx v Otdelenii Russkogo Jazyka i Slovesnosti Imper. Akad. Nauk*, I] (1867), p. 96 [= nr. XL].

7. I. Ja. Porfir'ev "Nadpis' na čaši Solomona", *Apokrifičeskie skazanija o vetxozavetnyx licax i sobytijax* [= *Imper. Akad. Nauk, Sbornik ORJaS, 17, 1*] (1877), 240-241.

8. A. N. Petrov, *Apokrifičeskoe proročestvo carja Solomona o Xriste...* [= *Pamjatniki Drevnej Pis'-mennosti*, 104] (1894).

9. V. M. Istrin, "Iz oblasti drevne-russkoj literatury, II. Drevne-russkie slovari: 'Proročestvo Solomona'", *Žurnal Minist. Nar. Prosveščenija*, 349 (1903) 201-218, esp. pp. 209-210.

10. V. I. Lamanskij, *Slavjanskoe žitie sv. Kirilla kak religiozno-èpičeskoe proizvedenie i kak istoričeskij istočnik* (Petrograd, 1915), *passim*, esp. pp. 224; 228.

11. I. E. Evseev, "Slovesa svjatyx prorok, protivoiudejskij pamjatnik po rukopisi XV veka", *Drevnosti* [= *Imper. Moskovskoe Arxeol. Obščestvo, Slavjanskaja Kommissija, Trudy*] 4,1 (1907), *passim*, esp. pp. 160; 172,9-174,3.

12. P. Lavrov, *Kyrylo ta Metodij v davn'oslovjans'komu pys'menstvi* [= *Ukrajins'ka Akad. Nauk, Zbirnyk istor.-filol. viddilu*, 78] (1928), pp. 34-35; Idem, *Materialy po istorii vozniknovenija drevnejšej slavjanskoj pis'mennosti [Akad. Nauk SSSR, Trudy Slavjanskoj Kommissii*, I] (1930), p. XLVI.

13. T. St. Tomov, "Perseval, ili Romanъt za Grala", *Godišnik na Sofijskija Universitet, Istor.-filol. fakultet*, 36,1 (1939-1940), pp. 115-118, esp. p. 117.

14. Leningrad, Saltykov-Ščedrin Public Library, Coll. of the Sofiskij Sobor (Novgorod), nrs. 1418 and 1449.

15. For the list of the eleven manuscripts containing the expanded version, cf. Petrov, *Apokrifičeskoe proročestvo...* (as in note 8 *supra*), pp. 5-10; for the list of the six manuscripts of the *Sayings of the Holy Prophets* containing the Chalice story, cf. Evseev, "Slovesa svjatyx prorok" ... (as in note 11 *supra*), pp. 153-157; for the text in the manuscript Kiev, State Public Library of the Ukrainian SSR, Barsov Collection, nr. 8, cf. Lavrov, *Materialy* ... (as in note 12 *supra*), p. XLVI.

16. Cf. Petrov, *Apokrifičeskoe proročestvo...* (as in note 8 *supra*), p. 14, 34-38: *pьrvyi že stixъ gl(agole)tъ o r(o)ž(de)stvě, a vtoryi o jatъi i o večeri, a tretii o kr(e)stě i o raspętъi i o uspenii i o položenii vъ grobě i o vъskresenii.*

Other differences between separate narratives, regardless of version, are of lesser importance. The Chalice is explained as symbolizing either the Lord or the Virgin.[17] The number of alphabets in which the inscription is said to have been composed fluctuates between two and three: on three occasions, the third line is said to have been written in an additional alphabet, the Greek one, a script with which Solomon was hardly conversant.[18] While the identity of the wise man who "read and explained" the inscription fluctuates as well — in two texts (represented by seven manuscripts) he is not mentioned at all,[19] in others, he appears as an anonymous 'Philosopher',[20] is given the name of Cyril[21] and is said to have christened Prince Vladimir or have been in Rus' 'before'[22] — these fluctuations do not convey any information beyond that contained in *Vita Constantini* or in the east Slavic Cyrillo-Methodian tradition.

Faced with the peculiar position of the passage of Solomon's Chalice in the *Vita*, where it is sandwiched in between two references to Constantine's missions, and with the existence of separate narratives — with and without exegesis — about that Chalice scholars could have been expected to ask such questions as these:

Is the story of the Chalice in *Vita Constantini* an integral part of the *Vita*, from which all the "separate narratives" are derived, or is it an interpolation disturbing the plan of the work, and perhaps having a common source with "separate narratives" about that Chalice? If it is an interpolation, what is that common source? If it is not, how do we reconcile the absence of the exegeses or *tolkovanija* from Chapter Thirteen with their presence in most of the "separate narratives" and in the *Sayings of the Holy* ⟨1809⟩ *Prophets?* Can the story's authenticity be con-

17. Cf. Evseev "Slovesa..." (as in note 11 *supra*), pp. 161-162.

18. Cf. Sreznevskij, *Svedenija* ... (as in note 6 *supra*), p. 96 [Coll. of the Sofijskij Sobor (Novgorod), nr. 1449]; Lamanskij, *Slavjanskoe žitie* ... (as in note 10 *supra*), p. 228 [Coll. of the Sofiskij Sobor (Novgorod), nr. 1450]; Lavrov, *Materialy* ... (as in note 12 *supra*), p. XLVI [Barsov Collection, nr. 8].

19. Petrov, *Apokrifičeskoe proročestvo* ... (as in note 8 *supra*) [Leningrad, Saltykov-Ščedrin Public Library, Op. I, nr. 18]; Evseev, "Slovesa ..." (as in note 11 *supra*), pp. 153-157 [six manuscripts].

20. Sreznevskij, *Svedenija* ... (as in note 6 *supra*), 96; Porfir'ev, *Apokrifičeskie skazanija* ... (as in note 7 *supra*), p. 240.

21. Lamanskij, *Slavjanskoe žitie* ... (as in note 10 *supra*), p. 228; Lavrov, *Materialy* ... (as in note 12 *supra*), p. xlvi.

22. Porfir'ev, *Apokrifičeskie skazanija* ... (as in note 7 *supra*), p. 240; Lamanskij, *Slavjanskoe žitie* ... (as in note 10 *supra*), p. 228; Lavrov, *Materialy* ... (as in note 12 *supra*), p. xlvi.

firmed or rejected if we examine its connections, if any, with other parts of the *Vita Constantini*? What was the factual foundation of the story: had St. Sophia's treasure ever possessed a "Solomonic" Chalice with a prophetic inscription? Assuming there was such a Chalice, what were the Semitic alphabets of the inscription? Would Constantine have been able to decipher them?

Finally, even assuming that the Chalice story is an integral part of the *Vita Constantini*, should we not ask whether it is original, that is, a report of an actual tour-de-force performed by Constantine the Philologist, or whether it is a literary device altogether invented or perhaps purloined by the *Vita's* ninth-century author from an earlier source and attributed to his hero?

Given the bulk of Cyrillo-Methodian literature, it is not surprising that each of these questions was asked on more than one occasion, each — except for the last question, which was only implied, and that only once.[23] In the scholarly ballot, integralists win hands down over interpolationists: only Lamanskij, following up Gorskij's lead, squarely rejected the Chalice story; he called it a later addition due to a biased South-Slavic corrector or adapter of the *Vita Constantini*; he made fun of his colleagues who attributed prodigious feats in oriental philology to Constantine during his stay in the Crimea; he offered the proof, obvious, but beside the point, that no Solomon's Chalice could exhibit Samaritan and Jewish scripts, since, so he said, the differentiation between the two is not earlier than the second century of our era, and he considered Constantine too good a scholar ever to have fallen for as obvious a trap as a forged inscription.[24]

Unfortunately, proof that a relic is a fraud is no proof that it never existed, and it was hardly consistent of Lamanskij first to belittle Constantine's acquaintance with Semitic tongues, then to endow him with enough expertise to discern a forgery in Hebrew. Moreover, when Lamanskij impugned the *Vita's* credibility and claimed that it was riddled with interpolations, he did this to eliminate from it evidence unfavorable to his theory that Constantine's Khazar mission was in reality a mission to the "Russians".

Since subsequent research showed *Vita Constantini* to be surprisingly trustworthy, and Lamanskij's theory untenable, the rest of his

23. By Evseev, in "Slovesa ..." (as in note 11 *supra*), p. 166.

24. Lamanskij, *Slavjanskoe žitie* ... (as in note 10 *supra*), pp. 19; 20; 215-229, esp. pp. 216; 223; 224; 225; 228.

arguments, including suspicions he cast upon the Chalice story, found little credence. In Lamanskij's time, only Petrov pointed to the lack of logical connection between what preceded and what followed upon the Chalice story, cautioned that it was premature to assume that separate narratives telling this story were dependent on Chapter Thirteen of the *Vita Constantini*, and urged the search for the origin of the prophetic lines on Solomon's Chalice.[25] In ⟨1810⟩ our day, only Picchio was disturbed by the fact that the bulk of Chapter Thirteen inserted a pause into the *trama narrativa* of the *Vita*.[26]

The integralist majority either brought strong arguments against the late date of the passage in which the Chalice story occurred[27] — this was unimpeachable, as long as no further conclusions were drawn from such arguments — or accepted that story as narrating an actual event and attesting to Constantine's philological interests.[28] Consistently enough, integralists assumed that the existence of a Solomonic Chalice — whether authentic or spurious, was not made clear — in St. Sophia in the ninth century was "thinkable"[29] or likely;[30] curiously enough, they did this on the basis of express evidence offered by Procopius and Evagrius — and thus easily accessible to the Byzantines — to the effect that the spoils of the Temple of Jerusalem, brought by Titus to Rome, by Genseric to Carthage and by Belisarius to Constantinople were *not*

25. Petrov, *Apokrifičeskoe proročestvo* ... (as in note 8 *supra*); pp. 4-5; 5-10; 11; cf. also reviews of Petrov's work in Žurnal Minist. Nar. Prosveščenija 295 (October, 1894), 429; *Vizantijskij Vremennik*, 2 (1895), 473 (by I. Sokolov).

26. R. Picchio, "Compilazione e trama narrativa nelle 'Vite' di Constantino e Metodio", *Ricerche Slavistiche*, 8 (1960), 61-95, esp. p. 80.

27. Lavrov, *Kyrylo ta Metodij* ... (as in note 12 *supra*), pp. 34-35: the passage in VC 13 goes back to the earliest layer of Church Slavonic, since it contains the old West Slavic word *sъnьmъ*. Parallel texts replace this word by *sborъ, zborъ, soborъ*.

28. E.g. T. Lehr-Spławiński, "Wann entstand die erste slavische Schrift (Glagolica)?", *Wiener Slawistisches Jahrbuch*, 12 (1965), 5-12, esp. p. 5; *idem*, "Przed misją morawską", *Tъržestvena sesija za 1100 godišninata na slavjanskata pismenost*, 863-1963 (1965), 49-54, esp. p. 49.

29. J. Bujnoch, transl., *Zwischen Rom und Byzanz. Leben und Wirken der Slavenapostel Kyrillos und Methodios* ... [= *Slawische Geschichtsschreiber*, 1] (1958), p. 169, n. 135.

30. F. Dvornik, *Les légendes de Constantin et de Méthode vues de Byzance* (1933), p. 209-210.

kept in the capital, but moved from there to the Church of the Holy Sepulchre in Jerusalem by Justinian.[31]

Answers to others questions usually depended on the scholars' integralist or interpolationist positions; regardless of position, some of these answers were naive, others astute. Here are the samples: the alphabets of the inscription were indeed Hebrew and Samaritan; Constantine-Cyril could decipher them, since he knew Hebrew and learned the Samaritan script in Kherson;[32] the absence of the exegeses to inscription lines from Chapter Thirteen shows that the *Vita* shortened its (Cyrillian?) source, and that, therefore, Constantine-Cyril's name should be attached to the exegeses as well;[33] the story of Constantine's Samaritan studies (VC 8) either shows that Chapter Thirteen ⟨1811⟩ is an integral part of the *Vita*; or was invented to prepare the Chalice passage in that chapter.[34]

The story in Chapter Thirteen (a) was borrowed from a mediaeval anti-Jewish tract (no longer extant);[35] or (b) it was part of an early Christian commentary to *Proverbs* 9, 1-11, since it appears in this context in the Slavic *Sayings of the Holy Prophets*. Furthermore, an early (also no longer extant) version of the *Sayings* was probably used (in what language, may we ask) by the compiler of the *Vita Constantini*, and the part of these hypothetical *Sayings* containing the Chalice story is thus a source for the *Vita's* Chapter Thirteen.[36] Finally, whatever the sources of

---

31. Procopius, *De Bello Vandalico*, II, 9,5-9 [= I, 456,18-457,12 ed. Haury]; Evagrius, IV,17 [= pp. 167-168 ed. Bidez-Parmentier]. Cf. A. Couret, *La Palestine sous les Empereurs grecs*, 326-636 (1869), p. 185. — I know only one source asserting that the spoils of Jerusalem, taken by Titus, went to Rome and hence to the Church of St. Sophia in Constantinople: it is the second (post-1204) version of Antonij the Novgorodian's *Pilgrimage*, cf. Antonij of Novgorod, *Kniga Palomnik*, ed. X. Lǫparev, in *Pravoslavnyj Palestinskij Šbornik*, 17,3 [= nr. 51] (1899), p. 11; cf. *ibidem*, p. xx.

32. N. K. Nikol'skij, "K voprosu o sočinenijax, pripisyvaemyx Kirillu filosofu", *Akad. Nauk SSSR,* Izvestija *po russkomu jazyku i slovesnosti*, (1928), 435; J. Vašica, *Literární památky epochy velkomoravské* 683-885 (1966), pp. 221-222.

33. Nikol'skij, "K voprosu..." (as in the preceding note), p. 440 and n. 1. I find it difficult to understand how anyone should want to add this lucubration of dubious value to Constantine's already swollen literary dossier.

34. Cf. Vašica, *Literární památky* ... (as in note 32 *supra*), p. 221, and Lamanskij, *Slavjanskoe žitie* ... (as in note 10 *supra*), p. 30, respectively.

35. Lamanskij, *Slavjanskoe žitie* ... (as in note 10 *supra*), p. 223.

36. Evseev, "Slovesa ... " (as in note 11 *supra*), pp. 161; 163; 167; 166.

Chapter Thirteen may be, the Chalice story is a translation from the Greek, done in all likelihood in the Slavic South. This last guess was due to Evseev and to the indomitable Lamanskij,[37] and we shall presently see that these two scholars were on the right track.

The assumption that the inscription on Solomon's Chalice was actually read and deciphered by Constantine led to one special conclusion. This conclusion was drawn by Roman Osipovič; briefly, it is that the three prophetic lines which we read in Chapter Thirteen are a Slavic translation of Constantine's own (but, again, no longer extant) Greek rendering of the inscription; that this Slavic translation is, if not by Constantine himself, then by an anonymous Great Moravian author and that, when reconstructed, it turns out to be poetry, since reconstruction reveals that the prophetic lines have a regular syllabic and strophic form and contain *paronomasiae*, a device characteristic of poetic riddles.[38]

Plainly, the *Vita*'s assertion that Constantine was the man who deciphered the inscription, and the modern theory agreeing with this and postulating that the Slavic lines rendering it are poetry, could be better tested, if we had the source of the Slavic text at our disposal. Logic, Lamanskij, Evseev, and Roman Osipovič told us that this source had to be Greek; however, as long as it could not be actually produced, we were not certain; nor were we immune to dangers of speculation.

The point of this note is to produce the source, or — to be cautious at first — the well-nigh perfect parallel to two out of three lines written on the Solomon Chalice. It occurs in *Scurialensis* Ψ. III. 7, a parchment manuscript of the eleventh century, consisting of 321 folios. On fols. 3-315^{r} we read the works of Ps.-Dionysius the Aeropagite, Ps.-Athanasius, Leontius of Byzantium, Gregory Thaumaturgus, Theodore Abucara, Maximus the Confessor, Anastasius Sinaita, and John Chrysostom. Fols. 315^{r}-320^{v} (fol. 321$^{r\text{-}v}$ *vacat*), however, are a *farrago* of texts, ranging from a computation of the date for the end of the world (one thousand years after Christ's First Coming, a chiliastic solution which I know from no other Byzantine source), ⟨1812⟩ through patristic and conciliar excerpts, the letter of Pontius Pilate to Emperor

37. Evseev, "Slovesa ... " (as in note 11 *supra*), p. 166; Lamanskij, *Slavjanskoe žitie* (as in note 10 *supra*), p. 225.

38. R. Jakobson, "Stixotvornye citaty v velikomoravskoj agiografii", *Slavistična Revija*, 10 (1957), 111-118, esp. pp. 112-113; 114-115. Vašica, *Literární památky* ... (as in note 32 *supra*), p. 222, merely states that the Chalice prophecy is in verse.

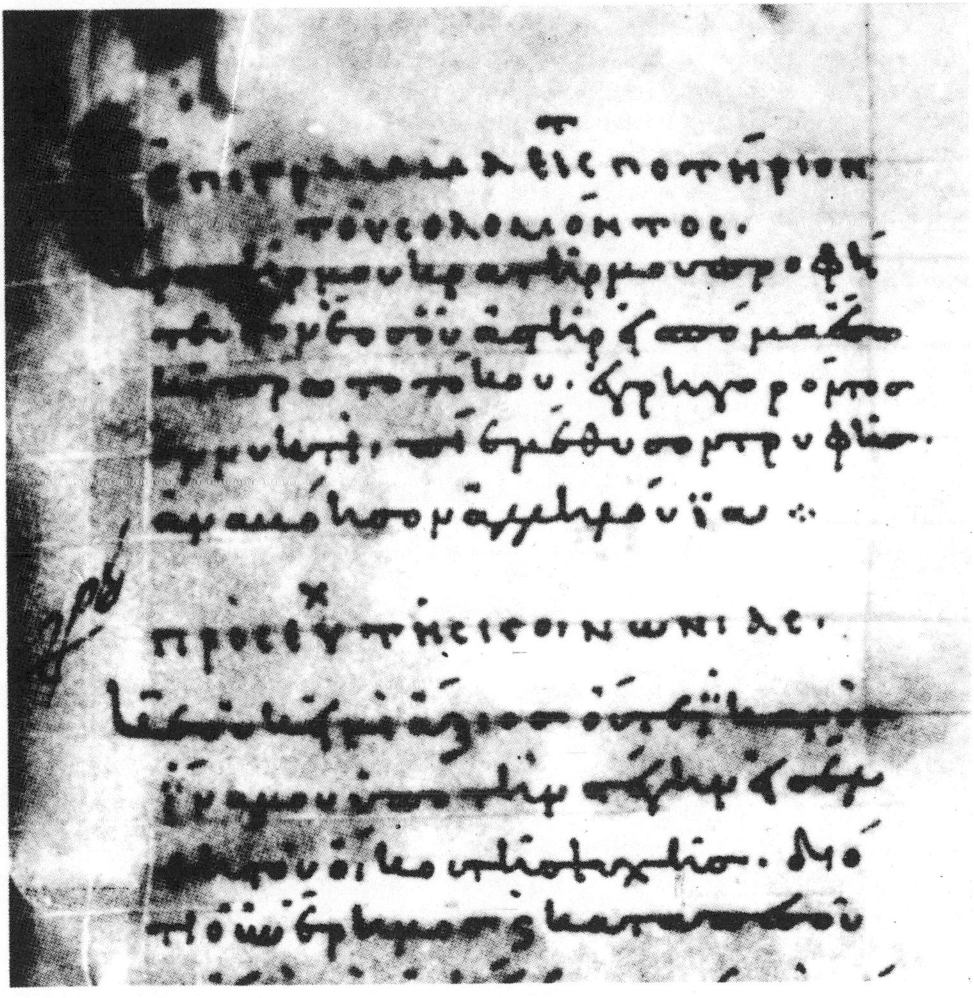

Fig. 1. Scurialensis Ψ. III. 7, fol. 317[r], a: Inscription on Solomon's Chalice.

Claudius[39] and an oracle on Corinth, to prescriptions and unguents against podagra or paralysis, and opening formulae for letters.

Folios like these, difficult to identify and promising small scholarly dividends, repel authors of catalogues: thus fols. 315-320 of the *Scurialensis* were omitted not only from Miller's *Catalogue*,[40] but also from the excellent — but avowedly unfinished — typewritten description of that manuscript by Father Grigorio Andres, Librarian of the Escurial.[41] As a result, the prophetic inscription on Solomon's Chalice, which occurs on fol. 317ʳ of the hodgepodge, remained hidden for too long. For the sake of clarity, the Greek text (cf. fig. 1) will be presented here along with the relevant two lines of the inscription as they stand in the *Vita Constantini*.

a 'Επίγραμμα εἰς τ(ὸ) ποτήριον τοῦ	
b Σολομόντος	
1 Κρατῆρ μου κρατῆρ μου προφήτευσον ἕος οὗ ἀστῆρ, εἰς πομα ἔσω	1 *Čaša moja, čaša moja, proricai donьdeže zvězda; vъ pivo bǫdi*
3 Κ(υρίο)υ πρωτοτόκου ἐγρηγορόντος ἐν νυκτί·	3 *gospodevi prъvěnьcu bъdęštu*
	4a *noštьjǫ [Po semь že drugyi granъ: na*
	4b *vъkušenъje gospodьnje sъtvorjena drěva*
πίε μέθυσον τρυφῆς,	4c *inogo] pьi i upьi sę veselьjemь*
5 ἀναβόησον ἀλληλούϊα.	5 *i vъzъpьi alliluja.*

b read Σολομῶντος 1 read κρατήρ read κρατήρ 2 read ἕως read ἀστήρ read ἔσο 4 for combination of πίνω and μεθύω in the Septuagint, cf. III *Kings* 16:9; 21 (20):16; Jeremiah 28 (51):7; and especially *Canticum* 5:1; Jeremiah 32:13 (25:27).

Except for the phrase *na vъkušenъje — inogo*, which has no counterpart in the Greek, and except for the two "*i*" in lines 4c and 5, every Slavic word corresponds to one, and only one, Greek word. Except for one

39. Cf. C. Tischendorf, *Acta Apostolorum Apocrypha* (1851), pp. 16-18.

40. E. Miller, *Catalogue des manuscrits grecs de la Bibliothèque de l'Escurial* (1848), devotes pp. 433-434 to our *Scurialensis*.

41. My thanks go to Father Andres for kindly having put his description of the Scurialensis Ψ. III. 7 at my disposal.

pair, *veselьjemь* : τρυφῆς,[42] the Slavic equivalents of the Greek in this one-to-one correspondence are routine. To put it simply, the Slavic is a word-by-word translation from the Greek. That Greek, not Slavic is the original language of the prophetic lines is an assumption dictated by common sense;[43] moreover, it appears from the combination πίε μεθυσον which ⟨1815⟩ imitates the usage of the Septuagint, while *pъi i upьi sę* alludes to nothing in particular.

Now the Greek original is in prose. It would be too much of a coincidence if a Slavic translator of a Greek prose text relied — as our translator did — on the technique of one-to-one correspondence, and came up with poetry; it would be equally unlikely if a translation, employing routine Old Church Slavic equivalents of the Greek words, should turn out to be replete with *paronomasiae*. I conclude that the Slavic text, at least those two prophetic lines for which we have the Greek counterpart, is not poetry. Its form was dictated by a mechanical choice of Slavic equivalents for Greek words, not by a conscious use of poetic devices.

In the *Scurialensis*, the inscription is transmitted anonymously. Strictly speaking, this leaves space for the assumption that what we have before us is the postulated Greek text of Constantine's translation, from which the name of the decipherer had been dropped. The date of the manuscript, eleventh century,[44] does not preclude such a theory, but I must reject it as too far-fetched; in my opinion, the story of the Solomon Chalice in the *Vita Constantini* is a borrowing; it comes into it from a context which originally had nothing to do with its hero; this story was introduced as proof of Constantine's superior intellectual powers, and as a complement to stories told about him elsewhere in the *Vita*: computing the "generations until Moses" (VC 9); computing the "seventy weeks" that is "four hundred and ninety years" from Daniel to Christ and quoting prophecies about Christ's coming (VC 10); and, finally, learning Jewish and Samaritan scripts in Kherson (VC 8).

42. Usually, *veselije* stands for ἀγαλλίασις, εὐφροσύνη, εὐωχία of the Greek; for other equivalents, cf. *Slovník jazyka staroslověnského*, 4 (1961), p. 181.

43. Istrin, "Iz oblasti ..." (as in note 9 *supra*), p. 210, considered the presence of the Chalice story in one version of the *Saying of the Holy Prophets* as proof that the *Saying* were of *non-Greek* origin. He must have been nodding when he wrote these lines.

44. Father Andres dates the main body of the *Scurialensis* to the eleventh century, fols. 317^r-320^r to the twelfth; I prefer the earlier date for both parts of the manuscript and hope that fig. 1 will bear me out.

Comparison with the text of the *Scurialensis* suggests that the version of the prophecy available to the Slavic hagiographer was the result of some transformation. In the *Scurialensis*, the prophecy corresponds to two lines of the Slavic text and refers to two events only: Nativity and Last Supper. As prophecies go, it is clear and to the point. In the *Vita*, the prophecy is expressed in three lines, and the exegeses tell us that these lines refer to Nativity, Last Supper, Crucifixion, Entombment, and Resurrection[45] — a cramming of all the main events in Christ's life into a slightly enlarged text of the inscription. Most Slavic versions of the prophecy have three lines but only two languages,[46] a discrepancy which suggests that the two-event prophecy of the *Scurialensis* is closer to the original version.

To say that the Solomon story is alien to the text of the *Vita* is not to prove that it is a later interpolation. The latter does seem plausible; however, the use of the word *sъnъmъ* for "assembly" gives an archaic tinge to the prophetic lines.[47] The Chalice ⟨1816⟩ story of Chapter Thirteen might have been inserted in the ninth century as a patch among many, making up the varicolored quilt of the *Vita*. While it is not clear when this patch became a part of the *Vita*, it is clear that it was borrowed from Byzantine literature.

I wish to go a step further. The Greek text of the Chalice inscription belongs to the lowly, rather than exalted, level of Byzantine letters. It is here that the *Quellenforscher* meets with difficulties. When he studies the exalted level, he deals with a body of piously preserved and readily accessible texts, which have suffered no considerable losses since the ninth century. On that level, dependence is easier to detect[48] than on the lowly level, where the extent of the scribes' and collectors' care was much smaller and the degree of loss between Constantine-Cyril's and our

45. Cf. note 16 *supra*. In the *Sayings of the Holy Prophets*, cf. Evseev, "Slovesa ..." (as in note 11 *supra*), pp. 172-174, we see an even later stage of exegetic growth: there, the prophetic lines are explained as referring to: 1. The Virgin, Christ, the Star of the Magi, Last Supper; 2. Gethsemane, Passion, Crucifixion, the Cross, Descent into the Limbo; 3. Pilate and the Jews.

46. All versions, except the three mentioned in note 18 *supra*.

47. For this argument of Lavrov's, cf. note 27 *supra*.

48. Thus, in the past forty years, Grivec, Gnidovec, and Vavřínek have established and discussed the influence of Gregory Nazianzen upon the *Lives* of the Slavic Apostles. Cf. V. Vavřínek, "Staroslověnské životy Konstantina a Metoděje a panegyriky Řehoře z Nazianzu", *Listy Filologické*, 85 (1962), 96-122 (bibliography).

days, much greater. What has been preserved is concealed, sometimes inaccessible.

Under these circumstances, tracking down the source of a passage like the Chalice inscription, or of a longer excursus like Constantine-Cyril's disputations at the Arab and Khazar courts, is a matter of accidental finds. The Greek text of the Chalice inscription was just such an accidental find, and my subsequent attempts at discovering parallels to it — mostly in Solomonic literature — desultory. Until further luck strikes, I shall be content to say that in examining our inscription we should keep an eye on four categories of Byzantine texts: the legends of Solomon, a ruler said to have been provided by a servant-demon with a magic cup made of a ruby-like stone, to have stumbled upon inscriptions and to have attempted to discover the time of the Coming of the Messiah;[49] anti-Jewish polemics, which made use of chronological computations and showed how Old Testament figures testified to the Advent of the Anointed;[50] both *Catenae* and anonymous commentaries on the *Pro-*

49. Cf. C.C. McCown, *The Testament of Solomon... (1922), p. 84** [= Recension C, XI, 7-9], where the magic cup is called κύλικα (*acc.*). Is the word κύλιξ, which may have stood for "chalice" in some Greek version of the Chalice story, behind the surprising expression *kelьja Solomonja*, "cell of Solomon" in one Slavic variant of the story (Petrov, *Apokrifičeskoe proročestvo* ... [as in note 8 *supra*], p. 13), where the context clearly indicates that *kelьja* should mean "cup"? According to the *Testament*, Solomon's cup was made of λίθον λυχνίτην. In the version offered by the Barsov manuscript (Lavrov, *Materialy* ... [as in note 12 *supra*], p. XLVI) *luxnitъ* is the fifth one among the stones making up Solomon's Chalice. — On inscriptions which Solomon found (one of them — in Greek! — he could not decipher) and on his attempts to predict the time of the Messiah, cf. L. Ginzberg, *The Legends of the Jews*, IV (1947), pp. 164-165; VI (1946), p. 282.

50. "Nine hundred and nine years". This number is a headache, since it does not tally with any Byzantine *computus*, nor can it be reconciled with the earliest Slavic computistic work, the *Istorikija* by Constantine Presbyter (*scripsit* ca. 894 and followed the system of the *Chronicon Paschale*, cf. V. N. Zlatarski, "Najstarijat istoričeski trud v starobъlgarskata knižnina", *Spisanie na Bъgar. Akademija na Naukite*, 27 [1923], 132-182 and A. Vaillant, "Les dates dans la chronologie de Constantin le Prêtre," *Byzantinoslavica*, 9 [1947-48], 186-191). I submit the following emendation, born out of despair: in VC 13, read *θ* сътъ п*θ*-ро and *θ* сътъ п*θ* лѣтъ instead of *θ* сътъ и *θ*-ро and *θ* сътъ и *θ* лѣтъ respectively. By changing и into п — palaeographically, not much of a surgery, at least in Cyrillic —, we obtain nine hundred and eighty nine years instead of nine hundred and nine. This brings us in full agreement with the system of Patriarch Nicephorus' *Breviarium*, a text with which Slavic bookmen of the ninth and tenth centu-

verbs; and forged ⟨1817⟩ prophetic inscriptions. Two of the latter were fabricated in 780-781, and under Leo VI (d. 912) respectively, that is, at a distance of several decades before and after the composition of our *Vita*. Both referred to Christ, and both were purportedly written — entirely or in part — in a foreign language.[51]

The Story of Solomon's Chalice may teach us little about Constantine's knowledge of Semitic languages, the *realia* of the cult of relics in ninth-century Byzantium, and ninth-century Slavic poetry. It does remind the students of the *Vita Constantini* once again that this earliest work of Slavic literature draws upon Greek sources; it also teaches us to keep in mind not only the learned, but also the more popular level of Byzantine letters.

---

ries were familiar (witness Constantine Presbyter, cf. Zlatarski, *ibidem*, p. 160). Thus: Adam-Exodus, 3829 years; Exodus-David, 630 years; David-Solomon, 40 years; twelfth year of Solomon, 12 years; total, 4511 years; Adam-Christ, 5500 years; *ergo*, twelfth year of Solomon-Christ, 989 years, *q.e.d.*

51. 1. Constantine VI and Irene's time: C. Mango, "A Forged Inscription of the Year 781", *Zbornik radova Vizantološkog instituta*, 8,1 (1963), 201-207, esp. p. 205 (inscription probably in Greek and Latin); on other forged "pagan" inscriptions foretelling the Coming of Christ, cf. *ibidem*, p. 207. — 2. Leo VI's time: the Synaxarium for October 17 (sarcophagus of Lazarus found in Citium [Cyprus] with inscription "in a foreign tongue"). Cf. R. J. H. Jenkins, B. Laourdas, C. A. Mango, "Nine Orations of Arethas ...", *Byzantinische Zeitschrift*, 47 (1954), esp. pp. 6-7.

XXII

Muscovy's Conquest of Kazan: Two Views Reconciled

The war of conquest presents the conqueror with two major problems: first, the isolation of the adversary by diplomacy and his liquidation by force; second, the justification of such aggression to his own supporters and to the outside world. Two tasks of the historian follow: the first is to fit into an understandable pattern what happened before, during, and after the conquest; the second is to tell us how the conquerors explained why the conquest should have happened, why it had to happen as it did, and — whenever there is evidence — how the conquered viewed the same sequence of events.

Thc Muscovite conquest of Kazan has lent itself well to a re-study from both points of view. When it comes to telling us what happened, we shall read a narrative not limited to the vantage point of most available sources, that is, of Muscovy, but one which takes into account the interplay, on the territory occupied by the successor states to the Golden Horde, of the sedentary and nomadic entities. These entities formed a whole of which Moscow was only one, and, as it turned out, the strongest, component.

As for the justification of conquest, Kazan — the first major non-Slavic unit to be absorbed by Muscovy — is an instructive case, since it offered a special challenge to the Muscovite ideologists. For a long time the gathering of Russian lands, Muscovy's patrimony, was the principal reason Muscovite bookmen advanced for her expansion. This reason had begun, at first sight at least, to outlive its usefulness. By the mid-sixteenth century the "Great Russian" lands had been gathered, and neither Kazanis nor Cheremissians could pass for Russians, whether White or Little. To meet this challenge, Muscovite bookmen sacrificed elegance but not ingenuity, since, along with some new arguments, they

---

This discussion section is based on a session, "Muscovite Imperialism and Kazan," held April 1, 1967, at the second national convention of the American Association for the Advancement of Slavic Studies, Washington, D. C.

managed to apply the old one to Kazan as well. Like Lithuanian possessions or Novgorod in an earlier century, Kazan turned out to be a patrimony — *otchina*, or, in a language more understandable to the Tatars, *iurt* — of the Muscovite princes. Moreover — so one later claim went — originally this Kazan patrimony had been inhabited by Russians.

⟨542⟩ Since the task of the historian who tells us what happened in the steppe or in diplomatic correspondence with it is different from that of his colleague who tells us what happened on the writing desk of a Muscovite cleric, findings of the two are apt to differ. The voice of the diplomat and trader, including that of the Tatar trader, both in horses and men, tends to sound matter-of-fact; the voice of the propagandist, bemoaning the fate of his Christian brethren led into captivity, will be strident.

Treatment of the sources by the two kinds of historians will tend to differ as well. What for one of them is a lucubration of little value — in the present case, *Kazanskaia istoriia*, or an official chronicle — is a mirror of political thought for the other. What for one of them appears as a reliable source, stripped of verbiage — diplomatic correspondence or instructions for negotiators — is less productive for the other and will be used by him chiefly for the specious ideological arguments which it contains.

However, differential use of sources for different purposes does not imply their evaluation in descending order of "goodness." An official Muscovite chronicle is not inferior to a Muscovite diplomatic document in yielding truth. If it were, the future historian would be justified if, on reading the sober text of the Soviet-American Cultural Agreement, he wondered what all the talk of the Cold War had been about. The historian's preference in choosing his sources is related to the kind of truth about the past he is pursuing. In short, the papers of Professors Keenan and Pritsak and that of Professor Pelenski complement each other.

Professors Keenan and Pritsak rely on comparative Turcology. Their case is strong, as it rests on the remarkable linguistic, cultural, and institutional uniformity of Turkic peoples, and the novelty and importance of the findings by the two contributors from Harvard reside in their use of this method. In order to describe developments among the successor states of the Golden Horde, they have been well advised to adopt the synchronic bicultural view — for that, rather than polyculturalism, is what is involved when we compare the Muscovite with the Turkic systems in the middle of the sixteenth century. In order to describe the crescendo of Muscovite justifications for the conquest of

Kazan, Professor Pelenski has been well advised to remain within the Muscovite culture, and there is virtue rather than sin in his sticking to the monocultural point of view. There is virtue, too, in further exploring the foreign — read Byzantine — roots of arguments appearing in Muscovite texts and stressing their generally medieval antecedents.[1]

⟨543⟩ The polycultural point of view, impatience with the propaganda of the Muscovite religious establishment, and putting one's trust in diplomatic documents are approaches laudable in themselves; moreover, each of them helps to modify the propositions about Kazan advanced by conventional history. All of them combined, however, cannot entirely do away with the following three of these propositions: that — at least in the last twenty years or so of the khanate's existence — Muscovy's relations with the khanate were on the whole hostile; that the conquest of Kazan was envisaged for some time before 1552 in various milieus of Muscovy; and that the religious issue did carry a measure of weight in the confrontation with the khanate.

Now the particulars. What happened to Kazan was a conquest (*vziatie*, say the contemporaries). Kazan, an imperfectly sedentary entity, was absorbed, in an especially drastic fashion,[2] by an expanding sedentary state with superior resources, superior methods of exploiting the

---

1. Example: When in his prayer at the coronation ceremony of 1547 Metropolitan Macarius asked God to "subdue unto him [i.e., Ivan IV] all barbarian nations," his words could have been invested with an anti-Tatar meaning by those who listened to him (see Professor Pelenski's article, p. 575, and note 70). Originally, however, the passage had nothing to do with Tatars or with Russia, since Macarius' prayer was a translation of the Patriarch's prayer at the Byzantine Emperor's coronation. At the corresponding spot of the Greek, we read *hypotaxon autō panta ta barbara ethnē*. See J. Goar, *Euchologium sive rituale Graecorum* (1730), p. 726; P. Schreiner, "Hochzeit und Krönung Kaiser Manuels II. im Jahre 1392," *Byzantinische Zeitschrift*, LX (1967), 77, lines 14-15; and, for Slavic texts, E. V. Barsov, "Drevne-russkie pamiatniki sviashchennogo venchaniia Tsarei na tsarstvo," *Chteniia v Imperatorskom Obshchestve istorii i drevnostei rossiiskikh* (ChOIDR), 1883, Book 1, pp. 27-28, 34, 51.

2. In January 1553 Ivan IV wrote to the Nogai Mirza Ismail: "God ... put Kazan into our hands. And such men as were in the city of Kazan, all of them died by our sword. As for their wives and children, our men led them into captivity" (*Prodolzhenie Drevnei rossiiskoi vivliofiki*, IX [St. Petersburg, 1793], 64). However, the parallel texts in letters to other mirzas, sent out at the same time, have a mitigated version: "And whoever insulted us (in Kazan), all of them died by our sword" (*ibid.*, pp. 61, 67, 69, 71).

subject populations, and superior military technology.[3] Since the two had had a common past, they understood each other extremely well. For all that, the relations between them were not on the whole peaceful. Between 1534 and 1545, chronicles, monastic charters, and lives of saints record one or more Kazani incursions a year on Muscovite territory.[4] Admittedly, it would have been difficult for the Tatars to stop raiding, since this was one of the three principal ways in which they kept their economy going, the other two being trade and the taxing of sedentary or semisedentary populations. This is why, if for no other reason, the Muscovite government could not be satisfied indefinitely with installing a vassal khan in Kazan; if not propagandistic writings, then such actions as the construction of the Russian cities of Vasil'sur'sk (1523) and Sviiazhsk (1550) on Kazan territory should give food for thought. These were conscious steps. The second of them was followed by the attempt at transforming the city of Kazan itself into another, ready-made, Sviiazhsk; this failed and the conquest came.[5] Vasil'sur'sk and Sviiazhsk were to Kazan what Anadolu Hisar and Rumeli Hisar, the two strangling fortresses on the eastern and western banks of the Bosporus, built ⟨544⟩ by the Ottomans in 1395 and 1452 respectively, were to Constantinople; the construction of Rumeli Hisar was a preliminary to the conquest of the city, and contemporaries were well aware of this.

By 1550 at least one other social group besides the ecclesiastics seems to have been backing the outright liquidation of Kazan. Ivan Peresvetov, we all agree, was the spokesman for the *dvoriane*, or "warriors" as he called them. He considered Kazan the crucial problem in Muscovite foreign policy and had his straw man Petr the Voevoda designate the Kazan khan as Ivan IV's "worst enemy." Peresvetov advocated taking the khanate and, in so doing, indulged in no nonsense

---

3. Example: In 1524 there was only one master gunner in the city of Kazan; see S. M. Solov'ev, *Istoriia Rossii s drevneishikh vremen* (Soviet ed.), III (Moscow, 1960), 270. About 1521 Vasilii III was rumored to have sent thirty thousand *pishchali* (small firearms) and *several* master gunners as a form of military aid to the ruler of Persia; see *Sbornik Imperatorskogo russkogo istoricheskogo Obshchestva* (SRIO), XCV (1895), 706.

4. See the list of incursions in S. O. Shmidt, "Predposylki i pervye gody 'Kazanskoi voiny' (1545-1549)," *Trudy Moskovskogo Gosudarstvennogo Istoriko-Arkhivnogo Instituta*, VI (1954), esp. 229-34.

5. The grand old man Solov'ev made a similar juxtaposition as early as 1855; see Solov'ev, III, 269. In general, his treatment of the Kazan affair is superb. For the attempt at making Kazan into another Sviiazhsk, see note 11 below.

about liberating poor Christian prisoners: "Such a [profitable] land, should it even be a friendly territory, one should not suffer it [to exist] on account of the great profit [that could be derived from it]."[6]

In the sixteenth century Christianity's conflict with Islam was more than a mere slogan of the over-eloquent members of the Muscovite ecclesiastical establishment. The Tverian merchant Afanasii Nikitin — whom I shall use here, since I have no Muscovite *gost'* trading among the Kazanis or the Nogais to quote — was not a priest, nor was the "warrior" Peresvetov, or the Crimean khan who used the religious conflict in his diplomatic game; to be sure, Sil'vestr was a priest of the Annunciation Cathedral, but when he wrote about Christianizing the newly acquired territory, he wrote as a politician.

Afanasii, who traveled through Moslem lands about 1470, was obsessed with retaining his religious — which also meant his national — identity. In his travelogue the subject comes up over and over again. He doubted his ability to withstand the lure of Islam. He had adopted a Moslem name, that of Hodja Iusuf the Khorasani. He did pray for the Russian land, but he did it in a Turkic *koine*. He felt guilty; he was neither fish nor fowl. That he counted his years of travel by Easters, that in his Turkic prayer he declared that he had found no place in the world equal to *urus yeri* — the Russian land — and that in the end he clung to Christianity is beside the point. It is important that this merchant should have devoted so much space to the plight of his mind, torn between the two religions, and so little to his commercial transactions. Despite his complaints, things must have gone more smoothly in Afanasii's business than in his spiritual life.[7]

Before the fall of Kazan Ivan Peresvetov said that baptizing the Tatars should go hand in hand with conquering the khanate.[8] Professor Pelenski reminds us that after the fall, Sil'vestr, a member of the ruling council, openly called for the baptism of the Cheremissians and "all the

6. See *Sochineniia I. Peresvetova*, ed. A. A. Zimin (Moscow and Leningrad, 1956), pp. 177, 183; for parallel passages in other versions of Peresvetov's text, see *ibid.*, pp. 204, 208, 242, 245. See also A. A. Zimin, *I. S. Peresvetov i ego sovremenniki* (Moscow, 1958), pp. 377-79, 384.

7. V. P. Adrianova-Peretts, ed., *Khozhenie za tri moria Afanasiia Nikitina 1466-1472* gg. (Moscow and Leningrad, 1958), esp. pp. 18, 20, 22-23, 25, 27 ("God alone knows the right faith").

8. *Sochineniia I. Peresvetova*, pp. 162, 182, 196, 208.

Agarenes," ⟨545⟩ that is, Muslims, and generally advocated the use of force by Orthodox rulers in baptizing conquered peoples.[9]

Sources do not afford more than one or two glimpses into the use of ideological arguments by the Moslem side. When they do, we see that they raise the religious issue. About 1520 the issue was exploited in order to foment trouble over Kazan between Moscow and the religiously straitlaced Istanbul. On that occasion the Crimean khan Muhammad-Girei had asserted in his correspondence with Sultan Selim I that while Kazan was his *iurt*, Vasilii III had set up Shah-Ali, his own puppet khan, there; he "allegedly had the mosques there destroyed and his own Christian churches erected there, and allegedly had bells hung up there." The Muscovite envoy to Istanbul was instructed to tell the Sultan that all this was a lie. The mosques were standing, no church construction had been ordered, and no bells were ringing in Kazan.[10]

In 1551, at Kazan's eleventh hour, the puppet Khan Shah-Ali refused to carry out the last detail of the task assigned to him by Ivan IV. What made him balk was religion. The Khan asked to be allowed to abdicate rather than acquiesce in the Muscovite annexation of the *Gorniaia Storona*, until 1550 part of the khanate, and satisfy the demand for "strengthening" Kazan with a Russian garrison, perhaps even with Russian settlers. Acquiescence would mean complete loss of internal support; but yielding to the second demand was impossible as a matter of principle: "I am a Muslim; I shall not act against people of my own faith."[11]

1480, so Professor Keenan tells us, has nothing to do with the "Tatar Yoke." There is a point to this *obiter dictum*, and the point has been made before; however, only seventy years after 1480, on the eve of Kazan's fall, an important Muscovite thought otherwise. This is worth noting, not only because in evaluating an event it is useful to ask what contemporaries or near contemporaries felt about it but also because *pop* Sil'vestr — for he, or another dignitary close to Ivan IV, is our impor-

9. Letter to Prince Aleksandr Borisovich Shuiskii-Gorbatyi, in D. P. Golokhvastov and Leonid, "Blagoveshchenskii ierei Sil'vestr i ego pisaniia," ChOIDR, 1874, Book 1, pp. 89, 99.

10. Instruction to Vasilii Mikhailovich Tretiak-Gubin, SRIO, XCV, No. 38, esp. 695-96.

11. Demand for "strengthening": *chtoby ukrepil gorod velikogo kniazia liudmi Ruskymi*. Khan's reply: *busurman de esmi ne khochiu na svoiu veru stati*. Nikon Chronicle, *Polnoe sobranie russkikh letopisei*, XIII (1904, reprint 1965), 173.

tant Muscovite[12] — suggested ⟨546⟩ that in the unfolding of God's plan — in the logic of history — 1480 was to be followed by better things, such as the fall of Kazan.

About 1550 "Sil'vestr" addressed Ivan IV and predicted, by means of doctored-up scriptural quotations, that God would destroy the strength of *pagan* tsars and that the *pagan* cities would "not be closed" to Ivan IV.[13] The pagan cities, I submit, stood for Kazan. The same writer quoted four events in world history which had preceded the anticipated triumph of Ivan. The first was the slaughter of a hundred and fourscore and five thousand warriors in Sennacherib's army under the walls of Jerusalem at the hand of the angel of the Lord; the second and the third, the long Arab siege of Constantinople under Constantine IV Pogonatus (674-78) and the Arab siege of Constantinople under Leo III the Isaurian (717); finally, the fourth event was the confrontation between, on the one hand, the haughty Tsar of the Great Horde, Ahmed, who said unto himself, "I shall kill all the Russian princes and will be the sole ruler upon the face of the earth," and, on the other, the humble Great Orthodox Ruler, Great Prince Ivan Vasil'evich, the Autocrat of

12. The text I am using is a letter to Ivan IV transmitted anonymously in the so-called *Sil'vestrovskii Sbornik* and published in Golokhvastov and Leonid, pp. 69-87. For discussion of authorship, attribution of the letter to Sil'vestr, and date of 1550, see Zimin, *I. S. Peresvetov*, pp. 50-61; for attribution of the same letter to Metropolitan Macarius, see I. I. Smirnov, *Ocherki politicheskoi istorii russkogo gosudarstva 30-50-kh godov XVI veka* (Moscow and Leningrad, 1958), pp. 233-39. I wish to add that the letter contains a quasi-quotation or two from the prayer pronounced by Metropolitan Macarius at the Coronation of Ivan IV in 1547; compare esp. p. 69 (*suditi liudem svoim v pravdu i nishchim tvoim istinnoiu i sudom pravednym*) with Barsov, pp. 28 and 51 (*da sudia liudi tvoia pravdoiu i nishchiikh tvoikh sudom*). Such a textual reminiscence would rather speak in favor of Macarius' authorship.

13. See Golokhvastov and Leonid, p. 70. The pertinent quotation is Isaiah 45:1-3, from which the name of King Cyrus was removed; the sentence was adapted to Ivan IV, and the words "kings" and "cities" changed into "pagan tsars" and "pagan cities" respectively. Isaiah 45:1-3, unchanged, is quoted in a similar context, namely in Chapter 3, "About inheriting enemy cities," of the "Chapters about consolatory exhortations ⟨addressed⟩ to Tsars, and, if you wish, to magnates." The author of the "Chapters" is, according to its latest editor, A. I. Klibanov, Ermolai-Erazm. If the date of the "Chapters" is indeed 1553, as Klibanov plausibly conjectures, then "the enemy cities" in question is Kazan. Cf. A. I. Klibanov, "Sbornik Sochinenii Ermolaya-Erazma," *TODRL*, XVI (1960), 182-186, 204.

All Rus', in short, Ivan III. The outcome of the showdown was that the tribe of Ahmed disappeared without trace.

Of the four events only one was Russian. When "Sil'vestr" had to select an occurrence in Russian history whose sequel was to be Kazan's fall, he did not choose the *Kulikovo Pole* of 1380, but the *Stoianie* on the Ugra of a hundred years later. He put it side by side with Biblical and Byzantine victories won by the People of God against the infidel. By his choice "Sil'vestr" was demonstrating to Ivan IV that Ugra was a world-historical event, as the fall of Kazan would be. He said one more thing. After the *Stoianie* on the Ugra "the Lord ... lifted the horn of the Orthodox great princes and liberated them from the impious pagan tsars." In the mind of a statesman close to Ivan IV, 1480 had had a great deal to do with the "Tatar Yoke."[14]

To intimate that Muscovy's attempts on Kazan were dysfunctional phenomena marring what were on the whole peaceful relations, that these relations were but little affected by religious animosities, and that the stand-off on the Ugra of 1480 was not as important as we have been told it was is to use a healthy device for awakening the adherents of conventional history from their slumber and making them think again. To do no more than this, however, is to administer historical smelling salts, not the real stuff of history.

The reader should be reassured at this point. The exciting quality of the ⟨547⟩ papers to which now he is about to turn resides in the fact that they do not limit themselves to serving the smelling salts. Telling us why Simeon Bekbulatovich was made "tsar" under Ivan IV (because he was a Chinggisid),[15] the explanation of how the *karachi* system worked, the suggestion about the two establishments in Muscovy are all real stuff. So

14. Golokhvastov and Leonid, p. 71. See esp. *pravoslavnykh velikikh kniazei Gospod' ... ot nechestivykh poganykh Tsarei svobodi.* In the letter to Prince Gorbatyi, *ibid.*, p. 93, "Sil'vestr" quotes the wise "Demokrit" not in the form in which it appears in various Old-Russian *Pchely* but verbatim as it occurs in Vasian Rylo's famous letter "*na Ugru*" of 1480. For other borrowings from Vasian Rylo by "Sil'vestr" (including the quotation from Isaiah 45: 1-3, which, however, is not doctored up in Vasian), see Zimin, *I. S. Peresvetov*, p. 53, n. 190.

15. This explanation elegantly supplements the "plot theory" discussed by Jack M. Culpepper, "The Kremlin Executions of 1575 and the Enthronement of Simeon Bekbulatovich," *Slavic Review*, XXIV, No. 3 (Sept. 1965), 503-6.

are Professor Pelenski's erudition and the various improved restatements of earlier observations, such as that on *Kazanskaia istoriia's* producing "local Russians" as original inhabitants of Kazan, that on the spurious character of the *iarlyk* of Ahmed Khan, and that on the meaning of the term *belyi tsar'*. After the three papers which follow, the study of Muscovy's relations with the steppe will not be the same again.

XXIII

Rozważania nad "Szachami" Jana Kochanowskiego

I

Poemat łaciński Marka Hieronima Vidy *Scacchia ludus*, czyli *Gra w szachy*,[1] cieszył się dużą popularnością w kołach literackich na przestrzeni trzech stuleci, począwszy od w. XV, kiedy został napisany, aż do XVIII, gdy zachwycał grających w szachy profesorów. Szachy świetnie nadawały się na temat gatunku heroikomicznego, jaki reprezentuje utwór włoskiego poety. Utarło się mniemanie, że sama forma utworu, jego sceneria mitologiczna i wergiliańskie heksametry kontrastują w sposób komiczny z niby-potyczkami "niby-bohaterów" i "trup komediantów." Utwór Vidy był szeroko tłumaczony, parafrazowany czy plagiowany w całej Europie.[2] Powiedziano nawet, że Aleksander Pope pomysł opisu gry w karty w *Puklu porwanym (The Rape of the Lock)* zaczerpnął z poematu Vidy. Ze wszystkich jednak utworów na Vidzie wzorowanych poemat Jana Kochanowskiego jest najdoskonalszy i z pewnością najbardziej twórczy.

⟨342⟩ *Szachy* Kochanowskiego ukazały się około r. 1562-1566.[3]

---

1. Najcelniejsze omówienie poematu w pracy: T. v. Heydebrand u.d. Lassa, *Zur Geschichte und Literatur des Schachspiels*. München 1897, s. 184 n. (pierwotna wersja *Szachów* Vidy pochodzi z r. 1513; wyd. 1, nieautentyczne — 1525; wyd. 2, skrócone, służące za podstawę licznych wydań następnych — 1527). Najlepsza bibliografia wydań w: A. v. d. Linde, *Geschichte und Literatur des Schachspiels*. T. 2. Berlin 1874, s. 258-264.

2. Linde (*op. cit.*) podaje najkompletniejszy wykaz przekładów i naśladownictw. Wśród znanych autorów, którzy korzystali z dzieła Vidy, znajduje się G. Marino — włączył on *quasi*-przekład utworu Vidy do pieśni XV *Adone*. Na Vidzie i Marinie wzorował się z kolei W. Jones, przyjaciel Boswella i Johnsona, autor angielskiego klasycznego poematu szachowego *Caïssa or the Game of Chess* (w: *Works*. T. 4. 1799).

3. Zob. *Bibliografia literatury polskiej*. "Nowy Korbut", t. 2. (1964), s. 334, 364-365.

Nie ma w nich rekwizytów mitologicznych i niezbyt komicznych naśladowań z Wergiliusza,[4] owych szafranowych wschodów słońca i Wener, do których humanista włoski przyrównuje króla szachowego. W *Szachach* zmieniono ramy obrazu: zamiast zgromadzenia bóstw na Olimpie — oglądamy dwór królewski; partnerami szachowymi są nie bogowie, lecz dwaj możni konkurenci do ręki królewny. Dla spotęgowania napięcia fabuły Kochanowski wprowadza elementy, których brak we wzorcu łacińskim: często wtrąca polskie porzekadła i aluzje do rodzimych podań. Dzięki temu formalne ćwiczenie literackie w gatunku heroikomicznym przekształca się w dzieło sztuki, które naprawdę bawi.

Badacze literatury polskiej podkreślali już te walory *Szachów*. Ostatnio zaś przyjął się pogląd, że jest to najdojrzalszy utwór młodzieńczy poety.[5] Można by jednak podjąć próbę wyjścia poza te uogólniające oceny. Tematem dziełka, które rozważymy, są przecież szachy, a zatem zostało ono napisane w przekonaniu, że czytelnicy posiadają jakąś znajomość tej gry. W wieku XVI przesłanka ta miała istotne podstawy, co potwierdza *Il Cortegiano* Castiglione'a czy *Dworzanin polski* Górnickiego.[6] Zmierzch popularności szachów w społeczeństwie i niedocenianie tego przez historyków literatury — to zjawiska znacznie późniejsze.

Szachy stanowią małe arcydzieło polskiej literatury renesansowej. Czy istotnie zdołaliśmy ogarnąć intencję utworu, zrozumieć należycie wszystkie ustępy? Jako czytelnicy odnosimy korzyść wtedy, gdy odkrywamy możliwie jak najwięcej warstw znaczeniowych dzieła literackiego i reagujemy na nie. Jako badacze dzieła literackiego musimy rozważyć to, co było istotne dla autora i współczesnej publiczności. To właśnie mając na uwadze, zajmę się utworami Vidy i Kochanowskiego pod kątem gry w szachy.

Scacchia ludus bawi nas jako dzieło literackie, lecz z punktu widzenia gry w szachy jest właściwie nieciekawe. Z całości utworu wydzielić można tylko przepisy gry (które są niemal identyczne z obecnymi) i kilka posunięć. Jest oczywiste, że dla Vidy szachy posłużyły jedynie jako pretekst do przedstawienia scenek komicznej rzezi i popisania się

4. Częściowe zestawienie zapożyczeń poematu Vidy z Wergiliusza w: V. Cicchetelli, *Sulle opere poetiche di M. Vida*. Milano 1904, s. 187-189, zwłaszcza s. 189, przypis 2.

5. Zob. K. Budzyk, *Szkice i materiały do dziejów literatury staropolskiej*. Warszawa 1955, s. 223.

6. *Il Cortegiano*, II, 31; por. *Dworzanin polski*, II.

znajomością *Eneidy*; gdy idzie bowiem o samą grę, jej zakończenie, tj. zwycięstwo jednego z partnerów, nie mogło być bardziej banalne: na ⟨343⟩ ostatek zostają trzy figury; białego króla spychają na brzeg szachownicy i zapędzają w matnię czarny król i królowa (hetman). Wszyscy naśladowcy Vidy, z jednym tylko wyjątkiem, podają takie samo zakończenie, bądź też w ogóle rezygnują z definitywnego rozwiązania gry.

Wspomniany wyjątek stanowi Kochanowski. Jego zakończenie, które obejmuje ponad 1/4 utworu, liczącego około 600 wierszy, jest zupełnie odmienne. Już sam ten fakt powinien być wskazówką, że poeta polski przypisywał jakieś znaczenie motywowi gry w szachy w swoim małym eposie. Gdyby pomysł gry miał mu służyć wyłącznie do przedstawienia fantastycznych bojów, mógłby był wówczas zadowolić się rozwiązaniem Vidy, podobnie jak inni autorzy.

Czy szachowe innowacje Kochanowskiego coś tedy znaczą? Innymi słowy, czy na podstawie utworu, postępując krok za krokiem, można odtworzyć położenie figur i dalszy przebieg gry prowadzący do mata? Jeden z XVI-wiecznych czytelników *Szachów* daje do zrozumienia, że jest to niemożliwe.[7] Podobne stanowisko zajął niedawny wydawca i komentator dzieł Kochanowskiego. Uważa bowiem, że poeta potraktował ruchy figur szachowych "swobodnie, bez troski o ścisłość".[8] Pogląd ten zasługuje na sprawdzenie.[9]

⟨344⟩ U Vidy gra kończy się przed zachodem słońca. Natomiast Kochanowski woli zostawić nas w niepewności: o zachodzie słońca partia jest prawie rozegrana i wszystko zdaje się wskazywać na to, że Fiedor, jeden z pretendujących do ręki królewny, dostanie mata w następnym posunięciu. Fiedor nie widzi wyjścia, by więc odwlec to, co jest nieunik-

---

7. W egzemplarzu "prawdziwej" edycji (z r. 1585) J. Kochanowskiego, znajdującym się obecnie w Landesbibliothek w Stuttgarcie (Slav. u. Ung. Dicht. add.), widnieje następująca uwaga, wpisana atramentem na ostatniej (103) stronicy *Szachów*:

> Rozum okazał i obrotne mowi
> W igrzisku [?] szachow tilko graiacz [?] słowi
> Skad sie też [?] żaden szachow nie nauczi
> ani metu da, ani też dokuczi.

8. J. Krzyżanowski, w edycji: J. Kochanowski, *Dzieła polskie*. T. 1. Wybrał, wstępem i przypisami opatrzył... Warszawa 1952, s. 325.

9. W niniejszym przekładzie posłużono się nazwami figur i notacją szachową według podręcznika T. Czarneckiego *Nauka gry w szachy* (Warszawa 1950), jedynie dla "Hetmana" — zgodnie z intencją Kochanowskiego — zachowując nazwę "Królowa". Poniżej zestawienie terminów, w którym uwzględniono naz-

nione, nalega na odłożenie ostatecznej rozgrywki do następnego dnia. Kochanowski opisuje wówczas położenie figur na szachownicy w sposób następujący:

469 Naprzód Król czarny (aby każdy wiedział)
Rochu się trzymał, który w kącie siedział.

Już sam w. 470 ogranicza możliwe pozycje czarnej wieży do dwóch, mianowicie do dwóch narożników szachownicy. Umiejscowiłem wieżę w narożniku a1 po stronie króla.[10] Jeśli idzie o czarnego króla, który "Rochu się trzymał", istnieją trzy możliwości, lecz tylko jedna z nich jest realna, mianowicie b1. Dalszy ciąg cytowanego urywka brzmi następująco:

471 Przed Królem stał Koń w piątym polu prawie,
A Pieszek w szóstym i na tejże ławie.

"Ława" oznacza rząd pionowy;[11] wypadnie nam zatem umieścić skoczka na polu b5, a piona na b6. Następny wiersz brzmi tak:

---

wy potoczne (w nawiasach) użyte przez Krzyżanowskiego, nazwy angielskie z oryginału artykułu i odpowiadające im terminy w *Szachach* Kochanowskiego.

Nazwa figury	*Odpowiednik Angielski*	*Określenia Kochanowskiego*
Król	King	Król, Pan, Wódz
Królowa	Queen	Pani, Królowa, Królewska Miłośnica, Baba, Jędza, Murzynka (tj. Czarna Królowa)
Wieża	Rook	Roch, Słoń
Goniec (Laufer)	Bishop	Pop, Biskup, Kapłan, Ksiądz, Mnich, Fenrych
Skoczek (Koń)	Knight	Rycerz, Jezdny, Koń
Pion (Pionek)	Pawn	Pieszek, Pieszy, Piechota, Drab, Dworzanin, Królewski Sługa, Panna Służebna

10. Wykluczone jest, aby czarna wieża zajmowała narożnik h1 po stronie czarnej królowej, ponieważ na podstawie w. 473 wiadomo, że czarny pion stojący na polu b6 ma przy sobie drugiego piona z prawej strony. "Prawy" oznacza: po stronie czarnej (por. w. 200, gdzie "Rycerz", tj. goniec, zagraża równocześnie "prawej Wieży" i królowi; z uwagi na to, że żadna z tych dwu figur nie wykonała poprzednio ruchu, "prawa Wieża" może oznaczać tylko wieżę h8 po stronie królowej). Gdybyśmy przesunęli ten układ figur na stronę królowej (tzn. na prawą stronę szachownicy), drugi pion musiałby stanąć na polu h5, lecz problemat wymaga, aby rząd pionowy h był wolny od przeszkód.

11. Ponieważ szereg drugi jest obstawiony figurami ciężkimi (biała królowa i biała wieża).

473 A wedle niego [ti. obok czarnego piona] drugi w prawej stronie.

Na podstawie paralelnego urywka możemy wywnioskować niezawodnie, że dla czarnych figur strona "prawa" oznacza stronę królowej[12] (tj. prawą stronę szachownicy); postawimy przeto drugiego piona na polu c6. W dalszym ciągu tekst mówi:

474 Ten miał nad sobą Popa ku obronie.

"Pop" oznacza "Biskupa" (gońca). Zestawiając ten wers z w. 478 widzimy, że dla czarnych "pod" znaczy tyle co 'w wyższym szeregu', a "pod" w tymże wierszu — 'bezpośrednio pod'. Wobec tego interpretuję ⟨345⟩ wyraz "nad" jako 'w szeregu bezpośrednio niższym', tj. gdzieś w szeregu piątym. Lecz "ku obronie" znaczyć może tylko to, że goniec osłania piona; pozostaje więc nam wyłącznie pole d5. Wróćmy znowu do tekstu:

475 Król biały patrzał na swego Szampierza
Przez Draba i przez Czarnego Rycerza.

"Szampierz" znaczy 'przeciwnik'. Co więcej, w *Szachach* Kochanowskiego zawsze znaczy 'król barwy przeciwnej'. Pion musi być czarny, ponieważ z poprzedniego urywka (w. 441 n.) wynika, że białe nie miały już pionów. Biały król może spoglądać na czarnego króla "przez czarnego Rycerza" (skoczka), unikając przy tym zagrożenia tylko wtedy, gdy stoi na polu b8. Ciąg dalszy tekstu brzmi:

477 A swego Rochu posadził na stronie[13],
Pod Królem czarnym, na wtórym zagonie.

"Wtóry zagon" jest równoznaczny z drugim szeregiem.[14] "Na stronie" jest niejasne. (Białą) wieżę ulokowałem w polu najbardziej oddalonym (od białego króla, tj. w rzędzie h). Właściwie dokładna pozycja białej wieży nie ma znaczenia, pod warunkiem że stoi ona w drugim szeregu i "na stronie". Powróćmy znowu do tekstu:

479 Na tymże rzędzie też Królowa była,
A jednym okiem na Księdza patrzyła.

12. Zob. przypis 10.

13. "A swego Rochu [tj. białą wieżę] posadzil [biały król] na stronie".

14. Por. w. 97: "Gdzie też na zagon ostateczny padnie" (o pionie, który przemienia się w królową).

"Rząd" oznacza szereg poziomy.[15] "tenże rząd", czyli "rząd" zajmowany przez białą wieżę, oznacza szereg drugi. "Patrzeć jednym okiem na" to tyle co zagrażać, wiadomo zaś, że królowa (hetman) atakuje bądź ruchem gońca, bądź wieży. "Ksiądz", czyli "Biskup" (goniec), jest oczywiście czarny (białe nie mają już gońca). Pozycję jego znamy: d5. Jedynym więc polem, w którym może stać biała królowa, jest pole d2. Omawiany przez nas fragment zamyka dwuwiersz:

481 Tym obyczajem oba ufy stały,
A czarnej przodek zeznawał Król biały.

Wiemy zatem, że następne posunięcie należało do czarnych.

Spójrzmy na odtworzony układ figur (rys. 1).[16] Sytuacja czarnych przedstawia się groźnie. Na szczęście czarnym przysługuje pierwsze posunięcie. Gdyby białe miały pierwszeństwo, następny ruch przyniósł⟨346⟩by czarnym mata, przy czym istnieją aż cztery różne sposoby sfinalizowania gry. Jednakże wszystko nie było jeszcze stracone, ponieważ partię rozegrać miano dopiero następnego ranka.

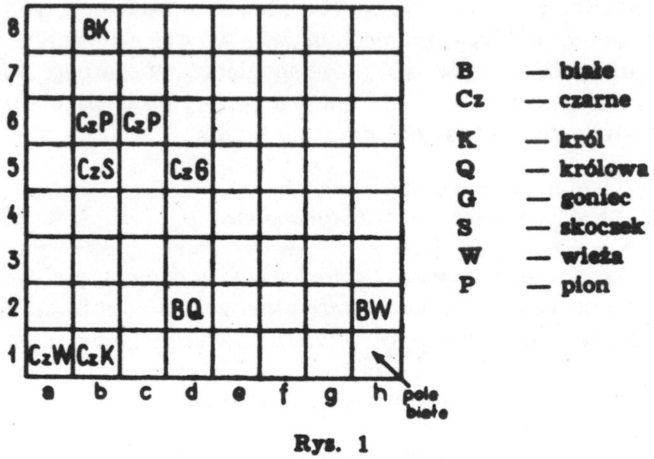

Rys. 1

15. Por. np. w. 153: "Wtóry rząd wszytek zastąpili".

16. Układ figur zgodny jest z konwencją średniowieczną: gracze ówcześni częstokroć patrzyli na szachownicę od strony figur czarnych. Zob. H. J. R. Murray, *A History of Chess*. London 1913, s. 224.

Gdy gracze i widzowie opuścili salę, przyszła królewna Anna, której losy rozstrzygnąć miał wynik gry, przyjrzała się położeniu figur na szachownicy —

507 I rzecze: "Dobry Rycerz jest od zwady,
Popu też nieźle zachować od rady;
Dać za miłego wdzięczną rzecz nie szkodzi,
Piechota przed się jako żywo chodzi".

Komnata była strzeżona, królewna nie mogła więc zmienić układu szachów; zrobi natomiast coś innego:

511 Obróci Rochu na Króla rogami,
I sama wynidzie zalawszy się łzami.

Jakie są "rogi" wieży, wyjaśnimy później. Tymczasem wystarczy powiedzieć, że królewna zwróciła wieżę w stronę białego króla, pozostawiając jąprzy tym na dotychczasowym miejscu.

Słowa i zachowanie się królewny były mniej zagadkowe dla czytelników współczesnych Kochanowskiemu, aniżeli nam się teraz wydają. Wypowiedź Anny zrozumieli mniej więcej tak: "Zachowaj skoczka i gońca, wykonaj ruchy pionami, poświęć najbardziej wartościową figurę" (tj. wieżę). Skierowanie wieży w stronę króla znaczyć miało "szachuj wieżą".

Następnego ranka grę podjęto na nowo. Pomimo przygnębienia Fiedor, gracz — jak sądzono — pokonany, zauważył zmianę położenia wieży. Stróże powiedzieli mu, kto poruszył wieżę poprzedniego wieczoru, powtórzyli także słowa królewny. Co mogła znaczyć tajemnicza wypo⟨347⟩wiedź? Fiedor skupił się i nagle wszystko wydało mu się jasne. W tym miejscu niektóre wydania *Szachów* podają, że Fiedor zawołał:

577 "A niechaj nie mam za wygraną k'temu,
Jeśli trzecim szciem mat nie będzie twemu"[17].

Wszyscy są zaintrygowani, Fiedor zaś przystępuje do wykonania swego planu.

17. Sprawę wątpliwej autentyczności tych wierszy poruszam w przypisie 33 (d).

a Roch jednym skokiem
Usiadł Królowi tuż pod samym bokiem[18].
Co czynisz, głupi? Mierzi cię ta trocha?
Chcesz darmo stracić tak wdzięcznego Rocha?[19]

Fiedor nie jest głupi, gdy oddaje dobrowolnie wieżę. Zmusza przeciwnika do zabicia szachującej wieży; biały król nie ma innego wyjścia — czytamy:

Tu próżno szukać jakiej inszej rady,
Przyjdzie do końca z Rochem patrzyć zwady;
Folgować darmo, bo tak Króla dusi,
Że mu rad nie rad Król wziąć gardło musi[20].
Wtym Drab przyskoczy, Król ustąpi kroku[21],
Przypadłszy drugi poimał ji z boku (rys. 2)[22],

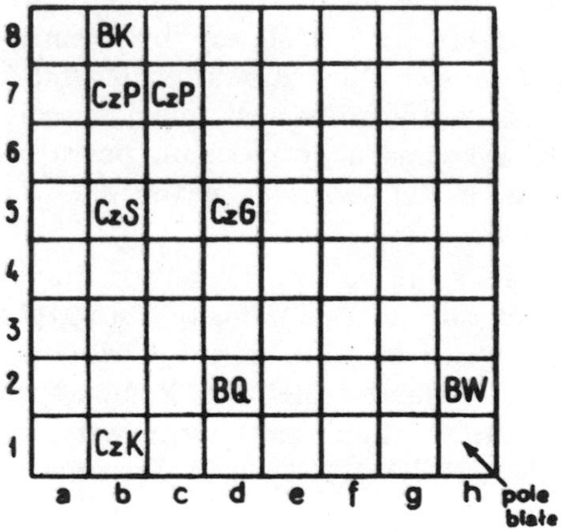

Rys. 2

18. Pierwsze posunięcie Fiedora: wieżą szachuje króla z pozycji a8.

19. Wieża nie jest broniona.

20. Biały król zabija wieżę.

21. Drugie posunięcie Fiedora: szachuje pionem z pozycji b7; biały król cofa się na pole b8 — innej możliwości nie ma.

22. "Drugi", tj. drugi pion; "z boku" — 'z ukosa', tak jak bije pion; trzeci ruch Fiedora: daje mata pionem, przesuwając go z pola c6 na c7.

⟨348⟩ *Passus* zamyka poeta dwuwierszem:

591 To było tej gry sławnej dokonanie,
Prawie nad wszytkich ludzi domniemanie.

Warto więc było potraktować poważnie szachową terminologię Kochanowskiego. W porównaniu z mdłym zakończeniem gry u Vidy — rozbudowany finał w utworze polskiego poety nabiera, w układzie artystycznym *Szachów*, cech dominujących. Celem zagadki szachowej, rozwiązanej w trzech posunięciach, było nie tylko wytworzenie napięcia, lecz także i jego rozładowanie. Napięcie rosło, a następnie ustępowało przez to, że umiejący grać w szachy czytelnicy (w w. XVI było ich niemało) śledzili krok za krokiem wskazówki autora, niezbyt zresztą trudne do odszyfrowania, a na koniec mogli posmakować rozwiązania dość prostego problematu.[23] Czytelnik lub krytyk, który zadowala się heroikomicznymi opisami bitew i pojedynków — nie ogarnia całości zamysłu poety, bo nie dostrzega istotnych elementów intencji utworu, stąd wiele piękna uchodzi jego uwagi. "Czytamy rzeczy piękne, lecz nie odczuwamy ich w pełni, dopóki nie nadążamy za autorem".[24]

II

Dokładne zbadanie elementów gry szachowej w utworze Kochanowskiego jest jeszcze bardziej pożyteczne dla badacza zajmującego się krytyką tekstu (edytora). Aby odtworzyć rzeczywiście poprawną postać tekstu, ten rodzaj badań łączyć należy ze szczegółową analizą najwcześniejszych drukowanych utworów poety. Dwa urywki *Szachów* posłużą do zobrazowania tej tezy — idzie nam tutaj wyłącznie o ilustrację.

W nowszych wydaniach *Szachów*, łącznie z ostatnim,[25] w. 441-444 mają następujące brzmienie:

---

23. Ta część wywodu została opracowana i wygłoszona, zanim dowiedziałem się, że co najmniej pięciu autorów próbowało już wcześniej zrekonstruować zagadkę szachową Kochanowskiego — J. S. Bandtkie (1826), M. Dzieduszycki (1856), W. Korotyński (1884), S. Witkowski (1892), i K. Nitsch (1923), przy czym każdy z nich udoskonalił dzieło swego poprzednika. Miło mi stwierdzić, że moje rozwiązanie zasadniczo pokrywa się z wynikami uzyskanymi przez Nitscha.

24. J. Keats, list z 3 V 1818 (w edycji M. Buxtona Formana [wyd. 3. Oxford 1948]: s. 142).

25. Np. J. Kochanowski, *Dzieła wszystkie*. Wydanie pomnikowe. T. 2. Warszawa 1884. — K. Nitsch, *"Szachy" Jana Kochanowskiego*. Lublin 1923. — Krzyżanowski, *ed. cit.*, s. 70.

441 A Pop tymczasem z Rycerzem wyciekli,
Ostatek wojska białego wysiekli,
Rycerz nie zginął i Roch się obronił,
Ale najbarziej Król małżonki chronił:

⟨349⟩ W tej wersji białym pionkom prócz króla zostaje królowa, wieża i skoczek, co jest sprzeczne z innymi wypowiedziami. W wersach następujących po tym urywku, aż do w. 469-482, gdzie poeta opisuje położenie figur przed zawieszeniem gry, nie ginie żadna figura; pamiętamy zaś, że kiedy partnerzy wstawali od stołu, białe miały tylko króla, królową i wieżę, nie miały natomiast skoczka.

Niektórzy wydawcy *Szachów* podają wariant tekstu nie zawierający tej nieścisłości. Tak jest np. w "prawdziwym" wydaniu zbiorowym dzieł poety z r. 1585.[26] Pierwszy dwuwiersz brzmi tutaj tak samo jak w urywku cytowanym wyżej, lecz w następnym czytamy:

443 Krom Rochu, bo ten mężnie się stawił,
A Król na ten czas królową się bawił.

Czytelnik, który gra w szachy, z pewnością uzna ten wariant za lepszy, ponieważ eliminuje zbędnego skoczka. Redakcja ta nie przypadła jednak do gustu wydawcom: po pierwsze dlatego, że w. 443 jest wadliwy rytmicznie; powodem drugim, i ważniejszym — tak przynajmniej utrzymuje się od czasu ukazania się "wydania pomnikowego" z r. 1884, stanowiącego rodzaj "wulgaty" — jest przekonanie, że wersja mniej techniczna z punktu widzenia gry w szachy musi być poprawniejsza pod względem tekstologicznym; tak można wyczytać w pierwszym oddzielnym wydaniu *Szachów* z lat 60-ych XVI wieku.[27] Tymczasem jednak tak nie jest, podobnie zresztą jak w wypadku innych często powtarzanych sądów. Obydwie edycje oddzielne *Szachów*; jedna z lat

26. Informacje podstawowe, niezbędne dla odróżnienia "prawdziwego" wydania Kochanowskiego z r. 1585 od wydań "nieautentycznych" ("*spuriae*") z tegoż roku (tj. z datą 1585, lecz w rzeczywistości drukowanych później), zawiera: K. Piekarski, *Bibliografia dzieł Jana Kochanowskiego. Wiek XVI i XVII.* Wyd. 2, rozszerzone. Kraków 1934, zwłaszcza przedmowa i s. 2-6.

27. Kochanowski, *Dzieła wszystkie*, t. 2, przypis 195 (do w. 444). Wynika to również z wypowiedzi Krzyżanowskiego, *ed. cit.*, s. 372.

1560-ych,[28] a druga z r. 1585,[29] podają w. 443-444 w brzmieniu następującym (warto zwrócić uwagę na nieobecność błędu rytmicznego w w. 443):

443 Krom Rochu, bo ten mężnie się zastawił,
A Król na ten czas Królową się bawił[30].

⟨350⟩ Redakcja ta jest zasadniczo wspólna wszystkim trzem najdawniejszym przekazom tekstowym *Szachów*,[31] powinna zatem znaleźć się ponownie w utworze. Szachistom propozycja ta wyda się pożądana, przyszłemu zaś wydawcy — jak sądzę — konieczna.

W wersach 451-454 biała królowa gotuje się do zadania ostatecznego ciosu osaczonemu w rogu czarnemu królowi. Zamysł ten wymaga, by szereg drugi, najbliższy polu, na którym stoi czarny król, obsadzić białą wieżą. Oto odpowiedni *passus* tekstu, wspólny wszystkim nowszym wydaniom:

451 A żeby Pana tym rychlej pożyła,
Rząd wszytek po nim Rochem zasadziła.
Sama już po nim cicho sie przykradnie,
Skąd mogła Króla już podchodzić snadnie.

O zadaniu powierzonym białej wieży znowu jest mowa w w. 477-478. To, że inicjatywę tego manewru przypisuje się tutaj białemu królowi, a nie królowej, nie ma większego znaczenia:

477 A swego Rochu posadził na stronie,
Pod Królem czarnym, na wtórym zagonie.

---

28. Jedyny dotychczas rozpoznany egzemplarz znajduje się w zbiorach Bibl. Kórnickiej (Cim. 2580); opis u Piekarskiego (*op. cit.*, nr XXV, 1). Pragnę złożyć podziękowanie profesorom Stanisławowi Frybesowi i Bogdanowi Horodyskiemu za udostępnienie mi mikrofilmu tej edycji.

29. Opis u Piekarskiego (*op. cit.*, nr XXV, 3). Korzystałem z facsimile tej edycji z roku 1884.

30. Udokumentowana przekazem pisemnym redakcja "zastawił" sprawia, że koniektura "⟨tam⟩ stawił" (Krzyżanowski, *ed. cit.*, s. 327) staje się zbędna.

31. Do r. 1934 istniał jeszcze w Polsce (w zbiorze prywatnym) jeden egzemplarz oddzielnego wydania *Szachów* sprzed r. 1572 (zob. Piekarski, *op. cit.*, s. XXX-IX); po wojnie — do r. 1958 próby odnalezienia tego egzemplarza nie powiodły się.

Pamiętamy, że terminy "zagon" (w. 478) i "rząd" (w. 452) są wymienne i obydwa służą do określenia szeregów poziomych, oznaczonych cyframi arabskimi. W obydwu przypadkach wieża stoi i w drugim szeregu, i "pod" królem, tj. w szeregu sąsiadującym z polem zajmowanym przez króla. "Pod Królem" w w. 478 znaczy dokładnie to samo co 'po nim' (tj. po królu) w w. 452.

Względy szachowe przemawiają za tym, by przywrócić "po⟨d⟩ nim" w w. 452, uzyskując w ten sposśb całkowitą zgodność pomiędzy wersami 452 i 478. Tym samym eliminuje się także powtórzenie "po nim ... po nim" w w. 452 i 453.

Redakcja "po⟨d⟩ nim" była problematyczną koniekturą, gdy zaproponowano ją po raz pierwszy.[32] Nie tylko odbiegała od tekstu przyjętego we wszystkich nowszych wydaniach, lecz nie znajdowano także dla niej odpowiednika ani w "prawdziwej" edycji dzieł Kochanowskiego z r. 1585, ani w osobnym wydaniu *Szachów* z tegoż roku. Dopiero konfrontacja ⟨351⟩ z pierwszym oddzielnym wydaniem *Szachów* z lat 1560-ych dowiodła, że proponowana tu redakcja nie jest wcale koniekturą. W wydaniu tym w. 451 i następne podano następująco:

A żeby Pana tym rychlej pożyła,
Rząd wszytek pod nim Rochem zasadziła.
Sama tuż po nim cicho sie przykradnie,

Uważne prześledzenie przebiegu rozgrywki szachowej w utworze Kochanowskiego oraz ponowne zbadanie najwcześniejszych edycji *Szachów* może ułatwić filologom udoskonalenie powszechnie uznawanego tekstu poematu i może nawet okazać się pomocne w rozwiązywaniu niektórych zagadnień krytyki tekstu.[33]

32. Na posiedzeniu Modern Language Association w Waszyngtonie w grudniu 1956.

33. Sama logika szachowa nie stanowi oczywiście dostatecznego kryterium wyboru wariantu tekstu. Co najmniej jedno z "nieautentycznych" wydań Kochanowskiego z r. 1585, to mianowicie, którym posługiwał się Nitsch (*op. cit.*), zawiera warianty wyraźnie korygujące niekonsekwencje szachowe w utworze. I tak:
a) w. 335: biała królowa zabija czarnego "Draba" (tj. piona) zamiast "Popu" (gońca). Jeżeli utwór ma także sens szachowy, zastąpienie gońca inną figurą jest nieodzowne, ponieważ czarne straciły już jednego gońca (w. 308-314). Gdybyśmy zatrzymali w w. 335 redakcję "Popu", czarne nie miałyby już ani jednego gońca, a przecież czarny goniec pojawia się znowu w w. 474, w opisie

III

⟨352⟩ Odtworzona sytuacja szachowa w poemacie Kochanowskiego zasługuje również na zbadanie przez historyków literatury. Dociekania na temat źródeł zagadki szachowej w tym utworze mogą bowiem doprowadzic do odszukania wcześniejszych wersji opowieści o królewnie Annie i jej fortelu.

Badacze literatury podkreślają, iż zagadka szachowa w poemacie Kochanowskiego jest własnym pomysłem poety,[34] zakładając widocznie,

sytuacji na szachownicy po odłożeniu gry do następnego dnia.

b) W. 205: "białego" zamiast "czarnego" w oddzielnych wydaniach *Szachów* 1562-1566 i 1585 oraz w "prawdziwym" wydaniu Kochanowskiego, bo przecież białe straciły wieżę.

c) W. 204; "i z Słoniem" zamiast "i z Koniem" (tj. skoczkiem); wzorując się na Vidzie, Kochanowski opisuje wieżę jako "Słonia z wieżyczką".

d) W. 557: n.: dwuwiersz zapowiadający mata w trzech posunięciach przydaje klarowności ekspozycji. Jednakże fragmentu tego brak w trzech wcześniejszych wydaniach *Szachów* (łącznie z "prawdziwą" edycją z r. 1585).

e) W. 203: "Koniem" zamiast "ku niem" (jak w "prawdziwej" edycji z r. 1585) stanowi inne nieco zagadnienie, ponieważ redakcja "Koniem" występuje również w dwu wydaniach oddzielnych z lat 1560-ych i z 1585. "Koniem" istotnie należy do tekstu, a ponadto lepiej oddaje sytuację na szachownicy, gdyż skoczek atakując wieżę oddala się równocześnie od króla (wbrew interpretacji Krzyżanowskiego, *ed. cit.*, s. 326).

W związku z pierwszymi czterema wariantami, które poprawiają zgodność wewnętrzną *Szachów*, nasuwa się pytanie, czy przypisać je samemu Kochanowskiemu czy jego przyjacielowi i wydawcy — Januszowskiemu. Chcąc tę kwestię rozstrzygnąć, trzeba by sięgnąć do oddzielnego wydania *Szachów*, wydrukowanego przed r. 1572 (zob. przypis 31). Odpowiedź na postawione tutaj pytanie wykraczałaby poza ramy samych *Szachów*. Gdybyśmy założyli, że poprawki wprowadził autor, a nie drukarz, który musiałby być szachistą, trzeba by jedno z wydań Januszowskiego z r. 1585 uznać za autentyczne, a tym samym przyjąć je za podstawowy tekst poety. Ten krok byłby jednak ryzykowny. W. Weintraub (*Jakiego Kochanowskiego znamy*? "Język Polski" 1930, z. 3), który porównał pewne partie pośmiertnego wydania Kochanowskiego z r. 1585 (*Monomachia, Pamiątka*) z wcześniej ogłoszonymi drukiem poszczególnymi utworami poety, wykazał w sposób przekonywający, że Januszowski rozmyślnie, a niezbyt fortunnie "poprawiał" teksty Kochanowskiego. Sądzę, że temat *Szachów* dostarcza obiektywnego kryterium do podjęcia delikatnej sprawy Januszowskiego (zob. o nim np. S. Dobrzycki, *Ze studiów nad Kochanowskim*. Poznań 1929, s. 43 n. — Krzyżanowski, *ed. cit.*, s. 426 n.).

34. Zob. M. Dzieduszycki, *Szachy w Polszcze*. "Czas" 1856, dodatek miesięczny za lipiec-wrzesień, s. 27, 32. — S. Witkowski, *Stosunek "Szachów" Kochanowskiego do poematu Vidy "Scacchia ludus"*. "Rozprawy Wydziału Filologicznego AU" t. 18 (1892), s. 31 n.

że zapożyczenie motywu szachowego ujmie coś z wielkości autora. Sam wątek niektórzy uważają za oryginalny,[35] inni natomiast szukają powiązań z różnymi źródłami, jak np. księga Olafa Magnusa z XVI w. o ludach skandynawskich (ojcowie badali charakter konkurentów swoich córek, każąc przyszłym zięciom grać w szachy) czy *Gesta Romanorum* (gdzie epizod z Wespazjanem i Aglae mówi o labiryncie i lwie pożerającym konkurentów królewny, a także o jej pomocnej wskazówce).[36] Jeden z historyków literatury zamyka omówienie tych teorii uwagą o jałowości "polowania na wpływy",[37] utrzymując, że problem powinien znaleźć rozwiązanie na wyższej płaszczyźnie, przy czym określa drugą część *Szachów* jako nowelę — gatunek charakterystyczny dla późnego renesansu.

Jeżeli jednak spojrzymy na utwór Kochanowskiego pod kątem gry w szachy, otrzymamy inną perspektywę. Prawdą jest, że Kochanowski wzoruje się na Vidzie, kiedy opisuje nowoczesną formę gry, "*alla rab*⟨353⟩*biosa*," która rozwinęła się we Francji i Włoszech około roku 1500. Natomiast te partie utworu, w których oddala się od swego modelu, noszą niekiedy znamiona gry opartej na przepisach obowiązujących w średniowieczu, przed reformą szachową. Tu właśnie leży klucz do rozumienia niektórych wierszy. Np. w pewnym momencie Kochanowski powiada o "Popie" (gońcu): "A kogo by tak zły człowiek nie zdradził!" (w. 236), nie podając żadnej motywacji dla tego rodzaju uwagi. Dlaczegoż by dostojnik kościelny ("Pop") miał być zdrajcą? Dlatego że "alfil", średniowieczny przodek gońca (szachowego "biskupa"), nosił miano zdrajcy z powodu podstępnego, skaczącego ruchu. W tekstach średniowiecznych "*alficus*" nosi określenie "*tanquam insidiator*" lub "*quasi fur speculator*", który podchodzi znienacka, "*decipit invigiles*".[38] W dwóch miejscach *Szachów* mowa jest

35. Dzieduszycki, *op. cit.*, s. 31. — Witkowski, *op. cit.*, s. 34, 38. — J. Łoś, recenzja Nitschowskiego wydania *Szachów*. "Język Polski" 1923, z. 2. — H. Sobczakówna, *Jan Kochanowski jako tłumacz*. Poznań 1934, s. 13.

36. Zob. J. Krzyżanowski, *Nieco o "Szachach" Jana Kochanowskiego*. W: *Od średniowiecza do baroku. Studia naukowo-literackie*. Warszawa 1938, s. 163-166. Autor referuje poglądy wcześniejsze i przedstawia propozycje własne.

37. *Ibidem*, s. 167. Uczeni rzadko obstają przy tym, kiedy im samym udaje się odszukać zródło.

38. Zob. A. v. d. Linde, *Quellenstudien zur Geschichte des Schachspiels*. Berlin 1881, s. 49. Według Krzyżanowskiego (*Nieco o "Szachach" Jana Kochanowskiego*, s. 174) nazwa "Pop" w odniesieniu do gońca należy do polskiej terminologij szachowej. Lecz "Pop" jest nazwą alfila w czeskich

o głodnym królu, który "skoczył" do kuchni.[39] Ruch ten zwykło się tłumaczyć jako roszadę, ale w tekście Kochanowskiego nie znajdujemy nic, co wskazywałoby jednoznacznie na ten ruch. Roszada była innowacją, której datę trudno ustalić dokładnie, lecz prawdopodobnie wprowadzono ją mniej więcej w czasach Kochanowskiego. Sądzę jednak, że poeta miał raczej na myśli "skok królewski" ("*saltus*"), tj. posunięcie zgodne z przepisami gry średniowiecznej.[40] W zagadkowym epizodzie z królewną Anną bohaterka obraca "rogi" wieży (w. 511). Komentatorzy twierdzą że idzie tutaj o kły słonia. Ale kły nie są przecież rogami. Co więcej, słoń noszący wieżyczkę jako symbol wieży szachowej jest wynalazkiem literackim Vidy. Zarówno w wiekach średnich jak i w czasach Kochanowskiego wieża miała elementy zbliżone do rogów, widoczne i na rycinach przedstawiających samą wieżę, i w schematycznych wykresach (zob. rys. 3-6).[41]

Rys. 3

Rys. 4

Rys. 5

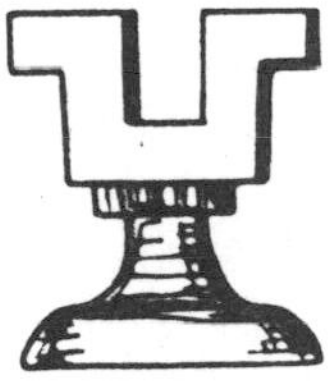
Rys. 6

tekstach o szachach z w. XIV i XV, jak podaje Č. Zírbt (*Dějiny hry šachové*. Praha 1888, s. 14, 16, 23 n.). Wiadomo zaś, który z dwu narodów był w tym czasie odbiorcą w sensie kulturalnym. Sądzę, że użycie w *Szachach* terminu 'Pop" zamiast "Biskup" (goniec) jest zapożyczeniem z czeskiego.

39. Zob. w. 91, n. 189 n. Por. u Vidy w. 217 n.

40. Zob. A. v. d. Linde, *Das Schachspiel des XVI. Jahrhunderts*. Berlin 1873, s. 12, 16.

41. Rys. 3: wieża z rękopisu należącego do zbiorów R. Cottona, Cleop. B. IX (XIII w.); rys. 4: jedna z "figur szachowych św. Ludwika" (XIV-XV w.), według Murraya (*op. cit.*, s. 767, 769); rys. 5-6: wieże z podręczników szachowych Luceny (1491) i Damiana (1512).

W *Szachach* zagadnienie sprowadza się do gry turniejowej, a zatem ‹354› reprezentuje linię rozwojową typową dla średniowiecznego problemu szachowego w Europie.[42] W literaturze średniowiecznej nie brak zresztą licznych prób dokładnego odtwarzania ruchów figur szachowych.[43]

Jeżeli istotnie niektóre partie *Szachów* mają inspirację średniowieczną, nie jest wówczas wykluczone, że znaleźć by można wcześniejszy problemat szachowy oraz motyw literacki podobny do tego, jaki występuje w utworze Kochanowskiego. Analogia taka rzeczywiście istnieje i znana jest jako "problemat Dilārām" (nazwę swą zawdzięcza imieniu bohaterki). Proweniencja tego problemu, jak zresztą wielu innych zadań szachowych znanych w średniowiecznej Europie, jest muzułmańska, autorstwo zaś przypisuje się mistrzowi z X wieku. Bez względu na to, jakie było naprawdę jego pochodzenie, problemat ten pojawia się po raz pierwszy w rękopisie arabskim z r. 1140 i znaleźć go można w licznych zbiorach orientalnych, począwszy od w. XII aż do

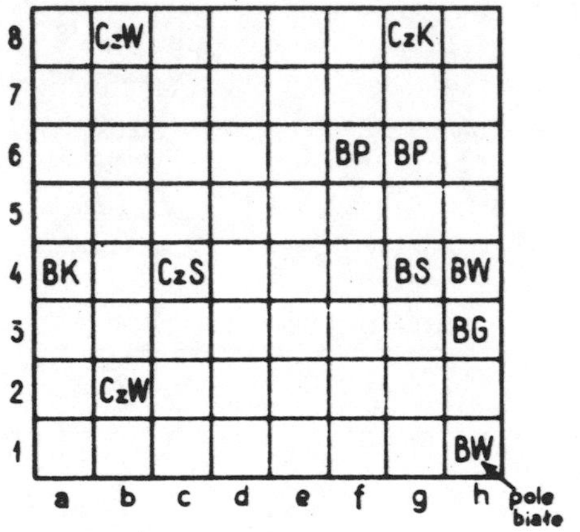

Rys. 7

42. T. v. Heydebrand u. d. Lasa, *Bemerkungen über das mittelalterliche Schach.* "Festschrift des akademischen Schachklubs München" 1896, s. 38. — Murray, *op. cit.*, s. 656.

43. Zob. imponującą listę w: F. Strohmeyer, *Das Schachspiel im Altfranzözischen.* W zbiorze: *Abhandlungen* [...] *Adolf Tobler* [...] *dargebracht.* Halle/Saale 1895, s. 393. — *Eschez amoureux.* Zob. Murray, *op. cit.*, s. 479.

XVIII.[44] Na Zachodzie pierwszy odnaleziony zapis pochodzi z r. 1283; zanotowano go wówczas aż czterokrotnie w tej samej pracy.[45] Okazuje się, że w średniowiecznej Europie pomysł Dilārām cieszył się taką popularnością że powstało ponad 200 blisko spokrewnionych sytuacji turniejowych, począwszy od takich, które wymagają tylko dwu ruchów.[46]

⟨355⟩ Problemat Dilārām w swej klasyczenej postaci (rys. 7) ma następujące rozwiązanie:

Ruch 1.	biała wieża	h4-h8 (szach królowi)
	czarny król	g8:h8 (zabija wieżę)
2.	biały goniec	h3-f5 (szach otwarty przez odsłonięcie wieży h1)
	czarna wieża	b2-h2 (zasłania swego króla)
3.	biała wieża	h1:h2 (bije czarną wieżę i szachuje)
	czarny król	h8-g8
4.	biała wieża	h2-h8 (szach)
	czarny król	g8:h8 (zabija wieżę)
5.	biały pion	g6-g7 (szach)
	czarny król	h8-g8
6.	biały skoczek	g4-h6 (mat)

Na pierwszy rzut oka wydawać się to może zbyt odległe od problematu Kochanowskiego. Lecz porównanie wykazuje, że podstawowe elementy sytuacji są w obydwu problematach jednakowe: król zwycięskiego gracza jest zepchnięty na brzeg szachownicy i zagrożony matem w jednym posunięciu; następny ruch należy do zwycięzcy; sekret zwycięstwa leży w pierwszym ruchu i polega na dobrowolnym poświęceniu wieży zwycięzcy (oddanie aż dwóch wież, jak u Arabów, jest niepotrzebnym podkreśleniem manewru); gracz pokonany musi bić wieżę; ostateczne zwycięstwo wymaga wprowadzenia do akcji pionów.

Dalsze dzieje pomysłu Dilārām na Zachodzie notują liczne odchylenia od oryginału. Barwa figur została zmieniona, figury problematu przesunięto z jednej strony szachownicy na drugą, a przeładowaną nieco koncepcję arabską uproszczono przez zmniejszenie liczby figur i posu⟨356⟩nięć.[47] I tak włoskie zbiory zadań szachowych pochodzące z

44. Zob. np. Linde, *Quellenstudien...*, s. 359, nr 121. — Murray, *op. cit.*, s. 286, nr 83, na podstawie piętnastu rękopisow i s. 311.

45. *Libro del Acedrex*, wykonana na polecenie Alfonsa X. Zob. Linde, *Quellenstudien...*, s. 49; s. 107, nr 54; s. 108, nr 57; s. 113, nr 90; s. 115, nr 100.

46. Murray, *op. cit.*, s. 312.

47. Zob. Linde, *Geschichte und Literàtur des Schachspiels*, t. 1, s. 276.

XV w. zawierają warianty bliższe rozwiązaniu Kochanowskiego, tj. z jedną wieżą i bez skoczka gracza pokonanego.[48]

Najbliższą jednak paralelę średniowieczną do sformułowania Kochanowskiego, a także i taką, która — jak mniemam — przekona czytelnika, znajdujemy w słynnym rękopisie cottońskim (ze zbiorów Roberta Cottona), pochodzenia anglo-normańskiego lub francuskiego z XIII wieku.[49] Wśród rozmaitych zadań dwa są oparte na pomyśle Dilārām. Jedno z nich prowadzi do mata w pięciu posunięciach (rys. 8):

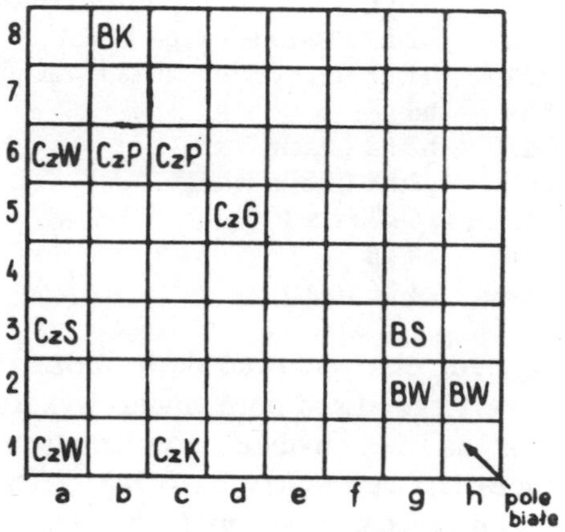

Rys. 8

48. LINDE, *Quellenstudien...*, s. 183. — MURRAY, *op. cit.*, s. 663.

49. HEYDEBRAND u. LASA, *Zur Geschichte und Literatur des Schachspiels*, s. 122 n. — LINDE, *Quellenstudien...*, s. 191 n., zwłaszcza s. 195, nr 9; s. 196, nr 16; s. 204 n. — MURRAY, *op. cit.*, s. 579 n., zwłaszcza s. 586, nr 9; s. 588, nr 19.

50. Białą królową, która stała w polu g2 (zamiast białej wieży), trzeba było przesunąć, gdyż w przeciwnym wypadku zagrażałby jej czarny goniec d5. Przy średniowiecznych zasadach gry wieża mogła pozostać na polu g2, ponieważ czarny alfil (goniec) nie mógł sięgnąć poza f3. Umieszczenie królowej w polu d2 zapobiega matowi w dwóch posunięciach, bo jeżeli w drugim posunięciu (pierwsze było czarną wieżą: a1-a8, szach, zlikwidowany zabiciem wieży przez króla b8:a8) czarny pion przesuwając się: c6-c7, powoduje szacha odkrytego (od gońca d5), wówczas biała królowa zabija gońca: g2:d5, a następny ruch pionem przynosi mata. — Z chwilą gdy biała królowa zajęła pole d2, czarny król musiał uchodzić; umieszczenie go w polu b1 wymagało najmniej przesunięć.

1. czarna wieża a6-a8 (szach białemu królowi)
   biały król b8-a8 (zabija wieżę)
2. czarny skoczek a3-b5 (szach otwarty wieżą odsłoniętą przez skoczka)
   biały król a8-b8

Jeżeli zamiast ruchu białym królem gracz zasłoni króla białą wieżą g2-a2, wówczas

3. czarny pion b6-b7 (szach)
   biały król a8-b8
4. czarny pion c6-c7 (mat)

⟨357⟩

Gdy problemat z rękopisu cottońskiego w tym stadium zestawimy z sytuacją w *Szachach* po odłożeniu gry do następnego dnia, wtedy okaże się, że z dziewięciu figur w partii rozgrywanej między Borzujem a Fiedorem aż siedem ma dokładne odpowiedniki w trzecim ruchu problematu cottońskiego. Obydwa zadania są finalizowane w trzech posunięciach, obydwa wymagają identycznego rozwiązania. Pozostałe trzy ruchy w rękopisie cottońskim (te same, które doprowadziły do zakończenia gry w *Szachach*) są następujące:

3. czarna wieża a1-a8 (szach)
   biały król b8-a8 (zabija wieżę)
4. czarny pion b6-b7 (szach)
   biały król a8-b8
5. czarny pion c6-c7 (mat) (rys. 9 i 10 [=1])

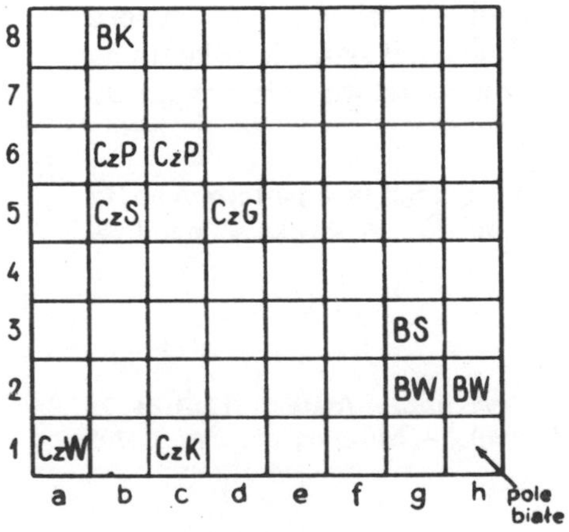

Rys. 9

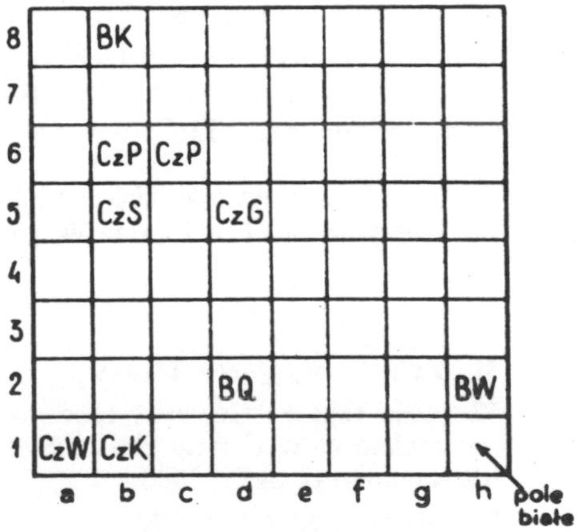

Rys. 10 (= rys. 1)

Okazuje się więc, że zagadka szachowa opisana w utworze Kochanowskiego jest uproszczonym wariantem problematu Dilārām. Z chwilą kiedy uprzytomnimy sobie, że Fiedor i Borzuj grali, "*alla rabbiosa*", rękopis cottoński zaś opiera się na średniowiecznych przepisach gry, znajdziemy wówczas wytłumaczenie odmiennej nieco pozycji pozostałych dwóch figur u Kochanowskiego.[50] Inne, mniej ważne rozbieżności tego ⟨358⟩ wariantu wyjaśnić można równie łatwo. W wersji Kochanowskiego zwycięstwo uzyskuje się szachując jednym pionem i zadając mata drugim. Taka sytuacja ma formę postulatu w zbiorach zadań szachowych powstałych około r. 1500, lecz sama koncepcja jest także zapożyczona z wcześniejszych wzorów muzułmańskich; w wariancie Dilārām manuskryptu cottońskiego z XIII w. natrafiliśmy właśnie na "*echec del un poun e mat del altre*".[51]

Sytuację Dilārām naśladowano jeszcze od czasu do czasu na Zachodzie w w. XVI[52] i była ona prawdopodobnie powszechnie znana graczom za czasów Kochanowskiego. Trudno więc znaleźć bezpośredni prototyp tej zagadki szachowej. Znacznie łatwiej było wykazać, że Kochanowski nie wymyślił sytuacji opisanej w *Szachach*, lecz opracował w swoim utworze najsłynniejszy problemat szachowy wieków średnich.

To stwierdzenie jednak nie wyczerpuje zagadnienia. Jestem również przekonany, że Kochanowski przejął także i opowieść, która tradycyjnie towarzyszy problematowi Dilārām. W świecie muzułmańskim powiastka dołączona do problematu jest udokumentowana przekazem pisemnym stosunkowo późno (znaleziono ją w rękopisach z XV, XVI i XVII w.),[53] a więc znacznie później niż zapis samego problematu, ale nie znaczy to, że opowieść powstała dopiero wtedy. Wśród wczesnych wariantów tej powiastki najdokładniej można oznaczyć datę wersji poety perskiego Firdausiego. Najstarszy rękopis jego utworu został skopiowany w roku 1503.[54] Firdausi umieścił sytuację Dilārām na czele zbioru problematów szachowych. Cytuję z tekstu dołączonego do wspomnianej zagadki:

> Dilārām była ukochaną hodży [...], pewnego razu partnerem hodży przy szachach był człowiek przystojny i roztropny; stawką w grze była

51. Zob. Linde, *Quellenstudien...*, s. 387, 204.

52. Zob. rkps P. Guarina, *Liber de partitis scacchorum* (data: 1512), fol. 26 (oglądałem go w Clevelandzkiej Bibl. Publicznej). — Murray, *op. cit.*, s. 705 (rkps niemiecki, ok. r. 1600).

53. Murray, *op. cit.*, s. 280.

54. *Ibidem*, s. 178.

nałożnica. Przeciwnik hodży był już o krok od wygranej, bo gdyby następny ruch należał do niego, byłby dał mata. Hodża przeraził się. Widząc to, Dilārām nagle zawołała: "Oddaj obie wieże, nie oddawaj mnie". Hodża zrozumiał i zaszachował czerwoną wieżą [...] [w dalszym ciągu Firdausi opisuje rozwiązanie gry]. Dilārām ocaliła go[55].

⟨359⟩ Według innej, podobnej wersji w rękopisie perskim z XVI w. Dilārām, ulubiona żona ostatecznego zwycięzcy (króla), dała mu zbawienną wskazówkę w wierszu:

O Królu, poświęć swe Wieże, a zachowaj Dilārām,
Posuń Gońca i Piona, a Skoczek da mata[56].

Wszystkie zasadnicze elementy opowieści o Dilārām pojawiają się w epizodzie z królewną Anną: wygraną w grze jest piękna kobieta (u chrześcijan musiała być córką królewską zamiast jednej z czterech żon czy nałożnicy; ale i Arabowie znali również bardziej niewinną wersję opowieści, czego dowodzi nazwa "problemat dziewczęcia" w odniesieniu do sytuacji Dilārām w rękopisie z r. 1572); mężczyzna, którego ona kocha, jest u progu porażki; punkt zwrotny w grze następuje dzięki trafnej wskazówce kobiety; sedno rady tkwi w napomnieniu, aby przegrywający partner w pierwszym ruchu poświęcił własną wieżę.

Te analogie w powiastce o królewnie Annie są pochodzenia wschodniego, i to stosunkowo świeżej daty. Oczywiście lepiej byłoby znaleźć zachodnią, wcześniejszą wersję motywu Dilārām. Tutaj napotykamy jednak trudności, bo na Zachodzie zachowały się tylko dwa zbiory, w których zadania szachowe mają oprawę literacką.[57] W literaturze europejskiej można natomiast bez trudu rozpoznać pewne elementy opowieści o Dilārām w XIII i w drugiej połowie XVI wieku.

Manuskrypt cottoński jest jednym z dwu zbiorów zawierających wstawki poetyckie. Po problemacie pierwszym następuje około 60 wersów tekstu objaśniającego, wierszowanego.[58] Czytamy tam, że partnerami przy szachach są dwaj baronowie, z których jeden stawia rękę swej córki, drugi zaś własne życie. Domyślić się można, że córka kochała

55. Tekst turecki i przekład niemiecki w: Linde, *Quellenstudien...*, s. 403 n.

56. G. Walker, *Chess in the East*. "Chess-Players Chronicle" t. 4 (1843), s. 184. Zob. Linde, *Quellenstudien...*, s. 49, przypis 1. Na temat opowieści zob. także *La bella Dilaram*. "L'Italia Scacchistica" t. 17 (1927), s. 191.

57. Heydebrand u. Lasa, *Zur Geschichte und Literatur des Schachspiels*, s. 122.

58. Tekst w: Murray, *op. cit.*, s. 583 n.

przeciwnika ojca, ale dla jej ukochenego gra przybrała obrót fatalny: już miał dostać mata, gdy panienka weszła do sali, w której odbywała się gra, ujrzała ukochanego w opresji i ogarnęła ją rozpacz. Rzekła wówczas:

> Głupi jest ten, kto w grze w szachy ryzykuje głowę, tępy zaś jest ten, kto nie potrafi przewidywać dalej niż dziewiąte posunięcie ani dostrzec tego, co może mu pomóc[59].

⟨360⟩ Po tych słowach, bardziej jeszcze tajemniczych niż wypowiedź królewny Anny, panna odeszła do swoich komnat. Baron zamyślił się głęboko ("*mult estudia*") i dostrzegł rozwiązanie — mata w dziewięciu posunięciach — które uratowało mu życie i zyskało rękę panienki.

Chociaż schemat szachowy ilustrujący tę powiastkę nie jest wariantem Dilārām, zauważono, że wiersze w rękopisie cottońskim są bardzo zbliżone do motywu Dilārām.[60] Wydaje się że na Zachodzie opowieść o Dilārām dość często odłączano od problematu, z którym była związana na Wschodzie.

Krótkie teksty, występujące w rękopisie cottońskim łącznie z dwoma problematami typu Dilārām, są mniej wyraźne, ale nie mniej ciekawe. Wiersze dołączone do sytuacji, która, jak przekonaliśmy się, jest niemal identyczna z zagadką w *Szachach*, zawierają następujące pouczenie: "bo kto nie odda rzeczy ulubionej, ten nie dostanie rzeczy upragnionej".[61] Drugi wariant problematu Dilārām zawiera podobną dewizę: "*qui non dat quando amat, non accipit omne quod optat*".[62] Oddanie, "rzeczy ulubionej" oznacza poświęcenie wież w czasie gry. "Rzecz upragniona", dla której trzeba ponieść ofiarę, "kiedy się jest zakochanym", to — jak sądzę — piękne dziewczę, w wierszach zaś rękopisu cottońskiego odnajduję echa powiastki o Dilārām. Co więcej,

59. W. oryginale:

Puis dit "mult est fols e bricun
Ke sa teste met en raancun
As esches si bien ne purueit
Vltre le neofime tret e aparceit
Quele chose aider le porra"

60. Heydebrand u. Lasa, *Zur Geschichte und Literatur des Schachspiels*, s. 126.

61. Murray, *op. cit.*, s. 586: "*Kar ki ne done chose amée: Ne prendra chose desirée*".

62. *Ibidem*, s. 588.

obydwa dwuwiersze przypominają mi wskazówkę królewny Anny dla Fiedora: "Dać za miłego wdzięczną rzecz nie szkodzi" (w. 509). Na zakończenie swego dowodu przytoczę jeszcze jeden nikły ślad opowieści o Dilārām w źródle zachodnioeuropejskim, w rękopisie niemieckim sporządzonym około roku 1600. W tekście objaśniającym uproszczoną sytuację Dilārām mowa jest o dziewczęciu: "Rycerz zabije Konia na życzenie panny, [...] rycerz zdobędzie pannę".[63]

Zagadka szachowa Kochanowskiego to z pewnością wariant problematu Dilārām. Związek problematu z opowieścią o Dilārām jest dowiedziony w świecie muzułmańskim, w średniowiecznej zaś Europie uważam go za prawdopodobny. Założenie, iż Kochanowski samodzielnie wymyślił epizod z królewną Anną, tak bardzo podobny do opowieści o Dilārām, nie wytrzymuje próby, chyba że będziemy zbytnio wierzyć w zbieg okoliczności. Moim zdaniem, druga część *Szachów* opiera się na powiastce o Dilārām. Epizod nowelistyczny w utworze Kochanowskiego uważam za zapożyczenie z okresu średniowiecza. Pod tym względem *Szachy* nie różnią się od wielu innych utworów renesansowych.

Opowieść o Dilārām jest motywem wędrującym i trudno odszukać bezpośrednie źródło, na którym oparł się Kochanowski. Nie jest wykluczone, że poeta nie słyszał nigdy imienia Dilārām. O powiastce razem z problematem mógł dowiedzieć się od jakiegoś szachisty. Z chwilą wprowadzenia na Zachodzie reformy szachowej (około r. 1500) popularność problematu Dilārām dobiegała kresu. W przebraniu królewny Anny ukazuje się Dilārām w poezji europejskiej po raz ostatni, ale za to w swej krasie najpełniejszej.

Z angielskiego przełożyła *Maria Gottwald*

63. *Ibidem*, s. 705: "*ein Ritter soll ein Ross erstossen durch einer Jungfrawen willen, ein Knab der soll springen, ein Ritter soll ein Jungfraw gewinnen*".

XXIV

Preface to Ivan Dujčev *Slavia Orthodoxa*

When the Byzantine scholar's descriptive job is done and he turns to giving grades to the civilization which is the subject of his study — when he has to assess Byzantium's contributions to European culture — he usually singles out three Byzantine achievements: preserving and transmitting Greek classical texts to the West; Byzantine art; and civilizing the elite, and through it the lower layers, of South and East Slavic medieval society. When we ask ourselves which of these three contributions is most operative today, we should reverse this sequence. The knowledge of Greek Classics has ceased to be a badge of distinction in the West for over a century and monstrous formations like *cinerama* proclaim the ignorance rather than the prestige of Greek among those who seek to determine our tastes today; the interest in Byzantine art has increased considerably over the past seventy years, but mostly among art historians and, lately, among the clientele for expensive coffee-table books.

On the other hand, civilizing the Orthodox Slavs is Byzantium's most enduring contribution to the making of our world. Byzantium is present in the fabric of South and Eastern Slavic culture today; present in the Balkan and Eastern European landscape through the monuments which it inspired, present in forms of the Orthodox worship, increasingly vestigial in the East, though not yet eradicated there; present in the modern languages of the Orthodox Slavs, in the Balkans mainly through lexical borrowings, in Eastern Europe more through idioms and syntagmas taken over from Church Slavonic.

Everywhere among the Orthodox Slavs national histories and Byzantine history either coincide or are intertwined for long stretches of time. What Byzantine impact is felt among the Slavs today is only the remnant of a much more extensive penetration, concealed under the subsequent layers of Turkic and Western influences. However, for a scholar it is not enough to agree on the magnitude of Byzantium's impact; he must show in the smallest detail what it was, in which cultural spheres it revealed itself, and through what channels it penetrated into the receiving societies. Only a handful of specialists today have taken up this challenge. Their task is first of all technical; in addition, it requires a delicacy of judgment, since the civilization of the Orthodox Slavs is a functioning one, and the anatomy of their body cultural requires vivisection rather than autopsy.

First among the technical requirements to be met by the ideal student of the subject is a familiarity with all epochs and levels of Greek. He must be equipped to detect Byzantine calques, puns and allusions both in Church Slavonic and ⟨ii⟩ in various vernaculars; he must be ready to translate every phrase of his Slavic sources back into the Byzantine Greek before moving to the next one. He must be intimately acquainted with Byzantine texts, not so much those through which the modern Western reader acquaints himself with the achievements of Byzantine high culture — Procopius, Psellos, Anna Comnena — as those which made up the daily reading of Byzantine literati through whom these texts were in turn transmitted to the Slavs. This means Patristic texts, to be sure, but above all monkish literature, the *farrago* of *Apophthegmata Patrum*, collections of sayings, gnomologia, dogmatic excerpts, and purely accidental stuff, much of it still buried in manuscripts, since all of this provided the daily spiritual nourishment for the Slavic Orthodox reader. Our student's experience of texts must enable him to spot a Byzantine commonplace in Slavic garb and to abstain from using it as a piece of information on a concrete event or social fact. He must be at home in the Byzantine artistic tradition and its local reflections among the Slavs. He must be an efficient, sometimes compulsive bibliographer, for he must have the ability to get at what is recondite, when it comes both to the sources themselves and to scholarly literature about them. The medieval Orthodox Slavic — and Moldavian — world must be his own backyard; particularly Bulgaria, an area saturated with Byzantine culture and a relay point in the passage of Byzantine influences to Moldavia, the Ukraine, and Muscovy; and Russia, the chief depository of medieval Slavic texts and objects.

In terms of judgment, our ideal student must steer clear of two pitfalls: that of identifying Byzantium with medieval Greece and that of endowing the Slavs with an overdose of autochtonous achievements and the peculiar ability of "creative absorption" and "selective reception" of Byzantine cultural values. Short of prohibiting the practice in the field to Orthodox Slavs and Greeks alike, we should recommend to our student a chance of viewing his task for a time from a geographical vantage point outside both the Orthodox Slavic and post-Byzantine areas.

Professor Dujčev comes closer to satisfying all of these ideal specifications than any scholar alive today, and the collection of sixteen essays in Russian and one in Czech which the reader is about to begin perusing is the proof of this. In one of them [VI][1] he explains an enigmatic passage in the Slavic translation of Josephus Flavius' "Jewish War" by reconstructing its Greek model ; in another [X] he assigns to an element of a story in the *Paterikon* of the Kiev Caves Monastery its place among analogous Byzantine stories, culled from most obscure contexts; and he closes the essay with a warning that this element has no historical value, since it goes back to a *topos*, and a *topos* is no foundation for conclusions on the everyday life of a given epoch [X, 92]. The two surveys of recent Bulgarian works dealing with early Slavic and early Russian literatures [XIII; XV] remind us once again of the debt specialists owe in their daily labours to that master of Byzantine and Early Slavic bibliography. Devotion to bibliography helps, instead of hindering, Professor Dujčev to draw large-scale historical pictures. The discussion of Bulgarian illuminated manuscripts of the ⟨iii⟩ fourteenth century against a background of Bulgarian political and social history of the time is one of them [XII]; it is in line with his interest in the artistic vehicle through which Byzantine influences penetrated into Bulgaria. Another is the superb synthetic treatment of the relations between the Moravian and Pannonian Slavs on the one hand and the Turanian and Slavic Bulgarians on the other; it gives meaning to two periods: that of the *Imperium Avaricum* in the seventh century and that of Car Boris, Cyril and Methodius and their successor in Bulgaria, Clement of Ochrid, in the ninth [XVII]. The study of the centers in which cultural contacts and exchanges occurred between Byzantines and Slavs — Professor Dujčev establishes fifteen such centers — is a third panoramic view, but one in which each detail stands out with clarity [V].

In the specious luxuriance of the Cyrillo-Methodian studies — mostly foliage without fruit — that were called forth by the recent anniversaries of the two Apostles, those by Professor Dujčev are in a class apart, for they contain discoveries or new interpretations, especially of Byzantine models, for concrete passages in the Lives of the Thessalonican brothers. Only three or four among the hundreds of practitioners in the field can occasionally claim similar success. Although many of Professor Dujčev's Cyrillo-Methodian articles have been assembled in another volume,[2] the present collection contains information welcome to the student of the Saints and their milieu; sources on the

1. References in brackets are to the number of an essay and its page.

2. *Medioevo bizantino-slavo, II. Saggi di storia letteraria* [Storia e letteratura, 113] (Rome, 1968).

Cult of Trees among the Slavs [I, 10-12]; recent Bulgarian views concerning the glagolitic alphabet and the implications of its use for the original text of the *Vita Methodii* [XIII, 602; 604]; mention of Cyril and Methodius in the calendar appended to Ostromir's Gospels [XIV, 590]; the bibliography on the antipodes theory rejected by the *Vita Constantini* and on Wiching's career [XVII, 24 n. 73; 31]; finally, reference to those Byzantine clerics in Car Boris' Bulgaria who were hostile to Slavic liturgy [XVII, 34]. Only one observation is controversial — about Constantine as a "young Bulgarian Slav"; on this point a number of Professor Dujčev's colleagues, myself included, would respectfully dissent.

What is true of the excellence of Professor Dujčev's techniques is true of the clarity of his conceptual framework. His Byzantium appears as a multinational empire, at various times comprising large segments of Slavic population [V, 107]. It follows that in the later Middle Ages the Orthodox Church, with Constantinople being merely her spiritual center, took care of a flock which was Slavic in its majority; in short, for much of Byzantine history Byzantine culture transcended the notion of Hellenism and the boundaries of the Byzantine state. As he illustrates these points, Professor Dujčev is far from slighting the Greek components of Byzantium. He looks for Byzantine, rather than for Turanic proto-Bulgarian, roots of certain features attested in the mixed Bulgarian society of the ninth century [I]. Turning to the fourteenth century Balkans, he tells us how hesychastic centers sprang up on both Greek and Bulgarian soil, how hesychasts of Slavic and Greek tongues lived and wrote side by side, and how thoroughly Greek modes of thought and Greek ⟨iv⟩ linguistic structures permeated contemporary literary production in Slavic [V, 127; XII].

The views of a scholar so remote from parochialism have been acclaimed, and his presence eagerly sought, by colleagues everywhere; in Sophia as well as in Athens, in Paris as well as in Rome (it is there that Professor Dujčev received much of his early training), in Washington as well as in Moscow and Leningrad. As his scholarly travels have spanned continents, he has enjoyed direct access to disparate sources out of which he has composed his unified picture of *Slavia Orthodoxa*. The discussion of one such remote source, the *Tomić Psalter*, provides some of the most illuminating pages reprinted here [XII, 16-19].

We are grateful to Professor Dujčev for putting together his Russian and Czech studies, not readily available in a middle-sized Western library, for convenient use, not only by his colleagues and admirers in the field, but also by Slavicists at large. Since the seventeen articles of this volume are only about a twentieth part of his output, numbering more than three hundred and fifty items, we hope that he will assemble a volume of essays forming another thematic or linguistic unit.[3] Our gratitude goes also to Variorum Reprints for the idea of assembling the *membra disiecta* of a scholar's output by means of a process which assures speedy publication and readability. We wish this idea the best of success.

3. Such an item as "Pismo na carigradskija patriarx' Nikolaj Mistika do arxiepiskopa na B'lgarija," *Prometej*, 3 (1939), 26-28, is a good candidate for a next volume of Professor Dujčev's selected essays.

XXV

The Cambridge and Soviet Histories of the Byzantine Empire

The Cambridge Medieval History. Volume 4: *The Byzantine Empire*. Part. 1: *Byzantium and Its Neighbours*. Part. 2: *Government, Church and Civilisation*. Edited by J. M. Hussey et al. Cambridge and New York: Cambridge University Press, 1966-67. Part. 1: xl, 1168 pp. Part. 2: xlii, 517 pp.

Istoriia Vizantii v Trekh Tomakh. An SSSR, Institut Istorii. Edited by S. D. Skazkin et al. Moscow: "Nauka," 1967. Vol. 1: 523 pp. Vol. 2: 471 pp. Vol. 3: 507 pp.

The Cambridge Medieval History is a household word for medievalists and sends its message in a familiar language.[1] The Soviet *Istoriia Vizantii* is more intriguing, for it is unprecedented in Soviet historiography, in both format and size. Moreover, it is couched in a language inaccessible to the majority of Western readers. Hence my remarks will be more useful if they stress the characteristics of the Soviet work.

Some points, however, will not be stressed here. Were we dealing with the comparison of histories written in the remote past, we would be greatly interested in discovering the "true" views of their authors — which was the true Procopius, that of the *History* or that of the *Anecdota*? Given the nature of things, I shall not ask such questions about the authors of our histories.

Furthermore, I shall not refer expressly to historical materialism, nor shall I correlate the dates of the preparation or publication of the Soviet history (its first volume was sent to the printer in May 1966, its third appeared in November 1967) with political events in Russia. To be absolutely fair, I would also have to speculate on the effects which Harold Wilson's return to power in 1964 may have produced on the writings of Miss Hussey — patently an unprofitable undertaking.

On contributors to both works I shall say only that while the fourth volume of Cambridge history was an international venture and hardly

1. In subsequent notes the abbreviation *CMH* refers to vol. 4, part 2.

drained the collective energies of Western Byzantinists, the Soviet history was a national enterprise. Although it drew upon scholars from only three Soviet cities (Moscow, Leningrad, and Sverdlovsk) it did involve a sizable proportion of Byzantinists active in the Soviet Union.

The two works differ in some features of organization. The principle of division adopted in the Cambridge history is topical, and chronological within some of the topics; this made it possible to group chapters on law, music, spirituality, literature, science, and art together in the second volume, the only one that concerns us here. The principle of division adopted by the Soviet history is chronological, and topical only within each chronological unit.[2] Since in practice the Soviet history distinguishes four periods in ⟨625⟩ Byzantine history as a whole — the fourth to the seventh century, the seventh to mid-ninth century, the mid-ninth to the end of the twelfth century, and the thirteenth to the fifteenth century[3] — the same topic, say scholarship and education, is treated in it four times. Both systems have their advantages and shortcomings; and since the difficulties inherent in both apply to any attempt at a classifying treatment of any civilization, I shall not pursue the subject further.

2. The following chapters of the Soviet history deal with Byzantine intellectual history: Volume 1, chap. 17 (pp. 379-94), "Byzantine Science and Education in the IV-VII Centuries" (E. E. Granstrem, Z. V. Udaltsova); chap. 18 (pp. 395-408), "Neo-Platonic Philosophy of the IV-VI Centuries" (K. V. Khvostova); chap. 19 (pp. 409-34), "Byzantine Literature of the IV-VII Centuries" (S. S. Averintsev); chap. 20 (pp. 435-80), "Byzantine Art of the IV-VII Centuries" (A. V. Bank, E. E. Lipshits). Volume 2, part, 1, chap. 6 (pp. 80-102), "Byzantine Culture Between the End of the VII and the First Half of the IX Centuries" (Granstrem, Averintsev, A. Ia. Syrkin, Lipshits). Volume 2, part 2, chap. 16 (pp. 354-68), "Science and Education" (Granstrem, A. P. Kazhdan); chap. 17 (pp. 369-86), "Literature" (Kazhdan); chap. 18 (pp. 387-420), "Art" (Lipshits, Bank). Volume 3, chap. 14 (pp. 219-33), "Science and Education" (Lipshits); chap. 15 (pp. 234-56), "Philosophy and Theology" (M. Ia. Siuziumov); chap. 16 (pp. 257-73), "Literature" (Averintsev); chap. 17 (pp. 274-88), "Architecture and Painting" (Lipshits); chap. 18 (pp. 289-302), "Applied Arts" (Bank); chap. 19 (pp. 303-41), "Specificity of the Social Development of the Byzantine Empire: Byzantium's Place in World History" (Udaltsova). See, in addition, the first chapter of each volume and part, which deal with sources and thus discuss individual Byzantine authors.

3. This is the division followed throughout in single chapters of the Soviet history. In the final chapter, however, Z. V. Udaltsova distinguishes only three periods in Byzantium's history: fourth to mid-seventh century, the mid-seventh to the beginning of the thirteenth century, and the Latin conquest to the end of the empire (3:304).

In the technique of exposition, the second part of the Byzantine volume of the Cambridge history is neither fish nor fowl. Essays — sometimes brilliant, sometimes lacking in depth — appear alongside chapters which attempt full coverage. At best, the latter are valuable reference tools; at worst, they belong to the genre of a Sears, Roebuck catalogue. The technique adopted in the Soviet history is sometimes that of abstract statements, founded on what a Western reader regards as aprioristic truths. Fortunately, however, in the chapters on literature and art the technique is not that of coverage but of teaching by example. The choice of representative *exempla* is conventional: When fifth to sixth-century Ravenna is treated, we read a detailed description of the Mausoleum of Galla Placidia, the two Baptisteries, and the churches of San Apollinare Nuovo and San Vitale (1:456-65). This method, outdated by the availability of first-rate reproduction in our time, has not yet been superseded when it comes to acquainting a nonspecialist with the art of a given epoch or area, especially if — as in the Soviet Union — neither the author nor the reader has easy access to the monuments themselves or to good reproductions of them. In literature, where the counterpart of visual reproduction in translation, the method is even more justified. Accordingly, the Soviet history devotes more than one page to recounting the contents of a representative *Vita* of a saint (2:88-89, 372 [Life of Basil the Younger], 373-74), or as many as two pages each to vignettes of outstanding literary figures: ⟨626⟩ Michael Psellos, Johannes Italos, Theodoros Metochites, Nikephoros Gregoras, and Demetrios Kydones (2:361-63, 365-66, 3:225-30). In short, the Cambridge history, while not claiming to be a reference work, is not apt to be read in one sitting. The authors of the Soviet history offer their readers more incentive for continued perusal.

As often happens in collective enterprises of this kind, what the two works have in common are their flaws. On occasion, both works offer outdated information.[4] The date of Metochites's birth is off by ten years,[5] that of the Chora mosaics by almost twenty, that of the Deesis in Saint Sophia by a century (the latter two flaws are in the Soviet history alone),[6] and that of the church in Constantinople now known as

---

4. In some instances, correct answers were available in print long before, say, 1965; sometimes such answers were being formulated at the time of printing. In the latter case no blame should be cast upon the authors of these histories.

5. *CMH*, pp. 240, 246, 276; *Ist. Viz.*, 3:222. Metochites was born in 1270.

6. Chora: *Ist. Viz.*, 3:261. The date of 1303 proposed there is a misunderstanding. "Ca. 1320" is the dating accepted today. St. Sophia Deēsis: *Ist. Viz.*,

Kalenderhane by three centuries.[7] Second, on occasion both works indulge in empty statements, an overly apologetic tone, and a tendency toward the "hard sell," no longer necessary in a mature discipline like ours. Since this is a harsh statement, it must be substantiated by a few examples — first from the Cambridge history: the rigidity of Byzantine legal developments is more apparent than real (p. 55); the repetition of formulae in Byzantine music is no proof of the lack of creative imagination, but rather the outcome of the integration of art and theology (p. 160); Byzantine religious poetry contains, along with artificial elements, passages of genuine literary merit (p. 210); Byzantine etymology was of no value, although "it would be unfair to blame the Byzantines for this" (p. 248); Photius was a theologian of note, although he took a great deal of his *Amphilochia* word for word from other sources (p. 218); without Leo the Mathematician of the ninth century, the revival of mathematical studies in the West would have been almost inconceivable (p. 265).

The Soviet history's *captatio benevolentiae* is aimed at a different ear. It sees in Neo-Platonism a natural reflection of ideological changes in its period (1:395); it describes the liturgical poetry of the Byzantines as popular in spirit (1:426-27, 3:328); it hears a folkloristic tone in the writings of the seventh-century John of the Ladder (1:429), a tone which very few of that author's Western readers would detect; it praises the painters of the Menologium of Basil II for borrowing details from surrounding reality (2:402), and ⟨627⟩ the artists of the eleventh-century mosaics at Hosios Lukas for being inspired by everyday life, but gives the antique motif of the Bath of the Child in the Nativity scene there as an example of such inspiration (2:405). It sees fine psychological characterizations of each of the persons represented in the mosaics of John II and Irene, and of their son Alexius in Saint Sophia — too subtle an insight into these conventional faces (2:408). One of the authors of the Soviet history lets her enthusiasm run away with her when she claims that Demetrios Kydones's horizon was close to that of the most prominent representatives of the Italian Renaissance (3:230). Finally, once, but only once, the Soviet history slips into the Hellenic hypothesis to which

---

3:278; for the date of 1260-80, generally accepted today, see, for example, O. Demus, *Die Entstehung des Paläologenstils in der Malerei* [= *Berichte zum XI. Internationales Byzantinisten-Kongress München* 1958, vol. 4, part. 2], pp. 16 and 29-30, n. 67.

7. *CMH*, p. 332 (Akataleptos, ninth-early tenth century); *Ist. Viz.*, 2:392 (late ninth century); investigations of the church which have been going on since 1966 support the twelfth-century date for its central structure.

the Cambridge history is beholden throughout,[8] and sees no change between Aristophanes and one — phallic — passage in the fourteenth-century animal story of the Quadrupeds (3:267).

In the interest of constructing a harmonious whole, both works sometimes give too positive an answer to moot questions. Thus they create the impression that the Quadrivium was a regular feature of the Byzantine educational system throughout the early and middle periods,[9] although our first definite evidence for a textbook reflecting the system dates only from the eleventh century, even if the term *mathēmatikē tetraktys* occurs in the ninth.[10]

My next point purportedly involves the mind, but also tends to arouse the emotions: it is the comparison of both histories' conceptual framework. Neither of the works contains programmatic statements; the Cambridge history, by the nature of things as they are over here, the Soviet history, because it has no preface and plunges right into its subject. However, one does not have to read far ahead in order to sense that the Soviet contributors are applying certain conceptions to all of their material, while the Westerners ⟨628⟩ have not consciously posed any conceptual questions at all.[11] Hence the Soviet work gives the impression

---

8. On this hypothesis — which I would prefer to call fallacy — which assumes that after the seventh century the Byzantine Empire, including its territories in Asia Minor, came to be a Greek empire and, in terms of culture, an heir to classical and Hellenistic Greece, and which further assumes that this empire was ethnically Greek, encompassing, to be sure, several minorities, notably the Armenians, see my review of the first part of the Cambridge history, "New Cambridge History of the Byzantine Empire," *Slavic Review*, 27, no. 1 (March 1968) : 109-18, esp. p. 110.

9. *CMH*, pp. 265, 266-68 (but "Stephen's" text may be as late as 800!), 268, n. 1, 270, and 272 (*CMH*'s first sure information on the Byzantine Quadrivium); *Ist. Viz.*, 2:83, 354-55.

10. I have in mind a teaching system, rather than the theory of a fourfold division of mathematics, which is attested in introductory courses of philosophy (e.g., Ammonius) about the year 500. See Aubrey Diller, "The Byzantine Quadrivium," *Isis*, 36 (1945-46): 132; for *mathēmatikē tetraktys*, cf. *Vita Nicephori* by Ignatios (ninth century), p. 149, 27, ed. De Boor. Allusions to a teaching program similar to the Quadrivium do occur in other ninth-century Lives of saints (e.g., the Slavic *Vita Constantini*, § 4). The next occurrence of the term *tetraktys tōn mathēmatōn* known to me dates from the twelfth century (Anna Comnena, *Alexias*, Prooemium, 1, cf. *CMH*, p. 194). For later examples see, for example, V. Laurent in the edition of Pachymeres's Quadrivium in *Studi e Testi*, 94 (1940): xvii-xxiv.

11. In all fairness, it must be reported that Dr. Kazhdan, a Soviet critic of the

of regularity, and of greater editorial uniformity; the reader of various chapters soon detects the same general principles which presumably operate in various aspects of Byzantine civilization — above all in art and literature. The Cambridge history has a more haphazard choice of topics — for instance, it devotes no special attention to education, a recurring feature of the Soviet work. It contains factual contradictions and fortuitous repetitions — for some reason it refers several times to Leo the Mathematician's artificial singing birds.[12] The illustrative material of the English work is superior in quality; however, in selecting, it reflects preserved monuments — hence the prevalence of sacred topics. When secular monuments are chosen, such as the mosaics of the Great Palace in Constantinople, the selection is dictated by aesthetic considerations. In the Soviet history, illustrations — even of the same monuments as those used by its English counterpart — are selected instead for their technological or social content: a water mill, an anchor, a fishing scene, a goat being milked, workers tilling the land or pruning vines (1:78-79, 88, 2:239, 243, 245). The Soviet history's conceptual position is both conveyed and detectable through key words recurring in the body of its text. There are two series of them: those with bad and those with good connotations. Categories such as generalized, symbolic, spiritualistic,[13] conservative, and self-effacing are undesirable things; they are complementary to such categories as individualized, realistic, rationalistic, democratic,[14] everyday life, plebeian,[15] humanistic, and conscious of self, which are desirable things. When reality does not fit neatly into one of the two series, the category of "contradiction" is introduced.[16] The historical development in literature and the arts, especially between the

Cambridge history, did detect in it a common and, in his opinion, unduly valued point of view — namely, that Byzantium was a centralized monarchy or "beneficial autocracy." See A. P. Kazhdan, "The Byzantine Empire," *Past and Present*, 43 (1969): 158-69.

12. Examples of factual contradictions: Romanus the Melode was both a Jew (p. 143) and a Syrian (p. 254); on page 202 Barlaam was victorious in his dispute with Gregoras, but on page 277 Gregoras was victorious. Manasses's Chronicle was composed in fifteen-syllable verses (p. 236, correct) and in twelve-syllable verses (p. 250). On Leo's automata: *CMH*, pp. 302, 328, 355. The Soviet history is equally impressed by these automata, but at least it mentions them with cross-references: 2:28, 86, 96.

13. *Ist. Viz.*, 2:384, 403, 407, 411, 412, 414, 3:274-75, 285, 329.

14. *Ist. Viz.*, 1:434, 458, 2:100, 102.

15. *Ist. Viz.*, 1:428.

16. *Ist. Viz.*, 1:381, 402, 458, 2:81, 84, 361, 401, 3:325.

ninth and twelfth centuries, moved from one set of categories to the other, but was arrested by the catastrophe of 1204 (2:386, 411; cf. 3:330).

Moreover, the Soviet history regularly correlates changes in culture and world outlook with changes in the social structure of the empire. Such a procedure, standard in Soviet scholarship, causes some discomfort to the ⟨629⟩ uncommitted reader; he does not object to correlation in itself — he himself practices it on occasion — but to correlation without proof. He may remember from his epigraphical readings that fifth-century Aphrodisias was a city harboring pagan intellectuals of Neo-Platonic tinge,[17] but he is not satisfied with a flat statement to the effect that while Christianity served the needs of a centralized state, Neo-Platonism objectively served the needs of the conservative, urban, slave-owning patriciate (1:396, 398, 404, 408). He knows that Palamas and Kantakouzenos were allies, but wishes there were some proof for the statement that Palamism was the ideology of reaction, that it spread defeatist moods of thought, and that it was helped by foreign intervention and the defeat of popular movements in the forties of the fourteenth century (3:235, 249). He feels cornered by the statement that Palamism was an ideology of acquiescence to the Turkish conquerors, while anti-Palamism was an ideology of concessions to the Italian trade capital (3:249). He is bewildered when he learns that with the development of feudalism the interior structure of church buildings underwent an evolution: inner partitions formed badly communicating rooms, thus reflecting the rise of social differentiations (2:94-95).

The uncommitted reader does not object to the use of general categories, only to those which strike him as anachronistic. Even Dr. Kazhdan's excellent contributions in the Soviet history suffer from his search for signs of religious and social skepticism and irreverence in texts where I, for one, find none (2:376, 378, 382-83). Not in the tenth-century dialogue, *Philopatris*, which does not mock, but rather praises, the Trinity;[18] not in the twelfth-century *Timarion*, where the seating of

---

17. Louis Robert, "Deux Épigrammes d'Aphrodisias de Carie et Asklépiodotos," *Hellenica*, 4 (1948): 115-26.

18. See *Ist. Viz.*, 2:376, and *Philopatris*, §§ 12-13. The text describes the puzzlement of Kritias; being a pagan and a "fall guy," he at first does not comprehend the dogma of the Trinity, but is set straight by Triephon, who had been converted by Saint Paul himself. As the text purports to be by Lucian, all is couched in pagan terms, but intermingled with concealed quotations from the Psalms and the Credo.

Emperor Theophilus beside the pagan judges of the Nether World reflects the legend of Theophilus the Benefactor and the Just Judge (*dikaiokritēs*) — a legend, incidentally, published by a Russian prerevolutionary scholar.[19] The uncommitted reader finds it hard to reproach the twelfth-century historian Niketas Choniates for not criticizing the class structure of society, for speaking with scorn of popular masses, and for condemning popular uprisings,[20] since he still has to be shown a Byzantine author who *praises* such uprisings.

⟨630⟩Finally, when the uncommitted reader comes across such *epitheta ornantia* as "valiant Russes" and "conceited Normans" put side by side in one paragraph where both peoples are actually doing the same thing, namely, attacking the empire (3:321-22), when he learns that Russian masters infused Byzantine art with the creative genius of the Russian nation, and introduced optimism, humanism, and sympathy for the simple man into it (3:339), or that Byzantine anticlerical satirical works penetrated into the popular strata of nations influenced by Byzantium and contributed to the development of free thought there (3:341), he hears echoes of a past which he hoped would never recur in Soviet historiography.

Fortunately such nuggets are not representative of the body of the Soviet history's chapters on culture. Rather than flog a dead horse, I wish to make three points on the conceptual framework of both histories. First, eyebrow-raising statements, including those of the patriotic variety, occur primarily in the chapters by older contributors to the Soviet history and are counterbalanced by "unpatriotic" ones. Second, the Cambridge history has its own blinkers.[21] The third point, somewhat controversial, is that though citizens of the Soviet state suffer from handicaps as historians, they, and especially the Russians among them, enjoy certain unique advantages when writing about Byzantine culture.

Ad primum: When the Soviet history describes the vestment of the fifteenth-century Greek Metropolitan of Moscow, Photius, it notes not

19. *Ist. Viz.*, 2:382. Cf. W. Regel, *Analecta Byzantino-Russica* (St. Petersburg, 1891), pp. xix and 40-43. The legend is also reflected in the Byzantine Chronicles. Thus Theophilus's having been an iconoclast has nothing to do with his choice as judge in *Timarion*, and no comic device is involved in that choice.

20. *Ist. Viz.*, 2:386. Cf. p. 381 (the very concept of equality was alien to Theodoros Prodromos [twelfth century]).

21. This is above and beyond the preconceptions which struck Dr. Kazhdan (see note 11 above).

only that the vestment has portraits *both* of the Emperor John VIII and of Prince Vasilii Dmitrievich but also that John VIII and the Byzantines are the only ones to have halos and enjoy a prominent position (3:293). We are also expressly informed that the fifteenth-century revetment of Our Lady of Vladimir is by Byzantine artists, not Russian, "as was previously attested by some scholars" (3:299).[22] Finally, the church of Saint Sophia in Kiev is discussed in one of the chapters on Byzantine art (2:405-6).[23]

Ad secundum: In the 1923 edition of the Cambridge history, J. B. Bury assigned to Byzantium the role of bulwark of Europe against Asiatic aggression, the latter being patently a bad thing (pp. xv-xvi). Bury must have known that Byzantium was not interested in being the bulwark for any power, but only in expansion or survival; however, this self-centered metaphor could be accepted in the twenties of this century, the period of unchallenged Western domination. It is more astonishing to hear the same expression of parochialism eight times in the new edition of the Cambridge history. It, too, assigns to ⟨631⟩ Byzantium the role of bulwark of Christendom against the onslaughts from the East, against inundation by Islam, or by the Arab Flood — all of them bad forces, by implication and by choice of metaphor (pp. 45, 363-64, 366-67, 374); it praises Byzantium for having preserved the classical legacy "for Europe" — not for "the world," or for "us" — and it equates the Europe thus defended with Western Europe (pp. 247, 262; cf. pp. 265, 374). As for peoples of Eastern Europe, the Russians are said — on some unspecified genetic authority — to have been of a simple and less independent stock than the Greeks or the Hellenized Anatolians (p. 374). On the whole, the Soviet history is free from such self-serving constructions. It does go along with the bulwark theory, at one single point, but does so with a difference. It says that for centuries the Byzantine Empire, *like Old Rus'*, served as a barricade for Western Europe and broke the onslaught of Turkic and Mongol hordes moving in from the East (3:322).

Ad tertium: Living in a centralized state as a member of its cultural elite gives one certain insights into the characteristics of Byzantine culture. One takes for granted that higher education in Byzantium was controlled by imperial power; one realizes that jurists were needed in the

---

22. The statement concerning the Byzantine origin of the revetment is credited to M. M. Postnikova-Loseva.

23. However, Saint Sophia is regarded as an achievement of both Byzantine and Old Russian art.

state apparatus (Soviet history, 1:388). When it comes to imperial power itself, one is able to go beyond the Cambridge history's mere listing of the ruler's prerogatives, for one has an idea, based on parallel experience, of how traditions and groups around the emperor shaped his activity and limited his autocracy (juxtapose *CMH*, p. 10, with the Soviet history, 3:157-59, 312-13). Finally, when describing the general traits of Byzantine literature between the seventh and ninth centuries, one can tell the local reader that these traits developed within the framework of Christian ideology, that scriptures determined the movement of thought, that parallels to all events were sought in the Bible, that quotations from the Bible and Church Fathers were the best expressions of one's own views, that literature and art were didactic in character, and that the creative task was not to reflect and explore the world, but to propagate aprioristic ideals, to edify and to expose vices (Soviet history, 2:81). The reader has but to substitute appropriate terms for "Christian," "Bible," and "Church Fathers," and he is on familiar ground.

He is also on familiar ground when he is told that a centralized state needed a centralized ideology, and that Christianity, rather than Neo-Platonism, was the ideology for such a state (Soviet history, 1:396). The awareness of the power of "scientific" ideology may have determined the inclusion in the Soviet history of two chapters on Byzantine philosophy, a topic absent from the Cambridge history. The Soviet contributor's previous training enabled him to consider the Neo-Platonist Proclus's Triad as an anticipation of Hegel's thesis, antithesis, and synthesis, a parallel which would hardly have occurred to a Western Byzantinist (1:399, 401, 408).

⟨632⟩ To formulate the purpose of Byzantine art as subduing the soul to the all-embracing power of the state — as one contributor to the Soviet history does — may be too much of a good thing, but it is paralleled, and may have been suggested, by the use made of art in her country (3:337).

The fact that he is living in a multinational empire helps a Soviet scholar to realize the multinational character of Byzantine culture: he receives the message through the Byzantine monuments of Armenia, Georgia, and the Ukraine and has no trouble applying the same principle to literature.[24] While the Cambridge history subscribes to the fiction of

24. See *Ist. Viz.*, 1:453, on the "polyethnic" character of Byzantine art. Cf. 3:325, 341, on multinational roots of Byzantine civilization, and on contributions to it made by Slavs, Armenians, and Georgians.

the "Greek-speaking East,"[25] the Soviet history's chapter on early Byzantine literature reasonably distinguishes, along with the predominant Graecophone current, works in Latin, Syriac, and Coptic (1:409). And when it comes to the system of education, the Soviet history is able to go beyond the Greek horizon and refer to the fifth- and sixth-century statutes of the Syriac school at Nisibis, the earliest known statutes of a medieval institution of higher learning (1:392).[26]

The Russian scholar speaks a language which still embodies, through the mediation of Old Church Slavonic, many elements of Byzantine Greek. Hence he is able to offer translations of Byzantine literature which surpass in faithfulness and texture those made in any other language known to me. Since that scholar shares with his reader a culture greatly influenced by Byzantium, he is able to make his point by drawing on analogies or information familiar to both.[27] The charm of the Soviet history's literary chapters and their superiority to that by the late Franz Dölger, a great specialist on the subject, consist simply in this: their author gives superb translations of Byzantine poets — whether of Gregory of Nazianzus, John of Damascus, Theodore of Studios, or the poetess Kassia; and he is able to draw not only upon Church Slavonic translations of Byzantine ecclesiastical hymns but also on poetic reworkings of ⟨633⟩ similar texts by modern Russian poets, Pushkin and Aleksei K. Tolstoy (1:413, 421, 2:88).

I do not wish to overwork the categories of ideology and cultural vantage point; if external pressures are not too strong, it is not they, but the living individual's competence, talent, and enthusiasm which deter-

25. *CMH*, p. 1. Cf., however, page 34 for the sensible observation that the Byzantine bureaucracy and church contributed, through the official use of Greek, to the Hellenization of foreign elements in the empire; page 139 for liturgy in multinational ecclesiastical communities; and page 206 for the crushing of indigenous languages on Byzantium's periphery by central authority.

26. For translations of the text see, for example, E. Nestle, "Die Statuten der Schule von Nisibis aus den Jahren 496 und 590," *Zeitschrift für Kirchengeschichte*, 18 (1898): 211-29, and F. X. E. Albert, "The School of Nisibis; Its History and Statutes," *Catholic University Bulletin*, 12 (1906): 160-81. Incidental intelligence: these first statutes uphold, *inter alia*, the principle of autonomy in academic governance.

27. *Ist. Viz.*, 2:371 (on the fate of *Stephanitēs and Ichnelatēs* in Old Russian literature); 3:265 (parallel between the *Rhodian Love Songs* and the Russian seventeenth-century popular novel [*Lubochnyi roman*]); 3:268 (parallel between the *Porikologos* and the story of Ersh Ershovich). Less felicitous is the parallel, drawn on page 266, between couplets in politic verse and the *chastushki*.

mine the quality of his work. On the whole, the best chapters, whether in the Cambridge or the Soviet history, are those by specialists on specialized subjects. Here the Cambridge history is easily superior in three fields: law, music, and science. It is not only that the Soviet history has no separate chapters devoted to these topics: the very names of Scheltema, Wellesz, and Vogel are a guarantee of that superiority.

Vogel's chapter on science in the Cambridge history is the best overall treatment of the subject anywhere. He is precise and reliable: he tells us, to give but one footnote, that the Byzantines took over the system of decimal fractions in the fifteenth century — that is, soon after its invention in Samarkand in 1427 (p. 279, n. 3). This footnote is a better testimony to Byzantine versatility than many an empty statement about change under the cover of conservatism.

In art, André Grabar is pitted against Mrs. Lipshits, whose achievements lie in other fields. The result is that the most convincing sociological assessment of Byzantine art — of its propagandistic character, of the role of government and church as the two main sources for commissions, and of the patronage by the Byzantine elite — stands not in the Soviet history but on the first two pages of Grabar's chapter. When it comes to minor arts, however, Mrs. Bank, a curator at the Hermitage, who was able to draw on objects in Soviet collections, offers a most informative presentation. The Leningrad paleographer, Mrs. Granstrem, gives a "materialistic," but correct, explanation of the revolutionary change from the uncial to the minuscule script — disappearance of the papyrus, the high price of parchment, and the concomitant need for writing in smaller letters and using ligatures (2:86) — while the very term minuscule is absent at least from the index to the second volume of the Cambridge history.

In literature, S. S. Averintsev's talent and enthusiasm are coupled with empathy for Byzantine texts and authors, with able stylistic and formal analyses, and with wide-ranging juxtapositions — such as that of Palladius's *Historia Lausiaca* with the *Fioretti* of Saint Francis of Assisi and that of the Life of Saint Anthony with Flaubert's work (1:413, 421). Taken together, they outweigh Dölger's experience and tip the scales in favor of the Soviet scholar.

Having distributed praise and blame, I turn to my last point. It has to do with the awareness shown by each side of the other's scholarship. Judging by items quoted, the Cambridge history comes in a poor second. The bibliog⟨634⟩raphies of the second volume are some one hundred pages long; yet they register only eight Soviet works by seven authors. The Soviet history's footnotes — it has no bibliography of its own —

contain, except for art, numerous references to the most recent Western literature.

It follows that despite a few instances of antiquated views, the Soviet history's main text does incorporate new results attained in the West. Here, however, a subtle selectivity is at work: new finds — such as those of stained glass in the Pantocrator Church in Constantinople by Peter Megaw — are reported, but, in this instance at least, the reader is not told who made them (2:418).[28] The main text of the Soviet history gives uneven treatment to the names of foreign scholars. Discussing Theodoros Metochites, that text speaks of his "most recent investigator, Georg Beck." One the next page, however, it refers to another student of Metochites merely by saying, "the *author*" of one of the most recent investigations correctly notes..." (3:225-26). Ostensibly, the criterion for the admission of a modern scholar into the Soviet history's general index is the occurrence of his name in the text or in the footnotes of the work. Yet André Grabar, quoted in both, has not been included. It is also of interest to report that only a few American scholars are found in the index of the Soviet history, although several of them are well represented in its footnotes.

Neither the Cambridge nor the Soviet history reflects the present stage of thinking on Byzantine culture in its own constituency. The Soviet history comes somewhat closer, perhaps because at least half of its contributors are even today under fifty years of age. Still, whoever wants to acquaint himself with the latest word in Soviet scholarship on Byzantine culture should turn not to the Soviet history but to Alexander Kazhdan's *Byzantine Culture* of 1968.[29] This small but remarkable book looks for the principles which explain Byzantine culture as a functioning system, tells us what Byzantines ate and drank (mostly bread, pulse, and wine), and operates with such terms as "model," "alienation," and "vertical [we would say "upward"] mobility" — all notions familiar to recent Western historiography, but not often heard in Western works on Byzantinology and never encountered in the Cambridge history. The latter work, seventeen years in the making, was written by luminaries who stood out, to be sure, in their time; by 1967, however, many of them were Emeriti Professors and Sometime Fellows of this or that, and much of the Cambridge history was antiquated before its first word was printed. The younger generation of Western Byzantinists has still the chance, and the duty, to say what it thinks about Byzantine culture.

28. Cf. A. H. S. Megaw, "Notes on Recent Work of the Byzantine Institute in Istanbul," *Dumbarton Oaks Papers*, 17 (1963): esp. 349-64.
29. *Vizantiiskaia kul'tura (X-XII vv.)* (Moscow, 1968).

XXVI

The Date and Author of the So-Called Fragments of Toparcha Gothicus

I

In 1819 the famous Hellenist, Karl Benedikt (Charles-Benoît) Hase published an annotated edition of Leo Diaconus.[1] Since that historian dwelt at length on the wars waged between the Russes, the Bulgarians and the Byzantines in the seventies of the tenth century, it appeared natural that the edition should have been dedicated to Count Nicholas Rumjancev, chancellor of the Russian Empire. In his notes to Leo, Hase,[2] a keeper of Greek manuscripts at what was then the Bibliothèque

---

1. *Leonis Diaconi Caloënsis Historia, scriptoresque alii ad res Byzantinas pertinentes... E Bibliotheca Regia nunc primum...edidit...et notis illustravit Carolus Benedictus Hase...* [= Corpus Byzantinae Historiae, 34] (Paris, 1819). This edition was reprinted, with some omissions, as Part XI of the Bonn Corpus in 1828. On both editions, cf. N. M. Panagiotakes (Panayotakis), Λέων ὁ Διάκονος, Α' Τὰ Βιογραφικά, Β' Χειρόγραφα καὶ ἐκδόσεις (1965) (the same work appears also in Ἐπετηρὶς Ἑταιρείας Βυζαντινῶν Σπουδῶν, [1965]), 111-26. Professor Nicholas Panayotakis has prepared a new edition of Leo Diaconus, and I drew upon his results and used his suggestions on several occasions in this paper.

2. For a recent appreciation of Hase (May 11, 1789 - March 21, 1864), with good bibliography, cf. A. Kollautz, "Jacob Philipp Fallmerayers Briefwechsel mit Karl Benedikt Hase und Oerstedt über die Geschichte des Kaisertums von Trapezunt," *Südostforschungen*, 18 (1959), 281-350, esp.281-99. Among other works, cf. H. Rassow, "Zur Erinnerung an Carl Benedikt Hase," *Weimarische Beiträge zur Literatur und Kunst...* (Weimar, 1865), 145-54; Ch. M. Brunet de Presle, "M. Hase, et les savants grecs émigrés à Paris sous le premier empire et sous la restauration," *Revue des cours littéraires de la France et de l'étranger,* 2,20 (April 15, 1865), 317-26, translated, with some omissions and additions, in M. P. Bretos (Vretos), ed., Ἐθνικὸν Ἡμερολόγιον τοῦ... ἔτους 1867, 206-31; A. R. Rhangabe, "Ἡμερολόγιον τοῦ Ἑλληνιστοῦ Ἀσίου (Hase)," in M. P. Bretos (Vretos), ed., Ἐθνικὸν Ἡμερολόγιον τοῦ... ἔτους 1868, 72-83, esp.

Royale of Paris, made frequent use of unpublished texts. Some of these texts were part of the permanent holdings of the Paris library; some had come there from abroad during the Revolutionary and Napoleonic Wars and remained under Hase's jurisdiction only temporarily, since they were returned to their original homes by 1815.

At one point in his narrative, Leo Diaconus mentions the taking of Kherson in the Crimea by Prince Vladimir in 989, and this gave Hase the opportunity to print three previously unpublished, and unknown, Greek fragments which, in his opinion, had a bearing upon that event. The first Fragment ⟨118⟩ related how a party headed by its narrator crossed the frozen Dnieper and traveled through the steppe in the midst of a winter snowstorm; the second dealt with an attack launched at the approach of winter by some barbarians upon the area (or, rather, town) ruled by the narrator which was called the Klimata; the third Fragment reported the success of the narrator in repulsing that attack and spoke of an assembly composed of his (non-Greek?) allies, of the narrator's journey to a ruler holding sway to the north of the Danube, and of that ruler's investing the narrator once more with the government of the Klimata.

As the contents of the three Fragments are difficult to render in a concise form, the reader is offered a facsimile of their full text as it ap-

72-75; M. Guigniaut, "Notice historique sur la vie et les travaux de Charles-Benoist Hase," *Mémoires de l'Institut National de France, Académie des Inscriptions et Belles-Lettres,* 27 (1877), 247-73; O. Heine, ed., *Briefe von der Wanderung und aus Paris* (Leipzig, 1894) [= substantially the same author's "Eine Wanderung nach Paris (1801)," *Deutsche Rundschau,* (1880), 145-55, 287-304, and "Aus der Zeit des Consulats," *Deutsche Rundschau,* 29 (1881), 124-35, 424-37]; K. A. von Hase, *Unsre Hauschronik. Geschichte der Familie Hase in vier Jahrhunderten* (Leipzig, 1898), esp. 77-111, 335-36 (with unpublished letters from the family archives); Ch. Joret, *D'Ansse de Villoison et l'hellénisme en France pendant le dernier tiers du XVIII*[e] *siècle* [= *Bibliothèque de l'École des hautes Études,* 182] (1910), esp. 422-24, 514; C. Pitollet, "*Le Père Hase.*" *Histoire de la venue en France de l'allemand qui refusa Anatole France au baccalauréat* (Brussels, 1922); J. Kalitsunakis, "'Αδαμάντιος Κοραῆς καὶ Κ. Β. Hase," Πρακτικὰ τῆς 'Ακαδημίας 'Αθηνῶν, 8 (1933), 49-69; S. B. Kougeas, "'Ο Hase εἰς τὴν 'Ελλάδα," Νέα 'Εστία, 14 (1933), 530-33. The manuscript Paris *Nouvelles acquisitions françaises* 6480, fols. 58[r]-62[v], contains the following five obituaries of Hase: *Le courrier du dimanche,* March 27, 1864; *Journal général de l'instruction publique,* March 30, 1864; *Le moniteur universel,* April 1, 1864; *Beilagen zu der Allgemeinen Zeitung,* April 1, 1864; *Beilagen zu der Allgemeinen Zeitung,* April 5 and 6, 1864.

peared in the *editio princeps* of 1819;[3] the text is followed by my own English translation.

254 NOTÆ PHILOLOGICÆ ET HISTORICÆ

τῆς Χερσῶνος ἅλωσιν] Hæc est illa Chersonis a Wladimiro Magno occupatio, quam Nestor Annal. 105. B. version. Scher. a. Christi 988 accidisse auctor est. Ad illustrandas res temporum illorum pertinent fortasse epistolæne dicam an commentarii fragmenta, servata in Cod. sæc. x exeuntis, S. Basilii, Phalaridis, S. Gregorii Nazianzeni epistolas varias continente. In hoc igitur Codice, qui fuit Bibliothecæ Regiæ, possessor, qui et legationem circa Danaprim (vide infra 254. D.) obivit, et oppido præfuit (257. D), litteris minutis perplexisque admodum, nec multo quam Cod. ipse recentioribus folia duo vacua illevit, multis verbis mutatis, inductis, superscriptis, ut dubitare non queas, eum hunc Cod., ut est exiguæ molis, in expeditionibus secum portasse, pagellisque ejus vacuis ad epistolas commentariosque meditandos esse usum. Dabo fragmenta quo ordine sunt in Cod. : tametsi legationem, de qua statim, non nisi post bellum (vide alterum fragmentum 256. D.) accidisse facile dicas. Prius sic incipit imperfecte, de Danapris trajectu, glacierum fragmentis lintres transmittentium infestantis : Pag. 108. C. C

Epistola Græci cujusdam, sæc. XI. circa Danaprim iter facientis.

. . δυσχερῶς κατήγετο, καίτοι μὴ πλείους τριῶν ἀνδρῶν ἑκάστου σφῶν δεχομένου· οὕτω πάνυ φαυλότατα ἦν. Ἀλλ' οὐδὲ ταῦτα ὅμως χώραν εἶχε παρὰ τῷ ῥεύματι· πολλὰ γὰρ αὐτῶν ἐπὶ μεγίσταις πάγαις δυσὶ συνηράσσετο καὶ ξυνέπιπτε· καὶ ὁσαχοῦ τοῦτο ξυμβαίη, ἐκπηδῶντες[a] τοῦ πλοίου οἱ ἐν αὐτῷ[b] τῷ πάγῳ καθῆντο, καὶ ὡς ἐφ' ὁλκάδος ἐφέροντο. Ἔνια δὲ αὐτῶν καὶ κατέῤῥαξεν ὑποβρύχια· οὕτως ἄρα χαλεπαίνων ὁ Δάναπρις ἐτύγχανεν. Ἡμεῖς δὲ αὐτοῦ χαλεπώτερον καὶ ἐπὶ πλεῖστον προσεδεχόμεθα, καὶ ἦμεν ὥσπερ ὀργιζόμενοι κατ' αὐτοῦ, τῷ μὴ πεπῆχθαι. Καὶ οὐ πολλάς που ὕστερον ἡμέρας τὸ ὕδωρ ἁπανταχῆ πέπηκτο, καὶ ἐπὶ μέγα ἦν ἰσχυρόν· ὡς καὶ πεζῇ καὶ ἵπποις ἀφόβως ἰέναι κατὰ τοῦ ῥεύματος, καὶ ἀγῶνας ὡς ἐπὶ πεδίων ἀνδρικῶς ἀγωνίζεσθαι. Καὶ καθάπερ τις θαυματοποιὸς ὁ Δάναπρις ἐδείκνυτο, βαρὺς μὲν καὶ χαλεπὸς τὸ πρὶν αἰωρούμενος[c], καὶ μονονουχὶ τοὺς εἰς αὐτὸν ὁρῶντας πάντας φοβῶν· μετὰ δὲ μικρὸν ἀνεπαύσατό τι, καὶ τοσοῦτον μαλακισθῆναι, ὡς ὑφ' ἁπάντων

[a] Codex. ἐκπηδόντες.
[b] Videtur deesse aliquid vel hic, vel post οἱ.
[c] Codex. ἠωρούμενος.

. . difficulter applicabant [lintres], tametsi unaquæque earum non ultra ternos homines caperet : adeo erant mirabiliter exiles. Quanquam ne sic quidem locum invenire poterant in fluctu, multis earum duobus maximis glaciei frustis collisis atque contritis : quod quoties accidebat, exilientes e lintre qui inerant, in glacie considebant, ac velut super oneraria navi vehebantur. Aliæ lintres vel hauriebantur fluctibus : tam infestum tunc se declarabat Danapris. Nos vero ibi ægre diuque exspectavimus, velut succensentes flumini, quod non esset glaciatum. Nec multos dies post, erat aqua tum undique gelu constricta, tum mirifice firma : ut pedites equitesque intrepide per fluxum commearent, certaminaque tanquam in campis strenue ederent. Ita quasi præstigiatorem aliquem se Danapris præbebat, prius violenter ac sæve elatus, et prope dicam aspicientibus universis terrorem injiciens : mirumque eundem brevi tempore submissum fractumque adeo videri, ut D

3. In subsequent notes, the Fragments will be cited by the page of the Paris edition, reproduced here in facsimile.

A illuderent et conculcarent omnes quasi subterraneum factum, et in latibulum aliquod a se ipso absconditum. Neque enim tantum aquas manantes referebant fluenta, quantum montes asperos et petrosos ostendebant. Et subter fluens liquor quanam in re aquæ vel par vel similis poterat videri!

παίζεσθαί τε καὶ καταπατεῖσθαι, ὑπόγειός τις ὥσπερεὶ δεικνύμενος, ἀπὸ καταδῦναί τινα ἑαυτὸν κατακρύψας. Οὐ γὰρ ὕδασιν οὕτω νάουσιν ἐῴκει τὰ ῥεύματα, ἀλλ' ὄρη σκληρά[a] τινα καὶ λιθώδη μᾶλλον ἐδείκνυτο. Τί γὰρ ἴσον ἢ ὅμοιον τὸ καταρρεόμενον ἐκεῖνο καὶ ὕδατι;

[a] Hæc non [illegible] [illegible] [illegible] etc.

II. Ita mœstitia nostra in hilaritatem conversa est: complosis manibus proxime accessimus, per æquor equitantes. Transgressi nullo negotio cum in vicum Borion venissemus, ad corpus reficiendum B jumentaque curanda nos convertimus, quæ ipsa ex majori parte aut erant invalida, aut defecerant. Confectis ibi diebus aliquot necessariis ad vires reparandas, accingebamus nos Maurocastrum profecturi. Sed jam paratis rebus omnibus, cum nihil aliud obstaret, ipsa media nocte (quanquam maturius profectum oportebat), flante tunc aquilone gravissimo, hieme omnium sævissima se præcipitante, ut facile crederes, impervia esse itinera, nec obdurare sub dio ullum, propeque fieri non posse, ut qui tecto non servaretur interitum effugeret, tunc, C inquam, formidine commoti subsistere ibidem nosque continere statuimus. Cujus consilii auctor apud sodales ego exstiti: non esse ullo modo domibus exeundum, nedum abnoctandum inde: quod princeps sidus (Saturnum vocamus) jam ad vesperum in conspectum se dabat, inque similitudinem naturæ ejus immutabatur aër. Transibat enim tunc Saturnus circa initia aquarii, sole brumalia signa permeante. Quare tempestas, ubi semel occœperat, ad majorem semper sævitiam progressa est, ut quæ prius terrifica nobis visa fuerant, cum subsequentibus collata D ludus prorsus viderentur: tam luculenter se hiems quoquoversum diffuderat. Ibi diebus compluribus confectis, vix tandemque cogitatio aliqua domum redeundi subiit animum, aëre quoque sereniore se repræsentante.

β'. Ὅθεν ἡμῖν τὸ κατηφὲς εἰς χαρὰν μεταβέβλητο· καὶ χεῖρας ἀνακροτήσαντες ἐγγὺς προσήειμεν, κατὰ πέλαγος ἱππασάμενοι. Ἀπονητί τε διαβάντες καὶ κατὰ τὴν κώμην γενόμενοι τὴν Βορείων, πρὸς εὐωχίαν ἐτραπόμεθα καὶ ἵππων ἐπιμέλειαν, ἀπειρηκότων καὶ αὐτῶν καὶ καταπεπονημένων ὡς πλεῖστα. Κἀπειδὴ ἡμέρας ὅσον ἀναλαβεῖν ἑαυτοὺς διατρίψαντες, ὡς πρὸς τὸ Μαυρόκαστρον χωρεῖν ἐπειγόμεθα. Ὡς δ' ἕτοιμα ἦν ἡμῖν τότε πάντα, καὶ ἐμπόδιον ὑπῆρχεν οὐδέν, περὶ μέσας νύκτας αὐτὰς (ὅτε καὶ πρωϊαίτερον ἡμᾶς ἐξορμῆσαι ἐχρῆν), ἄρκτου τότε βαρύτατα πνεούσης, καὶ χειμῶνος πάντως μᾶλλον χαλεπωτάτου καταρραγέντος, ὡς ἀβάτους μὲν τὰς ὁδοὺς εἶναι, μηδένα δὲ ὑπαίθριον ζῆν, σχεδὸν δὲ ἀδύνατον εἶναι τὸν μὴ στέγῃ συζώμενον περιεῖναι, δείσαντες ἀναπαύεσθαι καὶ ἠρεμεῖν ἔγνωμεν αὐτοῦ· ἐμοῦ τοῦτο τοῖς συνήθεσιν εἰπόντος, ὡς οὐ δεῖ τῆς οἰκίας ὁπωσοῦν ἐξιέναι, οὐδὲ ἀπονυκτερεῦσαι ἡμᾶς ἐνθένδε γενέσθαι· τοῦ πρώτου τῶν ἄστρων ἑσπέριον φάναι ἤδη ποιοῦντος, καὶ πρὸς αὐτὸν ἐκεῖνον μετατρεπομένου τοῦ περιέχοντος (Κρόνου δὲ καλουμένου[b]). Καὶ γὰρ ἔτυχε περὶ τὰς ἀρχὰς αὐτὸς διϊὼν ὑδροχόον, ἡλίου κατὰ τὰ χειμερινὰ διατρέχοντος. Ὁ μὲν οὖν χειμὼν ἀρξάμενος ἀεὶ προὔβαινε χαλεπώτερος, καὶ ἐντεῦθεν τὰ πρότερον ἡμῖν δόξαντα φοβερὰ παιδιαὶ καθάπαξ πρὸς τὰ μετὰ ταῦτα ἐδόκει· οὕτως ἄρα λαμπρῶς ὁ χειμὼν διέσχε πανταχοῦ. Ἡμέρας δὲ διατρίψαντες ἱκανάς, μόλις ὀψέ ποτε καὶ τῆς πρὸς τὰ οἰκεῖα μνήμη τις ἐπανόδου εἰσῄει, εὐδιεινοτέρου καὶ τοῦ περιέχοντος δεδειγμένου.

Maurocastrum oppidum.

[b] Aut verba τοῦ πρώτου [illegible] [illegible] [illegible] [illegible] [illegible] [illegible] Κρόνου δὲ [illegible] [illegible].

III. Itaque egressi sumus, ab incolis splendide stipati: omnes me manibus complosis approbant, me tanquam necessarium unusquisque suum respicit, mihi maxima precatur. Hoc die stadia LXX, neque illa integra, emensi sumus, idque prægressis ante nos aliis, qui maximam vim nivis jam dimoverant. Postridie ejus diei statim a principio difficillime pro-

γ'. Καὶ δὴ ἐξῄειμεν, δορυφορούμενοι παρὰ τῶν ἐγχωρίων διαφανῶς, πάντων εἰς ἐμὲ τὰς χεῖρας ἀνακροτούντων, καὶ βλεπόντων ὡς πρὸς οἰκεῖον αὐτοῦ ἕκαστος[c], καὶ τὰ μέγιστα εὐχομένων. Τότε μὲν οὖν οὐδὲ πάντας αὐτοὺς ἑβδομήκοντα σταδίους παραμείψαμεν, καὶ ταῦτα πρὸ ἡμῶν ἄλλων διαβεβηκότων καὶ τὸ πολὺ τῆς χιόνος ἐκκρουσαμένων. Τῇ δ' ὑστεραίᾳ

[c] Sic Cod.

ἀρξάμενοι χαλεπώτατα προήειμεν, ὥσπερ ἐπὶ πελάγους ἀποπαλαίοντες κατὰ τῆς χιόνος. Οὐ γὰρ δὴ γῆ τις ἐδόκει εἶναι, οὐδὲ χιὼν συνήθης· ἀλλ' οἱ μὲν ἵπποι μέχρις τραχήλου οὐχ ἑωρῶντο· τὰ δ' ὑποζύγια, καίπερ τελευταῖα ἀκολουθοῦντα ἡμῖν, διεφθείρετο, καὶ αὐτοῦ πολλὰ καταλέλειπτο. Τετράπηχυς γὰρ ἡ χιὼν ἐλέγετο, καὶ χαλεπῶς διαβατὴ ἦν. Πολλοὶ δὲ καὶ τῶν ἀκολούθων ἀφώρμησαν οἴκαδε, μεῖζον ἢ κατ' ἀνθρωπίνην δύναμιν τὸ ξύμβαν οἰηθέντες. Καὶ ἦν γάρ τι τοῦ ἀξυντρόφου τὸ χαλεπόν, πολλαχόθεν τῶν δυσχερῶν ἐπιόντων· χιόνος μὲν βαθείας οὕτω καὶ πυκνῆς κάτωθεν, ἀέρων δὲ βαρυτάτων ἄνωθεν ἐμπνεόντων. Ἀνακωχῆς δ' οὐδαμόθεν προσδοκωμένης, οὐδ' ὅθεν τις ἀμείνω σχοίη τεκμαιρομένης (τὰ γὰρ πάντα ἀνωφελῆ καὶ ἀνόνητά πως ἐν τοῖς τότε δεινοῖς ἐδέδεικτο), οὐκ ἦν πυρὰ καῦσαι, οὐδ' ἀναπαύσασθαι πρὸς ἀκαρῆ χρόνον[a] ἡμῖν ἡ χιὼν ἐνεδίδου.

gradiebamur, tanquam in pelago contra A
nivem luctantes. Nulla terra hic videbatur esse, neque nix usitata: equi ad collum usque non apparebant: jumenta, quamvis extremo agmine subsequentia, interibant, multaque ibi relinquebantur. Etenim dicebatur nix cubitorum IV altitudine, eratque difficillima transitu. Ita multi ex comitibus domum se contulerunt, quod calamitatem vim humanam superare arbitrabantur. Atque erat profecto insueta ærumna, miseriis undique fere ingruentibus: infra tam alta et spissa nix, superne flantes venti inclementissimi. Neque ulla sperari poterat malorum B
intercapedo, nec unde quis meliorem statum assequeretur (omnia inutilia et infructuosa esse his in malis apparebat), nulla erat facultas ignes accendendi, nec requiescere vel minimum spatium permittebat nobis nix.

δ'. Εὐναὶ δὲ τὰς νύκτας αἱ ἀσπίδες προσήεσαν[b]· πάντα ἡμῖν ἐκεῖναι καὶ κλῖναι καὶ ἐπικλίνια νομιζόμεναι τὰ λαμπρότατα. Ἐν γὰρ αὐταῖς τὰ σώματα ἀνεπαυόμεν ἐπὶ πυρᾷ, καὶ ταύτῃ οὐ λαμπρᾷ. Ὕπνον[c] δὲ καὶ τὰ ἐξ ὀνείρων φαντάσματα, ὥσπερ φοβηθέντα ἐκεῖνα, πάντα ἀπέστησαν. Ἀντεῖχε δ' οὐδεὶς ἄλλου κάλλιον[d]· πάντες δ' ὡς ἐν κοινῇ συμφορᾷ ὁμοίως καὶ ψυχὰς καὶ σώματα διετέθεντο. Ἐμακάριζέ τις τοὺς τεθνεῶτας, ὡς τοῦ φροντίζειν ἄρα καὶ τοῦ πονεῖν ἀπαλλάττοντας· ἐσχετλίαζεν ἄλλος κατὰ τῶν ἐσομένων, ποίοις ἄρα καὶ αὐτοὶ δεινοῖς τὸ ζῆν συμμετρήσουσιν. Οἱ δὲ πρόσκοποι ἐξέκαμον καὶ αὐτοί, ὑπὸ τοῦ πολλοῦ κακοῦ νικηθέντες, καὶ περιιέναι οὐκ ἴσχυον, ἀσαφῶς οὕτω πορευόμενοι κατὰ τῆς χιόνος. Τὸ δὲ δὴ χαλεπώτατον, ὅτι καὶ διὰ πολεμίας ἐπορευόμεθα γῆς, καὶ οὐδ' ἐκ τούτου ἀδεᾶ ἡμῖν καθειστήκει τὰ πράγματα, ἀλλ' ἐν ὁμοίῳ τό, τε τοῦ χειμῶνος καὶ τὸ τῶν πολεμίων ἐφοβούμεθα κακόν.

IV. Accedebant noctu scuta pro cubilibus: hæc pro omnibus habebamus, et pro stragulis et pro opertoriis splendidissimis. In illis enim corpus ad ignem, nec illum splendidum, refocillabamus. Somnum visa per quietem occurrentia, quasi timentem C
illa quoque, universum fugaverant. Neque quisquam magis quam alius ad ærumnas obduruerat: omnes erant ut in communi calamitate æque et animo et corpore afflicti. Alius beatos prædicabat mortuos, ut jam sensu doloribusque liberatos: lamentabatur alius posteros, quibus miseriis oppressi illi quoque vita essent defuncturi. Item labori succubuerant exploratores nostri, vi mali victi, nec per nivem incerto gradu errantes progredi poterant. Omnium autem acerbissimum erat, quod per regionem hosticam iter faciebamus, neque inde erant res nostræ D
periculo vacuæ, sed pariter hiemis hostiumque violentia timebatur.

[a] Supra scriptum est χρόνον, idemque poena inductum.

[b] Sic Cod. non [illegible];

[c] Cod. Ὕπνος.

[d] Hic scripta erant hæc tria alia: [illegible] omnia poena inducta sunt.

Hic imperfecte desinit fragmentum prius. Sequitur post quadraginta circiter folia alterum, eadem intricatissima manu, quod, ut est loco in Cod. posterius, ita præcedenti subjungo: tametsi fortasse ad tempus antecedens pertinet. Gens, cui dux ille, quisquis est, oppidum sibi commissum tradiderit, quæ sit, viderint docti, temporum partiumque illarum cognitionem cum prudenti judicio conjungentes. Rem in Chersoneso Taurica geri declarat mentio Clematum 258. B. facta: scriptura est ligata, quam vocant, sæc. X aut XI.

Ἀρχὴν γὰρ δὴ τότε τοῖς βαρβάροις πολεμεῖν ἔγνωμεν[e]· ἤ, εἰ δεῖ τι τἀληθὲς φάναι,

Omnino enim tunc barbaris bellum inferre decrevimus: aut, si vera fateri

δείσαντες

[e] Scriptum est hic, et posterius inductum: Καὶ διὰ τοῦτο γὰρ [illegible] καὶ βάρος τοῦ ἔργου.

A oportet, recessimus ab illis metu, ne ipsi
priores ab iis opprimeremur, statuimusque iis quantum possemus repugnare.
Æque enim universos diripiebant inhumanissime et pessundabant, ut quædam
belluæ in omnes impetum facientes.
Nulla his inerat vel erga conjunctissimos
continentia, nec ratione ulla aut justi
discrimine in patranda cæde volebant
uti : sed Mysorum prædam, quod aiunt,
ipsorum regionem reddere malo ac pernicioso consilio meditabantur. Evanuerat superior eorum æquitas et justitia :
quas præcipue colentes tropæa antehac
B maxima statuerant, adeo ut civitates et
gentes ultro accederent illis. Gliscebant
nunc, quæ velut e perpendiculo (quemadmodum aiunt) a virtutibus illis distant,
injustitia et intemperantia adversus subditos : neque ornare et ex re ipsarum
administrare civitates dedititias, sed redigere in servitutem et exscindere constituerant. Conquerentes de dominis
incolæ, seque nihil mali commisisse
liquido demonstrantes, nihil amplius
proficiebant, quam ut morte non afficerentur. Vis nimirum tanta malorum ingruerat, ut res humanæ quasi ruina aut
C voragine aliqua inopinata ac fatali perculsæ obrutæque horrendum in modum
viderentur. Erant exinanita hominibus
oppida plus x, pagi plane deserti non
minus quingentis : vicinitates denique et
confinia nostra velut tempestate obruebantur : incolæ innocentes, pactis juratis
traditi, manibus obtruncabantur gladiisque hostilibus.

δείσαντες τὸ μὴ φθῆναι ὑπ' αὐτῶν ἀναιρεθέντες, ἀπέστημεν, καὶ αὐτοῖς τὸ δυνατὸν ἀντιτετάχθαι διενοήθημεν, πάντας ὁμοίως λεηλατούντων καὶ διαφθειρομένων ἀπανθρωπότατα, ὥσπερ τινὰ θηρία κατὰ πάντων τὴν ὁρμὴν ἐνδεικνύντα. Οὐδὲ γὰρ τῶν οἰκειοτάτων φειδώ τις εἰσῄει αὐτοῖς, οὐδὲ λογισμῷ τινὶ ἢ κρίσει δικαίᾳ τὸν φόνον εἰργάσθαι προὔθεντο· ἀλλὰ τὴν Μυσῶν[a] λείαν καλουμένην θέσθαι τὴν αὐτῶν[b] γῆν κακῶς καὶ ἀσυμφόρως μεμελετήκεσαν. Ἀντέστραπτο γὰρ τὸ πρὶν αὐτοῖς ἴσον καὶ δίκαιον· ἃ δὴ περὶ πλείστου τιμῶντες τὸ πρότερον τρόπαιά τε τὰ μέγιστα κατωρθώκεσαν, καὶ πόλεις καὶ ἔθνη αὐτεπαγγέλτως προσῄεσαν αὐτοῖς. Νῦν δ' ὥσπερ ἐκ διαμέτρου ἀδικία τούτοις καὶ ἀμετρία κατὰ τῶν ὑπηκόων ξυνέστηκε. καὶ πόλεις ὑπηκόους, ἀντὶ τοῦ θεραπεύειν καὶ συμφερόντως εὐνομεῖν, ἀνδραποδίζειν καὶ διαφθείρειν ξυνέθεντο. Σχετλιαζόντές τε κατὰ τῶν ἡγεμόνων, καὶ ὡς οὐκ ἀδικοῖεν βεβαίως δεικνύντες οἱ ἄνθρωποι, οὐδὲν μᾶλλον ἴσχυον τοῦ μὴ τεθνάναι. Φορὰ γάρ τις, ὡς ἔοικεν, ὑπὸ κακίας ξυμβέβηκεν, ὡς περικλύζεσθαι τὰ τῶν ἀνθρώπων καὶ φοβερώτατα συγκεχῶσθαι δοκεῖν, ὡς ἐκ συμπτώματος ἤ τινος χάσματος παραλογωτάτου καὶ χαλεποῦ. Πόλεις μὲν γὰρ πλείους ἢ δέκα ἀνθρώπων ἐξεκενώθησαν, κῶμαι δὲ οὐκ ἐλάττους πεντακοσίων παντελῶς ἠρημώθησαν· καὶ ἁπλῶς, τὰ γείτονα καὶ πλησιόχωρα ἡμῶν ὥσπερ ἐκ χειμῶνος ἐπικλυσθέντα ἐγένοντο, ἄνθρωποί τε, ἠδικηκότες μηδὲν, προβληθέντες ἐπ' ὀμωσίᾳ, χειρῶν ἔργον καὶ ξίφους ἐγένοντο.

a Cod. Μυσῶν.

b Sic : prius scripserat ἡμῶν, sed id induxit.

Chersonesus Taurica populata sæc. X vel XI.

II. Ejusmodi pestem, generatim omnes misere conculcantem, cum aliquamdiu per infelices conterminos nostros
obambulasset, postremo ad præsidium
D meum quoque fortuna infesta adduxit.
Quam quia jam antehac eram veritus,
in magna cura versabar, ne accideret
improviso, nec latente impetu continuo
res nostras everteret. Deinde, ubi perspicuum aderat periculum, omnesque
palam fatebantur, in discrimen nos vitæ
venisse, ego tunc quidem perniciem
quam aptissime poteram repuli, quamvis
in extremum pæne periculum adductus.
Verum inde abruptis commerciis bellum
inter nos et barbaros ortum est, in quo
neque communicabant amplius nobiscum (tametsi sexcenties de compositione
ad illos mittebam), nec sine præliis mutuis res gesta est. Ita bellum continuo

β'. Τὸν δὴ τοιοῦτον ὄλεθρον καὶ κοινῇ πάντας κακῶς διαφθείραντα, καὶ περιελθόντα τοὺς παλαιπώρους ἡμῶν ἀστυγείτονας, καὶ πρὸς τὴν ἐμὴν ἀρχὴν τελευταίως ἡ πονηρὰ τύχη προσῆξεν, ὑφορώμενον μὲν ἐμοὶ καὶ πρότερον, καὶ πολλὴν ποιουμένῳ πρόνοιαν, μὴ ἄν ποτε ἐξαπιναίως ἐμπέσοι, μηδ' ἐκ τοῦ παραχρῆμα λαθὼν τὰ καθ' ἡμᾶς λυμήναιτο. Ὡς δ' ἀφῖκτο καθαρῶς ὁ κίνδυνος, καὶ πᾶσιν ἀνωμολόγητο φανερῶς, ὡς τὰ περὶ ψυχῆς νῦν ἡμῖν κινδυνεύεται, τὸν μὲν τότε ὄλεθρον σοφῶς τ' ὡς εἶχον ἀπεκρουσάμην, ἐμοῦ καίπερ τὰ ἔσχατα παρὰ μικρὸν κινδυνεύσαντος. Τὸ δὲ ἀπὸ τούτου, πόλεμος ἡμῖν ἀκήρυκτος καὶ βαρβάροις ἐγένετο, ἐν ᾧ οὔτε ἐπιμίγνυον ἔτι παρ' ἡμῖν (εἰ καὶ μυριάκις περὶ σπονδῶν ἐκηρύκευον), οὔτε ἀμαχητὶ πρὸς ἀλλήλους ἦμεν. Καὶ ὁ μὲν πόλεμος εὐθὺς ἤρξατο, ὁ δὲ χειμὼν ἐγγὺς ἦν

258 **NOTÆ PHILOLOGICÆ ET HISTORICÆ**

[a] *Hæc omnia inducta, reposita, iterum partim inducta. Ubi asteriscum notavi, in Cod. est* χειμῶν. *Num* χειμερινῶν, κ. [illegible];

[b] *Hic subsequuntur illa, postea inducta:* Ἀλλ' [illegible] [sic] [illegible] [sic] [illegible]

[c] *F.* [illegible] οἰκῆσαι, *instaurare.*

[e] Castrum Clematum [vid. Bandur. Imp. Orient. I. 113. B.]

[d] *Subest verbum aliud inductum, ut legi nequeat.*

[e] *Sequitur hic* [illegible], *quod oblitus est inducere scriptor.*

[f] *Codex,* ἀποβαλόντες.

[g] *Sic Codex. Vid. supra B not. b.*

[h] *Sic Cod.*

[i] *Hic primo sequuntur illa:* [illegible] *Deinceps illa iterum inducta.* [illegible] *quæ in textum recepi.*

ἐμβαλεῖν· ἔτι γὰρ οὐ πολὺ τῶν . . [a] ὁ ἥλιος ἀπῆν. Ἀλλ' οἱ μὲν βάρβαροι, στρατῷ παρασκευασθέντες ἱκανῷ, ἐσέβαλον εἰς τὴν γῆν ἡμῶν, ἱππικῷ τε ἅμα καὶ πεζῷ, νομίσαντες ὡς ἅμα βοῇ παραλήψεσθαι ἡμᾶς, τῇ τε τοῦ τείχους ἀσθενείᾳ, τῇ τε ἡμῶν ὀρρωδίᾳ. Καὶ οὐκ ἀπεικὸς ἦν αὐτοῖς ταῦτα οἴεσθαι, οὕτως ἐπὶ κατεσκαμμένῃ πόλει τὴν οἴκησιν ποιουμένων ἡμῶν, καὶ ὡς ἀπὸ κώμης μᾶλλον ἢ πόλεως τὰς προσβολὰς ποιουμένων [b]. Ἡ γῆ γὰρ προκατέσκαπτο παρ' αὐτῶν τῶν βαρβάρων καὶ ἱκανῶς ἐξηρήμωτο, ἐκ βάθρων αὐτῶν καταβαλλόντων τὰ τείχη· καὶ τότε ἀρχὴν ἐμοῦ πρώτου πάλιν οἰκῆσαι [c] τὰ Κλίματα διανοησαμένου. Τοιγάρτοι φρούριον μὲν τὸ πρῶτον ἐκ τῶν ἐνόντων ἐξῳκοδόμησα παρ' αὐτήν, ὡς ἐκ τούτου ῥᾳδίως καὶ τὴν ἄλλην ἅπασαν πόλιν οἰκισθήσεσθαι . . .

exarsit, impendebatque hiems : non multum enim a.. sol aberat. Sed barbari, comparato amplo exercitu, cum equitibus militibusque in regionem nostram irruperunt, nos momento expugnatum iri rati, cum ob murorum infirmitatem, tum ob trepidationem nostram. Neque erat absonum eos hoc sperare, quod in diruto oppido commorabamur, magisque ex vico, ut ita dicam, quam ex urbe eruptiones faciebamus. Vastata enim prius fuerat ab ipsis barbaris regio, et solitudo mera facta, muris solo æquatis: ego autem tunc demum habitare denuo Clemata [e] primus constitueram. Quare in principio juxta oppidum pro facultatibus feceram castellum, quod inde facile reliquam quoque civitatem instaurari posse . . . A B

Sequuntur in folio alio abrupta illa, superioribus subjungenda:

Καὶ τὸ μὲν ἀνῳκοδόμητο τάχει πολλῷ, καὶ περιέφρακτο τάφρῳ· καὶ ἅμα τούτων*[d] καὶ ὁ πόλεμος ἤρξατο. Μεμέριστο δὲ τὸ φρούριον κατὰ συγγενείας, καὶ κατέθεντο ἐν αὐτῷ τὰ σπουδαιότερα· ὅσα δὲ περιττὰ, ἔξω που κατὰ τὸν ἄλλον τῆς πόλεως περίβολον ἔκειτο. Ὤκειτο γὰρ ἤδη καὶ ἡ πόλις ἅπασα· τὸ δὲ φρούριον ὡς ἐν μεγάλῳ κινδύνῳ σώσειν ἡμᾶς ἐξητοίμαστο [e]. Ἀλλ' οἱ μὲν βάρβαροι τότε πολλοὺς αὐτῶν ἀποβαλόντες [f] καὶ καταισχυνθέντες [g] ἀπήεσαν πρὸς νύκτα, φυλάξαντες τὸ περίορθρον· ἐγὼ δὲ ἅμα ἕῳ τὸν στρατὸν ἀντεξῆγον πολεμησείων. Ἦσαν δέ μοι τότε ἱππεῖς μὲν ὀλίγῳ πλείους ἑκατόν, σφενδονῆται δὲ καὶ τοξόται ὑπὲρ τ'.. Οὐδαμοῦ δὲ τῶν βαρβάρων ὄντων, τὰ τῷ καιρῷ μοι σύμφορα ἐξηρτύετο, τεῖχος μὲν τὸ παλαιὸν ἀνεγείρων [h], καὶ διδάσκων τοὺς ἐμοὺς εὖ παρεσκευάσθαι πρὸς τὰ πολέμια. Πρὸς δὲ τοὺς ἡμῖν προσέχοντας δρόμῳ κήρυκας ἔπεμπον, καὶ μετεκαλούμην αὐτούς, σκεψόμενος περὶ τῶν ὅλων [i]. Ἀφιγμένων δὲ ἁπανταχόθεν, καὶ ἐκκλησίας ἐκ τῶν ἀρίστων γενομένης, ἃ μὲν εἶπον ἐγὼ τότε, καὶ ὡς οἵων δεσποτῶν μᾶλλον ἀντιποιεῖσθαι προσήκει, καὶ πρὸς οἵους ἐλθόντας τίνα ὠφέλειαν πειρᾶσθαι ἀπ' αὐτῶν εὑρίσκειν, καὶ τί ποιητέον ἐστί, καὶ τἄλλα πάντα, ὅσα τότε εἶπον ἐγώ, ἃ καὶ πλείους μᾶλλον τιμησαίμην, μακρὸν ἂν εἴη πάντα ἐφεξῆς λέγειν βούλεσθαι. Οἱ δέ, εἴτε ὡς μηδέποτε βασιλικῆς εὐνοίας ἀπολελαυκότες, μηδ' Ἑλληνικωτέρων τρόπων ἐπιμελούμενοι, αὐτονόμως δὲ μάλιστα ἔργων ἀντιποιούμενοι, εἴτε ὅμοροι ὄντες πρὸς τὸν κατὰ τὰ βόρεια τοῦ Ἴστρου βασιλεύοντα, μετὰ τοῦ

Idque propere et instauratum fuerat, et fossa circummunitum : unaque cum his* bellum quoque incepit. Divisum erat per cognationes castellum, resque pretiosiores in eo depositæ : minus necessariæ extra per reliquum oppidi ambitum erant collocatæ. Habitabatur enim tunc urbs jam tota : castellum autem præparatum fuerat, ut in magno periculo nobis saluti esset. C At barbari tunc, multis suorum amissis, cum ignominia noctu recesserunt, servato diluculo : primo mane ego prælii cupidus copias contra eduxi. Erant mihi tunc equites paulo plures quam centum, funditores et sagittarii supra CC. Barbari cum nusquam apparerent, quæ apta huic tempori essent a me adornata sunt, murus vetus erectus, edocti mei, quomodo recte se instruerent ad bellum. Eos autem qui ditionis nostræ erant, nunciis cursim missis accersivi, de rerum summa in consilium ire volens. D Undique cum advenissent, concione optimatum coacta, quos tunc ego sermones habuerim, qui domini potius essent expetendi, ad quos venire quamque commoditatem conari oporteret ab illis percipere, quid denique faciendum esset, et cætera universa tunc a me dicta, quæ ipse quoque reliquis omnibus præstabiliora duxissem, longum esset singula ordine dicere velle. Illi, seu quod nunquam benevolentiæ Imperatoriæ fructum ullum cepissent, seu quod, Græcanicam vitæ rationem parum curantes, instituta ad arbitrium ipsorum facta maxime requirerent, sive quod regi ad septentrionem Istri dominanti contermi-

IN LEONIS DIACONI LIB. X. 259

A nantes, præterquam quod ille exercitu magno valeret vique bellica efferret sese, ab illius vitæ ratione propriis moribus non differrent : idcirco statuerunt pacisci cum illis seque dedere, me autem negotium perficere publicitus omnes decreverunt. Ita profectus sum ad servandas fortunas nostras, eumque talem deprehendi, qualem desiderare quis maxime posset. Atque ita, ubi colloquio brevi, ut poteram, totum negotium transegeram cum eo, ille rem majorem, plus quam ullam, reputans, mihi Clematum imperium iterum volens lubensque omne tradidit, addidit-
B que etiam præfecturam totam, et ex ipsius regione reditus annuos idoneos largitus est.

στρατῷ ἰσχύειν πολλῷ καὶ δυνάμει μάχης ἐπαίρεσθαι, ἤθεσί τε τοῖς ἐκεῖ τὰ παρὰ σφῶν αὐτῶν οὐκ ἀποδιαφέροντας, ἐκείνῳ καὶ σπείσασθαι καὶ παραδοῦναι σφᾶς ξυνέθεντο, κἀμὲ τὰ τοιαῦτα πράξειν κοινῇ πάντες ἐπεψηφίσαντο. Clematenses ultro se dedunt.
Καὶ ἀπῄειν, ἵνα τὰ ἡμέτερα σώζων, καὶ ἐνέτυχον αὐτῷ ὡς εὔξαιτ' ἂν μάλιστά τις. Καὶ, ὡς δυνατὸν ἐν βραχεῖ λόγῳ πᾶν συμπεράνας αὐτῷ, ἐκεῖνος μὲν παντὸς μᾶλλον* μεῖζον τὸ πρᾶγμα ἐλογίσατο, ἐμοὶ δὲ τὴν τῶν Κλημάτων ἀρχὴν αὖθις ἀσμένως πᾶσαν ἔδοτο, καὶ προσέθηκε καὶ σατραπείαν ὅλην, ἔν τε γῇ τῇ αὐτοῦ προσόδους ἐπετείους ἱκανὰς ἐδωρήσατο. * Sic Cod.

Desinit hic præclarum illud plenumque rerum novarum fragmentum : quod si commentatio scriptiove, unde manat, integra ætatem tulisset, næ tunc haud paulo plus, quam nunc, sciremus de historia Chersonesi Tauricæ in tenebris, ut ita dicam, jacente ab a. 950, circa quem Constantinus Porphyrogeneta scripsit, usque ad colonias Genuensium in hos tractus sæc. XIII. deductas. Speremus certe, excussis per alias bibliothecas codd. Græcis medii ævi, lucem novam huic quoque historiæ parti oblatum iri : idque ut confidamus fore faciunt Ill. Comitis *Nicolai* de Romanzoff magnificentia, liberalisque ac generosus animus, quo incitatus cum reliquas disciplinas omnes fovet, tum maxime historiam patriæ locupletari cupit et ornari.

⟨123⟩ *Translation*

Fragment 1

[Leo Diaconus, pp.254C-256D, Paris ed., = pp. 496-498, Bonn]

...they [i.e., the boats] would land (κατήγετο; float down?) with difficulty, although each of them held only three men; of so flimsy ⟨a construction⟩ were they. But even they found no place (?) in the current, for many of them would be crushed between two huge floes and would threaten to collapse; and whenever this happened, those in the boat would jump out of it, sit on the floe, and float on it as if on a towed boat (ἐφ' ὁλκάδος). And some of the boats did break down and sink, so violent happened to be the Dnieper's anger. And we waited there, very distressed (? χαλεπώτερον), for quite a long time, and we were angry at the river, as it were, because it would not freeze over. And a few days later the water froze over everywhere (ἁπανταχῇ) and was mightily firm, so that one could fearlessly walk on foot and ride on horseback through (on top of?) the current (κατὰ τοῦ ῥεύματος), and contend in games in a manly fashion as if ⟨one were⟩ on a plain. And the Dnieper appeared as a sorcerer of sorts, at first rising (? αἰωρούμενος) in heavy anger and instilling fear into almost everyone beholding it; but soon thereafter, it relented somewhat and was so much mel⟨124⟩lowed that it ⟨permitted⟩ everyone to make fun of it and to trample upon it; it appeared to be subterranean, as it were, and to have settled down in some hole. For its flow did not resemble running waters, but rather hard and rocky mountains. For in what respect was that which flowed underneath (τὸ καταφερόμενον ἐκεῖνο; rushed down?) identical with or resembling water?

Hence our despondency turned into rejoicing and, having burst out in great applause, we approached it (προσίεμεν), having ridden over the surface of the sea. We crossed it without hindrance, and, having arrived at the village of Borion, we turned to food and drink and took care of our horses, which, too, were in great want (? ἠπορημένων) and fatigued. We spent there as many days as were necessary to regain strength, and we were anxious (ἠπειγόμεθα; hastened?) to move on Maurokastron. But as we were ready ⟨to break up⟩ and no obstacle remained, around midnight (for it was appropriate that we should start our journey rather early) a northern wind started to blow with great violence, and such a heavy storm broke out that the roads were considered impassable and no one ⟨was given a chance⟩ to survive outdoors. ⟨Consequently,⟩ we were seized with fear and decided to make a halt and to wait quietly on the spot. I told my companions (συσσίτοις) not to leave their houses under any circumstances or to sleep out, for the first of the stars was in its vespertine phase and the surrounding air (τοῦ περιέχοντος) — it was called Saturn — was turning to be like it. ⟨This star⟩ happened to be moving about the beginnings of ⟨the sign of?⟩ Aquarius, while the sun was traversing the winter ⟨part of the zodiac?⟩. The storm, having begun, continued to increase in force, and it turned out that what we had previously considered bad ⟨weather⟩ now appeared to us as mere child's play in comparison: so completely (? λαμπρῶς) did snow spread (extend?) everywhere. We spent quite a few days ⟨there⟩, and finally and reluctantly (? μόλις ὀψέ ποτε) began to think of a return journey to our own homes, especially since the surrounding air had cleared.

Accordingly, we left, with the natives accompanying us in a splendid (? διαφανῶς) procession. They all applauded me; each one of them considered me a ⟨particular⟩ friend of his and wished me the best of luck. On that day (? τότε) we covered less than seventy stadia, although other people had gone ahead of us and cleared (? ἐκκρουσαμένων) most of the snow. The next day, however, we moved forward with the greatest difficulty from the very beginning, struggling with the snow as if it were a sea. It seemed that the earth had disappeared, and that the snow was of a peculiar nature; the horses ⟨sank and⟩ were invisible up to their very necks; and the beasts of burden, although they brought up the rear end, were perishing, and many of them remained ⟨lying⟩ on the spot. For it was said the snow was four cubits deep, and hardly passable. Moreover, many of those who accompanied us left for their homes, considering the phenomenon to be beyond human strength. In fact, the distress was unusually great (οὐ ξυντρόφων), since difficulties beset ⟨us⟩ on all sides: down below there was deep and dense snow; up above, heavy winds were blowing. We did not expect respite from any direction, nor could we guess from where an improvement could come for us (since all ⟨measures⟩ proved ⟨125⟩ to be vain and no avail in our straits at that time); there was no way we could kindle a fire, nor did the snow leave us the smallest (? ἀκαρῆ) room for resting.

We had shields for beds at night; they were everything at once for us: splendid beds and bed-covers (? ἐπικλίνια). We provided rest for our bodies upon them next to a skimpy fire. We lacked both sleep and dreams, the latter having fled from us as if they, too, had been seized by fear. No one appeared more resistant than his neighbor, but all showed the same ⟨poor⟩ disposition of soul and body, the calamity being the same for all. One man blessed the dead, for they had been relieved both of preoccupation and trouble; another bewailed the survivors (ἐσχετλίασεν κατὰ τῶν ἐσομένων; complained against the future?), ⟨considering⟩ in what misery they were to live (τὸ ζῆν ἐκμετρήσουσιν; die?). As for the scouts (πρόσκοποι), they, too, succumbed to exhaustion, overcome by the snow. What was worse, we were advancing through enemy country, and for that reason our situation was not without danger; and the evil of the snow was equaled by that of the enemy.

FRAGMENT 2

[Leo Diaconus, pp. 256D-258B, Paris ed., = pp. 500-502, Bonn]

To begin with, we decided then to fight the barbarians; or, rather, truth to tell, we retreated, fearing that they may destroy us first, and resolved to oppose them ⟨defensively⟩ according to our possibilities, as they pillaged and destroyed everyone indiscriminately and most brutally, showing their animal impetus against everyone. For they did not spare even the closest ⟨of kin⟩ (? οἰκειοτάτων), nor were they guided by any thought or principle of justice in their slaughter; but they applied themselves to turning their own country into a "Mysian Wasteland," as the saying has it. For their former sense of equity and justice had turned upside down; and yet it was the observance of these very qualities which in the past led them to great victories, and made whole cities and peoples submit to them voluntarily. Now, however, the opposite, as it were, ⟨occurred⟩: they acted toward their subjects with injustice which was beyond all measure. Instead of taking care of the subject cities and administering them justly and to their advantage, they decided to enslave and destroy them. The subject populations complained against their rulers (? σχετλιάζοντες κατὰ τῶν ἡγεμόνων), and clearly proved that they had committed no transgression; nevertheless, they were not able to escape death. For it seemed that an evil impulse (? φορά) came about in such a fashion as to engulf the affairs of these people and confound them most dreadfully, as if a most unusual and dire accident ⟨had happened⟩ or a gulf ⟨had opened under them⟩. Indeed, more than ten cities were made empty of inhabitants, and not less than five hundred villages were utterly laid waste. In short, areas neighboring and lying close to us turned out to be devastated as if by a storm, and innocent ⟨126⟩ people, protected by oaths (? προβληθέντες ἐπ' ὀμωσία), fell victim to sword-holding hands.

Such a calamity, which had destroyed everyone and befell our unhappy neighbors, ill fortune did finally bring to the area under my own rule as well; I had suspected ⟨its coming⟩, and had taken great care that it should not befall us unexpectedly and cause us harm by its surreptitious and sudden ⟨arrival⟩. When the danger did clearly come, and when it was patently recognized by all that our very lives were at stake, I was able to repulse the calamity on that particular occasion, using as much judgment as I could, even if I exposed myself to well-nigh mortal dangers. From then on we waged an all-out (ἀκηρυκτί) war with the barbarians, during which they held no commerce with us (although I offered them truce on numerous occasions); rather, all our encounters resulted in armed clashes. And the war started at the very approach of winter; for the sun was no ⟨longer⟩ far from.... The barbarians, having mustered considerable forces, invaded our territory both with cavalry and with foot soldiers, convinced that they would take us over (? παραλήψεσθαι ἡμᾶς) at the very first war cry, on account both of the weakness of the wall and of our own cowardice. This was not an unreasonable expectation on their part, since we were dwelling in a town razed to the ground and making our sallies (προσβολάς) as if from a village rather than from a town. For prior to this event the land had been laid waste and made into a desert by the barbarians, who tore the walls down to their very foundations, and I was the first to have thought of inhabiting (providing with settlers?) Klimata. Accordingly, as the first task I had a keep built near the town from the available material, ⟨considering⟩ that from there (ἐκ τούτου; afterwards?) it would be easy to settle the remaining part of the town.

Fragment 3

[Leo Diaconus, pp. 258B-259A, Paris ed., = pp. 503-504, Bonn]

And the keep had been very speedily rebuilt and girded with a moat; and at the same time as this...the war began. ⟨Our⟩ keep was divided into sections according to clans (κατὰ συγγενείας), and they deposited their necessaries there; what was not indispensable was stored outside, in the remaining area (περίβολον; within the circuit wall?) of the town. For by then the whole town was inhabited, and the keep had been readied to save us in supreme danger. And the barbarians, having suffered heavy losses and having been put to shame, retreated with the approach of night, waiting for the dawn (? φυλάξαντες τὸ περίορθρον). As for me, I led out my troops at sunrise, spoiling for the fight (πολεμησείων). At that time, I had slightly over a hundred horse at my disposal, and over three hundred slingers and archers. As the barbarians were nowhere to be seen, I attended to things appropriate for the occasion: I had the old walls reerected and drilled my troops in preparing themselves for battle. And I was sending couriers to allies (? πρὸς τοὺς ἡμῖν προσέχοντας) and summoning them to me in ⟨127⟩ order to hold council (?) about the general situation. They arrived from every direction, and a council (ἐκκλησία) of notables was held. It would take too much space if I wanted to recount in detailed sequence what I said on that occasion: which rulers they should adhere to, to which ⟨rulers⟩ they should flock and which advantage they should attempt to obtain from them, and what should be done, and all the other things which I said at that time and which I value exceedingly highly. But they, either because they had never ⟨before⟩ enjoyed imperial benevolence and were not attached to the more refined Hellenic way of life (Ἑλληνικῶν τρόπων), but rather were accustomed to a way of life of their own, or because they were neighbors of the emperor (βασιλεύοντα) who ruled to the north of the Danube, and who (?) had large troops at his disposal and boasted military power, and because they did not differ in their own customs from those of those people, decided to conclude with them (ἐκείνων; read ἐκείνῳ?) a treaty of submission, and unanimously voted that I do the same. And I set out so that our cause be not lost, and was received by him in the most propitious circumstances imaginable. I expounded the whole case to him in terms as succinct as possible; he viewed the matter as being of utmost importance and, right away and very readily, he invested me with the full rule over Klimata, and added a whole satrapy (σατραπείαν ὅλην) to boot; moreover, he granted me considerable yearly income from his own territory.

II

If we disregard a free Russian translation of the Fragments which appeared in 1820,[4] a mere mention of them as noteworthy made in 1846,[5] and a page or two, teeming with inexactitudes, devoted to them in 1848 and 1855,[6] our text remained unexploited until 1862, when the renowned anti-Normanist Gedeonov treated it in the fifth section of his *Studies on the Varangian Question* and assigned it to the time of Prince Svjatoslav (d. 972 or 973).[7] Since Gedeonov's study, the Hase Fragments have given rise to a considerable volume of scholarly literature, an astonishing fact in view of the brevity of the Greek text, which amounts to slightly less than five in-folio columns of the Paris edition, or to four full pages of the Bonn Corpus. This volume of literature is easier to explain, however, if one considers the rarity of narrative sources pertaining to Russia's earliest history, ⟨128⟩ the passion all historians have for the study of origins, and the tantalizing promises held out by the Fragments themselves. They allude to a mysterious ruler; they speak of two (or three?) kinds of no less mysterious barbarians; they contain astronomical indications, and refer to certain place names, unfortunately

4. D. P. Popov, *Istorija L'va D'jakona Kalojskogo i drugie sočinenija vizantijskix pisatelej* (St. Petersburg, 1820), esp. 192-97. Popov's book, which I was able to inspect in the Lenin Library, is a straight translation of Hase's preface, edition, and (abbreviated) notes, made at the suggestion, and with the financial help, of Count Rumjancev; cf. e.g. the Count's letter to Academician Krug of December 15, 1819, Lenin Library, *Otd. rukopisej,* folder R.A. 6.4, letter no. 65.

5. A. Starčevskij, "O zaslugax Rumjanceva okazannyx otečestvennoj istorii," *Žurnal Ministerstva Narodnogo Prosveščenija,* 49 (1846), pt. V, 33-34.

6. V. V. Këne [= B. V. von Köhne], *Izsledovanija ob istorii i drevnostjax goroda Xersonisa Tavričeskogo* (1848), 220-22 (time: before Vladimir, during the wars waged by John Tzimisces with the Saracens). It was A.A. Kunik who drew von Köhne's attention to the Fragments in 1846. E. Muralt, *Essai de chronographie byzantine,* I (1885), 569, identified the narrator with the governor of Kherson and dated the Fragments to 988.

7. S. Gedeonov, "Otryvki iz izsledovanij o varjažskom voprose," I-XII, *Zapiski Imp. Akademii Nauk*, 1 (1862), Appendix no. 3, Sec. V, 66-70.

few in number, that either are known from other sources, even if it is difficult to localize them, or are quite unknown.

Thus, in the course of the last one hundred and ten years the most prominent practitioners of Russian history and Byzantinology have tried their hand at unlocking the Fragments' secret. In the past fifty years, not only several Russian scholars, but also their Rumanian, Bulgarian, and Greek colleagues have devoted studies to Hase's discovery;[8] and few, if any, shared the philosophical resignation of the Ukrainian historian Hruševs'kyj, who declared in 1913 that he would "dwell upon the Fragments no more," in view of their "utter obscurity."[9]

Of obscurity, the Fragments offer a great deal. To begin with, it enwraps the identity of the narrator: as late as 1871 he was still called *Anonymus*. His anonymity was not complete, since the epithet *Tauricus*, given him by Academician Kunik, connected him with the Crimea; but in 1874 Kunik went a step further, declaring the *Anonymus* to have been a Byzantine official of Greek, if local, origin, and christened him *Toparcha Gothicus*.[10] Under this name, or that of the Greek Toparch, he has been known in learned literature ever since, for nobody seems to have taken seriously Uspenskij's intimation that the narrator was none other than the patrician Petronas, of the Emperor Theophilus' time.[11] The title toparch, however, remains arbitrary, as it does not occur in the Fragments themselves. Moreover, Kunik's solution was contradictory, since no Byzantine official, let alone a Byzantine Greek, was likely to have been called a toparch.[12] The difficulty was sidestepped by those

8. Modern literature dealing with the Fragments of *Toparcha Gothicus* is given in Appendix I *infra*, where individual titles are quoted in full. In subsequent footnotes, all titles listed in that Appendix appear in abbreviated form.

9. Hruševs'kyj, *Istorija...* (as in Appendix I [b]), 464 note.

10. A.A. Kunik, "O zapiske bezymjannogo tavričeskogo (Anonymus Tauricus)," *Otčet o četyrnadcatom prisuždenii nagrad grafa Uvarova 25 sent. 1871 g.* (1872), 106-10. For Kunik's work of 1874, cf. Appendix I (a).

11. Uspenskij, "Vizantijskie..." (as in Appendix I [a]), 3-12, 28, 41.Uspenskij was aware that his hypothesis involved a drastic redating of the construction of the Khazar fortress of Sarkel on the Don by Petronas: instead of 838, this fortress would have been built in 903, the time to which Uspenskij assigned the Fragments. For a sharp and witty rebuttal of Uspenskij, cf. V. Vasil'evskij, "O postroenii kreposti Sarkela," *Žurnal Ministerstva Narodnogo Prosveščenija,* 265 (October, 1889), 273-89; pp. 282-85 are devoted to our Fragments.

12. Seen by Nystazopoulou, "Note..." (as in Appendix I [c]), 321-25. The only exception to Miss M.G. Nystazopoulou's rule appears to be Ἐπιδημία Μάζαρι (fifteenth century), which uses τοπάρχαι in the sense of "local Byzantine gover-

who considered the narrator to have been not a Greek but a Goth writing in Greek, especially since toparchs "of Gothia" in the Crimea are attested in the ninth century. This, again, corresponded to Hase's own interpretation, and tied our Gothic official to the Crimea.[13]

⟨129⟩ Unfortunately, the scene of the events is another of the Fragments' obscure points. To be sure, the events took place somewhere between the Dnieper, which the narrator crossed (but where was Borion, the otherwise unknown crossing point? at the rapids or below them? if at the rapids, why did the narrator choose such a difficult spot for the crossing? and from which bank to which was the crossing made?), and the Danube, to the north of which was the residence of the ruler whom he visited. But, if it was the Crimea, as suggested by the occurrence of the word Klimata in the Fragments (but were these Klimata a town or a region? and were they in fact the Crimean Klimata? might they not have been identical with Sarkel, built by Petronas for the Khazars about 838? or with *Klima Mestikon* in Thrace?), why did the narrator's party return to Maurokastron, which, as far as anybody knew for sure, was situated at the mouth of the Dniester? Consequently, the action of the Fragments has also been variously set on the Don, on the right bank of the Dniester in Bessarabia, in northern or southeastern Bulgaria, somewhere on the Danube (Paristrion?), or, south of that river, in northern Dobrudja.

The barbarians who appear in the Fragments present insoluble puzzles as well. Barbarians of one kind attacked the narrator's territory; barbarians of another kind were asked to assume a protectorate over his subjects. The attacking barbarians had treated kindly the populations under their control in the past, but turned against them at the time of the action described in the Fragments. The protecting barbarians were powerful and differed little in customs from the narrator's own subjects or allies. Were the attacking barbarians Huns, Khazars, Pečenegs, Hungarians, Black Bulgarians, Bulgarians, or Russes? And if Russes, then which: Normans, the controversial Azov Russes, or some Slavic autochtones, such as the Uličians? Were the protecting barbarians Khazars, Russes, Bulgarians or Pečenegs? Or was there only one kind of barbarians instead of two? Were the narrator's own subject Goths, Bulgarians, Pečenegs, or Byzantines? Each of these possibilities has been

---

nors in the Peloponnesus," cf. e.g. J.Fr. Boissonade, *Anecdota Graeca,* 3 (Paris, 1831), 178, 181. *Mazaris,* however, was just trying to impress the reader with a Lucianesque equivalent of ἄρχοντες τόπων.

13. A.A. Vasiliev (as in Appendix I [b], 105-106; 123-24, with sources.

proposed and in turn rejected, and scholarly energies for a time were diverted by the struggle between the Normanists and the anti-Normanists: what to several nineteenth-century Normanists was a protectorate by Scandinavian Russes over their ethnic relatives, the Goths, was to one twentieth-century anti-Normanist a protectorate by Russian Slavs over their ethnic relatives, the Bulgarians.

The powerful and generous ruler whose empire extended to the north of the Danube has been assumed to have been of the same stock as the protecting barbarians. But of which stock? Most scholars saw him as a prince of Rus', though even here dissenting votes were cast in favor of making him the Bulgarian Tsar Simeon, a Bulgaro-Slavic princeling, a Pečeneg chieftain, even the Byzantine emperor himself. If the ruler was a prince of Rus', which one was he? To some, he was Oleg of the ninth and tenth centuries; to others, Igor, Svjatoslav, or Vladimir (Hase's own candidate) of the tenth; and one Rumanian scholar opted for as late a ruler as Jaroslav the Wise (d. 1054).

The choice of prince clearly depended on the Fragments' date, and here some hope of certitude was held out, since, at the time when the narrator's party ⟨130⟩was caught by the winter storm near the Dnieper, the planet Saturn was in the evening phase at the beginning of Aquarius (but was it the beginning of the sign or of the constellation?). Unfortunately, the hope was vain, since Saturn is in Aquarius about every thirty years — for instance, in the years 903 (time of Oleg), 932 (time of Igor), 962 (time of Svjatoslav), 992 (time of Vladimir and the Bulgarian Tsar Samuel), 1021 and 1051 (time of Jaroslav the Wise and of the Pečeneg uprising in the Balkans) — and none of the astronomical experts summoned to assist historians could change anything in that. The most reliable basis for dating the Fragments was the editor's own remark that they were autograph notes, jotted down — perhaps in the course of the journey — by the narrator himself on (two?) empty folios of a manuscript he owned. In his edition of Leo Diaconus, Hase assigned that manuscript to the late tenth or early eleventh century.[14]

14. Hase's index to Leo is clear on the autograph character of the Fragments, *s.vv. autographus*, Paris ed. p. 285 = p. 571, Bonn; *codex*, 291 = 578; *inediti*, 300 = 591; cf. also Hase's introductory remark to the Fragments, 254B = 496. However, Hase did vacillate on the manuscript's date; cf. his index *s.vv. inediti*, 300 = 591, and introductory remark, 245B = 496 (tenth century); *Chersonesi*, 290 = 576. *Graeci*, 299 = 589; *historiae*, 299 = 590, and marginal remarks, 254C, omitted from the Bonn ed. (eleventh century); *Chersonesi*, 290 = 576, *Ister*, 303 = 594, *Russi*, 318 = 615, and introductory remark to Fragment 2,

Finally, no agreement could be reached on the time sequence of the Fragments. Many scholars accepted Hase's suggestion that the chronological order was Fragments 2, 3, 1; others were satisfied that the sequence in which they appeared in the edition and, according to the editor, on the freestanding folios of the manuscript was also the sequence of the events which they described.

In sum, after more than a century of research on the Fragments, scholars have produced various clusters of solutions. To give two examples, one cluster for place, time, narrator's subjects, attacking barbarians, protecting barbarians, ruler of the north was: Crimea, shortly before 965, Goths, Khazars, Norman Russes, Svjatoslav;[15] while another was the Danube region, 993, pro-Byzantine Bulgarians, anti-Byzantine Bulgarians, Russes, Vladimir.[16] The only consensus which has been reached in the last hundred and fifty years as to the meaning of the narrator's story is that the Fragments are mysterious, enigmatic, obscure, and controversial.

In the face of such disarray, little profit can be expected from discussing the literature of the subject any longer;[17] instead I shall follow the advice recently proffered by a distinguished Soviet scholar who advocates the discovery of some new evidence, for it alone, she rightly believes, can assist us in settling the dispute which has lasted for such a long time.[18] The evidence I ⟨131⟩ intend to submit here has to do with one manuscript of the Fragments published by Charles-Benoît Hase, with his correspondence and with his secret diary.

2651 = 500, marginal remark, 257C, omitted from the Bonn ed. (tenth or eleventh century).

15. Kunik, "O zapiske..." (as in Appendix I [a]), 61, 64, 90, 124.

16. Levčenko, "K voprosu..." (as in Appendix I [a]), 313, 325, 332-34.

17. The divergent views summarized above have been distilled from works quoted, directly or indirectly, in Appendix I.

18. Z.V. Udal'cova, *Sovetskoe...* (as in Appendix I [c]), 118. Already in 1899, Vasil'evskij confessed in a letter to Westberg: "From time to time I come upon the idea that it would not be a bad thing if one investigated the papers which Hase left after his death, and which are preserved in the Bibliothèque Nationale," cf. Westberg, "Zapiska..." (as in Appendix I), 78. Had Vasil'evskij's suggestion been followed right away, the dispute concerning the Fragments might well have been settled by now.

III

From the very beginning, scholarly study of the Fragments was handicapped by a piece of bad luck: when Hase published his notes to Leo Diaconus, he had to report that the manuscript in which the Fragments were originally discovered was no longer in the Bibliothèque Royale; they were found, he said, *in...codice qui fuit Bibliothecae Regiae*. Scholars wondered little about this, for it was general knowledge that between the years 1797 and 1815 hundreds of Greek manuscripts arrived in Paris and were subsequently returned to Italy and other parts of Europe, such as Vienna and Munich. The conclusion they most often drew from Hase's information was that he had copied the Fragments sometime before 1815. The fact remained, however, that the particular manuscript which contained the Fragments never turned up. Attempts, reported by Kunik, to discover its fate by writing to the Paris library were of no avail; neither was the search undertaken later by Krumbacher.[19]

When I set out to find the missing manuscript some years ago, I gave myself a fair chance of success. For one thing, Hase made a number of hints about the source of the Fragments: it was a manuscript containing the letters of St. Basil, St. Gregory of Nazianzus, and Phalaris; it dated from the tenth or eleventh century; it was of small format. This considerably limited the number of manuscripts to be examined. Secondly, manuscripts Paris *Supplément Grec* 898-900 contain lists in Hase's own handwriting of those authors whose works were contained in manuscripts that had entered the Paris library for a time and had been returned by 1815. From those manuscripts one had only to select collections of the letters of Basil, Gregory, and Phalaris. The sample thus obtained would exclude manuscripts from countries never conquered by Napoleon, thereby limiting the possibilities even further. Thirdly, there had to be in Paris a master list of manuscripts returned after 1815 to various European libraries. Finally, several specialized manuscript catalogues not available in Kunik's, Vasil'evskij's, Westberg's, or Krumbacher's day did exist by the 1960's; such were, in particular, the recent studies of the manuscript tradition of the correspondence of Basil the

19. Kunik, "O zapiske..." (as in Appendix I [a]), 66; Krumbacher, *Byzantinische Zeitschrift*, 10 (1901), 657. In a letter written to Westberg in 1898, Krumbacher stated that he believed the search for the lost manuscript of the Fragments to be more important than the study of the source itself, cf. Westberg, *Die Fragmente...* (as in Appendix I), 13.

Great and Gregory of Nazianzus.[20] If extant, the manuscript containing the Fragments would be listed in these studies.

It turned out that I overestimated my chances. The lists of Paris *Supplément Grec* 898-900 did yield three manuscripts — *Palatinus Graecus* 356 (Heidelberg), ⟨132⟩ *Palatinus Graecus* 129 (Heidelberg), and *Vaticanus Graecus* 1353 — containing letters of Basil, Gregory, and Phalaris. But of these only one, *Palatinus Graecus* 356, included all three authors, and it did not meet Hase's other specifications for the source of his Fragments, since in his own estimation, it dated from the fourteenth century and was not of small format.[21] The master list (in two volumes) of manuscripts returned from Paris after 1815 was located in the Bibliothèque Nationale, but all that remained of these volumes was their excellent Louis Philippe bindings; everything between the covers had disappeared.[22] Thus, I was reduced to drawing up a list of my own, mostly on the basis of Paul Gallay's inventory of the manuscripts of Gregory of Nazianzus.[23] It contained twenty-four "suspects," from the Escorial, Florence, London, Madrid, Milan, Modena, Munich, Paris,

20. Cf. especially Anders Cavallin, *Studien zu den Briefen des Hl. Basilius* (Lund, 1944) and two works by Paul Gallay: "Liste des manuscrits des lettres de Saint Grégoire de Nazianze," *Revue des études grecques*, 57 (1944), 106-24; and *Les manuscrits des lettres de Saint Grégoire de Nazianze* (Paris, 1957), esp. 15 note 1.

21. Combine Paris *Supplément Grec* 898, card 73^{r}, and Paris *Suppl. Gr.* 899, card 363^{r}, for *Vaticanus Graecus* 1353: Paris *Suppl. Gr.* 898, cards 73^{r} and 164^{r}, for *Palatinus Graecus* 129 (this is the famous miscellaneous, mistakenly called the "Planudean excerpts", cf. my article, "Some Autographs of Nicephorus Gregoras," *Zbornik Radova Vizantološkog Instituta SAN*, 8,2 [1964], esp. 447-50); Paris *Suppl. Gr.* 898, cards 75^{r} and 164^{v} and *Suppl. Gr.* 899, card 363^{r}, for *Palatinus Gr.* 356. In Paris *Suppl. Gr.* 898, cards 222^{r-v} 223^{r} and Paris and *Suppl. Gr.* 900, card 532^{r}. Hase noted that *Palatinus Gr.* 129 contains excerpts from Isocrates and Themistius. Hase made detailed descriptions of *Vaticanus Gr.* 1353 and the two *Palatini* in Paris *Suppl. Gr.* 811, fols. 1^{r}-22^{r}, 151^{r}-52^{v} and 206^{r}-28^{r}, respectively. On fol. 228^{r} he described *Palatinus Gr.* 356 as *codex... saec. XIV compilatus*. On fol. 206^{r} Hase gives the manuscript's size as *in folio parvo* which is still large when compared with "*in* 4." or "*in* 8."— terms which he used when indicating the size of other manuscripts described in Paris *Suppl. Gr.* 811. In fact, *Palatinus Gr.* 356 measures approximately 26 by 18 centimeters.

22. I saw the bindings on July 11, 1960, and remember the astonishment of Mademoiselle Marie-Louise Concasty, the keeper of Greek manuscripts at the Bibliothèque Nationale, who brought them to me herself. In 1970 even the bindings could no longer be located.

23. See note 20 *supra*.

Rome, Strasbourg, Venice, and Vienna.[24] Except for the Madrid manuscript, at present kept in Salamanca, all of them were inspected, either in the original or on microfilm, and the result was negative.

The possibility still remains — although I judge it to be a remote one — that the culprit has eluded the scholars' search and is lurking on the shelf of some library. Another possibility is simply that the manuscript has been destroyed. A distinguished expert on Hase expressed the view that Hase might have sent ⟨133⟩ it by ship, together with more than one hundred copies of his Leo edition, to his patron Count Rumjancev, residing in St. Petersburg. We know — or are told — that this ship, the frigate "le Mercure," sank with its whole cargo, which, incidentally, would account for the fact that the Paris edition of Leo is now a bibliographical rarity; the manuscript of the Fragments could have met with the same fate.[25]

24. *Scorialensis* Ψ-II-12 (12th c.); *Laurentiani Conventi Soppressi* 177 (11th c.), 627 (13th c.); *Laurentiani* IV, 14 (10th c.), LVII,7 (11th c.), LXXXVII,16 (13th c.); *Matritensis, Biblioteca del Palacio Real*, 43 (olim 7) (11th c.); *Ambrosianus Gr.* H 257 inf. (=1041 Martini-Bassi) (13th c.); *Mutinensis Gr.* III H 1 (=229 Puntoni) (11th c.); *Monacensis Gr.* 497 (11th-12th c.); *Parisini Gr.* 506 (10th c.), 3014 (13th c.); Paris *Coislin* 237 (11th c.); Paris *Suppl. Gr.* 763 (11th c.), 1020 (11th c.); *Angelicanus* C-4-14 (*Passioneus*) (11th c.); *Vaticani Gr.* 424 (13th c.), 434 (13th c.), 485 (13th c.), 712 (13th c.) 2209 (10th-11th c.); *Argentoratensis Gr. 21* (12th-14th c.); *Marcianus Gr.* LXXIX (12th c.); *Vindobonensis Theol. Gr.* CXLII (11th c.). In addition, I inspected *British Museum Additionals* 32643 (13th-14th c.) and 36749 (10th c.), and, of course, *Vaticanus Gr.* 1353 and the *Palatini Gr.* 129 and 356; cf. note 21 *supra*. My original net was purposefully cast too wide and it included the Escorial and Madrid, not documented among the following places of origin of foreign manuscripts which arrived in Paris between 1796 and 1809: Belgium, the *Ambrosiana*, Modena, Bologna, Monza, Verona, Venice, the *Vaticana*, parts of Pope Pius VI's private library, the *Laurentiana*, libraries of Piedmont, Turin, Munich, Salzburg, Potsdam, the Gymnasium of Elbing, Wolfenbüttel, and Vienna; cf. V.L. Delisle, *Le cabinet des manuscrits de la Bibliothèque Nationale*, II (1874), 33-34. The Turin library was severely damaged by fire in 1904; however, no manuscript destroyed on that occasion corresponded to Hase's specifications; cf. Fr. Cosentini in G. Mazzantini, A. Sorbelli, and L. Ferrari, *Inventari dei manoscritti delle biblioteche d'Italia*, 28 (1922, reprinted 1952), 13-45. Finally, there remains France itself, outside of Paris. Strasbourg yielded one suspect, acquired in 1910; there is no full list of Strasbourg manuscripts which burned in the fire of 1870. But could not Hase's manuscript have belonged to a monastery in the vicinity of Paris? If it did — and was not lost after 1815 — it should have been on the lists by Cavallin and Gallay.

25. The total edition of Leo was four hundred copies. On the one hundred and

According to prevailing opinion, these no longer extant Fragments were either an autograph draft of a report or autograph pages from a private diary.[26] Such texts are not intended for publication as literature. Thus, at first sight there was no chance of finding another copy of the Fragments in some extant Greek manuscript. Clearly, the next best thing to inspecting the missing manuscript was to examine its closest relative, the *apographon* which Hase made of the Fragments. It survives in Paris *Supplément Grec* 858, the printer's copy of the Leo Diaconus edition, and is, in fact, written in Hase's own hand.

IV

At present, the text of Hase's Fragments, his translation, and his explanations appear on folios 315^r and 347^r-351^r of the printer's copy.[27] Folio 315^r (fig.1) is taken up entirely by Hase's prefatory remark describing the manuscript from which he copied the Fragments; this remark gives two scanty references to the first two Fragments, surmises that the narrator was the manuscript's owner, and announces the first Fragment. Folios 347^r-351^r contain the rest. These latter folios, which include all of the Greek text, seem to have been sent to the printer later than the prefatory remark on the Fragments and the notes of the remaining parts

twenty-five (or one hundred and fifty) copies originally sent out to Russia and on the shipwreck, cf., e.g., Hase to Böttiger, letter of March 10, 1820, in Hase, *Unsre Hauschronik...* (as in note 2 *supra*), 105; cf. also letter of November 18, 1819 by Count Rumjancev to the (later) Kievan Metropolitan Evgenij (Bolxovitinov), in *Perepiska mitropolita Kievskogo Evgenija s... grafom...Rumjancevym...*, I (Voronež, 1868), 23. Subsequently, Rumjancev received fifty copies of Leo, cf. Rumjancev to Evgenij, letter of August 17,1820, *ibid.*, 34. The Lenin Library's Rumjancev Archive still possesses five copies of that second shipment, of which I was shown four. — The supposition that Hase may have sent the manuscript containing the Fragments to Rumjancev on the ill-fated ship was made independently by the late Michael Lascaris and Dr. Arnulf Kollautz, a student of Hase's correspondence; cf. Nystazopoulou, "Note..." (as in Appendix I [c]), 320; and Dr. Kollautz in personal letters of May 12, 1960, and March 16, 1971. If Hase did send his patron a manuscript which was on deposit at the Paris library, he was guilty of irregular procedure.

26. Cf., e.g., Westberg, "Zapiska..." (as in Appendix I), 257-58.

27. For the text of the Fragments in the printer's copy, cf. figs. 1, 3-11. The reader will be able to follow the statements of Section IV by comparing these figures with the facsimile of the Paris edition reproduced on pp. 118-123 *supra*.

of Leo Diaconus, because folio 315^r — that of the prefatory remark — was originally numbered 218, while folio 352^r, the first one after the Fragments, bears the crossed-out number 219, has a message to the printer — "voici le reste des notes sur Léon..." — and begins with the note which in Leo's printed text immediately follows the Fragments.

When we compare the handwritten with the printed version of Hase's prefatory remark, we realize that he was more hesitant as to the characteristics of the ⟨134⟩ original manuscript than the printed edition reveals: concerning the manuscript's date, he first wrote that it was *saec. XI*, then changed it to *X exeuntis* — no doubt a routine perplexity familiar to all paleographers. Hase also hesitated about the contents of the manuscript: he wrote *S. Basilii, Phalaridis, S. Gregorii Nazianzeni epistulas varias*, and this is all we read in the printed text; in the printer's copy, however, he continued with *Isocratisque et Themistii orationes aliquot*, but crossed it out, probably desirous of not overburdening the reader with superfluous detail. More interestingly, he was not sure about the size of the manuscript: at first he wrote *ut est medi* (intending *mediae*), but then crossed out *medi* and substituted *exiguae molis*, which stands in the printed version. Finally, Hase was not quite sure as to the time when the manuscript was last in the Royal Library: he first wrote *fuit olim* (which means not only "once upon a time," but also "long ago," and is the opposite of *nuper*, "recently") *Bibliothecae Regiae*, but then crossed out *olim*, and this shortened formulation is what we read in the printed text. The last two vacillations can hardly be lapses of memory, but perhaps Hase dealt with border cases — the manuscript could have been of small to middle size or bulk and could have been in the library as many as three years before 1818, which was neither *olim* nor *nuper*.

When it comes to Hase's views on the substance of the Fragments, it is now the printed text which reveals more hesitation than his original remarks in the printer's copy. In these remarks, Hase showed a more detailed conception of the Fragments' setting: they were clearly to be dated to the time of Vladimir the Great and the narrator was a Greek. The decision as to whether the attacking barbarians[28] were in fact Russes Hase left up to Academician Philip Krug, the prominent expert in early East European history and, incidentally, the intermediary between Hase and his patron Count Rumjancev. Still, in introducing the second Frag-

28. Hase must have meant the attacking barbarians in his introduction to the second Fragment in the printer's copy, for he wrote on fol. 348v: *Gens, quacum dux ille, quisquis est, consociationem dissolvisse scribit*.

ment Hase wondered why neither Vladimir nor, generally speaking, (another) "Russian king" was mentioned in the Fragments (but what of the third Fragment's ruler?), and thus implied that the Russian hypothesis was not the only one to be considered. There were indications that the barbarians may have been Pečenegs, but this, too, presented difficulties, for it was hardly possible that a Greek should have praised their equity and justice. Of all this, there is almost no trace in the printed text: in the prefatory remark, *Graecus* was replaced by the neutral *possessor*; in the introduction to the second Fragment, the innocuous phrase "may learned men, combining knowledge of those times and places with prudent judgment, consider who these people [i.e., the barbarians] may be," replaced mention of Vladimir, Russians, Pečenegs, the Greek narrator and Academician Krug in the printer's copy.[29]

⟨135⟩ In thus hesitating to commit his own interpretation of the Fragments to print, Hase exercised a scholar's prudent judgment. There were, however, two more occasions on which Hase hesitated, and Paris *Supplément Grec* 858 suggests that prudence may have deserted him on both of them.

The first occasion has to do with the number of Fragments. At the beginning of the prefatory remark on folio 315^{r} (fig. 1), Hase first wrote *pertinet ... commentarii fragmentum*, then changed *-et* to *-ent*, *- um* to *-a*, and continued with *duo*, to which he added *luce dignissima* above the line. Further on in the same remark, he wrote *dabo haec duo fragmenta*,

29. Compare the introduction to the second Fragment, p. 256D with Paris *Suppl. Gr.* 858, fol. 348v (fig. 6). In transcribing two sections eliminated from the final draft of the printer's copy, I use italics; I indicate with Roman type Hase's own deletions within the passages, and I place his insertions between slashes — ∖ ∕. Concerning the nationality of the barbarians (in the printer's copy they are the attacking barbarians; in the printed edition, they are the protecting barbarians), Hase originally wrote: ∖*qui sint*∕ an sint Russi, *illi*; Hase's major deletion, comprising four lines of the printer's copy, can be deciphered as follows: ∖*eorumque in primis*∕ inter quos *Philipp*um ∖*s*∕ *Kru*gum primario loco esse puto; *miror tamen* ∖*nec*∕ nec *Vladimirum Magnum, ad cuius tempora epistolam* ∖*facile referas*∕ referri possit, *neque omnino alium Russorum regem verbo commemorari*: Ad Patzinacos autem *Gentem* illam *septentrionem versus ab Istro habitare suadent quae* ∖*leguntur*∕ continuo post in ora No[a] [that is, in note "a" in the lower left margin of fol. 348v, which runs as follows: [a]hic *scrip*ta ∖*um*∕ erant ∖*est hic et*∕ *posterius inductum*: Καὶ διὰ τοῦτο γὰρ καὶ βόρεια τοῦ Ἴστρου. Remarkably enough, Hase makes no reference to the occurrence of the same phrase in the main text of the *third* Fragment] *ea*que *in Patzinacos cadere possunt, quorum tamen miram* [?] *aequitatem et iustitiam unquam laudari* ∖*a Graeco*∕ *potuisse, ut fit....*

which he changed into *dabo fragmenta ambo*, and his *ambo*, "both," clearly shows that at that point he had only two Fragments in mind for publication. In both of these places the printed edition has only the words *pertinent ... commentarii fragmenta* and *dabo fragmenta* respectively; thus it leaves the number of Fragments undetermined. Since all censors do nod on occasion, the traces of Hase's original intention were not entirely eliminated from the printed text. Introducing the second Fragment in the printer's copy on folio 348ᵛ (fig. 6), Hase first wrote *fragmentum illud ... sequitur ... aliud*, but changed *illud* to *prius* and *aliud* to *alterum. Prius* and *alterum* were left in the printed edition, although *alterum*, strictly speaking, means "second of a set of two." Moreover, in the printer's copy Hase distributed his two Fragments between two empty folios, one on each folio. This assignment of *folia duo vacua* remains in the printed edition, although the present number of Fragments is three, and the third Fragment is said to have stood *in folio alio* (cf. fig. 9), thus, on a third one, not accounted for in Hase's prefatory remark.[30]

These inconsistencies aside, Paris *Supplément Grec* 858 itself leaves no doubt that the number of Fragments which Hase originally intended to publish — and had originally discovered — was two. Folio 351ʳ (cf. fig. 11) contains Hase's closing remark on the Fragments as a whole (*desinit hic praeclarum illud ... fragmentum*), in which he regrets that the complete work of the narrator has not come down to us, hopes that further researches among unpublished manuscripts contained in "several" (or, after correction, "other") libraries will throw new light on Russian history, and is confident that the liberality of Count Rumjancev will make discoveries possible. However, these spirited closing remarks appear on folio 351ʳ, not under the *third* and final Fragment, but under the final words of the *second* one, πόλιν οἰκισθήσεσθαι, translated by Hase in a parallel column as *⟨ci⟩vitatem instaurari posse*. The third Fragment is an insertion; it is prefaced by the words *sequuntur in folio alio abrupta illa, quae* ⟨136⟩ *superioribus subjungenda esse autumo*, and occurs on the previous folio, 350ʳ-350ᵛ (cf. figs 9 and 10). The top of the recto of that folio contains the following instruction to the printer concerning the third Fragment: "à insérer à la page 258B après les mots *civitatem instaurari posse*." Page 258B is that page of the Paris edition of Leo on which we read the end of the *second* Fragment today; and *civitatem instaurari posse* are, as we just learned, the last words of Hase's Latin ver-

30. Westberg perceived this contradiction, but did not know what to make of it. Cf. "Zapiska..." (as in Appendix I), 258.

sion of that second Fragment. The bottom of folio 350^{v} (i.e., the end of the third Fragment in Paris *Supplément Grec* 858) displays the following message, also for the printer: "Ici suit le texte déjà imprimé," meaning the closing remarks to the Fragments as a whole. This last message, together with the reference to page 258B, unmistakably shows that Hase inserted his third Fragment when the previous two and the closing remark to the whole had already been printed. At that stage in the printing of the notes to Leo, Hase did not know — or had forgotten — that the third Fragment existed.

The reader of the printed text may doubt this conclusion, since in the introduction to the second Fragment, as it stands in the edition of 1819, Hase does not refer to the ⟨*Gens, cui dux...*⟩ *oppidum sibi commissum tradiderit*, and this act of "handing over" to the *protecting* barbarians is in fact described in the third Fragment. Here again, Paris *Supplément Grec* 858, folio 348^{v} (fig. 6), clarifies the matter: the words *oppidum... tradiderit* are a later change made on proofs; the printer's copy does not have them. It says, as we have already seen,[31] *consociationem dissolvisse scribit* instead, and thus merely alludes to the *attacking* barbarians and to the beginning of the *second* Fragment. By the time Hase wrote the introduction to the second Fragment in the printer's copy, he seems not yet to have suspected that his third Fragment would reveal the existence of the protecting barbarians or, for that matter, of the ruler holding sway to the north of the Danube.

Hase, then, must have discovered the third Fragment or found it in his papers at the last moment, when the notes to Leo were already being printed. In order to establish the point at which his find occurred, we must determine when the printing of the notes to Leo took place.

Correspondence between Hase, his former teacher Böttiger, and his patron Count Rumjancev helps to answer this query. The printing of the notes started in all probability *after* April 3, 1816, for Hase's letter to Böttiger written under that dateline stated that Leo Diaconus would now be "really" published. An advance of three thousand francs extended to Hase by Count Rumjancev on the strength of a recommendation by Professor Krug and other support which he would receive from the French Ministry of the Interior would enable him to cover the cost of printing Leo in the Royal Printing House. The whole work, Hase hoped, would appear toward the end of the year. The notes to the work contained many excerpts from "our *inedita*."[32]

31. In note 28 *supra*.

32. I used the full text of Hase's letter to Böttiger, kindly lent to me by Dr. Ar-

⟨137⟩ The notes to Leo were being printed by July 7, 1816. On that day Hase wrote Rumjancev: "on s'occupe maintenant de l'impression des notes, et l'on m'assure qu'avant la fin de l'année tout sera terminé."[33] Thus, the third Fragment was discovered by Hase in the manuscript — or rediscovered by him among his earlier notes — sometime in 1816 at the earliest. However, the same letter suggests with high probability that not only this discovery, but the discovery of the first two Fragments as well occurred *after* July 7, 1816.

Hase's letter is a reply to a message sent by Count Rumjancev to "Mr. Haser [sic] à Paris," of which we possess only a draft. The draft, in the Count's own hand, is undated, but, as Hase answered it "forthwith," it is clear that Rumjancev's clean copy was sent to Paris a month or so before July 1816.[34] The Count, passionately interested in the study of the origins of Russian Christianity and in the location of the city of Surož in the Crimea, appealed for help to the indefatigable student of *inedita*: "...je vous invite très instament Monsieur," he wrote, "à rechercher parmi les manuscripts inédits des auteurs Bisantins [sic] ceux dans lesquels peuvent être consignés quelques faits relatifs à l'Histoire de ma Patrie, ce sera me rendre un service essentiel, et je ne demande pas mieux que de le reconoitre."

---

nulf Kollautz; for an excerpt from it, cf. Kollautz, "Jacob..." (as in note 2 *supra*), 289. — It is difficult to determine when the printing of Leo's *text* began. In his letter to Rumjancev dated February 16, 1815 (Lenin Library, *Otd. rukopisej*, folder Fond 255.18.38), Hase wrote: "L'impression de Léon commence cette semaine." If Rumjancev subscribed to the edition for one thousand rubles, then, Hase announced optimistically, "rien ne s'opposera à ce que l'ouvrage ne soit terminé et mis en vente vers le mois de septembre prochain," i.e., September 1815. In the Preface to Leo (Paris ed., p. VI = p. XVII, Bonn) Hase stated that the printing of Leo as a whole had lasted for two years. Thus, it must have begun in 1816 at the earliest.

33. Hase to Rumjancev, Lenin Library, *Otd. rukopisej*, folder R.A.7.12, letter np. 9, p. 8. Cf. Appendix II B and fig. 22.

34. Draft: Lenin Library, *Otd. rukopisej*, folder Fond 255.5.34, Letter no. 9, dated "[1813 ?]" by the librarians. In the draft, Rumjancev queried Hase on the so-called Anonymus Banduri on the conversion of the Russes (in *Colbertinus* 4432), on Lives of St. Ignatius, on the baptism of Vladimir the Great, on Surož (which he believed to be in the Crimea or on the Taman' peninsula), on the Church of Gothia, and on ecclesiastical lists of the eighth century. In the letter of July 7, 1816, Hase gave information on ecclesiastical lists, on Lives of St. Ignatius, on Anonymus Banduri (*Colbertinus* 4432, "now" no. 3025), and on Surož. The quotation which follows in my text is on p. 1 of Rumjancev's draft. Cf. Appendix II A and fig. 13.

"Reconoitre" meant money, and all biographers of Hase dwell on his weakness for gold. Yet, in his reply Hase had to disappoint the Count. He did submit to him a short memorandum about Surož, based on Le Quien and Banduri, among other authorities, in which he identified that city with Sarat and Sudak, both of which he located in the Crimea; otherwise he had only to say: "Reduit par conséquent aux auteurs Grecs je m'estimerois heureux toutes les fois quand dans ceux- ci et dans le nombre de notes historiques et géographiques que j'ai recueillies en examinant les ouvrages inédits de notre Bibliothèque, il se trouvera quelques détails qui peuvent aider les recherches de V.E.

"Je n'ai point voulu retarder l'envoi de ma petite dissertation [This is the memorandum on Surož contained in the first part of the letter], mais j'espère que dans une quinzaine de jours je pourrois vous faire parvenir la totalité des épreuves de Léon, dont le tirage est achevé [There follows the sentence, already quoted, announcing that the notes to Leo were still being printed.]. Il me tarde de faire connaître à l'Europe savante combien je suis pénétré des sentiments de ⟨138⟩ reconnaissance et de respect avec lesquels j'ai l'honneur d'être Monseigneur de votre Excellence le très humble et très obéissant serviteur C. B. Hase."[35]

Unless Hase was withholding his discovery of the Fragments or had forgotten it, by July 7, 1816, he possessed no knowledge of any details contained either in an unpublished manuscript or in historical and geographical notes which he had previously collected that were related to any facts concerning the history of Russia.[36] From this letter we may conclude at least two things: first, that by July 7, 1816, Hase was actively engaged in historical researches on the Crimea and used Banduri and Le Quien,[37] second, and most important, that by July 7, 1816, Hase was

35. Hase to Rumjancev, 7-8. Cf. Appendix II B and figs. 21-22.

36. Beyond, that is, information furnished about Surož by the otherwise unknown writer "Maxime Catélianus," of Hase's memorandum, cf. pp. 170-71 *infra*.

37. Hase continued to work for the Count on the localization of Surož and the geography of the Crimea well into the year 1817: Rumjancev to Krug, letter of September 10, 1817 (Lenin Library, *Otd. rukopisej*, folder R.A.6.2, no. 25): "... je ne puis pas vous dire assez l'extreme satisfaction que m'a fait eprouver la très belle lettre de M. Hase et ses annexes... la petite carte de la Crimée est très curieuse, elle me fait perdre mon procès Monsieur et vous fait gagner le votre en determinant si bien la place de Soldaia... je voudrai [sic] bien que toute la carte fut gravée, veuillez en écrire à M. Hase." Hase's map may have been the result of Krug's inquiry: cf. Krug to Hase (?), letter of January 14, 1817 (Lenin

still unaware of the Fragments, Consequently, he promised only that he would be happy to communicate any text of this kind to the Count if he were to find one like it someday.

By a stroke of luck, Hase did subsequently find our Fragments, and the find occurred in two stages: he sent two Fragments to the printer first — this he did after June 10, 1817[38] — and was later able to insert the third into the proofs of the notes to Leo. Hase's closing remarks, put in the printed edition at the end of the last Fragment but written before its discovery, praised Rumjancev's efforts to enrich *historiam patriae*; just possibly, this was an echo of that part of the Count's letter in which he mentioned "l'Histoire de ma Patrie." Hase's stroke of luck, postdating July 1816, perhaps even June 1817, occurred either before May 1818, since on May 1, 1818, Rumjancev announced to Academician Krug his wishes concerning the distribution of copies of Leo "as soon as Mr. Hase will have sent them to me," or at least before October 10, 1818, when Rumjancev could pass the following good news to Krug: "je viens de recevoir je ne scais par qui un seul examplaire [sic] de Léon le Diacre auquel il manque sa préface. Mr. Haser [sic] me mande que... il n'obtiendra des presses l'ouvrage complet qu'à la fin de l'année."[39]

Here we have a serious puzzlement. By Hase's own statement, repeated twice in his Preface, the manuscripts appropriated during the Revolutionary and Napoleonic Wars left, or were about to leave, the Paris library in 1815; and we know from elsewhere that the earliest restitution of manuscripts appropriated during the Revolution and the Empire (the ones from Vienna) occurred on ⟨139⟩ September 21, 1814, and the latest (the ones from Bologna and the Vatican) on October 23, 1815.[40] Consequently, the manuscript in which Hase discovered the

Library, *Otd. rukopisej*, folder R.A.8.19, no. 9), concerning the geographical treatise by "the monk Bacon," and various place names, e.g., *Castella Gothorum* near Kherson. Cf. also note 165 *infra*.

38. Cf. Hase's note to the printer in Paris *Suppl. Gr.* 858, fol. 249r: "J'enverrai la suite après-demain, Jeudi. Ce mardi 10 Juin." Tuesday, June 10 gives the year 1817. Fol. 249r contained the commentary to Leo, p. 71D. The Fragments form the commentary to p. 108C.

39. Lenin Library, *Otd. rukopisej*, folders R.A.6.3., no. 46 and R.A.6.4., no. 61. However, Leo was late in arriving and this caused the Count a great deal of distress; cf. the complaints by Rumjancev to Krug, letters of July 16 and August 2, 1818, quoted in part in note 166 *infra*.

40. Hase's Preface: Paris ed., pp. XII and XVII = pp. XXIV and XXVII-XXVIII, Bonn; for precise dates, cf. Delisle, *Le cabinet...* (as in note 24 *supra*), 35-36.

Fragments was in all probability no longer there after July 1816. How could Hase have copied the Fragments from an original which had already been removed? Of course the manuscript could have remained in Paris for a while, upon Hase's own request, and Hase, who in his Preface gratefully acknowledged the prolonged stay of one such manuscript (this time with indication of its call number),[41] may have forgotten or neglected to mention the manuscript source of his Fragments in the same connection. If so, this manuscript must have remained in the Royal Library until shortly before the appearance of the advance copy of Leo's edition in the second half of the year 1818. Here, however, comes another serious puzzlement. If the manuscript did remain behind for some time — say, until 1817 — why did Hase first state in the printer's copy (which cannot be later than 1818) that it had been in the Royal Library *olim*, "quite a time ago," rather than say, *nuper*, "recently"?[42] And why did he hesitate in the printer's copy about the size and contents of a manuscript which presumably he was able to inspect at the time of writing his entry on the Fragments?

We have, then, two choices. Either we must assume that Hase wrote that entry from his own notes, made sometime between 1802 (when he began working on Leo's edition)[43] and 1815 (when the

---

41. Paris ed., p. XVII = pp. XXVII-XXVIII, Bonn. The manuscript in question was *Vaticanus Gr.* 163; at Hase's request, it was not among the various objects which *repentino anni* 1815. *tempore... Parisios olim convecta undique repeterentur*. Thus *olim* refers to the *arrival* in Paris of various manuscripts from abroad.

42. Especially since he did use the very word *nuper* in his Preface when referring to information he had drawn from manuscripts which had left Paris in 1815. Cf. Paris ed., p. XVII = p. XXIII, Bonn: cum *plurima essent* nuper *in Biblioteca Regia, multa supersint ad hanc diem*.

43. Hase to Böttiger, letter of July 27, 1802: this winter, Hase intends to work on Leo Diaconus. Böttiger to Hase, letter of August 14, 1802: asks for more details on Leo, invites Hase to write a piece on him, to be published in the *Merkur*. Hase to Böttiger, letter of 17 Messidor X (= 1802): Leo Diaconus is on Hase's program for the winter. References to authors who mentioned or worked on Leo: Fabricius, Du Cange, Combefis, de Pages, Gibbon. The edition of Leo would be dedicated to Böttiger. Hase has already copied a large part of Leo's first book. Hase to Böttiger, letter of 7 Nivose XI (= December 28, 1802): except for the last two books, Leo has been copied and translated into Latin. In all likelihood, the work will be printed in the Paris Corpus. Hase has collected, read and copied in part material from more than twelve manuscripts in the Bibliothèque Nationale for his notes to Leo; list of the authors and texts excerpted (no mention of the Fragments). I am indebted for knowledge of this cor-

manuscript of the Fragments in all probability left Paris), had forgotten about the existence of these notes on July 7, 1816, and forgot, even after that date, that he had copied three rather than two Fragments, but in the last moment was able to furnish the printer with the mislaid third Fragment (which, incidentally, is a logical and complete continuation of the second); or else we must look for another explanation.

⟨140⟩ The second occasion on which prudence may have deserted Hase has to do with the way in which certain parts of the Fragments' text are treated in the printer's copy. What follows will be technical, but indispensable for our line of reasoning.

Folio 347v, lines 3-4, of Paris *Supplément Grec* 858 (cf. fig. 4) contains the passage of the first Fragment in which the narrator and his party cross the Dnieper and arrive at the locality Borion. There, Hase first wrote κατὰ τὴν πόλιν γενόμενοι τήν, left a third of the next line empty, and continued with πρὸς εὐωχίαν. Subsequently, he crossed out τὴν πόλιν, "city," wrote κώμην, "village," above the line and filled the empty space with the word Βοριών. Since, however, Borion is a short word, an appreciable blank remained between that insertion and the following words πρὸς εὐωχίαν.

Hase himself provided a plausible, if indirect, explanation for the subsequent insertion of a proper name into his copy of the first Fragment: the script of the original manuscript, he pointed out, was intricate.[44] It could be argued, therefore, that at first reading he experienced difficulty in deciphering the name of the locality on the Dnieper — especially since this locality was otherwise unattested — and left a blank in his copy; this blank he filled on second reading. However, Hase's correction of τὴν πόλιν to κώμην is less easy to explain. Changes of this kind are more likely to have been made by the author than by the copyist of a Greek text. This is because πόλις, "town, city," and κώμη, "village," while they belong to the same semantic category, do not look much alike in writing, not even in intricate minuscule script.

---

respondence to Dr. Kollautz, who kindly provided me with the relevant typescripts. Cf. also Hase to Fries, December 28, 1802: "ich habe den unglückliche Gedanken gehabt, mich mit der Herausgabe zweier byzantinischen Autoren zu befassen, die ich im Mssc. auf der NB vorfand.... Die Arbeit wird mir unglaüblich lästig... ich bin indessen schon zu weit gegangen...." One of the two authors must have been Leo. For the text of the letter, cf. Kollautz, "Jacob..." (as in note 2 *supra*), 287.

44. Introductory remark to Fragment 2: *eadem intricatissima manu*, Paris ed., p. 256D = p. 500, Bonn; cf. *litteris minutis perplexisque admodum*, 254B = 496.

More noteworthy still is Hase's Latin translation of our passage on folio 347ᵛ. He first wrote *cum in oppidum Baxam venissemus*, without leaving any blank space between *oppidum* and *venissemus* or hesitating as to the spelling of "Baxa." Subsequently, he crossed out *oppidum Baxam*, "town of Baxa," and wrote *vicum Borion*, "village of Borion," above the line. The following question arises: how did Hase know that the locality was called Baxa if he was translating (either directly from the original manuscript, or from a transcript made of it by himself and set in the parallel column in the printer's copy) a Greek passage in which he could not at first decipher that locality's name?

Folio 347ᵛ offers one more peculiarity: in lines 17-18, the Latin translation had the words *quod iam prius fieri opportebat*. Hase crossed these words out, and with good reason, for no Greek text corresponds to them in the parallel column.

In the third Fragment, on Folio 350ʳ (fig. 9), Hase wrote a rather long passage, starting with τεῖχος μὲν τὸ παλαιόν and ending with περὶ τῶν ὅλων, at the bottom of the column, and indicated by the reference sign ♀ that the passage should be inserted into the main text between ἐξηρτύετο and 'Αφιγμένων. It is not quite obvious how a copyist could have omitted so many words from his original since no *homoeoteleuton* is involved. Moreover, there is no discontinuity in narrative between the words ἐξηρτύετο and 'Αφιγμένων. To top it all off, in a note which started with the words *hic primo leguntur illa*, Hase told the reader that ⟨141⟩ at the point of the original manuscript to which the note itself referred (*hic* = "here") he read some expunged words, which were followed (*inde*) by the word 'Αφιγμένων. In other words, Hase saw no *non*-expunged text whatsoever between the word to which his note was appended and 'Αφιγμένων. To the reader of the printed text, the annotated word is ὅλων — the end of the inserted passage — but originally it was ἐξηρτύετο, the last word before the insertion. For it is to ἐξηρτύετο that Hase first attached our note, marked by an exponential "d" in the printer's copy. Only later did he change "d" to "e" and assign the note to the words περὶ τῶν ὅλων.[45] It follows that initially Hase took a close look at the very spot of the original manuscript which must have contained the twenty-nine words of the inserted passage and did not see them at all.

45. In the printed text of the Paris ed., p. 258D, this note, already assigned to the words περὶ τῶν ὅλων, is marked by an exponential "i"; cf. p. 503, note †††, Bonn.

The printer's copy of the third Fragment exhibits the following three corrections: on folio 350ʳ, line 14, πλείονες was changed to πλείους; on folio 350ᵛ, line 9, ἀποδιαφέρεσθαι to ἀποδιαφέροντες; and on the same folio, line 12, ξυν was crossed out and followed by ἐπεψηφίσαντο. These corrections may merely reflect vacillations of Hase the copyist, faced with the task of resolving intricately written abbreviations. If so, Hase disappoints us as a professor of palaeography (a position to which he was appointed in late 1815 or 1816),[46] for in manuscripts of the tenth to eleventh century there is no abbreviation for -νες, only for -ους; none for -σθαι or -τες, only for -αι- or -ες; none for συν- (let alone for the Attic ξυν-), only for ἐπι-.

Finally, some differences in wording and word sequence exist between the Greek text of Paris *Supplément Grec* 858 [S] and the printer edition [P]. Thus: παρημείψαμεν σταδίους (S, fol. 348ʳ, line 6): σταδίους παρημείψαμεν (P, p. 255D); ἄλλων πρὸ ἡμῶν (S, *ibid.*, line 7): πρὸ ἡμῶν ἄλλων (P, *ibid.*); τοῖς δεινοῖς (S, *ibid.*, line 26): τοῖς τότε δεινοῖς (P, p. 256B); ὅτι (S, fol. 349ʳ, line 16): ὡς (P, p. 257B); ὄλεθρον (S, *ibid.*, line 2 *ab imo*): ὄλεθρον καὶ (P, p. 257C); ἀκηρυκτὶ ἡμῖν (S, fol. 349ᵛ, line 12): ἡμῖν ἀκηρυκτὶ (P, p. 257D). These final revisions by Hase patently were made on proofs, hence in 1816 or later. But on what basis? With the help of his own notes rather than by collating these proofs with the manuscript, for by 1816 that manuscript was, in all probability, no longer in Paris. Whatever the basis for Hase's revisions may have been, he disappoints us as a copyist, for he was negligent on at least six occasions (three of which had to do with word order) in transcribing quite a short text. By comparison, he reversed the word order only four times [47] in copying the *History* of Leo Diaconus, which occupies one hundred and seventy-four Bonn pages.

Thus, again, we have two choices. Either the *oppidum Baxa* of Hase's Latin version goes back to his earlier reading of the Greek manuscript — a reading which was later discarded and replaced by the blank for the locality's name on folio 347ᵛ of Paris *Supplément Grec* 858 — and Hase's corrections of the Greek (both those which still exist in the printer's copy and those which were made later on proofs), although barely distinguishable from stylistic changes ⟨142⟩ made by an author striving for Attic elegance, are in fact traces of a copyist's conscientious labor; or, again, we should look for another explanation.

---

46. Cf. note 133 *infra*.
47. Cf. Panayotakis, Λέων ὁ Διάκονος... (as note 1 *supra*), p. 120.

V

Until now we have been studying the external aspects and history of the only manuscript of the Fragments of *Toparcha Gothicus* which is accessible to us. We shall turn now to a scrutiny of the Fragments' internal evidence; it will serve as a countercheck to the examination of our text's material aspects. This scrutiny will proceed from lower to higher matters: from words to literary parallels, and from there, to *realia* and to the Fragments' conceptual framework.

VOCABULARY. In the five columns of the Paris edition (or on the four pages of the Bonn format), the Fragments offer at least nine oddities: five mistakes in accentuation or grammar and four *lexeis athesauristoi*. The mistakes are (a) χιῶνος (repeated four times) instead of χιόνος; (b) τὸ ξύμβαν instead of τὸ ξυμβάν; (c) ἄμεινα, possibly intended as a plural variation for ἄμεινον, although the neuter plural of ἄμεινον is ἀμείνονα or ἀμείνω; (d) εὗναι instead of εὐναί; and (e) τελείονι (*sc.* δυνάμει), while the correct comparative is τελειοτέρᾳ; this is an error, unless one wants to argue that Hase's tenth- or eleventh-century manuscript had πλείονι, which its editor misread for a non- existent word.[48]

The Fragments' four *lexeis athesauristoi* are: ἀποδιαφέροντες; ἐπικλίνια, "bed-covers"; ἐπ' ὁμωσία; and προκατέσκαπτο.[49] By com-

48. Χιῶνος, Paris ed., p. 255D = 498,6, Bonn, 256A *bis* = 498,8, 15, 256C = 498,31; τὸ ξύμβαν, 256A = 498,13-14; ἄμεινα, 256B = 498,17; εὗναι, 256B = 498,20; τελείονι, 258D, note "i" = 503, note †††; in all instances the printed text faithfully reproduces the errors of Paris *Suppl. Gr.* 858. Hase may have been aware that χιωνώδης, 255C-D, note "b' = 497, note****, was an error, for he placed a "[sic]" after that word. — Nystazopoulou, "Note..." (as in Appendix I [c]), 326, noticed two of the Fragments' mistakes. Professor Papazoglou-Ostrogorski, who kindly drew my attention to the erroneous χιῶνος, was furthermore disturbed by the *absence* of articles in the phrases ψυχὰς καὶ σώματα διετίθεντο, 256C = 498,26, and in ἄνθρωποί τε, 257C = 501,17. Conversely, Professor Panayotakis found the *presence* of the article in front of the "Mysian booty," τ ὴ ν Μυσῶν λείαν καλουμένην, 257A = 501,1, contrary to classical, Byzantine, or even modern Greek usage. Both colleagues were struck by ἄρκτου... βαρύτατον πνεύσαντος, 255B = 497,24-25, since ἄρκτος meaning "northern wind" seems to be unattested, and βαρύτατον as well as ἀέρων... βαρυτάτων ἄνωθεν ἐμπνεόντων, 256B = 498,16, remind one of *schwere Winde* rather than of anything Greek.

49. 'Αποδιαφέροντες, Paris ed., p. 259A = p. 503,35-36, Bonn; ἐπικλίνια, 256B = 498,22; ἐπ' ὁμωσία (remarkably, it appears without iota subscript in the

parison, Leo Diaconus and Agathias of Myrine have ten *lexeis athesauristoi* and eight *hapax legomena* in the whole of their respective histories.

Hase did excerpt the Fragments in the index to his Leo edition. There he referred to them forty-one times, and on three occasions listed orthographic peculiarities of the Fragments' manuscript.[50] It is remarkable that the very man ⟨143⟩ who by 1818 had collected thousands of lexical items and who was soon to become a renowned lexicographer should have failed to record any of the Fragments' four *hapaxes* in the same index, although he made sure of recording there the other *lexeis athesauristoi* of his edition. They include words derived from late texts (comparable to the Fragments in date) used by Hase in the notes to Leo such as βλύσις, which he culled from Theophylactus of Bulgaria.[51] Moreover, Hase did not quote any of the Fragments' four *hapax legomena* in the reedition of Stephanus' dictionary, a work of which he was one of the editors,[52] although unattested words, both from

---

Paris ed., 257C = 501,18; προκατέσκαπτο, 258A = 501,38. Ed. Kurtz realized that ἀποδιαφέρω was otherwise unattested, cf. Westberg, *Die Fragmente...* (as in Appendix I), 73.

50. *S. vv.: autographus*, Paris ed., p. 285 = p. 571, Bonn; *Borion*, 287 = 573; *Chersonem*, 290 = 576; *Chersonesi, sexies*, 290 = 576; *Clemata, bis* 290 = 577; *codex*, 291 = 578; *Danapris, ter*, 293 = 581; *fossa*, 298 = 587; *Graecorum, quater*, 298-299 = 588-589; *Graeci, bis*, 299 = 589; *historiae*, 299 = 590; *inediti*, 300 = 591; *Ister, bis*, 303 = 594; *Itacismi*, 303 = 594; καταισχυνθέντες 304 = 595; *Maurocastrum*, 307 = 600; Μυσῶν 309 = 602; *nix, bis*, 311 = 606; *proverbia*. 316 = 612; *Romanzoff*, 317 = 614; *Russi, bis*, 318 = 614; *Saturnus*, 319 = 615; *scuta*, 319 = 616; σκληρά 320 = 617; *Taurica*, 322 = 620; *Vladimirus*, 324 = 622. Orthographic peculiarities of the original text of the Fragments are introduced into the index *s.vv. Itacismi*, 303 = 594: *velut* αἰωρούμενος *et* ἑωρούμενος *permutata*, 254D = 497,9; καταισχυνθηθέντες, 304 = 595: κ. *vox nihili*, 258C = 503,17; σκληρά, 320 = 617: σ *et* σκιερά confusa, 255A = 497, 14.

51. Paris ed., p. 249B = p. 489,21, Bonn. The example came from the (still unpublished) commentary to Psalm 35(36):9-10.

52. Hase was to be the chief editor of the new *Thesaurus* by Stephanus, to be published under the auspices of Firmin Didot; cf. the title page of the first volume of the new edition, dated 1831. Although by 1833 he was no longer a central figure in the preparation of the *Thesaurus*, cf., e.g., the letter of M. J. Müller to Thiersch, in Kollautz, "Jacob..." (as in note 2 *supra*), 289, he continued the collaboration throughout his life. It is attested by the title pages of all eight volumes of Stephanus' *Thesaurus* and by new entries in the later volumes, signed with his name. He died (on March 21, 1864) while working at his desk, on

Leo proper and from his own notes to this author, are recorded there; such are (besides βλύσις) βλυστάνω, περινάω, πολυχεύμων, περιγειότης. They appear in the New Stephanus with explicit references to Hase's Leo, and new entries pertaining to them are in most cases followed by Hase's name.

The *hapaxes* of the Fragments spice up an otherwise monotonous fare, since the narrator repeats the same words or idioms over and over again. Δείκνυμι (especially the pluperfect ἐδέδεικτο) appears eight times, six times in the first Fragment alone, usually as an elegant variation for "was";[53] χαλεποῦ, χαλεπαίνων, χαλεπώτερον, and the like occur ten times, all but one in the first Fragment;[54] συναράσσειν and καταράσσειν three times, in different contexts; [55] the rare τοῦ περιέχοντος is used twice;[56] and the same is true of χεῖρας ἀνακροτεῖν, "applaud," as an expression of joy — once it is applied to the narrator's retinue who reacted in this way to the freezing of the Dnieper, once to the friendly and childlike barbarians who gave a spontaneous farewell to his party.[57] Περικλύζεσθαι and ἐπικλυσθέντα appear in close vicinity, as do ἀντιποιεῖθαι and ἀντιποιούμενοι, κατεσκαμμένη and προκατέσκαπτο.[58] Σχετλιάζειν κατά τινος is a remarkably rare construction, and wc shall return to it again; yet it, too, occurs twice in the Fragments.[59] Πόλις and κώμη are juxtaposed or opposed in two occasions,[60] and this ⟨144⟩ peculiarity of the narrator's style reappears in Hase's own scribal hesitation between the πόλις and the κώμη Borion. Finally, the narrator reveals his habit — shared by Byzantines, but also by authors of all times who write in a language not their own — of

---

which were discovered the final pages of the New Stephanus; cf. M. Guigniaut, "Notice historique..." (as in note 2 *supra*), 272.

53. Paris ed., p. 254D = p. 497,9, Bonn; 255A *bis* = 497, 12-13, 15; 255C, note b = 497, note****; 255D = 498,1; 256B = 498,19; 257A = 500,42; 257B = 501,10.

54. Paris ed., p. 254D *ter* = p. 497,3 *bis*, 9, Bonn; 255B = 497,25; 255C = 497,34; 256A *ter* = 498,7, 12, 14; 256C = 498,32; 257C = 501,14.

55. Paris ed., p. 254C = p. 496,42-43, Bonn; 254D = 497,2; 255B = 497,25.

56. Paris ed., p. 255C = p. 497,32, Bonn; 255D = 498,1.

57. Paris ed., p. 255A = p. 497,17, Bonn; 255D = 498,2-3.

58. Περικλύζεσθαι, ἐπικλυσθέντα, Paris ed., p. 257B, C = p. 501,12, 17, Bonn; ἀντιποιεῖσθαι, ἀντιποιούμενοι, 258D = 503,27 32-33; κατεσκαμμένη, προκατέσκαπτο, 258A = 501,36, 38.

59. Paris ed., p. 256C = p. 498,28, Bonn; 257B = 501,9.

60. Paris ed., p. 257C = p. 501,14-15, Bonn; 258A = 501,37.

amassing rare or precious words and *flosculi*: διόδους in the sense of "roads"; συσσίτοις; ἀποκοίτους; τοῦ περιέχοντος meaning "air"; οὐ ξυντρόφων, "unusual"; αὐτεπαγγέλτως; περίορθρον; and πολεμησείων.[61] These latter two words offered Hase another chance to adduce our Fragments in the New Stephanus, since both relevant entries in that dictionary do contain additions (mostly from Byzantine authors such as Synesius, translator of Achmes, Constantine Manasses, and Thomas Magister) which are signed with his name. Yet, he made no more use of that chance than he did in the case of the Fragments' *hapaxes*.

TEXTUAL PARALLELS. Literary parallels to the Fragments used as evidence here derive exclusively from texts with which Hase was acquainted or which go back to Hase himself. This is a matter of positive knowledge, even for Aeschines, whom Hase did not quote in print.[62]

I. The following eighteen examples, of which seventeen deal with passages and one with a cluster of words, indicate that Thucydides was foremost among the narrator's models:

I. 1. Fragment 1, ed. Hase, p. 245D: τὸ ὕδωρ... ἐπὶ μέγα ἦν ἰσχυρόν	Thucyd. II:97:4: ἐπὶ μέγα ἦλθεν ἡ βασιλεία ἰσχύος
2. *Ibid.*, p. 255D: οὐδὲ πάντας αὐτοὺς ἑβδομήκοντα σταδίους παρημείψαμεν	*Ibid.*, II:5:2 ἀπέχει δ' ἡ Πλάταια τῶν Θηβῶν σταδίους ἑβδομήκοντα
3. *Ibid.*, p. 256A: τετράπηχυς γὰρ ἡ χιὼν ἐλέγετο καὶ χαλεπῶς διαβατὴ ἦν	*Ibid.*, II:5:2: ποταμὸς ἐρρύη μέγας καὶ οὐ ῥᾳδίως διαβατὸς ἦν

61. Διόδους, Paris ed., p. 255B = p. 497,26, Bonn; συσσίτοις, 255C = 497,29; ἀποκοίτους, 255C = 497,30; τοῦ περιέχοντος, 255C, D = 497, 32, 498, 1; οὐ ξυντρόφων, 256A = 498,14; αὐτεπαγγέλτως, 257B = 501,5; περίορθρον, 258C = 503,18; πολεμησείων, 258C = 503, 19. Πολεμησείων occurs at least twice in Leo Diaconus, cf. 60,3 and 104,11, Bonn. — The Fragments display the same characteristics which Hase in his Preface detected in Leo and in Byzantine writers generally: elegant variation, use of pretentious instead of simple words, rare expressions, and repetitious vocabulary: cf. Paris ed., pp. VIII-IX = pp. XIX -XX, Bonn, esp. *deinde, idem vocabulum. aliquot lineis interjectis, libenter iterari*. In short, the narrator writes in a tenth-century Byzantine style as Hase understood that style.

62. For a quotation from Aeschines, cf. Hase's notes in Paris *Suppl. Gr.* 1347, fol. 111r (soon after 1821?). (*Ibid.*, fol. 132r, and in Leo Diaconus, p. 213B, he quoted the Pseudo-Platonic Axiochos, attributed in his time to Aeschines Socraticus.) On other texts, see pp. 174-75 *infra*.

4. *Ibid.*, p. 256A: πολλοὶ δέ... μεῖζον ἢ κατ' ἀνθρωπίνην δύναμιν τὸ ξύμβαν οἰηθέντες· καὶ ἦν γάρ τι τῶν οὐ ξυντρόφων τὸ χαλεπόν	*Ibid.*, II:50:1: χαλεπωτέρως ἢ κατὰ τὴν ἀνθρωπείαν φύσιν προσέπιπτεν ⟨*sc.* ἡ νόσος⟩ ἑκάστῳ καὶ ἐν τῷδε ἐδήλωσε μάλιστα ἄλλο τι ὂν ἢ τῶν ξυντρόφων τι
5. *Ibid.*, p. 256B: τὰ γὰρ πάντα ἀνωφελῆ καὶ ἀνόνητά πως ἐν τοῖς τότε δεινοῖς ἐδέδεικτο	*Ibid.*, II:47:4: πάντα ἀνωφελῆ ἦν
⟨145⟩ 6. *Ibid.*, p. 256C: οἱ δὲ πρόσκοποι ἐξέκαμον καὶ αὐτοί, ὑπὸ τοῦ πολλοῦ κακοῦ νικηθέντες	*Ibid.*, II:51:5-6: καὶ οἱ οἰκεῖοι ἐξέκαμνον ὑπὸ τοῦ πολλοῦ κακοῦ νικώμενοι
7. Fragment 2, ed. Hase, p. 257A: ἀνατέτραπτο τὸ πρὶν αὐτοῖς ἴσον καὶ δίκαιον	*Ibid.*, II:44:3: οὐ γὰρ οἷόν τε ἴσον [in the Bredenkamp edition, Leipzig, 1799: ἰσόν] τι ἢ δίκαιον βουλεύεσθαι
8. *Ibid.*, p. 257D: τὸ δὲ ἀπὸ τούτου, πόλεμος ἡμῖν ἀκηρυκτὶ καὶ βαρβάροις ἐγένετο, ἐν ᾧ οὔτε ἐπεμίγνυον ἔτι παρ' ἡμῖν	*Ibid.*, II:1:1: ἄρχεται δὲ ὁ πόλεμος ἐνθένδε ἤδη 'Αθηναίων καὶ Πελοποννησίων καὶ τῶν ἑκατέροις ξυμμάχων, ἐν ᾧ οὔτε ἐπεμίγνυντο ἔτι ἀκηρυκτεὶ παρ' ἀλλήλους
9. *Ibid.*, p. 258A: νομίσαντες ὡς ἅμα βοῇ παραλήψεσθαι ἡμᾶς	*Ibid.*, II:81:4: ἐνόμισαν αὐτοβοεὶ ἂν τὴν πόλιν ἑλεῖν
10. *Ibid.*, p. 258A: ὡς ἀπὸ κώμης προσβολὰς ποιουμένων	*Ibid.*, II:18:1: προσβολὰς παρεσκευάζοντο τῷ τείχει ποιησόμενοι
11. Fragment 3, ed. Hase, p. 258C: βάρβαροι... ἀπέῃσαν πρὸς νύκτα, φυλάξαντες τὸ περίορθρον	*Ibid.*, II:3:4: φυλάξαντες ἔτι νύκτα καὶ αὐτὸ τὸ περίορθρον
12. *Ibid.*, p. 258C: τὰ τῷ καιρῷ μοι σύμφορα ἐξηρτύετο, τεῖχος μὲν τὸ παλαιὸν ἀνεγείρων	*Ibid.*, II:3:3-4: ἵν' ἀντὶ τείχους ᾖ, καὶ τἆλλα ἐξήρτυον ᾗ ἕκαστον ἐφαίνετο πρὸς τὰ παρόντα ξύμφορον ἔσεσθαι
13. *Ibid.*, p. 258C: διδάσκων τοὺς ἐμοὺς εὖ παρεσκευάσθαι πρὸς τὰ πολέμια	*Ibid.*, I:18:3: πολεμοῦντες... εὖ παρεσκευάσαντο τὰ πολέμια
14. *Ibid.*, p. 258D: ἃ μὲν εἶπον ἐγὼ τότε, καὶ ὡς οἵων δεσποτῶν μᾶλλον ἀντιποιεῖσθαι προσήκει, καὶ πρὸς οἵους ἐλθόντας τίνα ὠφέλειαν πειρᾶσθαι ἀπ' αὐτῶν εὑρίσκειν, καὶ τί ποιητέον ἐστί, καὶ τἆλλα πάντα, ὅσα τότε εἶπον ἐγώ... μακρὸν ἂν εἴη πάντα ἐφεξῆς λέγειν βούλεσθαι	*Ibid.*, II:36:4: [Pericles' Funeral Oration]: μακρηγορεῖν ἐν εἰδόσιν οὐ βουλόμενος, ἐάσω· ἀπὸ δὲ οἵας τε ἐπιτηδεύσεως ἤλθον... καὶ μεθ' οἵας πολιτείας καὶ τρόπων ἐξ οἵων μεγάλα ἐγένετο, ταῦτα δηλώσας πρῶτον εἶμι

15. *Ibid.*, pp. 258D-259A: μετὰ τοῦ στρατῷ ἰσχύειν πολλῷ καὶ δυνάμει μάχης ἐπαίρεσθαι	*Ibid.*, II:97:5: ἰσχύι δὲ μάχης καὶ στρατοῦ πλήθει πολὺ δευτέρα
16. *Ibid.*, p. 259A: παραδώσειν σφᾶς ξυνέθεντο	*Ibid.*, II:4:7: ξυνέβησαν... παραδοῦναι σφᾶς αὐτούς
17. *Ibid.*, p. 259A: ἐμοί... τήν... ἀρχὴν ἀσμένως πᾶσαν ἔδοτο	*Ibid.*, VI:12:2: ἄρχειν ἄσμενος αἱρεθείς

18. Finally, the third Fragment shares with chapters ninety-six and ninety-seven of Thucydides' Second Book, chapters which occupy less than two ⟨146⟩ Teubner pages, a remarkably large cluster of the same words, regardless of the differences in contents between the two texts:

Third Fragment		Thucydides, Book Two
p. 258D:	τοῦ Ἴστρου	96:1: τοῦ Ἴστρου
	ὅμοροι ὄντες	96:1: εἰσὶ δ' οἱ Γέται... ὅμοροι
	αὐτονόμων	96:2: τῶν αὐτονόμων
		96:3 and 4: αὐτονόμους
	κατὰ τὰ βόρεια	96:4: πρὸς βορέαν
	βασιλεύοντα	97:3: βασιλεύσας
p. 259A:	προσόδους	97:5: προσόδῳ
	δυνάμει μάχης	97:5: ἰσχύι δὲ μάχης

The eighteen parallels just adduced settle the question of our text's genre: autograph or not, the Fragments are a literary work, utilizing at least one literary source; they are not travel notes jotted down hurriedly during the journey itself.[63] Whoever proposes the contrary must claim that the narrator carried Thucydides' text with him in his luggage rather than in his head on his trek through the steppe, and that he was influenced by the historian to the extent of covering, on one stormy day, exactly the same number of stadia — seventy — which Thucydides in his Second Book gives as the distance between Plataea and Thebes.

Although our list of Thucydidean material in the Fragments is the fullest to date, the find itself is not new: Vasil'evskij observed one of the

63. This was sensed by F. Uspenskij as early as 1904; cf. "F. Vestberg..." (as in Appendix I [a]), 244. Of course, Uspenskij, who argued for a ninth- or early tenth-century date for the Fragments, asserted that they were not autograph, cf. *ibid.*, 246, 248, 252, 253. That the Fragments were not a diary was also stated by Levčenko, "K voprosu..." (as in Appendix I [a]), 300-301. Levčenko, however, was aware of the Fragments' dependence on Thucydides.

parallels as early as 1876,[64] and Melikova pointed out several others in 1919.[65] Not many scholars, however, seem to have given an explanation for these parallels. Those who did saw in them either a reflection of the narrator's own affinity for the most tragic parts of Thucydides' *History* — which helps us little in establishing the Fragments' date — or proof of the quality of the literary education possessed by a Byzantine official of the late tenth century.[66]

On superficial inspection the latter interpretation can be defended. Although the extent of the Fragments' use of Thucydides as a model seems unparalleled in Byzantine literature of the ninth and tenth centuries, Byzantine historians of other periods, from Procopius and Agathias in the sixth century to Chalcocondyles and Critobulus in the fifteenth, imitated Thucydides in their writings. Even in the middle of the tenth century, the *Suda* and Constantine Porphyrogenitus' *Excerpta de Legationibus* and *De Virtutibus et Vitiis* quoted ⟨147⟩ from his *History*, and one Byzantine scholar established a particular recension of his text.[67]

However, attributing the Fragments' Thucydidean borrowings to a Byzantine of the tenth century poses difficulties. Byzantine historians turned to Thucydides for three purposes: they used him as a source for vocabulary, as a source for *flosculi*, and — primarily — as a model in treating their own subject matter. Faced with the plagues of 542 and 1347, respectively, Procopius and Cantacuzenus turned to Thucydides' Second Book to borrow from his description of the plague of 430 B.C. Agathias helped himself to the account of the siege of Plataea in order to depict that of Onoguris. Procopius and others used Thucydidean speeches, battles, character portraits, or debates of their own; not to speak of the appearance of Thucydides' opening words in many a Byzan-

64. Vasil'evskij, "Zapiski..." in *Trudy*, II (as in Appendix I), 164.

65. S. V. Melikova, "Gotskij toparx i Fukidid," *Izvestija Rossijskoj Akademii Nauk*, 6th Ser., XIII (1919), 1063-70. Melikova offers a few parallels not included in the present list.

66. Cf. Melikova, "Gotskij..." (as in preceding note), 1068 and 1070; Levčenko, "K voprosu..." as in Appendix I [a]), 300.

67. Cf. C. de Boor, *Excerpta Historica iussu Imp. Constantini Porphyrogeniti confecta*, I,2 (1903), 436-38; A. Kleinlogel, *Geschichte des Thukydidestextes im Mittelalter* (Berlin, 1965), 102, 104, 158, 169. Hase thought that Leo Diaconus did not use Thucydides; cf. Preface, Paris ed., p. IX = p. XX, Bonn. This was an error; compare, e.g., Leo Diac., *Hist.*, 21,9-11, Bonn with Thucydides, III:82:4.

tine's *prooemium*. Exceptions to this practice are very rare.[68]

In the Fragments, the narrator does use Thucydidean words and idioms; when it comes to content, however, his procedure is peculiar. In parallels 8-12, 14, and 16 borrowings do correspond more or less to the subject matter. However, in parallel 1 a kingdom is juxtaposed with water; in parallel 3, snowdrifts with a river; in parallel 4, a storm with the plague; and in parallel 15 the statement in the Fragments is the opposite of Thucydides'. The narrator needed Thucydides' passages for his own sentences and word clusters, regardless of their substance; he did not need them as much for stories of similar content.[69] In exploiting Thucydides, the narrator did not go out of his way: his parallels are almost entirely derived from a single book of Thucydides, the Second, and we saw that a large cluster of borrowed words comes from two of that book's chapters — ninety-six and ninety-seven.

Besides Thucydides the narrator's memory, his luggage, or his library at home appears to have contained other authors, even some who lived after the time to which Hase ascribed his manuscript. The parallels are as follows:

II. Fragment 1, ed. Hase, p. 255C:	Aeschines, *De falsa leg.*, cap. 127:
ἐμοῦ... τοῖς συσσίτοις εἰπόντος, ὡς οὐ δεῖ ἀποκοίτους ἡμᾶς... γενέσθαι	κἂν φῶσιν ἀπόκοιτόν με τουτωνὶ πώποτε τῶν συσσίτων γεγονέναι

⟨148⟩ Ἀπόκοιτος is rare, and its appearance in close proximity to σύσσιτος is rarer still. The very passage of Aeschines which contains these two words appears as an additional entry *sub verbo* ἀπόκοιτος in the New Stephanus, reedited by Hase. The addition is unsigned, but we know of other unsigned additions to the New Stephanus which Hase

68. A brief bibliography: H. Braun, "Procopius Caesariensis quatenus imitatus sit Thucydidem," *Acta Seminarii philologici Erlangensis*, 4 (1886), 161-221 (oldest and best); H. Lieberich, *Studien zu den Proömien in der griechischen und byzantinischen Geschichtsschreibung*, I-II (Munich, 1899-1900); G. Franke, *Quaestiones Agathianae* [= *Breslauer Philologische Abhandlungen*, 46] (1914); J. Dräseke, "Thukydides' Pestbericht (II, 47-53) und dessen Fortleben," *Jahresbericht des deutschen philologischen Vereins*, 40 (1914), 181-89; A. Cameron, "Herodotus and Thucydides in Agathias," *BZ*, 57 (1964), 33-52; *eadem, Agathias* (Oxford, 1970), 60-64.

69. This is to say that while the narrator did what Hase held against middle-Byzantine writers — *eorum* [i.e., classical authors'] *phrases undique arreptas ad verbum transferebant in propria scripta*, cf. Preface, Paris ed., p. IX = p. XX Bonn — he did it somewhat more clumsily.

presumably made himself, since they are drawn from his edition of Leo Diaconus.[70]

III. Fragment 1, ed. Hase, p. 255C-D, combined with the words of note "b": καὶ πρὸς [τὴν ἑαυτοῦ φύσιν] αὐτὸν ἐκεῖνον μετατρεπομένου τοῦ περιέχοντος, [φύσει ψυχρότατος καὶ χιωνώδης (sic) δοκῶν,] Κρόνου δὲ καλουμένου. καὶ γὰρ ἔτυχε περὶ τὰς ἀρχὰς αὐτὸς διιὼν Ὑδροχόου	Ptolemy, *Apotelesmatica*, p. 39,12-17, eds. Boll-Boer: τῷ μὲν τοῦ Κρόνου ψυκτικῷ ὄντι μᾶλλον τὴν φύσιν... ἐδόθη ὅ τε Αἰγόκερως καὶ ὁ Ὑδροχόος, μετὰ τοῦ ταῦτα τὰ δωδεκαμόρια ψυχρὰ καὶ χειμερινὰ τυγχάνειν *Ibid.*, p. 152, 22-23: ὁ τοῦ Ἑρμοῦ ἀστὴρ τῷ τοῦ Κρόνου πρὸς τὸ ψυχρὸν συνοικειούμενος
IV. 1. Fragment 1, ed. Hase, pp. 254D-255A: τὸ ὕδωρ ἁπανταχῇ πέπηκτο... ὡς καὶ πεζῇ καὶ ἵπποις ἀφόβως ἰέναι... οὐ γὰρ ὕδασιν οὕτω νάουσιν ἐῴκει τὰ ῥεύματα, ἀλλ' ὄρη σκληρά [σκιερά] τινα... ἐδέδεικτο... προσίεμεν, κατὰ πέλαγος ἱππασάμενοι. ἀκωλύτως δὲ διαβάντες...	Agathias, *Hist.*, 5:11:6 = ed. Keydell, p. 177,21-28: τὰ μὲν ῥεῖθρα... ἐπήγνυτο εἰς βάθος καὶ ἦσαν ἤδη σκληρὰ καὶ βάσιμα καὶ ἱππήλατα... Ζαβεργὰν δέ... τὰς δίνας εὐκολώτατα διαβαίνει... καὶ μηδενὸς αὐτῷ κωλύματος γιγνομένου... Σκυθίαν παραμειψάμενος... προσέβαλλεν.

Agathias' description of the crossing of the Danube by Zabergan's Kutrigur forces in March 559 may, but need not, have influenced the narrator's picture of the frozen Dnieper. The case is less ambiguous with the next set of passages:

2. Fragment 1, ed. Hase, p. 256D: ἐσχετλίασεν ἄλλος κατὰ τῶν ἐσομένων	Agathias, *Hist.*, 4:11:1 = ed. Keydell, p. 136,27-28: τῷ ἄχθεσθαι κατὰ τῶν στρατηγῶν
3. Fragment 2, ed. Hase, p. 257B: σχετλιάζοντές τε κατὰ τῶν ἡγεμόνων	

The Fragments' construction σχετλιάζειν κατά τινος is absent from dictionaries.[71] Agathias provides the closest parallel to this *unicum* (this

70. For entries from Leo in the New Stephanus (sixty of them), cf. Panayotakis, Λέων ὁ Διάκονος... (as in note 1 *supra*), 127 note 5. Of these, only four are signed with Hase's name; however, in nearly one-half of the total his name is mentioned.

71. Leo Diaconus has σχετλιάσας twice, once with ἐπί and a dative, once with an accusative, cf., *Hist.*, 106,17, 139,23, Bonn.

parallel includes the people against whom the dissatisfaction is directed). In turn, Agathias' own construction, ἄχθεσθαι κατά τινος, seems unique or at the very least quite rare: I was not able to find it elsewhere, and Keydell included it as noteworthy in his succinct *Index Graecitatis*. Consequently, unless we assume independent in⟨149⟩vention, we may claim with some probability that Agathias' passage did inspire our narrator.

4. Fragment 1, ed. Hase, p. 256B: οὐδ' ἀναπαύσασθαι πρὸς ἀκαρῆ[72] χώραν [χρόνον] ἡ χιὼν ἐνεδίδου	Agathias, *Hist.*, 4:18:6 = ed. Keydell, pp. 145,31-146,1: ὥσπερ ἐκ συνθήματος ἐν ἀκαρεῖ χρόνου τοῦ συνοίσοντος ἐστοχασμένοι
	Ibid., 2:9:6 = ed. Keydell, p. 52,11-12: οὐδὲ τοῦ... ἀμφιγνοῆσαι τὰ ποιούμενα χώρα ἐγίγνετο
	Ibid., 2:21:4 = ed. Keydell, p. 68,6-7: πλὴν οὐ γεγένηται χώρα τῷ Θεοδώρῳ
	Ibid., 4:14:5 = ed. Keydell, p. 140,24: χώραν παρέσχον ἐκείνῳ
5. Fragment 1, ed. Hase, p. 256C: τὸ δὲ χαλεπώτατον, ὅτι καὶ διὰ πολεμίας ἐπορευόμεθα γῆς	Agathias, *Hist.*, 3:9:13 = ed. Keydell, p. 95,7-8: ἀλλὰ πρὸς Λάζους παραταττόμενοι, καὶ ταῦτα ἐν πολεμίᾳ γῇ

The narrator also shares with Agathias a number of words and forms, such as αὐτεπαγγέλτως, ἀνατέτραπται, ἀνακωχή, διαφανῶς, παραμείβομαι, μηδὲν ἠδικηκότας, περίορθρον, βαρβαρικώτερον (cf. the Fragments' Ἑλληνικωτέρων τρόπων, p. 258D), and Vasil'evskij pointed out some of them.[73] True, most of those words occur in Thucydides as well, and it is the latter who may have determined the narrator's choice. However, since the rare αὐτεπαγγέλτως is absent from Thucydides, I should like to attribute it to Agathias' influence.

72. It is worth noting that in Leo Diaconus, *Hist.*, 17,5, Bonn, Hase wrote ἀκαρῆ, keeping the spelling of the Paris manuscript: ἀπονητί τε καὶ ἀκαρῆ. In that passage, as in the Fragments, the adverb stands alone. Whenever Leo combined it with ἐν, Hase wrote ἀκαρεῖ.

73. Vasil'evskij, "Zapiska..." in *Trudy*, II (as in Appendix I), 152, 156-57, 160.

V. 1. Fragment 1, ed. Hase, p. 255A: ὅθεν ἡμῖν τὸ κατηφὲς εἰς χαρὰν μεταβέβλητο	Leo Diaconus, *Hist.*, ed. Hase, p. 79A, Paris ed. = p, 128,1-2, Bonn: τῆς δὲ χειμερινῆς κατηφείας εἰς ἐαρινὴν αἰθρίαν μεταβαλούσης *Ibid.*, p. 31C, Paris ed. = p. 51,6-7, Bonn: ἐπεὶ δὲ τὴν τοῦ χειμῶνος κατήφειαν ἐαριναὶ τροπαὶ πρὸς γαληνιῶσαν μετεσκεύαζον ἱλαρότητα
2. Fragment 2, ed. Hase, p. 257A: ἀλλὰ τὴν Μυσῶν λείαν καλουμένην (indicating that a proverb is meant here) θέσθαι	Leo Diaconus, *Hist.*, ed. Hase, p. 46A, Paris ed. = p. 75,3, Bonn: λείαν Μυσῶν θέμενος *Ibid.*, p. 70D, Paris ed. = 114,25, Bonn: λείαν ἐτιθει Μυσῶν

⟨150⟩ In itself, the occurence of the same well-known proverb in two texts edited by the same scholar does not warrant special notice. What does make the coincidence noteworthy is the combination, in both texts, of the same verb (θέσθαι, θέμενος, ἐτιθει) with the proverbial saying. This combination is quite rare. Usually, Μυσῶν λεία is connected with εἶναι, γίγνεσθαι, ἔχειν, ποιεῖν, ποιεῖθαι, ἐργάζεσθαι, κατεργάζεσθαι, ἀποδείκνυσθαι. I found only two examples of τιθέναι connected with Μυσῶν λεία, in Theodore Prodromus' and Nicetas Eugenianus' verses. In fact, these two cases are only one, since Nicetas imitates Theodore.[74]

3. *Ibid.*, p. 257C: ἄνθρωποί τε, ἠδικηκότες μηδέν	*Ibid.*, p. 26D, Paris ed. = p. 43, 11-12 Bonn: ἐμοὶ δὲ τούτων εἰδηκότι μηδέν

---

74. Prodromus: *Rhodanthe and Dosicles*, I:26, ed. Hercher, *Erotici Scriptores Graeci*, II (1859), 289; Eugenianus: *Drosilla and Charicles*, I:22, *ibid.*, 437. Hase also noted the proverb Μυσῶν λείαν (with the verb ποιεῖσθαι) in his edition of the second *Dialogue* of Emperor Manuel II (with a Mohammedan); cf. *Notices et extraits des manuscrits de la Bibliothèque Imperiale*... 8, 2 (1810), 375; furthermore, he quoted it (with the verb κατεργάζεσθαι) in a passage from Ἐπιδημία Μάζαρι, cf. *ibid.*, 9,2 (1813), 189. — For the proverb itself, cf. Leutsch-Schneidewin, *Paroemiographi Graeci*, II, p. 38, who adduce our passage of Fragment 2 (this is, to my knowledge, the only quotation from the Fragments in a modern philological work); cf. also J. Fr. Boissonade, *Anecdota Graeca*, 3 (Paris, 1831), 113 note 1.

However, the *codex unicus* of Leo has here τοῦτον ἠδοκ... δέν, and Hase made the following felicitous — and surely correct — conjecture on the margin of page 26D: *ut possis legere* τοῦτον ἠδικηκότι, *nihil illum laedenti.* Thus, in this passage of Leo, Hase proposed writing ἠδικηκότι μηδέν, which, but for the case, is precisely what the Fragments' narrator wrote in his own notes.

4. *Ibid.*, p. 257D: ἀνωμολόγητο... ὡς τὰ περὶ ψυχῆς νῦν κινδυνεύεται	*Ibid.*, p. 15D, Paris ed. = p. 26,14, Bonn: διηγωνίζοντο, περὶ ψυχὴν κινδυνεύοντες

Again, Hase proposed "*f(ortasse)* ψυχῆς" in the margin of page 15D, which was precisely the construction used by the Fragments' narrator in the same phrase.[75]

VI. 1. Fragment 1, ed. Hase, p. 256B: οὐκ ἦν πυρὰ καῦσαι	*De Velit. Bell.*, ed. Hase, p. 136B, Paris ed. = p. 211,10, Bonn: καὶ πυρὰ πλεῖστα ἀνάπτειν; cf. *ibid.*, p. 164D, Paris ed. = 254,20, Bonn: πυρὰ... ἀνάψαι πολλά
2. Fragment 2, ed. Hase, p. 257A: τρόπαιά τε τὰ μέγιστα κατωρθώκεσαν	*Ibid.*, p. 118C, Paris ed. = p. 185,8, Bonn: μέγιστα κατ' αὐτῶν ἀνεστήσατο τρόπαια; cf. *ibid.*, p. 154B, Paris ed. = p. 238,20, Bonn: μεγάλα... ἐργάσῃ τρόπαια
⟨151⟩ 3. *Ibid.*, p. 257C: χειρῶν ἔργον καὶ ξίφους ἐγένοντο	*Ibid.*, p. 133C, Paris ed. = p. 207,5-6, Bonn: πολλούς... ἔργον μαχαίρας ποιήσονται
	Ibid., p. 151D, Paris ed. = pp. 234, 25-235,1, Bonn: πολλοὺς αὐτῶν μαχαίρας ἔργον ποιήσῃς
4. *Ibid.*, p. 258A: ἀπό... πόλεως προσβολὰς ποιουμένων	*Ibid.*, p. 165A, Paris ed. = p. 255,4, Bonn: ἐν τῷ μέσῳ ἱστάμενοι τὴν προσβολὴν ποιήσωνται

75. Professor Panayotakis provided the following list of words and expressions from Leo which are close to words or phrases found in the Fragments: ἀπανταχῆ (Paris ed., p. 254D = p. 497,6, Bonn), 103,6, Bonn; αὐτοβοεὶ αἱρεῖν (cf. ἅμα παραλήψεσθαι, 258A = 501,34), 7,3, 29,18, 43,2, 52,10, 55,5, 66,8, 71,22, 131,10, 135,2, 171,7; διχῆ (258B, note b = 501, note****), 110,22; ἔργον μαχαίρας or αἰχμῆς (cf. χειρῶν ἔργον καὶ ξίφους, 257C = 501,18), 12,9, 14,15, 29,17, 56,17, 74,20; μέγιστα τρόπαια (257A = 501,4), 158,3; ὅμοροι (258D = 503,33), 62,12, 99,19, 150,16.

5. *Ibid.*, p. 258B, note "b": διχῆ τὸν στρατὸν παρατάξαντες [i.e., the narrator]	*Ibid.*, p. 131D, Paris ed. = p. 204,4-5, Bonn: ὁ στρατηγός... διχῆ τὸν λαὸν αὐτοῦ διέλῃ; cf. *ibid.*, p. 149A, Paris ed. = p. 230,20, Bonn: ταύτας τοίνυν διχῆ διελὼν [i.e., ὁ τοῦ ὅλου στρατεύματος ἀρχηγός]; *ibid.*, p. 160A, Paris ed. = p. 247,17-18, Bonn: συναγαγὼν... τό... στράτευμα καὶ διχῆ αὐτοὺς διελὼν
VII. Fragment 1, ed. Hase, p. 255C: τοῦ πρώτου τῶν ἄστρων ἑσπέριον φάσιν ἤδη ποιοῦντος... (Κρόνου δὴ καλουμένου)	Psellus, *De omnif. doctr.*, 134 = p. 70, 6-7, ed. Westerink: ὧν πρῶτος ἐστὶν ὁ τοῦ Κρόνου λεγόμενος ἀστήρ[76]
	Paris *Suppl. Grec* 811, fol. 224ᵛ, description of *Palatinus Graecus* 356 in Hase's own hand: *Breve excerptum... de septem planetis... initium fol.* 169 *recto*: ἐν τῇ πρώτῃ ζώνῃ τοῦ οὐρανοῦ Κρόνος ἐστίν
	Ptolemy, *Apotelesmatica*, pp. 143,19-144,4, edd. Boll-Boer: πρῶτον γὰρ ἐπὶ ἀστέρων ὁ μὲν τοῦ Κρόνου... δυτικός... ὑπάρχων... τῇ... κράσει τὸ μᾶλλον ἔχοντας [i.e., people] ἐν τῷ ξηρῷ καὶ ψυχρῷ ⟨ποιεῖ⟩

That Saturn was the "first" of the stars was implied ever since that planet was assigned the outermost or "highest" position in the sequence of spheres. Accordingly, in the *Epinomis* the list of the three outer planets begins with Saturn; and Ptolemy in the *Almagest* calls the sphere of Saturn "the largest" and that of Jupiter "the second." Similar instances can be multiplied, and include Theodore Metochites, whose astronomical work Hase quoted and described in detail.[77] However, I found no examples, other than the three just adduced, of ⟨152⟩ Saturn being explicitly called "the first of the stars." The source of Psellus is

76. The parallel was also pointed out by Vasil'evskij, "Zapiska..." in *Trudy*, II (as in Appendix I), 150.

77. *Epinomis*, 987c 3-5; *Almagest*, IX:1 = II, 115, ed. Halma (1816) = II, 206,19-20, ed. Heiberg; cf. Geminus, *Elementa*, I,24, ed. Manitius; Cleomedes,

either Stobaeus or Pseudo-Plutarch, *De placitis philosophorum*.[78] Thus, the narrator may have been influenced by Stobaeus; however, the tenor of our Fragment seems closer to Psellus than to either of his two presumed sources. Hase's note in Paris *Supplément Grec* 811 is a part of his description of *Palatinus Graecus* 356. At the time of Hase's writing, the *Palatinus* was in Paris; the note is thus prior to 1815.

VIII. Fragment 3, ed. Hase, p. 259A: ἐκεῖνος μὲν παντὸς μᾶλλον μεῖζον τὸ πρᾶγμα ἐλογίσατο	*Timarion*, ed. Hase (1813), p. 195, 10-12: στομίῳ... προσηγγίσαμεν... μείζονι μᾶλλον ἢ κατὰ τὰ φρεάτεια

To the word μᾶλλον Hase appended the note: *Sic Cod.*, drawing attention to this unusual combination of two comparatives. In the index of *Timarion*, p. 161, Hase entered: μᾶλλον *cum comparativo*, 195, 12. Again, there is nothing remarkable about the use of μᾶλλον with a comparative in two Byzantine texts edited by the same author. But the combination of μᾶλλον with the same word in both cases presents more of a coincidence.

One more set of passages will conclude our discussion of Greek parallels to the Fragments.[79] These passages form a category apart, since they come from Hase's original Greek writings: from his secret diary, preserved in Paris *Supplément Grec* 1363 (see figs. 24-27) and in an excerpt published in 1868,[80] and from a letter to Saint-Martin.

IX. 1. Fragment 1, ed. Hase, p. 255C: πρὸς αὐτόν [*sc.* the "cold" planet Saturn]... μετατρεπομένου τοῦ περιέχοντος [*sc.* the air]	Paris *Suppl. Grec* 1363, p. 119 (entry for July 23, 1843): ἦν πρωῒ νεφώδης ὁ περιέχων... ὕστερον δὲ κατηνέχθη ὑετός

30, ed. Ziegler; Metochites, *Intr. Astr.*, I,13 = e.g., *Vaticanus Gr.*, 1365, fol. 32v. Hase's description of the *Vaticanus* is in Paris *Suppl. Gr.* 811, fols. 24r-38r.

78. Stobaeus: I:24:11 = I, p. 203 ed. Wachsmuth; Ps.-Plutarch: II:15 = Diels, *Doxographi Graeci*, pp. 344,17-345,3.

79. This is not to say that other parallels to the Fragments are difficult to find. By way of example, I mention three passages from Synesius' *Letter* 4 (description of an adventurous journey by sea): σχετλιαζόντων δὲ ἡμῶν, ed. Hercher, *Epistolographi Graeci*, 640a (cf. Fragments, Paris ed., pp. 256C, 257B = pp. 498,28, 501,9, Bonn); ἡμῶν δὲ ἐξ ἀπειρίας χεῖρ' ἐπικροτούτων *ibid.*, 643d (cf. Fragments, 255A, D = 497,17, 498,2-3); ἐγχρίμψαντες ἀκαρῆ πέτρα *ibid.*, 643d (cf. Fragments, 256B = 498,20). Hase quotes from Synesius' *Letters*: cf., e.g., his Leo, Paris ed., p. 211A = p. 435, Bonn.

80. On Hase's diary, its copyists Dübner and Reinach, and the excerpt published by Rhangabe, cf. pp. 167-169; Appendix III, and figs. 24-27.

Ibid., p. 255D: εὐδιεινοτέρου καὶ τοῦ περιέχοντος δεδειγμένου	*bid.*, p. 17 (entry for March 20, 1821): ἐχαιρόμην ὅτι οὐκ ἦν εὐδία
	Ibid., p. 44 (entry for August 1, 1830): ἔτι εὐδίας καὶ καύσεως A. R. Rhangabe in Ἐθνικὸν Ἡμερολόγιον τοῦ... ἔτους 1868, p. 78 (entry for June 29, 1837): ἀναλαμπούσης πάλιν τῆς εὐδίας

⟨153⟩ Ὁ περιέχων [*sc.* ἀήρ] is a rare term for "air, atmosphere, weather."[81] Yet, it not only occurs twice in the Fragments, but also reappears in Hase's own Greek prose. The Fragments' εὐδιεινοτέρου is echoed by εὐδία of the diary.

2. Fragment 1, ed. Hase, p. 256D: εὖναι δὲ νύκτα αἱ ἀσπίδες προσῄεσαν	Paris *Suppl. Grec* 1363, p. 32 (entry for October 11, 1829): ἦν σφόδρα κεκμηκώς, ὥστ' ἐμὲ εἰς ἐδνην ἰέναι ἤδη περὶ ἑνδεκάτην ὥραν (cf. fig. 27)

Ἐδνην does not exist in Greek; moreover, this word has no accent in Paris *Supplément Grec* 1363. The sense postulated for it in the context of Hase's entry is "bed." I submit that δ in ἐδνην is the copyist's (Reinach's or Dübner's) error for ύ, upsilon with an acute. We thus obtain εὔνην, "bed" (instead of the correct εὐνήν), for Hase's original. This would mean that both he and the Fragments' narrator committed precisely the same error in Greek accentuation.

3. Fragment 1, ed., Hase, p. 255B: ὡς ἀβάτους τὰς διόδους οἴεσθαι	Paris *Suppl. Grec* 1363, p. 11 (entry for October 4, 1814): Συνουσία σὺν τῇ κόρῃ τῆς διόδου [i.e., *fille de la rue*]
	Ibid., p. 42 (entry for July 28, 1830): ἐν μεγίστῃ καύσει... ἐδείπνησα ἐν διόδῳ (*de l'Opéra*?)
	Ibid., p. 44 (entry for July 30, 1830): ἐν καύσει ἐδείπνησα ἐν γωνίᾳ τῆς διόδου *Choiseul*

81. Examples of this meaning are given in the New Stephanus, *s.v.* Granted, the term is documented for one genuine tenth-century text, Genesius, *Regum*, 101, 4-5, Bonn: exposed to the cold, an ascete σφοδρῶς ὠχριᾷ καὶ τῇ πυκνώσει τοῦ περιέχοντος ὀδυνηρῶς φρικιᾷ.

Ibid., p. 99 (entry for July 7, 1840): μετὰ δὲ δεῖπνον ἐν διόδῳ ξυνεγενόμην τῇ...

Δίοδος, familiar from Thucydides, usually means "passage"; in the Fragments and in Hase's diary, however, the meaning is the concrete one of "road, street, avenue."

4. Fragment 1, ed. Hase, p. 255A: καὶ χεῖρας ἀνακροτήσαντες ἱκανῶς, προσίεμεν	Paris *Suppl. Grec* 1363, p. 62 (entry for December 9, 1833): Πριάττης, ὃς ἦν ἱκανῶς φορτικός
Fragment 2, ed. Hase, p. 258A: ἡ γῆ... ἱκανῶς ἐξερήμωτο	*Ibid.*, p. 77 (entry for December 29, 1836): ἐδίδαξα, οἶμαι, ἱκανῶς καλῶς
	Ibid., p. 99 (entry for July, 7, 1840) ἡμῶν δειπνούντων ἱκανῶς καλῶς
	Ibid., p. 123 (entry for January 9, 1844): ἐν τῇ Ῥωμαικῇ [i.e., modern Greek] ἀκροάσει ἦσαν ἀκροαταὶ ἱκανῶς πολλοί, ὅσον ὀκτώ

⟨154⟩ Both in the Fragments and in the diary ἱκανῶς means "quite, quite a...," in German, *ziemlich*. Hase himself attributed such a meaning to ἱκανῶς in a similar context; this is apparent from his lecture notes for the years 1818-64 in Paris *Supplément Grec* 1347. While explaining, on page 31, the modern Greek sentence διήλθομεν μέχρι τοῦδε τὴν καὶ ἐν ἑαυτῇ ἱκανῶς σκοτεινὴν ἱστορίαν, he wrote "assez" above ἱκανῶς.

The following two words, which do not occur with great frequency in Greek, appear both in the Fragments and in Hase's own writings:

5. Fragment 1, ed. Hase, p. 256B: Ἀνακωχῆς δ' οὐδαμόθεν προσδοκωμένης	Paris *Suppl. Grec* 1363, p. 43 (entry for July 29, 1830): ...ἀνακωχὴ ὅπλων... [i.e., armistice]
6. *Ibid., p. 254D:* τὸ ὕδωρ ἁπανταχῆ πέπηκτο	Paris, *Nouvelles Acquisitions Françaises* 9115, p. 115, Hase's letter to Saint-Martin: Ἄσιος [i.e., Hase] ...ὁ... ἁπανταχῆ πονήρως πράττων.[82]

82. Cf. also Fragment 1, ed. Hase, 256B: οὐκ ἦν πυρὰ καῦσαι, and the derivatives of καίω which appear in Hase's diary. Paris *Suppl. Gr.* 1363, 87

The Fragments' narrator hesitated between the ordinary συν- and the ξυν-, which was Attic, and therefore Thucydidean as well. ξυν- was for him the norm, and the instances of συν- should be considered as oversights. The sequence of Fragment 1, page 254C — ...συνηράσσετο καὶ ξυνέπιπτε· καὶ ὁσαχοῦ τοῦτο ξυμβαίη ... — is a convenient illustration of this distribution. Given the subject matter treated in Hase's diary, his entries contain doublets such as συνουσία and ξυνουσία, συνεγενόμην and ξυνεγενόμην, and combinations such as ξυνεγενόμην οὖν τὴν δυστυχεστάτην συνουσίαν. These together with less vivid terms such as ξυνήντησα, ξυντυχία, ξυγγραφή, ξυνειλήφθησαν, ξυνέλευσις, and ξύν, show that in the course of his career Hase treated συν- and ξυν- in a manner quite similar to that in which the narrator used this prefix in the Fragments, with Hase's preference, too, going to the Attic form.

In the preceeding catalogue of parallels, those coming from Psellus and *Timarion* are admittedly more tentative than those derived from Thucydides or Leo Diaconus. If there is any merit to them, however, the accepted dating of the Fragments will have to be revised, since Psellus died in the seventies of the eleventh century and the author of *Timarion* wrote in the twelfth.

Similarities between Hase's Greek and that of the narrator are more perplexing, for they take us down to the nineteenth century. They include the use of the same rare term, the likely occurrence of the same error in accentuation, and a similar treatment of ξυν-. These similarities may be fortuitous. If they are not, they still may be due to the Fragments' influence upon the Greek of their discoverer. However — we must admit the possibility — the reverse may be true as well.

⟨155⟩ REALIA. We pass now to the Fragments' unusual *realia*. Among these, I shall single out two toponyms and the reference to the planet Saturn.

1. As far as one can make out, the Κλίματα that had been destroyed by the barbarians and resettled and fortified by the narrator was a town, and Hase himself understood it in this way.[83] It has been recently observed that this meaning for Κλίματα is unique in a Byzantine text, either with reference to the Crimea or to any other area, and

(November 29, 1838): ὥστ' ἐμοὶ καυθῆναι φρικτῶς πως τὸ δακτύλιον, and καῦσις, "heat," pp. 42, 44, 45, 159 (entries dating from 1830 to 1857).

83. Cf. Hase's index to Leo, *s.vv. Clemata*, Paris ed., p. 290 = p. 577, Bonn: *C. castrum; fossa*, 298 = 587: *castrum Clematum; Taurica*, 322 = 620: *in T. Chersoneso castrum Clematum.*

already a hundred years ago, the meaning of this word in the Fragments struck Vasil'evskij as peculiar.[84] His way out of the difficulty was to identify the narrator's residence at Κλίματα with the *town* Κλέμαδες mentioned in Procopius' *De Aedificiis*. This caused Vasil'evskij to place the Fragments' action in Bulgaria; while a Rumanian scholar who likewise accepted the meaning "town" for Κλίματα located it in Capidava (modern Calachioi) in Dobrudja.[85]

What appears as an unparalleled usage of Κλίματα to modern scholars was a plausible interpretation to a reader of, for instance, Anselmo Banduri's edition of Constantine Porphyrogenitus' *De Administrando Imperio*, published in 1711. In Chapter forty-two of his work, Constantine speaks twice of the κάστρα τῶν Κλιμάτων near Kherson, and Banduri translates it by *urbes Climatum* on both occasions. Accordingly, on Banduri's map of the Empire the southern tip of the Crimea shows four small circles, arranged in a crescent, under the caption *Climata*.[86] These circles represent towns, each of which could presumably be called Klimata. Such an understanding of the term κάστρα τῶν Κλιμάτων was current in standard eighteenth- and early-ninenteenth-century works on the historical geography of the Black Sea coast. Charles de Peyssonnel adopted it when he said in 1765 "je croirois que c'est aux environs de Baly-Klava [Balaklava] qu'étoient les κάστρα τῶν Κλιμάτων, urbes Climatum, de Constantin Porphyrogénète. C'est en effet dans cet endroit-là que M. de l'Isle les a placées dans sa carte de l'Empire d'Orient, composée d'aprés le Theme [i.e., *De Thematibus*] de ce prince."[87] On maps inserted opposite pages 87 and 107 of his work, Peyssonnel places the legend *urbes Climatum* west of Mangup in the southwest Crimea.

84. Nystazopoulou, "Note..." (as in Appendix I [c]), 324 note 7, with bibliography; Vasil'evskij, "Zapiska..." in *Trudy*, II (as in Appendix I), 197, 200.

85. Vasil'evskij, "Zapiska..." in *Trudy*, II (as in Appendix I), 202-205. Cf. Procopius, *De Aedif.*, IV:4 (= p. 124,7, ed, Haury). We know nothing about Κλέμαδες, cf. V. Beševliev, *Zur Deutung der Kastellnamen in Prokops Werk "De Aedificiis"* (1970), 114. The Rumanian scholar is Petre Diaconu, "Zur Frage...," 330-41, and "Despre datarea...," 1228; cf. also Condurachi-Bărnea-Diaconu, "Nouvelles recherches...," 158 (all three articles as in Appendix I [c]).

86. Anselmo Banduri, *Imperium Orientale...*, II (Paris, 1711), "*Animadversiones in Constantini Porphyrogeniti libros de Thematibus, & de Administrando Imperio...*," map between pp. 32,33.

87. Charles de Peyssonnel, *Observations historiques et géographiques sur les peuples barbares qui ont habité les bords du Danube et du Pont-Euxin* (Paris, 1765), 92-93.

However, the closest parallel to the meaning of "town" for the Klimata of the Fragments occurs not in Peyssonnel, but in a work by a lady follower of his. Mrs. Maria Guthrie, formerly Acting Directress of the Imperial Convent for the Education of the Female Nobility of Russia, "performed a tour" of ⟨156⟩ the Crimea in the years 1795-96 and conveyed her impressions in ninety-three letters which she addressed in French to her husband, Matthew Guthrie, M.D., in St. Petersburg. Dr. Guthrie translated these letters into English, rounded them out with historical, geographic, and numismatic information and published them, after his wife's death, in London in 1802.[88]

Speaking of Climata in her Letter XXXIII, Mrs. Guthrie simplified the statement of Peyssonnel, her guide "in all doubtful cases," by changing his phrase into the singular. In the opening sentence of the letter, she declared: "We next visited the town of Balaklava, the Urbs Climatum of Constantinus Porphyrogenitus." Further along in the same letter, she described a fort nearby and concluded: "This mountain fort, probably placed on the site of the antient Greek city of Klimatum [note the use of the singular again], must in all ages have been a place of refuge for the merchants and their goods, who, when the enemy appeared, probably left the open lower town for the protection of the fortified city on the hill."[89] Finally, the map of the Crimea appended to her book displays an *urbs Climatum*, again in the singular, near Balaklava and not far from the southernmost tip of the peninsula (cf. fig. 28).

Given the close parallel in meaning between the Klimata of the Fragments and the "Greek city of Klimatum" of Mrs. Guthrie, it is important to note one coincidence: Hase was using her book in 1816. In the memorandum on Surož-Sudak which he addressed to Count Rumjancev on July 7 of that year, Hase referred to "Madame Guthrie (*A tour through Taurida* etc. London 1802.4. p. 127)" who "assure qu'elle [i.e., the city of Sudak] étoit déja en 786 siège d'un Archeveché."[90] The reference was correct.

We shall return to Mrs. Guthrie shortly in connection with another place name occurring in the Fragments. A fourth eighteenth-century

88. *A Tour, Performed in the Years 1795-6 Through the Taurida, Or Crimea, The Antient Kingdom of Bosphorus, The...Republic of Tauric Cherson...by Mrs. Maria Guthrie...described in A Series of Letters to Her Husband, The Editor, Matthew Guthrie, M.D....* (London, 1802).

89. *A Tour...* (as in preceding note), 109 and 112; the reference to Peyssonnel as "guide" appears *ibid.*, 25. Incidentally, the layout of Mrs. Guthrie's city shows some similarity to the Klimata of the third Fragment.

90. Hase to Rumjancev, 6; cf. Appendix II B and fig. 20.

treatise, the *Memoria Populorum*, by Johann Gotthilf Stritter, dating from 1774, will close our discussion of the Klimata. It took over Banduri's translation of chapter forty-two of *De Administrando Imperio*; with it went the term *Climatum urbes*, duly glossed τα καστρα των κλιματων.[91] No wonder that Hase, who knew and quoted all four works — those of Banduri and Guthrie in the letter of 1816 to Rumjancev[92] — understood the Fragments' Κλήματα to have been a town or, to be ⟨157⟩ more precise a *castrum*. In so doing, he simply followed the interpretation of Constantine Porphyrogenitus' text offered in the learned literature at his disposal. Hase placed the Κλήματα near Kherson, because the term, which occurs thirteen times in Constantine Porphyrogenitus (eleven times in *De Administrando Imperio* and twice in *De Thematibus*), appears ten times in immediate connection with the place name Kherson.[93] What would appear more natural to a reader of a hitherto unknown text illustrating Leo Diaconus' words Χερσῶνος ἅλωσιν than to encounter the term Κλήματα in that text? or more natural to a *falsarius* than to put it there and endow it with a meaning current at his own time?

Whoever casts suspicion on the Fragments' toponyms owes an alternative explanation for two traits which give our text a ring of authenticity: the itacistic spelling Κλήματα and the appearance of the city of Maurokastron in the first Fragment. The spelling with η is easily disposed of. Hase did not have to consult *Parisinus Graecus* 2009, an im-

91. J. G. Stritter, *Memoriae populorum olim ad Danubium, Pontum Euxinum... incolentium, e Scriptoribus Historiae Byzantinae...*, II (St. Petersburg, 1774), 1042.

92. Cf. *Notices et extraits des manuscrits de la Bibliothèque du Roi...*, 11, 2 (1827), 284 note 3 (Hase quotes and discusses Peyssonnel's *Observations*); Hase to Fallmerayer, letter of May 15, 1825, cf. Kollautz, "Jacob...." (as in note 2 *supra*), 314 (quotation from Peyssonnel's *Traité sur le commerce de la Mer Noire*, II [1787], 7); *Notices et extraits des manuscrits de la Bibliothèque Impériale...*, 8, 2 (1810), 267 note 1 (Hase states that he used Stritter's *Memoriae*); Hase to Rumjancev, letter of July 7, 1816, 4-5 (reference to Banduri), and 6 (reference to Mrs. Guthrie) (cf. Appendix II B and figs. 18-20); marginal note 1 in the Paris ed., p. 258B = p. 503, note*, Bonn (reference to Banduri's *Imperium Orientale*, I, 113B).

93. *De Administrando Imperio*: 1,28 [= p. 48] ; 10.5, 8, 11,10, 11, 12 [= p. 64]; 37,38-39 [=p. 168]; 42,8 [= p. 182]; 42,72, 82, 86 [= p. 186], eds. Moravcsik and Jenkins, 2nd ed., Dumbarton Oaks Texts, I (Washington, D.C., 1967); *De Thematibus*: 1,56 [= p. 86]; 12,3 [= p. 98], ed. Pertusi. Constantine Porphyrogenitus is the only author known to me *besides* our narrator to have used the term "Klimata" as a toponym.

portant manuscript of *De Administrando Imperio* showing Κλήματα throughout, since Banduri, whom he quoted, conveniently informed him that *caeterum apud eundem Constantinum scribitur* κλῆμα *ut* κλίμα... *et ita varie scriptum... passim reperitur apud Auctores.*[94]

At first, the difficulty with Maurokastron appears to be serious, since this place is impeccably attested in a twelfth-century manuscript as the seat of an (ephemeral?) metropoly νέας ῾Ρωσίας.[95] Whatever the exact location of that Maurokastron and the time of its elevation to the metropolitan rank may have been, both are close to the place and time of the Fragments. Consequently, the appearance of that place name in our text does constitute an argument for its genuineness. In providing alternative explanations for the occurrence of Maurokastron in the Fragments, I shall leave aside the fact that the manuscript which mentions the metropoly of Maurokastron, Paris *Coislin* 211, folio 261^{v}, was

94. On the spelling in *Parisinus Gr.* 2009, cf., e.g., the index to *De Adm. Imp.*, (as in previous note), 323, *s.v.* κλίματα; cf. Banduri, *Imperium Orientale...* (as in note 86 *supra*), 33.

95. Cf. E. Honigmann, "Studies..." (as in Appendix I [b]), 158-62 (date of foundation: between 1060 and 1064). Recently, in an ingenious theory, A. Poppe took the Maurokastron of Paris *Coislin* 211, fol. 261v to be a Greek *calque* for Černigov (*černъ* = black), and connected with that manuscript's entry a short-lived Rus' metropoly attested in one source for the seventies of the eleventh century; cf. A. Poppe, "Russkie mitropolii..." (as in Appendix I [c]), esp. pp. 97-101; *idem*, "L'organisation diocésaine de la Russie aux XIe-XIIe siècles," *Byzantion*, 40 (1970, published in 1971), esp. 180-81, and "Uwagi o najstarszych dziejach kościoła na Rusi. III...," *Przegląd Historyczny*, 56 (1965), esp. 557-60. If accepted, Poppe's theory would remove the Maurokastron of the Coislin manuscript from any discussion of the Fragments, since nobody has ever claimed that the narrator's party was returning *north* to Černigov rather than to a Maurokastron situated somewhere *south* of Borion. Tempting as I find it, I hesitate to accept the theory. While it is clear that ᾿Ασπρόκαστρον translated *Bělgorodъ*, it is less clear why Μαυρόκαστρον should have translated *Černigovъ* which, after all, is not *Černъ gorodъ*. Further, the untranslated form Τζερνιγῶγα occurs as early as the tenth century. Finally, the designation νέα ῾Ρωσία (puzzling in any case) is less likely for Černigov, one of the oldest Rus' towns, than for a place at the mouth of the Dniester. Pending the appearance of further evidence on behalf of the Černigov theory, I shall assume that the Maurokastron of the Coislin manuscript was on the Dniester, as Honigmann did, but that it was not ephemeral; it seems to have changed its name, to have been demoted to a bishopric, and to have continued as τὸ ἀσπρόκαστρον, εἰς τὸ στόμιον τοῦ ἐλίσσου ποταμοῦ [= the Dniester], which by the mid-fourteenth century was the bishopric of the metropoly of ῾Ρωσία τῶν Κυάβων, also called Μεγάλη ῾Ρωσία. Cf. *Parisinus Gr.* 1356 (date: 1342-1347?), fols. 294r-v.

accessible to Hase and shall merely remind the reader that Maurocastrum (with the variants Moncastro, Malvocastro, Maocastro, and the like) does occur in Western documents and on medieval maps, starting from 1290 and 1318 respectively, where it is put at the mouth of the Dniester.[96] In particular, the Catalan atlas of 1375 displays the spelling *Mavro Castro*; it was discovered in the Paris library in 1803 or 1804, that is, at a time when Hase was already regularly frequenting the establishment in which he was to find permanent employ one or two years later.[97] In addition to manuscript maps, *Mavro Castro* on the Dniester was adduced in printed works of Hase's time: the example I came across is Count Jan Potocki's book which dates from 1796.[98]

In Hase's view, however, the context of the Fragments pointed to the Crimea; it is therefore arguable that the narrator's Μαυρόκαστρον should be looked for there rather than near the Dniester. A Crimean Μαυρόκαστρον was a relatively recent settlement, but its name, connected with Karasubazar in the Crimea, was quoted in a famous eighteenth-century geographical encyclopedia.[99] On the other hand, *Maurum Castrum* is mentioned, along with Caffa and Sodaia (Sugdaea), as one of the Franciscan establishments in *Tartaria Aquilonaris*. Although it is probable that Maurokastron on the Dniester was meant

96. A clear presentation of the evidence involved is given by Brătianu, "Vicina II..." (as in Appendix I [b]).

97. Cf. J. A. C. Buchon and J. Tastu, "Notice d'un atlas en langue catalane, manuscrit de l'an 1375, conservé parmi les manuscrits de la Bibliothèque Royale, sous le n° 6816, fonds ancien, folio maximo," *Notices et extraits des manuscrits de la Bibliothèque du Roi...*, 14, 2 (1841), esp. 82. Hase was appointed to a permanent position in the manuscript division of the Bibliothèque Nationale in September 1805: cf. Delisle, *Le cabinet...*, II (as in note 24 *supra*), 280.

98. *Mémoire su un nouveau Peryple* [sic] *du Pont Euxin* (Vienna, 1796), 8.

99. A. F. Büsching, *Grosse Erdbeschreibung...*, IV [= *Das Asiatische Russland und die Krimische Tartarei*] (1784), 348: "10) Kara-Su oder Karabasar... die Griechen haben sie vormals Μαυρον Καστρον gennant." For other editions, cf. Büsching's *Erdbeschreibung...* (8th ed., 1787), 1225, and Thounmann, *Description de la Crimée...* (Strasbourg, 1786), 43: "10) Kara-sou ou Karasubasar, appelée autrefois par les Grecs Mavron-Kastron"; Thounmann seems originally to have written his description of the Crimea for Büsching's work; cf. his *Description...*, 2. For the statement that Karasubasar in the Crimea was a recent Tartar town, perhaps later than the sixteenth century, cf. Bertier-Delagarde, "K voprosu..." (as in Appendix I [b]), 7. In 1837, the inhabitants of Karasubazar no longer remembered their town's having been called Mavron Kastron; cf. P. Keppen [= P. I. Köppen]. *Krymskij Sbornik. O drevnostjax južnogo berega Kryma i gor Tavričeskix* (St. Petersburg, 1837), 337-38.

there as well,[100] eighteenth-century works did connect this Franciscan establishment with the Crimea.[101] Even the Franciscan document which displays that name in what could be viewed as a Crimean context was accessible to Hase, since one version of it was printed in the ninth volume of Wadding's standard *Annales Minorum*, which appeared in 1734.[102]

---

100. Implied in V. Laurent, "Un évêché fantôme ou la Bitzina taurique," *Echos d'orient*, 38 (1939), 91-103, esp. 102-103, and in Brătianu's "Vicina II..." (as in Appendix I [b]), 162.

101. Both Büsching and Thounmann (as in note 99 *supra*) state in their passages on Kara(su)bazar [= Mavron Kastron] that as early as the beginning of the fourteenth century Franciscans had a monastery there.

102. Lucas Wadding, *Annales Minorum...* 9 (2nd ed., Rome, 1734), 159-235. esp. 232-33: *Vicaria Aquilonis habet duas Custodias,* 1) *Custodia Gaezariae... Sclata. Barason* [read *Carasou*?]. *Maurum. Castrum. Vicena. Cimbulum. Tana. Saray.* Hase could have known from Peyssonnel's *Observations...* (as in note 87 *supra*) 84, if not from other sources, that "Gazaria" was the name of the Crimea, at least in the fourteenth century. Evidence for, and difficulties connected with, the localization of Maurokastron may be summarized as follows: A. Most scholars place Maurokastron at the mouth of the Dniester, adducing incontrovertible evidence — namely, Genoese and Venetian documents, portulans, and travelers' accounts ranging in date from the late thirteenth to the fifteenth century. This localization, however, presents two difficulties: 1) the form "Blacktown," *Mauro*castrum, is neither the earliest nor the most frequently used term; rather, for the port on the Dniester, the variants *Malvo-, Mon-, Mao-* predominate; 2) from the early fourteenth century on, the name "Blacktown" began to compete with that of "Whitetown," Ἀσπρόκαστρον, Akkerman, Bělgorod, Bellegrad, Album Castrum, and by the late fifteenth (?) century was supplanted by it; cf. esp. N. Bănescu, "Maurocastrum - Mo(n) castro - Cetatea Albă," *Academia Română, Memoriile secțiuni istorice*, 3rd Ser., 22, Mem. 6 (1939), 1-14; M. Nystazopoulou-Pélékidis, "Venise et la mer Noire du XIe au XVe siècle," Θησαυρίσματα, 7 (1970), 41-43 and note 107 (for the occurrence of Μαυρόκαστρον in a late portulan, cf. A. Delatte, *Les portulans grecs...* [1947], 291). B. Other scholars placed a Maurokastron in the Crimea, relying on Büsching's and Thounmann's information, on various lists of Franciscan establishments, and on our Fragments — none of them, to my knowledge, quoted Mrs. Guthrie. Only one author, J. Bromberg, used a Venetian document of 1435 (usually adduced to put Maurokastron at the mouth of the Dniester) to locate "Blacktown" in the Crimea. On the strength of such evidence, the Crimea Maurokastron was usually equated with Karasubazar or Mangup; Bertier-Delagarde, "K voprosu..." (as in Appendix I [b]), 18-19, was the only one to seek our narrator's Μαυρόκαστρον in Černaja Dolina (Karadere) between Taman' and Perekop.

This second localization presented more serious difficulties than the first. Büsching's and Thounmann's information was not documented; the Franciscan lists reflected two stages in the organization of Franciscan provinces and

⟨159⟩ However, we can go one step beyond these suppositions, for Mrs. Guthrie comes to our rescue again, in a passage which seems to have escaped the students of Maurokastron. Having arrived in Karasubazar, she had the following to report: "I now address you from the Tartar city of Karasubazár....This Tartar city seems to stand on the site of antient Portacra....It was the Mavron Kastron of the Byzantine writers, and then a city of the first rank on the peninsula; nay, even in the Time of the Tartars it still contained large well-built churches, probably erected by the Goths and Genoese...."[103] That the "Byzantine writers" who located Maurokastron in the Crimea are nowhere to be found is of no concern to us here. In 1816, Hase quoted Mrs. Guthrie's

---

presented the Qypčaq Empire (i.e., the *Tartaria Aquilonaris*) as comprising the mouth of the Dniester; the Fragments were ambiguous and thus helped to confuse rather than to clarify the issue; and the Venetian document of 1435 did not refer to the Crimea. Cf., in addition to works quoted in note 100 *supra*, F.K. Brun (Bruun), "Černomorskie Goty i sledy dolgogo ix prebyvanija v južnoj Rossii," *Zapiski Imp. Akademii Nauk*, 24 (1874), 30-31; *idem*, "Černomor'e. Sbornik izsledovanij po istoričeskoj geografii Južnoj Rossii, II," *Zapiski Imp. Novorossijskogo Universiteta*, 30 (1880), 216-17; W. Tomaschek, *Die Goten in Taurien* [= *Ethnologische Forschungen über Ost-Europa und Nord-Asien*, 1] (1881), 37 (hesitates between the Dniester and Karasubazar); J. Bromberg, "Du nouveau sur les princes de Theodoro-Mangoup en Gothie Criméenne," *Byzantina-Metabyzantina*, 1 (1946), 65-74 (with references to two previous — also untenable — articles by the same author). As a curiosity, I quote the compromise solution of P. Golubovskij, cited by Westberg, "Zapiska..." (as in Appendix I), 80, who put the Maurokastron of the first Fragment at Kara-Kerman, on the Southern Bug. — In a note to his Greek translation of Nicholas Costin's *Moldavian Chronicle*, Hase stated: "'Ασπρόκαστρον [le Château-Blanc] des Grecs est la ville d'Akkirman, située sur la rive droite du Dniester, à son embouchure dans la Mer Noire...," cf. *Notices et extraits des manuscrits de la Bibliothèque du Roi...* 11, 2 (1827), 338 note 2 [the same text in the printer's copy of Costin in Paris *Suppl. Gr.* 859, p. 295]. Thus, in the years 1822-1827 Hase did not connect Maurokastron with 'Ασπρόκαστρον-Akkerman on the Dniester, although he could have learned from Peyssonnel's work, which he quoted and criticized in the very notes to Costin's chronicle, that the old name of Akkerman was Moncastro: cf. *Observations...* (as in note 87 *supra*), 145. Hase's note to Costin's 'Ασπρόκαστρον and the fact tht he did not quote the Fragments on that occasion suggest that he connected the Μαυρόκαστρον of Fragment 1 with the Crimea. A third Μαυρόκαστρον may have been encountered by Hase: the name of the citadel, or of both castle and town, of Koloneia in the Pontus (today's Şebin-Karahisar). It is mentioned in Attaleiates, *Hist.* 125,6, Bonn, and in Scylitzes Continuatus, 679, 16, Bonn. Hase made frequent use of Scylitzes in his work on Leo.

103. *A Tour...* (as in note 88 *supra*), Letter LXII, p. 196.

work. I attribute great weight to this coincidence and believe that when the narrator ⟨160⟩ of the Fragments set Maurokastron as a goal on his trek through the snow-covered steppe, the goal he had in mind was a "city of the first rank on the peninsula" — of Crimea.

2. The following story can be pieced together from the astronomical passage of the first Fragment and its variant readings: in the midst of winter, about midnight, the narrator's party was about to leave Borion for Maurokastron; however, a formidable storm set in making the journey impossible. The narrator advised his party to remain indoors, since at that point, as he himself "could show from ⟨the observation of?⟩ the stars," Saturn was in its vespertine phase and stood at the beginnings of the sign of Aquarius.[104] At the same time, the sun was making its course through the winter signs, τὰ χειμερινά.

In this astronomical story, three statements are unexceptionable: that Saturn was in its vespertine phase — this Saturn obviously can do, and the terminology used by the narrator, if not usual, is paralleled, for instance, by Ptolemy's *Apotelesmatica*;[105] that Saturn was at the beginnings of Aquarius — this Saturn does about every thirty years; that the sun was in the winter signs — the sun is there every winter. After that — if we want to take the story literally — we meet with difficulties. "Vespertine phase" means the time of a star's last visibility on the western horizon after sunset, that is, the point in time just preceding the one when the sun, in consequence of its own apparent movement along the ecliptic, comes too close to the planet and drowns that planet in its light. For Saturn still to be thus visible on the western horizon, its elogantion from the sun should be no less than roughly fifteen to twelve degrees. So, if the narrator's Saturn was at the beginnings of Aquarius, the sun must have been somewhere in the second half of Capricorn.[106]

104. That the sign, rather than the constellation, was meant, is assured by the expressions τὰς ἀρχάς, usually connected with the first degree of a zodiacal sign; cf. Ptolemy, *Almagest*, XIII:9.

105. The usual term is δύσις. For ἑσπέριος φάσις, cf. Ptolemy, *Apotelesmatica*, 2:11:7 = p. 99,24-25, eds. Boll and Boer; cf. also Theodore Metochites, *Intr. Astr.*, I:82: διὰ τοῦτο ἐπὶ μὲν τῶν τριῶν τούτων ἀστέρων, ἑῷαί τε φάσεις πρῶται λέγονται καὶ ἑσπέριαι ἔσχαται; *ibid.*, I:83: ⟨ἀστέρες⟩ ποιοῦνται τὰς φάσεις ἐν τῇ ἀρχῇ ἑκάστου δωδεκαμορίου, *Vaticanus Gr.* 1365 (catologued by Hase; cf. note 77 *supra*), fols. 218v,222v.

106. According to Ptolemy, when Saturn is in 1° of Aquarius, its elongation from the sun must be 12°26′ for the latitude of Phoenicia; cf. *Almagest*, XIII:10 [= II, 606, ed. Heiberg].

This would still, of only loosely, correspond to its "running through" the winter signs.[107] The second half of Capricorn puts us sometime about the end of December, and since the narrator's party was near the banks of the (lower?) Dnieper, the sun set for them sometime around half-past four o'clock.[108] Saturn, being in its vespertine phase, would have to set about an hour later, as its elongation was roughly fifteen degrees from the sun. However, the time of the scene described in the Fragment is midnight, and in December, an observer, standing on the banks of ⟨161⟩ the Dnieper, presumably not too far from the Crimea, cannot possibly see Saturn in its vespertine phase at midnight, for at that hour and latitude the setting Saturn's elongation from the sun would be more than one hundred degrees, not fifteen. We must conclude either that the Fragment's description of the winter storm was written in the comfort of the narrator's study and that his mention of both midnight and Saturn's vespertine phase, which he himself "had *shown* from the stars," was retrospective and due to a lapse in memory, or that midnight in our passage should not be connected at all with the description of Saturn's position.[109] At the very least, the astronomical passage of the Fragments is of little or no value for establishing their chronology[110] and

107. For an imprecise usage, cf., e.g., Ptolemy, *Apotelesmatica*, 1:12:2, 18:4, 19:1, 4, 7, = pp. 33:10, 39:10 (Capricorn *and* Aquarius are χειμερινά) 41:8, 42:1, 43:4, eds. Boll and Boer.

108. Cf. the table of sunsets for the latitude 48°28′ (that of Dnepropetrovsk) between December and February of the years 874-1110 in Westberg, *Die Fragmente...* (as in Appendix I), 126; cf., e.g., Ptolemy, *Almagest*, II, 13 [= I, 186-7 ed. Heiberg]: greatest length of daylight for the *Clima* of Borysthenes is sixteen hours, hence sunset during the winter solstice is at 4:00 P.M.

109. This was the conclusion of Westberg, *Die Fragmente...* (as in Appendix I), 109, who based his case chiefly on the astronomical analysis of the first Fragment.

110. Left to themselves, astronomers, approached by various students of the Fragments, were able to produce only an open-ended series of dates about twenty-nine and one-half years apart. To assign the Fragments to a given time in the series, they needed additional information of two kinds: (a) on the meaning of astronomical terms in the Greek text, and (b) on data of a non-astronomical character, ranging from the century of the Fragments' original manuscript to the actual day on which the Dnieper usually froze over. Astronomers were provided with both kinds of information by the very historians who had consulted them in the first place. Secure in their possession of tables and diagrams, historians received back from their scientific colleagues merely their own preconceptions, both historical and terminological, in correctly tailored astronomical dress. Thus Uspenskij's expert, the Odessa Professor Kononovič, agreed with him that

should not be taken too literally.[111]

⟨162⟩ Conceptual Framework. At least two expressions in the Fragments do not correspond to the outlook which modern scholars posit for the mind of a tenth-century Byzantine author. In treating both expressions I shall belabor the obvious.

Saturn could have been observed in the *constellation* of Aquarius at the end of 903 — Uspenskij's preferred date for the Fragments — and proved it by means of a diagram; cf. Uspenskij, "Vizantijskie..." (as in Appendix I [a]), 42. Píč entrusted the same problem to Dr. Seydler, fed him his own interpretation concerning the setting of Saturn about midnight (cf. Fragment 1, p. 255B-C), and obtained the desired result of 991 as the Fragments' date; cf. Píč, *Der Nationale...* (as in Appendix I [a]), 84 and 85 note. Westberg eliminated midnight from the data with which he provided his two informants, Professor Wislicenus from Strasbourg and Dr. Seyboth from the leading Russian observatory of Pulkovo and was offered the year 963, corroborated by three tables and six diagrams. This happened to be the dating preferred by Westberg's mentor Kunik in 1874; cf. Westberg, *Die Fragmente...*, 109-18, 6 and "Zapiska...," 77 (both as in Appendix I). Vasil'evskij did the most reasonable thing: about 1876, he learned that Saturn would be in the *sign* of Aquarius in 1877, counted back, and came up with the years 993-996 and 964-967 as likely dates for the Fragments (he opted for the earlier one). Vasil'evskij's results, obtained "without any help of astronomy," were about as good as professional computations. Cf. Vasil'evskij, *Trudy...* (as in Appendix I [a]), 205-206. I shall close this list by quoting my own astronomer, Professor Otto Neugebauer: "As a source for historical chronology," he wrote, "the text [i.e., the astronomical passage of the Fragments] is obviously valueless since one may keep adding or subtracting multiples of 30 years to the above given dates [i.e., 903, 932, 962, 992, 1021, etc.]. The cause of the misunderstanding of the astronomical data by Westberg or his 'Beraters' lies in the fact that ⟨they⟩ did not know that 'Aquarius' never can mean the constellation but only the zodiacal sign." (Letter of September 22, 1961). The error of the astronomers was excusable, since they were led into it by historians. The Fragments' astronomical passage, the astronomers were led to believe, was a record of direct observation, made in the "deserted Steppe of the Pontus," and astronomers claimed that it was virtually impossible to determine the boundaries of a *zodiacal sign* from such observation; cf. Seyboth in Westberg, *Die Fragmente...* (as in Appendix I), 111-12. To my knowledge, the only scholar after Vasil'evskij who assumed that the Fragments referred to the *sign* of Aquarius, was Šangin, "Zapiska..." (as in Appendix I [b]), 122. He used an astrological text of A.D. 464, counted forward, and obtained February 971 as the date of our text. — For keen observations on the circular character of the "astronomical proof" adduced by students of the Fragments, cf. Uspenskij, "F. Vestberg..." (as in Appendix I [b]), 254-55.

111. If the narrator wrote in his study, his astronomical passage could have been inspired, *exempli gratia*, by Ptolemy's *Almagest*, XI:6, where the position of

The first of the Fragments' debatable phrases has to do with the term "Hellenic." The allies, or subjects, of the narrator preferred to submit to the ruler holding sway to the north of the Danube rather than to the narrator himself — and through him, presumably, to the Emperor of Byzantium — in part because they were not imbued with the "more pure Hellenic way of life." The Fragments' words Ἑλληνικώτεροι τρόποι, as a positive term and a sign of adherence to a high civilization, are redolent of Plutarch and Isocrates, whom Koraes — an acquaintance of Hase's — had just published in 1807, or of Pachymeres, who lived about the year 1300.[112] They are unparalleled, either in their positive connotation or in their application to things Byzantine, in any tenth-century text familiar to me. Today, everyone knows what any Byzantine narrator in the tenth century must have known, but what was difficult to realize at the beginning of the nineteenth: that, ever since the Church Fathers and certainly since the end of the sixth century, the terms "Hellene" and "Hellenic" were endowed with a negative connotation and came to mean "pagan" — even the pagan historian Zosimus used "Hellene" in this way — or at best "secular." Procopius' infrequent use of "Hellene" in the sense of a contemporary "inhabitant of Greece" and the early Byzantine term "Hellenic" with reference to the Greek language are isolated, neutral examples which do nothing to change the picture.[113] The same applies to the "Hellenic arts" occurring in the ninth-century Slavic *Vita Constantini*,[114] or to the remark by Constantine Porphyrogenitus about a high dignitary turned monk who was "not

Saturn on December 22, A.D. 138 at 8:00 p.m. (τῷ β' ἔτει 'Αντωνίνου κατ' Αἰγυπτίους Μεχὶρ ς' εἰς τὴν ζ' πρὸ δ' ὡρῶν ἰσημερινῶν τοῦ μεσονυκτίου) is described, in part, as being in 9°4' of Aquarius: τότε δὲ ὁ τοῦ Κρόνου ἀστήρ... ἐπέχων ἐφαίνετο Ὑδροχόου μοίρας θ' καὶ ιε'. The second volume of the *Almagest*, containing Book XI, was published by Abbé Halma in Paris in 1816. The passage in question is on p. 284 of the Halma edition [= II, 414,5-11, ed. Heiberg]. Hase worked on Ptolemy's *Syntax* and *Hourly Tables*, cf. Paris *Suppl. Gr.* 710, pp. 493, 495.

112. Cf. Pachymeres, *Hist.*, I, 360,9-11, Bonn: ὃν... μετεμφίασε πρὸς τὸ Ἑλληνικώτερον, meaning "had him dress in a Greek fashion."

113. Cf. Lechner, *Hellenen und Barbaren im Weltbild der Byzantiner...* (1954), esp. 10-12; P.K. Chrestou, Αἱ περιπέτειαι τῶν ἐθνικῶν ὀνομάτων τῶν Ἑλλήνων (Thessalonica, 1960), 21-28.

114. Chapter IV:2. ed., e.g., F. Grivec-F. Tomšič, *Constantinus et Methodius Thessalonicenses, Fontes* (1960), 99: Constantine, the future Apostle to the Slavs, learned "astronomy, music, and all the other Hellenic arts (*jelinьskyimъ xǫdožьstvomъ*).

privy to the Hellenic Muses."[115] Both cases are simply references to profane or grammatical learning, not to a superior way of life. Leo Diaconus — whether he was the narrator's contemporary or just his *livre de chevet* — offers a good example of what the phrase Ἑλληνικὸς τρόπος meant in a tenth-century text, even one written in high style: there, it applies to the bloody funerary sacrifices of the Russian idolaters, means "the pagan way," and is plainly a bad thing.[116] We have to wait until the twelfth and thirteenth centuries for the reappearance of the terms "Hellenes" and "Hellenic" to denote contemporary ⟨163⟩ Byzantines and "Byzantine ways," respectively, and for them to acquire a positive connotation.[117]

The oddity of finding the term Ἑλληνικωτέρων τρόπων in a tenth-century Byzantine text did not escape the perspicacious Vasil'evskij, who postulated the meaning "pagan [i.e., Russian] ways" for these words.[118] Vasil'evskij's instincts were right, but again, as when he considered Κλήματα to have been a town, he proposed the wrong remedy, for within the Fragments' context, Ἑλληνικωτέρων τρόπων must mean "the more refined Hellenic way of life." Since we cannot remove the incongruity by modifying the Fragments' meaning, we must once more consider modifying their date.

The way in which the participle βασιλεύοντα is used in the third Fragment is the second of the Fragments' conceptual anachronisms. The ruler whose territory, lying to the north of the Danube, adjoined that of the narrator's subjects or allies was a barbarian. Yet, when the narrator

115. *De Cerimoniis*, 457, 1-8, Bonn. Lechner, *Hellenen...* (as in note 113 *supra*), 52-53, attributes too much importance to this quotation, which concerns only Magister Leo's inferior style and his solecisms.

116. Leo Diaconus, *Hist.*, esp. 150,1, Bonn = Paris ed., p. 92D. Although Hase translated Ἑλληνικὸν τρόπον by *Graecorum more*, he knew that Ἑλληνικός meant "pagan," for he rendered Ἑλληνικοῖς ὀργίοις in the same passage by *gentilium sacris* and illustrated it in his notes (Paris ed., p. 245 = pp. 484-485, Bonn) by the story of an unbaptized Scythian (i.e., Russian) boy. For this story, going back to the collection of Paul of Monembasia, see F. Halkin, *Bibliotheca Hagiographica Graeca* (3rd ed., 1957), no. 1449e; *idem, Auctarium BHG* (1969), 305 (*ad* no. 1449e).

117. Cf., e.g., Lechner, *Hellenen...* (as in note 113 *supra*), 56-70; A. E. Bakalopoulos, Ἱστορία τοῦ νέου Ἑλληνισμοῦ, I (1961), 67-77 (bibliography); cf. the English edition of the same work, *Origins of the Greek Nation* (1970), 36-43; Chrestou, Αἱ περιπέτειαι... (as in note 113 *supra*), 46-49.

118. "Zapiska..."' in *Trudy*, II (as in Appendix I), 179-80. Vasil'evskij also quoted the relevant passage of Leo Diaconus.

described the power of that ruler, he used the verb βασιλεύειν: κατὰ τὰ βόρεια τοῦ Ἴστρου βασιλεύοντα. This was the perspective of fifth-century Athens or sixth-century Byzantium, not of the year 1000. In Thucydides, neither βασιλεύς nor βασιλεύειν was preempted for the Persian or Spartan kings alone: Lybians or Sicilians, but above all barbaric northern neighbors of the Hellenes, Macedonians, Molossians, Thracians, Lyncestians, and Odrysians, were ruled by βασιλεῖς, whose power was exercised by βασιλεύειν. The Second Book of Thucydides' *History* which, as we already know, greatly impressed the Fragments' narrator, offers a number of examples of this usage.

In the sixth century, Procopius and Agathias, both imitators of Thucydides, followed a similar pattern: the Goths, the Franks of Gaul, the Lazes of the Caucasus, or the Hepthalite Huns either had their βασιλεῖς or lived in territories called βασιλεῖαι, and the Byzantine emperor, whenever it was necessary to differentiate him from these rulers in unofficial language, was called βασιλεὺς ὁ μέγιστος.[119] Such a permissive treatment of βασιλεύς and related words was possible until that term acquired official status as the principal component in the titulature of the Byzantine emperors themselves. This happened under Heraclius, and from then on until late Byzantine times there could be, on the part of the Byzantines, occasional and grudging concessions of the imperial title to the Carolingians or the Bulgarians, but never to anonymous barbarian kinglets. Texts reflect this attitude and in no century more eloquently than in the tenth, the putative date of the Fragments. The story these texts tell is but a chapter in the history of Byzantine imperial ideology, and this history has been pieced together and admirably told by scholars of our day.[120] In Hase's time, on the other hand, no one could have had a systematic notion of By⟨164⟩zantine imperial ideology. Hase's frame of reference was provided precisely by authors he quoted in his work on Leo; and in these authors — Thucydides, Procopius, and Agathias — βασιλεύς and βασιλεύειν do occur along with such exotic names as Sitalkes, Elemundus, Teia, Chlotharius, or Gubazes.[121]

---

119. Agathias, *Hist.*, 4:9:3 [= p. 134,7, ed. Keydell].

120. By Bréhier, Dölger, Ohnsorge, Ostrogorski, and Treitinger.

121. Thucydides, e.g., II:21:29; Procopius, e.g., *De Bello Goth.* IV:9:8, 10:2, 27:19 [= II, p. 526,16, 531,2 638,5-6, ed. Haury]; Agathias, *Hist.*, Book I:3:1, 2, 4, 5:1, 6:2, 8:4, 20:10, Book II:2:2, 18:6, Book III:2:3, 14:3, 15:3, 4, 8, Book IV:3:3, 4:3, 6:3, 7:7 *bis*, 9, 9:9 *bis*, 13:4 [= pp. 12, 16, 24, 13,3 15,11, 17,8, 20,9, 37,1, 42,3, 64,31, 85,12, 102,19, 103,22, 28, 104,6-7, 125,32, 127,3, 129,28,

However, the Fragments' northern ruler was not a Thracian, Goth, or Laz, but presumably a "Russian," Here a modern work again comes in handy, as did Mrs. Guthrie's *Tour*. This work endowed rulers of Rus' in the tenth and eleventh centuries with German equivalents of imperial titles; again, we know that in 1816 Hase quoted it for Count Rumjancev's benefit. In his memorandum on Surož, where he discussed, among other things, the place name Tmutarakan' on the Taman' peninsula opposite the Crimea, Hase referred to "Histoire ancienne d'Asov et de la Crimée dans le Recueil de Müller volume II cahier I p. 71 [sic] S. Pétersbourg 1736.8."[122] In giving this reference, Hase made a slight error. He must have meant page 77, for it is on this page in the first fascicule of the second volume of Müller's *Sammlung* that the names Tmutracan, Tamatarcha, and Ταμάταρχα are discussed. Page 77 alone, which Hase doubtless read, contains four references to "Czar Jaroslaw" or "Czar Wsewolod," and the preceding page 76 says about Vladimir the Great, Hase's own candidate for the ruler holding sway to the north of the Danube, "er sey der erste unter den Russischen Kayseren gewesen, welcher Asov erobert." Everybody knows that the Greek equivalent for "Czar" and "Kaiser" is βασιλεύς; but did everybody know in Hase's day that from the Byzantine point of view there were no βασιλεῖς of the Russes in the tenth or the eleventh century? If not, it follows that, while the Fragments' attribution of βασιλεύειν to a barbarian, possibly one from Rus', appears jarring to a modern reader,[123] it was quite acceptable

131,21, 23, 33, 135,4, 10, 138,28, ed. Keydell]. If Hase read the chapter on the theme of Kherson in Constantine Porphyrogenitus' *De Thematibus* — and it is probable that he did, since he was interested in Kherson and quoted *De Thematibus* in his notes to Leo, Paris ed., p. 193A = p. 408, Bonn — he found there βασιλεύειν and ἐβασιλεύετο applied to Bosporan kings, ruling over Kherson and the Klimata. Cf. *De Thematibus*, 12,3 and 14 [= pp. 98-99, ed. Pertusi].

122. Hase's letter to Rumjancev, 3-4; cf. Appendix II (b) and figs. 17-18; the reference is to Gerhard Friedrich Müller, *Sammlung russischer Geschichte, Erstes Stück, Zweyter Band* (St. Petersburg, 1736), 77.

123. The term βασιλεύοντα in the third Fragment disturbed several earlier scholars: Kunik (especially in his late years), Buračkov, Uspenskij, Miljukov, and Braun. They all considered it inappropriate or too pretentious in connection with Princes Igor and Svjatoslav, but they all found their way out of the impasse. Kunik and Braun connected the word with Vladimir (a relative of the Byzantine emperor, or even emperor himself, witness the Greek conciliar decree of 1551!). Uspenskij's and Miljukov's task was easier, since in their opinion the fragments had nothing to do with Russian history, and the ruler of the North was the Bulgarian *c(ěsa)r'*, that is, βασιλεύς, Simeon. Finally, Buračkov rea-

to a scholar of Hase's time.[124]

⟨165⟩ If the foregoing discussion of the Fragments' internal evidence has not damaged our text's credibility, those who believe in its authority will not be disturbed by its minor oddities, such as the unattested village of Borion; the narrator's information — based on direct knowledge and therefore hardly a result of legendary inflation — that ten whole cities and five hundred villages (settlements which must thus have sheltered about sixty thousand people) were destroyed in the area under his jurisdiction, or in close proximity to it, by barbarians whom he managed to repulse with four hundred troops;[125] the narrator's account of his soldiers sleeping on their shields;[126] not to mention the use of ἐκ

---

soned as follows: since a tenth-century Greek, familiar with the terminology of his time, could not have called Igor τόν... βασιλεύοντα, the toparch, narrator of the Fragments, was not a Greek, but "a Khersonite, a Steppe-dweller, living along the banks of the Dnieper." Cf. Westberg, *Die Fragmente...*, 122; Uspenskij, "Vizantijskie...", 28; *idem*, "F. Vestberg...," 262; Miljukov, "Vremja...," 282; Buračkov, "O zapiske...", 245 (all as in Appendix I and I [a]).

124. In the course of the discussion which followed the presentation of my paper on the Fragments at the Thirteenth International Congress of Historical Sciences in Moscow (1970), my colleague G. G. Litavrin drew the attention of the assembly to the fact that the anonymous *Hortatory Speech to an Emperor*, a source of the second half of the eleventh century, refers to the son of a βασιλεὺς Βαραγγίας, that is, Harald, the son of the King of Norway. Cf. *Cecaumeni Strategicon*, eds. Wassilewsky and Jernstedt, p. 97,2. — The few eleventh- or twelfth-century examples of the use of βασιλεύς, βασιλικός in connection with contemporary non-Byzantines have mostly to do with Armenians or "Persians" (Turks). Such usage was classical. When the *Vita Pancratii*, cod. *Athous Laurae* Δ58, fols. 206r and 208r speaks of Ἀκυλίνος... βασιλεὺς Καλαβρίας, this is because tha action occurs in mythical times. I chanced upon only one close parallel to the usage of the Fragments, but it dates from the twelfth century: cf. Manasses, *Comp. Chron*, 3524 = p. 151, Bonn: ἦν δ' ὁ Χαγάνος βασιλεὺς Σκυθῶν τῶν προσαρκτίων (Hase used Manasses). The defenders of the Fragments' authenticity might wish to quote a *graffito* which recently came to light in St. Sophia of Kiev. There, the death of "our Emperor," *c(ěsa)rja naš[e]go*, is mentioned together with the date of 1054. However, this rare use represents the Kievan, not the Byzantine, point of view. Cf., e.g., S. A. Vysockij, *Drevne-russkie nadpisi Sofii Kievskoj* (1966), 39-41.

125. Levčenko, "K voprosu..." (as in Appendix I [a]), 325, realized that there was no place for ten cities and five hundred villages on the narrow coastal strip of the Crimea occupied by the theme of Kherson. His solution to the difficulty was to move the scene of events elsewhere.

126. To serve as beds, the shields must have been long, and Leo Diaconus, Paris ed., p. 82B = p. 133, 15-16, Bonn, does speak of shields (θυρεούς) that reached

βάθρων with the verb καταβάλλειν, in the manner of Thucydides and Procopius, although in later Byzantine texts ἐκ βάθρων is usually coupled with that verb's exact opposite, ἀνεγείρειν or the like;[127] or the appearance of σατραπεία as a term for a tenth-century administrative unit.[128] I shall therefore rest my case and turn to the summation.

VI

Until now, scholarly discussion of the Fragments has proceeded from the following four assumptions: the original manuscript of the narrator's story was roughly contemporary with the writing of the Fragments themselves; it is lost or has not yet been rediscovered; its date falls within two centuries, the tenth ⟨166⟩ and eleventh; the identity of the narrator of the Fragments is unknown. I propose that from now on we retain only the first of these assumptions, and substitute the follow-

---

down to the feet (ποδήρεις). However, these were Russian shields, and the fact that Leo described them in detail suggests that their shape seemed unusual to a Byzantine. As for Byzantines themselves — and the narrator's troops were Byzantines — they seem to have had small round shields shortly before the time of Manuel I, for we are told that that ruler had the round shields of his army changed to ποδήρεις; cf. Cinnamus, *Hist.*, 125,4-8, Bonn.

127. Cf., however, Leo Diaconus, 33,10, Bonn: ἐκ βάθρων κατεριπώσαντι; 69,2: ἐκ βάθρων ἀνετράπη.

128. Constantine Porphyrogenitus, *De Thematibus*, I, 67-68 [= p. 63, ed. Pertusi], uses σατραπεία and σατράπης, but the time he describes is that of the ancient Persians and Macedonians. Professor Hans-Georg Beck has brought to my attention the Greek text of the *Constitutum Constantini* (it may go back to about the year eight hundred), in which Constantine addresses πᾶσι τοῖς σατράπαις (chapter 11, transmitted in *Vaticani Gr.* 81 and 1115; cf., e.g., W. Ohnsorge, *Konstantinopel und der Okzident*, II[1966], 108); however, the author of the *Constitutum* strives to imitate the language of the fourth century. — Vasil'evskij, "Zapiska..." in *Trudy*, II (as in Appendix I), 188, adduced two examples of the use of the related words σατράπης, σατράπευσις by Nicetas Choniates (132,17, 166,3, Bonn) with reference to the Serbian and Hungarian rulers, respectively; he added, "one could find many more examples of this usage," but provided none. — The occurence of σατράπης in two works of *ca.* 1400, Manuel II's *Dialogue* (e.d. Trapp, cf. index *s.v.* "Bajezid I" and "Murad I") and 'Επιδημία Μάζαρι (e.g., J. Fr. Boissonade, *Anecdota Graeca*, 3 [Paris, 1831], 135, 161, 181) may be discounted; for one thing, the term designates sovereign foreign, including Ottoman, rulers; for another, both *Mazaris* and the *Dialogue* were known before 1818 to Hase, cf. note 74 *supra*; for Hase's quoting a passage containing σατράπης from the *Dialogue*, cf. his edition (note 74 *supra*), 322 note 3.

ing statements for the remaining three: the original manuscript of the Fragments is not lost; it is Paris *Supplément Grec* 858; its date falls within two years, 1816-18; the identity of the narrator is known — he is Charles-Benoît Hase.

The Fragments contain features unparalleled in the tenth century. Nothing, or next to nothing, for the historian's purpose can be safely inferred from them,[129] and such vagueness is a trait associated with documents of doubtful authenticity. On the other hand, every one of the Fragments' few factual elements either was available in Hase's time or is otherwise unattested. Several other parts of our text can be correlated with the state of learning about the year 1800, and particularly with the erudition of the Fragments' discoverer. Their vocabulary and contents tally with Charles-Benoît Hase's lexicographic strengths and weaknesses, with the range of his reading in classical and Byzantine authors, and with what was known in his day about the historical geography of the Black Sea, Byzantine *realia*, and the Byzantines' view of the world. The great deal of attention which the Fragments pay to snow storms, to four cubit deep snowdrifts, and to the frozen Dnieper — in a word, to the Russian winter — reflects a pre-Romantic, rather than Byzantine, sensibility, and just possibly echoes Napoleon's retreat from Moscow in 1812, an event whose hardships were not forgotten in Paris by 1818.

However, all this shows no more than that Hase could conceivably have written the Fragments. To go further, we need answers to two queries: was Charles-Benoît Hase in fact able himself to have composed the Fragments? and, if he was, why did he do so?

The first question consists of two parts, dealing, respectively, with Hase's ability to produce the Greek of our text, and with character traits that could have prompted him to this kind of action. His mastery of Greek of all epochs could be claimed on general grounds alone. After Villoison's death in 1805, and until approximately 1830, Hase was one of the three outstanding Hellenists of France and the only one to combine intimate knowledge of the classics with that of Byzantine and post-Byzantine authors.[130] Between 1810 and 1823, he amassed impressive

---

129. This phrase has been borrowed from Sir William Ramsay, *The Church in the Roman Empire before A.D. 170* (1904), 178, who describes with brilliant insight the telltale traits of forged documents.

130. Cf. Guigniaut, "Notice historique..." (as in note 2 *supra*), 272 (along with Boissonade and Letronne). Boissonade was at home among Byzantine authors, but did not excel in modern Greek.

credentials in the postclassical Greek field: he composed a preface to Johannes Lydus' *De Magistratibus* which remains exemplary to the present day; he edited Lydus' *De Ostentis*; he worked not only on Leo Diaconus, *De Velitatione Bellica, Timarion*, Psellus, and Manuel II's *Dialogues*, but also on excerpts from a Greek translation of the Moldavian Chronicle by Nicholas ⟨167⟩ Costin, dating from the seventeenth century.[131] Hase's knowledge of modern Greek, acquired in his student days at Jena, was his principal, if unexpected, asset in gaining entrée to Parisian salons[132] and by 1816 had earned him a post at the École des Langues Orientales Vivantes.[133]

Fortunately, we can go beyond generalities, for we have evidence of Hase's capacity to produce original texts in a mixture of classical, high-style Byzantine, and *katharevusa* Greek. Thus, he appended the following facetious signatures to his letters, one to Saint-Martin, the other to Dureau de La Malle: Ὁ παιδείας ἁπάσης ἐστερημένος καὶ δυσπραγὴς ἐν μοναχοῖς Ἄσιος, ὁ οὐ κατὰ τοῦτο μέν τινος ὑπερφέρων, κατὰ δ' ἐκεῖνο φέρ(ων) τὰ δεύτερα, ἀλλ' ἁπανταχῇ πονήρως πράττων, καὶ δυσδαίμων, καὶ πάσης κακίας σωλήν,[134] and, in imitation of monocondyle script, δι' αἰῶνος ὁ σὸς ὁ καὶ coquin

131. "Notice d'un manuscript de la Bibliothèque du Roi, contenant une histoire inédite de Moldavie composée en Moldave par Nicolas Costin...," *Notices et extraits des manuscrits de la Bibliothèque du Roi...* 11, 2 (1827), 274-394. Costin's text was ready by 1822: Hase to Böttiger, letter of April 28, 1822, in Kollautz, "Jacob..." (as in note 2 *supra*), 290.

132. As a nation, Hase wrote to a friend in 1801, the French were easy to dazzle. "Comment? même le Grec moderne?" everyone exclaimed upon hearing that he knew that language. Cf. Heine, *Briefe...*, pp. VI, 64, and Kalitsunakis, "'Αδαμάντιος...," 49-69, esp. 51 and 64 (both as in note 2 *supra*). In fact, the first person who provided Hase with a working recommendation — to Villoison — was the Greek Kodrikas, at that time dragoman of the Turkish Embassy in Paris, with whom Hase began to "rattle on" in modern Greek. Cf., e.g., Heine, *Briefe...*, 60. Hase ended up giving lessons in modern Greek to Villoison (to whom this arrangement afforded a delicate way of offering Hase a subsidy, since, as the latter himself gracefully acknowledged, Villoison knew modern Greek better than his teacher), cf. Heine, *Briefe...*, 60, 63, 71; Joret, *D'Ansse...* (as in note 2 *supra*), 422-24.

133. Cf., e.g., Brunet de Presle, "M. Hase...", 317-26, esp. 321; Heine, *Briefe...*, p. VIII; Kollautz, "Jacob...," 290-91 and note 20 (all as in note 2 *supra*). At the École, Hase was in charge of modern Greek and palaeography.

134. Cf. Paris, *Nouvelles acquisitions françaises* 9115, p. 115. Dureau de la Malle wrote a *Géographie physique de la Mer Noire, de l'intérieur de l'Afrique et de la Méditérannée* (Paris, 1807). Hase owned this book; cf. the catalogue of

χρηματίσας[135] (cf. figs. 23 A and B). He also offered his own translation of a passage of Pliny's into Lydus' hypothetical Greek.[136]

The other piece of evidence, which we have already quoted, is by far the more extensive and consists of excerpts, amounting to 177 pages, from Hase's secret diary, composed almost entirely in this kind of Greek. The extracts from the diary's full text are preserved in Paris *Supplément Grec* 1363 and were originally made by Johann Friedrich Dübner, who was the guardian of Hase's papers. Dübner was copied (and possibly further abridged) by Salomon Reinach in 1913, and this is the manuscript that we possess. As for Hase's original, it has either disappeared, or is preserved but remains to be identified, in some (East German?) archive.[137] Although its inaccessibility is regrettable, since the full text of the diary might offer a new clue to the Fragments' authenticity, the excerpts alone will suffice for our purpose. They show the ease with which Hase ⟨168⟩ handled his Greek or shaped it to express the intimate details of his life as a lover, a gourmet, a scholar, and a catty member of the academic and library milieu of Paris.[138]

An intimate encounter with a *fille de joie* was entered συνουσία σὺν τῇ κόρῃ τῆς διόδου. For a refined technical detail in the same area of endeavor a dual was used: συνεγενόμην γυναιξὶ δυσίν, ὄλισβον ἐχούσαιν. Fear of the consequences attending upon συνουσία appeared, classically enough, as μέγας φόβος περὶ ἀφροδισιακοῦ πάθους, but the contraption to prevent the latter is denoted by a neologism, ἐκσπασμάτιον τῶν Γάλλων.[139]

---

books to be auctioned after his death, *Catalogue des livres...et des manuscrits anciens grecs et orientaux, des chartes, etc... composant la bibliothèque de feu M. C.-B. Hase...* (Paris, 1864), 72.

135. Cf. Paris *Suppl. Gr.* 925, fol. 8v.

136. Paris *Suppl.Gr.* 859, fol. 64r (Hase's manuscript of his edition of Lydus' *De Ostentis*). Cf. Hase's printed edition, *Joannis Laurentii Lydi de Ostentis Quae Supersunt* (Paris, 1823), 34-35. Hase offered this translation as a partial substitution for a lacuna in Lydus' text. He did it *imitans...cum usum peculiarem saec. VI, tum maxime proprietatem, interdum etiam stuporem Lydi.*The imitation is successful.

137. For details on Hase's diary and its fate, cf. Appendix III.

138. Even as a young man Hase liked to make notes in Greek, not only when he wrote down his secrets, but also when he summarized lectures in history which he attended in Jena; cf. Guigniaut, "Notice historique...," 251; Heine, *Briefe...*, V (both references as in note 2 *supra*).

139. Paris *Suppl. Gr.* 1363, pp. 11 (October 4 and 5, 1814), 16 (August 30, 1819), 17 (August 8, 1821); cf. figs. 25-26.

"I ate at the Véfour" is rendered by βεφουροδειπνήσας; "oysters and beefsteak" by ὄστρεα καὶ πίφθεκ; "calf's liver sauté" by ἧπαρ μόσχου ἀλλόμενον; "in the *Journal des débats*" by ἐν τῇ ἐφημερίδι τῶν λογομαχιῶν; "tricolore" by φλάμουρον τριχρώματον; "guardes mobiles" by κινητὴ φυλακή; the law against *le cumul*, or the combining of salaries for several positions held simultaneously, by νόμος κατ' ἐπισωρεύσεως; "ministers" by μεσάζωντες (this was a Byzantinist's felicitous choice); "senators" by δημογέροντες; and Victor Hugo's *Notre Dame de Paris* by Παναγία τῶν Παρισίων (Hase found it depressing).[140] On occasion, Hase's — like our narrator's — Greek seems to have contained impurities. Thus, under September 24, 1814, he wrote: Ὁ Ναπολέων [Napoléon-Louis Bonaparte must be meant here] σφόδρα ἔκλαυσε περὶ πενίας· μὴ λαβεῖν τὴν μητέρα [Queen Hortense] τοὺς [here is the slip — he should have written τάς] τεσσαράκοντα μυριάδας φρ.[141]

The foregoing quotation shows the value of Hase's secret diary for the history of his time, and one day some student of nineteenth-century scholarship will exploit it in its entirety and reveal Hase's complaints against Tischendorf on account of the latter's δεισιδαιμονία καὶ προπέτεια ἐν τῷ διαλέγεσθαι, or his entry on the ἐπιστολὴ τοῦ πανούργου καὶ ἀμαθοῦς Abbé Migne.[142] For us, the importance of the contents of Paris *Supplément Grec* 1363 lies in the light which they throw on Hase's character, and on the habits prevalent not only in *le monde* but also in the scholarly world in which he moved. Amorous exploits and love of money aside, Hase's was a rather permissive world by our standards. In this world, Champollion the Younger secretly sold papyri and parchments of the Bibliothèque Nationale; a "frightful accusation" was leveled against Champollion the Elder, who reputedly had a small clan-

140. Paris *Suppl. Gr.* 1363, pp. 18 (April 7, 1822), 11 (April 2, 1814), 176 (July 29, 1863), 26 (May 15, 1826), 43 (July 29, 1830), 138 (February 26, 1848), 140 (June 13 and 26, September 19, 1848), 51 (April 26, 1831).

141. Paris *Suppl. Gr.* 1363, p. 11 (September 24, 1814); cf. fig. 25. Other examples of mistakes in Greek in the diary: pp. 6 (February 4, 1813): ἀνέψιον; 32 (August 9, 1829): ἐπάνοδος ἐλεεινός, κυανεῷ; 68 (February 8, 1835): οὐχ οἰός τε ἦν ἕπεσθαι αὐτάς (as in Latin); 122 (November 20, 1843): ἐν τ ῷ ἀκροάσει; 127 (January 6, 1845): προτιθήσεται νόμος. Of course, some of these mistakes may have been committed by copyists of the diary.

142. Paris *Suppl. Gr.* 1363, p. 105 (February 9, 1841); cf. also p. 11 (February 18, 1842): ἦλθε καὶ ὁ ἀνόητος Κώστας [= Tischendorf] λέγων μωρὰ πολλὰ περὶ ἀφιερώσεως τῆς Κ.Δ. πρὸς ἀρχιεπίσκοπον Παρισίων; on Migne, cf. p. 170 (January 12, 1861).

destine side door through which he en⟨169⟩tered into the manuscript section of the same library;[143] one Fétis had stolen πολυαρίθμητα βιβλία ἡμῖν τε [Bibliothèque Nationale] καὶ ἐν Μαζαρινικῇ [Bibliothèque Mazarine]; Rochette, Hase's collaborator on Leo, was accused of doing the same with some medals (in the Cabinet des Médailles?); Quatremère (called Τετραμήτωρ in the diary) was angry at the library when he was required to return thirty-seven manuscripts he had kept for thirty years; Hase himself and E. Miller, the celebrated Hellenist and palaeographer, both employees of the library, cut out, or intended to cut (κόψομεν), folio 119 from a Greek manuscript of Ephraem Syrus; and one Chrétin was rumored to have forged inscriptions of the city of Nerac.[144] A member of such a milieu did not have the same inhibitions which prevent present-day scholars from producing forgeries. And Hase did not have to run the risk of being exposed immediately by his peers, since by 1818 he had few, if any, equals in the knowledge of Byzantine texts.

Inhibition and motivation are two sides of the same coin. Whoever deals with Hase's motivations — the subject of the second query raised at the beginning of the present section — enters a murky area, and it is best to make our stay there as brief as possible.

Hase was an outsider who made good against great odds in foreign and difficult surroundings. Success under such circumstances engenders insecurity, defiance, and hybris. Today, we are convinced that Hase succeeded because he deserved to succeed; he himself was not sure of this, at least not at the beginning of his Parisian career. At first he wondered what his French protectors saw in him and attributed his salvation to his knowledge of modern Greek.[145] Even in his mature years, he was haunted by visions of "Nemesis" and imminent fall, for he had been "too lucky."[146] His success endured, however; gradually Hase must

143. Paris *Suppl. Gr.* 1363, pp. 55-56 (March 22 and May 9, 1832), 106, 107 (June 5 and 13, 1841), 137 (February 9 and 10, 1848); cf. p. 139 (March 11, 1848) ἀντίγραφα λείποντα.

144. Paris *Suppl. Gr.* 1363, pp. 61, 67 (July? 24, 1833 and November 12, 1834), 53, 54 (November 10, 1831 and January 21, 1832), 145 (November 13, 1849), 110 (January 12, 1842, 69, 71, 73 (April 2, October 8, 1835 and Janaury 26, 1836).

145. Heine, *Briefe...* (as in note 2 *supra*), 64.

146. Paris *Suppl. Gr.* 1363, p. 62 (December 2 and 10, 1833): ἐφοβούμην δ' ἀεί ποτε περὶ τοῦ μέλλοντος, πεπεισμένος ὅτι ἐν τῷ ἐρχομένῳ ἔτει πάθω [sic] μεγάλην τινὰ καταστροφήν, ὡς ὢν ἄγαν εὐτυχής. Dübner continues in his summary: Und diese Gedanken öfter, und Furcht von der "Nemesis;" wieder: φοβούμενος πως περὶ Νεμέσεως.

have come to believe that it was due not only to the gullibility of his new milieu but also to his own excellence. Yet, in his own mind this remained a moot point; consequently, people around him had to be tested and defied. Hence, the young Hase's signing one of his drawings *Rubens pinxit*;[147] hence his philological jokes made at parties at the expense of his hosts;[148] hence his later flaunting of his concubine in the face of one of his colleagues.[149]

⟨170⟩ Hybris may have followed upon defiance. As he was the best, he could afford the Fragments at the expense of these *messieurs pétropolitains* for whom he held little respect throughout his life. They had to rely on a Westerner for information about their own past and they deserved scorn for their self-centeredness because, as he wrote Miller in 1848, they "ne s'intéressent qu'aux ῾Ρῶς."[150] As early as 1814, Hase had a low opinion of Russian officers. And all that Dübner's summary of Hase's diary says about the Russian Minister of Education, Norov, an amateur scholar and one of Tischendorf's protectors, was

---

147. Drawing in the letter to Wilhelm Erdmann dated October 12, 1801; cf. Heine, *Briefe...*, 34. On tall stories (*Mythen*) which Hase and Erdmann in their youth loved to tell to their philistine hosts, cf. Hase, *Unsre Hauschronik...*, 87, 90 (both references as in note 2 *supra*).

148. Hase to Erdmann, letter of 15 Brumaire 1801; cf. Heine, *Briefe...*, 73; repeated in C. Pitollet, "*Le Père Hase...*", 45 (both references as in note 2 *supra*).

149. Story of Marquis de Belleval (time: about 1860), told in Pitollet, "*Le Père Hase...*," 55, and repeated in Kollautz, "Jacob...," 291-92 (both references as in note 2 *supra*): "ce n'est pas ma femme, Mossieur, c'est ma concubine!" — Cf. Philipp Anton Déthier, *La main divine dans l'histoire, ou essai pour déblayer cette science...* (Constantinople, 1869), 4: "feu M. le Professeur Haase [sic]... sur une demande qui lui fut faite dans les salons d'une dame distinguée de Paris, qui s'informait, pourquoi il ne s'était pas marié, donna la réponse singulière que, pour lui, s'attacher à une personne de préférence... cela lui semblait une injustice pour les autres personnes du beau sexe." I wish to thank Professor Cyril Mango for providing me with this passage.

150. E. Miller, review of L. Delisle's *Le cabinet des manuscrits de la Bibliothèque Impériale...* I-II (1868-1874) in *Journal des savants* (February 1876), 104-105: Hase advised Miller to look for Byzantine *inedita* in the Vatican Library: "quel bonheur, si vous pouviez découvrir quelque fragment inédit où il s'agirait des Tauroscythes, des Petchénègues (Πατζινάκαι), des peuplades Slaves au Nord du Pont-Euxin, car ces messieurs pétropolitains ne s'intéressent qu'aux ῾Ρῶς." The relevant passage angered, and was excerpted by, Vasil'evskij, "Zapiska..." in *Trudy*, II (as in Appendix I), 144 note 1.

that he had a "kalmukoid" face.[151] Rumjancev may have been naive; still, he was the Chancellor of the Empire, hence an important man. To ingratiate oneself further with such a person — no matter by what means — and to flex one's own philological muscle at the same time must have been a great temptation.

We know — or, at least, have good grounds to suspect — that Hase yielded to such a temptation on at least three occasions. The first of them was provided by the city of Surož, which he discussed in the memorandum, by now familiar to us, included in the letter to Rumjancev of 1816. There, he made use of an unpublished text, preserved "in our Library," that is, in Paris, in a "manuscript of the letters of Patriarch Athanasius I," in which an "otherwise unknown" writer (of the fourteenth century?), "Maxime Catélianus," spoke of having landed in a Crimean town called Sarat.[152] This piece of recondite information could only have come from a source that has since disappeared, since no manuscript of Patriarch Athanasius I's correspondence (or, for that matter, his other writings) available to us, either in Paris or elsewhere, contains a letter by "Catélianus,"[153] and Catélianus himself remains as unknown in our day as he was in Hase's.[154]

151. In 1814 Hase met again with Wilhelm Erdmann, the friend of his youth. Since their parting, Erdmann had become a Russian officer, and entered Paris with the Allies. Erdmann himself recalls that Hase told him in the Café de Mille Colonnes, frequented by Russian officers: "My dear friend, it is a terrible thing for me to see you among those Scythians and Sarmatians"; cf. *Unsre Hauschronik*... (note 2 *supra*), 104. Cf. fig. 25 for the entry of April 2, 1814 in Hase's diary, concerning eating oysters and beefsteak with Erdmann. On Norov, see Paris *Suppl. Gr.* 1363, p. 166 (March 15, 1859).

152. Hase's letter to Rumjancev, 5; cf. Appendix II B and fig. 19.

153. To make sure, I leafed through *Parisinus Gr.* 137 (and Paris *Suppl. Gr.* 971, Carton 114, no. 11, pp. 107-57, containing La Porte-du Theil's extracts from Athanasius' correspondence in that manuscript); *Parisini Gr.* 1351A, 1356, 1357A, 1388; Paris *Suppl. Gr.* 516; through the xerox copy of *Vaticanus Gr.* 2219; and I consulted the modern description of *Neapolitanus Gr.* 64 (II B 26) [= the beginning of *Parisinus Gr.* 137] in G. Pierleoni, *Catalogus Codicum Graecorum Bibliothecae Nationalis Neapolitanae*, I (1962), 188-90. Dr. Alice-Mary Talbot, an authority on Athanasius' correspondence, did not encounter the name Maxime Catélianus in manuscripts of Athanasius' letters (letter of June 20, 1970). In addition, Mlle M.-L. Concasty informs me that the card catalogue of authors established for internal use at the Cabinet des manuscrits of the Bibliothèque Nationale does not contain the name.

154. The family name is known from post-Byzantine times: cf; Dionysius Catelianus (Κατηλιανός), d. 1629, Bishop of Cythera. A number of Dionysius

⟨171⟩ According to this elusive writer, Sarat, which he reached after suffering shipwreck — only to go to Caffa the next day — was "une ville...située sur un rocher à peu de distance de la mer."[155] This unknown Crimean Sarat, Hase proposed, was identical with the Sarat of Constantine Porphyrogenitus and the same as the modern Crimean town of Sudak. By a happy coincidence Hase had only to turn over page 127 of the book by our acquaintance Mrs. Guthrie — the very page quoted in his memorandum to Rumjancev — to find the following description of the site of Sudak: "There are now only some ruins to be seen of this once-flourishing city, with the remains of an old fort...placed on a mountain close by the shore, which seems to have been constructed by the Genoese, whose antient works inclose a large space, and run all the way up to the top of the rock."[156] Hase, I believe, did turn to page 128 of Mrs. Guthrie's book, and the close agreement between the description of Sudak by a modern eyewitness and that given by "Catélianus" of Sarat-Sudak must have heightened his confidence, for he asked the Count in the next sentence of his memorandum: "V.E. ne pense-t-Elle pas qu'aux environs de cette dernière ville [i.e., Caffa] il n'y a guères que Soudak à qui conviennent toutes ces particularités [i.e., those pertaining to "Catélianus"' Sarat] ?"

Incidentally, Catélianus' unattested Crimean town of Sarat, which conveniently confirmed the hypothetical locale of Constantine Porphyrogenitus' attested, but otherwise not identified Sarat, reflected Hase's own scholarly thinking, not that of our time. In spite of the fact that Constantine mentions that name in close connection with the name "Kherson," modern scholars place the Emperor's Sarat not in the Crimea but in present-day Rumania, and identify it not with a town but with the river Sereth.[157]

Catelianus' letters (including one to Maximus Margunius) were published by Joh. Lamius (Giovanni Lami) in *Deliciae Eruditorum* (Florence, 1740), 62-104. The same (?) Dionysius, this time spelled "Catilianus," is mentioned in Montfaucon's *Palaeographia Graeca* (1708), 93, 98, a work which Hase quoted in his edition of Leo, pp. 188-89.

155. Hase to Rumjancev, 5; cf. Appendix II B and fig. 19.

156. Guthrie, *A Tour...* (as in note 88 *supra*), 128.

157. Cf. R. J. H. Jenkins *et al.*, eds., *Constantine Porphyrogenitus, De Administrando Imperio, II, Commentary* (by G, Moravcsik) (1962), 155, and Diaconu, *Les Petchénègues* (as in Appendix I [c]), 35-36. — M. G. Nystazopoulou, Ἡ ἐν τῇ Ταυρικῇ πόλις Σουγδαία... (Athens, 1965) — the latest work on Sugdaea-Surož-Sudak — is understandably silent on Sarat and "Catélianus."

In a letter to the Metropolitan of Kiev Evgenij (Bolxovitinov), dated January 17, 1821, Count Rumjancev himself informs us of another dubious find by Hase: "After his return from Genoa, Milan and Venice to Paris, Mr. Hase writes to me that he found only two hitherto unpublished manuscripts in the famous libraries of these places: 1) The Embassy of Andronicus III Palaeologus the Younger to Trebizond in 1338, which contains geographical information on the Abasgians and Circassians, and Mr. Hase concludes that this information may have some value particularly for Russian history...."[158]

⟨172⟩ An embassy of 1338 is unknown to historians of Trebizond or of Andronicus III.[159] However, a long passage in Nicephorus Gregoras referring to the marital irregularities of Basil II, Emperor of Trebizond (1332-40) and son-in-law of Andronicus III, could have given an imaginative reader the idea that at about that time an embassy might well have been sent to Trebizond by the irate father-in-law.[160] Hase not only read Gregoras and described his manuscripts before 1819, but declared in the preface of the Paris edition of Leo that he had several unpublished books of Gregoras "ready for print."[161] It is noteworthy, however, that when he discussed the very "Trapezuntine" passage of Gregoras (which he looked up in *Parisinus Graecus* 1723) in his letter to Fallmerayer of September 30, 1823, he failed to inform that historian of the Empire of Trebizond about his find, made only three years earlier.[162]

---

158. *Perepiska...* (as in note 25 *supra*), 40.

159. It is unknown both to past historians of Trebizond, and to the most recent one, Dr. Anthony Bryer, who has been working for more than a decade on the history of the Pontic area and with whom I discussed the matter. The "embassy of 1338" is not mentioned in Ursula V. Bosch, *Kaiser Andronikos III. Palaiologos...* (1965), pp. 150-51 (chapter on Andronicus' relations with the Empire of Trebizond).

160. Nic. Gregoras, *Hist.*, XI:8:1 = I, 548,24-549,19, Bonn. Basil II married the (illegitimate) daughter of Andronicus III Palaeologus in September 1335, had a son by his mistress in October 1337, married that mistress in July 1338, and died in April 1340. Cf. Michael Panaretos, Περὶ τῶν Μεγάλων Κομνηνῶν, ed. Lampsidis, Ἀρχεῖον Πόντου. 22 (1958), 64-65.

161. On descriptions of *Vaticani Gr.* 116, 1085, and 1086, made before 1815, cf. Hase to E. Miller, letter dated December 6, 1848, in *Journal des savants* (as in note 150 *supra*), 104; description of Gregoras' Treatises on the astrolabe (Paris *Suppl. Gr.* 13) in Paris *Suppl. Gr.* 1003, fols. 15r-16r; Gregoras ready for print: Preface, Paris edition, p. XIX = pp. XXX-XXXI, Bonn.

162. Cf. Kollautz, "Jacob..." (as in note 2 *supra*), 306.

The last piece of information about a remarkable project on which Hase was embarked not later than 1819-20 comes from Academician Krug, Hase's assiduous correspondent and intermediary between him and Count Rumjancev. In a note on works in the field of history that had appeared or were about to appear in Russia between the years 1815 and 1820, Krug announced that "Professor Hase in Paris" was to publish a volume containing several Greek and Latin *inedita* concerning the history of Eastern Europe, Russia, and the Pontic seashore from the thirteenth to the fifteenth centuries. Among these *inedita* there was to be a rhymed chronicle, entitled *Libri duo de Bellis hierosolymitanis, versibus politicis graecobarbaris*. This chronicle, contained in *Cod. Reg. Graecus* 2898, dealt with, among other things, the partition of Byzantium by the Latins, the Empire of Trebizond, and the Genoese trade in the Black Sea.[163] We must assume that Krug received his information from Hase, either directly or through Count Rumjancev. Hases announced volume of *inedita* never appeared, but, luckily for our purpose, we are on firm ground with *Parisinus Graecus* 2898. The manuscript does in fact exist, and does contain a slip, in Du Cange's handwriting, which says in part: *Anonymi de Bellis Hierosolymitanis Libri II versibus politicis* — its identity is thus established beyond doubt. However, the manuscript consists of nothing beyond the Greek translation of Boccaccio's *Theseis* and the Chronicle of Morea (this is the poem "On the Jerusalem War"),[164] and neither of these works says anything concerning the Pontic ⟨173⟩ regions (a part of which belonged to the Russian Empire) or the Genoese Black Sea trade (which fell within the scope of Count Rumjancev's interest in the medieval history of the Crimea).[165]

Even if we should ascribe the Trapezuntine embassy of 1338 and the Genoese trade in the Chronicle of Morea to a misunderstanding on the part of Rumjancev or Krug, "Maxime Catélianus" and the Crimean

163. Ph. Krug, *Forschungen in der älteren Geschichte Russlands*, II (1848), 742.

164. Cf. description and mention of this manuscript in J. Schmidt, *The Chronicle of Morea...* (1904, reprint 1967), pp. XVI-XVII, and E. Follieri, *Il Teseida neogreco, libro I*, (1959), 3 and note 1.

165. On Rumjancev's interest in the history of the Crimean Tartars and in the Genoese colonies on the Black Sea, cf. E. E. [= A. A.] Kunik's Preface to Krug's *Forschungen...* (as in note 163 *supra*), I (1848), p. CLXXII, repeated in *Žurnal Ministerstva Narodnogo Prosveščenija*, 65 (1850), pt. V, p. 9. Cf. also Krug to Rumjancev, no date (Lenin Library, *Otd. rukopisej*, folder R.A.8.19, no number): report of a conversation with Köhler on excavations that could be carried out in the Crimea and financed by the Count. More than forty tumuli awaited the spade there.

town of Sarat remain embarrassing, for we are informed of these in Hase's own handwriting. All three pieces of infomation are connected with the *messieurs pétropolitains* and all date from the years 1816-20. Within such a context, our Fragments would be the most extravagant of Hase's practical jokes.

This is not to say that the usual considerations could not have played a part in the deed which I am attributing to Hase. He loved money and honors, and the tactful (and innocent) Count Rumjancev provided him with both: with seventeen thousand rubles, all told,[166] through the intermediary of Academician Krug, and with a St. Vladimir medal, if only of the fourth class[167] — a decoration apparently bestowed upon foreign scholars, among others, for their services to the Russian cause. Yet, Hase could as easily have earned both the money and the medal without the Fragments.

VII

By now, two models stand side by side, both explaining the origin and the meaning of Hase's Fragments. In the first model — implied

166. Ikonnikov, *Opyt...* (as in Appendix I [b]), I, 1, p. 200 and note 5. Unfortunately, this statement cannot be corroborated, since Ikonnikov's reference to *Žurnal Ministerstva Narodnogo Prosveščenija*, 49 (1846), pt. V, p. 56 is faulty, the last page of part V being 50. It is possible, however, to account for 9,000 francs and rubles of that sum: 3000 francs for Leo were mentioned by Hase himself (cf. p. 136 *supra*); 6000 rubles (?) were paid to him by Rumjancev in advance for an edition of Psellus which never appeared; cf. Rumjancev to Krug, letter of July 16, 1818 (Lenin Library, *Otd. rukopisej*, folder R.A.6.3, no. 53, p. 2); "je suis bien affligé de ne voir point paroitre Leon le Diacre et de n'avoir pas reçu de reponse à ma lettre à Mr. Hase auquel j'avais fait remettre les six mille francs [sic] qu'il desiroit avoir pour faire l'edition de Psellus." Cf. Rumjancev to Krug, letter of August 2, 1818 (*ibidem*, folder R.A.6.4, no. 54, p. 2); "je m'afflige beaucoup je ne vous le cache pas d'etre sans nouvelles de Mr. Haser [sic], il ne m'a pas accusé la reception des six mille R. [thus: rubles] que je lui ai fait passer avant que de quitter Petersbourg pour l'edition de Psellus. et l'apparition de Leon le Diacre, est trop desirée pour être retardée si longtems au reste tout cela Monsieur n'est que pour nous deux."

167. The medal was bestowed upon Hase by His Majesty for his edition of Leo; cf. *Syn Otečestva* (of 1820 ?), 82 (in a review of Popov's translation, cf. note 4 *supra*; I read the review in Lenin Library, *Otd. rukopisej*, folder *Polt.* 33.39); Ikonnikov, *Opyt...* (as in Appendix I [b]) I, 1, p. 162 note 1. Hase asked Rumjancev to obtain a Vladimir medal for his assistant during the work on Leo, Chardon de la Rochette (the one who was to be φεύγω£ κλοπῆς in 1832; cf. p. 169 and note 144 *supra*). The Count wisely refused.

rather than expounded here — their discoverer appears as a scrupulous scholar. In 1816 Count Rumjancev asked Hase to search for unpublished sources pertaining to early Russian history. Hase made such a search, chanced upon the Fragments in a late-tenth-century manuscript, since lost or unidentified, and, at a late stage ⟨174⟩ in the printing of his Leo Diaconus, inserted his find into the notes to this author. For all its importance, the meaning of his discovery for early Russian history — if indeed it bears upon Russian history at all — remains mysterious.

The second model is the one which we have nearly finished constructing here. According to it, Hase wrote the Fragments piecemeal — the third one as an afterthought, which enabled him to introduce a northern (read: Russian) ruler, whose absence struck him when he was introducing the second Fragment, and to improve the image of the Russes by changing them from attacking into protecting barbarians. He wrote the Fragments on the basis of what he knew. By 1820 he was sent, perhaps with the assistance of Count Rumjancev, on a mission to Italy "à l'effet de compléter mes matériaux pour la continuation de l'histoire byzantine";[168] he must have started with this subject at an earlier date. His letter to Rumjancev and other letters attest that in 1816 and 1817 he was engaged in the study of the medieval geography of the Crimea. As for the Greek authors whose phrases are blended into the Fragments or provide parallels to them, Hase knew them all, and recalled their idioms.[169]

This is certainly true of Thucydides, the narrator's principal literary model. About January 1818 Hase quoted him, including Book Two, in his lecture notes; under February 13, 1813, he made the following entry in his Diary: Ναπολέων τοῦ Θουκυδίδους ἤρξατο.[170] Thus, a

168. Ikonnikov, *Opyt...*, (as in Appendix I [b]) I, 1, pp. 200-201, asserts that Rumjancev sent Hase to Genoa, Milan, and Venice; Hase himself said that he visited these cities at the expense of the (French) government; Hase to Böttinger, letter of April 28, 1822, in Kollautz, "Jacob..." (note 2 *supra*), 290.

169. In the Preface to Leo, Hase offered the following self-appraisal: there was no Greek author, whether sacred or profane, of any consequence, who wrote between the time of Theodosius and the fall of the empire, *quem non ita tractarim, ut non aliqua eius pars in memoria mea penitus insideret* (Paris ed., p. XVIII = p. XXIX, Bonn).

170. Notes: Paris *Suppl. Gr.* 1347, fols. 172r and 185r (for date, cf. fol. 185v); cf. fol. 201r. Diary: Paris *Suppl. Gr.* 1363, p. 6, cf. fig. 24. Other entries on lessons given to one or both Napoleons (τοῖν ἀνάκτοιν, τὼ ἄνακτε) on pp. 5 (September 23, 1812), 7 (February 24 and June 27, 1813), 8 (July 29, 1813), 9 (March 28, 1814).

few years before 1818 Hase began to teach the Athenian to Napoléon-Louis Bonaparte, then nine years old, and he may have continued this task until March 7, 1815, the day on which he gave the last lesson to the boy prince and to his younger brother, the future Napoleon III.[171] In the course of the instruction Hase must have gone through Book Two, with which the Peloponnesian War proper begins, and have parsed its sentences one by one. No wonder that by about 1816-18 he shared with the Fragments' narrator an intimate knowledge of Thucydidean vocabulary and phraseology.

According to another entry in the diary, Hase returned a copy of Stobaeus to his amanuensis Sypsomo on September 5, 1817.[172] He quoted Agathias repeatedly, and Ptolemy's *Apotelesmatica* occasionally, in his own notes to Leo Diaconus. As for Leo, Psellus, and the authors of *Timarion* and *De Velitatione Bellica*, by 1818 Hase had printed, or said that he was about to print,[173] all or ⟨175⟩ some of their works. The excerpt from *Palatinus Graecus* 356 is a Hase autograph anterior to 1815. And obviously he was familiar with his own diary.

In the course of composing the text of the Fragments, Hase, who in later years was able to unmask the notorius forger of Greek manuscripts, Simonides,[174] and consequently was aware of the pitfalls to which a falsifier is exposed in his work, proceeded with caution. He must have put a number of alternative formulations down on paper. Plainly, he could not use all of them in his final version. However, he did not reject

171. Paris *Suppl. Gr.* 1363, p. 12: ἡ τελευταία ἀκρόασις παρὰ τοῖν ἀνάκτοιν, ἀπερχομένοιν.

172. Paris *Suppl. Gr.* 1363, p. 14.

173. This was the case with Psellus; cf. Hase's Preface to the Paris edition, pp. XVII and XIX (= pp. XXVIII, XXX, Bonn) (*habeo...prelo...parata Michaelis Pselli Annales*); cf. Rumjancev to Evgenij, letter of September 13, 1817: "Now Hase, upon my request, will approach the printing of Psellus and George Hamartolus"; letter of August 17, 1820: Hase promised that the edition of Psellus would be ready by the end to the year; cf. *Perepiska...* (as in note 25 *supra*), 8, 34. Hase himself hoped to keep his promise: Paris *Suppl. Gr.* 1363, p. 104 (June 1, 1820): "Will in der Imprimerie Royale den Psellus anfangen lassen." Psellus never appeared, except for some excerpts published, on the basis of Hase's papers, by E. Miller in *Recueil des historiens des Croisades, Historiens Grecs*, I (Paris, 1875), 3-99. — At an earlier date, Hase described writings of Psellus contained in *Palatinus Gr.* 356 and Paris *Suppl. Gr.* 249; cf. Paris *Suppl. Gr.* 811, fols. 210r, 211r-212v, 216v-217v, 219r-v and 1003, fol. 307r.

174. Hase, *Unsre Hauschronik...*, 109; for a similar story, cf. *Le Courrier du dimanche* of March 27, 1864 (both references as in note 2 *supra*).

the discarded wordings outright; they reappeared as the mysterious manuscript's own variant readings in the margins of his 1819 edition and thus lent a cachet of genuineness to his find.[175] The Fragments' unique words are absent both from the index to Leo Diaconus and from the New Stephanus, since the man who coined these words himself was not apt to register them as *hapax legomena*, either because he was not aware of having produced *hapaxes* or out of scholarly *délicatesse*.

The actual inspiration for Hase's manuscript *qui fuit Bibliothecae Regiae* was one or both of the fourteenth-century *Palatini Graeci* 356 and 129 which had actually been in the library until 1815 and which Hase described in detail in Paris *Supplément Grec* 811, folios 206ʳ-228ʳ and 151ʳ-152ᵛ, respectively.[176]

If Hase wrote the Fragments himself, it follows that they mean what he said they meant, and that his own commentary provides the standard by which we should judge solutions to the Fragments' puzzles put forward by modern scholars since 1848. Hase's own, and therefore authoritative, story is this:[177] the narrator of the Fragments was a Greek; his direct subjects, too, were Greeks; the ruler of the north was Vladimir the Great; the Fragments are autograph; the narrator wrote — or at least made his journey to the Dnieper region — toward the end of the tenth or at the beginning of the eleventh century, in any case before 1015, the year of Vladimir's death; the most likely date for the narrator's journey is 991 or thereabouts, because that year meets the requirements of the astronomical data contained in the first Fragment and is, moreover,

175. Hase's corrections of the Fragments' itacisms (ἐκπηδόντες to ἐκπηδῶντες, ἑωρούμενος το αἰωρούμενος, Μεισῶν to Μυσῶν) look especially convincing. Yet, this is the very kind of error to which he drew particular attention when describing Leo's manuscript: Paris ed., p. XI = p. XXII, Bonn.

176. Hase's description of *Palatinus Gr.* 356 duly registers letters of Phalaris, Saint Gregory of Nazianzus and Saint Basil as entries following one upon another (in places 12, 13 and 14, respectively); cf. Paris *Suppl. Gr.* 811, fol. 207v-208r. In his description of *Palatinus Gr.* 129, excerpts from Themistius and Isocrates are mentioned one after another, cf. *ibid.*, fol. 151v.

177. Hase's own views on the Fragments' meaning can best be inferred from his remarks in the margins of the Paris edition and from his index to Leo. Three examples shall suffice here: cf. the marginal remark, Paris ed., p. 254C, omitted from the Bonn ed., and the index to Leo *s.v. Graeci*, 299 = 598: *Epistola Graeci cuiusdam, saec. XI circa Danaprim iter facientis*. Cf. further Hase's index *s.vv. codex*, 291 = 578: *c. a Graeco aliquo notis autographis... locupletatus; Russi*, 318 = 615: *Russorum (si de illis agitur in epistola anonymi saec. X aut XI) aequitas et iustitia in subditos*.

⟨176⟩ close to the taking of Kherson in 989, an event with which Hase connected the Fragments; in his original conception, prior to the writing of the third Fragment, the barbarians who had once been just were the Russes; in the final conception Russes were the protecting barbarians; the other barbarians may have been Pečenegs; barbarian *razzias* occurred in the Crimea; Maurokastron was in the Crimea; Klimata was a city on that peninsula, and Borion, a village near the banks of the Dnieper.[178]

The first model for the Fragments' origins and meaning has been accepted in every study devoted to this text; the second, by no one, at least not in so many words. For it appears that one scholar expressed doubt as to the Fragments' authenticity, but did so only in an indirect fashion. In his *History of Byzantine Literature*, Karl Krumbacher spoke of the "unsolved puzzle" of the Fragments' manuscript, of the "somewhat mysterious information" Hase gave about that manuscript, and of the "remarkably skillful and even humoristically tinged" language of the Fragments.[179] On another occasion, he was more explicit. He referred, using spaced lettering and an exclamation point, to the Fragments' description of "a snowstorm in the interior of Russia" — a natural phenomenon, he added, known to modern readers through two of Leo Tolstoi's stories — called this description a "nordisch-winterliches Stimmungsbild," and went on to discuss the "remarkable report" of the Gothic Toparch, not without drawing the reader's attention to the fact that all efforts, including his own, to rediscover the manuscript of the Fragments had utterly failed.[180] This was saying as

---

178. If Hase followed Mrs. Guthrie's information and itinerary as closely as I believe he did, Borion should be the Berislav of her map (cf. fig. 28), even though Berislav was on the right bank of the Dnieper and Borion should have been on the left. Mrs, Guthrie's Letter XII was sent "From Bereslave, at the Trajectus Crassi, on the Borysthenes." This was the point at which her party crossed the river, in order to proceeed to Perekop: "The small town of Bereslave, which stands on this pass, has nothing to recommend it but its fine view of the Dnieper, which we crossed here in a floating wooden bridge"; cf. *A Tour...* (as in note 88 *supra*), 43 and 45. I imagine the route taken (or intended) by the Fragments' narrator to have been Berislav-Karasubazar-Balaklava.

179. *Geschichte der byzantinischen Litteratur* (2nd ed., 1897), 268-69. — Two scholars, Vasiliev, *The Goths...* 120, and Levčenko, "*K voprosu...*," 292 (as in Appendix 7, [b] and [a], respectively), touched upon the question of the Fragments' authenticity by firmly rejecting any doubts that they were genuine.

180. Review of Westberg's *Die Fragmente...*, in *BZ*, 10 (1901), 657-58.

much as irony would permit. However, those who did not wish to hear Krumbacher's gentle hint disregarded it, or took his humor at face value.[181]

But neither the impressive number of scholars supporting the Fragments' authenticity nor Krumbacher's different stand on the matter should determine our choice between the two models presented here; that choice must rest on the arguments which each model is able to muster on its behalf. Before Mrs. Guthrie's *Tour* entered the discussion of our text, the strongest argument in support of the conventional view of the Fragments was the occurrence in them of the name Maurokastron, independently attested in a twelfth-century manuscript. Now that we can invoke Mrs. Guthrie to explain that occurrence, the ⟨177⟩ strongest argument in defense of the Fragments' authenticity is simply the honest scholar's assumption that a colleague — like everyone — is innocent unless proven guilty. The strongest argument in support of the view suggested here is the makeup of Paris *Supplément Grec* 858, with the peculiarities of the Fragments' language, sources, and conceptual framework serving as corroborative evidence.

Folios 315^r and 347^r-351^r of Paris *Supplément Grec* 858, Hase's letter to Count Rumjancev, his familiarity with Mrs. Guthrie's and Müller's books, the unusual scholarly information with which he repeatedly provided the Count, and the diary of Paris *Supplément Grec* 1363 create a strong case for Hase's authorship of the Fragments, and I confess that nothing short of the appearance of the medieval manuscript containing them will remove my doubts as to their tenth-century date. The proposition that the Fragments are a modern work, if accepted, will simplify the study of medieval Russian history by removing from its pages an illusory Russian protectorate over the Crimea and from its sources a conundrum which has something to do with Russia but nothing to do with the Middle Ages.

181. Westberg, *Die Fragmente...* (as in Appendix I), 12-13, quoted from a letter which Krumbacher wrote to him in 1898: "The way in which Hase mentions this manuscript [the lost manuscript of the Fragments] always struck me as peculiar, and I made a gentle hint to this effect [in the *History of Byzantine Literature*]." This quotation does not reappear in the parallel passage of Westberg's Russian reworking of *Die Fragmente...*; cf. *Vizantijskij Vremennik*, 15 (1908), 82-83.

APPENDIX I
A Bibliographical Note

A *bibliographie raisonnée* of the older literature on *Toparcha Gothicus* is to be found in the following three works, which are also basic studies on the subject: V. G. Vasil'evskij, "Zapiska grečeskogo toparxa," *Žurnal Ministerstva Narodnogo Prosveščenija*, 185 (June 1876), 368-434 (reprinted in that author's *Trudy*, II [1912], 136-212); F. Westberg, *Die Fragmente des Toparcha Goticus (Anonymus Tauricus) aus dem 10. Jahrhundert* [= *Zapiski Imperatorskoj Akademii Nauk*, VIIIe Série, *ist.-filolog. otdel.*, 5, 2] (1901) (reprints the Greek text); *idem*, "Zapiska Gotskogo Toparxa," *Vizantijskij Vremennik*, 15 (1908), 71-132, 227-86. For mere bibliographies, consult M. E. Colonna, *Gli storici bizantini dal IV al XV secolo, I. Storici profani* (Naples, 1956), 157, and G. Moravcsik, *Byzantinoturcica*, I (2nd ed.; 1958), 551.

In this note, I shall list three further categories of items dealing with *Toparcha Gothicus*: (a) some writings previous to 1958, quoted in the works just mentioned, but deserving special notice; (b) works which do not occur in Westberg's second article, or have appeared between 1908 and 1957, but have not been included in the bibliographies by Colonna and Moravcsik; (c) articles which have appeared since 1957.

(a) N. Lambin, "O Tmutorokanskoj Rusi," *Žurnal Ministerstva Narodnogo Prosveščenija*, 171 (January 1874), 58-95, esp. 79-95; A. Kunik, "O zapiske gotskogo toparxa," *Zapiski Imperatorskoj Akademii Nauk*, 24 (1874), 61-160; P. Buračkov. "O zapiske gotskogo toparxa," *Žurnal Ministerstva Narodnogo Prosveščenija*, 192 (1877), 199-252; J. L. Píč, *Der nationale Kampf gegen das ungarische Staatsrecht...* (Leipzig, 1882), 83-85; F.I. Uspenskij, "Vizantijskie ⟨178⟩ vladenija na severnom beregu Černogo Morja v IX-X vv." *Kievskaja Starina*, 25, nos. 5-6 (1889), 253-94 (also as a pamphlet with independent pagination, cited in notes to the present study); P. N. Miljukov, "Vremja i mesto dejstvija zapiski grečeskogo toparxa," *Trudy vos'mogo Arxeologičeskogo S'ezda v Moskve* 1890, III (1897), 278-89 (reprints the Greek text) (cf. *Vizantijskij Vremennik*, 5 [1898], 549-51); Ju. Kulakovskij, "Zapiska grečeskogo toparxa," *Žurnal Ministerstva Narodnogo Prosveščenija*, 340 (April 1902), 449-59; F. I. Uspenskij, "F. Vestberg, Kommentarij na zapisku gotskago toparxza," *Zapiski Imp. Akademii Nauk po istor.-filol. otdeleniju*, VIIIe Série, vol. VI, 7 [= *Otčet o sorok četvertom prisuždenii nagrad Grafa Uvarova*] (1904), 243-62; M. Levčenko, "K voprosu o 'zapiske grečeskogo toparxa,'" in *idem, Očerki po istorii russko-vizantijskix otnošenij* (1956), 291-339 (this is a slight reworking of the same author's "Cennyj istočnik po voprosu russko-vizantijskix otnošenij v X veke," *Vizantijskij Vremennik*, 4 [1951], 42-72); G. G. Litavrin, "Zapiska grečeskogo toparxa," *Iz istorii srednevekovoj Evropy* (Moscow, 1957), 114-30.

(b) A. Starčevskij, "O zaslugax Rumjanceva, okazannyx otečestvennoj istorii," *Žurnal Ministerstva Narodnogo Prosveščenija*, 49 (1846), part V, pp. 33-34; E. Muralt, *Essai de chronographie byzantine*, I (1855), 569-70; I. Zabelin, *Istorija russkoj žizni ...*, I (1876), 310 note 1; J. L. Píč and A. Amlacher, "Die Dacischen Slaven und Csergeder Bulgaren," *Sitzungsberichte der K. böhmischen Gesellschaft der Wissenschaften* (1888), 227-67, esp. 238-39; V.S. Ikonnikov, *Opyt russkoj istoriografii*. I-II (1891-1908; reprint 1966), cf. I, p. 200; II, p. 119 note 1; N. Iorga, *Studiĭ istorice asupra Chilieĭ şi Cetăţiĭ-Albe* (1899), 26-27; S. P. Šestakov, "Očerki po istorii Xersonesa v VI-X vekax po R.Xr." [= *Pamjatniki Xristianskogo Xersonesa*, 3] (Moscow, 1908), esp. 78-82; M. Hruševs'kyj, *Istorija Ukrajiny-Rusy*, I (1913, reprint 1954), 462-64 and note 4; Ju. Kulakovskij, *Prošloe Tavridy* (1914), 85 and note 2; F.I. Uspenskij, "Pervye stranicy russkoj letopisi i vizantijskie perexožie skazanija," *Zapiski Odesskogo obščestva Istorii i Drevnostej*, 32 (1915), esp. 225; A.L. Bertier-Delagarde, "K voprosu o mestonaxoždenii Mavrokastrona zapiski gotskogo toparcha," *Zapiski Odesskogo Obščestva Istorii i Drevnostej*, 33 (1910), 1-20; J. Brutzkus, "Pis'mo xazarskogo evreja ot X v.," *Evrejskaja mysl'*, 1 (1922), 31-71, esp. 58-68 (reprinted under the same title as a separate pamphlet [Berlin, 1924] , cf. 32-42); N. Bănescu, "Les premiers témoignages sur les Roumains du Bas-Danube," *Byzantinisch-neugriechische Jahrbücher*, 3 (1922), 287-310, esp. 306-10; V. A. Parxomenko, "Novye tolkovanija zapiski gotskogo toparxa," *Izvestija Tavričeskogo obščestva istorii, arxeologii i ètnografii*, 3 (1929) (inaccessible to me); F. Dvornik, *Les légendes de Constantin et de Méthode vues de Byzance* (1933, reprint 1969), 186-87; G. I. Brătianu, *Recherches sur Vicina et Cetătea Albă* (1935), 99-101; A. A. Vasiliev, *The Goths in the Crimea*, (1936), 119-31; J. Bromberg, "Toponymical and Historical Miscellanies...," *Byzantion*, 12 (1937), 169, and *ibid.*, 13 (1938), 35 note 2 and 52; V. V. Mavrodin, "Slavjano-russkoe naselenie nižnego Dona i severnogo Kavkaza v X-XI vekax," *Učenye Zapiski Gosudarstvennogo Leningradskogo Pedagogičeskogo Instituta im. Gercena*, 11 (1938), 231-73, esp. 251; A. N. Nasonov, "Tmutarakan' v istorii ⟨179⟩ vostočnoj Evropy X veka," *Istoričeskie Zapiski*, 6 (1940), 79-99, esp. 81 note 4 and 92-93; M. A. Šangin, "'Zapiska grečeskogo toparxa' kak istočnik o vojne russkix na Balkanax 970 g. i zimoj 971 g.," *Istoričeskij Žurnal* (1941, no. 9), 120-23; G. I. Brătianu, "Vicina II," esp. "VI. Maurocastron et Asprocastron," *Revue historique du sud-est européen*, 19 (1942), 155-66;

E. Honigmann, "Studies in Slavic Church History," *Byzantion*, 17 (1945), 160-61; V. V. Mavrodin, *Obrazovanie drevnerusskogo gosudarstva* (1945), 205 and 260-61; *idem, Drevnjaja Rus'* (1946), 194-95; E. V. Vejmarn and S. F. Strželeckij, "K voprosu o Slavjanax v Krymu," *Voprosy Istorii* (1952, no. 4), 94-99, esp. 98-99; M. A. Tixanova, "Doros-Feodoro v istorii srednevekovogo Kryma," *Materialy i issledovanija po arxeologii SSSR*, 34 (1953), 328 note 1; D. M. Dunlop, *The History of the Jewish Khazars* (1954), 165 and 244 note 45; B. Câmpina, "Le problème de l'apparition des états féodaux romains," *Nouvelles études d'histoire présentées au Xe Congrès des Sciences Historiques, Rome, 1955* (1955), 181-207, esp. 189-90 (cf. N. Bănescu's criticisms in *Byzantinische Zeitschrift*, 52 [1959], 195); M. V. Levčenko, "Problema russko-vizantijskix otnošenij v russkoj dorevoljucionnoj, zarubežnoj i sovetskoj istoriografii," *Vizantijskij Vremennik*, 8 (1956), 7-25, esp. 11, 13-14, and 22. M. A. Šangin's *Vizantijskie istočniki o vojne Svjatoslava s grekami*, a manuscript preserved in the Archives of the Leningrad section of the Institute of History, was inaccessible to me; cf., e.g., Levčenko, "K voprosu..." (as *supra*), p. 302 note 2, and P. O. Karyškovskij in *Vizantijskij Vremennik*, 6 (1953), 37 note 2.

(c) M. A, Šangin and A. F. Višnjakova, "Iz kommentarija k 'Zapiske grečeskogo toparxa,'" *Vizantijskij Vremennik*, 14 (1958), 99-102; D. L. Talis, "Iz istorii russko-korsunskix političeskix otnošenij v IX-X vv.," *Vizantijskij Vremennik*, 14 (1958), 103-15, esp. 105-06 and 108 note 22; B. D. Grekov, *Kiev Rus'* (1959), 623-24; A. L. Jakobson, *Rannesrednevekovyj Xersones* [= *Materialy i issledovanija po istorii SSSR*, 63] (1959), esp. 54 and note 2; C. Cihodaru, "Observaţii critice asupra însemnărilor toparhului bizantin," *Academia R. P. Romîne, Filiala Iaşi, Studii şi cercetări ştiinţifice, Istorie*, 12, 2 (Jassy, 1961), 259-72 (dates the Fragments to 1050-51); P. Diaconu, "Zur Frage der Datierung des Steinwalles in der Dobrudscha und der Lokalisierung der im Berishte des griechischen Toparchen geschilderten Ereignisse," *Dacia*, N. S., 6 (1962), 317-35 (the same article in Rumanian, "Despre datarea valului de piatră din Dobrogea şi localizarea evenimentelor din nota toparhului grec," *Studii*, 15, 5 [1962], 1215-35 [dates the fragments to *ca.* 992]); M. N. Tixomirov, *Istočnikovedenie istorii SSSR*, I (1962), 145; P. Xr. Petrov, "Vosstanie Petra i Bojana v 976 g. i bor'ba Komitopulov s Vizantiej," *Byzantinobulgarica*, 1 (1962), 121-44, esp. 122 and 142-44; C. Cihodaru, "Precizări necesare în legătură cu datarea valului de piatră din Dobrogea şi însemnările toparhului bizantin," *Studii*, 16, 5 (1963), 1123-35 (refutes Diaconu); M. G. Nystazopoulou, "Note sur l'anonyme de Hase improprement appelé Toparque de Gothie," *Bulletin de correspondance hellénique*, 86 (1962), 319-26 (good recent bibliography; cf. V. Laurent in *Byzantinische Zeitschrift*, 55 [1962], 349); *Tusculum-Lexikon* (Munich, 1982), 806-07, *s.v.*, "Toparcha Gothicus"; *Sovetskaja Istoričes⟨180⟩kaja Ènciklopedija*, V (1964), *s.v.* "Zapiska grečeskogo toparxa"; L. Jončev, ed. and trans., "Zapiska na gotskija toparx," *Grъcki izvori za Bъlgarskata istorija*, 5 [= *Izvori za Bъlgarskata istorija*, 9] (1964), 296-302 (reprints parts of Greek text); P. Diaconu, "Din nou despre valul de piatră din Dobrogea şi nota toparhului grec," *Studii şi cercetări de istorie veche*, 16 (1965), 189-99, 384-94; C. Cihodaru, "Alte precizări în legătură cu valul de piatră din Dobrogea şi cu însemnările toparhului bizantin," *Anuarul Institului de Istorie şi Arheologie*, 2 (Jassy, 1965), 261-80; N. M. Panagiotakes (Panayotakis), Λέων ὁ Διάκονος..., Α' Τὰ βιογραφικά, Β' Χειρόγραφα καὶ ἐκδόσεις (1965) (the same work in Ἐπετηρὶς Ἑταιρείας Βυζαντινῶν Σπουδῶν, 34 [1965]), esp. 121-22; Em. Condurachi, I. Barnea, P. Diaconu, "Nouvelles recherches sur le *Limes* byzantin du Bas-Danube aux Xe-XIe siècles," *The Proceedings of the XIIIth International Congress of Byzantine Studies* (1967), 179-93, esp. 187-88; A. V. Poppe, "Russkie mitropolii konstantinopol'skoj patriarxii v XI stoletii," *Vizantijskij Vremennik*, 28 (1968), 101 and note 65; Z. V. Udal'cova, *Sovetskoe vizantinovedenie za 50 let* (1969), 117-18; Petre Diaconu, *Les Petchénègues au Bas-Danube* [= *Bibliotheca historica Romaniae*, 27] (1970), esp. 33 note 81 and bibl. on 140-41; *Radjans'ka Encyklopedija Istoriji Ukrajiny*, II (1970), 182, *s.v.* "Zapyska hrec'koho toparxa"; I. Ševčenko, "Date and Author of the So-Called Fragments of Toparcha Gothicus," *Association Internationale des Etudes Byzantines, Bulletin d'information et de coordination*, 5 (1971), 71-95; H. Ahrweiler, "Les relations entre les Byzantins et les Russes au IXe siècle," *ibid.*, esp. 68-70; I. Ševčenko, Preface to the reprint of Westberg, *Die Fragmente...* (1972). — The typewritten thesis by M. Nystazopoulou, *La Chersonèse taurique à l'époque byzantine* (cf. Ahrweiler, "Les relations..." [as *supra*] , 56 note 5), inaccessible to me, is being reworked for publication.

APPENDIX II

Correspondence between Rumjancev and Hase[182]

A. [Rumjancev to Hase, draft, probably of April-June 1816, Lenin Library, *Otdel rukopisej*, folder Fond 255.5.34, no. 9; see figs. 13-14 *infra*]

---

182. In the transcription of the texts, no account was taken of deletions, orthographic idiosyncrasies, and mistakes. I wish to thank Professor Benjamin Uroff and Mrs. O. S. Popova for their help in obtaining the microfilms and

à Mr Haser à Paris

[p. 1] je vous fait mes remerciments de m'avoir ecris. Vôtre souvenir m'a flatté et je vous scais beaucoup de gré de vous occuper à completter la Collection des Bysantins, Mr Krug m'a montré la feuille d'Epreuve et j'en ai été satisfait. vous allez acquerir des droits à la reconoissance et vous en aurez de particuliers à la mien(n)e

je suis charmé d'aprendre que vous proposez de nous don(n)er entre-autres l'edition de George Hamartolus dont s'est servi Nestor et je vous invite très instament Monsieur à rechercher parmi les manuscripts inédits des auteurs ⟨181⟩ Bisantins ceux dans lesquels peuvent être consignés quelques faits relatifs à l'Histoire de ma Patrie, ce sera me rendre un service essentiel et je ne demande pas mieux que de le reconoitre.

Banduri, nous dit peu sur la Conversion des Russes à la Religion Chretien(n)e mais il se pouroit tres bien que le manuscript de la bibliotheque de Colbert N. 4432. dans lequel il paroit avoir puisé ces notions, contien(n)e davantage. Ne voudriez vous pas Mr avoir la bonté de parcourir ce volume et de vous assurer s'il ne contient point encore quelque chose qui soit relatif aux Russes? et si vous y faites pareilles découvertes je vous serai infiniment obligé de me les comuniquer au prealable sans retard.

S'il existe parmi les manuscripts qui sont à la Bibliotheque une vie un peu elargie du Patriarche St Ignace il seroit possible d'y retrouver quelques notions plus précises, sur des Russes qui abord⟨è⟩rent dit' on le lieu de son Exile et y troublerent ses pieuses ocupations, renverserent ses autels.

Coment les bisantins ne nous ont ils point transmis les details de la conversion de Wladimir au 10me siecle tandis que l'un d'entre eux cite cependant le secours que l'Empereur Basile recut de Wladimir et qu'il employa contre les rebelles adherents de Bardas Phocas. il doit nescessairement se trouver quelque part dans quelqu'un des Bysantins inedits des notions Historiques sur le Bapteme et le mariage de Wladimir peut être vous est il reservé d'en enrichir nôtre Nestor.

[p. 2] je ne mets com(m)e vous le voyez nulle reserve à mes importunités, en voici une nouvelle preuve.

je vous consulte Mr pour scavoir si les vastes conoissances que vous avez des Bisantins ne vous metent pas dans le cas d'eclaircir ce que c'etoit dans l'Empire d'orient que la ville de Sur ou Souroje que l'on trouve cité dans nos analles en plus d'une occasion, voici ce qui peut

---

reproductions of texts printed here, and the authorities of the Lenin Library, for allowing me to inspect these and other pieces of correspondence, in the summer of 1970.

vous mettre sur la voye.

Nôtre Eglise chôme le 15. de Dec(em)bre la Fête d'un St Etiene qui au 8me siecle etoit *Archevêque* de cette ville de la domination des Emp. Grecs; C'est un des Prelates dont le rôle [?] s'est signalé sous le Regne de Leon l'Isaurien en faveur des Images, et je suis frapé je l'avoue de ne l'avoir point retrouvé dans les differents receuils des Vies des Saints que l'Eglise Latine reconoit pour tels.

nos legendes, disent que né en Capadoce ils e presenta à l'age de 15. ans à Constantinople sous le Regne de Theodose l'adramitain; que le Patriarche Germain le consacra Archeveque de Sur ou Souroje. qu'il s'y rendit *par mer* et qu'au bout de 5 ans, il convertit au christianisme non seulement tous les habitants de la ville mais ceux de la contrée environante.

notez je vous prie Mr. que nos legendes disent, que ce Prelat fut particulierement protegé par l'Imperatrice Epouse de Constantin Copronime, qui sollicita et obtint de son Mary que ce fut lui qui tint sur le fonds de baptême leur fils, Leon qui devint ensuite Empereur.

Ce qui peut nous assister encore Mr c'est la relation d'un Voyage d'un de nos archeveques no(m)mé Pimin qui en 1389. sortant d'azov le 1. Juin pour se rendre à Constantinople, a passé le 5. Juin devant Caffa et Sur ou Souroje.

il en resulte nescessairement que le Sur ou Souroje, qui fait l'objet de ma curiosité etoit ou bien en Crimée sur la même côte que Caffa ou bien sur la côte ⟨182⟩ opposée dans l'Isle de Taman. Cette ville peut avoir porté chez les Bisantins un nom different, mais sa place geographique est à peu près determinée et peut être me doneriez vous moyen de la fixer tout à fait, en retrouvant dans les Bisantins, un archeveque Etiene protegé par l'Imperatrice fem(m)e de Constatin Copronime qui si ma mémoire ne me trompe etoit une Kosare, il est bon de vous dire aussi que dans la vie de ce Saint tel quelle est dans nos menées c'est un nom(m)é philarethe qui à sa mort lui succede dans son Archeveché; les actes des Conciles, Iconoclastes ou ceux des assemblées des Evêques qui leur etoient contraires ne portent ils pas des signatures de l'un ou l'autre de ces Archevêques et en ce cas, coment leur Archeveché y est il designé.

n'y avoit il pas en Crimée une Eglise des Goths? et ou se trouvoit son siege? y'a t'il quelque part un nomenclateur de touttes les metropoles chretienes qui au 8me siecle se trouvoient dans les limites de l'Empire d'orient. Soit quelles reconn⟨u⟩ssent com(m)e précedement la Hierarchie des Patriarches de Constantinople ou qu'a cause du Schisme des Iconoclastes elles se fussent rangées à cette Epoque sous la domination des Papes.

j'eprouve Mr je l'avoue quelque confusion de vous être si indiscret;

je trouble par cette lettre des occupations utiles et plus avantageuses dans leurs resultats, mais le veritable scavoir est toujours indulgent vous devez l'etre.

B. [Excerpt from letter of Hase to Rumjancev, dated July 7, 1816, Lenin Library, *Otdel rukopisej*, folder R. A. 7.12, no. 9, pp. 3-8; see figs 15-22 *infra*]

[p. 3] ... La question sur la position géographique de Sur ou de Sourage pourroit devenir le sujet d'un mémoire curieux. Voulant répondre sur le champ à Votre Excellence, je réunis ici peut-être un peu précipitamment ce que je pense à ce sujet. Que mes conjectures semblent admissibles ou non à V. E., Elle fera de ces matériaux épars l'usage qu'Elle voudra.

D'aprés l'itinéraire de l'Archevêque Pimine nous devons supposer que Sourage se trouvoit à peu de distance du detroit de Caffa, soit en Crimée, soit sur la côte opposée de l'Asie.

Je ne crois pas qu'il faille le chercher dans le pays des Abasges, la *Zichia* des Byzantins. D'abord, nous nous éloignerions trop du détroit; ensuite dans tout le tour du Pont-Euxin la cote depuis l'ile de Taman jusqu'à Dioscurias est précisément celle que les Empereurs d'Orient ont possédée le moins de temps. Ils n'y pouvoient déja plus rien au sixième siècle (Procope *Bello Gotthic*. I. 572. *B*.), et si Basile II s'en rendit maître vers 1022 (Cedren. II. 718.D.), sa domination ne fut certainement pas de longue durée. Les garnisons des Grecs, dispersées sur cette côte éloignée, habitée par des peuples sauvages et belliqueux, devoient être bientôt accablées, n'ayant pas, comme en Crimée, de larges bras de mer pour leur defense.

Je ne cherche pas non plus Sourage dans l'île de Taman. Nous connaissons le nom du siège métropolitan établi dans cette contrée; c'est celui de *Tmutarakan* en Russe (Histoire ancienne d'Asov et de la Crimée, dans [p. 4] le Recueil de Müller volume II cahier I p. 71. S. Pétersbourg 1736. 8 et le Mémoire du ⟨183⟩ M. le Comte de Mussin-Puschkin sur l'inscription de Gleb, figurée aussi dans le voyage de Pallas de l'an 1793 et 1794. Tom. II p. 184 de l'édit. Allemande), et *Tamatarcha* (Ταμάταρχα) ou *Metracha* (Μετραχά) chez les Byzantins. Le premier de ces deux noms se trouve dans Constantin (*De administrando imp.* 113. E. F.), le second dans Le Quien *Oriens Christianus* I, 1326. A. Il y' avoit en outre, du moins pour quelques temps, un evêché à Phanagoria (Le Quien, *ibid*.).

Il ne reste donc que la Crimée, et c'est dans la partie méridionale de cette presqu'ile que je me flatte de rencontrer la ville de Sourage [= Surož]. Je crois 1) qu'elle étoit connue chez les Grecs sous le nom de

Sarat, Σαράτ. 2) qu'ayant pris de l'accroissement vers le treizième siècle, elle est la Soldaja des Genois, et par conséquent le Soudak d'aujourd'hui, dont les ruines, les fortifications, et la position singulière ont attiré l'attention de presque tous les voyageurs modernes. Voici, Monseigneur, les raisons sur lesquelles j'appuye mes deux conjectures.

1. "La contrée des Patzinaques," dit Constantin (*De administrando imp.* 112 F. [ch. 42,62-64 = p. 184, eds. Moravscik- Jenkins]), "comprend tout le pays depuis la Russie et le Bosphore, jusqu'à Cherson, Sarat, Burat, et les trente divisions." Les Patzinaques occupoient donc tout l'intérieur de la presqu'ile, à l'exception de la côte escarpée qui en borde la côte méridionale. Les *trente divisions* sont les mêmes que les *trente Climata* (Banduri *Adnimadvers. in Constantin. De administr. imp.* [p. 5] 112 F.), près du Cap Balaclava. Je ne connais point Burat, qui était peut-être aux environs de Nikita, et Sarat, en suivant la côte, me semble tomber naturellement sur le Soudak d'aujourd'hui.

2. Ce qui me fait croire surtout à l'identité de Sarat et de Soudak, c'est une lettre inédite conservée dans notre Bibliothèque. Elle est écrite par Maxime Catélianus, personnage inconnu d'ailleurs. Ce monument curieux de l'impéritie des marins grecs au quatorzième siècle ne porte point de date; mais comme il se trouve au milieu des lettres du Patriarche Athanase (1289-1311 [rather: 1289-93; 1303-09]), on peut présumer qu'il est addressé à ce Prélat; d'ailleurs, la précision de son époque n'est pas d'une importance majeure pour nos recherches. V. E. verra que Catélianus, obligé de quitter Anchiale (était-ce parce que les Bulgares menaçaient ou avaient pris cette ville?), fit naufrage sur les côtes escarpées de la Crimée, qu'il gagna une ville nommée Sarat située sur un rocher à peu de distance de la mer, et qu'il se rendit à Caffa le lendemain. V. E. ne pense-t-Elle pas qu'aux environs de cette dernière ville il n'y a guères que Soudak à qui conviennent toutes ces particularités?

Mais, me dira-t-on, quand même il seroit constant que Sarat est le nom grec de Soudak, comment prouver l'identité de Soudak et de Sourage? Voici, Monseigneur, des rapprochements qui peuvent au moins conduire à une hypothèse:

3. Il est fait mention chez les auteurs Arméniens d'un bourg nommé indistinctement Sour-gat et Sou-dak, et qui certainement n'est autre chose que [p. 6] le Soudak des modernes. Sour-gat, d'après les Arméniens, était situé dans la partie Orientale de la Crimée, distant de cinq milles géographiques de Caffa. Etienne Arontz, Archevêque Arménien, rapporte (Géographie, Partie II. Tome ⟨184⟩ II p. 329.) qu'une colonie Arménienne s'y établit après la ruine de la ville d'Ani, saccagée par les Mahométains vers l'an 1320 de J.C.

4. Soudak est d'ailleurs une ville, si non antique, du moins bien

antérieure à l'arrivée des genois en Crimée. Madame Guthrie (*A tour through Taurida* etc. London 1802. 4. p. 127.) assure qu'elle était déja en 786 siège d'un Archeveché. Ce fait, s'il étoit constaté, seroit décisif en faveur de mon hypothese; mais j'avoue que je n'ai pu découvrir l'autorité d'après laquelle Madame Guthrie l'avance.

5. Ajoutons à ces inductions la route de Pimine qui, ayant passé Caffa, se dirigea probablement vers l'ouest dans la direction de Constantinople; se porter de Caffa vers Anapa ou Sotchouk-Kalé, auroit été revenir sur ses pas. Or, Soudak ou Soldaja etoit alors la seule ville considérable qu'il y eut sur la côte depuis Caffa jusqu'au cap Balaclava.

6. Il parait enfin que le nom Tartare Sou-dag, *montagne Sou*[a], est derivé du mot Sur, et qu'il renferme encore la première syllabe de celui de Sourage. Comme je me méfie toujours un peu des hypothèses fondées sur la seule conformité des sons, je ne remarquerois [p. 7] pas cette ressemblance, si elle était isolée; mais jointe aux autres faits elle ajoute, si je ne me trompe, un degré de probabilité à ma conjecture.

J'avoue cependant qu'il reste quelques difficultés que je ne saurois resoudre à moi seul. Il peut surtout paraître singulier que les Grecs qui parlent si souvent des Evêchés de Cherson (Le Quien, I. 1329.) et de Bosporus (*ibid.* I. 1827.), ne fassent jamais mention de l'Archeveché de Sarat. Dirions-nous que l'Evêché de Bosporus et l'Archeveché de Sarat ne sont peut-être qu'un seul, et que le siège de ces Prélats se trouvant établi, à différentes époques, tantôt dans l'une tantôt dans l'autre de ces deux villes, les Byzantins les aient toujours nommés Evêques de Bosporus en quel lieu que fût leur résidence?

Quoiqu'il en soit, Monseigneur, je crois avoir rendu probable au moins l'identité de Soudak et du Sarat de Constantin. Quant à celle de Sarat et de Sourage, c'est à V. E. de voir si ma conjecture s'accorde avec les particularités rapportées dans les annales Russes de cette dernière ville. Peut-être pourrois-je donner un degré de probababilité de plus à mon opinion en consultant des ouvrages Russes et Allemands; mais je me trouve dans une Bibliothèque, et je puis dire dans une ville, où il n'y a presque point des premiers, et peu des seconds. Reduit par conséquent aux auteurs grecs je m'estimerois heureux toutes les fois quand dans ceux-ci et dans le nombre de notes historiques et géographiques que j'ai recueillies en examinant [p. 8] les ouvrages inédits de notre Bibliothèque,

---

a. Je dois faire observer cependant, que le mot Tartare *dag*, montagne, s'écrit par un g, et que le nom de Soudak, chez les auteurs Arabes, se termine par un k; ainsi la signification de ce mot n'est peut-être pas celle que je dis là, mais la ressemblance entre *Sou* et *Sour* existe toujours.

il se trouvera quelques détails qui peuvent aider les recherches de V. E.

Je n'ai point voulu retarder l'envoi de ma petite dissertation, mais j'espère que dans une quinzaine de jours je pourrois vous faire parvenir la totalité des épreuves de Léon, dont le tirage est achevé. On s'occupe maintenant de l'im⟨185⟩pression des notes, et l'on m'assure qu'avant la fin de l'année tout sera terminé. Il me tarde de faire connaître à l'Europe savante combien je suis pénétre des sentimens de reconnaissance et de respect avec lesquels j'ai l'honneur d'être

Monseigneur
de votre Excellence
le très humble et très obéissant serviteur
C. B. Hase

Paris ce 7 juillet
1816

APPENDIX III
Note on Hase's Secret Diary

The full text of Hase's diary, of obvious interest both for establishing the truth about the Fragments of *Toparcha Gothicus* and for re-creating the history of his milieu, is unavailable at present. After Hase's death on March 21, 1864, his diary must have been examined by his relatives.[183] They realized that its contents should not be divulged and that the precept τὰ ἐν οἴκῳ μὴ ἐν δήμῳ fully applied to it. However, Ch. M. W. Brunet de Presle, Hase's former student, friend of long standing, and immediate successor at the École des Langues Orientales Vivantes, had access to at least a part of the full text of the diary, for he made available to A. R. Rhangabe (Rhagkabês) its pages concerning Hase's trip to Greece in 1837. These Rhangabe published in 1868.[184]

Hase willed his scholarly correspondence to his old school, the Gymnasium in Weimar.[185] People at the Gymnasium expected to receive

---

183. Hase's estate (as opposed to his papers) went to his niece, Frau Peucer, wife of a minister; cf. Hase, *Unsre Hauschronik...* (as in note 2 *supra*), 111.

184. For these details, cf. A.R. Rhangabe, " 'Ημερολόγιον... " (as in note 2 *supra*), and S. B. Kougeas, " 'Η προέλευσις τῆς ὑπὸ τοῦ Hase Παρισιακῆς συλλογῆς πατριαρχικῶν καὶ μοναστηριακῶν ἐγγράφων," 'Ελληνικά 20 (1967), 12-17 (Kougeas, too, published some passages from the Diary). Rhangabe and Kougeas erroneously dated Hase's journey to June-July 1840; however, Paris *Suppl. Gr.* 1363, p. 90 shows unmistakably that Hase spent the evening of July 7 of that year in Paris: while pp. 79-80 of the *Supplément*, with entries from June-July 1837, are a summary of the text published by Rhangabe.

185. Cf., e.g., Hase, *Unsre Hauschronik...* (as in note 2 *supra*), 111.

his diary as well, but by October 30, 1864, Hase's "Diaries had not yet come from France over to us."[186] According to a late and unreliable source, Hase's scholarly papers went to the Library of Jena University.[187]

This leaves Paris *Supplément Grec* 1363, which entered the Bibliothèque Nationale from Solomon Reinach's library.[188] The manuscript is in Reinach's own hand and is based on Johann Friedrich Dübner's[189] summary of the diary, ⟨186⟩ the full text of which the latter clearly must have possessed, at least for a time. We know from elsewhere that Dübner kept some of Hase's papers, which had been deposited with him by the members of Hase's family. However, Dübner died after a short illness in 1867, and all the papers found in his possession, including those of Hase, were sold at that time.[190]

Supplément Grec 1363 was written (perhaps with further omissions) by Solomon Reinach in 1913; Reinach, who himself searched for the original diary, left the following notes on pages 1-4 of the *Supplément*:

p. 1 [Reinach's hand]:

Sur Hase

Chantepie, bibliothécaire à l'Ecole normale, m'a dit autrefois qu'Adert, professeur à Genève, possédait une copie des mémoires de Hase. Cette copie ne parut pas à la vente d'Adert et les renseignements que Cartier, conservateur des Musées de Genève, essaya d'obtenir pour moi à ce sujet, se réduisirent à rien. Vers la fin de 1912, j'appris de Paul Mayer que feu Guardia, le grammairien avait possédé une autre copie.

---

186. Rassow, "Zur Erinnerung..." (as in note 2 *supra*), 146.

187. Pitollet, "*Le père Hase...*" (as in note 2 *supra*), 60.

188. Description of the manuscript in Ch. Astruc and M.-L. Concasty, *Le Supplément Grec, Tome III*, nos 901-1371 (1960), 685.

189. Dübner (1802-1867) was another classical scholar and editor (e.g., of the Greek anthology) of German origin established in Paris. However, he did not achieve success comparable to Hase's. On him, cf., e.g., P. and V. Glachant, *Papiers d'autrefois...* (Paris, 1899), chapter "Frédéric Dübner, d'aprés sa correspondance inédite," 195-264. Dübner and Hase worked together on the New Stephanus; however, their relationship was not without strain: Dübner, disappointed by his more illustrious colleague, who refused to intervene with the minister on behalf of Dübner's efforts to reform the teaching of Greek in French secondary schools, spoke of "le méprisable Hasius," *ibid.*, 222.

190. Cf. E. Miller in *Journal des savants* (January 1875), 17.

Confondant Guardia avec son collaborateur polonais, Wierzsewski [Wieruszewski?], je crus qu'il était conservateur du musée d'Alger. J'écrivis à Carcopino, successeur de Gsell à Alger; il apprit de Wierzewski[sic] que la fille de Guardia avait épousé Brunon, professeur à l'École de Pharmacie de Rouen. J'écrivis alors à Delatigny à Rouen, qui m'a dit qu'il était lié avec Brunon. Une recherche faite par le dernier fit retrouver la copie, que M. et Mme Brunon ont déposée chez moi le mercredi 5 février 1913, en m'autorisant à en faire usage comme bon me semblerait. Avec cette copie est une lettre de F. Hoefer, une notice sur Hase, et un très mauvais essai de résumé des mémoires.

La copie est faite d'un trait, sur papier bleu à entête: MAISON D'EDUCATION DIRIGÉE PAR M. L'ABBE A.J. DELBOS, VERSAILLES. M. Gaston Destrais (de Versailles), le 12 février 1913, me fait savoir que l'abbé Alexis Joseph Delbos, né à Agen le 4 mars 1804, figure pour la 1ère fois au recensement de 1849 comme prêtre et chef d'institution. Il avait à lui toute la maison, ou professaient deux prêtres, Lefeuvre Michaël et Maillet Casimir. Le reste de la maison logeait 7 internes et deux domestiques. En 1851 il figure comme *parti* et l'on perd sa trace à Versailles.

D'après Froehner (11 mars 1913) la copie serait de Dübner et proviendrait de la bibliothèque Adert de Genève. L'original serait resté dans la famille de Hase à Weimar ou aux environs. Dübner avait communiqué à Froehner la phrase qui le concerne; c'est cette phrase que je lui ai envoyée à mon tour et qui m'a valu sa réponse. [by another hand: voir 5 nov. 1845]

⟨187⟩ [p. 2 of the manuscript contains Reinach's excerpts on Hase from the encyclopedias of Brockhaus and Larousse]

p. 3 [Reinach's hand]:

Lettre à M. le docteur Guardia
Brunoy le 20 juillet 1876
Mon cher ami

J'ai mille pardons à vous demander du retard que j'ai mis à vous rapporter le singulier *Diarium* de Hase. J'avais entrepris, sur votre invitation, d'en faire quelques extraits, mais j'y ai renoncé après m'être aperçu que, elimination faite des détails personnels les plus scabreux, le tout se réduisait à peu près à zéro. Ce sera néanmoins un document *caractéristique* du personnage, et comme tel il pourrait avoir de l'intérêt.

Tout à vous,
F. Hocfcr

P.S. Les notes ci jointes, très rapidement crayonnées témoignent du travail d'élimination que j'avais commencé.

(Ces notes ⟨sont⟩ sans valeur et prouvent que Hoefer ne savait bien ni l'allemand ni le grec).

[p. 4 of the manuscript contains Reinach's note on Hortense de Beauharnais; then, among others, the following]: "J'ai rendu le Ms. original à Brunon en l'avertissant qu'il était sans valeur et devrait aller à l'enfer à la Nationale..."

In spite of Mayer's information, it seems that there was only one copy of the summary made by Dübner, the copy which passed from Adert to Guardia, then to his daughter Mme Brunon, and thence to Reinach. Several passages of the copy which was given to Reinach unmistakably show that it is a summary, and that Dübner had been the epitomator; Reinach himself (or another reader) noted this on several occasions. Thus on page 28, after the entry for September 8, 1827, we find: "preuve évidente que le ms. est un résumé." On page 131, the entry for November 5, 1845 runs as follows: "Ὁ Δύβνερ, διαλεγόμενος περὶ Καρόλου Ἰωάννου Hofmann τοῦ ὑβριστικοῦ (den ich völlig vergessen habe)." In the margin, Reinach [?] remarked in pencil: "signature."[191] The few pages published by Rhangabe are the only rendering of the full text of the diary known today; this can be demonstrated by comparing them with the corresponding passages of the summary in *Supplément Grec* 1363.[192]

In sum, although the chances of rediscovering the full text of Hase's diary are remote, the scholar is offered a few clues for reasonable action: he should search among the papers of Brunet de Presle, consult the Goethe- und Schiller-Archiv in Weimar which preserves materials willed by Hase to the Weimar ⟨188⟩ Gymnasium,[193] explore the library of Jena University, try to discover the fate of Dübner's papers, and pur-

---

191. Cf. also Paris *Suppl. Gr.* 1363, p. 113 (entry for August 12, 1842): Ἔδραμον πρὸς τὸν ἅγιον [probably an equivalent of sacré] Δυβνερ, ᾧ χρῆ διαδέξασθαι [read: διαλέξασθαι]: (Dies [?] keine Erinnerung). In the margin Reinach's (?) remark in pencil: "c'est donc Dübner qui résume."

192. Compare Rhangabe, " Ἡμερολόγιον..." (as in note 2 *supra*) 83 with Paris *Suppl. Gr.* 1363, p. 80. Both have the following entry for July 13: χαίρω δ' ἐγὼ ὅτι ἐκ τῆς Ἑλλάδος ἀναφέρω αὐτὸν τὸν χρυσοῦν σταυρόν [a decoration from the king of Greece], ἄνευ πόνου τινός.

193. However, my inquiry to the Nationale Forschungs- und Gedenkstätten der klassischen deutschen Literatur in Weimar elicited the reply that the Goethe- und Schiller-Archiv was in possession only of *letters* addressed to Hase between 1821 und 1864. The authorities of the Archive were not able to ascertain the whereabouts of Hase's other papers (letter of November 26, 1970).

sue the story of Hase's niece Frau Peucer and of the archives of the Hase family.[194]

The remaining clues are contained in Reinach's own story on page 1 of *Supplément Grec* 1363: by 1913, the original full text of the diary was believed to have remained with Hase's family in Weimar or thereabouts. As for Dübner's copy, it was given back to Brunon in 1913, and, if it has survived, it is in the possession of his heirs, for Brunon seems not to have followed Reinach's suggestion and entrusted the diary to the *Enfer* [locked section of pornographica] of the Bibliothèque Nationale; it is not there at present.[195]

194. Several pieces used in Hase, *Unsre Hauschronik...* (as in note 2 *supra*), were kept in this archive. Cf., e.g., note 1 to p. 77 (on p. 325).

195. I owe this information to Mlle M.-L. Concasty (letter of April 5, 1971). She also inquired about the Dübner copy at the Bibliothèque Municipale of Rouen (where Brunon lived) with no success.

PLATES

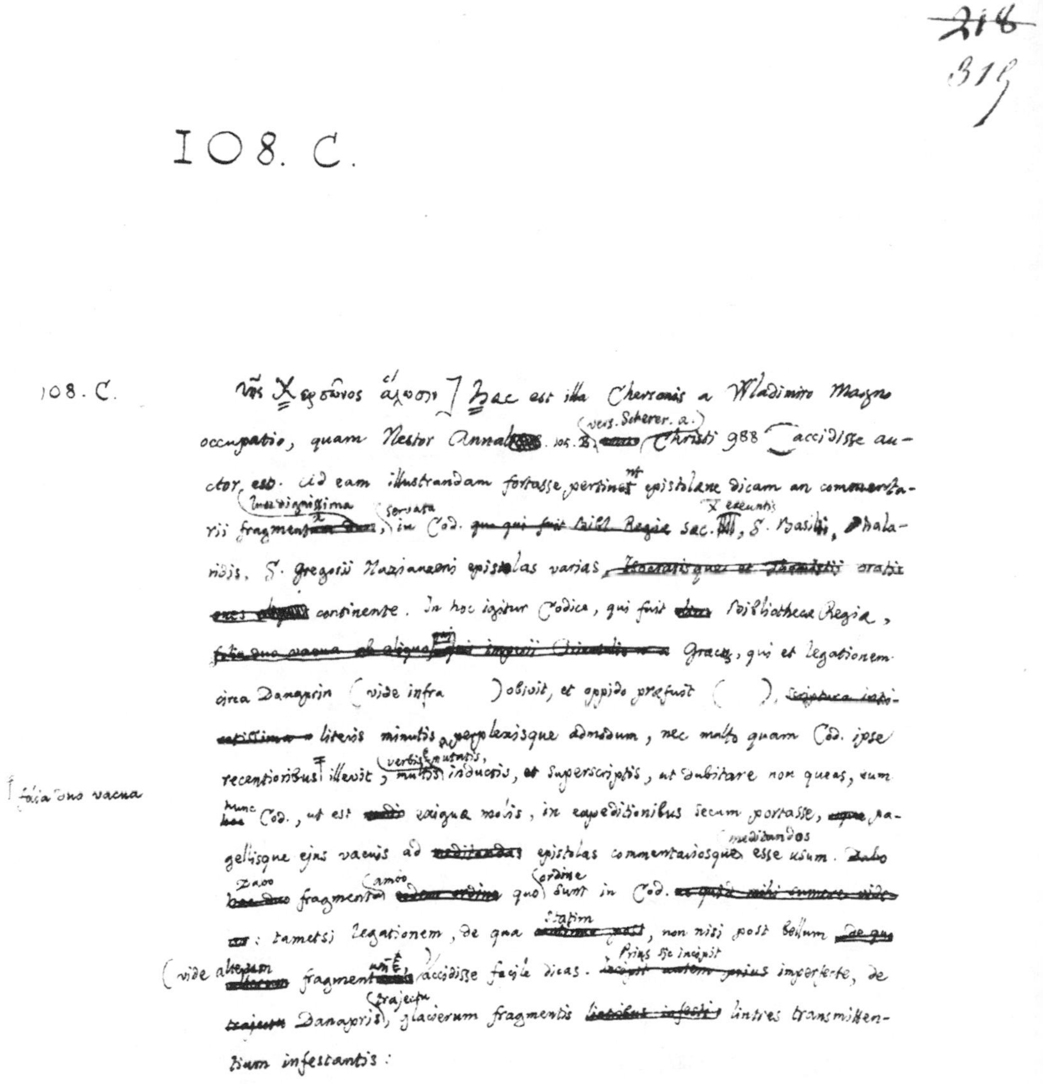

~~218~~ 315

108. C.

108. C. τῆς Χερσῶνος ἅλωσιν] Haec est illa Chersonis a Wladimiro Magno occupatio, quam Nestor Annal[illegible] (vers. Scherer. a.) Christi 988 accidisse auctor est. Ad eam illustrandam fortasse pertinent epistolae dicam an commentarii fragmenta incertissima, servata in Cod. [illegible] Bibl. Regiae saec. X exeuntis, S. Basilii, Phalaridis, S. Gregorii Nazianzeni epistolas varias [illegible] continente. In hoc igitur Codice, qui fuit Bibliothecae Regiae, [illegible] Graecus, qui et legationem circa Danaprin (vide infra) obiuit, et oppido praefuit ( ), [illegible] literis minutis perplexisque admodum, nec multo quam Cod. ipse recentioribus illevit, verbis mutatis, inductis, et superscriptis, ut dubitare non queas, eum hunc Cod., ut est exigua molis, in expeditionibus secum portasse, paginisque ejus vacuis ad epistolas commentariosque meditandos esse usum. Duo fragmenta [illegible] quo ordine sunt in Cod. [illegible]: tametsi legationem, de qua statim, non nisi post bellum (vide alterum fragmentum) accidisse facile dicas. Prius sic incipit imperfecte, de trajectu Danapris, glacierum fragmentis lintres transmittentium infestantis:

folia duo vacua

1. Paris *Supplément Grec* 858, fol. 315r. Printer's Copy of the Fragments = Paris Edition, p. 254B–C

(316)

~~219. C.~~

316

...ιστης, ἀπεδιώχθη τὸ βάρβαρον αὐτῆς ὅμιλ-
...ας τῶν τῆδε μερῶν, ὑποχωρῆσαι ὅθεν εἰ-
...πιδαῆς. Καὶ τὰ μὲν τῆς τότε γεγενημέ-
...νης ἀπροσδοκήτου καὶ θηριώδους ἐπιδρομῆς
...τω συνελέρθη.

ipso die repulsa est, reversique unde immoverat, coacta. Et quae tunc obvenerat improvisa atque atrox invasio, in hunc modum finem ~~cepit~~ cepit.

fol. 90 verso.

De ciborio sive umbraculo altaris aliunde educto columnisque quatuor innixo, copiosius Ducangius, Glossar. Graeci T. 653. D. ~~[illegible]~~ Constantinop. Christ. ~~[illegible]~~ 50. A — 55. A.‡ Tempus autem, quo ~~[illegible]~~ Sclavini Thessalonicam sic tentaverunt, ~~[illegible]~~ incidere videtur in ~~[illegible]~~ ~~[illegible]~~ circa a. 584: vide J. Chr. von Engel Geschichte des Ungrischen Reichs und seiner Nebenländer T. 259. B. Paucisque annis post, ut prodit ~~[illegible]~~ unde haec delibavimus ~~[illegible]~~, Avarorum princeps, legatis ad Mauricium Imp. missis, τὸν τὸ τηνικαῦτα τῶν Ἀβάρων ἡγούμενον, στείλαντα πρέσβεις πρὸς τὸν τῆς εὐσεβοῦς λήξεως, καὶ τὰ σκῆπτρα τῆς Ῥωμαίων ἀρχῆς κατέχοντα τότε Μαυρίκιον, fol. 97 recto, cum non posset inter eos quicquam convenire, omnem Sclavinorum gentem in Thessalonicam effudit. ~~[illegible]~~ Nam erat tunc tota haec natio in ditionem ejus: ὑπέκειτο γὰρ αὐτῷ τηνικαῦτα τὸ ἔθνος ἅπαν, ~~[illegible]~~ quod ~~affirmat~~ confirmantur, quae Engelius loco cit. T. 258. C. de ~~[illegible]~~ Sclavinis post a. 573 Avarorum imperio ~~[illegible]~~ subjectis acute disputat. Sequitur (in fol. 98) longa narratio ~~[illegible]~~ ~~[illegible]~~ → de Thessalonica bis sub Mauricio Imp. acerrime oppugnata, semel (tunc) a Sclavinis, iterum ab ipsis Avaris, deque civitatis post varias summasque angustias improvisa liberatione. Qua omnia ~~[illegible]~~ ante a. 602, quo casus est Mauricius, ~~acta~~ gesta, ab coaetoque teste perscripta (qui ideo alius esse debet ac Joannes II archiepiscopus Thessalonicensis, [illegible] circa a. 680 florens), ut supplementum historiae Theophylacti Simocattae in aliquo subsequentium voluminum, ~~[illegible]~~ ut diximus, si res nostra siverint, ~~[illegible]~~ proferemus.

‡ Descript. S. Sophiae 573. D. et Reiskius Comment. ad Const. Porphyr. Ceremon. aul. Byz. II. 64. A. 78. B. De templo decantatissimo Thessalonicensi S. Demetrii ~~[illegible]~~ circa allegata idem Ducangius D. ~~[illegible]~~ Comnena 252. D.

2. Paris *Supplément Grec* 858, fol. 316ʳ. Printer's Copy of Hases's Notes to Leo = Paris Edition, pp. 262D–263B

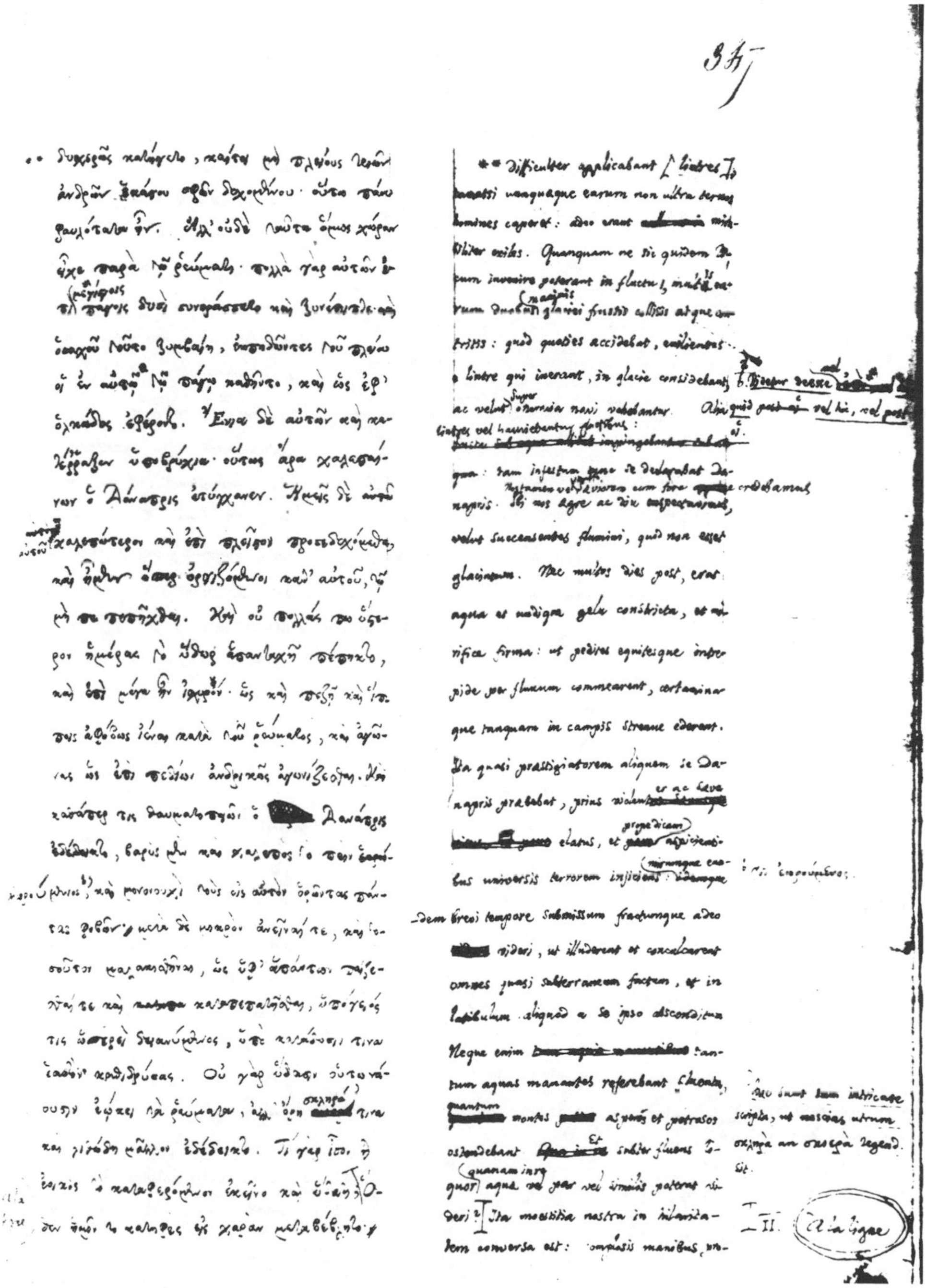

3. Paris *Supplément Grec* 858, fol. 347r. Printer's Copy of the Fragments = Paris Edition, pp. 254C–255A

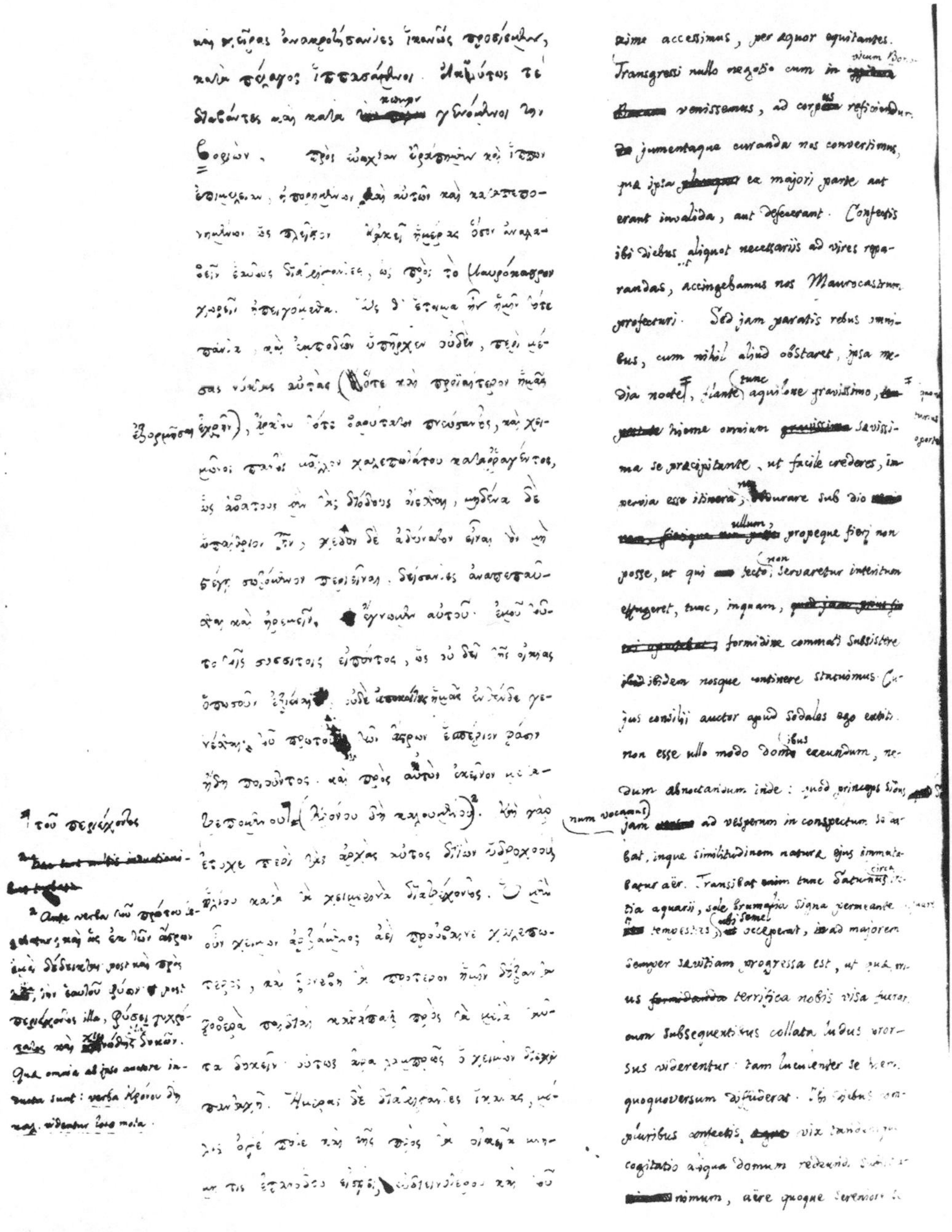

4. Paris *Supplément Grec* 858, fol. 347ʳ. Printer's Copy of the Fragments = Paris Edition, p. 255A–D

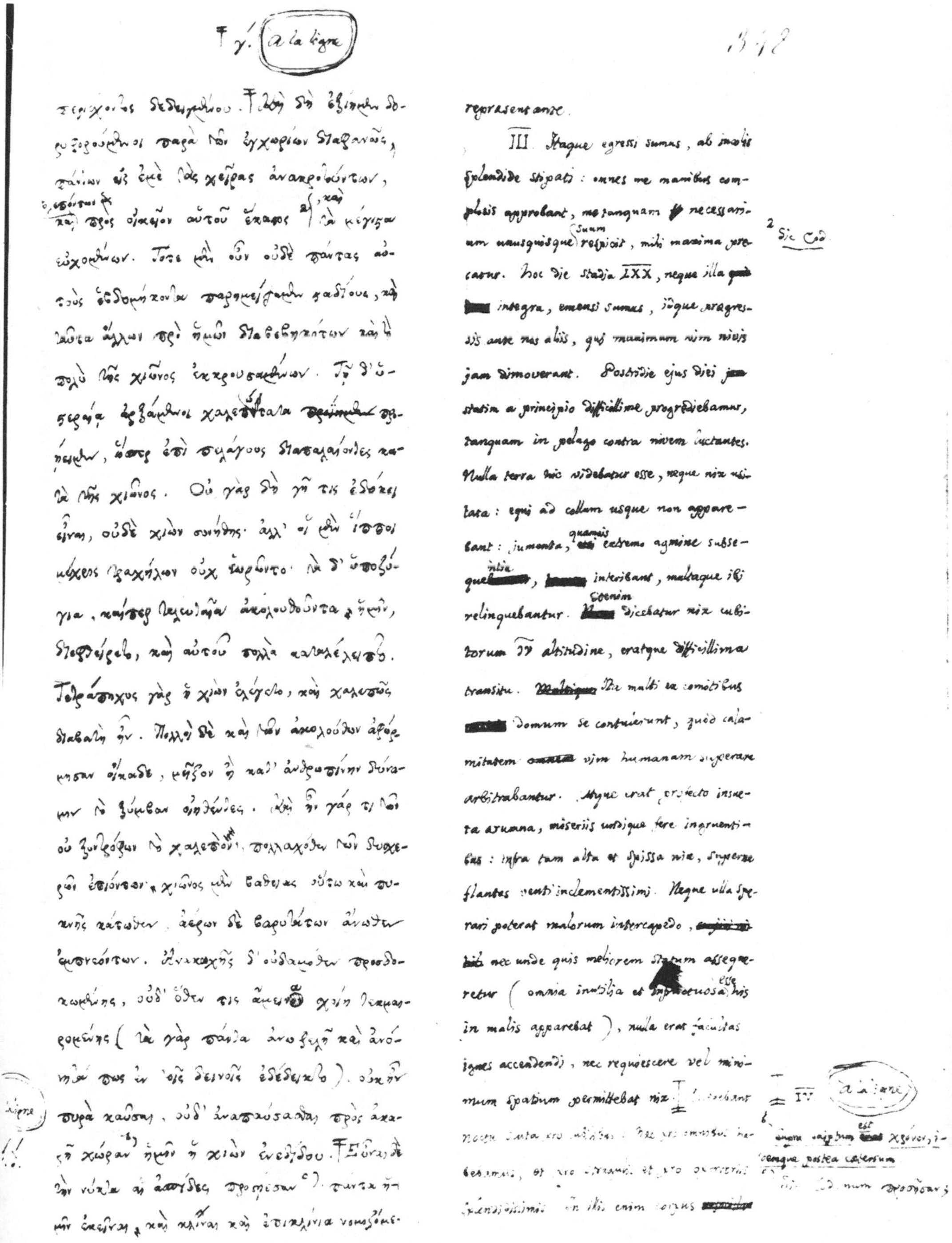
348

repraesentante.

III. Itaque egressi sumus, ab incolis splendide stipati: omnes me manibus complosis approbant, me tanquam necessarium unusquisque suum respicit, mihi maxima precantur. Hoc die stadia LXX, neque illa integra, emensi sumus, idque praegressis ante nos aliis, qui maximam vim nivis jam dimoverant. Postridie ejus diei statim a principio difficillime progrediebamur, tanquam in pelago contra nivem luctantes. Nulla terra hic videbatur esse, neque nix usitata: equi ad collum usque non apparebant: jumenta, quamvis extremo agmine subsequentia, interibant, multaque ibi relinquebantur. Enim dicebatur nix cubitorum XV altitudine, eratque difficillima transitu. Ita multi ex comitibus domum se contulerunt, quod calamitatem vim humanam superare arbitrabantur. Atque erat profecto insueta aerumna, miseriis undique fere ingruentibus: infra tam alta et spissa nix, superne flantes venti inclementissimi. Neque ulla sperari poterat malorum intercapedo, nec unde quis meliorem statum assequeretur (omnia inutilia et infructuosa esse his in malis apparebat), nulla erat facultas ignes accendendi, nec requiescere vel minimum spatium permittebat nix.

5. Paris *Supplément Grec* 858, fol. 348r. Printer's Copy of the Fragments = Paris Edition, pp. 255D–256B

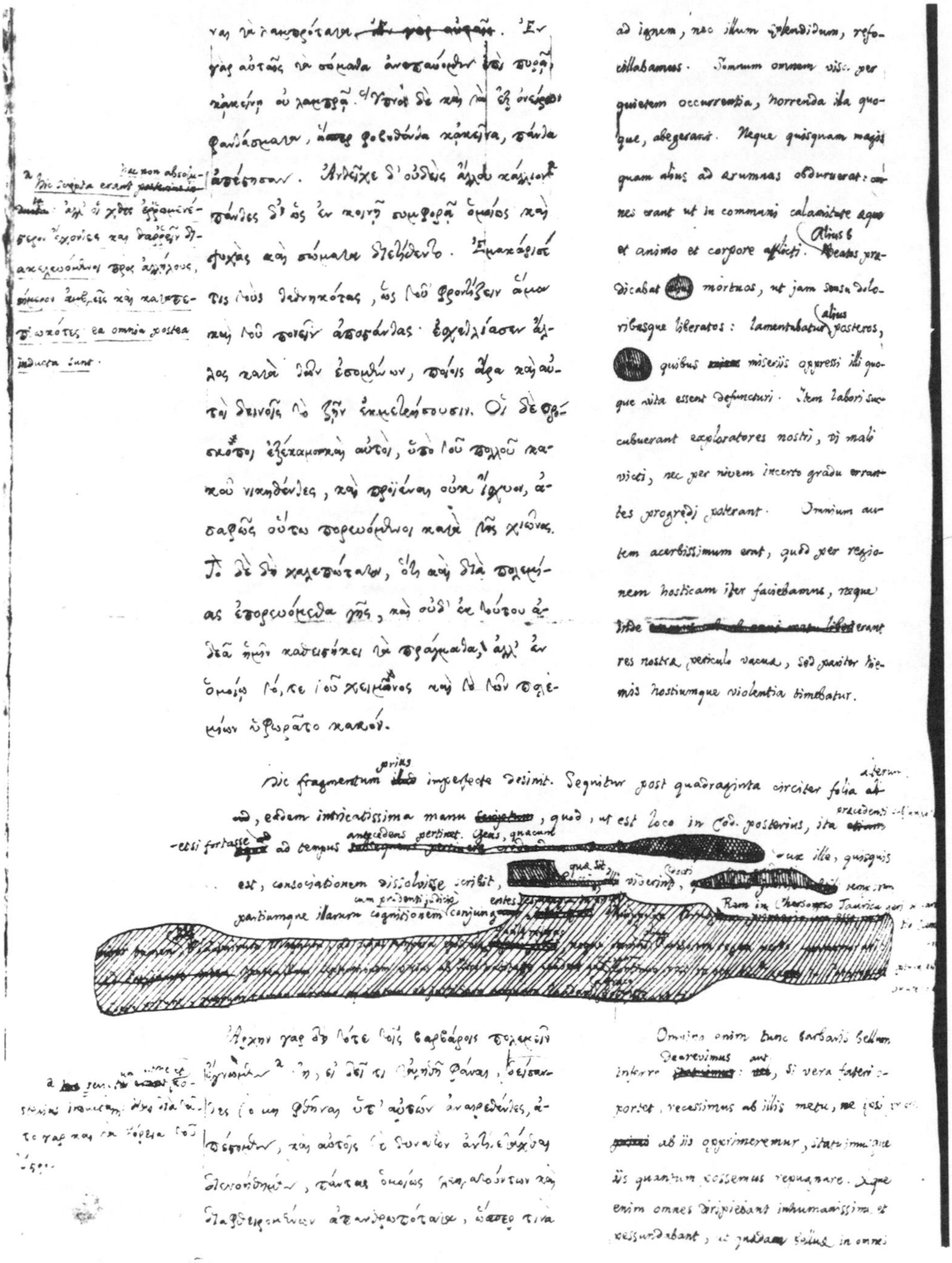
ad ignem, nec illum splendidum, refocillabamus. Somnum omnem visc. per quietem occurrentia, horrenda illa quoque, abegerant. Neque quisquam magis quam alius ad aerumnas obduruerat: omnes erant ut in communi calamitate aeque et animo et corpore afflicti. Alius beatos praedicabat [illegible] mortuos, ut jam sensu doloribusque liberatos: lamentabatur alius posteros, [illegible] quibus miseriis oppressi illi quoque vita essent defuncturi. Item labori succubuerant exploratores nostri, vi mali victi, nec per nivem incerto gradu errantes progredi poterant. Omnium autem acerbissimum erat, quod per regionem hosticam iter faciebamus, neque tute … erant res nostra, periculo vacua, sed pariter hiemis hostiumque violentia timebatur.

Sic fragmentum prius imperfecte desinit. Sequitur post quadraginta circiter folia alterum, eadem intricatissima manu …, quod, ut est loco in Cod. posterius, ita praecedenti … ad tempus antecedens pertinet. … [illegible]

Omnino enim tunc barbaris bellum inferre decrevimus aut, si vera fateri oportet, recessimus ab illis metu, ne … ab iis opprimeremur, statuimusque iis quantum possemus repugnare. Atque enim omnes diripiebant inhumanissime et vexabant, ut …

6. Paris *Supplément Grec* 858, fol. 348v. Printer's Copy of the Fragments = Paris Edition, pp. 256B–257A

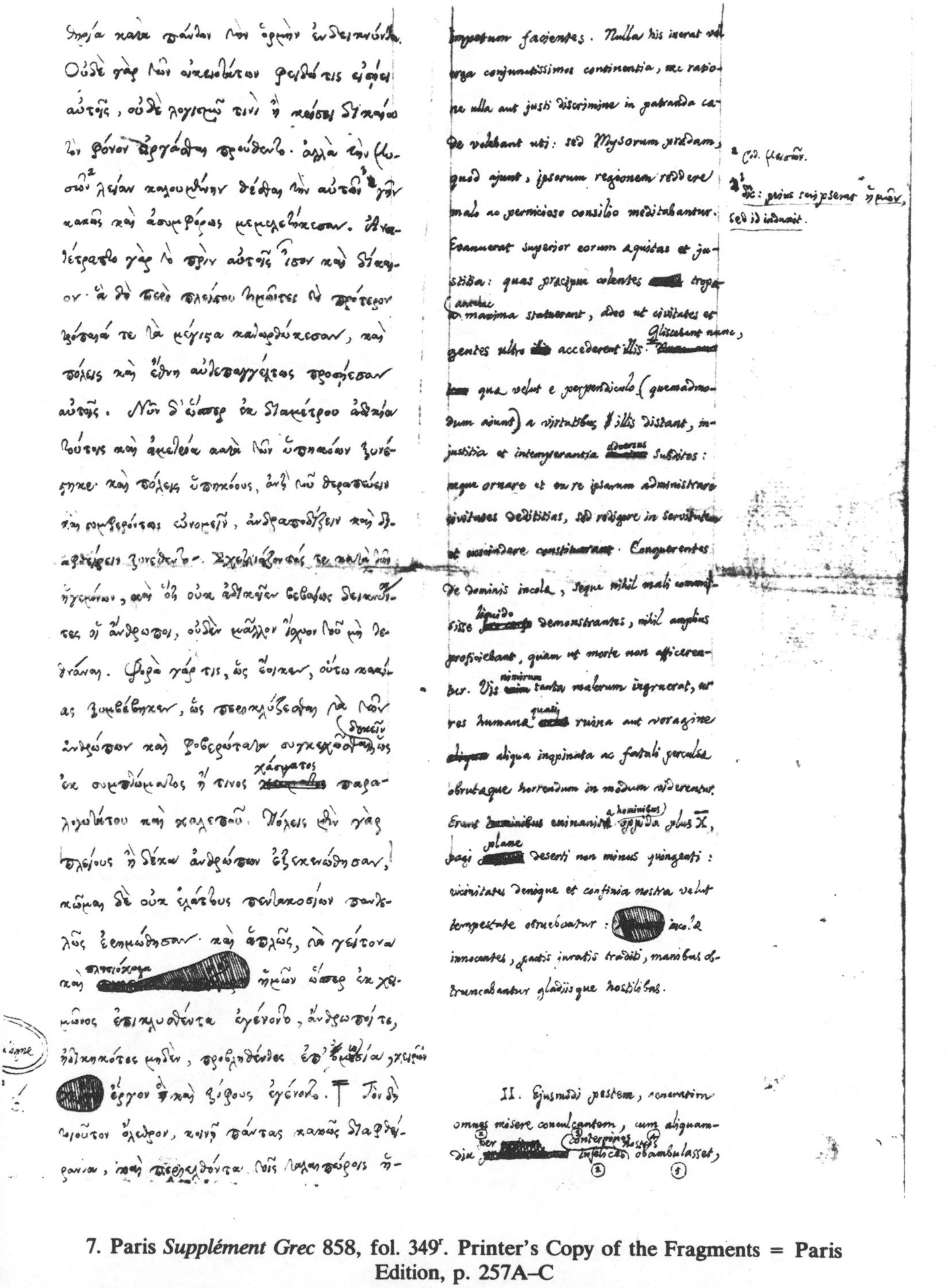

7. Paris *Supplément Grec* 858, fol. 349r. Printer's Copy of the Fragments = Paris Edition, p. 257A–C

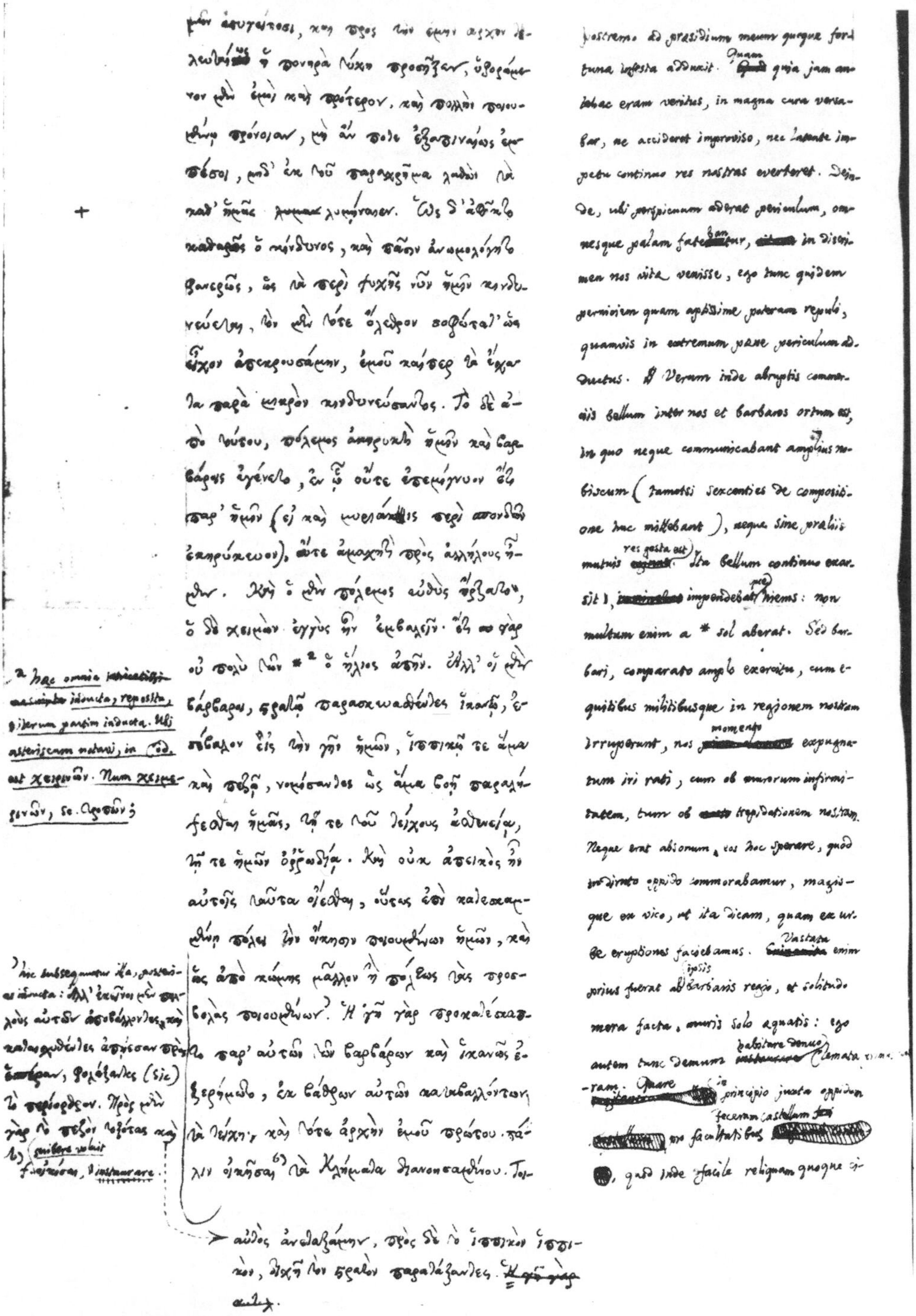

8. Paris *Supplément Grec* 858, fol. 349v. Printer's Copy of the Fragments = Paris Edition, p. 257C–258B

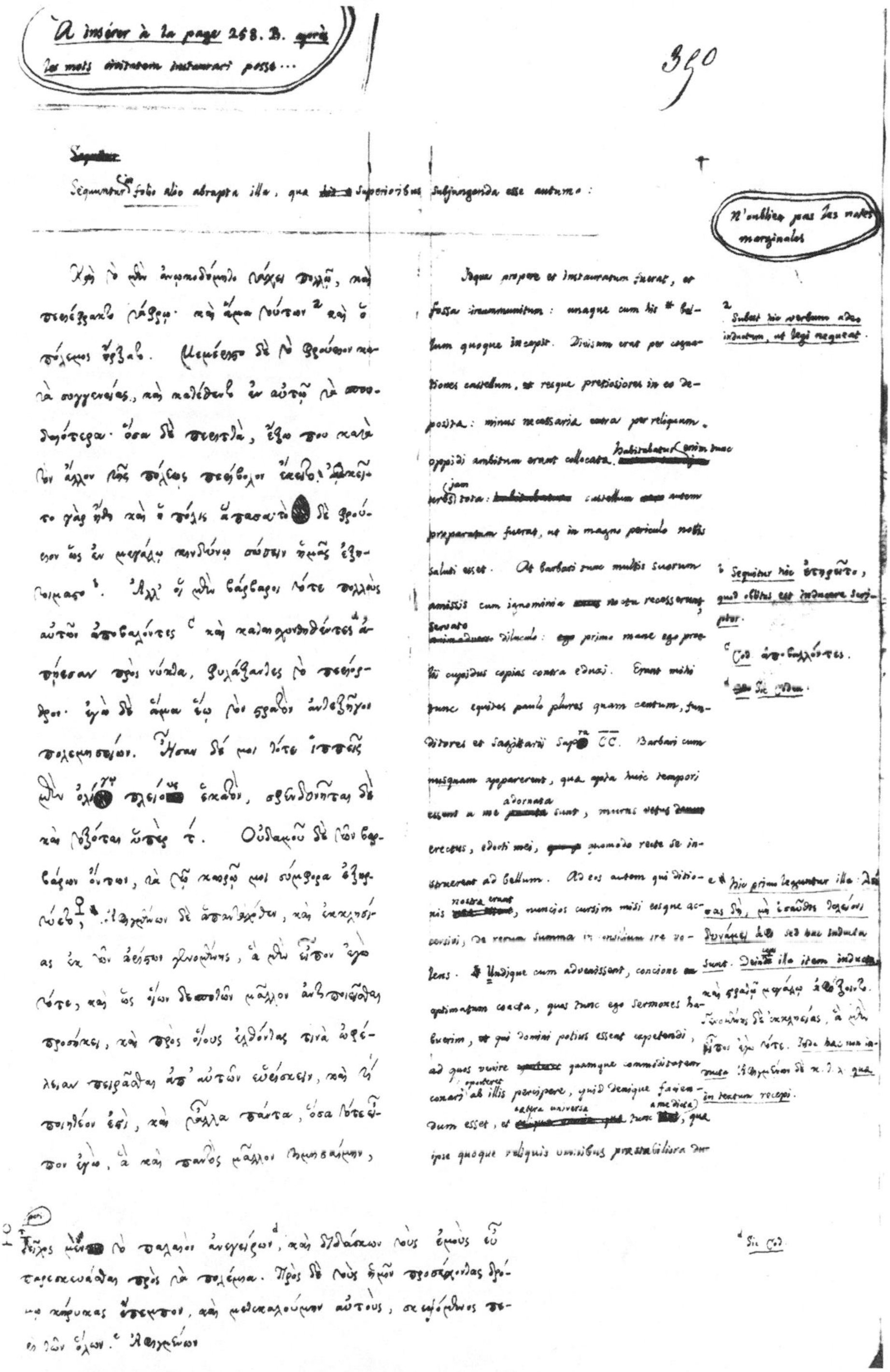

9. Paris *Supplément Grec* 858, fol. 350[r]. Printer's Copy of the Fragments = Paris Edition, p. 258B–D

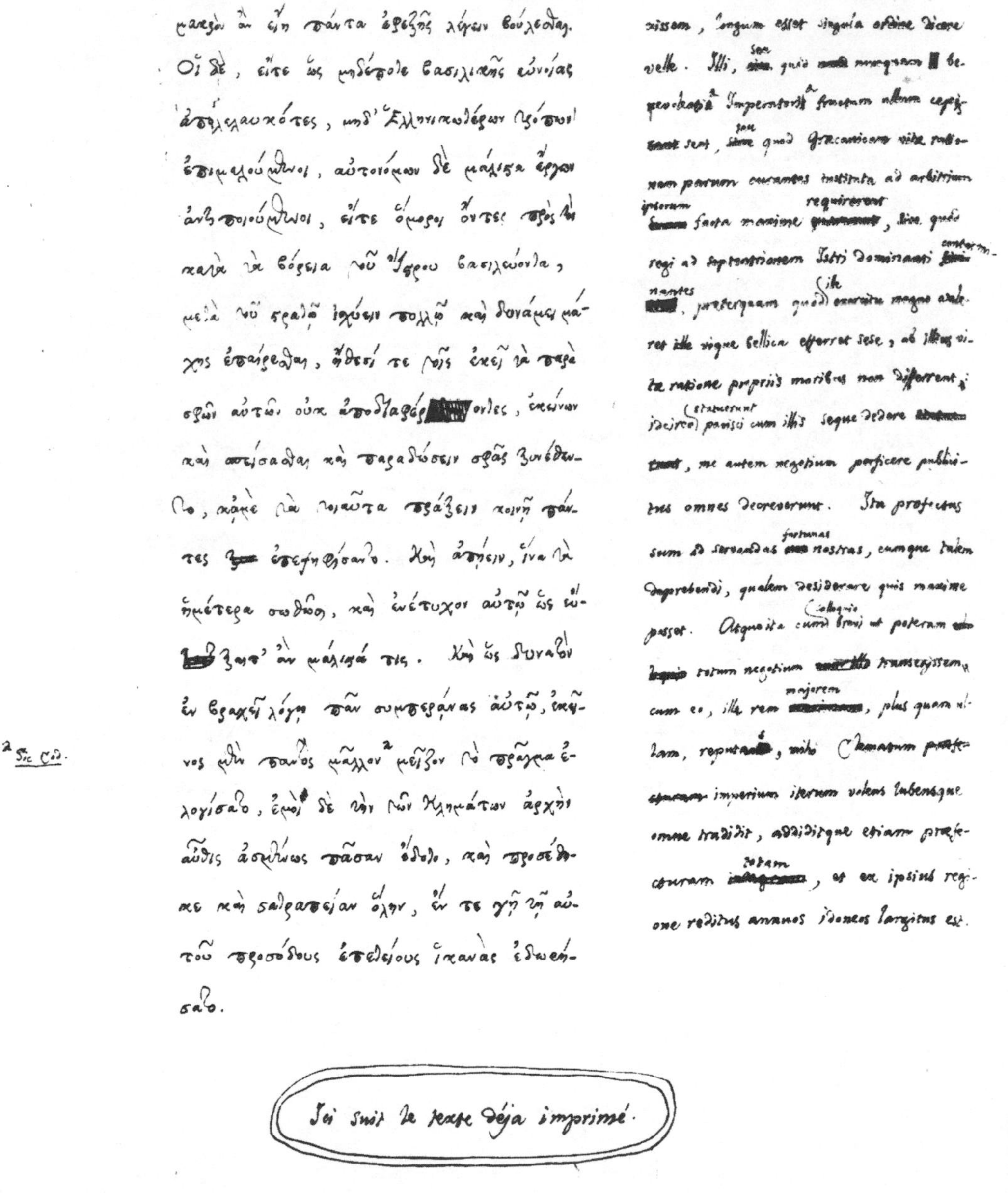

μακρὸν ἂν εἴη πάντα ἑξῆς λέγειν βούλεσθαι. Οἱ δέ, εἴτε ὡς μηδέποτε βασιλικῆς εὐνοίας ἀπολελαυκότες, μηδ' Ἑλληνικωτέρων ἐθῶν ἐπιμελούμενοι, αὐτονόμων δὲ μάλιστα ἔργων ἀντιποιούμενοι, εἴτε ὅμοροι ὄντες πρὸς τὸν κατὰ τὰ βόρεια τοῦ Ἴστρου βασιλεύοντα, μετὰ τοῦ στρατοῦ ἰσχύειν πολλῷ καὶ δυνάμει μάχης ἐπαίρεσθαι, ἤθεσί τε τοῖς ἐκεῖ τὰ παρὰ σφῶν αὐτῶν οὐκ ἀποδιαφέρ[redacted]οντες, ἐκείνῳ καὶ σπείσασθαι καὶ παραδώσειν σφᾶς συνέθεντο, κἀμὲ τὰ τοιαῦτα πράξειν κοινῇ πάντες [redacted] ἐψηφίσαντο. Καὶ ἀπῄειν, ἵνα τὰ ἡμέτερα σωθῇ, καὶ ἐνέτυχον αὐτῷ ὡς εὔ[redacted]ξαιτ' ἂν μάλιστά τις. Καὶ ὡς δυνατὸν ἐν βραχεῖ λόγῳ πᾶν συμπεράνας αὐτῷ, ἐκεῖνος μὲν παντὸς μᾶλλον[a] μεῖζον τὸ πρᾶγμα ἐλογίσατο, ἐμοὶ δὲ τὴν τῶν κλιμάτων ἀρχὴν αὖθις ἀσμένως πᾶσαν ἔδωκε, καὶ προσέθηκε καὶ σατραπείαν ὅλην, ἥ τε γῇ τῇ αὐτοῦ προσόδους ἐτησίους ἱκανὰς ἐδωρήσατο.

[a] Sic Cod.

vissem, longum esset singula ordine dicere velle. Illi, sive quia nunquam [redacted] beneficia Imperatoris fructum ullum ceperant, sive quod Graecanicae vitae rationem parum curantes instituta ad arbitrium ipsorum facta maxime requirerent, sive regi ad septentrionem Istri dominanti conterminantes, praeterquam quod ille exercitu magno valeret ille atque bellica efferret sese, ab illis vitae ratione propriis moribus non differrent, idcirco pacisci cum illis seque dedere statuerunt, me autem negotium perficere publice omnes decreverunt. Ita profectus sum ad servandas fortunas nostras, eumque talem deprehendi, qualem desiderare quis maxime posset. Atque ita cum brevi ut poteram colloquio totum negotium transegissem cum eo, ille rem majorem, plus quam ullam, reputavit, mihi Climatum praefecturam imperium iterum volens lubensque omne tradidit, addiditque etiam praefecturam totam, et ex ipsius regione reditus annuos idoneos largitus est.

Ici suit le texte déjà imprimé.

10. Paris *Supplément Grec* 858, fol. 350ᵛ. Printer's Copy of the Fragments = Paris Edition, pp. 258D–259B

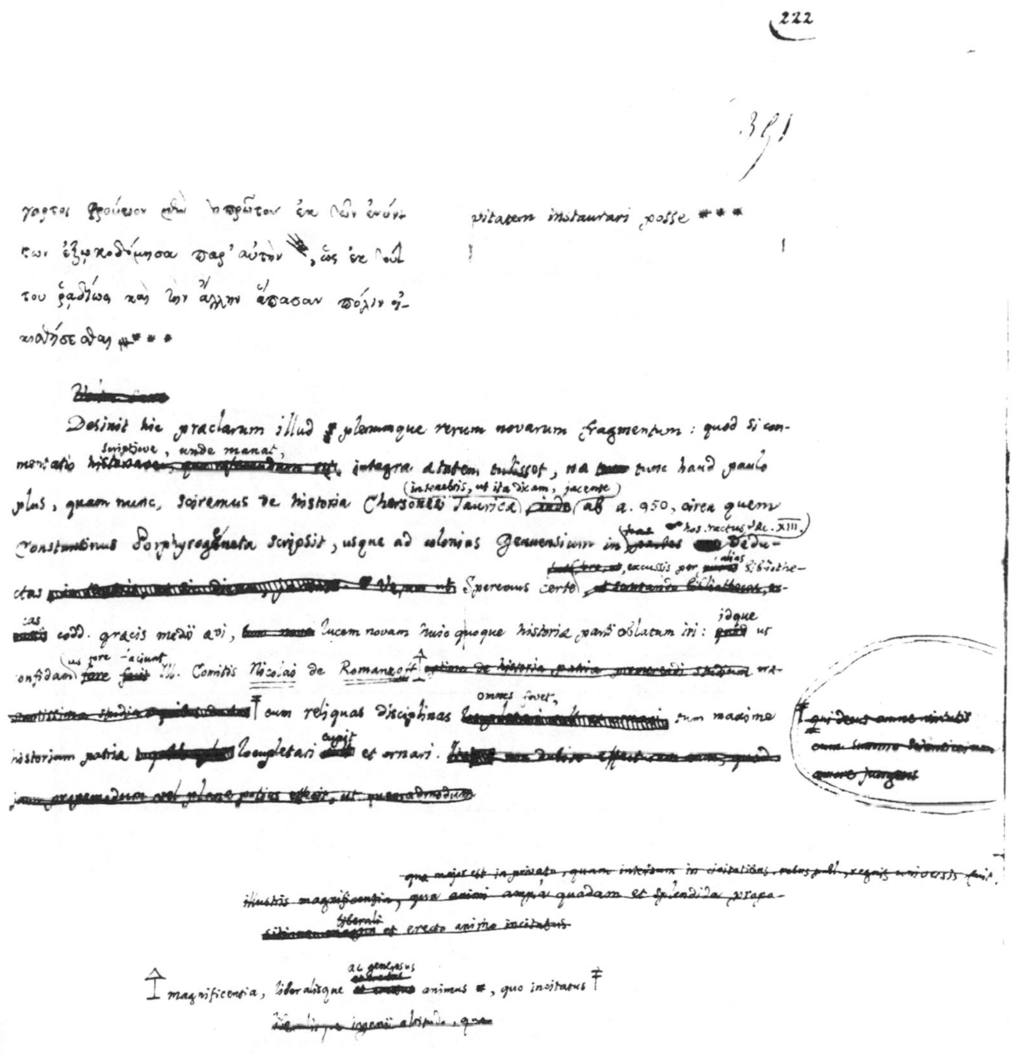

11. Paris *Supplément Grec* 858, fol. 351[r]. Printer's Copy of the Fragments = Paris Edition, p. 258B and 259B

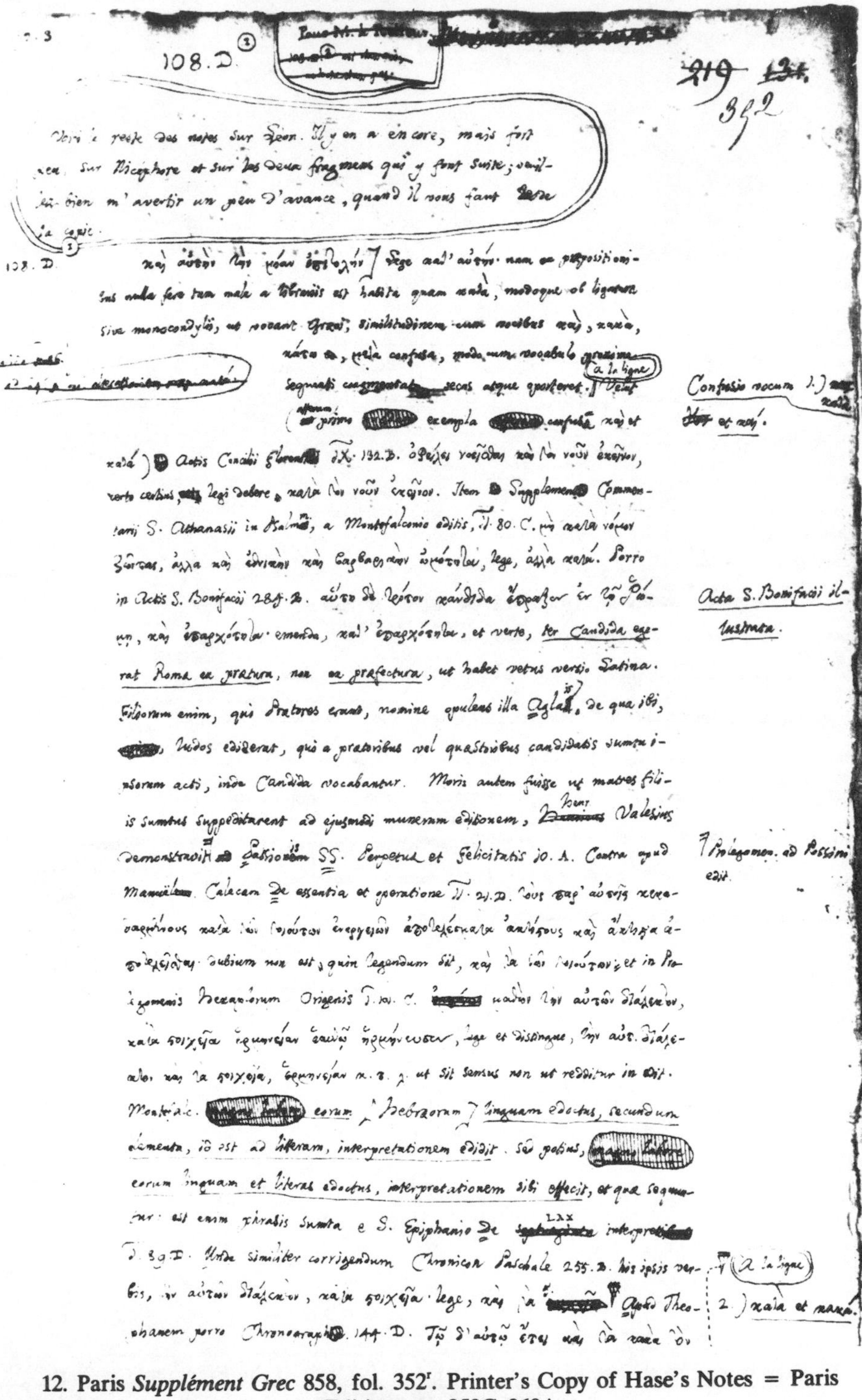

108. D.

Voici le reste des notes sur Léon. Il y en a encore, mais fort peu, sur Nicéphore et sur les deux fragments qui y font suite; veuillez bien m'avertir un peu d'avance, quand il vous faut de la copie.

108. D. καὶ αὐτὸν τὴν νέαν [illegible]] lege καθ' αὐτόν. nam ex praepositionibus nulla fere tam male a librariis est habita quam κατὰ, modoque ob ligaturas sive monocondylia, ut vocant Graeci, similitudinem cum vocibus καὶ, κατὰ, κάτω, μετὰ confusa, modo cum vocabulo proximo (à la ligne) sequenti coagmentata, secus atque oporteret. Veluti (alterum [redacted] exempla [redacted] confusi καὶ et κατὰ) in Actis Concilii Florentini [illegible] 132. B. ὀφείλει νοεῖσθαι καὶ τὸν νοῦν ἔχοντα, verte certius, legi debere, κατὰ τὸν νοῦν ἔχοντα. Item in Supplemento Commentarii S. Athanasii in Psalmos, a Montefalconio editis, II. 80. C. μὴ κατὰ νόμον ζῶντας, ἀλλὰ καὶ ἐθνικὴν καὶ βαρβαρικὴν [illegible], lege, ἀλλὰ κατά. Porro in Actis S. Bonifacii 284. B. αὐτὸ δὲ τρίτον κάνδιδα ἔπραξεν ἐν τῇ Ῥώμῃ, καὶ ἐπαρχότητα· emenda, κατ' ἐπαρχότητα, et verte, ter Candida egerat Romae ex praetura, non ex praefectura, ut habet vetus versio Latina. Filiorum enim, qui Praetores erant, nomine opulenta illa Aglais, de qua ibi, [redacted] ludos ediderat, qui a praetoribus vel quaestoribus candidatis sumtu ipsorum acti, inde Candida vocabantur. Moris autem fuisse ut matres filiis sumtus suppeditarent ad ejusmodi munerum editionem, Henr. Valesius demonstravit ad Passionem SS. Perpetuae et Felicitatis 10. A. Contra apud Manuelem Calecam de essentia et operatione II. 21. D. τοὺς παρ' αὐτῆς [illegible] κατὰ τῶν τοιούτων ἐνεργειῶν ἀπολελεσμένα [illegible] καὶ [illegible] ἀπολελεῖσθαι· dubium non est, quin legendum sit, καὶ τὰ τῶν τοιούτων; et in Prolegomenis Hexaplorum Origenis I. xv. C. [redacted] καθὼς τὴν αὐτῶν διάλεκτον, κατὰ στοιχεῖα ἑρμηνείαν ἑαυτῷ ἡρμήνευσεν, lege et distingue, τὴν αὐτ. διάλεκτον καὶ τὰ στοιχεῖα, ἑρμηνείαν κ. τ. λ. ut sit sensus non ut redditur in Edit. Montfalc. [redacted] eorum [Hebraeorum] linguam edoctus, secundum elementa, id est ad literam, interpretationem edidit. sed potius, [redacted] eorum linguam et literas edoctus, interpretationem sibi effecit, et quae sequuntur: est enim phrasis sumta e S. Epiphanio de LXX interpretibus II. 39. D. Unde similiter corrigendum Chronicon Paschale 255. B. his ipsis verbis, ἐν αὐτῶν διαλέκτῳ, κατὰ στοιχεῖα· lege, καὶ τὰ [redacted] (à la ligne) Apud Theophanem porro Chronographum 144. D. Τῷ δ' αὐτῷ ἔτει καὶ τὰ κατὰ τὸν

219 131. 352

Confusio vocum 1.) καὶ et καί.

Acta S. Bonifacii illustrata.

Prolegomen. ad Possini edit.

2.) κατὰ et κατά.

12. Paris *Supplément Grec* 858, fol. 352r. Printer's Copy of Hase's Notes = Paris Edition, pp. 259C–260A

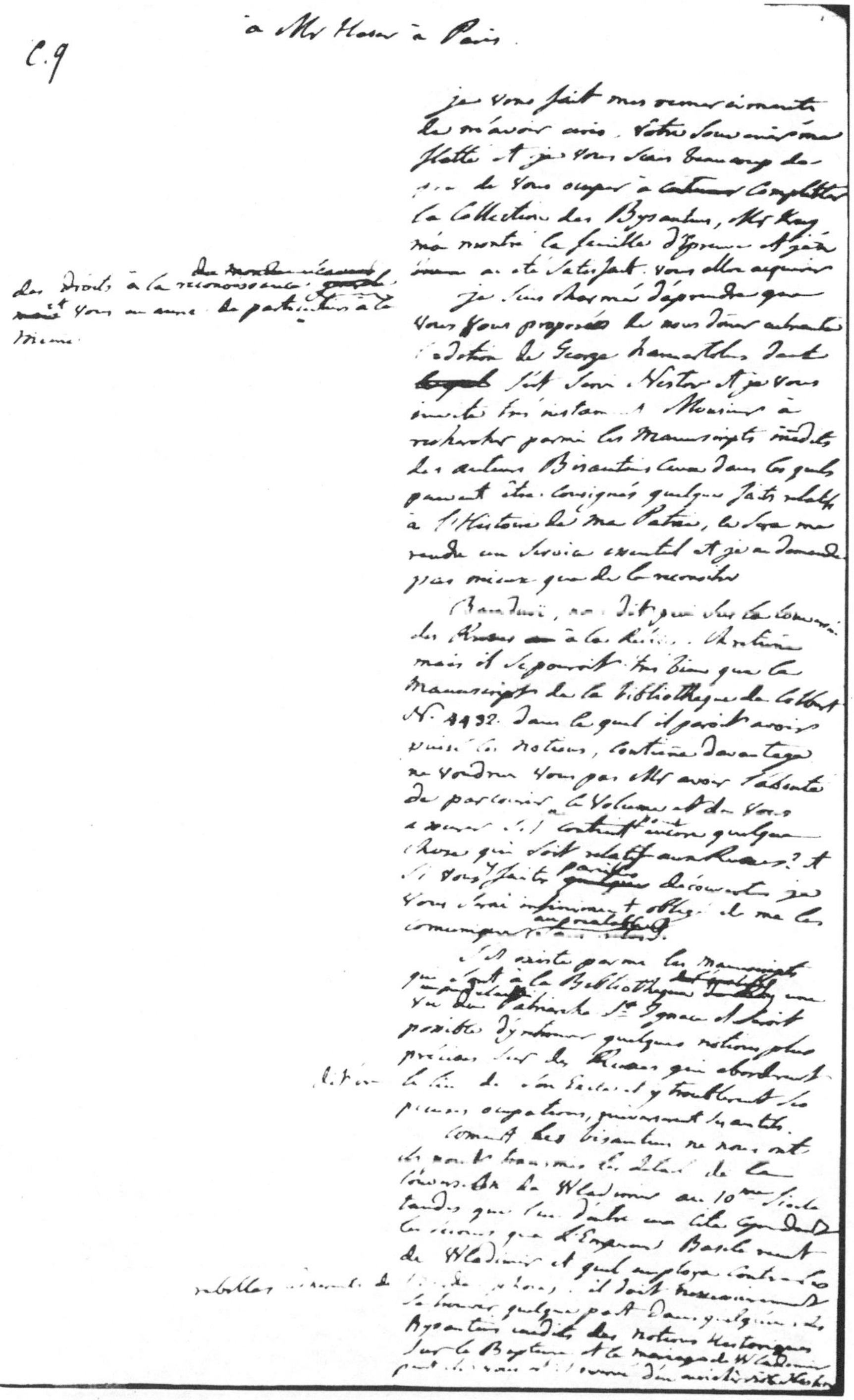
C.9

à Mr Hase à Paris.

13. Lenin Library, *Otdel rukopisej*, Fond 255.5.34, no. 9. Draft of Rumjancev's Letter to Hase, p. 1

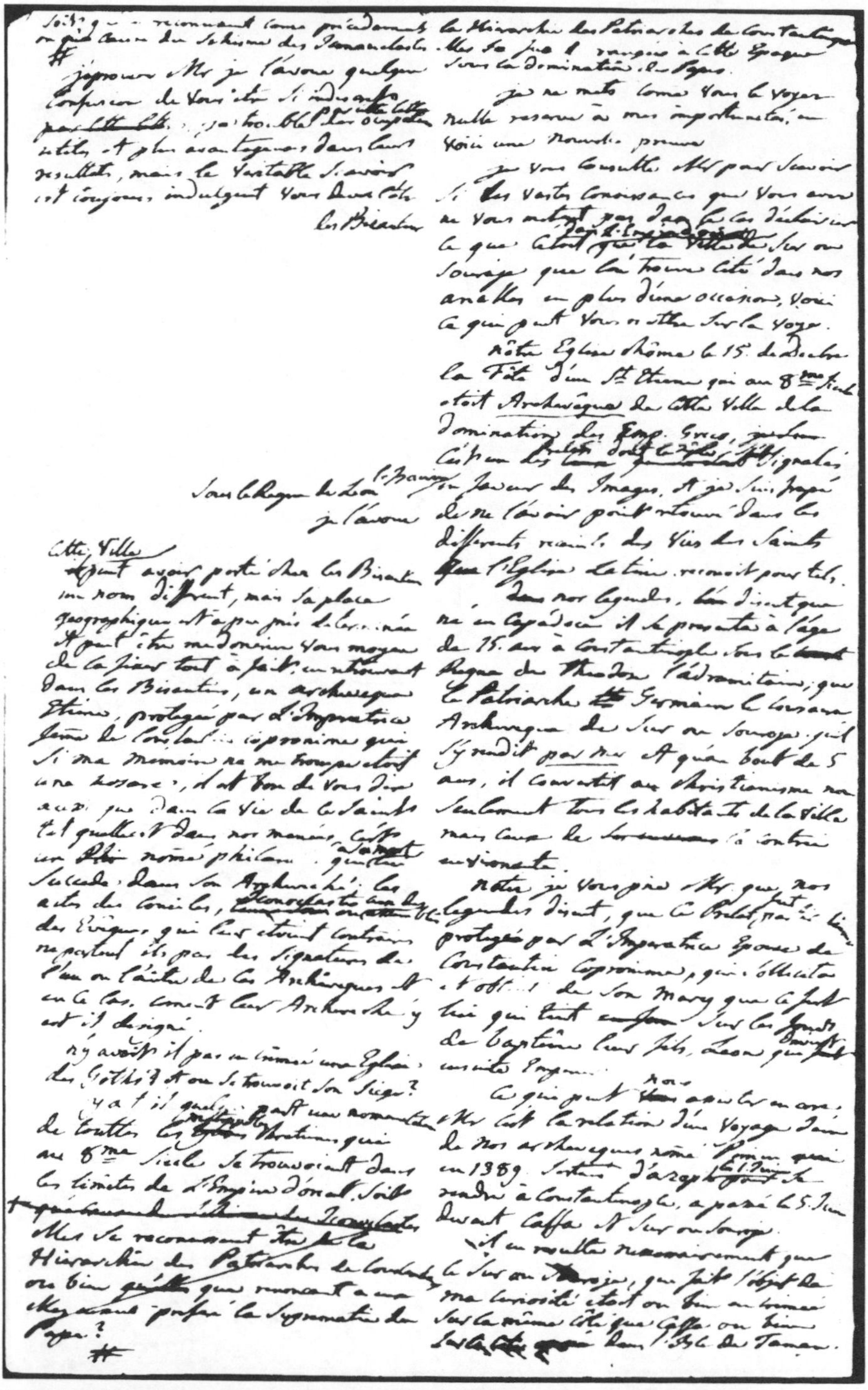

Soit qu'ils reconnaissent comme précédemment ce qui avant du Schisme des Iconoclastes. #

J'éprouve Mr je l'avoue quelque confusion de vous être si indiscret ; j'ai troublé par cette lettre des occupations utiles et plus avantageuses dans leurs résultats, mais le véritable savoir est toujours indulgent vous dans cette [illegible] les Bizantins

Sous le Règne de Léon l'Isaurien je l'avoue

Cette Ville doit avoir porté chez les Bizantins un nom différent, mais sa place géographique n'a pu être déterminée et peut être me donneriez vous moyen de la fixer tout à fait, en retrouvant dans les Bizantins, un archevêque Etienne, protégé par l'Impératrice femme de Constantin Copronime qui si ma mémoire ne me trompe étoit une Kosare ; il est bon de vous dire aussi que dans la Vie de ce Saint tel qu'elle est dans nos mains, c'est un [illegible] nommé Philaret qui [illegible] succède dans son Archevêché ; les actes des Conciles, [illegible] des Evêques qui leur étoient contraires ne portent ils pas les signatures de l'un ou l'autre de ces Archevêques et en ce cas, comment leur Archevêché y est il désigné.

N'y avoit il pas en Crimée une Eglise des Gothis ? et où se trouvoit son Siège ?

Y a t il quelque part une énumération de toutes les communautés chrétiennes qui au 8me siècle se trouvoient dans les limites de l'Empire d'orient. Soit [illegible] Mr se reconnaissant être de la Hiérarchie des Patriarches de Constantinople ou bien qu'elles [illegible] ayant passé sous la domination du Pape ? #

la Hiérarchie des Patriarches de Constantinople Mr. Je suis à ranger à cette Epoque sous la domination du Pape.

Je ne mets comme vous le voyez nulle réserve à mes importunités ; en voici une nouvelle preuve.

Je vous consulte Mr pour savoir si les vastes connaissances que vous avez ne vous mettent pas dans le cas d'éclaircir ce que c'était que la ville de Sur ou Souroge que l'on trouve cité dans nos annales en plus d'une occasion ; voici ce qui peut vous mettre sur la voie.

Notre Eglise chôme le 15. de Décembre la Fête d'un St. Etienne qui au 8me siècle étoit Archevêque de cette Ville de la domination des Emp. Grecs, [illegible] signalés en faveur des Images, et je suis frappé de ne l'avoir point retrouvé dans les différents recueils des Vies des Saints que l'Eglise latine reconnoit pour tels.

Dans nos légendes, l'on dit que né en Capadoce il se présenta à l'âge de 15 ans à Constantinople sous le Règne de Théodose l'Adramitain ; que le Patriarche St Germain le consacra Archevêque de Sur ou Souroge ; qu'il s'y rendit par mer et qu'au bout de 5 ans, il convertit au Christianisme non seulement tous les habitants de la ville mais ceux de la contrée environnante.

Notez je vous prie Mr que nos légendes disent, que ce Prélat fut [illegible] protégé par l'Impératrice Epouse de Constantin Copronime, qui sollicita et obtint de son Mary que ce fut lui qui tint [illegible] sur les fonds de baptême leur fils, Léon qui fut ensuite Empereur.

Ce qui peut nous aider encore Mr c'est la relation d'un Voyage d'un de nos archevêques nommé Pimen qui en 1389 sortant d'azof [illegible] pour se rendre à Constantinople, a passé le 5 Juin devant Caffa et Sur ou Souroge.

Il en résulte nécessairement que le Sur ou Souroge, qui fait l'objet de ma curiosité étoit ou bien en Crimée sur la même côte que Caffa ou bien [illegible] dans l'Isle de Taman.

14. Lenin Library, *Otdel rukopisej*, Fond 255.5.34, no. 9. Draft of Rumjancev's Letter to Hase, p. 2

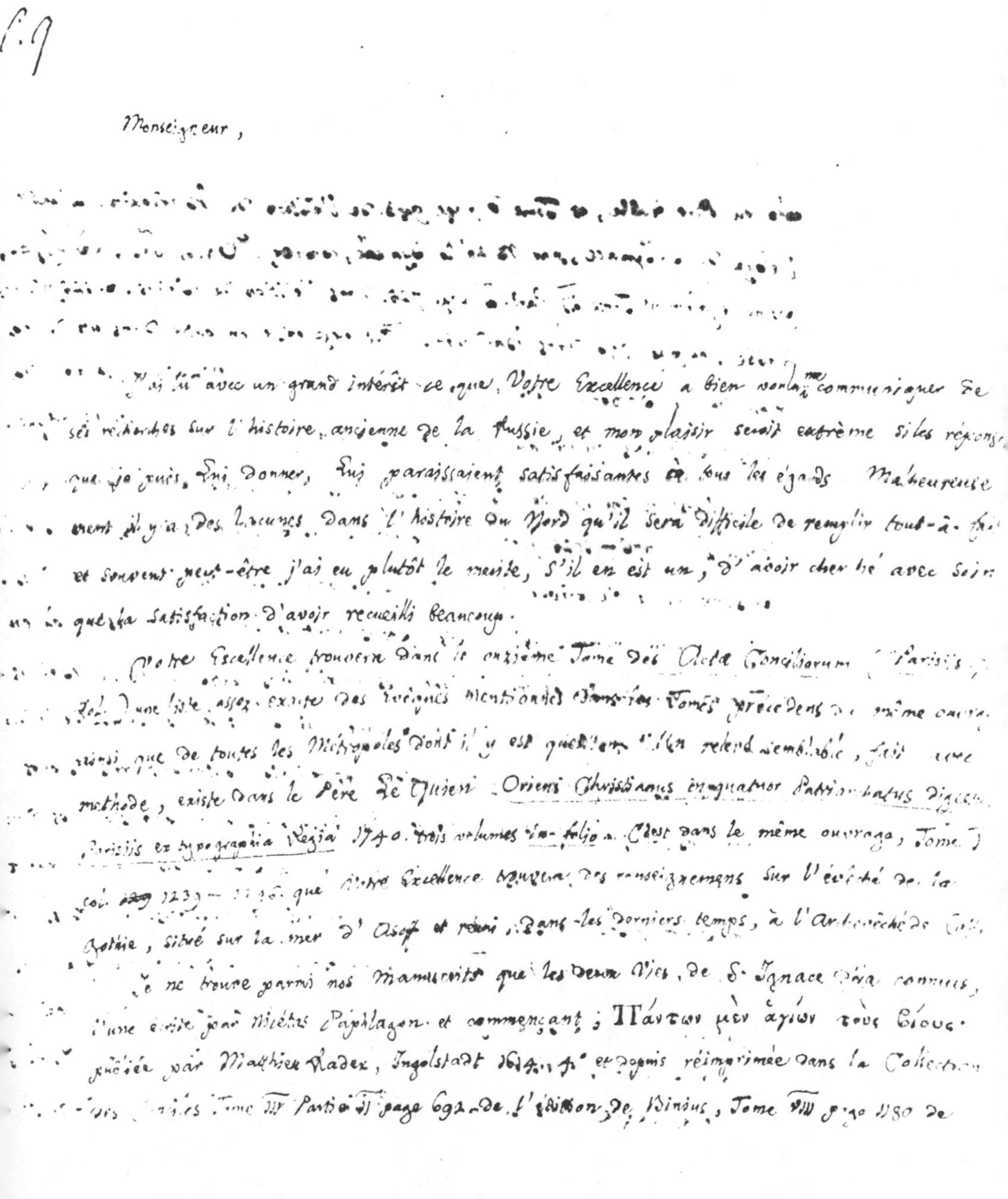

C. 9

Monseigneur,

[illegible]

J'ai lu avec un grand intérêt ce que Votre Excellence a bien voulu me communiquer de ses recherches sur l'histoire ancienne de la Russie, et mon plaisir seroit extrême si les réponses que je puis lui donner lui paraissaient satisfaisantes à tous les égards. Malheureusement il y a des lacunes dans l'histoire du Nord qu'il sera difficile de remplir tout-à-fait et souvent peut-être j'ai eu plutôt le mérite, s'il en est un, d'avoir cherché avec soin que la satisfaction d'avoir recueilli beaucoup.

Votre Excellence trouvera dans le onzième Tome des Acta Conciliorum (Parisiis, fol.) une liste assez exacte des évêques mentionnés dans les Tomes précédens du même ouvrage, ainsi que de toutes les Métropoles dont il y est question. Un relevé semblable, fait avec méthode, existe dans le Père Le Quien Oriens Christianus in quatuor Patriarchatus digestus, Parisiis ex typographia Regia 1740. trois volumes in-folio. C'est dans le même ouvrage, Tome I col. 1239 – 1240 que Votre Excellence trouvera des renseignemens sur l'évêché de la Gothie, situé sur la mer d'Asof et réuni dans les derniers temps, à l'Archevêché de [illegible]

Je ne trouve parmi nos Manuscrits que les deux Vies de S. Ignace déjà connues, l'une écrite par Nicétas Paphlagon et commençant : Πάντων μὲν ἁγίων τοὺς βίους. publiée par Matthieu Rader, Ingolstadt 1614 in 4° et depuis réimprimée dans la Collection des Conciles Tome VIII Partie II page 692 de l'édition de Binius, Tome VIII page 1180 de

15. Lenin Library, *Otdel rukopisej*, R.A.7.12, no. 9. Hase's Letter to Rumjancev, p. 1

celle du Père Labbe, et Tome V page 943. de l'édition de Hardouin. L'autre est l'éloge de S. Ignace, par Michel le Syncelle, commenç. Ὁ νέος οὗτος καὶ μέγας, imprimé également Tome VII Part. II page 725. dans l'édition de Binius, p. 1259 dans Labbe, et page 1010 dans Hardouin. Cet éloge existe en outre dans un de nos MSS. venu de la Sorbonne, avec une peroraison différente de l'imprimée, et avec des variantes importantes quant au texte, mais qui n'ajoutent aucun fait historique.

L'histoire inédite de Psellus, quoiqu'elle commence par le long regne de Basile II (976 – 1025) et qu'elle contienne des particularités intéressantes sur la personne et la vie privée de ce Prince, n'offre absolument rien sur les Russes qui n'y sont même nommés qu'une fois, précisément à la même occasion où en parle Zonare II. 221. B. ils fournissoient des auxiliaires contre le rebelle Bardas Phocas.

Le Manuscrit 4482. de Colbert, portant maintenant le No. 3025. de la Bibliothèque du Roi, est un petit in-4.° d'environ 80 feuillets, contenant trois discours de Libanius, et quelques pièces de vers. Le fragment sur la conversion des Russes suit immédiatement après celles-ci, et commence par les mots, κατὰ καὶ τὰ τοῦ σεβάσματος τούτων, comme dans Banduri Animadvers. ad Constantinum Porphyrog. de admin. imp. II. 112. La fin est également la même que dans l'imprimé, et l'examen le plus attentif m'a convaincu que non seulement la copie donnée par Banduri, mais encore l'analyse du Manuscrit dans le Catalogo Bibliothecae Regiae Pars secunda (Parisiis e typographia Regia 1739. Fol.) pag.

16. Lenin Library, *Otdel rukopisej*, R.A.7.12, no. 9. Hase's Letter to Rumjancev, p. 2

597 sq., sont exactes.

La question sur la position géographique de Sur ou de Sourage pourrait devenir le sujet d'un mémoire curieux. Voulant répondre sur le champ à Votre Excellence, je réunis ici peut-être un peu précipitamment ce que je pense à ce sujet. Que mes conjectures semblent admissibles ou non à V. E., Elle fera de ces matériaux épars l'usage qu'Elle voudra.

D'après l'itinéraire de l'Archevêque Simine nous devons supposer que Sourage se trouvait à peu de distance du detroit de Caffa, soit en Crimée, soit sur la côte opposée de l'Asie.

Je ne crois pas qu'il faille le chercher dans le pays des Abasges, la Zichia des Byzantins. D'abord, nous nous éloignerions trop du Détroit; ensuite, dans tout le tour du Pont-Euxin la cote depuis l'île de Taman jusqu'à Dioscurias est précisément celle que les Empereurs d'Orient ont possédée le moins de temps. Ils n'y pouvoient déjà plus rien au sixième siècle (Procope Bello Gothico. T. 572 B.), et S. Basile II s'en rendit maître vers 1022. (Cedren. II. 718 D.). Sa domination ne fut certainement pas de longue durée. Les garnisons des Grecs dispersées sur cette côte éloignée, habitée par des peuples sauvages et belliqueux devaient être bientôt accablées, n'ayant pas, comme en Crimée, de larges bras de mer pour leur défense.

Je ne cherche pas non plus Sourage dans l'île de Taman. Nous connoissons le nom du siège métropolitain établi dans cette contrée; c'est celui de Tmutarakan en Russie (Histoire ancienne d'Asow et de la Crimée, dans

17. Lenin Library, *Otdel rukopisej*, R.A.7.12, no. 9. Hase's Letter to Rumjancev, p. 3

le Recueil de Müller Volume II cahier I p. 71. St. Pétersbourg 1736. 8.) et le Mémoire
de Mussin-Puschkin sur l'inscription de Gléb, figurée aussi dans le Voyage de Pallas de l'an 1793 et 1794 Tom
II p. 184. de l'édit. Allemande), et Tamatarcha (Ταμάταρχα) ou Metrakha
(Μετραχά) chez les Byzantins. Le premier de ces deux noms se trouve dans
Constantin (De administrando imp. 113. E. F.), le second dans Le Quien Oriens
Christianus T. 1326. A. Il y avoit en outre, du moins pour quelque temps, un
evêché à Phanagoria (Le Quien, 1512).

Il ne reste donc que la Crimée, et c'est dans la partie méridionale de
cette presqu'île que je me flatte de rencontrer la ville de Sourage. Je crois
1.) qu'elle étoit connue chez les Grecs sous le nom de Sarat, Σαράτ. 2.)
qu'ayant pris de l'accroissement vers la treizième Siècle, elle est la Soldaia
des Génois, et par conséquent le Soudak d'aujourd'hui, dont les ruines, les
fortifications, et la position singulière ont attiré l'attention de presque tous
les voyageurs modernes. Voici, Monseigneur, les raisons sur lesquelles
j'appuye mes deux conjectures.

1.° „La contrée des Patzinaques," dit Constantin (De administrando imp.
F.) „comprend tout le pays depuis la Russie et le Bosphore, jusqu'à
„Cherson, Sarat, Burat, et les trente Divisions." Les Patzinaques occupoient
donc tout l'intérieur de la presqu'île, à l'exception de la côte ... qui
en borde la côte méridionale. Les trente Divisions sont les mêmes que les
trente Climata (Banduri Animadvert. in Constantin. De administr. im...

18. Lenin Library, *Otdel rukopisej*, R.A.7.12, no. 9. Hase's Letter to Rumjancev, p. 4

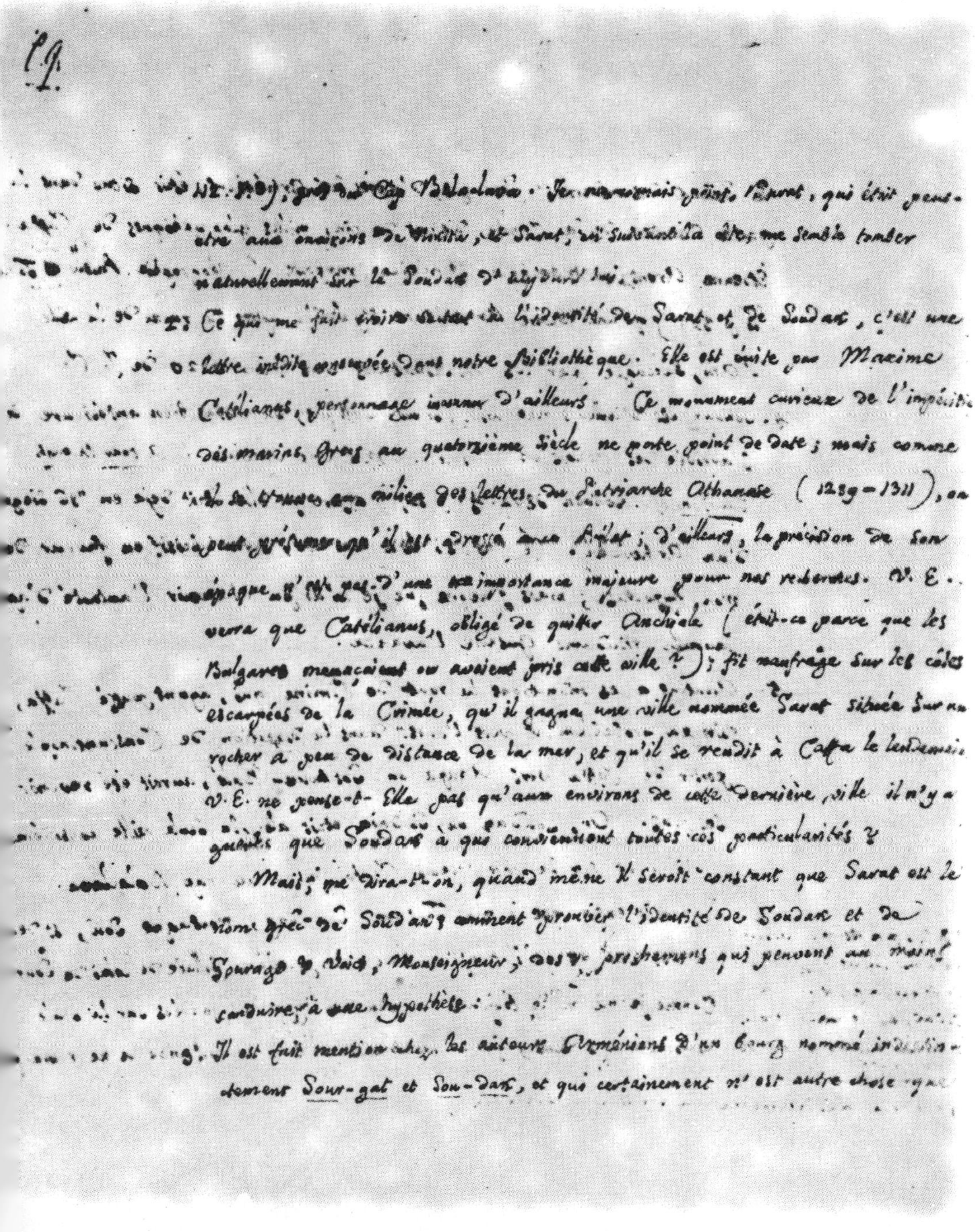

[illegible] Balaclava. Je n'examinerais point, [illegible], qui était peut-être aux environs de [illegible], et Sarat, [illegible] me semble tomber naturellement sur le Soudac d'aujourd'hui [illegible].

Ce qui me fait croire [illegible] de l'identité de Sarat et de Soudac, c'est une lettre inédite [illegible] dans notre Bibliothèque. Elle est écrite par Maxime Catilianus, personnage inconnu d'ailleurs. Ce monument curieux de l'[illegible] des marins Grecs au quatorzième siècle ne porte point de date; mais comme [illegible] au milieu des lettres du Patriarche Athanase (1289–1311), on peut présumer qu'il est adressé à ce Prélat; d'ailleurs, la précision de son époque n'est pas d'une importance majeure pour nos recherches. V. E. verra que Catilianus, obligé de quitter Anchiale (était-ce parce que les Bulgares menaçaient ou avaient pris cette ville?); fit naufrage sur les côtes escarpées de la Crimée, qu'il gagna une ville nommée Sarat située sur un rocher à peu de distance de la mer, et qu'il se rendit à Caffa le lendemain.

V. E. ne pense-t-Elle pas qu'aux environs de cette dernière ville il n'y a guères que Soudac à qui conviendroient toutes ces particularités?

Mais, me dira-t-on, quand même il seroit constant que Sarat est le nom grec de Soudac, [illegible] l'identité de Soudac et de [illegible]. Voici, Monseigneur, [illegible] qui peuvent au moins conduire à une hypothèse:

Il est fait mention chez les auteurs Arméniens d'un bourg nommé indistinctement Sour-gat et Sou-dac, et qui certainement n'est autre chose que

19. Lenin Library, *Otdel rukopisej*, R.A.7.12, nó. 9. Hase's Letter to Rumjancev, p. 5

le Soudak des modernes. Sour-gat, d'après les Arméniens, étoit situé dans la partie Orientale de la Crimée, distant de cinq milles géographiques de Caffa. Étienne Arontz, Archevêque Arménien, rapporte (Géographie, Partie II Tome II p. 329) qu'une colonie Arménienne s'y établit après la ruine de la ville d'Ani, saccagée par les Mahométans vers l'an 1320 de J. C.

4. Soudak est d'ailleurs une ville, si non antique, du moins bien antérieure à l'arrivée des Genois en Crimée. Madame Guthrie (A tour through Taurida &c. London 1802. 4° p. 127) assure qu'elle étoit déja en 786 siège d'un Archevêché. Ce fait, s'il étoit constaté, seroit décisif en faveur de mon hypothèse; mais j'avoue que je n'ai pu découvrir l'autorité d'après laquelle Madame Guthrie l'avance.

5. Ajoutons à ces inductions la route de Simine qui, ayant passé Caffa, se dirigea probablement vers l'ouest dans la direction de Constantinople; se porter de Caffa vers Anapa ou Soudjouk-Kalé, auroit été revenir sur ses pas. Or, Soudak ou Soldaja étoit alors la seule ville considérable qu'il y eut sur la côte depuis Caffa jusqu'au cap Balaclava.

6. Il paraît enfin que le nom Tartare Sou-dag, montagne Sou, est dérivé du mot Sour; et qu'il renferme encore la première syllabe de celui de Sourage. Comme je me méfie toujours un peu des hypothèses fondées sur la seule conformité des sons, je n'attacherois point d'importance à ce remarque ...

[margin:] ...s faire observer cependant, ...mot Tartare Dag, montagne, ...r un g, et que le nom de ..., chez les auteurs Arabes, ... par un K; ainsi l'étymologie de ce mot ... n'est peut-être pas celle ... de là, mais la ressemblance entre Son et Sour existe toujours.

20. Lenin Library, *Otdel rukopisej*, R.A.7.12, no. 9. Hase's Letter to Rumjancev, p. 6

pas cette ressemblance, si elle étoit isolée; mais jointe aux autres faits elle ajoute, si je ne me trompe, un degré de probabilité à ma conjecture.

J'avoue cependant qu'il reste quelques difficultés que je ne saurois resoudre à moi seul. Il peut surtout paraître singulier que les Grecs qui parlent si souvent des Evêchés de Cherson (Le Quien T. 1329.) et de Bosporus (ibid. T. 1327.), ne fassent jamais mention de l'Archevêché de Sarat. Dirions-nous que l'Evêché de Bosporus et l'Archevêché de Sarat ne sont peut-être qu'un seul, et que le siège de ces Prélats, se trouvant établi, à différentes époques, tantôt dans l'une tantôt dans l'autre de ces deux villes, les Byzantins les aient toujours nommés Evêques du Bosporus en quel lieu que fût leur résidence?

Quoiqu'il en soit, Monseigneur, je crois avoir rendu probable au moins l'identité de Soudak et du Sarat de Constantin. Quant à celle de Sarat et de Sourage, c'est à V. E. de voir si ma conjecture s'accorde avec les particularités rapportées dans les annales Russes de cette dernière ville. Peut-être pourrois-je donner un degré de probabilité de plus à mon opinion en consultant des ouvrages Russes et Allemands; mais je me trouve dans une Bibliothèque, et je puis dire dans une ville, où il n'y a presque point des premiers, et peu des seconds. Réduit par conséquent aux auteurs Grecs je m'estimerois heureux toutes les fois quand dans ceux-ci et dans le nombre de notes historiques et géographiques que j'ai recueillies en examin-

21. Lenin Library, *Otdel rukopisej*, R.A.7.12, no. 9. Hase's Letter to Rumjancev, p. 7

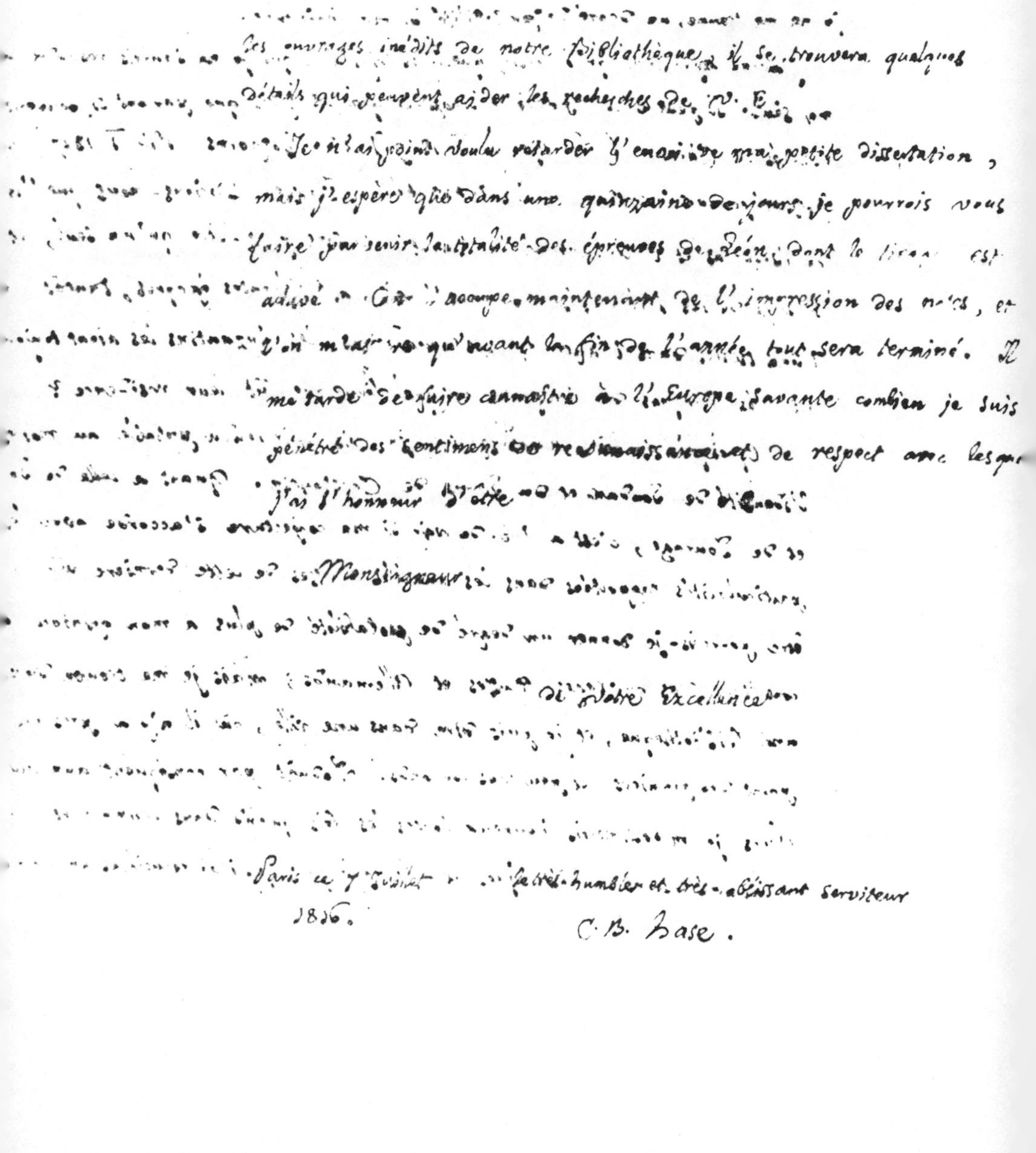

les ouvrages inédits de notre Bibliothèque, il se trouvera quelques
détails qui peuvent aider les recherches de V. E.
Je n'ai point voulu retarder l'envoi de ma petite dissertation,
mais j'espère que dans une quinzaine de jours je pourrois vous
faire parvenir la totalité des épreuves de Léon, dont le texte est
achevé. On s'occupe maintenant de l'impression des notes, et
j'ai lieu de croire qu'avant la fin de l'année tout sera terminé. Il
me tarde de faire connoître à l'Europe savante combien je suis
pénétré des sentimens de reconnoissance et de respect avec lesquels
J'ai l'honneur d'être
Monseigneur
de Votre Excellence
Paris ce 7 Juillet
1816.
le très-humble et très-obéissant serviteur
C. B. Hase.

22. Lenin Library, *Otdel rukopisej*, R.A.7.12, no. 9. Hase's Letter to Rumjancev, p. 8

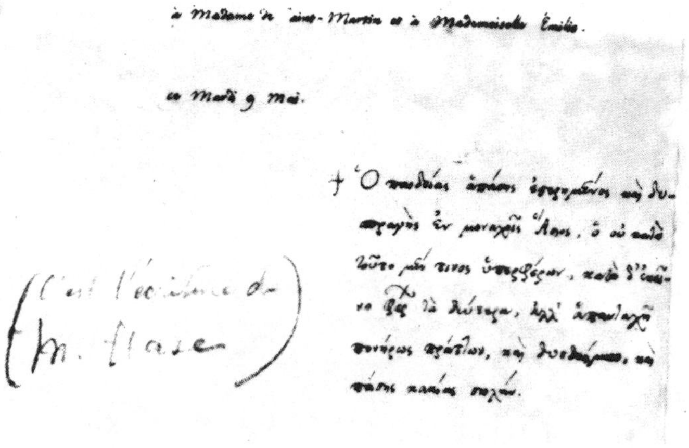
à Madame de Saint-Martin et à Mademoiselle Émilie.

ce Mardi 9 mai.

(C'est l'écriture de M. Hase)

23A. Paris *Nouvelles acquisitions françaises* 9115, p. 115. Signature from Hase's Letter to Saint-Martin

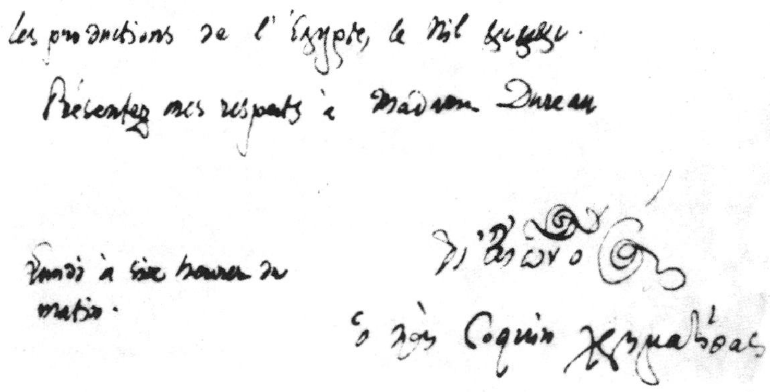
Les productions de l'Égypte, le Nil &c &c.

Présentez mes respects à Madame Dureau

Lundi à six heures du matin.

23B. Paris *Supplément Grec* 925, fol. 8ᵛ. Signature from Hase's Letter to Dureau de La Malle

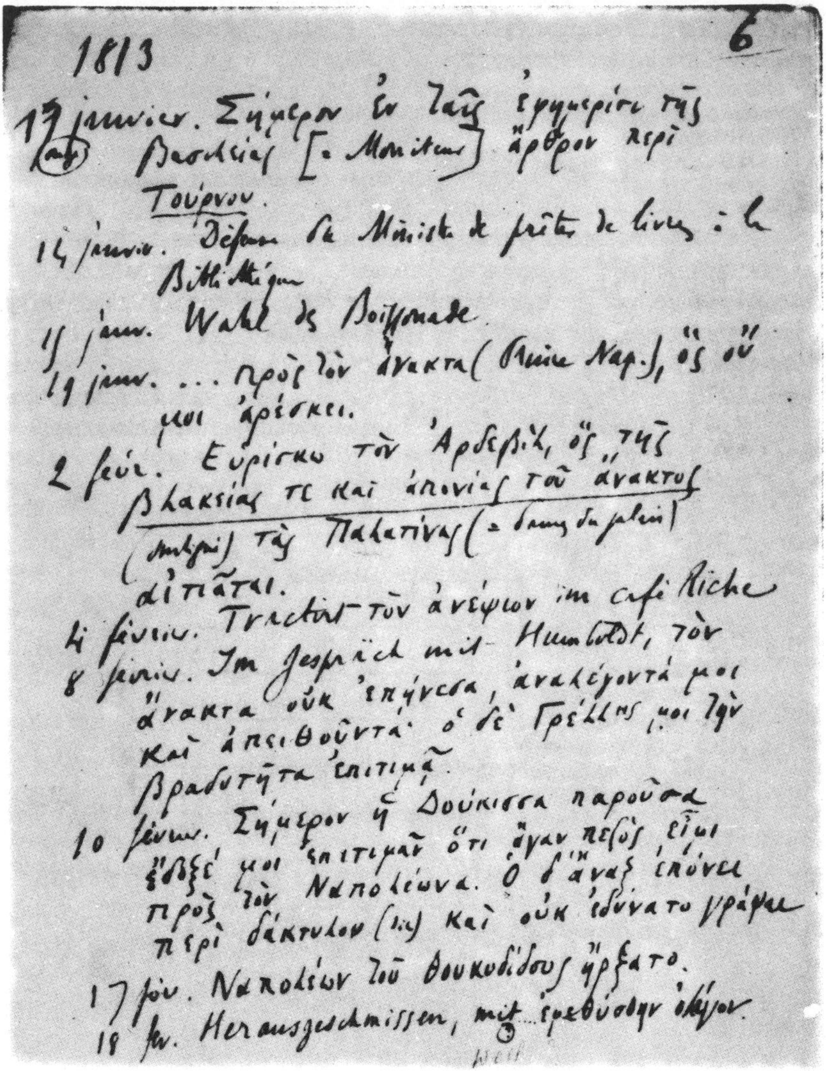
1813 6

17 janvier. Σήμερον ἐν ταῖς ἐφημερίσι τῆς Βασιλείας [= Moniteur] ἄρθρον περὶ Τούρνου.

14 janvier. Défense du Ministre de prêter de livres à la Bibliothèque

15 janv. Wahl de Boissonade.

19 janv. ... πρὸς τὸν ἄνακτα (Prince Nap.), ὃς οὔ μοι ἀρέσκει.

2 févr. Εὑρίσκω τὸν Ἀρδεβίλ, ὃς τῆς βλακείας τε καὶ ἀπονίας τοῦ ἄνακτος (...) τῆς Παλατίνας (= dames du palais) αἰτιᾶται.

4 févr. Tractat τῶν ἀνεψιῶν im café Riche

8 févr. Im Gespräch mit Humboldt, τὸν ἄνακτα οὐκ ἐπῄνεσα, ἀναλέγοντά μοι καὶ ἀπειθοῦντα· ὁ δὲ Γρέλλης μοι τὴν βραδυτῆτα ἐπιτιμᾷ.

10 févr. Σήμερον ἡ Δούκισσα παροῦσα ἔδοξέ μοι ἐπιτιμᾶν ὅτι ἄγαν πεζὸς εἶμι πρὸς τὸν Ναπολέωνα. Ὁ δ᾽ ἄναξ ἐκόνει περὶ δάκτυλον (sic) καὶ οὐκ ἐδύνατο γράφειν

17 févr. Ναπολέων τοῦ Θουκυδίδου ἤρξατο.

18 févr. Herausgeschmissen, mit ... ἐρεθύσθην ὀλίγον.

24. Paris *Supplément Grec* 1363, p. 6. Hase's Secret Diary

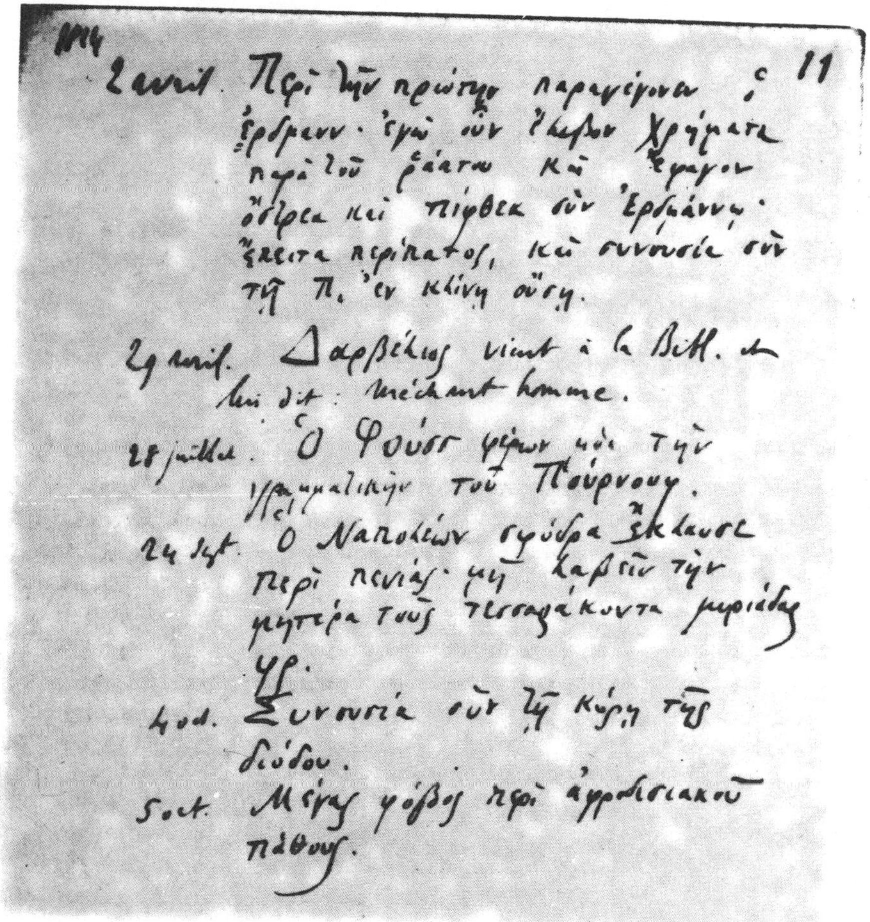

25. Paris *Supplément Grec* 1363, p. 11. Hase's Secret Diary

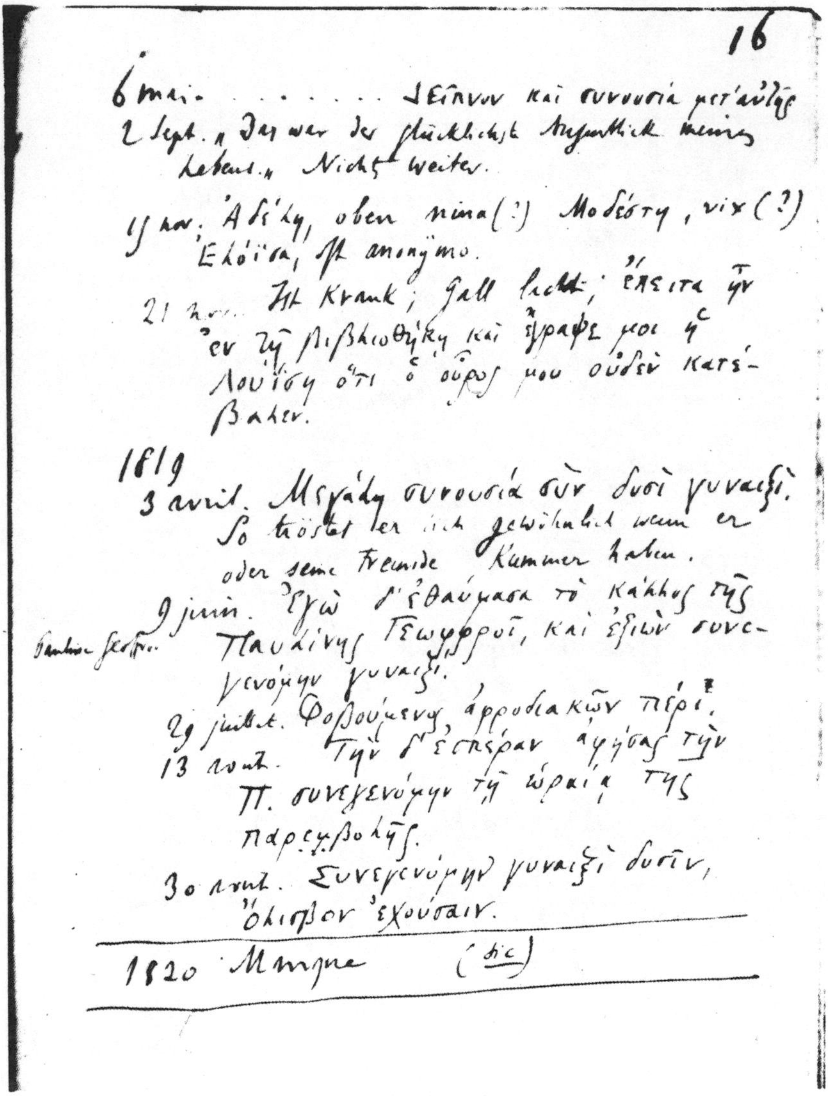

16

6 mai. . . . . δεῖπνον καὶ συνουσία μετ' αὐτῆς

2 Sept. „Das war der glücklichste Augenblick meines Lebens." Nichts weiter.

15 nov: Ἀδέλη, oben nina(?) Μοδέστη, vix(?) Ἐλόϊσα, oft anonymo.

21 nov. Ist krank; gall leicht; ἔπειτα ἦν ἐν τῇ βιβλιοθήκῃ καὶ ἔγραψε μοι ἡ Λουΐση ὅτι ὁ οὖρος μου οὐδὲν κατέβαλεν.

1819

3 avril. Μεγάλη συνουσία σὺν δυσὶ γυναιξί. So tröstet der sich gewöhnlich wenn er oder seine Freunde Kummer haben.

9 juin. Ἐγὼ δ' ἐθαύμασα τὸ κάλλος τῆς Παυλίνης Γεωφροῦ, καὶ ἐξιὼν συνεγενόμην γυναιξί. (Pauline Geoffroy)

29 juillet. Φοβουμένη, ἀφροδισιακῶν πέρι.

13 août. Τὴν δ' ἑσπέραν ἀψάμενος τὴν Π. συνεγενόμην τῇ ὡραίᾳ τῆς παρεμβολῆς.

30 août. Συνεγενόμην γυναιξὶ δυσίν, ὄλιβον ἐχούσαιν.

1820 [illegible] (sic)

26. Paris *Supplément Grec* 1363, p. 16. Hase's Secret Diary

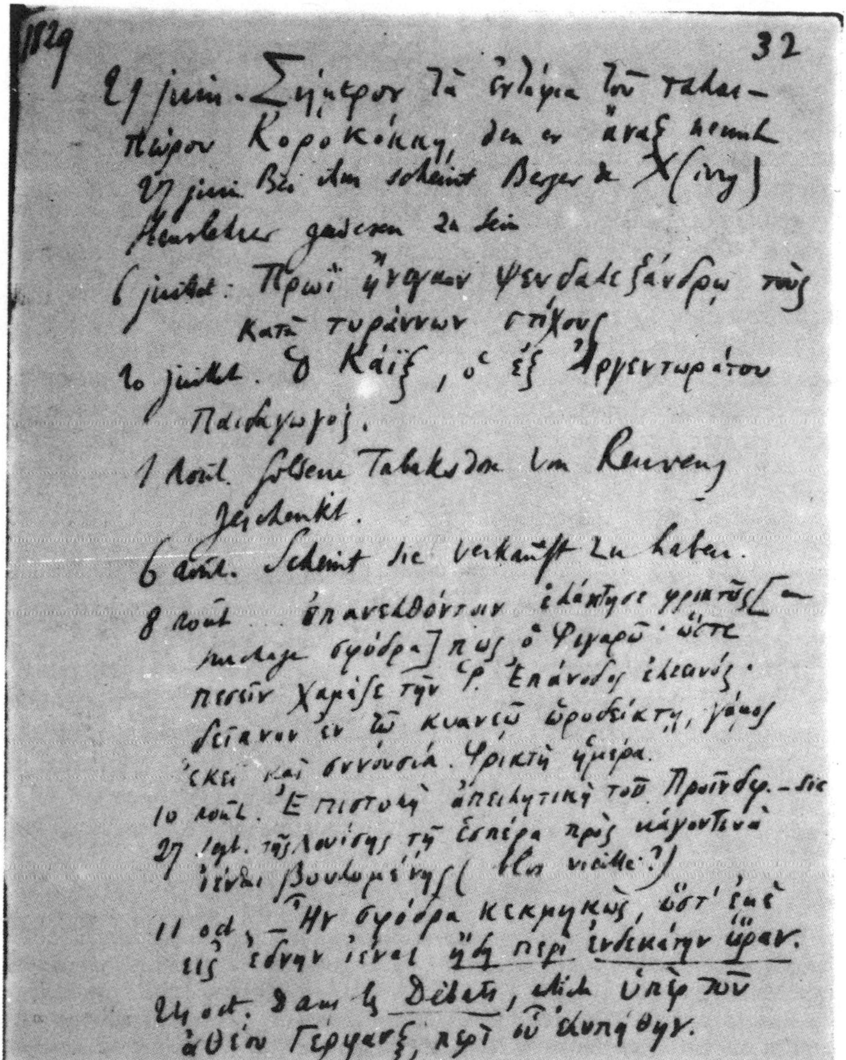

27. Paris *Supplément Grec* 1363, p. 32. Hase's Secret Diary

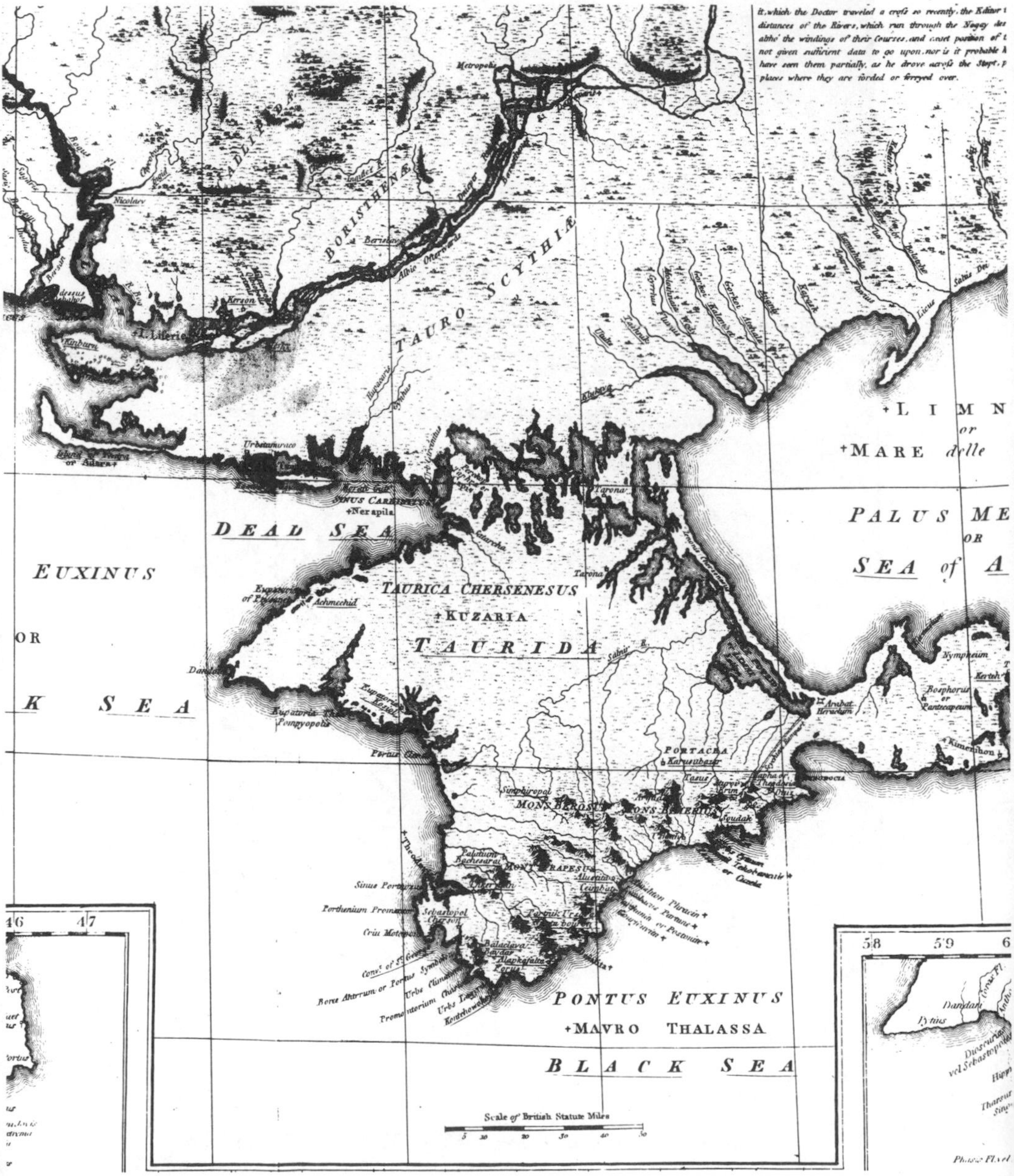

28. Map of the Crimea from Maria Guthrie, *A Tour. . . Through the Taurida. . .* (1802), detail

XXVII

On the Social Background of Cyril and Methodius

Since hardly a single facet of the *Lives* of Cyril and Methodius has remained unexplored in the course of the past hundred and twenty-eight years,[1] scholars have made inquiries into the milieu that produced the Apostles of the Slavs. However, they dwelt mostly on one aspect of the

1. In subsequent notes, *Vita Constantini* and *Vita Methodii* will be quoted as VC and VM, respectively. — A hundred and twenty-eight years bring us back to 1843. It should be restated that the credit for acquainting scholars with VC and VM belongs to A. V. GORSKIJ, "O sv. Kirille i Mefodii," *Moskvitjanin* (1843, Part 3, nr. 6), 405-434, since Gorskij was the first to print an analysis and a detailed summary of the *Lives* as we know them today, that is, as two separate texts. Two earlier scholars could claim priority over Gorskij, but they offered the contents of VC and VM without knowing the existence of the *Lives* themselves. (a) It is the merit of A. L. VON SCHLÖZER (*Nestor. Russische Annalen in ihrer slavischen Grundsprache*, 3 [1805], pp. 149-242, esp. 233-241) to have alerted the European scholarly community to the importance of the printed Slavic Menologium upon which he had chanced (p. 234: Wie werden die Ausländer...über diesen Fund staunen!), as it was Josef DOBROVSKÝ's "most fateful error" to have downgraded the value of Schlözer's find (in *Cyrill und Method, der Slaven Apostel* [1823], pp. 7-9, and Josef Dobrovský, *Cyril a Metod, Apoštolové slovanští* in *Spisy a projevy Josefa Dobrovského*, XII, 1948, pp. 23-24; cf. commentary by J. Vajs, *ibidem*, p. 101). However, although VC and VM were the two main sources of Schlözer's text, this text was but a compilation inserted (under the date of May 11) by Saint DIMITRIJ SAVYČ TUPTALENKO, later Metropolitan of Rostov (1651-1709), into the third volume of his *Kniga Žitij Svjatyx*, Kiev, Monastery of the Caves, 1700, cf. facsimile of title page in Xv. Titov, *Materialy dlja istorii knyžnoji spravy na Vkrajini v XVI-XVIII vv.* in *Ukrajins'ka Akad. Nauk. Zbirnyk istor.-filoloh. viddilu*, 17, 1924, p. 453 (Schlözer himself used the third ed. [Moscow, 1759], cf. *Nestor...*, p. 233). Thus Schlözer was only technically wrong when he viewed the text which he had found as "a Russian legend" (Nestor..., 234, cf. p. 242), and Dobrovský (*Cyrill und Method...*, p. 9) had a point in calling it *neueres Machwerk*; however, Saint Dimitrij (incidentally, ethnically a Ukrainian) was but an editor, and his late *Machwerk* consisted to a large extent of valuable ninth-century West and South

problem: they debated ⟨342⟩ whether Thessalonica and Macedonia were Slavic or Greek in the ninth century;[2] or else, they asked whether Cyril and Methodius themselves were Greeks or Slavs, and if the latter, what kind of Slavs.[3] In short, most of the effort spent on investigating Cyril's and Methodius' milieu had to do with that milieu's ethnic character, and the results obtained corresponded to the questions asked. Scholars were able to show, sometimes with excessive clarity, that by the ninth century, the Thessalonican region (if not perhaps the city itself) was heavily Slavicized; on the other hand, when it came to determining the ethnic origin of two individuals called Cyril and Methodius, the pro-Greek fac-

---

Slavic material. (b) The very first scholarly work to have contained a few quasi verbatim quotations or Russian translation from the *Lives*, was V. N. Tatiščev's *Istorija rossijskaja* (Part two, printed in 1773-4, but written by 1750; cf. the modern edition by the Soviet Academy of Sciences, 2, 1963, p. 35, cf. pp. 210-212). However, Tatiščev's main source was the Russian Primary Chronicle, *s.a.* 898, and the Menologium to which he referred in a note (*Čet'ja-Mineja*, cf. p. 210) must have been Dimitrij Rostovskij's *Kniga Žitij svjatyx* again: like Dimitrij's, Tatiščev's Menologium put the information on Constantine-Cyril under May 11, while all the other *Minei-Čet'i* containing VC or VM *in extenso* placed them under February 14, October, or April 6, respectively. Cf. M. Popruženko and St. Romanski, *Bibliografski pregled na slavjanskite kirilski istočnici za života i dejnostta na Kirila i Metodija*, 1935, pp. 27-35. In any case, Tatiščev did not use the two *Lives* in their original form. Dimitrij Rostovskij no doubt used at least the VC in compiling his entry under May 11 (he copied the Chilandar manuscript of VC, cf., e.g., Popruženko-Romanski, o. c. p. 31). He thus deserves some praise, since it is through his compilation that long portions of VC first appeared in print; but the saintly author's intent was edification, not scholarship.

2. Under the rubric "Constantine's and Methodius' Country of Birth", G. A. Il'inskij, *Opyt sistematičeskoj Kirillo-Mefod'evskoj bibliografii*, 1934, lists 6 entries (nr. 47, p. 63); M. Popruženko and St. Romanski, *Kirilo-metodievska bibliografija za 1934-1940 goda*. (1942), 6 entries (= nr. 26, pp. 53-54); and the forthcoming Cyrillo-Methodian bibliography by Dr. Josef Hahn, 27 entries and 8 reviews (nr. 61). I am indebted to Dr. Wilhelm Fink of Fink Verlag, Munich, for putting the galley-proofs of Dr. Hahn's book at my disposal. — Cf. also Tachiaos, Ἡ ἐθνικότης Κυρίλλου... (as in n. 4 *infra*), p. 103, n. 49.

3. Under the rubrics "Names, Origin, and Nationality of Cyril and Methodius," Il'inskij, *Opyt*... (as in the preceding note), lists 11 entries and 4 reviews (nr. 48, pp. 63-64); Popruženko-Romanski, *Kirilo-metodievska*... (as in the preceding note), 12 entries and 3 reviews (nr. 27, pp. 54-56), and Hahn (as in the preceding note), 31 entries and 20 reviews (nr. 62). Even the "Bъlgarska kirilometodievska bibliografija za perioda 1944-1962," *Xiljada i sto godini slavjanska pismenost* 863-1963 (1963), quotes two articles on the subject (p. 526 and n. 64 and 65).

tion won out and has been enjoying a comfortable lead, although opinions on this topic continue to vary up to the present day.[4]

As there have been no new sources to feed this ethnocentric discussion, it has by now reached a point where it seems more profitable to shelve it for awhile, to respond to changes in scholarly perspective which have meanwhile occurred in other fields of historical inquiry, and to put the question thus: What position did the milieu into which Cyril and Methodius were born occupy in the social and cultural spectrum of ninth-century Byzantium? In attempting ⟨343⟩ a reply to this vast question, I shall be able to quote hardly more than ten pertinent sources and refer to only six individuals, other than members of Cyril's and Methodius' family, by name. This sample, so small as to be irrelevant in the eyes of the most indulgent of sociologists, should appear large enough to students of *Cyrillo-Methodiana*, for in their work they are accustomed to even slimmer pickings.

The high social status of the brothers' family — at least in the minds of their hagiographers — can be inferred from the two *loci classici*

4. Cf., as most recent examples, (a) I. Dujčev, "Graeci amantes eum a puero," *Studien zur Geschichte Europas*, 3, *Wiener Archiv für Geschichte des Slaventums und Osteuropas*, 5 (1966), 15-19 and V. Tъpkova-Zaimova, "Solunskite slavjani i proizxodъt na Kiril i Metodii," *Konstantin-Kiril filosof, jubileen sbornik po slučaj 1100 godišninata ot smrъtta mu* (1969), pp. 63-68 (Cyril and Methodius were Slavs); (b) A. A. Tachiaos 'Η ἐθνικότης Κυρίλλου καὶ Μεθοδίου κατὰ τὰς σλαβικὰς ἱστορικὰς πηγὰς καὶ μαρτυρίας, in I. E. Anastasiou, ed., Κυρίλλῳ καὶ Μεθοδίῳ τόμος ἑόρτιος ἐπὶ τῇ χιλιοστῇ καὶ ἑκατοστῇ ἐτηρίδι, 2 (1968), pp. 83-132 (they were Greeks). Cf. also D. P. Bogdan, "La vie et l'oeuvre des frères Constantin-Cyrille et Méthode," *ibidem*, esp. pp. 40-41 (lists adherents of the pro-Slavic and the pro-Greek factions). — My own position is determined by the realization that in the opinion of their own contemporaries (both Latin and Slavic) Cyril and Methodius were either Greeks or non-Slavs. It is safe to assume that on the point of the Thessalonican brothers' ethnic background their contemporaries were better informed than we are. There remains that argument for Cyril's and Methodius' Slavic origin which has to do with the Slavic translation of the Gospels and Psalter (attributed in VM XV, 4 to both brothers). The argument is in two (somewhat contradictory) parts: (a) the translation is of high quality (inference: only Slavs with a mastery of Greek could have made it); (b) it exhibits peculiarities and short-comings (these are demonstrable: cf., e.g., V. Pogorelov in *Studi bizantini e neoellenici*, 5 [1939], 534-540; hence Greek was a language foreign to the translator). Therefore I assume that (if the texts which we possess go back entirely to Cyril's and Methodius' time), the brothers were Byzantines of Greek background leading — very expertly — a translation team which comprised Slavs as well.

of their *Lives*. The first refers to Methodius: "He was of no mean descent, on both sides, but rather of a very good and honorable ⟨lineage⟩, known earlier to God and the Emperor, and to the whole region of Thessalonica."[5] The second passage deals with Constantine: "It is the wont among the sons of rich people to engage in roving hunts; thus one day Constantine took his falcon and went out with them into the fields."[6]

Noble origin of both father and mother; imperial favor; local prominence; pastimes of the leisurely rich — all these traits point with certainty to a wealthy parental home, but, with the exception of the falcon episode, none of them goes beyond the imprecision of a hagiographic *topos*.[7] Fortunately, the *Vita Constantini* does offer one bit of hard information on our subject. It occurs in a third passage which speaks of the military rank held by Constantine's father: "There lived in the city of Thessalonica a certain man, rich and of noble birth, Leo by name, holding the rank of *drungarios* under the command of a *strategos*."[8] This helps us to assess the social stratum to which the parents of the

5. VM II, 4: *bě že roda ne xuda otъ obojǫdu, nъ velьmi dobra i čьstьna, znajema prъvěje bogomь i cěsarjemь i vьsejǫ Solunьskojǫ stranojǫ.* In subsequent notes, I shall quote VC and VM after the edition by P. A. Lavrov, *Materialy po istorii vozniknovenija drevnejšej slavjanskoj pis'mennosti* (1930, reprint 1966), but normalize the spelling and adopt the subdivision of chapters into sentences from F. Grivec-F. Tomšić, *Constantinus et Methodius Thessalonicenses, Fontes* [*Radovi Staroslavenskog Instituta*, 4] (1960).

6. VC III, 10: *Jedinojǫ že otъ dьnьi, jakože obyčai jestъ bogatičištemъ glumljenьje tvoriti lovitvojǫ, izide sъ nimi na polje, jastrebъ (var.: kragui) svoi vъzьmь. Bogatičišьtь* is a *hapax legomenon* in OCS, but its meaning offers no difficulty. As for *glumljenije*, it occurs twice in OCS in addition to the present passage: once it corresponds to ῥεμβασμός 'wandering about'. Hence *glumljenije tvoriti* appears to correspond to ῥέμβεσθαι 'rove, roam', an appropriate term to describe hunting in the fields. *SJS*, s. v., arrives at the meaning "delectatio" for *glumljenije* in our passage without indication of any other source. — [F. Grivec translates "delectari venatione", J. Vašica "bavit se lovem", 'enjoy hunting'. — Rd.].

7. In his otherwise valuable article, Mr. Tachiaos may not have sufficiently discounted the topical character of VM III when he stated that Constantine and Methodius "belonged to the aristocracy of the second most important city in Byzantium", cf. *op. cit.* (in note 4 *supra*), pp. 102-3. This is, in my opinion, to assess the social standing of the brothers a bit too highly.

8. VC II, 1: *Vъ Solunьscě že gradě bě mǫžь někyi* (var: *jeterъ*), *dobrorodьnъ i bogatъ, imenьmь Lьvъ, prědrъžę sanъ drǫgarьskъi podъ stratigonıь.*

Thessalonican brothers belonged and provides a fixed point from which to measure the extent of the brothers' own social ascent.

By the ninth century, a *strategos* was either the military and administrative head of a land province, or *thema* — and the *thema* of Thessalonica is attested ⟨344⟩ probably by ca. 836, surely by 856[9] — or the commander of a fleet, called *thematic* fleet. Both kinds of *strategoi* had *drungarioi* under their command;[10] to decide which kind of *drungarios* Leo was, we should keep three things in mind: (a) *Vita Constantini* says nothing about Leo's naval service; (b) Thessalonica seems to have had no *thematic* fleet with a *strategos*; (c) it did have a "provincial" fleet, but its chief officers had titles other than *strategos*. I shall therefore assume that the *strategos* "under" whom Leo served was the military governor of the land *thema* of Thessalonica, and that Leo himself was a *drungarios* in the thematic land army.[11] For our purposes, this is an important distinction, since the social status of the army *drungarios*, as reflected in his pay, *roga*, was lower than that of his naval counterpart, the ratio of the respective *rogai* being 3:20 by the year 910-11.[12]

---

9. Cf., e.g., A. Pertusi, ed., CONSTANTINE PORPHYROGENITUS, *De Thematibus* [*Studi e Testi*, 160] (1952), p. 168.

10. Cf., for the dry land *strategos* and *drungarioi* under him, e.g., J. B. BURY, *The Imperial Administrative System in the Ninth Century...* (1911), p. 139, 3-10; for the naval *strategoi* and their *drungarioi*, e.g., H. AHRWEILER, *Byzance et la mer* (1966), pp. 32; 69, n. 4; 96; 34; 48; 58 and J. FERLUGA, "Niže vojno-administrativne jedinice tematskog uređenja," *Zbornik radova Vizantološkog Instituta*, 2 (1953), esp. pp. 69-73.

11. On the *drungarios* of the army, cf. H. GELZER, *Die Genesis der byzant. Themenverfassung* [*Abhandlungen der philol.-hist. Kl. der Sächs. Gesellschaft der Wissenschaften*, 5] (1899), esp. p. 144; Ju. KULAKOVSKIJ, "Drung i drungarij", *Vizantijskij Vremennik*, 9 (1902), 1-30 (still by far the best); A. Vogt, *Basile Ier...* (1908), p. 344 (some errors); F. DVORNÍK, *Les légendes de Constantin et Méthode vues de Byzance* (1933, reprint with additions, 1969), pp. 18-19 (some further bibliography); G. STADTMÜLLER, *Michael Choniates, Metropolit von Athen...* [*Orientalia Christiana*, 32, 2] (1934), pp. 301-2; St. P. KYRIAKIDES, Παρατηρήσεις ἐπὶ τῆς ἐξελίξεως τῆς θεματικῆς διαιρέσεως τῶν Βυζαντινῶν..., in the same author's Βυζαντιναὶ Μελέται, II-V (1937), esp. pp. 275-277; H. GLYKATZI-AHRWEILER, "Recherches sur l'administration de l'Empire byzantin aux IXe-XIe siècles," *Bulletin de correspondance hellénique*, 84 (1960), 2-3; 80-81 (useful); *Eadem, Byzance...* (as in note 10 *supra*), e.g., pp. 62-63.

12. Const. Porph., *De Cerim.*, 662, 15 and 21 Bonn. Bury, *The Imperial...* (as in note 10 *supra*), p. 42, last line, failed to make the distinction when he lumped various quotations from *De Cerimoniis* together.

To define the social and cultural status of an army *drungarios* about the year 840 (Leo was still alive by the year 834),[13] we must limit ourselves to sources as close as possible to this date, since the position of the rank deteriorated in the course of the tenth century. Thus by 949 the 205 *drungarioi* of the *thema* of Charpezikion (east of the Euphrates) were paid only three *nomismata* in gold, while the 428 simple soldiers of that *thema* were paid two.[14] Moreover, the military treatises of the later tenth century do not mention *drungarioi* at all.

The sources known to me which fall into the period ca. 840-ca. 910 are seven in number: (a) Ibn Hurdādhbeh, *Liber viarum et regnorum*, date: ca. 840;[15] ⟨345⟩ (b) *Tacticon* Uspenskij, date: 845-856;[16] (c) The *Kletorologion* of Philotheos, date: 899;[17] (d) *Tactica* of Leo VI, date: 904-912[18] (we must remember, however, that Leo VI is heavily dependent on the so-called *Tactica* of Mauricius which dates from ca. 600;[19] consequently, the information in the *Tactica* of Leo VI sometimes reflects the reality of the sixth-seventh century rather than that of the ninth); (e) The order of battle for the Cretan expedition of 911, preserved in Constantine Porphyrogenitus' *De Cerimoniis*;[20] (f) Georgius

13. This is to be inferred from VC III, 1 (the seven-year-old Constantine talks to his father and mother; Constantine was born in 827).

14. Const. Porph., *De Cerim.*, 667, 10-11; 669, 9-10 Bonn. Cf. *ibid.*, 662, 21-22 (time: reign of Romanus Lecapenus).

15. Ed. M. J. de Goeje, *Bibliotheca Geographorum Arabicorum*, 6 (1899), esp. p. 84; cf. also Gelzer, o. c. (in note 11 *supra*), p. 114. Henceforth IH.

16. Ed. in *Izvestija rus. arxeolog. Inst. v Konstantinopole,* 3 (1898), 98-137. On the date of the *Tacticon*, cf., in the last place, G. Ostrogorski, "Taktikon Uspenskog i Taktikon Beneševića...", *Zbornik Radova Vizantol. Instituta,* 2 (1953), esp. p. 48. Henceforth TU.

17. Ed. Bury, *The Imperial...* (as in note 10 *supra*). Henceforth, P.

18. Ed. Migne, *PG*, 107, cols. 669-1120 and, for *Constitutiones* I-XI, by R. Vári, *Leonis Imp. Tactica*, I [*Sylloge Tacticorum Graecorum*, 3] (1917). Henceforth TL.

19. Ed. J. Scheffer, *Arriani Tactica et Mauricii Artis Militaris libri duodecim...* (1664, repr. 1967); cf. the new ed. by H. Mihăescu, Mauricius, Arta Militară [= Scriptores Byzantini, 6] (1970); on the date and author of this text, cf., in the last place, the posthumous article by A. Dain, "Urbicius ou Mauricius," *Revue des études byzantines*, 26 (1968), 123-136. Henceforth TM.

20. II, 24 = 651,13 - 660,12 Bonn. Henceforth DC. [Among the papers of the late Professor Romilly Jenkins, now preserved at Dumbarton Oaks, there is an edition with introduction, English translation, *index verborum* and beginnings of a commentary, of chapters 44 and 45 of the second book of *De Cerimoniiis*.]

Monachus Continuatus, *Vitae*; this chronicle dates from 963-969, but its most relevant passage goes back to a source dated soon after 838;[21] (g) *Vita S. Mariae Iunioris*, date of interpolated redaction: after 976; date of original redaction: ca. mid-tenth century, but the relevant passages reflect the time of Basil I's reign (d. 886).[22] The "famous *drungarios*" Stephen praised in the iambic inscription of the seaport Attaleia (modern Antalya), dated 909-10, must have been a naval *drungarios* and does not belong here.[23]

These seven sources yield the following picture: By 838 a *drungarios* must have enjoyed a high status, for Georgius Continuatus singles out Constantine the *drungarios* (along with only five other names) from among the important people taken prisoner after the fall of Amorium, and mentions him (correctly) after the two officers of higher rank (a patricius and stratege and a turmarch), respectively (GMC, 805, 15-19 Bonn). The theoretical chain of command was *strategos — turmarches — drungarios — comes — centurio* — other lower officers — ⟨346⟩ ⟨soldier⟩;[24] the actually attested chain of command, ⟨strategos⟩ — *turmarches — drungarios — comes* — soldier (DC 656, 10-16 Bonn); when a *drungarios* was promoted in the nineties of the ninth century, he advanced to the rank of *turmarches*.[25] Thus, while Leo did serve *podъ stratigomъ*, he was in fact two ranks below him.[26]

21. 805, 15-19 Bonn. Henceforth GMC.

22. Ed. H. Delehaye in *Acta sanctorum Novembris*, 4 (1925), pp. 692-705 and, in excerpts, G. Balasčev, "Novye dannye dlja istorii grekobolg. vojn pri Simeone," *Izvestija Rus. arxeol. Inst. v Konstantinopole*, 4 (1899), 189-220, esp. pp. 190-205, and P. Tivčev in *Fontes Graeci Historiae Bulgaricae*, 5 [*Izvori za bъlgarskata istorija*, 9] (1964), pp. 75-81 (bibliography). Cf., in the last place, C. A. Mango, "The Byzantine Church at Vize (Bizye) in Thrace and St. Mary the Younger," *Zbornik Radova Vizantološkog Instituta*, 11 (1968), 9-13. Henceforth VMI.

23. Ed. G. E. Bean, *Belleten*, 22 (1958), nr. 42 = pp. 44-46 (earlier bibliography). On the other hand, John, the imperial *strator* and *drungarios* of Koloneia (modern Şebinkarahisar) is of interest to our study, cf., e.g., Consul J. G. Taylor, in the *Journal of the Royal Geographic Society*, 38 (1868), 294-295 (best fascimile), F. Cumont, in École Française de Rome, *Mélanges d'archéologie et d'histoire*, 15 (1895), 286 and 294 (wrong reading), and S. Bénay in *Échos d'Orient*, 4 (1900-01), 93-94. For additional information on the Koloneia inscription, I am indebted to Dr. Anthony Bryer.

24. TL, Appendix, XXXV = Migne, *PG*, 107, cols. 1097D-1100A.

25. VMI, p. 692E with 694B and 697C.

26. We might assume that by using the word *podъ stratigomъ* the author of VC

On paper, the army *drungarios* commanded a *drungos* of a thousand horse (under special circumstances, this contingent was allowed to swell to three thousand, but to no more); the army of an important theme, the *Anatolikon*, was supposed to have a strength of four thousand, and have four *drungarioi* among its officers.[27] In practice, contingents under a *drungarios*' command must have been smaller, at least by 911, when ten *drungarioi* and 965 *stratiotai*, soldiers, were mustered up by the theme of Sebasteia (modern Sivas) (DC, 656, 14-15 Bonn). Thus on that occasion a *drungarios* could not have commanded more than a hundred soldiers. The discrepancy between the *Tactica* of Leo VI and the *De Cerimoniis* is due, I surmise, to Leo's work being out of date: the depreciation of the rank of *drungarios* must have set in by 911. At that time, the *drungarioi* had only a slight superiority over the next lowest rank, that of *comites*, commanders of a *bandon*, which, in theory, was a unit of two or three, but no more than four, hundred horse:[28] in the list of advance payments (travel expenses? διὰ τοῦ προχρέου) for the Cretan expedition of 911, we find ten *drungarioi* and eight *comites*, and the ratio of pay is 6:5.[29] The difficult passage in Philotheos' *Kletorologion*: δρουγγάριοι τῶν βάνδων, κόμητες ὁμοίως, is best explained by assuming that by 899 the two ranks, that of the *drungarios* and that of the *comes* commanding a *bandon*, began to be

---

wanted to point out Leo's exceptional position, and to remind his readers, familiar with army rules of their time, that he was *immediately* subordinated to the *strategos*. I prefer, however, to interpret the hagiographer's words as an attempt to present Leo in the best light, and yet to remain technically correct.

27. IH, p. 84 ed. Goeje; cf. TL, IV : 42 = Migne, *PG*, 107, col. 708CD = Vári, IV : 44, p. 68; IV : 45 = Migne, *PG* 107, col. 709A = Vári, IV : 47, p. 70; XVIII : 149 = Migne, *PG*, 107, col. 988AB; Appendix, XXXIV = Migne, *PG*, 107, col. 1110B.

28. IH, ed. de Goeje, p. 84; cf. A. Dain, *L'"Extrait tactique" de Léon VI le Sage*, (1942), p. 93, n. 4 and TL, IV : 41 = Migne, *PG*, 107, col. 708C = Vári, IV : 43, p. 67; IV : 45 = Migne, *PG*, 107, col. 709A = Vári, IV : 47, p. 70; Appendix, XXXIV = Migne, *PG*, 107, col. 1100B.

29. DC, 656, 14-15 Bonn. In the work mentioned in n. 20 *supra*, Prof. Jenkins explains our term by referring to πρόχρεια, payment in advance, prepayment in half, as in the Rhodian Sea-Law, ed. W. Ashburner (Oxford, 1909), § 32, 5 = p. 30; cf. *ibidem*, translation and commentary *ad locum*, p. 108. — However, by 904 Drungarios Nicephorus Kaminas must have carried enough weight to have dared refuse the crossing of the Halys (Kızıl Irmak) to *cubicularius* Samonas, confidant of Emperor Leo VI: GMC, 864, 1-3 Bonn. and R. J. H. Jenkins, "The 'Flight' of Samonas," *Speculum*, 23 (1948), 217-235, esp. 217 and 227.

fused into one.[30] In the account of the Cretan expedition of 949, we hear of *drungarioi* ⟨347⟩ and *comites* as one group; and in another place of the same account, the *comites* are altogether absent from the enumeration of payees, and the *drungarioi* are directly followed by *stratiotai* (DC, 666, 19-20; 667, 10; 669, 9 Bonn). On the other hand, Constantine Porphyrogenitus' *De Admin. Imperio* (date: 949-952) is silent on the territorial subdivision of a *thema* corresponding to a *drungos*. In this text, the territory of a *thema* is divided into *turmai* (under a *turmarches*), and the *turmai* directly into *banda*.[31] Thus by the middle of the tenth century, a development occurred for which parallels exist in institutional history: the actual function of the lower rank (command of a *bandon*, both as a military and territorial unit) was combined with the name of the higher one (*drungarios*), hence δρουγγάριοι τῶν βάνδων. The term δρουγγαροκόμητες reflects the final stage of the fusion.[32] As our main interest is limited to the ninth century, I leave out the question of the later survival of δροῦγγος as a term for a territorial subdivision.[33]

Whether the rank of *drungarios* began to lose importance already by the middle of the ninth century and whether by that time army *drungarioi* exercised territorial rule or were stationed in subdivisions of a *thema*, we do not know for sure, although there is some evidence to corroborate the latter assumption. When he was still *drungarios*, Nicephorus, the husband of St. Mary the Younger, resided in a village, and it was only after his promotion to the turmarchate that he and his wife moved up to the town of Bizye (today's Vize), v. VMI, 693B and 694A. On the other hand, the information that during Tsar Symeon's war with Byzantium Nicephorus' son Baanes, who was probably *drungarios* by that time, commanded the Byzantine contingent which "recently" had moved to Selymbria (today's Silivri) is too vague to be of use here: Baanes may have been forced to retreat to a fortified place which had nothing to do with his regular territorial assignment.[34] This

30. P, p. 139, 10 and 5. Bury's explanation in P, p. 42: "*Drungarioi* of all the ten *banda*, comites of one *bandon* each" is too contrived.

31. To be inferred from *De Admin. Imperio*, § 50, 90; 102-108; 133-134 = pp. 236-237, edd. Moravcsik-Jenkins; on a *bandon* of Lampe in Phrygia, ef. L. Robert, *Villes d'Asie Mineure* (2nd ed., 1962), p. 357.

32. Cf., e.g., DC, 494, 9-10, where they appear to be in command of *banda*, and 663, 6-7, Bonn (date: reign of Romanus Lecapenus), where each *drungarios* appears to be in command [?] of two or three soldiers.

33. Cf. Stadtmüller, *Michael Choniates*, (as in note 11), p. 303.

34. Combine VMI, pp. 701CF and 703F.

assignment seems even to have been Bizye, or its environs, for Baanes is said to have had close spiritual ties with Theodore the turmarch. Thus we can presume that this Theodore was Baanes' immediate superior; we know that Theodore had taken over the *turma* of Baanes' father; consequently, Theodore commanded the *turma* of Bizye, and Baanes must have been stationed near him.[35]

Leo is said to have lived (*bě*) in Thessalonica; he may therefore have belonged to the *strategos'* entourage, although, *pace* modern scholars, we know nothing ⟨348⟩ of that governor's "headquarters."[36] Warfare in the ninth century was an intermittent affair, and Turmarches Nicephorus, the husband of Mary the Younger, went away on campaigns only intermittently (VMI, p. 694D); the manpower per unit was increased, and officers called in or recruited, for a given campaign. *Drungarioi* may have been among such "reserve" officers mobilized *ad hoc*: in any case, they were not high enough to be appointed centrally, but were recruited by the local *strategos*; only holders of the next-highest rank, that of a *turmarches*, were appointed by the Emperor.[37] Thus an army *drungarios* could spend part of his time (except perhaps for the spring and summer campaign months) in peaceful pursuits, for instance in administering his property in what, in the case of Nicephorus, was a village, in the case of his son Baanes, a provincial town, and in the case of Leo, the capital of a theme.

Army *drungarioi* do figure in the aulic hierarchy, but they rank low there. About the year 850, they were listed hundred ninety-eighth out of a total of two hundred ten ranks, while our Leo's ultimate superior in the *thema*, ὁ πατρίκιος καὶ στρατηγὸς Θεσσαλονίκης, occupied the twenty-third place on the same list.[38] By 899, the army *drungarioi* belonged to the fourth, or lowest, class of officials, and were assumed to have been mere officers not endowed with a nobiliary title.[39]

35. VMI, p. 704A. In 904, *drungarios* Nicephorus Kaminas may have been assigned to a point (bridge? ford?) controlling the crossing over the Halys (cf. n. 29).

36. The modern scholars are Kulakovskij (as in note 11), p. 17 and Ahrweiler (as in note 10), p. 63 and the tantalizing note 1.

37. TL, IV : 43 = Migne, *PG*, 107, 708D = Vári, IV : 45, p. 68 and VMI, p. 694A, where Drungarios Nicephorus takes over a *turma* "by the command of the Emperor."

38. TU, pp. 129 and 115 (I accept the correction of TU, p. 129, proposed by Bury in P, p. 43, from ὁ δρουγγάριος τῶν θεμάτων to οἱ δρουγγάριοι τ.θ.).

39. Cf. P, p. 153, 23-24 and, for the meaning of ἄπρατοι used there, R.

To fill the posts of commanding officers (including *drungarioi*) Leo VI (following in the steps of Onasander) recommended choosing people of proven loyalty to the Empire — a reasonable precaution, since in the ninth century both the Empire and its army were multinational — of noble descent (εὐγενεῖς κατὰ... τὸ γένος) and of wealth (οὐδὲν κωλύει καὶ εὐπορωτάτους αὐτοὺς εἶναι).[40] Thus when the *Vita Constantini* calls Leo *dobrorodьnъ* (that is, εὐγενής, noble, the only attested Greek equivalent of that word)[41] and *bogatъ*, wealthy, it does more than repeat a hagiographic *topos*; it uses terms ⟨349⟩ which were applied to army officers, including *drungarioi*, at that time. Moreover, when the same *Vita* speaks of *sanъ drǫgarьskъi*, it is using correct language: *sanъ* corresponds, *inter alia*, to ἀξία, ἀξίωμα of the Greek[42] and δρουγγάριοι are explicitly listed among the holders of ἀξιώματα (P, p. 139, 4 and 10).

It is difficult to say how wealthy an average *drungarios* was in the ninth century. We have some information on the wealth of Nicephorus (d. ca. 922), [43] but this information pertains mostly to the period after ca. 895, when Nicephorus had become a turmarch, at which time his fortunes had presumably further improved. He hailed from a χωρίον, that is, a rural settlement, in Thrace[44] and, as we saw, was stationed in a

---

Guilland, *Recherches sur les institutions byzantines*, I, [= *Berliner byzantinistische Arbeiten*, 35] (1967), pp. 158-161. The *Tacticon* (date: 975-979) recently discovered (and soon to be published) by Professor Oikonomides does not list the δρουγγάριοι τῶν θεμάτων, for it does not deal with officials of lower rank at all. I owe this information to the kindness of Professor Oikonomides.

40. TL, IV : 3 = Migne, *PG*, 107, col. 700 BC = Vári, p. 50; Onasander, *ed*, Vári, lines 157-160. Insistence on noble origin of officers is absent from TL's other main source, TM, dating from about the year 600. This reflects the rise of the Byzantine provincial gentry, which was in full swing by the ninth century. On this point, see the paper, "Observations on the Aristocracy in Byzantium," by George Ostrogorsky, to appear in *Dumbarton Oaks Papers*, 25 (1971), esp. p. 48, and A. P. Każdan in *Zbornik Radova Vizantološkog Instituta*, 11 (1968).

41. Cf. *Slovník jazyka staroslověnského*, I, Praha 1966, s. v.

42. Cf., e.g., *Codex Suprasliensis*, p. 99, 8, ed. Severjanov, corresponding to *Analecta Bollandiana*, 1 (1882), 449, 10; *ibidem*, p. 291, 26, corresponding to *Acta Sanctorum Maii*, 3 (1680), p. 19*.

43. Combine Balasčev, (as in note 22), p. 209 (Bizye beleaguered from ca. 921 to after 925) and Delehaye, (as in note 22), p. 691A (Nicephorus died towards the beginning of the siege of Bizye).

44. VMI, p. 692E. For the meaning of χωρίον, cf. e.g. F. Dölger, *Beiträge zur Geschichte der byzant. Finanzverwaltung* ... [= *Byzantinisches Archiv*, 9]

κώμη, that is, a village, as long as he was *drungarios*. While still in this rank, he enjoyed enough prestige to marry a bride from a noble Armenian family, whose relatives enjoyed the favor of Basil I;[45] and the bride brought him a comfortable enough dowry, since she was able to cover the considerable expenses of her charities without drawing on her husband's assets (VMI, p. 694D). Incidentally, Nicephorus' son Baanes, also a *drungarios*, was able to conclude an advantageous marriage as well.[46] As *turmarches*, Nicephorus ruled over an extensive household, with servants and stewards (VMI, pp. 693A; 695B; 695F-696A), and when he decided to remove, by force if necessary, the body of his deceased wife from the cathedral church at Bizye, he could muster up forty men, presumably from his own household (VMI, p. 699A). The family of Nicephorus must have enjoyed social prestige in Bizye, for when his wife was on her deathbed, all the prominent ladies of the town called to take their last leave of her (VMI, p. 696E). Finally, Turmarch Nicephorus himself died a rich enough man to afford a marble sarcophagus for his body.[47]

There is little direct evidence concerning the cultural level of the army *drungarioi*; the indirect evidence, however, is discouraging. Even after his promotion to the rank of *turmarches*, Nicephorus beat his wife, and her biographer quotes her husband's blows among the causes that brought about her death (VMI, p. 696CD). In his *Tactica*, Leo VI recommends that *turmarchai*, ⟨350⟩ officers of the rank directly above that of *drungarios*, should be literate, *if possible* (εἰ δυνατόν, εἰδότας τὰ γράμματα).[48] If this passage of the *Tactica* reflects the situation prevalent in the ninth century,[49] it would follow that literacy, meaning ability to carry on or at least read official correspondence in Greek, was not a necessary prerequisite for becoming an army *drungarios*. We have

(1927), p. 66; G. Ostrogorskij, "La commune rurale byzantine," *Byzantion*, 32 (1962), esp. pp. 144; 162, n. 3.

45. Cf. VMI, p. 692D; Nicephorus himself was probably a Greek, judging by the names of his brother and sister, cf. VM1, p. 695B.

46. With a "prominent" lady, cf. VMI, p. 703F.

47. VMI, p. 702E. However, either Nicephorus was not wealthy enough to be able to support close relatives in need, or he was a callous person, for his brother Alexius lived in abject poverty while Nicephorus was still alive: VMI, p. 700B.

48. TL, IV : 43 = Migne, *PG*, 107, col. 708D = Vári, IV : 45, p. 69.

49. This is not clear, for TL almost literally copies TM, I : 4, pp. 30-31, ed. Scheffer = p. 58, 21 ed. Mihăescu.

no information on Nicephorus' literacy, either as *drungarios* or as *turmarches*; his wife Maria, who seems to have had a socially more prominent background than her husband, could read the Psalter (VMI, p. 694B). However, when their pious son, Drungarios Baanes, sang matins, vespers, and canons in honor of the Mother of God, he did it "without using a book at all for this purpose" (VMI, p. 704C). These words are ambivalent, since they may merely mean that Baanes did not need, rather than that he was not able, to refer to a written text. In any case, literacy was not a matter of course in a family like that of Nicephorus, for it is expressly stated that his other son Stephen-Symeon "became familiar with letters" (γράμματα... γέγονεν ἔμπειρος), an achievement which opened the gates of the imperial palace to him (VMI, p. 704C).

We should conclude that Drungarios Leo was an officer of middle rank[50] in the land army of a western, that is, less important, theme.[51] He held a position which was to decline in the course of the century that followed his death, but which, to judge by the passage of Georgius Continuatus on the prisoners of Amorium, was still very reputable about the year 840. From the vantage point of the Constantinopolitan court protocol, Leo's was a minor station in life; in Thessalonica itself, however, he must have enjoyed considerable influence, as Turmarch Nicephorus did in Bizye; and he may very well have been a man of noble origin and of substance. He did leave an inheritance to Constantine (VC III, 25); however, since his wife feared for her son's material future after Leo's death, this inheritance could not have been too large.[52] As for Leo's literary culture, it was in all probability quite rudimentary.

As sons of such a father, Constantine and Methodius did enjoy a head start in life; however, they made great advances, both socially and (even more) culturally, in the course of their respective careers. As a *drungarios*, Leo ⟨351⟩ ranked hundred ninety-eighth in the aulic hierarchy; as a former head of a *kъnęženije* (ἀρχοντία?) his elder son

50. In IH, p. 118, Gelzer likened this rank to that of a German major of ca. 1900. In "The 'Flight' of Samonas" (as in note 29), pp. 217 and n. 1; 227 and in the work referred to in n. 20, Jenkins translated δρουγγάριος by "colonel", which was perhaps too generous a rendering. — The same rendering is used in the latest book by F. Dvorník, *Byzantine Missions Among the Slavs* (1970), p. 53.

51. Both in TU and in P, the Western themes and officials rank below the Eastern themes and their officials.

52. VC II, 6. "I care for nothing, save only for this child and how he will be provided for (*kako imatъ byti ustroenъ*)."

Methodius, had he remained a layman, would have ranked hundred and thirty-seventh, a jump of sixty-one rungs of the ladder.[53] Thus Leo's son Methodius went far beyond Nicephorus' son Baanes, who died as *drungarios*, that is, in a rank inferior to that of his father. As for Leo's younger son Constantine, he succeeded much more brilliantly — not only than his own father, but also than Stephen-Symeon, the other son of Nicephorus with whom his career offers some similarity: while Stephen "learned the letters," found his way into the imperial palace (as a scribe in some bureau, we presume) and on account of his amiable character found favor with people whom the hagiographer vaguely calls "the mighty" (VMI, p. 704C), Constantine enjoyed literary fame beyond the confines of the Empire, was a protégé of Logothete Theoktistos (until his murder in 856 the vizier of the Empire), and claimed the personal friendship of Patriarch Photius.[54]

---

53. Cf. TU, p. 126. A word of caution: although it is not generally realized, neither the correspondence *kъnęženije*: ἀρχοντία nor the meaning of ἀρχοντία assumed here are actually attested in our sources.

54. Another valid approach to the social background of a person is through that person's genealogy. This was the path taken by K. G. Bonis (Mpŏnes), Οἱ ἅγιοι Κύριλλος καὶ Μεθόδιος οἱ τῶν Σλάβων Ἀπόστολοι καὶ ἡ βασιλικὴ τοῦ ἁγίου Δημητρίου Θεσσαλονίκης.... Μελέτη πρώτη in Κυρίλλῳ καὶ Μεθοδίῳ τόμος ἑόρτιος (as in n. 4 *supra*), 1 (1966), pp. 251-289. The author provided his article with the subtitle "Contribution to the Clarification of the Problem of the Saints' Family..." and found that Leo the *drungarios* was Prefect of the City of Thessalonica and first cousin of Theodore of Studios. Since the method which Professor Bonis followed in arriving at his conclusions is as startling as the conclusions themselves, his article is quoted here merely for the sake of curiosity. The same, I fear, applies to Professor Bonis' Οἱ Ἕλληνες ἱεραπόστολοι τῶν Σλάβων Κύριλλος καὶ Μεθόδιος, ὑπὸ τὸ νέον φῶς τῆς ἐπιστήμης. Μελέτη δευτέρα, in Ἐπιστημονικὴ Ἐπετηρὶς τῆς Θεολογικῆς Σχολῆς τοῦ Πανεπιστημίου Ἀθηνῶν, 16 (1967); cf. also K. Bonis, *Die Slavenapostel* (1969).

XXVIII

Michael Cherniavsky 1922-1973

When Michael Cherniavsky, Andrew Mellon Professor of History at the University of Pittsburgh, and adjunct professor of history at Columbia University, died suddenly at his home in Pittsburgh on July 12, 1973, he was fifty years old. Born in Harbin into a family of émigrés from Russia, Cherniavsky received his early education in English-speaking establishments in China: Tientsin Grammar School and St. John's University in Shanghai. He arrived in this country in 1939 and enrolled in the University of California at Berkeley, from which he obtained all his degrees. His studies at Berkeley were interrupted by his war service with the U.S. Army Air Force Intelligence in the Southwest Pacific between 1942 and 1945, and his academic career began in 1951, the year in which he obtained his doctorate.

The two determinants of Cherniavsky's thinking, writing, and teaching were also among the determinants of his actions and his adult life-style. They were the personal and intellectual impact of Ernst Kantorowicz — first as teacher and later as life-long friend — and the passion for the Russian Revolution. It was Kantorowicz's political theology, his interest in history's great figures, and in the ruler cult, and his skillful handling of artistic sources in elucidating abstract concepts of the Middle Ages that informed Michael's work on early Russian history — his treatment of the princely saints, his preoccupation with the myth of power, the attention he paid to the Old Believers' pictorial propaganda, and his fascination with the rulers' portraits in the Annunciation Cathedral. Michael's chief contribution to scholarship lies in his application of the tenets elaborated by Kantorowicz to that segment of ancient Rus's and Muscovy's past where investigators too often wander among imaginary reconstructions of the various *izvody* of chronicle accounts, or are on an obligatory, if futile, search for class struggles. The proof of Michael's passion for the Russian Revolution, its antecedents, and its aftermath is in his other writings: his book *Prologue to Revolution: Notes of A. N. Iakhontov on the Secret Meetings of the Council of Ministers, 1915* (1967), his earlier brilliant essay "Corporal Hitler, General Winter and the Russian Peasant," *Yale Review,* Summer 1962 (pp. 547-58), and his other musings on the Soviet style of war. This proof is also in the kind of basic questions Michael would raise: while Kantorowicz would discuss historical causality in general, Michael would imply the regularity of the historical process in his search for the preconditions of a revolution.

It was not a simple matter to reconcile these two determinants: the teachings of Kantorowicz, the patrician and the rifle-carrying fighter against the Spartakists in Berlin and the Räterepublik in Munich in 1919, who never made clear what kind of existence was to be attributed to the ideas whose history he pursued, and the writings of a Shaposhnikov, or the deeds of a Frunze, neither of whom should have had any doubts about the relation between the base and the superstructure. Yet ⟨865⟩ Michael did produce such a reconciliation. To see how he did it in conceptual terms, we have only to turn to his short essay of 1968 ("The Charismatic Figure in History," *Civilization,* ed. A. Taylor, pp. 588-90). The essay quotes the myth of Frederick II, Kantorowicz's hero. Of the three charismatic personalities it singles out, one of them, Alexander the Great, is universal. The second, Julius Caesar, was treated as such in a book by Gundolf, a member of the Stefan George circle and young Kantorowicz's protector. But the third was Michael's own choice. It was Lenin. From his fascination with the Revolution came the involvement in the Berkeley Oath Controversy (1950), and, later on, in the teach-ins. However, by 1970, the year of the last-but-one of Michael's seven trips to the Soviet Union, fascination had begun to turn into sadness caused by disappointment with the Soviet present.

In 1951,when Kantorowicz moved from Berkeley to the Institute for Advanced Study in the wake of the Oath Controversy, Michael became his research assistant in Princeton. There followed the nine quiet years (1952-61) at Wesleyan University, during which he wrote two of his best-known articles, "Holy Russia: A Study in the History of an Idea," *American Historical Review,* 63 (1958): 617-37, and "Khan or Basileus: An Aspect of Russian Mediaeval Political Theory," *Journal of the History of Ideas,* 20 (1959): 459-76, and his most important work, *Tsar and People: Studies in Russian Myths* (1961, reprinted in 1970). The reward for this writing presented itself in 1961 in the form of an appointment at the University of Chicago, where he remained until 1964, and where his friendship and intellectual collaboration with Leopold Haimson took its final shape. The first connection with Columbia came in 1964 — at various times he was visiting scholar at the Russian Institute, visiting professor, and, starting in 1969, adjunct professor of history. In the same year, 1964, there began a number of transfers: to Rochester (1964-69), to Albany (1969-72, where he was Leading Professor), and finally to Pittsburgh. These transfers meant an ascent as well. Albany and Pittsburgh were name chairs; and the Mellon Professorship, Michael's last title, ranks among the more prestigious in the country.

Although he moved a great deal in his post-Chicago years, both inside and outside the country, he managed to write two outstanding pieces: "The Old Believers and the New Religion," *Slavic Review,* 25 (1966): 1-39, and "Ivan the Terrible as Renaissance Prince," *Slavic Review,* 27 (1968): 195-211. His part-time base in New York brought him in touch with publishing firms; he became a scholarly organizer on a big scale — an editor for Prentice-Hall and for Random House. For all this activity, he was working on new subjects. The national consciousness of medieval Russia was one of them ("Political Culture and the Emergence of National Consciousness in Early Modern Russia," *James Schouler Lectures in History and Political Science, 1972,* to appear); the iconography of the Annunciation Cathedral in the Kremlin, a project for which he was collecting material during his last trip to the Soviet Union in 1973, was another. He taught brilliantly and, through his seminar at Columbia, became more influential than any of his contemporaries in forming a new generation of sudents of early Russian history. He was appreciated abroad — in 1971 he was visiting professor at the École Pratique des Hautes Études — and written about at home. He was among the leading historians interviewed in Norman Cantor's *Perspectives on the European Past: Conversations with Historians* (1971).

⟨866⟩ Seen from the outside, the twenty-two years between 1951 and 1973 were years of ascent and success. It is best to stop short of exploring the landscape in which he was lost in the end.

XXIX

Ljubomudrějšij Kỳr" Agapit Diakon: On a Kiev Edition of a Byzantine *Mirror of Princes*

I

In 1711, Anselmo Banduri published his *Imperium Orientale*. Along with several Byzantine works of prime importance, this book offered the seventy-two *Hortatory Chapters* by Agapetus[1] with a Latin translation. Banduri's text, repeatedly reprinted, is still the standard edition of the *Chapters*. About their author, Banduri had this to say:

> Now, concerning Agapetus, the author of the present small book, who claims to have been deacon of the Most Holy Great Church of God, that is, of Saint Sophia, and who, judging by his manner of speech and style, was a Greek, I have nothing to report.[2]

1. For basic bibliography on Agapetus, and the analysis of his *Hortatory Chapters*, cf. Ihor Ševčenko, "A Neglected Byzantine Source of Muscovite Political Ideology," *Harvard Slavic Studeis*, Vol. II (1954), pp. 141-179 (this was reprinted in M. Cherniavsky, ed., *The Structure of Russian History...* [New York: 1970], pp. 80-107), and Patrick Henry, "A Mirror for Justinian: the *Ekthesis* of Agapetus Diaconus," *Greek, Roman and Byzantine Studies*, Vol. III (1967), pp. 281-308. To bibliographical items contained in these two articles, add: G. Downey, *Constantinople in the Age of Justinian* (Norman, Oklahoma: 1960), pp. 49-52; B. Rubin, *Das Zeitalter Justinians*, Vol. 1 (Berlin: 1960), pp. 171, 427-429; Ihor Ševčenko, "On Some Sources of Prince Svjatoslav's *Izbornik* of the Year 1076," *Orbis Scriptus, Festschrift für Dmitrij Tschižewskij zum 70. Geburtstag* (Munich: 1966), pp. 723-738; F. Dvornik, *Early Christian and Byzantine Political Philosophy: Origins and Background*, Vol. II (Washington, D.C.: 1966), esp. pp. 712-715; *Repertorium Fontium Historiae Medii Aevi*, Vol. II (1967), p. 141; G. Downey, *Justinian and the Imperial Office* [= *Lectures in Memory of Louise Taft Semple, Second Series*] (Cincinnati: 1968), esp. pp. 12-16; W. D. Schmitt in *Studia Byzantina*, Vol. II (1973), pp. 17 and 23; R. Romano, "Un'inedita parafrasi metabizantina della *Scheda regia* di Agapeto Diacono," *Atti dell'Accademia Pontaniana, Nuova Serie*, Vol. XXII (1973), pp. 1-15 (with bibliography).

2. Anselmus Banduri, *Imperium Orientale...*, Vol. I (1711), p. iv (*Praefatio*): *De*

⟨2⟩ Today, some two hundred and sixty-five years after Banduri, we have even less to say about Agapetus as a person. The study of the manuscripts of the *Chapters* carried out at the beginning of this century has shown that their title, in which Agapetus is designated as Deacon of the Great Church of Saint Sophia, occurs only in one branch of the tradition.[3] Thus, the link between Agapetus and Saint Sophia may be the result of a later conjecture, rather than a reflection of the original circumstances.

We are thus left with the acrostic of the *Chapters* — a reliable source of information, since it is woven into the body of the work itself. It states that Agapetus was a Deacon and that the person addressed was an emperor by the name of Justinian.[4] That this emperor was the Great Justinian (527-565), rather than Justinian II (685-695; 705-711) can be gathered from chapters seventeen and thirty-four of Agapetus: both these chapters imply that the addressee reached the pinnacle of power only after holding other offices. This was precisely the case of Justinian I, whereas Justinian II was born to the purple and was crowned Emperor at the age of sixteen, perhaps even fourteen, in 685 at the latest.[5]

Even with the question of the addressee thus settled, doubt might arise as to the epoch in which Agapetus lived, since all of the numerous manuscripts of the *Chapters* — close to ninety of them were listed in 1906, but their number is close to one hundred — are late in date. By and large, they belong to the fifteenth, sixteenth and eighteenth centuries.[6]

Agapeto autem huius libelli auctore, qui se Sanctissimae Dei Magnae Ecclesiae, hoc est, Sanctae Sophiae, Diaconum profitetur, et quem oratio et stylus Graecum fuisse arguunt non est quod dicam.

3. A. Bellomo, *Agapeto diacono e la sua Scheda Regia* (Bari: 1906), esp. pp. 40-44 (mention of Saint Sophia only in "Category III" of manuscripts). Bellomo's book should be read along with the devastating review by K. Prächter, *Byzantinische Zeitschrift*, Vol. XVII (1908), pp. 152-164, who calls our author Deutobold Mystifizinski (p. 162).

4. Cf., e.g., the title of *Palatinus Graecus*, 228, fol. 264r: *Tō theiotatō kai eusebestatō basilei hēmōn Ioustinianō Agapētos elakhistos diakonos.*

5. Cf. Agapetus 34, translated by James White (1564): "So thou most famous Emperor, albeit thou hast obtained governance after governance, and is come to the highest honor..." On Justinian II's youth and accession to the throne, cf. C. Head, *Justinian II of Byzantium* (Madison, Wisconsin: 1971), pp. 21, 27.

6. The following tabulation has been made on the basis of Bellomo (as in note 3 above), pp. 13-14. If we discount the *Florilegia*, and the five manuscripts ambivalently described by Bellomo as "antico," we obtain the following distribution: the earliest extant and quasi-complete manuscript of Agapetus' text,

By itself, ⟨3⟩ the direct tradition of the *Chapters* does not rule out the possibility that they might be a work of literary fiction, rather than an address to a living Emperor.

The indirect tradition of the *Chapters* removes this doubt. One of the Slavic versions of Agapetus is earlier than the year 1076;[7] excerpts from Agapetus have been inserted into Greek manuscripts of *Florilegia* dating from as early as the eleventh century.[8] In the second half of the ninth century, Photius (or some contemporary of his) made extensive use of the ⟨4⟩ *Chapters* in an analogous work, written in the name of Emperor Basil I, ostensibly for the edification of his son Leo VI.[9] Finally, the Greek version of the story of *Barlaam and Joasaph* contains two long portions on rulership, which exhibit literal coincidences with

Palatinus Graecus 228, is attributed, perhaps too optimistically, to the thirteenth century; it is the only one to be given so early a date; six manuscripts come from the fourteenth century; thirty-two from the fifteenth; thirteen, from the sixteenth; one from the seventeenth; at least three, from the eighteenth; and twenty (from Athos) are attributed to the eighteenth and nineteenth centuries. The sum total of manuscripts known to Bellomo in 1906 was eighty-two and six fragments. However, his list is far from complete. To give but one example, it omits the nine Agapetus manuscripts which are kept in the Library of the Rumanian Academy of Sciences; all of these manuscripts are of the eighteenth century, and some of them offer a translation in modern Greek, or a commentary. Cf. C. Litzica, *Biblioteca Academiei Române. Catalogul manuscriptelor greceşti* (Bucharest: 1909), Nos. 240 (with commentary by Sebastos Kyminites, cf. note 72 below); 630 (with a translation in modern Greek); 636; 657; 699; 700 (all four provided with an interlinear translation); 709 (with an interlinear paraphrase); 726 (text incomplete); 733 (text incomplete). Thus, the bulk of the preserved Greek manuscripts of Agapetus is post-Byzantine; several of them (at least five) were copied in the West. I know only two parchment manuscripts of Agapetus: *Palatinus Graecus* 228 and *Vaticanus Graecus* 1014 (fifteenth, not thirteenth century, as Bellomo contends, p. 23).

7. Cf. my "On Some Sources..." (as in note 1 above), pp. 724-728.

8. Cf. *Laurentianus Plut.* 7:15 (eleventh century), fols. 137r-137v (Chapter 21); *Monacensis Graecus* 429, the so-called *Melissa Augustana*, fol. 89r (Chapter 21); in its choice of sayings, the *Melissa* is similar to the *Laurentianus*; the Munich manuscript of the *Melissa* is dated to 1346, but the time of compilation of the collection itself is 10th-13th centuries, cf. C. Wachsmuth, *Studien zu den griechischen Florilegien* (1882), p. 109. I have not seen the *Bodl. Baroccianus* 143 (11th-12th century), fol. 191r (quoting Chapter 21).

9. Best edition in K. Emminger, *Studien zu den griechischen Fürstenspiegeln*, III (Munich: 1913), pp. 50-73; cf. also Migne, *PG*, 107, col. xxi-lvi. On Photius' authorship, cf. my "A Neglected Byzantine Source..." (as in note 1 above), pp. 163-164.

passages of Agapetus. *Barlaam and Joasaph* depends directly on Agapetus, rather than on a source shared with him and lost for the convenience of speculating scholars.[10] And the middle of the eighth century seems to be the most likely of the various proposed datings for this Byzantine version of the Buddha legend.[11] Agapetus' *Chapters*, then, are attested three, or even two, centuries after their purported date. And within these intervening centuries, we know no occasion which would lend itself to the creation of a *pseudepigraphon* involving the name of Justinian the Great; Justinian's legend belongs to later times.

Within the reign of Justinian I, Agapetus himself provides us with the *terminus ante quem* for the composition of his work: his seventy-second and last chapter invokes Christ's help for the Emperor and his spouse, and Theodora, Justinian's famous wife, died in 548. As for the *terminus post quem* for the *Chapters*, common sense advises us to put it soon after the beginning of Justinian's sole rule in 527, a natural occasion for the submission of a gratulatory tract, which was self-serving to boot — Agapetus' admonitions that the Emperor show liberality towards "his subjects" have a transparent purpose. The sixth chapter of Agapetus strengthens the ⟨5⟩ assumption: it praises the advantages possessed by a man who is able to carry out his plans, and continues: "since God has graciously given thee the power of which your counsel (*hē agathē sou boulēsis*) was in need for our sake," the Emperor should both will and act in a manner pleasing to God.[12] Justinian, Agapetus implies, has just ascended the throne and was now able to carry out his designs.

The contents and intention of Agapetus' seventy-two chapters — a

---

10. Here I differ from the opinion of K. Prächter, "Der Roman Barlaam und Joasaph in seinem Verhältnis zu Agapets Königsspiegel," *Byzantinische Zeitschrift*, Vol. II (1893), pp. 444-460, cf. esp. p. 449ff.

11. This is to say that in the controversy about the eighth or the eleventh century dating of the Greek version, over which eminent authorities took opposite stands (F. Dölger being on one side, and P. Peeters and S. Der Nersessian on the other), I adopt the view of Franz Dölger, cf. his study, *Der griechische Barlaam-Roman: Ein Werk des H. Johannes von Damaskus* [= *Studia Patristica et Byzantina*, 1] (Ettal: 1953).

12. White's translation of chapter six: "Nothinge maketh so muche a man good and honest, as to be hable to do timely all that hee willeth; bothe to will forsoth, and to do that is humaine and gentle, because therefore power is given to thee of God, the whiche thy good wyll, for us, did neede. Will all, and do all, as pleaseth him, which hath given to thee the same power."

Mirror of Princes exalting the Emperor's divine might, setting some limits to it, and giving him advice — have been repeatedly discussed, most recently by Patrick Henry III.[13] Here, I shall merely adduce some of our author's representative statements: The Emperor is sovereign over all and a universal ruler — he is at the helm of the ship of state encompassing the whole world (chapter 2) and is like unto God in the extent of his earthly power (chapter 21). He received his power from God "to the similitude" (i.e., after the likeness) "of the heavenly Kingdom" (chapter 1). This means that he is the imitator of God on Earth, and that the Heavenly Kingdom is the model for his state. He should imitate Gods in his own actions as well: through practice of *philanthrōpia* — love for his subjects and protection of the poor — through impartiality and fairness in exercising justice, and through the choice of righteous counselors rather than flatterers, for he will be accountable to God for their deeds. True, nobody on earth can force the Emperor to observe the Laws; however, he should follow them by exercising self-control and thus give a good example to his subjects (chapter 27). Though his power be Godlike, the Emperor is reminded that he is a mere man: he should "not forget that he is made of earth when he ascendeth from dust to the place of Estate" (i.e., his throne); "and after, within a shorter time, discendeth into dust againe" (chapter 71).

For the rest, it will be sufficient to make three points: 1) that ⟨6⟩ the *Chapters* draw on commonplaces of Hellenistic political theory, and that among their identifiable sources are a tag from Plato's *Republic* 473d, Isocrates' (or Pseudo-Isocrates') *Ad Nicoclem* and *Ad Demonicum*, St. Basil's *Regulae* and *Sermons*, Gregory of Nazianzus' *Sermons* and *Letters*, Gregory of Nyssa — all these culled more likely from a *Florilegium* than from the originals and, of course, the Holy Writ;[14] 2) that, among his contemporaries, Agapetus is paralleled by the author (Petrus Magister?) of the treatise *On Political Science*,[15] whom, however, he does not approach either in depth or in breadth; and 3) that

---

13. "A Mirror for Justinian..." (as in note 1 above).

14. For Agapetus' sources, cf. e.g., the works by Bellomo (as in note 3 above), Prächter (as in notes 3 and 10 above), and Patrick Henry (as in note 1 above); to which add B. Keil, "Epikritische Isokratesstudien," *Hermes*, Vol. XXIII (1888), pp. 346-391, esp. pp. 367-369.

15. Ed. A. Mai, *Scriptorum Veterum Nova Collectio*, Vol. II (1827), pp. 590-609. Cf. Dvornik, *Early Christian...* (as in note 1 above), Vol. II, p. 706 and V. Val'denberg in *Byzantion*, Vol. II (1926), pp. 55-76.

the main device by which he alternately charms and annoys the reader is stylistic: division of the subject matter into short chapters, often tripartite in structure, and, within the chapters themselves, use of parallel clauses grouped in identical patterns and delimited by *paromoea* or straight rhyme.

It is to these stylistic traits that Agapetus owed his popularity in schools, particularly in the West, during the Renaissance and early modern times, so that his *Chapters* became a textbook for the teaching of Greek grammar to speakers of Greek and foreigners alike. In a fair number of manuscripts, copied in the West as well as in Byzantium, Agapetus was provided with extensive schedographic, or parsing, commentaries,[16] exhibiting common traits with the writings of the influential Byzantine grammarian, lexicographer and editor of the classics, Manuel Moschopoulos (fl. ca. 1300). The didactic uses of the *Chapters* were praised in the preface to Agapetus' ⟨7⟩ earliest printed editions.[17]

II

Agapetus' thought, such as it was, did exercise some influence in the West during the sixteenth and seventeenth centuries — but his impact as a political and moral theorist was most pronounced among the Orthodox of the post-Byzantine period, above all among the Eastern Slavs and the Rumanians. This impact may be measured by the large number of Slavic manuscripts of our text (at least ten can be readily quoted,[18]

16. As examples, I quote *Parisinus Graecus* 2553 (15th century), fols. 153^r-198^v, with a Latin translation by a later (16th century?) hand, following the printed editions of the years 1509 (Kalliergis, *editio princeps*) or 1518 (Froben ed.); and *Monacensis Graecus* 83 (15th-16th century), fols. 264^r-292^v.

17. In the preface of the *editio princeps* (1509), Zacharias Kalliergis stated that the translation of Agapetus (which followed upon the Greek) was made literal on purpose, with people in mind who had to use Latin translations in their readings of Greek, on account of the dearth of teachers of that tongue: *penuria praeceptorum viva voce instituentium*. Froben repeated this point in his preface to the Basle edition of 1518 (p. 67); the Latin translation of Agapetus was made literal for the sake of inexperienced boys who would find in Agapetus a marvelous tool for learning Greek: *ob imperitiores et maxime studiosos pueros, qui ex hoc genus libellis mirum dictu, quam feliciter et facile Graecam sibi linguam comparent*.

18. Nine manuscripts are listed in Ja. S. Lur'e, *Ideologičeskaja bor'ba v russkoj publicistike konca XV-načala VXI veka* (1960), pp. 476-477, notes 242-244. On the eighteenth-century manuscript having once belonged to Paisij Velyčkovs'kyj (1722-1794), cf. note 73 below.

although a systematic search should reveal more), by the considerable influence Agapetus exercised upon Eastern Slavic political writings, and, finally, by the fact that before the introduction of print the Slavs produced two different translations of the *Chapters*,[19] separated from each other by as much as four hundred years. The later of the two translations circulated ⟨8⟩ in excerpts, of which we know at least two different versions.[20]

---

19. The earlier translation is represented by Moscow, *Gosudarstvennyj istoričeskij muzej, Sinod.* 202 (15th century), fols. 33^{v}-47^{v}, cf. A. Gorskij and K. Nevostruev, *Opisanie slavjanskix rukopisej moskovskoj Sinodal'noj biblioteki*, Vol. II, No. 2 (Moscow: 1859), esp. pp. 621-622, and by the same library's *Sinod.* 991 [= *Uspenskie Čet'i-Minei* of Macarius], fols. 692^{r}b-696^{r}b, cf. Arkhimandrite Iosif, *Podrobnoe oglavlenie Velikix Četiix-Minej vserossijskogo mitropolita Makarija...* (Moscow: 1892), pp. 502-503 (in the "Tsar's copy" of Macarius' *Minei*, the same translation is to be found in fols. 928ff of the February volume, cf. A. V. Gorskij and K. I. Nevostruev, in *Čtenija v Imp. Obščestve istorii i drevn. rossijskix...* [1886, book 1], pp. 136-137); the later translation, by Moscow, Lenin Library, *Volokolamskoe sobr.*, 158/522 (16th century), fols. 305^{r}-323^{r}, cf., e.g., Hieromonk Iosif, "Opis' rukopisej perenesennyx iz biblioteki Iosifova monastyrja v biblioteku Moskovskoj Duxovnoj akademii," *Čtenija v Imp. Obščestve istorii i drevn. rossijskix...* (1881, book 3), pp. 169-171, and by Moscow, Lenin Library, *Volokol. sobr.* 134/489 (16th century), fols. 325^{v}-334^{v}, cf. Hieromonk Iosif, *ibidem*, pp. 101-107, esp. pp. 104-105. The earlier translation is divided into sixty-seven chapters, compared with seventy-two of the Greek Agapetus. In fact, this translation omits only two chapters of the Greek (31 and 52); it shortens some further chapters of the original, but numbers them as separate units. The difference of five between Greek and Slavonic is due to the fact that on occasion the number sequence was disturbed, or two or more chapters of the Greek were counted as one. The later translation has seventy-three chapters instead of seventy-two. This is due to an error at the end, common to all manuscripts known to me: there is no chapter number 71 in the Slavic, hence Agapetus 71 = Slavic 72 and Agapetus 72 = Slavic 73. I have only a tentative conclusion on the relationship between the two translations: on occasion the two are so close (cf., e.g., Agapetus 12 and 61 = early translation, 56) that the recent translation may be a revised version of the earlier one. However, the recent translation is closer to the Greek and sometimes offers better sense than the earlier one (cf. Agapetus 28, 32, 39, 63); hence, the translator or editor of that translation must have had the Greek original before his eyes. On the two translations of Agapetus, cf. also V. Val'denberg, "Nastavlenie pisatelja VI v. Agapita v russkoj pis'mennosti," *Vizantijskij vremennik*, Vol. XXIV (1923-1926), pp. 27-34, esp. pp. 28-30 (some inexactitudes).

20. One form of the excerpts is represented by Moscow, Lenin Library, *Volokolamskoe sobr.*, 164/530 [F. 113/530], fols. 183^{v}-194^{r}, cf. Hieromonk

I assign the earlier translation — certainly ante-dating the year 1076, by which time it was reflected in one of Prince Svjatoslav's *Miscellanies* — to tenth-century Bulgaria, and to the reign of Symeon the Great (893-927), or his successor Peter (927-969). If my attribution, which I proposed some years ago,[21] should turn out to be correct — as I believe it will — this version of Agapetus would be the earliest known Old Church Slavonic translation of a secular Greek text.

⟨9⟩ Agapetus' concepts and *copia verborum* go beyond those of the Scriptures and liturgical and hagiographical texts which make up the canon of Old Church Slavonic language and letters. It follows that for the Slavicist, both the technique and the vocabulary of the early Slavic translation transcend the value of the *Chapters'* contents.

The picture which emerges from the study of the Slavic Agapetus' vocabulary is as follows: in the process of translating, the Slavic bookman moved with some freedom and on the whole showed a commendable grasp of the Greek, but he had to falter when he faced technical terms, for instance those of rhetoric, such as *deinotēs*, "forcefulness," to which nothing could yet have corresponded in tenth-century Slavic.[22] When it comes to vocabulary, the translation is close to the *Codex Suprasliensis* and rounds out our knowledge of the Old Church Slavonic canon. Thus, to give but three examples, it offers, first, words which we could postulate, but not attest, for the earliest period,[23] secondly, a Turkic (Danube-Bulgarian) borrowing, which hitherto was known only from late texts, but was attributed by scholars — as it turns out, correctly — to the earliest layer of Old Church Slavonic,[24] and thirdly, it reflects a

---

Iosif, "Opis' rukopisej..." (as in the preceding note), pp. 182-186. It contains chapters 5, 8, 21-24, 28-29, 32, 39, 44, 46-48, 51, 53, 55, 57, 61, 64, 67, 68-69, 72, (=71), 73 (=72). The other form is reflected in *Sofijsk*, manuscript of the former Ecclesiastical Academy of St. Petersburg (now in State Public Library), No. 1480 (16th century). It has a different selection of chapters, cf. Val'denberg, "Nastavlenie..." (as in the preceding note), pp. 28-29. Both forms of excerpts are from the more recent translation.

21. In "On Some Sources..." (as in note 1 above), pp. 729-730.

22. Agapetus 42 *deinotēta* is translated by *svar"*, "battle, fight" in the early Slavic version, chapter 38. *Svar"* occurs in that meaning in the *Codex Suprasliensis*.

23. So *ošinovenije* for *apokhē*, "abstinence," Agapetus 66 (= Slavic version, chapter 60). This word is unknown to dictionaries, but cf. *ošiti sę* = *apekhesthai*, "abstain from."

24. This is *kurěl'ky* (Slavic version, chapter 30), rendering *eidos*, "form, shape, kind" (Greek Agapetus, 34). Cf. O. Pritsak, "Bolgarische Etymologien I-III,"

stage during which such basic terms of State and Church as "ruler," "subject," or "piety," did not yet have firmly established equivalents in Old Church Slavonic.[25]

⟨10⟩ As for the contents of the Slavic Agapetus' message, I treated his influence upon Slavic political writings, including those of the formative period of Muscovite political ideology, in some detail on two previous occasions,[26] and shall not repeat here the texts and authors, ranging from the eleventh century to the eighteenth, who used Agapetus to bolster up the ruler's power, or to combat each other.[27]

Ural-Altaische Jahrbücher, Vol. XXIX (1957), pp. 212-213 (Slavic examples from 14th-17th centuries). Another early Turkic borrowing occurring in our Slavic Agapetus is *tikor'*, *tik"ri*, "mirror" (chapters 7 and 23 = Greek Agapetus 9 and 24). For this word, which occurs in the *Codex Suprasliensis*, cf. Z. Gombocz, *Die bulgarisch-türkischen Lehnwörter in der ungarischen Sprache* [= *Mémoires de la Société finno-ougrienne*, 30] (1912), p. 134 = No. 217 (Čuvaš *t'ögor* = mirror).

25. *Arkhōn*, "ruler, official," occurs four times in Agapetus (chapters 71, 10, 66, 30); it is rendered by four different equivalents in the early Slavic translation, *knęz, vlastelin", vladušča, bolęrom"* (chapters 66, 10, 60, 28; *boljarin"* for *arkhon* has not been hitherto attested in Old Church Slavonic). *Hypēkoos*, "subject" occurs seven times (chapters 65, 47, 36, 49, 48, 20, 27); in Slavic it is rendered by six different equivalents: *vručenii, ljudina, pod" vlast'ju, svoim" ljudem", pokorivym* (not attested in this meaning in the exhaustive entry of the *Slovník jazyka staroslověnského*), *pokornikom"* (word not attested in *SJS*) (chapters 61, 47, 32, 44, 20, 25). *Eusebeia*, "piety," occurs twice (chapters 5, 15). It is rendered in two different ways: *bl(a)gyja věry* and *dobroč'stija* (chapters 5, 15). Not even in the later Slavic version is the standardization of the term *hypēkoos* complete: this version's usual rendering is *podvlastnyi*, but on two occasions (chapters 20 and 27) it gives *područnik"*. Only the Kiev printed edition of 1628 renders the term throughout by *poslušnyj* in the main text, while the glossator substitutes *poddanyj* in six out of seven instances.

26. "A Neglected...Source..." and "On Some Sources..." (both as in note 1 above).

27. The fate of Agapetus in Russian texts was pursued in my Columbia University seminar of 1958, and independently by A. A. Zimin and Ja. S. Lur'e, *Poslanija Josifa Volockogo* (Moscow: 1959), cf. esp. pp. 183-184; 260-262; and by Ja. S. Lur'e, *Ideologičeskaja bor'ba...* (1969), esp. p. 475 and n. 239; p. 479; we made the same findings. One further, and to my knowledge unpublished, gleaning: The chapter *K sud'jam"*, "To the Judges," of the juridical collection *Měrilo pravednoe*, ed. Tixomirov, pp. 38-39 = fols. 19^v-20^r, is but a garbled and reshuffled rendering of the Agapetian cento contained in the *Admonition to the Rich* of the *Izbornik* of 1076, fols. 24^v-28^v; thus Agapetus did shape, if to an unknown degree and unbeknownst to his readers, the outlook of secular judges of Rus' as well. On Agapetus in the *Testament* of Ivan IV, see p. 29 below. The

⟨11⟩ III

Among printed translations of Agapetus, the first Slavonic one was published in Kiev in 1628.[28] It occupies a place apart, for in it — as in many of the cultural endeavors undertaken in Kiev at the time of the early Ukrainian revival — East meets West. The best bibliological description of the 1628 print is by Titov;[29] I shall translate it here, putting my additions and corrections between square brackets:

> In the very year of 1628 the presses of the Lavra issued a book, the printing of which was completed towards the end of 1627 (the book's dedication to Peter Mohyla [this statement is in error, cf. note 39 below], who at that time was only '*proizbrannu s G(ospodo)m" v predstatelstvo starěišea pastvy postničestvujuščix*,' bears the date of December 1, 1627), and which was entitled '*Ljubom(u)drějšago Kyr" Agapita diakona... glavizny poučitel'ny*' [read *poučitelny*]. The book's dimensions are almost the same as those of '*prep. avvy Dorofea poučenija dušepolezna*,' that is, *in quarto*: surface of printed page = 17 cm. in length (including upper border and the catchwords) by 12 cm. in width (including lateral border). The book is small, containing six unnumbered pages (frontispiece and dedication to Peter Mohyla [but cf. note 39 below] and twenty-two pages paginated at the top (odd pages being numbered at the right, even pages, at the left). The normal number of lines per page is twenty-seven, and the number of letters per line, thirty-seven. Signatures (consisting each of four

excellent Soviet 1965 edition of Svjatoslav's *Izbornik* of 1076 does not note Agapetian passages in that manuscript. (This was done, however, in the review of that edition by M. Labunka, *Revue d'histoire ecclésiastique*, 63 [1968], pp. 1149-1150). In general, not everyone took this find into account: thus, V. P. Adrianova-Peretc, "Aforizmy Izbornika Svjatoslava 1076 g. i russkie poslovicy," *Trudy Otdela drevnerusskoj literatury...*, Vol. XXV (1970), pp. 7, 11 continued to use the Agapetian passages of *Izbornik* as a source for Kievan proverbial sayings. N. A. Meščerskij's interesting article, "K vorposu ob istočnikax Izbornika 1076 goda," *ibidem*, Vol. XXVII (1972), pp. 321-328, does not address itself to Agapetus.

28. *Ljubom(u)drějšago Kÿr" / AGAPITA DIAKONA, / Blažennějšemu / i bl(a)g(o)č(e)stivějšemu / CARJU IOUSTINIANU: / Pače že vsěm" Pravedno xo/tęščim" nad strast'mi carstvovati. / GLAVIZNY POUČITELNY, / Po Kraegranesiju Ellinski Izloženy. / Slavenski že Pr"věe Napečatany, / V" S(vja)toj Velikoj Čjudotvornoj / Lavrě PEČERSKOJ Kievskoj / Stavropigionu S(vja)tějšag(o) Patriarxi vselen(skago): / arxiep(i)s(kopa) Konstantinopolskogo Novog(o) rima / Lěta G(ospod)nę axki.*

29. Xv. [=F. I.] Titov, *Materijaly dlja istoriji knyžnoji spravy na Vkrajini v XVI-XVIII vv...* (Kiev: 1924), No. 31 = pp. 193-194. The next best description is by *Idem, Tipografija Kievo-Pečerskoj Lavry...*, Vol. I (1916), p. 172.

folios or eight pages) are numbered at the bottom. The frontispiece of the book stands out by its simplicity, but also by its beauty. It is a felicitous reworking of the Strjatyn frontispiece (*Služebnik* of the Caves Monastery of 1620 and the *Nomocanon* of 1620); its borders accommodate portraits: on the left (counting from above) those of St. Vladimir (bust), St. Boris (bust) and Blessed Theodosius (full figure) [holding a scroll with the words: *G(ospod)i imę Pre(svja)tya B(ogorodi)ca*]; on the right (again, counting from above) those of St. Ol'ga (bust), St. Gleb (bust) and Blessed Anthony (full figure) [holding a scroll with the words: *G(ospod)i da bǫdet na městě*]. At center bottom is the picture of the Great Church of the Caves; on both sides, pictures of its nearer ⟨12⟩ and farther Caves. [In the right lower corner of Anthony's portrait there stands a monogram, to be resolved as L. T. These letters are the initials of the engraver.[30]] On the verso of the frontispiece is the representation of the Dormition of the Virgin (the cut is 11 cm. long and 8.5 cm. wide) [this woodcut, copied from p. 409a of the *Menaion* printed in Venice by Božidar Vuković in 1538, was also used in Lavra prints of 1619 and 1620; it may have been chosen by Pamvo Berynda[31]]; above it is a verse '*Agg(e)li uspenie Pr(ě)č(i)stya viděvše udivišasę, kako D(ě)va v"sxodit" ot zemlę na nebo*,' and below it, [a quotation identified as coming from the] *Song of Songs*, chapter [3], verses 7 and 8. Page 1, top, displays a head piece (wrestling nymphs [sirens?]); red ink is used in the title and on p. 1. On p. 21 at bottom there is the following entry '*Lěto Bytia mira, zrlst (7136* [= 1628]) *Indiktia ai. S(o)lncu krug kd. Luny ai. Ključ X Vissekstovoe Lěto v ručě b*: S: B: M^{m} [in reality, m^{n}, see page 13 below: t.]; and on p. 22 (left without pagination) [as a filler, we read an excerpt *On Confession* attributed to Gregory of Nazianzus, *inc. ne medli ispovědati...*, it is followed by the list of *Errata*] at bottom, under a line, stand the initials P.B.; in all likelihood, they are those of Pamvo Berynda. [Next to P.B., there is a crescent with a star; this emblem appears next to Berynda's initials in other prints and woodcuts[32]]. The paper is the same as that used in Dorotheus' *Teachings*;

---

30. On L. T., cf. D. A. Rovinskij, *Podrobnyj slovar' russkix graverov XVI-XIX vv.*, Vol. II (Moscow: 1895), pp. 600-601 (our print = no. 7); it is to be supplemented by P. Popov, "Materijaly do slovnyka ukrajins'kyx hraveriv," in *Ukrajins'ka knyha XVI, XVII, XVIII st.*, [= *Trudy Ukrajins'koho Naukovoho Instytutu Knyhoznavstva*, 1] (1926), No. LXXII = pp. 294-295. Cf. also *Istorija ukrajins'koho mystectva*, (1967), pp. 355-356. L. T., active between the 1620's and the 1640's, worked both in L'viv (Lemberg) and in Kiev.

31. G. I. Koljada, "Pamvo Berynda — arxitipograf," *Kniga: Issledovanija i materialy*, Vol. IX (1964), pp. 133-134; D. Medaković, *Grafika srpskix štampanix knjiga XV-XVII veka* [= *Srpska Akad. Nauka, Pos. Izd., CCCIX*] (Belgrade: 1958), P1. LIV, 2 and p. 206.

32. Cf. Koljada, "Pamvo..." (as in the preceding note), pp. 125-127, 139.

no watermark could be ascertained. We used the copy of the Lavra Library (V^7/115), which is lacking four pages following upon the frontispiece; these pages are preserved in the copy of the Imperial Public Library of St. Petersburg [the Saltykov-Ščedrin Library] (II.7.2).[33]

⟨13⟩ The "printer" (that is, probably, maker-up and type-setter) of our text was Stephen Berynda, a relative, perhaps the brother,[34] of the more famous Pamvo, the lexicographer. This can be deduced from the letters *S: B: mn: T* which stand in the left lower corner of page 21, an abbreviation to be resolved as "*Stefan Berynda, mnij Tÿpograf,*" "Stephen Berynda the most humble printer." A similar, if more explicit, signature, was used by Stephen in the *Preface* to the *Various Teachings* by Dorotheus of Gaza, a work, as we already know, closely connected with our print. There, we read: *Stefan Berynda, mnij v Tÿp(ografěx'')*.[35]

The "corrector," meaning editor or translator, of the new Slavonic version was none other than Peter Movilă (Mohyla), future Metropolitan of Kiev, but late in 1627 still Abbot-elect of the Monastery of the Caves. He combined the tradition of his native Moldavia with Polish culture, study in the West, devotion to his new Ukrainian milieu, and championship of the Orthodox cause.[36]

33. For other descriptions of our print, cf. S. O. Petrov, Ja. D. Birjuk and T. P. Zolotar', *Slavjanskie knigi kirillovskoj pečati XV—XVIII vv. Opisanie knig... v Gosudarstvennoj publičnoj biblioteke USSR* (Kiev: 1958), No. 96, with references to the earlier works by Sopikov, Undol'skij-Byčkov-Viktorov, Karataev and Titov. To these, add S. T. Golubev, *Kievskij mitropolit Petr Mogila...*, Vol. I (Kiev: 1883), p. 400 = No. 24 (correct attribution of the translation to Mohyla; erroneous indication that the preface was dedicated to the "new arkhimandrite," i.e., Mohyla); Picot, "Pierre Movilă..." (as in note 36 below), p. 120 = No. 1 (correct attribution of the translation to Mohyla; mention of libraries owning the print).

34. "Perhaps a relative:" cf. Maslov, "Drukarstvo..." (as in note 41 below), p. 47; Titov, *Tipografija...* (as in note 29 above), p. 215; "apparently brother:" M. Myxajlenko, "Pro kyjivs'ki starodruky XVII i počatku XVIII st. (1616-1721)," *Bibliolohyčni visti* (January-March, 1924), p. 85 and V.V. Nimčuk, *Leksykon slovenoros'kyj Pamvy Beryndy* (Kiev: 1961), p. x.

35. Cf. Titov, *Materijaly...* (as in note 29 above), p. 192. Cf. also *ibidem*, p. 188: *Stefan Berynda, Tÿp(ograf'')* [= *Postface* to Pamvo Berynda's *Leksykon*]. On Stephen as "printer," and on the wide meaning of the term *tÿpograf''*, cf. Titov, *Tipografija...* (as in note 29 above), pp. 116, 130, 144, 146, 168, 214-216, 475. Cf. also Maxnovec', *Ukrajins'ki...* (as in the next note),pp. 214-215.

36. For a good first approach to Mohyla (1596-1647), cf. the bibliography of his works, contemporary sources and secondary literature in L. Je. Maxnovec',

The claim that Mohyla was the translator, or at least the editor, of the Kiev print rests on the concluding sentence of the *Preface*, which ⟨14⟩ runs as follows:

Ispravi že sę ot Ellinskago Idiomate s" mnogim opastvom V" Bl(a)g(o)č(e)stii siajuščǫ B(o)gopriemcu Tezoimennago Mogily Dakijskix Zeml' Načalnika Otrasliǫ, Tvr"doimennago Pr"vopr(e)st(o)lnika tezoimennǫ. Proizbrannu s" G(ospodo)m" v Predstatelstvo starějšęa Pastvy Postničestvujuščix. Admittedly, the sentence is obscure. Are *siajuščǫ, ostrasliǫ* and *tezoimennǫ* datives, as *proizbrannu* surely is, or are they instrumentals? In the first case, we would have a long dative absolute, and the sentence would merely mean that the text of Agapetus was collated with a Greek text when Mohyla, a scion of the ruling family of "Dacia" was Abbot-elect of the Kievan Lavra. In the second case, Mohyla himself would have been the editor. The latter interpretation is the only correct one, and can be sufficiently supported by two arguments. First, a parallel can be adduced from a strictly contemporary Lavra print in which the formula *ispravi sę ot*, "was corrected on the basis of," is followed by the name of the "corrector" in the instrumental. In the *Postface* of Dorotheus' *Various Teachings*, Stephen Berynda stated: *Ispravi že sja sie ot drevnjago istinnago i slavnogo Ellinogrečeskago dialektu, vsečestnym ieromonaxom kyr Iosifom"...*, "The present work was corrected on the basis of the true and glorious Helleno-Greek dialect by the Most Venerable Hieromonk Lord Joseph..." Secondly, *otrasliǫ* must be an instrumental, since *ot"rasl'*, "scion," is feminine. The dative *B(o)gopriemcu* "the one receiving God," goes with *tezoimennago*, "homonymous with."[37] The combination contains a message: *bogopriim'c'*, a cliché based on the Greek *theodokhos*, is an epithet of the old man Symeon of the Gospel who received Christ in his arms. This epithet occurs both in Greek patristic

Ukrajins'ki pys'mennyky..., Vol. I (Kiev: 1960), pp. 415-427, to which add: E. Picot, "Pierre Movilă (Mogila)," in E. Legrand, *Bibliographie hellénique... au dix-septième siècle*, Vol. IV (1896), pp. 104-159; A. Jabłonowski, *Akademia Kijowsko-Mohilańska...* (Cracow: 1899-1900); A. Malvy and M. Viller, *La Confession Orthodoxe de Pierre Moghila...* [= *Orientalia Christiana*, 10] (1927); T. Ionesco, *La vie et l'oeuvre de Pierre Movila, métropolite de Kiev* (Paris: 1944); E. N. Medynskij, *Bratskie školy Ukrainy i Belorussii v XVI-XVII vv.* (Kiev: 1954); R. Łużny, *Pisarze Kręgu Akademii Kijowsko-Mohylańskiej a literatura polska...* (Cracow: 1966).

37. The terms *t'zoimenit", t'zoimenit'n",t'z", t'z'n"* are constructed with a dative, cf. F. Miklosich, *Lexicon, sub verbis.*

writings and in Church Slavonic,[38] and — here is the message — the name of Mohyla's father, the Moldavian hospodar, *was* Symeon. Thus the closing sentence of the *Preface* should be translated as follows:

> ⟨15⟩ It was emended with great care on the basis of the Hellenic idiom by the scion, resplendent in piety, of Mohyla, the ruler of Dacian Lands homonymous with the one who received God [= Symeon]; his ⟨own⟩ name being identical with that of the holder of the first throne, ⟨a man of⟩ firm name [= Peter]; ⟨it happened⟩ when he had been elected to the rule over the flock of ascetic Elders.

In short, for the purposes of the edition of 1628, the Slavic Agapetus was collated with the Greek original by Mohyla.[39] It is less likely that the *Preface to the Pious Reader* comes from Mohyla. It is mannered, and its contorted sentences remind one more of a bookworm's style than that of a *grand seigneur*. If Mohyla had written it, he would not have referred to himself as a man "resplendent in piety;" he would have simply signed it, as he did when he dedicated a *Preface* to the *Pentecostarion (Cvětnaja Triod')* of 1631 to his brother Moses.

We just saw that in his description of our print, Titov speculated that the letters PB which we read at its last (unnumbered) page stand for Pamvo Berynda, in 1628 the "chief printer" (*arxitypograf"*) of the Lavra. Titov's hypothesis has been since confirmed.[40] Pamvo could have penned that highly ornate *Preface* himself. He did relish veiled and complicated circumlocutions when giving dates and names (including his own) in publications in which he himself participated.[41] Moreover, the *Preface* considers the translation of Agapetus as a sequel to the *Various Teachings* of Dorotheus of Gaza (sixth-century), a book dedicated to

38. For reference, cf. *Slovník jazyka staroslověnského*, s.v. *bogopriim'c'*; F. Miklosich, *Lexicon...* s.v. *bogoprijem'c'* (*Vita* of Symeon by Domentijan) and A. W. H. Lampe, *A Patristic Lexicon...*, s.v. *theodokhos*, 3 (Methodius of Olympus, Cyril of Jerusalem).

39. To say this is to correct the misapprehension of Titov who, as we just saw, thought that our print was "dedicated to Peter Mohyla." To repeat, the error goes back to Golubev, *Kievskij mitropolit...* (as in note 33 above), p. 400, who speaks of "the preface *for* the new arkhimandrite." Picot, "Pierre Movilă..." (as in note 36 above), p. 120, and Maxnovec', *Ukrajins'ki pys'mennyky...* (as in note 36 above), p. 416, attribute the translation to Mohyla.

40. By Koljada, "Pamvo...' (as in note 32 above).

41. Cf., e.g., S. Maslov, "Drukarstvo na Ukrajini v XVI-XVIII st.," *Bibliolohyčni visty* (January-March 1924), p. 46, with references.

Mohyla and published in the same year of 1628, and Pamvo Berynda was instrumental in the publication of Dorotheus.[42]

⟨16⟩ The author of the *Preface*, whatever his identity may have been, was the spokesman for the Abbot-elect of the Monastery of the Caves. Since the *Preface* connected Agapetus with the edifying work of Dorotheus,[43] it followed that Agapetus' function, too, was that of edification. Mohyla — like the editors of our text in the sixteenth-century West — directed his message to wide circle of recipients. The title page of the Kiev edition stated that Agapetus' *Chapters* were addressed to Justinian, "or rather to all those who desire to rule over passions in a righteous manner;" and the first part of the *Preface to the Pious Reader* aimed at the simple layman. "And do not say," the author of the *Preface* writes in that first part, "that the latter [i.e., the *Teachings* of Dorotheus] are rules to be followed only by monks, while the former [i.e., the *Chapters* of Agapetus], by Rulers, rather than by their subjects. Do not be misled, O Beloved One ... for the True Emperor is not the one who rules over a multitude of people, while he is ruled by passions, but rather the one who rules over himself and his passions. And, according to the testimony of two Apostles, the King of Kings created 'Ruler and Priest' not only those who hold the helm of the Universe or of the Church, but all those who live in Piety and Virtue ... Accept readily Love, that bond of perfection, from the Beloved One [the pun is explained in the margin: "from Agapetos"], since he was a faithful counselor of Emperors, so that you may begin to rule in this world and to go on ruling for all time to come."

In the second part of the *Preface*, however, the author — again in

42. Cf. Titov, *Materijaly...* (as in note 29 above), No. 31 = p. 192, end of the text of the *Postface to the Reader* in the Dorotheus print: Pamvo Berynda was the moving spirit behind the enterprise, and took part in the preparation and the printing of Dorotheus' Slavonic text. In considering the authorship of the *Preface* to our Agapetus, we might keep in mind Joseph (Kirillovič?), protosynkellos of Alexandria and pilgrim to Palestine and Sinai. It was Joseph who compared the text of Dorotheus with the Greek original. Cf. Titov, *Materijaly...*, p. 192; *Tipografija...*, p. 173. Golubev, *Kievskij mitropolit...* (as in note 33 above), Vol. I, p. 400 prudently speaks of the collective authorship of "the community of the Caves Monastery."

43. Beginning of the *Preface*: "Accept, O pious reader, after *ot dara B(o)žia* [pun explained in the margin: "Dorofea"] ... *darovaniax"...i* [= also] *ot V"zljublennago sv(ja)ščennoslužitelę* [pun explained in the margin: "Agapita ierodiakona"] *D(u)šepoleznaa v"kratcě k" Pravděimennomu* [pun on the name of Justinian] *Samodr"žcu izložennaę nakazania*.

the ⟨17⟩ tradition of the sixteenth-century West — apostrophizes those in authority, both ecclesiastics and laymen:

> You, too, who have been honored with dignities in the hierarchy of the Church; you, Pious Emperors crowned by God [is the Tsar of Moscow meant here?]; and you, Officials who wield worldly powers,[44] accept the Precepts of this servant [again, the pun is explained in the margin: "diakona"] Beloved of God, which were composed in a laconic style, and which are fittingly worthy of you. If you look into them as into a Mirror, you will see there the true and appropriate image of wise administration and of the Christian and Just Kingdom, and will know God, the recompense you owe Him, and the instability inherent in gathering earthly wealth; and you will learn for what reason He handed to you dominion on earth....

What follows occupies almost the whole last page of the *Preface*. The contents of the message are simple: the *Preface* was written on December 1, 1627; in carrying out this task, the corrector of the Slavic text used the Greek original (*ispravi že sę ot Ellinskago Idiomate*); his name was Peter Mogila (Mohyla), Abbot-elect of the Lavra of Kiev.

On the other hand, the form of these subscriptions, written in high Old Church Slavonic style,[45] is of surprising intricacy. A while ago, we were able to follow the writer when he called the editor, "the offspring of Mogila by the same name, the Chief of the Dacian Lands [i.e., Moldavia]," we had to think for a moment when this editor was further called "homonymous with the firmly named first holder of the throne," that is, Peter (since *petra* means stone in Greek, stones are hard, or firm, and *pr''vopr(e)st(o)lnik''* corresponds to *protothronos* of the Greek, an epithet of Apostle Peter and his successors); but in order to understand the very first subscription,[46] ⟨18⟩ we must mentally translate it back into Greek, word for word. Only then does il appear to us that *dělatelnica*

44. *Konec''* (genitive plural); probably a cliché based on the Greek *telé* "magistrates, powers," since *telos* usually means "end," in Slavonic *kon'c'*.

45. The language of the title page and *Preface*, too, is Church Slavonic; the only traces of Ukrainian are in the genitive form *Patriarxi* on the title page and in the first running title of the *Preface, Pred''slovie Do Čitelnika* (the other running title has the Church Slavonic form *k'' Čitatelju*).

46. *Dan'' v'' dobrodetělnoj Dělatelnici Pr''vonačalnyę S(vja)tolěpnago Žitel'stva v'' Rossii S(vja)tyę Dvoica s'' Vyšše dannago Iskupnika i B(o)ž(e)st''v(en)nago daęnia, B(o)ž(e)st''v(en)nago že Kÿota upokojenia Žilišča. Ot Neveščest'v(en)nago ognę v'' veščest''v(en)nom'' est(e)stvě javlenia, minuvšim'' sto šest'desęt'' i dvom'' desęticam'' i sedmim'' lětom k''sim''

(ergastērion) is the printing shop; that *žitelstvo* is the way of life (*politeia*); that *Rossia* is Rus', because such is the form of that land in Greek; that the "Holy Twosome" are first, Anthony of the Monastery of the Caves, since *iskupnik*, "redeemer" is a pun on that Saint's name, provided one knows that in Greek *Ant-ōnios* may be interpreted as one buying (*ōneomai*) in exchange (*anti*); and, second, Theodosius, alluded to as *B(o)ž(e)st"v(en)nago daęnia*, "Divine offering;" furthermore, that *kÿota upokoenia* refers to the Dormition of Virgin Mary, since Mary was the *kibōtos*, or Ark, which contained Christ; and that *žilišča*, "dwelling," means monastery, since one of the Greek equivalents of that Slavic word happens to be *monē*, which also means "monastery."[47]

These subscriptions, let alone the *Preface*, adhere so closely to Greek models not because they are a translation from the Greek. Patently, no translator would have replaced the proper names Antonios or Agapetos by "Redeemer" or "the Beloved One"; moreover, he would have rendered *diakonos* by *diakon"* rather than by *služitel'*. The subscriptions are a display of élite erudition, a bond among the initiates who were in fact familiar with the "Hellenic idiom." But how many people in Kiev of 1627 outside of the Lavra printing press could savor all the nuances of this display? We shall never know, nor shall we know what turn the cultural trends would have taken in the Ukraine without the Civil War of 1648. What we do know, is that these virtuoso allusions to Greek models of Old Church Slavonic were part of the answer which the Orthodox gave to the Jesuit reliance on Latin; and it is worth pondering that Agapetus was summoned to rescue the Orthodox cultural cause.[48]

⟨19⟩ IV

Mohyla — perhaps in concert with Pamvo Berynda — approached the task of publishing Agapetus as a modern scholar would, and con-

---

priloživšim"sę. [i.e., A.D. 1627] *Dekam(brija): ā, dnę. Tekušču že rečennomu Kyrio-Pasxa Lětu.* There follows the sentence, just discussed, about Mohyla's involvement in "correcting" the text of Agapetus.

47. The reader, incidentally, was already offered parts of the same message on the title page woodcut. There, he saw Saints Theodosius and Anthony, and the *verso* of that page displayed for him the scene of the Virgin's Dormition.

48. Latin, of course, was making its inroads into Orthodox ranks. Mohyla — and his milieu — knew it very well, and I suspect that the choice, in our subscription, of the feminine *dělatelnica* rather than of the regular Church Slavonic *dělatelišče* for the Greek neuter *ergastērion* was influenced by the feminine gender of *officina*, the usual Latin term for the printing shop.

sulted all the tools available to him: the two Slavic versions,[49] and the Greek text; the latter must have come to Kiev from the West, in the form of one of the printed editions available at the beginning of the seventeenth century. The following four observations suffice to show that the Greek model of the Kiev text was a printed edition of Agapetus.

1. The title on page 1 closely follows the Greek title of the printed editions, e.g., those of 1509 and 1518; the title of the new translation is slightly different, that of the old one, completely divergent from that of the Kiev text.

2. The colophon formula of the Kiev print (p. 21) agrees with analogous formulae of Greek printed editions like those of 1518 (p. 100) or 1592 (p. 19):

KT	Greek editions
Konec". Izloženie Poučitelnoe agapita Diakona K" Iustinianu Kesaru, jaže u Ellin" Carskij (naricaet" sę) svitok"	*Telos ektheseōs parainetikēs Agapētou diakonou, hētis par' Hellēsi basilika onomazetai skhedē*

3. In Agapetus 53, the Kiev text omits a clause absent from the printed editions, but present in both manuscript Slavic translations, and in some Greek manuscripts:

KT	NT	OT
da pročee ot B(og)a propovědan" budeši, s" Věncem" nepobedimago C(a)rstva Stęži i Věnec" bl(a)gotvorenia k" niščim" ⟨20⟩	*daže ubo i ot b(o)ga proslavišis(ę) i ot b(o)gamudryx" vosxvališis(ę), s věncem nepobědimago c(a)rstvia stęži i věnec' bl(a)gotvorenia eže k niščim*	*togo bo radi i ot b(og)a poxvalen" budeši i ot dobrě smyslęščix proslavlen". S věncem' nepobědimago tvoego c(a)rstvija iměi ⟨i⟩ věenec' eže na niščix m(i)l(o)st'.*[50]

49. On the two Slavic versions, cf. pp. 7-10 above. Henceforth, in the headings of parallel columns I shall call them "old translation" [OT] and "new translation" [NT] respectively; the Kiev text will be called KT. V. Val'denberg, "Pečatnye perevody Agapita," *Doklady Akademii nauk SSSR* (1928, No. 13), pp. 283-290, esp. pp. 284-285 gives a basically correct account of the relationship between KT, OT and NT.

50. Froben's printed Greek text of 1518 has, like KT, *hina toinyn para theō anakērykhthēs, meta tou stephanou tēs aēttētou basileias ktēsai kai to stemma tēs tōn penētōn eupoiias*, while between *anakērykhthēs* and *meta* the *Monacensis*

4. In Agapetus 4, the Kiev text reproduces an error found in a number of the printed Greek editions, while both Slavic versions follow the correct reading; the error was due to the confusion between *domata*, "houses" (wrong), and *dōmata*, "gifts" (correct):

KT	NT	OT
i iže Diadimoju oblečenii i iže pod domom" povr"ženii	*i iže diadimoju ob'vęzaemii i iže daniix rad(i) predležaščii*	*i v" věnci xodęščei i darmi počtenii.*[51]

The Kiev text is the most literal of the three Slavic renderings of Agapetus. This applies both to its choice of vocabulary — thus in Agapetus 1 it has *c(a)rstvia* for the Greek *basileias*, "Empire," while the two Slavic versions have *vlasti* — and, regrettably, to its word order — thus it managed to render Agapetus 3 without changing the sequence of a single word of the Greek. The beginning of this chapter runs as follows:

KT	NT	OT
B(o)ž(e)st"vnomu učeniju i pr"vomu čl(ově)ci eže poznati koždo sebe naučaem" sę	*b(o)ž(e)stvennomu učeniju i pervomu naučaemsę čl(ově)ci eže komu koždo sam sę poznati*	*b(o)žestvenoe učen'i pervoe č(lo)v(ě)ci sut eže razuměti čemu o nem učimi esmi* [Greek text misunderstood].[52]

Except for the word order, the Kiev text of the foregoing passage is virtually ⟨21⟩ identical with the new translation. This is not an isolated occurrence, as will be seen from some random examples:

Agapetus 4:

KT	NT	OT
brenie bo imut"vsi rodu praotca no o blagosti da počitaem" sę nravom"	*bernie bo imějut' vsi rodu praotca no o bl(a)g(o)sti da proslavlęemsę nravov*	*bern'e bo imut' vsi rodu praděda no dobrymi veličaimy sę nravy*

Graecus 551, fol. 123ᵛ adds, with OT and NT, *kai para tōn eu phronountōn, anarrhēthēs*, "so that thou mightst be acclaimed by people well disposed ⟨towards you⟩."

51. Froben edition of 1518: *kai hoi diadēmata perikeimenoi kai hoi dia domata prokeimenoi*. The Latin translation in the same edition has *cubicula*.

52. *Theion mathēma kai prōton hoi anthrōpoi to gnōnai tina heauton didaskometha*, "We men are taught this divine and first lesson: for each of us to know himself."

Agapetus 7:

KT	NT	OT
zemnyx" iměnij nepostoannoe bogatstvo ibo bl(a)gix" del" bl(a)g(o)d(a)t' k" tvoręščim" v"zvraščaet" sę	*zemnyx imenii nepostoanoe bogat'stvo dobryx bo del" bl(a)g(o)dati k" tvoręščim v"zvraščajutsę*	*zemnago iměn'ja nestojaščee b(og)at'stvo... bl(a)gim" bo delom" darove na tvoręščim" ix v"zvraščajutsę.*

Agapetus 8:

KT	NT	OT
Ne pristupen ubo esi čl(ově)kom" vysoty radi nižnago Carstva, bl(a)gopristupenže esi trebujuščim" dr"žavy radi vyšnęa vlasti. I otvr"zaeši ušesa	*nepristupim ubo esi čl(ově)kom vysoty radi zemskago c(a)rstva, bl(a)gopristupim že byvaeši trebujuščim deržavy radi gornia oblasti. i otverzeši ušesa*	*nepriložen ubo esi čl(ově)kom vysoty radi c(a)rstvija zemnago, krotok že budi trebujuščim deržavy radi gornęja vlasti. i otverzai uši...*

Thus we may assume that the translator of the Kiev text knew and used the new Slavic translation. In other — admittedly much fewer — cases, however, his rendering is closer to the working of the old translation: in Agapetus 1, *hylakēn* "barking," is rendered, as in the old translation, by *laanie*, while the new translation has *brexanie*; in Agapetus 2, *asphalōs*, "securely," is translated by *tvr"dě*; the old translation, too, has *tverd"* or *tverdo*, while the new translation uses *opasně*.

⟨22⟩ In its choice of words, the Kiev text is purist and shows occasional preference for rare and authentic Church Slavonisms: thus in Agapetus 1 we read *otrěeši* for *otženeši* of both Slavic versions, and *vynu* for *besprestani* (new translation) or *vsegda* (old translation); even the modern sounding *vesla* in Agapetus 2, as opposed to *kormila* of the new translation and to *pravilo* of the old, belongs to the canon of old Church Slavonic. Departures from the Greek are rare — in Agapetus 7, the Kiev text renders *dromon* "course" by *vremennoe tečenie*, as opposed to *tečenie* alone of both Slavic versions. Rare, too, are individual errors in the Kiev text. One of them, in Agapetus 1, must be due to haplography:

KT	NT	OT
iže pače simi tebe [this makes no sense]	*pače vsex semu te*	*pače vsego semu te...*[53]

53. *Hyper hapantas ton toutou se.*

Another error, in Agapetus 53, is due to a misreading of the Greek *kalōn* "good deeds" for *kakōn* "evil deeds"; hence the Kiev text's *dělanie zlyx"*, as opposed to the correct *delanie blago* of the new translation and *dělex dobryx* of the old. Both errors have been corrected in the list of *Errata* on the (unnumbered) p. 22 of our print.

In sum, the Kiev text is a new, and usually quite literal, translation from the Greek; its vocabulary is archaizing; its author consulted both the new and the old Slavic translation in his work, but relied more on the new than on the old in his formulations.[54] It follows that when a wordding in the Kiev text differs from both Slavic versions, this wording does not go back to any Slavic manuscript, but is to be dated to the time of the translator of our print, that is, to about 1627. This point is worth retaining; I shall return to it at the end of the present introduction.

The crowded margins of our print were used to accommodate various kinds of information. These include the Greek acrostic and its Slavic translation, each couple of letters standing next to the beginning of the relevant ⟨23⟩ chapter; summaries of selected chapters;[55] references to the Old and New Testament paralleling the contents of single chapters;[56] finally, variant readings, or glosses, to our text. The latter afford an insight into the philological kitchen of the Lavra printing press. Moreover, as the term *ispravi sę* "was corrected," is ambiguous, we cannot be sure whether Mohyla's own contribution was limited to these variants or whether Mohyla should be credited with the revision of the text proper, and the glosses should be assigned to some learned member of the Lavra's editorial staff, such as Pamvo Berynda, a man with a bent for lexicography. In any of these eventualities, the glosses deserve a closer look.

The glossator proposed fifty-two variant readings to the printed text. In his work, he used the same tools as did the editor of the text. He relied on the new and old Slavic translations, on the vulgate Latin translation (which he consulted in one of the numerous printed editions

54. Similar suggestions were already made by Val'denberg, "Pečatnye perevody..." (as in note 49 above), pp. 284-285.

55. Examples: Chapter 6 [= p. 3] *vsegda/blagougod/naa B(og)u i xotě(ti) i tvori(ti)*; chapter 9 [= p. 4] *C(a)rskaa d(u)ša/kakova/imat(") byt(i).*

56. Examples: Chapter 8 [= p. 3] is appropriately glossed with a reference to Matth. 18:77 [i.e. 18:23-35]. Both texts illustrate the principle that God will treat us as we shall treat our neighbor; both use the word *klevrět"*, "fellow-slave." In chapter 14 [= p. 5], the word *gnoj* "corruption, filth" is glossed by Job 17:14, where *gnoj* occurs as well.

of Agapetus prior to 1628)[57] and on his own judgment; when he did think for himself, he attempted, with varying success, to move closely to the Greek.

Ten of the glossator's variant readings were drawn from, or coincided with, the new Slavic translation;[58] six of the glosses were drawn from, or coincided with, the old one.[59] In four cases, it is difficult ⟨24⟩ to say whether the new or the old translation was the source of a gloss.[60]

There are only three incontrovertible instances of the glossator's dependence on the Latin translation,[61] but they suffice to prove that a Latin text was available to him. We thus may claim Latin influence upon the glossator in a number of further instances, two of which are quite convincing.[62] We can attribute at least nine more glosses to the influence

57. For proofs that the Kiev editor had a printed edition of Agapetus at his disposal, cf. p. 19 ff above.

58. Examples: Page 3 (= Agapetus 6 *epeidē*): text *elma*; gloss *poneže*; new translation *poneže*; old translation *elma*. Page 3 (= Agapetus 7 *epirrheōn*): text *pritiča*; gloss *tekušče*; new translation *tekuščee*; old translation *priticaja*. Page 11 (= Agapetus 34 *phronēma*): text *razuměnie*; gloss *mudrova[nie]*; new translation *m(u)drovanie*; old translation: *m(u)drost'*.

59. Examples: Page 5 (= Agapetus 13 *abebaiou*): text *neizvěstnago*; gloss *ne[utvr''žden]ago*; new translation *nepostoannago*; old translation *neutveržena*. Page 7 (= Agapetus 19 *therapeia*): text *ugoždenie*; gloss *služba*; new translation *ugoženie*; old translation *služba*. Page 20 (= Agapetus 70 *parapempousa*): text *predsylajušči*; gloss *[pre]pušč[ajušči]*; new translation *preposylaet'*; old translation *prepuščajušču*. However, of the six glosses coinciding with the old translation, two may have been influenced by the Latin: Page 5 (= Agapetus 15 *meterkhetai*): text *prexodit*; gloss *mimoide[t]*; Latin translation *transit*; new translation *prexodit'*; old translation *mimoxodit'*. Page 12 (= Agapetus 41 *eunoousi*): *drugom''*; gloss *bl(a)govolny[m'']*; Latin translation: *bene sentientibus*; new translation *drugom*; old translation *bl(a)gorazumnym''*.

60. Examples: Page 12 (= Agapetus 40 *epieikeian*): text *pravosti*; gloss *krot[osti]*; both new and old translation *krotost'*. Page 16 (= Agapetus 54 *epitattein*): text *zaveščevati*; gloss *povelě[vati]*; new translation *povelěti*; old translation *povelěvati* (here the presumption is in favor of the old translation).

61. Page 11 (= Agapetus 35 *eunoias*): text *prięzni*; gloss *bl(a)govolenia*; Latin translation: *benevolentiae*; new translation: *ljub'vi*; old translation: *dobroum'ja*. Page 12 (= Agapetus 40 *authadeian*): text *dr''zost'*; gloss *upor*; Latin translation *pertinacem*; new translation *gordosti*; old translation *ljutost'*. Page 14 (= Agapetus 45 *egenou*): text *byl'' esi*; gloss *rodilsę*; Latin translation: *natus es*; new translation: *byl'' esi*; old translation: *moščen esi*.

62. Page 14 (= Agapetus 48 *kataphronōn*): text *preobydęi*; gloss *[pre]zira[ęi]*; Latin translation: *contemnendo*; new and old translation: *preobidę*. Page 14 (=

of the Latin; among them, those which replace *poslušnyj* ("subject": a cliché for *hypēkoos*) of the text by the Ukrainian (via Polish) *poddanyj* (six out of seven cases)[63] deserve special mention. The substitutions may ⟨25⟩ have been influenced by the Latin translation's regular use of *subditus* at the corresponding places. However, this substitution may have been made independently; for it must be remembered that *poddanyj* (and its variants) is a cliché formed after *subditus* in Polish, Ukrainian and Russian,[64] and was in current Ukrainian usage by the sixteenth century.

The remaining twenty marginal readings can be labeled as the glossator's original contributions. Eight of them were attempts to move closely to the Greek original. Some of these attempts were acceptable if unnecessary;[65] others were a distinct step backwards.[66] This leaves us with twelve "original" glosses for which we can postulate no model. Some may reflect the glossator's desire to make the text more understandable, as when he proposed *ladia, čoln"* for the text's (and both Slavic versions') *korabec"*, "small ship" or the like; when he wrote *služitel [korabnyj]* for *korabnik*, "sailor"; or when he replaced the rare *klevrětom"*, "fellow-slaves," of the text (and of both Slavic translations) by the more common *ravnoslužaščy[m"].*[67] It would be idle to

---

Agapetus 48 *akataphronēton*): text *ne preobidenno*; gloss *[ne pre]ziraem[o]*; Latin translation: *haud aspernabilem*; new and old translation: *ne preobidimu*.

63. Cf. Kiev text, pp. 9 (= Agapetus 27); 11 (= Agapetus 36); 14 (= Agapetus 47); 14 (= Agapetus 48); 14 (= Agapetus 49); 19 (= Agapetus 65).

64. Cf., e.g., M. Vasmer, *Ètimologičeskij slovar'...*, III (Moscow: 1971), p. 296.

65. Examples: Page 5 (= Agapetus 15 *politeias*): text *žitelstva*; gloss *graždan*[stva]; Latin translation *vitae*; new translation *žitel'stva*; old translation (best): *žit'ja*. Page 15 (= Agapetus 51 *deomenous*): text *trebujuščix"*; gloss *prosę[ščix"]*; new translation: *trebujuščix*; old translation: *trebujuščaja*. Cf. also p. 1 (Agapetus' Title *eusebestatō*): text *blagočestivomu*; gloss *[blagočestiv]ějš[emu]* (however, the new translation, too, has *bl(a)goč(e)stivějšemu*).

66. Examples: Page 3 (= Agapetus 5 *arkhei* "he begins"): text *obladae(t)*; gloss *načalstvu[et"]* (*arkhei* understood as "he rules"); new translation (best): *načinaet'*; old translation: *vladět'*. Page 12 (= Agapetus 39 *prothymian* "willingness"): text *usr"die*; gloss *predložen[ie]*; new traslation: *userdie*; old translation: *spěšen'e*. Page 17 (= Agapetus 59 *proanastellontes* "curbing beforehand"): text *predustavlęjuščie*; gloss *[pred]posyla[juščie]* (connecting this verb with *stellō* "send"); new translation *predstavlęjušče*; old translation (best): *v"zderžajušče*.

67. Page 3 (= Agapetus 2 *skaphos*); page 4 (= Agapetus 10 *nautēs*); page 18 (= Agapetus 64 *homodoulois*).

speculate on the reasons for other substitutions, such as the ⟨26⟩ gloss *mal[ost']* for *xudost'*, "worthlessness" of the three Slavic versions.[68]

V

So much for the sources used in the constitution of the Kievan text of Agapetus. At this point, two further queries come to mind; both have to do with this text's influence. One concerns the impact of the *Hortatory Chapters* on Mohyla's own writings; the other, the possible use of the 1628 edition in Wallachia and Moldavia. The latter question is itself a part of the larger problem of Agapetus' fate in Rumanian lands. Unfortunately, no clear-cut answer can as yet be given to either of these questions.

Three years after the appearance of Agapetus, Mohyla dedicated the Lavra *Pentecostarion (Cvětnaja Triod')* to his brother Moses (hospodar of Moldavia in 1630-1632 and 1633-1634). Mohyla's *Preface* is interspersed with Greek phrases in Greek type — in order, we surmise, to impress the addressee both with his brother's knowledge of Greek and with the technical capabilities of the Lavra press. The *Preface* contains a miniature *Mirror of Princes*, composed by Mohyla himself for the benefit of his ruling relative. The *Mirror* is divided into fifteen chapters, of which five refer to matters politic, and ten to matters sacred. We may postulate the influence of Agapetus in this arrangement by chapters, but the references and parallels in Mohyla's *Mirror* are all scriptural. To be sure, some thoughts are Agapetian; thus, when the fifth "politic" chapter states that "the duty of any ruler is to wage war against enemies but to spare the innocent" it gives the same message as that of Agapetus' chapter 28, but Mohyla's formulation is closer to Virgil's tag *parcere subiectis et debellare superbos* [*Aen.* VI: 853] than to Agapetus' sentences.[69] This fits well with what we know of the Metropolitan's intellectual equipment.

Mohyla, the "*voevodič*" of Moldavian lands," was intimately involved with the movement of ideas, teachers, texts and printing presses from Kiev ⟨27⟩ and L'viv to his ancestral lands. What we know at present about Agapetus in Rumania is little, but even this little justifies some speculation. Agapetus does not seem to have been used in the *Admonitions* which the Voyvode of Wallachia Neagoe Basarab (1512-1521)

68. Page 5 (= Agapetus 14 *to outidanon*).

69. For the text of Mohyla's *Preface* to the *Pentecostarion* of 1631, cf. Titov, *Materijaly*... (as in note 29 above), No. 38 = pp. 263-266.

had issued in Greek and Slavic for his son Theodosius.[70] However, the Rumanian *Preface* to a translation of John Chrysostom's *Sermons*, published in 1691 and addressed to hospodar Constantin Brăncoveanu, does contain quotations from our author; and a full Rumanian translation of Agapetus — which was never printed — is preserved in two manuscripts, both coming from Rîmnic in Wallachia; the earlier of them dates from the nineties of the seventeenth century. The model for the Rumanian translation is said to have been a Slavic, rather than Greek, Agapetus; this presumably since the scribe of the earlier manuscript, one Vlad, was a translator from Slavic.[71] All this, again, fits well with what we know about the chronology of East Slavic influence in Rumanian lands.[72] Of course, ⟨28⟩ even if the source of the Rumanian translation was Slavic, it may have been a manuscript rather than a print; in fact, we know at least one Slavic Agapetus manuscript in Rumanian lands: it belonged to the library of the Ukrainian ascetic Paisij Velyčkovs'kyj, a library which he left in the Neamţ monastery in Moldavia,[73] but its date

70. For the Slavic text, combine P. P. Panaitescu, *Cronicile Slavo-Romîne din sec. XV-XVI publicate de Ion Bogdan* (Bucharest: 1959), pp. 218-263 with G. Mihăilă in *Romanoslavica*, Vol. XVI (1967), pp. 359-375; old Rumanian translation (with indication of sources) in F. Moisil and Dan Zamfirescu, *Învăţăturile lui Neagoe Basarab...* (Bucharest: 1971); cf. also Dan Zamfirescu, *Neagoe Basarab şi Învăţăturile către fiul său Theodosie, problemele controversate* (Bucharest: 1973), with discussion of Neagoe's sources. [See also *Addendum* on p. 525]

71. The above information is culled from A. Duţu, *Les livres de sagesse dans la culture roumaine* (Bucharest: 1971), chapter 2: "Le miroir des princes," pp. 97-153. This chapter is an enlarged version of the same author's "Le 'Miroir des Princes' dans la culture roumaine," *Revue des Etudes Sud-Est Européennes*, Vol. VI (1968), pp. 439-479 and was in turn reprinted, with some changes, in the Rumanian version of the book, *Cărţile de înţelepciune în cultura română* (Bucharest: 1972), pp. 65-103. The two manuscripts containing the Rumanian Agapetus are ms. rom. 3190 and 1788 of the Rumanian Academy of Sciences.

72. Cf. P. P. Panaitescu, "L'influence de l'oeuvre de Pierre Mogila, archevêque de Kiev, dans les Principautés roumaines," *Mélanges de l'Ecole Roumaine en France*, Vol. V (1926), pp. 3-97. In spite of geography, Ukrainian influence in Wallachia preceded that in Moldavia. On Greek manuscripts of Agapetus in Rumanian lands, cf. note 6 above and C. Dima-Drăgan, *Biblioteca unui umanist Roman...* (Bucharest: 1957), p. 155 (*Vindobonensis Suppl. Gr.* 87, written in 1700; it once belonged to the *Stolnic* Constantine Cantacuzino).

73. Cf. A. I. Jacimirskij, "Slavjanskie i russkie rukopisi rumynskix bibliotek," *Sbornik Otdelenija russkogo jazyka i slovesnosti Imp. Akad. nauk*, Vol. LXXIX (1905), p. 555.

is eighteenth century, thus too late to have served as a model for the Rumanian translator of about the second half of the seventeenth.

On the other hand, we do know that a Slavic version of another Byzantine Mirror of Princes printed "in Russia" was the source of a Rumanian translation preserved in a manuscript, apparently of the eighteenth century.[74] The work was the *Hortatory Chapters* of Pseudo-Basil I, addressed to Emperor Leo VI; given the cultural context, this printed source was in all probability the Kievan Lavra edition of 1680, although in theory two other editions could have served as models: the bilingual one of Ostrog (1607) and that of Moscow (also of 1680).[75] The parallel offered by the impact produced by the Slavic print of Pseudo-Basil lends plausibility to the thought that the Rumanian Agapetus of the Rîmnic manuscripts may have been translated from the Kiev print of 1628. The last word on this matter belongs to Rumanian scholars.

In closing, a few words on the fate of the Kiev text among the Russians: the translation revised by Mohyla was reprinted, with slight ⟨29⟩ changes adapting it to Russian linguistic usage of the time, in Moscow in 1660.[76] Although the relation of the Kiev text to the subsequent four

74. Cf. Duțu, *Les livres de sagesse...* (as in note 71 above), p. 112.

75. On the bilingual Ostroh edition, cf. K. Koperžyns'kyj, "Ostroz'ka drukarnja...," *Bibliolohyčni visty* (January-March, 1924), p. 81; Petrov, Byrjuk and Zolotar', *Slavjanskie knigi...* (as in note 33 above), No. 50; and the excellent, unfortunately only mimeographed, work by T. A. Bykova, *Katalog izdanij ostrožskoj tipografii...* (Leningrad: 1972), No. 20. On the Moscow edition of 1680, cf. A. S. Zernova, *Knigi kirillovskoj pečati, izdannye v Moskve v XVI-XVII vekax...* (Moscow: 1958) No. 358. For the Kiev edition, cf. V. S. Sopikov-V. N. Rogožin, *Opyt rossijskoj bibliografii*, Vol. I (1904), No. 1431; Karataev, No. 863. Cf. also on the three editions, I. P. Erëmin in *Istorija russkoj literatury*, Vol. II, Part 2 (1948), pp. 148-149.

76. It appeared as a part of the *Anfologion* of 1660, pp. 82-114. Title on p. 82: *Izloženie glavizn" poučitelnyx" / napisannoe : ot agapita diakona / s(vja)tějšia B(o)žia Velikia c(e)rkve / egože kraegranesie takosę imat: / Bl(a)žennějšemu, i Bl(a)gočesti/vomu c(a)rju našemu Iustinianu, / agapit xudějšij diakon"*. I used the British Museum copy. The dependence of the Moscow text on that of Kiev was already seen by Val'denberg, "Pečatnye..." (as in note 49 above), pp. 285-286. For the *Anfologion*, earlier bibliographical references to it, and Soviet libraries containing it, cf. A. S. Zernova, *Knigi kirillovskoj pečati, izdannye v Moskve v XVI-XVII vekax...* (Moscow: 1958), No. 287 [however, Zernova failed to realize the Kiev origin of the Agapetus text in *Anfologion* and attributed all of that book's translations to Arsenij Grek].

Russian translations of Agapetus has not been investigated in detail, it is safe to assume that these translations are independent from it.[77]

Thus at first sight, the influence of the Kiev Agapetus in Muscovite lands seems limited to the Moscow reprint. We must report, however, one additional, and puzzling, point. It has to do with the appearance of a passage from Agapetus in the *Testament* of Ivan IV. That *Testament* contains the following, explicitly announced, quotation:

> *jako že inde rečeno est': podobaet ubo carju tri sija vešči iměti, jako bogu ne gnevatisja i jako smertnu ne voznositisja i dolgoterpelivu byti k sogrešajuščim.*[78]

The most recent study of the *Testament* stated that the provenance of this quotation had not been cleared up.[79] In fact, two out of "these three things" which a ruler should possess have been lifted from Agapetus 21.[80] ⟨30⟩ The puzzling fact is that the sequence of words in the *Testament's* Agapetian passage agrees not with that of either the old or new Slavic manuscript translations, but with that of the Kiev (and Moscow) printed editions, which closely follow the word-order of the Greek:

Testament	KT	NT	OT
podobaet ubo carju... jako bogu ne gnevatisja i jako smertnu ne voznositisja	*podobaet" ubo tomu i aki B(o)gu ne gněvatisę i aki smr"tnu ne v"znositisę*	*podobaet ubo emu jako i sm(e)rtnomu ne prevoznositis(ja) i ako b(o)gu ne gněvatis(ja)*	*podobaet' ubo emu jako sm(e)rtnu ne v"znositis(ę) i aky b(o)gu ne gněvatisę.*[81]

77. I did not see any of these later translations, dating from 1766, 1771 (two) and 1827 respectively (the latest one was made for scholarly purposes). On these points, cf. Val'denberg "Pečatnye..." (as in note 49 above), pp. 286-290; even he could not find the edition of 1766.

78. Cf. L. V. Čerepnin, *Duxovnye i dogovornye gramoty velikix i udel'nyx knjazej XIV-XVI vv.* (Moscow: 1950), p. 432 (= fol. 16ᵛ of the only extant copy).

79. G. Stökl, *Testament und Siegel Ivans IV [= Abhandlungen der Rheinisch-Westfalischen Akademie der Wissenschaften*, 48] (1972), p. 83 and n. 35. Not having recognized the quotation, Professor Stökl misunderstood the relevant passage.

80. This was already seen by Val'denberg (as in note 19 above), p. 32.

81. Judging by the one manuscript accessible to me, Agapetus excerpts, too, have the sequence of NT and OT for chapter 21: cf. *Volokol.* F113/530 (as in note 20 above), fol. 184ᵛ: *podobaet ubo emu jako i smertnomu ne prevoz-*

Now, according to the somewhat contradictory internal evidence, Ivan IV's *Testament* seems to have been composed in 1572 or in 1564.[82] In any case, the tsar died in 1584, almost half a century before the appearance of the Kiev text. This text, as we remember, is a new creation; thus it has no history going beyond, say, the year 1620. To point to the affinity between the Agapetian passage of the Kiev and Moscow prints, on the one hand, and the *Testament*, on the other, is to call for a careful reexamination of the latter text's authenticity. Apparently, no serious thought has ever been given to this task, in spite of the admittedly unsatisfactory textual evidence for our document and of the peculiarities of its structure.[83] ⟨31⟩ This task cannot be undertaken here.[84]

In Byzantium, authors of political and paraenetic literature had an opportunity to draw upon Agapetus for about nine hundred years. Somewhat surprisingly, they made only modest use of this opportunity.[85] Medieval Slavic lands were more receptive; there, the disciples of the Byzantines — those in the south as well as those in the east — heavily relied on *Hortatory Chapters*, and the authors of the Kiev edition, who

---

nositis(ę) i jako B(o)gu ne gnevatis(ę). The sequence of the Greek text is that of KT and the *Testament*, cf. Froben edition of 1518: *khrē toinyn auton kai hōs theon mē orgizesthai kai hōs thnēton mē epairesthai.*

82. Stökl, *Testament...* (as in note 79 above), pp. 19 and 40.

83. This impression is left by the few perfunctory passages in Stökl, *Testament...* (as in note 79 above), pp. 20 and 33 with n. 101. Cf., however, the review of Professor Stökl's book by Edward Keenan, *Slavic Review*, Vol. XXXIII, No. 3 (March 1974), pp. 129-130, who strongly suspects the genuineness of the *Testament*.

84. Here, I must sound a note of caution. The agreement in word order between the *Testament* and the Agapetus editions of 1628 and 1660 may be the result of an accident, the scribe — or rather the *dictator* — of the document quoting from memory. Furthermore, as I discovered no other examples of the use of Agapetus in the *Testament*, I cannot rule out the chance that it quotes some third source in which the fragment of Agapetus 21 had already been garbled, or which adhered to the Greek word order. I omit other theoretical, but unlikely possibilities (direct access to Greek, interpolation). In short, by itself, the Agapetus fragment of the *Testament* does not prove that the document is spurious. But it should prompt some investigation.

85. Cf. texts quoted on pp. 3-4 above. The only Byzantine *Mirror of Princes* which made extensive use of Agapetus was the collection of *Precepts* by Emperor Manuel II for his son John VIII, cf. esp. Precepts 8, 31, 39, 60, 95 (= Migne, *PG*, 156, cols. 324; 340; 344-345; 357; 381) with Agapetus 8, 25, 66, 28, 13.

presented Agapetus in Church Slavonic garb and made use of medieval Slavonic translations of the deacon carried on the same Byzantine tradition.

However, Agapetus' heyday came after the fall of Byzantium, and much of his success happened in the West. Here Agapetus profited from the introduction of print and, starting in the early sixteenth century, acquired new champions, a new — didactic — purpose, and a new reading public. The *editio princeps* of May 11, 1509 was printed by Greeks from Crete established in Venice, but between the sixteenth and eighteenth centuries, Agapetus' *Hortatory Chapters* went through numerous editions — about sixty of them — by non-Greeks and appeared not only in classical tongues — Greek and Latin — but also in vernacular languages — German, English, Italian, French and Spanish.[86]

⟨32⟩ Seen in this perspective, the first printed edition of the Slavic Agapetus ceases to be an accident: it was just one more text of a Greek author who, for over a century, had been popular in the West. To be sure, the print of 1628 was a sign of a Byzantine revival; but it also was an echo of what was going on in contemporary European publishing.

ADDENDA

I. *Ad* p. 521, note 70:

On the vexed question concerning the language of the original version cf., most recently, P. Ş. Năsturel, "Remarques sur les versions grecque, slave et roumaine des 'Enseignements du Prince de Valachie Neagoe Basarab à son fils Théodose'," *Byzantinisch-neugriechische Jahrbücher*, Vol. XXI (1971-1974, printed in 1975), pp. 249-271 (original version was in Greek, but its practically simultaneous Slavic reworking became the official text).

II. To the Editors of *Recenzija*:

In my *Ljubomudrějšij Kyr" Agapit Diakon*... [Supplement to *Recenzija*, Vol. V, No. 1 (Fall-Winter 1974)], pp. I-II (= remarks concerning the facsimile reproduction), I surmised that the Kiev copy of the 1628 edition of Agapetus' *Hortatory Chapters*, the first pages of which served as basis for the facsimile, once belonged to the Library of the Suprasl' Monastery near Białystok (Poland). My surmise rested on the words *Monastirja Bělostoc'kogo* contained in the ownership note jotted down (in an early eighteenth century hand?) at the end of

86. On printed editions and translations of Agapetus , cf., e.g., S. F. G. Hoffmann, *Lexicon bibliographicum sive index editionum et interpretationum scriptorum Graecorum*..., Vol. I (Leipzig: 1832), pp. 92-96 (most complete, if not exhaustive; registers sixty-one editions).

Kiev copy (cf. p. xxxi of the facsimile). As a school friend of Professor Jan Białostocki whose ancestors in the male line came not from the city of Białystok, but from Volhynia, I should have known better.

In fact, the *Monastryr' Bělostoc'kij* was situated in what subsequently became the village of Bilyj Stok (Belostok, Białystok), about 30 kilometers northwest of Luc'k, today the capital of the Volhynian *oblast'*. It was founded ca. 1636, and was the residence of a bishop. Thus in all probability the Kiev copy always remained on Ukrainian territory. On the *Bělostoc'kij* monastery, cf. e.g., V. V. Zverinskij-N. P. Sobko, *Materialy dlja istoriko-topografičeskogo izslědovanija o pravoslavnyx monastyrjax v Rossijskoj Imperii...*, Vol. III, *Monastyri zakrytye do carstvovanija Imperatricy Ekateriny II* (St. Petersburg: 1897), no. 1496 (with precious information on documentary evidence); and *Słownik geograficzny Królestwa Polskiego...*, Vol. I (1880), p. 202.

I wish to make two additional remarks with reference to the main part of my introduction.

1. On p. 500 and note 11, I dated the Greek version of the story of Barlaam and Joasaph — and, consequently, the excerpts from Agapetus which it contains — to the eighth century. Subsequently, I became acquainted with the still unpublished work of Dr. Victor Tiftixoglu (Munich) who again compared the Georgian and Greek versions of the story and who mustered serious arguments on behalf of a later date (presumably ca. 1000) of the Greek version. For our purposes it would mean that parts of the Greek *Barlaam and Joasaph* (which indeed depends directly on Agapetus) should not be used as a proof that Agapetus was quoted by a Byzantine writer as early as the eighth century. For a recent and succinct presentation of the thesis that the Greek version depends on the Georgian one, which in turn was made about the year 1000, cf. the introduction by D. M. Lang to G. R. Woodward and H. Mattingly, [*St. John Damascene*], *Barlaam and Ioasaph* [The Loeb Classical Library, 34] (London-Cambridge, Mass.: 1967), esp. pp. XX-XXXII.

2. *Ad* p. 523, note 77: For a description of the two Russian Agapetus translations of 1771 (by S. Pisarev and the Ukrainian scholar Vasyl' Ruban), cf. *Svodnyj katalog russkoj knigi graždanskoj pečati XVIII veka, 1725-1800*, Vol. I (1963), p. 22.

Ihor Ševčenko

FACSIMILE

The facsimile of the Kiev edition of Agapetus is based on two copies of our print. Most of it (up to and including page 20) reproduces the copy of the Library of the Academy of Sciences of the USSR, Leningrad, Section of Rare Books, Inventory Number 1115. Pages 21 to the end come from the copy of the State Public Library of the Ukrainian SSR, Kiev. This substitution was indicated, since the last page of the Leningrad copy is damaged at the bottom and thus lacks the crucial information on Stephen Berynda's having been involved in the production of our text.

One of the previous owners of the Kiev copy was a Polish nobleman who took down the names of some military units, their commanders, and their disposition. His notes run as follows (doubtful readings are provided with question marks): *Commenda(n)tem woyska ImP: W(oyewody): Ruskie(g)o/ImP. Starosta Osiecki/Quatermagister Jacek Sucharski/ImP. Chorąże(g)o: Stacyę [?] wzieli[?] Chorągiew / Wiell[?]: ImP: Czesznika Koronnego/ Namiesnikiem był P. Kosieracki wybierał/P. Siwierski.*

The Polish text is followed by ownership notes in Church Slavonic. It results from them that the Kiev copy belonged to a "monastery of Białystok" and was bound together with the *Various Teachings* of Dorotheus. The last line of the Slavonic entry reproduces the beginning of a *troparion* of the Service of the Vespers,[1] which is repeated at the Feast of Annunciation.[2]

The Slavonic note, in what looks like an eighteenth century hand, runs as follows: *Syja kniga ggl(ago)lemaja Dorofej/Monastirja Bělostoc'kogo/ B(ogorodi)ce Děvo raduisja obradovannaja.* The only monastery "of Białystok" known to me is the famous Suprasl' (Supraśl) monastery near that town. It not only was *sub vocabulo* of the Virgin but was called the Monastery of the Annunciation, an event which is the subject of the last line of the entry in Church Slavonic. We may, therefore, surmise that the Kiev copy once belonged to the Library of the Suprasl' Monastery, historically a foundation of the Kiev Lavra.

I wish to thank the Directors of the Leningrad and Kiev Libraries and Messrs. G. M. Proxorov and H. N. Lohvyn for their help in procuring microfilms of the respective copies of the Kiev Agapetus. I am also indebted to Mr. E. Kasinec for his bibliographical assistance.

---

[1]For the Greek counterpart of this *troparion*, cf., e.g. *Hōrologion to Mega... hypo Bartholomaiou Koutloumousianou...*, 9th ed. (Venice: 1860), p. 126. For the Church Slavonic text, cf., e.g. *Velikij Sbornik*, Vol. I (Jordansville: 1951), p. 14, where we read the usual *blagodatnaja* instead of *obradovannaja* (in Greek, *kekharitōmenē*); however, our *troparion* is reproduced with the word *obradovannaja* on a woodcut of the Virgin of Kupjatyči, cf. Titov, *Materijaly...* (as in note 29 above), p. 239.

[2]For the use of this *troparion* in services connected with the feast of the Annunciation, cf., e.g., *Mēnaion tou Martiou* (ed. Phōs, Athens: 1961), pp. 173, 183, 185, 188, 189.

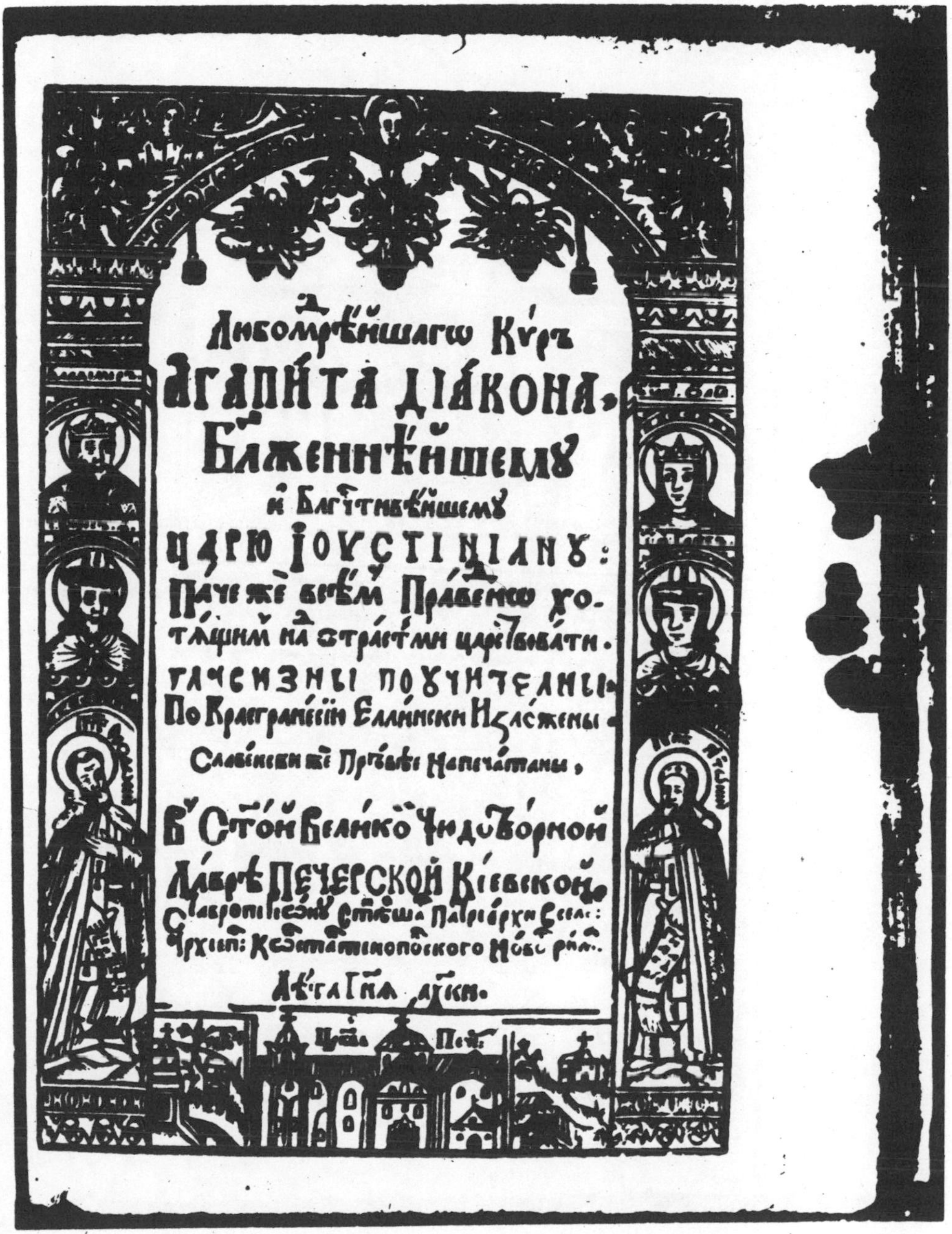
Любомудрѣйшагѡ Кѵръ
Агапита Діакона,
Блаженнѣйшему
и Благочестивѣйшему
Царю Іоустініану:
Паче же всѣмъ праведнѡ хотѧщимъ на земли царствовати.
Главизны поучителны.
Славенски же пре[в]еде[н]ы напечатаны,
В Стой Великой Чудотворной
Лаврѣ Печерской Кіевской,
Ставропігіи святѣйшагѡ Патріархи Вселенскаго:
Архіеп: Константинопольского Новаго Рима.

iv

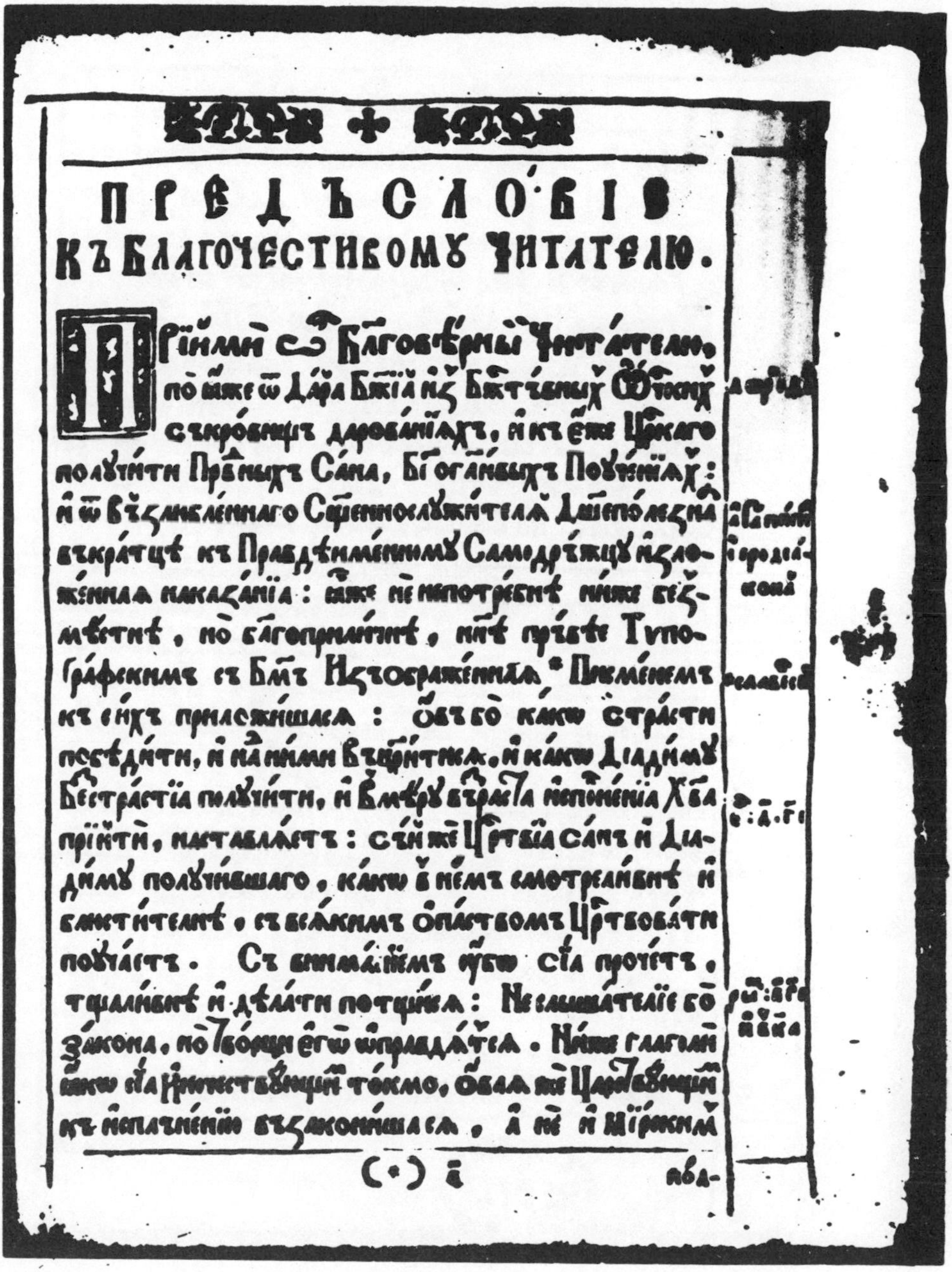

ПРЕДЪСЛОВІЕ
КЪ БЛАГОЧЕСТИВОМУ ЧИТАТЕЛЮ.

Пріимали есте благовѣрныи читателю, по ниже ѿ дара Бжіа изъ Бжтвенных ѿческих съкровищъ дарованіахъ, и къ еже Црьскаго получити Прѣвных Сана, Богоданных Поученіах: и ѿ Възлюбленнаго Сщенносложителя Душеполезна въкратцѣ къ Правдѣимленнимъ Самодръжцу изложеннаа наказаніа: иже не непотребнѣ ниже безмѣстнѣ, по благоприличнѣ, нынѣ прѣвѣте Тупографскимъ съ Бжіимъ Изъображенніа * Премѣненемъ къ сихъ приложишася: овъ бо како страсти побѣдити, и на ниже Вѣдритѣла. и како Діадиму Бестрастіа получити, и Въ Вѣру вѣрна Напоменія Хва пріяти, наставляетъ: сей же Црьтвіа Санъ и Діадиму получившаго, како в немъ смотрелнѣ и блюстителнѣ, съ всяким опаствомъ Црьтвовати поучаетъ. Съ вниманіемъ убо сіа прочетъ, трилѣнѣ и дѣлати потщися: Не слышателіе бо закона, по Творци его ѡправдатся. Ниже глаголи како сіа Христіанствующим токмо, обаче Царствующим къ исполненію възлюбившася, а не и мірскимъ

(·) в

пова-

v

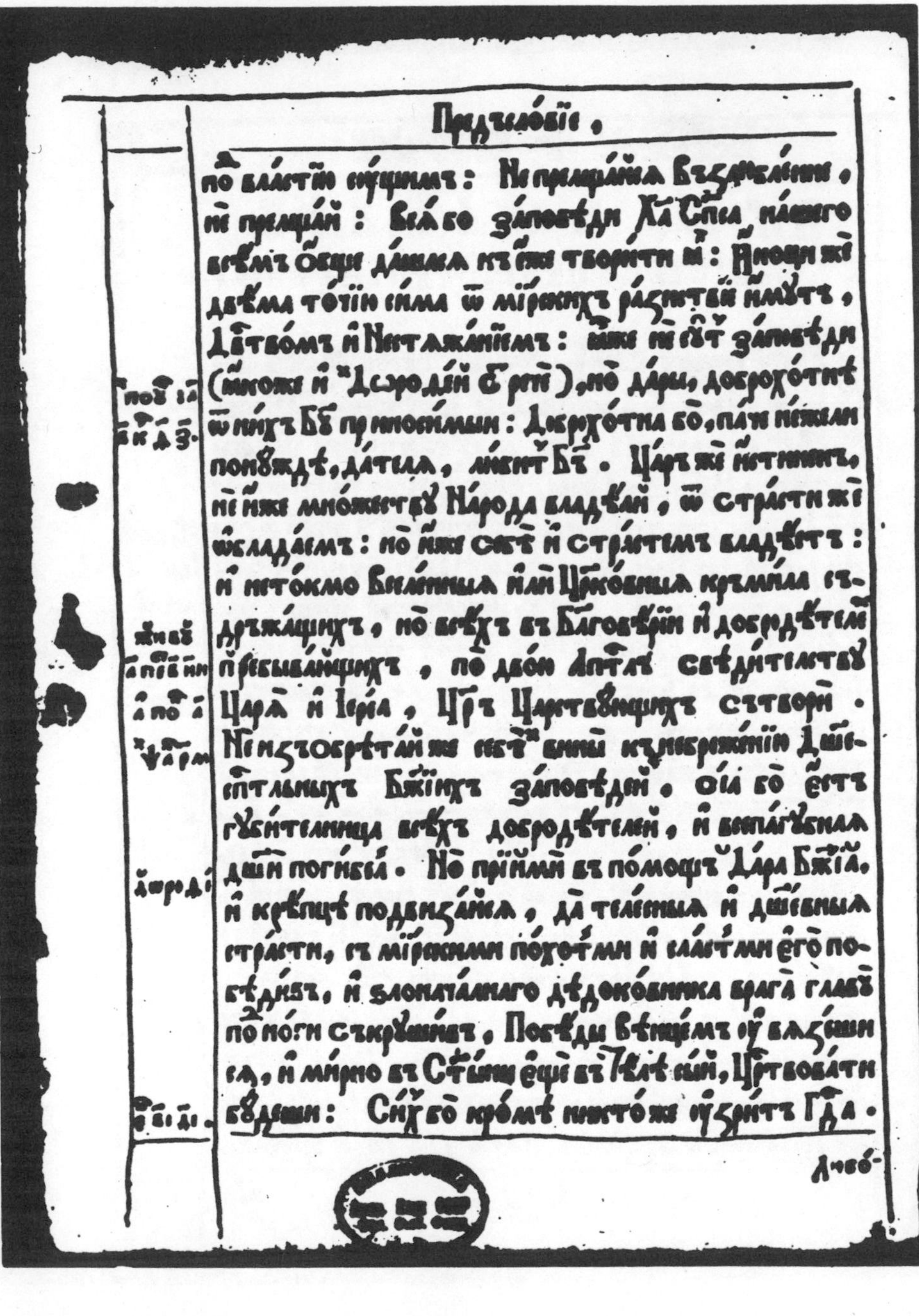

Предсловіе.

по власти сущимъ: Не премудрая Вѣзаблѣнии,
не премудрии: Вся бо заповѣди Христа Спаса нашего
всѣмъ общие дадашася къ сему творити ихъ: Иноци же
двѣма тотію сима от мирскихъ разнятся имутъ,
Дѣвствомъ и Нестяжаніемъ: иже не суть заповѣди
(якоже и Добродѣй Оретъ), но дары, доброхотнѣ
от нихъ Богу приносимыи: Доброхотна бо, паче же и
повсюду, дателя, любитъ Богъ. Царь же истинныи,
не иже множеству народа владѣяй, от страсти же
обладаемъ: но иже себе и страстемъ владѣетъ:
и не токмо Вселенныя или Церковныя кормила съ-
держащихъ, но всѣхъ въ Благовѣрии и добродѣтели
пребывающихъ, по двою Апостолу свидѣтелству
Царя и Іерея, Царь Царствующихъ сътвори.
Не изъобрѣтай же себѣ вины къ небреженію душе-
спасителныхъ Божіихъ заповѣдей. Сія бо есть
губителница всѣхъ добродѣтелей, и всепагубная
души погибель. Но пріимый въ помощь Дара Божія,
и крѣпцѣ подвизайся, да телесныя и душевныя
страсти, съ мирскими похотьми и сластьми его по-
бѣдивъ, и злопагубнаго древокозненика врага главу
подъ ноги съкрушивъ, Побѣды вѣнцемъ увязшися,
и мирно въ Святыни еще въ тѣлѣ сый, Царствовати
будеши: Сихъ бо кромѣ никтоже узритъ Господа.

Любо-

До Читѣлника.

Любовь твоѧ ѡ Короли сказъ съвершенїа, ѿ Бъзлю-
бленнаго (Короля Вѣрна Совѣтника Царѧ) оусердно
прїимай, аще Прѣвѣчне Цр̃твовати здѣ начнешъ, и
въ безконечныѧ вѣки хощеши, Кромѣ бо Любвѣ,
нетокмо всѧ Добродѣтели (аще и бѫдѹтъ), но
и Мѹчитела конечна, по Апл̃ѹ, ничтоже естъ.

Агапит

а кг і г, ан: іс.

Прїимѣте и вы иже Бм̃ъ въ Їерархїи
Црковной Санове постовленныи Правителїе, и Бго-
вѣнчанныи Блг̃тивыи Царїе и Властели Мѵрскихъ
концевъ държащїи, сего Бголюбезнаго Слѹжителѧ
прикладѣте вамъ достойнаѧ, Лаконїцки съста-
вленнаѧ Поѹченїѧ, в нихъ же прилѣжно въззрающе
аки въ зрцалѣ мирнаго строенїа, и Хртїанскаго
Правѣднаго Царствованїа истинный и свойственный
образъ оузрѣвше, Бга и длъжное емѹ ѿ васъ
въздаянїе, и самыхъ себѣ, и непостоянное временнаго
богатства събранїе познаете: и того ради вамъ
ѿ него на земли Властелское правленїе врѹченно е,
наѹчитесѧ: и бодрѣно съ опаснымъ вниманїемъ
въ страсѣ Бжїимъ врѹченное вамъ Хво словесное
стадо пасти, аки слово ѡ немъ въздати хотѧще
нелицемѣрномѹ Сѹдїи, потщитесѧ: Силнїи бо
силно истѧзани (по Прркѹ) бѫдѹтъ.

Дїакона

ѳ: ѕі ві

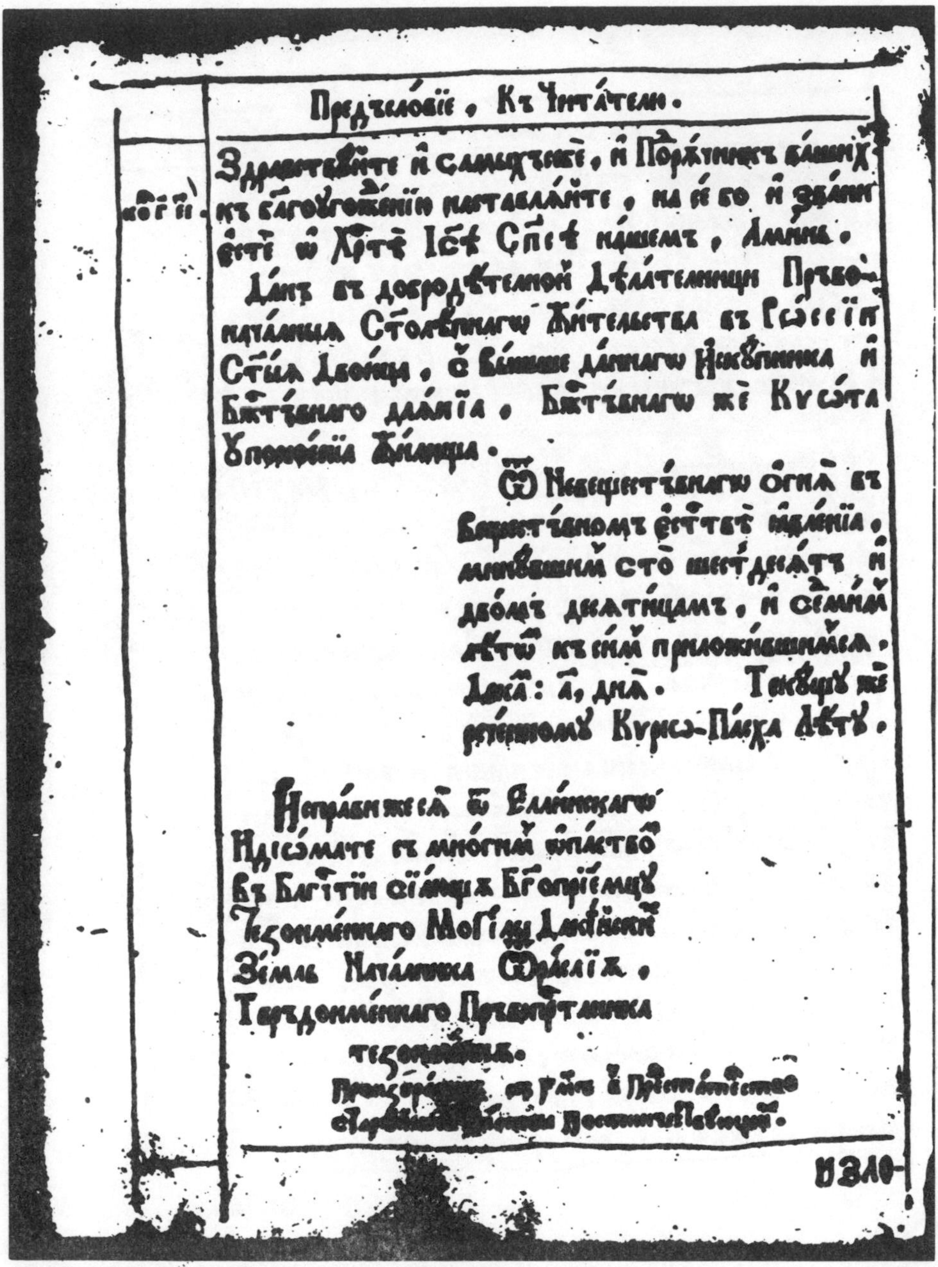

Предсловіе, Къ Читателю.

Здравствуйте и сами у себе, и подружіе ваших къ благоугожденію наставляйте, на се бо и звани есте о Христе Іисусе Спасе нашемъ, Аминь.

Даны въ добродѣтелной дѣлателницы Прьвоначалника Столпнаго Жителства въ Россіи

Святыя Двоица,

От Невещественнаго огня въ вещественном естестве явленія, минувшим сто шестдесят и двум десятицам, и семмым лѣтом къ сим приложившимся. Декабря: а, дня.

Курсо-Паска лѣту.

Исправижеся от Еллинскаго Идіомате съ многим опаством

Земли

Изложеніе
главизн поучителных,
начертаное
от Агапита діакона.
Свѧтѣйшїа Бж҃їа великїа Црк҃ве.
Ихже краегранесїе тако сѧ имать:
Блаженнѣйшему, и благочестивому
Царю нашему Іоустиніану,
Агапит худѣйшїй діакон.

Честь всѧкоа превыше имѣѧй
Достоинство Царю, почитай паче
всѣх тебе удостоившаго Бг҃а. зане
и по подобїю нб҃снагw Црствїа даде ти
Скипетръ земнаго началства, да члвѣки научиши
правды храненїю, иже на нѧ неистовающихъ сѧ
отженеши лаанїа, свщеннми от него Царствоваем законы,
и иже под собою Царствуя законне.

а Нико-

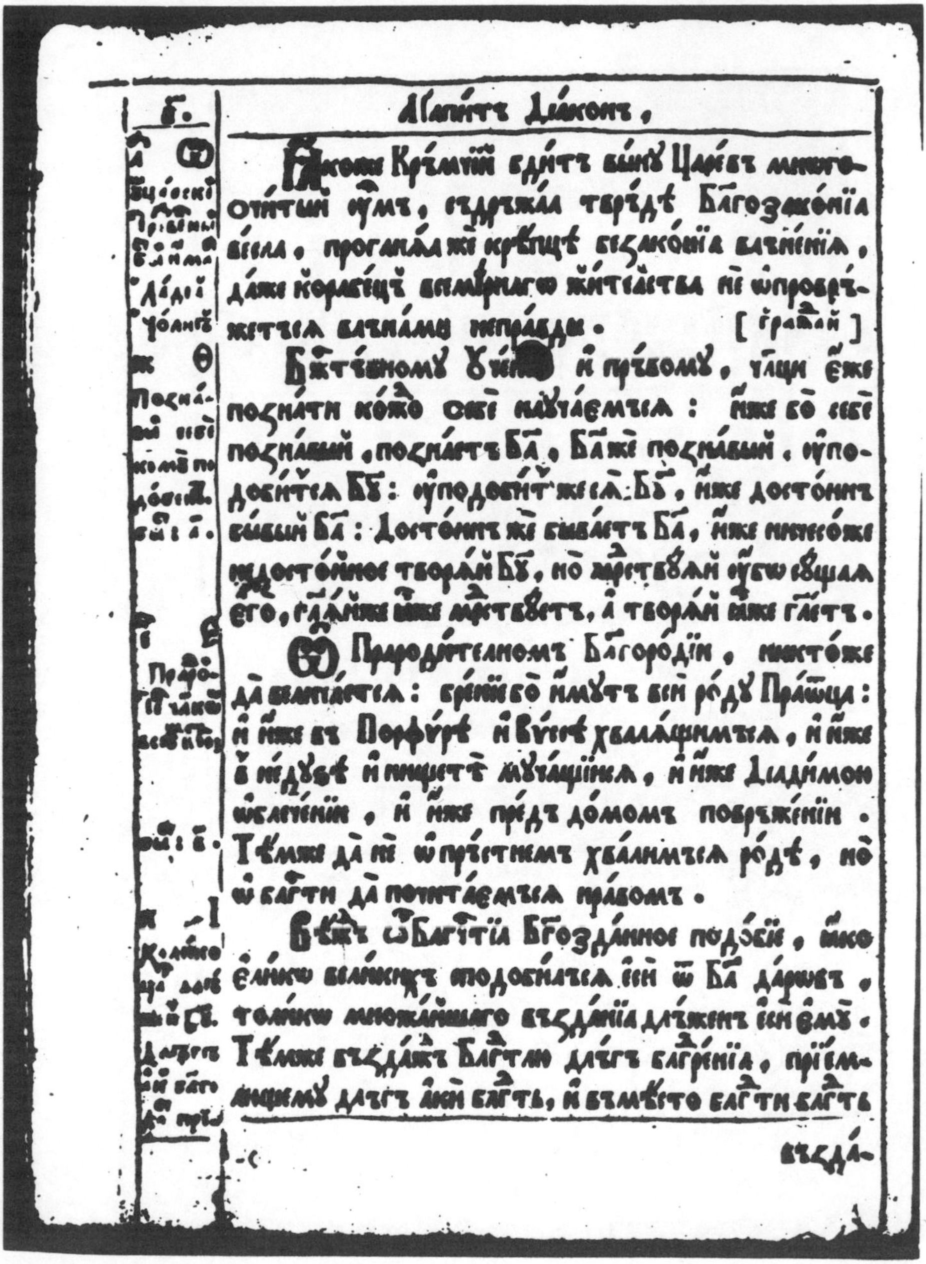

Агапитъ Діаконъ.

Окормы кръмчій единъ всемꙋ царевъ многоочитый ѹмъ, съдержа твердѣ благозаконіа весла, прогоняя же крѣпцѣ беззаконіа влъненіа, да же корабль всемирнаго жителства не ѡпровръжется влънами неправды. [гранай]

Въ жителномꙋ ѹченію и правомꙋ, учащи еже познати кождо себе научаемься: иже бо себе познавый, познаетъ Бга, Бга же познавый, уподобится Бгу: уподобится же сея Бгу, иже достоинъ бывый Бга: Достоинъ же бываетъ Бга, иже ничесоже недостойное творяй Бгу, но мудрствуяй убо вещая его, глаголяй иже мудрствуетъ, а творяй иже глетъ.

Прародителномъ благородіи, никтоже да величается: бреніе бо имутъ вси роду праѡтца: и иже въ Порфуре и Вуссе хвалящимся, и иже в недузе и нищете мучащійся, и иже диадимои ѡбложеніи, и иже предъ домомъ повръженіи. Темже да не ѡ пръстнемъ хвалимься роде, но ѡ благости да почитаемься правомъ.

Въ елико ѡ благостіи богозданное подобіе, яко елико величайшихъ сподобихъся вси ѿ Бга даровъ, толико множайшаго въздаяніа длъжени есмы ему. Темже въздаяй Блгодателю длъгъ благодаренія, пріемлющемꙋ длъгъ аки благъ, и въ место благти благъ

възда-

въздающему: тѣмъ бо паче и благостемъ обладаеш, и якоже долгъ благодѣтельства въздаетъ. Благодаренiя же възыскуетъ от насъ, не еже глаголы благими произношенiе, но еже вещми благостынными приношенiе.

Никтоже тако благоизволена творитъ тако, яко мощи убо иже хощетъ творити, паче же тако любезная и хотѣти и творити. Елма убо от Бога тебѣ дарована сила, еяже требоваше насъ ради благости хотѣнiе, вся и хощи и твори якоже угодно естъ, иже сiе тебѣ давшему.

Земныхъ имѣнiй непостоянное богатство, рѣчныхъ струй подражаетъ временное теченiе: въ малѣ убо притичая имѣти мнящимъся, помалѣ же претичая къ инымъ отходитъ: самое же благотворенiя сокровище постоянно естъ стяжавшимъ е, ибо благихъ дѣлъ благость къ творящимъ възвращается.

Не приступенъ убо еси тѣкымъ высоты ради нижняго Царства: благоприступенъ же еси требующимъ, державы ради вышняя власти: и отверзаеши уши иже нищетою одръжимымъ да обрящеши Божiй слухъ отверзтъ: яковiи бо аще будемъ нашимъ клевретомъ, таковаго къ намъ обрящемъ Владыку.

Д.

Агапитъ Діаконъ.

м Т Цр҃скаѧ дш҃а какова има быти

Ѹ многопечалнои Царевои души, аки зерцалу обретатися достоитъ, да Божественными лучами присно облистаетъ, и вещей суды оттуду научаетъ ся: ничтоже бо тако творитъ подобающая съзирати, яко еже хранити ону всегда чисту.

у Ѿ *служітели царево съгрѣшнїе болши всѣх. Исправлеиїе нестаѧзанїа

Якоже въ Плавецехъ егда убо *Корабникъ погрешитъ, малу наноситъ съплавающимъ пагубу, егда же самъ Кръмчій, всемъ сътворитъ Кораблю погибель: Такожде и въ Граде, аще убо некто от иже под властію съгрешитъ, не толико общее елико себе обидитъ: егда же самъ Князь, всемъ гражданомъ съделоваетъ пагубу. Сей убо великія казни пріиметъ, аще что презритъ от подобающихъ. Съ многимъ опасствомъ, и да глаголетъ вся и да творитъ.

и К чловечских вещей неравенство

Кругъ некій человечкіа обращаетъ вещи, иногда инако носа сія и обносяща: и симъ неравенство естъ, еже ничесомуже от настоящихъ втожестве пребывати. Достоитъ убо тебе държавный Царю, въ обратіемъ сихъ пременении непревратенъ имети благочестія помыслъ.

л Ласкателе ѿвраща

Отращайся ласкателей прелестныхъ словесъ, якоже врановъ хищныхъ нравовъ: Очи бо телесемъ ископываютъ они: Сіи же, души

пе

Іѹстиніанѹ царю. г.

помрачаютъ помышленія, не ѡставляюще зрѣти ѿпадса
вещей истиннѹ: или бо похваляютъ иногда слад.
гажденію достойная, или порицаютъ множицею
похваламъ лѹчшая: да ѿ обоихъ едино ѿ нихъ
погрѣшаетъся. или злое похваляемо, или
доброе ѹкаряемо.

Равномѹ быти достоитъ всегда царевѹ мѣро- I
ванію: еже бо влагатися вещей преложеніамъ,
ѹма неизвѣстнаго знаменіе бываетъ. а еже крѣпцѣ ѿстрастій
въ добрыхъ ѹтвръдитися, якоже благочестивая ваша
ѹтвръдися дрьжава, и ниже къ грьдыни превъзно-
ситися, ниже къ печали низноситися ѹтвръжден-
ныхъ есть крѣпцѣ, и незыблемѹ имѹщихъ дѹшю.

Аще кто ѿтнщенно имать помышленіе ѿ Б
человѣческія прелести, и видитъ хѹдость своего
естества, краткое же и скорое здѣшнаго живота,
и съпряженіи плъти гной, въ грьдыни не впадетъ
брегъ, аще и въ достоинствѣ бѹдетъ высоцѣ.

Пачеже всѣхъ царствія славныхъ, благочестія вѣнецъ V А
царя ѹкрашаетъ. ибо богатство ѿходитъ, а
слава преходитъ. Слава же божественнаго жителства,
безъсмрътными вѣки съпротязаетъся, и забытія
превышше оныхъ имѹщихъ поставляетъся.

Зѣло мнитъ ми ся безмѣстно быти, якоже С Г

л г богатѹ-

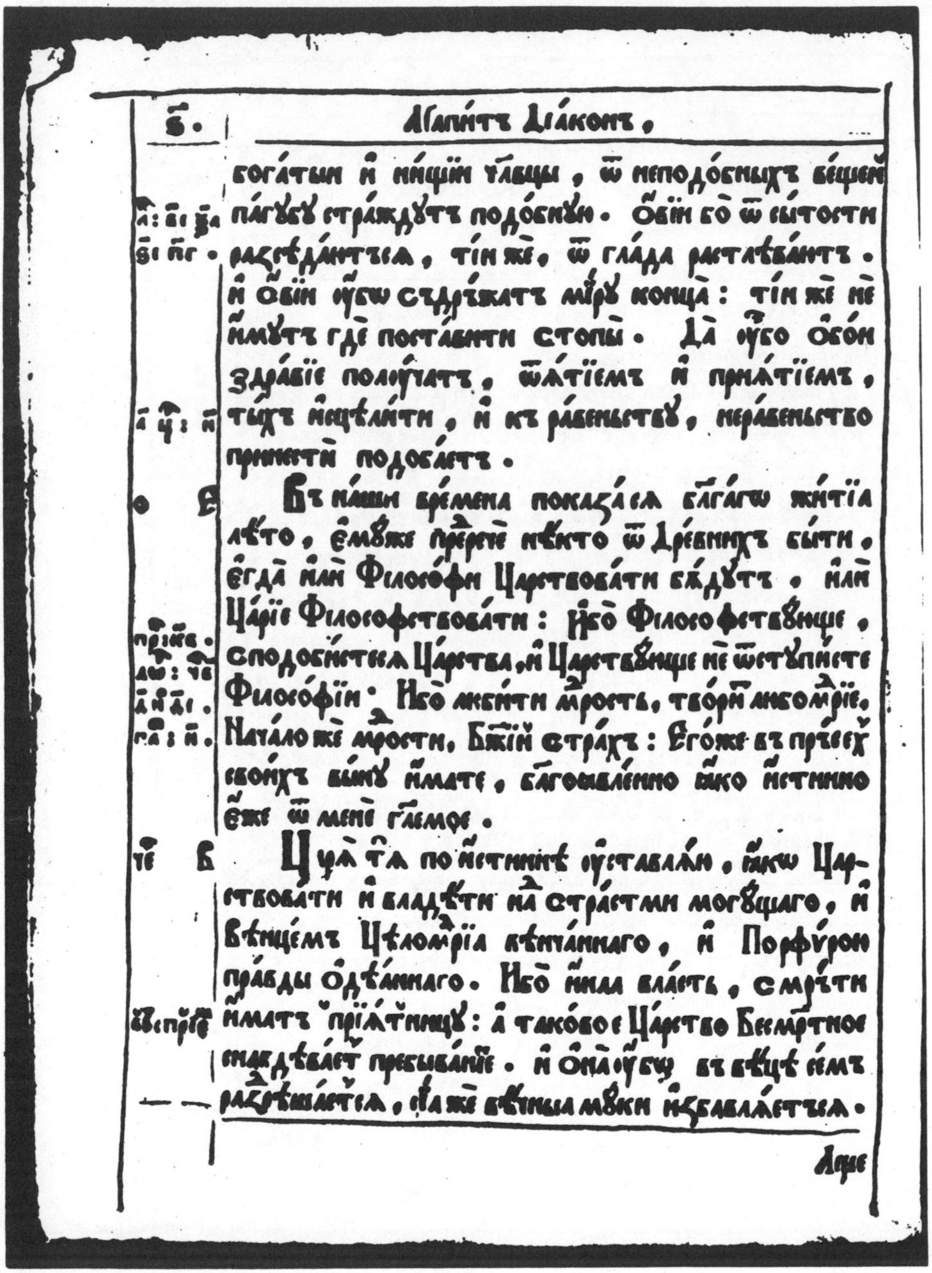
ѕ. Агапитъ Діаконъ.

богатыи и нищіи человѣцы, отъ неподобныхъ вещей
л: ві ѕа пагубѣ страждутъ подобнѣи. Овіи бо отъ сытости
ѕі пг. разсѣдаютъся, тіи же, отъ глада растаеваютъ.
и овіи убо содрѣжатъ миру конца: тіи же не
имутъ гдѣ поставити стопы. Да убо овои
здравіе получатъ, отъятіемъ и пріятіемъ,
а ч: п тѣхъ исцѣлити, и къ равенству, неравенство
привести подобаетъ.
о В Въ наши времена показася благаго житія
лѣто, еже древле прорече нѣкто отъ древнихъ быти.
егда или Философи царствовати будутъ. или
Царіе Философствовати: Ибо Философствующе,
пріте. сподобистеся Царства, и Царствующе не отступисте
лю: че Философіи. Ибо любити мудрость, твори любомудріе.
а н аі. га: и. Начало же мудрости, Божій страхъ: Егоже въ прсехъ
своихъ всегда имате, благословенно яко истинно
еже отъ мене глаголемое.
те Б Царства по истиннѣ уставляй, яко Царствовати и владѣти надъ страстми могущаго, и
вѣнцемъ цѣломудріа вѣнчаннаго, и Порфурою
правды одѣяннаго. Ибо иная власть, смерти
евс прве имать пріятницу: а такового Царство Безсмертное
сподобляетъ пребываніе. И она убо въ вѣцѣ семъ
разрушается, сія же вѣчныя муки избавляется.

Аще

Іоустиніанꙋ Царю. ѕ.

Аще ѿ всѣхъ хощеши приплодити честь, бꙋди всѣмъ благъ обще. Ничтоже бо тако къ благоволенію привлачитъ, якоже благотворенія благъ, даемыя требꙋющимъ: ибо страха ради бываемое ꙋгожденіе, преѡбразꙋемо есть ласканіе, притворенной чести именемъ прелщающе оному внимающихъ. Е т

Честно вправдꙋ есть ваше Царство, яко на сꙋпостаты ꙋбо показꙋетъ власть, послꙋшнымъ же, подаетъ человѣколюбіе. И побѣждающе оныхъ силою орꙋжія, безорꙋжною любовію своихъ побѣждаетъся. Елико бо звѣри и овчати средне, толико обоимъ отмѣняетъся различное. С и

Сꙋществомъ ꙋбо тѣлесѣ, равенъ е всякомꙋ человѣкꙋ царь: властію же достоинства, подобенъ е иже надъ всѣми Богꙋ. не имать бо на земли себе высочайшаго. Подобаетъ ꙋбо томꙋ и яко Богꙋ не гнѣватися, и яко смертнꙋ не възноситися: аще бо и образомъ Божіимъ почтенъ есть, но и прахꙋ перстномꙋ съплетъся, имже наꙋчаетъся, иже къ всѣмъ равенствꙋ. Т е

Пріемли иже блага совѣтовати хотящихъ, но не ласкати всегда тщащихся: Ѻви бо полезное съзираютъ въ истиннѣ: ѻви же, къ Л о

мна-

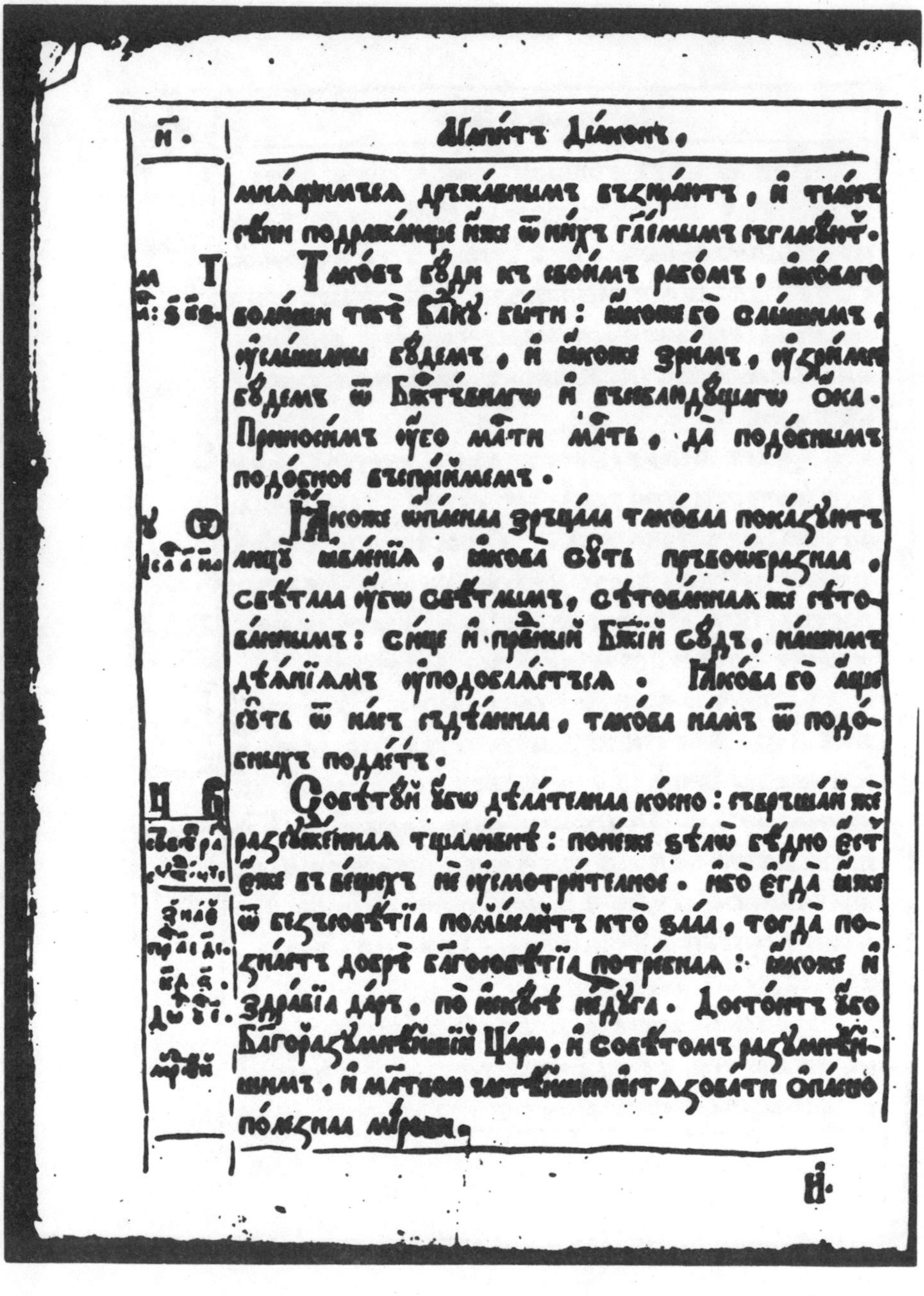
н҃.

Агапитъ Дїаконъ.

мнѧщимсѧ дръжавнымъ взираютъ, и тѣломъ свойми подражающе иже ѿ нихъ глаголемымъ вѣщаютъ.

Таковъ буди къ своимъ рабомъ, яковаго молиши тебѣ Бога быти: якоже бо слышимъ, услышани будемъ, и якоже зримъ, узримы будемъ ѿ всевидѧщаго и всенадзирающаго ока. Приносимъ убо мати мать, да подобнымъ подобное воспрїимемъ.

Якоже ѡпасная зерцала таковаѧ показуютъ лицу ѡбразы, якова суть первообразнаѧ, свѣтлаѧ убо свѣтлымъ, сѣтованнаѧ же сѣтованнымъ: сице и правый Бжїй судъ, нашимъ дѣянїямъ уподоблѧетсѧ. Якова бо аще суть ѿ насъ содѣѧннаѧ, такова намъ ѿ подобныхъ подаетъ.

Совѣтуй убо дѣлателнаѧ косно: соверша́й же разсмотренная тщаливѣ: понеже ѕѣлѡ бѣдно есть еже въ бѣдахъ не усмотрителное. Ибо егда иже ѿ безсовѣтїя помышлѧетъ кто ѕлаѧ, тогда познаетъ добрѣ благосовѣтїя потребнаѧ: якоже и здравїя даръ, по ѧвѣ недуга. Достоитъ убо Благоразумнѣйшїй Царю, и совѣтомъ разумнѣйшимъ, и мл҃твою частѣйшею испытовати ѡпасно полезнаѧ мірови.

Н.

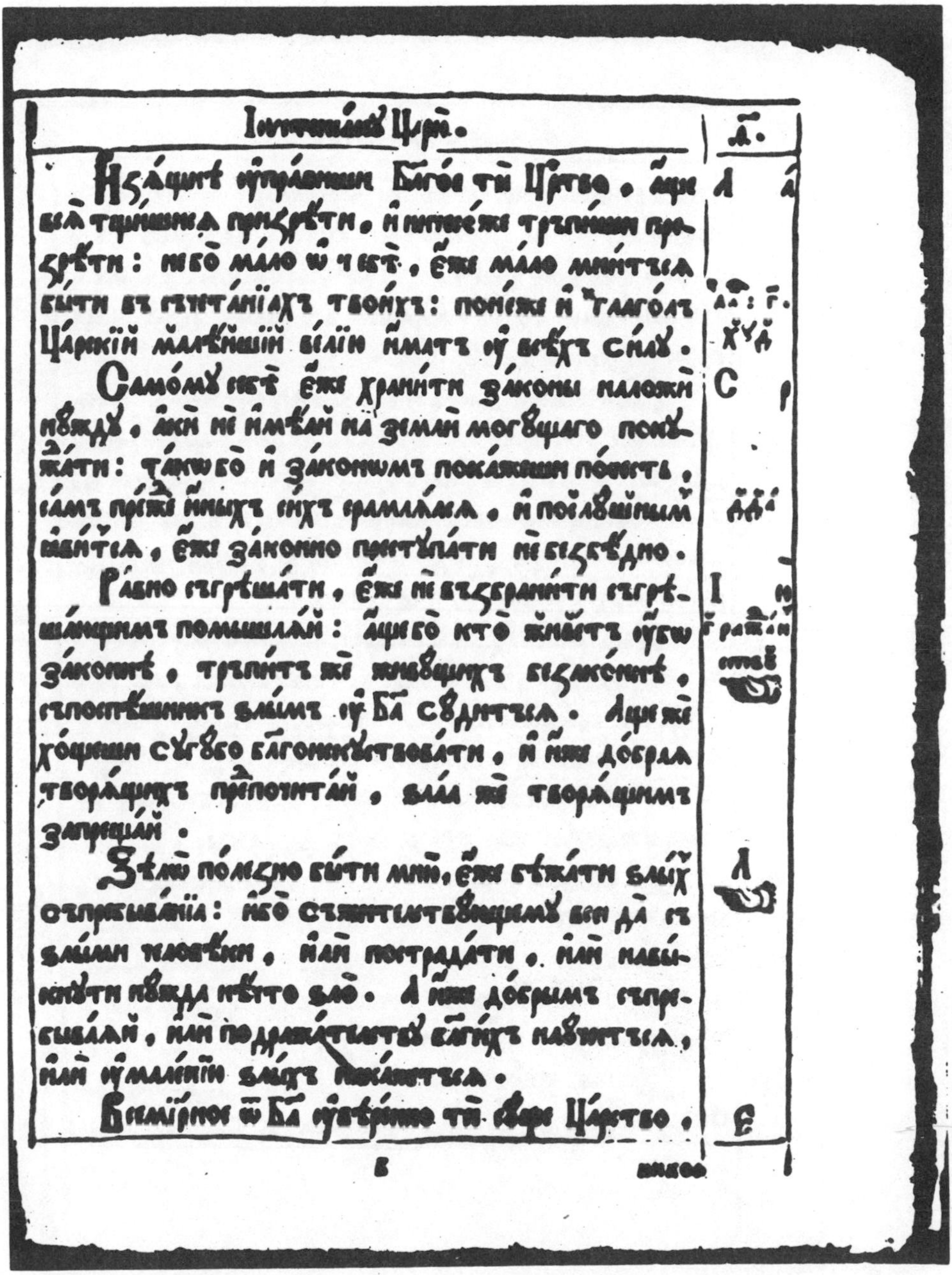
Іустиніанꙋ Црю.

Изрядное оуправленїи Богое ти Црство, аще
вся тщимшися прикрѣти, и ниже тръпнши про-
зрѣти: нибо мало ѿ чесѣ, еже мало мнитъся
быти въ съчетанїахъ твоихъ: понеже и глаголъ
Царскїй малѣйшїй велїю имать оу всѣхъ силꙋ.

Самомꙋ вѣсѣ еже хранити законы налоѫи
повждꙋ, аки не имѣвай на земли могꙋщаго пону-
ждати: такожбо и закономъ покаѧвши почесть,
самъ прежде иныхъ сихъ срамляюся, и поѧвльшимъ
являтъся, еже законно преступати небезбѣдно.

Равно съгрѣшати, еже не възбранити съгрѣ-
шающимъ помышлай: аще бо кто живетъ оубо
законнѣ, тръпитъ же живущихъ беззаконнѣ,
съпоспѣшникъ злымъ оу Ба сꙋдится. Аще же
хощеши съꙋщество благоникѣствовати, и иже добрая
творящихъ прѣпочитай, злая же творящимъ
запрещай.

Зѣло полезно быти мнѣ, еже бѣжати злыхъ
оупрѣбыванїя: ибо съ[illegible] всѣхъ да съ
злыми человѣки, или пострадати, или навы-
кнꙋти повсюда нѣчто зло. А иже добрымъ съпре-
бывалай, или подражати тѣмъ благихъ навыкнетъся,
или оумаленїи злыхъ покажется.

Всемирное ѿ Ба оувѣренное ти [illegible] Царство,

В

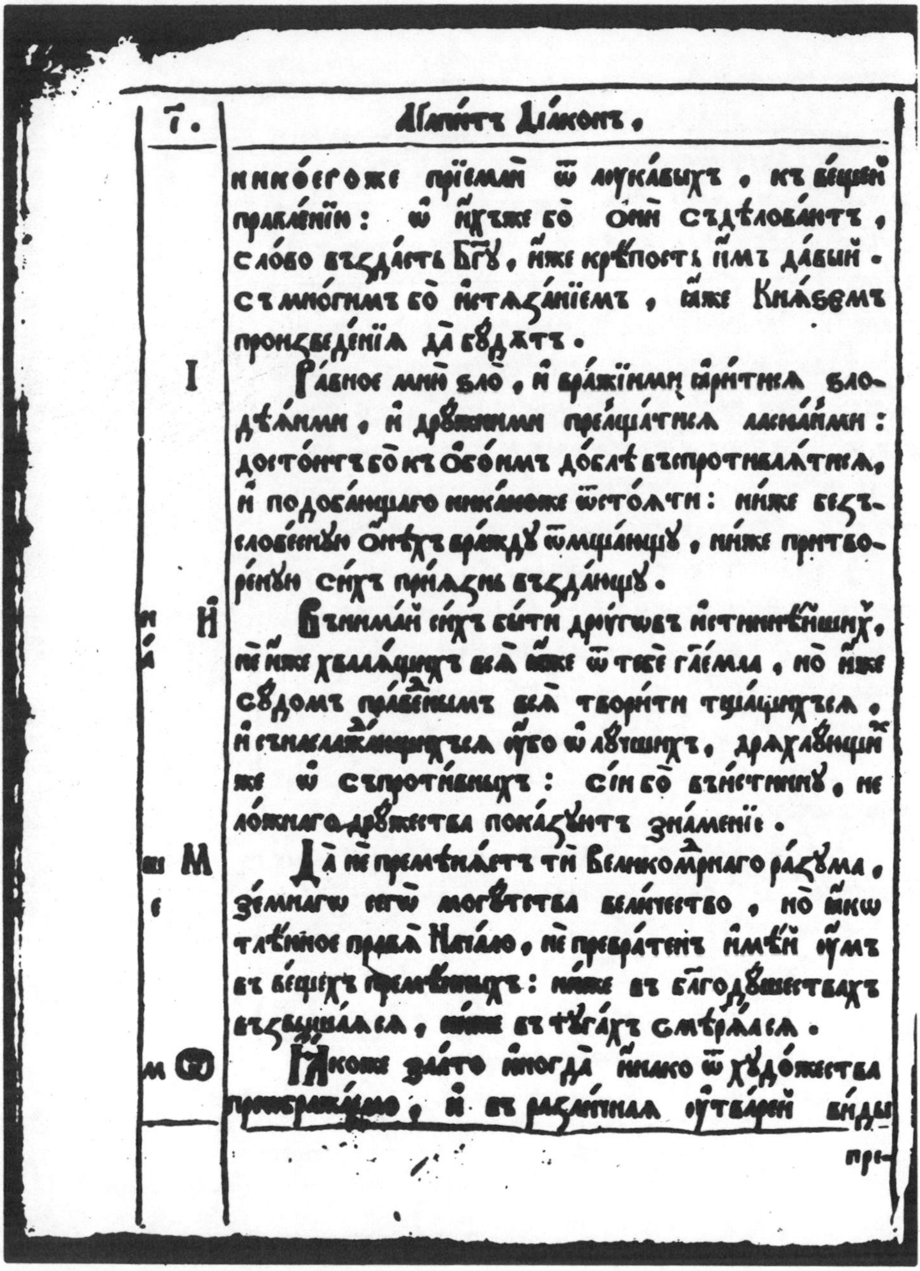

г. Агапитъ діаконъ.

никоегоже пріемлй ѿ лукавыхъ, къ вещей
правленію: ѿ нихже бо они съдѣловаютъ,
слово въздастъ Бгу, иже крѣпость имъ давый.
съ многимъ бо истязаніемъ, иже княземъ
произведеніа да будутъ.

I Равное мнѣ бло, и вражінмаѧ прѣтиса бло-
дѣяніи, и дружнимми прелщатиса ласкаями:
достоинъ бо къ обоимъ добле въпротиватиса,
и подобающаго никакоже ѿстояти: ниже безъ-
словесный онѣхъ вражду ѿмщающу, ниже притво-
реннѣй сихъ приязнь въздающу.

Н Вънимай сихъ быти другихъ истиннѣйшихъ,
не иже хвалящихъ вса иже ѿ тебе глемаа, но иже
судомъ праведнымъ вса творити тщащихся,
и сънаслаждающихся убо ѿ лучшихъ, досаждающи
же ѿ сътворенныхъ: сіи бо въистинну, не
ложнаго дружества показуютъ знаменіе.

М Да не премѣняетъ ти великомирнаго разума,
земнаго сего могутства величество, но яко
тлѣнное правлениа начало, не превратенъ имѣй умъ
въ вещехъ превеликихъ: ниже въ благодушествахъ
възношаласа, ниже въ тягахъ смѣраласа.

Ѡ Якоже злато иногда инако ѿ художества
преображаемо, и въ различнаа утварей виды
пре-

претворяемо, еже есть пребываетъ, и премѣненія не терпитъ: Такоже и ты Благопохвалнѣйшій Царю, иное от иныхъ пріемля начало, достигъ же и самую горнѣйшую честь, самъ пребываеши, не въ тѣхъ же вещехъ, неизмѣнное имѣя въ добрыхъ разумѣніе. митрові

Н у Неправдивъ тогда Царствовати крѣпце, егда не хотящими Царствуеши человѣки: еже бо неволею покаряемое, крамолитъ время пріемлюще: а еже свѣязи привязаній владѣемое, известное имать къ владѣющему благопокореніе. отверг(шимъ) ... благово(лен)ія

І І Да державу Царства сотвориши пріснопаматное, елико имаши гнѣвъ на погрѣшившихъ согрѣшившихъ, толико имѣти и на себе согрѣшившаго неправды. Никтоже бо можетъ сущаго на толицѣй власти наказовати, аще не размышленіе само от самаго согрѣшившаго подвигнится.

О о Иже велію власть пріемый, подателя власти да подражаетъ по силѣ. Аще бо нѣкако образъ носитъ иже надо всѣми Бога, и тѣмъ содержитъ сущаго надо всѣми Начала: въ семъ найпаче Бога подражаетъ, еже ничтоже вмѣняти от еже помиловати предпочтителнѣйше.

Ѵ ѵ Пяти злата и каменія честна благотворенія

в в богато-

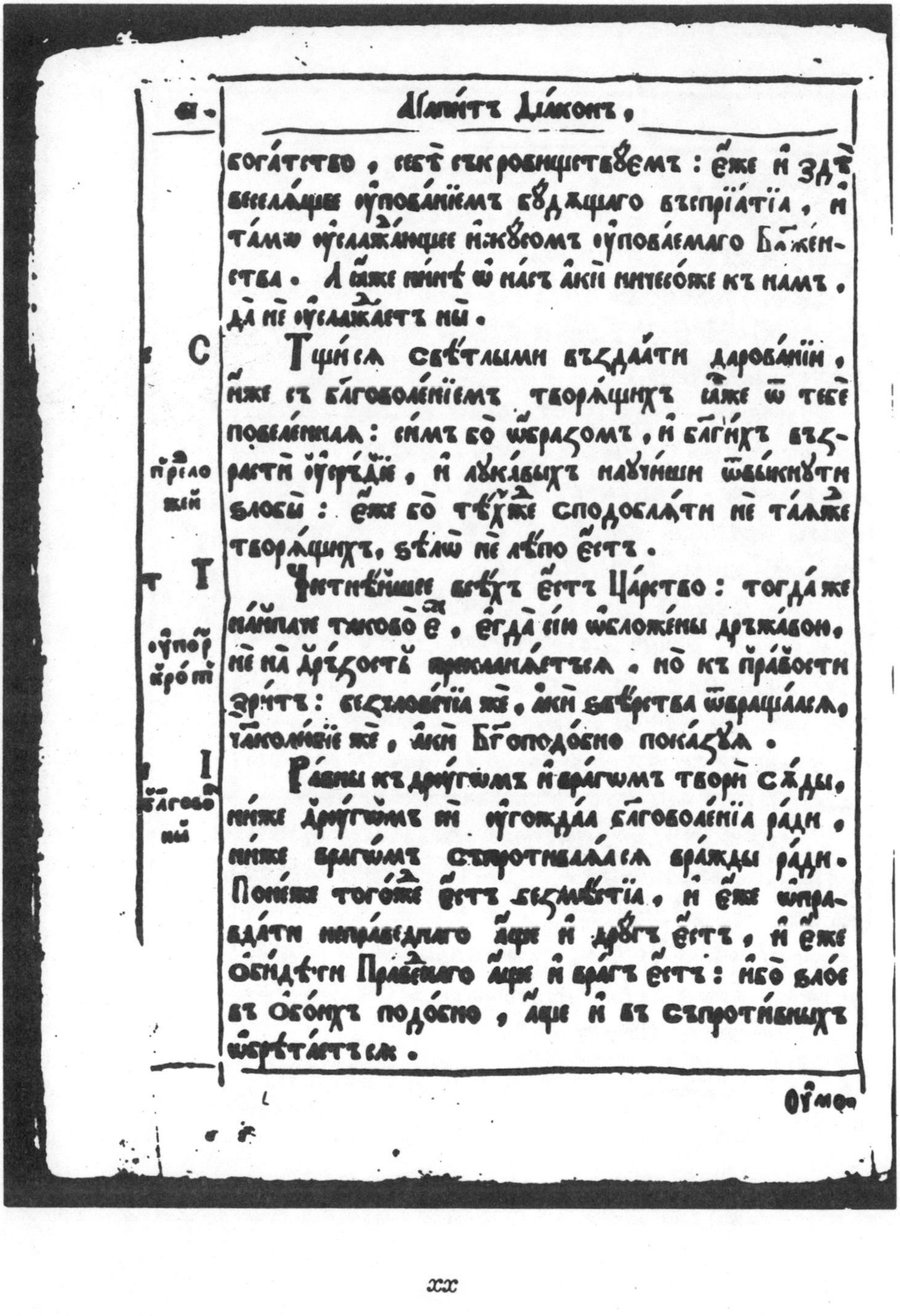

Агапитъ Дїаконъ,

богатство, себе сокровищствуемъ: еже и зде
веселящее упованїемъ будущаго восприятїя, и
тамо услаждающее искусомъ уповаемаго блажен-
ства. А еже нынѣ от насъ аки нитесоже къ намъ,
да не услаждаетъ ны.

Тщися свѣтлыми воздаяти дарованїи,
иже съ благоволенїемъ творящихъ яже от тебе
повелѣнная: симъ бо образомъ, и благихъ воз-
расти усердїе, и лукавыхъ научиши отвыкнути
злобы: еже бо тѣхже сподобляти не таяже
творящихъ, зѣло не лѣпо есть.

Честнѣйшее всѣхъ есть Царство: тогдаже
наипаче таково е, егда сии облажены державою,
не на дерзость преклоняетъся. но къ правости
зритъ: безсловесїя же, аки звѣрства отвращаяся,
чл҃колюбїе же, аки Бг҃оподобно показуя.

Равны къ другомъ и врагомъ твори суды,
ниже другомъ ни угождая благоволенїя ради,
ниже врагомъ сопротивляяся вражды ради.
Понеже тогоже есть безсловесїя, и еже опра-
вдати неправеднаго аще и другъ есть, и еже
обидѣти праведнаго аще и врагъ есть: ибо злое
въ обоихъ подобно, аще и въ сопротивныхъ
обрѣтается.

Оумо

Іустиніа́нꙋ Царю̑. | Гі.

Оумовнима́телнѣ Сꙋдїа́мъ достои́тъ послꙋ-
ша́ти веще́й: неꙋдо́бно бо̑ е̑стъ Пра́вды обрѣ́теніе.
оудо́бнѣ отбѣга́ющей ѿ и҆́же не ѕѣлѡ̀ внима́ющихъ.
а҆́ще же̑ и҆ гла̑ющихъ ѡстава́ше си́лность, и҆ гла́емыхъ
презрѣ́вше оувѣща́ніе въ глꙋбинꙋ̀ оумышле́ніа себѣ̀
вло́житъ: си́це пострѣпа́тъ е҆́же ѿ ни́хъ некомое.
и҆ сꙋгꙋ́баго грѣха̑ оубѣ́жатъ: ни́же са́ми до́брое пре-
да́юще, ни́же и҆̑нымъ то̑ твори́ти и҆сколающе.

Равночи́селныѧ ѕвѣзда́мъ а҆̑ще стѧ́жеши
и҆справле́ніа, нико́гдаже побѣди́ши Бж҃їю бл҃гть.
Е҆́лика бо̑ а҆̑ще кто̑ прино́ситъ Бꙋ҃, ѿ е҆го́выхъ,
е҆го́ваѧ прино́ситъ е҆мꙋ̀: И҆ ꙗ҆́кѡ не оудо́бъ е҆́стъ
превъзы́йти на̑ Сл҃нци свое́й сѣ́нь. предваря́ющꙋю
при́сно а҆̑ще и҆ ѕѣлѡ̀ спѣша́щагося, си́це и҆ не̑ пре-
въсходи́мꙋю Бж҃їю бл҃гты́ню, бл҃готворе́ніами не̑
превъзы́йдꙋтъ ча̑щи.

Не̑ и҆знꙋри́телно е҆́стъ бл҃готворе́ніа бога́тство:
внегда́ бо да́ѧти прие́млетъсѧ. и҆ внегда̑ расточа́ти
събира́етъсѧ. Сі́а и҆мѣ́ай въ дш҃и твое́й Бога́то
дарова́ти Царю̑, дава́й всѣ́мъ неща́дно, прося́щимъ
ѿ тебе̑: не́нщетна бо̑ и҆мѣ́еши ѿ си́хъ въздаѧ́ніа,
е҆гда̑ пойдетъ вре́мѧ дѣ́ломъ въздаѧ́ніа.

Ма́ніемъ Бж҃їимъ Ца́рство прі́емъ, подража́й
того̑ дѣ́лы бл҃ги́ми, зане̑ ѿ ни́хъ бл҃готвори́ти

в Г мог-

Н ... Правдꙋ неꙋдоб обрѣтенїа
І ... : бл... непобѣдимъ никогда.
А а
Н

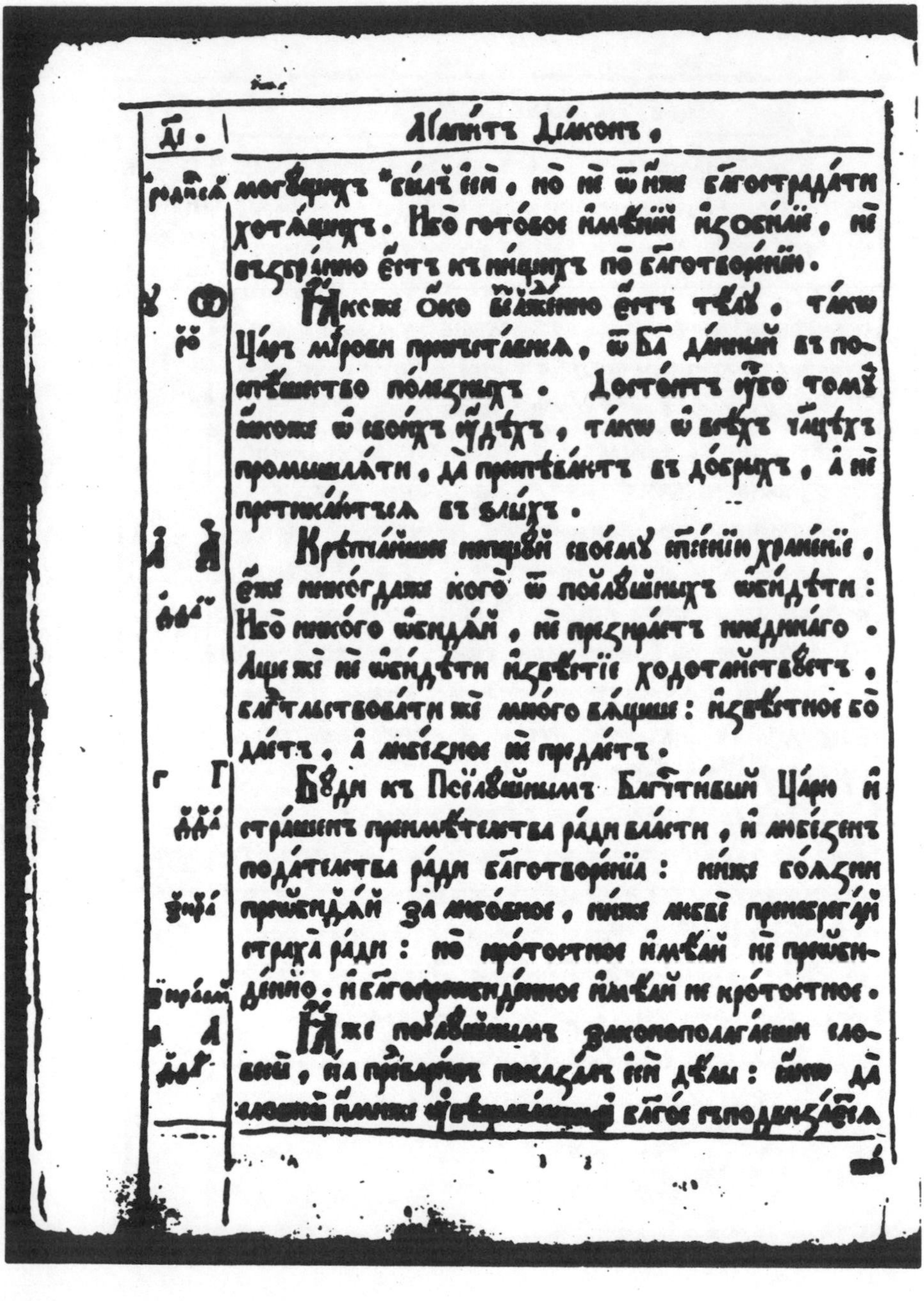

Агапитъ Діаконъ.

могꙋщихъ быти есй, но не ѿ иныхъ благострадати хотѧщихъ. Нбо готовое имѣнїй изобилїе, не возбранно есть къ нищихъ по благотворенїю.

Якоже око ѡбложенно есть тѣлꙋ, такѡ Царь мїрови приставленъ, ѿ Бга данный въ поспѣшество полезныхъ. Достоитъ ꙋбо томꙋ якоже ѿ своихъ ꙋдѣхъ, такѡ ѿ всѣхъ тщетхъ промышлѧти, да преспѣваютъ въ добрыхъ, а не претыкаютсѧ въ злыхъ.

Крѣпчайшее наипервѣй своемꙋ спасенїю храненїе, еже никогдаже кого ѿ посланшихъ ѡбидѣти: Нбо никого ѡбидѧй, не презираетъ никаднаго. Аще же не ѡбидѣти извѣстїе ходотайствꙋетъ, благодарствовати же много блаще: извѣстное бо даетъ, а любезное не предаетъ.

Бꙋди къ повелѣвшимъ благоѧтнѣйшїй Царю и страшенъ премѣнетелства ради власти, и любезенъ подателства ради благотворенїа: ниже болѣзни превиндѧй за любовное, ниже любве пренебрегай страха ради: но кротостное имѣѧй не превзыденно, и благоприемлемое имѣяй не кротостное.

Яже повелѣвшимъ законоположенїя словеса, на прѣварѣ показанъ есй дѣлы: якоже да словесный планиже ꙋпреїраблѧемый благое сподобилса

Іустиніану Царю. | еі

жи́тїе. Та́ко бо бл҃гопокорена ѿбы́тъсѧ твоѧ̀ дръ-
жа́ва и҆ гл҃ющи дѣла́телем, и҆ дѣла́ющи словесем.
Ва́щшее ли́бо Царю пре́тихїи, и҆же прїа́ти ѿ П п
тебѣ бл҃гти ма́лщихъ, не́жели тща́щихъсѧ да́ры
тебѣ приноси́ти: ѻнѣмъ бо длъжникъ възда́нїа
съставлѧ́ешиса, сїи же тебѣ Бг҃а длъжника творѧ̀,
приклонѧ́ющаго ѿиже къ ни́мъ бываемаа, и҆ възда-
ющаго бл҃ги́ми възда́нми. Бг҃олюбе́зный и҆ тако-
любный твоӣ ра́зумъ.
Слънцу оубѡ дѣло є҆ е҆же ѡ҆свѣща́ти лꙋчами Н н
тва́рь: Царе́вы же добродѣтель, е҆же ми́ловати
требующихъ: ѻнаго же свѣтлѣйшїй е҆сть Благо-
утробный Царь, ѻнобо оуступаетъ въспрїемнице-
ствомъ но́щи: ѻвъ же, не оуступаетъ въпохище-
нїи злыхъ, но свѣтомъ истинны изобличаетъ
та́йныда непра́вды.
И҆же пре́жде тебе Царе́й власть оукраша́ше: Ты же Т т
сїю Дръжа́вне. свѣтлѣйшую сътворилъ еси, ти́хо-
стїю растворѧ́а власти вели́чество, и҆ бл҃гтїю побѣ-
жда́а приносѧ́щихъ ти стра́хъ. Тѣмже при-
ста́нищу твоеа ти́хости, вси прите́каша и҆же ма́ти
требующїи и҆ нищеты волнѣ свобо́жшиса, бл҃гры́ла
ти пѣ́нїи възсыла́ютъ.
Вели́ко могуститкомъ всѧ̀ превъсходи́ши. О о

твоа

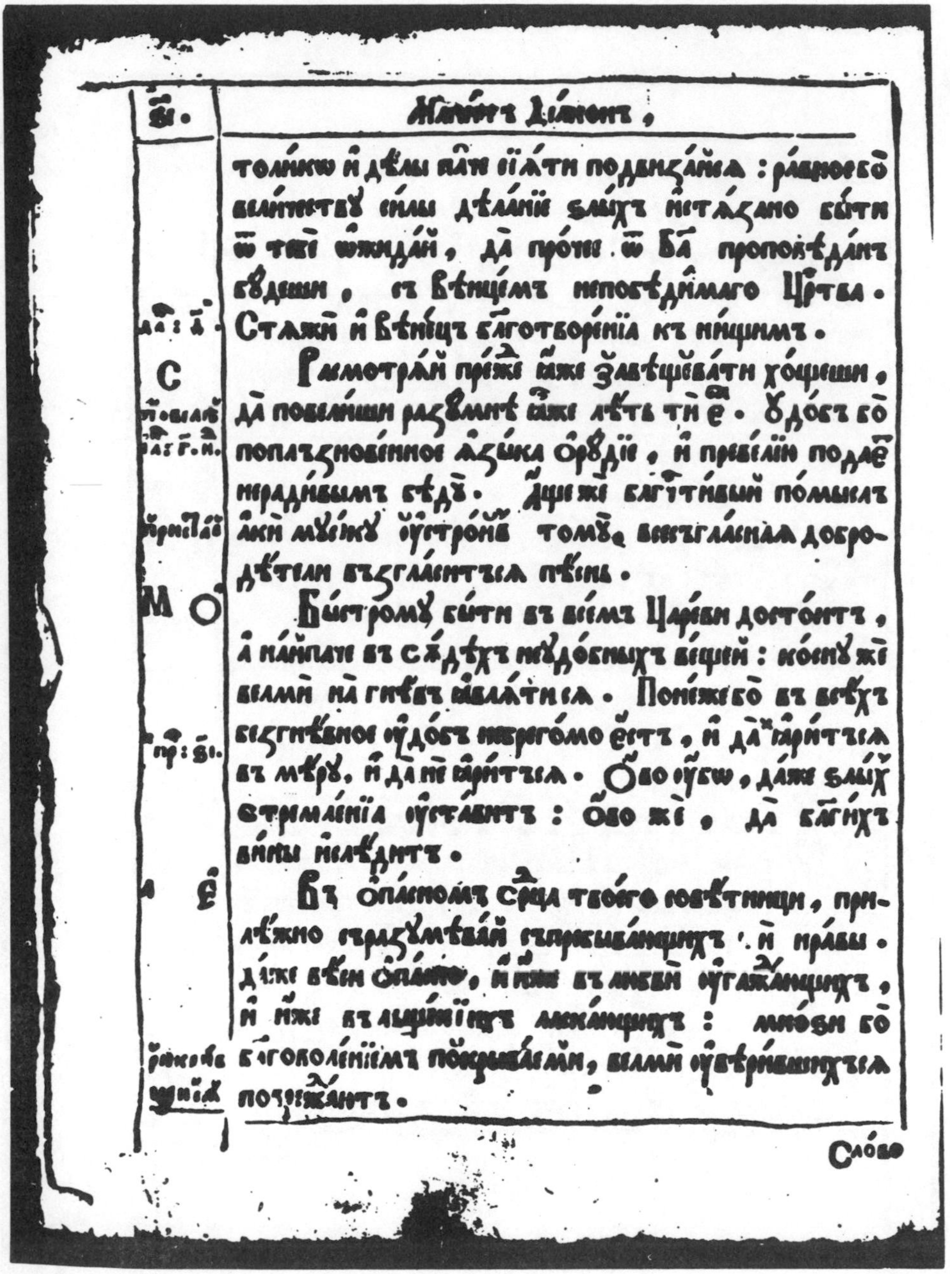

Агапитъ Дiаконъ.

толико и дѣлы паче сiяти подвизайся : равно бо
величеству силы дѣланiе благихъ истязано быти
от тебе ожидай, да противу от Бога проповѣдаинъ
будеши, съ вѣнцемъ непобѣдимаго Царства.
Стяжи и вѣнецъ благотворенiя къ нищимъ.

Разсмотряй прежде иже завѣщевати хощеши,
да повелиши развмотрѣ иже лѣть ти есть. Удобъ бо
поползновенное языка орудiе, и превелiю подаетъ
нерадивымъ бѣду. Аще же благочтивый помыслъ
аки мусiку устроиши тому, всесогласная добродѣтели возгласитъся пѣснь.

Быстрому быти въ всемъ Цареви достоитъ,
а наипаче въ судѣхъ неудобныхъ вещей: ко сему же
зѣло не на гнѣвъ обладатися. Понеже бо въ всѣхъ
безгнѣвное удобъ недерегомо есть, и да каритъся
въ мѣру, и да не каритъся. Ово убо, да же злыхъ
стремленiя уставитъ: ово же, да благихъ
вины исслѣдитъ.

Въ опасномъ сердца твоего совѣтници, при-
лежно сразумѣвай сопротивляющихъ, и правы.
даже вѣси опасно, и иже въ любви утаевающихъ,
и иже въ лицемѣрiи лишающихъ : многи бо
благоколѣнiемъ покрываеми, зѣло увѣрившихся
поврежаютъ.

Слово

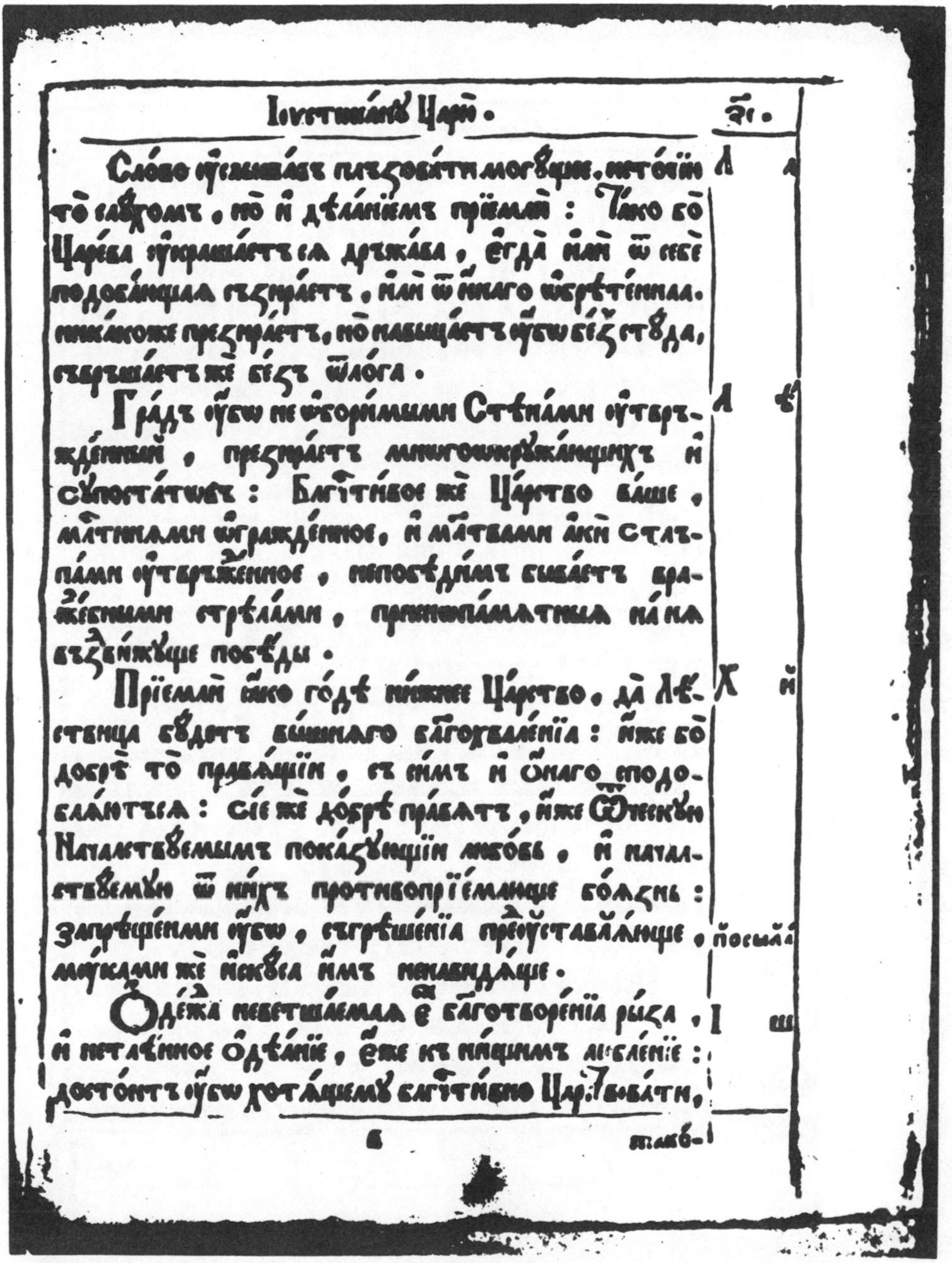

Іустиніанꙋ Царю. ві.

Слово ѹбѣжавшаѧ пръзовати могꙋщее, нетокмо то слꙋхомъ, но и дѣланием приемлѧй: Ꙗко бо Царева ѹкрашаетъ сѧ държава, егда или ѿ себе подобающаѧ съзираетъ, или ѿ иного обрѣтеннаѧ. никакоже презираетъ, но навыцаетъ ѹбо без стꙋда, съвръшаетъ же безъ ѿлога. Л а

Градъ ѹбо не оборимыми стѣнами ѹтвръжденный, презираетъ многоокрꙋжающихъ и сѹпостатовъ: Благочестивое же Царство ваше, молитвами огражденное, и молитвами аки стлъпами ѹтвръжденное, непобѣдимъ бываетъ вражиими стрѣлами, приснопамѧтныѧ на на възвѣнжшѧ побѣды. Л в

Приемлѧй ѹбо Господь нижнее Царство, да лѣствица бꙋдетъ вышнего благохваленія: иже бо добрѣ то правѧщіи, съ ними и оного сподобляютъ сѧ: сіе же добрѣ правѧтъ, иже отеческꙋю наслѣдꙋемымъ показꙋющіи любовь, и наслѣдꙋемꙋю ѿ нихъ противоприемлющіе болѣзнь: запрещеніемъ ѹбо, съгрѣшенія предѹставлѧюще, мꙋками же искꙋса имъ неввидѧще. Х и посла

Одежда невѣтшаемаѧ е благотворенія риза, и нетлѣнное одѣяніе, еже къ нищимъ млъбленіе: достоитъ ѹбо хотѧщемꙋ благочестно Царьствовати, I ш

в таков-

нг. Агапитъ діаконъ,

таковыми одеждами украсити душу: Нищелюбіа бо
одеянъ Порфурою, и Нбснаго Цртва сподобится.

С Скипетръ Цртвіа ѿ Ба пріемъ, смотри како
угодиши иже ти давшему то: И яко на всѧ тѧки
ѿ него препочтенный, вящше всехъ спешися пре-
почтити его. Сіа же почесть вменяетъся пре-
велія, аще яко себе иже ѿ него създанныя блюдеши,
и яко длъгъ възложеніе благотворенія исплъняеши.

Т Тещи чсо къ вышней помощи всякъ длъженъ
естъ тѧкъ, иже спсенія желаяй: Царь же првее
всехъ, яко пекійся ѿ всехъ. ѿ Ба бо хранимый
и супостатомъ одолеваетъ добле, и своихъ
утвръждаетъ тщаливне.

О Бъ убо никогоже требуетъ, Царь же единаго
Ба: подражаяй проче, иже никогоже требующаго,
и нещадно даваяй просящимъ млть, не ѿпасно
подаяніи испытуя ѿ своихъ рабехъ, но всемъ подаа еже
къ житію прошенія: много бо лутше естъ до-
стойныхъ ради миловати, и недостойная, нежели
достойныя лишати, недостойныхъ ради.

С Прощенія проса съгрешеніемъ, Прости и ты,
иже въ тѧ съгрешающимъ, зане оставленіи про-
тиво даетъся оставленіе: и еже къ клевретомъ
нашимъ примиреніе, къ Бу дръзновеніе и привоеніе.

Іоустиніанꙋ Царю. Д і.

Достоитъ иже непорочно Црьствовати хотѧщемꙋ сѧ, Д д
и ꙗже ѿ внѣ безславіа хранитисѧ, и себе прежде оныхъ
стыдѣтисѧ: да еже ꙗвленнѣ съгрѣшати оныхъ
ради оудръжитъсѧ, и еже наединѣ съгрѣшати пресвѧтыи
ѿ себе възбранитъсѧ. Аще бо пославшимъ срама дїакон
достоины ꙗвлѧтъсѧ, много вѧщше Царь достоинъ того бꙋдетъ.

Невѣжды оубо быти злобѣ глю, еже творити І і
зла и мꙋцѣ достоинаа: Начальника же лꙋкавство,
еже творити добраа и спасенію виновнаа. Небо
злыхъ ѿтꙋжденіа ѡправдаетъ Властителѧ, но
добрыхъ подаанїе, вѣнчаетъ сицеваго. Да не тъчїю
протее помышлѧетъ еже оудалитисѧ злобы, но
да и правдꙋ пріати потщитсѧ.

Санѡвъ свѣтлостьми неоумолѧетъ сѧ Л л
смръть: на всѣхъ бо всеꙗдныѧ своѧ налагаетъ страшна
зоубы. Тѣмже прежде оного неоумолимаго при-
шествіа, преложимъ на нбса имѣніи богатство.
Никтоже бо ꙗже въ мірѣ събираетъ, тамо ѿшедъ
ѿнашаетъ, но вса на земли ѡставль нагъ слово
полагаетъ ѡ житіи своемъ.

Господинъ оубо е надъ всѣми Царь: рабъ же К к
съ всѣми е Бжїй. тогда же наипаче наречетсѧ
Господинъ, егда самъ себѣ владѣетъ, и безмѣстнии

в г слов. Агапитъ Дїаконъ.

властемъ не работаетъ: но съпоборника имѣѧ
благочтиваа помысла непобѣдимаго самодръжца
безсловесныхъ страстей, иже всѣхъ матерь похоти
вооружїемъ цѣломудрїа низлагаетъ.

о О Имже образомъ сѣнни тѣлесемъ послѣдуютъ,
сице душамъ грѣси сшествуютъ, явственѣ
дѣанїа изъобразующе. Сего ради нѣсть на
судѣ отрещися: сами бо когождо свѣди-
тельствуютъ вещи, не гласа испущающе, но такова
являюще, якова же ими сдѣлашася.

н N Корабля по мори шествующаго подражаетъ
шествїе, краткое настоящаго житїа устроенїе,
Пенющаѧ нас иже того пловцевъ лстяще, и помалу
потлазающе теченїе, и въ свой когождо пред-
путь бываюющи конецъ. Аще убо сїа суть, мимо-
текущемъ мимоходящаа мїру вещи, и прѣтекущемъ
на ятте въ вѣки вѣкомъ пребывающаа.

ѕ О Грядый и превъзносливый человѣкъ, даже
аки инецъ высокорожный възноситъся, но да
помышляетъ плѣти съставъ, и да упокоитъ
срѣдца превъзношенїе. Аще бо и бысть начальникъ
на земли. да не невѣсть быв от земля, от
прѣсти на Престолъ възходя, и въ онъ по времени
нисходя.

Зрящеса

Іустиніану Царю. | ка.

Тщися убо, непобѣдимый Царю, и якоже на лѣствицу восходити начинающіи, не прежде ставают на горнемъ степени, донелѣже верха достигнутъ степенемъ: такоже и ты имѣй добрыхъ восхода, яко да и вышнего Царствія созданіе воспріимлеши: еже ти да подастъ Хс҃, съ супружницею Цр҃тъ, Царствующим и Царствуемымъ, во вѣки: Аминь. С

КОНЕЦЪ.

Изложеніе поучителному Агапита діакона къ Іустиніану Кесарю, иже у Еллинехъ царскій (нарицаемый) свиток.

Лѣто бытія міра, з҃рмв. Індікта, ді. Слнцу кр҃у, кд. Луны ді. Клю҃, Х. Високостное. Лѣто отъ ржс҃тва, в.

е: Б: м: Ї

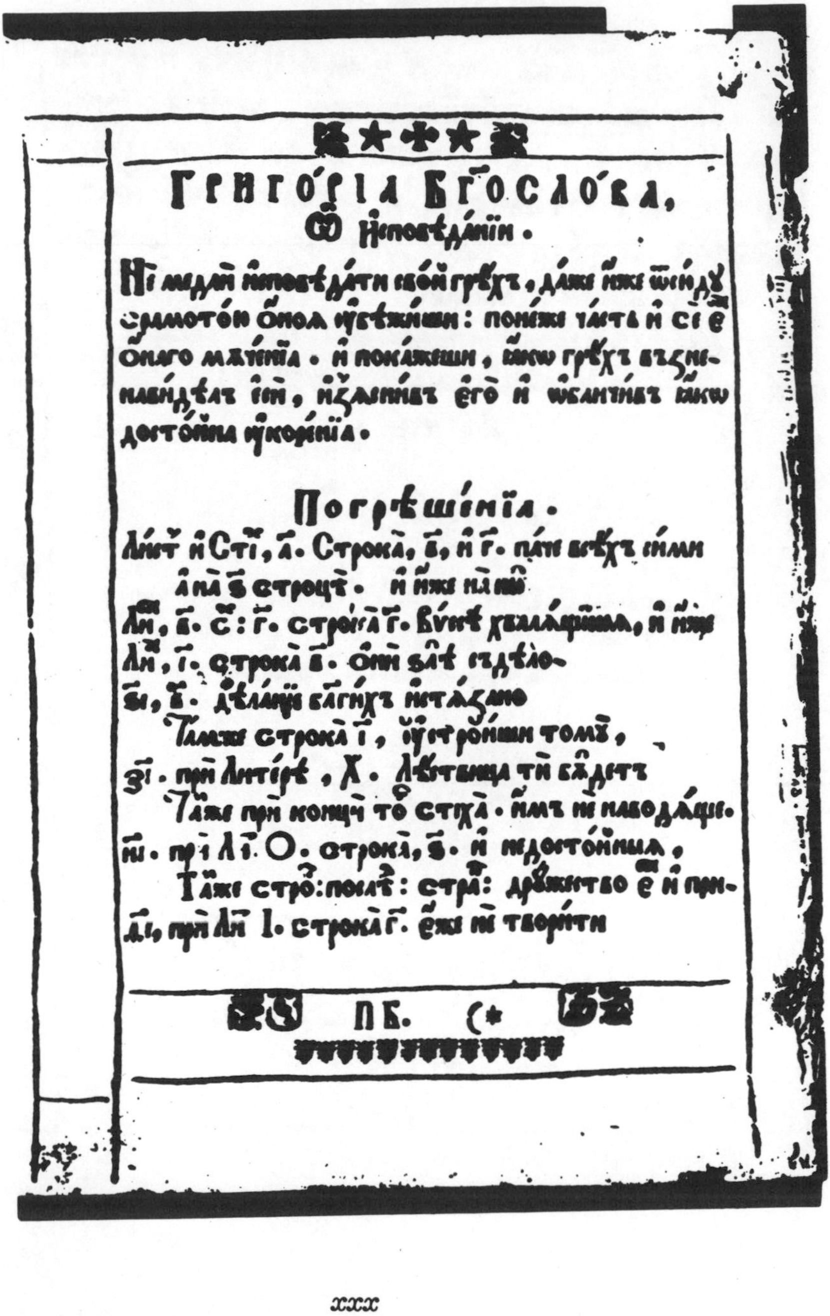

ГРИГОРІА БГОСЛОВА,
Ѿ исповѣданіи.

Не медли исповѣдати свой грѣхъ, даже иже ѿ сихъ срамотой оного избѣжиши: понеже часть и се есть оного мученія. и покажеши, яко грѣхъ возненавидѣлъ еси, изъявивъ его и обличивъ яко достойна укоренія.

Погрѣшенія.

Лист и Сті, а. Строка, в, и г. пате всѣхъ силли
ана в строцѣ. и иже на нѣ
Ли, в. с: г. строка г. вѵнѣ хвалареника, и иже
Ли, і. строка в. они бл҃е сздѣло-
ви, в. дѣлающе благихъ истазано
Таже строка і, устроиши тому,
зі. при литерѣ, х. лѣствица ти будетъ
Таже при концѣ то стиха. имъ не наводаще.
ни. при лі. О. строка, з. и недостойница,
Таже стро: послѣ: стра: дружество е и при-
лі, при ли і. строка г. еже не творити

ПБ.

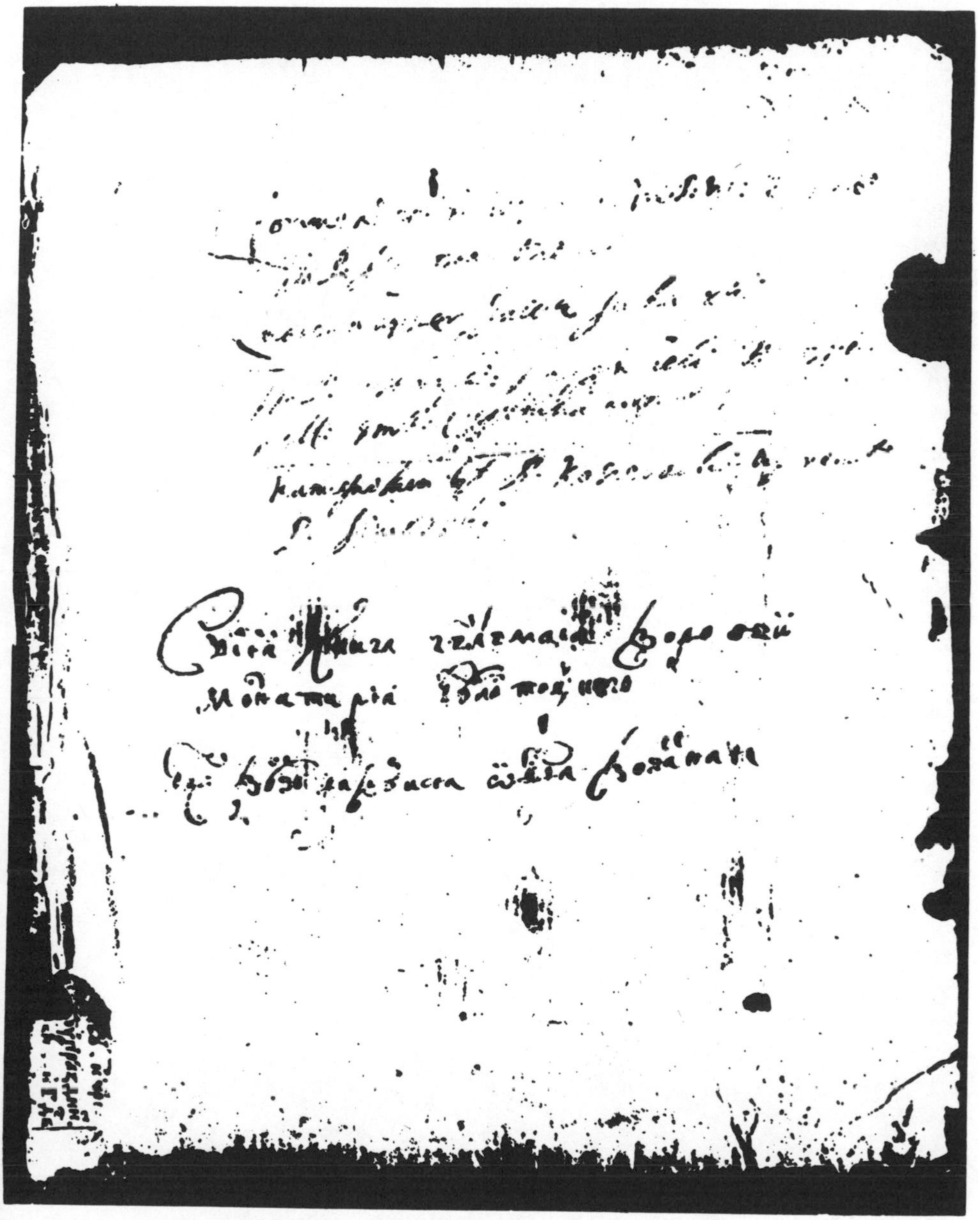

XXX

Preface to F. Westberg, *Die Fragmente des Toparcha Goticus*

I

Exactly one hundred years ago, Academician Kunik ranked the so-called Fragments of Toparcha Gothicus, at that time called *Anonymus Tauricus*, among "first-rate sources of early Russian history."[1] Very little — only six items — had been written on the Fragments between their publication by Karl-Benedikt (Charles-Benoît) Hase in 1819 and Kunik's verdict of 1871. And even these few items, except for Gedeonov's remarks of 1862, were either inconsequential, or inspired by Kunik himself, who had known our text since 1846. After 1871, however, secondary literature on the Fragments assumed impressive proportions. The new phase started with Kunik's own long study of 1874, followed by other statements of his, both published and unpublished, which registered his changing views on the subject. Soon, other leading Russian historians and Byzantinists, some surpassing Kunik in stature, took up the challenge of the Fragments: Ilovajskij, Vasil'evskij, Uspenskij, and in our century, Vasiliev and Levčenko; occasionally, a distinguished foreigner, such as Tomaschek or Hruševs'kyj, would join the company.

The popularity of the subject has continued unabated in the most recent past: between 1958 and 1970, some twenty-five articles, by Russian, Bulgarian, Romanian, or Greek authors, were devoted to it entirely or mentioned it in passing.[2] This volume of scholarly literature might

1. A.A. Куник, "О Записке безъимянного таврического (Anonymus Tauricus)", Отчет о четырнадцатом присуждении наград Графа Уварова 25 сентяб. 1871 года (1872), pp. 106-110, esp. p. 108. — The following abbreviations shall be used in this Preface: BB (in the text, *VV*) = Византийский Временник; Записки АН = Записки Императорской Академии Наук по историко-филологическому отделению; ЖМНП = Журнал Министерства Народного Просвещения.

2. A complete bibliography of works on the Fragments subsequent to the present reprint and its reworking by Westberg in BB, 15 (1908), can be compiled on

seem astonishing in view of the brevity of the Greek text, which amounts to not quite twelve columns in the present reprint (pp. 14-26). The scholarly interest in our text is easier to explain, however, if we consider the tantalizing promises held out by the Fragments themselves. They allude to a mysterious ruler; they speak of two (or is it three?) kinds of no less mysterious barbarians; they contain astronomical indications, and refer to certain placenames, unfortunately few in number, that either are known from other sources, even if it is difficult to localize them, or are quite unknown.

Of all the studies dealing with the Fragments, the most thorough and convenient is Friedrich Westberg's re-edition of the Greek text, accompanied by several translations and a commentary. This is the present reprint.

We know little about its author. He was born in 1864 (the very year in which Hase, the Fragments' discoverer, died) and may have belonged to a family which provided Riga with members of its German municipal council down to the late nineteenth century.[3] He wrote on four groups of topics: Oriental sources concerning the Slavs; the Longobards; our Fragments and subjects related to them; and — unexpectedly — the chronology and topography of the Old and New Testaments. On several occasions, he published a study first in German and then republished it (in a slightly altered form) in Russian. His work on the Fragments followed the same pattern; the German version, reprinted here, dates from 1901; the Russian variant, somewhat enlarged, appeared in 1908.[4] Even with such doublets, Westberg's bibliography contains a mere dozen positions, all dating from the years 1898-1913.[5] No details are available

---

the basis of *A Bibliographical Note* printed as Appendix I. in my fully documented study of the Fragments, cf. *Dumbarton Oaks Papers*, 25, (1971). This *Note* gives references to selected works and to *raisonnées* and simple bibliographies prior to 1958; it also lists all items devoted to the Fragments between 1958 and 1971.

3. Inferred from G. Westberg, *Deutschland und das Baltikum. Ein genealogischer Versuch* (Hamburg, 1921), p. 14.

4. BB, 15 (1908), 71-132; 227-286.

5. "Ibrâhîm-ibn-Ja'kûb's Reisebericht über die Slavenlande aus dem Jahre 965," Записки АН, 3, 4 (1898); "Beiträge zur Klärung orientalischer Quellen über Osteuropa," Известия Имп. Академии Наук, 11, 4 (1899), 211-245; 275-314; the present reprint; Комментарий на записку Ибрагима ибн-Якуба о Славянах [= Имп. Академия Наук, истор-филол. отд., submitted at the meeting of March 21, 1901] (1903) (a reworking of "Reisebericht"); "Zur

to me on his scholarly activity between 1913 and his death in 1920.[6]

Under the circumstances, we must extract information on Westberg's scholarly profile and biography from his own writings and from those by his reviewers. Topics which Westberg treated throughout his career were a bit too varied, even disparate, for a regular member of the academic profession. He was more adept in tackling concrete scholarly difficulties, whatever their content may have been, and trying out congenial procedures — such as computing calendar dates, land distances, and using astronomy — on them, than in pursuing a given historical subject for its own sake. Westberg's mind was that of a problem-solver, and the Fragments may have attracted him precisely because they were a puzzle which had withstood the probings of scholars in the past.

⟨viii⟩ It seems that Westberg never attained professorial rank. Between 1890 and 1915 he was Senior Teacher of History and Geography in the town *Realschule* of Riga; he was a student of medieval Russian and German history, rather than an Orientalist, although he acquainted himself with the principles of Arabic in order to work on Ibrahim-ibn-Ja'kub and must have known some Hebrew; he possessed "notions of cosmography;" in his opinions on the origins of Rus', he was a Normanist (this was not surprising, considering his German background)[7] —

Wanderung der Langobarden," Записки АН, 6, 5 (1904); "Zur Topographie des Herodot. I," *Klio*, 4 (1904), 182-192; Zur Topographie des Herodot. II." *ibidem*, 6 (1906), 259-268 (mostly about Scythia and the Crimea); "О Житии св. Стефана Сурожского," ВВ, 14 (1907), 227-236; "Записка готского топарха," *ibidem*, 15 (1908), 71-132; 227-286 (a reworking of the present Reprint); "К анализу восточных источников о Восточной Европе," ЖМНП, N.S., 13 (January-February, 1908), 364-412; *ibidem*, 14 (March, 1908), 1-52 (a reworking of "Beiträge"); *Die Biblische Chronologie nach Flavius Josephus und das Todesjahr Jesu* (Leipzig, 1910); *Zur Neutestamentlichen Chronologie und Golgothas Ortslage* (Leipzig, 1911) (Jesu's date: 12 B. C. — April 3, 33 A. D.); Review of K. Dieterich's *Byzantinische Quellen zur Länder- und Völkerkunde*, BB, 20 (1913), 21-23. Cf. *Byzantinische Zeitschrift*, 8 (1899), 581-2; 9 (1900), 706; 10 (1901) 657-58; 12 (1903), 694; 17 (1908), 627-28; 18 (1909), 647; 19 (1910), 566; 20 (1911), 550; 22 (1913), 613; *Die biblische Chronologie...* has Westberg's bibliography after p. 202. — Westberg also contributed to *The Jewish Encyclopedia*.

6. Cf. *Die Religion in Geschichte und Gegenwart*, 5 (2nd ed.; 1931), col. 1882, s.v. Westberg, Friedrich.

7. Cf. Записки АН, 6, 2 (1902), 21; ВВ, 15 (1908), 72; Известия Имп. Академии Наук, 4 (1899), 219.

but above all, he was a protégé, devotee and follower of the eccentric antiquarian, "Protestant monk," and life-time student of the Fragments, academician Arist Aristovič Kunik.[8] Westberg discussed with Kunik matters pertaining to Ibrahim-ibn-Ja'kub and followed his views on that author;[9] and his conception of the Fragments' meaning was largely that of Kunik.[10]

In 1900, Westberg won the minor Uvarov prize, worth five hundred rubles, for his study of Ibrahim.[11] Apparently encouraged, he entered the competition once more in 1902 with his Russian reworking of the Commentary to the Fragments. This time, he had to be satisfied with honorable mention.[12] The jury did no injustice to Westberg, for he excelled more through industriousness, exemplified by his extensive correspondence with other scholars in the field, whose replies he quoted, and through fullness of coverage, exemplified by the excessive number of astronomical charts appended to his study, than through critical acumen.

For all that, bad luck may have marred Westberg's second attempt at the Uvarov prize. In the text submitted to the jury, he criticized the famous Byzantinist Feodor Uspenskij for explaining the Fragments through "hypotheses overly bold and often contradicted by historical evidence."[13] This stricture was justified, but Westberg could not have

8. Cf. Vasil'evskij's obituary of Kunik in Известия Имп. Академии Наук, 10, 3 (March, 1899), xv-xxvi, esp. pp. xv, xxv.

9. Записки АН, 6, 2 (1902), 220, 229: cf. ЖМНП, N.S., 14 (March, 1908), 35: незабвенный академик Куник.

10. The date of the Fragments was 963 [Kunik said: shortly before 965]; at that time, three powers vied for influence on the territory governed by the Toparch: the Khazars [Kunik's barbarians], the Grand Prince of Kiev [Kunik's prince] and the Byzantine Emperor [obvious]. "How wonderfully does it all fit Tauria [Kunik's locale of the Fragments] in the tenth century!" (Cf. the present reprint, pp. 6, 80; BB, 15 [1908], 77). This conception was not the one offered by Kunik either in 1871 (when he dated the Fragments to 940) or towards the end of his life (when he placed them in Vladimir's time), but the one Kunik presented in his basic article of 1874.

11. Cf. Записки АН, 6, 2 (1902), 21-24; 219-234 (reviews by Baron v. Rosen and T. D. Florinskij).

12. Записки АН, 6, 7 (1904), 14-16.

13. I assume that this criticism stood in the manuscript text which Westberg submitted to the jury, since it occurs both in the present reprint, anterior to the competition (p. 11), and in the reworking printed subsequently to it: cf. BB, 15 (1908), 81.

foreseen that Uspenskij would be designated as the main reviewer of his work. In his lengthy appraisal, Uspenskij repaid the criticism in kind — again, justifiably so — and stuck by his own "overly bold" suppositions. However, gentleman that he was, he did recommend Westberg for the minor Uvarov prize, and stated that, were there ever a need for a new edition of the Fragments with translation and commentary, Westberg's work should be included in such a re-edition almost in its entirety.[14]

It never occurred to Westberg to question our text's authenticity. He reprinted *in extenso* the entry on Toparcha Gothicus from Krumbacher's *Geschichte der byzantinischen Litteratur*, where the language of Hase's discovery was characterized as "auffallend gewandt und sogar humoristisch gefärbt." Westberg further reprinted, in all innocence and without comment, a passage from Krumbacher's reply to his letter of 1898. The reply reported second thoughts about Hase's procedure, thoughts which, Krumbacher said, he had "ganz zart angedeutet" in his *History of Byzantine Literature*; in the same reply, Krumbacher stated that he would welcome with more enthusiasm the proof of the existence of the Fragments' lost manuscript than he would an investigation, however penetrating, of the text itself. Subsequently, Westberg may have realized the implications of Krumbacher's comments, for he omitted the relevant passage of the reply from his enlarged Russian version of our reprint. In that version, Westberg did report Krumbacher's review of the reprint, but said nothing about Krumbacher's ironical references to Tolstoj and to the "nordisch-winterliches Stimmungsbild" conveyed by the Fragments.[15]

We must not blame Westberg for his unquestioning faith, for until 1970, no student of the Fragments explicitly stated that they might not be genuine. Krumbacher limited himself to ironical hints and never came out with an open attack on the Fragments. Two or three scholars openly despaired of ever solving the puzzle of the Gothic Toparch;[16] two others — a surprisingly small number — at least mentioned the question of our

14. Cf. Ф. И. Успенский, "Ф. Вестберг, Комментарий на записку готского топарха," Записки АН, 6, 7 [= Отчет о сорок четвертом присуждении наград Графа Уварова] (1904), 243-262, cf. esp. p. 257. The present reprint implements Uspenskij's suggestion.

15. The present reprint, pp. 12-13 and BB, 15 (1908), 82-83; for Krumbacher's review, cf. *Byzantinische Zeitschrift*, 10 (1901), 657-58.

16. W. Tomaschek, *Die Goten in Taurien*, (1881), p. 33; Ю. Кулаковский, "Записка греческого топарха," ЖМНП, 340 (April, 1902), 453; 457-58; Uspenskij, "Ф. Вестберг..." (as in note 14 *supra*), p. 256.

text's genuineness, but did it only in order to reject any doubts on that point outright.[17]

In retrospect, it appears remarkable that scholars pondered so little over the Fragments' credentials. No matter how convinced they may have been that our text was genuine, the rules of their craft called for an examination of those credentials, and ⟨ix⟩ that for two reasons. First, historical information contained in the Fragments was extremely meager, and what was offered was so vague that forty or one hundred and ten years of research respectively (depending on whether we stop our count with Westberg or go down to our own time) led to most diverse solutions as to the Fragments' locale, time, protagonists. The locale was sought anywhere between Thrace in the Balkans and the Don river; the time, fixed between about the year nine hundred and the middle of the eleventh century; the Gothic Toparch (incidentally, neither the title nor the ethnic attribution is mentioned in the Fragments themselves) was considered to be a Greek, a Goth, or an unspecified steppe-dweller; the ruler of the north was identified as a Russian prince (Igor, Svjatoslav, Vladimir the Great, or Jaroslav the Wise), a Bulgarian Tsar or a Pečeneg chieftain; the Toparch's subjects were either Goths, Bulgarians, Pečenegs or Byzantines, and the barbarians (either of the attacking or the defending kind) were said to have been Huns, Khazars, Pečenegs, Hungarians, Black Bulgarians, Bulgarians, or Russes (if the latter, then either Normans, the controversial Azov Russes, or Uličians), depending on the scholar. The only consensus which students of our text were able to reach either by Westberg's or our own time was that the Fragments were enigmatic, mysterious, obscure and controversial. Westberg's own monograph is a good witness to this, for it opens with the words, "Die rätselhaften Fragmente." Students of the Fragments should have remembered that vagueness, poverty of information and obscurity are traits associated with documents of doubtful authenticity.

The second reason which required a thorough examination of the Fragments' credentials is more weighty than the first one, but it can be given in one sentence: the original (tenth or eleventh century?) manuscript of the Fragments, discovered, used and described by Hase, was seen by nobody but himself. By his own words, it was no longer in evidence in 1818, and has never turned up since. Until recently, the only

---

17. A.A. Vasiliev, *The Goths in the Crimea* (1936), p. 120; М. Левченко, "К вопросу о 'Записке греческого топарха'" in the same author's Очерки по истории русско-византийских отношений (1956), p. 292.

text of the Fragments used by scholars — and Westberg was no exception — was the one printed in the notes to the Paris or the Bonn editions of Leo Diaconus published by Hase and dating from 1819 and 1828 respectively.

After a study of Paris *Supplément Grec* 858, written in Hase's own hand, and containing our Fragments, I have come to the conclusion that this text was composed — rather than discovered — by Karl-Benedikt Hase between 1816 and 1818. Hase, I claim, did it in part to satisfy the scholarly interests of Count Nicholas Rumjancev, the Chancellor of the Russian Empire, and financial supporter of his publishing ventures, including the edition of Leo Diaconus, and in part to make a private test of his own virtuosity and to perpetrate a joke at the expense of the Russian amateur-scholars whom Hase held in low esteem.

For detailed arguments in support of this assertion, I must refer the reader to my fully documented study on the subject.[18] Here, I shall merely give a list of those considerations which, without touching upon Hase's personality and scholarly habits, create a strong presumption for his authorship of the Fragments.

1. The original manuscript of our text, which, as Hase himself obliquely stated, left Paris not later than 1815, either has been lost or has never existed. A search among twenty of the twenty-four extant manuscripts which roughly correspond to Hase's own description of the manuscript allegedly containing the Fragments, failed to produce that text. At the same time, two manuscripts closely corresponding to Hase's specifications for the original manuscript of the Fragments, were in fact studied and described by Hase.

2. The Paris *Supplément Grec* 858 is the printer's copy of his edition of Leo Diaconus. On folios 315^r and 347^r-351^r, this copy contains the three Fragments of the Toparcha Gothicus. *Supplément Grec* 858 shows with all desired clarity that as late as 1818, Hase was aware of — and intended to print — only *two* Fragments. The question arises: how did he find the third Fragment in 1818, if, as he himself hinted and all scholars assumed, the manuscript containing all three Fragments had left his hands in 1815? Moreover, the Fragment as they stand in *Supplément Grec* 858 exhibit a number of corrections and insertions of the kind

18. Cf. *Dumbarton Oaks Papers*, 25 (1971). In the present introduction, I borrowed a few passages from that study, especially its footnotes 110 and 123. — For a summary presentation of my views on the Fragments, cf. *Association internationale des études byzantines, Bulletin d'Information*, 5 (1971), 71-95.

which is usually ⟨x⟩ associated with the work of an author, rather than a mere copyist or editor, of a Greek text. Finally, the comparison between the printer's copy in *Supplément Grec* 858 and the printed text of Hase's notes on the Fragments shows that the latter hesitated as to the contents, date, and even material characteristics, such as the size, of the purported original manuscript of that text.

3. It appears from the correspondence between Count Rumjancev, Hase and Academician Krug that Hase had no knowledge of, or was concealing, the Fragments' existence as late as July 1816, that is, almost a year after the departure from the Bibliothèque Nationale of the last lot of manuscripts appropriated by the French during the Revolutionary and Napoleonic wars. Yet, it was presumably in one of these manuscripts restituted in 1814 or 1815 that Hase had found our text. On the other hand, the same correspondence indicates that, by 1816 and in response to Rumjancev's queries, Hase was engaged in research on the historical geography of the Crimea, in his own opinion the locale of the Fragments.

4. The Fragments occupy only five columns of the Paris edition (or, as we have seen, twelve columns of the present reprint); yet, they contain five mistakes in accentuation or grammar and four *lexeis athesauristoi*. This incidence of nine oddities is abnormally high for so short a Greek text, were it genuine. Hase did not mention the four unattested words of the Fragments either in the index of his Leo Diaconus, or in the new edition of the Stephanus dictionary, although he introduced other *hapaxes* into both of them. These *hapaxes* were from late texts, comparable in age to the purported date of the Fragments, and were quoted in his edition of Leo Diaconus.

5. Hase intimated that the Fragments were autograph notes, jotted down by their author during the journey across the steppe. Yet, our text shows extensive dependence on literary sources, the foremost of which (offering eighteen parallels) is Thucydides, the very author whom Hase taught to Napoléon-Louis Bonaparte, and perhaps to his younger brother, the future Napoleon III, between 1813 and 1815. Other literary parallels include Ptolemy's *Apotelesmatica*, Agathias, Leo Diaconus, *De Velitatione Bellica*, Psellos, and *Timarion* — all authors or texts which Hase either edited or knew intimately. One text offering lexical parallels with the Fragments is Hase's secret diary written in Greek, an abridgment of which has been preserved in Paris *Supplément Grec* 1353; in addition to several rare words (such as ὁ περιέχων, "air," cf. the present reprint, pp. 16, 17) the diary seems to share with the Fragments the same mistaken accentuation of a Greek word (ευνη instead of the correct εὐνή, cf. the present reprint, pp. 18; 48).

6. The narrator of the Fragments considers Κλίματα to have been a town, or a *castrum* (cf. the present reprint, pp. 23; 26; 65-66; 75-77; 83-85). This meaning for Klimata is unique in a Byzantine text, either with reference to the Crimea or to any other area; on the other hand, the view that Klimata were *urbes*, or even an *urbs*, was current in eighteenth-century learned literature used by Hase. In particular, Mrs. Maria Guthrie, whose book, published in 1802, Hase quoted in his letter to Rumjancev of 1816, spoke of *urbs Climatum* and of the "Greek city of Klimatum."

The enigmatic toponym Maurokastron of the Fragments (cf. the present Reprint, pp. 16; 42; 49-54) was known to eighteenth-century scholars, and Hase demonstrably used several of their works. These scholars placed Maurokastron either at the mouth of the Dniester or in the Crimea. In Hase's own view, the context of the Fragments pointed to that peninsula, and, among other authors, Mrs. Guthrie informed him that the Crimean town of Karasubazar, which she visited, was "the Mavron Kastron of the Byzantine writers."

7. Two expressions in the Fragments clash with the frame of reference which modern scholars postulate for the mind of a tenth-century Byzantine. The first is Ἑλληνικώτεροι τρόποι, a more "Hellenic way of life," as a positive term and a sign of adherence to a high civilization (cf. the present reprint, pp. 25; 71-72); the second, the participle βασιλεύων, applied to the presumably tenth-century Rus' ⟨xi⟩ ruler who governed to the north of the Danube (cf. the present reprint, pp. 25; 72-73). Both expressions were quite acceptable to a scholar of Hase's time and erudition. He could not yet have had any systematic notion of Byzantine imperial ideology, but could, and did, read in G. F. Müller's *Sammlung russischer Geschichte*... (1736) the epithets "Czar" and "Kayser" applied to Vladimir the Great, Jaroslav, and even Vsevolod.

8. Between 1816 and 1820, Hase gave, either to Count Rumjancev himself or to his friend Academician Krug, three other pieces of suspect scholarly information, all of them connected with the Crimea or the Black Sea — areas of special interest to the Count.The first has to do with a text — identified by Hase but no longer to be found — which described the journey of an otherwise unattested writer "Maxime Catélianus" to the equally unattested town of Sarat in the Crimea; the second, with an unknown manuscript which referred to the equally unknown embassy sent by Andronicus III to Trebizond in 1338 and offered, so Hase told Rumjancev, information of value for Russian history; the third, with a chronicle (this time actually preserved in Paris), which allegedly contained, among other things, material on the Genoese

trade in the Black Sea; this chronicle turns out to be the *Chronicle of Morea*, which once speaks of Genoese warships, but in the Bay of Arta, not in the Black Sea.

II

If the Fragments are indeed a modern forgery, then the main value of Westberg's monograph is historical and methodological. Armed with insight which Westberg lacked, the modern scholar can analyze the weaknesses of what that author saw as his main contribution to the study of the Fragments. Considering himself something of a cosmographer (an opinion fully shared by Kunik, cf. the present reprint, pp. 6 and 1), Westberg believed that he had "fully" and "once and for all" succeeded in establishing the Fragments' precise date by means of scientific astronomy. He upbraided Vasil'evskij, Píč and Uspenskij for coming up with artificial constructions, proposing results contrary to "astronomical computations," providing astronomers with falsely understood information, or being unable to cope with the astronomical section of his own monograph. He even rejected Kunik's late hypothesis about Vladimir as the Fragments' ruler, because astronomical computations were against it (cf. the present reprint, pp. 115; 117; 8; 10; 83; 122; and *VV*, 15 [1908], 84).

The trouble with Westberg's scientific proof was that it was no proof at all, for the strictly astronomical indications of the Fragments, three in number (Saturn in the vespertine phase, Saturn at the beginnings of Aquarius, the Sun in the winter signs, cf. the present reprint, pp. 16; 43-45; 109-118) do not suffice to fix an absolute time for our text. What ensued in the cooperation between scholars, including Westberg, and professional astronomers, was a series of misunderstandings, with reciprocal good will and courtesy obscuring the issue. Left to themselves, astronomers were able to produce only an open-ended series of dates, each separated by about twenty-nine and a half years, that is, by the intervals between Saturn's returns to the same point of the ecliptic. To assign the Fragments to a given time in the series, they needed additional information of two kinds: first, on the meaning both of the astronomical terms and of particular phrases occurring in the Greek text (how could the narrator "show from the stars" that Saturn was in Aquarius? Was Aquarius a constellation or a sign? Was the Toparch's observation, if it was one, made at midnight?); second, on data of non-astronomical character, ranging from the century of the Fragments' original manuscript to the actual day on which the Dnieper usually froze over.

Astronomers were provided with both kinds of information by the very historians who had consulted them in the first place. Secure in their possession of tables and diagrams, historians did not realize that they obtained from their scientific colleagues merely their own preconceptions, both historical and terminological, in scientific disguise. Thus Uspenskij's expert, the Odessa Professor Kononovič, agreed with him that Saturn could have been observed ⟨xii⟩ in the *constellation* of Aquarius at the end of 903 — Uspenskij's preferred date for the Fragments — and proved it by means of a diagram.[19] Píč entrusted the same problem to Dr. Seydler, fed him his own interpretations concerning the setting of Saturn about midnight, and obtained the desired result of 991 as the Fragments' date.[20] Westberg wisely eliminated midnight from the data with which he provided his two informants, Professor Wislicenus from Strasbourg and Dr. Seyboth from the leading Russian observatory of Pulkovo, and was offered the year 963. This conclusion, supported by three tables and six diagrams, also happened to be the dating preferred in 1874 by Westberg's mentor, Academician Kunik (cf. the present reprint, pp. 109-118; 6).

Vasil'evskij did a reasonable thing: about 1876, he learned that Saturn would be in the *sign* of Aquarius in 1877, counted back, and came up with the years 933-936 and 964-967 as likely dates for the Fragments (he opted for the earlier one). Vasil'evskij's results, obtained "without any help of astronomy," were about as good as professional computations.[21] Professor Otto Neugebauer whom, emulating Westberg, I consulted on the matter, wrote the following: "As a source for historical chronology the text [i. e., the astronomical passage of the Fragments] is obviously valueless since one may keep adding or subtracting multiples of thirty years to above given dates [i. e., 903, 932, 962, 992, 1021, etc.]. The cause of the misunderstanding of the astronomical data by Westberg or his 'Beraters' lies in the fact that ⟨they⟩ did not know that 'Aquarius' ⟨in a text like the Fragments⟩ never can mean the constellation but only the zodiacal sign" (letter of September 22,

19. Ф. И. Успенский, "Византийские владения на северном берегу Черного Моря в IX-X вв.," *Киевская Старина*, 25 (n. 5-6) (1889), 253-294 (also separately as a pamphlet, where the relevant passage is on p. 42).

20. J. L. Píč, *Der nationale Kampf gegen das ungarische Staatsrecht...* (Leipzig, 1882), pp. 81-85 and note.

21. В. Г. Васильевский, "Записка греческого топарха," ЖМНП, 185 (June, 1876), 428-29, reprinted in the same author's Труды, 2, (1912), pp. 205-206.

1961). The error of the astronomers was excusable, since they were led into it by historians. Westberg's informers, for instance, were first told that the Fragments' astronomical passage was a record of direct observation, made during a difficult journey through the "deserted Steppe of the Pontus;" but astronomers maintained that it was virtually impossible to determine the boundaries of a *zodiacal sign* from such observation (cf. the present reprint, pp. 111-112); on the other hand, it was easy to locate a constellation just by looking at the sky.

To my knowledge, the only scholar after Vasil'evskij who assumed that the Fragments referred to the *sign* of Aquarius, was Šangin;[22] he used an astrological entry of 464 A.D., counted forward, and obtained February 971 as the date of our text. In his review of Westberg's prize essay on Toparcha Gothicus, Uspenskij had an easy task in pointing to the vicious circle which imprisoned those students who attempted to offer an astronomical proof for the date of the Fragments.[23]

The reader who adopts my view on the Fragments' authenticity can undertake one further methodological exercise: he can observe how, whenever Westberg and other students were puzzled by the Fragments, they failed to consider what even in their time was an arguable alternative — that the Fragments were a forgery; instead, they either abstained from pursuing the problems posed by our text's contradictory passages, or resorted to hypotheses which made matters even more involved than they had been before.

For all his faith in the Fragments, Westberg did point to their obscurities and incongruities. Sometimes, he would just throw up his hands, for instance when he admitted that to ask why the author of our text gave the name "areas to the north of the Danube" to the Russian state was to ask a question to which no satisfactory answer was possible (the present reprint, p. 56). The problem of the Toparch's nationality, he thought, was moot (cf. the present reprint, p. 75; in *VV*, 15 [1908], 130 he declared that it was insoluble). On other occasions, Westberg merely listed the difficulties inherent in the Fragments themselves or in Hase's commentary to them, without following up their implications. Examples: he was aware of the confusion in Hase's statements about the number of the Fragments and even used the word "Widerspruch" in

22. М. А. Шангин, "'Записка греческого топарха' как источник о войне русских на Балканах 970 г. и. зимой 971 г.," Исторический Журнал (1941, n. 9), 122.

23. Uspenskij, "Ф. Вестберг..." (as in note 14 *supra*), pp. 254-55.

describing Hase's *modus operandi* (cf. the present reprint, p. 86), but drew no conclusion from his observation. He (or rather his philological adviser and fellow scholar from Riga, Eduard Kurtz), also saw that the innocent looking ἀποδιαφέρω was unknown to dictionaries (cf. the present reprint, p. 73), but left it at that.

⟨xiii⟩ In most cases of detected difficulties, however, Westberg (or his mentors, Kunik and Kurtz) dealt with obscure and problematic passages of the Fragments by proposing remedies which were worse than the ills they intended to cure. Thus he changed the faulty εὖναι ("beds," with an error in accentuation) to εὖνοι and proposed the nonsensical rendering "benevolently did the shields approach" (cf. the present reprint, pp. 18 and 48);[24] he corrected the non-existent ἐπ' ὀμωσία into the *hapax* ἐπωμοσία (cf. *ibidem*, pp. 21 and 60-61 and *VV*, 15 [1908], 110); he followed Kunik's explanation that the anachronistic term Ἑλληνικώτερος with its positive connotation must have been known to the Toparch from "some now lost ancient Greek text" (cf. the present reprint pp. 71-72 and *VV*, 15 [1908], 125). The other anachronistic term was βασιλεύων. It could conceivably point to Vladimir (cf. the present reprint, pp. 25: 72-73); however, βασιλεύων was not βασιλεύς, hence, the Fragments' ruler of the North was Svjatoslav (cf. the present reprint, p. 122).

Westberg was aware that no one except the narrator of the Fragments used the toponym Klimata to denote a city; nevertheless, he adopted this meaning, at least for the second Fragment, for, so he argued, we know too little about the history of the Crimea in the tenth century to exclude such a meaning (cf. the present reprint, p. 84); the narrator's return from Kiev or another northern residence of the Russian prince must have happened close to a February 1; however, at that time the narrator could no longer have observed Saturn's setting after sunset, an observation attested in the first Fragment; hence, Westberg argued, the Toparch must have made two separate journeys to Kiev (cf. the present reprint, pp. 80-81).

Westberg was not the only student of the Fragments who stopped before the brink. His critic, Uspenskij, too, was struck by incongruities occurring in that text and formulated them clearly. If there were mountains of ice at one spot of the Dnieper, he asked, why did the Toparch's party decide to cross it exactly at that spot? If horses sank up to their necks in the snow, how could they move at all? The Toparch was a

24. This unfortunate change was criticized right away by Kulakovskij, "Записка..." (as in note 16 *supra*), pp. 458-59.

Byzantine; yet nothing in what he said or did indicated that he was a member of a Christian society.

One line of reasoning followed by Uspenskij is especially instructive. In the tenth century, the Toparch turned for help to a ruler holding sway to the north of the Danube, instead of appealing first to the Byzantine Kherson. "We are dealing here with a blatant anachronism," exclaimed Uspenskij; after all, during the tenth century, Byzantium's position in the Crimea was quite assured. At this point one might expect Uspenskij to have cast some doubt upon a text wich exhibited such a blatant anachronism. All in vain. He concluded that, since the Fragments could not have referred to the tenth century or to the Crimea, they either were to be dated to the ninth century, or their locale was to be moved to the Danube or the Don.[25]

Levčenko, to quote one of the more recent scholars, realized that the southern coastal strip of the Crimea (the area of Constantine Porphyrogenitus' Klimata and Kherson) was too narrow to hold ten cities and five hundred villages, allegedly destroyed by the attacking barbarians — a piece of information which Westberg accepted without batting an eyelash (cf. the present reprint, pp. 21 and 58). However, Levčenko's solution to the difficulty was to move the scene of action to the more spacious Bulgaria.[26]

I shall close this list of methodological *exempla* with the participle βασιλεύων occurring in the third Fragment. Both Westberg and several of his predecessors and contemporaries felt uncomfortable about that term. Kunik (especially towards the end of his life), Buračkov, Uspenskij, Miljukov, and Braun considered its use inappropriate or too pretentious in connection with Princes Igor and Svjatoslav, but they all found their ways out of the impasse. Kunik and Braun connected the participle with Vladimir (surely a relative of the Byzantine Emperor, Vladimir was even called Emperor in the Greek conciliar decree of 1551!). Uspenskij and Miljukov had an easier task, since in their view the Fragments had nothing to do with Russian history and the βασιλεύων of the North was the Bulgarian *c(ěsa)r'*, that is, βασιλεύς, Symeon. Finally, Buračkov reasoned as follows: since a tenth-century Greek, familiar ⟨xiv⟩ with the terminology of his time, could not have called Igor βασιλεύων, the Toparch was not a Greek.[27]

25. Uspenskij, "Ф. Вестберг..." (as in note 14 *supra*), pp. 245-46; 257-62.

26. M. Levčenko, "К вопросу..." (as in note 17 *supra*), p. 325.

27. Cf. the present reprint, p. 122; Uspenskij, "Византийские владения..." (as

Westberg's monograph is not the most novel or penetrating treatment of the so-called Fragments of Toparcha Gothicus — that epithet must be reserved for Vasil'evskij's work of 1876.[28] However, among all the studies which have taken the Fragments at their face value, Westberg's is the most detailed investigation. With the present reprint at his disposal, the student of Russo-Byzantine relations will be in a better position to assess the value of arguments which are now challenging the authenticity of Hase's enigmatic find.

---

in note 19 *supra*), p. 28; *idem*, "Ф. Вестберг..." (as in note 14 *supra*), p. 262; П. Н. Милюков, "Время и место действия записки греческого топарха," Труды восьмого Археологического Съезда в Москве 1890, 3 (1897), p. 282; П. Бурачков, "О записке готского топарха," ЖМНП, 171 (January, 1874), p. 245. — The defenders of the Fragments' authenticity might wish to invoke the *graffito* recently discovered in St. Sophia of Kiev, in which the death of "our Emperor," *c(ěsa)rja naš[e]go*, is mentioned under the year 1054. This might give them an opportunity for connecting the "ruler of the North" with Jaroslav the Wise, or at least for pointing to the — unfortunately non Greek — use of "imperial" terminology in Kiev. Cf., e. g., С. А. Высоцкий, Древне-русские надписи Софии Киевской (1966), pp. 39-41.

28. "Записка...," referred to in note 21 *supra*.

ADDITIONAL NOTE:

The *Personal der Kaiserlichen Universität zu Dorpat nebst Beilage*, e.g., 1885, Semester II, p. 41, and 1889, Semester I, p. 43, lists the following information on Westberg: He was born in Kurland, enrolled at Dorpat University in the second semester of 1884 (student number 12415), with history as a field of concentration. At first, he lived in the first district of Dorpat, Scharrenstrasse 7, in the house of one Hübbe; later, he changed his address to the third town district, Jamasche Strasse 16, a house owned by one Emmerich. Westberg graduated sometime in 1889, for he is listed among those students who passed the Teacher's Certificate (*Lehrerprüfung*) in history between February 1 and September 1 of that year.

The following item should be added to Westberg's bibliography given in note 5 above: "Eine gefährliche Strömung der modernen Pädagogik," *Pädagogischer Anzeiger für Russland*, 4 (1912), 395-97. There, Westberg turned against new currents and advocated sticking to old-fashioned discipline. It appears from this article that by ca. 1912 Westberg had taught at the *Stadtrealschule* of Riga for twenty-two years. Thus he came there ca. 1890, probably from the interior of Russia (cf. *"ich, der bis dahin nur mit innerrussichen Schulverhältnissen vertraut war"*), thus merely a year after his graduation in 1889.

XXXI

Francis Dvornik

Francis Dvornik was born on August 14, 1893, in the Moravian village of Chomýž. As the young boy grew, his abilities became so obvious that he was destined for a priestly career — the usual way of social ascent at that time. He died at the age of 82, on November 4, 1975, in the very place of his birth, the family home in his native village, while on a visit from the United States. His funeral was celebrated by two bishops and 120 priests; presidents of academies sent their telegrams of sympathy and his obituaries appeared in the leading papers of the world. Scholars, prelates, and laymen everywhere paid homage to a man who changed our views of the history of Byzantium, of the Slavs and of the Church of Rome; provided broad syntheses of Slavic civilization from its beginnings to the early modern period; and traced the development of Byzantine political ideas from their beginnings in the ancient Orient to their reflections in post-Byzantine Eastern Europe.

Dvornik's scholarly output is not only unusually large — some 18 books and monographs, not counting translations and revised editions; over 130 articles; and over 60 book reviews — but also fairly variegated, ranging from a monograph on St. Wenceslas through a history of ecumenical councils. However, Dvornik in his writings never departed from three major subjects, all of them interconnected: the early relations between Byzantium and the Slavs, culminating in the story of the mission of Cyril and Methodius; the relations between Orthodoxy and Rome, culminating in the story of the Photian schism and undertaken in the hope that objective scholarly work would further the cause of the unity of churches; and, finally, the medieval roots of later developments in East-Central Europe.

Three factors in Dvornik's biography and personality influenced the choice of these topics and the way in which he treated them. First, his Moravian origin, which made him familiar with Cyril and Methodius. Their mission had been destined for Moravia; their tradition had contributed to the 19th-century national revival in the Bohemian and Slovak lands; and Dvornik's Czech scholarly predecessors, such as Safařík and Pastrnek, had excelled in research on the Slavic Apostles. The second factor was his being a priest. This turned his attention to the contacts between the Eastern and the Western churches — again a tradition which in the Czech lands went as far back as the last years before the fall of Byzantium. Indeed, as a Catholic ecclesiastic, he was intimately involved in the cause of union, but in an irenic spirit and in a tradition of openness towards the East, prevailing in his native land; and his formal education as a seminarian provided him with a technique of clear articulation of larger units of thought, a quality which informed his subsequent writing. Third, Dvornik was endowed with an innate understanding of politics and had some passion for it, having participated in his younger years in the political life of his country, both at home and, subsequently, as an emigrant. This explains his tendency to study the ecclesiastical problems of the Middle Ages primarily in terms of political conflicts and struggles for territory and revenues rather than as doctrinal conflicts or intellectual confrontation.

Even his common sense, which contributed to his success as a scholar, and his unerring discernment of what was essential and what adventitious may be attributed to his early background. But the central qualities of his greatness — intelligence, the ability to view history in large interconnected units, and sheer passion for writing — were his own, not his environment's.

In 1912 Dvornik entered the Cyrillo-Methodian Theological Faculty at Olomouc. He was ordained a priest in 1916 and took care of his German-speaking rural flock for some years afterwards. In 1919 he enrolled in the Charles University of Prague, and a year later he moved to Paris. It was at the Sorbonne, under the guidance of the great Charles Diehl, that he received his formation as a Byzantinist. He did not neglect, however, his Slavic studies, which he pursued at the Institut des Études Slaves, nor his interest in matters politic, for in 1923 he obtained a diploma from the École des Sciences Politiques. His thesis for the Doctorat-ès-Lettres appeared in 1926. Its title *Les Slaves, Byzance et Rome* indicated the direction his research was to take for the rest of his life; and its publication assured the young scholar's fame. The book dealt with the impact of the Slavic invasions upon church organization in the Balkans; with the Cyrillo-Methodian mission; and with the competition between Rome, Constantinople, and the Frankish empire over Bulgaria, whose territory coincided in part with the ecclesiastical province of Illyricum. Two years later, in 1928, Dvornik became Professor at the Charles University. His attention now turned to one of the main pieces of evidence used in his thesis, namely, the Slavic *Lives* of Cyril and Methodius. The result of his research appeared in 1933 under the title *Les légendes de Constantin et de Méthode vues de Byzance* (reprinted in 1969). It was the first of the two greatest achievements of his scholarly life. The book's title announced the author's method — a study of the *Lives* not from the point of view of Moravia, the destination of the apostles, but rather of Constantinople, where their mission originated and where it was conceived. The book's aim may have been to counter the doubts cast upon the *Lives* by Western scholars, in particular the famous Berlin Professor Alexander Brückner, but the approach was valid, for the *Lives* are, in fact, specimens of Byzantine as much as of Slavic literature. Dvornik not only established the reliability of these two earliest literary documents written in Slavic but also enriched our knowledge of ninth-century Byzantine political and cultural history. All his subsequent writings on Cyril and Methodius were elaborations upon his insights of 1933, integrating the results of later textual and archaeological research into the framework established by him at that time.

The second outstanding achievement of Dvornik's scholarly work was his reopening of the Photian question, one of the *causes célèbres* of medieval history. Ever since the Middle Ages, Photius has been blamed for the schism that rent the garment of the Church, and yet Photius was a learned man and a teacher of Cyril, Apostle of the Slavs. The figure of this ninth-century patriarch had loomed large in Dvornik's previous books. Now he was to become the subject of a rehabilitation. The book *The Photian Schism, History and Legend* was essentially completed in French by 1939 but did not appear until 1948, when it was published in England. In it Dvornik told what has since become a familiar story — now that his views have been generally accepted — but what 30 years ago was a challenge to the prevailing image of the patriarch. Far from being an intruder on the patriarchal throne and a rabid adversary of Rome, twice excommunicated by the Pope, Photius was a moderate who had made peace with his predecessor and who was not excommunicated by the Pope for a second time. These notions, as well as the claim that the anti-Photian council of 869-70 was ecumenical, were, so Dvornik showed, medieval elaborations. At one point in his book Dvornik made a veiled suggestion that Photius, an Orthodox saint, might deserve canonization by the Catholic Church as well. The Catholic Church absorbed these novel views, even if she took her counsel before doing so. For one thing, other Catholic scholars began to come independently to conclusions similar to those of Dvornik, even if their writings lacked the breadth of his overall view; for another, Rome's attitude towards the East was changing. At the end, the once embarrassing opinions of Monsignor Dvornik were given sanction, for he was appointed an adviser to the Preparatory Commission of the Second Vatican Council.

We may owe the preservation of the Photius manuscript to Dvornik's keen political sense. The events of 1938 found him abroad, and after the occupation of Prague by Hitler in 1939 he severed his connection with Czechoslovakia. He escaped from France to England in 1940 with his manuscript and spent the war years and those immediately following the war dividing his time between his duties as a chaplain to a nunnery evacuated to Sussex and his studies in the British Museum: there, he reworked his Photius and wrote his book *The Making of Central and Eastern Europe*. In this work, published in 1949, he concerned himself with the fact that a large Slavic state never arose in East-Central Europe; as a consequence, a bridge between East and West was lacking, and Kievan Rus', in spite of its early contacts with the West, turned to its Byzantine mentor. The book dealt with the period between the 10th and the 13th centuries, but preoccupations of the early post-war years were not, perhaps, absent from the author's mind.

In 1948 Dvornik was invited to Dumbarton Oaks as a Visiting Professor and thus was brought into the orbit of Harvard. His permanent appointment at Dumbarton Oaks in the following year, when he became Professor of Byzantine History, ushered in the final, long, stable and serene period of his life. He was able to devote himself to his writing; and he produced a number of major books, all connected with the central themes of his research, notably *The Idea of Apostolicity in Byzantium and the Legend of the Apostle Andrew* (1958), *The Ecumenical Councils* (1961), *Byzance et la Primauté Romaine* (1964), *Early Christian and Byzantine Political Philosophy. Origins and Background* (1966), *Byzantine Missions Among the Slavs: Ss. Constantine-Cyril and Methodius* (1970). At the same time he gave unstinting service to Dumbarton Oaks and Harvard. He concerned himself particularly with the needs of the Dumbarton Oaks library — then in a period of rapid growth — and he was a frequent participant in the annual symposia, two of which he directed or helped to direct. Twice, in 1951 and 1956, he taught courses in Cambridge; and this experience made him aware of the need for a comprehensive work on Slavic history for English-speaking readers. His two volumes *The Slavs: Their Early History and Civilization* and *The Slavs in European History and Civilization*, published in 1956 and 1962 respectively, were based on his Harvard lectures.

His retirement in 1964 brought no change in his circumstances or in the rhythm of his work. He remained in residence at Dumbarton Oaks, ever helpful to colleagues, visitors and staff. He was a man without affectation, straight-forward and warm hearted, tolerant and extremely generous. Though he appreciated the honors showered upon him in the later part of his life, he retained the simplicity of a *curé de campagne*. But this *curé* offered his guests the most exquisite French wines and refined repasts and provided the young in trouble with comfort and wise counsel, remembered for its clarity and its moderation. No wonder that he sensed a moderate in Photius.

XXXII

George Ostrogorsky

GEORGE ALEXANDROVIČ OSTROGORSKY died in Belgrade on October 24, 1976, at the age of seventy-four. With him disappeared one of the last members of a group of scholars who had spent their youth in pre-Revolutionary Russia, left it because of the Revolution, continued their studies in the West, settled there, and acquired world-wide reputations in their respective branches of Byzantinology.

Ostrogorsky was born on January 19, 1902, in St. Petersburg. His father was principal of a secondary school and a writer on pedagogical subjects. Ostrogorsky completed his secondary education in a St. Petersburg classical *gymnasium*, and thus acquired knowledge of Greek early in life. He began his university studies abroad, in Heidelberg (1921), where at first he devoted himself to philosophy, economics, and sociology, though he also took courses in classical archeology. As important as his topics are the names of his teachers: Karl Jaspers, Heinrich Rickert, Alfred Weber, and Ludwig Curtius. His interest in history, especially Byzantine history, was awakened by a young Dozent by the name of Percy Ernst Schramm. After studying various aspects of Byzantinology in Paris in 1924-25 (where Charles Diehl, Gabriel Millet, and Germaine Rouillard were his teachers), Ostrogorsky received his doctorate from the University of Heidelberg in 1925 with a dissertation in which he combined his interests in economics and Byzantine history. Entitled "Die ländliche Steuergemeinde des byzantinischen Reiches im X. Jahrhundert," the thesis was published in the *Vierteljahrschrift für Sozial- und Wirtschaftsgeschichte* 20 (1927; reprint, Amsterdam, 1969). He taught as *Privatdozent* in Breslau from 1928 to the fateful year of 1933, when he moved to Belgrade. There he was invited to occupy the Chair for Byzantinology. Ostrogorski made Yugoslavia his permanent home and taught at Belgrade for forty years, retiring from the University in 1973. He was made a corresponding Member of the Serbian Academy in 1946 and a Regular Member in 1948. In the latter year an Institute of Byzantinology was created within the Academy; Ostrogorsky assumed its direction and remained at its helm until his death. He was chief editor of the Institute's house organ, the *Zbornik Radova Vizantološkog In-*

stituta, through its sixteenth volume which appeared in 1975. He also supervised the monograph series of the Institute of which the choice items were his own study *Pronija* (1951) and the multivolume collection of Byzantine Sources for the History of the Nations of Yugoslavia.

Ostrogorski repaid in more than one way the hospitality he met with in his new country: he created a new generation of Yugoslav Byzantinists, broadened the horizons of Yugoslav historians by the example of his personal research, and provided for them closer contacts with the world scholarly community. Under his guidance the Belgrade Institute became, along with Munich, Paris, and Dumbarton Oaks, a leading center of research in the field of Byzantinology. Ostrogorsky remained faithful to Belgrade to the very end, although over the years suggestions were made that he take up residence in an American or Soviet center of Byzantine studies.

To non-specialists Ostrogorsky is best known as the author of the standard *History of the Byzantine State* (*Geschichte des byzantinischen Staates*, Handbuch der Altertumswissenschaft XII, 1, 2), a work which saw three German editions (1940, 1952, 1963), two English ones (1957, 1968), and translations into some ten other languages. The fame of the *History* is fully deserved: it has a conception of its own, especially reflected in its periodization (the periods being 324-610; 610-1028; 1028-1453); it is written elegantly and with a great economy of means; and the text is supplemented ⟨775⟩ by well-chosen information on sources and pertinent secondary literature, thus providing a point of departure for research on particular topics. Today, the *History* remains the standard reference work on political, social, and institutional developments in the Empire.

To the specialist Ostrogorsky is known as the author of an extensive œuvre comprising some 180 titles. If one sets aside some technical articles (such as his famous investigation of the chronology of Theophanes in *Byzantinisch-Neugriechische Jahrbücher* 7 [1930]), the bulk of his production forms three main clusters: the first, heralded by his doctoral dissertation; comprises writings on social, economic and institutional history, topics which had been favored by pre-Revolutionary Russian Byzantinology; the second, adumbrated by his Habilitationsschrift on *Iconoclasm*, consists of works on religious and imperial ideology of Byzantium; finally, the third deals with Byzantino-Slavic, especially Byzantino-Balkan, relations.

In the field of social history Ostrogorsky's outstanding contributions deal with the history of the *pronoia* — a land grant, bestowed originally *ad vitam* in exchange for services that usually were military in character (*Pour l'histoire de la féodalité byzantine* [Brussels, 1954]) —

and the history of the Byzantine peasantry, as revealed especially by the Acts of Mount Athos and by inventories of peasants (*praktika*) dating from the late Byzantine period. In these studies, Ostrogorski assumed the existence of a specific Byzantine variety of feudalism. In the field of institutional and administrative history, he was the proponent of an early date for the creation of the so-called *theme* system in the Empire (he put the formation of the earliest *themes* in the time of the Emperor Heraclius), though he also followed the development of the system to its crystalization in the ninth century. In the field of state ideology Ostrogorsky devoted some attention to the coronation ceremonial; his chief merit in that field, however, is the reconstruction of the medieval concept of the hierarchy of states, with the universal Byzantine emperor at its head ("Die byzantinische Staatenhierarchie," *Seminarium Kondakovianum* 8 [1935], 509-520, and "The Byzantine Emperor and Hierarchical World Order," *The Slavonic and East European Review* 35 [1956]). In the field of Byzantino-Slavic relations, he did not neglect the Empire's impact upon Kievan Rus' (see his articles on St. Vladimir and on Princess Olga, written in 1939 and 1967 respectively), but most of his production dealt with the relations between Byzantium and Serbia. His principal achievements in this category were a study on the Chronicle of the Serbian Princes in Constantine Porphyrogenitus (1949); the Serbian chapters in his book *Pronija* (1951); an article on Stephen Dušan and his nobles in their struggle against Byzantium (1951; reprinted in *Byzantion* 22 [1952-53]); and last but not least his monograph on the Serbian principality of Serres after Dušan's death (1965).

The world of learning rewarded Ostrogorsky with what he once called "undeservedly numerous honors": honorary doctorates from Oxford (1962), Strasbourg (1968), and the Sorbonne (1972), as well as membership in the German Order *Pour le mérite* in Arts and Sciences (1966), and in a number of Academies, including the *Académie des Inscriptions* (1970), the Austrian Academy of Sciences (1971), and our own Mediaeval Academy of America (1964).

Ostrogorsky traveled and lectured widely, from Edinburgh to Palermo, from Moscow to Berkeley. Twice (in 1957 and 1969) he came to America for extended stays at Dumbarton Oaks, where he participated in three Symposia. He must have found his sojourns at Dumbarton Oaks rewarding, for he included three articles written for the symposia, and published in *Dumbarton Oaks Papers* 13 (1959) and 19 (1965), in an "Abridged Bibliography" of his, containing only 23 items ("Byzantium in the Seventh Century"; "Byzantine Cities in the Early Middle Ages"; "The Byzantine Background of the Moravian Mission").

Ostrogorsky's scholarly methods were traditional. The basis of all his work was a painstaking analysis of sources, whether narrative or archival; what was unusual was ⟨776⟩ the breadth of the conclusions which he was able to draw from evidence referring to concrete cases, such as that offered by chancery pieces or Athonite charters. His views on changes in the seventh century and on the character of what he called Byzantine feudalism are at the center of today's scholarly debate.

The impression Ostrogorsky conveyed as a man was first and foremost one of gentleness. The Belgrade Institute was a large family of which he was the revered central figure; and warmth and peace are terms that best describe his home where he and his wife Fanula (a historian in her own right) dispensed hospitality to visitors from abroad. However, when it came to scholarly convictions, Ostrogorsky revealed himself to be made of stern stuff. He defended his views methodically and laid bare the weaknesses of his opponents. A case in point is his spirited polemic with Henri Grégoire as to whether or not there was an expedition of Prince Oleg against Constantinople (*Seminarium Kondakovianum* of 1939 and 1940 respectively).

The clues to Ostrogorsky's greatness as a Byzantinist must be sought partly in his Russian culture and in his long stay in Yugoslavia (a country whose past was intimately connected with Byzantium) and partly in his intellectual links with the world at large. Throughout his life Ostrogorsky remained attached to his Russian background and retained his love for Russian literature — he even said that had he remained in Russia he would have studied that literature rather than Byzantium — and it is worth noting that the first and the last items of his bibliography were written in Russian. The legacy he left to Yugoslavia is the flourishing state of Byzantinology in that country, and the legacy he left to the world is his *History of the Byzantine State*.

XXXIII

Remarks on the Diffusion of Byzantine Scientific and Pseudo-Scientific Literature among the Orthodox Slavs*

I

Translations of non-literary texts from the Greek produced by or for Orthodox Slavs in the Middle Ages may have appeared to these Slavs as part of a unique undertaking. But from the vantage point of Byzantium, which was the repository or source of the originals, translations into Slavonic were merely comparable to those into Armenian, Syriac, Arabic or Latin. One difference, however, should be mentioned at the very outset. Some Orthodox Slav nations, such as the Bulgarians (to single out those who did most of the early translating), were living in immediate cultural and political proximity to the Empire for a long time, and Orthodox Slavs as a whole were certainly more influenced in their culture and literature by Byzantium than were Islam or Western Christianity, and even ⟨322⟩ perhaps the Syrian Christians. With these Slavs, translated literature by far outranked original works in bulk, prestige and popularity.[1] Yet the Orthodox Slavs translated fewer of the scientific

---

* A short draft of this paper was distributed as a supplementary paper at the Colloquium on the Transmission of Knowledge organized under the directorship of Professor John Murdoch at Dumbarton Oaks, Washington, D.C. in the Spring of 1977. The paper was designed to offer, for purposes of comparison, information on Slavonic sources to non-Slavists, especially Arabists and Western medievalists, dealing with problems of translations in their own fields. The text was rewritten and its notes enlarged in 1980. In this paper, the term 'Middle Ages' covers the period down to the seventeenth century. This has to do with the peculiarities of the history of Eastern Europe and the Balkans. Within this time-span, 'Eastern Europe' means Orthodox Eastern Europe. Due to the nature of our evidence, the term 'scientific' will be used rather loosely.

1. In 1903, Academician A. I. Sobolevsky began his fundamental work on translations in Muscovite Rus' with the following two short sentences, set out for emphasis as separate paragraphs: 'In Ancient Rus', translated literature was of a considerably greater importance than original literature. It was incomparably

and philosophical works available in Byzantium than did the Syrians, Arabs or Latins.[2]

The reason for such a state of things cannot be due to a lack of appropriate models, for in the ninth and tenth centuries (which is precisely when the first Slavonic translations from Greek came into being) Byzan-

---

richer than original literature': 'Perevodnaya literatura Moskovskoy Rusi XIV-XVII vekov' (*Sbornik Otdeleniya russkogo yazyka i slovesnosti Imperatorskoy Akademii nauk*, 74, 1, St Petersburg, 1903, p. v. (hereafter *SORYaS*)).

2. For access to editions of many relevant Slavonic translations, and to critical studies on them, see I. U. Budovnits, *Slovar' russkoy, ukrainskoy, belorusskoy pis'mennosti i literatury do XVIII veka*, Moscow, 1962, and L. Ye. Makhnovets', ed., *Ukrayins'ki pys'mennyky, bio-bibliohrafichnyy slovnyk*, vol. 1, Kiev, 1960. Since most of the works of concern to us circulated in Eastern Europe or have been preserved in east Slavonic manuscripts, recent general treatises on the early history of science in 'Russia' (a term which includes Byelorussia and the Ukraine as well) are relevant to us; on the whole, the earlier the date of a publication, the more useful it is for our purposes. The best is still the pioneer work by T. I. Raynov, *Nauka v Rossii XI-XVII vekov*, Moscow, 1940, as it is based on primary sources, is free from patriotic fervour and contains ample paraphrases of translated texts. B. E. Raykov, *Ocherki po istorii geliotsentricheskogo mirovozzreniya v Rossii*, 2nd edn, Moscow-Leningrad, 1947, is sober: see especially pp. 11-45 and 66-104. On the other hand, N. A. Bogoyavlensky, *Drevnerusskoye vrachevaniye v XI-XVII vv.*, Moscow, 1960, while he deserves praise as a bibliographer, is better as a physician than as a literary and cultural historian, since he finds signs of 'national experience' in *translated* treatises anterior to the seventeenth century and tends to date them early; similarly, V. K. Kuzakov, *Ocherki razvitiya yestestvennonauchnykh i tekhnicheskikh predstavleniy na Rusi v X-XVII vv.*, Moscow, 1976, stresses original contributions and favours the early modern period; the book is not in close touch with the sources at all times; it also contains inexactitudes and reticences (for those, see e.g. pp. 37, n. 19; 44; 50). N. A. Meshchersky, *Istochniki i sostav drevney slavyano-russkoy pis'mennosti IX-XV vekov*, Moscow, 1978, does not deal with our category of texts. Several essays gathered in *Yestestvennonauchnyye predstavleniya drevney Rusi. Sbornik statey*, Moscow, 1978, are valuable and pertinent to our topic. Among works in western languages, the most informative and realible survey is by M. D. Grmek, *Les Sciences dans les manuscrits slaves orientaux du Moyen Âge* (Les Conférences du Palais de la Découverte, Série D., N. 66), Paris, 1959. The unpublished Oxford D. Phil. thesis by W. F. Ryan, *Astronomical and Astrological Terminology in Old Russian Literature* (1969): Press-mark Bodley, M. S. D. Phil. d. 4861, based on vast manuscript material, is excellent and offers more than its title announces. See also articles by Ryan on particular points, quoted in notes 6 and 38 below. A. Vucinich, *Science in Russian Culture*, I: *A History to 1860*, Stanford, 1963; London, 1965, 463 pp., devotes only seven pages to the period before the seven-

tine scholars produced an impressive scientific revival. That revival, an integral part of what some years ago was called the ⟨323⟩First Byzantine Humanism,[3] is attested both by the production of standard scientific texts (the dated manuscripts of Ptolemy, 813-20, and Euclid, 888, come immediately to mind) and by the activity of individuals, such as Leo the mathematician, the putative teacher of the Apostle of the Slavs, Cyril.

The fact that Orthodox Slavs, who translated so much from the Greek, chose little from among scientific, technical and philosophical works available in Byzantium should be correlated with another fact: that translators into Syriac, Latin and even Arabic depended on a longer local cultural tradition, which included translating habits, while the Southern (and certainly Eastern) Slavs had no literary past (as distinct from literacy) prior to the second half of the ninth century. However, even this correlation does not explain why relatively little scientific material was translated in the *subsequent* centuries of the Slavo-Byzantine cultural symbiosis and why, with a very few exceptions, Slavonic translations post-dated their Byzantine originals by two to seven centuries.[4]

---

teenth century: see a critical review article by W. F. Ryan, 'Science in Medieval Russia: Some Reflections on a Recent Book' (*History of Science*, 5, Cambridge, 1966, pp. 52-61 [p. 53: a short list of translated works; pp. 58-61: a succinct, but good bibliography on the subject]). F. J. Thomson 'The Nature of the Reception of Christian Byzantine Culture' (*Slavica Gandensia*, 5, Ghent, 1978, pp. 107-39) draws up a *corpus* of translations coming from Byzantium and thus discusses texts of interest to us (see esp. pp. 113-15, 118-19, 124 n. 23, 134 n. 122). Thomson's valuable statements suffer from an anti-Orthodox bias.

3. The term was coined by P. Lemerle in his *Le Premier humanisme byzantin*, Paris, 1971; see my review of this excellent work in *American Historical Review*, 79, New York, 1974, pp. 1531-35.

4. I. P. Yerëmin, 'O vizantiyskom vliyanii v bolgarskoy i drevnerusskoy literaturakh IX-XVII vv.' in *Slavyanskiye literatury, Doklady sovetskoy delegatsii. V. mezhdunarodnyy s"yezd slavistov (Sofiya, sentyabr' 1963)*, Moscow, pp. 5-13 (German summary, pp. 12-13), repeated in id., *Literatura drevney Rusi*, Moscow-Leningrad, 1966, pp. 9-17, explained this pattern of delayed reception by saying that Bulgarian and 'Old Russian' bookmen wished to assimilate the early Christian literature together with its classical heritage rather than absorb contemporary Byzantine works. To say this is to postulate for the tenth to twelfth centuries a positive attitude towards the classics and a capacity to differentiate between 'early Christian' and 'Byzantine' that no Slav *littérateur* (and only a few Byzantine writers), of the time possessed. Instances of relatively quick reception of Byzantine works by the Slavs are few; most of them date from the late Byzantine period. Here belong (a) the *Profession of the Faith* by Michael

II

In our search for an explanation, we may find it convenient to apply to Orthodox Slavs in general, and to our subject in particular, the ⟨324⟩ theory of selective adaptation, originally proffered by Soviet scholars assessing the extent to which Byzantine culture had been assimilated in Kievan Rus'. According to their theory, the selection of cultural values and contents taken over by a society on the receiving end is determined by the needs of that society. As long as we are willing to substitute the term 'equipment' for 'needs', the theory seems useful, for it tells us by implication that in assessing the relationship between a giving and a receiving culture, it is as important to be aware of what was *not* assimilated as it is to render account for what was.[5]

During the Middle Ages, no major work of Greek antique philosophy or science (which the Byzantines considered a part of their own body of knowledge) was translated by Orthodox Slavs in its entirety. For example, the earliest translation of a pseudepigraphic text (incidentally, unconnected with Byzantium and only minimally connected with Greece) which purported to contain Aristotle's precepts found its

---

Synkellos (d. 846) and a *Short Chronicle* (extending down to the year 920), both transmitted in the *Miscellany* of 1073 (see. p. 332 below). The first of these texts must have existed in Slavonic by the early tenth century; the second was obviously translated before 1073; (b) *Disputation Between Panagiotes and the Azymite* (on which see p. 337 below) and several polemical, homiletic or hagiographical writings dealing with the leading figures of the Hesychastic movement (fourteenth century). Translations of all these texts are attested in Serbian and East Slavonic manuscripts of the fourteenth and fifteenth centuries; (c) The *Syntagma* (an alphabetically arranged collection of Canon Law and *Responsa*) by Matthew Blastares, written in 1335 and translated in Serbia towards the middle of the fourteenth century. On a fourteenth-century Bulgarian manuscript of this translation see Y. N. Beneshevich in *SORYaS*, 6, 4, 1901, pp. 150-74, 181-227. For details on Hesychastic works (by Gregory the Sinaite, Nicephorus Kallistos Xanthopoulos, Philotheos Kokkinos, Gregory Palamas, Nil Kabasilas, David Anthypatos, Patriarch Kallistos), see Sobolevsky, 'Perevodnaya literatura' (see n. 1), pp. 15, 17-21; see also *Starine*, 9, Zagreb, 1877, pp. 13-14 (Nic. Kallistos in a fifteenth-century Serbian manuscript). Further examples of late Byzantine works translated by the fourteenth century in Thomson. 'The Nature of the Reception' (see n. 2 above), pp. 118-19.

5. Raynov, op. cit. (n. 2), pp. 20 and 100, spoke not only of 'needs' or 'interests', but also of the 'capabilities' of Old Russian thought in selecting and absorbing translated texts. In this apt formulation Raynov has had few, if any, followers in more recent Soviet literature on the subject.

way into Muscovy only in the sixteenth century[6] and the earliest (and partial) translation from Greek into Russian of the authentic Aristotle dates from the mid-eighteenth century.[7] Technical and philosophical writings were not a special case, for (with the exception of Josephus Flavius or of George of Pisidia's *Hexaemeron*, on which see p. 335 below) no sophisticated ancient Greek or Byzantine work of history or literature was accessible to ⟨325⟩ the Orthodox Slavonic reader not privy to Greek or non-Slavonic languages until modern times.

In short, unless one posits the unlikely, namely, a vast and selective disappearance of texts, it would seem that Orthodox Slavs, who at an early date managed to produce works of applied technology such as impressive architecture, and later on to compete ideologically with their

6. The work is the *Secreta secretorum* (in Slavonic *Taynaya taynykh*, improperly called *Aristotelevy vrata*), 'Aristotle's' precepts to Alexander useful for rulers and high officials, with astrological, hygienic and dietetic passages, translated (at the end of the fifteenth or in the early sixteeth century) from the Hebrew, surely outside of Muscovy, somewhere in the Grand Duchy of Lithuania. The *Taynaya taynykh* was copied in Russia down to the eighteenth century (total number of MSS: 20). Edition and discussion in M. N. Speransky, *Iz istorii otrechennykh knig*, IV: *Aristotelevy vrata ili Taynaya taynykh* (Pamyatniki drevney pis'mennosti i iskusstva, CLXXI), St Petersburg, 1908, esp. pp. 100, 128-30. See also Sobolevsky, 'Perevodnaya literatura' (see n. 1), pp. 419-29; M. N. Speransky, '"Aristotelevy vrata" i "Taynaya taynykh"' (*SORYaS*, 101, 3, 1928, pp. 15-18: the two texts are not identical); W. F. Ryan, 'A Russian Version of the *Secreta secretorum* in the Bodleian Library' (*Oxford Slavonic Papers*, 12, Oxford, 1965, pp. 40-48); id., 'Aristotle in Old Russian Literature' (*The Modern Language Review*, 63, 3, London, 1968, pp. 650-58); id., 'Drevnerusskiy perevod zhizneopisaniya Aristotelya Diogena Laertskogo' (*Slavia*, 37, Prague, 1968, pp. 349-55 (translation of this appendix to *Taynaya taynykh* was made probably from the Latin)); id., 'The Onomantic Table in the Old Russian *Secreta secretorum*' (*Slavonic and East European Review*, 49, London, 1971, pp. 603-6).

7. The translation was of the Second Book of *Politics*; it was due to H. Poletyka (incidentally, a Ukrainian), and was printed in 1757. Two other 'Slavonic' translations from Aristotle (*Economics* and Book One of *Physics*) were made before that, in 1676 and at the end of the seventeenth century respectively; however, the first of them was done in Moscow from 'the Latin and the Polish tongues', and the second (perhaps in Kiev), from the Latin. Moreover, both these translations remained in manuscript. On all this, compare the excellent Appendix 'K istorii aristotelevskoy traditsii na Rusi', in V. P. Zubov, *Aristotel'*, Moscow, 1963. On p. 7, Zubov regrets that he has been unable to follow in detail the fate of Aristotle's heritage among the Western and Southern Slavs; this on account of the absence of preliminary works of synthetic character.

Byzantine mentor, did not absorb much of the scientific and philosophical literature available in Byzantium.

III

The earliest Slavonic literature is essentially a translation literature, and its language, Old Church Slavonic, is replete with calques from the Greek. As for the earliest original works of Orthodox Slavs, which date from the late ninth and early tenth centuries — the *Lives* of Constantine and Methodius, the treatise *On Letters* by monk Khrabr, the earliest dodecasyllable poems — they, too, go back in part to Greek models or contain passages translated from the Greek. It is difficult to give the precise extent of the earliest translation activity and to localize it. It has been asserted, although it is neither as yet provable nor *a priori* likely, that some translating of liturgical texts was done for the benefit of the Slav invaders settled on Byzantine territory; we are on safer ground for a later period, since we are expressly told of some preparations made in anticipation of the Byzantine mission to Moravia (863). One early original text — the *Life* of Constantine-Cyril — seems to have been written by someone more familiar with Rome than with Slavonic Moravia, perhaps even in Rome itself.

The great period of translation was the tenth century; it produced much of the stock on which Orthodox Slavs drew throughout the Middle Ages. This period was also that of the first texts of interest to our subject. The place in which this first vast translation activity unfolded was the Bulgaria of Tsars Symeon (d. 927) and Peter (d. 969). Scholars advance the claims of the eleventh-thirteenth century and of Kiev to being the next period and place of translations; and some thirty works were once believed to have been translated in the Kievan realm. As time goes on, these claims are being whittled away, and I am afraid that little can be said with confidence about translations made in Yaroslav the Wise's (d. 1054) Kiev.[8]

⟨326⟩ A further intensification of translating activity occurred in the Balkans in the fourteenth century. In Bulgaria, it coincided with the cultural efflorescence under Tsar John Alexander, and the spiritual and intellectual ferment (of Byzantine origin) in the Church, the leading

8. For the optimistic view, compare A. I. Sobolevsky, 'Osobennosti russkikh perevodov domongol'skogo perioda' (*SORYaS*, 88, 3, 1910, pp. 162-77); see, however, the cautionary and just remarks by Meshchersky, 'O nekotorykh istochnikakh' (see n. 25), pp. 35-36.

figure of which was Patriarch Euthymius of Trnovo, the leader of the so-called Trnovo School.[9] Fourteenth- and early fifteenth-century Serbia also produced translations, owing to the favourable cultural climate which existed during the reigns of Stephen Dušan, Lazar, and Stephen Lazarević.

Some intellectuals belonged to both national milieux. At the beginning of the fifteenth century, one of them, Constantine Kostenečki, was a Bulgarian active at the Serbian court after the collapse of his own country under the Turkish onslaught; in addition to being a translator himself, he was concerned with the problems of translation.

But in Eastern Europe of that period, contributions to translation literature (whether from the Greek or from other languages) were slim. We have to wait until the sixteenth, and above all, the seventeenth century for the appearance there of new translations from sacred, patristic, Byzantine and early modern Greek texts, or reworkings of old ones. This happened in Kiev and in Muscovy; in the seventeenth century the latter employed many scholars from Byelorussia and the Ukraine, for these were well versed in Greek.[10]

IV

Although the bulk of translated literature was spiritual and ecclesiastical in all the periods just singled out, there was a difference in emphasis across time. Liturgical texts and excerpts from the Holy Writ made up almost all the literary effort in the late ninth century, but even at that time a book of the Sayings of the Fathers, the exact nature of which is still controversial, and a *Collection of Canon Law*, are said to have been translated by the elder of the two Apostles of the Slavs, Methodius.[11]

---

9. Among recent works on that school, see *Tărnovska knizhovna shkola, 1371-1971*, Sofia, 1974 (proceedings of a symposium).

10. For details see Sobolevsky, 'Perevodnaya literatura' (see n. 1), pp. 283-382. The outstanding text critics and translators are Maksim the Greek (Trivolis) and Epifaniy Slavynets'ky, a lexicographer and 'the father of Slavonic-Russian bibliography', in the sixteenth and seventeenth centuries respectively.

11. *Vita Methodii*, chapter 15. A recent brilliant — if unconvincing — attempt to identify the *otьčьskyje kъnigy* of the *Vita* is by F. W. Mareš, 'Welches griechische Paterikon wurde im IX. Jahrhundert ins Slavische übersetzt?' (*Anzeiger der phil.-hist. Klasse der Österreichischen Akademie der Wissenschaften*, 109, Vienna, 1972, pp. 205-21). His solution: The *Dialogues* of Gregory the Great. I suspect that some more conventional *paterikon biblion* (this title is repeatedly attested in Byzantine texts) is meant in this passage of the *Vita Methodii*.

⟨327⟩ The tenth century, the golden age of translation literature, saw works of Church Fathers, theological works, *Lives* of saints, two extensive chronicles — the total number of such Byzantine chronicles ever translated into Church Slavonic is six — *florilegia* and even a number of works treating natural sciences, and therefore relevant to us, being translated in Bulgaria. The needs of the developing Church and State hierarchies called for legal texts, and they were among the earliest non-literary translations. In canon law, the first such translation (that of the *Nomokanon* of John Scholastikos) is assigned to the late ninth century and, as we have seen, attributed to the pen of Methodius; while the second, that of the *Collection of XIV Titles*, dates from about 900.[12] An early collection of secular laws, based on Byzantine texts, is also dated by some to the very earliest period.[13] Other translations of legal texts (such as the *Syntagma* of Matthew Blastares) were made in the mid-fourteenth century, at the time of the great legal activity in Stephen Dušan's Serbia.

In matters of political ideology, Byzantium, whether envied, emulated or resented, remained a model for Orthodox Slavs. The 'Mirror of Princes' by a sixth-century deacon of the Great Church, Agapetus, was the very first secular Greek literary text translated into Slavonic (again, most probably in tenth-century Bulgaria). This text, along with its twin, the *Admonitions* of Emperor Basil I to his son Leo VI, found its way into *florilegia* and influenced the political ideology of Muscovy, and of the Moldavian and Wallachian principalities.[14]

V

When we come to study the transmission of knowledge by means of translation literature, we need to know how well the translators (and in due course, the readers) understood their models, not just which models

12. See for example, J. Vašica, 'Metodějův překlad nomokánonu'(*Slavia*, 24, Prague, 1955, pp. 9-41), and, on the Slavonic *Nomocanon* of *c.* 900 (earliest manuscript: the so-called *Yefremovskaya Kormchaya* of the twelfth century), Ya. N. Shchapov, *Vizantiyskoye i yuzhnoslavyanskoye pravovoye naslediye na Rusi v XI-XIII vv.*, Moscow, 1978, pp. 49-100.

13. J. Vašica, 'Origine Cyrillo-Méthodienne du plus ancien code slave dit "Zakon sudnyj ljudem"' (*Byzantinoslavica*, 12, Prague, 1951, pp. 153-74).

14. I. Ševčenko, 'Agapetus East and West: The Fate of a Byzantine "Mirror of Princes"' (*Revue des études sud-est européennes*, 16, Bucharest, 1978, pp. 3-44, esp. pp. 28-30).

they chose. There is a consensus among scholars that the very first translations, those connected with the Apostles of the Slavs and their direct disciples, escaped the strait-jacket of literalness and were quite commendable. However, these praiseworthy products are of little interest for our purposes, because of their predominantly sacred and liturgical content. Later translations, starting with those of the tenth century, never attained the level of those produced at the ⟨328⟩ outset of this Slavonic literary activity — but it is in this later period that the texts of concern to us were produced.[15]

Slavonic translators were aware of the problems of their craft; on two occasions at least, their leading representatives left remarks which border on a theory of translation. But these remarks were rudimentary. At the beginning of the tenth century, John the Exarch of Bulgaria, who may have been relying on theoretical statements of Constantine-Cyril himself, used some technical terms of Greek rhetoric and quoted from Pseudo-Dionysius the Areopagite to the effect that translations should not be literal, but rather according to sense. Unfortunately, the translation of the relevant Pseudo-Dionysian passage is difficult to understand without reference to the original; and in practice, John clung for the most part to the principle of a one-to-one correspondence between original and translation. What troubled him greatly was that Greek nouns of a given gender could not always be translated by Slavonic nouns of the same gender.[16]

In the fifteenth century, Constantine Kostenečki was, to borrow Vatroslav Jagić's words, rather a Greek than a Bulgarian or a Serb

15. On the high quality of the early translations, see, e.g., my 'Three Paradoxes of the Cyrillo-Methodian Mission' (*Slavic Review*, 23, 2, Chicago, Ill., 1964, esp. pp. 231-32, 234-35). On errors in the 'second-generation' translations of the tenth century, see A. Leskien, 'Zum Šestodnev des Exarchen Johannes' (*Archiv für slavische Philologie*, 26, Berlin, 1904, pp. 1-70); K. H. Meyer, 'Altkirchenslavische Studien, I: Fehlübersetzungen im Codex Suprasliensis' (*Schriften der Königsberger Gelehrten Gesellschaft*, 15/16, Königsberg, 1939, pp. 64-95). Meyer's judgement is milder than Leskien's.

16. Relevant text of John the Exarch in V. Jagić, *Codex Slovenicus rerum grammaticarum*, St. Petersburg-Berlin, 1896, reprinted Munich, 1968, pp. 32-36 (Preface to the translation of *De orthodoxa fide* by John of Damascus). Same text in A. Vaillant, *Textes vieux-slaves* (Textes publiés par l'Institut d'études slaves, VIII, 1-2), Paris, 1968, I, pp. 72-76 (text); II, pp. 59-62 (commentary). Vaillant (see e.g. *Textes vieux-slaves*, I, pp. 63-64; II, pp. 52-54, with earlier bibliography) re-published a fragment of a preface to the Lectionary (the so-

⟨329⟩ by his education, way of thinking and mode of expression. Thus he must have understood his Greek originals well. But in his theory of translation (the basis of which he took over from the Trnovo School) Constantine advocated too slavish an adherence to models. As he was a pedant, the application of his theory led to results not much different from those obtained by John the Exarch.[17]

There were some exceptions. In the fourteenth century, Dimitriy Zograf, the translator of the poem of George of Pisidia on Creation, interpreted according to the sense (such as he saw it) when faced with difficult words in George's iambics; he also coined a few felicitous periphrases and even attempted — on two occasions at least — to render

---

called *Hilferding Fragment*), badly preserved in an eleventh-twelfth-century manuscript and declared it to be a Slavonic translation of an original preface composed in Greek by Constantine-Cyril himself. As there are literal coincidences between the *Hilferding Fragment* and John the Exarch's *Preface*, Vaillant concluded that John was copying the Apostle of the Slavs. Since 1964, doubts have arisen in my mind concerning Vaillant's thesis (once I was more positive on the point of Cyril's authorship of the *Fragment*, see *Slavic Review*, 23, 1964, p. 230). Is not the author of the *Hilferding Fragment* too unsophisticated to have been Constantine himself? That author admits to have followed, as far as possible, the principle of literal translation; he, too, is greatly troubled by the trivial differences in gender between Greek and Slavonic nouns of the same meaning; and he mistranslates a clause in St Paul's First Epistle to the Corinthians 14. 19 (granted, one can always saddle the clumsy Slavonic translator of Constantine's with this error). The Greek rhetorical terms behind John Exarch's *strašьnъ* and *čьstьnъ* seem to be *phoberos* and *semnos* respectively. Numerous works by E. M. Vereshchagin deal with the translation technique of Constantine-Cyril and Methodius as he reconstructs it from the earliest text of the Slavonic gospels, rather than with the earliest translation theory: see e.g., his *Iz istorii vozniknoveniya pervogo literaturnogo yazyka slavyan*, I: *Perevodcheskaya tekhnika Kirilla i Mefodiya*, Moscow, 1971, and II: *Var'irovaniye sredstv vyrazheniya v perevodcheskoy tekhnike Kirilla i Mefodiya*, Moscow, 1972; 'Kyrills und Methods Übersetzungstechnik: drei Typen der Entsprechung zwischen griechischen und slavischen Wörtern' (*Zeitschrift für slavische Philologie*, 36, Heidelberg, 1972, pp. 373-85); the author uses modern terminology, but relies for a good deal of his material on Berneker's famous article of 1912/13 in praise of Constantine's art.

17. Text of Constantine Kostenečki's *Skazanie o pismenekh* in Jagić, *Codex Slovenicus* (see n. 16), pp. 95-129 (in a single manuscript); Russian summary, ibid., pp. 200-29; Jagić's judgement on Constantine, ibid., p. 81. Text of the abbreviated (but more widely known) version of the *Skazanie*, reduced almost entirely to orthographic matters, in B. St. Angelov, *Iz starata Bъlgarska, ruska i srъbska literatura*, vol. II, Sofia, 1967, pp. 200-30, esp. 211-22.

a Greek pun by a Slavonic one.[18] Another case in point, coming from the same century, is the translator of the Zonaras Chronicle (probably an intelligent Bulgarian), who succeeded in giving simplified but reasonably free renderings and did slavicize proper names.[19] But, to judge by other translations and by the *Narration on the Book of Saint Dionysius the Aeropagite*, the overall picture was bleak: in one passage, the *Narration*, apostrophizing the reader of the Slavonic version of Pseudo-Dionysius, made him exclaim in bewilderment and despondency: 'No one is able to understand what is written in Saint Dionysius.'[20]

VI

Throughout their Middle Ages, Orthodox Slav literati did encounter certain names of antique philosophers, some of their sayings — authentic or not — and statements — often disapproving — ⟨330⟩ concerning their doctrines. The names and sayings were those of Thales, Parmenides, Democritus, Pythagoras, Socrates, Plato or Aristotle; the statements

18. For the text of the Slavonic George of Pisidia and relevant studies, see n. 36 below. Examples of translations *ad sensum*, sometimes offering correct, even graceful, solutions and sometimes being ways out of difficulty: in v. 371 (of the Migne edition) 'the most important stars' is rendered by 'the notable planets'; in v. 963 'the flame of Aetna', by 'inextinguishable flame'; in v. 1117 'Homer's fictions', by 'Homer's fables'; in v. 1125, 'long-lived crow', by 'longwinded crow'. Skilful periphrase: in v. 672 'verdure' is expressed by 'flowers of the field'. Felicitous pun: in v. 1441 'the raving Mani (*Manenta ton memēnota*)' is translated by 'Mani the deluded (*Manentu omanenomu*)'. See also v. 1394 for a similar pun. On the other hand, the translator omits some sophisticated passages altogether, for instance a harangue against the neoplatonist Proclus, an apostrophe of Plato and Aristotle and a final prayer beseeching God to bestow victories and world rule upon the Emperor (Heraclius).

19. Cf. M. Weingart, *Byzantské kroniky v literatuře církevněslovanské*, vol. I, Prague, 1922, pp. 84-127; less positive appreciation in A. Jacobs, *Zonaras-Zonara. Die byzantinische Geschichte bei Joannes Zonaras in slavischer Übersetzung*, Munich, 1970, esp. pp. 89-90.

20. These words are adduced, from a manuscript of the last quarter of the sixteenth century (MS No. 184 of the Yegorov collection, Lenin Library, Moscow), by A. I. Klibanov, 'K probleme antichnogo naslediya v pamyatnikakh drevnerusskoy pis'mennosti' (*Trudy Otdela drevnerusskoy literatury* [hereafter *TODRL*] 13, Leningrad, 1957, pp. 178-79); see also Prokhorov, 'Korpus' (see n. 22), pp. 353-54, 360.

were about Plato's ideas,[21] his doctrine of assimilation to God (*homoiōsis theō*) dear to the Church Fathers, the tripartite division of the soul, or about human anatomy. Neo-Platonic notions were accessible as well. Some of these things were learned through translations of Gregory of Nazianzus (earliest manuscript: eleventh century), through the version of the *Corpus* of Pseudo-Dionysius the Areopagite (made in the Balkans under Serbian patronage in 1371 and introduced into Moscow soon afterwards),[22] through (tenth-eleventh century) translations of Byzantine low-brow chroniclers such as Malalas or George the Monk, or even through the Alexander Romance, or a rendering of some Byzantine (ninth century?) reworking of Aristotle.[23] However, most of the information of a scientific and philosophical character came to Orthodox Slavs from works to which we are turning now.

VII

Two of the three earliest dated Slavonic manuscripts (written in 1073 and 1076 respectively) are *florilegia* or *Miscellanies* (the third, and the earliest, dated manuscript is a Gospel).[24] Both of them are connected

21. On slight knowledge about Plato in Old Rus', see D. Čiževky, *Aus zwei Welten*, The Hague, 1956, pp. 45-65; id., *Antychna literatura v stariy Ukrayini*, Munich, 1956, pp. 9-10.

22. An early copy of monk Isaiah's translation of the Pseudo-Dionysian *Corpus* (with Maximus the Confessor's commentary), now in the Lenin Library, Moscow (*GBL,MDA,* fund. [f. 173], nr. 144), is by the hand of Metropolitan of Kiev and Moscow Kiprian (a Bulgarian, d. 1406). Another, Serbian, copy of that translation (now in the Saltykov-Shchedrin Library, Leningrad) is close in date to 1371. At least fifty manuscripts of Isaiah's translation have been preserved in Russian libraries (a word of caution: about half of them were copied late, in the seventeenth century). See G. M. Prokhorov, 'Korpus sochineniy s imenem Dionisiya Areopagita v drevnerusskoy literature' (*TODRL*, 31, 1976, pp. 356-61, esp. pp. 351-52, 354).

23. I am referring to the elusive original of John the Exarch's 'anthropological' passage in *Hexaemeron*, 226d7-235b28, ed. Aitzetmüller (see n. 34), vol. VI, 1971, pp. 172 ff.; this passage goes back somehow to Aristotle's *Historia animalium*: see A. Leskien, 'Der aristotelische Abschnitt im Hexaemeron des Exarchen Johannes' in *Zbornik u slavu Vatroslava Jagića*, Berlin, 1908, pp. 97-111; Kristanov and Dujčev, *Estestvoznanieto* (see n. 34), p. 571.

24. For a report on recent work in Slavonic *florilegia* and their Greek models see W.R. Veder in *Polata k"nigopis'naya*, 3, Nijmegen, 1980, pp. 54-63 (summary of the Symposium on Middle Greek and Slavonic Literatures held in Thessaloniki

with the Kievan court; both of them are parchment manuscripts (one of them *de luxe* and made for a princely patron), and the models of both — that of the de luxe *Miscellany* of 1073 certainly, that of the *Miscellany* of 1076, quite likely — were created in tenth-century Bulgaria.[25] While only slightly more than one half ⟨331⟩ of the sources of the *Miscellany* of 1076 have been identifield, I assume that eventually nearly all of them

in May 1979). The present paper takes only a few categories of *florilegia* into account; for a proposed classification of the full material, see Veder, ibid., p. 57.

25. (a) Miscellany, or *Izbornik*, of 1073 (of importance to our topic); facsimile edition by T. S. Morozov, *Obshchestvo lyubiteley drevney pis'mennosti*, vol. 55, St Petersburg, 1880; partial edition (stopping at about f. 75) with parallel Greek text by E. V. Barsov in *Chteniya v Imperatorskom Obshchestve istorii i drevnostey rossiyskikh* (hereafter Chteniya OIDR), Moscow, 1882, book 4; best description in A. V. Gorsky and K. I. Nevostruyev, *Opisaniye slavyanskikh rukopisey Moskovskoy Sinodal'noy Biblioteki*, II, 2, Moscow, 1859, no. 161, pp. 365-405. For recent bibliography, see n. 27 below. (b) Miscellany, or *Izbornik*, of 1076 (of no direct relevance to our topic): good diplomatic edition by V. S. Golyshenko *et al.*, *Izbornik 1076 goda*, Moscow, 1965; recent literature in T. Rott-Żebrowski, *Pismo i fonetyka Izbornika Światosława z 1076 roku*, Lublin, 1974, pp. 221-25, who, however, missed the important article by Horace G. Lunt, 'On the *Izbornik of 1076', Studies in Slavic Linguistics and Poetics in Honor of Boris O. Unbegaun*, New York, 1968, pp. 69-77. Among works published after 1974, see N. A. Meshchersky, 'O nekotorykh istochnikakh "Izbornika 1076 goda" v svyazi s voprosom o proiskhozhdennii ikh perevodov' in *Kul'turnoye naslediye drevney Rusi. Istoki, stanovleniye, traditsii*, (Festschrift for D. S. Likhachev), Moscow, 1976, pp. 34-38 (rightly points out that preexisting Church Slavonic translations underwent secularization and 'Kievization' in the *Izbornik* of 1076); L. I. Sazonova, 'Ritmiko-sintaksicheskiye elementy v "Izbornike 1076 goda"', ibid., pp. 38-42; N. N. Rozov, 'Kak "sdelana" vstupitel'naya stat'ya "Izbornika 1076 goda"', ibid., pp. 43-46 (off target); id., 'Izbornik 1076 goda kak pamyatnik istorii russkoy knigi', *Izvestiya Akademii nauk SSSR, seriya literatury i yazyka*, 35, Moscow, 1976, pp. 545-54 (critique of the simplistic interpretations by Budovnits; relation between make-up and contents of the *Izbornik*); id., *Kniga drevney Rusi*, Moscow, 1977, pp. 23-34 (claims originality and 'broad erudition' for the compiler of the *Izbornik*; proposes identity of scribes for the *Izborniki* of 1073 and 1076); D. Freydank, 'Der Izbornik von 1076 und die Apophthegmata Patrum' (*Zeitschrift für Slawistik*, 21, Berlin, 1976, pp. 357-65); W. R. Veder, 'Welche Paterika lagen vor 1076 in slavischer Übersetzung vor' (*Slovo*, 28, Zagreb, 1978, pp. 25-34); and T. N. Kopreyeva, 'Novyye dannyye dlya izucheniya teksta Izbornika 1076 goda' in *Problemy istochnikovedcheskogo izucheniya rukopisnykh i staropechatnykh fondov. Sbornik nauchnykh trudov*, Leningrad, 1979, pp. 92-112 (this important article introduces a manuscript whose contents closely parallel those of the *Izbornik* of 1076 and help fill some of its gaps).

will turn out in the last analysis to be Byzantine. 'In the last analysis', for the *Miscellany* of 1076 is not itself a direct translation from the Greek, but a compilation drawing upon already available (and sometimes abbreviated) translations.[26] No such uncertainties and need for distinguishing nuances exist with respect to the *Miscellany* of 1073. We know of at least nine Greek manuscripts, two of them of the tenth century (Coislin 120 and Vat. Gr. 423) which are close to or virtually identical with it in content ⟨332⟩ (this is especially true of Vat. Gr. 423). Thus the manuscript evidence alone disposes of recent claims that individual entries of this earliest translated *florilegium* were *selected* and arranged (presumably in Bulgaria) to meet the intellectual and ideological needs of the Bulgarian élite of the tenth century, and that this selection was undertaken by the Bulgarian Tsar Symeon himself, perhaps with the assistance of John the Exarch.[27]

---

26. The evidence for this was provided by my analysis of Agapetus excerpts in the *Izbornik* of 1076, where they occur under the disguise of an 'Admonition to the Rich' and virtually reproduce an independently attested earlier translation, done probably in Bulgaria: see I. Ševčenko, 'On Some Sources of Prince Svjatoslav's *Izbornik* of the Year 1076' in *Orbis Scriptus, Dmitrij Tschiżewskij zum 70. Geburtstag*, Munich, 1966, pp. 723-38. For a further indication (contained in Sofia, National Library, MS Slavonic 1037) that the Agapetus excerpts of the *Izbornik* of 1076 reproduce analogous excerpts made from an earlier translation in Bulgaria or at least in the Balkans, see my 'Agapetus East and West' (see n. 14), p. 28, n. 86. More recently, W. R. Veder produced new evidence for the use of previously translated excerpts (from the *Paterika*) by the compiler of the *Izbornik* of 1076. See his 'Welche Paterika' (as in the preceding note), esp. p. 33. D. Freydank has the merit of having established that another passage of the *Izbornik* of 1076 (attributed in that manuscript to Nilus of Ancyra) is a translation of a part of the Preface to Palladius's *Lausiac History*. It is regrettable that he should have proposed a 'Russian' (curiously enough using a 'hyper-Bulgarian form'!) as a translator; asserted that the translation was made especially *for* the *Izbornik*; and related the nuances of the translation to the concrete social situation in eleventh-century Kiev, in the sense of I. U. Budovnits's theory of 'social conciliation' (a theory fortunately abandoned by at least one recent Soviet scholar: see Rozov, 'Izbornik' [see n. 26], pp. 547-48). See also D. Freydank, 'Interpretation einer griechisch-kirchenslavischen Übersetzung im *Izbornik* von 1076' (*Zeitschrift für Slawistik*, 12, 1967, pp. 38-48).

27. On nine Greek manuscripts close to or virtually identical in contents and arrangement with the *Izbornik* of 1073, see Veder in *Polata k'nigopis'naya* (see n. 24), p. 59. E. È. Granstrem, following Nikol'sky, spoke of sixteen manuscripts: see her 'Vizantiyskoye rukopisnoye naslediye i drevnyaya slavyano-russkaya literatura', in *Puti izucheniya drevnerusskoy literatury i pis'mennosti*, Leningrad, 1970, p. 146, n. 17. I stated as early as 1957 (*Speculum*, 32 [1957], Cam-

The contents of the *Miscellany* of 1073 are essentially patristic, and range from excerpts from St Basil through the interpolated version of *Questions and Answers* of Pseudo-Anastasius the Sinaite (the recension in eighty-eight questions),[28] John Chrysostom, Maximus Confessor, a short Chronicle (similar to a section of that attributed to Patriarch Nicephorus but not identical with it), to the Confession of the Faith by the ninth-century Michael Synkellos. But the *Miscellany* of 1073 does also contain several pieces of philosophic, scientific and medical interest: *On the Essence and Nature* and *On Categories* by Theodore of Rhaithou (i.e. of Pharan? *c.* 600?); on *Stylistic Devices* by the Grammarian George Choiroboskos (*c.* 800?); and a treatise, attributed to John of Damascus, *On the Months According to the Macedonians* (as well as Romans, Jews, Hellenes and Egyptians; it also gives brief dietetic prescriptions for each month).[29]

bridge, Mass., p. 539) that MS Vat. 423 was possibly the closest model of the *Izbornik* of 1073 (it is). This was apparently rediscovered twenty yeras later by B. Peychev, 'Cod. Vat. Gr. 423 — Ein Analogus dem Izbornik J. 1073 (*Palaeobulgarica*, 1, Sofia, 1977, p. 78). (Granstrem was aware of Vat. Gr. 423 by 1970: see her 'Vizantiyskoye rukopisnoye naslediye' as in the present note, p. 146 and n. 18). The Greek text of Vat. Gr. 423 is being prepared for publication by Mario Capaldo. Proceedings of a 1973 conference on various aspects of the *Izbornik* of 1073 were published under the title *Izbornik Svyatoslava 1073 g. Sbornik statey*, Moscow, 1977. For our purposes, see the good chapters by Simonov (pp. 170-84, on numerals), Girshberg (pp. 185-203, on signs of the Zodiac) and Pyotrovskaya (pp. 317-31, on differences between the *Short Chronicle* of the *Izbornik* and that attributed to the Patriarch Nicephorus). On the other hand, chapters by D. Angelov and E. I. Georgiev (pp. 256-72) ignore the fact that the *Izbornik* reproduces a single model and display the unfortunate tendency towards connecting its individual entries and the process of its compilation with Bulgaria. V. Putsko's 'Ob istochnikakh miniatyur Izbornika Svyatoslava 1073 goda' (*Études balkaniques*, 16, 1, Sofia, 1980, pp. 101-19), discusses Byzantine pictorial models, but does not deal with miniatures of astronomical character: see p. 119, n. 53. See also Rozov, *Kniga drevney Rusi* (as in n. 25 above), pp. 20-23 (stress on alleged original contributions of *Izbornik's* scribe) and figs. 2-3 after p. 64 (facsimiles of pages with zodiacal signs).

28. For bringing clarity on these *Questions and Answers* we are indebted to the late M. Richard; see his 'Florilèges spirituels, florilèges grecs', *Dictionnaire de spiritualité...*, 33-34, Paris, 1962, pp. 500-2, and 'Les Véritables "Questions et réponses" d'Anastase le Sinaite', *Institut de recherche et d'histoire des textes, Bulletin*, 15, Paris, 1967-68, pp. 39-56.

29. *Miscellany* of 1073, fols 223^{r}-236^{r}; 237^{v}-240^{v}; 250^{v}-251^{v} (with pictures of zodiacal signs). On excerpts from Choiroboskos (now again dated to *c.* 750-825, see Bühler-Theodoridis in *Byzantinische Zeitschrift*, 69, Munich, 1976, p. 399)

⟨333⟩ Texts such as that by Theodore 'of Rhaithou' gave the tenth-century Bulgarian reader access to introductory material on Aristotelian philosophy and necessitated the creation of a technical terminology, parts of which have survived in several Slavonic languages to the present day. Texts such as the treatise attributed to John of Damascus introduced some rudimentary concepts of astronomy (Sun, Moon and the other five planets with their names and symbols; information on their sequence; the zodiacal signs and their relation to the months during which the sun traverses them). Misunderstandings could hardly be avoided in this first attempt — 'planets' are once translated as 'deceivers', according to the root 'to cause to err' of their Greek name, while fixed stars appear as 'non-deceivers';[30] in one passage the Greek names of the

---

see J. Besharov, *Imagery of the Igor' Tale in the Light of Byzantino-Slavic Poetic Theory*, Leiden, 1956, and the analysis of the *Miscellany's* relevant text in my review of her work, *Speculum*, 32, 1957, pp. 538-43. See also B. St. Angelov, *Iz starata...II* (as in n. 17 above), pp. 89-105 (useful but uncritical; Greek and Slavonic texts; other Slavonic manuscripts containing Choiroboskos) and chapters on Choiroboskos in the collection *Izbornik Svyatoslava 1073 g.* (as in n. 27 above), pp. 99 ff. and 139 ff. For a discussion of incidental medical and dietary passages in the *Izbornik* of 1073, see N. S. Tikhonravov, 'Svyaz' pozdneyshikh lechebnikov s Izbornikom Svyatoslava 1073 goda', *Letopisi russkoy literatury i drevnosti*, 1, Moscow, 1859, p. 150 (on the survival of the entry *On the Months* in a seventeenth-century medical collection); Cheban, 'K voprosu' (as in n. 57 below), pp. 101-3; and Bogoyavlensky, *Drevnerusskoye vrachevaniye* (as in n. 2 above), pp. 137-48 (who, alas, considers the *Izborniki* of 1073 and 1076 to be two 'variants' of one and the same text and sees in both a source for the study of the 'medico-sanitary traditions of the Russian nation').

30. In a section of *Question* 19 by Anastasius the Sinaite, entitled 'From [Gregory] the Theologian, on Love of the Poor', the *Izbornik* of 1073, f. 116ᵛ, has *lьstivyikhъ nekyikhъ i nelьstьnyikhъ sъkupy i raskhody*, which corresponds to *planētōn de tinōn kai aplanōn synodous kai hypochōrēseis* of the Greek, cf. *Vaticanus Gr.* 423, fol. 203ʳ (Jacobus Gretser, *Opera omnia...*, XIV, Regensburg, 1770, 2nd part, p. 277). The *Izbornik's* translation is not unique, as it is paralleled in the Epistle of Jude 13, where *asteres planētai* is rendered by *zvězdy lьstnyye* and *zvězdy lьstivny* in the Šišatovac and Christinopol Apostles respectively: see F. Miklosich, ed., *Apostolus e codice monasterii Šišatovac*, Vienna, 1853, p. 216 and Ae. Kałużniacki, ed., *Actus Epistolaeque Apostolorum Palaeoslovenice ad fidem codicis Christinopolitani saeculo XII° scripti*, Vienna, 1896, p. 106. The mechanical translation in Jude 13 should cast some doubt on the attribution of the Slavonic version of this Epistle to Methodius himself. For fixed stars, *aplaneis asteres*, appearing as 'non-deceiving stars', see, in addition to *Izbornik* of 1073, fol. 116ᵛ, N. S. Tikhonravov, *Pamyatniki otrechennoy literatury*, vol. II, Moscow, 1863; reprint, The Hague-Paris, 1970, p. 412, and

twelve signs of the Zodiac were taken for the names of Macedonian months. But in other passages of the *Miscellany* the usual translation for 'planets' was *planity*, a word which has been retained (in the form *planida*) in popular modern Russian;[31] modern Russian also retained most of the names for the zodiacal signs occurring in the text of the *Miscellany*.

From the tenth century on, such *florilegia* became one channel through which Orthodox Slavs received inklings of wisdom literature, ⟨334⟩ of scientific notions, and of the antique mode of thought and through which they became acquainted with the names and utterances of antique authors. The actual process of transmission and diffusion still remains unclear in its details. For one thing, various kinds of independently translated collections, including the *Gnomic One-liners* by Menander and the Wisdom Books of the Old Testament were included into the *florilegia*; for another, the translations or recensions were made in Bulgaria, Serbia, apparently in Kievan or Halyč Rus' (twelfth-thirteenth century?) and possibly later in Moldavia. Furthermore, the same or similar collections were translated more than once in different areas of Orthodox Slavdom (such as Bulgaria and Kiev), and the process of absorption extended from the tenth to the seventeenth century.[32]

However, we know enough to be able to identify the models of the main types of the later translated *florilegia*; they were the *Sacra parallela* attributed to John of Damascus, and the *Melissa* (The Bee, in Slavonic

Ryan, *Astronomical and Astrological Terminology* (see n. 2), pp. 144-45, who adduces four further examples, drawn from Russian *Sborniki* of the fifteenth to seventeenth centuries. *Lьstivyi* is to be added to Ryan's list of thirteen equivalents for 'planet' (pp. 132-45).

31. *Planida* also occurs in several seventeenth-century Russian cosmographical and astrological manuscripts: see Ryan, *Astronomical and Astrological Terminology* (see n. 2), p. 189, and Sobolevsky, 'Perevodnaya literatura' (see n. 1), pp. 133-34. The standard modern Russian *planeta* is a seventeenth-century borrowing from Latin. On *planit, planita, planida* and *planeta* see N. I. Lepskaya, 'K istorii slova planeta' in *Ètimologicheskiye issledovaniya po russkomu yazyku*, vol. 5, Moscow, 1966, pp. 49-59.

32. On later *florilegia*, M. N. Speransky, 'Perevodnyye sborniki izrecheniy v slavyanorusskoy pis'mennosti. Issledovaniye i teksty' (*Chteniya OIDR*, 199, Moscow, 1901, no. 4; 212, 1905, no. 1; 213, 1905, no. 2 (also published separately, Moscow, 1904; reprint of the Serbian material, Munich, 1970) is still unsurpassed. On Kiev or Halyč Rus' as the place of the earliest translation of the *Bee (Pchela)*, see id., *Iz istorii russko-slavyanskikh literaturnykh svyazey*, Moscow, 1960, pp. 42-44.

Pčela) of Pseudo-Anthony; the latter text itself consisted of an interpolated recension of the *Loci communes* of Pseudo-Maximus the Confessor combined with a text which lies behind that part of the *Sacra parallela* which was devoted to Virtues and Vices.[33] The arrangement of the Slavic *florilegia*, like that of their main models, was in part alphabetical and in part topical.

VIII

The other, and wider, channel through which secular information, more or less technical in nature, reached the Slavonic reader was provided by translations of miscellaneous works dealing with natural history, geography, meteorology and astronomy; such works treated these topics tangentially, if sometimes at length. What follows is the list of the most important among the relevant items.[34]

⟨335⟩ 1. Two works by John the Exarch, an older contemporary of Tsar Symeon of Bulgaria: a partial translation of John of Damascus's *On the Orthodox Faith* (which also introduced astronomical and Aristotelian terms into Slavonic) and the *Hexaemeron*, a compilation based mostly on Basil the Great, but also on Severianus of Gabala, Theodoret of Cyrrhus, and on some adaptation of Aristotle's *Historia animalium*.

2. The *Christian Topography* of Cosmas Indicopleustes (sixth century), translated at an uncertain date (the earliest manuscript: late fifteenth century). The translation is to be assigned most likely to Bulgaria,

---

33. See Speransky, 'Perevodnyye sborniki' (see n. 32); M. Richard, 'Les "Parallela" de Saint Jean Damascène', in *Actes du XIIe Congrès international des études byzantines*, vol. II, Belgrade, 1964, pp. 485-89; and id., 'Florilèges spirituels' (see n. 28), pp. 492-94.

34. To save space, I omit bibliographical references to the best known of these items: John the Exarch, Ps.-Caesarius, Cosmas Indicopleustes, and the *Physiologus*. For convenient access to relevant parts of these texts and references to editions, see Tsv. Kristanov and I. Dujčev, *Estestvoznanieto v srednovekovna Bъlgarija, sbornik ot istoricheski izvori*, Sofia, 1954, and the reference works by Budovnits and Makhnovets' quoted in n. 2 above. For the text of John the Exarch's *Hexaemeron* see now R. Aitzetmüller, *Das Hexaemeron des Exarchen Johannes*, I-VII, Graz, 1958-75. For a good detailed résumé of the scientific parts of John's *Hexaemeron*, cf. G. S. Barankova, 'Ob astronomicheskikh i geograficheskikh znaniyakh' in *Yestestvennonauchnyye predstavleniya drevney Rusi* (see n. 2), pp. 48-62.

but was popular in other areas of Orthodox Slavdom: thus the bulk of its manuscripts is in East Slavonic, a fact which is quoted to support claims that Cosmas was translated in Kievan Rus'.

3. The four *Dialogues* of Pseudo-Caesarius, a sixth-century text translated probably in Tsar Symeon's Bulgaria. The *Dialogues*, which hardly reach the level of St Basil's *Hexaemeron*, touched upon problems of metereology, condemned astrology but dealt with some astronomy and geography, and discussed earthquakes.

4. The *Physiologus*: the version closest to the Greek model was produced at an early date in Bulgaria from the second — that is, fifth-sixth century — recension of the original. Like the *Christian Topography*, the *Physiologus* is well represented in East Slavonic manuscripts.[35]

5. A somewhat abbreviated translation of George of Pisidia's (seventh century) *Hexaemeron or On the Making of the World*, an iambic poem in 1,894 lines. The translation, done by Dimitriy Zograf in 1385, survives in numerous East Slavonic manuscripts, ranging from the fifteenth to the eighteenth century. An entry repeated in a number of them states that the poem was translated into 'the Russian tongue', but peculiarities of spelling point to the Bulgarian, or at least South Slavonic, origin of the version. The Slavonic title, *Praise to God About* (or: *On Account of*) *the Making of All Creation*, is a more apt summary of the contents of George's work than is the Greek title of *Hexaemeron*. The poem is in fact a series of considerations on the Works of God in Nature, including the Animal Kingdom; information on the latter is derived from tidbits in Aristotle's and Aelian's *Historiae animalium*.[36]

⟨336⟩ The next two items are adduced here with some reservations.

6. *Book of the Holy Secrets of Enoch*. Of this Christian *apocryphon*, continuing the Jewish *Enoch*, we have only three Slavonic

35. On a version of the *Physiologus* preserved only in South Slavonic manuscripts, see Grmek, *Les Sciences dans les manuscrits* (see n. 2), p. 30 and n. 76.

36. For the Slavonic text of George of Pisidia's poem see I. A. Shlyapkin, *Shestodnev Georgiya Pisida v slavyano-russkom perevode 1385 goda* (Pamyatniki drevney pis'mennosti i iskusstva, XXXV), St Petersburg, 1882. See also the study by id., 'Georgiy Pisidiyskiy i yego poema o mirotvorenii v slavyano-russkom perevode 1385 goda' (*Zhurnal Ministerstva narodnogo prosveshcheniya*, 269, St. Petersburg, June 1890, pp. 264-94; esp. p. 270, n. 1 on manuscripts; pp. 287-89 on South-Slavonic origin of the translation; pp. 274-75, list of lines in the Greek which were omitted in the Slavonic). See P. Nikitin, 'Zamechaniya k tekstu "Shestodneva" Georgiya Pisidiyskogo' (*Zhurnal*

versions preserved in a dozen manuscripts; the Greek original, which was still available in Byzantium in the thirteenth century, is now lost. The short Slavonic version is the earliest and closest to its model: it is a genuine translation made (in Macedonia?) perhaps as early as the tenth century. As for the first Slavonic reworking of that translation, it was done in the Balkans in the late fifteenth century, and contains vast interpolations.

The claim of the short Slavonic version to a place in our list rests on Enoch's having traversed the seven heavens on his journey towards the Lord, and having described them one by one. The fourth heaven is that of the Sun and the Moon; Enoch computes the movements of these luminaries in and out of the 'gates' on the ecliptic and comes up with 364 days for the duration both of the Solar and the Lunar year. These archaic figures reproduce those of the Jewish *Enoch*. The claim of the first Slavonic reworking of *Enoch* to being listed here rests on its astronomical and calendarial corrections and interpolations: the duration of the Solar and Lunar years is changed to 365 and one quarter (the Julian calendar's system) and 354 days respectively; and the reviser introduced a parameter important for the computation of Easter date (the 'Great Cycle' of 19 × 28 or 532 years). In the last analysis, these insertions were of Byzantine origin, but they were made up of elements already available to the reviser through previous Slavonic translations.[37]

It is doubtful whether any Slavonic reader used the *Book of Enoch*

Ministerstva narodnogo prosveshcheniya, 255, January 1888, Section of Classical Philology, pp. 1-29) who makes use of the Slavonic translation to emend the Greek original. The most recent and thorough discussion of the relation between the Slavonic version of George and its model is the monograph by Giuseppe Fermeglia, 'Studi sul testo delle due versioni (slava ed armena) dello *Hexaemeron* di Giorgio Pisida', *Memorie dell'Istituto Lombardo — Accademia di Scienze e Lettere, Classe di Lettere — Scienze morali e storiche*, 28, fasc. 2, Milan, 1964, pp. 227-332, esp. pp. 229-31 (on the nationality of the translator: *non liquet*) and pp. 236-42 (on the errors of the Slavonic translator). I received N. Radošević, *Šestodnev Georgija Piside i njegov slovenski prevod* (Vizantološki Institut Srpske Akademije Nauka i Umetnosti, Posebna izdanja, 16), Belgrade, 1979, too late to be able to profit from it in the present paper, but see pp. 99-124 (a chapter discussing the Slavonic translation) and pp. 131-33 (English summary of that chapter).

37. For the edition of the *Book of Enoch* and excellent discussion of its textual and linguistic aspects, see A. Vaillant, *Le Livre des secrets d'Hénoch, texte slave et traduction française*, 2nd edn, Paris, 1976, esp. chapter VI of text, pp. 11-17 and 91-93. On computistic elements in our text, cf. J. K. Fortheringham, 'The Easter Calendar and the Slavonic Enoch' (*Journal of Theological Studies*, 23,

for astronomical or computistic information. *Enoch*, however, is a ⟨337⟩ legitimate quarry from which to extract later terminology and misunderstandings concerning the names of stars.[38]

7. *Disputation* (in Slavonic: *Prěnie*) *Between Panagiotes and the Azymite*, a late thirteenth-century anti-Latin tract, translated in the Balkans relatively soon after its appearance (the earliest dated Slavonic manuscript: 1384). In the first part of the tract (which in some Greek versions takes the form of questions and answers), the Orthodox puts his adversary, an 'Azymite', that is, adherent of the unleavened bread (and a Cardinal!) to shame by showing off knowledge about the number and sequence of heavens; the sublunar sphere; the rising and setting of the sun; the distance between heaven and earth; the depth of the sea; the respective sizes of the sky, the land, and the seas; terrestrial Paradise; and the causes of thunder and lightning. One source for the bizarre notions displayed by the spokesman for the Orthodox is the *Book of Enoch*; other sources are obscure, but all reflect views circulating among semi-educated Byzantines of the time.[39]

IX

I am aware of only four works or categories of works known in translation that were *in their entirety* devoted to scientific or parascientific matters. These are:

London, 1921, pp. 49-56) who was perplexed to find so late an element as the cycle of 532 years in an early *apocryphon*. But, as we just saw, the cycle appears in a section interpolated in the fifteenth century.

38. See W. F. Ryan, 'Curious Star Names in Slavonic Literature' (*Russian Linguistics*, 1, Dordrecht, 1974, pp. 139-50, esp. pp. 138-39, 144-46).

39. Slavonic text of the *Disputation* in A. N. Popov, *Istorikoliteraturnyy obzor drevne-russkikh polemicheskikh sochineniy protiv latinyan (XI-XV vv.)*, Moscow, 1875 (reprint, London, 1972), pp. 251-86; see also Prince P. V. Vyazemsky in *Pamyatniki drevney pis'mennosti*, 4, Moscow, 1879, pp. 37-65 (not inspected by me). Passages on thunder and lightning also in Peretts, 'Materialy' (*Zapiski* [see n. 43], pp. 4-5). Greek texts: A. Vassiliyev, *Anecdota Graeco-Byzantina*, 1, Moscow, 1893, pp. 179-88 (truncated text); M. N. Speransky, 'K istorii preniya Panagiota s Azimitom' (*Vizantiyskiy Vremennik*, 2, Moscow, 1895, pp. 521-30 (pp. 527-30: a fragment going beyond the text of Vassiliyev)); N. Th. Krasnosel'tsev, '"Preniye Panagiota s Azimitom" po novym grecheskim spiskam' (*Letopis' Istoriko-filologicheskogo obshchestva pri Imp. Novorossiyskom Universitete*, 6 [Vizantiyskoye otdeleniye, 3], Odessa, 1896, pp. 295-328 [fullest text]).

1. The so-called *Novaković Fragments* (forty-six in number) on cosmography and geography preserved in three manuscripts, two of them Serbian, of the fifteenth and sixteenth centuries. It is quite likely that Constantine Kostenečki (see p. 328 above) was their compiler; what is certain is that he used them in the geographical excursus included in his *Life of Stephen Lazarević*. Since 1939 we have known the *Fragments* to be a translation of parts of the *Solutiones breves* attributed to Michael Psellos, with added passages from Psellos's *De Omnifaria doctrina* and of some elements from the *Hexaemeron* of ⟨338⟩ Basil the Great.[40] These *Fragments*, of slight value in themselves, made the concept of the sphericity of the earth again accessible to the Orthodox Slavonic reader (in the wake of St Basil the concept had been already offered to that reader by John the Exarch).

2. A short metrological fragment (about measures of length, capacity, time and weight) contained in a Serbian miscellany of 1441-42. It goes back to a Byzantine model, although it is not clear whether it is a straight translation or a compilation based on Greek materials.[41]

3. Short astrological tracts, or, more appropriately, divinatory writings, based on natural phenomena:[42]

---

40. The discovery belongs to C. Giannelli, 'Di alcune versioni e rielaborazioni serve delle "Solutiones breves quaestionum naturalium" attribuite a Michele Psello,' *Studi bizantini e neoellenici*, 5, 1, Naples, 1939, pp. 445-68; repeated in Giannelli's *Scripta Minora* (*Studi bizantini e neoellenici*, 10), 1963, pp. 1-25. Recent discussion and edition of the *Fragments* (basis: three manuscripts) in B. St. Angelov, *Iz starata...II* (see n. 17), pp. 164-90.

41. Cf. S. Ćirković, 'Metrološki odlomak Goričkog Zbornika' (*Zbornik radova Vizantološkog instituta*, 16, Belgrade, 1975, pp. 183-89).

42. For the convenience of non-Slavists, the titles of these tracts will be given here in their Greek form. For a brief but lucid survey of Byzantine models of this type of treatise, see L. Delatte, 'Note sur les manuscrits astronomiques du Mont Athos,' *Annuaire de l'Institut de philologie et d'histoire orientales et slaves*, 11, Brussels, 1951 (Mélanges H. Grégoire, 3), pp. 107-12 (basis: 150 late manuscripts, dating from the sixteenth century on). More diffuse and partly antiquated, but still informative, are those sections of M. A. Andreyeva's articles on *Brontologia* and *Selēnodromia* that offer new Slavonic texts and deal with their sources. See her 'Politicheskiy i obshchestvennyy element vizantiyskoslavyanskikh gadatel'nykh knig' (*Byzantinoslavica*, 2, 1930, pp. 47-73; sources are discussed on pp. 49 ff.); ibid., 3, 1931, pp. 430-61 (pp. 453-54: *Gromovnik* from the Hodoš manuscript, dated by Andreyeva to the fifteenth century); ibid., 4, 1932, pp. 65-84 (pp. 76-83, two *Gromovniki* of the eighteenth century); *eadem*, 'K istorii vizantiysko-slavyanskikh gadatel'nykh knig' (*Byzantinoslavica*, 5, 1933-34, pp. 120-61).

a) *Selēnodromia* (in Slavonic: *Lunniki*), establishing propitious or evil days for a given activity (whether related to agriculture, building, war, health, or public matters) depending on the day of the lunation, on the position of the moon in the Zodiac or on its brilliance and shape (especially of the crescent).

b) *Brontologia* (in Slavonic: *Gromniki* or *Gromovniki*), offering divination by the time of thunder (sometimes measured in terms of phases of the moon) or by the region of the sky where thunder and lightning occur.[43]

⟨339⟩

c) *Zōdiologia*, determining the fate of boys and girls born under a given sign of the Zodiac.[44]

d) *Kalendologia* (in Slavonic: *Koljadniki*), determining the character of the year (its seasons, abundance or scarcity of produce, epidemics) according to the day of the week coinciding with the first of January or with the day of Christmas.[45]

e) *Dōdekaetērides*, or prognoses for twelve years according to the zodiacal sign 'reigning' in a given year.

f) A composite treatise (given the title *On the Course* [or Period] *of the Year and on the Changes of Air* in the manuscript and that of

43. Two basic works on Slavonic *Brontologia* and *Selēnodromia* are V. N. Peretts, 'Materialy k istorii apokrifov i legend, I. K istorii Gromnika...' (*Zapiski istoriko-filologicheskogo fakul'teta Imp. Sankt-Peterburgskogo universiteta*, 54, 1, St Petersburg, 1899, esp. pp. 1-80 [pp. 54-80: texts]); and id., 'Materialy k istorii apokrifov i legend. K istorii Lunnika' (*Izvestiya ORYaS*, 6, 3, St Petersburg, 1901, pp. 1-126: pp. 60-72, text of an early *Lunnik*); ibid., 6, 4, 1901, pp. 103-31 (pp. 104-7, edition of an early *Lunnik*; Byzantine counterparts of this text appear in Oxford, Bodleian, MS Barocci 206, f. 130r-130v; in *Catalogus codicum astrologorum graecorum* [hereafter CCAG], vol. 3, Brussels, 1901, pp. 32-39: and ibid., vol. 11, 2, 1932, pp. 157-62). See also Tikhonravov, *Pamyatniki*, vol. II (see n. 30), pp. 361-76 (texts); V. Jagić, 'Opisi i izvodi iz nekoliko yuzhnoslovinskikh rukopisa, XVI,' *Starine*, 10, 1878, pp. 119-24 (Slavonic and Greek texts).

44. See Jagić, *Starine*, 10, 1878, pp. 124-26.

45. For texts, see Tikhonravov, *Pamyatniki*, 11 (see n. 30), pp. 377-81; Jagić, *Starine*, 10, 1878, pp. 115-18. For Byzantine counterparts of Slavonic *Kalendologia*, see e.g. Oxford, Bodleian, MS Barocci 206, f. 130r; Jagić, *Starine*, 10, 1878, p. 115; R. Wünsch, 'Zu Lydus de ostentis' (*Byzantinische Zeitschrift*, 5, 1896, pp. 419-20); *CCAG*, 7, 1908, p. 126; ibid., 10, 1924, pp. 151-52. Both in Greek and in Slavonic, *Kalendologia* are sometimes attributed to the prophet Esdras.

Astrologiya by its modern editor) that combines some straight astronomical notions about the number of heavens, the sequence of planets, and the sphere of fixed stars with astrological, calendarial, dietetic and medical lore.[46]

In actuality, pure Slavonic forms of these tracts are as rare as the pure forms of their Byzantine prototypes. Thus, *Gromovniki* often offer composite texts, in which phases of the moon, lunar and solar eclipses, haloes around the sun and the moon, comets, shooting stars, rain, hail, rainbows and earthquakes are quoted along with thunder and lightning as divinatory signs.

These Slavonic texts, displaying various degrees of contamination and recombination of astrological material, do no more than reproduce analogous forms of their Byzantine models (which sometimes bear the double title '*Brontologion* and *Seismologion*' and in turn go back to Arabic prototypes). A great deal of instability prevails in this kind of literature whether Byzantine or Slavonic: as there are practically as many redactions of a treatise as there are manuscripts of it, a close relationship between the Slavonic text and its Byzantine model is sufficiently established if we can claim quasi-identity for their structure and detect in both a reasonable proportion of divinations that are identical in substance and rather close in form.[47] ⟨340⟩ Translations of these Byzan-

46. For Slavonic *Dodekaetēris*, see Peretts, 'Materialy' (*IORYaS*, 6, 4, pp. 109-10); for Byzantine counterparts, see *CCAG*, 2, 1900, pp. 144-52 and ibid., 3, 1901, pp. 30-31. Text of *Astrologiya* in Tikhonravov, *Pamyatniki*, II (as in n. 30 above), pp. 398-421. The edition is based on three sixteenth-century manuscripts, but the text's terminology is archaic and its origin, surely Byzantine: see p. 398, *drimit*, which back to the Greek *drimytēs*, 'sharpness, pungency (of foods)'. For fragments from *Astrologiya* (after the main manuscript used by Tikhonravov), see Zmeyev, *Russkiye vrachebniki* (as in n. 58 below), pp. 240-42.

47. For a composite *Gromovnik*, see text no. 3 in Peretts, 'Materialy' in *Zapiski* (see n. 43), pp. 60-80, and its close relatives published by Andreyeva, 'Politicheskiy...' *Byzantinoslavica*, 3, 1931, pp. 455-60) and 'K istorii' (n. 42), pp. 156-59. For Byzantine counterparts of Slavonic composite *Gromovniki* closely related to Peretts, no. 3, see Oxford, Bodleian, MS Auct. T. 5. 8, fols. 18^r ff.; 55^v ff.; 95^r ff.; also *CCAG*, vol. 8, 3, 1912, pp. 172-79 (for October); ibid., vol. 10, 1924, pp. 154-55 (for October-December). See also Andreyeva, 'K istorii' (see n. 42), pp. 143-53. Other examples of composite *Gromovniki* are Peretts, 'Materialy' (*Izvestiya* (see n. 43), 6, 4, pp. 123-24 (time measured by the waxing or waning moon; Byzantine counterpart in *CCAG*, vol. 8, 3, 1912, pp. 169-71) and Jagić, *Starine*, 10, 1878, pp. 121-23 (Byzantine counterparts in Jagić, ibid., pp. 123-24; *CCAG*, vol. 8, 3, 1912, pp. 166-67 and ibid., 10, 1924, pp. 58-59,

tine astrological texts seem to have been done in the Balkans. The manuscripts (nineteen of the *Gromovniki* alone were known by 1899) are South Slavonic and Moldavian, as well as East Slavonic; the earliest preserved *Gromovnik* dates from the early fourteenth century; the earliest preserved *Lunnik* (the genre is represented by a dozen manuscripts), from the middle of the fifteenth. Starting with the sixteenth century, most of the new astrological texts (especially those circulating in the Orthodox lands of the Polish Commonwealth and in Muscovy) were of non-Byzantine origin.[48]

4. Short medical and pharmaceutical treatises. I list illustrative examples of translations from or adaptations of ancient Greek or Byzantine originals, all seemingly done by Serbs:[49]

a) *Narrative on Human Bodies and Elements* dealing with four humours and embryology and based on a Byzantine reworking of Hippocrates's *Peri physios anthrōpou* and *Peri physios paidiou*. It is preserved in a Serbian manuscript attributed by Jagić to the fifteenth century.[50]

b) The *Iatrosophia Concerning All Occasions*, a pharmaceutical treatise discovered in a fifteenth-century manuscript of Serbian provenance in the monastery of Chilandar (Mount Athos) in 1951.[51]

c) *Fragments* attributed — wrongly — to Galen (cf. *Galinovo na Ipokrata* in the title) and preserved in Russian manuscripts of the fifteenth-seventeenth centuries based on a Serbian ⟨341⟩ model.

60-62). For a composite *Lunnik*, see Peretts, 'Materialy,' *Zapiski* (see n. 43), pp. 54-56; for Byzantine counterparts to this *Lunnik's* first entries under the respective months (on the position of the moon), see *CCAG*, 8, 3, 1912, pp. 179-80; this text is close to the simple *Lunnik* published in Peretts, 'Materialy', *Izvestiya* (see n. 43), 6, 4, pp. 108 (divination by the position of the moon).

48. See Raykov, *Ocherki* (see n. 2), pp. 66-104.

49. For a fuller list of translated or adapted Serbian medical treatises, see R. V. Katić, *Medicina kod Srba u Srednjem veku* (Srpska Akademija Nauka, Posebna izdanja, 310), Belgrade, 1958, p. 42; see also id., *Srpska medicina od IX do XIX veka* (Srpska Akademija Nauka i Umetnosti, Posebna izdanja, 415), Belgrade, 1967, pp. 104-14, on the Chilandar medical MS 517 (sixteenth century) that uses ancient Greek and Byzantine along with Western sources.

50. See Jagić, 'Opisi i izvodi' (see n. 43), pp. 95-99. The text itself must be fairly recent, for it uses the Turkic term *bubrega* for 'kidney' (p. 95).

51. Published, e.g. in R. V. Katić, *Medicina kod Srba* (see n. 49), pp. 60-62. See also Grmek, *Les Sciences* (see n. 2), p. 37 and n. 94; cf. n. 88.

They seem to reflect some course of elementary instruction in medicine.[52]

X

Several items, occasionally discussed in modern treatises on the history of 'Russian' science, are absent from the inventory drawn up in the previous three sections. One or another of these items may marginally belong into our context; however, others do not, for they either are not scientific (no matter how generously one construes the term), or are not direct translations from the Greek.

The South Slavonic version of Severianus of Gabala's (*c.* 400) six homilies on the first six (in Slavonic: second to seventh) days of Creation is one of such marginal items. On balance, it contains too little material pertaining to natural science to justify its inclusion in our lists, even if Severianus himself insisted that not only the Doctrine of God (*theologia*), but also the Doctrine of Nature (*physiologia*) deserved treatment in his homilies on the Genesis. The omission is of little practical importance: as the Slavonic translation of Severianus was done quite early,

52. See Tikhonravov, *Pamyatniki*, II (see n. 30 above), pp. 405-10, and Zmeyev, *Russkiye vrachebniki* (n. 58 below), pp. 242-45. In the manuscript of the Trinity Sergius Lavra, no. 177, the medical fragments *Galinovo na Ipokrata* are a part of *On the Course of the Year*, or *Astrologiya*, concerning which see p. 607 and n. 46 above; this fact seems to have escaped some modern authors (see n. 61 below). A shortened version (with younger Russian linguistic traits) of *Galinovo na Ipokrata* occurs in a seventeenth-century collection of medical prescriptions (*Lechebnik*), ed. by M. Yu. Lakhtin, 'Starinnyye pamyatniki meditsinskoy pis'mennosti' (*Zapiski Moskovskogo arkheologicheskogo instituta*, 17, 1912, pp. 1-3). For a summary of *Galinovo na Ipokrata* see Bogoyavlensky, *Drevnerusskoye vrachevaniye* (n. 2 above), pp. 32-34. For the Greek character of the original, see Tikhonravov, *Pamyatniki*, vol. II, p. 408: "*spanost*' which is an exiguity of one's beard": this goes back to the Greek *spanos*, 'beardless person'. In view of the Serbian character of several medical manuscripts quoted here, it is perhaps legitimate to relate them to the best-known hospital of late Costantinople, the *Xenōn tou Kralē*, or 'Hospice of the ⟨Serbian⟩ King'. It was founded by King Milutin in the early fourteenth century, and staffed by him with 'his own people'. The hospital continued to flourish in the next century. It is conceivable that some professionally educated Serbian monks were active at the *Xenōn* along with the Greeks, and that they did some translating. On the hospital, see M. Živojinović, 'Bolnica Kralja Milutina u Carigradu' (*Zbornik radova Vizantološkog instituta*, 16, Belgrade, 1975, pp. 105-17, esp. p. 109).

some of his material was used by John the Exarch in his *Hexaemeron*, a work that occupies the place of pride in our second list.[53]

Works of divination based on random numerical procedures have little claim to inclusion in our lists, even though such works have occasionally attracted the attention of historians of science. Here belongs the Slavonic divinatory Psalter (earliest known manuscript: ⟨342⟩ *c*. 1100) and treatises on geomancy, in Slavonic, *rafli* (cf. the Greek *rample*, *ramplia*, a term which in turn goes back to the Arabic *raml*, for 'sand'), or their reflections in the Radzivill Chronicle.[54] Although the divinations (*gataniya*) of the Psalter are clearly Byzantine, they are in fact a set of hundred and fifty oracles of quite ancient origin, several of them repeating formulae used in Hellenistic oracles with ready answers.[55]

While all of the divinatory Psalter's *gataniya* are literal translations

53. On the six manuscripts (four East Slavonic, two Bulgarian) of Severianus's homilies (called *Hexaemeron*, or *Shestodnev* in Slavonic), see Sobolevsky, 'Perevodnaya literatura' (see n. 1), pp. 21-22. Detailed description of one manuscript in Gorsky and Nevostruyev, *Opisaniye* (as in n. 25 above), no. 203, pp. 628-32; five of the six homilies correspond to homilies two to six on Genesis by Severianus; one, the fifth, to a homily attributed to John Chrysostom.

54. For a facsimile of the earliest Psalter with divinations, consisting of two *membra disiecta*, the Bychkov Fragments, now in Leningrad, and Sinai codex Slavonic 6, see M. Altbauer and H. G. Lunt, *An Early Slavonic Psalter from Rus'*, I: *Photoreproduction*, Cambridge, Mass., 1978, esp. pp. ix-x. For Slavonic geomancy of Byzantine origin, see M. N. Speransky, *Iz istorii otrechennykh knig, I: Gadaniya po psaltiri* (Pamyatniki drevney pis'mennosti i iskusstva, 129), St Petersburg, 1899, pp. 59-76 (discussion, quite confused) and Appendix, pp. 15-20 (a geomantic tract in a Serbian redaction; I was able to identify the text of its Greek original as that published by A. Delatte, *Anecdota Atheniensia*, I, Liège-Paris, 1927, pp. 577-61). M. N. Speransky, 'Leos des Weisen Weissagungen nach dem Evangelium und Psalter' (*Archiv für slavische Philologie*, 25, Berlin, 1903, pp. 239-49, esp. pp. 245-49), had already published a Greek text related to his own geomantic tract without much awareness of the geomantic character of either. For geomantic signs on f. 228 of the Radzivill Chronicle, see, e.g. R. A. Simonov, *Matematicheskaya mysl' drevney Rusi*, Moscow, 1977, pp. 62-64, who thought that these signs meant abacus computations; this error was corected by A. V. Chernetsov, 'Ob odnom risunke radzivillovskoy letopisi' (*Sovetskaya arkheologiya*, Moscow, 1977, no. 4, pp. 301-6).

55. The Greek models of the Slavonic *gataniya* have been preserved in a fairly large number of Byzantine Psalters and at least one miscellaneous manuscript. I intend to publish these models elsewhere and thus simplify the prolix discussion in M. N. Speransky, *Iz istorii otrechennykh knig*, I (see preceding note), who did not find the Greek sources of the texts.

from Byzantine Greek, the Byzantine pedigree of some other candidates for inclusion in our inventory is far less certain. Still other relevant texts are not direct translations, but local imitations or compilations recombining previously translated Byzantine material.[56] Such items should be omitted altogether. In medicine, these range from one short but interesting and quite matter-of-fact dietetic fragment found in a sixteenth-century Russian manuscript,[57] to a class of medical and pharmaceutical collections similar to the Chilandar *Iatrosophia* listed above, but containing magical incantations and prayers in addition to medical prescriptions. These collections went by the names of *Lěchebniki*, *Travniki*, *Zel'niki* ('Herbals') or *Vertogrady* ('Gardens', cf. the Latin *Hortus* as title of medical works) ⟨343⟩ in the East, and *Lekaruše* in the Balkans. Preserved *Lěchebniki* and *Vertogrady* seem to be post-Byzantine: although it is claimed that the genre goes back to the late fifteenth century (or even earlier), the earliest datable Muscovite works of this class are of the sixteenth, and the manuscripts themselves, of the seventeenth century.[58] Moreover, except for some Greek terms and Greek (?) magical formulae, most of the immediate sources of these collections point to the Latin, German, or Polish West, rather than to Byzantium (e.g. prescriptions for the cure of the 'French disease', that is — syphilis).

---

56. I made an exception for the venerable *Izbornik* of 1076 (see p. 330 above) since my (and some others') belief in its being a compilation of previously existing translations may not be universally shared.

57. Published by S. Cheban, 'K voprosu o gigienicheskikh predpisaniyakh v drevnerusskoy literature' (*Zhurnal Ministerstva narodnogo prosveshcheniya*, N. S., 43, St Petersburg, January 1913, pp. 100-21; text on pp. 116-17). According to the editor, the text is surely a translation and was made, most probably from a Byzantine model, towards the end of the fourteenth century at the latest (this on account of two occurrences of archaizing imperfects in *-chǫt* . However, our fragment may, at least in part, be an original composition of East Slavonic provenance (preference given to river over lake fish implies conditions different from those of Greece and the Balkans); moreover, some of its vocabulary is decidedly late (e.g. such terms as the Turkic *izyum*, 'raisins', or the Romance *latuga*, 'lettuce').

58. See e.g. Cheban, 'K voprosu' (as in the preceding note), pp. 106 and 112. On *Lechebniki*, see Tikhonravov, 'Svyaz'' (as in n. 29 above); L. F. Zmeyev, *Russkiye vrachebniki. Issledovaniye v oblasti nashey drevney vrachebnoy pis'mennosti*, St Petersburg, 1896, describing 186 manuscripts, and Lakhtin, 'Starinnyye pamyatniki' (see n. 52 above). The candidate dissertation by V. F. Gruzdev, *Russkiye rukopisnyye lechebniki*, Leningrad, 1946, was inaccessible to me.

Furthermore, the category of works to be left out includes computistic writings, such as the calendar treatise by Kirik of Novgorod, dating from 1136,[59] or various Paschal Tables, whose authors merely relied on procedures borrowed from Byzantium. Finally, here belongs the so-called *Tolkovaya Paleya*, or *Old Testament With Commentaries*. In this compilation (of East Slavonic origin?), said to have been put together in the thirteenth century, passages pertaining to cosmology, anthropology and (in some versions) zoology were made up of pieces quarried from translations already quoted here: John the Exarch's *Hexaemeron*, Cosmas Indicopleustes, and the *Physiologus*.[60] In sum, it is better to run the risk of being too terse than to pad the evidence.[61]

---

59. Facsimile and modern Russian translation of Kirik's *A Doctrine by Means of Which One Can Know the Numbers* (i.e. make the computation) *of All Years* in *Istorikomatematicheskiye issledovaniya*, 6, Moscow, 1953, pp. 174-95. Its elements are Byzantine, but it is not a translation. On Kirik, see Simonov, *Matematicheskaya mysl'* (as in n. 54 above), pp. 93-108.

60. For the text of two versions of *Tolkovaya paleya* (based on manuscripts of the years 1406 and 1477 respectively), see *Paleya Tolkovaya po spisku sdelannomu v Kolomne v 1406 g., trud uchenikov I. S. Tikhonravova*, Moscow, 1892 and *Tolkovaya paleya 1477 goda...*, vol. I (Obshchestvo lyubiteley drevney pis'mennosti, XCIII), St. Petersburg, 1892. These two versions are essentially the same when it comes to natural sciences. On the controversy (waged mainly between Istrin and his disciples on one hand and Shakhmatov on the other) concerning the sources, date, and place of origin of the *Tolkovaya paleya*, see e.g. A. Karneyev, 'K voprosu o vzaimnykh otnosheniyakh Tolkovoy Palei i Zlatoy Matitsy' (*Zhurnal Ministerstva narodnogo prosveshcheniya*, 327, February 1900, pp. 335-36); ibid., February 1906, pp. 225-46 (by Istrin); ibid., November 1906, pp. 204-33 (by Istomin); A. Mikhailov, 'K voprosu o proiskhozhdenii i literaturnykh istochnikakh Tolkovoy palei' (*Izvestiya po russkomu yazyku i slovesnosti Akademii nauk SSSR*, vol. I, fasc. I, Leningrad, 1928, pp. 49-80). For the view localizing the *Tolkovaya paleya* among Southern Slavs, see M. N. Speransky, 'Istorijska Paleja, njeni prevodi i redakcije u staroj slavenskoj književnosti' (*Srpska Kraljevska Akademija, Spomenik*, 16, Belgrade, 1892, esp. p. 4). The so-called *Historical Paleya*, a truncated South Slavonic translation of a Middle-Byzantine paraphrase of the Old Testament (in Greek: down to Daniel; in Slavonic: down to David), is of no relevance to us, as it has no excursus dealing with natural science: see Speransky, *Iz istorii* (as in n. 32 above) pp. 104-47; D. Flusser, 'Palaea Historica, an Unknown Source of Biblical Legends' (*Scripta Hierosolymitana*, 22, Jerusalem, 1971, pp. 48-79: summary of contents).

61. Even our own lists contain some padding, for they include works read primarily for their moral and theological message rather than for information they conveyed on the movement of the Heavens, on Nature and on Philosophy. An example of padding can be adduced from the works of Kuzakov and

⟨344⟩ Even thus pruned, the inventory of our sections VII, VIII and IX does account for a majority of texts that dealt, in part or in whole, with philosophy, astronomy and natural sciences, and were available to Orthodox Slavs down to the sixteenth century.[62] Exact sciences are almost totally absent from our sample, and what was transmitted, was aimed at a general cultivated reader or, in the case of the *Disputation Between Panagiotes and the Azymite*, reflected information valued by Byzantine ecclesiastics of quite modest cultural level.

The vast majority of original translations for which we can establish a provenance come from the Balkans. Eastern Slavs were most active in copying, using, re-arranging and benefiting from the translations, but they were not among their foremost producers. The models of most relevant items — either those quoted in our lists or those eliminated from them — were Greek. The four accidental scientific texts translated from the Hebrew in the Grand Duchy of Lithuania (and done in the variant of the Slavonic literary language used in that state), and three or four translations from the Latin, done in Novgorod and Moscow, do not change the picture. But the very appearance of translations from languages other than Greek was a sign that about year 1500 Orthodox Slavs were responding to new impulses, at least in Eastern Europe.[63]

Bogoyavlensky (see n. 2 above): both authors discuss chronicles among sources for the history of science in Rus', just because chronicles record comets and eclipses of the Sun and the Moon, mention epidemics or individual illnesses, and contain incidental information on diet. Padding (of an unwitting variety, I assume) also occurs when passages from the same work, and the same manuscripts, are adduced as coming from different sources; these passages are thus paraded through the pages like the same soldiers marching over and over again across the stage in *Aida*: see Cheban, K voprosu' (see n. 57), pp. 108 and 110; Bogoyavlensky, *Drevnerusskoye vrachevaniye* (see n. 2), pp. 28 and 32.

62. In our period, Catholic Slavs sharply differed from the Orthodox in their scientific readings, as they did in most other matters. The demonstration for the Balkans comes from manuscripts of scientific content preserved in Croatia and Slovenia: see M. D. Grmek, 'Rukovet starih medicinskih, matematičko-fizičkih, astronomskih, kemijskih i prirodoslovnih rukopisa sačuvanih u Hrvatskoj i Sloveniji' (*Rasprave i gradja za povijest nauka*, I, Zagreb, 1963, pp. 259-343). Grmek's two hundred and eighty items are in their majority Latin or Italian, with German, French, Croatian, Slovenian and even Hungarian texts making up the rest. The catalogue offers only a few Slavonic fifteenth-century manuscritps in Glagolitic script (exorcisms, medical prescriptions, magic formulae), and even there Byzantine origins of the contents remain to be proven.

63. All translations from the Hebrew may date from the late fifteenth century. This is certainly true of at least one of the two logical treatises (*Logical Ter-*

The seventeenth and eighteenth centuries brought a flood of these new impulses; they reached Muscovy first through Polish and ⟨345⟩ Ukrainian mediation, then through direct contacts with the West. This spelled the end of Byzantine preponderance in non-religious fields, including the scientific one, although scientific and parascientific texts of Byzantine origin continued to be copied and read in miscellaneous manuscripts until the late eighteenth century.

The wider question for historians to ponder is whether the Byzantine heritage was irrelevant to the subsequent development of science among Orthodox Slavs, especially to its great blossoming in Russia, or whether — as seems more likely — the heritage of Byzantium did contribute the background of subject matter and habits of thought that somehow furthered that development.[64]

---

minology by Maimonides; *Logic* by Al-Gazali), for a 'heretical' *Logic* was known in Novgorod by 1489: see Brice Parain, 'La Logique dite des Judaïsants' (*Revue des études slaves*, 19, Paris, 1939, pp. 315-29, esp. p. 315). Among translations from Latin, that of the computistic and calendaric Book VIII of Guilielmus Durandus's *Rationale divinorum officiorum* (late thirteenth century) was made in Novgorod in 1495: see V. Beneshevich, "Iz istorii perevodnoy literatury v Novgorode kontsa XV stoletiya" (*SORYaS*, 101, 3, 1928, pp. 378-80). The famous *Lucidarius* was translated shortly after 1500.

64. I am indebted to Dr W. F. Ryan, Academic Librarian of the Warburg Institute, London, and to Mr J. S. G. Simmons, Research Fellow and Librarian at All Souls College, Oxford, for their criticism and help in matters of bibliography. I received the important review article by Heinz Miklas, 'Ergebnisse und Perspektiven bei der Erforschung der kirchenslavisch-griechischen Übersetzungstheorie und Übersetzungspraxis' (*Palaeobulgarica*, 4, 3, Sofia, 1980, pp. 98-111) and also *Polata k''nigopis'naja*, no. 4, Nijmegen, 1981 (fascicule devoted to *Paterika*) too late to make use of them in this paper.

XXXIV

Report on the Glagolitic Fragments (of the *Euchologium Sinaiticum?*) Discovered on Sinai in 1975 and Some Thoughts on the Models for the Make-up of the Earliest Glagolitic Manuscripts*

The manuscript finds made on Sinai in 1975 electrified several scholarly communities. In addition to fragments of Greek manuscripts, including over a dozen new folia of the *Codex Sinaiticus* and samples of hitherto unknown preminuscule script, these finds brought to the fore manuscript fragments in Syriac, in Cyrillic, and in Georgian. Unfortunately, access to these finds, let alone their publication, has met with considerable delay; to date, only two preliminary reports, both dating from 1980 and concerning the Greek manuscripts alone, have appeared in scholarly journals; one, by James Charlesworth, stresses biblical manuscripts; the other, more detailed, is by the noted paleographer, the late Linos Politis.[1] On Slavic finds, we have only rumors, and half a page of most rudimentary, if greatly exciting, data.[2] In October of 1981, at the Inter-

---

* An earlier version of this paper was delivered at a Bulgarian-American Conference held at Dumbarton Oaks, Washington, D.C., in November 1981.

1. James H. Charlesworth, "The Manuscripts of St. Catherine's Monastery," *Biblical Archaeologist*, 43, no. 1 (Winter 1980): 26-34 (for earlier mention of the 1975 finds in that journal, cf. fn. 5 on p. 33); Linos Politis, "Nouveaux manuscrits grecs découverts au Mont Sinai. Rapport préliminaire," *Scriptorium* 34 (1980): 5-17 and 9 plates.

2. W. R. Veder, reporting on the Second Summer Colloquium on Old Bulgarian Studies (Sofia, 1980) in *Polata K"nigopis'naja* 5 (October 1981): 31-32, reproduced a list of Sinai finds provided by Moshé Altbauer. Among its items are a complete Glagolitic homiliary and a complete Glagolitic psalter, both of undetermined age.

national Congress of Byzantine Studies in Vienna, His Eminence Damianos, archbishop of Sinai, announced that a summary catalogue of some of those finds — at least the Greek ones — was in proof and that after its appearance scholarly inquiries would be entertained on a first-come, first-served basis. As a result of ⟨120⟩ all this, my report is the best that I can offer under the circumstances.[3]

I

In 1979 I was allowed to inspect — and to retake — four photographs of non-Greek manuscript fragments that had come to the fore on Sinai in 1975. Among them were two photos apparently a recto and a verso of a folio, of a text identified as Georgian by those who first worked on the Sinai finds (plates 1 and 2, pp. 123-124). A glance at these photos suffices for any Byzantinist, let alone Slavicist, to realize that what was labeled as Georgian is, in fact, Glagolitic and that the new Glagolitic find belongs to the earliest period of Slavic writing. A conservative guess is that the date of the manuscript is no later than A.D. 1100.

At first, I, too, thought that we were dealing with a recto and verso of one folio, but I soon realized that one of the photos, showed two folia. A detail illustration makes this point clear: fig. 1 (pag. 125) shows some lines of another folio, lines that are visible through the hole in our verso and are disrupting the sequence in that verso's relevant text. Thus our fragments consist of two or more folia. From my present information I deduce that they contain no less than three and no more than six folia.[4] Thus, as far as I know, at most one-third of the newly-discovered fragments is at present accessible outside of Sinai.

We shall speak briefly about the partly visible folio later; first, however, let us turn to the contents of plates 1 and 2. I shall call them "folio X recto" and "last folio verso," respectively. Folio X recto contains two prayers of the service of the Third and the Sixth Hours, respec-

3. The Summary Catalogue of Greek manuscripts discovered in 1975 is by Dr. P. Nikolopoulos, Director of the National Library of Greece; the analogous checklist of Slavic manuscripts is in a planning stage (information of December 1981). I have been advised by the Sinai authorities that until such a checklist is ready, they will not provide me with photographs of the new Slavic finds (letter of November 1981).

4. In the list by Moshé Altbauer (see fn. 2 above), there is an item "f. 4 of the *Euchologium* Sin. Slav. 37...." This item seems to refer to our fragments. If Altbauer actually saw them, they would, then, consist of four folia.

tively. Last folio verso also contains two prayers, which belong to the service of the *lychnikon*, or the beginning of the Vespers. They are the prayers of the Sixth and of the Seventh Antiphon. These four prayers were recited secretly by the priest during the antiphonic ⟨121⟩ psalmody, that is, the alternate chanting of groups of psalms (which were called *antiphona*) or of verses of psalms alternating with refrains (also called *antiphona*), by two choirs.[5] The upper half of folio X recto contains the prayer of the bowing down of the head, recited at the close of the Third Hour (= Prayer 1). The lower half of folio X recto shows the beginning of the prayer of the First Antiphon of the Sixth Hour (= Prayer 2). The upper half of the last folio verso contains the end of the prayer of the Sixth Antiphon of the beginning of the Vespers (= Prayer 3). The lower half of the last folio verso contains the prayer of the Seventh Antiphon of the beginning of the Vespers (= Prayer 4).

The models of all four of these prayers can be identified. All are Greek. In order to increase the likelihood that I was dealing with genuine models, I chose Greek texts surely earlier than our fragments. They come from the *Barberinianus Graecus* 336, the earliest known Greek Euchologium, dating from the eighth century; unfortunately, it is still unpublished.[6] Greek equivalents of some or all of the four prayers of our fragments are also contained in a number of Euchologia dating from the tenth to the twelfth century and preserved in Leningrad, Sinai, Patmos, Athens, and Oxford.[7] Incidentally — and this is worth retaining for

5. Cf. L. Petit, entry "Antiphone dans la liturgie grecque," *Dict. d'Archéologie chrétienne et de Liturgie*, I, 2 (1924): 2461-88, especially 2477-80, and D. N. Moraites, s.v. Ἀντίφωνον, in Θρησκευτικὴ καὶ Ἠθικὴ Ἐγκυκλοπαιδεία, vol. 2 (1963): 944-45.

6. I wish to thank Dr. André Jacob, our chief authority on the *Barberinianus*, for kindly sending me transcripts of two relevant prayers (3 and 4) from the manuscript itself. The four prayers of the *Barberinianus* are translated or published in M. Arranz, S.J., "Les prières sacerdotales des vêpres byzantines," *Orientalia Christiana Periodica* 37 (1971): 93, 94 (= our Prayers 3 and 4); and idem, "Les prières presbytérales des Petites Heures dans l'ancien Euchologe byzantin," *Orientalia Christiana Periodica* 39 (1973): 39, 42 (= our Prayers 1 and 2).

7. The prayers are relatively common. What follows are random examples from sources not later than the twelfth century. For Leningrad Greek 226, cf. A. Jacob, "L'euchologe de Porphyre Uspenski...," *Le Muséon* 78 (1965): 173-214, especially p. 189, nos. 96 and 97; and p. 186, nos. 59 and 60; for Sinai Greek 958 (tenth century), cf. the texts printed in A. Dmitrievskij, *Opisanie liturgičeskix rukopisej xranjaščixsja v Bibliotekax pravoslavnago Vostoka*, II Εὐχολόγια

future use — the *Barberinianus* and the just mentioned tenth-century *Euchologium* of Leningrad — that is, manu⟨122⟩scripts relevant as sources of our fragments — are of South Italian provenance.[8] Below, I am offering the text of the four Slavic prayers in Latin transliteration, and juxtaposing them with their Greek models; the English translations are in each case renderings of the Slavic text.

Prayer 1

fol. X, recto, upper half

Prayer "of the bowing down of the head" at the end of the Third Hour

Barberinianus Gr. 336, pp. 46-47[10]

1a *NA GJU* (š) *· POKLO* (n) *LJU* (d) *TE* (b)
1b *GI PO* (p) *VTA* (i) *%*
Prikloni gï ůxo tvoė · ůsly
ši mo(l)tvǫ našjǫ, ï vsę po
klonьšęję tebě gla (v) *svoję, bla*
govi sti · sъxrani · v (š)[9] */. blago*
dětijǫ i štedrotami edinočę ˙/.

[ΕΥΧΗ Δ' ΗΓΟΥΝ ΤΗΣ ΑΠΟΛΥΣΕΩΣ Α'
inc.'Ο θεὸς ὁ τῇ σῇ εἰκόνι τιμήσας ἡμᾶς etc.;
then Καὶ τοῦ διακόνου "τὰς κεφαλὰς] ἡμῶν τῷ κυρίῳ" ἐκφω⟨νοῦντος⟩, ἐπεύχεται ὁ ἱερεύς·
"Κλῖνον κύριε τὸ οὖς σου καὶ ἐπάκουσον τῆς προσευχῆς ἡμῶν.

(Kiev, 1901), pp. 37 and 39; for Patmos, cf. *Patmiacus Gr.* 743 (a. 1180) (at least the two prayers of the *lychnikon*) [*Patmiacus Gr.* 104, which also has those prayers on fols. 3ʳ-3ᵛ, dates from 1233/4]; for Athens, cf. the texts printed in P. N. Trempelas, Μικρὸν Εὐχολόγιον, vol. 2 (1955), especially pp. 251-52; for Oxford, cf. *Bodleianus, ms. Auct.* E. 5.13 [= *Miscellaneus* 78 Coxe], fols. 46ʳ-46ᵛ (Vespers; late twelfth century).

8. For *Barberinianus's* Italo-Greek origin, see, e.g., A. Strittmatter, "The Barberinum S. Marci of Jacques Goar, Barberinianus Graecus 336," *Ephemerides Liturgicae* 47 (1933): 329-67; and H. Follieri, *Codices Graeci Bibliothecae Vaticanae Selecti...* (1969), no. 10 = pp. 19-20; on the same origin of Leningrad, Greek 226, cf. Jacob, "L'euchologe..." (as in fn. 7 above), pp. 175-76. A. F. Cereteli's old opinion that our manuscript is of "Syriac" type should disappear from secondary literature. Cereteli's own plate V, 1-2 easily refutes his hypothesis. Cf. his *Paleografičeskie snimki s nekotoryx grečeskix, latinskix i slavjanskix rukopisej Imp. Publ. Biblioteki* (St. Petersburg, 1914), p. 5 and plate V, 1-2.

9. In line 5, the abbreviation = *vъzglašenie*.

10. This is Strittmatter, "The Barberinum" (as in fn. 8 above), no. 93, published in Arranz, "Les prières presbytérales" (as in fn. 6 above), p. 39; cf. also Dmitrievskij, *Opisanie* (as in fn. 7 above), 37 (= Prayer 5); Jacob, "L'euchologe" (as in fn. 7 above), no. 96 = fol. 57ᵛ.

Plate 1 – Sinai fragment, folio X recto.

Plate 2 – Sinai fragment, last folio verso.

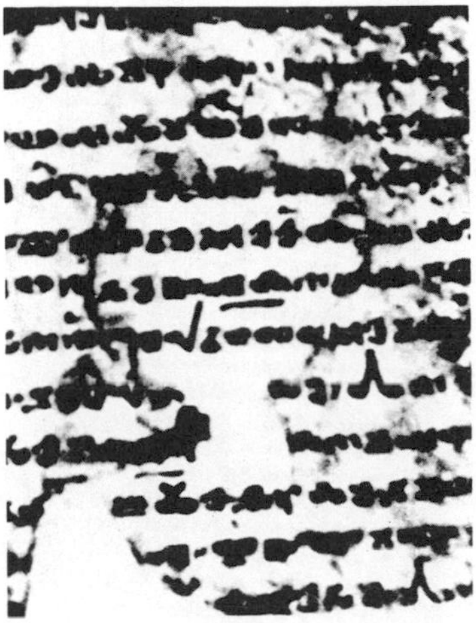

Fig. 1: Sinai fragment, last folio verso and folio (X plus A) verso, detail.

Fig. 2: *Euchologium Sinaiticum*, 100 b.

Figure 3: *Euchologium Sinaiticum*, 61 b.

Fig. 4: *Euchologium Sinaiticum*, 95 b.

Fig. 5: *Cryptoferratensis* B. α. IV, fol. 145r (a. 991).

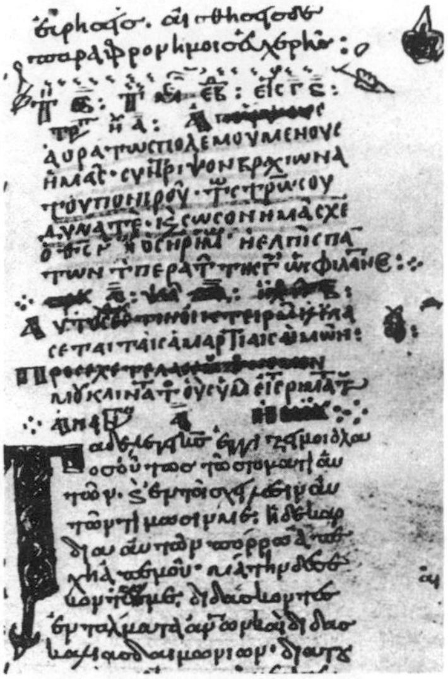

Fig. 6: *Vaticanus Reginensis Gr.* 75, fol. 49r (ca. a. 983).

Fig. 7: *Oxoniensis Bodl. Laud Gr.* 75, fol. 326v. (a. 976).

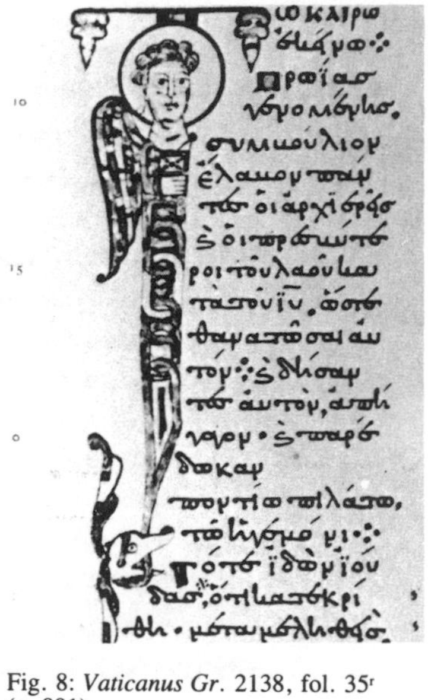

Fig. 8: *Vaticanus Gr.* 2138, fol. 35r (a. 991).

Fig. 9: *Oxoniensis Bodl. Gr.* 204, fol. 17^r.

Fig. 10: *Vaticanus Gr.* 2138, fol. 3^v and 26^r (a. 991).

Fig. 11: *Euchologium Sinaiticum*, 77 b.

Fig. 12: *Euchologium Sinaiticum*, 81 b.

Fig. 13: *Parisinus Lat.* 12.048 (Sacramentary of Gellone, end of the 8th century).

Fig. 14: *Cryptoferratensis* A.α.III, fol. 1ʳ.

Fig. 15: *Euchologium Sinaiticum*, 14 b.

Fig. 16: *Atheniensis Bibl. Nat.* 74, fol. 94ʳ.

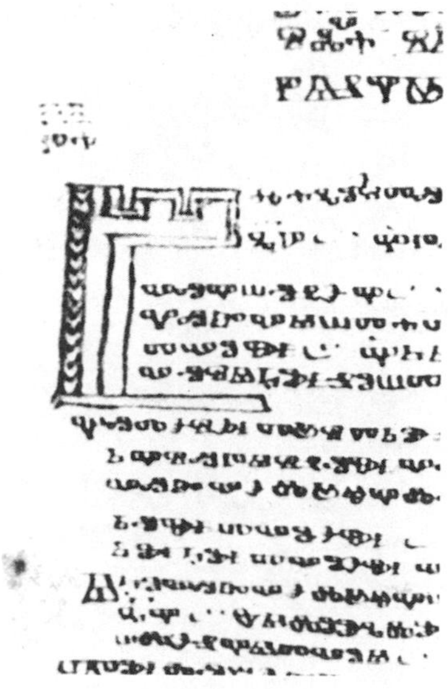

Fig. 17: *Psalterium Sinaiticum*, fol. 121ᵛ.

Fig. 18: *Patmiacus Gr.* 33, fol. 99ʳ.

Fig. 19: *Euchologium Sinaiticum*, 59 b.

Fig. 20: *Vaticanus Gr.* 866, fol. 404ᵛ.

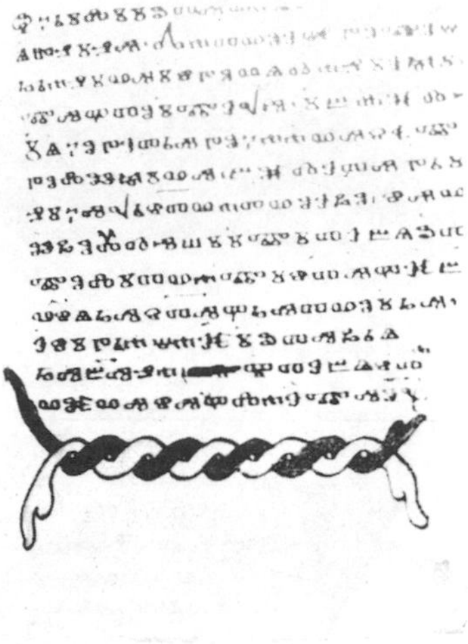

Fig. 21: *Euchologium Sinaiticum*, 80 a.

Fig. 22: *Vaticanus Gr.* 866, fol. 216r.

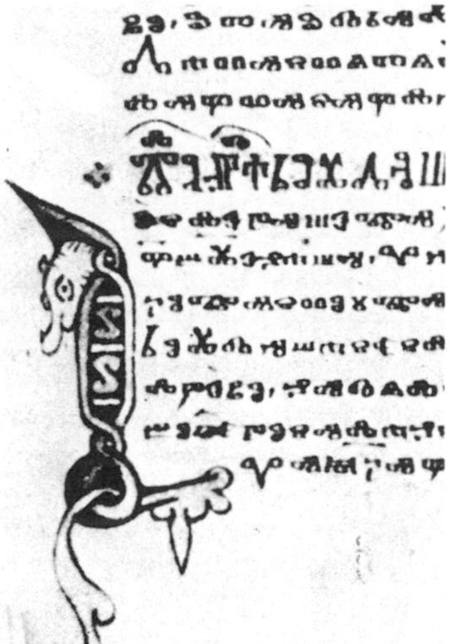

Fig. 23: *Euchologium Sinaiticum*, 32 b.

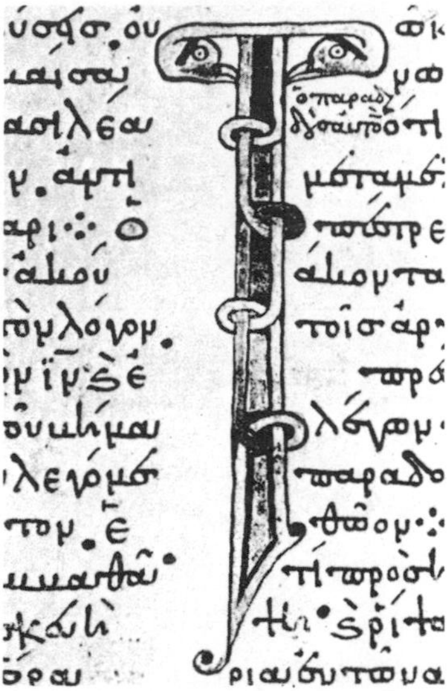

Fig. 24: *Vaticanus Gr.* 2138, fol. 29v (a. 991).

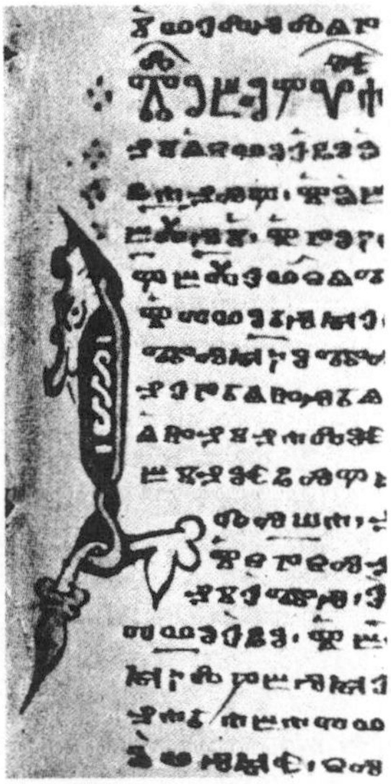

Fig. 25: *Euchologium Sinaiticum*, 23 a.

Fig. 26: *Codex Zographensis*, fol. 131ʳ.

Fig. 27: *Psalterium Sinaiticum*, fol. 123ʳ.

Fig. 28: *Codex Assemanianus*, fol. 157ᵛ.

καὶ πάντας τοὺς ὑποκεκλικότας σοι τὰς ἑαυτῶν κεφαλὰς εὐλόγησον, φύλαξον, ἁγίασον.

Ἐκφώ⟨νως⟩· "χάριτι καὶ οἰκτιρμοῖς καὶ φιλανθρωπίᾳ."

LET US BOW DOWN OUR ⟨HEADS⟩ UNTO THE LORD. PEOPLE: UNTO THEE, O LORD. PRIEST SEC(RETLY):

O Lord, incline Thy ear, and hear our prayer; and bless, sanctify, and preserve ⟨132⟩ all those who have bowed down their heads unto Thee. Au⟨dibly⟩: Through the Grace and Mercy of ⟨Thine⟩only bego⟨tten Son with Whom Thou art blessed, together with Thy Holy and Good and Life-giving Ghost, now and ever and unto the ages of ages⟩.

Prayer 2

fol. X, recto, lower half

Beginning of the prayer of the First Antiphon of the Sixth Hour

Barberinianus Gr. 336, p. 148[13]

l d
MO NA E GONĚ ·
i
ANTЬFONЪ'/.
i
Sty vlko · bže na · proste
ry prěčistěi svoi rǫ
cě na čestьněmь svo
èmь krstě · i rǫkopisa
nie grěxъ našixъ pri
gvoždь na nemь ì potrě

ΕΥΧΗ ΩΡΑΣ ϛʹ ΑΝΤΙΦΩΝΟΥ Αʹ
῞Αγιε δέσποτα ὁ θεὸς ἡμῶν ὁ κατὰ τὴν παροῦσαν ὥραν ἐν τῷ προσκυνητῷ σου σταυρῷ τὰς ἀχράντους σου χεῖρας ἐκτείνας καὶ τὸ τῶν ἡμετέρων ἁμαρτιῶν ἐν αὐτῷ προσηλώσας καὶ ἐξαλείψας χειρόγραφον, ἄφες ἡμῖν καὶ νῦν πᾶν ἁμαρτημάτων ὄφλημα, καὶ πάσης τῆς ἐξ ἔργων καὶ λόγων καὶ ἐνθυμήσεων

---

11. In lines 7/8 I conjecture *potrěb⟨ь⟩, i nyně* — required by ἐξαλείψας (a past participle), καὶ νῦν of the Greek — as the original reading.

12. In lines 12/13 our text reads *.nei zъlъ*. The Greek model has ἐνθυμήσεων πονηρῶν in this place. The *Slovník Jaz. Staroslověnského* (hereafter *SJS*), *s.v. pomyšlenije* quotes ἐνθύμησις as one of this word's equivalents. Cf. also *Euchologium Sinaiticum*, ed. Nahtigal (hereafter *ES*; for full title of the edition, cf. fn. 31 below), p. 72 a 16: *pomyšlenь i nepravedně*; ibid., p. 92 a 5: *otъ skvrъnenъ pomyšlenei; Freising Fragments*, III, 29: *uzeh nepraudnih del i nepraudnega pomislena*.

13. This is Strittmatter, "The Barberinum" (as in fn. 8 above), no. 94, published in Arranz, "Les prières presbytérales" (as in fn. 6 above), p. 42; cf. also Dmitrievskij, *Opisanie...* (as in fn. 7 above), pp. 37 and 1005; Jacob, "L'euchologe" (as in fn. 7 above), no. 97 = fol. 58ʳ.

bi nyně[11] · *ỏtъpusti namъ*
v^sěkъ dlъgъ grěx⟨o⟩vъny ·
svobodi ny ỏ⟨tъ⟩ v^sěko
go osọždenię̌ ⟨dě⟩ęnię̌
slovesъṇ ⟨——i pomyšl⟩ęnei[12]
zъlъ · da ḅ⟨———⟩ ęṃь

πονηρῶν κατακρίσεως ἐλευθέρους ἡμᾶς ἀνάδειξον, ἵνα ἐν καθαρᾷ καρδίᾳ [τὴν ὀφειλομένην σοι δοξολογίαν ἐν παντὶ καιρῷ προσφέρωμεν.]

PRAY(ER) AT THE 6 HOUR; ANTIPHON

Holy Lord our God, Thou who didst extend Thy immaculate arms on Thy venerable cross and didst nail to it the handwriting of our sins and blot it out; forgive us now all the debt of our sins; free us from all condemnation ⟨———⟩ evil deeds, words [?] ⟨and⟩ thoughts. So that we

⟨133⟩ Prayer 3

last folio, verso, upper half[14]

Vespers, end of the prayer of the Sixth Antiphon

Barberinianus Gr. 336, p. 92[17]

⟨*štedrota*⟩]
mi[15] *tvoimi ï miḷọstijọ tvoě*
jọ·ï posěti ṇąsъ tvoejọ bla
godětijọ · ï ḍąžḍị nam otъbě
gnọti i pročee otъ nastojęšta
ȧgo d^ne · ỏtъ bystryxъ ky
znei ï kovъ nep⟨ri⟩ězninъ·sъ
xrani životъ na⟨šь⟩ blagodě
tijọ staago tvoego dxa ˙/. v ˙/.[16]
milostijọ i čkljubiemь edin ˙/.

[ΕΥΧΗ ΕΣΠΕΡΙΝΗ ϛʹ
Κύριε, κύριε, ὁ τῇ ἀχράντῳ σου δυνάμει συνέχων σύμπαντα, ὁ μακροθυμῶν ἐπὶ πᾶσιν ἡμῖν καὶ μετανοῶν ἐπὶ ταῖς κακίαις ἡμῶν καὶ μακρύνων ἀφ' ἡμῶν τὰς ἀνομίας ἡμῶν, μνήσθητι τῶν οἰκτηρ]μῶν σου καὶ τοῦ ἐλέους σου, καὶ ἐπίσκεψαι ἡμᾶς τῇ σῇ ἀγαθότητι, καὶ δὸς ἡμῖν διαφυγεῖν καὶ τὸ λοιπὸν τῆς παρούσης ἡμέρας ἐκ

14. This prayer occurs in modern *Služebniki*, e.g., that of 1857, p. 2ᵛ, as prayer 5 rather than 6 in the *posledovanie večerni*. For earlier texts, cf. (a) the Novgorod (?) Euchologium of the fourteenth century owned by Metropolitan Ioan Teodorovyč, facsimile edition by P. Kovaliv, *Molytovnyk: Služebnyk, pamjatka XIV stolittja* (New York, 1960), fol. 37ᵛ (as prayer 6; this Euchologium's text goes back to that of our fragments), and (b) the printed *Služebnik* (Moscow, 1602), V̄, 2ᵛ-3ʳ (cf. A. S. Zernova, *Knigi Kirillovskoj pečati izdannye v Moskve v XVI-XVII vekax* [Moscow, 1958], p. 20 = no. 18; I used the Bodleian Library copy 4° L, 11, Th. BS; this text, numbered 6, goes back to a reworked, or perhaps new, translation adhering closely to the Greek).

15. In line 1, ⟨štedrota⟩mi, a word beginning on the recto of the last folio, is sure on account of οἰκτιρμῶν of the Greek model. In the same line, one could also read *mlostijọ* instead of *milostijọ*.

16. In line, 8, the abbreviation ≐ *vъzglašenie*.

17. This is Strittmatter, "The Barberinum" (as in fn. 8 above), no. 56, to ap-

τῶν τοῦ πονηροῦ ποικίλων μηχανημάτων, καὶ ἀνεπιβούλευτον τὴν ζωὴν ἡμῶν διαφύλαξον τῇ χάριτι τοῦ ἁγίου σου πνεύματος.
Ἐκφώνησις· Ἐλέει καὶ φιλανθρωπίᾳ.

through Thy ⟨Compas⟩sion and Thy Mercy; and visit us through Thy Grace ⟨134⟩ and grant that for the rest of this day as well we may escape the wily [?] contrivances and plots of the Enemy. Preserve our lives through the Grace of Thy Holy Ghost, etc. Aud⟨ibly⟩: Through the Mercy and Love of Mankind of Thy onl⟨y-begotten⟩ etc.

Prayer 4

last folio, verso, lower half[18]

---

pear as no. 60 in the forthcoming edition by Jacob; it is published in J. Goar, Εὐχολόγιον *sive Rituale Graecorum* (1647), p. 36 (2nd ed. of Venice [1730], p. 29), and translated in Arranz, "Les prières sacerdotales" (as in fn. 6 above), p. 93; cf. also Trempelas, Μικρόν (as in fn. 7 above), p. 251; Jacob, "L'euchologe" (as in fn. 7 above), no. 59 = fol. 39^{r}, and modern Greek Euchologia (e.g., ed. Zerbos [Venice, 1869], p. 14), where our prayer appears as no. 5.

18. A version close to this prayer occurs in modern *Služebniki*, e.g., that of 1857, p. 3^{r}, as prayer 6 rather than 7. For earlier texts, cf. the Euchologium ed. Kovaliv (as in fn. 14 above), fol. 37^{v}-38^{r} (as prayer 7); *Služebnik* of 1602 (as in fn. 14 above), V̄, 3^{r}-3^{v} (as prayer 7).
For purposes of comparison, I am transcribing our Prayer 4 after these two sources. As in our Prayer 3, the Euchologium ed. Kovaliv, for all its errors, offers a text going back to our fragments, while the text of 1602 reflects a reworked (or new) translation closely following the Greek. This text may represent the redaction of the *Služebnik* attributed to Metropolitan Cyprian. Cf., e.g., N. N. Rozov, "Russkie Služebniki i Trebniki," *Metodičeskie rekommendacii po opisaniju slavjano-russkix rukopisej dlja svodnogo Kataloga rukopisej...*, II, 2 (Moscow, 1976), pp. 315-16; 329 and fn. 20.
Euchologium ed. Kovaliv, fol. 37^{v}-38^{r}: *Be velikyi i čjudnyi. strojai člvka neizrečenьnoju svojeju blgostiju. batym promyšlenijemь. | i darovavъ namъ mira sego blgaja i obručivyi namъ obětovanoje crstvo. danymi uže namъ blgymi stvori namъ uklonitisę ot vsękogo zla. mimošedъšaja časti dne sego. dažь namь pročeje bes poroka sxraniti prestuju slavu tvoju. xvalęšče* etc.
Služebnik of 1602, V̄, 3^{r}-3^{v}: *mltva antifona z^{go}. Bže velikii i divnyi. iže neizrečennoju blgostyneju, i bogaty^{m} promyslomъ ustrojaę člčskii život iže i mirskaę nam blagaę darovavъ i poručivъ na^{m} obětovannoe crstvo, radi uže darovannyxъ namъ blgъ sotvorivyi nas, i nnešnęgo dne mimošedšuju častь, ot vsękogo uklonitisę zla. darui namъ i ostavšee bez' zaroka soveršiti pred stoju slavoju ti. slaviti* etc.

Vespers, prayer of the Seventh Antiphon

Barberinianus Gr. 336, pp. 94-95[29]

MÔ VEČERѢNIĮ ANѢFÔ Ž ·/.
Gi bže veliky · čjudno strǫję
čky vъ životъ neizdreče
nѣnojǫ b⟨lagost⟩ijǫ[19] *i boga*
tymь ⟨promy⟩šleniemь[20]
darova⟨vъ nam⟩ѣ[21] *mirѣs⟨kaa⟩*[22]
blagaá ⟨i porǫ⟩čei[23] *namъ obě*
tovanoe cr⟨st⟩vo · danymi
juže ⟨namъ b⟩lagy·şѣtvo
riv⟨y [?] *ny u⟩kloniti şę*[24] *otъ*
v^sego ⟨zъla ——⟩[25] *mimošьdъšjǫ*
ǫ čęş⟨tь d^ne ——⟩ ego ·[26] *daždi na*
mъ ⟨i pročee bes⟩pǫroka[27] *konьča*
tį ⟨prědъ stojǫ slavojǫ tv⟩ǫejǫ[28] *xva*

ΕΥΧΗ ΕΣΠΕΡΙΝΗ Ζ'
Ὁ θεὸς ὁ μέγας καὶ θαυμαστός, ὁ ἀνεκδιηγήτῳ ἀγαθωσύνῃ καὶ πλουσίᾳ προνοίᾳ διοικῶν τὴν τῶν ἀνθρώπων ζωήν, ὁ καὶ τὰ ἐγκόσμια ἡμῖν ἀγαθὰ δωρησάμενος καὶ κατεγγυήσας ἡμῖν τὴν ἐπηγγελμένην βασι⟨135⟩λείαν διὰ τῶν ἤδη κεχαρισμένων ἡμῖν ἀγαθῶν, ὁ ποιήσας ἡμᾶς καὶ τῆς νῦν ἡμέρας τὸ παρελθὸν μέρος ἀπὸ παντὸς ἐκκλῖναι κακοῦ, δώρησαι ἡμῖν καὶ τὸ ὑπόλοιπον ἀμέμπτως ἐκτελέσαι ἐνώπιον τῆς ἁγίας δόξης σου, ὑμνεῖν [σε τὸν ἀγαθὸν καὶ φιλάνθρωπον θεὸν ἡμῶν.
Ἐκφώνησις· Ὅτι ἐλεήμων καὶ.]

---

19. *SJS* quotes ἀγαθωσύνη as equivalent to *blagostь*, but not to *blagodětь* or *blagodatь*. The Greek prayer has ἀγαθωσύνη at the corresponding spot. Cf. *ES*, p. 20 b 11/12: *neizdrečeny* (= error!) *blagostiją*.

20. The reading in line 5 is assured by προνοίᾳ of the Greek prayer, usually rendered by *promyšlenije*, and by *bogatymъ promyšleniemъ* in *ES*, p. 20b 12/13.

21. The reading in line 6 is assured by the Greek (ἡμῖν... δωρησάμενος, a past participle) and by *darovavъ namъ* of the Euchologium ed. Kovaliv, fol. 38ʳ (for text, cf. fn. 18 above).

22. Reading suggested by *mirskaę* in *Služebnik* of 1602, V̄, 3ᵛ (for text, see fn. 18 above) and by *ES*, p. 90a 2/3 *pečalei mirъskyxъ*.

23. At first sight, ⟨porǫ⟩čei or ⟨izdrǫ⟩čei seems too short, for the lacuna here is longer than 4 or 5 letters, but the Greek model of this passage has only καὶ κατεγγυήσας. *SJS* gives ἐγγυᾶσθαι 'give surety', as one of the equivalents of *porǫčiti* and *izdrǫčiti/ati*. *ES*, p. 83 b 9 has *porǫčьnikъ*, corresponding to ἐγγυητής. The Euchologium ed. Kovaliv, fol. 38ʳ has *obručivyi*, Služebnik of 1602, V̄, 3ᵛ, *poručivъ* (for texts, cf. fn. 18 above). In sum, I opted for *porǫčei*.

24. The reading *sъtvorivy* (for ποιήσας) is doubtful. The usual rendering of ποιήσας in *ES* is *sъtvorъ or sъtvorei*. *Ukloniti sę* is sure, since the ἐκκλῖναι of the Greek prayer is regularly rendered by *ukloniti sę*.

25. *Zъla* is assured on account of the Greek and *ES*, p. 72 b 26 *izbavi mę gi otъ v^sego zъla*. This word alone seems too short to fill the gap; yet, the Greek has only κακοῦ, and the Euchologium ed. Kovaliv, fol. 38ʳ (for text, see fn. 18 above) has *vsękogo zla. mimošedъšaja časti*, essentially as in our text.

PRAY(ER), EVENING [?] ANTIPHON 7

O Lord great God, Thou Who wondrously managest men in life through ⟨136⟩ inexpressible go⟨odn⟩ess and bounteous ⟨pro⟩vidence; Who hast bestowed upon us the good things of the world ⟨and⟩ ⟨pled⟩gest to us the promised Kin⟨gd⟩om through the good things Thou hast given ⟨us⟩ already; Who hast cause⟨d us to a⟩void all ⟨evil——⟩ in the pa⟨rt of———day⟩ that has passed by; grant that we may also complete without blame that which remains of it ⟨in the face of T⟩hy ⟨holy glory⟩; to prai⟨se⟩

II

How should we assess the Slavic translations? The answer is that, on the whole, the Slavic faithfully follows its original but sounds natural at the same time — thus it displays a trait that is characteristic of the earliest translations. In the prayers of the Sixth Hour and of the Seventh Antiphon, the translations are freer than elsewhere; they do not follow the word order of the Greek, and in spots tend to be paraphrases. That is why I was unwilling to fill in all the gaps in the Slavic text in spite of having its Greek model at my disposal.

Let us single out some discrepancies between original and translation in the prayer of the Sixth Hour (= Prayer 2). In line 2, the words

---

26. The lacuna after *čęs*⟨tь⟩ is difficult to fill. On account of τῆς νῦν ἡμέρας of the Greek, one would expect ⟨*d҃ne nyněštьnjaj*⟩ego (*SJS* gives ὁ νῦν as a model for *nyněštьnъ*, and the *Služebnik* of 1602 reads *nnešnęgo dne*). The lacuna seems too short for this solution, however. Perhaps our text simply had *d҃ne sego*, as the Euchologium ed. Kovaliv, fol. 38ʳ does (for texts, cf. fn. 18 above).

27. The reading in line 13 is assured by the Greek model which had καὶ τὸ ὑπόλοιπον ἀμέμπτως. For *pročee*, cf. our folio (X + A) verso, line 5, and *ES*, p. 83 b 18 *i pročee životа moego*, where it stands for ὑπόλοιπον of the Greek. For *bes poroka* = ἀμέμπτως, cf. *SJS* s.v. *porokъ*. *Bes poroka* occurs in *ES*, p. 98a 22/23. Finally, the Euchologium ed. Kovaliv, fol. 38ʳ has *dažь namъ pročeje bes poroka sxraniti* (for full text, cf. fn. 18 above).

28. The reading in line 14 is based on the ἐνώπιον τῆς ἁγίας δόξης of the Greek prayer and on the two East Slavic parallel witnesses of fn. 18 above. There, the Služebnik of 1602 has *pred stoju slavoju ti,* while the *prestuju slavu tvoju* of the Euchologium ed. Kovaliv must be an error for *prědъ stoju slavoju tvojeju*.

29. This is Strittmatter, "The Barberinum" (as in fn. 8 above), no. 57, to appear as no. 61 in the forthcoming edition by Jacob; it is published by J. Goar, Εὐχολόγιον (1647), pp. 36-37 (2nd ed. of Venice [1730], p. 29), and translated in Arranz, "Les prières sacerdotales" (as in fn. 6 above), p. 94; cf. also Trempelas, Μικρόν (as in fn. 7 above), p. 252; Jacob, "L'euchologe" (as in fn. 7 above), no. 60 = fol. 39ᵛ, and modern Greek Euchologia (e.g., ed. Zerbos [Venice 1869], p. 15), where our prayer appears as no. 6.

'at the present hour' of the Greek are omitted in the Slavic. In line 4, the epithet προσκυνητῷ 'adorable', referring to the cross, is replaced by the more familiar *čěstьnětmь,* which usually corresponds to τίμιος 'venerable'. In lines 6/7, *prigvoždь* 'having nailed down' is a past participle, rendering the Greek participle προσηλώσας. The parallel *potrěbi* 'blot (or blotted) out', in line 7 is not a participle, however, even though its Greek equivalent ἐξαλείψας is. To restore the correspondence, I conjecture *potrěbь, i* 'having blotted out, and' as the original reading; this fits the Greek well, especially since we need an *i* before *nyně* to correspond to the καὶ νῦν of the Greek. Finally, in line 10 we read the imperative *svobodi* 'free', which is simple but adequate, whereas the Greek has the more ponderous ἐλευθέρους ἡμᾶς ἀνάδειξον 'proclaim us free'.

Before going any further, let us say a word about the verso of the ⟨137⟩ hardly visible folio, which I shall call "folio (X plus A) verso" (fig. 1). Only a few words on that folio are legible. We realize, however, that the first four visible lines are the end of a prayer, and that the penultimate legible line is the beginning of another prayer. The two capital letters, of which only the *az* is surely legible, indicate that a title is standing in between. If folio (X plus A) verso is connected with the last folio of our fragment, it must contain some earlier prayers of the beginning of the Vespers. There are, in fact, some similarities between the visible words of that folio and the Greek texts of the prayers of the Second and Third Antiphon of the Vespers.[30] There is no need to belabor the point, however, because sooner or later some scholar will inspect the whole fragment and put an end to the guessing. In the meantime, I am offering the transliteration of the visible part of folio (X + A) verso (= Prayers 5 and 6).

Prayers 5 and 6
fol. X + A verso, visible part
Vespers? Parts of Prayers of the Second and Third Antiphons?
(line numbers correspond to the lines of the last folio, verso of the fragments)

Pr. 5	4 *d̨enьna*	4 of the day [?]
	5 *pročee d^n̦⟨e⟩*	5 rest of the ⟨day⟩
	⟨v^se⟩go zъla b̦	⟨all⟩ evil

30. For Greek texts, cf., e.g., J. Goar, Εὐχολόγιον *sive Rituale Graecorum*, 2nd ed. (Venice, 1730), pp. 28-29 and 163-64; Trempelas, Μικρόν (as in fn. 7 above), pp. 249 and 250.

	ъ *crstvy*	Kingdom
	vacat	
	vacat . *A* vacat	
Pr. 6	10 ⟨*gi*⟩ *bže na*⟨*šь*⟩	10 ⟨Lord⟩ our God
	⟨———⟩ъ·*iz̨*	
	ę⟨———⟩ . . .	
	⟨———⟩.	
	14 ⟨———⟩	

⟨138⟩ III

We now turn to the search for the manuscript to which our fragment once belonged. I need not be a Sherlock Holmes to realize that another Sinai manuscript should be the prime suspect. Almost all available indicators point to the Glagolitic *Euchologium Sinaiticum* (*ES*), one of the oldest Slavic manuscripts in existence, still kept on Sinai.[31] We may start with external indicators. The first is the similarity in general appearance, let alone the similarity of initials (plate 1 and figs. 2 and 3, pp. 123, 125); the second, close similarity in dimensions — the *ES* measures 140 × 105 mm. and our fragment measures 148 x 105 mm.; the third is the fact that the *ES* is mutilated at the beginning, so that there is "room" for putting our fragment into its lost front part — in Greek Euchologia, this first part of the volume is liturgical and includes the very prayers contained in our fragments; the fourth indicator is the fact that other fragments securely or putatively connected with the *ES* have been taken from Sinai in the past — two leaves by Uspenskij in

31. Recent editions: J. Frček, *Euchologium Sinaiticum I-II*, in *Patrologia Orientalis* 24, 5 (1933, reprint 1974) and 25, 3 (1939, reprint 1976) [Greek parallels, French translation]; R. Nahtigal, *Euchologium Sinaiticum*, in *Akademija Znanosti in Umetnosti v Ljubljani, Filozof.-filol.-hist. Razred, Dela*, 1-2 (Ljubljana, 1941-42) [Facsimile; edition with commentary, bibliography]. Glossary: S. Słoński, *Index verborum do Euchologium Sinaiticum* (Warsaw, 1934). Succinct bibliography in F. Sławski, art. Modlitewnik Synajski, in *Słownik Starożytności Słowiańskich* 3, no. 1 (1967): 272-73. Cf. also A. Dostál, "L'eucologe slave du Sinai," *Byzantion* 36 (1966): 44-50; bibliographies in articles by E. Dogramadžieva and P. Penkova in *Slovansko Jazikoslovije, Nahtigalov Zbornik* (1977), pp. 47-66 and 375-87; and R. Mathiesen in the next note.

1853, one by Krylov in the same year, and one by Kondakov in 1881.[32] This shows that some loose leaves of that *Euchologium* were lying around in the nineteenth century, possibly in the very room where the new fragment was found, for that room served as a depository for damaged and disused material until the beginning of our century. Also, the fragments obtained by Uspenskij and possibly those brought by Krylov were from the first, or liturgical, part of the *Euchologium*, the very part into which our fragments would fit quite well.

⟨139⟩ Two internal indicators, too, point in the direction of the *ES*. The first of them is the quasi-identity of the hands in both manuscripts; the second, correspondences in morphology,[33] vocabulary,[34] phraseology,[35] and spelling, such as the consistent differentiation between *e* and *je*. Given the great similarities between the two documents, I relied on the *ES* in reading the difficult spots on the fragments' photographs and in my reconstructions of the damaged parts of the text.

Should we, then, view our fragments as belonging to the *ES* and assign them somewhere to the now lost beginning of the manuscript? In all probability, yes. Out of scholarly scruple, however, I will mention three features that must be explained before we definitely incorporate our fragment into the *ES*. The first of these is the apparent difference in the number of lines in both documents. The second is a slight difference in the tracing of the big initials, the big initial for *slovo* being always empty inside in the *ES* (contrast plate 1 with fig. 4, p. 125); and the

32. Cf. Frček, *Euchologium...I-II* (as in the preceding fn.), pp. 612-17; E. È. Granstrem, *Opisanie russkix i slavjanskix pergamennyx rukopisej...* (Leningrad, 1953), p. 78 (on *Glag*. 3, i.e., the Kondakov fragment)and pp. 78-79 (doubts that the Krylov fragment belongs to the *ES*); cf. also R. Mathiesen, "Uspenskij's Bifolium and the Chronology of Some Early Church Slavonic Translations," to appear in the Festschrift for Moshé Altbauer.

33. Cf., e.g., *daždi*, Prayers, 3, 3 and 4, 12, which is the only imperative form of the second person singular in the *ES*. This feature of *ES* has been singled out by H. G. Lunt, *Old Church Slavonic Grammar*, 6th ed. (The Hague, 1974), 16.22 = p. 122.

34. Only seven or eight words or signs for numerals of our fragments are not attested in *ES*. They are provided with an asterisk in the *index verborum* at the end of this article.

35. Cf., in addition to parallels quoted in notes 19, 20, 22, 25, 27 above, *rǫkopisanie grěxъ našixъ*, Prayer 2, 5-6, with *moixъ grěxъ... rǫkopisanie ES*, 83 b, 17; and *otъ nastojęštaago d̃ne*, Prayer 3, 4-5 with the same three words in *ES*, 89 b 22.

third, the sequence of prayers in the fragments. The fragments have the Hours prayers first and the Vespers prayers afterwards. This is the exact opposite of the sequence found in all the early Greek Euchologia known to me. Thus, in the *Barberinianus* the two prayers of the Hours on folio X recto of the fragment are numbered 93 and 94, while the two prayers of the Vespers on the last folio verso are numbered 56 and 57. In the catalogue of the Leningrad Euchologium, the respective numbers are 96 and 97 for the Hours and 59 and 60 for the Vespers. Thus what appears to be later in our fragments is earlier in the Greek Euchologia, provided, of course, that we have correctly established the sequence of the folia.[36] If we have, we may venture a ⟨140⟩ reason for this discrepancy. The early Greek Euchologia start with the Vespers and proceed to the Hours. The sequence is different in the early Greek Horologia. There, the Hours precede the Vespers, as they do in our fragments. So, while there is a 95 percent likelihood that our fragments belong to the *ES*, we should keep in mind the 5 percent possibility that they may come from some twin manuscript, say a Horologion.

IV

The conveyance of the Sinai Glagolitic fragments to Europe by Uspenskij and Krylov in the past century did cause a small sensation among Slavicists; later on, controversy ensued as to whether these fragments, by then available to European scholars, did or did not belong together with the faraway *ES*.[37] Today, some forty years after the appearance of the facsimile edition of the entire *ES* by Nahtigal, Slavicists are more blasé, but not blasé enough to forget how exiguous is the body of earliest Slavic non-scriptural texts. Therefore, the new find will be welcomed by friends of Old Church Slavonic literature and Slavic linguistics, both in Bulgaria and elsewhere, as well as by liturgiologists.

---

36. For sequences in the *Barberinianus* and in the Leningrad Euchologium, cf. fns. 10, 13, 17, 29 above, To obtain the sequence (a) prayers of the Vespers, (b) prayers of the Hours, for our fragments, we would have to refold our two folia the other way (with our first folio recto becoming the last folio recto, and the present last folio verso becoming the first folio verso) and assume that they once formed the inner part of the outermost *bifolium* of a quire, or better yet, of a *quinio* (this to accommodate some 37 prayers in between our prayer 4 and our prayer 1). Again all speculation is idle at this point, for inspection on the spot will one day provide the answer.

37. For the history of the controversy, Frček, *Euchologium...I-II* (as in fn. 31), pp. 614-16.

For the sake of Slavicists I report that our fragments do bring some new information. They offer the word *bystrъ* — strangely enough, attested in only one other Old Church Slavonic "canonical" manuscript, the *Supraslienśis* — with a hitherto unknown meaning of "wily" or "cunning" (Prayer 3, 5); they may provide the positive form of the adverb *čjudno* (Prayer 4, 2), otherwise unattested in the Old Church Slavonic canon; they enable us to add a couple of hitherto unknown Greek equivalents of known Old Church Slavonic words;[38] and they contain some new material illustrating the use of the *jers*.

All these points, however, are minor technicalities. I wish to touch ⟨141⟩ now upon a broader issue connected with the new find and ask: what were the models used for the make-up and ornament of early Glagolitic manuscripts?

V

The textual sources of our fragments are all Greek; let us call them eastern. When it comes to the fragments' ornament and general make-up, however, the models that can best be postulated — or, at least, the closest parallels that can be adduced — are western, namely, Italo-Greek. As our fragment and the *ES* are either the same thing or are twins, I shall use both of them as evidence. In the juxtapositions that follow, I made every effort to limit Italo-Greek comparisons to well-known manuscripts that are precisely dated between the ninth and the eleventh centuries and are expressly localized in Italy. While I will miss some good parallels because of this limitation, I will be able to avoid arguments as to whether an example I adduced is or is not South Italian. Understandably, as points of camparison, I have chosen features prevalent in Italo-Greek manuscripts but either rare in other Greek manuscripts, especially Constantinopolitan, or altogether absent from them.

In a nutshell, parallels between the two groups of manuscripts extend to, first, the habit of putting a layer of yellow, reddish or green paint over which titles, rubrics, or initials are written — this was done to help the reader find the right place (plate 1 and figs. 5-6, pp. 123, 126). The same function could be performed by drawing a line across a title

38. A word of caution on *čjudno*: in view of the masculine θαυμαστός of the model, it may be an error for *čjudnъ* or *čjudne* (voc. sg.). — New equivalents: in addition to *bystrъ* = ποικίλος, we have *neizdrečenъnǫjǫ*, Prayer 4, 3/4 = ἀνεκδιηγήτῳ, and *mirъs⟨kaa⟩*, Prayer 4, 6 = ἐγκόσμια; none of these equivalents is attested in *SJS*.

(fig. 7, p. 126). The second parallel is the use of inordinately large initials; such giants are absent from Constantinopolitan manuscripts (figs. 8-12, pp. 126-127). Like their Latin counterparts (fig. 13, p. 128), these initials sometimes "eat into" the body of texts, rather than stand outside of it (figs. 14-15, p. 128). The Italo-Greek initials are not only large, but also of a shape unusual in Byzantium proper, yet they are paralleled by Glagolitic initials (figs. 16-17, pp. 128-129). Third, the parallels between Italo-Greek and Glagolitic manuscripts include the use of wide interlaced bands or headpieces to separate parts of texts or to surround titles (figs. 18-19, p. 129). Fourth, they include the use of narrow braided bands for separation purposes (figs. 20-21, pp. 129-130). The fifth set of parallels has to do with ornamental features in the initials that are identical in both series of ⟨142⟩ manuscripts. I shall single out two such features: first, the S-shaped ornaments within initials (figs. 22-23, p. 130), and second, the use of eyes or animal heads with eyes and beaks as parts of the make-up of initials (fig. 3, 24-25, pp. 125, 130-131). The sixth point has to do with similarities in the color scheme between Italo-Greek and Glagolitic manuscripts, especially with the presence of greens in both groups. Unfortunately, the reader must accept this point on faith, because I am not able to reproduce any of the numerous examples of "early Glagolitic" greens — starting with the green of our fragment — in color and compare them with the greens of Italo-Greek manuscripts, such as, to quote an example, the Leningrad Greek 71, copied in Salerno in 1019-20; nor am I able to show combinations of yellow and ochre, non-typical for Byzantium proper, but occurring in such Gospel texts as Athens, National Library 74 (an Italo-Greek witness) and the *Codex Assemanianus*, respectively.[39]

This evidence suggests that Italo-Greek manuscripts offer the closest parallel to the make-up and ornament of at least one early Glagolitic witness, namely, the *ES* (if we consider our fragments as a part of that manuscript), or of two witnesses (if we consider these fragments as a part of a twin manuscript). However, I find my observation applicable to other witnesses as well: to the *Codex Zographensis*

39. For a color reproduction of Athens, Nat. Lib. 74, fol. 1^{v}, cf. A. Marava-Chatzinicolaou and Ch. Toufexi-Paschou, *Catalogue of the Illuminated Byzantine Manuscripts of the National Library of Greece*, vol. 1 (1978), fig. 74; for its initials in color, cf. ibid., figs. 76-79; for its braided headpieces, cf. figs. 82 and 85. For a color facsimile of the *Codex Assemanianus*, cf. now *Asemanevo evangelie, faksimilno izdanie* (Sofia, 1981), e.g., fols. 12^{v}, 13^{r}, 13^{v}, 23^{r}, 31^{v}, 44^{r}, 49^{v}, 51^{v}, 55^{r}.

(fig. 26, p. 629), to the *Psalterium Sinaiticum* (fig. 27, p. 629) and to the *Codex Assemanianus* (fig. 28, p. 629) — in short, to the majority of the earliest Glagolitic manuscripts. In other words, I am suggesting that the habits of the producers of the earliest books written in Old Church Slavonic reflect South Italian influences.

The proposition that an artistic influence emanated from South Italy towards the Balkan Slavs is paralleled by André Grabar's recent hypothesis according to which Italo-Greek illuminated manuscripts of the period influenced one aspect of the practice of illumination in Byzantium itself.[40] Thus my suggestion should appear less startling to ⟨143⟩ an art historian than it might to a Slavic philologist, whose main points of reference for our period are Byzantium, Macedonia, Bulgaria, Moravia, and the Franks. Nor is it, strictly speaking, novel, for in recent years, connections were occasionally established between Italo-Greek and early Slavic illumination and ornament. But these were *obiter dicta*, dealing with individual Greek or Slavic manuscripts, such as the few well chosen words on the *ES* and the Sinai Psalter by Kurt Weitzmann whose broad knowledge of East and West enabled him to put these manuscripts in their proper framework;[41] Guillou's and Tschérémisinoff's well-intentioned attempt based on an inappropriate example;[42] or a stray

40. Cf. A. Grabar, *Les manuscrits grecs enluminés de provenance italienne (IXe-XIe siècles)* (Paris, 1972), pp. 96-97; Italo-Greek manuscripts transmitted the Western composite initial to Byzantium (but *not* the "Latin" ornaments or the "colossal" initials with which we are dealing here; cf. ibid., pp. 92-93).

41. Kurt Weitzmann, *Illustrated Manuscripts at St. Catherine's Monastery on Mount Sinai* (Collegeville, Minnesota, 1973), p. 13.

42. Cf. A. Guillou and Katia Tchérémisinoff, "Note sur la culture arabe et la culture slave dans le katépanat d'Italie (X^e-XIe s.)," *Mélanges de L'Ecole française de Rome* 88 (1976): 677-92, especially 685-90, repeated with only a few changes in A. Guillou, "La culture slave dans le katépanat d'Italie," *Slavjanskie Kul'tury i Balkany* (Sofia), 1 (1978): 267-74. In both articles, the general cultural background is drawn with a master's pen; and the connection (made in the wake of Weitzmann) between the *ES*, the Sinai Psalter, and South Italy is to be applauded (even if, *pace* p. 690, these manuscripts were hardly *written* in South Italy); however, the main new piece of manuscript evidence adduced by the authors — namely, Athens, National Library 149 (Acts of the Apostles and the Epistles, rather than "Psalter") — does not quite belong in our context. True, the text of the manuscript itself, its original rubrics, headpieces and simple initials, are unmistakably by a South Italian scribe of the late tenth or early eleventh century. But all the titles in black ink are either added in spaces left empty by the original scribe, or rewritten over the original rubrics: cf. fols.56^v-57^r, where the original title of 57^r, + ΥΠΟΘΕCIC... THC ΔΕΥ, still reflected in mirror image on fol.

remark or two drowned among a plethora of ⟨144⟩ guesses on *Codex Assemanianus's* putative connections ranging from Coptic to Mycenaean.[43] What, I submit, is novel in my suggestion is that it points

---

56ᵛ, was erased, and a Greek title in black ink by a "Slavicizing" hand substituted for it. This hand is, however, to be dated to the fourteenth century; so are the Slavic titles and texts on scrolls, probably written by the same hand; so are the three miniatures of St. Peter and Paul. The spelling of the Slavic on the scrolls, too, points to the fourteenth century (and perhaps to Serbia); the paschal tables of fol. 159ʳ start with the year 1328; finally, the manuscript itself reached the Athens National Library from Bačkovo in Bulgaria. Thus Athens, National Library 149 is not a witness, along with the two early Glagolitic manuscripts from Sinai, for Slavic scribal artistic activity and bilingual culture somewhere in South Italy in the first half of the eleventh century; it reflects the activity of some center, situated in the Balkans in the fourteenth century, where a Slavic scribe mastered Greek script reputably well, and where bad miniatures were attempted. I am able to make only one valid statement of use to our topic in connection with the Athens manuscript: this manuscript attests to the movement of books from South Italy to the Balkans sometime between the eleventh and fourteenth century. For a description of the Athens, National Library 149, cf. Marava-Chatzinicolaou and Toufexi-Paschou, *Catalogue* (as in fn. 39 above), no. 8 = pp. 51-55 and figs. 62-71. Slight doubts that the Slavic miniatures of this manuscript are of the same period as its text were already expressed by Grabar, *Les manuscrits grecs* (as in fn. 40 above), 68 (with the assistance of L. Vranoussis).

43. V. Ivanova-Mavrodinova and L. Mavrodinova, "Ukrasata na starobъlgarskite glagoličeski rъkopisi," in *Paléographie et diplomatique slaves* [= Balcanica III, Etudes et documents, 1] (Sofia, 1980), trace (p. 195) "a few" examples of ornament in the *ES* back to Greek manuscripts from South Italy; V. Ivanova-Mavrodinova and A. Džurova, *Assemanievoto evangelie. Starobъlgarski glagoličeski pametnik ot X vek* [= a companion volume to the facsimile edition of the Codex] (Sofia, 1981), reproduce (p. 32) a passage from Weitzmann (as in fn. 41 above), state (pp. 19,20), on evidence unknown to me, that some textual traits of the *Assemanianus* are paralleled in Greek manuscripts from South Italy, and admit (p. 42) in the *Assemanianus* the existence, "though to a small degree," of elements similar to those of some western manuscripts. Otherwise, the authors range widely in their search for artistic sources of that manuscript. Their preferences go: to Bithynia (about whose ninth-century securely dated and localized *illuminated* manuscripts we know next to nothing), on the strength, I assume, of Cyril and Methodius's stay in the Mt. Olympus region there and on account of the "Bithynian milieu" cautiously postulated by Kurt Weitzmann in 1935 on the basis of one non-illuminated ornamented manuscript, cf. his *Die byzantinische Buchmalerei...* (Berlin, 1935), pp. 39-44 (incidentally, the ninth-century Bithynian manuscript in question was written in Kios-Gemlik, rather than in the unknown diocese τῆς βίου; in any case its ornament has nothing to do with either Glagolitic or South Italian ornament); to Cappadocia; to Syria-Palestine; to "Greek-Oriental Provinces," or to late Antiquity in

to a link between the bulk of the earliest Old Chuch Slavonic production and Byzantine Italy.[44]

Studying the make-up and ornament of ninth-to-eleventh century Italo-Greek manuscripts may be of help in narrowing down the date of their Glagolitic counterparts, including our newly discovered fragments from Sinai. Comparison with Italo-Greek manuscripts strengthens the impression that these fragments are not later than the end of ⟨145⟩ the eleventh century; they could be even earlier. I am not able to go beyond this guess in terms of absolute chronology. I do have a tentative idea, however, concerning the relative chronology of the main Glagolitic manuscripts. Again, I derive this chronology from their make-up and ornament, and am suggesting that our fragments, the *ES*, and the *Zographensis* come first, followed by the *Psalterium Sinaiticum* and the *Codex Assemanianus*, in that order. Thus, the *Assemanianus* would be the youngest, rather than the oldest, among the early Glagolitic manuscripts. This sequence runs counter to views prevalent in the secondary literature, but coincides with the most recent, and still unpublished, opinions of some Slavic linguists.[45]

---

general. Much of it repeats the conceptions, and the terminology, of before 1914. Yet even an untrained eye is struck by the western crown within the initial for V on fol. 74ᵛ of the *Assemanianus*. Furthermore, the Cyrillic entry on fol. 146ᵛ that mentions the feast of Saint Nicholas under May 20 (a "western" date, conditioned by the translation of the saint's relics to Bari in South Italy) should give food for thought.

44. Systematic work on ornaments in early Cyrillic manuscripts is still to be done. The examples offered by the old, but excellent plates in V. V. Stasoff (= Stasov), *Slavjanskij i vostočnyj ornament po rukopisjam drevnjago i novago vremeni* (St. Petersburg, 1887) suggest that the ornament and initials in the early (eleventh-twelfth centuries) Cyrillic manuscripts are close to the "South Italian" ornaments of early Glagolitic ones. Cf. plates I, 3 (Rumjancev Museum 961, fol. 2: braided band; red, green, yellow colors); I, 24 (*Codex Suprasliensis*, Ljubljana part), fols. 8 and 42 (braided bands); II, 1 (Rumjancev Museum 1690, fol. 68: wide interlaced headpiece); II, 2 (ibid., fol. 88: narrow interlaced band); II, 17 (ibid., fol. 55ᵛ: letter B with eye and beak); III, 1 (Rumjancev Museum 1685, fol. 26ᵛ: band with the S-motif); III, 2 (ibid., fol. 34: interlaced band); III, 4 (ibid., fol. 5ᵛ: interlaced band with the S-motif); III, 26 (ibid., fol. 2ᵛ: three S-motifs in letter B).

45. In the standard edition of the *Assemanianus* by J. Vajs and J. Kurz, *Evangeliarium Assemani, Codex Vaticanus Slavicus glagoliticus* vols. 1 and 2 (Prague, 1929 and 1955) our manuscript is dated to the end of the tenth or the beginning of the eleventh century; cf. vol. 1, p. vii and vol. 2, p. vii. In the two works quoted in fn. 43 above (and in other recent Bulgarian publications, too

There are several ways of interpreting the parallels in ornament between the Italo-Greek and early Glagolitic manuscripts. I give low priority to postulating common sources of influence for the two, because South Italian parallels alone explain matters in a better, and simpler, way than any such postulated sources, be they transalpine (whether insular or Carolingian)[46] or "Oriental" (read Syro-Palestin⟨146⟩ian).[47] A

---

numerous to be adduced here), the *Assemanianus* is said to be the earliest Old Bulgarian Glagolitic manuscript known to scholarship and is dated to the years 950-980, cf. Ivanova-Mavrodinova and Mavrodinova, pp. 190, 193; Ivanova-Mavrodinova and Džurova, pp. 11, 19, 23, 25, 56, 57, 65. The chronological sequence, based on ornament and proposed by the two Mavrodinovas (p. 193), is as follows: 1. The *Assemanianus*; 2. The *Zographensis* and the *Marianus*; 3. The *ES*; 4. The *Psalterium Sinaiticum*.

Professor Horace G. Lunt obtains the first rank among the linguists most recently advocating a late date for the *Assemanianus*. He considers it to be "surely the youngest" of the Old Chuch Slavonic gospel manuscripts and dates it to the second half of the eleventh century, or even to 1100. Cf. Lunt's three forthcoming studies: "On the Old Church Slavonic Codex Assemanianus," to appear in *Makedonski jazik* (Skopje); "On OCS Gospel Texts," to appear in *Byzantinobulgarica* (Sofia), and "On Dating Old Church Slavonic Gospel Manuscripts," to appear in *Studies in Slavic and General Linguistics* (Utrecht, 1982). Professor Robert Mathiesen, too, doubts the early date of the *Assemanianus* (communication by letter).

All artistic and linguistic considerations aside, the mid-tenth century date for the *Assemanianus* is unlikely on account of the mention of Theodora of Thessalonica in its *synaxarium* (fol. 152^{v}). As the Greek Theodora died in 892, her inclusion into a Slavic Synaxarium a mere sixty years after her death would be unusual.

46. Grabar, *Les manuscrits* (as in fn. 40 above), pp. 82-93, has listed Carolingian and insular influences in Italo-Greek manuscripts (influences reaching South Italy either directly, or through the mediation of Northern Europe or, finally, the city of Rome). It is impossible to show, for lack of evidence, direct Carolingian or insular influences on the earliest Slavic manuscripts produced, say, in Moravia or the area in which Methodius was active. Such influences would be possible to imagine; but could a tradition of illumination be created in a maximum of twenty years, to live on after direct contacts with the Franks had been interrupted?

47. Ivanova-Mavrodinova and Džurova, *Assemanievoto* (as in fn. 43 above), p. 42, assert that similarity of ornamental elements in the *Assemanianus* and some western manuscripts, respectively, is due to the "elementary truth" that Syro-Palestinian and Coptic elements played a role in the formation of Western art. Cf. also ibid., p. 61 and p. 62 where — in seeming disregard of geography — common (Syriac and "Egyptian") models are adduced to explain similarities between Italo-Greek and the nearby Croatian Glagolitic manuscripts.

higher priority should be assigned to historical and cultural explanations. The first is offered by channels for contacts between the Balkans and Italy.[48] The second explanation would postulate the existence of a Slavo-Greek milieu in late ninth-century Rome.[49] A third would deal with the missionary activity originating in Italy and spreading to the Balkans in the ninth century,[50] even if in our search for traces of the movement of people and books from South Italy across the Adriatic we should go beyond the earliest period and keep the tenth and eleventh centuries in mind as well.

In pursuing those explanations, we should consider the ornament of Glagolitic manuscripts as a "tracer" for contacts,[51] and should add ⟨147⟩ Byzantine Italy to Byzantium and the Latin West in our list of main areas from where cultural influences entered the Balkans between the ninth and eleventh centuries. Such a vast topic can be only suggested,

---

48. For an excellent, if short, statement on these contacts, cf. the two articles by A. Guillou quoted in fn. 42 above, with good bibliography (including studies by I. Dujčev and Guillou himself); cf. also the bibliography in A. Guillou, "L'Italie byzantine au XIe siècle. Etat des questions," in *L'art dans l'Italie méridionale, aggiornamento dell'opera di Emile Bertaux...* (Rome, 1978), p. 3ff.

49. If we could enlarge our meagre body of information on this milieu, we would move a long way towards explaining the familiarity with the ecclesiastical topography of the city of Rome, and with Roman affairs, displayed in the *Vita* of Constantine, Apostle of the Slavs. Whoever wrote the *Vita* knew Rome quite well.

50. This is more of a stab in the dark than an explanation. On missionary activity from the west, including impulses from Italy, cf. F. Dvorník, *Byzantine Missions among the Slavs...* (New Brunswick, 1970), especially chap. 3, pp. 73-104 and 346-62.

51. Peculiarities of texts preserved in the earliest Glagolitic manuscripts would be the best "tracers." Here, analysis has not progressed beyond general statements concerning the "western," i.e., Latin elements (read: Vulgate elements and Hebrew ones that had entered the Latin West) in the early Slavic translations of the Lectionary and the Psalter. Again, the term "western" turns scholars' minds either to mixed Byzantine models (thought to have absorbed those Latin and Hebrew elements), or to Moravia, where reworkings by Slavs are said to have been done under Latin influence. Cf. Vajs-Kurz, *Evangeliarium* (as in fn. 45 above), I:xxv, and J. Lépissier, "La traduction vieux-slave du psautier," *Revue des Etudes Slaves* 43 (1964): 59-72, especially 72. I know of only one scholar who connects the text of an early Glagolitic manuscript with Italy: according to Guillou-Tschérémisinoff, "Note" (as in fn. 42 above), p. 690, fn. 6, A. Jacob found that some prayers of the *ES* were "composed with the help of Italo-Greek manuscripts." Unfortunately, Dr. Jacob's findings, "in press" by 1976, are still inaccessible to me.

but not responsibly tackled in a first presentation of a mere two pages of an early Glagolitic manuscript. May this presentation meet with the approval of the Sinai authorities, and help expedite their plans to proceed with the full publication of the new finds, both Glagolitic and Cyrillic, that were made in their monastery.

Addendum to fn. 39: — J. Leroy, "Notes codicologiques sur le *Vat. gr.* 699," *Cahiers archéologiques* 23 (1974): 73-79, considers (p. 76 and fn. 25) initials containing a twisted cord to be characteristic of Italo-Greek manuscripts (cf., e.g., our fig. 10). Many initials in both the *ES* and other Glagolitic manuscripts are decorated in the same way (cf. our figs. 2 and 26). — For interlaced bands in the Italo-Greek manuscripts, cf. now E. Follieri, "Due codici greci... *Ottob. gr.* 250 e 251," in *Palaeographica Diplomatica et Archivistica, Studi in onore di Giulio Battelli* (Rome, 1979), pp. 159-221, especially figs. I and VI.

PHOTO CREDITS:
Plates 1 and 2 and fig. 1 — photo Ševčenko; figs. 2, 3, 4, 11, 12, 15, 19, 21, 23, 25 — R. Nahtigal, *Euchologium Sinaiticum*, in *Akademija Znanosti in Umetnosti v Ljubljani...*, 1-2 (Ljubljana, 1941-42), plates 100 b, 61 b, 95 b, 77 b, 81 b, 14 b, 59 b, 80 a, 32 b, 23 a; fig. 5 — L. Th. Lefort and J. Cochez, *Palaeographisch album...* (Louvain, 1943), plate 61; figs. 6, 24 — P. Franchi De'Cavalieri and J. Lietzmann, *Specimina Codicum Graecorum Vaticanorum...* (Berlin and Leipzig, 1929), plates 16, 17; fig. 7 — K. Lake and S. Lake, eds., *Dated Greek Manuscripts to the Year 1200*, vol. 2 (Boston, 1934), plate 101; fig. 8 — H. Follieri, *Codices Graeci Bibliothecae Vaticanae Selecti...* (Vatican, 1969), plate 32; figs. 9, 13, 20, 22 — André Grabar, *Les manuscrits grecs enluminés de provenance italienne (IXᵉ-XIᵉ siècles)* (Paris, 1972), figs. 134, 94, 127, 121; fig. 10 — Kurt Weitzmann, *Die byzantinische Buchmalerei des 9. und 10. Jahrhunderts* (Berlin, 1935), pl. XCII, figs. 584-585; fig. 14 — M. Bonicatti, "Aspetti dell'industria libraria mediobizantina negli 'scriptoria' italogreci e considerazioni su alcuni manoscritti Criptensi miniati," in *Atti del Terzo Congresso internazionale di studi sull'alto medioevo* (Spoleto, 1959), pp. 341-64, plate 3; fig. 16 — Anna Marava-Chatzinicolaou and Christina Toufexi-Paschou, *Catalogue of the Illuminated Byzantine Manuscripts of the National Library of Greece*, vol. 1: *Manuscripts of New Testament Texts, 10th-12th Century* (Athens, 1978), fig. 78; figs. 17, 27 — Moshé Altbauer, *Psalterium Sinaiticum: An Eleventh-Century Glagolitic Manuscript from St. Catherine Monastery, Mt. Sinai* (Skopje, 1971), fol. 121ᵛ, 123ʳ; fig. 18 — Microfilm, Patmos Monastery; fig. 26 — V. Jagić, ed., *Quattuor evangeliorum Codex Glagoliticus olim Zographensis nunc Petropolitanus* (Berlin, 1879), plate 1; fig. 28 — V. Ivanova-Mavrodinova and A. Džurova, *Assemanievo evangelie. Starobъlgarski glagoličeski pametnik ot X vek* (Sofia, 1981), fol. 157ᵛ.

APPENDIX

Index Verborum to the Sinai Fragments[52]

*A (= *numeral*, 1 [?]), 5:9 (*n.e.*)
antifonъ: antьfonъ, 2:1 (ἀντιφώνου); antъfon, 4:1 (*n.e.*)
azъ: *see* my

b⟨————⟩, 5:6
b⟨————⟩emь, 2:13
bez: ⟨bes⟩, 4:13 (ἀ————)
blago: ⟨b⟩lagy, 4:9 (διά... ἀγαθῶν)
blagodětь: blagodětiję (χάριτι), 1:5, 3:7; 3:2 (ἀγαθότητι)
blagosloviti: blagovi, 1:4 (εὐλόγησον)
blagostь: b⟨lagost⟩iję, 4:4 (ἀγαθωσύνῃ)
blagъ: blagaa, 4:7 (ἀγαθά)
bogatъ: bogatymь, 4:4 (πλουσίᾳ)
bogъ: bže (ὁ θεός), 2:2, 4:2, 6:10 (*n.e.*)
*bystrъ: bystryxъ, 3:5 (ποικίλων)

cěsarьstvo: cr⟨st⟩vo, 4:8 (βασιλείαν); crstv ⟨————⟩, 5:7 (*n.e.*)
čęs⟨tь⟩, 4:12 (μέρος)
čьstьnъ: čestьnemь, 2:4 (προσκυνητῷ)
člověkoljubije: čkljubiemь, 3:9 (φιλανθρωπίᾳ)
člověkъ: čky, 4:3 (ἀνθρώπων)
*čudьno: čjudno[?], 4:2 (θαυμαστός)

da, 2:13 (ἵνα)
darovati: darova⟨vъ⟩, 4:6 (δωρησάμενος)
dati: danymi, 4:8 (κεχαρισμένων); daždi, 3:3 (δός), 4:12 (δώρησαι)
dějanije: ⟨dě⟩ěnič, 2:11 (ἔργων)
dьnь: dˆne, 3:5 (ἡμέρας); dˆn⟨e⟩, 5:5 (*n.e.*)
dьnьnъ: denьna ⟨————⟩, 5:4 (*n.e.*)
dlъgъ, 2:9 (ὀφλημα)
duxъ: dxa, 3:8 (πνεύματος)

52. Words not attested in the *ES* are marked with an asterisk. Greek equivalents following a reference by prayer number and line are valid only for that particular reference, cf. the entry *blagodětь*. Equivalents following a Slavic word are valid for all the subsequent references, or until a new equivalent following a reference by prayer number and line makes its appearance, cf. the entry *našь*. *N.e.* = no equivalent in Greek. Dr. Donald Ostrowski helped to compile this index.

E (= *numeral*, 6), 2:1 (ς')
e⟨————⟩, 6:12
⟨————⟩ego, 4:12

jedinočędъ: edinočę ˙/., 1:6 (*n.e.*)
jedinosǫštьnъ: edin ˙/., 3:9 (*n.e.*)

glava: glav, 1:4 (κεφαλάς)
godina: godně, 2:1 (ὥρας)
gospodь: gi, 1:1 (*n.e.*), 1:2 (κύριε), 4:2 (*n.e.*); ⟨gi⟩, 6:10 (*n.e.*), gju, 1:1 (τῷ κυρίῳ)
grěxovьnъ: grěx⟨o⟩vъny, 2:9 (ἁμαρτημάτων)
grěxъ: grěxъ (*gen. plur.*), 2:6 (ἁμαρτιῶν)

xva⟨————⟩, 4:14 (ὑμνεῖν?)

i (καί), 1:3, 1:6, 2:5, 2:7, 3:1, 3:2, 3:3, 3:4, 3:9, 4:4; ⟨i⟩, 2:12, 4:7, 4,13, 3,6 (*n.e.*) (*n.e.*)
iz⟨————⟩, 6:11

konьčati, 4:13 (ἐκτελέσαι)
kovъ: kovъ (*gen. plur.*), 3:6 (*n.e.? Cf.* kyznь)
krьstъ: krstě, 2:5 (σταυρῷ)
kyznь: kyznei, 3:5 (kyznei i kovъ: μηχανημάτων)

ljudije: ljud, 1:1 (*n.e.*)

milostь: milostijǫ, 3:1 (ἐλέους), 3:9 (ἐλέει)
*mimoiti: mimošьdъšjǫǫ, 4:11 (παρελθόν)
mirьskъ: mirъs⟨kaa⟩, 4:6 (ἐγκόσμια)
molitva: mol (εὐχή), 2:1, 4:1; moltvǫ, 1:3 (προσευχῆς)
my; namъ (ἡμῖν), 2:8, 3:3, 4:7, 4:12, ⟨nam⟩ъ, 4:6; ⟨namъ⟩, 4:9; nasъ (ἡμᾶς), 3:2; ny, 2:10; ⟨ny⟩, 4:10

na, 2:1 (*gen.*), 2:4, (ἐν), 2:7 (ἐν)
našь: naš (*acc. plur. fem.*), (ἡμῶν), 1:1; naš (*voc. sg. masc.*), 2:2; na⟨šь⟩, 3:7, 6:10 (*n.e.*); našixъ, 2:6 (ἡμετέρων); našjǫ, 1:3 (ἡμῶν)
nastojati: nastoję̌staago, 3:4 (παρούσης)
neizdrečenъ: neizdrečenъnojǫ, 4:3 (ἀνεκδιηγήτῳ)
neprijazninъ: nep⟨ri⟩ězninъ (*gen. plur.*), 3:6 (τοῦ πονηροῦ)
nyně, 2:8 (νῦν)

*obětovati: obětovanoe, 4:7 (ἐπηγγελμένην)
onъ; nemь, 2:7 (αὐτῷ)
osǫždenije: osǫždenič, 2:11 (κατακρίσεως)
otъ, 3:4 (*gen.*), 3:5 (ἐκ), 4:10 (ἀπό); o⟨tъ⟩, 2:10 (*gen.*)

otъběgnǫti, 3:3 (διαφυγεῖν)
otъpustiti: otъpusti, 2:8 (ἄφες)

pokloniti: poklon (*imp. 1st pers. plur.*), 1:1 (*n.e.*; poklonьšęję, 1:3 (τοὺς ὑποκεκλικότας)
pomyšlenije: ⟨pomyšl⟩enei, 2:12 (ἐνθυμήσεων)
popъ: pop, 1:1 (ὁ ἱερεύς)
*porǫčiti: ⟨porǫ⟩čei[?], 4:7 (κατεγγυήσας)
porokъ: bes poroka, 4:13 (ἀμέμπτως)
posětiti: posěti, 3:2 (ἐπίσκεψαι)
potrěbiti: potrěbi (= potrěbь i?), 2:7 (ἐξαλείψας... καί)
prěčistъ: prečistěi, 2:3 (τὰς ἀχράντους)
prědъ: ⟨prědъ⟩, 4:14 (ἐνώπιον)
prigvozditi: prigvoždь, 2:6 (προσηλώσας)
prikloniti: prikloni, 1:2 (κλῖνον)
pročijь: pročee, 3:4 (τὸ λοιπόν), 5:5 (*n.e.*); ⟨pročee⟩, 4:13 (τὸ ὑπόλοιπον)
promyšlenije: ⟨promy⟩šleniemь, 4:5 (προνοίᾳ)
prostrěti: prostery, 2:2 (ἐκτείνας)

rǫka, rǫcě, 2:3 (χεῖρας)
rǫkopisanije, 2:5 (χειρόγραφον)

slava: ⟨slavojǫ⟩, 4:14 (δόξης)
slovesьnъ: slovesьn⟨————⟩, 2:12 (λόγων)
strojiti: stroję, 4:2 (διοικῶν)
svętiti: sti (*imp. 2nd pers. sg.*), 1:5 (ἁγίασον)
svętъ: staago, 3:8 (τοῦ ἁγίου); ⟨stojǫ⟩, 4:14 (τῆς ἁγίας); sty, 2:2 (ἅγιε)
svoboditi: svobodi, (ἐλευθέρους ἡμᾶς ἀνάδειξον)
svojь: svoemь, 2:4 (σου); svoi, 2:3 (σου); svoję, 1:4 (ἑαυτῶν)
sъxraniti: sъxrani, 1:5 (φύλαξον); 3:6 (διαφύλαξον)
sъtvoriti: sъtvoriv⟨ъ⟩[?], 4:9 (ὁ ποιήσας)
štedrota: štedrotami, 1:6 (οἰκτιρμοῖς); ⟨štedrota⟩mi, 3:1 (οἰκτιρμῶν)

taina [?]: vtai (*i.e.* vъ tainǫ?), 1:1 (*n.e.*)
ty: tebě, 1:4 (σοι); teb (*dat. sg.*) 1:1(*n.e.*)
tvojь (σου): tvoe, 1:2; tvoego, 3:8; tvoejǫ, 3:1; ⟨tv⟩oejǫ, 4:14; tvoimi, 3:1; tvoejǫ, 3:2 (τῇ σῇ)

uxo, 1:2 (τὸ οὖς)
ukloniti sę: ⟨u⟩kloniti sę, 4:10 (ἐκκλῖναι)
uslyšati: uslyši, 1:2 (ἐπάκουσον)
*uže: juže, 4:9 (ἤδη)

⟨————⟩ъ, 6:11

večerьnь: večerъnii, 4:1 (ἑσπερινή)

velikъ, 4:2 (μέγας)
vladyka: vlko, 2:2 (δέσποτα)
vьsěkъ: v^sěkъ, 2:9 (πᾶν); v^sěkogo, 2:10 (πάσης)
vьsь: v^sę, 1:3 (πάντας); v^sego, 4:11 (παντός); ⟨v^se⟩go, 5:6 (*n.e.*)
vъ, 4:3 (*acc.*?)
vъzglašenije: vš'/., 1:5 (ἐκφώ⟨νως⟩?), 3:8 (ἐκφώνησις),

zъlo: zъla, 5:6 (*n.e.); ⟨*zъla⟩, 4:11 (κακοῦ)
zъlъ: zъlъ (*gen. plur. neutr.*), 2:13 (πονηρῶν)

*Ž (= *numeral*, 7), 4:1 (Z)
životъ (τὴν ζωήν), 3:7, 4:3

XXXV

The Many Worlds of Peter Mohyla

To be in Kiev during the almost twenty years of Metropolitan Peter Mohyla's ascendancy in that city (1627-1646) must have been a heady experience for many a soul. The Orthodox at large were witnessing the rebirth of their Greek religion and of their Rus' nation. Select groups among them — teachers and students of Mohyla's college, well-established parents sending their sons there, or printers and editors at the press in the Monastery of the Caves (fig. 1, p. 684) of which Mohyla was abbot — could feel that they were playing an important part in bringing about that rebirth. Some helped by teaching, supporting, or learning the new "sciences," others by enlisting modern technology in the service of a sacred cause. In several quarters, spirits were uplifted and minds were expanding.

My essay will be devoted primarily to these two lively and optimistic decades in Kiev's intellectual life. It will deal with the early years of Mohyla and of his educational enterprise; with the intellectual horizons of the metropolitan and of the students in his newly created college in Kiev; and with the attitude the college and its founder displayed toward the Polish Commonwealth and the Cossacks. I shall only occasionally touch upon the subsequent history and influence exerted by Mohyla's college, which was raised to the rank of an academy toward the very end of the seventeenth century. I shall, however, close with some remarks on what Mohyla's school may have contributed to the growth of Ukrainian historical and national consciousness.* ⟨10⟩

---

* By way of experiment, I adopted the transcription rules proposed by O. A. Bevzo, "Pro pravyla drukuvannja istoryčnyx dokumentiv, pysanyx ukrajins'koju movoju v XVI-XVIII st.," *Visnyk Akademiji nauk URSR*, 1958, no. 2, pp. 12-26 (cf. esp. 23-25), for proper names and texts written in the vernacular. For titles of books and for texts written (or purporting to be written) in Slavonic, I used the simplified conventional transliteration (except for rendering of г by h rather than g). The terms *Rossija* and *rossijs'kyj* have been translated as "Rus'" and "Ruthenian," respectively, for in texts written in Mohyla's lifetime and within his jurisdiction these terms mean "Rus'" or "belonging to Rus'" within

I

The Kievan Epiphany *Bratstvo*, a religious confraternity of laymen and clergy, was founded in 1615. It obtained the rank of a *stauropēgion* — that is, a foundation directly protected by the patriarch of Constantinople — through a charter issued in 1620 by Theophanes, the patriarch of Jerusalem, who acted as Constantinople's plenipotentiary. The same charter sanctioned the Confraternity's school, which it called a school of Helleno-Slavonic and — significantly — Latin scripture. The year 1620, which saw the "illegal" re-establishment of an Orthodox hierarchy in the Ukraine and in Belorussia by the same Theophanes, was thus also a milestone for an educational upsurge in Kiev. The corresponding secular privilege for the confraternity was issued by the Polish king Sigismund III in 1629.

The directorship of the Confraternity school was an important post; it was held by people drawn from the ranks of the Orthodox intellectual elite. Iov Borec'kyj, the first metropolitan of Kiev of the restored hierarchy of 1620, was director between 1615 and 1619 and a superior of the school until 1631. Other prominent intellectuals, both laymen and ecclesiastics, among the officers of the school were Vasyl' Berezec'kyj the jurist, Meletij Smotryc'kyj (1618? 1626/28?), whose name is familiar to Slavic philologists, Kasijan Sakovyč, and Zaxarij Kopystens'kyj, archimandrite of the Monastery of the Caves. Such was the state of Orthodox education in Kiev when Peter Mohyla appeared on the scene, to strengthen and broaden the new concepts that were already making their way in that education.[1]

---

the Polish-Lithuanian Commonwealth, as opposed to *Moskva* 'Muscovy' and *moskovs'kyj* 'Muscovite'. To allow control and to avoid confusion with cases where "Rus'," "Ruthenian" translates *Rus', rus'kyj*, all renderings of the terms *Rossija* and *rossijs'kyj* are followed by the original form in brackets. Thus: "Ruthenian nation (*narodu rossijs'koho*)." To designate written languages of the time, I adopted "Ruthenian" for the relatively unified language written in the Polish-Lithuanian Commonwealth on the territories of Rus' (that is, in the Ukraine, in Belorussia, and in parts of Lithuania); "Slavonic" for what I would like to call Vulgar Church Slavonic — a language in principle obeying the grammar of Old Church Slavonic and based on its vocabulary, but permeated with morphological and lexical elements belonging to later stages of various Slavic languages, with the local language providing most intrusions.

1. On confraternities (brotherhoods) and their educational activity, cf., e.g., S. T. Golubev, *Istorija Kievskoj duxovnoj akademii, I. Period domogiljanskij* (Kiev, 1886) (inaccessible to me); K. V. Xarlampovič, *Zapadnorusskie pravoslav-*

⟨11⟩ Mohyla (in Roumanian Movilă, meaning "hill" or "mountain") came from the family of Moldavian hospodars.[2] Moldavia originally depended ecclesiastically on Halyč, and when the Poles, as successors ⟨12⟩ to the Halyč principality, extended their protectorate over Moldavia (by then inhabited by speakers of a Roumanian dialect) they insisted on maintaining Moldavia's ecclesiastical dependence on Halyč. Despite the establishment (in 1401) of a separate Moldavian metropolitan see with residence in Suceava (Sučava), Moldavia remained in touch with western Rus', partly because its vassalage to Poland was renewed (1402) and partly because in Moldavia the main language of administration and of the church was Slavonic — a vehicle that continued to be used (if to a lesser extent as time progressed) into the eighteenth century in official acts and in contacts with the Polish-Lithuanian Commonwealth. Polish, too, was introduced in Moldavia. The treaties of 1519 and 1527 between Sigismund I and Hospodar Stephen were written in that language, as was some of the correspondence of the L'viv burghers and the L'viv confraternity with the hospodars. Ruthenian had its share in this correspondence as well: for instance, Symeon Mohyla, the father of our Peter, wrote to the L'viv confraternity in that language.

nye školy XVI i načala XVII veka ... (Kazan', 1898), pp. 187ff.; E. N. Medynskij, *Bratskie školy Ukrainy i Belorussii v XVI-XVII vv. i ix rol' v vossoedinenii Ukrainy s Rossiej* (Moscow, 1954), and the two good works by Ja. D. Isajevyč, *Bratstva ta jix rol' v rozvytku ukrajins'koji kul'tury XVI-XVIII st.* (Kiev, 1966), and *Džerela z istoriji ukrajins'koji kul'tury doby feodalizmu* (Kiev, 1972). Some information on confraternities can be derived from several books mentioned in the next note. For the various charters of Patriarch Theophanes, cf. *Pamjatniki izdannye Vremennoju kommisieju dlja razbora drevnix aktov...*, vol. 2 (Kiev, 1846), nos. III-V, pp. 49-85 (cf. esp. 66, 70); for King Sigismund III's privilege, cf. ibid., no. VI, pp. 86-92. — On the later years of the Confraternity school and the early ones of that of Mohyla, cf. the interesting *Autobiographical Note* by Rev. Ihnatij Jevlevyč (Iewlewicz), ed. S. T. Golubev, in the *Universitetskie izvestija* of Kiev, 26, no. 5 (May 1886): 74-79. We learn from Jevlevyč (p. 75) that the Confraternity school had classes of *infima, grammatica*, and *syntaxima*, an indication that Western educational patterns had been introduced in Kiev before Mohyla.

2. For a first approach to the vast literature on Mohyla and his college and academy, cf. the references in L. Je. Maxnovec', *Ukrajins'ki pys'mennyky*, vol. 1 (Kiev, 1960), pp. 415-27, to which add the items cited in my "Agapetus East and West: The Fate of a Byzantine Mirror of Princes," *Revue des études sud-est européennes* 16 (1978): 30, fn. 96. Furthermore, cf. Hugh F. Graham, "Peter Mogila — Metropolitan of Kiev," *Russian Review* 14 (October 1955): 345-56 (here Mohyla is viewed from the All-Russian vantage point); V. S. Pakulin, entry "Mogila" in *Sovetskaja istoričeskaja ènciklopedija* 9 (1966), col. 537; A.

Religious polemical literature of the sixteenth and early seventeenth centuries, written in Ruthenian and Polish, also reached Moldavia, largely through the L'viv confraternity. In turn, many hospodars were benefactors of the confraternity, as they were of other Orthodox establishments outside their frontiers, for instance, the monasteries of Mount Athos and the Monastery of St. Catherine on Mt. Sinai.

The Mohyla family was granted the rights of indigenous nobility in the Commonwealth in 1593. In 1595 Jeremiah Mohyla became hospodar as a vassal of Poland; his brother Symeon, father of Peter, was a vassal hospodar as well. Peter Mohyla, who spent his childhood in Moldavia, is reported — in a single source of dubious authority — to have studied in France after his father's death in 1608. He moved to Poland when the fortunes of his family declined in Moldavia. In 1617 he was at the court of Hetman Żółkiewski; in 1621 he took part in the Battle of Xotyn' (Chocim) against the Turks at the side of the victorious Lithuanian grand hetman Chodkiewicz. He then moved to the Ukraine, bought landed property near Kiev, and entered monastic orders at the city's Monastery of the Caves in 1625.

In spite of this Western background and friendly stance toward

Žukovs'kyj, *Petro Mohyla j pytannja jednosty cerkov* [= Ukrainian Free University Series: Monographs, 17] (Paris, 1969) (bibliography); W. K. Medlin and Ch. G. Patrinelis, *Renaissance Influences and Religious Reforms in Russia* (Geneva, 1971), esp. pp. 124-49 (several inexactitudes); H. Kowalska, entry "Mohiła (Moghilă, Movilă) Piotr," in *Polski słownik biograficzny* 21, no. 3 (1976): 568-72 (level-headed; interested in Union negotiations; bibliography); A. Sydorenko, *The Kievan Academy in the Seventeenth Century* [= University of Ottawa Ukrainian Studies, 1] (Ottawa, 1977) (bibliography); H. F. Graham, entry "Mogila, Petr Simeonovich (1596-1647)," in *The Modern Encyclopaedia of Russian and Soviet History* 23 (1981): 9-12 (some bibliography); and Z. I. Xyžňjak, *Kyjevo-Mohyljans'ka akademija*, 2nd ed. (Kiev, 1981). Several works quoted in subsequent notes contain portrayals of the metropolitan. Among older publications, I wish to single out A. Martel, *La langue polonaise dans les pays ruthènes-Ukraine et Russie Blanche, 1569-1667* (Lille, 1938, but completed by 1931), esp. pp. 239-88, "L'Académie de Kiev," and 289-307, "Conclusion," for the sharpness of its sight, its ample recourse to sources (including Titov's *Materijaly*), and its plausible thesis that in Mohyla's time most of the Ruthenian Orthodox elite was loyal to the Polish Crown. Cf. the sympathetic, if guardedly critical, review of Martel by J. Šerex (George Y. Shevelov) in *Ukrajina* (Paris), 2 (1949): 99-107. In documenting statements by Mohyla or his circle, I made liberal use of Xv. Titov, *Materijaly dlja istoriji knyžnoji spravy na Vkrajini v XVI-XVIII vv. Vsezbirka peredmov do ukrajins'kyx starodrukiv* [= Ukrajins'ka akademija nauk, Zbirnyk istoryčno-filolohičnoho viddilu, 17] (Kiev, 1924).

Poland, the Mohyla family, including Peter, were ardent supporters of Orthodoxy. Some time after 1628, when Mohyla finally became archimandrite of the Caves Monastery, he set about establishing a school there. He intended to create an institution which would keep Eastern ⟨13⟩ Orthodoxy untouched and properly taught, but would avoid the drawbacks of Confraternity schools. Instruction at his school was to attain the level of Western — which in practical terms meant Polish — education and thus make unnecessary sending Orthodox youth to the West in quest of learning. In short, his school at the Caves Monastery was to be not so much a Helleno-Slavonic as a Latino-Polish one. That made his enterprise suspect to Orthodox zealots.

To avoid Orthodox attacks, in 1631 Mohyla secured the blessings of the patriarch of Constantinople for the foundation of what a contemporary witness described as a school of Latin and Polish sciences. When in the fall of the same year instruction began for the more than hundred pupils in the newly created school, located near the Caves Monastery, Kiev's Orthodox zealots spread unfriendly rumors about what was being taught there, and the teachers at the school were accused of pro-Uniate leanings. This upset the lower classes and when the Cossacks, too, learned about the accusations, Mohyla was in jeopardy: both his teachers and he himself were presumably threatened with death for introducing Latin and Polish in the school. As one of the teachers (and a future metropolitan of Kiev), Syl'vester Kossov, said in his *Exegesis* of 1635, Mohyla's opponents intended to stuff the sturgeons of the Dnieper with the teachers of the school — a bit of incidental information precious both to the intellectual historian and to the historical ichthyologist.[3] Acting with skill, Mohyla reached a compromise by agreeing to a fusion of his Caves school with that of the Kiev confraternity, situated in Kiev's Podil district; and for a number of years instruction was given in that part of the city. The fusion, implemented during the school recess of 1632, is attested in several documents, two of which involve the

3. For "better than one hundred" pupils in the first year of Mohyla's school, cf. the *Note* by Jevlevyč (as in fn. 1 above), p. 77. For the sturgeons, cf. *Arxiv Jugo-Zapadnoj Rossii*, pt. 1, vol. 8, 1 (Kiev, 1914), esp. p. 423 "Był ten szas [sic], żechmy się wyspowiadawszy, tylko ióż oczekiwali, póki nami ... dnieprowych jesiotrów nadziewać zechcą, abo póki iednego ogniem, drugiego mieczem na drugi świat zasłą." For a discussion of Mohyla's foes in the 1630s and an analysis of Kossov's apology of Mohyla's school, cf. Ju. Geryč, "*Exegesis* Syl'vestra Kosova (1635 r.)," in a number of issues of *Logos*, 9-12 (Yorkton, Sask., 1958-61). On Mohyla's and the teachers' lives being threatened by "ignorant popes and Cossacks," cf. also the testimony of Gabriel Domec'kyj, quoted in S. Golubev, *Kievskij mitropolit Petr Mogila ...*, vol. 1 (1883), p. 436.

Cossacks. In an important statement, dated 12 March 1632 from Kaniv, the Cossack hetman Ivan Petryžyc'kyj and the Zaporozhian Cossacks extended their protection over the school founded by Mohyla; in a letter of 17 March 1632, ⟨14⟩ the hetman bade the local Cossack *ataman* to support the union of the Confraternity's school with Mohyla's.[4]

The Latin character of the new school, offensive to the Orthodox zealots, was also repugnant to the Jesuits and to certain high officials of the Crown, including Vice-Chancellor Thomas Zamoyski, who were unwilling to yield the monopoly in higher learning to the benighted Ruthenians. The Jesuits, in particular, fearing competition for their own schools in the Ukraine (their first foundation, in Kiev's Podil, dated from about 1620), exerted pressure upon the government. Accordingly, in 1634 King Władysław IV ordered Mohyla to abolish the Latin schools and Latin printing presses under his jurisdiction and to use the rights granted him "with moderation."

In spite of this, a year later (1635), the king confirmed Mohyla's school in Kiev. Not as an academy, it is true; it would have no jurisdiction of its own and no subjects beyond dialectic and logic — that is, no theology — were to be taught there. However, the king yielded on the point of Latin and allowed liberal arts (*humaniora*) to be taught "in scholis Kijoviensibus ... Graece et Latine." Note the modest term *scholis*: it appears that an academy which would prepare an elite for service in Rus' was considered more inconvenient to the policies of the Catholic state than a re-established Orthodox hierarchy. The latter, it was continuously hoped, could be persuaded to join the Union, especially if a Uniate patriarchate of Kiev were created and the patriarchal throne were offered to Mohyla — a bait he refused to take, either in 1636 or in later years.[5] Mohyla's dream of an academy was not to be

4. For documents concerning the fusion, cf. *Pamjatniki* (1846) ... (as in fn. 1 above), nos. VIII-X, pp. 101-143; Petryžyc'kyj's statement of 12 March 1632 was later confirmed by Bohdan Xmel'nyc'kyj and his son Jurij, cf, ibid., p. 143. For Petryžyc'kyj's letter of 17 March 1632, cf., e.g. *Pamjatniki izdannye Kievskoju kommissieju dlja razbora drevnix aktov*, vol. 2, 2nd ed. (Kiev, 1897), pp. 421-22, reprinted in Žukovs'kyj, *Petro Mohyla* (as in fn. 2 above), p. 216. Cf. also the *Note* by Jevlevyč (as in fn. 1 above).

5. Cf. M. Andrusiak, "Sprawa patriarchatu kijowskiego za Władysława IV," *Prace historyczne w 30-lecie działalności profesorskiej Stanisława Zakrzewskiego* (L'viv, 1934), pp. 269-285, with sources. Cf. also M. Rechowicz, "Sprawa patriarchatu kościoła 'greckiego' na ziemiach dawnej Polski," *Ateneum Kapłańskie* 49 (1948): 346-52 (inaccessible to me) and A. H. Velykyj, "Anonimnyj projekt Petra Mohyly ...," *Analecta Ordinis S. Basilii Magni*, ser. 2, vol. 4 (Rome, 1963), pp. 434-97.

fulfilled in his lifetime, and his school remained the *Collegium Kijoviense Mohileanum* until the end of the century. For all that, it was the most important of the schools in the Ukraine under Mohyla's supervision, others being, for instance, those of Kremjanec' (Krze⟨15⟩mieniec) in Volhynia, and of Vinnycja in the Braclav palatinate (the Vinnycja school was transferred to Hošča around 1640). When Mohyla attempted to have his school named an academy, he was trying to give it equal status with the Jesuit schools, such as the Vilnius (Wilno) Academy. No wonder that Mohyla's college borrowed much from the Jesuit system — the enemy was to be fought with the enemy's weapons.

The college's top administration consisted of a rector and a prefect. The rector was also the abbot of the Monastery of the Epiphany Confraternity, a position implying rule over landed property. Consequently, the rector was the college's top budgetary officer; he also taught philosophy and, in a later period, theology. The prefect was the inspector and administrator in charge of supplies and feeding the students; as professor, he taught rhetoric. The regular teachers were assisted by the more gifted students, called *auditores*, who both explained the subjects to their fellow pupils before classes and supervised learning in the dormitory (*bursa*). In doing so, they were following Jesuit practice, but also continuing a mediaeval tradition and functioning somewhat as tutors in English colleges do today.

The curriculum, patterned on the Jesuit model, initially took five years to complete. The classes were called *infima*, *grammatica*, *syntaxima*, class of poetics, and class of rhetoric. The first three classes offered mostly instruction in languages: Greek, Latin, Slavonic and Polish; also catechism, ecclesiastical chant, and arithmetic. The poetics class taught what we would call literary theory today, literary genres, and mythology, since every contemporary speech, poem or other writing had to be heavily seasoned with mythological allusions. Most of the textbooks on poetics that remain date from a later period, but two of them are early, and come from 1637 and 1646, respectively. Some of these textbooks, incidentally, were composed by famous personalities such as Symeon Polockij, and Feofan Prokopovyč. All manuals of poetics were written in Latin and Polish with examples drawn both from such classical writers as Martial and from the Polish-Latin poet Matthew Sarbiewski. Later textbooks drew liberally on Polish Renaissance and Baroque poetry (Jan Kochanowski, Samuel Twardowski) for their examples.[6]

---

6. On the textbook of 1637 by A. Starnovec'kyj and M. Kotozvars'kyj (known only in a copy of 1910, rediscovered in 1968), cf. V. I. Krekoten', "Kyjivs'ka

⟨16⟩ In the class of rhetoric students were taught the rules of composing gratulatory speeches, speeches of thanks, greetings, farewells, and funeral orations. The earliest textbook (based on lectures given in 1635/36) used examples culled both from Erasmus of Rotterdam and Stanisław Orzechowski; the most important one, by Prokopovyč (1706), showed some anti-Polish cultural bias, but was written, like the overwhelming majority of Kiev manuals of rhetoric, in Latin.[7] Plays on biblical subjects were among the students' extracurricular endeavors; at first, they were both composed and performed by pupils. This activity, again patterned on Jesuit practice, was to continue and would culminate in the "tragedokomedia" *Vladimerъ* composed by Prokopovyč and performed by Kiev students as a welcome to Hetman Mazepa in July of 1702.

The class of dialectic provided training in scholastic disputations, an antiquated procedure consisting of questions and answers and subdivisions of the subject. Philosophy was taught according to Aristotle (or his commentators), and in Latin. It was subdivided into logic, physics, metaphysics, and ethics — again, hardly an innovative procedure, but no different from that adopted in most schools of the time. The course lasted three years. As for textbooks, the first one composed by Joseph Kononovyč-Horbac'kyj for the courses of 1639/40 (and still unpublished) was modestly called *Subsidium logicae*, perhaps reflecting the doubts as to whether philosophy was a permissible subject, but the third, written by Innokentij Gizel' for his courses of 1646/47 (it, too, is still unpublished), was called explicitly *Opus totius philosophiae*. Its last part dealt

---

poetyka 1637 roku," in *Literaturna spadščyna Kyjivs'koji Rusi i ukrajins'ka literatura XVI-XVIII st.* (Kiev, 1981), pp. 118-54 (pp. 125-154: Ukrainian translation of the text); cf. also *Radjans'ke literaturoznavstvo*, 1970, no. 10, p. 77, and I. Ivan'o, *Očerk razvitija èstetičeskoj mysli Ukrainy* (Moscow, 1981), pp. 77 and 83. On other textbooks, cf. R. Łużny, *Pisarze kręgu Akademii Kijowsko-Mohylańskiej a literatura polska ...* [= Zeszyty naukowe Uniwersytetu Jagiellońskiego CXLII, Prace historycznoliterackie, Zeszyt 11] (Cracow, 1966), pp. 22-107 (still the best), and D. S. Nalyvajko, "Kyjivs'ki poetyky XVII-počatku XVIII st. v konteksti evropejs'koho literaturnoho procesu," in *Literaturna spadščyna* (as in this fn., above), pp. 155-195.

7. For bibliographical description of textbooks of rhetoric produced in Mohyla's college and academy, cf. Ja. M. Stratij, V. D. Litvinov, V. A. Andruško, *Opisanie kursov filosofii i ritoriki professorov Kievo-Mogiljanskoj akademii* (Kiev, 1982), pp. 11-136 (127 items). Nine out of ten books of Prokopovyč's Latin textbook can now be read in Ukrainian translation; cf. V. I. Šynkaruk et al., eds., *F. Prokopovyč, Filosofs'ki tvory*, vol. 1 (Kiev, 1979), pp. 101-433 [Book IX, *On Sacred Eloquence*, has been omitted].

with God and the angels, perhaps a substitute for the absence of a course in theology. To learn this latter sublime subject, ⟨17⟩ more gifted pupils were sent to Catholic academies in Vilnius and Zamość or even abroad.[8]

II

Mohyla was consecrated as a Crown-approved metropolitan of Kiev in 1633. While introducing reforms into the liturgical practices of his church, he championed the return *ad fontes*; and the sources he had foremost in mind were Greek, even if sometimes they were located in the West — in Venice or even in Eton. Mohyla best expressed his postulate in the prefaces he wrote to the Service Book or Leiturgiarion (*Služebnyk*) of 1639 and to the Sacramentary or Euchologion (*Trebnyk*) of 1646, the last work issued by the Lavra press in his lifetime.

8. In his *Note*, Jevlevyč (as in fn. 1 above), p. 77, implies that a class of philosophy was taught in the united schools of the confraternity and Mohyla as early as 1632. He himself attended a three-year course in philosophy in Mohyla's college about 1640. For information on textbooks of philosophy produced in Kiev, cf. M. Stratij and others, *Opisanie kursov* (as in the preceding fn.), pp. 152-324 (cf. esp. pp. 152-65 on the texts by Kononovyč-Horbac'kyj and Gizel'); V. M. Ničik, "Rol' Kievo-Mogiljanskoj akademii v razvitii otečestvennoj filosofii," in V. D. Beloded and others, *Filosofskaja mysl' v Kieve* (Kiev, 1982), pp. 105-48 (in this chapter's title, "otečestvennyj" has the pre-1914 meaning of "Russian in the broad sense, including Ukrainian and Belorussian"; the main value of Ničik's exercise consists in quotations [in Russian translation] from hitherto unpublished Kievan textbooks on philosophy, logic, and rhetoric. The author deals predominantly with the late seventeenth and early eighteenth centuries); and I. S. Zaxara, *Bor'ba idej v filosofskoj mysli na Ukraine na rubeže XVII-XVIII vv. (Stefan Javorskij)* (Kiev, 1982), esp. pp. 55-62. For a Russian translation of parts of Gizel's *Opus totius philosophiae*, cf. Ja. M. Stratij, *Problemy natur-filosofii v filosofskoj mysli Ukrainy XVII v.* (Kiev, 1981), pp. 145-187. For Ukrainian translations of other textbooks on logic, philosophy, physics, rhetoric and poetics in the periodical *Filosofs'ka dumka*, between 1970 and 1979, cf. I. K. Bilodid, *Kyjevo-Mohyljans'ka akademija v istoriji sxidnjoslovjans'kyx literaturnyx mov* (Kiev, 1979), p. 75, fn. 70. — Information about the curriculum and organization of Mohyla's college has been culled mostly from A. Jabłonowski, *Akademia Kijowsko-Mohilańska* ... (Cracow, 1899-1900) (old but excellent; based on sources), and A. Sydorenko, *Kievan Academy* (as in fn. 2 above), pp. 107-134. Among other works cited in fn. 2 above (or accessible through that note), cf. also those by S. T. Golubev (especially his essay, "Kievo-mogiljanskaja kollegija pri žizni svoego fundatora, Kievskogo mitropolita Petra Mogily," *Trudy Kievskoj duxovnoj akademii* 31, no. 12 [1890]: 535-557) and by Xyžnjak.

In the preface of 1646, the metropolitan fended off attacks coming from the detractors of his publications, and stressed the basic agreement between the Rus' and Greek sacramentaries. In addition, he professed the aim of eliminating the errors contained in sacramentaries that had been printed in Vilnius, L'viv, and Ostroh at a time when ⟨18⟩ there was no Orthodox hierarchy — i.e., before 1620 — and when publishers were issuing books for "ill-gotten gains." Such faulty books perpetuated old customs and old prejudices; for instance, they contained a prayer for the midwife who swaddled the child. According to Mohyla, there was no New Testament authority for such a prayer: in passages devoted to the Nativity, the Evangelists implied that the Virgin Mary swaddled her son herself. What did a midwife have to do with all this?[9]

Mohyla declared that in his *Trebnyk* he would provide a standard text based on the Greek sacramentary, and that this text was to supersede all others. In a play on words, he appealed to his readers to stop using the useless usage books (*ponexaj zažyvaty nepotrebnyc' z Trebnykov predrečennyx*), and he castigated those who continued to refer to such sacramentaries.[10] In doing so he showed the same ⟨19⟩ attitude, the

9. Mohyla may have been technically right here, but pictorial representations of a midwife at Christ's birth do exist and go back to about the year 700. Moreover, a prayer mentioning the midwife at Christ's birth does occur in some Greek Euchologia; cf. S. Golubev in *Arxiv Jugo-Zapadnoj Rossii*, pt. 1, vol. 9 (Kiev, 1893), p. 104 and fn. 1.

10. Cf. Titov, *Materijaly* (as in fn. 2 above), no. 51, pp. 367-73. Cf. esp. pp. 370-71: "... I saw at all times that our enemies and the false brothers of Holy Orthodoxy weighed heavily upon and did violence to the Orthodox by various acts of malice and offense; and that they brazenly called our priests ignoramuses and ruffians when it came to dispensing and celebrating the Holy Sacraments and ⟨performing⟩ other liturgical functions. They clamored that Orthodox Rus' had turned heretic, that she was ignorant of the number, form, matter, intention and effect of the Holy Sacraments, ⟨that she⟩ was unable to render account of them, and ⟨that she⟩ followed divers ways in the performance of the Holy Sacraments. Having labored according to my lights on behalf of Jesus Who granted me strength, I took upon myself to lift ⟨the burden of⟩ such a heavy scorn by the Foe from the enlightened Orthodox congregation of the Holy Church of Rus' (*rossijs'koji*). By the Grace of God my labors were not in vain, as may be gathered by any enlightened and pious reader of the present book called the *Trebnyk*. If you read it, enlightened reader, you will recognize that it is a singular calumny ⟨to assert⟩ that Rus', in the persons of her prelates and other superiors, might be deficient in the requisite doctrine concerning her salvation, ⟨a doctrine received⟩ from the Holy Ghost Who is always present in the Holy Church. Church books, translated by the divinely inspired men from the Greek into the Slavonic tongue, and containing the true and sublime theology, are

same purifying and renovating spirit, and the same reliance on Greek standards that Patriarch Nikon was to show in Muscovy some years later.

For all such justified praises of the Greek as the appropriate source for improved Slavonic texts, Greek and Slavonic soon diminished in importance in Kievan printing and education, and the school of Mohyla became more and more Latinized and Polonized.[11] There were valid reasons for the shift. By the middle of the seventeenth century, Greek was no longer a language of modern thought, and Old Church Slavonic never had been. It was taught because it was the language of Orthodox ecclesiastical texts. The right of the Orthodox to use Latin and Polish in their teaching, however, continued to be challenged not only by the Orthodox zealots and by Catholics led by the Jesuits, but also by the Uniates. Mohyla had to reassert this right in the forties of the seventeenth century. In his *Lithos or Stone* (1644), he admitted that Rus'

---

proof of this... Whoever so wishes, should collate Greek manuscript *Euchologia* with our Rus' ones; he will find without fail that they are in essential accord concerning the performance and application of the seven Divine Ecclesiastical Sacraments." For Mohyla's preface to the 1639 edition of the Leitourgiarion or *Služebnyk*, cf. Titov, *Materijaly*, pp. 213-19. Cf. esp. p. 216 on "striving for gain" by printers of the previous Slavic books; p. 217 on the high value of Greek models and on Ruthenian and Muscovite service books and on the distinction between "our" and "Muscovite" service books (which, too, are considered to be of high value); and p. 218 for a quotation from St. Augustine and for an attack on L'viv printers.

11. The most vigorous Kievan statement in defense of the Slavonic language (both in the sense of Church Slavonic and in that of "Slavic in general") known to me stems from Zaxarij Kopystens'kyj, Mohyla's predecessor as abbot of the Monastery of the Caves. It dates from 1623; thus it is earlier than Mohyla's appearance on the scene. Even this forceful apology was written in Polonized Ukrainian. It comprised the following four points; that Slavonic was spoken by Japhet and his generation; that Slavonic is naturally appropriate for translating from the Greek; that Latin is poorer in that respect; and that Latin is inferior to Greek, especially in matters of philosophical and theological terminology. By comparison, Pamvo Berynda's incidental praises of the "deeply wise" and "broad" (Church) Slavonic tongue are mild and lack the anti-Latin sting. They were published in 1627; thus they were written when Mohyla was still only a monk at the Monastery of the Caves. For Kopystens'kyj, cf. Titov, *Materijaly* (as in fn. 2 above), no. 14, pp. 74-75; for Berynda, cf. ibid., no. 27, p. 178 and no. 28, p. 185. In terms of titles alone, out of 80 books published by the Lavra Press between 1616-1654, 12 were in Polish or Latin, but Polish items such as the *Paterikon*, the *Teratourgēma* and Mohyla's *Catechism* must have been issued in large editions.

needed a knowledge of Greek and Church Slavonic for religious purposes. But for political activity, he claimed, it needed not only Polish, but also Latin, because people of the Polish Crown lands used Latin as if it were their mother tongue. In both chambers of parliament, in the courts, in dealings with the Crown, in all political matters, Ruthenians, as citizens of the Crown, should know the languages without which one could not function in the state. It would be neither right nor decorous for a Ruthenian to speak Greek or Slavonic in front of a member of the Senate or of the Diet, for he would need an interpreter to accompany him wherever he went, and would be taken for a stranger or a simpleton. Even in explaining matters of faith, one should be able to give a reply in the language in ⟨20⟩ which one is asked the question, that is, either in straight Latin or in Polish with ample Latin admixtures.[12]

Consequently, by 1649 Greek was taught in the college only "in part" (*otčasti*). Such was the testimony of the notorious Paisios Ligarides, the patriarch of Jerusalem, who taught in the college for a while and who was to play a nefarious role in the downfall of Nikon, the patriarch of Moscow, several years later. Ligarides may have had a point. The preface to the *Eucharisterion*, the gratulatory tract offered Mohyla in 1632 by the school's pupils, contains an error in Greek, and the Greek fresco inscriptions done about 1643 in the Church of the Savior at Berestovo barely make sense (fig. 2, p. 685).[13] Even Mohyla's

12. *Arxiv Jugo-Zapadnoj Rossii*, pt. 1, vol. 9 (Kiev, 1893), pp. 375-77.

13. Ligarides may have been of the opinion that in his time the college had very few teachers who knew Greek, cf. Jabłonowski, *Akademia* (as in fn. 8 above), p. 102; Martel, *La langue polonaise...* (as in fn. 2 above), p. 281; this, however, is not borne out by the source quoted in both books as evidence for his alleged view, namely, *Pamjatniki...*, 2 (1846) (as in fn. 1 above), no. XIV, p. 190. — Fresco inscriptions at Berestovo: The scroll held by Prophet Zephaniah (cf. fig. 2, p. 685) exhibits the letters ΦΟΝИ И|ΜΕΡΑΣ Κ-|ΥΙΠΕΡ Κ-|ΑΙ CΚΑΙ|ΡΆΤΑΙΔ∀\|ΗΑΓΤΝИ|ꞁ ΕΡΑΣ-|ΑΛΓΙ'ΓΓ-|ΟΟ. Except for the first two words, this is gibberish. To understand it, we must turn to the late Greek painters' manuals, containing instructions about the portraits of the Prophets in the drum of the dome. There, we read, e.g.: "Prophet Zephaniah, an old man with a short beard, says: Φωνὴ ἡμέρας Κυρίου πικρὰ καὶ σκληρά· λέλεκται [*varia lectio*: τέτακται] οὖν αὔτη ἡμέρα σάλπιγγος," 'The voice of the day of the Lord is bitter and harsh; it has been called [*v.l.*: set up as] the day of the trumpet.' Cf., e.g., A. Papadopoulos-Kerameus, ed., Διονυσίου τοῦ ἐκ Φουρνᾶ Ἑρμηνεία τῆς ζωγραφικῆς τέχνης... (St. Petersburg, 1909), pp. 261-289. The errors on the Prophet scrolls are most probably due to local *amanuenses*. The names of the Prophets themselves are written correctly, probably by Greek painters — for there seems to be Greek inscriptional evidence in the Church of

own writing of 1631 exhibits some imperfections in Greek and it is only charity that allows us to call them typographical errors.[14] As for the Slavonic and Ruthenian languages, they must have been taught on the basis of local textbooks and dictionaries produced toward the end of the sixteenth century — such as Lavrentij Zyzanij's Grammar and *Leksis* (both printed in Vilnius in 1596) — or issued in the period of the Kiev Confraternity school, such as Meletij Smo⟨21⟩tryc'kyj's Grammar of 1619 and Pamvo Berynda's *Leksikon slaveno-rosskij*, the latter published in the Caves Monastery in 1627.

Polish, more than Latin, was becoming the literary vehicle in the college, even at the printing house of the Caves Monastery. In 1645, Mohyla supplemented the Ruthenian edition of his abbreviated catechism with a Polish one, and the Polish edition was published first. What is more, the two books about the virtues of, and the miracles performed by, the monks of the Caves Monastery throughout its history (the *Paterikon* by Sil'vester Kossov of 1635, and the *Teratourgēma* by Afanasij Kal'nofojs'kyj of 1638) were written in Polish. The preface to the latter work includes an allusion to Apuleius and Latin words and quotations, one of them from the *Ars Poetica* of Horace.[15] Thus the future linguistic coloring of the college, and later of the academy — which was to remain largely Latin and Polish until about the middle of the eighteenth century, even under Russian domination — developed within a few years of the date of its foundation.

III

Mohyla's educational enterprise reflected the interplay of cultural forces in seventeenth-century Ukraine. The ancestral faith survived in borrowed forms, and admiration for the church poetry of a John of Damascus coexisted with predilection for classical mythological trappings. However, Mohyla's college was what it was also because the man

---

the Savior that the painters of the 1643/44 restoration were Greeks: cf. words ἱστόρησε Γραικῶν δακτύλοις 'provided with pictures by the fingers of the Greeks,' in a fresco poem on one of the walls. The poem is difficult to read.

14. Titov, *Materijaly* (as in fn. 2 above), pp. 263, 264, 265. The error πεντεκοστάριον on p. 265 (instead of -ντη-) seems to indicate that in ecclesiastical and high style Greek, Mohyla — or his printer — pronounced both η and ε as [e], that is, not in the Byzantine, but in the Erasmian way.

15. Cf. *Arxiv Jugo-Zapadnoj Rossii*, pt. 1, vol. 8, 1 (Kiev, 1914), pp. 473-77, esp. p. 477, and Titov, *Materijaly* (as in fn. 2 above), esp. p. 523.

who created it was a man of many worlds. His experience and his contacts — or his plans — encompassed Warsaw, Cracow, possibly some other Polish or Western center of learning, but also Jassy (Iaşi), Constantinople, and even, if to a much lesser degree, Moscow. He could choose the level and language of discourse according to his addressee, and he could combine a Jesuit's sophistication with an Orthodox believer's simple faith in miracles performed by his religion.

It is of some importance to study the use of languages within the seventeenth-century Rus' elite. It appears that most members of that elite understood all four languages involved — Slavonic, Ruthenian, Polish, and Latin. Thus no one language or style was the sole vehicle at the speaker's or writer's disposal for conveying a particular message. A choice was involved, and that choice indicated the cultural commit- ⟨22⟩
ment or cultural position taken at a given moment. Thus, to his brother Moses, the hospodar of Moldavia, Mohyla wrote in almost pure Slavonic. The foreign quotations of his missive were all Greek, and all other quotations were scriptural. It is astonishing how well Mohyla mastered the Slavonic idiom, which he learned probably from teachers connected with the L'viv confraternity. However, the real concerns of the man and the time put a limit to his linguistic and conceptual mimicry. The missive's Slavonic, good as it was, contained words (such as *političeskaę* and *ceremonii*) that were outside of the Old Church Slavonic canon. When Mohyla described for his brother the duties of the ideal ruler, he was practicing a genre used in the Byzantine world since at least the sixth century. While listing these duties, Mohyla proclaimed that his brother, being a ruler, was to be a benefactor of the church — that was Byzantine enough. But he was also to be a benefactor of schools (*blahodětelju ... učilišč byti*) — this piece of advice I do not remember reading in any mirror of princes addressed to a Byzantine emperor.[16]

Another set of Mohyla's Slavonic writings deals with miracles performed in his own time in the Orthodox church; not exclusively in the Ukraine — for, after all, he was not a Ruthenian, just an Orthodox of many cultures — but also on Ukrainian territory. One of these miracles occurred in the household of his own servant, Stanislav Tretjak. Tretjak had just built a house and asked Mohyla to consecrate it. This Mohyla

16. For the text in question (Mohyla's dedication of the Pentēkostarion [*Cvětnaja Triodь*] of 1631 to Moses Mohyla), cf. Titov, *Materijaly* (as in fn. 2 above), no. 38, pp. 263-66, and D. P. Bogdan, "Les enseignements de Pierre Movilă adressés à son frère Moise Movilă," *Cyrillomethodianum* 1 (1971): 1-25, esp. 19-22.

did, and left some of the holy water behind. When he returned a year later, he was met by Tretjak and his wife, who had kept the water and who claimed that it had changed into wine. Mohyla tasted it. The taste reminded him, he wrote, of Wallachian wine (*vkus aki voloskoho vina*), and he wanted to make sure that no mistake had occurred. After all, the son of the hospodar of Wallachia and Moldavia would know his Wallachian wines. When the couple swore that the change was miraculous, Mohyla accepted their word, took the holy water with him, and still had it at the time of writing. The water "had a bouquet and taste of wine, and was not turning to vinegar."[17]

Stories such as this must have been meant for all Orthodox, not only for those of the Ukraine. When Mohyla addressed his own monks, ⟨23⟩ Kiev churchgoers, or the clerics of his jurisdiction, as he did in his inaugural sermon pronounced in Kiev's Lavra in March of 1632, or in his prefaces to the Service Book of 1639 and to the Sacramentary of 1646, he wrote in Polonized Ukrainian, using such Polish words as *daleko barzěj* 'much more', *pien'knaja* 'beautiful', and *preložonyje* 'superiors', but keeping the Ukrainian *ohon' musyt (byti)* 'fire must (be)', *pyšučy* 'writing', *ščo* 'what', and *ščoby* 'in order that'. This mixed language also contained elements of Slavonic, if unauthentic, appearance such as *jedinoutrobně* and *smotrěti*. Most scriptural quotations in the preface to the Sacramentary were in Old Church Slavonic, but some were in the Ruthenian literary language of the time, mixed with Slavonic.

When Mohyla addressed representatives of the Orthodox nobility, whether Bohdan Stetkevič, a Belorussian chamberlain, Theodore Suščans'kyj, a land-scribe of the Kiev palatinate, or Jeremiah Vyšnevec'kyj (Wiśniowiecki), a prince in danger of apostatizing from Orthodoxy, his Ruthenian language was heavily Polonized, his quotations were drawn from Lactantius or St. Augustine, his Christian similes heavily contaminated with bits of pagan wisdom, and his flattery was as artless as the recipient must have been undiscriminating. To his relative Prince Vyšnevec'kyj he wrote: "This venerable cross will be unto your princely grace what the mast was once unto Ulysses, which protected him from the Sirens, that is, the pleasures of this world."[18] We must duly report that Mohyla's reference to Ulysses attached to the mast (a prefiguration of the cross) harkened back to Greek patristic literature of

17. *Arxiv Jugo-Zapadnoj Rossii*, pt. 1, vol. 7 (Kiev, 1887), pp. 113-14.

18. Cf. Titov, *Materijaly* (as in fn. 2 above), no. 39, pp. 268-70, cf. esp. p. 269. Mohyla was dedicating the text of his inaugural sermon of 1632 to Vyšnevec'kyj.

the early fourth century, but we are more interested to note that in naming the hero from Ithaca he used the Latinizing *Ulessesovy*, not a derivative from the Greek *Odysseus*. And when Mohyla spoke of the ancestors of Theodore Proskura Suščans'kyj, a man whose young son, or at least relative, was a student at the college, he spun the following yarn, in which he must have believed as much as he did in Hercules or Apollo. The ancestry of Proskura went back to Vladimir the Great. One of his forebears served Anne, the daughter, so Mohyla seems to have said, of the Byzantine emperor and the wife of Vladimir. This forebear was given the *proskura* (*prosphora*, blessed bread eaten after communion) to be carried from church to palace, and ate it on the way. Hence the family nickname Proskura. ⟨24⟩ This nickname was attested by Rus' chroniclers, whom, of course, Mohyla failed to specify. Under Svjatoslav, prince of Kiev in 1059 (*sic*), the Proskuras received their coat-of-arms of cross and arrow as a reward for the exploits of one family member in a battle against the infidel Cumans (*hustym trupom pohanskym šyrokoje okryl pole* — at least most of this phrase sounded Ukrainian). We must skip four centuries for the next family exploit, assigned to the reign of King Alexander of Poland (ca. 1500). From then on, it is clear sailing until the time of the recipient of Mohyla's dedication.[19]

To church historians Mohyla is best known as the author or principal co-author of the *Orthodox Confession of Faith*, a treatise consisting of three parts (that corresponded to the three theological virtues) and containing about 260 questions and answers. It was discussed and partly emended at a synod in Jassy (Iaşi) in Moldavia in 1642, and its Greek version was approved by all the four Greek Orthodox patriarchs a year later. The *Confession* was first published in modern Greek in 1667; it had been elaborated in Kiev in 1640, however, and its original language and one of its sources were in all likelihood Latin.[20]

19. Cf. Titov, *Materijaly* (as in fn. 2 above), pp. 328-29, and no. 46, pp. 330-33, esp. 331-32. Suščans'kyj was the recipient of the vernacular adaptation of the Church Slavonic translation of the Homiliary wrongly attributed to Kallistos I, patriarch of Constantinople (1350-53; 1355-63); this adaptation was published by Mohyla in 1637 on the basis of the edition of Jev'je (1616). On some of the problems connected with the Slavic printed editions of the Homiliary by Ps.-Kallistos, cf. now D. Gonis, "Carigradskijat patriarx Kalist I i 'Učitelno Evangelie,'" *Palaeobulgarica* 6, no. 2 (1982): 41-55, esp. 53. The coat-of-arms of the Suščans'kyjs is reproduced on the verso of the Homiliary's title, cf. Titov, p. 194. Mohyla's source (indicated in the margin of p. 331) for the origin of that coat-of-arms was the Polish Chronicle of Stryjkowski, "p. 187."

20. That the *Orthodox Confession* was "originally written in Latin" (Λατινιστὶ

When it comes to vernaculars other than Ruthenian, Mohyla's ⟨25⟩ mastery of Polish, both scholarly and of the oratorical variety, is safely attested by his own published writings. Furthermore, there is evidence for Mohyla's knowing some modern Greek and handling it in print and, naturally enough, for his proficiency in spoken Roumanian, but no trace of his ever using Moldavian in writing. Such a find would be unlikely, both on account of the cultural situation of the time — practically speaking, the earliest books in Roumanian, printed by Ukrainian printers dispatched by Mohyla to Wallachia and Moldavia, date only from the 1640s — and on account of the family tradition. The frescoes in the church at Sucevița, founded and richly endowed by the Movilă family, are all in Slavonic.[21]

πρῶτον γεγραμμένη) is stated by Meletios Syrigos in his autograph manuscript. This is our only explicit evidence, but it is weighty: Syrigos was charged with emending the *Confession's* text and translated it into Greek in 1642. It is conceivable that the *Confession* could have been originally written in Polish; as yet, there is no proof for this thesis. That it should have been written in Ruthenian is the least likely of all. On the *Confession* and the question of its original language, cf., e.g., A. Malvy and M. Viller, *La Confession orthodoxe de Pierre Moghila métropolite de Kiev (1633-1646)...* [= Orientalia Christiana, 10] (Rome-Paris, 1927), esp. pp. li-lii (best); Žukovs'kyj, *Petro Mohyla...* (as in fn. 2 above), pp. 169-184 (compilative); R. P. Popivchak, *Peter Mohila, Metropolitan of Kiev (1633-47): Translation and Evaluation of His "Orthodox Confession of Faith" 1640* [= D.S.D. thesis no. 259 of the Catholic University of America] (Washington, D.C., 1975), pp. 17-18 (compilative; P. reports on the Polish theory by O. Bârlea [1947; inaccessible to me]). On the *Summa* by the Jesuit Canisius (d. 1597) as one source for the *Confession*, cf., e.g., M. Viller, "Une infiltration latine dans la théologie orthodoxe. La Confession orthodoxe attribuée à Pierre Moghila et le catéchisme de Canisius," *Recherches de science religieuse* 3, no. 2 (1912): 159-68 (textual parallels; dependence on Canisius in the choice of Scriptural quotations; parallels in the plan of both works; no wholesale borrowings).

21. Mohyla's "Spiritual Speech," given in Jassy before the wedding of Janusz Radziwiłł to Maria, daughter of the Moldavian hospodar Vasilie Lupul, was printed in Kiev in 1645 in Polish (except for Scriptural quotations, all of which were in Old Church Slavonic). Mohyla tells us, however, that he had delivered that speech in the hospodar's church "partly in the Polish, partly in the Wallachian language (*Wołoskim Ięzykiem*)." Cf. *Mowa duchowna przy szlubie Iaśnie Oswieconego P. Jego M. Pana Ianusza Radziwiła...*, reprinted in A. Mihăilă, *Contribuții la istoria culturii și literaturii române vechi* (Bucharest, 1972), esp. p. 199. I am indebted to Professor Andrzej de Vincenz for a copy of Mihăilă's reprint. For the Slavonic fresco inscriptions in Sucevița, cf., e.g., M. A. Musicesco, *Le monastère de Sucevița*, 2nd ed. (Bucharest, 1967) (further bibliography on p. 55).

In which language did Mohyla write when he did so for his private use? My guess is, in Polish and Ruthenian rather than Slavonic or Latin. It is in Polish that he jotted down notes about commissions he made to various goldsmiths in 1629 (though one such note and two entries he made in books are in Ruthenian). Moreover, it is worth noting that Mohyla chose to write or dictate a deeply personal text, his will, in Polish rather than in Ruthenian or Latin. In that document he richly endowed his beloved college and gave it his library of books in several languages collected throughout his lifetime (this library burned in the 1650s). For these good deeds of his he imposed upon the future generations the obligation of carrying on instruction in Kiev's schools just as it had been carried on in his lifetime under the privileges granted by His Royal Majesty, the Polish king.[22] ⟨26⟩

22. To help us decide what Mohyla's "intimate" written language — as opposed to the several languages in which he wrote for public consumption — may have been, we have the evidence of his autograph manuscript, published in *Arxiv Jugo-Zapadnoj Rossii*, pt. 1, vol. 7 (Kiev, 1887), pp. 49-189. It is a miscellany, consisting of: (a) a record (pp. 49-132) of miracles wrought by the Orthodox faith in Mohyla's time (we drew upon this record for the story of the Tretjaks); (b) pieces of liturgical poetry (pp. 133-70) composed by Mohyla (including the song in celebration of Władysław IV's ascent to the throne); (c) reflections (pp. 171-80) on monastic life; (d) lists (pp. 181-83) of contributors (with amounts contributed) to the work of restoration in St. Sophia and the Tithe church; (e) notes (pp. 184-85) concerning commissions to goldsmiths; and (f) a catalogue (pp. 186-89) of Latin books Mohyla bought in Warsaw in 1632/33. While the first two miracles (p. 49, localized in Pokuttja "beyond the Dnieper" and in Halyč) and the very last one (pp. 131-32, localized in a town near Thessalonica) are in Ruthenian, almost everything in between is in quite correct Slavonic. Mohyla's liturgical poetry is close to Old Church Slavonic (true, once, on p. 137, he did write *viroju* instead of *věrojǫ*). Reflections on monastic life are in Slavonic. Lists of contributors to repairs of St. Sophia and the Tithe church are in Ruthenian. Notes concerning goldsmiths are in Polish (one note of a similar content being in Ruthenian). Finally, the catalogue of books is in Latin. The choices of Slavonic for liturgical poetry and for reflections on monastic life and of Latin for the book catalogue were imposed by the subject matter. The choice of Ruthenian for the lists of contributors may have had to do with the fact that, with one exception, all these contributors were Ruthenian. These lists were hardly a private document. Moreover, neither the description of Orthodox miracles, nor the poetry, nor the treatise on monasticism could have been written down for private use. These pieces must have been intended for eventual dissemination, some of them in the Orthodox world at large, since their goals were apologetic, edifying, liturgical and, in one case, panegyric. (Thus, the stories of Orthodox miracles are not a "journal"; on the other hand, neither are they evidence for Mohyla's championship of Slavonic as *the* literary language of Rus'.) In sum, when I guess

IV

On Easter 1632, twenty-three pupils (*spudeov*) of the college, headed by their professor of rhetoric, and presumably the school's prefect, ⟨27⟩ Sofronij Počas'kyj, submitted to Mohyla a versified pamphlet of thanks called *Eucharisterion*.[23] The pamphlet, with a preface in prose

that Polish even more than Ruthenian was the likely vehicle for Mohyla's "private" written language, I do it on the strength of the fact that the most personal of the six documents in Mohyla's autograph manuscript was in Polish. On various written languages of Rus' in our period, cf. the classic (if antiquated) work by P. Žiteckij, *Očerk literaturnoj istorii malorusskogo narečija v XVII i XVIII vv.*, vol. 1 (Kiev, 1889), esp. pp. 15-51, 147-62, and its Ukrainian translation with L. A. Bulaxovs'kyj's updating preface: *Narys literaturnoji istoriji ukrajins'koji movy v XVII vici* (L'viv, 1941), esp. pp. 1-44, and 119-31; the reliable Martel, *La langue polonaise* (as in fn. 2 above), passim; the excellent essay by George Y. Shevelov, "L'ukrainien littéraire," *Revue des études slaves* 33 (1956): esp. pp. 73-76 (cf. its English translation in A. Schenker and E. Stankiewicz, eds., *The Slavic Literary Languages*, New Haven, 1980), and, for the same author's latest views, *A Historical Phonology of the Ukrainian Language* (Heidelberg, 1979), § 43:3 = pp. 566-71 (succinct but also well balanced). Interpretations in these works differ from the "functional" one offered here. In spite of its promising title, the chapter "Movna koncepcija Kyjevo-Mohyljans'koji akademiji," in Bilodid, *Kyjevo-Mohyljans'ka akademija* (as in fn. 8 above), pp. 48-84, is of little use to anyone interested in the interplay of languages in seventeenth-century Rus'. On reasons for the use of various levels of language in seventeenth-century prefaces, cf. the good observations by Sazonova, "Ukrainskie ... predislovija" (as in fn. 41 below), esp. p. 185. — For Mohyla's testament, cf. *Pamjatniki* ..., 2 (1846) (as in fn. 1 above), no. XI, pp. 144-81 and *Pamjatniki izdannye* ..., (1897) (as in fn. 4 above), no. XVI, pp. 429-39. The latter text was reprinted by Žukovs'kyj, *Petro Mohyla* (as in fn. 2 above), no. 21, pp. 244-47. For Mohyla's Ruthenian (or even Ukrainian) entries in books he owned, cf. the *Addendum* to this fn. at the end of the present article.

23. For the text of the *Eucharisterion*, cf. the facsimile in this issue, pp. 255-93; S. T. Golubev, "Priloženija k sočineniju: Istorija Kievskoj duxovnoj akademii, VIII," in *Universitetskie izvestija* of Kiev, 1886, no. 4, pt. 2, pp. 46-64; no. 5, pt. 2, pp. 65-69; Titov, *Materijaly* (as in fn. 2 above), no. 41, pp. 291-305; H. Rothe, *Die älteste ostslavische Kunstdichtung 1575-1647*, Zweiter Halbband (Giessen, 1977), pp. 293-315 (omitting the preface). Cf. also excerpts in O. I. Bilec'kyj, *Xrestomatija davn'oji ukrajins'koji literatury (do kincja XVIII st.)*, 3rd ed. (Kiev, 1967), pp. 191-192, and Bilodid, *Kyjevo-Mohyljans'ka akademija* (as in fn. 8 above), p. 26. For a partial versified translation into modern Ukrainian, cf. *Apolionova ljutnja: Kyjivs'ki poety XVII-XVIII st.* (Kiev, 1982), pp. 35-45 (where all poems are attributed to Stefan-Sofronij Počas'kyj). For secondary literature on the *Eucharisterion*, and a detailed discussion of its contents, cf. the article in this issue by N. Pylypiuk, pp. 45-70.

signed by the professor (who used two Greek quotations), had two parts. Both give an idea of the horizon of the young men beginning their study in the newly founded college and of the cultural values inculcated into them.

The first part of the pamphlet is entitled *Helikon*: Mohyla's grateful pupils erect that mountain of the Muses as a poetic act of gratitude to him. Their poem is also called the First Garden of Knowledge; eight "roots" appear in it, each of them described in verses signed by their student author, or at least reciter. The "roots" are Grammar, Rhetoric, Dialectic, Arithmetic, Music, Geometry, Astronomy, and Theology, that is, the mediaeval *trivium* and *quadrivium* in the usual sequence, plus theology. (The appearance of theology expressed the hopes and early aspirations of the school's authorities rather than subsequent reality, for, as we already know, the royal charter of 1635 did not grant the college the right of teaching that science.) *Helikon*, or *New Helikon*, in case we have not guessed it yet, is the school — or one of the schools — presided over by Mohyla (a pun also on his name, Movilă, i.e., "mountain" in Moldavian).

The second part of the pamphlet, also written in verse, is called *Parnass* — again the home of the Muses and of Apollo — or the Second Garden of Knowledge. It, too, was erected by the school's pupils in honor of Mohyla. The second garden has ten offshoots of knowledge, that is, the nine Muses plus Apollo. The existence of two mountains calls for an explanation and the one that comes readily to mind is that they represent the efforts of the pupils of the Confraternity and the Caves Monastery schools, respectively.

The language of both poems is heavily Polonized Ukrainian. Their ⟨28⟩ two concrete messages are the glorification of Christ, the Victor risen at Easter time, and the praise of Mohyla. Their two ideological messages seem to reflect the organizational compromise of 1631/32. They are, first, that Classics are good, but too classicizing an education is not a good thing; and, second, that the Uniates are certainly abominable.

The poems themselves say this in part: Grammar looks forward to the time when the Rus', the descendants of the famous Roxolanians (a Sarmatian tribe whose mention provided antique ancestry for the Ruthenians and erudite credentials for the poem's author), will equal the wise pagans in learning. Dialectic (likened, after a saying of "the Stagirite," to a sharp thorn) wishes that the thorn of wisdom would prick the sight of "the sad Uniate basilisks [who are] cruel asps." Thus Aristotle was put beside King David, since the "basilisks" and the "asps" alluded to Psalm 90 (91):13. Music quotes the pagans Diogenes and Orpheus —

along with the Byzantine John of Damascus. Geometry refers in the same breath to Xenophanes of Colophon and to Christ, "the highest Geometer," who rose from under the earth ("the earth" being *gē* or *gaia* in Greek; bear in mind that the various poems were both honoring Mohyla and celebrating Easter of 1632). Finally, in the poem on Theology, Mohyla is indirectly likened to Hercules. As the "assiduous Spaniard" had set up a marble pillar on the shores of the Western ocean to mark the outer limits of Hercules's labors, so the archimandrite erected a column on the banks of the Dnieper in the "Septentrional" zone (*pry berehax Dniprovyx pod sedmi triony*) to mark the beginning of the ocean of Theology. On that spot Mohyla will put an end to the Ruthenians' search and to their pilgrimages to faraway lands to study that science; may the good Lord grant that from now on they listen "to theologians of their own." The verses addressed to Apollo toward the end of the poem *Parnass* invite the pagan god to visit the Ruthenian lands (*krajev rossijs'kyx*), which are hungry for learning. However, toward the very end of *Parnass*, both Apollo and his sisters, the Muses, are chased away and the Virgin Mary is asked to take up her abode among the students of the college.

Two emblematic woodcuts adorn the tract.[24] One depicts Mohyla ⟨29⟩ himself standing on Helicon and holding the pastoral staff and the branch of wisdom; he is spurning the scepter and the crown, an allusion to his having given up his claim to the throne of Moldavia. The other woodcut represents Mucius Scaevola, the hero of a Latin legend set in the sixth century B.C., who is standing on Parnassus and putting his right hand into the fire. The scene is included because the Mohyla family claimed descent from this Roman hero, a speculation not unparalleled both in the history of humanism and of the Balkans.

This second woodcut sums up well the composite character of Mohyla's world. The hero of the woodcut is a Roman; he stands on a Greek mountain; with one exception, the explanatory legends are in Cyrillic script; but they contain Polonisms, such as the word *zvytjazcy* for "victor." The exception is something written in Greek letters on the

24. Cf. Titov, *Materijaly* (as in fn. 2 above), pp. 293-99; Žukovs'kyj, *Petro Mohyla* (as in fn. 2 above), pp. 50 and 84; Rothe, *Die älteste ... Kunstdichtung* (as in the preceding note), pp. 481 and 482 (= figs. 38 and 39). A search for parallels for these and similar woodcuts in sixteenth- and seventeenth-century emblem books might well repay the effort. Mohyla himself bought a Latin book of "Emblemata" in Warsaw in 1632, cf. *Arxiv Jugo-Zapadnoj Rossii*, pt. 1, vol. 7 (Kiev, 1887), p. 187.

left arm of Mucius Scaevola. The meaning of these letters seems to have escaped previous scholarship.[25] Yet they deserve a closer look, for they tell us about the degree of familiarity with the Greek in Mohyla's milieu. They read *skaia cheir* 'left hand', and thus offer an etymologically correct pun on the name of Scaevola, because *scaevus* and *skaios* mean the same thing, namely, "left(-handed)," in Latin and Greek. Scaevola, we remember, got the nickname "left-handed" after putting his right hand into the fire and thus permanently crippling it.

We can be virtually certain that the professor of rhetoric Sofronij Počas'kyj, author of the *Eucharisterions's* preface and perhaps of all its poems as well, was the same person as Stefan Počas'kyj, the student of the Confraternity school who recited the very first poem of the *Virši*, a tract published in 1622 by Kasijan Sakovyč to commemorate the funeral of Hetman Sahajdačnyj.[26] Ten years later, Počas'kyj must have remembered his role in this literary enterprise. In short, there is *prima facie* presumption that the immediate model for the *Eucharisterion*'s plan and structure was offered by Sakovyč's *Virši*. (In the wider scheme of things, of course, models for the *Eucharisterion* are to be looked for in contemporary textbooks of ⟨30⟩ poetics and in Polish Renaissance and Baroque poetry.) The choice of Easter for reciting the *Eucharisterion* may have been influenced by what the printers of the Lavra had done in 1630: their *Imnologia*, a collection of ten signed poems, was an Easter offering to Mohyla, in which each author blended the praise of Christ, the risen Victor, with that of the archimandrite.[27]

---

25. Titov, *Materijaly* (as in fn. 2 above), p. 305, merely remarked: "there is also an inscription on the left sleeve" of Mucius Scaevola. S. T. Golubev's description in *Universitetskie izvestija* of Kiev, 1886, no. 4, pt. 2, p. 59, lacks any reference to Scaevola's left arm.

26. For the text, cf., e.g., Titov, *Materijaly* (as in fn. 2 above), no. 11, pp. 37-50; Rothe, *Die älteste ... Kunstdichtung* (as in fn. 23 above), pp. 219-246 (on p. 246 references to other reprints, usually excerpts).

27. Cf. Titov, *Materijaly* (as in fn. 2 above), no. 35, pp. 234-39. With one exception in the middle, those poems of the *Imnologia* that are written in Polonized Ukrainian regularly alternate with those in Slavonic. This arrangement may have been intentional. Two tracts published a year after the *Eucharisterion* are close to it in structure and in some motifs, and may have been influenced by it. They are (1) the Εὐφωνία *veselobrmjačaa Na Vysoceslávnyj Thrón Mitrópolii Kievskoj ščaslíve vstupújučemu ... Kyr Petru Mohílě.... ot Tipohrafov v ... Čudotvórnoj Lavrě Pečérskoj pracújučyx ... dedikovánaja*; cf. Titov, *Materijaly* (as in fn. 2 above), no. 42, pp. 306-309; Rothe, *Die älteste ... Kunstdichtung* (as in fn. 23 above), pp. 315-22 (on p. 322 references to other reprints and excerpts); and (2) *Mnemosyne sławy, prac, i trudow ... Piotra Mohiły ... ná*

I know next to nothing of most of the youthful authors (or reciters) of the *Eucharisterion's* gratulatory poems. With two exceptions, such people as Theodor Suslo or Martyn Suryn are but colorful names to me. The exceptions are Vasylij Suščans'kyj-Proskura, who, as we have just surmised, was a son or a relative of the addressee of one of Mohyla's prefaces; and Heorhij Nehrebeckij, probably a relative of Father Constantine Niehrębecki, *namiestnik* of St. Sophia of Kiev and one of the executors of Mohyla's will.[28]

On the other hand, we know a great deal about some other officers or alumni of the college who were active or graduated during Mohyla's lifetime, since they are among the important intellectuals of the century: Epifanij Slavynec'kyj, who was a Hellenist recruited to Moscow by Patriarch Nikon; Arsenij Satanovs'kyj, an assistant to Slavynec'kyj, who also went to Moscow; and men who wrote both in Ukrainian and Polish and were authors of sermons and writers of ⟨31⟩ prominence in other fields as well: Joannikij Galjatovs'kyj, Lazar Baranovyč and Antonij Radyvylovs'kyj. Thus from its very beginnings, the college was both a producer of local intellectual leaders and a purveyor of talent abroad, above all to Moscow. It was to perform this double role for over a century.[29]

---

pożądány onego wiazd do Kiowá; od Studentow Gymnasium w Bráctwie Kiowskim przezeń fundowánego Świátu podána ...; cf. Rothe, *Die älteste ... Kunstdichtung* (as in fn. 23 above), pp. 323-43 (valuable as apparently the only full reprint; a few misunderstandings of the text). For an excerpt (in original and translation) from the *Mnemosyne*, cf. also Martel, *La littérature polonaise* (as in fn. 2 above), p. 287 and fn. 1. *Mnemosyne* deserves further study. — An echo of the *Eucharisterion* (or of notions popular at the time of its composition) can be heard in this passage of Kossov's *Exegesis*: "their Benevolences, the Sirs citizens of Kiev and of other counties began to fill our *horrea Apollinea* with their children, as with little ants, and to call ⟨these *horrea*⟩ Helicon, Parnassus, and to glory in them." Cf. *Arxiv* (as in fn. 3 above), p. 423.

28. Cf. *Pamjatniki ...*, 2 (1846) (as in fn. 1 above), p. 177; *Pamjatniki izdannye ...*, 2 (1897) (as in fn. 4 above), p. 435; Žukovs'kyj, *Petro Mohyla* (as in fn. 2 above), pp. 246-47. *Namiestnik* is Polish for *locumtenens*.

29. The role of Mohyla's college and academy as exporters of talent and printing know-how abroad and as a training ground for foreign students is a well-researched topic. K. V. Xarlampovič, *Malorossijskoe vlijanie na velikorusskuju cerkovnuju žizn'*, vol. 1 (Kazan', 1914), still remains a classic for Muscovy and Russia. For the most recent general survey, cf. "Kul'turni zvjazky Kyjevo-Mohyljans'koji akademii," in Xyžnjak, *Kyjevo-Mohyljans'ka akademija* (as in fn. 2 above), pp. 162-216 (discusses Muscovy and Russia, Belorussia, Moldavia and Wallachia, Serbia, and Greece). For Muscovy and Russia alone (and in a

V

Mohyla was a loyal subject of the Polish Crown. He composed a liturgical poem in Church Slavonic to celebrate the enthronement of "our great tsar Władysław ⟨IV⟩." Whenever he spoke of "our fatherland" (*otčyzna naša*), he meant the Polish-Lithuanian Commonwealth. This should not astonish us: Bohdan Xmel'nyc'kyj himself used the term *ojczyzna* in the same sense as late as 1656, at least for the benefit of the Polish Crown hetmans and the Polish king.[30] In Mohyla's own mind, the legitimacy of his being seated on the Kiev metropolitan's throne rested on three foundations: the inspiration by the Holy Ghost who moved the heart of His Majesty King Władysław IV; the blessing of the holy apostolic capital of Constantinople; and the will of the whole of the Ruthenian nation (*narodu rossij*⟨32⟩*s'koho*).[31] What he and his successor on the Kiev throne, Syl'vester Kossov, aspired to, but did not obtain, was equality for this Ruthenian nation within the framework of the Commonwealth. For all his Orthodoxy and in spite of the fact that in

later period), cf. F. B. Korčmaryk, *Duxovi vplyvy Kyjeva na Moskovščynu v dobu Het'mans'koji Ukrajiny* [= Shevchenko Scientific Society, Ukrainian Studies, 14] (New York, 1964). For Moldavia and Wallachia, cf. P. P. Panaitescu, "L'influence de l'oeuvre de Pierre Mogila, archevêque de Kiev dans les Principautés roumaines," in *Mélanges de l'Ecole roumaine en France 1926*, pt. 1 (Paris, 1926), pp. 3-95 (excellent); Žukovs'kyj, *Petro Mohyla* (as in fn. 2 above), pp. 113-15; and the bibliographical article by Dr. Cazacu, pp. 184-222 below. I shall adduce but two telling examples for Moldavian contacts: In 1640, Sofronij Počas'kyj, the moving spirit of the *Eucharisterion*, led some alumni and teachers of the college to Jassy, where they founded a school which continued for a few years. A year later, a printing press manned by Kievan printers was established there.

30. "Great tsar Władysław": *Arxiv Jugo-Zapadnoj Rossii*, pt. 1, vol. 7 (Kiev, 1887), p. 169 (caution: in the manuscript, the text of the poem is not in Mohyla's hand). "Fatherland": for the usage of Mohyla, cf., e.g., Titov, *Materijaly* (as in fn. 2 above), p. 333; for that of Xmel'nyc'kyj, cf. his letters addressed to the Crown hetmans and to King Jan Kazimierz, respectively, in A. B. Pernal, "Six Unpublished Letters of Bohdan Khmel'nyts'kyi (1656-1657)," *Harvard Ukrainian Studies* 6, no. 2 (June 1982): 223 and 225; for Markian Balaban laying down his life for "his beloved *otčyzna*, the Polish Crown," cf. Titov, *Materijaly*, p. 186 (the text dates from 1627).

31. Cf. Titov, *Materijaly* (as in fn. 2 above), no. 49, p. 359: *ja tedy v toj Rossijs'koj zemli z nadxnenja D(u)xa s(vja)t(o)ho do s(e)rdca Korolja jeho M(y)l(o)s(ty) Vladyslava Četvertoho, nam ščaslyve Panujučoho i vseho Narodu Rossijs'koho voleju, vzjavšy urjad Rossijs'kyj Arxierejs'kyj za bl(aho)s(lo)veniem s(vja)tijšeji stolyci Ap(o)s(to)l's'koji Konstantynopol's'koji....*

1640 he lavished fulsome praise on Tsar Mixail Fedorovič (to whom he applied for material assistance for Kiev's shrines and for permission — never granted — to found a special monastery in Moscow where Kievan monks could teach Greek and Slavònic to sons of boyars and to simple folk),[32] Mohyla remained politically anti-Muscovite. He praised his noble Ruthenian addressees or their ancestors for taking part in campaigns against Moscow in the service of the Polish king; the family of one of them he extolled for having waged war on Moscow under King Stefan Batory (Báthory); another addressee he commended for participating in the expedition to Moscow under the leadership of the young Władysław IV.[33] When the brother of Metropolitan Iov Borec'kyj, Andrew, presumably alluded in conversation with Mohyla to the possibility of a union between Muscovy and Rus', Mohyla is said to have replied that this alone was enough to have Andrew Borec'kyj impaled.[34] This loyalist attitude is a far cry from that displayed by the Borec'kyj brothers, by a man lower down on the social scale, the Belorussian Afanasij Filippovič, who traveled to Moscow and embarrassed Mohyla by his Orthodox intran⟨33⟩sigence, or, finally, by those Orthodox whom Kasijan Sakovyč accused of betraying the Polish Crown's secrets to Moscow before 1646.[35] Mohyla's points of reference were Kiev, Warsaw, Jassy, and

32. Cf. *Pamjatniki izdannye ...*, 2 (1897) (as in fn. 4 above), pp. 423-27; *Akty otnosjaščiesja k istorii Južnoj i Zapadnoj Rossii ...*, vol. 3 (St. Petersburg, 1861), nos. 18 and 33, pp. 27-29 and 39. Both documents are preserved only in contemporary Russian translation *s beloruskogo pisma*. Both were "read before the tsar." In 1640, Mohyla's *locumtenens*, Ihnatij, gave a detailed report in Moscow's *Posol'skij prikaz* on military and political events in the Ukraine, Lithuania, and Poland (he also repeated some gossip about relations between the Polish king and the Turkish sultan and about actions planned by the Habsburg emperor against the Swedes). He did not pass on any treasonous information, however. Cf. *Akty otnosjaščiesja...*, no. 22, pp. 32-34. On Mohyla's relations with Moscow, cf., e.g., V. Èjngorn, "O snošeniax malorossijskogo duxovenstva s moskovskim pravitel'stvom v carstvovanie Alekseja Mixajloviča," *Čtenija v Imp. Obščestve istorii i drevnostej rossijskix pri Moskovskom universitete* 165 (1893, bk. 2): 24-32.

33. Cf. Titov, *Materijaly* (as in fn. 2 above), pp. 332 and 339.

34. This story is reported by Pantelejmon Kuliš, "Otpadenie Malorossii ot Pol'ši (1340-1654), tom pervyj," *Čtenija v Imp. Obščestve istorii i drevnostej rossijskix pri Moskovskom universitete* 145 (1888, bk. 2, pt. 3): 179. Kuliš gives no precise reference; he only points to the *Glavnyj arxiv inostrannyx del* as the source of his information.

35. On Iov Borec'kyj's relations with Moscow and the Crown and on his tergiversations, cf., e.g., Èjngorn, "O snošenijax" (as in fn. 32 above), pp.

Constantinople, but hardly Moscow. To blame him for this, to impute that it was not so, or to call his religious policy a "Latin pseudomorphosis of Orthodoxy," is to disregard our evidence, to imply that the yardstick for measuring what is Orthodox is kept in Russia, and to indulge in anachronisms.[36] When it comes to Mohyla's theology, it is advisable to ⟨34⟩ keep the verdict of Mohyla's Orthodox contemporaries in mind. In 1642/43, Greek Orthodox patriarchs and hierarchs found his Orthodoxy in order: they scrutinized his *Orthodox Confession of Faith* and ended up by approving it. In this approved form, the document was highly valued and accepted as the official profession of faith by all the leaders of Orthodox churches of the seventeenth and eighteenth centuries, including Adrian, the last patriarch of Moscow before Peter I's

20-21; and K. Chodynicki's entry "Borecki, Jan" in *Polski słownik biograficzny* 2 (1936): 315-317. For Borec'kyj's brothers, cf., e.g., the supplication addressed in 1640 to Tsar Mixail Fedorovič by Iov and Andreas's sister in *Akty otnosjaščiesja* ... (as in fn. 32 above), no. 32, pp. 38-39. On Filippovič, cf. A. F. Koršunov, *Afanasij Filippovič: Žizn' i tvorčestvo* (Minsk, 1965) and the review of this book by F. Sysyn in *Kritika* 8, no. 3 (Spring 1972): 118-29. For Sakovyč's charges, and Mohyla's refutation, cf. *Lithos* ..., in *Arxiv Jugo-Zapadnoj Rossii*, pt. 1, vol. 9 (Kiev, 1893), p. 4 and fn. On the date of Sakovyč's charges, cf., ibid., S. Golubev's introduction, p. 134 and fn. 1.

36. I have in mind, *inter alia*, the grave indictment of Mohyla by the late Father G. Florovsky, for whom the "crypto-Romanism" and the "pseudo-morphosis of Orthodoxy" propagated by our metropolitan were "probably more dangerous than the Union itself." Cf. Father Florovsky's celebrated *Puti russkogo bogoslovija*, 2nd ed. (Paris, 1981), pp. 44-56, esp. p. 49, and *Ways of Russian Theology*, vol. 1 (Belmont, Mass., 1979) (a somewhat revamped and enlarged English version of *Puti*), pp. 64-85. The very brilliance of Father Florovsky's portrayal of Mohyla should not blind us to the fact that the author wrote not as an "unbiased" historian (for he did not believe that such a person could exist), but as a Russian theologian. Keeping this in mind, we may sympathize with Father Florovsky's disapproval of Mohyla. His casting doubt on Mohyla's Orthodoxy is another matter. Beginning with the seventeenth century, all Orthodox ecclesiastics who were not bound by Russian standards of confessional purity (and some who were) found few or no objections to Mohyla's *Confession* or to the Latin ingredients in it (assuming that they were aware of these ingredients); and they never impugned his Orthodoxy. Father Florovsky may have been right in viewing Mohyla's thought and reforms as alien to Russian theology, but was less justified in blaming their author for it. On my reading of the evidence, Mohyla (and the vast majority of upper-class educated Orthodox living in the Polish-Lithuanian Commonwealth in the first half of the seventeenth century) gave relatively little thought to Muscovy; they lived in a different world. Moscow was absent from the modern place-names adduced among various illustrative examples in Smotryc'kyj's Slavonic grammar of 1619; his list was limited to Kiev,

reforms, and Arsenij, enemy of Peter's reforms and metropolitan of Rostov in the 1750s, who considered Mohyla's catechism "more essential for the priest than philosophy."

What Mohyla's attitude toward Hetman Xmel'nyc'kyj would have been we cannot say, since his death on 1 January 1647, new style, came more than a year before Xmel'nyc'kyj's uprising, dubbed "civil war" in contemporary Polish sources. To form an educated guess on Mohyla's putative attitude, it will be helpful to remember that in a hagiographical piece dating from after 1629, he had a local saint frustrate the Zaporozhian Cossacks' plan to plunder the Moldavian city of Suceava; and that two of his first cousins were wives of Stanisław Rewera Potocki, the Polish palatine of Braclav and Cracow, and a third was married to the fiercely anti-Cossack Prince Jeremiah Vyšnevec'kyj.

At first, the uprising itself did not badly disrupt the teaching at the college — some of its important alumni graduated from it around 1649 or 1650 and serious war damage to its buildings occurred only in the fifties — nor did it stem the wave of Latin and Polish influence.[37] The will of the whole Ruthenian nation, to use Mohyla's own words — or at least of its Ukrainian branch — was favorable to the college. In 1651 and 1656 Hetman Xmel'nyc'kyj endowed the monastery of the Kiev confraternity

Cracow, L'viv, and Wilno (Vilnius). It follows that in terms of mere history, Mohyla is outside the ways of *Russian* theology; he belongs in Father Florovsky's book only tangentially — for instance, as a parallel to Patriarch Nikon and as a man who helped create the preconditions for the later invasion of Muscovy and Russia by Ukrainian and Belorussian clerical erudites and theologians. Cf. also Professor Sysyn's review article in this issue, pp. 155-187. [Father Florovsky's strictures against Mohyla and his school have their antecedents in nineteenth-century Russian historiography. To my knowledge, the only nineteenth-century Ukrainian historian unfriendly to Mohyla was Taras Ševčenko's younger contemporary, Pantelejmon Kuliš.]

37. Two examples: In *Rosa inter spinas*, a textbook of poetics dating from 1686 (the year of the official incorporation of Kiev into the Tsardom of Muscovy), students were given Polish examples culled from the cycle of poems by Samuel Twardowski; the cycle, written in 1634, was entitled "The Felicitous Expedition Against Moscow by the Most Serene Władysław IV." On *Rosa*, cf. Łużny, *Pisarze* (as in fn. 6 above), esp. pp. 37-38. As late as the 1690s, textbooks on rhetoric recorded Latin and Polish eulogies or funerary orations in honor of Xmel'nyc'kyj, cf. V. Peretc in *Čtenija v istoričeskom obščestve Nestora Letopisca* 14 (1890): 11-20. — The Latin legacy of Mohyla's college was so strong that some courses were taught in that language in the Russian Empire's ecclesiastical academies and seminaries as late as the 1840s. Cf. Golubev, "Kievo-mogiljanskaja kollegija..." (as in fn. 8 above), p. 544.

and "the schools attached to it" with the expropri⟨35⟩ated landed possessions of the Dominican fathers in and near Kiev,[38] those of the Jesuits and those of the Catholic bishop and chapter of Kiev; thus the college profited in the redistribution of the spoils. The Treaty of Bila Cerkva of 1651 expressly mentions the rights of the Kiev college. However, the chief — and highly valuable — assistance the Cossack uprising and its aftermath of 1654 gave the Mohyla college was indirect. It consisted in the expulsion of the Jesuits from the Ukraine: they were never to return to Kiev. In this way, serious competition to the college was eliminated, a competition which might have been a threat to it if the Jesuits were to stay. The potentially most advantageous decision connected with the Cossacks came to the college not through Xmel'nyc'kyj, but through Hetman Vyhovs'kyj and the Treaty of Hadjač of 1658. This treaty raised the college to the rank of academy and endowed it with the same prerogatives and liberties as "the Academy of the University of Cracow." It even provided that a second academy be erected in the Ukraine. Although this provision of the Hadjač treaty remained as unenforced as the others, it did give the teachers at the college a new impetus in their attempts to enhance their school's status. In 1670, Hetman Peter Dorošenko instructed his envoys to the negotiations with the Polish side in Ostroh to press for the establishment of an academy in the Ukraine. But it was the Russian Peter I who finally satisfied the Kievan teachers' wishes (1694 and 1701).

VI

For all its undeniable achievements, Mohyla's college did not produce original thought. This was not only because original thought is rare in human affairs, but also because the college's goal was fully to absorb existing, in this particular case, Western, cultural standards. Those who are catching up with established value systems strive for parity, not for

38. Dominicans: cf. I. Kryp"jakevyč and I. Butyč, *Dokumenty Bohdana Xmel'nyc'koho* (Kiev, 1961), no. 131, pp. 209-210 (on p. 210, references to earlier editions). In 1659, the Kiev *polkovnyk* V. Dvorec'kyj issued a detailed confirmation of Xmel'nyc'kyj's *universal* of 1651, cf. *Pamjatniki...*, 2 (1846) (as in fn. 1 above), no. XIX, pp. 213-22, and *Pamjatniki izdannye...*, 2 (1897) (as in fn. 4 above), no. XXIV, pp. 449-51. Jesuits: Kryp"jakevyč-Butyč, *Dokumenty* (as in this fn. above), no. 349, pp. 467-68 (on p. 468, references to earlier editions). In 1659, Tsar Aleksej Mixajlovič confirmed Xmel'nyc'kyj's *universal* of 1656, cf. *Pamjatniki izdannye...*, 2 (1897) (as in fn. 4 above), no. XXV, pp. 451-53.

originality. Involved contemporaries do not feel this to be a ⟨36⟩ drawback; those few who do gamble on original contributions coming after parity is achieved.

To be sure, a short-cut to original contributions does exist. It runs through changing the rules of the game: forgetting all about catching up and striking out on one's own instead (or in the wake of others who already have left the catching-up problems behind). In the history of learning and education, the challenge issued by the fledgling Collège de France to the Sorbonne a century before Mohyla is the case in point. Such short-cuts are taken only rarely in the course of civilization, however, and it would be unfair to Mohyla and to his successors to demand from them an act that was beyond their reach. The original contribution we might expect from Mohyla's college and academy is of a different kind. What went on there did affect the growth of a peculiarly Ukrainian consciousness. In that respect, however, the early college was the successful continuator of incipient trends rather than an initiator of new ones; and in later years its impact on national consciousness was not explicitly intended.

One contribution was made in the early period: intellectuals in the milieu of Mohyla (as well as in that of his immediate predecessors) rediscovered Kiev's early past. The roots of the Kievan present were traced back to that past, and historical continuity was established between the earliest Rus' and Kiev on the one hand and the Ukraine of the early seventeenth century on the other. Following in the tracks of Zaxarij Kopystens'kyj and of the *Virši* on Sahajdačnyj's funeral in 1622, Mohyla adopted the conception of the Kievan Primary Chronicle and traced the Rus' nation back to Japhet. That nation was called "the nation of Vladimir" by one student of his school.[39] Inscriptions in the Church of the Savior in Berestovo, restored by Mohyla in 1643/44, connect his name, the name of the metropolitan of all Rus' (*v'seę Rossii*), with that of the "autocrat" ruler of all Rus' (*vseę Rossii*) Vladimir the Great (who was thereby promoted to imperial rank) (figs. 3-4, pp. 686-7);[40] and we

39. For descent from "the noble" Japhet (and not from the "ignoble" Cham, as insinuated by the Polish critics), cf. Titov, *Materialy* (as in fn. 2 above), p. 268; for the "nation of Vladimir (*narodu Włodzimierza*)" who built 300 churches in Kiev "according to Stryjkowski," see Rothe, *Die älteste...Kunstdichtung* (as in fn. 23 above), p. 328, lines 21-22.

40. The Berestovo inscription of 1643 runs as follows: *Síju c(e)rkov' | Sozdà velíkij || i vseę Rossii knjaz | I samoderžec, S(vja)tyj || Vladímir: Vo s(vja)tom | Kr(e)ščé⟨n⟩ii Vasíli(j).* Po lě||*těx že Mnóhix, I po ra||zorénii ot bezbožnyx*

already know that in his genealogi⟨37⟩cal flatteries Mohyla traced the ancestry of his addresses back to the times of Vladimir the Great and invoked Rus' chroniclers in support of his statements. Finally, in the laudatory poems that the students of Mohyla's school and the printers of Kiev composed on the occasion of his enthronement in 1633, the Cathedral of Saint Sophia (later restored by him) commended (*polecaju*) to the newly installed metropolitan the walls that it had received from Jaroslav the Wise.[41]

⟨38⟩ This contribution, much as establishing historical continuities may appeal to us, was of limited importance. To realize this, we have only to recall that when financial need arose, Mohyla pointed out to the

---

Tatar || Proizvoléiniem [sic] B(o)žiim || obnovísę Smirénnym || Petrom Mohíloju arxiep(i)s(ko)pom Mitropolitom Kievski(m) Halickim I vseę̌ Rossii. Eksarxoju s(vja)taho || Ko(n)stantínopolskoho ap(o)s(to)lskaho pr(ě)s(to)la arximandrítom Pečerskim. Vo slávu Na Thavórě Preobrazšahos(ę) X(rist)a B(o)ha || slóva 1643. hodà | ot Sotvorenię že miru, 7151: [There follow some letters, probably *P, O, M, K, T, Ot, H*; are they the painter's signature?]. To my knowledge, this inscription is unpublished.

41. For tracing the ancestry of a Ruthenian aristocrat back to Kievan princes Svjatoslav, "Wlodzimirz, Boriss" and "Hlib," cf. Zaxarij Kopystens'kyj's preface addressed to Prince Stefan Svjatopolk Četvertens'kyj in 1623, Titov, *Materijaly* (as in fn. 2 above), p. 69, and Kal'nofojs'kyj's verses on the Četvertens'kyjs in *Teratourgēma* of 1638, Rothe, *Die älteste...Kunstdichtung* (as in fn. 23 above), p. 420. For comparing Prince Constantine Ostrožs'kyj to Vladimir and Jaroslav, cf. the poem in the Ostroh Bible (1581), reprinted in Rothe, ibid., pp. 5-6. For passages on St. Sophia's walls, cf. *Mnemosyne* in Rothe, ibid., poem 9, 13-20, pp. 334-335; poem 11, 3-6, p. 337; and Εὐφωνία *veselobrmjačaa* (as in fn. 27 above), p. 310 (Titov) and 319 (Rothe). The relevant passage of the Εὐφωνία is also reproduced in Bilec'kyj, *Xrestomatija* (as in fn. 19 above), p. 194. — For recent Soviet views on the rediscovery of Kiev's past in the Mohyla circle, cf. the two chapters by L. I. Sazonova, "Ukrainskie staropečatnye predislovija (bor'ba za nacional'noe edinstvo)" and "Ukrainskie staropečatnye predislovija (osobennosti literaturnoj formy)," in A. N. Robinson et al., eds., *Russkaja staropečatnaja literatura (XVI-pervaja četvert' XVIII v.)* (Moscow, 1981), pp. 129-52, 153-87 (several interesting observations on levels of language in the prefaces, on L'viv and Kiev prints as models used by Patriarch Nikon, on Suščans'kyj-Proskura, on invoking princely ancestry for the Ostrožs'kyjs and the Četvertens'kyjs and on the change in the character of the prefaces brought by the year 1654; p. 168, confusion on the meaning of *rossijs'komu rodu* or *naroda rossijs'koho* — these terms are taken to refer to "Russians in general"; p. 137, a charming slip going back to pre-1914: *južnorusskom krae* used with reference to places like L'viv, Vilnius and Kiev); and I. S. Zaxara, "Istorija Kyjivs'koji Rusi v ocinci dijačiv Kyjevo-Mohyljans'koji akademiji," in Ja. D. Isajevyč et al., eds., *Kyjivs'ka Rus': Kul'tura, tradyciji* (Kiev, 1982), pp.

autocrat Muscovite tsar that both "autocrat" rulers, Vladimir and Jaroslav the Wise, were the tsar's forebears;[42] or to juxtapose the Kiev intellectuals' search for roots of their Rus' with the impressive claims to antiquity and suzerainty that the less sophisticated compilers of the *Stepennaja kniga* had elaborated in Moscow three quarters of a century earlier. To be sure, there are similarities in both searches for roots. When Mohyla spoke of "seventeen generations" that had elapsed "since their graces, the Stetkevičs, were born to senatorial dignity,"[43] his device paralleled the conception of the *Stepennaja kniga*. However, Kievan intellectuals did little with the resources close to home, compared to what Muscovite bookmen had done with the faraway Kievan tradition. Before we find these intellectuals sadly wanting, we should consider the differences in the respective historical settings of Kiev and Moscow: the genealogies produced by the Kievan intellectuals addressed the mere remnants of the Ruthenian upper class, while those produced by the bookmen of Moscow supported the claims of a powerful and vigorous dynasty. This dynasty obtained final suzerainty over the city of Kiev in 1686, but its garrisons were present there as early as 1654. From the

89-92 (according to the author, professors of the academy invoked old Kievan traditions to promote the idea of unification with brotherly Russia — the new "reunited" state had to be as strong as Kievan Rus' had been in her day). Much better are the few sober pages by Ja. D. Isajevyč, "Rol' kul'turnoji spadščyny Kyjivs'koji Rusi v rozvytku mižslov"jans'kyx zv"jazkiv doby feodalizmu," in Ja. D. Isajevyč et al., eds., *Z istoriji mižslov"jans'kyx zv"jazkiv* (Kiev, 1983), esp. pp. 7, 10-14. — Two motifs of ideal genealogy used in the circle of Mohyla or in his college (as well as in other places) to enhance the image of Rus' and of Kiev have been left out of consideration here. In my view, they belong, originally at least, in a different context, that of establishing the legitimacy and antiquity of the Orthodox faith, and even its superiority over the Roman one. These are (1) the motif of "Roxolanian Sion," i.e., the Orthodox Church of Rus' with Kiev in her center as spiritual daughter of Jerusalem (a motif occuring before Mohyla's time, but used in his milieu or by his successor in the 1630s and 1650s); and (2) the motif of Kiev as the Second Jerusalem (a motif which is later and less frequenty attested, but better known to modern scholars on account of R. Stupperich's article of 1935, for which cf. fn. 44 below). This latter motif, an outgrowth of the first, was used for the benefit of two tsars: in 1654 by the spokesman of Hetman Ivan Zolotarenko near Smolensk (cf. *Akty otnosjaščiesja...* [as in fn. 32 above], vol. 14 [1889], no. 7, col. 176) and in 1705 [?] and 1706 by Prokopovyč in Kiev.

42. Cf. *Pamjatniki izdannye...*, 2 (1897) (as in fn. 4 above), pp. 425-426; *Akty otnosjaščiesja...* (as in fn. 32 above) no. 18, esp. pp. 28-29.

43. Cf. Titov, *Materijaly* (as in fn. 2 above), p. 338.

1670s Kiev professors, such as Innokentij Gizel', entered the ranks of the dynasty's ideologists; and the practice of establishing *direct* links between the Kiev of Vladimir and that of the college had soon to be abandoned. From then on, the whole panoply of speculations about Kiev's glorious past began to be used for the benefit of Kiev's new rulers and the term *rossijskij* began to acquire the meaning of "Russian." As late as July of 1705, Prokopovyč called Hetman Mazepa "a great successor" and a mirror image of Vladimir; ⟨39⟩ but on July 5 of 1706, during Peter I's visit to Kiev, the same Prokopovyč delivered a welcoming sermon in which he saw to it that both the hills of that Second Jerusalem and its Church of St. Sophia would sing the glories of the tsar *vseja Rossii*, the descendant and successor not only of Vladimir, but also of Jaroslav, Svjatoslav, Vsevolod and Svjatopolk, and the true embodiment of their virtues.[44] To judge by Gizel' and Prokopovyč alone, in the mature period of Mohyla's school its leading professors used history to promote the notion of All-Russian oneness as much as their predecessors used it to foster local patriotism.

The main, and the most lasting, contribution the college made to a specifically Ukrainian consciousness was an indirect one, and it began in Mohyla's lifetime. It consisted in the general raising of the level of Kiev's intellectual life, in imbuing Ruthenian youth with Western cultural notions, and thus in providing the elite with cultural self-confidence with respect to the Poles. These Western notions may appear to us, modern readers of the *Eucharisterion*, not to be of the highest order. A revolutionary change must have occurred from the local point of view, however, when a Ruthenian student spoke of Mt. Helicon rather than Mt. Thabor and listened to Horace rather than to the *Oktoix*. By combining its Western tinge and Latino-Polish message with Orthodoxy,

---

44. For Prokopovyč's flattery of Mazepa (*seho* [Vladimir's] *izobraženye pryjmy ot nas, jako toho ž velykyj naslidnyk ... Zry sebe samaho v Vladymeri, zry v pozori sam, aky v zercali ...*), see the Prologue to *Vladimerъ*, I. P. Eremin, ed., *Feofan Prokopovyč, Sočinenija* (Moscow and Leningrad, 1961), p. 152. The sermon of 5 July 1706, entitled "Slovo privětstvitel'noe na prišestvie vъ Kievъ Ego Carskago Presvětlago Veličestva...," is in *Feofana Prokopoviča...Slova i rěči poučitel'nyja, poxval'nyja i pozdravitel'nyja...*, vol. 1 (St. Petersburg, 1760), cf. esp. pp. 2-5, 10-11. Its text is discussed in R. Stupperich, "Kiev — das zweite Jerusalem. Ein Beitrag zur Geschichte des ukrainisch-russischen Nationalbewusstseins," *Zeitschrift für slavische Philologie* 12, no. 3/4 (1935): 332-55, cf. esp. pp. 333-36; and in Jury Šerech (G. Y. Shevelov), "On Teofan Prokopovič as Writer and Preacher in His Kiev Period," *Harvard Slavic Studies* 2 (1954), esp. pp. 216-21. Professor Shevelov stresses the sermon's religious, rather than political, aspects.

Mohyla's college performed a double task: it provided an alternative to the outright Polonization of the Ukrainian elite, and it delayed its Russification after 1686. It thus helped strengthen, or at least preserve, that elite's feelings of "otherness" from both the Poles and the Muscovites (and subsequently Russians), and created the basis for the later affirmative feelings of Ukrainian identity.[45]

⟨40⟩ Today, Mohyla and his college continue to serve as points of reference for scholars, both in Europe and in America, who trace the growth of civilization and of national traditions among Eastern Slavs in early modern times; thus when a student of the college wrote in 1633

Gdyż Europá, Azja i kraj Ameryká,
Z Płomienistą Lybią Mohiłow wykrzyka,[46]

his Baroque hyperbole had the makings of a true prophecy.

---

45. I discover with interest that Jabłonowski, *Akademia* (as in fn. 8 above), p. 248, made a similar assessment over eighty years ago.

46. *Mnemosyne*, in Rothe, *Die älteste...Kunstdichtung* (as in fn. 23 above), poem 13, lines 29-30, p. 340: "While Europe, Asia, and the country of America together with the flamboyant Libya [i.e., Africa] proclaim ⟨the glory of⟩ the Mohylas,..."

Addendum to footnote 22: We can still read entries that Mohyla made or dictated in two books he owned. The first of them stands on fol. 3ᵛ of the *Monacensis Slavicus* 1, a precious Gospel manuscript of Stephen the Great, dating from 1493. It is in a vernacular which can be considered Ukrainian and runs as follows (I do not expand the contractions; supralinear letters are put in parentheses):

> *Róku bo(ž) naro(ž)nia* a x l z [= 1637]: *Mča deka(b) kā: | Ja Pétrъ Mohyla arxyep(s)pъ Mytropoly(t) Kievskij | Halyckij i vsea Rossíy arxyma(n)dry(t) ѕ̄. lavry Ve(ly)kia | Pečersia* [sic] *Kievskia. Kupyle(m) sie stoe Eu(h)lie; Y(?)na | dalemъ věčno y neporušno v xra(m) Preč(s)toy B(d)cy Mo | nastyra Pečer(s)koho, h(d)e tělo moe polo(ž)no bude(t)*

The script of the note is so professional, and so different from that of the following entry, that it is difficult to assert that the note in question is an autograph. It must, however, reflect Mohyla's own words.

The second entry is in fol. 3ʳ of a Greek Leiturgiarion written by a nun Melania in L'viv in 1620. It is in Ruthenian, is surely an autograph, and runs as follows;

> *Petr Mohyla A(r)xiep(s)p Mytropoly(t) Kievskiy rukoju vl(as)noju*

Cf. P. P. Panaitescu, "Un autograf al lui Petru Movilă pe un tetraevanghel al lui Ştefan cel Mare," *Revista istorică Română* 9 (1939): 82-87 (facsimile on p. 84) and V. Brătulescu, *Miniaturi şi manuscrise din Museul de Artă Religioasă* (Bucharest, 1939), pp. 37-43 (facsimile on pl. IX).

Fig. 1. – The Lavra Printing Press, Southern View. Building Stages: 1701-1862; restored in 1954. (Photo Ševčenko 1970)

Fig. 2. – Church of the Savior at Berestovo. Scroll held by the Prophet Zephaniah. 1643/44. (Photo Ševčenko 1970)

Fig. 3. – Church of the Savior at Berestovo. Inscription Recording Restoration by Mohyla in 1643. Detail. (Photo Ševčenko 1970)

Fig. 4. – Church of the Savior at Berestovo. Inscription Recording Restoration by Mohyla in 1643. Detail. (Photo Ševčenko 1970)

SOURCES OF ARTICLES PUBLISHED IN THIS VOLUME

I. Byzantium and the Slavs.
E.g., *Harvard Ukrainian Studies* 8:3-4, pp. 289-303 (December, 1984)

II. An Important Contribution to the Social History of Late Byzantium.
Review of Georgije Ostrogorski *Pronija, Prilog istoriji feudalizma u Vizantiji i u južnoslovenskim zemljama* (Belgrade, 1951).
Annals of the Ukrainian Academy of Arts and Sciences in the U.S. 2:4 [6], pp. 448-59 (1952)

III. 'To the unknown Land': A proposed Emendation of the Text of the Igor' *Tale*.
Slavic Word 8:4, pp. 356-59 (December, 1952)

IV. Bars'ka Jevanhelija počatku XVII stolittja v Pierpont Morgan Library.
Naukovyj zbirnyk UVAN, 2, pp. 192-95 (1953)

V. Review of *Harvard Slavic Studies* 1 (1953).
Speculum 28:4, pp. 887-92 (October, 1953)

VI. A Neglected Byzantine Source of Muscovite Political Ideology.
Harvard Slavic Studies 2, pp. 141-79 (1954)

VII. Review of Mytropolyt Ilarion, *Podil jedynoji Xrystovoji Cerkvy i perši sproby pojednannja jiji, istoryčno-kanonična monohrafija.*
Südost-Forschungen 13, pp. 387-89 (1954)

VIII. The Definition of Philosophy in the *Life of Saint Constantine.*
For Roman Jakobson: Essays on the Occasion of His Sixtieth Birthday, 11 October, 1956, comp. Morris Halle, Horace G. Lunt, Hugh McLean, and Cornelis H. Van Schooneveld (The Hague, 1956), pp. 449-457

IX. Byzantine Cultural Influences.
Rewriting Russian History: Soviet Interpretations of Russia's Past, ed. C. E. Black (New York, 1956; 2nd ed. 1962), pt. 2: *The Application of Theory: Selected Examples,* chap. 6, pp. 143-97

X. Review of *Imagery of the Igor' Tale in the Light of Byzantino-Slavic Poetic Theory*, by Justinia Besharov.
Speculum 32:3, pp. 538-43 (July, 1957)

XI. Review of *Mediaeval Slavic Manuscripts: A Bibliography of Printed Catalogues*, by David Djaparidze.
Speculum 33:3, pp. 390-93 (July, 1958)

XII. Byzantine Elements in Early Ukrainian Culture.
Ukraine: A Concise Encyclopedia, ed. Volodymyr Kubijovyč (Toronto, 1963), Vol. 1, pp. 933-40

XIII. The *Civitas Russorum* and the Alleged Falsification of the Latin Excommunication Bull by Kerullarios.
Actes du XII Congrès International des Études Byzantines, Ochride, 10-16 septembre 1961 (Belgrade, 1964), vol. 2, pp. 203-12

XIV. Yaroslav I.
Encyclopedia Americana: International Edition (New York, 1964) vol. 29, p. 652

XV. New Documents on Constantine Tischendorf and the *Codex Sinaiticus*.
Scriptorium 18:1, pp. 55-80 (1964)

XVI. Review of *Obshchestvenno-politicheskaia mysl' drevnei Rusi* (*XI-XIV vv.*), by I. U. Budovnits.
American Historical Review 71:1, p. 138 (October, 1965)

XVII. Sviatoslav in Byzantine and Slavic Miniatures.
Slavic Review 24:4, pp. 709-13 (December, 1965)

XVIII. On Some Sources of Prince Svjatoslav's *Izbornik* of the Year 1076.
Orbis Scriptus: Dmitrij Tschiżewskij zum 70. Geburtstag, ed. Dietrich Gerhardt, Wiktor Weintraub, and Hans-Jürgen zum Winkel (Munich, 1966), pp. 723-38

XIX. George Christos Soulis, 1927-1966.
Slavic Review 25:4, pp. 720-22 (December, 1966)

XX. Russo-Byzantine Relations after the Eleventh Century.
Proceedings of the XIIIth International congress of Byzantine Studies, Oxford, 5-10 September 1966, ed. J. M. Hussey, D. Obolensky, and S. Runciman (London, 1967), pp. 93-104

XXI. The Greek Source of the Inscription on Solomon's Chalice in the *Vita Constantini*.
To Honor Roman Jakobson: Essays on the Occasion of His Seventieth Birthday (The Hague, 1967), pp. 1806-17

XXII. Muscovy's Conquest of Kazan: Two Views Reconciled.
Slavic Review 26:4, 541-547 (December, 1967)

XXIII. Rozważania nad *Szachami* Jana Kochanowskiego.
Pamiętnik Literacki 58:2, pp. 341-61 (1967)

XXIV. Preface to Ivan Dujčev, *Slavia Orthodoxa: Collected Studies in the History of the Slavic Middle Ages* (London, 1970), pp. i-iv.

XXV. The Cambridge and Soviet Histories of the Byzantine Empire.
Slavic Review 30:3, pp. 624-34 (September, 1971).

XXVI. The Date and Author of the So-Called Fragments of Toparcha Gothicus.
Dumbarton Oaks Papers 25, pp. 115-188 (1971)

XXVII. On the Social Background of Cyril and Methodius.
Studia Paleoslovenica (Prague, 1971), pp. 341-51

XXVIII. Michael Cherniavsky 1922-1973.
Slavic Review 33:4, pp. 864-66 (December, 1974)

XXIX. Ljubomudrějšij Kỳr" Agapit Diakon: On a Kiev Edition of a Byzantine *Mirror of Princes*.
Recenzija 5:1 — Supplement, pp. 1-32 (Fall-Winter, 1974)

XXX. Preface to the reprint of Friedrich Westberg, *Die Fragmente des Toparcha Goticus (Anonymus Tauricus) aus dem 10. Jahrhundert* [= Subsidia byzantina lucis ope iterata, 18] (Leipzig, 1975), pp. vii-xviii

XXXI. Francis Dvornik. (August 14, 1893-November 4, 1975) (with Ernst Kitzinger and John Meyendorff).
Harvard University Gazette, vol. LXXII, No. 20, February 18, 1977

XXXII. George Ostrogorsky (with William Huse Dunham, Jr. and Ernst Kitzinger), *Speculum* 53:3, pp. 774-76 (July, 1977)

XXXIII. Remarks on the Diffusion of Byzantine Scientific and Pseudo-Scientific Literature among the Orthodox Slavs.
Slavonic and East European Review 59:3, pp. 321-45 (July, 1981)

XXXIV. Report on the Glagolitic Fragments (of the *Euchologium Sinaiticum?*) Discovered on Sinai in 1975 and Some Thoughts on the Models for the Make-up of the Earliest Glagolitic Manuscripts.
Harvard Ukrainian Studies 6:2, pp. 119-51 (June, 1982)

XXXV. The Many Worlds of Peter Mohyla.
Harvard Ukrainian Studies, 8:1-2, pp. 9-44 (June, 1984)

INDEX

ADDENDA

Chapter I

For another example of the genre represented by this chapter, cf. N. V. Pigulevskaja, "Vizantija i Slavjane," in her *Bližnij Vostok, Vizantija, Slavjane* (Leningrad, 1976), 131–48. The essay by the distinguished orientalist is quoted here on account of both its (few) similarities with mine and its (more numerous) differences from it.

For the newer approaches, cf. Simon Franklin, "The Reception of Byzantine Culture by the Slavs," *The 17th International Byzantine Congress. Major Papers* (New Rochelle, N.Y., 1986), 383–97 who tackles the problem with the tools of Cultural Translation and Reception Theories and with the notion of cultural blockage. His (mostly Kievan) illustrative examples are analyzed both by new and traditional means. Cf. also Franklin's earlier "The Empire of the *Rhomaioi* as Viewed from Kievan Russia: Aspects of Byzantino-Russian Cultural Relations," *Byzantion*, 53 (1983), 507–37 (stresses Kievan cultural autonomy, for all the impulses Kiev received from far-away Byzantium).

Axinia Djurova, "L'intégration du monde slave dans le cadre de la communauté orthodoxe (IXe–XIIe siècles): Notes préliminaires," *Harvard Ukrainian Studies*, 12/13 (1988/1989), 643–71 operates with the notions of "active" or "creative" Reception, where Byzantine originals acquire new meanings in Slavic garb, and stresses the active role of Bulgaria in elaborating "structural prototypes" for Kiev.

For a comparative approach applied to hagiography, cf. Ivan Božilov, "L'hagiographie bulgare et l'hagiographie byzantine: unité et divergence," in E. Patlagean and P. Riché, edd., *Hagiographie, cultures et sociétés, IVe–XIIe siècles* (Paris, 1981), 535–57. The author combines the new with the traditional and the no longer current. He quotes or uses some of my general definitions of 1976 and divides his material into *Lives* of Byzantine saints in Bulgarian hagiography and *Lives* of Bulgarian saints in Byzantine hagiography; on the other hand, he still puts the *Lives* of Cyril and Methodius among Bulgarian documents and operates with the notion of "popular" *Lives*, rather than *Lives* written in low style.

Chapter II

George Ostrogorski's book *Pronija* subsequently appeared in a French translation by Henri Grégoire: *Pour l'histoire de la féodalité byzantine* (Brussels, 1954), XVI, 388 pp.

Chapter III

For those interested in parallels to the postulated <*zemli*> *neznaemě*, I can offer the expressions ξένην χῶραν ἄγνωστον (or χώραν ξένην καὶ ἄγνωστον). They occur in the tenth-century *Synaxarium* of Constantinople under April 19 and July 26 and refer to the travels of John, pupil of Gregory the Decapolite (ninth century) or John of the Old Lavra (no date) respectively. The two Johns both leave their native places, go to the "unknown <foreign> land" and end up in the Old Lavra of Chariton in Palestine. Cf. H. Delehaye, ed., *Synaxarium ecclesiae Constantinopolitanae* [=Propylaeum ad Acta Sanctorum Novembris] (Brussels, 1902), 616, 6–7 and 844, 5. Delehaye (*ibid.*, 1028, *ad* 843,24) assumed the two Johns to have been the same person. On the contrary, S. Vailhé in *Revue de l'Orient chrétien*, 9 (1904), esp. pp. 491–98 maintained that they were two different persons, and he may have been right. In any case this John or these Johns belong to the ninth century.

Chapter VI

Cf. four recent studies on Agapetus: Patrick Henry, III, "A Mirror for Justinian: the Ekthesis of Agapetus Diaconus," *Greek, Roman and Byzantine Studies*, 8 (1967), 281–308, cf. n. 7 (the author takes over and enlarges upon my observations on the relationship between Ps.-Philo and Agapetus); N. E. Kopasov, " 'Nastavlenie' Agapita i zapadnoevropejskaja političeskaja mysl' XVI–XVII vv. (Agapit i Èrazm)," *Vizantijskij vremennik*, 43 (1982), 90–97 (against my suggestion that Erasmus may have known, and been inspired by, Agapetus's "Mirror"); M. T. Djačok, "O meste i vremeni pervogo slavjanskogo perevoda 'Nastavlenija' Agapita," in E. K. Romodanovskaja, ed., *Pamjatniki literatury i obščestvennoj mysli èpoxi feodalizma* (Novosibirsk, 1985), 5–12 (against my attribution of Agapetus's first Slavic translation to Tsar Symeon's or Tsar Peter's Bulgaria; the author asserts—a doomed effort, I am afraid—that this translation was made in Rus' [mercifully enough "not later than 1076"] and that it is a product of "drevnerusskaja" literature); Renate Frohne, *Agapetus Diaconus, Untersuchungen zu den Quellen und zur Wirkungsgeschichte des ersten byzanti-*

nischen Fürstenspiegels (Dr. Phil. Dissertation, Tübingen, 1985) (on pp. 19–110 the author takes up, and enlarges upon—in part through new finds—my information on Agapetus's *Nachleben*). To Frohne's ample bibliography (pp. 255–71) add these two later items: R. Romano, "Retorica e cultura a Bizanzio: due *Fürstenspiegel* a confronto," *Vichiana*, N.S. 14, 3 (1985), 266–316 (on Agapetus and Theophylact of Ochrid, especially valuable for the latter); D. G. Letsios, Η " Ἔκθεσις κεφαλαίων παραινετικῶν" του διακόνου Αγαπητού. Μία σύνοψη της ιδεολογίας της εποχής του Ιουστινιανού γιά το αυτοκρατορικό αξίωμα, in Δωδώνη, 14, 1 (1985), 175–210 (bibliography on p. 176, n. 2).

Chapter VIII

I adduce two more definitions of philosophy of the "Cyrillian" kind, both coming from prominent, if somewhat earlier, contemporaries of the Slavic Apostle: 1. κἀν τούτοις πρὸς τὴν θείαν μίμησιν, ὅσον ἐφικτόν, ἀποτυπούμενος, cf. Theodore of Studios (d. 826), *Parva catechesis*, 18, 47–48 = p. 67 ed. Auvray; 2. ἡ φιλοσοφική (some manuscripts have φιλοσοφία) . . . τέλος <sc. ἔχει> τὸ ὁμοιοῦσθαι θεῷ κατὰ τὸ δυνατὸν ἀνθρώπῳ, cf. Michael Synkellos (d. 846), Μέθοδος περὶ τῆς τοῦ λόγου συντάξεως, ch. 7 = p. 163, 42–43 ed. Donnet.

Chapter X

George Choiroboskos, routinely assigned to the sixth century, has been dated again to a period after the mid-eighth century: cf. W. Bühler and Chr. Theodoridis, "Joannes von Damaskos *terminus post quem* für Choiroboskos," *Byzantinische Zeitschrift*, 69 (1976), 397–401. The grounds for this dating, first proposed by A. Papadopoulos-Kerameus in 1898, appear solid, based as they are upon the occurrence of quotations from John of Damascus, Cosmas of Jerusalem and Andrew of Crete in Choiroboskos's parsing Commentary on the Psalms, a work that is surely his; these quotations are unlikely to have been interpolated. Thus we would be faced with the somewhat surprising conclusion that Choiroboskos became so influential as quickly as a century or so after his death, as to have been anthologized in Greek miscellaneous manuscripts (the case in point being, e.g., the *Vaticanus graecus* 423 of the tenth century) and through them to have entered Bulgarian Slavic letters by about the year 900, and the literary milieu of Kiev, by the third quarter of the eleventh century (witness the *Izbornik* of 1073). This would be a relatively rare case of a "latest" Byzantine author's appearance among the Slavs (another rare parallel is offered by the presence of Michael Synkellos [ninth century] in the same *Izbornik* of 1073).

Two articles concerning ''On Figures'' by George Choiroboskos in the *Izbornik* of 1073 appeared in B. A. Rybakov, ed., *Izbornik Svjatoslava 1073 g.* (Moscow, 1977): 1. E. È. Granstrem and L. S. Kovtun, ''Poètičeskie terminy v Izbornike 1073 g. i razvitie ix v russkoj tradicii (analiz traktata Georgija Xirovoska)'' (pp. 99–108); 2. G. K. Vagner, ''Stat'ja Georgija Xirovoska 'O obrazex' v Izbornike Svjatoslava 1073 g. i russkoe iskusstvo XI v.'' (pp. 139–52). Granstrem and Kovtun paid little or no attention to *Izbornik*'s mistranslations (cf., e.g., p. 104, note 21); Vagner, too, did not ask to what extent the Slavic translator had misunderstood his Greek original. Nor did he stress the fact that *óbrazъ* ''image,'' is one of the Slavic renderings of τρόπος; instead, he postulated an opposition between the (Bulgarian) language of the *Izbornik*'s original compiler and the (Rus') language of its Kievan (and presumable ''interventionist'') copyist. Only by means of such a device was he able to juxtapose the grammatical ''images'' of Choiroboskos with the visual images of Kievan art.

Chapter XIII

Several years after the appearance of my article I realized that many of its results had been anticipated by W. Szcześniak, ''Rzekoma bytność legatów papieża Leona IX na Rusi,'' *Przegląd Historyczny*, 3, 2 (1906), 162–76. Reverend Szcześniak, using common sense, found no reasons for the Roman legates' detour to the ''far-away and barbarous Rus',''no echoes of such a detour in contemporary sources, and no time for making it on the part of the Papal delegation. The Papal legates were in a great hurry to return to Rome by the ordinary route that included the Italian Teate at the other end and followed the *Via Egnatia* from Constantinople. Reverend Szcześniak even proposed the Thracian Rusion as being the *civitas Russorum.* He stopped short, however, of questioning Cardinal Humbert's allegation that Michael Kerullarios had falsified the excommunication bull. If the almost total neglect of Reverend Szcześniak's article on the part of my colleagues—as far as I know, only V. T. Pašuto, *Vnešnaja politika Drevnej Rusi* (Moscow, 1968), 82 and 319, was aware of it, even though it is unclear whether he accepted its conclusions—can be excused by the *dictum* that *Polonica non leguntur*, this excuse hardly applies to myself, for I was educated in Warsaw.

Chapter XVIII

See *Addendum* to Chapter VI

Chapter XXI

The main reactions to my find were as follows: Roman Jakobson, "Poxvala Konstantina Filosofa Grigoriju Bogoslovu," in *Roman Jakobson, Selected Writings*, 6, 1 (1985), 207–39 (originally published in *Slavia*, 39, 3 [1970], 334–61), esp. pp. 231–39, granted that I "had the luck of finding a Greek text corresponding to the first of the three *quatrains* [in Jakobson's arrangement] and the two last lines of the second *quatrain* of the Old Slavonic inscription on the Chalice." He maintained, however, that this find constituted no proof against the poetic character of the translation. Professor Jakobson also denied that Chapter 13 of the *Vita Constantini* could have been an interpolation. To maintain the contrary, he said, is to neglect the artistic structure and symbolism of that text, and to miss the fact that we are dealing with a specimen of an outstanding literary composition. Finally, he proposed to read the number of years elapsed between Solomon's twelfth year and Christ as 990.

Riccardo Picchio, "Strutture isocoliche e poesia slava medioevale: a proposito dei capitoli III e XIII della *Vita Constantini*," *Ricerche Slavistiche*, 17–19 (1970–72), 419–45, esp. pp. 438–43, graciously took into account the publication of the Greek source of the Chalice inscription; entertained the possibility of interpolations in parts or in the whole of Chapter 13, or at least of later re-elaborations in it; but felt, in the light of his theory of tonic isocolism, that the whole of Chapter 13 was poetic, or reflected a sophisticated rhetorical structure. Professor Picchio also observed that—if some rearrangements are undertaken—the third line of the Chalice inscription combines Isaiah 25:2 with Ezekiel 34:24. In another article ("Chapter 13 of *Vita Constantini*: its Text and Contextual Function," *Slavia Hierosolymitana*, 7 [1985], 133–52), Professor Picchio analysed the textual tradition of Chapter 13 of *Vita*—it turned out to be complicated—compared it to the "apocryphal" version of the Chalice story and found it difficult to ascertain how the two fit together and, consequently, to decide what kind of interpolation may have occurred in *Vita*'s Chapter 13: we may perhaps be dealing with an interpolation consisting of an altered form of the original, an interpolation that was absorbed back into it. In his complicated argument, Professor Picchio attributed a great importance to quotations from Isaiah 35:2 and Ezekiel 34:24 constituting the third line of the Chalice inscription; they are somewhat garbled in both the *Vita* and the "apocryphal" traditions, but, according to him, must have stood in a "correct" form in the original text of Chapter 13.

Moshé Taube (Jerusalem) gave a lecture, "Remarks on Chapter 13 of the *Vita Constantini*," at Harvard University's Ukrainian Research Institute on December 11, 1986; it appeared under the title "Solomon's Chalice, the Latin Scriptures and the Bogomils" in *Slovo*, 37 (1987), 161–70. Professor Taube turned to those parts of the Chalice inscription (in lines two and three) for which the Greek text I produced offers no equivalents; he considered that one or two passages there could best be explained by the Latin Vulgate, and drew some general conclusions from this consideration. In particular, he interpreted *drěva inogo* as <the Cross made> "of one tree" (rather than "of the other tree" or "wood"). To this purpose, he invoked the passage in Ezekiel 37:19, where the Vulgate has *lignum unum*.

Finally, Ivan Dujčev provided a sympathetic summary of my find in *Harvard Ukrainian Studies*, 7 (1983), esp. 163–65.

To sum up, the reactions quoted above deal with (1) the poetic character of the Slavonic version of the Solomon inscription; (2) the question of whether Chapter 13 is interpolated, in part or in whole; and (3) with those parts of the inscription and the Chalice story for which no precise Greek equivalent has as yet been discovered.

Ad primum: I have little to say here, because statements that continue, after 1967, to claim poetic quality for the Slavonic Solomon inscription are not disprovable; consequently, they do not lend themselves to a refutation. I still fail to see how a Greek text in prose, translated word for word into Slavonic, can become poetry; certainly not on the lone strength of graphic devices applied to it by its modern students. My general view on the matter of the earliest Slavic poetry recorded in medieval texts is as follows: The only poetic form demonstrably used in the earliest Slavonic literature is the counterpart of the Byzantine twelve-syllable verse; such a view meets the requirements of common sense, since this verse was the most wide-spread Byzantine meter at the time. Common sense further requires that in the case of every other poetic form postulated for the earliest Slavonic texts we should look for corresponding Byzantine models, and show that they were consistently adapted. As yet, nobody has succeeded in doing this, and the recent meritorious work by Antonina Filonov Gove, *The Slavic Akathistos Hymn, Poetic Elements of the Byzantine Text and its Old Church Slavonic Translation* (Munich, 1988) is a case in point. Every other claim for poetic meter in the earliest Slavonic literature has been a modern construct, undertaken independently of historical context and probabilities.

Ad secundum: I continue to consider (and Professor Picchio, as I understand him, does, too) the Solomon story in the *Vita Constantini* to be an interpolation; but I now feel, without being able to prove it, that this interpolation came into being less likely in the process of the composition of the *Vita*, than at a later stage in the text's history.

Ad tertium: In my article I avoided speculation and concentrated on those parts of the Solomon inscription for which the Escurial manuscript offered Greek correspondences. In the more relaxed mood of an *Addendum*, I shall admit to the belief that the Escurial version is an abbreviation of a larger whole; that we have an idea of the whole through the Slavic versions; and that the whole's Greek form, including the three "verses" and their commentary (but not the computation of years between Solomon and Christ), will one day come to light. At least two things follow if one accepts this premise.

Firstly, we should applaud Professor Picchio for drawing our attention to the analogies between parts of the inscription and the two Old Testament passages (Isaiah 35:2 and Ezekiel 34:24); but we should see them as a part of the Chalice story, rather than as "keystones of <*Vita Constantini*'s> hagiographic construction," connected with the "spiritual salvation of the Slavs." Therefore, there is no need to correct the "errors," in these quotations (these "errors," I claim, were already present in the postulated Greek original), or to wonder why the "theologically funded interpretation" in Chapter 13 of the *Vita* left no trace in the East Slavic tradition. I suspect that this interpretation never existed.

Secondly, *pace* Professor Taube, *drěva inogo* does not correspond to *lignum unum* and does not mean "of one tree." This is not because of trivial difficulties: thus, *inъ* (let alone its genitive) is unattested in the meaning of "one" when it stands by itself (as opposed to being a part of *composita*)—we should not be swayed by one occurrence in a peculiar sixteenth-century manuscript; it is not quite true that in Ezekiel 37:19 *lignum unum* of the Vulgate has no counterpart in the Septuagint; and one must not use modern Russian *derevo* to discuss presumable ninth-century equivalents of *lignum*: in fact, in the three passages of Ezekiel 37 where we do have Greek and Slavic (e.g., the Ostroh Bible) parallels to *lignum unum* (verses 16, 17 and 19), we read ῥάβδον μίαν and *žezlъ* (not *drěvo*) *edinъ* respectively (only in verse 20 do we have *drěva* for ῥαβδοι, *ligna*). This is because Greek models offer a better solution.

The usual Greek equivalent of the Old Church Slavonic *drěvo* in the meaning of 'wood' is ξύλον (which may mean both 'wood' and 'tree'). Since in Christian Greek ξύλον has also the meaning of "Cross", the same meaning is repeatedly attested for *drěvo* (and, which is of no relevance to us here, for the Christian Latin *lignum*). Now let us return to the second line of the Chalice inscription—which is admittedly a prophecy about Christ—and assume that it, too, goes back to the Greek model. In that line, as elsewhere, *vъkoušenie* would render γεῦσις or βρῶσις; *na vъkoušenie . . . drěva* would correspond to εἰς γεῦσιν τοῦ ξύλου. This "taste of the tree" is in fact known from early Greek Christian literature. The late fourth-century *Apostolic Constitutions* 6:7:3 (=II, 312, 22 ed. Metzger) has τὸν Ἀδὰμ τῇ γεύσει τοῦ ξύλου τῆς . . . ἀθανασίας ἐστέρησεν, "<Satan> deprived Adam of immortality through the taste of the tree." For examples of "tasting of the Tree" in John Chrysostom, cf. Migne, *PG*, 53, col. 133; 54, cols. 611 and 617; 56, col. 531 (spurium); 62, col. 745 (spurium). Of course Adam tasted of the Tree of Knowledge, while the Lord (cf. *Gospodne* of our line) was to be crucified and thus was to taste of *another* tree or wood (*drěva inogo*), namely the Cross, the Tree of Life. This disposes of the modern "one tree" and vindicates the medieval Slavic (originally, we claim, Byzantine) exegesis *drěvo ino estъkr'st, a vъkoušenie raspętie* (cf., e.g., K. Kuev, ed., *Ivan Aleksandrovijat Sbornik of 1348 g.* [Sofia, 1981], 385). The contrast between the Tree of Knowledge and the tree or wood of the Passion—the other tree—is attested early as well. In the apocryphal Μαρτύριον τοῦ ἁγίου ἀποστόλου Ἀνδρέου ch. 5 (=II, 1, 12–13 ed. Bonnet) Apostle Andrew thus explains the salvation through the mystery of the Cross (διὰ τοῦ μυστηρίου τοῦ σταυροῦ): as the first man ushered in Death through the transgression of the tree (διὰ τῆς τοῦ ξύλου παραβάσεως), it was necessary that Death be expelled from among men through the tree of the Passion (διὰ τοῦ ξύλου πάθους); it was necessary that the tree of concupiscence (τὸ ξύλον τῆς ἐπιθυμίας) be eliminated by the tree of the Cross (διὰ τοῦ ξύλου σταυροῦ). For the expression "another," cf. John Chrysostom, *Hom.* 16, 6 *in Genesim* (Migne, *PG*, 53, col. 133–4): ἀπὸ τοῦ ξύλου τούτου ἐφ' ἕ τ ε ρ ο ν μεταγάγωμεν τὸν λόγον, ἀπὸ τοῦ ξύλου τούτου ἐπὶ τὸ ξύλον τοῦ σταυροῦ, "Let us transfer our discourse from this tree (i.e., Adam's Tree of Knowledge) to *another* <tree>; from this tree to the tree of the Cross." The Cross, then, was the "other tree" or wood, as the Byzantine interpreter in Slavic garb had rightly pointed out. For other cases in which John Chrysostom contrasts the Tree of Adam or of Paradise with the Tree of the Cross, cf. Migne, *PG*, 49, col. 396 (important passage) and 50, col. 702. That the Lord's *vъkoušenie* may possibly hearken back to βρῶσις as well, is suggested by another passage in the same chapter 5 of the *Martyrium* of Andrew, where one version has Christ receive the <bitter> taste (βρῶσιν δέξασθαι) of the bile (on the Cross) on account of the most sweet taste (βρώσεως) of the forbidden tree.

The case of "one tree" and the purported connections of Chapter 13 with the Vulgate may serve as a cautionary tale. Insufficient regard for the Byzantine context may lead to proposals that appear likely on general grounds (such as the Latin connections, in fact entertained by the Cyrillo-Methodian milieu), but rest on flawed evidence. For the earliest layer of Slavic letters the investigative rule is: look to Byzantium first, since Slavic parallels hardly exist at that period and non-Byzantine influences are few and far between—even when it comes to scriptural and liturgical material.

Elsewhere, T. St. Tomov, "Edna vъzmožna bъlgarska usporedica na legendata na Grala (iz žitieto na Konstantin-Kiril Filosof), in *Starobъlgarska literatura. Izsledvanija i materiali*, I (Sofia, 1971), 65–80, is among the more outlandish interpreters of Solomon's inscription.

The counting of years between Solomon and Christ is attested in Byzantine chronographical computations of years elapsed between the Creation and Christ, but the figures given in Greek texts known to me are always considerably higher than 909. As for "the twelfth year of Solomon" of Chapter 13, it, too, somehow hearkens back to Byzantine computations; either to their usual statement that Solomon began his reign at the age of twelve, or to a misunderstanding reflected at least in two manuscripts of Synkellos, to the effect that the king built the temple in the twelfth (rather than the second) year of his reign. Cf., e.g., A. A. Mosshammer, ed., *Georgii Syncelli Ecloga Chronographica* (Leipzig, Teubner, 1984), apparatus to p. 212, 8 and 10.

Chapter XXVI

In addition to the reviews and discussions of this article recorded in the bibliography of *Okeanos* [=*Harvard Ukrainian Studies*, 7] (1983), 19=no. 80 (cf. especially the two publications by Ivan Božilov), I shall quote four pieces *exempli gratia*; they reflect the respective positions of Soviet and Western scholarship concerning "Toparcha Gothicus". Eight years after the appearance of the "Toparch," E. È. Lipšic, discussing Soviet literature on the subject, wrote ("Vizantijskie pis'mennye istočniki," in V. V. Mavrodin et al., edd., *Sovetskoe istočnikovedenie Kievskoj Rusi* [Leningrad, 1979], 77–78) that "Toparcha Gothicus" was a source difficult to interpret, and the Soviet scholars had not yet arrived at a consensus as to its author, time, and to the place where this work had been written. A. N. Saxarov, "Vostočnyj poxod Svjatoslava i 'Zapiska grečeskogo Toparxa',"

Istorija SSSR, 1982, 3, 86–103, esp. pp. 94–103, connected the Fragments of the "Toparch" with Prince Svjatoslav's anti-Khazar expedition of the year 965, and even had the "Toparch" visit Kiev. Mr. Saxarov did cite my article (cf. p. 97 and note 47), but inexplicably derived from it the conclusion that I had "connected the events [described in the Fragments] with the conflict between Byzantium and Rus' at the time of Vladimir Svjatoslavič in the years 987–988." On the other hand, W. Buchwald, A. Hohlweg, O. Prinz, edd., *Tusculum Lexicon* (3rd ed., 1982), 806–07 (entry "Toparcha Gothicus") found that the Fragments "have now been shown to be a forgery." Finally, A. Grafton, *Forgers and Critics: Creativity and Duplicity in Western Scholarship* (Princeton, 1990), 42–43, drew on my article to characterize, in a brilliant page, Ch.-B. Hase as the creator of the Fragments.

The most up-to-date study on Ch.-B. Hase is by Pierre Petitmengin, "Deux têtes de pont de la philologie allemande en France: le *Thesaurus Linguae Graecae* et la 'Bibliothèque des auteurs grecs' (1830–1867)," in M. Bollack, H. Wismann, Th. Lindken, edd., *Philologie und Hermeneutik im 19. Jahrhundert*. II (Göttingen, 1983), 76–98. Cf. the guarded statement (p. 79 and note 18): "He <i.e., Hase> knew Greek manuscripts well and was an editor endowed with some genius, if he in fact himself composed the fragments of the 'Toparcha Gothicus,' these much controverted documents dealing with the earliest Russian history."

In 1989, owing to the generosity of the descendants of Ch.-B. Hase, Dr. mult. Alexander von Hase and Dr. Ulrike von Hase-Schmundt, I was appraised of the existence of two categories of Hase documents (they were discovered in the archives of the Hase family): autograph drafts of letters that Hase addressed to various people (including one to Count Rumjancev pertaining to the amulet [*zmeevik*] attributed to Volodimer Monomax's time, an amulet which apparently had been sent to Paris for Hase's expert appraisal), and the coveted autograph of the full text of a considerable part of Hase's secret Diary. The drafts of the letters start about the year 1810; the recovered part of the diary, hélas, begins only with the year 1835—too late to shed light on the genesis of the Fragments or at least on the process of the printing of the *History* of Leo Diaconus. There is still hope that the full autograph of the earlier part of the Diary will be discovered. In 1990, I learned from Dr. Alexander von Hase that hundreds of new drafts of letters by Hase had been found in that year. I had no opportunity to examine them. The documents I did inspect show Hase at his impish best: his texts are written in German, French, French in Greek letters, and in a Greek of his own making. Whatever the contribution of the new Hase documents to the solution of the Toparcha conundrum may turn out to be, they are of high and independent value for the history of nineteenth-century French and European scholarship and should be published either fully, or in the form of *regesta*.

Chapter XXVII

After completion of my article, I became aware of several references, both textual and epigraphic, to ninth-century *drungarioi*. These references do not radically modify my assessment of the social status enjoyed by Cyril and Methodius's father; still, their evidence suggests that this status may have been somewhat more comfortable than I had assumed. Here is the additional evidence:

1. In a passage of Theophanes Continuatus, *Hist.*, 3:5 = 89, 15–18 Bonn that is reminiscent of *Vita Methodii*'s chapter 2, we read that the father of the future Empress Theodora, wife of Emperor Theophilos (d. 842), was "not a man without distinction or one of the many when it came to his position in life, but a *drungarios* or, according to some, <even> a *turmarchēs*." The passage confirms what we have known all along, namely that the grade of *drungarios* was immediately subordinate to that of *turmarchēs*; in addition, it implies that the grade of *drungarios* enjoyed a sufficiently high social status in the second quarter of the ninth century to be invoked for the purpose of making Theodora, the provincial girl, presentable at court. This information was perhaps meant to counter the gossip that disparaged the imperial bride as a Paphlagonian country bumpkin.

2. Another case is that of Nicetas, a *drungarios* active in Lydia (in the Thracesian theme) before 837. In the original *Life* of Peter of Atroa, written ca. 847 (ed. V. Laurent, *La Vie merveilleuse de Pierre d'Atroa* [=Subsidia Hagiographica, 29] [Brussels, 1956]), our Nicetas appears anonymously and carries no title. He is described there as a rich man (cf. § 24, 32–33: ἦν γὰρ ὁ ἀνὴρ τῶν εὐπόρων) who had at least fourteen female servants (according to § 25, 6–8, fourteen of his servants were for a while possessed by the Devil). He had been an iconoclast (§ 24, 50–51), but repented and was cured by Peter of his paralysis. In the rewritten *Life* of Peter (date: 860–865, cf. V. Laurent, *La Vita retractata et les miracles posthumes de Saint Pierre d'Atroa* [Subsidia hagiographica, 31] [Brussels, 1958], 28–30) our man is a *drungarios*, is given the name of Nicetas and the epithet of ἔνδοξος (§ 109, 1 and 9–10). The mention of fourteen demoniac female servants whose miraculous cure "we have described" (§ 109, 4) makes certain that Nicetas is the same person as the wealthy former iconoclast of the original *Life* (§§ 24–25). Nicetas was sent by the *stratege* (of the theme) to the Mesonesos of Malagina.

3. In a passage in the *Vita* of the 42 Martyrs of Amorium (V. Vasil'evskij–P. Nikitin, edd., ''Skazanija o 42 amorijskix mučenikax,'' *Mémoires de l'Académie Impériale des sciences de St. Pétersbourg*, VIIIe Série, Classe historico-philologique, vol. VII, 2 [1905], 34, 8–16), relating the events of the year 845, we read the following story: One of the prisoners and potential future martyrs, a former iconoclast, had wavered in his resolve and had preferred physical survival to a martyr's crown. Another prisoner, Kallistos, the *dux* of Koloneia (today: Şebin-Karahissar), saw a *drungarios* of his standing by and bewailing his master's imminent death. Kallistos said: ''As I made you known to the earthly emperor, so I shall make you to enroll in the service of the eternal one.'' The *drungarios* agreed to stand in for the apostate ex-iconoclast and thus made the original number of forty-two martyrs complete again. We can conclude from this story that a mid-ninth century provincial *drungarios* could have been presented to the emperor, but was in a relationship of subservience to a *dux*, called his ''lord'' (κύριος, 34, 12).

4. Two inscriptions of the late ninth century mention *drungarioi* as co-founders or founders of churches. One, dating from 871, comes from the now destroyed church of Saint John Mankoutes in Athens, and is exhibited at present in the Byzantine Museum of that city. It commemorates the foundation of the church of Saint John the Baptist by the couple Constantine and Anastaso and ''their beloved child, John the *drungarios*;'' they willed ''all their possessions'' to that church. (Cf. A. Xyngopoulos in Εὑρετήριον τῶν μνημείων τῆς Ἑλλάδος, Α', Εὑρετήριον τῶν μεσαιωνικῶν μνημείων, I. Ἀθηνῶν, vol. II (1929), 85–87 (photograph). The other inscription, dated to 10 October 897, was found in Galatia, in Mas'ud Köy on the territory of Colonia Germa. It mentioned the construction of a church adorned with wall paintings and dedicated to the Saints Nicholas, Basil and Hypatios; the construction of the church occurred at the expense of a former *drungarios* and imperial *strator* Gregoras (ὑπ' ἐμοῦ . . . Γρηγορᾶ βασηληκοῦ στράτωρος κὲ δρουγαρήου γεγονότως). Cf. H. Grégoire, ''La Vie de Saint Blaise d'Amorium,'' *Byzantion*, 5, 1 (1929), 400–01, especially 401, n. 1 (improves upon the text in CIG, IV [1877], no. 8690).

These two inscriptions parallel that of John, the imperial *strator* and *drungarios* of Koloneia (see note 23 of my article; for one more publication of John's inscription, see Sideropoulos in Ὁ ἐν Κωνσταντινουπόλει Ἑλληνικὸς Φιλολογικὸς Σύλλογος, suppl. to vol. 17 [1886], 135). The three inscriptions indicate that a *drungarios*, or a family of which a *drungarios* was a member, were opulent enough to have a church built ''in <their> remembrance and for the remission <of sins>,'' as the Athens inscription puts it, although the atrocious spellings in the Gregoras and John inscriptions do not speak well of the educational level of those who executed them, and perhaps even of those who commissioned them.

The sober book by F. Winkelmann, *Byzantinische Rang- und Ämterstruktur im 8. und 9. Jahrhundert* [=*Berliner byzantinistische Arbeiten*, 53] (Berlin, 1985) offers ample material on our topic. After separating the more important "sea" *drungarioi* from their "land" counterparts, one gains the impression that the rank of the latter was not too elevated; cf. especially p. 57, where the seals of two land *drungarioi*, datable to the ninth century, give them the middling rank of *stratores*, considerably lower than that of *protospatharioi* (cf. however, an [earlier?] seal of Constantine "*spatharios* and *drungarios*," dated to the eighth-ninth centuries in K. Konstantopoulos, Βυζαντιακὰ μολυβδόβουλλα [Athens, 1917], p. 58 = no. 190).

By the eleventh century, *drungarios* lost its technical meaning and came to be used as a family name. Cf., e.g., an inscription of the year 1074 in the chapel of Saint Merkurios near the village of Hagios Markos on the island of Corfu, in P. L. Vocotopoulos, "Fresques du XIe siècle à Corfou," *Cahiers archéologiques*, 21 (1971), esp. pp. 152–53.

To the discussion (footnote 1 of the article) of the use Dimitrij Tuptalo made of the *Lives* of Constantine and Methodius and related materials in his *Kniga žitij svjatyx*, add now N. M. Dylevskij, "Žitie slavjanskix pervoučitelej Mefodija i Kirilla v obrabotke Dimitrija Rostovskogo," *Études Balkaniques*, 1 (1986), 105–13 and L. A. Jankowska, "'Žitie i Trudy' sv. Mefodija i sv. Konstantina-Kirilla v *Četьix-Minejax* sv. Dimitrija Rostovskogo," *Slavia Orientalis*, 37, 2 (1988), 179–221 (detailed; laudatory of Dimitrij).

Footnote 54 of my article provoked a spirited reaction on the part of Professor K. G. Bonis (Μπόνης). In two studies he restated his views on the alleged family ties between the Thessalonican brothers and the imperial house, and on the connection between the mosaics in the church of St. Demetrios in Thessaloniki and the members of the family or household of one Leo the *drungarios*, assigned to the ninth century and presumably the Saints' father. Professor Bonis also expressed grave reservations against my article as a whole. Cf. Συμβολὴ εἰς περαιτέρω ἔρευναν τοῦ προβλήματος τῆς καταγωγῆς τῶν ἱεραποστόλων τῶν Σλάβων Κυρίλλου καὶ Μεθοδίου, in Βυζαντινά, 13, 1 [=Δώρημα στὸν Ἰωάννη Καραγιαννόπουλο] (1985), pp. 427–51 and "Ein weiterer Beitrag zur

Frage der Abstammung der Slavenapostel Kyrillos und Methodios,'' Βυζάντιον, Ἀφιέρωμα στὸν Ἀνδρέα Ν. Στράτο, I (1986), 41–57. In one instance, at least, Professor Bonis attributed to me a view that is the opposite of the one I expressed. Contemporary sources, I said on p. 342, n. 4 of the article's original pagination, held that Constantine-Cyril and Methodius were either Greeks or non-Slavs; this was tantamount to saying that I, too, believed that they were Greeks. Professor Bonis concluded just the opposite: that I believed they were Slavs. Cf. Συμβολή, p. 434, n. 8 (Ἄρα κατὰ τὸν K. Ševčenko ἦσαν Σλάβοι!); cf. also ''Ein weiterer,'' p. 45, n. 8.

Such misunderstandings, based on a misreading of a foreign text, can easily be set straight. I am at a loss, however, when I read Professor Bonis's statement to the effect that my σλαβικὴ καταγωγή, my Slavic origins, render my conclusions doubtful *a priori* (Συμβολή, p. 441, n. 14). Even the Stalin Constitution, I am told, granted that no one should be held responsible for the sins of one's parents.

Professor A.-E. N. Tachiaos, *Cyril and Methodius of Thessalonica; the Acculturation of the Slavs* (Thessaloniki, 1989), 38 surmised that ''*Drungarius* Leo's family undoubtedly had powerful connections, through either friends or relations, with the higher echelons of Constantinopolitan society. The fact of the two boys' selection by the Emperor clearly demonstrates this.'' Unfortunately, the popular genre of the book did not allow Professor Tachiaos to substantiate his opinion.

Chapter XXIX

See *Addendum* to Chapter VI

Chapter XXXIV

Against my expectations, reactions to the *Report* have been few. The first of them, an indirect one, came from Francis J. Thomson, ''Early Slavonic Translations—an Italo-Greek Connection?'' *Slavica Gandensia*, 12(1985), 221–34. Relying on his remarkable command of sources, Professor Thomson considered a number of Greek texts that are connected in one way or another with South Italy and with it alone, and are represented in Slavic translations; he then raised the question of whether there had been literary contacts between South Italy and Bulgaria, and assuming that there had been such contacts, what forms they could have taken. He answered this question with a *non liquet*. It appears from the first sentence of Professor Thomson's article that his *position du problème* was influenced by the "comment" aroused by the presence of certain Italo-Greek traits in Glagolitic (he says "Bulgarian Glagolitic") codices. Unless I unduly flatter myself, the "comment" was my *Report*, given the fact that Professor Thomson's first endnote referred to Professor Weitzmann's article of difficult access that the *Report* adduced. Professor Thomson centered his search on contacts between South Italy and Bulgaria. This, I submit, was too narrow a perspective, at least when it comes to the make-up of Italo-Greek and Slavic manuscripts. A search that promises more fruitful results is one for connections between the two shores of the Adriatic, rather than between Italy and a lone Slavic group. The recently established presence of Italo-Greek traits in Greek manuscripts surely produced in Epirus puts matters in a wider context; influences from Italo-Greek centers emanated to various parts of the Balkans. One could even think of these influences reaching the Slavs indirectly, through a western Greek mediation. On Epirote manuscripts with Italo-Greek traits, cf. the paper given by Professor Diether Reinsch (Bochum) at the International Colloquium on Greek Palaeography held at Erice (Sicily) in September of 1989.

In contrast, Father Miguel Arranz, S. J., found that the Fragments identified in the *Report* represented a "sensational discovery." The noted liturgiologist took full cognizance of the *Report* in his "La tradition liturgique de Constantinople au IXe siècle et l'Euchologe slave du Sinaï," to appear (a) "in a Zagreb periodical," and (b) in a volume entitled *Slavenska misija svete braće Ćirila i Metoda*, II. *Kršćanska Europa u IX stoleću* (publ. by Kršćanska Sadašnjost, Zagreb—the author provided me with a typescript of the relevant parts of this essay in 1985); and in his "La liturgie de l'Euchologe slave du Sinaï," *Christianity among the Slavs. The Heritage of Saints Cyril and Methodius* [=*Orientalia Christiana Analecta*, 231] (Rome, 1988), 15–74, esp. pp. 16, 19–20, 71–72, 74. To be sure, his doubts were more pronounced than were mine on the matter of the "new folia" of Sinai (*Fragmenta Glagolitica* according to his terminology) being a part of the *Euchologium Sinaiticum*; he thought that the *Fragmenta* were earlier than the *Euchologium*. Moreover, Father Arranz was more decisive than I had been in rearranging the order of the Fragments. One should defer to his liturgiological expertise.

We now have a full description and facsimile reproduction of the Fragments, cf. I. C. Tarnanidis, *The Slavonic Manuscripts Discovered in 1975 at St. Catherine's Monastery on Mount Sinai* (Thessaloniki, 1988), esp. pp. 65–86 and plates pp. 185–90, 219–47. We thus know that the Fragments discovered in 1975 consist of 28 folia, of which the *Report* transcribed and discussed only fols. 1^{r}, a part of fol. 1^{v} and fol. 2^{v} (=pp. 74–76 in Tarnanidis; there, *ad* fol. 1^{r}, first line, change *naš<emъ>* to acc. sing. fem., and omit *sę*: it is our *heads* that we should incline, not *ourselves*; in the incipit of the prayer on fol. 1^r, instead of the unclear *v·št<i>* read *v<ъzgla>š<enie>*; same observation concerning "*v·št<i>*" in fol. 1^v and 4^v). Professor Tarnanidis proves that all the newly discovered folia (including folia 1–4) were originally a part of the preserved *Euchologium Sinaiticum*. He is aware of the *Report*, without pointing to the parallels between it and what he terms his discoveries and hypotheses (compare his pp. 72–73 with *Report*, pp. 139–40 and footnote 36). He promises, on p. 73, a commented edition of folia 1–4 of the Fragments. Until it appears, the *Report* should still be consulted.

For a detailed review of Professor Tarnanidis's work, cf. now R. Mathiesen, "New Old Church Slavonic Manuscripts on Mount Sinai," forthcoming in *Harvard Ukrainian Studies*, 15, no. 1/2 (June 1991).

Chapter XXXV

Another autograph remark by Peter Mohyla in vernacular (with the formula *rukoju vlasnoju*) is on fol. 1^r of Oxford, Bodleian Library, *MS Auct. T. 6. 1*. The manuscript is a 17th-century Greek musical anthology; the fact that Mohyla owned it is one more indication that he was familiar with Greek. Cf. Ralph Cleminson, *A Union Catalogue of Cyrillic Manuscripts in British and Irish Collections* (London, 1988), 220–21 = no. 145 and Fedor B. Poljakov in *Die Welt der Slaven*, 35, 2 = N.F. 14, 2 (1990), 308.

These reprints of articles, reviews, and other short pieces by the well-known Byzantinist, Ihor Ševčenko, are gathered together in one volume for the first time. The collection reflects the author's wide-ranging interests and his significant contributions to the study of the relationship between Byzantine and East Slavic culture. A number of the original articles have been provided with addenda by the author.

Among the articles are the author's now famous study, "Fragments of the Toparcha Gothicus," in which he demonstrates their nineteenth-century provenance at the hands of their "discoverer" Karl Benedikt Hase; the analysis of the impact on Muscovite political ideology of the writings of Deacon Agapetus; the discovery of the Greek prose original of the putative poem contained in the *Life* of the Slavic Apostle Cyril; and the find, made at St. Catherine's Monastery, of Constantine Tischendorf's letters regarding the transfer of the Codex Sinaiticus to St. Petersburg. Other articles include the author's studies on the impact of Byzantine elements in early Ukrainian culture and in some Kievan texts; and his observations on Byzantine social history at the time of the Slavic Apostles. Ševčenko offers these studies up as a challenge to the younger generation of scholars engaged in new approaches within these fields. Of further interest to Byzantinists and Slavists alike are the author's reviews and retrospectives, including retrospectives of